LEGAL
THESAURUS/
DICTIONARY

A Resource for the Writer
and the Computer
Researcher

William P. Statsky

LEGAL
THESAURUS/
DICTIONARY

A Resource for the Writer and the Computer Researcher

William P. Statsky

DELMAR
CENGAGE Learning

Detroit • New York • San Francisco • New Haven, Conn • Waterville, Maine • Lonon

Legal Thesaurus / Dictionary
William Statsky

For product information and technology assistance, contact us at
Cengage Learning Customer & Sales Support, 1-800-354-9706

For permission to use material from this text or product, submit all requests online at **cengage.com/permissions**
Further permissions questions can be emailed to

Library of Congress Control Number: 8429136

ISBN-13: 978-0-3148-5305-8

ISBN-10: 0-3148-5305-7

Delmar Cengage Learning
5 Maxwell Drive
Clifton Park, NY 12065-2919
USA

Cengage Learning products are represented in Canada by Nelson Education, Ltd.

For your lifelong learning solutions, visit
delmar.cengage.com

Visit our corporate website at **www.cengage.com**

Notice to the Reader
Publisher does not warrant or guarantee any of the products described herein or perform any independent analysis in connection with any of the product information contained herein. Publisher does not assume, and expressly disclaims, any obligation to obtain and include information other than that provided to it by the manufacturer. The reader is expressly warned to consider and adopt all safety precautions that might be indicated by the activities described herein and to avoid all potential hazards. By following the instructions contained herein, the reader willingly assumes all risks in connection with such instructions. The publisher makes no representations or warranties of any kind, including but not limited to, the warranties of fitness for particular purpose or merchantability, nor are any such representations implied with respect to the material set forth herein, and the publisher takes no responsibility with respect to such material. The publisher shall not be liable for any special, consequential, or exemplary damages resulting, in whole or part, from the readers' use of, or reliance upon, this material.

Printed in the United States of America
24 25 26 27 28 29 30 12 11 10 09 08

For Jessica:
Thirteen years and counting

Also by William P. Statsky

Case Analysis and Fundamentals of Legal Writing, 2d ed. St. Paul: West Publishing Company, 1984 (with J. Wernet).

Legal Research and Writing: Some Starting Points, 3d ed. St. Paul: West Publishing Company, 1986.

Legislative Analysis and Drafting, 2d ed. St. Paul: West Publishing Company, 1984.

Torts: Personal Injury Litigation. St. Paul: West Publishing Company, 1982.

Rights of the Imprisoned: Cases, Materials, and Directions. Indianapolis: Bobbs-Merrill Company, 1974 (with R. Singer).

Family Law, 2d ed. St. Paul: West Publishing Company, 1984.

Introduction to Paralegalism: Perspectives, Problems, and Skills, 3d ed. St. Paul: West Publishing Company, 1986.

Preface

There are a number of instances in which you may find yourself struggling for the "right" word. For example:

- while writing a legal memorandum, appellate brief, or other document;

- while searching a data base with a computer;

- while using the thousands of indexes in the tens of thousands of law books in a comprehensive law library.

If all you need is a synonym, this book should provide one for you. Yet the book is not simply a collection of synonyms. While a vast number are included, the scope of the entries is much broader. A substantial menu of related words and phrases is also provided. Since you sometimes will not know what you are looking for until you find it, you need a broad arena of connected words and phrases as candidates for the "correct" terminology.

The relatively recent emergence of computer-assisted research systems has lead to a new need to generate word options. In WESTLAW, for example, the publisher (West) has prepared a "Query Planner" on which you write down possible words and phrases before tackling the keyboard. You are encouraged to think of "all synonyms or alternatives" for the important words involved in the client's case. Similarly, the publisher of LEXIS (Mead Data) tells you to think of "alternative expressions" in its preliminary work sheet called, "Developing a Search Request". Users of research data bases are sometimes urged to identify "searchonyms" and to try them on the computer. A searchonym can include a synonym, an antonym, or some other related term.

The *Legal Thesaurus/Dictionary* can help you use such computer data bases by giving you ready access to a myriad of word alternatives.

In addition, the book provides definitions of the major words and phrases involved in the practice and study of law.

Appreciation is gratefully acknowledged to West Publishing Company for its permission to use and adapt definitions from *Black's Law Dictionary*. Similarly, Daniel Oran, a colleague on other writing ventures, was kind enough to allow me to draw material from his *Oran's Dictionary of the Law*. Special thanks are also due to the following individuals who assisted me in the massive task of compiling this book: Richard Nakamura, Joan Torkildson, Bill Gabler, Angela Grote, Commie Farrell, and John Lassiter.

WEST'S

LEGAL
THESAURUS/
DICTIONARY

A Resource for the Writer and the Computer Researcher

Aback, *adv.* **1.** Shocked (the client was taken aback by the decision). Surprised, unawares, thrown off guard, startled, amazed, astonished, bewildered, stunned, perplexed, flabbergasted, "floored." **2.** Backward (to move aback). Rearward, to the rear, back, behind, toward the back, regressively. *Ant.* Prepared; forward.

Abaction, *n.* **1.** Carrying away by violence. See larceny. **2.** Stealing animals.

Abandon 1. *v.* To surrender totally and intentionally (it is unethical to abandon a client). Desert, forsake, forswear, renounce, relinquish, refuse to perform, yield, totally withdraw, give up absolutely, repudiate, quit, resign, waive one's interest, turn one's back on, totally ignore, abjure, walk out on, abnegate, abdicate, cast aside, cast off, discard, turn away from, depart from, strand, maroon, leave in the lurch, vacate, retract, discontinue, leave aside, disown, reject. **2.** *n.* Wantonness (drove with abandon). Lack of restraint, absence of self-control, lawlessness, intemperance. *Ant.* Retain; moderation.

Abandoned, *adj.* **1.** Surrendered (abandoned property). Deserted, forsaken, forsworn, renounced, relinquished, repudiated, vacated, discarded, dropped, cast away, cast off, cast aside, discontinued, left, left behind, shunned, rejected, demitted, marooned, given up, neglected, outcast, desolate, destitute, forlorn, vacant, unoccupied. **2.** Dissolute (an abandoned life). Depraved, licentious, irreclaimable, profligate, shameless, incorrigible, reprobate, unprincipled, unrestrained, lost, loose, dissipated, wild, wicked, wanton, debased, corrupt, hardened, sinful, unconstrained, immoral, disreputable, unrepentant, demoralized, unfortunate, uninhibited, debauched, shameful, degraded, desperate, lewd, unchaste, amoral, vicious, hopeless, helpless, solitary, adrift, scorned. *Ant.* Claimed; virtuous.

Abandonee, *n.* A person to whom something is abandoned. See abandon (1).

Abandonment, *n.* The total and intentional surrender of property, persons, or rights (abandonment of spouse, child, copyright). Relinquishment, renunciation, abnegation, demission, resignation, desertion, denial, disavowal, departure, withdrawal, repudiation, rejection, abjuration, abdication, abrogation, forsaking, evacuation, apostasy, dereliction, defection, rescission, disownment, cession, decampment, flight, ceding, yielding, disaffection, cancellation, vacating, neglect. *Ant.* Acceptance.

Abase, *v.* To lower or humble (she refused to abase herself). Humiliate, bring down, debase, depress, reduce, degrade, disgrace, dishonor, demean, downgrade, cast down, discredit, denigrate, disparage, depreciate, devaluate, belittle, shame, malign, slander, smear, demote. *Ant.* Praise.

Abash, *v.* See embarrass, disparage, discredit, decry, slander.

Abatable nuisance A nuisance that can be diminished or eliminated. A nonpermanent interference with the use of land or with a right that is common to the public. See nuisance, abate, abatement.

Abate, *v.* **1.** To eliminate (abate a nuisance). Destroy, terminate, demolish, beat down, put down, bring to an end, put an end to, raze, lay low, remove, suppress,

1

abolish, annihilate, annul, invalidate, negate, nullify, quash, undo, vitiate, abrogate, cancel, repeal, rescind, abandon, revoke, vacate, defeat, discontinue, dissolve, exterminate, obliterate, quell, void. **2.** To diminish (the wind abated). Reduce, lessen, alleviate, decrease, moderate, mitigate, attenuate, allay, temper, lighten, limit, relieve, soften, subside, weaken, curtail, decline, diminish, modify, palliate, rebate, deduct, remit, lower, relax. *Ant.* Create; increase.

Abatement, *n.* **1.** Termination (abatement of a lawsuit; abatement of a nuisance). Destruction, obliteration, extermination, extinguishment, stoppage, abolition, quashing, defeat, eradication, annulment, quelling, revocation, end, ending, elimination, cancellation, crushing, abrogation, discontinuance, cessation, repression, suppression, nullification, invalidation, voidance, fade-out, check. **2.** Reduction (abatement of taxes; abatement of a legacy because of inadequate funds available). Decrease, cutback, lowering, lessening, discount, curtailment, limitation, remission, markdown, diminution, write-off, allowance, mitigation, subsidence, tempering, assuagement, decline, mollification, alleviation, slackening, modification, extenuation, softening, relief, weakening, falling-off, sinking, ebb, decay, shrinking, settling, palliation, fading, lightening, attenuation, waning. *Ant.* Enlargement; intensification.

Abator, *n.* **1.** Someone who illegally takes possession of land upon the death of the owner before the heir or devisee can take legal possession. **2.** Someone who abates a nuisance.

Abbreviate, *v.* To shorten (the editor abbreviated the names of the judges). Abridge, contract, condense, abstract, digest, brief, truncate, cut, cut down, prune, reduce, summarize, boil down, synopsize, compress, pare down, curtail, trim, lessen, epitomize, retrench, diminish, shrink, dock, narrow, clip, constrict. *Ant.* Enlarge.

Abbreviation, *n.* See abbreviate, digest (1), brief (2).

Abbroachment, *n.* Obtaining control of goods on the market by buying at wholesale and selling at retail. Forestalling a market.

Abdicate, *v.* To voluntarily renounce (abdicate the throne). Give up, leave, quit, vacate, resign, cede, forgo, relinquish, retire, withdraw, disown, demit, depart, part with, lay down, renounce all claim to, disclaim, yield, surrender, abandon, repudiate. *Ant.* Claim, assert.

Abdication, *n.* The voluntary renunciation of a privilege or an office (the attorney general later regretted her abdication). Surrender, abandonment, resignation, repudiation, retirement, waiver, demission, quitting, relinquishment, cession, disowning, desertion, withdrawal, abnegation, abjuration, yielding, ceding, vacating, rejection, disclaimer, disavowal, transfer.

Abdomen, *n.* A body cavity in a mammal containing the stomach, the kidneys, etc. Belly, gut, intestinal organ, ventricle, viscera. See also venter.

Abdominal, *adj.* Relating to the abdomen (abdominal pain). Visceral, intestinal, ventral, gastric, stomachic, digestive.

Abduct, *v.* To take away a child, wife, ward, or servant unlawfully (the patient was abducted). Kidnap, steal, steal away, shanghai, "snatch," pirate, commandeer, take away by force, take away surreptitiously, impress, conscript, bear off, carry away, carry off, expropriate, hijack, ravish, rape, seize, make off with, grab, run off with, run away with, capture, ensnare, appropriate, purloin, spirit away, transport, wrest from, deprive, lay hold of, arrogate. *Ant.* Return, restore.

Abduction, *n.* The unlawful taking away of a child, wife, ward, or servant (abduction of the heir by force). Kidnapping, child snatching, child stealing, withdrawing, subjugation, impressment, spiriting away surreptitiously, carrying away, ravishment, theft, confiscation, seizure, commandeering, hijacking, capture, expropriation, rape, arrogation. *Ant.* Restoration.

Abductor, *n.* Someone who abducts. Kidnapper, thief, robber, pirate. See also thief.

Aberrant, *adj.* See aberration, abnormal, deviant (1), anomalous.

Aberration, *n.* Deviation from the norm (noticeable aberrations in behavior). Abnormality, irregularity, nonconformity, anomaly, divergence, peculiarity, abortion, corruption, perversion, derangement, delusion, eccentricity, strangeness, insanity, lunacy, freak, monster, degradation, degeneration, distortion, freakishness. See also exception (3). *Ant.* Normality, standard.

Abet, *v.* To encourage someone to commit a crime (abet the conspirators). Aid, assist, help, promote, incite, back, instigate, prompt, procure, advocate, foment, support, request, goad, conspire, counsel, connive, cooperate with, arouse, command, facilitate, spur, stimulate, induce, urge, exhort, facilitate, prod, succor, sustain, give moral support to, "egg on," sanction, endorse, embolden, inspire, arouse, countenance, underwrite. *Ant.* Discourage, frustrate.

Abetment, *n.* The incitement of someone to commit a crime. See abet.

Abettor, *n.* A person who encourages or incites another to commit a crime (he was charged as an abettor). Collaborator, backer, helper, co-conspirator, conspirator, accomplice, accessory, instigator, promoter, advocate, assistant, prompter, associate, inducer, protagonist, partner, aider, confederate, coadjutor, right hand, underwriter. *Ant.* Antagonist, competitor.

Abeyance, *n.* Not finally settled; not being in force or use for a time (the decision was held in abeyance). In expectancy, not vested, in expectation, in the clouds, in pendenti (in suspension), in waiting, dormancy, interim, interval, intermission, in a state of temporary inactivity, latency, pause, quiescence, arrest, deadlock, inactivity, interregnum, recess, repose, respite, postponement, lull, stay, deferral, hiatus, remission, anticipation, contemplation, delay, reprieve, deferment, interruption, breathing spell, lapse, discontinuance. *Ant.* Action, continuity.

Abhor, *v.* To react with disgust (abhor the violence). Hate, despise, loathe, be revolted by, detest, abominate, execrate, scorn, reject, be nauseated by, recoil from, dislike, shun, view with horror. *Ant.* Admire.

Abhorrence, *n.* See abhor, contempt (2), odium, hostility.

Abhorrent, *adj.* See repugnant (1), contemptible; abhor.

Abide, *v.* **1.** To obey (they agreed to abide by the decision). Comply with, observe, accept the consequences of, conform to, carry out, carry into execution, live up to, yield to, heed, perform, observe, execute, acquiesce in, adhere to, follow, submit to, respect, agree to, acknowledge, discharge, fulfill, consent to, stand by. **2.** To tolerate (she could not abide the delay). Put up with, bear patiently, endure, suffer, brook, stand, "stomach," submit to. See also continue. **3.** To remain (abide with me). Stay, reside, "stick with," linger, live, dwell, sojourn. See also continue. **4.** To endure (time will abide). Last, be permanent, survive, persevere, persist. *Ant.* Disregard; resist; depart; die.

Abiding, *adj.* See permanent, perpetual.

Ability, *n.* **1.** The power to do something (the court's ability to enforce the order). Capacity, potential, strength, facility, faculty. **2.** The competence to do something (the ability to make decisions). Talent, capability, aptitude, fitness, proficiency, expertise, know-how, effectiveness, qualification, gift, adeptness, acumen, flair, genius, command, mastery, efficiency, ableness, expertness, adaptability, prowess, intelligence, knowledge, ingenuity, skill, endowment, mastery. *Ant.* Impotence; incompetence.

Ab initio, *adv.* From the beginning (the marriage was void ab initio). From the first act, in the first place, from its infancy, from the inception. *Ant.* Starting now, in the future.

Abject, *adj.* **1.** Deplorable (abject poverty). Complete, wretched, degrading,

3

pathetic, miserable, hopeless, terrible, inescapable, thorough, helpless, humiliating. **2.** Contemptible (abject coward). Immoral, mean, sordid, debased, despicable, low, vile, corrupt, dishonorable, fraudulent, disgraceful, hateful, groveling, ignoble, foul, odious, evil, depraved. See also contemptible. *Ant.* Honorable; admirable.

Abjudicate, *v.* To deprive one of something as a result of a judgment.

Abjuration, *n.* Formally giving up rights; a renunciation given under oath (abjuration of citizenship). Sworn denial, abandonment, relinquishment, rejection, abnegation, disowning, repudiation, discarding, recantation, disavowal, forswearing, rejection, revocation, defection, disaffirmation, renouncement, recall. *Ant.* Affirmation, confirmation.

Abjure, *v.* To give something up formally; to renounce under oath (he abjured all allegiance to the state). Repudiate, forswear, reject, retract, disown, disclaim, discard, disavow, revoke, renege, relinquish, recant, recall, abrogate, dismiss, deny, take back, withdraw, surrender, abandon, cede, abnegate, cast off, disdain, withdraw, desert, renunciate, apostatize, eschew, forgo. *Ant.* Certify, maintain.

Ablation, *n.* An excision. See amputate.

Ablaze, *adj.* See burn, fire (1).

Able, *adj.* Competent (able attorney). Qualified, knowledgeable, capable, skilled, gifted, experienced, intelligent, talented, expert, clever, accomplished, adroit, proficient, powerful, masterful, creative, superior, outstanding, versed, efficient, adequate, fit, endowed, brilliant, robust, vigorous, enterprising, first-rate, inventive. See also learned. *Ant.* Inept, useless.

Able-bodied, *adj.* Capable of performing the regular and ordinary duties of a job (able-bodied worker). Robust, healthy, in good health, strong, sturdy, fit, sound, well, well-conditioned, physically fit, in shape, in good condition, able, solid, muscular, well-built, fast, sturdy, brawny, powerful, sinewy, wiry, manly, hardy, lusty. *Ant.* Decrepit.

Ablution, *n.* Purification. See sanitation.

ABM Antiballistic missile.

Abnegate, *v.* To renounce (she abnegated her rights). Give up, relinquish, abjure, abandon, deny, surrender, forbear, reject, refuse, resign, decline, yield, abdicate, repudiate. *Ant.* Accept.

Abnormal, *adj.* Considerably irregular (abnormal reaction). Unusual, not average, not typical, atypical, aberrant, nonconforming, eccentric, anomalous, deviant, deviating, unnatural, singular, peculiar, strange, erratic, uncommon, queer, bizarre, odd, freakish, unexpected, extraordinary, unique, perverse, unconventional. *Ant.* Ordinary, normal.

Abnormally dangerous Extrahazardous (abnormally dangerous inmate). Extraordinarily dangerous, exceptionally hazardous, unusually dangerous, fraught with peril, inherently dangerous.

ABO The system of human blood typing that produces the blood types A, B, AB, and O.

Aboard, *adv.* On board a vessel or other mode of transportation. Inside, within, on deck.

Abode, *n.* Home, residence (the normal place of abode). Dwelling place, address, fixed place of residence, habitation, habitat, house, lodging, domicile, quarters, living quarters, headquarters, homestead, accommodations, apartment, tenement, "pad."

Abogado, *n.* (Span.) An advocate.

Abolish, *v.* To eliminate completely (the legislature abolished the court). Repeal, revoke, do away with completely, annul, abrogate, rescind, destroy, put an end to, declare null and void, render null and void, eradicate, erase, end, crush, extirpate, formally end, terminate, annihilate, dispense with, invalidate, void, set aside, extinguish, squelch, quash, repudiate, disestablish, demolish, subvert, negate, undo, abate, delete, discontinue, dissolve, overturn, overrule, override, vacate, retract, countermand, cancel, vitiate, supersede, expunge. *Ant.* Establish, create.

Abolishment, *n.* See reversal, rescission, abjuration, defeat (2), neutralization, elimination, abolition.

Abominable, *adj.* See repugnant, odious, gross (1), offensive, contemptible.

Abomination, *n.* See infamy, corruption, odium, debauchery.

Abolition, *n.* A complete elimination (abolition of slavery). Annihilation, termination, nullification, cancellation, rescission, rescinding, revocation, repeal, destruction, eradication, ending, abolishment, annulment, suppression, obliteration, vitiation, defeasance, disestablishment, extirpation, voidance, vacation, withdrawal, repudiation, countermand, reversal, retraction, dissolution, overthrow, subversion, invalidation, demolition, extermination, extinction. *Ant.* Establishment, restoration.

Aboriginal, *adj.* Relating to natives (aboriginal title). First, from the beginning, indigenous, native, primal, primitive, original, autochthonous, primordial, primeval. *Ant.* Recent, imported.

Abort, *v.* **1.** To terminate a pregnancy. Miscarry, give birth before viability. **2.** To fail to complete (abort the mission). Terminate, end, fail, fail to develop fully, halt, stop, call off, quell, fall short, come to naught, thwart, frustrate, arrest, prevent, fizzle, nullify, obstruct, cease, not reach, intercept. *Ant.* Deliver; finish.

Abortee, *n.* A woman who has had or is having an abortion.

Abortifacient 1. *n.* Something that is used to produce or cause an abortion, e.g., drugs. **2.** *adj.* Inducing or causing an abortion.

Abortion, *n.* **1.** The premature expulsion of the embryo or nonviable fetus from the uterus (abortion on demand). Miscarriage, aborticide. **2.** Failure (the hearing was an abortion). Fiasco, defeat, frustration, disaster, termination, aberration, disappointment, fruitless attempt, blunder. *Ant.* Full-term delivery; success.

Abortive, *adj.* **1.** Fruitless (an abortive venture). Unprofitable, profitless, unsuccessful, worthless, ineffective, failed, failing, unavailing, unfruitful, unproductive, unrewarding, ineffectual, miscarried, miscarrying, nugatory, idle, sterile, inoperative, barren, impotent. **2.** Incompletely or imperfectly developed (an abortive plan). Undeveloped, underdeveloped, rudimentary, untimely, immature, premature, stunted. *Ant.* Effective; consummated.

Abound, *v.* To overflow. Teem, exuberate, bristle, crowd, flourish, fill, thrive, overgrow, swell. *Ant.* Diminish.

About, 1. *adv.* Near in quantity or amount (about 680 pages of testimony). Approximately, approximating, nearly, close to, almost, more or less, around, well-nigh, circa, roughly, approaching, generally, virtually. See also "more or less." **2.** *prep.* Concerning (an affidavit about damages). Regarding, respecting, with reference to, with regard to, touching, having to do with, re. See also "in re."

About-face, *n.* Change of position or backtracking. See reverse, reversal.

Above 1. *adj.* Mentioned earlier (the above discussion). Aforementioned, abovementioned, former, previous, preceding, described earlier, said, supra. **2.** *adv.* Superior status (the court above). In a higher place, over, more powerful, higher in authority. **3.** *prep.* In excess of (above forty pages). Over, more than, exceeding, larger than, greater than.

Aboveboard, *adj.* See open (5, 7), honest, direct (6), explicit, outright, moral, bona fide.

Aboveground, *adj.* See surface (1).

ABP

ABP Arterial blood pressure.

Abrasion, *n.* See contusion, lesion, injury, wound.

Abrasive, *adj.* Causing irritation (counsel's abrasive behavior). Provoking, causing annoyance, rough, nasty, coarse, harsh, gnawing, cutting, biting. See also caustic. *Ant.* Soothing.

Abreast, *adj.* See informed, cognizant.

Abridge 1. *v.* To diminish (the order abridged the mayor's power). Lessen, curtail, minimize, narrow, cut, decrease, limit, truncate, subtract, trim, strip, deprive, divest. **2.** *adj.* Condensed (an abridged edition). Abbreviated, digested, shortened, summarized, synopsized, capsulized, scaled down, compressed, boiled down, abstracted, concentrated, *Ant.* Increase; expanded.

Abridgment, *n.* **1.** Reduction (abridgment of damages). Cutting down, lessening, decrease, curtailing, subtraction, limitation, restriction, diminution, restraint, contraction, retrenchment, narrowing. **2.** Summary (she prepared an abridgment of the testimony). Condensation, digest, shortened version, recapitulation, précis, epitome, synopsis, outline, brief, syllabus, abstract, compendium, conspectus, abbreviation, survey. *Ant.* Expansion; unabridged text.

Abroad, *adv.* Overseas. In a foreign land, out of the country, wandering, traveling, vacationing, away, at large.

Abrogate, *v.* To cancel (to abrogate the clerk's authority). Repeal, put an end to, end, terminate, annul, destroy, abandon, discard, reject, declare null and void, nullify, negate, quash, void, invalidate, abate, extinguish, obliterate, abolish, do away with, eliminate, rescind, set aside, reverse, undo, override, renounce, repudiate, abjure, withdraw, contradict, vacate, vitiate, disestablish, discontinue, veto, abnegate. *Ant.* Enact, establish.

Abrupt, *adj.* See caustic, impetuous, precipitate, sudden, rude.

Abscond, *v.* To flee in order to avoid legal process; to run away and hide in order to escape the consequences of something (the clerk absconded with the company files). Leave suddenly, leave clandestinely, escape, vanish, secretly flee, disappear, sneak away, slip away, bolt, take flight, depart hastily, secretly depart, travel covertly, withdraw, decamp, retreat, go, quit, desert, elude, make off, steal away, "split," lie concealed. *Ant.* Remain.

Absence, *n.* **1.** Failure to be present (absence of counsel). Nonpresence, nonappearance, nonattendance, truancy. **2.** Deficiency (absence of proof). Lack, want, unavailability, inadequacy, defect, scarcity, need, dearth, privation, vacuum, paucity, missing, omission, shortage, insufficiency, incompleteness. *Ant.* Presence; adequacy.

Absent, *adj.* **1.** Missing (absent without leave). Not present, away, abroad, gone, truant, off the premises, elsewhere, unavailable, out, nonattendant, being away from, at a distance from, not in company with, off somewhere. **2.** Inattentive (an absent expression). Absorbed in thought, preoccupied, blank, dreaming, lost, absorbed, distracted, removed, oblivious. *Ant.* Present; receptive.

Absent-minded, *adj.* See oblivious, careless, remiss, absent (2), negligent, reckless.

Absent without leave (AWOL) Not present at one's military position or assignment when there is no permission to be away, but without the intent to stay away permanently or to desert.

Absentee, *n., adj.* A person who is not present; pertaining to one who is not present (recorded as an absentee; absentee ballot, absentee landlord).

Absolute, *adj.* **1.** Unconditional (absolute authority). Free from all qualifications or restrictions, unrestricted, unqualified, total, unlimited, entire, utter, unbounded, unbound, unhampered, unimpeded, unrestrained, supreme, full, without exception, unreserved, arbitrary, autocratic, despotic, tyrannical, dictatorial. **2.** Complete (absolute nullity). Perfect, clear, whole, sheer, undiminished, comprehensive, undivided, genuine, untainted, utter, free from imperfection, unadulterated, ideal. **3.** Positive (absolute proof). Certain, affirmative, infallible, conclusive, decisive, exhaustive, final, whole, solid, comprehensive, explicit, unequivocal, unambiguous, demonstrative, accurate, confirmed, factual, reliable, sure, genuine, indubitable, unquestionable, commanding, independent, not dependent, autonomous, self-evident, self-determined, endless, infinite, consummate, best. *Ant.* Qualified; incomplete; vague.

Absolute liability Responsibility for an injury or damage regardless of whether it was caused innocently or through negligence or fault.

Absolutely, *adv.* **1.** To the fullest extent (absolutely sure). Completely, entirely, unconditionally, wholly, thoroughly, totally, categorically, without limit, fully, unqualifiedly, utterly. **2.** Positively (absolutely essential). Definitely, unquestionably, without doubt, beyond doubt, certainly, truly, in truth, affirmatively, actually, indeed, unequivocally, really, in reality, demonstrably, in fact, manifestly, indubitably, infallibly, explicitly, expressly, strictly, plainly, specifically, precisely, unambiguously, decidedly. *Ant.* Approximately; maybe.

Absolute nuisance A nuisance (i.e., an interference with the use of land or with a right that is common to the public) that will lead to liability regardless of how reasonable the defendant was in trying to avoid the interference.

Absolute privilege A defense that avoids liability for defamation irrespective of the motives of the defendant.

Absolution, *n.* An official declaration that the accused is innocent (absolution of the suspect). Exoneration, exculpation, acquittal, discharge, remission, clearance, cleansing, forgiveness, pardon, dispensation, indulgence, amnesty, release, dismissal of charge, liberation, freedom, vindication. *Ant.* Condemnation.

Absolve, *v.* **1.** To release from an obligation (she was absolved from her promise). Release, exempt, loosen, deliver, liberate, discharge, set free, excuse from, let out of. **2.** To free from guilt or blame (he is absolved of the minor charges). Acquit, exonerate, find innocent, clear, exculpate, vindicate, forgive, pardon, remit, excuse. *Ant.* Obligate; accuse.

Absorb, *v.* **1.** To drink in or assimilate (absorb the moisture). Sponge up, suck in, draw in, blot up, gather in, swallow up, digest, take in, incorporate, imbibe. See also inundate. **2.** To preoccupy or immerse (absorbed themselves in the trial). Enwrap, fascinate, rivet, mesmerize, seize. See also engage (2), enamor, consume. **3.** See centralize.

Absorbed, *adj.* See preoccupied, engaged.

Absorbing, *adj.* See intriguing, compelling, attractive, enjoyable.

Absorption, *n.* **1.** Assimilation (the absorption of the company). Appropriation, incorporation, devouring, destroying, consumption, engulfing. **2.** A collective bargaining term for the preservation of seniority rights when companies are merged.

Abstain, *v.* To hold back (abstain from any accusations). Refrain, resist, eschew, forbear, forgo, withhold, refuse, desist, decline, reject, turn down, discontinue, renounce, suppress, shun, spurn, abnegate. *Ant.* Indulge.

Abstemious, *adj.* See moderate (1), economical.

Abstention, *n.* The act of refraining (abstention from the work of the committee). Abstaining, nonparticipation, avoidance, nonindulgence, refusal, denying oneself, holding off, abstinence, eschewing, forbearance, inaction, self-deprivation, self-denial, restraint, withholding, self-mortification, puritanism, curbing, repression, suppression, shunning, spurning, curtailment. *Ant.* Indulgence.

Abstention doctrine A federal court can decline to exercise or postpone the exercise of its power or jurisdiction to hear a case in deference to the state court system. The federal court refrains from deciding the federal issues until the state court has resolved the state issues in the case.

Abstinence, *n.* See abstention, celibacy.

Abstract 1. *v.* To take away or remove (to abstract the funds). Steal, separate, disengage, detach, disunite, isolate, divide, part, appropriate, purloin, take dishonestly, seize, divert, disjoin, take out of context, eliminate, disassociate. **2.** *v.* To summarize (to abstract the documents). Abridge, condense, epitomize, synopsize, abbreviate, excerpt from, make an abstract of, make an outline of, compress, compact, shorten, reduce, digest, edit, cut down, curtail, prune. **3.** *n.* A summary (prepare an abstract of the file). Abridgment, outline, synopsis, digest, condensation, abbreviation, compendium, précis, epitome, extract, résumé, conspectus, syllabus, brief, sum and substance, capsule, draft, review, recapitulation, summary of salient points, compilation, analysis, consolidation, reduction, extract, prospectus, essence. **4.** *adj.* Theoretical (an abstract argument). Conceptual, remote, not concrete, unrelated, philosophical, metaphysical, intellectual, hypothetical, visionary, general, indefinite, ideal, impractical, pure. See also moot. **5.** *adj.* Obscure (an abstract approach). Complicated, difficult, hidden, vague, enigmatic, mysterious, impractical, abstruse, incomprehensible, attenuated. *Ant.* Unite; expand; complete text; concrete; clear.

Abstraction, *n.* **1.** The wrongful taking of something. See abstract (1), larceny. **2.** A generalization. Conceptualization, idea, theory, concept, generality, hypothesis, "pipe dream," impracticality, symbol, formula, notion, vague statement.

Abstract of title A summary of the documents and facts appearing in public records that affect title to land (e.g., prior deeds or conveyances of the land, liens, mortgages, covenants, wills, court orders).

Abstruse, *adj.* See obscure (1), complex (1).

Absurd, *adj.* Illogical (an absurd result). Irrational, could not have been intended, foolish, senseless, ridiculous, preposterous, unnatural, logically inconsistent, contradictory, idiotic, crazy, meaningless, unreasonable, ludicrous, unbelievable, nonsensical, incongruous, patently fallacious, stupid, drivel, infatuated, asinine, fatuous, inane, silly, moronic, anomalous, farcical, implausible, inconsistent, inconceivable. *Ant.* Rational.

Abundance, *n.* See sufficiency, excess, wealth, luxury, remainder (2), most, majority, mass (2), abundant.

Abundant, *adj.* Plentiful (abundant evidence). Ample, well-supplied, bountiful, bounteous, profuse, lavish, more than enough, sufficient, copious, replete, rich, teeming, overflowing, flowing, opulent, liberal, thick, much, lush, luxuriant, generous, extravagant, bristling, fruitful, productive. See also great (1), big, full, many, majority, mass (2), liberal (3). *Ant.* Scarce.

Abuse 1. *v.* To mistreat (abuse a child). Injure, degrade, oppress, harm, molest, debauch, wrong, damage, defile, malign, scold, disparage, berate, vilify, assail, flay, assault, batter, misemploy, misapply, misdirect, misappropriate, mismanage, mishandle, pervert, spoil, corrupt, debase, maltreat, revile, rail against, defame, libel, slander, rape, reproach, disgrace, dishonor, condemn, denounce, reprove, distort, exploit, pollute, victimize, ill use, ill treat, violate, prostitute, profane, desecrate, deceive, seduce, betray, disrespect, strike, wound, attack, torment, torture, persecute, belittle, ridicule. **2.** *n.* Misuse (abuse of discretion; abuse of confidence). Desecration, improper use, insult, condemnation, vituperation, invective, defamation, obloquy, billingsgate, insult, contumely, scurrility, opprobrium, denouncement, reproof, distortion, malfeasance, misfeasance, exploitation, maltreatment, misdirection, misappropriation, assault, battery, reproach, scorn, ridicule, aspersion, malversation, censure, denunciation, disparagement, belittlement, injury, damage. *Ant.* Assist; respect.

Abuse of discretion A decision that is manifestly unreasonable, arbitrary, biased, illogical, inconsistent, not supported by the evidence, or beyond the power of the decision maker. A decision that is clearly erroneous or unjust.

Abuse of process A tort that exists when there has been (a) a use of civil or criminal proceedings, (b) for an improper or ulterior purpose, (c) resulting in actual damage. Example: You have someone arrested in order to pressure him or her to repay a loan or to marry your child. The purpose of the criminal law is not to collect debts or to encourage marriage.

Abusive, *adj.* See offensive, caustic, malicious, hostile, derogatory, abuse.

Abut, *v.* To touch at one end (the two lots abut). Border on, adjoin, be contiguous, be adjacent to, be next to, reach, connect with, join, meet at one end, meet end to end, meet, touch, verge on, flank, attach, end at, lean against, conjoin, impinge, juxtapose.

Abutment, *n.* **1.** That which abuts or borders on something. Abutting, adjacency, contiguity, juxtaposition, adjoining, union, connection, attachment, joint, junction, contact, being contiguous, being adjacent. **2.** Support. Prop, bulwark, brace, buttress, rampart, pier, stay, terminal support.

Abuttals, *n.* End lines of land. See boundary.

Abutter, *n.* One whose property abuts, is contiguous, or joins at a border or boundary where no other land, road, or street intervenes.

Abysmal, *adj.* Deep or bottomless (abysmal shame). Boundless, immeasurable, vast, huge, enormous. See also big, extreme (1).

Abyss, *n.* A chasm or bottomless pit (fall into the abyss). Cavity, void, gorge, infinitude, limbo, depth, gully, crevasse, crack, chaos, inferno, hell.

Academic 1. *adj.* Speculative or theoretical. See hypothetical, abstract (4), moot. **2.** *adj.* Scholastic. Educational, scholarly, erudite, pedagogical, pedantic, formal, collegiate, studious, bookish, cultured. See also learned, literary (2), cultivated, demonstrative (1). **3.** *n.* See teacher, scholar, student.

Academician, *n.* See teacher.

Academy, *n.* See school.

Accede, *v.* **1.** To give one's agreement (accede to the request). Consent, agree, assent, acquiesce, yield, comply, concur, approve, cooperate, allow, permit, let, concede, grant, subscribe, admit, endorse, defer to, go along with, surrender to, abide by, acknowledge, respond affirmatively, capitulate, back down, obey, conform, grant, vouchsafe. **2.** To attain an office or position; to take control of (accede to the throne). Inherit, assume, succeed to, reach. *Ant.* Decline.

Accelerate, *v.* To cause something to happen sooner (when the future interest was accelerated, it vested earlier than originally contemplated). Hasten, quicken, step up, speed up, rush, spur, advance, dispatch, facilitate, augment, promote, stimulate, impel, intensify. See also precipitate (1), expedite. *Ant.* Delay, decelerate.

Accelerated depreciation Depreciating property in such a way that the deductions are greater during the early years of the life of the asset. Methods of this kind of depreciation include double declining balance and sum of the years' digits.

Acceleration, *n.* Speeding up, hastening, facilitation, shortening the time for the vesting in possession of an expectant interest. See advancement, advance (3).

Acceleration clause A clause in a contract (e.g., mortgage, promissory note) stating that if a certain event happens, the payment schedule under the contract is advanced. For example, a mortgage might provide that the entire loan must be repaid immediately if a single payment is missed or if the mortgaged property is transferred.

Accelerator, *n.* See catalyst.

Accent 1. *n.* Stress or intonation. Emphasis, pronunciation, accentuation, tone, articulation, speech pattern, modulation, enunciation. **2.** *v.* To stress or accentuate. Underline, italicize, mark, punctuate, highlight, underscore, intensify. See

Accent

also emphasize.

Accentuate, *v.* See accent (2).

Accept, *v.* **1.** To receive with approval or with the intent to retain (she accepted the goods). Take without protest, receive willingly, take possession of, secure, gain. **2.** To assent to (he accepts the offer). Acquiesce in, approve, adopt, embrace, accede to, concur, admit as satisfactory, authorize, endorse, ratify, sanction, honor, acknowledge, concede, believe, yield, accommodate oneself to, resign oneself to, go along with, suffer, tolerate, endure, reconcile oneself to, submit to, bear, undertake, assume responsibility for, assume, admit, avow. *Ant.* Reject.

Acceptable, *adj.* See admissible, proper, adequate, worthy, competent.

Acceptably, *adv.* See well (2).

Acceptance, *n.* Acquiescence (acceptance of guilt). Consent, approbation, approval, acknowledgment, favorable reception, endorsement, ratification, acceding, adoption, accession, agreement, reception, acquisition, affirmation, confirmation, recognition, resignation, toleration, sanction, satisfaction, submission. *Ant.* Rejection, opposition.

Acceptance of check The signed engagement of the drawee (usually a bank) to honor a draft (a document for the transfer of money) as presented.

Acceptance of deed Acts, conduct, or words that manifest an intent to take title to the property described in the deed.

Acceptance of goods There are three ways a buyer can accept goods: (a) by signifying to the seller that the goods are conforming or that the buyer will accept them in spite of their nonconformity, (b) by failing to make an effective rejection, and (c) by doing an act inconsistent with the seller's ownership.

Acceptance of offer The assent by the person to whom an offer has been made (offeree) to enter into a binding agreement with the person making the offer (offeror) according to the terms of the offer.

Accepted, *adj.* See common (1).

Acceptor, *n.* Someone who becomes liable on a draft by an acceptance of it. See acceptance of check.

Access, *n.* **1.** Opportunity to reach (access to the commissioner). Opportunity to communicate with, admittance, entrée, entrance, approachability, accessibility, availability. **2.** The availability of contact for a designated purpose (access in order to inspect the land and the records). Entry, approach, avenue, liberty to approach, passage, passageway, route, gateway, means of access, means of approach, right of entry, opening, inlet, path, ingress. *Ant.* Inaccessibility.

Accessible, *adj.* Easy to reach (an accessible court). Reachable, nearby, at hand, on hand, within reach, available, obtainable, achievable, attainable, vulnerable, persuasible, persuadable, easily influenced, susceptible, approachable, easily approached, public, unrestricted, securable, obliging, weak, unguarded, compliant, informal. *Ant.* Remote.

Accession, *n.* **1.** Increase, addition (the accession of two offices). Augmentation, accretion, increment, supplement, extension, appurtenance, accrual, accumulation, continuation, adjunction, adjunct, appendage, fixture, adhesion, annexation, attachment, combination, fastening, fusion, incorporation, amplification, broadening, developing, joining, merger, uniting, supplementation, expansion, growth, swelling, aggrandizement, widening. **2.** A country's acceptance of a treaty (Britain's accession). Assent, agreement, acceding, consent, concordance, concord, acquiescence, concurrence, acceptance. **3.** Taking control or possession of something (accession to office). Succession, elevation, inauguration, elevation, inheritance, investiture. *Ant.* Decrease; rejection.

Accessory, *n.* **1.** Someone who, without being present, helps another to commit a crime (accessory before or after the fact). Cohort, conspirator, co-conspirator, accomplice, conniver, comrade, consort, abettor, collaborator, particeps criminis, auxiliary, confederate, helper, facilitator, associate, assistant, contributor, aide, partner, coadjutor, colleague, encourager, participant, party, companion, planner, follower. **2.** Something added or joined; a subordinate part; an incident (computer accessories). Attachment, supplement, supplementary part, addition, adjunct, extension, appendage, accompaniment, subordinate element, subsidiary, concomitant, ancillary, auxiliary, accretion, increment, component, adornment, incidental, collateral, nonessential, secondary, contributory, adventitious, excess, complement, appurtenant.

Accessory after the fact A person, knowing that a crime has been committed, who receives, harbors, or conceals, the offender (the principal) in order to assist the latter to escape arrest or punishment.

Accessory before the fact Someone who procures, counsels, commands, abets, or encourages another (the principal) to commit a crime. The accessory before the fact is not present at the time and place of the crime.

Accessory building A structure that is detached from the main building on the land. An outbuilding; a subordinate structure.

Accessory contract A subsidiary contract (e.g., mortgage, suretyship) made to assure performance of another contract.

Accessory use In zoning law, the use of land in a way that is customarily incidental or subsidiary to the principal use of the land. For example, in a residential area, it may be an accessory use of land to park a commercial vehicle in the driveway of one's home if the vehicle is used to travel to and from work.

Accident, *n.* **1.** An unexpected occurrence (discovery by accident). Unforeseen event, chance occurrence, unintended occurrence, fortuitous event, fortuitous circumstance, unanticipated occurrence, hap, happenstance, undesigned event, contingency, chance, fortune, luck, fate. **2.** An unexpected misfortune (motor vehicle accident). Mishap, casualty, mischance, contretemps, miscarriage, unfortunate event, untoward occurrence, disaster, act of God, tragedy, catastrophe, cataclysm, calamity, affliction, adversity, collision, wreck, crash, misadventure, ruin, collapse, mistake, oversight, blunder. *Ant.* Plan, certainty; anticipated benefit.

Accidental, *adj.* **1.** Happening unexpectedly, happening by chance (accidental meeting). Fortuitous, unintentional, unforeseen, unplanned, unpremeditated, unexpected, freak, unanticipated, haphazard, adventitious, unwitting, undesigned, contingent, unthinking, serendipitous, casual, random. **2.** Nonessential. Accessory, supplemental, incidental, secondary, subordinate, collateral, superfluous, extraneous, dispensable, expendable, extra, circumstantial, parenthetical, irrelevant. *Ant.* Intended, planned; essential.

Accidental cause A causal entity that could not have been foreseen.

Accidental means (in insurance policy) Something that happens by chance or fortuitously without intention or design and which is unexpected, unusual, and unforeseen.

Accident arising out of employment (worker's compensation) An occurrence that is neither expected, designed, nor intentionally caused by the worker. A causal connection exists, however, between the occurrence and the job. There are four basic categories of accidents in the Worker's Compensation Act: (a) a sudden, unexpected traumatic event such as a fall or blow, (b) an unusual exertion in the course of work causing an unexpected and sudden injury, (c) an unusual pathological result of an ordinary condition of work, and (d) sudden and unexpected injury caused by failure of an employer to furnish medical care to an employee.

11

Accident-prone, *adj.* Having a tendency to become involved in accidents. See susceptible.

Acclaim, *v., n.* See honor (2), appreciate (3); tribute (2), acclamation.

Acclamation, *n.* Enthusiastic acceptance of something, usually without counting individual votes in favor of the acceptance (the amendment was approved by acclamation). Shouting approval, applause, burst of applause, plaudit, cheer, ovation, approbation, cry, outcry. See also indorsement (2), tribute (2). *Ant.* Boos, censure.

Acclimate, Acclimatize, *v.* See adapt, accommodate (2).

Accolade, *n.* See celebration (3), honor (3), acclamation, prize (1).

Accommodate, *v.* **1.** To do a favor or service (the clerk accommodated us by granting an extension). Assist, serve, oblige, supply, aid, provide, furnish, help out, indulge, lend a hand, abet, entertain, shelter, house, harbor, administer to, comfort, coddle, defer, yield. **2.** To adjust; to make suitable (the mediator was not able to accommodate the differences). Reconcile, conform, fit, suit, fashion, attune, harmonize, make consistent, coordinate, integrate, blend, acclimate, equalize, modify, bring into line, bring to terms, adapt, settle, balance, square. *Ant.* Impede; disorient.

Accommodated party One to whom the credit of the accommodation party (see this phrase) is loaned.

Accommodating, *adj.* Indulgent, obliging, agreeable, or yielding. See cooperative (2), conciliatory, flexible, malleable, amenable, permissive, charitable, benevolent.

Accommodation, *n.* **1.** A favor done for someone, usually without payment or consideration (e.g., signing a note to help someone secure a loan). Convenience, benefit, advantage, courtesy, kindness, help, aid, indulgence, assistance, service. **2.** An adjustment (reach an accommodation). Adaptation, settlement, agreement, concord, modification, reconciliation, harmonization, conformity, equalizing, balancing, reorientation, acclimatization. **3.** Lodging. See home (1), lodge (3). *Ant.* Hindrance; inflexibility.

Accommodation bill See accommodation paper.

Accommodation indorser See accommodation party.

Accommodation maker Someone who signs a promissory note or other instrument as a surety to lend his or her credit to another.

Accommodation note See accommodation paper.

Accommodation paper A promissory note or bill of exchange that is signed by a person in order to help someone else secure credit or a loan. The person signing is the accommodation party.

Accommodation party Someone who signs commercial paper (see this phrase) as maker, acceptor, drawer, or indorser for the purpose of lending his or her name to another party on the paper.

Accompany, *v.* To go with (the clerk accompanied us to the record room). Follow, escort, go along, be together with, associate with, convoy, chaperon, wait on, consort with, go hand in hand with, coexist, coincide, join, combine, link, affiliate, match, attach, occur with, be connected with, protect, support, conduct, guard, be near enough to be able to help, exercise supervision over, advise, counsel, guide, caution. *Ant.* Abandon.

Accompanying, *adj.* See accessory (2), auxiliary, supplemental.

Accomplice, *n.* A person who knowingly, voluntarily, and intentionally participates with someone else in the promotion, facilitation, or commission of a crime (he was tried as an accomplice to the robbery). Accessory, principal, abettor, aider and abettor, crime participant, agent, partner in crime, confederate, collaborator, assistant, cohort, contriver, conniver, supporter, ally, associate, conspirator, co-conspirator, co-defendant, fellow criminal, crony, colleague, advisor, instigator, inciter, particeps criminis, socius criminis, helper, confrere. *Ant.* Antagonist.

Accomplish, *v.* See attain, carry (5), complete (1), perfect (3), close (1), commit (2), discharge (2), perform, realize (2), conclude.

Accomplished, *adj.* See perfect (1), able, competent, learned, brilliant, qualified, apt (3, 4).

Accomplishment, *n.* See perfection (1), completion, act (3), performance (1).

Accord 1. *n.* An agreement or contract to settle an existing dispute; both sides agree to accept something other than what was originally claimed to be due (reach an accord). Compromise, settlement, adjustment, accommodation, conciliation, reconciliation, harmonization, arbitration. **2.** *n.* The state of agreement (the opinion was in accord with the views of the bar). Conformity, consonance, harmony, sympathy, unanimity, consistency, coherence, symmetry, unison, accordance, concurrence, rapport, concert, consent, understanding. **3.** *v.* To grant or concede (he was accorded the highest honor). Bestow, present, render, cede, allow, give, vouchsafe, yield, endow, bequeath. **4.** *v.* Misc. Correspond, agree, concur, harmonize, conform, approve, allow, acquiesce, consent, reconcile, accommodate, match, adjust, adapt, attune, parallel, resemble. *Ant.* Discord; disagreement; refuse.

Accordance, *n.* Agreement (in accordance with the court's order). Harmony, accord, conformity, consonance, concurrence, concert, unanimity, sympathy, consistence, coherence, symmetry, unison, rapport, consent, understanding. *Ant.* Violation.

Accord and satisfaction An agreement or contract to settle an existing dispute whereby both sides agree to accept something other than what they initially claimed was due. See accord. The accord is the agreement. The satisfaction is the execution or performance of the agreement which in effect eliminates the original dispute. The initial debt or claim is extinguished.

Accordingly, *adv.* See consequently.

According to, *prep.* Consistent with (according to custom). In accordance with, as indicated by, on the authority of, in line with, conformable to, in the light of. *Ant.* Contrary to.

Accost, *v.* **1.** To approach someone in an offensive way (the defendant accosted my client). Speak to suddenly, assail, approach boldly, confront, affront, assault, attack, insult, annoy, offend, outrage, bother, dare, pester, nab, buttonhole, hail, invade, harass, molest, badger, pursue, greet, address, salute. See also challenge. **2.** To solicit sex (the prostitute accosted the stranger). Proposition, lure.

Accouchement, *n.* Childbirth. Parturition, delivery, bringing forth, giving birth.

Account 1. *n.* A financial record or statement of debts, credits, transactions, etc. (a computer is used to help keep the accounts). Ledger, register, tally, report, inventory, score, computation, calculation, list of receipts and payments, record of debits and credits, record of business dealings, journal, bookkeeping, books, balance sheet, bill, invoice. **2.** *n.* A list of reasons or explanations (the account of the witness was unbelievable). Story, version, justification, interpretation, description, chronicle, history, enumeration, appraisal, brief, summation, summary, recapitulation, review, narrative, recital, rehearsal, detail, reckoning, elucidation, explication, commentary, rationalization, portrayal, report, exposition. **3.** *n.* Worth (the evidence was of no account). Note, importance, repute, reputation, distinction, consequence, quality, value, consideration, standing, rank, import, esteem. **4.** *v.* To provide an explanation or reckoning (the witness was not able to account for the inconsistency). Explain, clear up, assign the cause, interpret, answer for, elucidate, expound.

Accountability, *n.* Subject to be called to account (the lack of accountability in the decision-making process). Responsibility, amenability, answerability, liability, comprehensibility.

Accountable, *adj.* **1.** Responsible (accountable for one's actions). Liable, likely to be called to account, answerable, amenable, subject to pay, punishable, censurable, chargeable, beholden, duty-bound, legally obligated, under obligation, open to. See also actionable, bound (1). **(2)** Explainable (an accountable summary). Definable, describable, capable of being accounted for, explicable, translatable. *Ant.* Immune; inexplicable.

Accountable receipt A written acknowledgment that something (e.g., money) has been received and that a duty therefore arises under the agreement to respond (e.g., by delivering goods, by making payment).

Account annexed A simple method of pleading a common account; a pleading in account form (e.g., of goods sold and delivered).

Accountant, *n.* A person who is skilled in keeping financial records and accounts (the accountant performed an audit). Bookkeeper, auditor, controller (comptroller), C.P.A., teller, bursar, examiner. See also treasurer, recorder.

Account current An open or running account; an account that is periodically settled.

Account debtor The person who has obligations on an account.

Accounting, *n.* **1.** A bookkeeping system for recording business transactions, balancing debits and credits, settling accounts, maintaining internal control, etc. **2.** A statement or report on the financial condition of an enterprise. **3.** A settling of an account with a determination of what is owed. **4.** The payment of profits made from the unfair use by the defendant of the plaintiff's trademark or trade name.

Accounting identity A statement that two numerical things are equal by accepted definition (e.g., "assets equal liabilities plus stockholder's equity").

Account payable A regular business debt not yet paid; a debt owed by a business, usually on open account.

Account receivable A regular business debt not yet collected; a debt owed to a business, usually on open account.

Account render An action at common law when a person fails to make an accounting (e.g., if an administrator of an estate fails to render an account of expenses and payments, etc.).

Account rendered A statement of debts presented to the debtor by the creditor.

Account sales An account rendered by a sales agent, consignee, factor, or broker stating the sales of goods, the prices, the commissions, the expenses, and balance due the consignor or constituent.

Account stated An account that has been accepted as correct by the debtor and creditor; an agreement on the accuracy of the account stating the balance due.

Accouple, *v.* To join, unite, marry.

Accouter, Accoutre, *v.* See equip.

Accouterment, Accoutrement, *n.* See equipment.

Accredit, *v.* **1.** To acknowledge or recognize officially (the law school is accredited). Authorize, certify, license, endorse, empower, sanction, give official status, vouch for, qualify, authenticate, validate, approve, guarantee, commend, credit, recommend, attest. See also commission (5). **2.** To accept the credentials of a foreign envoy. **3.** To send an envoy to a foreign country with credentials. **4.** To attribute (the quote is accredited to Holmes). Credit, assign, ascribe.

Accreditation, *n.* See approval, clearance (3), commission (1), accredit.

Accretion, *n.* **1.** Growth in size by accumulation or addition (the deed did not cover accretions). Increment, growing to a thing, aggregation, increase by adhesion, concretion, enlargement, joining, uniting, attachment, appendage, increase, extension, augmentation, accession, supplement, accrual, building up, expansion. **2.** A growing together. Fusion, aggregation, coalescence, consolidation, adhesion. **3.** The gradual and imperceptible addition of soil to the shore of waterfront property. See alluvion, avulsion, reliction. **4.** The incorporation of employees to an already existing bargaining unit when there is such a community of interest among the entire group that the additional employees have no separate unit identity.

Accroach, *v.* **1.** To exercise power without authority; to infringe. See annex (2). **2.** To attract; to acquire.

Accrual, *n.* Something that is accrued; something that comes into existence or that grows in amount. Increase, enlargement, accretion, expansion, accumulation, growth, maturing.

Accrual basis A method of accounting that shows expenses incurred and income earned for a given period (e.g., a year), although such expenses and income may not have actually been paid or received during this period. For example, an amount is included in gross income when a right to receive it exists regardless of whether the amount has actually been received. See cash basis.

Accrual method of accounting See accrual basis.

Accrual of cause of action The time at which the right to bring the action or suit arises (e.g., when the breach of contract occurs, when the last act necessary to complete the tort occurs, when the injury occurs, when the plaintiff discovers the error that caused the injury). See cause of action, statute of limitation.

Accrue, *v.* **1.** To grow in amount (interest accrues monthly). Increase, augment, accumulate, gain, amass, expend, enlarge, total, redound, cumulate, add on, add to, acquire, appreciate, broaden, extend, escalate, multiply, swell, supplement, annex, build up, collect, advance, aggrandize. **2.** To come into existence (the right accrued). Vest, come into force, come to pass, become a present right, become complete, become a present demand, mature, become enforceable, fall due, become due, result, inure, take effect, arise, issue, develop, execute, perfect, ripen. *Ant.* Decrease; stagnate.

Accrued alimony and child support payments Payments for alimony and child support that are due but not yet paid. See arrearages.

Accrued expense An expense that has been incurred but not yet paid.

Accrued liability An expense that is recognized or chargeable but not yet payable.

Accruing, *adj.* In the early stages; developing. See inchoate.

Acculturation, *n.* **1.** A change in the culture of a group due to association with another culture. See civilization. **2.** The methods or process by which a culture is absorbed by an individual from birth.

Accumulate, *v.* To collect (the firm accumulated large debts). Pile up, amass, cumulate, bring together, stockpile, assemble, gather, aggregate, hoard, agglomerate, store, husband, save, garner, congregate, combine, multiply, compile, enlarge, accrue, acervate, expand, warehouse, treasure, conserve, reserve, cache, stow away, deposit, increase.

Accumulated earnings tax A tax imposed on corporations that accumulate their earnings beyond the reasonable needs of the business rather than distribute them as dividends to the stockholders.

Accumulated legacy That part of an estate which has not yet been paid to the beneficiaries.

Accumulation, *n.* **1.** Increase by additions (accumulation of property). Amassment, agglomeration, aggregation, assemblage, conglomeration, accrual, amount accrued, supply, store, congeries, cumulation, cumulus, heap, pile, stockpile, accretion, reserve, concentration, cluster, holdings, acervation. **2.** An accumulation of a fund by an executor or trustee occurs when he or she amasses rents, dividends, and other income received, treats it as capital, invests it, makes new

15

capital of the income derived therefrom, and then invests that capital. The capital and income procured in this way constitute accumulations. **3.** The separate property of a wife while living separately from her husband in a community property state.

Accumulation trust A trust in which the income is collected or accumulated for a period of time before being distributed to beneficiaries.

Accumulative, *adj.* Resulting from additions or accumulations (accumulative funds). Additive, cumulative, aggregative, augmentative.

Accumulative dividend A dividend on preferred stock which is to be paid before any distribution to holders of common stock. The dividend is accumulated before distribution to holders of common stock. See cumulative preferred dividend.

Accumulative judgment A second sentence that is to be added to the first. When the sentence imposed by the first judgment has been served, the defendant begins serving the sentence imposed by the second judgment. See consecutive sentences.

Accumulative legacy An additional gift of personal property in a will.

Accuracy, *n.* See veracity, fact, validity, precise, accurate.

Accurate, *adj.* Precise; free from errors; conforming to a standard (an accurate report). Correct, true, truthful, exact, strict, unerring, faithful, rigorous, trustworthy, right, particular, reliable, certain, careful, meticulous, scrupulous, proper, punctilious, perfect, faultless, verifiable, actual, factual, authoritative, sure, dependable, veracious, authentic, valid, bona fide, unquestionable, conscientious, scientific, unimpeachable, genuine, unambiguous, thorough. *Ant.* Defective, false.

Accursed, *adj.* Damned, cursed, condemned, or doomed. See abandoned (1), corrupt (1), base (2).

Accusation, *n.* A formal charge that a person has committed a crime or other misconduct (an accusation of fraud). Denouncement, denunciation, accusal, imputation, incrimination, gravamen, crimination, allegation, aspersion, inculpation, condemnation, censure, invective, recrimination, reprehension, citation, complaint, presentment, indictment, bill of indictment, information, arraignment, impeachment, filing of charges, preferring charges, reproach, insinuation. *Ant.* Exoneration.

Accusatory body An entity that determines whether enough evidence exists to accuse someone of a crime (e.g., grand jury).

Accusatory stage The stage of a criminal investigation during which the focus is on an individual who has been taken into custody and from whom a confession or incriminating statements are being sought.

Accuse, *v.* To bring formal charges against someone for a crime or other misconduct (accused of fraud). Call to account, blame, fault, find at fault, charge, arraign, indict, impeach, incriminate, criminate, inculpate, complain against, lodge a complaint against, inform against, reprove, reproach, rebuke, cite, challenge, tax, censure, criticize, denounce, upbraid, cast aspersions, impugn, defame, reprobate, prosecute, implicate, attack, denunciate, recriminate, involve, expose. *Ant.* Exonerate.

Accused, *n.* The person against whom criminal proceedings are instigated; the defendant in a criminal case; the target of a criminal investigation (the accused stood before the judge). Suspect, alleged culprit, alleged wrongdoer, suspected criminal, respondent. *Ant.* Accuser.

Accuser, *n.* A person who claims that a specific individual has committed a crime (confront her accuser). Accusant, informer, incriminator, plaintiff, prosecutor, recriminator, reviler, libelant, denouncer, indicter, complainant. *Ant.* Accused.

Accustom, *v.* To acquaint, ingrain, inure, or familiarize. See adapt, addict (2).

Accustomed, *adj.* **1.** Customary (the store's accustomed manner of doing business). Habitual, traditional, by habit, established, by established course of conduct, usual, often used, conventional, common, commonplace, normal, regular, set, routine, ordinary, prevalent, prevailing, expected, chronic, confirmed, fixed, natural, well-known, everyday. **2.** Familiar through repetition (lawyers are accustomed to jargon). Used to, inured to, given to, acclimated, habituated, seasoned, addicted, adapted, ingrained, familiarized, acquainted, prone, conditioned, hardened. *Ant.* Rare; unfamiliar.

AC/DC See bisexual.

Ace, *adj.* See expert (2).

Acequia, *n.* An irrigation canal; a ditch.

Acerbate, *v.* See harass, disturb.

Acerbity, *n.* Sharpness, sourness, or bitterness. Acidity, irascibility, acrimony, petulance, ill humor, virulence, irritability, rancor, peevishness.

Acervate, *v.* See accumulate.

Acetylene, *n.* A flammable or explosive gas.

Ache, *v., n.* See suffer (1), bemoan, cry (1), desire (1), pain, affliction.

Achievable, *adj.* See feasible.

Achieve *v.* See attain, complete, realize (2), close (1), commit (2), perfect (3), acquire, perform, conclude.

Achievement, *n.* Success, fulfillment, feat, or consummation. See completion, performance (1), perfection (1).

Acid, *n., adj.* See drug; caustic, biting, cutting, offensive, malicious.

Acidhead, *n.* A frequent user of LSD. See addict (1).

Acknowledge, *v.* **1.** To certify (she acknowledged the deed). Admit, admit as genuine, admit the truth of, recognize, profess, confess, avow, confirm, concede, assume responsibility for, authenticate, grant, own, uphold, declare valid, endorse, subscribe to, accept, allow, approve, acquiesce, consent, accede, yield, attest to, assent, take notice of, extend cognizance to, take cognizance of, ratify, defer to, testify, notice, realize, ascribe, divulge, reveal, proclaim, publish, bear witness, depose, vouch for. **2.** To express appreciation for (the lawyer acknowledged the favor). Be grateful for, express gratitude for, thank, reward, requite, repay, compensate. **3.** To take notice of (the judge acknowledged our presence). Recognize, respond, declare, accept, concede, approve, signal, notice. *Ant.* Repudiate; disregard.

Acknowledgment, *n.* **1.** An affirmation that something is genuine (acknowledgment of a deed). Confirmation, admission, concession, declaration, testimony, confession, avowal, ratification, profession, endorsement, authentication, validation, consent, certification. **2.** Recognition (acknowledgment of a debt). Verification, acceptance, assent, agreement, acquiescence, response, reply. **3.** See gratitude. *Ant.* Rejection.

ACLU American Civil Liberties Union.

Acme, *n.* See apex, altitude, extreme (3).

A coelo usque ad centrum From the sky to the center of the earth (describing the extent of one's ownership of land).

Acolyte, *n.* See assistant.

Acquaint, *v.* Familiarize, notify, make known. See introduce; acquaintance.

Acquaintance, *n.* **1.** Someone with whom you are familiar but not close or intimate (a former acquaintance). Companion, associate, colleague, confrere, casual friend, distant friend, person slightly known, comrade; relationship, dealings, fellowship. **2.** A personal knowledge of something (an acquaintance with computers). Familiarity, experience, awareness, knowledge, information, cognizance, training, consciousness, perception, understanding, apprehension, grasp, attachment, intimacy, association, affinity. *Ant.* Stranger; ignorance.

Acquainted, *adj.* Familiar (acquainted with the new rules). Known, known thor-

17

oughly, personally known, apprised, aware of, made aware of, briefed, informed, notified, conversant with, knowledgeable, told, communicated to, attuned to, advised, educated, enlightened, cognizant of, conscious of, associated with. *Ant.* Ignorant.

Acquest, *n.* An estate acquired newly or by purchase.

Acquêts, *n.* Property that has been acquired by purchase or gift, not by succession.

Acquiesce, *v.* To consent passively or without enthusiasm; to consent by implication, e.g., through silence (acquiesce in the removal). Accept grudgingly, endure, tolerate, suffer, submit, admit, concede, acknowledge, resign, yield, "stomach," "swallow," give in, defer, bend, bow, surrender, accede, relent, give way, "knuckle under," "throw in the towel," prostrate, succumb, comply, "bite the dust," capitulate. *Ant.* Object.

Acquiescence, *n.* Passive consent or submission; implied consent through the failure to object; conduct that would lead others to conclude that you consent or that you have waived your rights (the committee's acquiescence in the director's plan). Tacit consent, tacit approval, tacit assent, lack of disapproval, nonresistance, quiet approval, deference, concurrence, agreement, surrender, capitulation, submissiveness, acceptance, resignation, accession, allowance, acknowledgment, sufferance, compliance, willingness, stoicism, fatalism, obedience, forbearance, tolerance, passivity, docility, admission, sanction.

Acquire, *v.* To obtain; to gain ownership of; to secure by one's own efforts (acquire an interest). Procure, achieve, amass, attain, reach, get, reap, come into possession of, appropriate, win, earn, take over, purchase, realize, receive, collect, cultivate, capture, inherit, derive, garner, annex, exact, extort, wrest from. *Ant.* Release.

Acquired surplus The surplus that exists in one company that is purchased or taken over by another.

Acquisition, *n.* Obtaining ownership or possession; the thing obtained is also referred to as the acquisition (the acquisition of the asset; a rare acquisition). Procurement, obtainment, collection, amassing, gathering, acquirement, realization, purchase, accumulation, annexation, accession, increment, assumption, attainment, receipt, reception, confiscation, seizure, capture, takeover, expropriation, assets, possession, property, gain, prize, proceeds, gift, benefit, inheritance, find. *Ant.* Release.

Acquisitive, *adj.* Grasping (an acquisitive offense is a crime against ownership or possession). Greedy, acquiring, covetous, predatory, mercenary, materialistic, avid, accumulative, hoarding, sordid. *Ant.* Self-denying.

Acquit, *v.* **1.** To release someone from an obligation (to acquit her of any further responsibility under the contract). Discharge, exempt, forgive, unburden, satisfy, remit, deliver from, excuse, free, liberate. **2.** To declare that the accused is innocent of the crime (the jury acquitted him of rape). Exonerate, absolve, exculpate, vindicate, certify innocence, declare innocent, judicially discharge, declare not guilty, purge of an accusation, let off, pardon, grant amnesty to, condone. *Ant.* Hold to; convict.

Acquittal, *n.* **1.** A discharge or release from an obligation or engagement (e.g., a contract debt). **2.** A formal declaration or certification of innocence of a crime. See pardon, exoneration (1), acquit, exculpate.

Acquittance, *n.* A written discharge from an obligation.

Acre, *n.* A quantity of land: 4,840 square yards or 43,560 square feet or 160 square rods.

Acrimonious, *adj.* See caustic, biting, cutting, hostile, malicious.

Acrimony, *n.* See animus (2).

Acrobat, *n.* A person with skills of agility and body movement. Trapeze artist, gymnast, balancer, contortionist, stunt person, tumbler, tightrope walker.

Acrophobia, *n.* Fear of high places. See illness, disease.

Across, *adv., prep.* From one side to the opposite side of. From side to side, over, on or to the other side of, extending the width of, laterally, diagonally, crosswise, athwart, over, crossways, thwart, transversely, facing, fronting, opposite to, intersect.

Act 1. *n.* Something done voluntarily as opposed to convulsive movements or in reaction to coercive outside forces (the act of pulling the trigger). External manifestation of the will, expression of will, expression of purpose, execution of intent, exercise of one's own power, intentional conduct. **2.** *n.* A law passed by the legislature (Social Security Act). Statute, statutory law, edict, decree, legislation, resolution, joint resolution, mandate, measure, determination, resolve, enactment, ordinance, code, rule, regulation, precept, prescript, bill. **3.** *n.* A deed, something done (the act of winning). Performance, accomplishment, achievement, action, measure, consummation, effect, execution, exploit, feat, motion, move, movement, operation, transaction, work, undertaking, reality, step, commission, course, enterprise, maneuver, task, proceeding, job. **4.** *n.* A pretense (his fainting was an act). Fraud, sham, show, fake. **5.** *v.* To perform (you must act on the authority you have). Function, fulfill a function, operate, execute, carry into execution, transact, do, administer, carry into effect, exert energy, work, behave, conduct, enact, represent; portray, pretend, feign, play, play the part of, imitate, personate, impersonate, masquerade, simulate, stage, characterize, comport oneself, conduct oneself.

Acta publica Things of general knowledge and concern.

Acting, *adj.* Temporarily functioning as or substituting for (acting director). Provisional, pro tem, contingent, surrogate, ersatz, taking the place of, deputy, standing in the place of, filling in for someone else, representing. See also interim.

Acting within scope of employment See scope of employment.

Act in pais Something done out of court without being a part of the court's official proceedings.

Actio damni injuria Action for damages due to negligent or other wrongful acts.

Actio ex contractu A contract action.

Actio ex delicto A tort action.

Action, *n.* **1.** A proceeding in a court of law in which one seeks the redress of an alleged wrong (an action for defamation). Lawsuit, suit, case, legal proceeding, judicial proceeding, judicial redress, cause, action at law, litigation, inquisition, hearing, trial, contest, dispute, controversy, hearing, prosecution, process, procedure, claim, petition. **2.** Conduct; something done (unwarranted action). Performance, behavior, act, activity, reaction, transaction, accomplishment, operation, execution, deed, course of conduct, functioning, doing, thing, feat, implementation, achievement, exploit, motion, movement, mechanism, administration, enforcement, carrying out, engagement, work, job, business, play, exertion, agency, effort, force, influence, instrumentality, measure, battle, conflict, encounter, combat, contest.

Actionable, *adj.* Pertaining to that which can become the basis of a lawsuit; pertaining to that which can be remedied by a court action (actionable fraud). Justiciable, litigable, remediable, accountable, suable, responsible, chargeable, amenable, answerable.

Actionable per se Pertaining to words that are defamatory in themselves. Pertaining to defamation that can be established without pleading and proving special damages. Words that are actionable per se fall into four categories: Statements that (a) accuse plaintiff of a crime, (b) adversely affect the plaintiff's trade, calling, or profession, (c) accuse the plaintiff of having a loathsome disease, and (d) accuse the plaintiff of unchastity.

Actionable tort A wrong that fits within all of the elements of one of the available torts.

Action at common law An action governed by the common law rather than an action based on a statute, equitable remedies, or continental (civil) law.

Action at law A judicial proceeding to redress an alleged wrong, usually involving the right to a jury trial. See action (1).

Action ex contractu An action for the breach of a promise in a contract.

Action ex delicto An action of tort; an action arising out of fault, misconduct, or malfeasance; an action arising from a breach of duty growing out of a contract.

Action in equity An action seeking equitable remedy or relief.

Action in personam See in personam.

Action in rem See in rem.

Action malum in se See malum in se.

Action malum prohibitum See malum prohibitum.

Action of assumpsit See assumpsit (2).

Actio non datur non damnificato There is no action given to one who is not injured.

Action on the case Also called trespass on the case or case. An action on the case is an action to recover for injuries that were caused in a variety of ways: (a) where the injury resulted indirectly and consequentially, not directly or immediately; (b) where the injury resulted from acts that were not committed with force (or if force was used, the matter involved was not tangible); or (c) where the injury resulted from nonfeasance, negligence, or the failure to use proper skill in the performance of a contract. An action on the case was created to cover those injuries that could not be handled by a straight trespass action. For example, if someone threw a log on the road, the person hit by the log as it fell could sue in trespass (direct injury), but the person who later ran his or her car into the log would bring an action on the case (indirect injury).

Action quasi in rem See quasi in rem.

Action to quiet title An action in which the plaintiff asserts his or her title or interest in land and that the defendant's claim in the land is invalid; an action compelling an adverse claimant either to establish his or her claim or be forever estopped from asserting it.

Actio personalis moritur cum persona A personal action dies with the person. See survival action.

Activate, *v.* To trigger or ignite. See initiate, incite, animate, cause (2), provoke, muster, marshal (2), organize.

Activator, *n.* See catalyst.

Active, *adj.* **1.** Functioning (an active director). Working, performing, running, operant, operative, actively operative, in operation, in effective operation, acting, effectual, at work, occupied, engaged, going, live, in force, on duty, moving, in action, in actual process, in practice, in force, ticking, existing, existent. **2.** Producing an effect (active part). Causative, effective, powerful, forceful, influential, potent. **3.** Energetic (active force). Lively, animated, busy, industrious, forceful, assertive, alert, alive, imaginative, diligent, effective, burgeoning, dynamic, peppy, efficient, effectual, productive, profitable, influential, strong, ebullient, fervent, indefatigable, hardworking, untiring, vigorous, strenuous, buoyant, optimistic, carefree, agile, nimble, humming, bustling, stirring, bubbling, spirited, restless, earnest, eager, assiduous, consumed with, zealous, committed, aggressive, unremitting, enterprising. *Ant.* Inactive; impotent; stagnant.

Active negligence Negligence resulting from positive, affirmative acts or conduct, not from mere inaction or passiveness. See negligence, passive negligence.

Active trust A trust in which the trustee is under a duty to take active steps in the carrying out of the trust (e.g., invest assets, distribute profits). See dry trust, passive trust.

Activist, *n.* See partisan, advocate, nonconformist, entrepreneur, actor, promoter.

Activity, *n.* Movement, action, or progress (the board of directors reported little activity). Enterprise, exercise, undertaking, venture, exertion, concerted activity, life, labor, work, project, pursuit, application, assignment, scheme, campaign, process, operation, crusade, energy, industry, briskness, flurry, zeal, eagerness, agility, vitality, liveliness.

Act malum in se See malum in se.

Act malum prohibitum See malum prohibitum.

Act of attainder See bill of attainder, attainder.

Act of bankruptcy Conduct of a debtor that could force him or her into involuntary bankruptcy (e.g., transferring property, while insolvent, to some creditors in order to prefer them over other creditors).

Act of dominion See dominion.

Act of God An unusual event caused exclusively by nature; the cause of an injury exclusively due to nature, which could not have been avoided or prevented by the use of reasonable care. Examples: flood, tornado. See chance (1, 2).

Act of insolvency 1. Conduct that demonstrates that a bank is unable to meet its liabilities. 2. Conduct of a debtor that would justify the filing of involuntary bankruptcy proceedings against him or her.

Act of nature See act of God.

Act of state doctrine Courts of this country are precluded from inquiring into the validity of governmental acts of foreign governments that take place within their own territory.

Actor, *n.* 1. Plaintiff, litigant. Claimant, complainant, aggrieved party, petitioner, malcontent, accuser, party, party to litigation, adversary, intervenor, prosecutor. 2. Agent. Manager, pleader, patron, proctor, operator, factor, administrator, representative, stager, broker, steward, executor, proxy, commissioner. 3. A person who acts. Worker, doer, player, practitioner, participant, perpetrator, performer, thespian, impersonator, trouper.

Actrix, *n.* Female actor (e.g., female litigant, female agent). See actor.

Act and Resolutions; Acts and Resolves The session laws of a state legislature, printed chronologically.

Actual, *adj.* 1. Substantial (actual need). Factual, material, demonstrable, objective, concrete, tangible, reliable, indisputable, unimpeachable, undeniable, authentic, accurate, verifiable, legitimate, positive, genuine, bona fide, physical, categorical, precise, perceptible, nontheoretical, palpable, corporeal, based on fact, well-grounded, determinate, undoubted, confirmed, certified, certain, decided, prevailing, current, very, sure, hard, well-founded, exact, faithful, absolute, literal, official. 2. Existing (actual situation). Existing presently in fact, having a valid objective existence, existent, now existing, not imaginary, as represented, extant, de facto, at this moment, present day, here and now, present, living, live. *Ant.* Probable; fictitious.

Actual cash value Fair market value as measured by what a willing buyer would offer and what a willing seller would accept in a cash sale in an open and free market—not at a forced sale. In some contexts, actual cash value may also mean the cost of restoration or the replacement costs less depreciation.

Actual controversy A concrete dispute in which the underlying issues are not moot or premature, the interests of the parties are real and adverse, and the controversy is ripe for judicial determination; a justiciable controversy.

Actual damages Compensatory damages for actual loss or injury; damages in satisfaction of, or in recompense for, loss or injury actually sustained; all damages other than punitive or exemplary damages.

Actuality, *n.* Reality. See fact, verity.

Actualize, *v.* See attain, realize (2), make (1).

Actual malice 1. For purposes of an award of punitive damages, actual malice is ill will, the intent to injure, or a reckless disregard of another's rights. **2.** For purposes of a defamation action involving constitutional issues, actual malice is knowledge of falsity or a reckless disregard as to truth or falsity.

Actuarial, *adj.* Pertaining to the calculation of statistical risks, premiums, estate values, etc., for insurance purposes.

Actuary, *n.* A person skilled in mathematical calculations to determine insurance risks, premiums, etc. A statistician.

Actum, *n.* Something done; a deed.

Actuate, *v.* See initiate, incite.

Actus, *n.* **1.** An act or action. **2.** A right of way.

Actus reus The wrongful deed or act. When the actus reus is combined with the mens rea (guilty mind), a crime has been committed. For the crime of murder, for example, the actus reus is the homicide, and the mens rea is the malice aforethought.

Acumen, *n.* See judgment (2), comprehension, discretion (3), maturity, experience (1), common sense, learning, education.

Acute, *adj.* **1.** Perceptive, astute (acute observer). Discriminating, sensitive, keen, clear-sighted, ingenious, alert, aware, penetrating, probing, perspicacious, bright, intelligent, sage, discerning, foreseeing, clever, acuminate, intuitive, quick-witted, cutting, provident, trenchant, observant, pointed, piercing, poignant, knowledge-able, prudent, sapient, incisive. **2.** Severe, grave (acute pain). Intense, distressing, overwhelming, powerful, agonizing, very great, racking, deep, overpowering, dangerous, critical, crucial, serious, desperate, hazardous, precarious, threatening, urgent, perilous, pungent. *Ant.* Dull; innocuous.

Ad, (*Lat.*) At, by, for, near, on account of, to, until, upon, concerning.

Adage, *n.* See maxim.

Adamant, *adj.* See incorrigible, inflexible, wild (3).

Adapt, *v.* To adjust, to make suitable for use (the standard form was adapted to our state law). Acclimate, alter, accommodate, assimilate, conform, comply with, harmonize, reconcile, shape, fashion, modify, recompose, accustom, acclimatize, square, suit, arrange, qualify, compose, readjust, proportion, temper, match, model, modulate, remodel, regulate, settle, bring into correspondence, standardize, quadrate, convert, correlate, fit.

Adaptable, *adj.* See malleable, convertible, flexible, conciliatory.

Adaptation, *n.* See modification, accommodation (2).

Ad colligendum bona defuncti For collecting the goods of the deceased.

Ad curiam At a court; before the court.

Add, *v.* **1.** Attach. Connect, adjoin, include, append, annex, join, unite, affix, suffix, tack on, offer in addition, subjoin, superadd, superimpose. **2.** Increase. Extend, enlarge, aggrandize, augment, supplement, raise, amplify, magnify, encumber, intensify, saddle, clutter, burden. **3.** Total. Aggregate, tally, calculate, compute, reckon, sum up, figure, count, cast, estimate, score.

Ad damnum A clause (usually in the complaint) stating the amount of money that is claimed as damages for the alleged wrong committed.

Addendum, *n.* Something added, e.g., charts added at the end of an appellate brief. Appendix, supplement, addition, insertion, augmentation, extension, appendage, postscript, subscript, afterthought, added section to a writing, annexation, codicil, attachment, rider, adjunct, complement, appurtenance.

Addict, *n.,* **Addict,** *v.* **1.** *n.* A habitual or obsessive user of something, e.g., narcotics (drug addict). "Fiend," "dope fiend," "acidhead," "junkie," "head," "hophead," "freak," "mainliner," user, drunkard, drunk; believer, slave, fan, disciple, devotee, enthusiast, adherent, follower, "hound," habitué, acolyte, "buff." **2.** *v.* To habituate (addicted to drugs). Accustom, surrender to, dedicate, devote, predispose, wed, condition, attach. *Ant.* Nonuser; withdraw.

Addiction, *n.* See compulsion.

Addition, *n.* **1.** Something added. See increase, attachment (3), accessory (2). **2.** In insurance law, coverage for "additions" includes buildings added, joined, or appurtenant to other buildings. **3.** A title or description added to someone's name (Mary Jones, painter).

Additional, *adj.* See supplemental, extra, ancillary.

Additional servitude A new and additional servitude or easement on land taken by eminent domain for which additional compensation is required.

Additur, *n.* The court's power to increase the amount of a jury award. The process often works as follows: (a) the plaintiff wins a jury award that is deemed inadequate, (b) the plaintiff moves for a new trial, (c) the judge tells the defendant that a new trial will be ordered unless the defendant agrees to increase the verdict by a designated amount. The denial of the new trial is conditioned on the defendant's consent to the increase.

Addle, *v.* See confuse.

Add on clause A clause in an installment contract making earlier purchases security for new purchases.

Addone, Given to.

Address, **1.** *n.* Place of residence or business where a person can usually be reached by mail, phone, visit (current address). Abode, habitation, lodging, quarters, domicile, mailing address, location, locality, accommodations, business address, home. **2.** *v.* To speak or write to (address the jury). Approach, greet, court, talk to, salute, plead, petition, appeal, lecture, preach, apply to, accost, apostrophize, discuss with, hail, solicit, implore, entreat. **3.** *n.* A speech (foreign policy address). Lecture, discourse, sermon, dissertation, talk, statement, oration, harangue, appeal, invocation, petition, request, solicitation, suit. **4.** *n.* Skill (a research job performed with address). Adroitness, cleverness, ingenuity, ability, tact, discretion, dexterity, competence, dispatch, facility. **5.** *n.* That portion of a bill in equity describing the court where the bill is filed.

Adduce, *v.* To present or introduce (adduce evidence in support of). Offer, allege, advance, state, allude, disclose, mention, bring forward, produce, declare, submit, tender, propose, divulge, point out, illustrate, contend, proffer, urge, assert, cite, lay, suggest, evince, plead, assign, infer, quote, name.

Adeem, *v.* To take away; to revoke the bequest of a legacy. Withdraw, annul, cancel, abolish, repudiate, rescind, recall, abrogate. *Ant.* Create.

Ademption, *n.* A revocation or satisfaction of a gift in a will; this result is implied by the law from the acts of the person making the will (testator) before the death of the latter. From these acts, the law presumes an intent to revoke or satisfy. For example: Mary leaves Bill a specific horse in her will. Before Mary dies, she gives the horse to Bill, she sells it to Bob, or the horse dies. The legacy of the horse is adeemed. When Mary dies, Bill does not get a substitute for the horse. Extinction, recalling, retraction, cancellation, abnegation, renunciation, taking away, annulment, nullification, abolition, voidance, invalidation, repudiation, dissolution, negation, recanting, repeal. See also advancement.

Adept, *adj.* See expert (2), qualified, competent, effective, able, apt (3), erudite.

Adequate, *adj.* Sufficient (an adequate remedy at law). Fully sufficient, reasonably sufficient, commensurate, suitable, suited, equal to what is required, satisfactory,

Adequate

acceptable, passable, right, enough, effective, standard, proportionate, adapted, capable, qualified, competent, serviceable, ample, fit, fitting, fitted, requisite, up to standards, OK, okay, conclusive, convincing, up to par, worthy, up to snuff, allowable, admissible, presentable, tolerable, sufficing, effectual.

Adequate consideration Consideration that is equal to or reasonably proportioned to the value of that for which it is given; consideration that is not so grossly disproportionate to value as to offend against fair dealing.

Adequate remedy at law Adequacy is determined by comparing the remedy available at law with the remedy being sought in equity. The remedy at law is adequate if it is as plain, as complete, and as efficient to the prompt administration of justice as the remedy being sought in equity. If there is an adequate remedy at law, then the equitable remedy (e.g., injunction) will be denied.

Ad fidem In allegiance.

Ad fin., Ad finem, *adj., adv.* To the end.

Ad gravamen To the grievance or injury.

Adhere, *v.* **1.** To cling to (the seal adheres to the document). Be in league with, cleave to, stick, join, coalesce, cohere, hold fast, take hold, merge, consolidate, unite, fasten, bond, attach, link, combine, glue, cement, affix, fuse, weld, fasten, agglutinate, latch, tighten, secure, anchor, clamp. **2.** To be faithful (the court adhered to its earlier holding). Stand by, stand firm, be loyal, be constant, be attached, identify, champion, espouse, support, uphold, advocate, maintain loyalty, defend, preserve, abide, follow, endure, carry on, persevere, be steadfast, maintain, hold closely, hold firmly to. *Ant.* Detach; be disloyal.

Adherence, *n.* See coherence (2), adhesion (1), fidelity.

Adherent, *n.* A follower, fan, backer, or supporter. See advocate (1), accessory (1).

Adhesion, *n.* **1.** Adherence. Sticking to, attachment, accretion, cohesion, viscosity, union, fidelity, loyalty, association, faithfulness, alliance. See also coherence (2). **2.** The combining of bodily tissues. **3.** A country's agreement to accept part of a treaty.

Adhesion contract A contract that often has the following characteristics: (a) a standardized, form contract, (b) covering consumer goods and services, (c) the seller is in a superior bargaining position, (d) the buyer has no realistic opportunity to bargain over terms—the contract is offered on a "take it or leave it" basis, (e) the buyer has no realistic opportunity to shop elsewhere for a more favorable contract.

Adhesive 1. *adj.* Sticky, clinging, gummed, adhering, mucilaginous, gluey. **2.** *n.* A substance that adheres. Glue, cement, paste, mortar, solder, tap, wax, plaster.

Ad hoc, *adj., adv.* For this; for this special case or purpose only (an ad hoc committee). See provisional.

Ad hominem, *adj., adv.* To the person; appealing to the prejudices of a person; a personal attack.

Adieu, *interj., n.* Farewell. Good-by, bon voyage, adios, sayonara, leave, departure.

Ad infinitum, *adj., adv.* Without end (the judge's remarks went on ad infinitum). To any extent, without limit, to an indefinite extent, indefinitely, boundlessly, eternally, incalculably, endlessly, limitlessly.

Ad int., Ad interim, *adj., adv.* In the meantime; temporary.

Adios, *interj.* See adieu.

Adjacent, *adj.* Lying near or close by (adjacent objects may or may not be in contact with each other). Touching, neighboring, in the neighborhood of, adjoining, bordering, contiguous, next to, proximal, coterminous, attached, abutting, juxtaposed, beside, nigh, having a common border, linked, consecutive, successive, contacting, tangent, continuous, connecting, coterminous, proximate, alongside, meeting. *Ant.* Remote.

Adjective law The rules of practice and procedure; remedial laws; the rules by which the substantive law is administered; the legal machinery by which substantive rights and duties are enforced or made effective. Example: the service of process rules.

Adjoin, *v.* See border (2), abut, attach (2).

Adjoining, *adj.* Touching (adjoining lots). Abutting, contiguous, meeting, bordering, neighboring. See also adjacent.

Adjourn, *v.* To postpone or suspend until another time (the court adjourned at noon). Recess, defer, put over to a future time, put off, delay, hold over, interrupt, close, end, procrastinate, prorogue, break, suspend, protract, hold in abeyance, terminate, disband, disperse, dissolve. *Ant.* Convene.

Adjournment, *n.* See adjourn, interruption, cessation.

Adjudge, *v.* To make a decision (he was adjudged to be in contempt). Decide, judicially determine, pass on judicially, decree, settle, arbitrate, mediate, adjudicate, give judgment, render judgment, sentence, rule upon, assign, relegate, allot, arbitrate, sit in judgment, award, conclude, proclaim, ordain, order, pronounce judgment.

Adjudicate, *v.* To judge (when settlement efforts failed, they decided to ask the court to adjudicate the matter). Adjudge, decide, judicially determine, decree, settle, arbitrate, render judgment, sentence, rule upon, pronounce judgment, decree, umpire, referee.

Adjudication, *n.* A formal determination or judgment by a court of law. The word may also refer to a formal decision of an administrative agency acting pursuant to its quasi-judicial powers. Ruling, opinion, decision, holding, order, decree, judgment, pronouncement, disposition, finding, command, edict, resolution, sentence, arbitration, award, verdict.

Adjudicative facts Facts (in a dispute before an administrative agency) about the parties, their activities, business, and property. Adjudicative facts usually answer the questions of who did what, where, when, how, why, and with what motive and intent. Legislative facts, on the other hand, do not usually concern the immediate parties but are general facts that help the tribunal decide questions of law, policy, and discretion.

Adjudicatory proceeding A method of resolving factual disputes, usually within an administrative agency.

Adjunct, *n.* Something secondary or subordinate that is added (an adjunct to the proceeding). Incidental, supplement, accessory, auxiliary, secondary feature, appurtenance, complement, appendage, appendix, footnote, attachment, extension, augmentation, postscript, subsidiary, addendum, corollary. *Ant.* Principal.

Adjunction, *n.* Adding or attaching one thing to another. See accession (1).

Adjuration, *n.* A solemn statement; a sworn statement; an entreaty (adjuration of the witness). Solemn charge, solemn appeal, oath, address, plea, command, request, affirmation, avowal, vow, testimony, averment.

Adjust, *v.* **1.** To settle or arrange; to remove differences or discrepancies (to adjust the account). Harmonize, attune, tune, correct, rectify, balance, arrange, dispose, set in order, conform, straighten, regulate, regularize, repair, change, alter, reconcile, equalize, stabilize, align, calibrate, order, correlate, compromise, coordinate, reset, restore equilibrium, strike a balance, moderate, mediate, remedy, clarify, solve. **2.** To adapt (the measurements had to be adjusted). Make suitable for use, acclimate, alter, accommodate, conform, reconcile, convert, regulate, standardize, proportion, fashion, arrange, correlate, modulate. **3.** To pay a liquidated claim.

Adjustable, *adj.* See malleable, convertible, flexible.

Adjusted basis The cost or other basis of property (a) reduced for depreciation, depletion, and any item that represents a return of capital, and (b) increased by capital improvements, purchase commissions, zoning costs, legal fees in defending title, etc.

Adjusted gross estate The gross estate less deductions for administration expenses, funeral expenses, debts of the decedent, etc.

Adjusted gross income Gross income of an individual less certain deductions (e.g., business expenses, long-term capital gain deductions).

Adjustment, *n.* Settlement of a claim; a determination of the accuracy of a claim, whether it should be reduced, etc. (a satisfactory adjustment). Accommodation, straightening, justification, bringing into agreement, arrangement, reconciliation, agreement, understanding, negotiation, attunement, bargain, accord, compact. See also correction (2).

Adjustment bond A bond that is issued as part of a corporate reorganization.

Adjustment securities Stocks, bonds, and other securities issued as part of a corporate reorganization.

Adjutant, *n.* See assistant.

Ad legem At the law.

Ad lib, *adv.* Freely, impulsively, without deliberation. See spontaneous.

Ad libitum At will; as one pleases.

Ad litem For the suit, for purposes of this litigation (guardian ad litem).

Ad majus For the larger or greater.

Admeasure, *v.* See apportion.

Admeasurement, *n.* Apportionment; assignment of shares. Allotment, allocation, distribution, proportional distribution, parceling, meting out, measuring out, division, consignment, partition, assignment, sharing, dealing, dispensing, ration.

Admeasurement of dower 1. A writ brought by an heir (upon reaching majority) to rectify an assignment of dower made during minority by which the doweress received more than that to which she was entitled. 2. The settlement of a widow's dower right.

Admeasurement of homestead The identification at an execution sale of the portion of land to which a homestead exemption applies.

Adminicle, *n.* 1. Aid, support. 2. Evidence used to support other evidence; corroboration.

Adminicular, *adj.* Auxiliary; subordinate to; corroborative (adminicular evidence). Supportive, assisting, helping, confirmative, confirmatory, corroborating, corroboratory.

Administer, *v.* 1. To manage (administer the company). Direct, administrate, supervise, enforce, carry out, execute, run, govern, regulate, preside over, discharge the duties, take charge of the business or operation, manage the affairs, conduct, control, oversee, head, superintend, boss, dispose of, engineer, steer, settle, minister, guide, pilot, officiate, operate, reign, prosecute, implement, effectuate. 2. To give or supply (administer justice). Dispense, furnish, provide, deal out, hand out, parcel out, mete out, portion out, measure out, dole out, distribute, serve, apply, offer, tender, contribute, issue, assign, allot, consign, allocate, afford, inflict, impose, accord, bestow, impart, confer, extend. 3. To settle and distribute the estate of a dead person.

Administrate, *v.* See administer, manage, regulate, organize.

Administration, *n.* 1. The management of something, e.g., a government agency, a business, an estate (skills of administration). Direction, superintendence, execution, oversight, supervision, regulation, control, care, conduct, performance of duty, dispensation, ministration, handling, guardianship, settlement, government. 2. The executive department of the government (the Administration of Ronald Reagan). Policymakers, government, establishment, leadership, office-holders, hierarchy, bureaucracy, power structure, regime, authority, presidency. **3.** The act of giving or furnishing something (the administration of relief). Distribution, supplying, disposal, dispensation, offering. **4.** The management and settlement of the estate of a decedent.

Administration ad colligendum The right to manage an estate which is granted for the purpose of collecting and preserving the goods of the deceased that are about to perish (bona peritura).

Administration cum testamento annexo (CTA) Administration of an estate where no executor is named in the will, or where one is named but is unable to serve. Administration with the will annexed.

Administration de bonis non (DBN) Administration of that portion of an estate which was not administered by a prior executor or administrator, e.g., because of the death of the latter.

Administration letters The document that authorizes a person to manage the estate of someone who has died without leaving a valid will.

Administration of estate The management and settlement of an estate involving the collection of assets, the payment of debts and claims against the estate, the payment of estate taxes, and the distribution of the remainder of the estate to those entitled to receive it. The decedent is an intestate (someone who dies without leaving a valid will) or a testate (someone who dies leaving a valid will) where no executor is available.

Administration pendente lite Administration of an estate pending the resolution of a controversy over the will, e.g., its validity.

Administrative, *adj.* Executive; that which pertains to the carrying out of something else, e.g., a statute (administrative duties). Regulatory, managerial, managing, supervisory, ministerial, routine, administerial, organizational, directorial, directive, bureaucratic, governmental, hierarchical, superintending, regulatory, authoritative, guiding.

Administrative act A routine, ministerial, clerical, or necessary act that carries out something else.

Administrative agency A governmental body that carries out or administers the law, particularly the law passed by the legislature. Examples: City Sanitation Division, the FBI.

Administrative board An administrative agency, often one with quasi-judicial powers.

Administrative discretion The power of an administrative agency to choose among alternative courses of action based on beliefs, perceptions, inclinations, and preferences that are usually not susceptible of proof or disproof.

Administrative law 1. The law governing the conduct, powers, and procedures of administrative agencies. **2.** The laws created by administrative agencies.

Administrative Law Judge (ALJ) A hearing officer within an administrative agency; someone who presides over administrative hearings pursuant to an agency's quasi-judicial power.

Administrative order A resolution of a dispute before an administrative agency; a final disposition following an administrative hearing.

Administrative Procedure Act (APA) 1. A federal statute governing procedures before federal administrative agencies, e.g., participation in rule making, the conduct of hearings. **2.** A state statute with the same name, serving the same function for state administrative agencies.

Administrative remedy A procedure within an administrative agency for allowing someone to assert a right; a nonjudicial remedy provided by the agency itself. Generally, such remedies must be exhausted before the case can be taken to court.

Administrative tribunal An administrative agency that holds hearings and renders decisions on controversies within the agency.

Administrator, *n.* **1.** A manager (the plant administrator). Supervisor, director, custodian, head, officer, official, chief executive, executive, overseer, leader, boss, administrative head, curator, superintendent, foreman, governor, president, commander, steward, ruler, chairperson, dean. **2.** A person appointed by the court to manage or administer the estate of a decedent (the administrator paid the funeral bill). Personal representative, legal representative, representative of the estate, administratrix, executor, executrix, trustee, estate supervisor.

Administrator ad litem A special administrator appointed by the court to represent the estate of a decedent in a court proceeding.

Administrator cum testamento annexo (CTA) See administration cum testamento annexo.

Administrator DBN See administration de bonis non.

Administrator de bonis non (DBN) See administration de bonis non.

Administrator of estate See administration of estate.

Administrator pendente lite See administration pendente lite.

Administrator with will annexed See administration cum testamento annexo.

Administratrix, *n.* A woman who administers the estate of the deceased. See administration of estate.

Admirable, *adj.* See worthy, superior (2), elevated.

Admiralty, *n.* The law of the sea, the law pertaining to navigable waters, maritime law, e.g., contract and tort actions that arise out of commerce on the seas. See maritime.

Admiration, *n.* See approbation, affection (1), attachment (4), affinity (2).

Admire, *v.* See appreciate (3), adulate, enjoy, honor (2).

Admirer, *n.* See adherent, partisan, advocate, suitor.

Admissible, *adj.* Pertaining to that which can be allowed because it is relevant or pertinent to the matter at hand and should be considered (admissible evidence). Whether it is true or false will be determined separately. Unobjectionable, permissible, allowable, admittable, eligible, presentable, tolerable, acceptable, authorized, sanctioned. *Ant.* Inadmissible.

Admission, *n.* **1.** A statement (or conduct) of a party that is inconsistent with a position the party is taking in the litigation. **2.** A voluntary concession or confession (admission of guilt). Acknowledgment, profession, avowal, divulgence, revelation, disclosure, announcement, declaration, allowance, statement, affirmation, assent, acceptance, attestation, unveiling, exposure, making known. **3.** Entrance (restricted admission). Admittance, access, ingress, entry, passage, path, opening, incorporation, reception.

Admission against interest A statement made by one of the parties to an action which amounts to a prior acknowledgment that one of the material facts relevant to the issues is not as he or she now claims.

Admit, *v.* **1.** To accept as true or valid (she would not admit that the money was stolen). Concede, grant, acknowledge, confess, suffer, accede to, agree to, avow, own up to, assent, acquiesce, subscribe to, approve of, concur, proclaim, divulge, disclose, confide, announce, "come clean," profess, accept, confirm, declare, recognize, reveal. **2.** To give access to (admitted to the bar). Let in, receive, induct, grant access, include, welcome, entertain, shelter, house, harbor, install, license, inject, institute, inaugurate, incorporate, invest. *Ant.* Reject

Admittance, *n.* See entrance, permission.

Admix, *v.* See commingle.

Admixture, *n.* A mixture; something formed by mixing (an admixture of ideas). Combination, compound, blend, composite, association, conglomeration, jumble, union, fusion, amalgamation, assortment, potpourri, adulteration.

Admonish, *v.* **1.** To warn or caution (the jury was admonished by the judge not to discuss the case). Advise, forewarn, apprise, counsel, enjoin, put on guard, "tip off," make aware, alert, remind, acquaint, notify, inform, instruct, teach, advocate, urge. **2.** To criticize or censure (admonish the child). Rebuke, reprove, chide, chasten, exhort, discipline, "call down," call to account, deprecate, remonstrate, lecture, reprimand, correct, scold, chastise, disapprove, reprehend, reproach, upbraid, berate, reprobate, take to task, punish.

Admonishment, *n.* See correction (1), censure; admonish.

Admonition, *n.* **1.** A warning. Advice, forewarning, alert, instruction, lecture, reminder, cautionary statement, counsel, notification. **2.** A reprimand. Calling to account, scolding, reproach, punishment, chastisement, rebuke, remonstrance, upbraiding. See also censure (1).

Ad nauseum, *adv.* To the extreme, to the point of disgust, endlessly, forever.

Adolescence, *n.* The time between puberty and the age of majority (difficulty adjusting during his adolescence). Youth, minority, growing years, pubescence, prime, wardship, heyday, nonage. *Ant.* Adulthood.

Adolescent, *adj.* See juvenile (2).

Adopt, *v.* **1.** To go through a formal process of establishing a relationship of parent and child between persons who are not so related by nature. **2.** To follow (the judge adopted the theory). Embrace, espouse, choose, accept, assume, appropriate, affect, approve, ratify, take, take up, take on, take to oneself, attach oneself to, affiliate, arrogate, borrow, conform to, follow, utilize, usurp, employ, use, annex, admit, avow, assimilate, accept as one's own, select, select as one's own, make one's own, receive, approve, recognize, sanction, support, maintain, father, mother, foster, naturalize, elect. *Ant.* Abandon.

Adoptee, *n.* The person adopted.

Adoption by estoppel A child acquires the status of an adopted child when others are prevented from denying this status. No formal (statutory) adoption procedures are followed, but conduct or promises made by a person make it inequitable for this person (or his or her estate) to claim that the child does not have the status of an adopted child. An equitable adoption.

Adoptive parent Someone who adopts another person.

Adorable, *adj.* See attractive, beautiful.

Adoration, *n.* See love.

Adore, *v.* See adulate, enjoy (2), appreciate (3), honor (2).

Adorn, *v.* See clothe, furnish, beautify, color (3).

Adornment, *n.* See apparel.

Ad perpetuam In perpetuity.

Ad quod damnum 1. To what damage or injury; how will others be prejudiced. **2.** A writ to complain of an assessment of condemnation damages.

Adrift, *adv., adj.* Without aim or purpose; floating without anchor (set adrift). Afloat, astray, stray, loose, straggling, meandering, lost, perplexed, deviating, rambling, confused, roving, roaming, vacillating, wandering, disjoined, diffused, directionless, dispersed, scattered. *Ant.* On target.

Adroit, *adj.* See apt (3), expert (2), able.

Adulate, *v.* To idolize, worship, glorify, praise, deify, or exhalt. See also enjoy (2).

Adulation, *n.* See worship.

Adult, *n.* A person who has reached the age of majority (e.g., 21, 18). The age may differ depending on what the person is trying to do (e.g., vote, marry, administer an estate). Senior, of age, age of consent, man, woman, person of legal age; mature, fully grown. *Ant.* Minor, immature.

Adulterant, *n., adj.* That which makes something else inferior or impure.

Adulterate, *v.* To make inferior or impure (the substance had been adulter-

Adulterate

ated). Contaminate, corrupt, debase, pollute, alloy, defile, vitiate, spoil, dilute, water down, attenuate, deteriorate, make impure, sophisticate, tamper with, "doctor," denature, impurify, taint, weaken, devalue, depreciate, prostitute, cheapen, bastardize, infect, muddle, pervert, worsen, degrade, impair, warp, debilitate, denaturize. *Ant.* Purify.

Adulterated, *adj.* See corrupt (1).

Adulterator, *n.* Corrupter, counterfeiter.

Adulterer, *n.* A man who commits adultery.

Adulteress, *n.* A woman who commits adultery.

Adultery, *n.* Voluntary sexual intercourse by a married person with someone other than his or her spouse (divorce on the ground of adultery). Infidelity, cuckoldry, extramarital relations, illicit sexual relations, unfaithfulness, breaking of the vows, meretricious sexual relationship, fornication, criminal conversation, affair, tryst, enticement, seduction. *Ant.* Fidelity.

Ad valorem tax A tax calculated on the basis of the value of the property to be taxed.

Advance 1. *v.* To prepay; to fulfill an obligation before it is due. **2.** *v.* To loan; to supply on credit. Accommodate, provide, supply, furnish, contribute, give, pay. **3.** *v.* To move ahead. Proceed, progress, go forward, march, move, continue, propel, facilitate, expedite, stimulate, precipitate, accelerate, speed, hasten, quicken, forge, gain ground. **4.** *v.* To improve. Strengthen, support, promote, exalt, develop, prosper, elevate, dignify, further, benefit, foster, serve, assist, aid, help, enhance, heighten, upgrade, augment, enrich, abet, progress, succeed, aggrandize. **5.** *v.* To increase. Grow, gain, magnify, thrive, mature, elaborate, enlarge, intensify, multiply. **6.** *v.* To offer. Present, propose, advocate, urge, lay before, submit, hypothesize, posit, maintain, suggest, broach, tender, proffer, propound, give, bid. **7.** *n.* Promotion. Elevation, furtherance, exaltation, honor. **8.** *n.* Breakthrough. Invention, step forward, discovery, important development. **9.** *n.* See loan.

Advancement, *n.* **1.** An irrevocable gift from a parent (while living) to his or her child which anticipates what the child would inherit upon the death of this parent. The intention of the parent is to have this gift deducted from what the child would have inherited. **2.** Improvement. Progression, development, progress, promotion, enhancement, evolution, furtherance, growth.

Advance sheets 1. Unbound reporters containing court opinions that are printed in advance of the bound reporter volumes. When the bound volume comes out, the advance sheets are usually thrown away. **2.** The most recent pamphlet of *Shepard's Citations* giving the latest sheparadizing data.

Advantage, *n.* See benefit (1), aid (2), mileage (2).

Advantageous, *adj.* See gainful, beneficial, auspicious, instrumental, optimistic.

Advent, *n.* Coming, arrival, approach. See appearance (2).

Adventitious, *adj.* Accidental, occurring fortuitously (adventitious event). Incidental, not inherent, foreign, alien, supervenient, coming from without, extraneous, casual, random, haphazard, nonessential, supplemental, superficial, serendipitous. See also fortuitous, extrinsic (2). *Ant.* Inherent.

Adventure, *n.* **1.** A hazardous enterprise. Venture, hazard, risk, danger, challenge, jeopardy, peril, exploit, emprise, risky undertaking, trial, chance, fortune, pursuit, enterprise, gamble, experiment, episode, occurrence, incident, happening, event, feat; imperil, put in danger, expose to risks. **2.** Peril (as used in marine insurance). **3.** A shipment of goods in charge of an agent to be sold for the best price available. **4.** See legend.

Adventurous, *adj.* Heroic, brave, bold, daring, fearless, courageous, sturdy, intrepid. See also hazardous, dangerous.

Adversary, *n.* Opponent (a formidable adversary). Adverse party, litigant, opposing party, opposition, antagonist, disputant, combatant, competitor, rival, enemy, assailant, foe, contestant, opposer, challenger, opposite, other side, oppugner, party, contender, contester, resister. *Ant.* Comrade.

Adversary proceeding A proceeding, e.g., a hearing, in court or at an administrative agency in which opposing parties may contest a matter. *Ant.* Ex parte proceeding.

Adversary system A system of justice or a legal system where an impartial judge presides over a proceeding in which opponents present their case in the best light possible. The judge does not act as prosecutor as in an inquisitional system of justice.

Adverse, *adj.* **1.** Opposed, in opposition, having opposite interests, against (adverse claim). Opposing, counter, antagonistic, hostile, belligerent, conflicting, inimical, contrary, antithetical, incompatible, contradictory, at variance, oppugnant, counteractive, antipathetic, confronting, inconsistent. **2.** Unfavorable (adverse circumstances). Harmful, detrimental, unpropitious, unfortunate, negative, injurious, unfriendly, destructive, noxious, damaging, deleterious, untoward, unlucky, catastrophic, dangerous, disastrous, hurtful, disadvantageous, prejudicial, unsatisfactory, hindering, impeding, ruinous, corrosive, inauspicious, fractious, counteracting, discordant, obstructive, resistive. *Ant.* Parallel; propitious.

Adverse claim 1. An alleged right of one person asserted against the interest of another person. **2.** A claim to possession of land that is contrary to the rights of the title holder. **3.** A claim asserted against a trustee in bankruptcy.

Adverse interest Goals, needs, or claims of one person or group that are different from or opposed to those of another person or group.

Adverse party A party to an action whose interests are opposed to or opposite of the interests of another party to the action. See adversary.

Adverse possession A method of acquiring title to land without buying or paying for it in the traditional sense. The following is required: (a) actual possession or occupancy of the land that is (b) hostile to the current owner, (c) visible, open, and notorious, (d) exclusive, (e) continuous for a statutorily defined number of years, and (f) maintained under a claim of right as against everyone else.

Adverse witness 1. A hostile witness. **2.** A witness who gives evidence that is prejudicial to the party that produced the witness (which allows the party to impeach the witness).

Adversity, *n.* See affliction, misfortune, burden (2), failure, defeat.

Advert, *v.* See refer.

Advertise, *v.* To make known to; to announce publicly (advertise the firm's services). Notify, call attention to, apprise, propagate, publish, advise, inform, declare, bring to public attention, circulate, disseminate, trumpet, promulgate, publicize, promote, propagandize, proclaim, broadcast, "puff," post, diffuse, blazon, blaze, ventilate, report, transmit, spread, distribute, purvey, rumor, communicate, radiate, display, show, ballyhoo.

Advertisement, *n.* See notice (1), advertise.

Advice, *n.* **1.** An opinion or viewpoint offered as guidance (lawyer's advice). Counsel, legal counsel, recommendation, recommended course of action, suggestion, instruction, warning, alert, intimation, guidance, admonition, caution, advisement, direction, exhortation, rede, persuasion, proposal, advocacy, teaching, proposition, lesson, plan, scheme, wisdom. **2.** Information, notification (I received advice from the clerk that the case had been dismissed). Communication, word, news, report, communiqué, intelligence, message, notice, pointer, inside information, cue, tip, tip-off, account, tidings, enlightenment, facts, insight, data, memorandum.

Advisable, *adj.* Advantageous (the lawyer deemed it advisable). Practical, appropriate, wise, proper, profitable, useful, correct, beneficial, suitable, expedient, fitting, recommendable. *Ant.* Imprudent.

Advise, *v.* **1.** To recommend a course of action (she advised against incorporation). Counsel, give counsel to, give guidance, give an opinion, give advice, offer counsel, opine, admonish, suggest, guide, direct, caution, prescribe, advocate, persuade, instruct, teach, propose, consult, urge. **2.** To inform (this is to advise you that a claim has been filed). Notify, warn, forewarn, apprise, give notice, acquaint, tell, make known, communicate, announce, remind, alert, familiarize, convey, report, express, submit, enlighten.

Advise and consent The constitutional power and right of the U.S. Senate to advise the president on treaties and major presidential appointments and to approve or disapprove them.

Advisement, *n.* **1.** Careful consideration. **2.** The act of a judge in taking time to deliberate before making a decision (take under advisement).

Adviser, advisor, *n.* Confidant, guide, consultant, coach. See counsel (1), teacher.

Advisory *adj.* **1.** Giving nonbinding advice or counsel (advisory opinion). Counseling, suggesting, advising, recommendatory, consultative, consultatory, consulting, guiding, expert, professional, cautionary. **2.** *n.* A report giving information (small craft advisory). See report (1), record (2).

Advisory jury A jury whose verdict is not binding on the court. A jury used in a federal court when a right to a jury does not exist.

Advisory opinion An opinion of a court that is not binding. Unlike the normal opinion, which arises out of adversarial proceedings, the advisory opinion is usually requested by the legislature or by the chief executive.

Advocacy, *n.* Speaking, writing, or otherwise acting in support of or in opposition to something (advocacy of the plan). Pleading for, active espousal, promotion, championship, backing, endorsement, recommendation, defense, support, campaigning for, speaking out for, furthering, urging, pressing for, forceful persuasion.

Advocate 1. *n.* Someone who assists or argues for another (an advocate for the disadvantaged). Pleader, defender, lawyer, attorney, attorney at law, counsel, counselor, legal representative, representative, solicitor, barrister, legal adviser, spokesman, spokeswoman, spokesperson, "mouthpiece," supporter, champion, backer, propagandist, upholder, patron, intercessor, intermediary, negotiator, promoter, apologist, proponent, adherent, vindicator, propagator, abettor, espouser. **2.** *v.* To support or argue for (to advocate acceptance). Promote, recommend, champion, defend, advance, second, justify, propound, rally around, argue for, plead, plead for, plead the case of, plead the cause of, plead in favor of, speak for, side with, buttress, further, speak out for, speak in favor of, campaign for, unite with, stand up for, push for, press for, fight for, stand by, back, uphold, favor, endorse, propose, prescribe, encourage, urge, espouse, sustain, reinforce, subscribe, vindicate, propagate, contend for, vote for, exhort.

Aegis, *n.* See protection, auspices.

Aerial, *adj.* High, lofty. See remote (1), incorporeal, intangible (1).

Aerodynamics, *n.* The science of gases in motion.

Aeronaut, *n.* A pilot of aircraft. Flier, balloonist, aviator.

Aeronautics, *n.* The science that deals with the design and operation of aircraft. See navigate.

Aesthete, esthete, *n.* See expert (1), fake (3).

Aesthetic, esthetic, *adj.* Relating to beauty and good taste (aesthetic appreciation). Tasteful, referring to taste, beautiful, artistic, cultured, fastidious, refined, having artistic value, sensitive, discriminating, becoming, classical, delicate.

Affable, *adj.* See amicable, convivial, friendly, civil (3), conciliatory, accessible.

Affairs, *n.* Whatever a person may do (private affairs). Business, general operations, concerns, fiscal relations, practical concerns, responsibilities, duties, finances, activities, transactions, problems, personal problems, matters, cares, events, circumstances, episodes, occurrences, enterprises, functions, happenings, undertakings, projects, ventures, commitments, incidents; celebrations, social gatherings, ceremonies, festivities; romances, relationships, love affairs, liaisons, amour.

Affect, *v.* **1.** To act on (upon); to influence (the ruling will affect the project). Have an effect on, impress, change, enlarge, abridge, produce an effect, alter, modify, moderate, work upon, touch, strike, stir, sway, transform, move, bear upon, concern, regard, pertain to, relate to, interest, impinge on, impact, reach, prevail upon, induce. **2.** To feign (the new lawyer affected unconcern). Pretend, counterfeit, adopt, mimic, simulate, imitate, assume, arrogate.

Affectation, *n.* See pretense.

Affected, *adj.* See counterfeit, artificial, feigned, flamboyant, pompous.

Affected class 1. Persons who suffer the present effects of past job discrimination. **2.** Persons who constitute a class for purposes of bringing a class action.

Affecting commerce 1. In commerce. **2.** Having led or tending to lead to a labor dispute burdening or obstructing commerce or the free flow of commerce.

Affection, *n.* **1.** Fondness, attachment (genuine affection). Love, tenderness, tender feeling, tender passion, feeling, devotion, endearment, goodwill, inclination, partiality, regard, predisposition, kind disposition, solicitude, bias, bent, friendship, friendliness, warmth, liking, proclivity, propensity, kindness, penchant, passion, sentiment, concern, admiration, esteem, predilection. **2.** Disease (grave affection). Malady, ailment, sickness, illness, disorder, affliction, complaint, infirmity, condition, infection, indisposition, disturbance. **3.** Pawning or mortgaging something to assure the payment of money or the discharge of some other duty.

Affectionate, *adj.* Loving, passionate, caring, fond, partial, attached, doting, tender. See friendly, cooperative (2), charitable.

Affiance, *v.* **1.** To pledge, promise. **2.** To agree to marry; to engage.

Affiant, *n.* Someone who makes and files an affidavit. See deponent.

Affidavit, *n.* A written or printed declaration or statement of facts made voluntarily and confirmed under oath or affirmation before a person authorized to administer the oath or affirmation (the affidavit of the witness). Sworn statement, attestation, testimony, testimonial, deposition, avowal, declaration under oath, attested statement.

Affidavit of merits An affidavit stating that the defendant has a sound defense; an affidavit of defense.

Affidavit of service A sworn statement that a document (e.g., summons) has been exhibited or delivered to a designated person.

Affiliate 1. *n.* A branch; a company controlled by another company (an affiliate of General Motors). Division, subdivision, wing, subsidiary, unit, part, bureau, desk, department, chapter, office, local, component, arm, member, colleague, associate, auxiliary, assistant, partner. **2.** *v.* To join (the two firms affiliated on the case). Connect, unite, ally, associate, band together, incorporate, annex, attach, bring into close association, bring into close relation, combine, amalgamate, consolidate, merge, syndicate, federate, adopt, enter, register, enroll, enlist. **3.** *v.* To determine the paternity of an illegitimate child.

Affiliated, *adj.* See associated.

Affiliation, *n.* **1.** Being associated with a group or organization but not necessarily as a member thereof. See association, connection. **2.** Determining the paternity of an illegitimate child and the obligation to support it; a bastardy proceeding.

Affinity, *n.* **1.** The relationship that exists between a wife and her husband's blood relatives, or between a husband and his wife's blood relatives. Relationship by marriage, not by blood. Kinship, kindred, family tie, propinquity, heritage, connection, bond, clan, lineage, ancestry, consanguinity. **2.** Attraction, partiality (an affinity for computers). Fondness, propensity, sympathy, liking, inclination, friendliness, proclivity, fancy, leaning, bias, preference, predisposition, penchant, love, concern, regard, affection, bent, susceptibility. **3.** Likeness, similarity (an odd affinity between the opponents). Resemblance, parallelism, analogy, correlation, correspondence, compatibility, parity, similitude, homogeneity, symmetry. *Ant.* Consanguinity; antipathy; dissimilarity.

Affirm, *v.* **1.** To declare that a judgment, decree, or order of a lower tribunal is valid and must stand as rendered (the appellate court affirmed the judgment below). **2.** To approve or ratify (she affirmed the agent's contract). Confirm, endorse, certify, warrant, sustain, reassert, strengthen, substantiate, validate, corroborate, authenticate, acknowledge, uphold, concur, back up, vouch for, support, verify, substantiate, guarantee. **3.** To declare or assert (affirm his innocence). Maintain, claim, declare solemnly, testify, depose, vouch, contend, announce, say, state, allege, advance, adjure, propose, swear, asseverate, vow, assure, attest, proclaim, pronounce, aver, propound, enunciate, make a statement, make an assertion, assert positively, state positively, avouch, bear witness to, make an affidavit, insist, give evidence. *Ant.* Overturn; veto; be silent.

Affirmance, *n.* **1.** A declaration that a judgment, decree, or order of a lower tribunal is valid and must stand as rendered. **2.** The ratification or confirmation of a voidable or unauthorized act or contract by a party who is to be bound thereby. See affirmation, approval.

Affirmant, *n.* Someone who testifies on affirmation or affirms instead of taking an oath.

Affirmation, *n.* **1.** A solemn assertion or declaration which can be a substitute for an oath. **2.** Testimony, certification. Word, statement, sworn statement, assertion, avowal, averment, pronouncement, asseveration, adjuration, confirmation, establishment, acknowledgment, endorsement, approval, ratification, profession, deposition, allegation, assurance, assent, affidavit, verification, authentication, substantiation.

Affirmative 1. *adj.* Pertaining to that which establishes or declares something positively (an affirmative response). Categorical, emphatic, dogmatic, unequivocal, unqualified, absolute, express, explicit, declarative, definite, certain, positive, approving, corroborative, strengthening, confirmative, confirmatory, ratifying, concurring, agreeing, assenting, establishing, supporting. **2.** *n.* Yes; assent.

Affirmative action 1. Steps and programs that are designed to eliminate existing and continuing discrimination, to remedy the lingering effects of past discrimination, and to create systems and procedures to prevent future discrimination. **2.** Action taken by the National Labor Relations Board to correct wrongs that have been committed—remedial action, not merely punitive or disciplinary.

Affirmative charge An instruction to the jury that the defendant cannot be convicted under a designated count; removing an issue from the jury's consideration.

Affirmative defense A defense that raises matters not covered in the plaintiff's complaint and that will defeat the plaintiff's claim even if the plaintiff is able to prove all of the allegations in its complaint. Examples: contributory negligence, accord and satisfaction.

Affirmative easement An easement involving the giving of rights to use the land burdened with the easement when this use would otherwise be unlawful. See easement.

Affirmative pregnant An allegation in a pleading that implies a negative in favor of one's opponent.

Affirmative warranty An insurance warranty that asserts the existence of a fact at the time the policy is entered into. A promissory warranty, on the other hand, is an agreement that the insurer's duties shall be conditional on the future existence of certain facts.

Affix, *v.,* **affix,** *n.* **1.** *v.* To attach physically; to attach securely and permanently (affix your signature). Fasten, connect, annex, add, fix, unite, combine, join, subjoin, link, seal, button, gird, hood, staple, clip, buckle, sew, screw, append, adjoin, graft, incorporate, cohere, secure, bind, couple, cling to, set to, insert, tack, nail, enclose. **2.** *n.* Something added. Attachment, appendage, appendix, supplement, subscript, prefix, suffix. *Ant.* Detach (1).

Afflict, *v.* See harass, bemoan, suffer, cry (1); affliction.

Affliction, *n.* Causing continuing anguish or anxiety; the state of anxiety (endure the affliction). Misery, distress, adversity, calamity, disaster, grief, suffering, tribulation, trouble, sorrow, ordeal, misfortune, depression, catastrophe, wretchedness, trial, mishap, torment, plague, curse, woe, sickness, injury, persecution, torture, brutality, hardship, oppression, burden. See also anguish, anxiety, pain. *Ant.* Benefit, comfort.

Affluence, *n.* See wealth, property (1), luxury.

Affluent, *adj.* Rich, wealthy, comfortable, prosperous, well-to-do. See abundant.

Afforce, *v.* To add to or strengthen.

Afford, *v.* See provide, manage, furnish, bear, risk (2).

Affranchise, *v.* To set free from obligations. See liberate, enfranchisement.

Affray, *n.* The fighting of two or more persons in a public place. Fight, brawl, fracas, set-to, row, quarrel, conflict, battle, tussle, fisticuffs, commotion, riot, breach of the peace, disorderly conduct, clash, combat, fray, altercation, melee, tumult, scrimmage, contest, uproar, dissension, squabble, encounter, violence.

Affreightment, *n.* A contract to transport goods by ship.

Affront 1. *n.* An insult (a personal affront). Indignity, outrage, disgrace, injury, barb, discourtesy, insolence, contumely, slur, offense, slight, abuse, ill-treatment, "put-down," disrespect, wound, aspersion, humiliation, impertinence, wrong, provocation. **2.** *v.* To insult (to affront the witness). Offend, annoy, abuse, slight, wound, provoke, shame, displease, denigrate, chafe, irritate, ridicule, defame, degrade, damage, assault, disdain, sting, confront, vex, outrage, antagonize, pique, impugn, exasperate, humiliate, distress, confound, malign, confuse, wrong, disconcert, ill-treat, be offensive. *Ant.* Compliment; flatter.

Aficionado, *n.* Fan, devotee, enthusiast. See addict (1), champion (1).

A force et armis With force and arms.

Aforementioned, *adj.* See aforesaid.

Aforesaid, *adj.* Mentioned earlier in the statute, contract, or other document (the aforesaid clause). In a preceding part, already described, already identified, preceding, next before, prior, aforementioned, above mentioned, previously specified, named, such. *Ant.* Following.

Aforethought, *adj.* Thought of beforehand for any length of time, however short (malice aforethought). Premeditated, preconceived, forethought, prepense, predeliberated, preconsidered, deliberate, planned, designed, calculated, considerate, intended, reflective, studied, prepared, sober, calm. *Ant.* Spontaneous.

A fortiori, *adv.* With greater force, all the more so (if the earlier case is invalid, then a fortiori the later case is invalid). Still more conclusively, especially, with stronger reason, thus, accordingly, consequently, for a certainty, certainly.

Afraid, *adj.* Alarmed (afraid of the consequences). Terrified, frightened, apprehensive, panicky, fearful, edgy, tense, scared, jittery, anxious, uneasy, fainthearted,

Afraid

timid, intimidated. *Ant.* Calm.

Aft, *adv.* At or near the stern of a ship.

After, *adv., prep.* Later (shortly after; after long deliberation). Succeeding; subsequent to; inferior in point of time, priority, or preference; following, in consequence of, because of, behind.

Afterbirth, *n.* The placenta and fetal membranes expelled after childbirth.

Aftercare, *n.* Treatment during convalescence.

Afterlife, *n.* Future life. Eternity, perpetuity, Zion, afterworld, hereafter. See also heaven.

Aftermath, *n.* See consequence (1).

Afterthought, *n.* Second thought. Reconsideration, re-examination, reflection. See also review (2).

Afterward, *adv.* See subsequent.

Afterworld, *n.* See afterlife, heaven.

Again, *adv.* Anew. Afresh, once more, ditto, over, a second time, encore, repeatedly.

Against, *prep.* **1.** Contrary (against my wishes). In conflict with, versus, counter, at odds with, adverse to, directly opposite, contra, in opposition to, at cross-purposes, opposed to; counterbalance, match. **2.** Facing (against the wall). Fronting, toward, face to face, vis-à-vis, over against, in contact with, in full view of, upon, on.

Against the manifest weight of the evidence An opposite conclusion is clearly evident, or the verdict is palpably erroneous and wholly unwarranted.

Agape, *adj.* Astonished. Amazed, dazed, spellbound, stupefied, thunderstruck, dumbstruck, dumbfounded, agog, surprised, shocked, flabbergasted, aghast, horrified, appalled, stunned, awestruck, enthralled, excited, eager, breathless, alert. See also awesome.

Age 1. *n.* A length of time (our current age). Period, time, stage of time, life, stage of life, duration, duration of existence, epoch, era, eon, aeon, date, years, time, cycle, span, interval of years, generation, existence, period of existence, life span, season, phase, millennium, eternity. **2.** *n.* Old age. Advanced age, ancient, elderly, oldness, decline of life, declining years, ripe age, senescence, senility, superannuation, decrepitude, seniority, maturity, venerableness, patriarch, mellowness, vintage. **3.** *v.* To grow old (age with dignity). Mature, ripen, weather, wear, mellow, develop, season, wane, decline, deteriorate.

Agency, *n.* **1.** A relationship in which one person acts for another or represents another by the latter's authority (e.g., principal and agent, master and servant). **2.** A governmental body that carries out or administers the law. Bureau, commission, department, office, committee, authority, board, administration, bureaucracy, organization, establishment, delegation, desk. **3.** A business that acts on behalf of others. Firm, company, corporation, house. **4.** The means by which something is accomplished. Power, instrumentality, instrument, action, activity, force, intervention, operation, work, mechanism, function, management, causation, direction, influence, mediation, medium, representation, support, conduct, charge, command, handling, service, method, interaction, mission, mode of action, route, modus operandi, system, process, practice, course, procedure, steps, vehicle, intercession, procurement, effectiveness, doing, governance, superintendence.

Agency by estoppel An agency that arises when the principal's negligence allows others to believe that the agent possesses authority, which in fact does not exist.

Agency by operation of law An agency created by the law and not by agreement of the principal and agent. An agency by estoppel.

Agency in fact An agency created by agreement of principal and agent and not by operation of law.

Agency of the United States A department, division, or administration within the federal government.

Agency shop A union security device whereby to continue employment any nonunion employee is required to pay to the union sums equivalent to those paid by union members, either in an amount equal to both union dues and initiation fees or in an amount equal to dues alone.

Agenda, *n.* Things to be done (proposed agenda for the meeting). Program, memorandum of items of business, calendar, itinerary, schedule, business, docket, plan, organized list of events, proposal, proposition, timetable. See also schedule (1).

Agent, *n.* **1.** A person authorized to act for another; someone who conducts the business of another (a lawyer is the agent of the client). Representative, deputy, substitute, subagent, functionary, go-between, middleman, intermediary, factor, commissioner, surrogate, delegate, aide, advocate, emissary, negotiator, attorney, medium, proxy, servant, employee, broker, envoy, proctor, plenipotentiary, vicar, lieutenant, second, understudy, steward, sub, backup, stand-in, bench warmer, alternate, trustee, double, ambassador. **2.** That which produces an effect; a power (agent of destruction). Force, cause, instrument, means, agency, author, effective principle, vehicle, machine, element, doer, mover, actor, performer, operator, executor, promoter, perpetrator, worker, practitioner, executive.

Age of consent 1. The age at which people can marry without parental consent. See majority. **2.** The age at which a female can consent to sexual intercourse so that the male can avoid the charge of statutory rape.

Age of majority 1. Age of 18 or 21, depending on what the person is trying to do, the intent of the parties, the intent of the statute, etc. **2.** The age at which a person can no longer disaffirm a contract. **3.** The age at which one can vote, enter a will, etc. **4.** The age at which the right to be supported by parents often ends.

Age of reason The age at which a child is deemed capable of acting responsibly (often 7 years of age). Below age 7, a child is conclusively presumed to be incapable of committing a crime.

Agglomeration, *n.* See accumulation, collection.

Agglutinate, *v.* See attach (2).

Aggrandize, *v.* See promote, augment; enhance.

Aggrandizement, *n.* See increase, accumulation.

Aggravate, *v.* See harass, disturb, exacerbate, accost (1), provoke, outrage (2), attack; aggravated.

Aggravated 1. *adj.* Made worse (aggravated injuries). Heightened, inflamed, increased, worsened, made more severe, made more grievous, magnified, deepened, exaggerated, exacerbated, amplified, enlarged, augmented, sharpened, multiplied. **2.** *v.* Exasperated (he was aggravated by the attack). Provoked, irritated, annoyed, bothered, infuriated, offended, disturbed, enraged, angered, affronted, harassed. *Ant.* Improved; relieved.

Aggravated assault 1. Often, an assault with a deadly weapon or with the intent to kill, rob, or rape. **2.** An attempt to cause serious bodily injury to another or causing such bodily injury knowingly or recklessly under circumstances manifesting extreme indifference to the value of human life.

Aggravating, *adj.* See offensive, obnoxious, odious, blatant, aggravated.

Aggravation, *n.* Circumstances that increase the enormity of a crime or tort, adding to its injurious consequences; the circumstances go beyond the essential elements of the crime or tort itself. See aggravated, nuisance, annoyance, dissatisfaction.

Aggravation of damages

Aggravation of damages 1. Special circumstances that warrant an increase in the damage award, e.g., malice of the wrongdoer. **2.** An increase in the damages suffered in connection with a pre-existing injury.

Aggregate 1. *n.* Total amount (the aggregate of the damage). Entire number, complete whole, mass, total, sum, total, total amount, sum, body, amount, combination, collection, assemblage, composite, compound, gross amount, union, totality, whole, composite whole, conglomeration, entirety. **2.** *v.* To bring together. Accumulate, assemble, collect, gather, amass, cluster, cumulate, group, lump together, systematize, unite, conglomerate, compile, integrate, join.

Aggregate theory of partnership A partnership is the totality of persons engaged in a business and not an entity in itself as in the case of a corporation.

Aggregation, *n.* The combination of two or more elements in patent claims, each of which is unrelated and each of which performs separately and without cooperation, where the combination does not define a composite integrated mechanism. See aggregate.

Aggregation doctrine A rule that precludes a totaling of claims in order to reach the jurisdictional amount necessary to sue in a federal court.

Aggression, *n.* See assault, attack, infringement.

Aggressive, *adj.* See belligerent, hostile, contentious, litigious, disobedient, offensive, assertive, diligent.

Aggressor, *n.* The person who initiates the use of force; the person who provokes, invites, or seeks trouble. Attacker, assailant, raider, trespasser, invader, assailer, assaulter, belligerent, antagonist.

Aggrieve, *v.* See injure, provoke (2), bemoan, suffer, cry (1).

Aggrieved, *adj.* Having been injured; having been deprived of legal rights (aggrieved minority). Damnified, afflicted, wounded, wronged, ill-used, ill-treated, maltreated, mistreated, stung, beset, distressed, abused, imposed upon, offended, damaged, oppressed, misused, hurt, adversely affected, grieved, offended, persecuted, anguished, taken advantage of.

Aggrieved party Someone who suffers a substantial grievance; someone whose legal right is invaded; someone whose personal or property rights or interests are directly affected by a decree, order or judgment.

Aghast, *adj.* See agape.

Agile, *adj.* See active (3), flexible, malleable.

Aging; aging of accounts Classifying the accounts receivable according to the time that has elapsed since the date of billing or the due date (e.g., 30 days, 60 days).

Agitate, *v.* See provoke, exacerbate, intimidate, disturb, harass.

Agitation, *n.* See disturbance, confusion (1), emotion, passion.

Agitator, *n.* Someone who stirs up or disturbs things (outside agitator). Activist, social reformer, advocate, fomenter, instigator, incendiary, firebrand, inciter, demagogue, "rabble-rouser," militant, revolutionary, troublemaker. *Ant.* Peacemaker.

Aglow *adj.* See clear (3).

Agnate, *adj.* Having a common source; descended from the male side. See akin (1).

Agnostic, *n.* Doubter, skeptic, disbeliever.

Agog, *adj.* See agape.

Agonize, *v.* See suffer.

Agony, *n.* See anguish, anxiety, depression, affliction, pain.

Agrarian, *adj.* Relating to land (agrarian reform). Agricultural, agronomic, farming, cropraising, rural, pastoral, country, geoponic.

Agree, *v.* **1.** To come to an agreement (they agreed to incorporate). Come to an understanding, strike a bargain, bargain, covenant, contract, settle, compromise, come to terms, give mutual assent, exchange promises. **2.** To accept (they agreed to the plan). Assent, concur, comply, allow, suit, consent, acquiesce, approve, accord, concede, subscribe, correspond, accede, adapt, adopt, grant, endorse, affirm, confirm, sanction, stipulate, ratify, yield, pledge, promise, undertake, avow, acknowledge. **3.** To come into harmony (the balance sheets did not agree). Coincide, conform, match, tally, accommodate, reconcile, unite, settle, comport, blend, join, harmonize, "square."

Agreeable, *adj.* See attractive, enjoyable, cooperative (2), conciliatory, amicable, friendly, appropriate (3), charitable (2).

Agreed case A written statement of facts agreed to by the parties and submitted to the court so that a trial on these facts will not be needed. The court will then rule on the questions of law. The facts agreed upon are the ultimate, material facts of the case.

Agreement, *n.* **1.** A manifestation of mutual assent by two or more persons to one another; a meeting of the minds (agreement to sell). Bargain, contract, pact, deal, covenant, compact, settlement, arrangement, concordat, mutual understanding, treaty, obligation, commitment, pledge, engagement, undertaking, stipulation, mutual promise. **2.** Harmony; the absence of dissension (agreement between the accounts). Concurrence, unity, accord, conformity, uniformity, concord, parallelism, correspondence, concert, affinity, similitude, cooperation, consonance, assent, congruity, consent, understanding.

Agribusiness, *n.* Agriculture operating as big business.

Agriculture, *n.* Raising crops and livestock. Farming, cultivation, husbandry, agrology, agronomy, geoponics, tillage, gardening, soil conservation, horticulture.

Aid 1. *v.* To assist; to supplement the efforts of others. Support, help, act in cooperation with, promote, abet, foster, back, bolster, succor, advance, serve, encourage, advocate, further, second, benefit, accommodate, sustain, facilitate, reinforce, strengthen, rescue, cooperate, oblige, attend, uphold, ease, lend assistance. **2.** *n.* Assistance. Help, relief, succor, lift, support, benefit, cooperation, allowance, furtherance, patronage, charity, dole, donation, rescue, helping hand, subsidy, reinforcement, accommodation, facilitation, guidance, encouragement, maintenance, supplies. **3.** *n.* Assistant. Helper, auxiliary, associate, helpmate, backer, supporter, deputy, co-worker, attendant.

Aid and abet Assist, counsel, or incite someone to commit a crime. See aid (1), abet.

Aid bond Local government bonds that aid private industry engaged in a project that will benefit the public.

Aide, *n.* See aid (3), assistant.

Aider by verdict The curing or healing, by the verdict rendered, of a defect or error in the pleading that might have been objected to before the verdict. The facts that the jury logically needed to reach the verdict are assumed to have been properly alleged.

Ail, *v.* To worry. Distress, trouble, afflict, sicken, wound. See also suffer (1), pain.

Ailment, *n.* Bodily or mental indisposition; a slight disorder (recurring ailment). Illness, sickness, disability, weakness, disease, complaint, infirmity, malady, indisposition, condition, discomfort, infection, pain, hurt, ache, affliction, affection, syndrome. *Ant.* Fitness.

Aim 1. *v.* To act intentionally; to point intentionally; to direct a weapon at a distinct portion of an object (he aimed the gun at the car). Focus, take aim, level, train, beam, zero in, concentrate, give direction to, head, sight, fix. **2.** *v.* To try; to attempt (to aim for a retrial). Endeavor, essay, purpose, intend, want, wish, strive, crave, yearn for, aspire to, seek, mean. **3.** *n.* Intention, plan (our aim is to obtain a reversal). Purpose, design, intent, object, objective, scheme, goal, mark, desire, reason, aspiration, ambition, direction, wish, inclination, tendency, endeavor, determination, target, end, course, undertaking, desideratum, point.

Aimless, *adj.* See accidental (1), capricious, blind (1), casual, fortuitous, irregular.

Air 1. *n.* Atmosphere, sky, stratosphere, oxygen, wind. See also climate (1). **2.** *n.* See pretense. **3.** *v.* See express (2), proclaim, communicate. **4.** *n.* See environment, climate (2).

Aircraft, *n.* Plane. Airplane, jet, dirigible, glider, airliner, helicopter, blimp, rocket, satellite.

Air Force, *n.* See military.

Airing, *n.* See circulation.

Air piracy, *n.* See piracy, hijack.

Airplane, *n.* See aircraft.

Airport, *n.* Landing area. Airstrip, field, airdrome, runway; hangar.

Air raid, *n.* See attack (2).

Airstrip, *n.* See airport.

Airtight, *adj.* See incontestable.

Airy, *adj.* Ventilated, exposed. See immaterial, illusory.

Aisle, *n.* See passage (2), highway, course (1).

Ajar, *adj.* See open (3).

Akin, *adj.* **1.** Related by blood. Kin, kindred, having a common ancestor, cognate, of the same stock, consanguineous, agnate, affiliated, allied, of one blood, fraternal. **2.** Comparable. Alike, agreeing, corresponding, conforming, similar, analogous, like, related, matching, affiliated, identical, germane, connected, associated, parallel, resembling, relevant, linked, harmonizing, congenial, interchangeable, allied. *Ant.* Unrelated; unlike.

Alacrity, *n.* See speed (1).

Alarm *n.* See fear, consternation, apprehension (3); warning; provoke, intimidate.

Alarming, *n.* See hazardous, dangerous, precarious, distressing, imminent.

Albatross, *n.* See burden (1, 2).

Album, *n.* See record (2).

Alcohol, *n.* See liquor, intoxicating liquor.

Alcoholic, *n.* See drunkard; intoxicated.

Alcove, *n.* Niche. Cubicle, bay, recess, corner, nook, stall, cavity. See also cell, chamber (1), asylum (2).

Alderman, *n.* A member of the local legislative body. See legislator.

Aleatory contract A mutual agreement in which the advantages and losses depend on an uncertain event, e.g., an insurance contract. Performance depends on uncertain contingencies.

Alert, 1. *adj.* See circumspect, cautious, active (3), prompt (1), alive (2). **2.** *n.* See warning. **3.** *v.* See notify, publish.

Alertness, *n.* See caution (3).

ALI American Law Institute.

Alia Other things.

Alias, *n.* False name. Assumed name, pseudonym, also known as (a.k.a.), nom de guerre, sobriquet.

Alias execution A second writ of execution after the first one was returned without being successful in satisfying the judgment.

Alias summons A new summons issued when the original has not produced its effect because of a defect in the form or manner of service.

Alias writ A second or further writ that takes the place of an earlier writ that has not been effective.

Alibi, *n.* A defense alleging that the defendant was "elsewhere" at the time of the crime and therefore could not have committed it. Excuse, justification, explanation, reason, apology. See also pretext, pretense.

Alien 1. *n.* A foreign-born person who has not qualified as a U.S. citizen. Resident foreigner, noncitizen, unnaturalized person. See also stranger. **2.** *adj.* Strange, unfamiliar. Remote, foreign, distant, exotic, bizarre, estranged, separated, conflicting, contrary, hostile, adverse, antagonistic, contrasted, dissimilar, unlike, unconnected, unaffiliated, different, unrelated, inappropriate, inconsistent, unallied, not pertinent, extraneous, inapplicable, irrelevant, opposed, incompatible, incongruous, contradictory, outside. **3.** *n.* Stranger. Foreigner, outsider, newcomer, outlander, interloper, intruder, immigrant, emigrant, refugee. **4.** *v.* To convey; to transfer title. *Ant.* Citizen; natural.

Alienable, *adj.* See Transferable. Legally capable of being transferred to the ownership of another.

Alienage, *n.* The condition or status of an alien.

Alien and Sedition Acts Federal statutes of 1798 punishing those who criticized or defamed the government, giving the president the power to deport undesirable aliens, lengthening residency requirements to become a citizen, etc.

Alienate, *v.* **1.** To transfer; to transfer title (to alienate property). Convey, assign, demise, remise, consign, deed, sign over, make over, abalienate, give up, hand over, turn over, devolve, transfer ownership, relinquish, cede, surrender. **2.** To estrange; to make hostile (he alienated the judge). Make unfriendly, separate, divorce, disaffect, antagonize, divide, disengage, disunite, withdraw, withdraw the affections of, wean, aggravate, detach, set against, break off, sever, rupture, embitter, turn away, fall out, repel, incense, provoke. *Ant.* Retain; mediate.

Alienation, *n.* **1.** The transfer of property by conveyance, by will, etc. See exchange (2), conveyance (1). **2.** Rupture, schism, bitterness. See separation (2), hostility, animus. **3.** Mental derangement; insanity.

Alienation clause A clause in an insurance policy that voids the policy if the property being insured is sold.

Alienation of affections A tort consisting of (a) the intent of a third person to diminish the marital relationship between a husband and wife, (b) affirmative conduct in carrying out this intent, (c) affections (e.g., society, assistance, sexual relations) between the spouses are in fact alienated, and (d) the alienation was caused by the third person.

Alienee, *n.* A person to whom property is conveyed or transferred.

Alienist, *n.* A doctor specializing in mental diseases; a doctor who is an expert on the mental competence of witnesses.

Alienor, *n.* A person who transfers or conveys property.

Alight, *v.* Step down; come to rest on the ground (alight from the plane). Come down, dismount, disembark, touch down, set down, land, settle, descend, perch. See also landing (2).

Align, aline, *v.* See adjust (1, 2); adapt; ally (3), associate (1).

Alignment, alinement, *n.* **1.** An adjustment to a line. See adjustment, modification. **2.** The plan for a road. **3.** See association (3).

Alike 1. *adj.* Similar (alike in their methods). Analogous, resembling, like, akin, comparable, related, synonymous, tantamount, corresponding, kindred, homogeneous, equivalent, parallel, in like manner, closely allied. **2.** *adv.* Identically (by judge and jury alike). Equally, uniformly, evenly, similarly, all the same, in the same way, as duplicates. *Ant.* Different; separately.

Alimony, *n.* Support that one spouse pays another after they have been separated or divorced (monthly alimony). Maintenance, separate maintenance, support payment, sustenance, upkeep, allowance. See also means, maintenance (1), assistance.

41

Alimony in gross A single, definite, and determined sum of alimony not subject to change or modification. The amount, however, may be payable over a set period of time in installments.

Alimony pendente lite Alimony that is provided pending the outcome of the suit for divorce, legal separation, or separate maintenance. Temporary alimony.

Aline, align, *v.* See adjust (1, 2), adapt; ally (3).

Aliquot, *adj.* **1.** Contained in something else an exact number of times. **2.** Fractional; any definite interest.

Alive, *adj.* **1.** Having life (kept alive). Living, animate, existing, subsisting, quick, breathing, extant, functioning. See also conscious. **2.** Vigorous (alive with excitement). Vivacious, animated, vibrant, brisk, energetic, alert, spry, exciting, excited, dynamic, active, robust, spirited. *Ant.* Deceased; apathetic.

ALJ See Administrative Law Judge.

All, *adj., n., pron., adv.* The entire amount of something; the whole; all the individual components without exception. Aggregate, totality, everything, everybody, entirety, complete, full, universe, universal, each and every, utterly, sum, undiminished, any, any and all, utmost, perfect.

All-absorbing, *adj.* See central (2).

Allah, *n.* See God.

All-around, *adj.* See comprehensive.

Allay, *v.* See mitigate, assuage.

Allegation, *n.* A statement of fact that one expects to prove (allegation of wrongdoing). Assertion, statement, declaration, plea, affirmation, averment, testimony, contention, ipse dixit, charge, complaint, claim, accusation, imputation, incrimination, affidavit, inculpation.

Allegation of faculties A wife's statement on the property of her husband in reference to an alimony claim.

Allege, *v.* To state facts you expect to prove (she alleged that the car was stolen). Recite, claim, assert, charge, declare, affirm, avow, advance, maintain, plead, aver, adduce, set forth, accuse, attest, introduce, predicate, urge, cite, say, profess, contend, present, asseverate, avouch, propound.

Alleged, *adj.* Supposed, represented, declared, or affirmed. See putative, reputed, ostensible, doubtful.

Allegiance, *n.* The obligation of fidelity and obedience to the government in return for protection. Faithfulness, homage, fealty, loyalty, duty, obligation, devotion, submission, deference, subjection, subservience, subjugation, dedication, adherence, attachment, responsibility, commitment, pledge, support. *Ant.* Treason.

Allegory, *n.* See legend, symbol; symbolic.

Allen charge A supplementary instruction to a jury having difficulty reaching a decision, in which the judge tells the jurors that they should carefully listen to and be deferential toward each other's views. Also called a "dynamite" charge, a "shotgun" instruction, a "third-degree" instruction, and a "nitroglycerine" charge.

Allergy, *n.* Hypersensitivity. Weakness, vulnerability, sensitivity, susceptibility; aversion.

All events test For accrual method taxpayers, income is earned when (a) all the events have occurred that fix the right to receive the income, and (b) the amount can be determined with reasonable accuracy.

Alleviate, *v.* See mitigate, assuage; remedy, heal, cure (2).

Alleviation, *n.* See reduction; remedial.

Alley, *n.* See passage (2), highway, course (1).

All fours See "on all fours," analogous.

Alliance, *n.* **1.** Union through intermarriage; affinity. Family connection, relationship, nuptial tie, kinship. **2.** An association of states or nations. Federation, confederation, confederacy, coalition, fusion, pool, union, affiliation, combination, league, Anschluss, merger, partnership, syndicate, consortium, association, cartel. **3.** Treaty. Accord, compact, pact, covenant, entente, agreement, concordat, understanding.

Allied, *adj.* See associated; alliance.

All-important, *adj.* See crucial, important.

All-inclusive, *adj.* See comprehensive, complete (2), full.

Allocable, *adj.* Distributable. In analyzing accounts, the breaking down of a lump sum charged or credited to one account into several parts to be charged or credited to other accounts. See allocate, allot.

Allocate, *v.* To assign or distribute (allocate the tasks). Allot, earmark, mete, apportion, divide, admeasure, appropriate, deal, parcel out, consign, set aside, dispense, share, designate, classify, ration, administer, set apart, portion out, grant, assort.

Allocation, *n.* See distribution, division; allocate, allot.

Allocation of income 1. In trust accounting, the process by which income is distributed between principal and income. **2.** When two or more businesses are controlled by the same interests, the IRS may allocate or distribute income to prevent tax evasion.

Allocution, *n.* A formal inquiry by the judge of the defendant who has just been convicted of a crime as to whether the latter has any cause to show why sentence should not be imposed. The right to make a statement before sentence is imposed.

Allodial, *adj.* Free; owned without obligation.

Allodium, *n.* Absolute ownership of land; land not subject to any rent, service, or other tenurial right of an overlord.

Allograph, *n.* A writing or signature made for a person by another (the opposite of autograph).

Allonge, *n.* A piece of paper annexed to a bill of exchange or promissory note. Endorsements are written on this attached paper when no room is available on the instrument itself. Appendix, rider, supplement, addendum, postscript.

Allot, *v.* To divide, apportion, or distribute; to apportion shares, debentures, etc., to those who have applied for them. Allocate, assign, earmark, measure out, mete out, partition, classify, set apart, portion out, share, destine, prorate, appoint, specify, designate, ration, parcel out, dispense, dole out, deal, administer, give, grant, allow, award, provide, present, prescribe, ordain.

Allotment, *n.* **1.** A share, portion, or partition. Apportionment, allocation, appointment, ration, percentage, measure, part, "cut," fraction, allowance, assignment, quota, consignment, division, proportion, disposal, distribution, dispensation, disposition, grant, dole, deal. **2.** Land acquired by or awarded to individual Indians.

Allottee, *n.* A person who receives a share under an allotment.

All-out, *adj.* See complete (2).

Allow, *v.* **1.** To bestow (allow yourself enough time). Assign, grant, confer, give, allocate, allot, furnish, impart. **2.** To approve; to authorize (the judge allowed the extension). Accept, admit, concede, adopt, acknowledge, vouchsafe, endorse, support, acquiesce, agree, sanction, permit, license, grant, accredit, certify, qualify, sustain, charter, commission, empower, legitimize, legitimate, enable, defer. **3.** To tolerate (further delay will not be allowed). Endure, suffer, bear, consent, yield, submit, permit, withstand, brook, countenance, undergo.

Allowable, *adj.* See admissible, legal, adequate.

Allowance, *n.* **1.** Portion assigned or bestowed. See allotment (1). **2.** Acceptance, admission, or authorization. See approval. **3.** Tolerance. See endurance. **4.** Family support. See maintenance (1); compensation. **5.** See benefit. **6.** Deduction, exemption. See discount (1).

Alloy, *n.*, **alloy,** *v.* See compound (3); pollution; debase.

All right, *adv.* See adequate, competent, safe (2), fit (1), healthy.

Allude, *v.* See refer, intimate (6).

Allure, *v.* See entice, entrap, seduce.

Alluring, *adj.* See attractive, beautiful, enjoyable, intriguing, compelling; entice.

Allusion, *n.* See reference, citation (2), insinuation, suggestive.

Allusive, *adj.* See suggestive.

Alluvion, *n.* Accretion; the process of gradual and imperceptible increase of the earth on the shore due to the movements of the water. See accretion.

Ally, *n.*, **ally,** *v.* **1.** *n.* One nation that has joined an alliance with another (a faithful ally). **2.** *n.* An associate (an ally at the firm). Partner, confederate, assistant, colleague, coalitionist, confrere, coadjutor, supporter, cooperator, aide, helper, auxiliary, friend, affiliate, co-worker, accessory, abettor, accomplice, collaborator. **3.** *v.* To unite (ally yourself with experts). Band together, join, align, combine, connect, associate, league, marry, unify, affiliate, federate.

Alma mater, *n.* See school (1).

Almanac, *n.* See record (2).

Almighty, *adj.* See absolute, dominant, God.

Almost, *adv.* See about (1), hardly.

Alms, *n.* See charity (1), donation, assistance (2), bounty (2).

Almsgiving, *n.* See bounty (2); charitable (1).

Alone, *adj.*, *adv.* **1.** By oneself. Sole, singly, apart from others, without others, single, unassisted, of one's own power, solo, separately, only. **2.** Unique. Unparalleled, peerless, unmatched, incomparable, singular, unequaled, matchless. **3.** Isolated. Solitary, deserted, abandoned, unaccompanied, detached, apart, desolate, removed, separate, forlorn, forsaken, lonely, private.

Along, *prep.*, *adv.* Lengthwise. In a line with, following the line of, along the side of, from one end to the other, parallel to the length of, on the border of, next to, side by side.

Aloof, *adj.* See indifferent, remote (1), neutral, apathetic; reserve (4).

Aloud, *adv.* Audibly, loudly, noisily, plainly, resoundingly, or distinctly.

Alpha, *n.* See commencement.

Alphabetize, *v.* See file (3), group (2).

Also, *adv.* In addition, in like manner, besides, as well, likewise, similarly, too, this too, withal, along with, including, further, furthermore, moreover, and, plus.

Altar, *n.* Table, mound, platform; shrine, temple, sanctuary. See also holy, religion, God.

Alter, *v.* To make a change in; to change partially; to modify without altering its identity (alter the document). Transform, vary, moderate, shift, twist, turn, increase, decrease, remake, transmute, reshape, reform, recast, adjust, "doctor," reduce, accommodate, adapt, refashion, tamper, temper, remodel, permute, revise, reconstruct, modulate, rearrange, diversify, accustom, metamorphose, mutate, reorganize, deviate, invert. See also convert.

Alterable, *adj.* See convertible.

Alteration, *n.* **1.** Making a thing different from what it was before without destroying its identity. See change (1), modification, conversion; alter. **2.** Writing or erasing on a document or instrument that changes its language or meaning.

Altercate, *v.* See argue, debate (1), fight (2), contend (1).

Altercation, *n.* A heated or angry dispute (an altercation over the bill). Quarrel, wrangle, wrangling, fight, scrap, brawl, affray, row, broil, strife, scene, fracas, scuffle, bickering, dispute, discord, contention, argument, disturbance, jarring, "rhubarb," intense debate, combat, contest, squabble, clash, "spat," conflict, war of words, melee, jangle, dissension, remonstrance, "falling out," feud.

Alter ego, *n.* **1.** Second self. Double, the other "I," the other self, double, stand-in. See also consort (1). **2.** In corporate law, the doctrine of alter ego allows the court to disregard the corporate entity (pierce the corporate veil) and hold the individual responsible for acts knowingly and intentionally done in the name of the corporation. See instrumentality rule, piercing the corporate veil.

Alternate 1. *v.* Rotate. Platoon, alter, interchange, vary, reciprocate, take turns. **2.** *n.* Substitute or back-up. See agent (1), surrogate.

Alternative, *n., adj.* Choice between two things, courses, or propositions; the option that may be selected. Pick, preference, election, decision, recourse, selection, conclusion, other choice, substitute, replacement, back-up, resource, reserve.

Alternative pleading Alleging facts in a pleading (e.g., complaint) that are not necessarily consistent. Pleading statements in the alternative, any one of which would be sufficient independently.

Alternative remainders Remainders in which disposition of the property is made in the alternative, one to take effect only if the other does not, and in substitution of it.

Although, *conj.* Notwithstanding. In spite of, even though, even if, despite the fact that, albeit, however. See nevertheless.

Altimeter, *n.* A device to determine height or elevation.

Altitude, *n.* Elevation or summit. Height, top, pinnacle, zenith, acme, crown, supremacy, apogee, tip, crest.

Altogether, *adv.* Completely, thoroughly, totally. See entire.

Altruism, *n.* See benevolence, bounty (2).

Altruistic, *adj.* See humanitarian, benevolent, charitable (1).

Always, *adv.* Without exception. Forever, every time, regularly, unceasingly, without end, perpetually, eternally, incessantly, inevitably, interminably.

Amalgam, *n.* See compound (3), amalgamation (2).

Amalgamate, *v.* See combine, affiliate (2), amalgamation.

Amalgamation, *n.* **1.** Consolidation, combining. Interfusion, intermarriage, merger, coalescence, blending, commingling, mixture, mixing, fusing, association, confederation, federation, integration, incorporation, compound, conjunction, co-mixture. **2.** The union of two or more corporations into one corporate body.

Amass, *v.* See accumulate, hoard.

Amateur, *n.* Novice. Layman, dabbler, nonprofessional, dilettante, neophyte, tyro. See also beginner. *Ant.* Expert.

Amaze, *v.* Astonish. Stagger, astound, stun, dumfound, shock, flabbergast, stupefy, awe. See also surprise (1); agape.

Amazement, *n.* See surprise (2), consternation; agape.

Amazing, *adj.* See extraordinary, appalling, intriguing, attractive; agape.

Ambassador, *n.* See delegate (2).

Ambiance, ambience, *n.* See environment, climate (2).

Ambidexter, *n., adj.* **1.** Able to use both hands. **2.** An attorney who is paid by both sides. **3.** A juror who is paid by both sides. **4.** Someone who works both ends. See deceptive, fraud.

Ambience, ambiance, *n.* See environment; aura.

Ambiguity, *n.* That which is doubtful or uncertain (ambiguity in the statute). Double meaning, equivocation, double talk, indefiniteness, ambivalence, uncertainty, obscurity. See also vagueness. *Ant.* Clarity.

Ambiguity upon the factum An ambiguity as to the foundation of the document itself as opposed to doubt on the meaning of a certain clause in it.

Ambiguous, *adj.* Doubtful or capable of more than one meaning (ambiguous clause). Equivocal, abstruse, cryptic, enigmatic, unclear, uncertain, vague, indeterminate, problematic, obscure, in doubt, at issue, puzzling, perplexing, indefinite, foggy, questionable, borderline, not specific, undefined, dubious, two-edged, double-edged, cloudy, circuitous, nebulous, deceptive, misleading. *Ant.* Plain.

Ambit, *n.* Boundary; the limits of a power. Limit, enclosing line, border, perimeter, range, rim, realm, orbit, circumference, circuit, margin, sphere, periphery, bounds, domain, extent, province, jurisdiction, dominion, confines.

Ambition, *n.* Drive, push, zeal, force, spirit, energy, or enthusiasm. See aim (3), intent (1); ambitious.

Ambitious, *adj.* Enterprising. Eager, avid, zealous, industrious, aggressive, forceful, driving, hungry, "pushy," avaricious, greedy, scheming, selfish. *Ant.* Timid.

Ambivalence, *n.* See doubt (2), conflict (1).

Ambivalent, *adj.* See doubtful (1), ambiguous.

Amble, *v.* See walk.

Ambulance chasing Soliciting business by or for an attorney, e.g., seeking out people who have been recently injured in order to offer attorney services.

Ambulate, *v.* See walk.

Ambulatory, *adj.* Revocable (ambulatory will). **1.** Subject to change, capable of alteration, mutable, not fixed, reversible, changeable, modifiable, variable, amendable, permutable. **2.** Walking, moving (ambulatory exercise). Mobile, itinerant, nomadic, pedestrian, peripatetic, up and about. *Ant.* Irrevocable; stationary.

Ambush 1. *n.* A surprise attack from a concealed position. Ambuscade, pitfall, lure, lying in wait, waylaying. **2.** *v.* To attack unexpectedly. Snare, trap, bushwhack, lure, entrap, ensnare, assault, assail.

Ameliorate, *v.* See improve, advance (4), remedy (2), amend (1), benefit (2).

Ameliorating waste Waste committed by the tenant that in fact improves the land.

Amelioration, *n.* **1.** Improvement. Elevation, advancement, reform. See amendment (1), betterment (2). **2.** Mitigation. Alleviation, remedy, mending, cure. See also mitigate.

Amenable, *adj.* **1.** Accountable (he held himself amenable to the orders of the court). Answerable, responsible, subject to answer to the law, liable, liable to answer, liable to punishment, liable to be called to account. **2.** Responsive (amenable to suggestions). Accessible, obedient, receptive, submissive, adaptable, malleable, flexible, agreeable, pliant, yielding, plastic, acquiescent, cooperative, compliant, open-minded, complaisant, willing, persuadable, reasonable, favorably disposed, accommodating, docile, elastic, manageable, pliable, supple, timid, deferential, obsequious, flaccid, passive, corrigible, educable, reformable, willing to listen, tractable, impressionable, obliging, sympathetic.

Amend, *v.* **1.** To improve (amend the condition). Correct, remedy, repair, reform, purify, rectify, better, cleanse, mend, make better, perfect, ameliorate, refine, upgrade, meliorate, emend, polish, redeem, redress. **2.** To change (amend the proposal). Revise, alter, enlarge, add, develop, transform, refashion, revamp, rewrite, rework, modify, adjust, edit, qualify, commute, convert.

Amendment, *n.* **1.** Improvement. Correction, remedy, repairing, reformation, rectification, betterment, perfection, clarification, amelioration, refinement, redemption, redressing, purification. **2.** A change. Revision, alteration, enlargement, addition, development, transformation, revamping, reworking, rewriting, modification, adjustment, editing, qualification, variation, conversion, metamorphosis, exchange. **3.** Legislation. Statute, act, measure, bill, rider, resolution, clause. **4.** Attachment. Supplement, appendix, appendage, addendum, postscript. *Ant.* Deterioration (1); status quo (2).

Amends, *n.* Payment or satisfaction for a wrong (to make amends for the inconvenience). Reparation, compensation, indemnity, indemnification, restitution, atonement, retribution, remuneration, redress, restoration, quid pro quo, recompense, requital, expiation, return, damages, rectification, reimbursement, settlement, relief, quittance, propitiation, recoupment, adjustment, vindication, peace offering, apology, acknowledgment.

Amenity, amenities, *n.* **1.** Features of property that make it agreeable or pleasant (among the amenities of the apartment were the location, the view, the access to transportation, etc.) Enhancement, attraction, convenience, facility, accommodation, enjoyableness, charm, luxury, lure, appeal, refinement. **2.** A negative easement that restrains the owner of property from doing on or with the land that which would otherwise be lawful. **3.** Civility (he possessed the requisite amenities). Manners, courtesy, gentility, graciousness, amiability, gentleness, politeness, social grace, good breeding, urbanity, protocol, sociability. See also ceremony. *Ant.* Disadvantages (1); rudeness (3).

A mensa et thoro See divorce a mensa et thoro.

Amerce, *v.* To punish by fine or penalty. Discipline, judge, condemn, punish, impose a punishment, mulct, penalize, chastise. *Ant.* Reward.

Amercement, *n.* A fine or punishment. Deprivation, mulct, pecuniary penalty, condemnation, chastisement.

American rule The winning party in litigation cannot obtain the costs of attorney fees from the losing party unless authorized by statute or unless the losing party acted in bad faith, vexatiously, wantonly, or for oppressive reasons.

Ami, amy, *n.* Friend, amicus.

Amiable, *adj.* See amicable, convivial, friendly, attractive, cooperative (2), benevolent.

Amicable, *adj.* Mutually agreed to by the parties; friendly (an amicable demand). Harmonious, amiable, agreeable, consenting, accommodating, obliging, peaceable, cordial, willing, submissive, benign, civil, polite, pleasant, understanding. See also benevolent, friendly, convivial. *Ant.* Hostile, adversary.

Amicus curiae, *n., adj.* Friend of the court. A nonparty who advises or makes suggestions to the court. An amicus curiae brief is the document containing this advice that is submitted to an appellate court.

Amiss, *adj., adv.* See wrong (2, 3), erroneous.

Amity, *n.* See peace, harmony (1); companionship.

Ammunition, *n.* Bullets. Explosives, powder, bombs, cartridges, fuzes, gunpowder, torpedoes. See also arms, gun, weapon.

Amnesia, *n.* Loss of memory. A state of forgetfulness, inability to remember.

Amnesty, *n.* A collective or general pardon from the state (they were all granted amnesty for their crimes). Forgiveness, absolution, release, remission, discharge, acquittal, exoneration, waiving, dismissal, immunity, excuse, clemency, reprieve, mercy, leniency, exemption, forgetting, oblivion, dispensation, liberation, moratorium. *Ant.* Condemnation, prosecution.

Among, *prep.* In the group of; amid (the property is to be divided among the heirs). Intermingled with, between, mingled with the same group, in company with, in association with, in the class of, with one another, in the midst of, by all, by many of.

Amoral, *adj.* Neither moral nor immoral. See neutral, indifferent, callous, bad (2).

Amorous, *adj.* Loving, ardent, sexual. See passion.

Amorphous, *adj.* See indeterminate, indefinite, ambiguous, abstract, obscure (1).

Amortization, *n.* The liquidation of a debt by installments or by payments into a sinking fund. The allocation (and charge to expense) of the cost or other basis of an intangible asset over its estimated useful life. The process of writing off the cost of an intangible asset to the periods benefited. Examples of amortizable intangibles include patents, copyrights, and leasehold interests. Intangible assets with an indefinite life (e.g., goodwill) are not amortizable. Reduction of a debt or fund, discharge, liquidating a debt or claim.

Amotion, *n.* Removing something or someone from a position or office. Eviction, removal, putting out, turning out, carrying away, ouster.

Amount, *n.* **1.** Total (the amount of the damages). Sum, sum total, aggregate, magnitude, volume, enumeration, whole quantity, whole, extent, reach, range, account. **2.** Any quantity (the amount of your involvement). Measure, bulk, mass, volume, enumeration, parcel, estimation, expanse. **3.** The full effect or result. Significance, consequence, outcome, import, substance. **4.** The total of principal and interest.

Amount in controversy The amount sued for; the amount claimed; the value of the right asserted by the plaintiff. The amount needed to establish diversity jurisdiction in a federal court.

Amount realized The amount realized by a taxpayer on the sale or exchange of property. The measure of this amount is the sum of the cash and the fair market value of any property or services received.

Amphetamine, *n.* Stimulant. See drug (2).

Amphitheater, *n.* See auditorium.

Ample, *adj.* See abundant, adequate, considerable (2).

Amplification, *n.* See increase, attachment (3), accumulation, accretion; clarification; decoration, puffing.

Amplify, *v.* See add (1, 2), augment, comment (2), extend (1); exaggerate.

Amplitude, *n.* Immensity. Magnitude, profusion, largeness, abundance, plentitude. See also extent, scope, range.

Amputate, *v.* To cut off. Remove, sever, dismember, excise, mutilate, clip, prune. See also cut. *Ant.* Join.

Amuck, *adv.* See wild (3).

Amuse, *v.* To please. Gratify, entertain, divert, exhilarate. See also satisfy (2), pander (2), delight; interest (5).

Amusement, *n.* Entertainment. Pleasurable occupation, diversion, pastime, merriment, fun, relaxation, enjoyment, play, frolic, recreation, avocation, junket, cheer, gaiety, joviality, mirth, escapade, gratification. See also sport (1, 2). *Ant.* Boredom.

Amusing, *adj.* See comic, facetious, enjoyable, attractive; intriguing; amusement.

Anachronistic, *adj.* See obsolete.

Analgesic, *n.* Pain-relieving medication.

Analogize, *v.* See compare (1).

Analogous, *adj.* Similar in some respects (an analogous case). Comparable, matching, resembling, cognate, allied, alike, correspondent, associated, in the same mold, congruent, congruous, interchangeable, homogeneous, parallel, equivalent. See also correlative, like, akin (2); parity, relative, related. *Ant.* Dissimilar, disparate.

Analogue, *n.* See correlate (2); analogy, parity.

Analogy, *n.* Alikeness; partial similarity (reasoning by analogy). Comparability, likeness, parallelism, affinity, similitude, resemblance, correlation, connection. See also correspondence (1), parity, comparison.

Analysis, *n.* See examination, inquiry (1), classification (1), assay (1), reason, clarification.

Analytic, analytical, *adj.* Probing. Organized, inquiring, questioning, testing, critical, systematic, problem-solving. See also logical.

Analyze, *v.* See canvass (1), clarify, construe, investigate, reason (3), argue.

Anarchist, *n.* Someone who believes in the absence of government and in the overthrow of government by force. Rebel, anarch, renegade, mutineer, malcontent, iconoclast, terrorist, revolutionary, syndicalist. See also insurgent, nihilist. *Ant.* Conservative.

Anarchy, *n.* The absence of government (the state of anarchy). Lawlessness, mobocracy, mob rule, chaos, reign of terror, disorder, nihilism, tumult, confusion, riot, insurrection, bedlam, mutiny, apostasy, pandemonium, disorganization, misrule, turmoil. *Ant.* Control, discipline.

Anathema, *n.* Excommunication, curse (anathema to the spirit). Censure, abomination, condemnation, malediction, damnation, execration, banishment, reprobation, imprecation, fulmination, ban, proscription, denunciation, reprobation. *Ant.* Blessing.

Anatomical, *adj.* See corporal; anatomy.

Anatomy, *n.* The study of the structure of organisms. Biology, zoology, botany; bones, frame, build, body, composition. See also examination, inquiry (1).

Ancestor, *n.* The person from whom one is descended. Forefather, forebear, forerunner, progenitor, precursor, originator, predecessor, begetter, antecedent, primogenitor, genitor, patriarch, parent, procreator, sire; prototype, precedent.

Ancestral, *adj.* See hereditary.

Ancestry, *n.* The persons within one's line of descent (unknown ancestry). Family, lineage, line, geneology, blood, bloodline, pedigree, origin, heredity, stock, race, extraction, house, birth, ancestral line, tribe, clan, seed, parentage, dynasty, history, background, genesis, kinship, stirps, predecessors, parents, derivation, ascendants, consanguinity.

Anchor 1. *n.* A heavy iron used to keep a vessel stationary. Safeguard, kedge. See also foundation (2), security (2), mooring. **2.** *v.* See attach (2), affix (1).

Ancient, *adj.* Old. Primitive, aged, hoary, primeval, prehistoric, remote, primal, elderly, ageless, classical, dated, antiquated, antique, old-fashioned, archaic, obsolete, outmoded, sinking, antediluvian, out of date, waning, immemorial, superannuated, fossilized, timeworn, senile, wasting, fading, moldering, forgotten, venerable, traditional. *Ant.* Contemporary.

Ancient lights Windows that have had outside light for over a given length of time (e.g., 20 years) cannot be blocked off by an adjoining landowner in some states. Both the windows and the rule about blocking them are called ancient lights.

Ancient writings or documents A document that is more than 30 years old (or 20 years in some states) with nothing suspicious about it. The document is presumed genuine if it has come from a proper place of custody.

Ancillary, *adj.* Auxiliary, aiding (ancillary proceeding). Accessory, supplementary, subordinate, subsidiary, attendant upon, adjunct, contributory, helping, subservient, complementary, secondary, dependent, collateral, additional, supporting, upholding, concomitant, incidental, extraneous, attendant, accompanying, cooperative. *Ant.* Primary, principal.

Ancillary administration A proceeding in a state where a decedent had property, but which is different from the state where that person lived and had his or her main estate administered.

Ancillary jurisdiction Once federal jurisdiction properly attaches to the primary case before the federal court, the latter also has jurisdiction over certain subsidiary or subordinate disputes, even though it might not independently be able to proceed to adjudicate them.

And, *conj.* See also.

Androgynous, *adj.* Having both male and female characteristics. Unisex; bisexual.

Anecdote, *n.* See report (1), account, legend, narrative evidence.

Anemic, *adj.* Pale. Wane, pallid, colorless, ashen, faded, bloodless, white, feeble, weak, languid, subdued. See also exhausted, slight (2), thin. *Ant.* Robust.

Anesthetic, *n.* See narcotic, drug, medicine, treatment.

Anew, *adv.* Over again (begin anew). De novo, once more, in a new way, in a different way, freshly, new, encore.

Angel, *n.* Spirit. Cherub, saint, seraph, archangel. See also patron.

Angel dust, *n.* An illegal hallucinogen; phencyclidine.

Angelic, *adj.* See clean (1).

Anger, *n., v.* See wrath, annoyance, passion, animus (2); harass, provoke, disturb, exacerbate, outrage (2).

Angle, *n.* See grade (2).

Angry, *adj.* Irate. Infuriated, peeved, offended, mad, upset, indignant, furious, piqued, incensed, enraged, exasperated, provoked, inflamed, vexed, irritated. See also aggravated (2), wild, violent. *Ant.* Calm.

Angst, *n.* See anxiety.

Anguish, *n.* Extreme distress; great mental or physical suffering (untold anguish). Torment, torture, grief, misery, affliction, anxiety, severe pain, excruciating pain, suffering, heartache, remorse, pang, woe, rack, paroxysm, deep sorrow, disquiet, care, soreness, sting, burden, discomfort, pathos, solicitude, blow, worry, bane, trepidation, throe, travail, heavy heart, dolor, tribulation, irritation, twinge, trial, spasm, shock, disquietude. *Ant.* Consolation.

Anguishing, *adj.* See bad (4).

Animadversion, *n.* See censure (1).

Animal 1. *n.* Any living organism with the power of voluntary motion. Often, however, the word is meant to exclude humans. Living being, creature, beast, brute, whelp, quadruped, bird, mammal; calf, cow, dog, cat, camel, canary, capon, cattle, cheetah, chicken, colt. See also corporal. **2.** *adj.* Coarse, vulgar. Monstrous, carnal, physical, brutal, beastly, demonic, canine, instinctive, obscene, barbarian, fiendish, savage, carnivorous.

Animate, *v.* To motivate. Create, enliven, energize, stimulate, fortify, rouse, galvanize, quicken. See also refresh, incite, challenge (2), initiate.

Animated, *adj.* See ardent, emotional, strong (2).

Animator, *n.* See catalyst.

Animosity, *n.* See hostility, animus (2).

Animus, *n.* **1.** Intention (the offense must contain a separate animus). Design, will, mind, soul, animating spirit, animating purpose, disposition, inclination, motive, resolve, resolution, temper. **2.** Animosity (antilabor animus). Enmity, hostility, prejudice, bias, rancor, opposition, acrimony, grudge, antipathy, ill will, invidiousness. See also malice, wrath. *Ant.* Instinct; partiality.

Animus furandi The intent to steal.

Annals, *n.* See record (2).

Annex, *v.*, **annex,** *n.* **1.** *v.* To join together (the certificate should be annexed to the application). Tie, bind, attach, subjoin, add, unite, affix, connect, tack on, merge, link, incorporate, append, supplement, fasten, combine, include, postfix, expand. **2.** *v.* To take over (the county annexed the lake). Appropriate, seize, "grab," steal, arrogate, usurp, expropriate, confiscate, accroach, assume, impound, sequester. **3.** *n.* An extension (I'll meet you in the annex). Addition, attachment, wing, appurtenance, expansion, branch, continuation, ell.

Annexation, *n.* **1.** Merging or attaching one thing to another. See merger, combination. **2.** The takeover of something (e.g., territory). See appropriation (1).

Annihilate, *v.* See abolish, rescind, annul, destroy, kill, erase.

Annihilation, *n.* See abolition, rescission, elimination.

Anniversary, *n.* See annual (1).

Annotate, *v.* See clarify, comment (2).

Annotated, *adj.* Organized by subject matter with commentary or references.

Annotation, *n.* Explanatory commentary (read the annotation in *American Law Reports*). Notes, explanation, critical commentary, interpretation, remarks, elucidation, exposition, footnotes, explication, illustrations, marginalia, appendix, exegesis, scholium, construction, glossary. See also clarification, comment (1).

Announce, *v.* See proclaim, pronounce, assert.

Announcement, *n.* See declaration, communication, report (1).

Annoy, *v.* See harass, disturb, accost (1), outrage (2), exacerbate, provoke, assault, attack; annoyance.

Annoyance, *n.* Exasperation, discomfort (continuous annoyance). Vexation, aggravation, nuisance, harassment, molestation, provocation, irritation, irritant, incitement, hassle, headache, ire, trouble, pestering, torment, affront, disturbance, ruffling, enraging, harm, inconvenience, bedevilment, bother, thorn, agitation, nettling, taunting, persecution, grievance. See also pain, burden. *Ant.* Consolation.

Annual 1. *adj.* Of or pertaining to a year (annual recertification). Yearly, returning every year, occurring once a year, anniversary, perennial, seasonal. **2.** *n.* A publication that comes out once a year (the board's report is an annual). Annals. See record (2).

Annual percentage rate The true cost of borrowing money expressed in a standardized, yearly way to allow the consumer to understand the credit terms and to "shop" for credit.

Annuitant, *n.* One who receives an annuity. See beneficiary, recipient.

Annuity, *n.* A fixed sum payable to a person at specified intervals for a specific period of time or for life (life insurance annuity). Allowance, income, payment, pension, subsidy, retirement, stipend, appropriation, allotment.

Annul, *v.* To nullify (to annul a marriage). See annulment (1). Make void, reduce to nothing, annihilate, abolish, do away with, cancel, destroy, abrogate, quash, undo, dissolve, invalidate, rescind, revoke, void, repeal, overrule, countermand, set aside, retract, neutralize, eliminate, negative, erase, vacate, counteract, extinguish, negate, reverse, blot out, terminate, vitiate, repudiate, dispose of, efface, disestablish, supersede, withdraw, renege, abjure, override, disavow. *Ant.* Create, perform.

Annulment, *n.* **1.** A declaration that a marriage never existed; a declaration that an attempted marriage is invalid or void. **2.** Nullification. Annihilation, abolition, cancellation, destruction, abrogation, quashing, undoing, dissolution, invalidation, revocation, repeal, retraction, neutralization, elimination, vacation, extinguishment, reversal, termination, vitiation, repudiation, effacement, withdrawal, abjuration, disavowal, rescission, voidance, suspension, recantation, obliteration, negation. *Ant.* Validation.

Annunciate, *v.* See proclaim, pronounce, assert.

Annunciation, *n.* See declaration.

Anoint, *v.* To consecrate. Crown, sanctify, canonize, enthrone, hallow. See also dedicate, honor (2), approve; holy, religious.

Anomalous, *adj.* Unusual, irregular (anomalous behavior). Deviating from the common rule, exceptional, abnormal, singular, erratic, strange, aberrant, peculiar, unnatural, eccentric, atypical, foreign, incongruous, deviant, heterodox, anomalistic, curious, inconsistent, discordant, different, unique, monstrous, bizarre, awry, misplaced, unconventional, inappropriate, unsuited. *Ant.* Uniform, natural.

Anomaly, *n.* See deviation, eccentricity, caprice.

Anonymous

Anonymous, *adj.* Nameless, unknown source (a tip from an anonymous caller). Unnamed, pseudonymous, unrecognized, uncredited, unsigned, unattributed, authorless, incognito, unacknowledged, unidentified, unspecified, innominate. *Ant.* Named.

Another, *adj.* Additional. A second, extra, one more, supplemental, distinct, different, separate, variant.

Answer 1. *n.* A pleading in which a response is made to the claim of another party (file an answer). Defense, counterclaim, reply, plea, countercharge, recrimination, rebuttal, denial, rejoinder, refutation. **2.** *n.* An acknowledgment (it took ten days to receive the answer). Response, reply, retort, return, confirmation, reaction, exchange, retaliation. **3.** *n.* The solution (the only answer is to litigate the dispute). Resolution, determination, finding, interpretation, key. **4.** *v.* To take responsibility for (she will answer for his debts). Be liable for, suffer for, be obligated for, be accountable for, be answerable for, be surety for. **5.** *v.* To respond (I have not answered the charge). Reply, acknowledge, retaliate, confirm, debate, contest, counter, rebut, retort, deny, confute, return, rejoin, defend, controvert. **6.** *v.* To be sufficient (the qualifications of the witness answer the requirements). Fulfill, satisfy, be adequate, serve, be enough, measure up, pass muster, conform, correspond, suit, suffice, fill, meet, correlate.

Answerable, *adj.* See accountable (1).

Antagonism, *n.* See hostility, collision (2), animus (2), malice.

Antagonist, *n.* See adversary, enemy, assailant.

Antagonistic, *adj.* See hostile, contradictory.

Antagonize, *v.* See alienate (2).

Ante 1. *prefix* Before, prior to. **2.** *n.* See pool (3), purse (1).

Antecedence, *n.* See precedence.

Antecedent 1. *adj.* Prior in point of time (antecedent negligence). Preceding, earlier, pre-existing, previous, preliminary, anterior, former, foregoing, first. **2.** *n.* Forerunner (the typewriter is the antecedent of the word processor). Precursor, predecessor, ancestor, harbinger, father, mother, cause. **.3.** *n.* Antecedents. Forefathers, primogenitors, lineage, house, stock, ancestry, pedigree, family. *Ant.* Succeeding; descendant.

Antecedent debt A debt that is prior in time to another transaction. In contract law, this earlier debt may furnish consideration for a new contract to pay.

Antedate, *v.* **1.** To place a date on a document that is earlier than the date the document was written (to antedate a check). Affix an earlier date, predate, date before the true time, backdate, misdate. **2.** To precede (Justice Story antedates Justice Holmes). Antecede, forerun, anticipate, come first, pave the way, pre-exist, preface, herald, usher in, presage, happen before. *Ant.* Follow, come after.

Antenuptial, *adj.* Made before marriage. An antenuptial agreement or settlement is a contract made by people about to be married which settles the matters of support and property division in the event of the death of one of the parties or the dissolution of the marriage. Prenuptial, premarital.

Anterior, *adj.* See antecedent (1), prior.

Anthology, *n.* See book (4).

Anthropometry, *n.* The science of measuring the human body.

Antic, *n.* Prank. Caper, lark, horseplay, trick, escapade, practical joke, stunt, sport, romp.

Anticipate, *v.* **1.** To foresee (the storm could not have been anticipated). Prognosticate, foreknow, prophesy, predict, foretell, presage, forecast, intuit, preconceive, divine, portend, herald, foretaste, augur, predetermine. **2.** To expect and prepare for (to anticipate the judge's arrival). Watch for, contemplate, count on, consider in advance, guard against, apprehend, look forward to, hope for,

52

envision, meet in advance, await, assume, dread.

Anticipation, *n.* **1.** The act of doing a thing before its proper time or simply doing it before something else. **2.** The right to pay off a mortgage before it comes due without paying a "prepayment penalty." **3.** The right under some contracts to deduct some money (usually equal to the current interest rate) when paying early. **4.** In patent law, a person is anticipated if someone else has already patented substantially the same thing. See anticipate; likelihood, hope (2), chance (3), probability, presumption. **5.** See apprehension, anxiety, anguish.

Anticipatory breach of contract A repudiation of a contract duty before the time fixed in the contract for the performance of that duty.

Anticlimax, *n.* Letdown. Disappointment, comedown, disillusionment. See also failure (1).

Antidote, *n.* See cure (1), medicine (2), treatment, correction (2); medical.

Anti-dumping, *adj.* See dumping.

Anti-lapse statute Prevents a lapse (termination) of a clause in a will which would otherwise occur if the person who was to receive property under the clause dies before the testator (the one who wrote the will).

Antipathy, *n.* See hostility.

Antiquated, *adj.* See old, obsolete.

Antique 1. *n.* Artifact. Find, rarity, fossil, curio, object d'art, trinket. **2.** *adj.* Old-fashioned. See old, obsolete, obsolescent.

Anteroom, *n.* See chamber (1).

Anti-semite, *n.* One biased against Jews. See bias.

Antiseptic, *adj.* See clean (2), sanitary.

Antisocial, *adj.* See hostile.

Antithesis, *n.* See reverse (2), contradiction, opposite, contrast, opposition.

Antithetical, *adj.* See contradictory, opposite, contrary, inconsistent.

Antitrust, *adj.* Concerning the prevention or regulation of monopolies, price fixing, and other unlawful restraints on trade and commerce.

Anxiety, *n.* Apprehension, tension, or uneasiness that stems from the anticipation of impending danger or the fear of the unknown. Foreboding, care, distress, suffering, dread, tension, anguish, disquiet, disquietude, worry, misgiving, alarm, angst, torment, torture, misery, concern, solicitude, pain, presentiment, doubt, mistrust, suspense, uncertainty, fretfulness, eagerness. *Ant.* Calm, serenity.

Anxious, *adj.* See concerned, active (3), apprehensive, afraid, suspicious (2); jealous; anxiety, anguish.

Any, *adj., adv., pron.* See all.

A.P.A. See Administrative Procedure Act.

Apart, *adv.* See alone, separate (1), private.

Apartheid, *n.* Sanctioned or mandated racial segregation. See segregation, bias, prejudice; separation (2).

Apartment, *n.* See home (1).

Apathetic, *adj.* Cold. Unfeeling, uncaring, emotionless, impassive, spiritless, inert, dull, dispassionate, detached, aloof. See also indifferent (2), callous, lazy.

Apathy, *n.* See indifference; ennui; apathetic.

Ape, *v.* See copy (2); mock (1).

Aperture, *n.* See break (3).

Apex, *n.* The highest point. Top, acme, apogee, crest, pinnacle, peak, summit, zenith, tip, climax, vertex, heights, crown, crowning point, head, culmination, extremity, extreme, ultimate, consummation, utmost, realization, limit, prime, attainment. *Ant.* Bottom, depth.

Aphonic, *adj.* See mute.

Aphorism, *n.* See maxim.

Aplomb, *n.* See self-confidence, restraint (2), balance (5), composure.

Apocryphal, *adj.* See fictitious, counterfeit (2), false, deceptive, deceitful.

Apogee, *n.* See apex.

Apologetic, *adj.* See contrite.

Apologist, *n.* See advocate (1).

Apology, *n.* See acknowledgment (1), amends, defense.

Apoplexy, *n.* A sudden loss of consciousness, sensation, and voluntary motion due to an escape of blood or serum into the brain or spinal cord.

Apostasy, *n.* A renunciation of principles. Defection, desertion, backsliding, abandonment, repudiation, falling away, treason, betrayal, disloyalty, heterodoxy, perfidy, withdrawal, succession. See also rebellion, defiance, insubordination; heresy.

A posteriori From the effect to the cause (a posteriori reasoning). Inductive, empirical, from the particular to the general. *Ant.* A priori.

Apostle, *n.* Missionary. Proselytizer, evangelist, minister, disciple, propagandist, witness, pioneer. See also deputy, messenger, advocate.

Apothecary, *n.* Pharmacist. Druggist, chemist.

Appall, *v.* See outrage (2)

Appalled, *adj.* See agape.

Appalling, *adj.* Frightening. Ghastly, alarming, intimidating, terrible, grim, horrible, awful. See also repulsive, odious.

Apparatus, *n.* Machinery. Appliance, contraption, paraphernalia, tool, outfit, gear, engine. See also instrument (2), equipment, device.

Apparel, *n.* Garments. Vestments, attire, wardrobe, uniform, cover, adornment, dress, outfit, costume "duds," array, robes, habit. See also clothes.

Apparent, *adj.* **1.** Capable of being clearly seen or understood (an apparent defect). Perceptible, unmistakable, discernible, visible, unconcealed, clear, obvious, evident, distinct, manifest, overt, patent, plain, lucid, prominent, flagrant, blatant, noticeable, uncovered, glaring, unveiled, conspicuous, tangible, express, definite, identifiable, self-evident, recognizable. **2.** Seeming (it was an apparent victory, although all of the facts are not yet in). Ostensible, probable, presumptive, presumable, likely, conceivable, expected, alleged, illusory, deceptive, pseudo, plausible, superficial, external, outward, unreal, hopeful, prospective, contemplated. *Ant.* Ambiguous; unlikely.

Apparent authority Authority of an agent that exists because the principal knowingly or negligently permits the agent to exercise it, or because the principal holds the agent out as possessing it.

Apparition, *n.* See ghost, demon.

Appeal **1.** *n.* Asking a higher tribunal to review the decision of an inferior tribunal (notice of appeal). Petition, appellate review, reexamination. **2.** *n.* A call for help (the appeal went unnoticed). Entreaty, request, supplication, solicitation, prayer, adjuration, address, suit, plea. See also application (1). **3.** *n.* Attraction (the evidence had considerable appeal). Fascination, interest, allure, magnetism, draw, pull, charm. See also market (3). **4.** *v.* To make a request (she appealed for help). Implore, beg, beseech, plead, entreat, pray, apply, sue, invoke, resort, adjure, supplicate.

Appeal bond A bond submitted by the person bringing an appeal which will cover the costs of the opponent if a determination is made that the appeal had no merit or that it was not prosecuted with effect.

Appealing, *adj.* See cogent, attractive, enjoyable, beautiful, outstanding (2), intriguing, compelling.

Appear, *v.* **1.** To come formally and properly before a tribunal (he appeared solely to contest the court's jurisdiction). Enter an appearance, submit oneself to, attend the court proceeding, present oneself. **2.** To become clear (it appears from the evidence that a trial would be a waste of time). Be manifest, be clear, emerge, show, seem, look, be plain, be obvious, materialize, be visible, arise, come into view, strike one as being, be patent, arrive, present itself, issue, emanate, surface, give the appearance of, come to light, loom. *Ant.* Vanish; become doubtful.

Appearance, *n.* **1.** Formally and properly coming before a tribunal (she filed a notice of appearance as his attorney). **2.** Coming into view (the appearance of the cancer). Manifestation, emergence, materialization, sight, introduction, arrival, publication, advent, exhibition, occurrence, exposure, display, picture, perspective, image. **3.** External look (the witness gave the appearance of being knowledgeable). Form, demeanor, presence, countenance, manner, expression, guise, air, face, semblance, mien, show, pretense, visage, pretext, color, look, profile, exterior, embodiment, comportment, aspect, bearing, behavior, presentation, deportment, style, character, shape, posture, physiognomy. *Ant.* Departure.

Appease, *v.* See mitigate, assuage, accommodate, yield (1), pander (2), delight.

Appellant, *n.* The person or party who brings the appeal. Challenger, appealer, contender, dissatisfied party, aggrieved party.

Appellate, *adj.* Concerning appeals (an appellate court).

Appellate jurisdiction The power of an appellate court to review the decision of an inferior tribunal to determine whether this tribunal made any errors of law.

Appellate review The process by which a higher court determines whether a lower tribunal has committed any errors of law in a particular case. A review of the decisions made below.

Appellation, *n.* See name (1), alias, mark.

Appellee, *n.* The person against whom an appeal is brought. See respondent.

Append, *v.* To add or affix (we should append the document to the application). Attach, supplement, annex, tag, tack, connect, join, fasten, include, insert. *Ant.* Detach, omit.

Appendage, *n.* Something added as a supporting component (the argument was not part of the original presentation but was added later as an appendage). Accessory, attachment, appendix, corollary, addition, accompaniment, supplement, adjunct, appurtenance, concomitant, collateral, codicil, subsidiary, extension, allonge, annex, branch, postscript, incidental, extra, appendant, companion, nonessential, appliance, epilogue, suffix, extremity.

Appendant 1. *adj.* Attached. Annexed, added, subordinate, appended, pendant, supplemental, auxiliary, concomitant, subsidiary, subjoined. **2.** *n.* That which beyond memory has belonged to something more important or worthy. **3.** *n.* Attachment. Appendix, addition, appurtenance, extension, adjunct.

Appendix, *n.* Something added (an appendix to the brief). Addition, supplement, rider, codicil, epilogue, appendage, continuation, pocket part, extension, supplementation, insertion, complement, appurtenance, postscript, adjunct, back matter, annex. *Ant.* Main body.

Appertain, *v.* To belong to (the duties that appertain to the presidency will be examined at a later time). Be pertinent to, have relation to, apply to, refer to, affect, pertain, regard, be applicable to, be connected with, be part of, be characteristic of, be dependent upon, involve, have reference to. See also concern (1). *Ant.* Be irrelevant to.

Appetite, *n.* See desire (4), affinity (2).

Appetizing, *adj.* See delectable, attractive, enjoyable.

Applaud, *v.* See honor (2), recommend, appreciate (3); acclamation.

Applause, *n.* See acclamation, approval.

Appliance, *n.* See apparatus, instrument (2), equipment.

Applicable

Applicable, *adj.* Capable of being applied (an applicable holding). Relevant, to the point, usable, fitting, acceptable, pertinent, adaptable, germane, useful, apropos, compatible, appropriate, right, apt, befitting, suitable, pointed, apposite. *Ant.* Irrelevant, inapplicable.

Applicant, *n.* Someone who applies for something (an applicant for letters of administration). Supplicant, solicitor, aspirant. See also candidate, petitioner.

Application, *n.* **1.** A petition; a request for something (an application for benefits). Requisition, entreaty, solicitation, appeal, inquiry, demand, motion, proposal, submission, proposition, bid, presentation, prayer. **2.** Relevance (the testimony has no application to the issue). Function, utilization, operation, pertinence, appositeness, germaneness, aptness, utility, bearing, fitness, meaning, significance. **3.** Diligent attention (application to your legal studies). Effort, resolution, diligence, perseverance, dedication, commitment, tenacity, industry, attentiveness.

Apply, *v.* **1.** To make a formal request (to apply for leave to amend). Petition, entreat, solicit, appeal, inquire, demand, move, propose, bid, pray, audition, seek, call for, press, coax, plead, ask, clamor, sue, canvass, endeavor to obtain, campaign, make suit, beseech, beg, supplicate, implore, urge, importune. **2.** To have relevance (the case does not apply). Be suitable, fit, be pertinent to, pertain to, refer to, be connected with, have reference to, have a bearing on, involve, affect, connect, have to do with, be appropriate, suit, impinge on, hold good for, hold true for. **3.** To persevere (she applied herself and passed the examination). Be diligent, dedicate, commit, be attentive, devote, concentrate, study. **4.** To put into practice (apply what you have learned). Put to use, employ, execute, utilize, exercise, administer, carry out, put into operation. *Ant.* Ignore; be irrelevant; resign; waste.

Appoint, *v.* **1.** To select (he was appointed chairperson). Designate, prescribe, nominate, name, assign, commission, delegate, deputize, install, elect, invest, choose, authorize, license, sanction, empower, establish, proclaim. **2.** To determine (the judge appointed a time for a new hearing). Arrange, establish, decide upon, fix, prescribe, set, ordain, command, impose, order, direct, require, decree. **3.** To furnish (they appointed the new law office with the latest computer equipment). Supply, equip, provide. *Ant.* Discharge; neglect; dismantle.

Appointee, *n.* The person selected. Beneficiary, deputy, emissary, commissioner, representative, agent, delegate, envoy. See also nominee.

Appointment, *n.* **1.** The selection of a person to carry out a responsibility (a power of appointment). Assignment, designation, nomination, commissioning, deputation, installation, election, authorization, establishment, naming, ordination, allotment, certification. **2.** Position (your appointment as commissioner takes effect immediately). Job, post, office, station, assignment, situation, spot, place, employment, profession, occupation, undertaking. **3.** Engagement (your appointment is at noon). Date, meeting time, interview. *Ant.* Cancellation (1).

Apportion, *v.* To divide and distribute proportionally (Congress apportions representatives among the states). Allot, distribute, share, share in just proportions, earmark, administer, assign, allocate, designate, dispense, partition, measure out, parcel out, subdivide, prorate, assort, demarcate, disseminate, mete, dole out, separate, admeasure, dispense, split, ration, consign. *Ant.* Assemble, collect.

Apportionment, *n.* **1.** Dividing and assigning in just proportion (the apportionment of responsibility). Allocation, distribution, allotment, rationing, assignment, proration, demarcation, subdivision, partition, separation, parceling out, earmarking, appointment, administration, consignment, measuring out, division, appropriation. **2.** The process of allocating legislators or representatives among several areas or political subdivisions. **3.** The allocation of a charge or cost (e.g., taxes)

56

among several parties. **4.** The distribution of legal responsibility for a transaction or tort.

Apposite, *adj.* See appropriate (3).

Appraisal, *n.* A valuation of something (property appraisal). Estimate, evaluation, setting a price on, assessment, survey, calculation, measurement, computation, judgment, rating, assay, opinion, appraisement.

Appraise, *v.* To fix a price for something (the stock is appraised at $100). Set a value upon, identify the true value, value at what it is worth, valuate, survey, count, calculate, measure, compute, rate, assay, weigh, account, approximate, price, gauge, inspect, scrutinize, review, examine. See also judge (3), assess.

Appraisement, *n.* A valuation of property. See appraisal.

Appraiser, *n.* Someone who evaluates (appraises) property.

Appreciable, *adj.* Capable of being perceived (an appreciable difference between the two briefs). Perceptible, perceivable, recognizable, considerable, measurable, noticeable, comprehensible, discernible, detectable, ascertainable, visible, assessable, substantial, tangible, calculable, concrete, sizable, evident, pronounced, clear, plain, definite, material, patent, conspicuous, manifest, undeniable, obvious, notable, discoverable. *Ant.* Indistinguishable, negligible.

Appreciate, *v.* **1.** To increase in value (the land appreciated over the years). Raise, advance, enhance in value, improve, inflate, upgrade, gain. **2.** To understand (it is difficult to appreciate the anxiety he went through). Perceive, comprehend, realize, be sensitive to, know, be conscious of, be aware of, apprehend, recognize, conceive, notice, be cognizant of, sympathize, detect, estimate justly, fathom. **3.** To value (no judge is more widely appreciated). Esteem, honor, admire, applaud, praise, respect, acclaim, venerate, revere, cherish, like, treasure, prize. *Ant.* Depreciate; misjudge; despise.

Appreciation, *n.* **1.** Increase in value (you will have to pay taxes on the appreciation). Inflation, rise in value, accumulation, accrual, price increase, growth, realization, addition, escalation, advance, multiplication, increased monetary worth. **2.** Awareness (we need a greater appreciation of the time required). Perception, understanding, comprehension, realization, conception, recognition, apprehension, detection, sensitivity, sympathy, cognizance, appraisal, consciousness, valuation, estimation, calculation, measuring, weighing, judging, savoring. **3.** See approbation, affection (1). **4.** See gratitude. *Ant.* Depreciation; ignorance.

Appreciative, *adj.* Grateful. Conscious, indebted, thankful, obliged, full of gratitude, beholden, gratified. See also benevolent; happy.

Apprehend, *v.* **1.** To be aware of; to have knowledge of (a reasonable ground to apprehend danger). Perceive, comprehend, appreciate, fathom, realize, be apprised of, discover, view, discern, see, know, grasp, sense, take in, absorb, imagine, regard, be conscious of, surmise, feel, intuit. **2.** To arrest (she was apprehended in Baltimore). Seize, capture, take into custody, restrain, constrain, detain, take prisoner, confine, hold, incarcerate, imprison, jail. **3.** To fear (to apprehend that hostages will be taken). Suspect, dread, forebode, be afraid of, have a presentiment of, mistrust, distrust, worry. *Ant.* Misconceive; release; be hopeful.

Apprehension, *n.* **1.** Knowledge or belief (apprehension of a harmful or offensive contact). Understanding, perception, awareness, appreciation, comprehension, cognition, recognition, realization, discovery, discernment, intuition, image, view, impression, notion, judgment, observation. **2.** Seizure (the apprehension of the defendant at the scene of the crime). Arrest, capture, restraint, constraint, detention, confinement, incarceration, imprisonment, jailing, taking into custody, internment. **3.** Fear (filled with apprehension over the possible verdict). Foreboding, anxiety, worry, misgiving, dread, concern, suspicion, uneasiness, premonition, suspense, stress, edginess, strain, tension, excitement, awe, doubt, disquiet, disquietude, alarm, dismay, premonition of trouble, qualm, agitation, consternation, trepidation, uncertainty, indecision, on pins and needles, expectation, solicitude. *Ant.* Ignorance; liberation; confidence.

Apprehensive, *adj.* Anxious. Fearful, alarmed, distressed, worried, restless, scared, disturbed, nervous, jittery, edgy, uneasy, concerned, distrustful. See also afraid, suspicious (2); apprehend, apprehension. *Ant.* Calm.

Apprentice, *n.* See intern, assistant, artisan, amateur, beginner, employee; articled.

Apprise, *v.* To give notice (she was apprised of the sale at the meeting). Inform, tell, communicate, point out, advise, make aware, make known, publish, advertise, report, warn, disclose, reveal, make acquainted, enlighten, make cognizant of, brief, admonish, teach, declare, divulge. *Ant.* Keep secret.

Approach 1. *v.* To come nearer in place or time (he tried to move out of the way as the car approached). Come within range, draw nearer, move toward, advance, meet, verge, converge, approximate, drift, gain upon, come, be at hand, come forward, be in sight of, verge on, confront, be in proximity of. **2.** *v.* To resemble (few judges approach her talents). Approximate, be comparable to, be similar to, equal, match, be like, parallel, compare, meet. **3.** *v.* To make overtures to (have you approached them about a settlement). Make a proposal to, make advances to, take a first step toward, sound out, introduce, propose, recommend, suggest, offer, mention, propound. **4.** *v.* To begin (approach the negotiations with an open mind). Commence, initiate, enter upon, embark upon, set about, undertake. **5.** *n.* An access (the right of approach at sea). Way, passage, passageway, path, entry, driveway, pathway, ingress, route, avenue, adit. **6.** *n.* Method of handling (the court's new approach to products liability). Attitude, procedure, method for dealing with, technique. *Ant.* Withdraw; diverge; ignore; terminate; exit.

Approachable, *adj.* See accessible.

Approaching, *adj.* See comparable; approach.

Approbation, *n.* Praise, approval (he did not anticipate such approbation for her work). Commendation, sanction, acceptance, acknowledgment, esteem, congratulation, acclaim, endorsement, support, favor, admiration, regard, appreciation, ratification. *Ant.* Condemnation.

Appropriate 1. *v.* To make something your own (he appropriated what he saw). Seize, exercise dominion over, take possession of, expropriate, impound, commandeer, confiscate, usurp, claim, plunder, embezzle, steal. **2.** *v.* To designate money for a particular purpose (Congress appropriated funds for the agency). Earmark, allocate, apportion, allot, assign, authorize, set apart, devote. **3.** *adj.* Fit and proper (the grant of an injunction is appropriate in this case). Fitting, suitable, congruous, correct, apt, apropos, accurate, well-suited, pertinent, relevant, opportune, germane, to the point, timely, agreeable, convenient, applicable, befitting, seemly, becoming, commensurate, tailor-made, meet, satisfactory, accommodating, admissible, proportionate, felicitous, apposite, practicable, advantageous, merited, sufficient, decent, advisable, felicitous, eligible, reasonable, consonant, rightful, consistent. *Ant.* Cede, relinquish; withhold; unsuitable.

Appropriation, *n.* **1.** The act of taking something over, of making it your own (an appropriation of plaintiff's property). Seizure, exercising dominion, taking possession, conversion, expropriation, impoundment, confiscation, usurpation, plundering, embezzlement, stealing, accroachment, divestment, annexation, capture, arrogation, acquisition, assumption, purpresture, piracy, pillage, raid, displacement, levy, deprivation, dispossession. **2.** The designation of money for a specific purpose (the legislature rejected the increased appropriation for the dam). Allocation, earmarking, apportionment, allotment, assignment, authorization, dispensation, budget, setting apart, funding, endowment, grant, stipend, allowance, devotion. **3.** See invasion of privacy. *Ant.* Relinquishment.

Approval, *n.* The act of acceptance (approval of the plan was conditioned on available funding). Confirmation, ratification, sanction, consent, endorsement, acquiescence, license, blessing, imprimatur, nihil obstat, permission, affirmance, toleration, charter, commission, immunity, accreditation, carte blanche, stamp, concurrence, liberty, indulgence, encouragement, approbation, agreement, compliance, mandate, authorization, validation, assent, condonation, connivance, accord, verification, adoption, support, affirmation, permit, allowance, favor, authentication, countenance, backing, commendation. *Ant.* Opposition, rejection.

Approval sale An agreement that passes title when the buyer indicates that the goods are acceptable.

Approve, *v.* To consider acceptable; to sanction (the judge would not approve the extension). Be satisfied with, confirm, ratify, be favorable toward, consent, admit the propriety of, authenticate, assent, endorse, acquiesce, license, bless, agree, comply, authorize, validate, adopt, support, affirm, permit, allow, favor, back, countenance, accept, certify, recommend, uphold, maintain, sustain, esteem, appreciate, concur, advocate, subscribe, value, justify, affirm. See also commission (5). *Ant.* Condemn, repudiate.

Approximate 1. *v.* To estimate (the witness was asked to approximate the distance). Make a rough calculation, reckon, guess. **2.** *v.* To come close to (the drawing approximates reality). Border on, verge, approach, closely resemble, be in the neighborhood of, lean toward, converge, mimic, duplicate, simulate, imitate, look like. **3.** *adj.* More or less (the approximate distance was 10 feet). Estimated, proximate, approaching, inexact, nearly accurate, relative, coming near, surmised, resembling. *Ant.* Calculate precisely; conflict with; precise.

Approximately, *adv.* See more or less, about; approximate (3).

Approximation, *n.* **1.** When the terms of a charitable trust have become impossible or impractical to observe, a court can alter the terms to fulfill the donor's general charitable intent. **2.** An estimate (we had to be satisfied with an approximation of the distance). Rough calculation, estimation, approach, proximity, neighborhood, resemblance, convergence, correspondence, propinquity, similarity.

Appurtenance, *n.* That which belongs to something else; something physically secondary to a primary part but serving a useful or necessary function in connection with the primary part (the light fixtures were appurtenances). Something annexed, accessory, adjunct, appendage, auxiliary, incidental, attachment, supplementation, annex, supplement, branch, accession, extension, addendum, appendix, addition, dependency.

Appurtenant, *adj.* belonging to (an appurtenant easement is attached to and passes with the dominant tenement). Accessory, incident to, adjunct, appended, annexed, appertaining, connected, ancillary, attached, subsidiary, auxiliary, dependent.

A priori, *adj., adv.* From what goes before; prior to investigation. Speculative, conjectural, presumptive; from cause to effect; from the general to the particular, because certain facts exist other facts will follow as a consequence.

Apropos, *adj.* See appropriate (3), apt (1), pertinent, cogent.

Apt, *adj.* **1.** Suitable, appropriate (the witness made some apt remarks that helped establish causation). Fit, fitting, apropos, relevant, pertinent, germane, congruous, timely, applicable, to the point, felicitous. **2.** Inclined (the witness is apt to say something rash). Predisposed, liable, prone, likely, given to, disposed, tending, susceptible, subject. **3.** Gifted (an apt student). Quick to learn, intelligent, competent, talented, bright, clever, teachable, ingenious, brilliant, skillful, adroit, astute, capable, adept. **4.** Having the requisite qualifications;

suited to its purpose. *Ant.* Irrelevant; unlikely; dull; incapable.

Aptitude, *n.* See ability, facility (3), gift (2), power.

Aquatic, *adj.* Pertaining to water (aquatic rights). Marine, oceanic, pelagic, nautical.

Arable, *adj.* Fit for cultivation (arable land). Plowable, farmable, fecund, fertile, tillable. *Ant.* Barren.

Arbiter, *n.* A referee, someone chosen to resolve a dispute (his bias disqualified him from being an arbiter). Umpire, judge, arbitrator, intermediary, interceder, mediator, moderator, adjudicator, reconciler, authority, master, determiner, ruler, dictator. See also authority (4). *Ant.* Bystander.

Arbitrage, *n.* The simultaneous purchase and sale of the same or an equivalent security or commodity in different markets in order to profit from price discrepancies.

Arbitrament, *n.* The decision of an arbitrator. Award, arbitration, judgment, opinion.

Arbitrary, *adj.* **1.** Capricious (no reasons were given for the court's arbitrary decision). Irrational, irresponsible, whimsical, unreasonable, subjective, random, inconsistent, fanciful, frivolous, erratic, at pleasure, in bad faith, illogical, nonrational, determined by no rule or law. **2.** Absolute (an arbitrary ruler). Tyrannical, despotic, dictatorial, unlimited, domineering, autocratic, summary, totalitarian, imperious, overbearing. *Ant.* Responsible; limited.

Arbitrate, *v.* **1.** To submit a dispute to arbitration (labor and management agreed to arbitrate). **2.** To render a decision as an arbitrator (the AAA arbitrated the dispute submitted to it). Decide, resolve, adjudicate, umpire, settle, referee, pass judgment, bring to terms, determine, decree. **3.** Reconcile. Mediate, moderate, intervene, conciliate, intercede, settle, harmonize, propitiate. See also negotiate.

Arbitration, *n.* **1.** The submission of a dispute to an impartial third party as an alternative to traditional litigation in court. The disputants agree in advance to abide by the decision of the arbitrator. (When negotiations broke down, the parties agreed to try arbitration.) **2.** The decision of an arbitrator (an arbitration award). Judgment, arbitrament, resolution, adjudication, settlement, determination, decree, conciliation, intervention.

Arbitrator, *n.* Someone to whom matters in dispute between two or more parties are submitted for final determination (the arbitrator found that a violation had occurred). Arbiter, umpire, judge, adjudicator, referee, decider, intervenor, mediator.

Arc, *n.* Curve. Arch, bend, half-moon, dome, curl, crescent, bow, semicircle; vault, doorway, span.

Arcade, *n.* **1.** Porch, gallery, cloister, portico, archway, colonnade, piazza. **2.** See market (1).

Arcane, *adj.* See hidden, obscure, ambiguous.

Arch, *n.*, *adj.* See arc; chief (2).

Archaic, *adj.* See ancient, obsolete.

Archenemy, *n.* See enemy, adversary.

Archetype, *n.* The original from which copies are made. Prototype, predecessor, ancestor, paradigm, exemplar, paragon, ideal, classic, mold, standard. *Ant.* Copy, imitation. See also model, instance.

Archipelago, *n.* A group of islands. See island, sea.

Architect, *n.* Someone who devises plans for buildings and supervises their construction. Designer, drafter, draftsman, planner, creator, artist, innovator, founder, builder, originator, inventor, author, prime mover, engineer, pioneer, organizer, generator, maker, former, contriver.

Architecture, *n.* See building, environment, design, constitution (2).

Archives, *n.* **1.** Place where old documents are stored (the Indian treaties can be found in the archives). Library, registry, depository, museum, file room, bank. **2.** Documents that are stored (historical archives). Papers, records, memoranda, ledgers, statistics, memorabilia, public papers, annals, minutes, rolls, registers, muniments.

Archivist, *n.* See recorder, caretaker, manager.

Archway, *n.* See entrance; arc.

Arctic, *adj.* See cold (2).

Ardent, *adj.* Impassioned. Passionate, intense, zealous, zestful, eager, high-strung, fervent, hot, burning, fiery. See also emotional, strong (2).

Ardent spirits Intoxicating liquors; distilled liquors.

Ardor, *n.* See passion; conviction (3); life (3), vigor, spirit.

Arduous, *adj.* See onerous, serious, difficult, severe, extreme, draconian.

Area, *n.* **1.** A particular territory or surface (the area was inadvertently left out of the deed). Region, section, zone, quarter, terrain, expanse, district, tract, locality, space, precinct, neighborhood, belt, lot, vicinity, environs, milieu, surroundings, province, borough, parish, barrio, colony, ghetto, estate, place, plot. **2.** Sphere of interest or activity (in the area of negotiation, she had no equal). Realm, arena, domain, orbit, field, province, department, bailiwick, jurisdiction, breadth, compass, scope.

Arena, *n.* **1.** Stadium. Gymnasium, pavilion, coliseum, rink, ring, forum, auditorium, hall, bowl, circus, stage. See also facility (2), building (1). **2.** See area.

Arguable, *adj.* Debatable (an arguable claim). Disputable, at issue, open to argument, questionable, contestable. See also controversial, moot, debatable. *Ant.* Undeniable.

Argue, *v.* To contend or debate. Contest, claim, remonstrate, plead, refute, challenge, wrangle, bicker, discuss, controvert, analyze, expostulate, protest, hold, reason, allege, advance, urge, oppose, stress, proclaim, dissuade, assert, propound, fight, haggle, feud. *Ant.* Concede.

Argument, *n.* **1.** Position; inference drawn from premises (argument of counsel to the jury). Line of reasoning, case, plea, pleading, refutation, argumentation, evidence, grounds, defense, contention, proof, theme, thesis, demonstration, submission, statement, rebuttal, discussion, discourse, assertion, claim. **2.** Dispute (the argument was bitter and endless). Disagreement, fight, quarrel, altercation, controversy, polemic, bickering, dissension, division, feud, wrangling, clash, brouhaha, imbroglio, misunderstanding, hostility, squabble, spat, war of words, schism, ruckus, hassle, embroilment. **3.** A summary.

Argumentation, *n.* See argument.

Argumentative, *adj.* Quarrelsome; given to debate or dispute; containing conclusions as well as facts (the pleading is argumentative because it contains arguments as well as statements of fact). Combative, polemic, apologetic, disputatious, dialectic, petulant, controversial, debatable, opinionated, cantankerous. See also belligerent, hostile, contentious (1), litigious. *Ant.* Conciliatory.

Arid, *adj.* Dry. Baked, sterile, parched, waterless. See barren, fallow, dormant, dead.

Arise, *v.* **1.** To appear; to come into being (a cause of action arises when the act is complete; an injury arising out of employment). Originate, occur, emanate, spring up, emerge, come into existence, commence, begin, become manifest, become visible, accrue, proceed from, take origin, ensue, come to light, be derived, present itself, become operative, result from, flow from, proceed from, be dependent on, grow out of, derive, start, take place, happen, evolve, materialize. **2.** To stand up (arise from the bench). Wake up, ascend, rise, mount, climb. *Ant.* Disappear; fall.

Arising out of See accident arising out of employment; arise.

Aristocracy, *n.* Nobility. Upper class, elite, gentry, society, noblesse, cream, gentility, patrician, Brahmin, gentleman, lady, lord, blue blood, intelligentsia.

Aristocratic, *adj.* Polished, cultured, delicate, well-bred, fashionable. See civil (3).

Arm, *n.*, *v.* See extremity; arms; strengthen, augment, equip, clothe; branch (1).

Armada, *n.* A fleet of ships. See vessel (1).

Armament, *n.* See arms, weapon, ballistics.

Armed, *adj.* Equipped with weapons or with whatever is needed for the occasion (armed neutrality; armed with facts and figures). Under arms, panoplied, prepared, furnished, fortified, outfitted, geared, ready, provided, strengthened, reinforced. *Ant.* Unarmed, unprepared.

Armed forces, *n.* See military (2).

Armed robbery Taking another's property by force while armed with a deadly weapon. See robbery.

Armistice, *n.* A suspension of fighting. Truce, cease-fire, moratorium. See also reprieve, interruption, cessation, abeyance; compact (1), concord (1).

Armor, *n.* See protection; shield (1).

Armory, *n.* A place where arms are stored. Arsenal, warehouse, depot, magazine.

Arms, *n.* Weapons; that which is used to defend oneself. Ammunition, firearms, munitions, armament, bombs, rifles, pistols. See also weapon, gun.

Arm's length At a distance; as between two strangers who are looking out for their individual self-interests (an arm's length transaction; a husband is not allowed to deal with his wife at arm's length).

Arm-twisting, *n.* See coercion; constrain (1).

Army, *n.* See military, sailor, group (1).

Aroma, *n.* Pleasant odor. Fragrance, smell, incense, scent, perfume, trace, bouquet, savor, redolence, balm. See also manifestation.

Aromatic, *adj.* See fragrant.

Arousal, *n.* See awakening.

Arouse, *v.* See animate, incite, bait (3), initiate.

Arraign, *v.* To bring an accused before a court to hear the criminal charges and to enter a plea of guilty, not guilty, etc. (she was arraigned immediately after her arrest). Charge, accuse, incriminate, criminate, denounce, inform against, summon, file charges, prosecute, denunciate, cite, impute, censure, criticize, assail, rebuke, impugn. *Ant.* Exonerate.

Arraignment, *n.* Bringing the accused before a court to hear the criminal charges and to enter a plea of guilty, not guilty, etc. (her counsel at the arraignment). Formal accusation, prosecution, incrimination, denouncement, charging, implication. See also arraign, indictment. *Ant.* Exoneration.

Arrange, *v.* See plan, prepare, settle, establish, organize.

Arrangement, *n.* See order (4), plan (1), composition, classification (1), organization (2), production, manufacture.

Arrangement with creditors A plan whereby the debtor settles with his or her creditors or obtains more time to repay debts. Under the Bankruptcy Act, the court can supervise such plans. Composition with creditors.

Arrant, *adj.* See complete (2).

Array 1. *n.* A group of persons summoned to be jurors; the list of jurors impaneled. **2.** *n.* Collection (array of troops). Congregation, arrangement, aggregation, display, organization, marshaling, assembling, exhibition, layout, classification, order, disposition, design. **3.** *v.* To place in order (the witnesses were arrayed against us). Marshal, assemble, group, dispose, amass, rank, muster, arrange, organize, deploy, place.

Arrearages, arrears, *n.* Unpaid debts (the arrearages amounted to $100; he was

$100 in arrears). Obligations outstanding, remaining balance, delinquency, overdue payments, liability, deficit, overdue debt, indebtedness, balance due, debit, deficiency. *Ant.* Prepayment.

Arrest 1. *n.* Taking someone into custody. Arrest involves the authority to arrest, the assertion of that authority with the intention to affect an arrest, and restraint of the person to be arrested. Apprehension, detention, capture, seizure, constraint, incarceration, "bust," internment, legal restraint, custodial detention. **2.** *v.* To deprive a person of his or her liberty by legal authority. Apprehend, take into custody, seize, jail, incarcerate, imprison, capture, "collar," "bust," hold, commit, secure, constrain, confine. **3.** *v.* To stop (the doctor was not able to arrest the cancer). Halt, block, end, retard, slow, avert, impede, thwart, subdue, abort, suspend, interrupt, delay, obstruct, curb, check, enjoin, prevent, stay, stall, hinder, detain, withhold. *Ant.* Free; start.

Arresting, *adj.* See compelling, extraordinary, outstanding (2), moving (1), intriguing, enjoyable, attractive.

Arrest of judgment A court's refusal to render a judgment; a court's decision to stay a judgment because of errors that have been discovered in the record.

Arrest warrant A written order signed by a judge or magistrate that commands a law enforcement officer to arrest a person and bring him or her before the court in order to answer the charges made in a complaint.

Arrival, *n.* See appearance (2), landing (2).

Arrive, *v.* See appear (2), enter (2), approach (1), realize (2).

Arrogance, *n.* Haughtiness. Pride, snobbery, vanity, presumption, conceit, insolence, chutzpah, audacity, self-importance, swagger, assurance, braggadocio. See also contempt, pretense.

Arrogant, *adj.* Haughty. Egotistical, pompous, vain, insolent, supercilious, conceited, fatuous, self-important, presumptuous, overbearing, imperious, disdainful, snobbish, proud, condescending, high and mighty, lordly. See also contemptuous.

Arrogate, *v.* See appropriate (1), encroach, seize (1), confiscate, attribute (1).

Arrogation, *n.* **1.** Claiming or seizing something without authority or right (the court's action amounted to an arrogation of legislative power). Appropriation, usurpation, taking, assumption, confiscation, adoption, attachment, requisition, preemption, accroachment, annexation, sequestration. **2.** The adoption of an adult. **3.** See attribution. *Ant.* Relinquishment.

Arsenal, *n.* **1.** A place to store arms. Warehouse, depot, armory, magazine, ammunition dump. **2.** A collection of weapons. Ammunition, firearms, arms, munitions, rifles, pistols.

Arson, *n.* The malicious burning of the house of another. Starting a fire or explosion with the purpose of destroying a building or an occupied structure of another, or damaging any property (even one's own) in order to collect insurance. Incendiarism, pyromania, destroying property by fire.

Art, *n.* **1.** The systematic application of knowledge and skill in producing a desired result (the art of cross-examination). Talent, mastery, expertise, skill, craft, facility, know-how, dexterity, science, profession, trade, knack, aptitude, competence, craftsmanship, workmanship. **2.** In patent law, the process or method used to produce a useful result. **3.** See masterpiece, opus. *Ant.* Incompetency.

Artery, *n.* See highway, conduit (2), course; vein (1).

Artful, *adj.* See deceptive, deceitful, evasive, artificial (2); apt (3), able, expert (2).

Article, *n.* **1.** A clause or provision in a document (the statute violates Article VI of the Constitution). Paragraph, portion, chapter, division, passage, section, proviso, proposition, stipulation, point, unit, term, topic, subject. **2.** Thing (all articles must be inspected). Commodity, item, res, object, effect, entity, being, matter, product, piece, substance. **3.** A set of propositions or rules (Articles of

Confederation; articles of incorporation). Term, principle, instrument, document, tenet, canon, precept, mandate, rubric. **4.** Monograph (an article in the newspaper). Theme, essay, study, piece, story, tract, critique, report.

Articled, *adj.* Bound by agreement (articled clerk). Under contract, indentured, apprenticed, obligated.

Articles of incorporation A certificate of incorporation. The document that establishes (incorporates) a corporation when it is filed with the appropriate governmental agency.

Articulate 1. *adj.* See clear (1), comprehensible, lucid (2). **2.** *adj.* Eloquent. Fluent, expressive, fluid, smooth, silver-tongued, facile, graceful, intelligible. **3.** *v.* See pronounce, declare, express (2); clarify, voice, communicate.

Articulation, *n.* See communication.

Artifact, artefact, *n.* See object (3), item, goods.

Artifice, *n.* Contrivance (the attempt to bypass the rule by mislabeling it is an artifice that any good lawyer will uncover). Device, trick, trickery, deception, stratagem, evasion, ruse, maneuver, move, strategy, plot, plan, hoax, subterfuge, dodge, guile, duplicity, machination, invention, cleverness, artificiality, chicanery, tactic, circumvention, pretext, delusion, slyness, distortion, ingenuity, fabrication, misrepresentation, guise, prevarication, finesse, fiction, fraud, deceit, screen, intrigue, wile, sham, loophole, conspiracy, cabal, falsification. *Ant.* Sincerity.

Artificer, *n.* **1.** A skilled worker. Mechanic, craftsman, machinist, artisan, operative. **2.** Inventor. Creator, designer, builder, originator, manufacturer, artist, architect.

Artificial, *adj.* **1.** Not natural; created by humans (the ditch is an artificial condition of the land). Synthetic, manmade, constructed, manufactured, unnatural, imitation. **2.** Not based on reality, forced (the theory consists of a string of artificial arguments). Contrived, spurious, specious, sham, phony, factitious, pretentious, overdone, fake, ersatz, strained, deceptive, theatrical, dummy, concocted, unreal, casuistic, sophistical, fictitious, illusory, synthetic, ungenuine, false, adulterated. *Ant.* Natural; genuine, actual.

Artificial insemination Injecting semen into a woman by a method other than sexual intercourse.

Artillery, *n.* See weapon, gun.

Artisan, *n.* Someone skilled in a trade, craft, or art. Craftsman, artificer, worker, mechanic, workman, skilled laborer, journeyman, master, handicraftsman, technician, operator, tradesman, master craftsman.

Artist, *n.* See artisan, expert (1), professional (2).

Artistic, *adj.* See aesthetic, attractive, expert (2), apt (3).

Artless, *adj.* See innocent (2), commonplace, awkward.

Art, words of See term of art.

Ascend, *v.* To go up; to pass up (ascend the ladder). Climb, advance, mount, rise, scale, escalate, incline, soar, pass upward, succeed to, inherit. *Ant.* Descend.

Ascendancy, *n.* See supremacy, authority (2), power, dominion.

Ascendant 1. *n.* A person with whom one is related in the ascending line: parent, grandparent, great-grandparent, etc. (the land came from her ascendants). Ancestor, sire, procreator, progenitor, genitor, primogenitor, forefather, forebear, antecedent. **2.** *adj.* Superior (an ascendant position in the firm). Dominant, preeminent, controlling, prevailing, eminent. *Ant.* Descendant; insignificant.

Ascent, *n.* **1.** Transference, transmission, or inheritance of an estate from ancestors to heirs in the ascending line. **2.** Movement upward (her ascent from associate to partner). Advancement, promotion, progress, progression, upgrading, climb, escalation, elevation, ascension, levitation. *Ant.* Descent, fall.

Ascertain, *v.* To find out (to ascertain the needs of the community). Determine, render certain, fix, estimate, clear away the doubt, investigate, identify, establish, settle, verify, resolve, conclude, grasp, discover, uncover, learn, ferret out, unearth, detect, certify, see, inquire, study, appraise, pinpoint, come to a conclusion, confirm, untangle, decipher, resolve, deduce, find out, fathom. *Ant.* Ignore, confuse.

Ascertainable, *adj.* Discoverable (an ascertainable loss of money or property as a result of the fraud). Establishable, discernible, verifiable, calculable, demonstrable, knowable, certifiable, determinable. See also appreciable.

Ascetic, *adj.* Self-denying (ascetic existence). Rigorous, abstemious, Spartan, frugal, abstinent, puritanical. See also strict (2). *Ant.* Indulgent.

Ascribe, *v.* See attribute, connect (2), characterize, attach (3).

Ashamed, *adj.* Embarrassed. Humiliated, sorry, humbled, mortified, chagrined, distressed, uneasy, degraded, bewildered, guilty, withdrawn, abashed, remorseful.

Asinine, *adj.* See absurd, juvenile, irrational, lunatic, dumb.

As is In its present condition (the goods are sold as is). Without warranty, as shown, in its existing physical condition, with all faults, with imperfection. *Ant.* Under warranty.

Ask, *v.* **1.** To inquire (ask the witness if she knows). Interrogate, question, examine, query, request information, quiz, grill. See also investigate, cross-examine. **2.** To petition (ask the court for an extension). Request, plead, implore, supplicate, entreat, beseech, pray, adjure, appeal, apply, sue, importune, beg. *Ant.* Answer; ignore, spurn.

Asleep, *adj.* See dormant, passive (1), oblivious.

Aspect, *n.* See appearance (3), attribute (2), characteristic (1), component.

As per In accordance with (it was sent as per your instructions). In accordance with the terms of, as requested, as indicated in the contract.

Aspersion, *n.* Damaging statement (the report cast aspersions on his integrity). Censure, slander, defamatory statement, scandal, reproach, mockery, denunciation, humiliation, detraction, obloquy, dishonor, slur, abuse, vilification, libel, distraction, discredit, attack, impugnment, vituperation, reflection, animadversion, invective, condemnation, affront, slight, denigration, reproof, derision, malediction, disparagement. *Ant.* Commendation.

Asphalt, *v., n.* See pave.

Asphyxiate, *v.* See suffocate.

Aspirant, *n.* See candidate, applicant.

Aspiration, *n.* See desire (4), hope (2), aim (3).

Aspire, *v.* See desire (1), hope (1), attempt (3).

Asportation, *n.* Carrying away or removing something (taking concealed goods out of the store was sufficient asportation to support a larceny conviction). Removal, displacement, transfer, carriage, transmission. See also carrying away.

Ass, *n.* Fool. Idiot, donkey, dunce, blockhead, jackass, "jerk," imbecile, lamebrain, moron, simpleton, sap, bonehead, lightweight. See also boor, idiot.

Assail, *v.* See attack (1), assault (3).

Assailant, *n.* A person who attacks. Attacker, aggressor, assailer, accoster, invader, aggressor, antagonist, challenger, maligner, ravager, adversary, vilifier. *Ant.* Aide, benefactor.

Assassinate, *v.* See kill (1).

Assassination, *n.* The murder of someone, often a public figure. Slaying, homicide, execution, killing, elimination, annihilation, silencing, massacre, slaughter.

Assault 1. *n.* A tort with the following elements: (a) an act, (b) an intent to cause a harmful or offensive contact, or an intent to cause an apprehension of a harmful or offensive contact, (c) the apprehension of imminent harmful or offensive contact to the plaintiff's own person, and (d) causation of the apprehension. A reasonable apprehension of an imminent battery. Assault is also a crime. The word "assault" sometimes means actual physical contact with the victim, so that under this meaning, the word is synonymous with battery. **2.** *n.* Attack. Seige, aggression, strike, offense, intrusion, incursion, onslaught, foray, invasion, violation, molestation, outrage, ambush, rape, injury, besiegement, thrust, storming, barrage, bombardment, torrent, shelling, combat, threat. **3.** *v.* To attack. Mug, batter, accost, set upon, assail, strike, lunge, lash, besiege, invade, storm, insult, abuse, charge, threaten, "mug," molest, harass.

Assay, *n.*, assay, *v.* **1.** *n.* An examination or trial to test the quality and quantity of metals (an assay of the components). Inspection, scrutiny, experimentation, analysis, diagnosis, investigation, exploration, appraisal, evaluation. **2.** *v.* To put to a trial; to examine the quality and quantity of metals. Inspect, scrutinize, investigate, explore, analyze, appraise, evaluate, judge, search, probe. **3.** *v.* To try, to attempt (the lawyer assayed to explain the theory). Endeavor, essay, undertake, exert oneself, strive.

Assemblage, *n.* 1. A collection of people (the assemblage in the hall became restless). Crowd, throng, assembly, array, association, gathering, body, multitude, pack, audience, congregation, caucus, tribe, committee, party, squad, company, ensemble, convention. **2.** Combining things together (an assemblage of evidence). Collection, aggregation, concentration, amassment, assembly, mobilization, accumulation, union, symposium, combination, cluster, cumulation, compilation, agglomeration. *Ant.* Individual; dispersion.

Assemble, *v.* See build, collect (1), produce (2), accumulate, converge, convene.

Assembly, *n.* 1. A gathering or meeting of people (a religious assembly). Congregation, convention, committee, community, crowd, association, conference, caucus, congress, conclave, body, group, assemblage, herd, throng, flock, mass, troop, council. **2.** One of the houses of the legislature in many states (the Assembly voted to repeal the measure). See legislature; legislator. *Ant.* Dispersion (1).

Assent 1. *n.* Agreement (the action of the clerk constituted an assent by the government). Consent, approval, authorization, admission, affirmation, acceptance, submission, accord, sanction, acquiescence, recognition, concurrence, permission, endorsement, ratification, concession, approbation, verification, corroboration, "OK," blessing, allowance, concordance, substantiation, concord, willingness. **2.** *v.* To agree (the lawyer assented to the proposal). Concur, approve, authorize, admit, affirm, accept, submit, sanction, acquiesce, endorse, ratify, verify, concede, allow, corroborate, subscribe to, embrace, permit, harmonize, yield, acknowledge, uphold, comply. *Ant.* Rejection; reject.

Assert, *v.* To declare; to state as true (the accused asserted her innocence). Insist upon, claim, maintain, swear, contend, profess, asseverate, propound, stress, announce, utter, avouch, advance, set forth, affirm, recite, annunciate, plead, espouse, aver, declare, offer, assure, advocate, pledge, say, defend, support, press, disseminate, broadcast, predicate, make felt. *Ant.* Negate, disclaim.

Assertion, *n.* A declaration or positive statement (the assertion that the drug caused the death is preposterous). Claim, contention, affirmation, proposition, proclamation, averment, allegation, avowal, asseveration, assurance, acknowledgment, dictum, argument, remark, predication, maintenance, defense, vindication, announcement, attestation, insistence, representation. *Ant.* Disclaimer.

Assertive, *adj.* Insistent (assertive personality). Confident, self-confident, bold, positive, aggressive, emphatic, decisive, dogmatic, strong-willed, self-assured, pushy, forceful, outspoken, opinionated, forward, domineering, presumptuous. *Ant.* Hesitant.

Assess, *v.* 1. To fix the value of something (the land was assessed at market value). Appraise, value, rate, estimate, ascertain, compute, measure, gauge, calculate, test, price, calibrate, reckon. See also judge (3). **2.** To charge with one's share (each member of the bar was assessed $10). Tax, levy, impose, demand. **3.** To evaluate (how would you assess your chances of obtaining a favorable verdict). Weigh, judge, consider, look over, appraise, measure, investigate, review, take stock of.

Assessed, *adj.* Imposed, appraised (assessed value. Calculated, levied, ascertained, computed, fixed, estimated, gauged.

Assessment, *n.* **1.** A determination of the value of something (an increase in the assessment of the land). Appraisal, valuation, rating, estimation, appraisement, assigned value, face value, measure. **2.** A determination of the share that is due from someone; an amount assessed (he could not afford his assessment). Tax, exaction, levy, impost, duty, capitation, imposition, periodic payments, toll, fee, surcharge, charge. **3.** Estimation (an assessment of the chances of winning). Evaluation, judgment, investigation, examination, measurement, review, gauging, estimation.

Assessor, *n.* A person who assesses or appraises the value of things (tax assessor). Charger, judge, estimator, collector, evaluator.

Asset, *n.* **1.** Anything of value; property (the judgment must be satisfied out of the defendant's assets). Resource, capital, estate, money, belongings, means, chattel, possessions, holding, fund, equity, valuable, wherewithal, goods, financial resource, inventory, reserve, wealth. **2.** Benefit (your prior experience will be an asset). Advantage, strength, qualification, boon, virtue, aid, plus, distinction, strong point, power, help. *Ant.* Liability; hindrance.

Asseverate, *v.* See certify.

Asseveration, *n.* A solemn declaration (his asseveration was witnessed). Avowal, affirmation, positive assertion, averment, deposition, assurance, protestation, proclamation, testimony, certification, acknowledgment, attestation, confirmation, profession, pledge, adjuration, vow.

Assiduous, *adj.* See indefatigable, diligent, strong (2).

Assign, *v.* **1.** To transfer ownership or rights (Jones assigned his policy to Smith). Turn over, grant, entrust, alienate, transmit, consign, surrender, sign over, convey, endorse, make over, negotiate. **2.** To allot (they were assigned the task of researching the liability issue). Allocate, apportion, relegate, mete out, award, dispense, distribute, consign, set apart, appoint, designate, entrust, commission, authorize, choose, name, delegate, ascribe, empower, fix, stipulate, particularize, point out. *Ant.* Maintain; hold back.

Assignable, *adj.* Pertaining to that which can be transferred or negotiated (an assignable mortgage). Consignable, conveyable, transmittable.

Assigned account A debt owed to a company that the company uses as security for its own debt to a bank. Also called pledged accounts receivable.

Assigned counsel An attorney appointed by the court to represent a poor person.

Assigned risk A risk that an insurer would not take on its own. The government requires the insurer to provide coverage in such situations, usually involving automobile insurance.

Assignee, *n.* The person to whom property or rights are transferred (Smith assigns his contract to Jones. Jones is the assignee; Smith is the assignor). Grantee, donee, transferee, recipient.

Assignment, *n.* **1.** The transfer of ownership or rights (assignment of wages to a creditor). Consignment, surrender, endorsement, negotiation, conveyance, alienation, cession, conferment, transmittal. **2.** Allotment (the senior attorney made the assignment of the research tasks). Allocation, apportionment, dispensation, distribution, designation, delegation, commission, authorization, allowance, meting out, division, selection, specification, doling out, dealing out. **3.** Task (my assignment was to collect all the assets). Responsibility, chore, duty, job, work, charge, function, homework, mission, instruction, obligation, part.

Assignor, *n.* The person who transfers property or rights (Smith assigns his cause of action to Jones. Smith is the assignor; Jones is the assignee). Transferor, grantor, donor.

Assigns, *n.* Assignees; persons to whom property or rights are transferred or assigned (the condition is binding on all your assigns). Transferees, donees, grantees, recipients.

Assimilate, *v.* See incorporate (2), absorb (1), adjust.

Assise, assize, *n.* **1.** An ancient court. **2.** An old writ (assise of nuisance). **3.** A verdict or finding of jurors pursuant to a writ of assise.

Assist 1. *v.* To help (he was assisted by a jailhouse lawyer). Aid, accommodate, support, serve, advocate, abet, benefit, cooperate with, succor, boost, relieve, administer to, encourage, minister to, foster, enhance, befriend, oblige, lend a hand, conspire with, connive with, endorse, maintain, nurture, comfort, patronize, back, second, subsidize, accompany, escort. **2.** *n.* Helping hand (he needs an assist in learning to shepardize). Boost, hand, aid, contribution. See also assistance (1). *Ant.* Impede; obstruction.

Assistance, *n.* **1.** Service or help provided (the defendant is entitled to effective assistance of counsel). Support, relief, benefit, succor, advocacy, protection, care, championship, accommodation, furtherance, cooperation, intercession, good offices. See also aid (2). **2.** Financial support (the foundation's call for assistance). Contribution, patronage, alms, subsidy, welfare, dole, sustenance, relief, charity. *Ant.* Hindrance.

Assistant, *n.* A helper or deputy (legal assistant). Aide, attendant, auxiliary, associate, abettor, confederate, accessory, second, ally, colleague, collaborator, disciple, clerk, accomplice, supporter, agent, apprentice, partner, subordinate, lieutenant, co-worker, underling, acolyte, adjunct, dependent, lackey, servant, hireling, cog, coadjutor, adjutant, subaltern. *Ant.* Opponent.

Assize, *n.* See assise.

Associate 1. *v.* To combine or join together (it is a mistake to associate your client with that plan). Connect, relate, attach, pair, unite, identify, link, correlate, affiliate, incorporate, wed, federate, league, mate, accompany, amalgamate, conjoin, syndicate, coalesce, confederate, synthesize, merge, group, ally, yoke, mingle, attribute, couple. **2.** *n.* A colleague or subordinate (she is an associate in the firm). Teammate, assistant, partner, copartner, confederate, auxiliary, aide, collaborator, co-worker, confrere, accomplice, comrade, ally, coadjutor, peer, compeer, mate, fellow, equal, acquaintance, confidant, intimate, buddy, friend. *Ant.* Divide; stranger.

Associated, *adj.* Affiliated (associated corporations). Connected, united, allied, combined, linked, confederated, federated, leagued, cooperating, coupled, joined, cognate, akin. *Ant.* Unrelated.

Association, *n.* **1.** An organization of people joined for a common purpose (the bar association). League, consortium, union, partnership, alliance, trust, company, corporation, coalition, affiliation, confederation, syndicate, guild, body, society, fraternity, sorority, club, group membership, clique, fellowship, cartel, pool, monopoly, chain, grange, house, firm, sodality, coterie, combine, congress, brotherhood, sisterhood, faction, sect, wing, ring, axis. **2.** A relationship (your association with the adversary will lead to an inference of support). Connection, involvement, participation, linkage, affiliation, acquaintance, collaboration, concert, bond, camaraderie, friendship, fraternization, intercourse, affinity, dependency, dealings, cooperation, kinship, alignment, intimacy. *Ant.* Separation; alienation.

Assort, *v.* See classify, group (2).

Assorted, *adj.* See separate (1), various.

Assortment, *n.* See classification, collection, multitude.

Assuage, *v.* To lessen the intensity of something (find out if anything is available to assuage the pain). Mitigate, calm, mollify, ease, allay, soften, temper, pacify, moderate, palliate, sooth, tranquilize, quiet, blunt, abate, dull, relieve, relax, slacken, qualify, reduce, quench, check, deaden, subdue, remedy, appease, satiate, silence, console, heal, satisfy. *Ant.* Aggravate, augment.

Assume, *v.* **1.** To take upon oneself (he assumed the mortgage upon purchase). Undertake, take to oneself, take over, take up, take on, accept, take responsibility for, attempt, venture, become bound, adopt. **2.** To suppose (we will assume for the moment that you were there). Presume, hypothesize, speculate, presuppose, infer, postulate, surmise, theorize, divine, predicate, take for granted, believe, apprehend, fancy, opine, deduce, deem, suspect, suppose, understand, conjecture, posit, grant, concede, imagine. **3.** To seize (they assumed power by force). Usurp, expropriate, take over, arrogate, annex, commandeer, confiscate, appropriate, preempt. **4.** To imitate (he assumed the guise of respectability). Simulate, adopt, impersonate, mimic, pretend, feign, appear as, counterfeit, affect, pose.

Assumed, *adj.* **1.** Hypothetical (assumed facts). Presupposed, supposed, considered true, given, conceded, conjectured, posited, understood, stated. **2.** Sham (assumed name). Feigned, false, bogus, fabricated, adopted, spurious, pseudo, phony, fictitious, so-called, make-believe, illusory, synthetic. *Ant.* Proved; authentic.

Assuming, *adj.* See arrogant.

Assumpsit, *n.* **1.** A promise or agreement. **2.** An action to recover damages for the nonperformance of a contract.

Assumption, *n.* **1.** The act of taking something upon oneself (assumption of a lease; assumption of a risk). Taking on, acceptance, adoption, undertaking, shouldering, becoming responsible for. **2.** A conjecture (the company will receive the contract on the assumption that its application is in order). Supposition, premise, presupposition, hypothesis, inference, surmise, belief, presumption, theory, guess, postulate, speculation. **3.** Seizure (the assumption of control of the board). Appropriation, expropriation, annexation, arrogation, confiscation, usurpation, exaction, taking. *Ant.* Rejection; proof; relinquishment.

Assumption of the risk A defense to a damage action. Elements: (a) The injured person knew of and appreciated the danger—there was an understanding of the risks, and (b) the injured person voluntarily chose to be exposed to the danger.

Assurance, *n.* **1.** A declaration tending to inspire confidence; the act of assuring (assurance of safety). Guaranty, pledge, word, averment, security, surety, warrant, warranty, vow, affirmation, promise, understanding, expectation, protestation, statement, profession, pact, oath, commitment, certification. **2.** The deed or document that conveys real property. **3.** Insurance (*Brit.*).

Assure, *v.* **1.** To state with certainty (she assured us that she had not provoked the attack). State positively, declare, assert, attest, aver, avouch, establish, profess, swear, asseverate. **2.** To make secure (the only way to assure compliance is to monitor performance). Insure, ensure, guarantee, secure, make certain, free from doubt, confirm, clinch, pledge, warrant, certify, underwrite, verify, corroborate, seal. *Ant.* Equivocate; confound.

Assured 1. *n.* A person who has been insured (state the name of the assured under the policy). Insured, covered person. **2.** *n.* Occasionally, the beneficiary under an insurance policy (the named assured). **3.** *adj.* Secure (the assured clear distance rule requires that a driver be able to stop a vehicle within the distance he or she can clearly see). Certain, reliable, indisputable, unquestionable, dependable, guaranteed, positive, absolute, undoubted. **4.** *adj.* Self-confident (an assured attorney). Confident, self-assured, self-controlled, unwavering, arrogant, presumptuous, brazen, overconfident, bold, assertive, complacent, vain. *Ant.* Dubious; insecure.

Assurer, *n.* A person or company that provides insurance. Insurer, indemnifier, underwriter.

Asterisk, *n.* A signal (*) to show an omission or a footnote reference.

Astonish, *v.* See amaze, surprise (1); agape.

Astonishing, *adj.* See extraordinary, appalling, serious (2), acute; agape.

Astonishment, *n.* See surprise (2), consternation.

Astound, *v.* See amaze, surprise (1); agape.

Astounding, *adj.* See extraordinary, appalling, serious (2), acute.

Astray, *adv.* See wrong (2, 3), wander.

Astringent, *adj.* See caustic, rude.

Astrologer, *n.* See oracle; augur, clairvoyance; witchcraft.

Astronomical, *adj.* See big, great.

Astute, *adj.* See prudent, acute, expert (2), able, deceptive, deceitful.

Asylum, *n.* **1.** An institution for the care of unfortunates (insane asylum). Home, hospital, eleemosynary institution, ward, sanatorium, sanitarium, farm. **2.** A hiding place (the criminal sought asylum in the warehouse). Refuge, sanctuary, shelter, covert, harbor, haven, security, reserve, retreat, hideaway, den, haunt, cloister, cave, resort, hideout, sanctum, port, arbor, protection.

At arm's length See arm's length.

At bar Before the court (the case at bar). Now being litigated, the instant case.

Ate, *v.* See eat.

At hand See close (6).

Atheism, *n.* Disbelief in God. Skepticism, irreligion, impiety, godlessness, unbelief, agnosticism, iconoclasm, materialism. See also apostasy.

Atheist, *n.* Someone who does not believe in God (a professed atheist). Nonbeliever, unbeliever, iconoclast, infidel, heretic, skeptic, heathen, pagan, nihilist, agnostic. *Ant.* theist.

Athlete, *n.* Competitor. Player, "jock," gymnast, sportsman, contestant, contender, amateur, professional, acrobat.

Athletic, *adj.* See able-bodied, healthy, tall.

Athletics, *n.* Sports. Events, games, acrobatics, gymnastics, exercises, competition, contests, Olympics, physical contact, training, calisthenics, workout.

At issue A case is at issue when the answer has been filed and no further pleadings are necessary, or at the point at which there has been an affirmation and a denial. In contention, in dispute, in issue, in controversy. See also controversial, issue of law, issue (3).

At large 1. Free; not limited to any specific place (the dog was at large). Unrestrained, unfettered, loose, released, independent, unconfined. **2.** An entire area rather than a designated district of the area (at large elections).

Atmosphere, *n.* See air (1), environment.

At odds See incompatible, inconsistent (1), contradictory, different, nonconforming; negative.

Atom, *n.* **1.** Electron, molecule, neutron, proton, ray, cathode, particle. **2.** See iota, scintilla.

Atomize, *v.* See break (2).

Atone, *v.*, **atonement,** *n.* See satisfy (1), satisfaction (1), redress, amend (1), amends, contrition.

At par See par (1), par value.

Atrocious, *adj.* See cruel, contemptible, outrage.

Atrocity, *n.* Outrageous conduct (the atrocity of his behavior). Barbarism, abomination, savage deed, horror, savagery, brutality, wickedness, ferocity, fiendishness, monstrosity, infamy, cruelty, truculence, scandal, hideousness, ruthlessness, inhumanity. See also outrage. *Ant.* Benevolence.

Atrophy, *n.* Degeneration of the body; wasting away (the injury ultimately led to atrophy). Emaciation, decay, weakening, enervation, marasmus. See also consumption (2).

Attach, *v.* **1.** To seize persons or property so that they will come under the custody and control of the court (attach the defendant's salary and inventory). Confiscate, garnishee, sequester, sequestrate, distrain, appropriate, take, impound, levy, press, impress, take possession of, secure. **2.** To fasten (attach the certificate to the application). Bind, tie, connect, join, affix, annex, subjoin, pin, weld, add, unite, adhere, merge, append, consolidate, combine, assemble, make fast, couple, nail, clip, staple, buckle, knit, zipper, snap, hook, screw, cement, agglutinate, engraft. **3.** To attribute (the judge attached no significance to the discrepancy). Ascribe, assign, accredit, apply, impute, connect, associate. *Ant.* Release; detach; disassociate.

Attaché, *n.* A person assigned to a diplomatic office. See delegate (2).

Attached, *adj.* **1.** Seized through a writ of attachment or other court order (an attached account). Confiscated, garnisheed, sequestered, secured, appropriated, taken, impounded, levied, replevied. **2.** Connected (attached buildings). Annexed, affixed, united, consolidated, merged, welded, combined, assembled, cemented, engrafted, agglutinated, subjoined, conjoined, joined. *Ant.* Released; detached.

Attachment, *n.* **1.** The seizure of persons or property so that they will come under the custody and control of the court (the retirement benefits were immune from attachment). Confiscation, garnishment, sequestration, appropriation, taking, impoundment, dispossession, distraint, divestment. **2.** The act of fastening (the attachment of the seal to the certificate). Annexation, affixing, union, connection, securing, insertion, appending. **3.** Something added (file the brief with all the attachments). Extra, appendage, appendix, addendum, accessory, codicil, rider, supplement, appurtenance, fixture, complement. **4.** Affection (his attachment to the commissioner is unwavering). Friendship, bond, fondness, admiration, esteem, respect, partiality, affinity, regard, predilection, loyalty, leaning, fidelity. *Ant.* Relinquishment; detachment; principal part; hostility.

Attachment bond Money that is put up to free property that has been attached. The bond substitutes for the property and guarantees that if the person who attached it wins in court, money will be available to pay the claim.

Attack 1. *v.* To set upon or assail (he attacked the decision). Charge, barrage, assault, lambaste, denounce, rush, advance, abuse, besiege, strike, invade, malign, revile, flay, take the offensive, lunge at, bear down on, waylay, molest, threaten, oppugn, storm, tackle, aggress, beleaguer, beset, raid, wallop, blow, box, smack, bomb, bombard. **2.** *n.* The action of attacking (the attack was intense). Assault, aggression, denouncement, onslaught, onset, offensive, charge, abuse, denigration, raid, incursion, strike, thrust, reprisal, blitz, foray. *Ant.* Retreat.

Attain, *v.* To arrive at or accomplish (attain the age of majority). Realize, actualize, procure, consummate, complete, reach, earn, achieve, perfect, effectuate, secure, effect, acquire, reap, win. *Ant.* Lose, forfeit.

Attainable, *adj.* See feasible, accessible, available.

Attainder, *n.* The loss of civil rights that occurs when a defendant receives the death sentence (e.g., a forfeiting of property). See bill of attainder.

Attainment, *n.* See completion, act (3), perfection (1), performance (1).

Attaint 1. *n.* Disgrace. Dishonor, defilement, humiliation, shame. **2.** *n.* A writ

71

to determine whether the jury has rendered a false verdict. **3.** *v.* To condemn to attainder.

Attempt 1. *n.* A crime consisting of the following elements: (a) an intent to commit the crime, (b) an overt act toward its commission, (c) the failure to complete the crime, and (d) the apparent possibility of committing it. **2.** *n.* An effort to do something (the attempt to have the verdict overturned). Try, undertaking, effort, struggle, endeavor, venture, experiment, essay, trial, enterprise, test. **3.** *v.* To try to accomplish something (he will attempt to establish a new cause of action). Venture, undertake, struggle, assay, essay, aspire, endeavor, hazard, strive, quest, aim, seek, begin, commence.

Attend, *v.* See assist (1), appear (2), visit, frequent (2).

Attendance, *n.* See presence (1), appearance (2).

Attendant 1. *n.* A person who assists someone else (the attendants on the floor of the Senate). Helper, assistant, aide, escort, companion, chaperon, auxiliary, steward, stewardess, servant, follower, waiter, waitress, valet, comrade, lackey, associate. **2.** *adj.* Resulting as a consequence (attendant hardships or circumstances). Concomitant, accompanying, connected, affiliated, associated, related, concurrent, following. *Ant.* Boss; unconnected.

Attention, *n.* See note (5), vigilance, interest (3), concentrate (1), notice (2).

Attentive, *adj.* See cautious; cognizant; civil (3).

Attenuate, *v.* To weaken (the medicine did little to attenuate the pain). Dilute, diminish, adulterate, impair, curtail, reduce, decrease, make thin, draw out, make slender, enfeeble, water down, rarefy, contract, constrict, deflate, narrow. *Ant.* Enlarge, fortify.

Attest, *v.* To bear witness; to affirm to be true or genuine (the witness attests the signature to the will; attested by oath). Certify, verify, solemnly declare, affirm, vouch for, assert, validate, authenticate, swear, aver, substantiate, confirm, endorse, declare, corroborate, testify, warrant, give evidence, demonstrate, indorse, asseverate, uphold, signify, manifest, evince, acknowledge, allege, depose, express, profess, take the stand, avouch, give testimony, depone. *Ant.* Refute, contradict.

Attestation, *n.* The act of witnessing the actual execution (making) of a document and subscribing (signing) one's name as a witness to that fact (the attestation of a will). Verification, certification, affirmation, authentication, averment, substantiation, endorsement, asseveration, corroboration, demonstration, confirmation, assurance, avouchment, adjuration, declaration, subscription, testimony, evidence, proof. *Ant.* Refutation.

Attesting witness Someone who signs a document for the purpose of proving and identifying it.

Attestor, *n.* A person who attests; an attesting witness.

Attic, *n.* Garret, loft, mansard, dormer.

Attire, *n., v.* See apparel, clothes, uniform (2); clothe.

Attitude, *n.* See manner, disposition (4), demeanor, behavior, carriage (3), climate (2), emotion.

Attorn, *v.* To transfer or turn over to another; to agree to become the tenant of the new owner. Assign, deliver, consign, confer, convey, cede, grant, relinquish.

Attorney, *n.* **1.** A lawyer. Counsel, legal representative, counselor, attorney at law, legal advisor, officer of the court, juris doctor, JD, legal practitioner, barrister, solicitor, advocate, member of the bar, prosecutor, attorney general, general counsel, defense attorney, learned counsel, jurist, "mouthpiece," shyster. **2.** A person who is authorized to act in place of another. Agent, attorney in fact, representative, substitute, proxy, factor, deputy.

Attorney-client privilege An evidentiary rule that confidential communications in the course of professional employment between attorney and client may not be divulged by the attorney without the consent of the client.

Attorney General, *n.* The chief attorney for the government. He or she is often called the corporation counsel in local governments.

Attorney in fact, *n.* Someone who is given authority through a power of attorney to do a particular nonlegal act. An "attorney in fact" need not be a member of the legal profession. Agent, substitute, proxy, factor, deputy, representative.

Attornment, *n.* See attorn.

Attract, *v.* See entice, entrap, enamor, interest (5), bait (3); attractive.

Attraction, *n.* See affinity (2), interest (4), amenity (1), appeal (3), bait (1).

Attractive, *adj.* Alluring (attractive nuisance). Inviting, appealing, beckoning, seductive, captivating, magnetic, tempting, enticing, fetching, pleasing, fascinating, enchanting, interesting, engaging, delightful, agreeable, winning, pleasant, handsome, elegant, prepossessing, bewitching, lovely, exquisite, enthralling, likable, desirable, entrancing. See also beautiful, intriguing, compelling, enjoyable. *Ant.* Dull, repulsive.

Attractive nuisance doctrine A duty of reasonable care is owed to prevent injury (a) to a trespassing child unable to appreciate the danger (b) from an artificial condition or activity on land (c) to which the child can be expected to be attracted. The torpedo doctrine, the turntable doctrine.

Attribute, *v.,* **attribute,** *n.* **1.** *v.* To consider as belonging to (the accident was attributed to a defective design). Associate, assign, accredit, impute, charge with, blame, link, trace to, ascribe, cause by. See also connect (2). **2.** *n.* Characteristic (she has all the attributes of a fine attorney). Trait, quality, ability, faculty, talent, gift, endowment, mark, property, peculiarity, idiosyncrasy, eccentricity.

Attribution, *n.* **1.** The act of ascribing or attributing. Assignment, association, imputation, tracing, reference, allusion, acknowledgment. See also citation (2). **2.** Assigning to one taxpayer the ownership interest of another taxpayer.

Attrition, *n.* Gradual and natural decrease. See reduction, erosion.

Attune, *v.* See adjust (1).

Atypical, *adj.* See abnormal, outstanding (2), special (1), extraordinary, original (3), deviant (1).

Au courant, *(Fr.)* See current (3).

Auction, *n.* A public sale of property to the highest bidder by one licensed and authorized for that purpose.

Audacious, *adj.* See adventurous, alive (2), courageous, ardent, arrogant, ambitious.

Audacity, *n.* See valor, spirit (2), arrogance, effrontery.

Audible, *adj.* Loud, hearable, intelligible. See clear (1) plain.

Audience, *n.* See assemblage (1), congregation; public (1).

Audit 1. *n.* A formal or official examination and verification of books of account by an auditor (the board of directors called for a special audit of the current fiscal period). Accounting, investigation, scrutiny, inspection, review. **2.** *v.* To examine and verify books of account formally or officially (she audited the books). Investigate, inspect, review, scrutinize, attest, check, research, certify, probe, monitor, balance, go over, oversee.

Audition, *n.* Tryout. See hearing, appraisal, assessment.

Auditor, *n.* Someone who is trained to examine financial records and accounts and to verify the accuracy of statements therein. See inspector, accountant.

Auditorium, *n.* Hall, theater, gallery, assembly hall, meeting place, arena, amphitheater, coliseum.

Augment, *v.* To increase or intensify (if the injury had not occurred, he would have augmented his salary by 50%). Enlarge, expand, grow larger, multiply, advance, appreciate, enhance, inflate, extend, build up, swell, amplify, widen, escalate, accelerate, heighten, deepen, aggravate, lengthen, puff up, cram, widen, raise, cumulate, bloat, stretch, magnify, bulge, supplement, thicken, amass, mushroom, balloon, aggrandize, reinforce. *Ant.* Diminish.

Augur, *v.* To be a sign of; to predict. Foretell, prognosticate, presage, harbinger, bode, intimate, forewarn, be an omen of, divine, forecast, indicate, signify. See also oracle, clairvoyance (2).

August, *adj.* See considerable (1), predominant.

Aura, *n.* Ambiance. Mood, tone, air, character, aroma, atmosphere, feel, karma, spirit, quality, emanation, sensation, essence. See also environment, climate (2).

Auspices, *n.* Support, sponsorship (he was allowed into the country under the auspices of the State Department). Patronage, backing, authority, aegis, advocacy, guidance, encouragement, control, oversight, aid, championship, security, influence, protectorship, countenance, management, wardship, favor, superintendence. See also charge (11).

Auspicious, *adj.* Favorable. Timely, opportune, propitious, hopeful, prosperous, seasonable, right, promising, appropriate, reassuring, lucky, rosy, encouraging, clear, bright. See also expedient (1). *Ant.* Ominous.

Austere, *adj.* See extreme (1), ascetic, strict (2), formal (3), grave (3), plain, caustic.

Australian ballot A system for voting in elections in which the names of candidates are printed and the vote of each citizen is secret.

Authentic, *adj.* Trustworthy, real (the will is authentic). Reliable, dependable, credible, creditable, truthful, accurate, factual, authoritative, verified, legitimate, confirmed, approved, genuine, bona fide, attested, original, unadulterated, true, veritable, convincing, solid, sound, sure, demonstrated, documented, literal, wellfounded, valid, validated. *Ant.* Counterfeit.

Authenticate, *v.* See certify, corroborate, ratify (2), prove, affirm, authorize, assure.

Authentication, *n.* The process of establishing the genuineness and authenticity of a writing; the process of establishing that an item of evidence is what it purports to be (authentication of the deed). Certification, verification, legitimation, documentation, confirmation, substantiation, attestation, corroboration, evidence, assurance.

Authenticity, *n.* See validity, legality, legitimacy.

Author 1. *n.* A writer; someone who writes an original literary composition (author of the torts treatise). Composer, scribe, man of letters, drafter, dramatist, novelist, essayist, biographer, journalist. **2.** *n.* An originator (author of our present troubles). Creator, source, origin, founder, parent, father, mother, architect, begetter, sire, contriver, prime mover, inventor, generator, planner, producer, progenitor, ancestor, first cause, inaugurator, beginner. **3.** *v.* To create something; to be the author of something (he authored the memo). Draft, write, compose, create, originate.

Authoritarian, *adj.* See arbitrary, strict (2), narrow (2), absolute (1).

Authoritative, *adj.* Commanding. See official (2), conclusive; rational.

Authorities, *n.* **1.** Those in control; those in power (the incident was not reported to the authorities). Government, police, administration, officials, directors, rulers, governors, bureaucracy, establishment, magistrates, commanders, executives. **2.** Sources relied on for a legal argument. The sources include statutes, cases, regulations, treatises, etc. (a table of authorities should be placed at the beginning of your brief). Precedents, citations, references, primary authority, secondary authority.

Authority, *n.* **1.** The power or right to act, to make decisions, to enforce decisions, to control (we challenged the board's authority to issue the subpoena). Jurisdiction, prerogative, authorization, dominion, strength, privilege, control, supremacy. **2.** Strength, influence (the clerk's authority had to be respected). Leadership, dominion, regime, prestige, title, sovereignty, administration, government, governance, importance, dominance, domination, sway, esteem, ascendancy, control, influence, mastery, force, regency, credibility, "clout," respect, seniority. **3.** Leader (the magistrate was the authority in town). Ruler, monarch, king, queen, head, governor, administrator, director, commander, emperor, czar, chairman, chairperson, chief, prince, autocrat, boss. **4.** Expert (Prosser is the leading authority on torts). Master, specialist, sage, scholar, connoisseur, judge, pundit, arbiter. **5.** A source relied upon for a legal argument (what is your authority for that theory). Precedent, statute, rule, ruling, holding, source, reference, citation, judgment, guide, document, decision, order, treatise, treaty, secondary authority, primary authority.

Authorization, *n.* See approval, license (1); authority.

Authorize, *v.* **1.** To empower (the employee was authorized to make the purchase). License, accredit, appoint, give permission, enable, commission, allow, invest, give leave, charter, depute, enfranchise, entitle, entrust, permit, direct, underwrite, grant permission, legislate. **2.** To sanction (the director must authorize all expenditures). Consent, confirm, certify, affirm, warrant, approve, support, tolerate, advocate, vouch for, assent, recommend, countenance, recognize, prescribe, endorse, legitimate, legitimize, legalize, solemnize, formalize, acquiesce, sanctify, sustain, subscribe. *Ant.* Prohibit.

Authorized, *adj.* See certified.

Auto, *n.* See vehicle (1).

Autocracy, *n.* Government by one person, the autocrat. Totalitarianism, dictatorship, despotism, absolutism, authoritarianism. See also tyranny. *Ant.* Democracy.

Autocrat, *n.* See tyrant, authority (3).

Autocratic, *adj.* See arbitrary (2), strict (2), absolute.

Autograph, *n.* See signature (1), mark.

Automatic, *adj.* Self-propelling. See spontaneous, mechanical, habitual; inevitable, involuntary; inherent, congenital.

Automation; automaton, *n.* Robot, machine, computer, puppet, zombie, automatic operation.

Automobile, *n.* See vehicle (1).

Autonomy, *n.* Self-government (the committee was given autonomy in hiring). Independence, self-rule, freedom, sovereignty, liberty, self-determination. *Ant.* Dependency.

Autopsy, *n.* An examination of a dead body to determine the cause of death. Postmortem, dissection, necropsy.

Autre vie Another's life. See estate pur autre vie.

Auxiliary, *adj.* Aiding, subsidiary (auxiliary police; auxiliary administration). Reserve, ancillary, additional, supplementary, back-up, assistant, helping, supportive, cooperative, subordinate, attending, aiding, subservient, abetting, collateral, cooperating, supplemental, dependent, contingent, complementing, secondary, accessory, appurtenant, contributing, contributory. *Ant.* Opposing, chief.

Avail 1. *v.* See capitalize (2), help (2); employ (2). **2.** *n.* See benefit (1).

Available, *adj.* Ready for immediate use (available income). Obtainable, within reach, accessible, at hand, attainable, reachable, securable, free, convenient, handy, suitable, serviceable, procurable, fit, receptive, vacant, on call, appropriate, fitting, beneficial. *Ant.* Unavailable, useless.

Avalanche, *n.* Deluge, landslide, bombardment, inundation, cascade, flood, torrent, quake, eruption. See also catastrophe, disaster.

Avant-garde, *n.* Innovator. Fashion, vanguard, pioneer, vogue, experimenter, modernity, originality, underground, trailblazer, leader, trend, front, imagination, now, contemporary, counterculture; progressive. See also novel, original.

Avarice, *n.* Excessive greed (the lawyer's avarice eventually led to his disbarment). Selfishness, craving, hunger, cupidity, covetousness, lust, avidity, rapacity, ambitiousness. *Ant.* Generosity.

Avaricious, *adj.* Greedy. Mercenary, rapacious, avid, selfish, acquisitive, possessive, mean, covetous, hoarding, gluttonous, insatiable, omniverous, grasping, envious, desirous, resentful, spiteful. See also jealous.

Avenge, *v.* To retaliate. Reward, compensate, requite, get even, repay, exact satisfaction. See also return (3); punishment, retaliation.

Avenue, *n.* See highway, course (1), conduit (2).

Aver, *v.* See assert.

Average, *adj.* **1.** The mean between two or more quantities (average salary). Median, middle, ratio, norm, par, center, mid, midmost. **2.** Typical (average ability). Common, commonplace, mediocre, tolerable, passable, ordinary, standard, fair, unexceptional, normal, prosaic, so-so, run-of-the-mill, moderate, garden variety, satisfactory. *Ant.* Maximum; superior.

Averment, *n.* A positive statement (averments in pleadings must be simple and direct). Allegation, statement of facts, affirmation, attestation, assertion, declaration, avowal, pronouncement, asseveration, remark, protestation, deposition, avouchment, adjuration.

Averse, *adj.* See hostile, adverse; suspicious, doubtful (1).

Aversion, *n.* See hostility, opposition, animus (2).

Avert, *v.* See avoid (2), arrest (3), block (2).

Aviation, *n.* Flying, aeronautics. Flight, gliding.

Aviator, *n.* See aeronaut.

Avid, *adj.* See ardent, avaricious, emotional, strong (2), ambitious.

A vinculo matrimonii See divorce a vinculo matrimonii.

Avocat, *n.* (*Fr.*) Advocate. Lawyer, barrister.

Avocation, *n.* Side interest; hobby (her avocation was hunting). Distraction, sideline, relaxation, pastime, diversion, recreation, entertainment, pursuit. See also amusement.

Avoid, *v.* **1.** To annul or cancel (to avoid a contract). Invalidate, vacate, destroy, annul, void, refute. See also rescind. **2.** To escape (to avoid a car; to avoid liability). Evade, elude, steer clear of, forsake, eschew, forbear, shun, boycott, sidestep, bypass, avert, dodge, withdraw, refrain, divert, prevent, prohibit, decline, ward off, retreat. See also circumvent. *Ant.* Validate; confront.

Avoidable, *adj.* Escapable (avoidable consequences). Refrainable, evadable, diversionary, diverting, preventable, stoppable. *Ant.* Unavoidable.

Avoidable consequences The damages that the injured party could have minimized. See mitigation of damages, doctrine of.

Avoidance, *n.* **1.** In pleading, avoidance is a statement admitting the facts in a pleading by the other side, but showing how these facts could not have their ordinary legal effect (confession and avoidance). **2.** Escaping or evading (avoidance of compliance). Deviation, evasion, dodging, bypass, abstinence, refraining, eschewal, abstention. **3.** Cancellation (avoidance of contract). Annulment, rescission, voidance, invalidation, quashing, nullification.

Avouch, *v.* See assert; acknowledge (1); guarantee (2).

Avow, *v.* See assert, acknowledge (1).

Avowal, *n.* An open declaration (avowal of guilt). Statement, testimony, affirmation, admission, pronouncement, proclamation, averment, protestation, assurance, word, confession, profession, acknowledgment, testimony, certification, corroboration, revelation, disclosure, assertion, authentication, contention, deposition, asseveration, verification, validation. *Ant.* Disclaimer.

Avulsion, *n.* **1.** The sudden and perceptible loss or addition to land by the action of water, or a sudden change in the bed or course of a stream. **2.** A tearing away. Separation by force, wresting, ripping.

Await, *v.* See anticipate (2).

Awake 1. *adj.* Conscious; alert, on guard. See conscious, cognizant, responsive, alive; cautious. **2.** *v.* To wake, rouse. See refresh, animate, incite, provoke.

Awaken, *v.* See animate, incite, provoke.

Awakening, *n.* Renaissance. Arousal, stimulation, rebirth, realization, revival, invigoration, animation, awareness, activation, resurrection, resuscitation, refreshment, renascence.

Award 1. *n.* The decision of a body or entity such as an arbitration board (appeal from the award). Decision, order, decree, grant, pronouncement, finding, determination, resolution, verdict, judgment. **2.** *n.* Prize. Honor, citation, remuneration, payment, gift, grant, medal, trophy, wreath. **3.** *v.* To grant; to adjudge (award an injunction). Adjudicate, judge, decree, decide, determine, settle, conclude, assign, allot, allocate, endow.

Aware, *adj.* See informed, cognizant, conscious.

Awareness, *n.* See cognizance (3).

Away, *adj., adv.* See absent, abroad.

Awe, *n.* **1.** Astonishment, amazement, bewilderment. See surprise (2), consternation. **2.** See apprehension (3). **3.** Respect. Reverence, adoration, veneration, solemnity.

Awesome, *adj.* Amazing. Overwhelming, shocking, impressive, fearful, intimidating, terrible, moving, formidable, sublime, horrible, tremendous, wondrous, alarming, dreadful, disquieting, astonishing. See also appalling, repulsive, agape.

Awful, *adj.* See bad (2), awesome, appalling, odious, repulsive, repugnant, offensive.

Awkward, *adj.* Blundering. Gauche, ungainly, artless, maladroit, inept, clumsy, uncouth, incapable, ungraceful, cumbersome, unfit, unmanageable, inelegant, embarrassing, indelicate, humiliating. See also backward; inconvenient.

Awning, *n.* Canopy. Cover, marquee, shelter, tent, booth, canvas. See also ceiling (2).

AWOL See absent without leave.

Awry, *adj., adv.* See wrong, erroneous, disproportionate.

Ax 1. *v.* See cut (1). **2.** *n.* Hatchet, pick, chopper, cleaver. **3.** *v.* See discharge (5).

Axiom, *n.* See maxim, principle (1), belief (2).

Axiomatic, *adj.* See manifest (1), certain (3).

Axis, *n.* **1.** Pivot. Shaft, stem, spindle, bar, axle, arbor, vertical, mandrel. **2.** See alliance (2). **3.** See center (1, 2).

B

Babble, *v.* To chatter. Prattle, gibber, chitchat, blab, rattle on, drivel, mumble, cackle, prate, ramble, blather, banter, blither. See also sound (5), noise.

Baby, *n.* See child, minor (1), infancy (1), juvenile (1).

Baby-sit, *v.* See mind (2), guard, oversee.

Bacchanalian, *adj.* See wild (2), lascivious, abandoned (2); debauchery; spree.

Bachelor, *n.* See single (2).

Back 1. *v.* To assume financial responsibility for; to endorse (the syndicate backed the venture). Support, countersign, finance, sponsor, assist, subsidize, abet, plead for, promote, approve, underwrite, validate, sanction, encourage, aid, succor, bolster, stand by, sustain, countenance, favor, warrant, advocate. See also recommend. **2.** *adj.* Delayed (back pay). Deferred, in arrears, behind, due, tardy, late, elapsed, past, prior, previous, earlier, gone, expired, overdue, obsolete. **3.** *n.* Rear part of the body (injury to the back). Spine, backbone, posterior, vertebrae. **4.** *adv.* In reverse direction (she fell back and injured her neck). Backward, to the rear, behind, toward the rear.

Backadation, *n.* See backwardation.

Backbite, *v.* See slander (2).

Backbiting, *adj.* See calumnious, libelous.

Backbond, *n.* A bond of indemnification given to a surety.

Backbone, *n.* See character (1), quality (2), resolution (4), endurance, spirit, self-confidence.

Backdating, *n.* Dating a document prior to the date it was prepared or drawn (backdating a check). Predating. *Ant.* Postdating.

Backdoor, *adj.* See clandestine.

Backer, *n.* See promoter, surety, champion (1), advocate (1); backing.

Backfire, *v.* To boomerang. Backlash, explode, rebound. See also fail (1); ricochet.

Background, *n.* See circumstances, context, experience (1), education, environment.

Backhanded, *adj.* See indirect, ambiguous, deceptive, deceitful.

Backing, *n.* Providing assistance (financial backing). Indorsement, patronage, sponsorship, promotion, support, sanction, cooperation, aegis, auspices, abetment, encouragement, approval, collaboration, championship, advocacy, subsidy, grant, allowance, aid, stipend, welfare, award, succor. *Ant.* Opposition.

Backlash, *n.* See reversal, backfire.

Backlog, *n.* See inventory (2), accumulation (1), reserve (2).

Backpedal, *v.* See depart (1).

Backslide, *v.* See regress, revert, lapse.

Back talk, *n.* See insubordination.

Backtrack, *v.* See revert, regress, depart (1), lapse; trace (2).

Backward, *adj.* **1.** Retarded. Dull, stupid, slow, feeble-minded, moronic, subnormal, undeveloped, unsophisticated, irrational. See also absurd. **2.** Shy. Self-effacing, bashful, timorous, reticent, timid, withdrawn, uncommunicative, unassuming, demure. **3.** See inverse.

Backwardation, *n.* Money paid to postpone the delivery of stock that has been purchased.

Backyard, *n.* See yard (2).

Bacteria, *n.* Germs. Microorganisms, parasites, virus, bacillus.

Bad, *adj.* **1.** Defective (bad design). Inferior, faulty, imperfect, below standard, incompetent, inefficient, shoddy, second-class, objectionable, unsuitable, unsatisfactory, below par, inadequate, poor, weak, lacking, adulterated, unfit, contaminated, tainted, worthless, ill-qualified, cheap, spoiled, incapable, deplorable, foul, ruined, useless, unproductive, second-rate, decaying, impure, base. **2.** Evil (bad character). Depraved, immoral, godless, dissolute, corrupt, dishonorable, amoral, venal, disgusting, degenerate, scandalous, disreputable, debauched, insidious, unprincipled, Machiavellian, heinous, atrocious, wicked, sinful, repulsive, obstreperous, delinquent, detrimental, undesirable, nefarious, sinister, inhuman, vile, cruel, satanic, flagrant, sordid, reprehensible, contemptible, ignoble, malevolent, profligate, abominable, abhorrent, villainous, despicable, destructive, vicious, improper, odious, detestable, grim, fraudulent, libertine, nasty, horrid, faithless, deceitful, irascible, criminal, accursed, poisonous, bestial, venomous, unwholesome, iniquitous, fiendish, baleful, damaging, wretched, coarse, unseemly, obnoxious, caustic, baneful. **3.** Incorrect (a bad decision). Unsound, doubtful, wrong, faulty, illogical, fallacious, unfounded, ungrounded, inconsistent, irrational, unreasonable erroneous, questionable, detrimental, mistaken, undependable, outrageous, misleading. **4.** Severe (a bad accident). Wicked, grave, harsh, grievous, searing, piercing, horrible, tormenting, intense, distressing, cruel, tragic, anguishing, excruciating, gnawing, wretched, harsh, racking, acute, unpleasant, disagreeable, nasty, torturing, regrettable, serious, pathetic. *Ant.* Superior; honorable; correct; innocuous.

Bad blood See hostility, animus (2), conflict (1), opposition.

Bad faith Conscious doing of wrong; dishonest purpose (she entered the contract in bad faith). Improper dealing, untrustworthiness, breach of faith, deception, double-dealing, dishonesty, insidiousness, fraud, meretriciousness, underhandedness, willfulness, willful failure, malice, intentional or gross recklessness, affirmative misconduct, conscious disregard, deliberate misleading, deliberate refusal, base, abjection, collusion, deceit, conspiracy, duplicity, falsehearted, treachery, perfidy, foul play. *Ant.* Good faith.

Bad fortune See casualty (1); chance (1), destiny, fate; ill-fated.

Badge, *n.* A distinctive mark (badge of honor). Token, mark, symbol, sign, stamp, insignia, brand, representation, label, identification, emblem, flag, logo, hallmark, attribute. See also characteristic, manifestation.

Badge of fraud A fact tending to throw suspicion upon a questioned transaction, raising an inference that it is fraudulent.

Badger, *v.* To annoy (the creditor badgered the debtor). Harass, provoke, hound, plague, press, antagonize, beset, browbeat, heckle, irritate, molest, torment, bait, pester, disturb, ruffle, vex, taunt, nag, importune, bother, pursue, abuse, trouble, aggravate, assail, rile, disquiet, pique, exasperate, distress, harry, persecute, irk, discountenance, bedevil, worry, hector, grate, coerce. *Ant.* Assist.

Bad luck, See misfortune, chance (1) destiny, fate; ill-fated.

Badmouth, *v.* To criticize. See disparage.

Baffle, *v.* See confuse, amaze, surprise (1).

Baffling, *adj.* See mysterious.

Bag, *n.* Sack. Container, receptacle, pouch, pocket, valise, tote, case, sac, satchel. See also vessel (2).

Baggage, *n.* Suitcases. Trunks, luggage, parcels. See also bag, effects, movables, equipment, cargo, freight.

Bail 1. *n.* The amount of money or property that is presented to the court by or on behalf of someone accused of a crime in order to allow him or her to be released from jail and to secure his or her appearance in court as the case proceeds (bail was set at $50,000). Security, collateral, deposit, pledge, surety, undertaking, indemnity, bond, bail bond, warranty, assurance bond. **2.** *n.* The person who furnishes the money or property that enables an accused to be released until the next court appearance. Surety, sponsor, bondsman. **3.** *v.* To obtain the release of someone by being responsible (security) for his or her appearance in court as the case proceeds. Post collateral, post bond, sponsor.

Bailable offense An offense for which an accused can be admitted to or be eligible for bail.

Bail bond A three-party contract that involves the state, the accused, and a surety under which the surety guarantees the state that the accused will appear in court as the case proceeds. If the accused does not appear, the surety must pay the state the amount of the bond.

Bailee, *n.* The person to whom personal property is entrusted under a contract of bailment (Bob leaves his car with the XYZ Parking Garage while he shops. The Garage is the bailee; Bob is the bailor). Transferee, recipient, consignee, assignee. *Ant.* Bailor.

Bailiff, *n.* **1.** A court officer who keeps order while the court is in session, watches over the jury and prisoners, etc. (the bailiff swore in the witness). Sheriff, sheriff's deputy, officer, marshal, constable. **2.** A person to whom some authority, care, guardianship, or jurisdiction is delivered, committed or entrusted (bailiff of the goods). Manager, overseer, supervisor, steward.

Bailiwick, *n.* The area within which someone has authority or skill (litigation was not his bailiwick). Jurisdiction, department, area, district, domain, field, circuit, specialty, territory, province, ward, expertise, realm, sphere, orbit, compass, center, base, "turf."

Bailment, *n.* A delivery of personal property to someone under an express or implied contract whereby the property is accepted and later redelivered after the purpose of the contract is fulfilled. (Sue stores her furniture at a warehouse. Their transaction is a bailment. Sue is the bailor; the warehouse is the bailee.)

Bailor, *n.* The person who delivers personal property to another under a contract of bailment. (Jim borrows Bill's book. Bill is the bailor; Jim is the bailee). Transferor, assignor, grantor, deliverer. *Ant.* Bailee.

Bailout, *n.* See rescue; abandonment.

Bailout stock Nontaxable preferred stock issued as a stock dividend.

Bait 1. *n.* Enticement (the offer to settle was bait to renegotiate a new contract). Appeal, allurement, temptation, decoy, lure, inducement, trap, draw, "come-on," attraction, seduction, blandishment, coaxing, solicitation, cajolery, fascination, invitation, snare, charm, spell, magnet, tantalization, tease. **2.** *v.* To pester (the prosecutor tried to bait the defense counsel). Annoy, worry, heckle, torment, badger, bedevil, persecute, harry, nag, antagonize, harass, "needle," "ride," aggravate, vex, threaten, arouse, taunt, deride, rouse, distract, gall, hector, irk, anger, pique, enrage, incense, instigate, enflame, goad, hound, incite, prod, ridicule, mock, tease, irritate, menace, browbeat, detract, provoke, distress. **3.** *v.* To entice (the insurance company baited the victim with a large settlement offer). Lure, tempt, induce, ensnare, entrap, attract, tantalize, intrigue, enthrall, inveigle, interest, draw, beguile, swindle, deceive, dupe, solicit, entreat, seduce, lobby, goad, importune, captivate, exhort, bias, pressure, predispose, urge, titillate. *Ant.* Discouragement; endear; deter.

Bait and switch A deceptive sales practice in which an offer is made not to sell the advertised product at the advertised price, but to draw a customer to the store to sell him or her a similar product that is more profitable to the advertiser-seller.

Bake, *v.* To cook. Roast, barbecue, toast, fry, warm, prepare, broil, simmer, griddle, percolate, braise, stew, grill, char, fire, heat, scald, boil.

Balance 1. *n.* What is left over (the will provided that the balance of the estate would go to the institute). Remainder, surplus, residue, residuum, extra, carry-over, surplusage, excess, remains, remnant, amount owed, outstanding portion, overplus. **2.** *n.* The difference between the debit and credit sides of an account; an equality between the total of the two sides of an account. **3.** *v.* To determine whether a difference exists between the debit and credit sides of an account; to equalize both sides. Calculate, total, equate, figure, contrast, offset, counterbalance, compare, tally, settle, weigh. **4.** *n.* Equilibrium (he was injured when the machine was no longer in balance). Uniformity, equivalence, stability, weight, symmetry, parity, counterpoise, equation, equality, proportion. See also harmony. **5.** *n.* Stability, poise (a person of skill and emotional balance). Sanity, self-confidence, self-restraint, self-control, reason, judgment, confidence, wisdom, dispassion, presence, composure, aplomb, judiciousness, consistency, discretion, prudence, acumen. *Ant.* Deficiency; imbalance; irrationality.

Balanced, *adj.* See fair.

Balance sheet See account (1).

Balcony, *n.* Platform, gallery. Terrace, portico, porch, extension, deck, loggia, veranda.

Bald, *adj.* See bare, plain, naked (1, 2).

Balderdash, *n.* Nonsense. Drivel, "bull," gobbledegook, folly, stuff, humbug, gibberish, bunk, double talk, foolishness, poppycock, asininity, moonshine, junk, trivia, baloney, hot air, claptrap, rubbish, trash. See also refuse, vacuity, prolixity; verbose.

Baleful, *adj.* See harmful, bad (2), malicious, corrupt.

Balk, *v.* See resist, impede, demur (2).

Balkanize *v.* See divide.

Ballad, *n.* See poem, music.

Ballistics, *n.* The study of firearms and other projectiles, e.g., to determine whether a given bullet was fired from a particular gun.

Balloon, *v.* See augment.

Balloon note A promissory note that calls for a substantial payment of principal at the end of the term—often the full balance remaining.

Ballyhoo, *v.* See advertise.

Balm, *n.* See aroma; ointment, medicine.

Baloney, *n.* See balderdash.

Bamboozle, *v.* See inveigle, deceive, betray (1), cheat (1).

Ban 1. *n.* A prohibition (the order imposed a ban on all demonstrations). Disallowance, prevention, interdiction, taboo, proscription, restriction, forbiddance, barring, injunction, embargo, exclusion, banishment, suppression, censorship, constraint. **2.** *v.* To prohibit (dynamiting was banned). Disallow, prevent, interdict, proscribe, restrict, forbid, bar, embargo, exclude, banish, suppress circumscribe, censor, constrain, check, thwart, abrogate, veto, enjoin, stop, estop, repress, stay, outlaw. **3.** *n.* An announcement. Public notice, proclamation, decree, pronouncement. *Ant.* Authorization; allow.

Banal *adj.* See commonplace (2), household, routine.

Banc Bench. En banc is the full bench or the full court as opposed to a smaller number of judges on the bench.

Band, *n., v.* See alliance, cabal (1), company (2), association (1); ally (3), collect (1).

Bandage, *n.* Dressing, band-aid. Gauze, ligature, compress, binding, cover, protection, tourniquet, pad.

Bandit, *n.* A robber or outlaw. See thief, wrongdoer.

Banditry, *n.* Organized robbery. See larceny.

Bandy, *v.* To toss about. Throw, hit back and forth, exchange, swap, shuffle, trade, barter, pass. See also circulate.

Bane, *n.* **1.** Torment (the attacks on her character were the bane of her existence). Curse, nuisance, calamity, disaster, ruin, plague, nightmare, pest, harm, poison, venom, scourge, evil, misery, anguish, death, downfall, pollution. **2.** A malefactor. *Ant.* Blessing; benefactor.

Baneful, *adj.* See harmful, lethal.

Bang, *v.* See collide (1).

Banish, *v.* See expel, bar (4), sequester; banishment.

Banishment, *n.* Punishment by exile (banishment from his native country). Expulsion, deportation, eviction, removal, excommunication, expatriation, discharge, ostracism, segregation, dismissal, abandonment, repudiation. *Ant.* Invitation.

Banister, *n.* Rail. Handrail, balustrade, guardrail, runner, baluster, support, rest.

Bank 1. *n.* A financial institution that receives money on deposit, cashes checks or drafts, makes loans, discounts commercial paper, and performs similar functions. Banking house, commercial bank, savings bank, exchequer. **2.** *n.* A place where money is stored. Depository, treasury, coffers, safe, reserve, storehouse, stockpile, savings, fund, vault, till, bursary, repository. **3.** *v.* To do business with a bank (he banks at Shaumut Bank). Make deposits, save, borrow, accumulate, amass. **4.** *n.* A mound, elevation of earth, slope, etc. (bank of the river). Embankment, pile, grade, mass, ridge, hill, dune, strand, shore.

Bankroll, *n., v.* See fund (2); capitalize (1), back (1), finance (1).

Bankrupt, *adj.* Being unable to pay debts as they are due; a debtor undergoing a federal bankruptcy proceeding (bankrupt estate; bankrupt company). Insolvent, impoverished, destitute, depleted, indigent, wiped out, "busted," penniless, exhausted, ruined, bereft, failed. *Ant.* Sound, solvent.

Bankruptcy, *n.* The inability to pay debts as they are due; the condition of being bankrupt (when the company was unable to meet its payroll, it was on the verge of bankruptcy). Insolvency, financial ruin, impoverishment, indigence, destitution, disaster, penury, failure, liquidation, defaulting. *Ant.* Solvency.

Bankruptcy, act of See act of bankruptcy.

Banner, *n.* See caption; symbol, badge, manifestation.

Banquet, *n.* Feast. Meal, repast, dinner, party, festival, symposium. See also ceremony.

Bantam, *adj.* See short (2).

Banter, *v., n.* See babble; joke; reply, answer.

Baptize, *v.* See initiate, call (4), name (2), induct, launch.

Bar 1. *n.* The court (the case at bar). Tribunal, bench, judiciary, assise, forum, sessions, court of law. **2.** *n.* Members of the legal profession (the bar voted to support the change in the rule). Lawyers, attorneys, counselors, counselors at law, counsel, solicitors, barristers, legal fraternity, advocates, jurists. **3.** *n.* An impediment (the damage issue presented the biggest bar to settlement). Barrier, obstacle, blockage, obstruction, hurdle, constraint, stumbling block, block, snag, restraint, difficulty, limitation, check, hindrance, injunction, ban, deterrent, wall, roadblock, congestion. **4.** *v.* To prohibit (she was barred from practicing dentistry). Ban, prevent, block, exclude, debar, forbid, blacklist, blackball, deny, suspend, ostracize, circumscribe, lock out, banish, disallow, stop, impede, exclude. **5.** *v.* To obstruct (the entrance was barred by the roadblock). Hinder, block, deter, impede, frustrate, barricade, thwart, chock, shut off, enjoin, seal, estop, restrain, fence, inhibit, constrain, oust, evict, eject. *Ant.* Benefit; allow; facilitate.

Barb, *n.* See affront (1).

Barbarian, barbaric, *adj.* See wild (3), gross (1), cruel, inhuman, base (2), violent, bad.

Barbarity, *n.* See cruelty, bestiality (2).

Barbecue, *v.* See bake.

Barber, *n.* Haircutter, hairdresser, coiffeur, beautician. See also merchant.

Bare 1. *adj.* Limited, mere (bare licensee). Plain, unrefined, unaccompanied, simple, straightforward, marginal, meager, bald, mean, austere, bleak, hollow, elementary, unadorned, laconic. See also naked. **2.** *v.* To divulge (in her opening statement, the attorney bared the facts of the conspiracy). Reveal, expose, exhibit, announce, vent, unveil, confess, unfold, declare, uncover, disclose, show, display, represent, air, make known, admit, denude, lay open. *Ant.* Embellished; conceal.

Barefaced, *adj.* See manifest (1), arrogant.

Barely, *adv.* See hardly.

Bar examiners Persons appointed to test individuals and determine their qualifications to practice law.

Bargain 1. *n.* An agreement (the bargain required a 10% increase). Contract, mutual understanding, accord, pact, compact, covenant, settlement, convention, concordat, arrangement, bond, treaty, pledge, stipulation, negotiation, entente, deal, transaction, indenture, accordance. **2.** *v.* To negotiate an agreement (they bargained until midnight). Barter, deal, dicker, arrange, come to terms, agree, contract, settle, haggle, promise. *Ant.* Disagreement; stall.

Bargain and sale A contract or bargain by the owner of property to sell it to another person for a consideration whereupon a use arises in the latter; a contract to convey.

Bargainee, *n.* The grantee of an estate in a deed of a bargain and sale.

Bargaining unit A group of employees who have banded together to improve their working conditions; a labor union authorized to engage in collective bargaining.

Barge, *n.* See vessel (1).

Barometer, *n.* See criterion.

Barracks, *n.* See habitation, home (1).

Barrage, *n.* See assault (2), attack (2), battery (2).

Barrator, *n.* Someone who commits barratry.

Barratry, *n.* **1.** The offense of stirring up quarrels or litigation (the lawyer was censured for barratry). See also champerty. **2.** An act committed by the master or mariners of a vessel for some fraudulent or unlawful purpose contrary to their duty to the owner, resulting in injury to the owner.

Barred, *v.* See bar (4, 5).

Barrel, *n.* See vessel (2).

Barren, *adj.* **1.** Childless (a barren couple). Infertile, sterile, issueless, without issue. **2.** Unproductive, ineffective (a barren argument). Inept, worthless, bare, void, empty, unprofitable, fallow, insufficient, inane, impotent, fruitless, jejune, tedious, vain, abortive, pointless, monotonous, profitless, stillborn, ineffectual, dreary, inadequate, unfruitful, uninteresting, useless, prosaic, dull, vapid, deficient, witless, unsuccessful, moronic, forlorn, unyielding, dry, unrewarding, idle, boring, incompetent, nugatory. *Ant.* Fertile; worthwhile.

Barretor, *n.* See barrator.

Barretry, *n.* See barratry.

Barricade, *n., v.* See blockade, block (1), check (1, 5), clog, hinder, impede, obstruct.

Barrier, *n.* See blockade, wall (1), obstruction; jetty.

Barrister, *n.* An English attorney with special skills and rights as a trial or litigation attorney. See attorney.

Barter

Barter, *v.* To exchange goods or services without the use of money (he bartered a new dictaphone for an old computer). Bargain, trade, market, "swap," traffic, negotiate, dicker, haggle, wrangle. See also deal (2).

Base 1. *adj.* Inferior (base metal). Impure, adulterated, debased, alloyed, poor quality, cheap, worthless, counterfeit, tawdry, spurious, artificial, false. **2.** *adj.* Sordid, corrupt (base motives). Immoral, dishonorable, repugnant, malicious, depraved, contemptuous, vile, iniquitous, mean, despicable, gross, dissolute, contemptible, abject, infamous, unprincipled, sordid, obnoxious, debauched, detestable, degenerate, abhorrent, profligate, invidious, incorrigible, sinister, culpable, cowardly, offensive, vulgar, obscene. **3.** *n.* That on which something rests (the base of the structure collapsed). Floor, support, bottom, foot, underpinning, groundwork, foundation, pedestal, substructure, footing, bed, prop. **4.** *v.* To form a foundation for (he based his theory of recovery on § 126 of the code). Establish, ground, depend, form, found, rest, bottom, predicate, construct, build, hinge, institute, proceed, model, derive. **5.** *n.* See division (2), base (2), military; sailor. *Ant.* Superior; noble; pinnacle.

Baseless, *adj.* Groundless (a baseless allegation). Unwarranted, empty, unsupported, false, untenable, uncorroborated, illogical, unreasonable, unfounded, gratuitous, indefensible, senseless, unjustifiable, idle, unsubstantiated, erroneous. *Ant.* Sound, factual.

Bashful, *adj.* Shy. Timid, withdrawn, reticent, demure, nervous, unassuming, diffident, embarrassed, self-conscious, self-effacing, blushing, retiring, unobtrusive, chary, reserved. *Ant.* Agressive.

Basic, *adj.* See fundamental, essential, organic (1), intrinsic, primary; original; clear, simple.

Basilica, *n.* See church.

Basin, *n.* See lake, sea (1).

Basis, *n.* **1.** The foundation of something (what is the basis of your damage claim). Ground, support, principle, authority, rationale, premise, hypothesis, essence, source, justification, footing, warrant, core, essential, base, root, substance, soul. **2.** The amount assigned to an asset for income tax purposes (capital improvements will increase the basis of your house).

Basket, *n.* See vessel (2).

Bassinet, *n.* See bed (1).

Bastard 1. *n.* A child born before its parents were married or born from those who never married (throughout history, bastards have not had all of the same rights as legitimate children). Illegitimate child, filius nullius, love child, natural child. **2.** *adj.* Inferior (bastard French). Impure, adulterated, false, imperfect, deficient, spurious, irregular, bogus, pretended, counterfeit, sham. *Ant.* Legitimate child; genuine.

Bastardize, *v.* **1.** To give evidence that would tend to establish the illegitimacy of a child (the court refused to accept testimony that would bastardize the infant). **2.** To degrade (you tend to bastardize the procedure when you use it to exert pressure in that way). Demean, prostitute, corrupt, pervert, pollute, cheapen, devalue, vitiate, dishonor, spoil, contaminate, distort, poison. See also debase (1). *Ant.* Enhance.

Bastardy proceeding A court proceeding to determine paternity and to compel support.

Bastion, *n.* Stronghold (bastion of freedom). Fortress, tower, pillar, Gibraltar, rock, citadel, bulwark, fortification, castle, garrison. See also defense (2).

Bat, *v., n.* See batter; bludgeon (1).

Batch, *n.* See collection (2), bulk (1), lot (3).

Bathe, *v.* To wash. Clean, shower, rinse, cleanse, douche, scrub, soak, launder,

84

tub. See also wash (1), water (2), submerge.

Bathetic, *adj.* See sentimental.

Bathroom, *n.* Toilet facility. Latrine, privy, water closet, rest room, "john," men's room, comfort station, washroom, powder room, lavatory, outhouse, commode.

Battalion, *n.* A military unit. See company (2).

Batter, *v.* To strike; to damage (the winds battered the fence). Mistreat, bruise, injure, smash, strike, hit, wallop, lash, box, pound, maul, shatter, pummel, fragment, smite, ruin, demolish, lacerate, disfigure, mutilate, deface. See also shoot, kill, attack, assault, beat, abuse, maim. *Ant.* Aid.

Battery, *n.* **1.** A tort with the following elements: (a) an act, (b) the intent to cause a harmful or offensive contract, (c) a harmful or offensive contact with the plaintiff's person, and (d) causation of the harmful or offensive contact. Battery can also be a crime. **2.** Unlawful touching; an attack. Striking, storming, aggression, assault, pounding, raid, foray, pummeling, beating, bombardment, siege, barrage, whipping, flogging, thrashing, hitting.

Battle, *n., v.* See war, combat, argument (2); compete.

Battleship, *n.* See vessel (1).

Bawd, *n.* See prostitute (1).

Bawdy, *adj.* See obscene, vulgar, common (3).

Bawdyhouse, *n.* A house of prostitution. Bordello, house of ill-repute, house of ill-fame, whorehouse. See also brothel.

Bay, *n.* See sea (1).

Bayonet, *n.* See weapon.

Bayou, *n.* See lake, sea (1).

Bazaar, *n.* See market (1).

Bazooka, *n.* See weapon.

BB gun, *n.* See weapon.

Beach, *n.* See shore.

Beacon, *n.* A signal or light. Landmark, beam, warning, guiding signal, guide, alarm, fire, smoke signal, mark, indicator, indicant, alert, flare; lantern, lighthouse, buoy, pharos, siren, radar, transmitter.

Beam 1. *n.* Board (support beams). Pole, plank, timber, stud, strip, rod, joist, girder, two-by-four, brace, wood, frame, support. **2.** *n.* Ray (beam of light). Streak, glare, flash, glow, stream, radiation, flare, shaft. **3.** *v.* To shine (the light beamed). Glow, emit, radiate, sparkle, incandesce, streak, glare, broadcast, transmit.

Bear, *v.* **1.** To produce (the account bears interest at 9%). Yield, generate, germinate, accrue, return, breed, create, supply, earn, fund, provide, furnish, offer, give, multiply, engender, propagate, reproduce, invent, bring forth, augment, surrender, bestow, contribute, cause, confer, gestate, develop, render. **2.** To support (the litigation division bore the brunt of the new cases). Sustain, shoulder, uphold, carry, champion, supply, maintain, tolerate, accept, weather, brave, undergo, experience, encounter, submit to, abide, suffer, persevere, brook, "stomach," carry, transport, digest, swallow, fare, fortify, cushion, nourish, acquiesce, countenance, go through, stand, aid, assist, succor, bolster. **3.** To acknowledge; to defray (to bear the expense). Admit, assume, vouch for, affirm, substantiate, authenticate, ratify, certify, prove, corroborate, endorse, pledge, indemnify, remit, incur, refund, guarantee, be answerable for, be responsible for, accept. *Ant.* Destroy; hinder; reject.

Bearable, *adj.* Tolerable. Manageable, endurable, livable, sufferable, admissible, supportable, passable, maintainable.

Bearer, *n.* Someone in possession of a document (the check was payable to bearer). Carrier, possessor, holder, courier, recipient, taker.

Bearer bond A bond payable to whoever has possession of the bond. Endorsement is not necessary to transfer ownership.

Bearing, *n.* See manner, demeanor, carriage (3), appearance (3); connection (2), association (2), relevant.

Beast, *n.* See animal; demon, tyrant, aberration, wrongdoer.

Beastly, *adj.* See base (2), wild (3), cruel, gross (1).

Beat, *v.* **1.** To inflict any unlawful physical violence (he beat his wife). Batter, hit, strike, whip, punch, flagellate, attack, trounce, abuse, bruise, afflict, maul, slap, flog, wallop, knock, hammer, lambaste, cudgel, thrash, pummel, belabor. **2.** To defeat (she beat her opponent at his own game). Conquer, subdue, vanquish, triumph over, overcome, crush, master, destroy, upset, checkmate, excel, undo, outclass, outflank, outmaneuver, surpass, suppress, overpower, subjugate, overwhelm, quell, outdo, rout, stop, eclipse, predominate, outrange. **3.** To pulsate (his heart beat at an irregular rate). Throb, pulse, palpitate, tremble, rock, twitch, shimmy, jerk, shudder, shake, vibrate, quake, quiver, fluctuate, undulate, waver. *Ant.* Console; lose.

Beating, *n.* See battery, attack.

Beau, *n.* Lover. Boyfriend, follower, Romeo, intimate, sweetheart, suitor, beloved, playboy, flame, swain. See also paramour, adherent.

Beautician, *n.* See barber.

Beautiful, *adj.* Good-looking. Shapely, exquisite, fair, comely, glamorous, engaging, becoming, sexy, pleasant, pretty, resplendent, handsome, gorgeous, enchanting, lovely, sightly, captivating, brilliant, slender, fine. See also attractive. *Ant.* Grotesque.

Beautify, *v.* To adorn. Embellish, grace, brighten, array, paint, polish, ornament, improve, enhance, dress up, furbish. *Ant.* Disfigure.

Beauty, *n.* Attraction. Grace, radiance, splendor, excellence, loveliness, glamour, artistry, proportion, charm, symmetry, comeliness, bloom, delicacy. See also appeal (3); benefit (1), aid (2).

Because, *conj., adv.* In view of the fact that. As a consequence of, consequently, by virtue of, inasmuch as, therefore. See also whereas.

Beckon, *v.* See summon (1), entice, entrap.

Becloud, *v.* See obscure (3), cloak.

Becoming, *adj.* See beautiful, attractive, appropriate (3).

Bed, *n.* **1.** Furniture for sleeping. Bunk, lounge, crib, berth, cot, hammock, couch, mattress, cradle, bassinet, sleeping bag, recliner. See also chamber (1). **2.** See base (3), floor (4).

Bedazzle, *v.* See amaze, obscure (3).

Bedevil, *v.* See harass.

Bedfellow, *n.* See ally (2), associate (2).

Bedlam, *n.* See confusion, anarchy, violence, riot, commotion.

Beef, *n.* See grievance, complaint.

Beer, *n.* See liquor.

Befitting, *adj.* See appropriate (3).

Befog, *v.* See obscure (3), cloak.

Befriend, *v.* To make friends with. Consort with, get acquainted with, embrace, welcome, stand by, fraternize with, assort, familiarize. See also help (2), benefit (2), favor (3), foster.

Befuddle, *v.* See obscure (3), confuse, amaze, distract (2); intoxicated.

Beg, *v.* See apply (1), petition (2), beseech, appeal (4).

Beget, *v.* To father. Sire, procreate, breed, reproduce, propagate, multiply, spawn, generate, conceive, impregnate. See also produce (2), engender.

Beggar, *n.* See pauper, tramp (1).

Begin, *v.* To initiate. Commence, originate, start, institute, embark, instigate, launch, beget, pioneer, spawn, establish, inaugurate, introduce, found, create, emerge, appear, open, arise, enter upon, broach, conceive, set in motion. *Ant.* Terminate.

Begin again, *v.* See continue (4).

Beginner, *n.* **1.** Novice. Apprentice, rookie, freshman, greenhorn, pupil, initiate, fledgling, recruit, trainee, student. See also amateur. **2.** See author (2).

Beginning, *n.* See commencement; commence, begin.

Beguile, *v.* See deceive, betray (1), cheat (1); divert, cloak, entertain, flirt.

Behalf, *n.* In the interest of (the attorney spoke in my behalf). Defense, benefit, support, advantage, account, protection, welfare, sponsorship, auspices, advocacy, assistance.

Behave, *v.* See act (5), perform.

Behavior, *n.* Conduct; the manner in which a person reacts (reprehensible behavior leading to punitive damages). Way of life, actions, course of conduct, manner of life, response, reaction, demeanor, beliefs, habits, decorum, attitude, comportment, deportment, pattern of life, bearing, style, mien, air, manners. See also carriage (3).

Behold, *v.* See witness (2).

Behoof, *n.* Advantage, benefit (to his use and behoof). Use, profit, service, good, advancement, well-being, avail, account.

Being, *n.* See person, character (4), object (3), entity, essence.

Belabor, *v.* See repeat, harass.

Belated, *adj.* See late (3).

Beleaguer, *v.* See harass, surround.

Belief, *n.* **1.** A persuasion of the truth or an assent of the mind to the truth of a declaration, proposition, or alleged fact (belief in the defendant's guilt). Conclusion, conviction, judgment, impression, deduction, presumption, supposition, hypothesis, assumption, position, thesis, inference, opinion, assurance, trust, confidence, reliance, theory, notion, view, guess, intuition, credence, understanding. **2.** Accepted principle (political beliefs). Credo, dogma, tenet, rule, philosophy, doctrine, maxim, precept, persuasion, faith, creed, religion, ethics, morality, canon, axiom, gospel, conviction, platform, teaching, way of thinking, manifesto, ideology, orthodoxy. *Ant.* Skepticism.

Believable, *adj.* Trustworthy (a believable witness). Colorable, plausible, well-founded, conceivable, credible, creditable, persuasive, unquestionable, rational, acceptable, imaginable, likely, tenable, substantial, impressive, solid, dependable, irrefutable, indisputable, reliable, sure, unimpeachable. *Ant.* See also convincing. Implausible, impeachable.

Believe, *v.* See accept (2), maintain (3), assert, trust (6).

Belittle, *v.* See disparage, harass, slander (2), condemn (3).

Bellboy, *n.* See servant (2).

Bellicose, *adj.* See hostile, belligerent, litigious, contentious.

Belligerency, *n.* **1.** The status of de facto statehood attributed to a body of insurgents by which their hostilities are legalized. **2.** Warfare. Aggression, combat, violence, bellicosity, militancy, tumult, enmity, siege, animosity, discord, riot, assault, melee, combativeness, pugnacity. *Ant.* Peacefulness.

Belligerent, *adj.* Militant (a belligerent attitude). Antagonistic, bellicose, unfriendly, inimical, cantankerous, pugnacious, argumentative, defiant, polemical, warring, quarrelsome, hot-tempered, truculent, threatening. See also hostile, litigious, contentious. *Ant.* Amicable.

Bellow, *v.* See proclaim, communicate; yell.

Belong, *v.* See own, possess; attached; inherent.

Belongings, *n.* See effects, possession (2).

Below, *adj., adv.* At a lower rank; a lower court. See under, infra.

Belt 1. *n.* A band worn or placed around something. Cord, strap, sash, ribbon, girdle, cincture, waistband, collar. **2.** *v.* See beat (1).

Bemoan, *v.* To lament. Grieve, mourn, cry, moan, bewail, weep over, regret, sigh, rue, groan. See also complain (2).

Bemuse, *v.* See obscure (3), absorb (2).

Bench, *n.* The seat where the judges sit; the court. Tribunal, bar, judiciary, judge, panel of judges, forum.

Bench conference A meeting at the judge's bench between the judge and the attorneys out of the hearing of the jury.

Bench mark, *n.,* **benchmark,** See measure (1); landmark (2); historic.

Bench warrant A process issued by the court for the attachment or arrest of a person to compel his or her attendance before the court.

Bend, *v.* See comply, grovel, cringe.

Bender, *n.* See spree; intoxicated.

Bene, Well; in proper form; legally; sufficiently.

Beneath, *adv., prep.* See under.

Benediction, *n.* See prayer (2).

Benefaction, *n.* See benevolence, gift (1), bounty (1), charity.

Benefactor, *n.* See patron (2), champion (1), advocate (1).

Beneficence, *n.* See benevolence, gift (1).

Beneficial, *adj.* Tending to the benefit of a person (beneficial purpose). Valuable, advantageous, aiding, worthwhile, favorable, productive, helpful, obliging, lucrative, propitious, rewarding, salutary, useful, serviceable, wholesome, for one's good, contributory, utilitarian, benign, usable, conducive, remunerative, serendipitous, prosperous, accommodating, promising, restorative, edifying, efficacious, functional, healing, practicable, cooperative, healthful, paying, fertile. *Ant.* Detrimental.

Beneficial enjoyment The enjoyment that a person has in an estate in his or her own right and not as a trustee for another.

Beneficial estate The person takes the estate solely for his or her own use and benefit and not as the mere holder of the title for the use of another.

Beneficial interest 1. Profit, benefit, or advantage resulting from a contract, or the ownership of an estate as distinct from the legal ownership or control of the estate. **2.** The interest of a devisee, legatee, or donee that is taken for his or her own use or benefit.

Beneficial owner 1. One who does not have title to property but has those rights in the property that are the normal incidents of owning the property. **2.** The cestui que trust who enjoys ownership of the trust but not legal title.

Beneficial use 1. The right to use and enjoy property to one's liking as distinguished from a mere right of occupancy. **2.** Such right to the enjoyment of property where the legal title to the property is in one person while the right to its enjoyment is in another.

Beneficiary, *n.* One who benefits from the act of another (beneficiary under a will; income beneficiary). One who receives an advantage, recipient, donee, inheritor, legatee, receiver, cestui que trust, heir, grantee, winner, pensioner.

Beneficiary heir One who has accepted the succession under the benefit of an inventory regularly made (Louisiana).

Benefit 1. *n.* An advantage (she had the benefit of knowing what the witness would say). Profit, fruit, privilege, gain, interest, help, avail, betterment, worth, blessing, advancement, usefulness, welfare, accommodation, utility, assistance, boon, reward, satisfaction, convenience, promotion, succor, account, service, favor, courtesy, good turn, utilization, satisfaction, aid, bonus, gratuity, offering, value, plus. **2.** *v.* To assist (everyone benefited from the experience). Help, profit, aid, serve, gain, avail, better, promote, subsidize, improve, succor, enhance, ameliorate, befriend, forward. *Ant.* Impairment; harm.

Benefit of clergy 1. An exemption for members of the clergy that allowed them to avoid being subject to the jurisdiction of certain secular courts. **2.** An exemption from capital punishment. **3.** Married, not merely living together.

Benefit society A corporation that exists to receive periodic payments from members and to hold the payments as a fund to be loaned or given to members needing financial help.

Benevolence, *n.* Doing helpful things for others that one is not under an obligation to do (everyone appreciated her benevolence). Desire to promote happiness, promotion of general happiness, charity, kindness, philanthropy, support, assistance, service, humanitarianism, charitableness, compassion, good will, beneficence, doing well, humanity, unselfishness, altruism, generosity, amiability, goodness, succor, agreeableness, tolerance, clemency, graciousness, self-sacrifice, liberality, indulgence. *Ant.* Unkindness, selfishness.

Benevolent, *adj.* Loving others and being actively desirous of their well-being (the trust had a benevolent purpose). Philanthropic, humane, humanitarian, charitable, altruistic, unselfish, generous, benignant, liberal, helpful, neighborly, amicable, paternal, maternal, eleemosynary, accommodating, well-meaning, hospitable, agreeable, amiable, empathetic, magnanimous, warmhearted, kind, open-hearted, obliging, considerate, supportive, understanding, thoughtful, compassionate, temperate, indulgent, sympathetic, affable, benign, sensitive, tenderhearted, comforting, kindly, feeling, gentle, solicitous, commiserative, tolerant, unstinting, gracious, decent. *Ant.* Malicious.

Benevolent association or corporation An organization having a charitable, philanthropic, nonprofit purpose, e.g., to promote the mental, physical, or spiritual welfare of people.

Benign, *adj.* See benevolent, charitable (1), amicable, harmless, good.

Benny, *n.* Amphetamine tablet used as a stimulant. See drug (2).

Bent, *n.* See disposition (4), style (3), direction (3), mode, bias.

Bequeath, *v.* **1.** To give personal property to another through a will (I bequeath to my sister all that I own). Will. **2.** To hand down; to endow (he bequeathed a tradition of integrity). Transfer, donate, leave, entrust, allot, distribute, confer upon, bestow, present, contribute, impart, consign, render, cede, leave to, dower, vest, remit, furnish, provide, invest, transmit, demise. *Ant.* Disinherit.

Bequest, *n.* A gift of personal property by will (he received a bequest of $20,000). Testamentary gift, endowment, grant, legacy, birthright, disposition, bestowal, allotment, heritage, bequeathal, devise, inheritance.

Berate, *v.* See blame (3), complain (2), reprimand, castigate, condemn (3).

Bereavement, *n.* See loss; anguish, anxiety, pain, affliction.

Bereft, *adj.* See destitute.

Berserk, *adj.* See deranged, insane, violent, hysterical.

Berth, *n.* See bed (1); dock (2), harbor (2, 3); lodge (2).

Beseech, *v.* To plead with (I beseech you to consider the consequences). Entreat, implore, supplicate, appeal to, importune, petition, urge, adjure, pray, beg, press, conjure, ask, solicit, invoke, insist, clamor.

Beset, *v.* See attack (1), harass.

Besides, *adv.* See moreover.

Besiege, *v.* See attack (1), charge (6), harass, surround.

Besmirch, *v.* See pollute, corrupt.

Best 1. *adj.* Of the highest quality (the best available evidence). Most suitable, most desirable, foremost, unrivaled, chief, distinguished, supreme, superior, exceptional, preeminent, exemplary, finest, unsurpassed, choice, extraordinary, paramount, incomparable, unparalleled, perfect, impeccable, peerless, transcendent, first-class, first-rate, fine, sterling, auspicious, strongest, most powerful, crowning, inimitable, select, superlative, outstanding, beyond compare, second to none, quintessential, consummate. **2.** *v.* To defeat (best her opponents). Conquer, triumph over, outdo, subdue, outclass, surpass, trounce, humble. *Ant.* Worst; succumb.

Best evidence rule A rule of evidence requiring that a party produce the most reliable proof of a fact that is available. For example, if a painting is available as evidence, a photograph of the painting will not do.

Bestial, *adj.* See wild (3), cruel, gross (1), obscene, base (2), carnal.

Bestiality, *n.* **1.** Sexual relations between a human and an animal. **2.** Savage or bestial behavior. Cruelty, inhumanity, brutality, barbarity, savagery, viciousness, ruthlessness, cannibalism. *Ant.* Compassion.

Bestow, *v.* To give or confer (the survivor has the power to bestow the remainder of the property). Grant, impart, donate, apportion, present, distribute, bequeath, assign, consign, allot, vest, award, spend, cede, invest, convey, furnish, endow, fund, accord, dispense, render, mete, settle upon, commit, administer, commission, authorize, empower, consent, license, indulge, proffer, release, supply. *Ant.* Acquire.

Bestowal, *n.* See endowment, bestow.

Bet 1. *n.* A contract by which two or more parties agree that a sum of money or other thing shall be paid or delivered to one of them on the happening or not happening of an uncertain event (a $2 bet). Wager, chance, gamble, raffle, lottery, risk, speculation, plunge. **2.** *v.* To wager or risk something (the boxer illegally bet against himself). Gamble, hazard, stake, speculate, chance, venture, parlay, pledge, lay, game, play.

Betray, *v.* **1.** To be a traitor to (she betrayed her country). Be disloyal, be unfaithful, be treacherous, dupe, deceive, play false with, trap, mislead, ensnare, beguile, abandon, "double-cross," deliver up, violate, entrap, inveigle, be disloyal, "sell out," trick, lead astray, debauch, decoy, swindle, victimize, defraud, desecrate, corrupt, defile, bamboozle, cozen, overreach, circumvent. **2.** To divulge (your action betrayed a confidence). Reveal, expose, unmask, exhibit, manifest, evince, uncover, bring to light, report, confess, inform, make known, show, indicate, betoken, air, impart. *Ant.* Be faithful; conceal.

Betrayal, *n.* **1.** Disloyalty (betrayal of the mission). Treachery, treason, perfidy, unfaithfulness, duplicity, deception, abandonment, corruption, undermining, double-dealing, rebellion, breach of faith, revolt, bad faith, chicanery. **2.** The act of disclosure (betrayal of a confidence). Exhibition, uncovering, unmasking, revelation, exposition, telling, violation. *Ant.* Loyalty; preserving.

Betroth, *v.* See engage (4).

Betrothal, betrothment, *n.* A mutual promise of marriage. Engagement, troth, betrothing, espousal, vow.

Better 1. *adj.* See superior (2). **2.** *v.* See improve, repair (1), correct (2). **3.** *n.* See beat (2), best (2).

Better, bettor, *n.* See gambler.

Betterment, *n.* **1.** An improvement on property that increases its value more than mere repairs, maintenance, or replacements (an appropriation was made for betterments). **2.** Making something better (betterment of society). Improvement, correction, amelioration, reformation, cultivation, enhancement, refinement, promotion, furtherance, advancement, rehabilitation. *Ant.* Deterioration.

Betting, *n.* The act of placing a bet or wager. See bet (1).

Bettor, *n.* See gambler.

Between, *prep.* See among; intervening.

Beverage, *n.* Drink. Liquid, soda, water, refreshment, libation, potion, dram, draft, cocktail, soft drink, soup, quencher. See also liquor, potable.

Bewail, *v.* See bemoan, suffer, cry (1).

Beware, *v.* To be careful. Watch, look out for, be wary, take precautions, be on the alert, mind, think twice, guard against, take heed, look first. See also warning, danger.

Bewilder, *v.* See obscure (3), confuse, surprise (1), amaze (1).

Bewildering, *adj.* See obscure (1), complex (1), extraordinary, appalling, serious (2), acute.

Bewilderment, *n.* See confusion, consternation.

Bewitch, *v.* See entice, entrap; conjure.

Beyond, *prep., adv.* See excess; extra, further (1).

Beyond a reasonable doubt The measure of proof needed for conviction in a criminal case: The factfinder must be convinced or satisfied to a moral certainty. Absolute certainty is not required. On the other hand, reasonable doubt means more than a vague suspicion.

B.F. Bonum factum; a good or proper act, deed, or decree; approved.

BFP See bona fide purchaser.

BIA Bureau of Indian Affairs.

Biannually, *adv.* Twice a year (the report must be filed biannually). Semiannually.

Bias 1. *n.* A predisposition to decide a question in a certain way (Smith has a bias because he is related to the defendant). Inclination, bent, prepossession, preconceived opinion, proclivity, partiality, close-mindedness, prejudice, narrow-mindedness, leaning, slant, preference, favoritism, proneness, tendency, penchant, partisanship, susceptibility, bigotry, intolerance, prejudgment, unfairness, dogmatism, distortion. **2.** *v.* To be swayed or influenced (the witness was biased, since she was employed by the plaintiff). Distort, bend, warp, incline, slant, indoctrinate, dispose, predispose. *Ant.* Impartiality.

Bible, *n.* Scriptures. Holy Writ, Good Book, the Word, New Testament, Old Testament. See also manual (2), authority (4, 5).

Bibulous, *adj.* See intoxicated.

Bicameral, *adj.* Having two chambers or houses in the legislature. *Ant.* Unicameral.

Bicker, *v.* See argue.

Bickering, *adj.* See contentious (1).

Bicycle, *n.* See vehicle (1).

Bid 1. *n.* An offer by a prospective purchaser to pay a designated price for property that is about to be sold at auction. An offer to perform a contract for a designated price. (He submitted the lowest bid.) Proposal, offer, tender, proffer, proposition, submission, price, quoted price. **2.** *v.* To make an offer (she bid $25). Offer, tender, advance, propose, suggest, quote. **3.** *v.* To command (the judge bids you to stand). Direct, order, dictate, demand, adjure, enjoin, require, summon, charge, insist. See also command (3).

Bidding, *n.* See command (1), summons, citation (1).

Biennial, *adj.* Occurring every 2 years; lasting 2 years (a biennial election).

Biennium, *n.* A 2-year period.

Bifurcate, *v.* To divide into two parts (bifurcate the trial into the liability and the damage issues). Separate, branch, partition, split, bisect, diverge, part, cleave. *Ant.* Unify.

Bifurcated trial A case in which certain issues are tried separately (e.g., guilt and punishment; liability and damages).

Bifurcation

Bifurcation, *n.* See separation.

Big, *adj.* Large. Considerable, sizable, substantial, extensive, abundant, appreciable, astronomical, huge, immense, grand, towering, majestic, enormous, massive, ample, mammoth, colossal, grandiose, vast, prodigious, heavy, obese, spacious, titanic, tremendous, wide. See also great (1), outstanding (2).

Bigamous, *adj.* Involving bigamy (bigamous marriage).

Bigamy, *n.* Knowingly entering a second marriage when the first marriage still exists. Bigamy is a crime and a ground for an annulment.

Big brother, *n.* See backer, champion, patron, advocate; tyrant; manager; government.

Big-hearted, *adj.* See benevolent, charitable (1), kind.

Bigot, *n.* A prejudiced person (from her opinions, she was clearly a bigot). Racist, sexist, chauvinist, dogmatist, zealot, fanatic, extremist, monomaniac, Archie Bunker. *Ant.* Tolerant person.

Bigoted, *adj.* See narrow (2); bigot.

Bigotry, *n.* See bias (1), prejudice (1), discrimination.

Bike, *n.* See vehicle (1).

Bilateral, *adj.* Having or involving two sides (bilateral divorce). Reciprocal, two-sided, mutual. *Ant.* Unilateral.

Bilateral contract A contract in which both contracting parties are bound to fulfill obligations reciprocally toward each other; a contract with rights and duties on both sides; a contract with mutual promises between the parties.

Bilingual, *adj.* Pertaining to expression in two languages.

Bill, *n.* **1.** A proposed law (the legislator introduced the tax bill in the Senate). Proposed statute, proposed legislation, draft, measure. **2.** Invoice (the bill will be sent along with the goods you purchased). Account, account payable, record, statement, charges, tally, reckoning, fee, debt, debit, score, balance due, cost, tab, tabulation.

Billboard, *n.* See placard.

Billet, *n.* **1.** The soldier's quarters in a civilian's house. Lodging accommodations, housing, shelter, berth, installation. **2.** A ticket that authorizes the soldier to occupy a civilian's house.

Billing, *n.* See notice (1), bulletin, account (1).

Billingsgate, *n.* See profanity, slander (1).

Bill of attainder A legislative act that applies either to named individuals or to easily identifiable members of a group in such a way as to inflict punishment on them without a judicial trial. If the punishment is death, the act is a bill of attainder. If the punishment is less than death, the act is a bill of pains and penalties.

Bill of exceptions A formal statement in writing of the objections or exceptions to a judge's rulings taken by a party during a trial.

Bill of exchange A three-party document in which the first party draws an order for the payment of a sum certain on a second party for payment to a third party at a definite future time. A draft.

Bill of lading A document evidencing receipt of goods for shipment issued by a person engaged in the business of transporting and forwarding goods (including airbills).

Bill of pains and penalties See bill of attainder.

Bill of particulars A more detailed or specific statement of the claims brought by one party against another (civil case), or of the charges brought by the prosecutor against the defendant (criminal case).

Bill of rights The first ten amendments to the U.S. Constitution.

Billy, *v.* See bludgeon (1).

Bimonthly, *adj.* Happening every two months. Semimonthly, fortnightly.

Bin, *n.* See vessel (2).

Binary, *adj.* Twofold. See two, dual, double.

Bind, *v.* **1.** To obligate (the agreement binds you and your spouse). Oblige, burden, impose, force, engage, constrict, encumber, charge, pledge, warrant. See also commit (3). **2.** To fasten or secure (bind the extension to the wall). Hook, attach, bundle, unite, connect, weave, enchain, join, rope, bond, gird, tie, pinion, cement, paste, glue. **3.** To confine (bound by tradition). Restrain, restrict, strap, fetter, handcuff, immobilize, limit, choke, chain, impede, impress. **4.** To bandage (bind the wound). Encircle, wrap, dress, tie up. *Ant.* Release; loosen; liberate; unwrap.

Binder, *n.* **1.** A statement of the major terms of an insurance contract which gives temporary protection to the insured until a formal policy is issued. **2.** A deposit to secure the right to purchase property. Pledge, stake, installment, assurance, security, collateral, guaranty, token.

Binding, *adj.* Enforceable (a binding agreement). Obligatory, mandatory, valid, compelling, coercive, incumbent, final, unconditional, indissoluble. See also compulsory. *Ant.* Unenforceable.

Binding over See bound over.

Bind out, *v.* To place one under a legal obligation to serve another (to bind out an apprentice).

Binge, *n.* Orgy. Bacchanalia, fling, revelry, party, spree, feast, carnival. See also debauchery.

Bingo, *n.* See gambling, bet (1).

Biodegradable, *adj.* See perishable.

Bioethics *n.* The study of the ethical implications of medical and biological developments.

Biography, *n.* Memoirs. History, autobiography, account, story, life story. See also confession, record.

Biology, *n.* The study of living organisms. See science.

Biopsy, *n.* The study of tissue from a living organism. See inquiry (1), examination.

Bipartisan, *adj.* Supported by both parties. See conciliatory.

Bipartite, *adj.* Consisting of or divisible into two parts (a bipartite agreement). Bifurcated, separate, bisected, disjoined, disconnected, disunited, divided, subdivided, severed. *Ant.* Unified.

Birth, *n.* **1.** The act of being born (birth of a child). Childbirth, nativity, arrival, parturition, confinement, bearing, birthing. **2.** The beginning of something (birth of a nation). Commencement, origin, creation, inception, start, genesis, source, fountainhead, debut, emergence, embryo, opening, onset, rise, inauguration, introduction, origination, nascency. **3.** Lineage (of noble birth). Descent, pedigree, extraction, ancestry, blood, stock, breed, heritage, race, family, line, parentage, bloodline, succession, heredity, background, house, stirps, forebears. *Ant.* Death; conclusion.

Birth control See Contraceptive.

Bisect, *v.* To cut in two. See cut (1), divide; contact (4), connect.

Bisexual, *adj.* Attracted sexually to both sexes. AC/DC; androgynous; hermaphrodite.

Bishop, *n.* See Clergy.

Bit, *n.* See iota, part (1).

Bitch, *v., n.* See complaint (2); prostitute (1); grouch.

Bite, *v.* See cut (1).

Biting, *adj.* Penetrating. Piercing, acid, scathing, sarcastic, trenchant, cutting, sharp-tongued, smarting, withering, sharp, acrimonious. See also caustic.

Bitter, *adj.* See caustic, hostile, angry, mortal (2), malicious, disaffected.

Bitterness, *n.* See hostility, wrath, annoyance.

Bizarre, *adj.* See odd (1), anomalous.

Blab, *v.* See babble; disclose.

Blabber, *v.* See babble.

Black acre A fictitious name that teachers and writers use to indicate a parcel of land. Also: white acre.

Blackball, *n.* See exclusion, ban (1), expulsion, removal (2), boycott, segregation, censorship.

Black code Laws of southern states regulating slavery.

Black letter law The basic principles of law; the fundamentals in any area of law.

Blacklist, *n.* See bar (4), boycott; censorship.

Black lung, *n.* Pneumoconiosis due to coal dust.

Blackmail, *n.* An unlawful demand of money or property under a threat to do bodily harm, to damage property, to accuse of a crime, or to expose someone. Extortion, ransom, protection, "shakedown," coercion, bribe, bribery, "hush money," payoff, tribute, exaction.

Black market Illegal buying and selling; a business operating independent of government regulation.

Blackout, *n.* See restraint (1), censorship.

Black sheep, *n.* See offender, wrongdoer.

Blacktop, *v.* See pave.

Blade, *n.* See weapon.

Blame 1. *n.* Responsibility for a fault or wrong (she accepted the blame). Onus, accountability, liability, imputation, charge, burden, ascription, assignment, assignation. **2.** *n.* Condemnation (the jury placed the blame on the defendant). Censure, rebuke, renunciation, castigation, criticism, reproof, accusation, reprobation, damnation, reproach, disapproval, obloquy, incrimination, disparagement, fault, admonition, sin, shortcoming, misdeed, guilt, stricture, remonstrance, recrimination, complaint, disapprobation, animadversion, disapproval, wrong, defect. **3.** *v.* To find fault with, to accuse (the judge blamed defense counsel for the delay). Hold responsible, censure, castigate, rebuke, renounce, denounce, criticize, damn, incriminate, admonish, upbraid, arraign, reprove, berate, reprobate, scold, indict, impugn, reprimand, chastise, reproach, chide, disapprove, impeach, fault, deprecate, ascribe, disparage. *Ant.* Vindication; praise; exonerate.

Blameless, *adj.* Innocent (a blameless victim). Guiltless, unblemished, faultless, unsullied, irreproachable, unimpeachable, unspotted, stainless, sinless, ethical, pure, virginal, immaculate, above suspicion, sincere, inviolate, true, chaste, undefiled, inviolable, honorable, creditable, spotless, clear, not guilty, untainted, uncorrupted, unoffending, impeccable, virtuous, sterling, above reproach, without fault, beyond criticism, unobjectionable, innocuous, vindicated, moral. See also innocent. *Ant.* Implicated, guilty.

Blameworthy, *adj.* Deserving blame (blameworthy conduct). At fault, culpable, wrongful, censurable, guilty, reprehensible, delinquent, iniquitous, ignoble, immoral, reproachable, nefarious, discreditable, condemnable, contemptible, contemptuous, venal, corrupt, unworthy, depraved, criminal, negligent, indefensible, erring, devious, impeachable, tainted, sinister, odious, contumelious, questionable, accusable. *Ant.* Innocent, spotless.

Bland, *adj.* See amicable, commonplace (2), moderate (1).

Blank, *adj.* See bare (1), void (3), vacant.

Blank check, *n.* See carte blanche (2).

Blanket, *adj.* See comprehensive; blind (3), cloak; wrapper, vessel (2), package.

Blaring, *adj.* See blatant (2).

Blasé, *adj.* See casual (3), indifferent, apathetic, remote (1).

Blaspheme, *v.* See desecrate, attack (1).

Blasphemous, *adj.* See profane, irreverent; blasphemy.

Blasphemy, *n.* Contempt or reproach in written or oral form directed against God or sacred matters. Sacrilege, desecration, cursing, irreverence, apostasy, profaneness, iconoclasm, heresy, execration, swearing, mockery, defilement, profanation, outrage, violation, iniquity, irreligion, wickedness, degradation, imprecation, impiety. See also profanity; irreverent. *Ant.* Reverence.

Blast, *n., v.* See noise, attack (1), eruption.

Blatant, *adj.* **1.** Conspicuous (a blatant violation of the rules; a blatant defect). Obvious, clear, overt, unmistakable, plain, manifest, glaring, naked, bald, patent, public, exposed, prominent, noticeable, discernible, well-known, outstanding, sheer, outright. **2.** Offensive (once he became blatant, everyone moved away). Obtrusive, vulgar, boisterous, noisy, loud, crude, piercing, ill-mannered, cheap, harsh, crass, clamorous, obstreperous, rowdy, scurrilous, uncouth, brazen, assertive, rough, rude, gaudy, common, bellowing, vociferous, screaming, piercing, coarse, demeaning, blaring, indelicate, ribald, ill-bred, unseemly. *Ant.* Latent, subtle, tasteful.

Blather, *v.* See babble.

Blaze, *n.* See fire (1), conflagration, light, storm, eruption; burn, engrave.

Blazing, *adj.* See blatant.

Bleak, *adj.* See bare (1), barren (2), dismal.

Bleep, *n.* See noise.

Blemish, *v., n.* See impair, pollute; cloud (1).

Blend, *v., n.* See commingle, combine, coalesce, cohere (1), amalgamate; compound (3), mixture.

Bless, *v.* See honor (2), anoint, dedicate; recommend, back (1).

Blessed, *adj.* See happy, fortunate.

Blessing, *n.* See approval, gift, windfall.

Blight, *n.* See affliction, corruption, disease, calamity.

Blimp, *n.* See aircraft.

Blind 1. *adj.* Careless (blind faith). Obtuse, imperceptive, stupid, shortsighted, unreflecting, heedless, indiscriminate, myopic, dense, ignorant, neglectful, unconscious, insensitive, thoughtless, mindless, unenlightened, benighted, purblind, injudicious, insane, senseless, unaware, unversed, uncritical, unreasonable, irrational, naive, impetuous, bovine, incognizant, insouciant, unobservant, sightless, visionless, dim, rash, dull, nescient. **2.** *adj.* Hidden (a blind cover). Concealed, covered, unrevealed, undisclosed, unknown, anonymous, obstructed, blocked, remote, private, dim, dark, obscure, camouflaged, unsuspected, covert, screened, latent, undetected, masked, shrouded. **3.** *v.* To render invisible or unclear (blinded by the snow). Blur, veil, cloud, blanket, shroud, conceal, seclude, screen, dim, muddle, eclipse, cloak, camouflage, befog. *Ant.* Rational; overt; clarify.

Blink, *v.* See ignore, connive.

Blip, *v.* See censor (3).

Bliss, *n.* See happiness, emotion, passion.

Blister, *v.* See burn.

Blistering, *adj.* See hot (2).

Blithe, *adj.* See casual (3), happy.

Blither, *v.* See babble.

Blitz, *n.* See campaign, attack.

Blizzard, *n.* See storm.

Bloat, *v.* See augment.

Bloc, *n.* See alliance (2), cartel (1), gang.

Block 1. *n.* An obstacle (a block in the road ahead). Obstruction, bar, impediment, hindrance, restraint, impasse, snag, interference, barrier, jam, blockage, pack, hurdle, constraint, hitch, deterrent, cul-de-sac, congestion, stoppage. **2.** *v.* To obstruct (she tried to block passage of the bill). Retard, impede, hinder, jam, prevent, thwart, frustrate, deter, blockade, stop, curb, arrest, stem, clog, intercept, restrain, check, ban, prohibit, hamper, proscribe, avert, restrict, bar, halt, detain, preclude, suppress, withhold, stifle, rein in, postpone, quell, put down, overturn, foil, eclipse, dam, repulse, encumber, foreclose. **3.** *n.* A group. See body (3), combination. *Ant.* Facilitation; open; individual.

Blockade, *n.* Action taken against an enemy nation so as to prevent supplies and people from entering or leaving the nation. Encirclement, barricade, blockage, siege, barrier, cordon, sealing off, obstruction, containment, confinement, surrounding, closure, impediment, strangulation, hindrance. See also close (2).

Blockage, *n.* **1.** An obstruction (the blockage prevented all access). Barrier, impediment, hurdle, jam, congestion, impasse, deterrent, hindrance, restraint, constraint. See also blockade, block (1). **2.** A recognition in tax law that in some instances a large block of stock cannot be marketed and turned into cash as readily and as advantageously as a few shares. This is taken into consideration in determining the value of the stock.

Blockhead, *n.* See idiot.

Blood, *n.* **1.** Family line (royal blood). Ancestry, heritage, lineage, stock, race, breed, genealogy, kindred, line, pedigree, heredity, nationality, affinity, consanguinity, clan, stirps, kinship, derivation, extraction, line, next of kin, birth, relations, relatives, house, descendants, progeny, posterity. **2.** Temperament (hot blood). Passion, temper, constitution, character, spirit, humor, makeup, disposition, mettle, mood, state of mind, nature.

Blood bath, *n.* See murder, assassination, kill.

Blood grouping test A test to determine who could *not* possibly be the father of a child.

Bloodshed, *n.* See assassination, murder, kill, violence.

Bloodsucker, *n.* See parasite.

Bloodthirsty, *adj.* See wild (3), gross (1), predatory, cruel, deadly, violent, mortal (2).

Bloom, *v., n.* See develop, mature (1), advance (3, 4, 5); prime (3), apex.

Blooper, *n.* See error.

Blossom, *v., n.* See develop, mature (1), advance (3, 4, 5); prime (3), apex, culmination.

Blot, *v.* See impair, pollute, slander, cancel.

Blouse, *n.* See clothes.

Blow, *v., n.* See calamity, catastrophe; attack (1), batter; collision (1).

Blowup, *n.*, **blow up,** *v.* See eruption; augment.

Bludgeon 1. *n.* A heavy club or stick, often weighted at one end by metal, used as a weapon (the bludgeon was found at the scene). Cudgel, bat, billy, racket, mallet, cane, baton, blackjack, mace, truncheon. **2.** *v.* To inflict injury with a heavy club or stick (bludgeoned to death). Hammer, pummel, club, bash, "clobber," strike. **3.** *v.* To coerce. Intimidate, harangue, bully, bluster, browbeat, terrify, terrorize.

Blue, *adj.* See obscene; depression.

Blue blood, *n.* See aristocracy.

Blue-collar, *adj.* Pertaining to wage earners who often engage in manual labor. See employee.

Blue jeans, *n.* See clothes.

Blue laws, *n.* Laws regulating Sunday entertainment activities, work, and commerce.

Blueprint, *n.* A detailed plan, drawing, or outline (blueprint for action). Master plan, sketch, design, prospectus, scheme, proposal, conception, draft, strategy, game plan. See also map, record.

Blue-ribbon, *adj.* See special (1), exceptional, outstanding (2).

Blues, *n.* See depression (1).

Blue sky laws State statutes that regulate offerings and sales of securities.

Bluff 1. *v.* To deceive by pretense or the appearance of strength (bluff your opponent). Fool, mislead, lie, delude, cozen, pretend, simulate, trick, dupe, dissemble, defraud. See also cloak. **2.** *n.* A sham (a bluff to pressure you into selling). Pretense, lie, deception, trick, fraud, fake, boast, bravado, bluster, humbug, braggadocio. **3.** *n.* A high, steep bank, as by a river, the sea, or a plain; a bank or a bankhead with a broad, steep face (a high bluff by the ocean). Cliff, bank, ridge, promontory, slope, palisade, peak, knoll, precipice. See also mountain. **4.** *adj.* Outspoken (a bluff nature). Rough and hardy, candid, burly, crude, straightforward, frank, good-natured, open, direct, brusque, crusty, short, unconventional, abrupt, blunt. *Ant.* Rectify; truth; suave.

Blunder 1. *n.* A careless mistake (the misdelivery was a blunder). Error, indiscretion, slip, folly, omission, abortion, inadvertence, stupidity, gaffe, solecism, faux pas, oversight, fumble, fiasco, lapse, misstep, flaw, gaucherie. **2.** *v.* To make a careless mistake (he blundered into the cement). Stumble, stagger, flounder, misjudge, miscarry, botch, fumble, miscalculate. See also err. *Ant.* Triumph, achievement; be correct.

Blunt, *adj.* See rude, sudden, abrasive, caustic.

Blur, *v.* See obscure (3), confuse, conceal, impair, pollute.

Blurt, *v.* See communicate, voice (2), publish.

Bluster, *v., n.* See bludgeon (3), coerce; boast; pretense, artifice.

Board 1. *n.* A group of persons with managerial, supervisory, or investigatory functions and powers (the board of directors of the company). Commission, body, committee, panel, trustees, bureau, council, tribunal, directors, court, judiciary, directorate, executive branch, conclave, cabinet, presidium, group, management. **2.** *n.* Meals (room and board). Food, provisions. **3.** *v.* To get on (board the ship). Climb, embark, mount, enplane, entrain, enbus. See also enter (2).

Boarder, *n.* See tenant (1), guest (1).

Boarding house, *n.* See hotel.

Boarding school, *n.* See school (1).

Boast, *v.* To brag. Trumpet, gloat, swagger, glow, blow one's horn, bluster, glory, strut, flatter oneself, crow, vaunt, flaunt, show off, sound off. See also exaggerate, overrate; puffing; pompous, arrogant; pretense. *Ant.* apologize.

Boastful, *adj.* See arrogant.

Boat, *n.* See vessel (1).

Boatswain, *n.* A sailor who superintends the work of the crew. Foreman, supervisor, manager, overseer, superintendent, boss, chief.

Bobsled, *n.* See vehicle (1).

Bode, *v.* See augur.

Bodice, *n.* See clothes.

Bodiless, *adj.* See incorporeal.

Bodily 1. *adj.* Pertaining to or concerning the body (bodily injury). Human, carnal, somatic, organic, living, corporeal, fleshly, animal. **2.** *adj.* Physical (bodily pain). Having substance, substantial, tangible, perceptible, real, factual, solid, concrete, existent, existing, visible, tactile, actual, palpable, manifest. **3.**

Bodily

adv. As a group (they were accepted bodily). En masse, collectively, completely, entirely, wholly. *Ant.* Mental; spiritual; individually.

Body, *n.* **1.** The main part (the body of the memo). Substance, essential part, central part, essence, core, structure, principal portion, center, heart. **2.** A person. The person can be natural (a human) or artificial (a corporation). Individual, human being, human, creature. **3.** A group of persons or things considered as a whole (governing body; a body of laws). Mass, group, collection, company, party, aggregation, aggregate, entity, troupe, conglomeration, assemblage, assembly, bulk, corps, corpus, mob, multitude, throng, federation, faction, coalition, congress, block, league, clique, association, coterie, band, corporation, society, array, set, bundle, cluster, party, bunch. **4.** A corpse (the body was never recovered). Remains, cadaver, carcass, corpus delicti, skeleton, "stiff." **5.** Torso (she could not move her body). Physique, frame, trunk, figure, build, flesh and bones.

Bodyguard, *n.* See guardian, attendant (1), keeper, coterie.

Body heirs, bodily heirs Lineal descendants, progeny, issue, heirs begotten or borne.

Body language See gesture, manifestation.

Body politic, body corporate 1. A social compact by which the whole people covenants with each citizen, and each citizen with the whole people, that all shall be governed by certain laws for the common good. **2.** A municipal corporation, school district, county, or city. **3.** State or nation. See nation. **4.** Public associations.

Boggle, *v.* See amaze, surprise (1); avoid (2).

Bogus, *adj.* Sham (bogus money; bogus check). Imitation, spurious, quasi, phony, ungenuine, fraudulent, counterfeit, feigned, pseudo, dummy, pretend, forged, synthetic, artificial. *Ant.* Bona fide, real.

Bohemian, *n., adj.* See vagabond (2); artisan, author (1); odd (1).

Boil, *v.* See rage; bake.

Boil down, *v.* See condense.

Boilerplate, *n.* Standard language in legal documents that is identical in documents of a like nature; language often used in documents having a definite meaning in the same context without variation (two thirds of the deed is boilerplate). Uniform language, stereotyped language, accepted language, conventional language, standardized language, customary language, stock language.

Boisterous, *adj.* See wild (3), incorrigible; noisy.

Bold, *adj.* See courageous, explicit, adventurous, ambitious, ardent; rude.

Boldfaced, *adj.* See obvious, naked (2); rude.

Boldness, *n.* See valor, courage.

Bolshevism, *n.* See communism.

Bolster, *v.* See aid (1).

Bolt, *n., v.* See lock; run (2), flee.

Bomb, *n., v.* See weapon, arms, ballistics; attack (1).

Bombard, *v.* See attack (1).

Bombastic, *adj.* See pompous, arrogant.

Bombshell, *n.* See shock, surprise (2).

Bona, *n.* (*Lat.*) Goods, property, possessions.

Bona fide, *adj.* In good faith (bona fide effort). Sincere, true, genuine, without fraud, without deceit, honest, aboveboard, open, actual, innocent, real, not feigned, candid, trustworthy, ingenuous, legitimate. See also de facto. *Ant.* Dishonest.

Bona fide purchaser (BFP) One who has purchased property for value without any notice of defects in the title of the seller.

Bonanza, *n.* See windfall, bounty (1).

Bond 1. *n.* A certificate or evidence of a debt in which the entity that issues the bond (a company or a governmental body) promises (a) to pay the bondholders a specified amount of interest for a specified amount of time and (b) to repay the loan on the expiration date. Certificate of indebtedness, debenture, promissory note, obligation. **2.** *n.* An obligation to pay a designated amount of money if a certain act is not done (the appellant had to post a bond). Warrant, warranty, security, assurance, surety, guarantee, guaranty, promise, pledge. **3.** *n.* An agreement. Covenant, compact, contract, bargain, treaty, concordat, arrangement, word. **4.** *n.* Connection (a strong bond between them). Link, nexus, tie, knot, affinity, union, attraction, attachment, liaison, relation, relationship, fealty, loyalty, adherence, binding force, glue, cement, fastener, allegiance, ligature, ligament, cordon, binding. **5.** *v.* To join. Hold together, merge, unite, glue, coalesce, weld, link, couple, blend, fuse, consolidate, combine, cohere, attach, knot, connect.

Bondage, *n.* Slavery; involuntary personal servitude (freed from bondage). Enslavement, restraint, serfdom, bonds, yoke, vassalage, confinement, imprisonment, helotry, thralldom, kidnapping, detention, internment, chains, entombment, manacles, forced labor, subjection, reins, subjugation. See also servitude. *Ant.* Independence.

Bond coupon Part of a bond that is cut and surrendered for payment of one of successive payments of interest.

Bond creditor A creditor whose debt is secured by a bond.

Bonded, *adj.* Secured by a bond (a bonded employee). See bond (2).

Bondsman, *n.* A person who has entered into a bond as surety; one who furnishes a bond (bail bondsman). Surety, guarantor, voucher.

Bone, *n.* Calcified tissue of the skeleton. Ossicle, cartilage; cavity, marrow.

Bonehead, *n.* See idiot.

Bonfire, *n.* See fire (1), conflagration.

Bonification, *n.* A waiving of taxes, especially on export goods.

Bonnet, *n.* See clothes.

Bonus, *n.* Something extra; a consideration or premium paid in addition to what is strictly due (annual bonus). Fringe, gift, tip, dividend, honorarium, perquisite, bounty, present, surplus, gratuity, boon. See also compensation, reward. *Ant.* Penalty.

Boob, *n.* See idiot, ass, boor.

Book 1. *v.* To enter charges against someone (the police immediately booked her). Accuse, prefer charges, arrest, indict. See also charge (3). **2.** *v.* To list or record in a book. Register, inscribe, log, enroll, schedule, enumerate, catalog, index, post, write down, note. **3.** *n.* To schedule (the hotel booked his reservation). Engage, hire, reserve, charter, program, slate, bill, procure, line up, contract for. **4.** *n.* Bound sheets of paper with writing on them (a lengthy book). Treatise, text, work, volume, pamphlet, monograph, tract, brochure, manual, opus, publication, primer, reader, speller, workbook, reference, source, tome.

Booking, *n.* The step taken after an arrested person is brought to the police station, which may involve entering relevant facts on the police "blotter," fingerprinting, etc. See book (1, 2).

Bookkeeper, *n.* A person who records the financial accounts and transactions of a business. Accountant, record keeper, someone who keeps the books, clerk, examiner, inspector, teller. See also controller.

Bookkeeping, *n.* See account (1), clerical (2).

Bookmaker, *n.* Someone who makes or collects bets for others. Gambler, "bookie." See also gambling.

Book value The going-concern value for a company, which is arrived at by adding all assets, deducting all liabilities, and dividing that sum by the number of shares of outstanding common stock. The valuation at which assets are carried on the books.

Bookworm, *n.* See scholar.

Boom, *n.* See noise.

Boomerang, *n.* See return (2), reverse, ricochet.

Boon, *n.* See benefit (1), bounty (1), windfall.

Boor, *n.* A crude person. Oaf, churl, hick, clown, clodhopper, rube, peasant, brute, ox, klutz, bungler, slob, lug, yokel, bumpkin.

Boorish, *adj.* See rude.

Boost, *v.* See advance (4), strengthen, augment, defend (1), aid (1); honor (2); tribute (2).

Booster, *n.* See patron, advocate.

Boot, *n.* See ouster, clothes.

Booth, *n.* See enclosure.

Bootlegger, *n.* Someone who makes, stores, or transports alcoholic beverages for sale in violation of the law. Runner, moonshiner, smuggler, one who operates on the black market. See also contraband.

Bootstrap sale 1. Using the assets or cash of a business to acquire that business. **2.** Converting ordinary income from a business into capital gain from the sale of corporate stock.

Booty, *n.* Property captured from the enemy at war. Spoils, plunder, takings, loot, prize, pillage.

Booze, *n.* See liquor, alcoholic liquor.

Bordello, *n.* See brothel, bawdyhouse.

Border 1. *n.* Boundary line (cross the border). Edge, frontier, brink, margin, periphery, rim, fringe, borderland, perimeter, brim, extremity, ambit, demarcation line, confine, verge, circumference, outskirt, selvage, end. **2.** *v.* To join; to adjoin (Canada borders the United States). Neighbor, connect, flank, verge on, surround, embrace, encircle, frame, conjoin, bound, confine, be next to, abut, attach, edge, delimit, define, circumscribe, delineate, unite, impinge on, touch, demarcate. *Ant.* Interior.

Borderline, *adj.* See marginal.

Bore, *v., n.* See harass; nuisance, boor.

Boredom, *n.* Tedium, monotony, malaise, repetition, doldrums, weariness, routine, dullness. See also exhaustion, ennui.

Boring, *adj.* See commonplace (2), pedestrian (2), household, ordinary; boredom.

Born, *adj.* **1.** Being delivered or expelled from a mother's body; brought into life. Begotten, delivered, given birth to. **2.** By birth or nature (a born litigator). Innate, natural, inborn, hereditary, intuitive, inbred, intrinsic, inherent, ingrained, congenital, genetic, native, inherited, instinctual, organic, connate, endowed from birth. *Ant.* Learned (2).

Borough, *n.* A town or township with a municipal charter. A political subdivision of a state. See area (1), division (2), zone.

Borrow, *v.* **1.** To solicit and receive money or other property from another with the intention and promise to repay or return it (borrow $500 from the bank). Seek the use of, use, receive as a loan, take on credit. **2.** To adopt and use as one's own (the author borrowed ideas from Justice Cardozo). Imitate, plagiarize, appropriate, copy, usurp, cite, paraphrase, steal, arrogate, simulate, mirror, abstract, acquire, take, commandeer, pilfer, filch, quote. *Ant.* Lend; create.

Bosom, *n.* See center, interior.

Boss, *v., n.* See manage; manager, master (1).

Botany, *n.* The science of plants. See science.

Botch, *v.* See blunder.

Both, *adj.* See two.

Bother, *v.* See harass, disturb, accost (1), outrage (2), exacerbate, provoke, assault, attack; concern (2).

Bottle, *n.* See vessel (2).

Bottleneck, *n.* See obstruction; impede, hinder.

Bottom, *n.* See base (3).

Bottomless, *adj.* See perpetual.

Bottomry, *n.* A contract by which the owner of a ship borrows money for equipment or for repairs of the ship. The ship becomes the security for the loan.

Boudoir, *n.* See chamber (1).

Boulder, *n.* See rock, mountain.

Boulevard, *n.* See highway, course (1).

Bounce, *v.* See ricochet, jump; evict, oust.

Bound 1. *adj.* Being obligated (bound by the decision; bound by the contract). Compelled, constrained, limited, burdened, accountable, tied, necessitated, obliged, required, answerable, forced, determined, engaged, committed, indebted, liable, responsible. **2.** *adj.* Fastened (bound prisoners). Tied, secured, in bonds, handcuffed, restrained, fettered, restricted, shackled, manacled. **3.** *adj.* Certain (the effort is bound to fail). Destined, doomed, fated, sure, assured, positive, determined, predetermined, compelled, required. **4.** *n.* Boundary (the bounds of the estate). Confine, range, border, outskirt, rim, limit, periphery, extremity, realm, territory, domain, district, region, province, orbit, area. *Ant.* Unrestrained; unrestricted; uncertain; interior.

Boundary, *n.* The separation that marks the division between two things (e.g., two adjoining properties). Border, dividing line, mete, limit, confine, perimeter, edge, frontier, rim, enclosure, periphery, fringe, verge, brink, margin, borderland, partition, fence, line of demarcation, ambit, extremity, pale, mark, circumscription, termination, terminus, terminal, barrier, contour, frame, acme, apogee, outline, compass, environs.

Boundless, *adj.* See perpetual, permanent, incalculable.

Bound over 1. The act by which a court requires a person to promise to appear for trial or to furnish bail. **2.** Transferring a case to a grand jury after finding probable cause that the accused committed the crime.

Bounds, *n.* External or limiting lines of any object or space. See bound (4), boundary.

Bounteous, *adj.* See abundant, benevolent.

Bountiful, *adj.* See abundant, benevolent.

Bounty, *n.* **1.** An additional benefit (each received a bounty of $400). Reward, grant, bonus, gratuity, donation, largess, blessing, premium, aid, benefaction, subsidy, concession, tip, remuneration, bonanza, honorarium, tribute, boon, prize, emolument, perquisite, token. **2.** Generosity (the bounty of the foundation). Philanthropy, altruism, beneficence, charity, munificence, succor, goodness, assistance, liberality, almsgiving. *Ant.* Greed.

Bourbon, *n.* See liquor.

Bourgeois, *adj.* See conventional, commonplace (2).

Bout, *n.* See contest (2), conflict; term (1); spree.

Boutique, *n.* See market (1).

Bow, *v.* See acquiesce, comply; grovel, cringe, flatter, pander (2).

Bowdlerize, *v.* See censor (3).

Bowl, *n.* See vessel (2).

Box, *n., v.* See vessel (2), package, cell; batter, sport.

Boxcar, *n.* See vehicle.

Boy, *n.* See child, juvenile; man; servant, employee.

Boycott 1. *n.* A concerted refusal to do business with a particular person or business in order to obtain concessions or to express displeasure with certain practices of the person or business (consumer boycott). Blacklisting, blackballing, embargo, avoidance, withholding patronage, forbearance, interdiction, ostracism. **2.** *v.* To refuse to participate (he boycotted the meeting). Shun, ignore, blackball, blacklist, abstain, spurn, ostracize, reject, shut off, outlaw, interdict, forbear, ban, desist, avoid, picket, scorn, rebuff, slight. *Ant.* Patronage; participate.

Boyfriend, *n.* See suitor (2), intimate (5); man.

Brace, *v.* See affix (1), sustain (3), strengthen, augment, defend (1), aid (1), build (1).

Bracket, *n.* See class, classification (2).

Brag, *v.* See boast.

Braggadocio, *n.* See pretense, arrogance, showoff.

Braggart, *n.* See showoff, boor, ass.

Brain, *n.* See mind (1), ability, reason (2), comprehension.

Brain death (a) Unreceptivity and unresponsiveness to externally applied stimuli and internal needs, (b) no spontaneous movements or breathing, (c) no reflex activity, and (d) a flat electroencephalograph reading after a 24-hour period of observation.

Brainwash, *v.* See influence (2), educate, discipline (4), imbue; coerce.

Branch 1. *n.* A subdivision (a branch of the union). Part, section, subsidiary, local, chapter, unit, division, affiliate, bureau, wing, office, department, desk, arm, agency, portion, member, offshoot, lodge. **2.** *v.* To separate into different directions (the accident occurred where the road branches). Diverge, bifurcate, divide, radiate, fork, angle. See also part (3). *Ant.* Whole; unite.

Brand 1. *n.* A mark used to identify a product or service (the brand was easily identifiable). Label, emblem, logo, trademark, trade name, stamp, sign, hallmark, earmark, blaze, badge, insignia, tag, motto, impress, imprint, inscription, symbol, identification. **2.** *n.* Kind (the judge did not appreciate her brand of humor). Quality, type, grade, class, sort, make, line, ilk, character, species, nature, variety. **3.** *v.* To stigmatize (his antics branded him a troublemaker). Disgrace, defame, stain, blemish, discredit, censure, expose, denounce, blacken, defile, vilify, shame, tarnish, disparage, malign, taint, impugn, soil, sully, deprecate. See also characterize. **4.** *v.* See engrave.

Brandeis brief An appellate brief in which economic and social studies are included along with legal principles.

Brandish, *v.* To wave threateningly (the defendant brandished her gun at the plaintiff). Swing, exhibit, wield, dangle, flaunt, shake, emblazon, flourish, display, parade. *Ant.* Lower.

Brandy, *n.* See liquor.

Brash, *adj.* See rude; careless, reckless, impetuous, sudden.

Brat, *n.* See child, juvenile, delinquent, wrongdoer.

Bravado, *n.* See valor, pretense, arrogance.

Brave, *adj.* See courageous, adventurous, ardent, assertive, ambitious; challenge (1); reckless.

Bravery, *n.* See valor; courageous.

Brawl, *n.* A noisy quarrel in a public place leading to the disturbance of the peace. Uproar, feud, imbroglio, fracas, scrap, altercation, melee, row, affray, squabble, disturbance, brannigan, brouhaha, scuffle, wrangle, commotion, broil, riot, scramble, embroilment, rumpus, fisticuffs, rampage, dogfight, donnybrook, slugfest, eruption.

Brawny, *adj.* See able-bodied, healthy.

Brazen, *adj.* See rude, offensive.

Breach 1. *n.* The breaking or violation of an obligation or a law (breach of contract). Infringement, disregard, transgression, evasion, nonfulfillment, nonperformance, trespass, repudiation, infraction, break, contravention, nonobservance, delinquency, neglect, dereliction, encroachment, distortion, default, nonadherence. **2.** *n.* Rupture (a breach in the wall). Split, chasm, gap, rift, gash, opening, fissure, rent, flaw, crack, crevice, fracture, hole, cleft, fault, void, gulf, schism. **3.** *v.* See break (1), encroach, interfere, attack (1), assault (3). *Ant.* Compliance; closure; comply.

Breach of close The unlawful entry on another's soil, land, or close.

Breach of contract The failure, without legal excuse, to perform any promise one is contractually obligated to perform.

Breach of the peace A violation or disturbance of the public tranquillity and order. Riot, fracas, uproar, melee, row, brannigan, rumpus, donnybrook, slugfest, dogfight, scrap. See also brawl.

Breach of warranty The failure or falsehood of an affirmative promise or statement; the nonperformance of an executory stipulation.

Bread, *n.* See cash; food.

Breadth, *n.* See scope, measure (1), extent.

Break 1. *v.* To violate (to break an agreement). Breach, neglect, betray, infringe, transgress, contradict, disregard, oppose, cancel, annul, mutilate, disobey, defy, ignore, slight, renege, shirk, contravene, overlook, infract, disdain, vacate, revoke, impede. **2.** *v.* To fracture (he broke his leg). Split, rupture, sever, tear, snap, pulverize, chip, cut, fragment, splinter, puncture, crack, rip, crush, demolish, shatter, atomize, section, divide, lacerate, wound, injure, burst, fissure. **3.** *n.* A crack or interruption (break in the chain of causation). Breach, rift, hole, opening, rupture, fracture, snap, fissure, shattering, rent, gap, separation, tear, hiatus, pause, lapse, aperture, disruption, schism, cleavage, gulf. *Ant.* Comply; repair; consistency, continuation.

Breakable, *adj.* Fragile. Weak, brittle, frail, unstable, feeble, flimsy. See also tender (5). *Ant.* Sturdy.

Break down, *v.*, **breakdown,** *n.* See collapse, debacle, defeat.

Breaking, *n.* Forcibly separating, parting, disintegrating, or piercing any solid substance. Using any act of force to gain entry with a criminal intent.

Breaking a close Unlawful entry upon land.

Breaking and entry Common-law burglary: Breaking and entering the dwelling of another with the intent to commit a felony therein. Statutes have modified this definition in many states.

Break off, *v.* See cease.

Breakout, *n.*, See escape.

Breakthrough, *n.* See advance (8), discovery.

Breakup, *n.* See debacle.

Breakwater, *n.* See jetty.

Breath, *n.* Respiration. Inhalation, exhalation, breathing, gasp, wind; inhale, breathe, snuff, sneeze, sniffle, smell, whiff. See also life; aroma, fragrant.

Breathalyzer test A test to determine the content of alcohol in someone suspected of operating a motor vehicle under the influence of liquor.

Breathtaking, *adj.* See moving (1), compelling, attractive, touching, intriguing, extraordinary, outstanding (2), great, emotional, wild.

Breed, *v.* See beget, raise.

Breve *n.* A writ.

Brevet, *n.* The promotion of an officer without an increase in pay.

Brevia, *n.* (*Lat.*) Writs.

Brew, *v.* See devise (3), create.

Bribe, 1. *n.* A gift of money or of something else of value given to influence the conduct of the receiver (the senator solicited the bribe). Lure, payoff, kickback, payola, subornation, lubrication, "grease," hush money, corrupt gratuity, corrupt money, illegal gift, seduction, allure, incitement, inducement. See also graft, gratuity (2). **2.** *v.* See corrupt (2).

Bribery, *n.* The offering, giving, receiving, or soliciting of anything of value to influence the action of an official in discharge of a legal or public duty. Abuse of office, breach of trust, payoff, graft, corrupt money, corrupt payment, corruption, allurement, simony, prostitution of public trust, corrupt influence, illegal inducement.

Bridal, *adj.* See nuptial, marital.

Bridge, *v., n.* See connect; connection; intersection; highway.

Bridle, *v.* See restrain, control, check (1, 5), circumscribe (1), clog (2).

Brief 1. *n.* A written statement or argument prepared by counsel concerning a case in court (appellate brief; trial brief). **2.** *n.* A summary of something (a brief of a case). Synopsis, outline, abstract, résumé, digest, sketch, epitome, précis, excerpt, conspectus, extract, abridgement, abbreviation, core, compilation, prospectus, roundup, review, short version, survey, rundown, recapitulation, restatement, compendium, profile. **3.** *adj.* Concise (a brief response). Succinct, compact, terse, trenchant, thumbnail, to the point, exact, condensed, laconic, abridged, compendious, epigrammatic, short, abrupt, abbreviated, limited, compressed, straightforward, pointed, elliptical, reduced. **4.** *adj.* Momentary (a brief hearing). Quick, cursory, short-term, ephemeral, evanescent, transitory, transient, temporary, passing, fast, fleeting, volatile, mercurial, elusive, meteoric, perishable, impermanent, fugitive, permutable, short-lived, precarious. *Ant.* Full text; protracted; lengthy.

Briefed, *adj.* See familiar (1).

Brigade, *n.* See company (2); military.

Bright, *adj.* See beautiful, clear (3), attractive; light, brilliant.

Brilliance, *n.* See clarity; light; brilliant.

Brilliant, *adj.* **1.** Highly intelligent or inventive. Gifted, expert, intellectual, creative, brainy, capable, astute, masterful, quick, cerebral, precocious, accomplished, quick-witted, sharp, sagacious, alert, perceptive, deft, sage, erudite, masterful, educated, remarkable, competent, penetrating, shrewd. **2.** See clear (3).

Bring, *v.* See convey (3), get (1).

Bring about, *v.* To procure (bring about an agreement). Bring to pass, complete, accomplish, cause, effectuate, generate, give rise to, originate, perform, occasion, secure, actualize, carry through. *Ant.* Fail.

Bring together, *v.* See compile, collect.

Brink, *n.* See verge, border (1), boundary.

Brisk, *adj.* See active (3).

British thermal unit (BTU) The amount of heat required to raise a pound of water one degree Fahrenheit.

Brittle, *adj.* See breakable, weak.

Broad, *adj.* **1.** Wide in range (a broad ruling). Not limited, all-embracing, comprehensive, universal, blanket, sweeping, extensive, liberal, far-reaching, inclusive, extended, large, spacious, unlimited, wide-ranging, general, nonspecific, catholic, ample, blanket, encyclopedic, roomy, hospitable, undetailed, diffuse, indefinite, vague, indeterminate, composite, widespread, full. **2.** Obvious (a broad hint). Evident, clear, plain, open, frank, straightforward, pronounced, candid, glaring, sincere, striking. *Ant.* Narrow; obscure.

Broadcast, *v.* See publish, circulate.

Broaden, *v.* See augment, extend (1), widen.

Broad-minded, *adj.* See open (6, 7), liberal (2).

Brochure, *n.* See book (4), bulletin.

Broil, *v.* See bake.

Broken, *adj.* **1.** Financially ruined (broken man). Impoverished, bankrupt, insolvent, indigent, destitute, defeated, vanquished, fallen, crushed, humbled, failed. **2.** Violated (broken commitment). Transgressed, delinquent, nonobservant, infringed, contravened, encroached. **3.** Fractured (broken line). Damaged, ruptured, shattered, defective, injured, mangled, cracked, divided, lacerated, pulverized, severed, disintegrated, splintered, rent, torn, destroyed, out of order, nonfunctioning, ruined, spoiled, erratic, incomplete, deranged, inconsistent, irregular, dilapidated, run-down, disconnected, unsteady, fragmentary, spasmodic. *Ant.* Wealthy; intact.

Broker, *n.* An agent who arranges contracts for a fee (real estate broker; insurance broker). Go-between, dealer, factor, intermediary, middleman, negotiator, medium, jobber, interceder, mediator, attorney in fact, representative, emissary, proxy, deputy, link, commission agent, matchmaker. *Ant.* Principal.

Brokerage, *n.* **1.** The business or occupation of a broker. **2.** The wages or commissions of a broker. Fee, compensation, remuneration, emolument, charges.

Brood, *v.* See deliberate (1); mope, bemoan, cry (1), suffer.

Brooding, *adj.* See preoccupied, engaged; mope, bemoan, suffer.

Brothel, *n.* House of prostitution. Bawdyhouse, house of ill fame, cathouse, whorehouse, bordello, parlor house, bagnio.

Brotherhood, *n.* See association (1), union (1), gang.

Browbeat, *v.* See intimidate, coerce, compel.

Browse, *v.* To scan, examine cursorily, peruse, or check out. See observe (3); investigate.

Bruise, *v., n.* See hurt, injure; injury, contusion, lesion, wound.

Brusque, *adj.* See rude, caustic.

Brutal, *adj.* See cruel, wild (3), gross (1), inhuman.

Brutality, *n.* See cruelty.

Brute, *n.* See boor, wrongdoer.

BTU See British thermal unit.

Bucket, *n.* See vessel (2).

Bucolic, *adj.* See idyllic, country (2), innocent, happy.

Buddy, *n.* See associate (2), intimate (5).

Budge, *v.* See move (2).

Budget 1. *n.* A plan for the coordination of resources and expenditures (the budget is prepared once a year). Schedule, program, blueprint, spending plan. **2.** *n.* The amount of money set aside for a specific purpose (the budget for yellow pads). Allocation, allotment, allowance, funds, appropriation, provision, estimate, ration, share, quota, reserve, total, aggregate, account. **3.** *v.* To schedule (budget your time). Program, estimate, allocate, apportion, arrange, cost out, docket, portion.

Buffer, *n.* See protection.

Buffoon, *n.* See boor, idiot.

Bug, bugging, 1. *n., v.* A form of electronic surveillance by which conversations may be secretly overheard and recorded. Wiretap, listen in, listen stealthily, snoop, monitor, spy. See also inspection; eavesdrop. **2.** *v.* See harass. **3.** *n.* See defect. **4.** *n.* See disease; germ.

Buggery, *n.* See sodomy.

Buggy *n.* See vehicle (1).

Build, *v.* **1.** To amplify (she built her law practice into a major firm). Increase, strengthen, develop, augment, expand, enlarge, reinforce, enhance, intensify, accelerate, raise, supplement, multiply, brace, heighten, evolve, achieve, parlay, elevate, harden, aggrandize, extend. **2.** To construct (they build computers). Create, manufacture, fashion, fabricate, assemble, originate, make, sculpture, engineer, erect, raise, produce, devise, establish, set up, form, forge. See also compose (2), construct. *Ant.* Undermine; suspend, destroy.

Builder, *n.* One whose occupation is the planning and construction of buildings and other structures. Contractor, carpenter. See also entrepreneur, patron, backer, producer, owner, employer.

Building, *n.* **1.** A structure enclosing a space within its walls (the building collapsed). Edifice, house, quarters, station, construction, establishment, abode, erection, frame, office, business, fabric, superstructure, lodge, residence, domicile, headquarters, dwelling, address, site, lodging, premises. **2.** The process of construction (building a foundation). Production, formulation, manufacturing, making, framing, composition, structuring, architecture, sculpturing, engineering, designing, preparation, development, organization, installation, assembling, devising, forging, creating, originating, implementation, execution.

Built, *adj.* See made (1).

Bulge, *v.* See augment, protrude.

Bulk, *n.* **1.** The entire quantity or a substantial part (a bulk sale). Aggregate, total, block, lot, mass, chief part, main part, most, majority, batch, cluster, accumulation, volume, size. See also corpus. **2.** Extent (the bulk of the documents was overwhelming). Size, magnitude, volume, mass, dimensions, density, weight, measure, massiveness, enormity, greatness, largeness, sum, quantity, substance, number, body, totality, bigness, greatness.

Bulkhead, *n.* See jetty.

"Bull," *n.* See balderdash, prolixity.

Bulldoze, *v.* See coerce, intimidate.

Bullet, *n.* See weapon, ammunition.

Bulletin, *n.* An official publication or notice; an ongoing publication (*Internal Revenue Bulletin*). Announcement, statement, notification, communication, record, information, communiqué, intelligence, dispatch, brochure, pamphlet, monograph, review, journal, entry, memorandum, circular, flyer, poster, handbill, news report.

Bullheaded, *adj.* See inflexible, contumacious.

Bullion, *n.* Uncoined gold or silver. See coin, currency, money.

Bullpen, *n.* A place of close confinement in a jail or prison. A place for temporary detention. See jail.

Bully, *v., n.* See coerce, intimidate; wrongdoer, boor.

Bulwark, *n.* See protection, wall, asylum.

Bum, *n.* See tramp, vagabond (2).

Bump, *v., n.* See push, collide; bumping; collision (1).

Bumping, *n.* **1.** Failing to board ticketed passengers due to an oversale of tickets by the airlines. **2.** Displacement of a junior employee's position by a senior employee.

Bumpkin, *n.* See idiot, boor; backward.

Bunch, *v., n.* See collect (1), accumulate, pack (1); collection (2), package, multiplicity.

Bundle, *n., v.* See package, collection (2), assemblage (1).

Bungalow, *n.* See home (1), building (1).

Bungle, *v.* See blunder.

Bungler, *n.* See idiot, boor.

Bunk, *n.* See bed; balderdash.

Bunker, *n.* See vessel (2), protection, home (1).

Buoyant, *adj.* See happy, active (3); life (3).

Burden 1. *n.* The onus or responsibility (burden of proof). Duty, obligation, liability, requirement, mandate, charge, engagement, assignment, necessity, pressure, encumbrance. **2.** *n.* Something difficult to bear (the burden of defeat). Anxiety, adversity, weight, strain, hardship, stress, oppression, ordeal, tribulation, albatross, millstone, misery, affliction, brunt, impediment, imposition, sorrow, handicap, trouble, vexation. **3.** *v.* To obligate (he burdened his estate). Encumber, tax, make responsible for, saddle with, vex, overload, hamper, charge, impede, clog, weigh, afflict, oppress, hinder, handicap. *Ant.* Freedom; joy; liberate, exonerate.

Burden of evidence See burden of going forward.

Burden of going forward The responsibility of a party during the trial to present evidence on an issue in order to make or meet a prima facie showing on that issue. The burden of evidence. See burden of producing evidence.

Burden of persuasion The responsibility of a party with the burden of proof to convince the trier of fact (judge or jury) of all of the elements of its case.

Burden of producing evidence The obligation of a party to introduce evidence sufficient to avoid a ruling against him or her on the issue. This burden is met when the party with the burden of proof has introduced sufficient evidence to make out a prima facie case.

Burden of proof The duty of affirmatively proving a fact or facts in dispute on an issue. The duty of establishing a fact or facts by the requisite amount of proof (e.g., preponderance of the evidence, clear and convincing evidence).

Burdensome, *adj.* See difficult (2), onerous, inconvenient, severe, extreme, draconian.

Bureau, *n.* A division of the government or other organization (Bureau of Prisons). Department, committee, unit, administration, branch, office, service, commission, agency, ministry, authority, board, subdivision, post.

Bureaucracy, *n.* **1.** An organization consisting of a chain of command, specialty departments, regulations, red tape, etc. Process of government, government, government by bureaus, administration, agencies, management, system, bureaus, authorities, government officialdom. See also civil service. **2.** Red tape, regulations, forms, rules, "runaround," officialism. See also red tape.

Bureaucrat, *n.* See administrator, official (1), officer, incumbent (1).

Burgeon, *v.* See develop (1).

Burgh, *n.* See municipality.

Burglar, *n.* A person who commits burglary. Thief, stealer, plunderer, housebreaker, gangster, robber, purloiner, prowler, bandit, second-story man, felon, trespasser, looter. See also offender, wrongdoer.

Burglary, *n.* Breaking and entering the dwelling house of another in the nighttime with the intent to commit a felony therein. Statutes have modified this definition in many states (e.g., breaking may not be required, any kind of structure can be burglarized at any time of day). Stealing, plundering, robbery, housebreaking, purloining, pilfering, looting, marauding, thievery, felony, unlawful entry, purloinment. See also larceny.

Burgundy, *n.* See liquor.

Burial, *n.* The act or process of burying a deceased person. Interment, entombment, sepulture, sepulcher, obsequies, rites, funeral, inhumation. See also autopsy, mortuary.

Burlesque

Burlesque, *adj., n.* See odd (1); obscene; clown, comic; mock (1); caricature, joke.

Burly, *adj.* See able-bodied, healthy.

Burn, *v.* To damage or injure by fire or similar substance (the fire or acid burned his foot). Incinerate, blaze, flame, combust, char, tan, brown, conflagrate, singe, scar, gut, scald, smolder, enkindle, kindle, inflame, roast, carbonize, ignite, simmer, overheat, consume, radiate, spark, be ablaze, incandesce, flash, reduce to ashes, parch, fuel, blister. *Ant.* Extinguish.

Burning, *adj.* See ardent, emotional, caustic, strong (2); crucial, critical (1).

Burnout, *n.* See illness, affliction.

Bursar, *n.* See treasurer, accountant, controller.

Burst, *v., n.* See attack (1), batter; eruption.

Bury, *v.* See conceal, cloak; burial.

Bus boy, *n.* See servant (2), employee.

Bushel, *n.* **1.** Unit of measurement: 32 quarts; 4 pecks; 35.24 liters; 2,150.42 cubic inches. **2.** See vessel (2).

Bushes, *n.* See shrubbery, woods.

Bushwhack, *v.* See ambush, attack (1).

Business, *n.* **1.** One's work (she is in the construction business). Trade, occupation, profession, employment, vocation, craft, career, job, livelihood, mission, practice, undertaking, calling, line, activity, endeavor, means of support, specialty, assignment, pursuit, field, walk of life, venture, industry, shop, concern, affairs, station. **2.** Commerce (career in business). Industry, manufacturing, trade, ventures, merchandising, marketing, buying and selling, dealing, bargaining, trading, commercial intercourse, bartering. **3.** A commercial enterprise (businesses are taxed). Store, shop, corporation, company, office, undertaking, enterprise, firm, venture, cartel, establishment. **4.** Matter, affair (the business at hand). Task, topic, chore, responsibility, issue, subject, situation, procedure, point, problem, question, case, theme, thesis, concern, transaction.

Business entry rule An exception to the hearsay rule allowing the introduction into evidence of entries made in the usual course of business even if the person who made the entries is not in court.

Business guest One invited to a business establishment as a guest to whom a duty of care is owed. See Guest.

Business invitee One who is impliedly or expressly invited to the premises for transacting business and to whom a duty of care is owed. See invitee.

Businesslike, *adj.* Orderly, methodical, systematic. See efficient, diligent.

Business purpose A justifiable business reason (not mere tax avoidance) for carrying out a transaction. See purpose (1).

Business records exception An exception to the hearsay rule allowing original, routine records (whether or not part of a business) to be used as evidence even though they are hearsay.

Business trust A form of business organization in which the property is placed in the hands of trustees who manage and deal with it for the benefit and use of beneficiaries. Massachusetts trust, common-law trust. See also company (1), association (1).

Business visitor One who is invited or permitted to enter or remain on the premises of another for a purpose directly or indirectly connected with the business dealings between them. See visitor, guest, invitee.

Bust, *v.* See arrest (1); break (2).

Busy, *adj.* See active (1, 3), diligent, engaged.

Busybody, *n.* See interloper; intermeddle; officious, prying.

Busywork, *n.* Makework. See assignment (3), labor, function, job.

"But for" test A test for causation in tort law. "But for" what the defendant did or failed to do, would the plaintiff have been injured? (Useful in limited circumstances.) See causation, cause; except (2).

Butcher, *v., n.* See kill (1); blunder; merchant.

Butler, *n.* See servant (2), employee.

"Butt in," *v.* See interfere, intermeddle.

Buttress, *v.* See aid (1), carry (2), strengthen, equip, defend (1), confirm (1), sustain (3), build (1).

Butts and bounds A phrase used in conveyancing to describe the end lines or circumscribing lines of a certain piece of land. Metes and bounds.

Buy, *v.* **1.** To acquire the ownership of property by giving the agreed price or consideration or by agreeing to do so (buy the land). Purchase, secure, trade, obtain, procure, pay for, bargain for, redeem. **2.** To bribe (the commissioner was bought). Corrupt, suborn, pay off, palm, hire, buy off. *Ant.* Sell.

Buy and sell agreement An agreement among partners or owners of a company that if one dies or withdraws from the business, his or her share will be bought by the others or disposed of according to a prearranged plan.

Buyer, *n.* One who buys. Purchaser, vendee, emptor, customer, invester. See also patron, client (2). *Ant.* Seller.

Buy in, buying in Buying property at auction, at a tax sale, or at a mortgage foreclosure sale by the original owner or by someone with an interest in the property.

By-bidder, *n.* Someone employed by the seller to bid on property, not to become a purchaser but to stimulate others to make bids.

Bylaws, *n.* Regulations or rules adopted by organizations for their own government. Ordinances, canons, prescripts, standards, laws, orders, precepts.

By operation of law Effected or brought about by some positive legal rule.

Bypass, *v., n.* See avoid, circumvent; highway.

By-product, *n.* See effect (1), consequence (1).

Bystander, *n.* One who stands near; someone who is not directly concerned or involved (duty owed to the injured bystander). Spectator, observer, beholder, looker-on, onlooker, eyewitness, watcher, viewer, passerby, audience, reporter, attender, kibitzer. See also witness (2). *Ant.* Participant.

C

Cab, *n.* See vehicle (1).

Cabal, *n.* **1.** A small association formed for the purpose of intrigue (the cabal met in secret). Clique, ring, league, band, gang, faction, confederacy, union, coalition, junta. **2.** An intrigue (an antigovernment cabal). Scheme, plot, connivance, racket, plan, collusion, complicity. See also conspiracy.

Cabaret, *n.* See inn.

Cabin, *n.* See home (1).

Cabinet, *n.* **1.** An advisory board or counsel of a chief executive (the Reagan cabinet). Council, ministry, committee, directors, official advisors, assembly, panel, administration. **2.** See closet, alcove.

Cable, *n.* See communication (2); chain (1); rope, thread; vehicle (1).

Cache, *n.* **1.** Hiding place (the arms were kept in the cache). Hideout, crypt, vault, warehouse, repository, depository, storehouse, store, locker. **2.** Something hidden (a cache of arms). Stockpile, hoard, collection, reserve, accumulation, treasure, fund.

Cachet, *n.* See characteristic (1).

Cackle, *n.* See noise.

Cad, *n.* A knave, dastard, or villain. See boor, wrongdoer, crook.

Cadaver, *n.* A dead body. Remains, carcass, "stiff," deceased, body, bones. See also corpse.

Cadet, *n.* See sailor; military; scholar.

Cadger, *n.* See pauper.

Cadre, *n.* See group (1).

Caesarean section, *n.* Incision into abdominal wall and uterus to reach the fetus.

Café, *n.* See inn.

Cafeteria, *n.* See inn, commissary (2).

Cage, *n., v.* See vessel (2); jail, cell; chain (2); confine.

Caged, *adj.* See captive.

Cahoots, *n.* See collaboration.

Caisson, *n.* See vessel (2); vehicle (1).

Cajole, *v.* See persuade; entice, entrap, cheat (1).

Calamitous, *adj.* See fatal, bad, deleterious, adverse (4); calamity.

Calamity, *n.* An extreme misfortune (the earthquake was a calamity not covered by the insurance policy). Disaster, catastrophe, tragedy, act of God, shock, mishap, cataclysm, blow, grievous loss, adversity, casualty, affliction, scourge, fatality, hardship, reverse, ill fortune, misery, bad luck, distress, collapse, tribulation, destruction, mischance, wreck, staggering setback, burden, trial, ruin, ruination, heartache, anguish, stroke, ill, evil, blight, undoing, downfall. *Ant.* Blessing.

Calculable, *adj.* See ascertainable.

Calculate, *v.* **1.** To compute (calculate the damages). Figure, ascertain, add up, reckon, measure, assess, count, caste, determine, tally, subtract, divide, multiply, appraise, work out, value, place a value on, account, enumerate, quantify. **2.** To estimate (calculate the risks). Predict, judge, forecast, consider, evaluate, gauge, survey, deduce, infer, imagine.

Calculated, *adj.* Intended by design to produce a certain effect or result (a calculated decision). Premeditated, thought-out, intended, determined, considered, planned, deliberate, willed, aimed, directed. See also conscious (2). *Ant.* Haphazard.

Calculating, *adj.* See devious; cautious.

Calculation, *n.* See estimate (1), census.

Caldron, *n.* See vessel (2).

Calendar, *n.* **1.** A list of cases awaiting trial or other action by the court. Docket, trial list. See record (2). **2.** A system of dividing time into years, months, weeks, and days. Almanac. See record (2). **3.** A schedule (the calendar of events). Program, agenda, timetable, menology, log, record, chronicle, register, diary, annals, journal, table, chronology, history, list, order.

Calendar year The period from January 1 to December 31 inclusive.

Calf, *n.* See animal (1).

Caliber, *n.* See quality, capacity (2).

Calibrate, *v.* See adjust (1).

Calisthenics, *n.* See athletics.

Call 1. *v.* To make a request or demand (called to testify). Command, instruct, requisition, insist on, prescribe, order, require, petition, appeal, adjure, entreat, beseech, implore, solicit, press, supplicate, bid, pray, ask, invite, appeal to. **2.** *v.* To assemble (call for a bench conference). Summon, subpoena, convene, collect, ask to come, call for, convoke, muster, unite, mobilize, gather, draft, rally, hail, page, congregate, beckon. **3.** *v.* To demand payment (to call a note). **4.** *v.* To characterize (they called it an infraction of the rules). Name, designate, label, term, classify, identify, denominate, christen, baptize, entitle, tag, dub, define, style, describe, phrase, nominate, title. **5.** *v.* To proclaim (call a strike). Announce, decree, declare, signal, report, herald. **6.** *n.* An option to buy a specified number of shares of stock. **7.** *n.* A demand for payment. **8.** *n.* A visible, natural object or landmark designated in a conveyance of land that is a limit or boundary to that land. **9.** *n.* A demand by a company for persons to fulfill their promise to buy stock. **10.** *n.* See citation (1).

Callable, *adj.* Subject to be called and paid for before maturity (callable bonds). Redeemable, retrievable, reclaimable.

Call girl, *n.* See prostitute.

Calligraphy, *n.* See handwriting.

Calling, *n.* Occupation, mission (her calling was the law). Profession, vocation, business, trade, employment, walk of life, craft, pursuit, career, work, office, position, specialty, line, métier, forte, field, activity, enterprise, job, undertaking, livelihood, lifework, situation, berth, stint, station, assignment, task, aptitude, art, subject, sphere, practice, specialization.

Callous, *adj.* Hardened, insensitive (a callous disregard for his safety). Unfeeling, heartless, compassionless, obdurate, blunt, indifferent, tough, cold, uncaring, inured, apathetic, adamant, unyielding, impassive, impervious, unsympathetic, relentless, brutal, inflexible, unresponsive, unmoved, intolerant, cruel, indurated, ruthless, churlish, surly, merciless, severe, crotchety. *Ant.* Compassionate.

Callow, *adj.* See juvenile (2).

Call to mind See recall (3), recognize (1); recollection, memory.

Calm, *adj., v.* See quiet (1, 2), patient (3), deliberate (3), reasonable, cautious, composure; stabilize, mitigate, assuage.

Calumnious, *adj.* Derogatory, defamatory (a calumnious report). Libelous, slanderous, false, malicious, pejorative, vituperative, scurrilous, abusive, insulting, contumelious, detracting, invidious, scandalous, maligning, traducing, disparaging, debasing, malevolent, opprobrious, assailing, stigmatizing, backbiting, critical, humiliating, slighting, damaging, smearing, contemptuous, insinuating, caustic, disrespectful, outrageous. *Ant.* Laudatory.

Calumny, *n.* See slander.

Camaraderie, *n.* See company (3), goodwill (2), affinity, community (3), companionship.

Camel, *n.* See animal (1).

Camera, *n.* A judge's chamber. See in camera.

Camouflage, *v.* See conceal, cloak, disguise.

Camp, *n.* See home; military; division (2).

Campaign, *n.* An organized effort to promote a cause or person (a campaign for prison reform). Endeavor, operation, battle, crusade, strategy, action, undertaking, venture, plan, quest, movement, drive, attack, blitz, tactics, course of action, design, expedition, mobilization, struggle, organization.

Campbell, Lord See Lord Campbell's Act, wrongful death action.

Camper, *n.* See vehicle (1).

Campfire, *n.* See fire (1).

Campus, *n.* See school (1).

Can, *n.* See vessel (2).

Canal, *n.* See river, conduit (2).

Canard, *n.* See rumor, slander; fiction.

Canary, *n.* See animal (1).

Cancel, *v.* **1.** To obliterate (they cancelled the contract). Strike out, cross out, destroy, expunge, erase, revoke, recall, annul, void, invalidate, rescind, abandon, repeal, surrender, waive, terminate, render null and void, quash, avoid, negate, abort, suspend, reverse, withdraw, blot out, abrogate, set aside, countermand, recall, call off, drop, end, relinquish, disavow, abjure, veto, break off, abnegate, dispense with, vitiate, retract, renege, deny, overrule, override, dismiss, exterminate, eradicate, excise. **2.** To neutralize (the remorse tended to cancel the hostility). Atone for, counterbalance, offset, countervail, allow for, redeem, make up for, repay, balance out. *Ant.* Enact.

Cancellation, *n.* Destruction of the force, effectiveness, or validity of something (the tearing constituted a cancellation of the will). Abrogation, annulment, destruction, expungement, revocation, invalidation, rescission, abandonment, recision, repeal, termination, negation, abortion, suspension, withdrawal, retraction, vitiation, extermination, eradication, countermand, waiver, deletion, reversal, discontinuation, dissolution, liquidation, dismissal, renunciation, repudiation, extinction, elimination, relinquishment, excision, recall, counterorder, erasure. *Ant.* Implementation.

Cancelled check A check that bears the notation of cancellation of the drawee bank as having been paid and charged to the drawer.

Cancer, *n.* See disease.

Candid, *adj.* See outright, open (4), direct (6), blatant; honest.

Candidate, *n.* One who seeks an office, privilege, or honor; one who is put forward by others for an office, privilege, or honor (a candidate for judge). Nominee, aspirant, runner, solicitant, applicant, hopeful, campaigner, contestant, entrant, challenger, officeseeker, contender, competitor.

Candor, *n.* Openness, sincerity, frankness, forthrightness, boldness, bluntness, free speaking, honesty, plain speaking, simplicity. See honest, honor (3), outright.

Canine, *n.* See animal (2).

Canister, *n.* See vessel (2).

Cannabis, *n.* See drug (2).

Cannibalistic, *adj.* See wild (3), cruel, gross (1), base (2), obscene.

112

Cannon, *n.* See weapon, arms, ballistics.

Canny, *adj.* See careful, cautious, apt (3), able, deceptive.

Canoe, *n.* See vessel (1).

Canon, *n.* **1.** A law (canons of professional responsibility). Rule, ordinance, legislation, statute, act, code, requirement, mandate, imperative, decree, edict, dogma, doctrine, commandment, command, precept, dictate, order, prescript, prescription, instruction, general rule. **2.** Principle, standard (the canons of behavior). Yardstick, maxim, criterion, bench mark, model, ethic, pattern, formula, verity, touchstone, norm, test.

Canonize, *v.* See anoint, honor (2), approve.

Canon law Ecclesiastical law; Roman church jurisprudence.

Canons of construction rules, principles, or guidelines that can be of help in interpreting statutes, regulations, wills, and other written documents.

Canopy, *n.* See awning, ceiling (2), protection.

Cantankerous, *adj.* See inflexible, callous, arbitrary, rude, contentious (1), contumacious, difficult (3).

Canteen, *n.* See market (1); inn; military.

Canton, *n.* See district.

Canvass, *v.* **1.** To examine and count the votes cast in an election in order to determine authenticity (to canvass the returns). Scrutinize, investigate, review, analyze, inquire into, pursue, evaluate, dispute, audit, count, follow up, consider, study, inspect, debate, dissect, explore, probe, poll, pursue. **2.** To solicit votes, contributions, opinions, etc. (to canvass the neighborhood). Survey, appeal for, petition, sift, invite, entreat, press, implore, urge.

Canyon, *n.* See valley, abyss, crevice.

Cap, *v.* See complete (1), cover, culminate.

Capability, *n.* See ability, capacity.

Capable, *adj.* **1.** Having the capacity or ability (capable of doing serious bodily harm). Having the power, fitting, susceptible, open, subject, prone, accessible, admitting, predisposed to, likely to, receptive to. **2.** Competent (a capable paralegal). Intelligent, qualified, able, worthy, effective, clever, skillful, gifted, adroit, accomplished, deft, fit, proficient, talented, experienced, brilliant, ingenious, expert, sagacious, learned, adequate, suited, effectual, potent, strong, worthy, smart, versed, masterful. *Ant.* Incapable.

Capacitate, *v.* See enable, qualify (1).

Capacity, *n.* **1.** Legal qualification or competency to do something; the ability to understand the nature and effects of one's acts (capacity to contract; capacity to sue). Power, license, faculty, facility, aptitude, ability, capability, authority, right, authorization, liberty, privilege, sanction, leave, jurisdiction, prerogative. **2.** Skill (a judge of formidable capacity). Understanding, competence, aptitude, acumen, potentiality, talent, endowment, forte, propensity, caliber, stature, sense, gift, readiness, know-how, experience, expertise, judgment, sufficiency, genius, brains, mind, bent, discernment, strength, sagacity, perspicacity. **3.** Occupation or function (the judge spoke in her capacity as chairperson). Post, office, assignment, duty, responsibility, service, job, place, position. *Ant.* Incapacity.

Cape, *n.* See clothes.

Caper, *n.* See antic.

Cap gun, *n.* See weapon.

Capias, *n.* (*Lat.*) "That you take." A name for a category of writs that requires an officer to take the body of the defendant into custody. For example, "capias ad respondendum" is a judicial writ that commands the sheriff to take the defendant and bring him or her to court in order to answer the charges of the plaintiff.

Capita, *n.* Head, person, body. See per capita.

Capital

Capital, *n.* **1.** Accumulated assets used for the production of profit (without capital, the corporation could not expand). Resources, funds, credits, cash, reserves, possessions, property, liquid assets, working capital, available means, wherewithal, balances, income, money, wealth, principal, stock, holdings, receipts. **2.** An owner's equity in a business (a loan against capital). Investment, interest, allotment, portion, stake. **3.** The sum total of corporate stock. *Ant.* Debts, liabilities.

Capital case, crime, or offense One for which death is the possible punishment.

Capital expenditure Expenditure for long-term betterments or additions that is chargeable to the capital asset account and is added to the basis of the property improved.

Capital gain Profit (gain) realized on the sale or exchange of a capital asset.

Capitalist, *n.* See entrepreneur, financier, employer, owner, manager.

Capitalization, *n.* The total amount of the various securities issued by a corporation. See capital, capitalize.

Capitalize, *v.* **1.** To supply with investment funds (the company was capitalized beyond its expectations). Finance, sponsor, stake, subsidize, invest, "bankroll," back, promote, aid, advance, contribute, furnish support, provide money for, provide capital for, set up. See also fund (1). **2.** To convert a periodical payment into an equivalent capital sum. To compute the present value of an income extended over a period of time. **3.** To use to one's advantage (he capitalized on his opponent's failure to file). Benefit, profit, exploit, utilize, take advantage of, avail oneself of, employ, convert to good use, make capital of, "milk," seize the chance, manipulate. *Ant.* Withdraw; bypass, ignore.

Capital punishment Punishment by death. Death sentence, execution.

Capital stock All shares representing ownership of a business, including preferred stock and common stock. The amount fixed by the charter to be subscribed and paid in or secured to be paid in by the shareholders.

Capital surplus Property paid into a corporation by the shareholders in excess of capital stock liability.

Capitation tax A tax or imposition upon the person. A per capita tax. See tax (1).

Capitulate, *v.* To acknowledge defeat (the union negotiators would not capitulate). Surrender, succumb, yield, give up, submit, give in, relent, accede, cede, "cave," come to terms, acquiesce, concur, soften, recant, bow, retract, assent, comply, resign.

Capitulation, *n.* See abandonment, abdication, concession (2); capitulate.

Capper, *n.* A decoy or lure for the purpose of swindling (a capper was used to obtain the funds). Deception, trick, trickery, chicanery, bait, shill, disguise, trap, inducement, camouflage, allurement.

Cap pistol, *n.* See weapon.

Caprice, *n.* The disposition to change one's mind impulsively; a sudden change of mind; an illogical notion (the verdict was so excessive as to indicate unaccountable caprice). Whim, arbitrariness, quirk, eccentricity, fancy, craze, notion, fad, vagary, conceit, peculiarity, freak, crotchet, fantasy; unreasonableness.

Capricious, *adj.* Impulsive; not based on standards (the warden's denial was capricious). Whimsical, erratic, illogical, vacillating, fickle, impulsive, unpredictable, volatile, variable, mercurial, irresponsible, unreasonable, fanciful, freakish, uncertain, arbitrary, flighty, indecisive, wavering, inconsistent, inconstant, unstable, lawless, frivolous, undisciplined, irresolute, unsystematic. *Ant.* Decisive, consistent, responsible.

Capsize, *v.* To turn over. Overturn, overthrow, keel over, upset, tip over, flip over, turn turtle, upend.

Captain, *n.* See manager, chief (1), sailor; military.

Caption, *n.* The heading or introductory part of a pleading, court opinion, memo, or other document which identifies what it is, who is involved, the court or agency, etc. Title, inscription, rubric, imprint, legend, headnote, preface, superscription, banner, flag, designation, annotation, identification.

Captious, *adj.* See difficult (3), critical (2), contentious, querulous, litigious, disobedient.

Captivate, *v.* See entice, entrap, interest (5), bait (3).

Captivating, *adj.* See moving (1), compelling, touching, intriguing, attractive, enjoyable, irresistible.

Captive 1. *adj.* Not at liberty to depart with ease (captive audience). Confined, caged, imprisoned, penned, enslaved, incarcerated, locked up, oppressed. **2.** *n.* A prisoner (no captives were taken by the hijacker). Hostage, internee, convict, inmate, victim, bondman, slave, thrall. *Ant.* Independent; free person.

Captivity, *n.* See restraint (1).

Capture 1. *n.* The taking of property or persons by force, threats, or strategy (the capture of the fleet). Seizure, apprehension, ensnaring, arrest, trapping, appropriation, occupation, recovery, catching. **2.** *v.* To take property or persons by force, threats, or strategy (she was captured by the police in Boston). Seize, apprehend, take, ensnare, arrest, appropriate, catch, subdue, impress, incarcerate, restrict, imprison, corner, grasp, trap, take prisoner, take captive, take into custody, take possession of, attach, confine. *Ant.* Relinquishment; release.

Car, *n.* See vehicle (1).

Carat, *n.* A measure of weight for precious stones equivalent to $3\frac{1}{6}$ grains Troy, or 200 milligrams.

Caravan, *n.* See vehicle (1); convoy, group (1).

Carbon, *n.* See copy (1).

Carcass, *n.* See cadaver, corpse, body (4).

Cardinal, *adj.* **1.** Of the greatest importance (the cardinal principle). Chief, pivotal, foremost, prime, dominant, basic, central, outstanding, head, necessary, indispensable, principal, vital, essential, leading, major, fundamental, intrinsic, paramount, key, main, focal, first, preeminent, primary, elemental, elementary, material, overriding, utmost, preponderant, commanding, absolute, supreme, predominant, top, crowning, prevailing. **2.** See clergy. *Ant.* Secondary, subordinate.

Care 1. *n.* Watchful attention; the manner in which a reasonable person will act in the face of risks (he approached the animal with care). Concern, diligence, discretion, caution, prudence, regard, security, vigilance, solicitude, conscientiousness, prudence, circumspection, alertness, wakefulness, heed, thought, discrimination, scrupulousness, consideration, interest, carefulness. **2.** *n.* Worry (the cares of management). Distress, concern, anxiety, mental distress, grief, suffering, burden, perplexity, trouble, stress, strain, load, responsibility, sorrow, pressure, heartache, apprehension, tribulation, anguish, onus, disquietude, tension, solicitude, unease. **3.** *n.* Protection (the child was placed in the care of the state). Guardianship, control, oversight, custody, superintendence, surveillance, charge, supervision, responsibility, guidance, tutelage, vigil, keeping, ministration, attention. **4.** *v.* To be concerned (he did not care what happened to the employee). Be worried, bother about, be interested, be uneasy, be apprehensive, mind, bother, regard, heed, be troubled, be solicitous. *Ant.* Carelessness (1); delight (2); ignore (4).

Careen, *v.* See lean.

Career, *n.* Occupation or profession (her career as an attorney). Business, line, employment, calling, vocation, craft, trade, inclination, work, livelihood, pursuit, post, office, specialty, walk of life, métier, job, activity, lifework, position. *Ant.* Hobby.

Carefree, *adj.* See casual (3), innocent (2), happy, festive, juvenile (2), active (3), indifferent (2), debonair, safe (2).

Careful, *adj.* Cautious (a careful design). Prudent, attentive, mindful, wary, heedful, alert, foresighted, painstaking, provident, discreet, guarded, observant, vigilant, scrupulous, solicitous, circumspect, particular, precise, thoughtful, conscientious, exact, critical, meticulous, accurate, steady, correct. *Ant.* Reckless.

Carefulness, *n.* See caution (3).

Careless, *adj.* Not watchful; the absence of care (careless driving). Negligent, unreasonable, irresponsible, unwary, inattentive, heedless, neglectful, thoughtless, incautious, indiscreet, reckless, unmindful, unconcerned, uncaring, sloppy, unthinking, inconsiderate, unobservant, remiss, disregardful, inadvertent, oblivious, lax, unfit, slack, rash, slipshod, absentminded, imprudent, injudicious, casual, wasteful, cursory, superficial, hasty, precipitate, impetuous, lackadaisical. *Ant.* Cautious.

Caress, *v.* To fondle. Hold, embrace, pat, stroke, kiss, cuddle, touch, hug, snuggle, rub, massage, pet, squeeze, feel, paw, partake, nudge, graze, brush.

Caretaker, *n.* One who takes care of a person, property, or an estate (the will appointed him caretaker of the account). Attendant, custodian, administrator, superintendent, warden, curator, overseer, manager, guard, keeper, gatekeeper, steward, porter, watchman, janitor, jailer, archivist, governor, supervisor, minister, sentry. See also conservator, fiduciary (1).

Carfare, *n.* See fare, charge (9), fee (1), price.

Cargo, *n.* Goods transported on a truck, train, ship, or other carrier. Freight, load, haul, merchandise, lading, burden, shipment, consignment, capacity, baggage, payload, provisions, contents, carload, truckload, freightload, trainload, commodities, stock.

Carhop, *n.* See servant, employee.

Caricature, *n.* A distorted representation. Travesty, spoof, exaggeration, parody, mockery, cartoon, takeoff, lampoon, burlesque, farce, satire, portrait. See also imitation, slander (1).

Caring, *n.* See love, affection, concern; affectionate.

Carload, *n.* See cargo.

Carnage, *n.* See murder, homicide, assassination.

Carnal, *adj.* Pertaining to the bodily passions (carnal abuse). Sexual, lustful, fleshly, sensual, salacious, prurient, animal, libidinous, lascivious, lewd, bestial, erotic, lecherous, gross, concupiscent, wanton. See also obscene, physical. *Ant.* Spiritual.

Carnal abuse An act of assault or debauchery of the female sexual organs via the genital organs of the male, short of penetration.

Carnal knowledge Sexual intercourse. Coitus, copulation, penetration, rape, coupling, venereal act, sex act, consummation, coition, fornication.

Carnival, *n.* See celebration (2), amusement.

Carnivorous, *adj.* See predatory.

Carouse, *v., n.* See dissipate (1); spree.

Carp, *v.* See complain (2), quibble.

Carpenter, *n.* See builder, architect, laborer.

Carpet, *n.* See rug.

Carping, *adj.* See contentious (1), critical (2), difficult (3).

Carriage, *n.* **1.** Transportation of goods, freight, or passengers (the business of carriage). Carrying, portage, truckage, shipment, conveyance, transference. **2.** A vehicle to carry things (he rode in a carriage). Coach, wagon, car, cart, chaise, conveyance, buggy. See also vehicle (1). **3.** Posture (a judge of stately carriage). Stance, attitude, appearance, demeanor, behavior, cast, deportment, manner, bearing, conduct, air, mien, presence, comportment, poise.

Carrier, *n.* An individual or company engaged in transporting passengers or goods for hire. Porter, transporter, runner, conveyor, bearer, ferrier, forwarder, shipper. See also messenger.

Carry, *v.* **1.** To bear; to transport (carry the liquid). Remove, convey, cart, haul, take, convoy, bring, tote, transfer, lug, shift, transplant, transmit, propel, lift, deliver, "schlep," ferry. **2.** To support (the check carried him through the month). Sustain, uphold, buttress, prop, maintain, shoulder, bear up, bear, underpin, undertake, fortify, strengthen, reinforce. **3.** To communicate (the reporter carries judicial highlights). Publish, print, offer, disseminate, transmit. **4.** To result in (the crime carries a 10-year sentence). Conclude, end, culminate, eventuate. **5.** To succeed (the argument carried the day). Achieve, complete, gain, prevail, triumph, accomplish, score, win, influence, conquer. **6.** To have as a characteristic (her opinion carried great weight). Merit, deserve, qualify, entitle, earn, garner, acquire, yield, win.

Carry-back, *n.* A provision in the tax law that permits a taxpayer to apply the net operating loss in one year to recompute the tax owed in several preceding years.

Carrying, *n.* See conveyance (2).

Carrying away The act of removal by which the crime of larceny is completed and which is essential to it (taking and carrying away the property of another). Asportation, expropriation, commandeering, purloining, removing, transporting, abducting, conveying, kidnapping, shanghaiing, dragging away.

Carrying charge Charge made by the creditor, in addition to interest, for providing installment credit. Overhead, operating cost, expense.

Carrying out, *n.* See commission (4).

Carry out, *v.* See commit (2), comply, conduct (2).

Carry-over, *n.* Net operating loss for one year that may be used or applied in following years. See remainder, residue.

Carry through, *v.* See complete (1).

Cart, *n., v.* See vehicle; carry (1).

Carta, *n.* A charter or deed (Magna Carta).

Carte blanche, *n.* **1.** A blank sheet of paper that is signed. **2.** Unlimited authority (the broker was given carte blanche in making the purchase). Free reign, free license, unconditional power or authority, free hand, full powers, full discretion, permit, sanction, passkey, blank check, liberty. See also freedom. *Ant.* Narrow instructions.

Cartel, *n.* **1.** A combination of producers of any product joined together to control the production, sale, and price of the product in order to obtain a monopoly (costs doubled because of the actions of the cartel). Syndicate, alliance, trust, block, union, coalition, consortium, association, merger, amalgamation, bloc, affiliation, league, federation, confederation, pact, consort, combine. **2.** An agreement between enemies while the hostilities continue (a cartel to exchange prisoners). Accord, mutual understanding, concordat, compact, bargain, covenant, stipulation, convention.

Carton, *n.* See vessel (2).

Cartoon, *n.* See caricature, imitation.

Cartridge, *n.* See ammunition; vessel (2).

Carve, *v.* See divide, cut; engrave.

Cascade, *n., v.* See river; fall (2).

Case, *n.* **1.** An action or lawsuit (the case of Smith v. Jones). Suit, litigation, cause, action at law, suit in equity, controversy, dispute, proceeding, judicial proceeding, contest, matter, hearing, inquiry, debate, process, trial. **2.** See action on the case. **3.** An occurrence or example (a case of misidentification). Instance, happening, phenomenon, occasion, illustration, affair, paradigm, sample, adventure, concern, model, event, chance, exemplification, representation, specimen, episode, business, circumstance, situation. **4.** A statement of arguments (she stated her case first). Reasons, reasoning, position, argumentation, thesis, rationale, evidence, hypothesis, exposition, ground, foundation. **5.** State of affairs (if that is the case, we should settle). Set of circumstances, situation, status, standing, posture, course of events, predicament, dilemma, condition, plight, set of facts, factors, reality. **6.** See wrapper, package, vessel (2).

Case agreed on See agreed case.

Case and controversy Claims or contentions of litigants brought before the court for adjudication by regular proceedings established for the protection or enforcement of rights, or for the prevention, redress, or punishment of wrongs. If the judicial power is capable of acting on the claim or contention of a party, it is a case or controversy. See actual controversy, justiciable.

Case in chief That part of a trial in which the party with the initial burden of proof presents its evidence and then rests.

Case of first impression See first impression.

Cash, *n.* Money or its equivalent. Currency, legal tender, change, capital, notes, assets, funds, specie, ready money, coin, coinage, bills, "bread," means, resources, reserves, medium of exchange, pecuniary assets, negotiable check, treasure, wherewithal.

Cash basis A system of accounting that treats as income only that which is actually received and as an expense only that which is actually paid out. *Ant.* Accrual basis.

Cash flow The cash generated from property. The amount of cash left over after all payments are made.

Cashier 1. *v.* To dismiss with dishonor (the engineer was cashiered). Discharge, fire, disbar, "sack," remove from office, oust, expel, unseat, unfrock, displace, depose. **2.** *n.* See teller, bookkeeper, clerk (2), accountant, treasurer.

Cashier's check A check drawn by a bank upon itself and issued by an authorized officer of the bank, directed to another person evidencing the fact that the payee is authorized to demand and receive from the bank, upon presentation, the amount of money represented by the check.

Cash market value See fair market value.

Cash value The price in ready money (no deferred payments) that property would bring at a private sale, not at a forced or auction sale.

Cask, *n.* See vessel (2).

Casket, *n.* See vessel (2); burial.

Cast 1. *v.* To deposit formally (cast a ballot). Register, record, vote, select, make a choice, establish, mark. **2.** *v.* To discard (cast all suspicion aside). Dismiss, ignore, reject, "deep six," throw away, shed, hurl, propel, disband, pitch, heave, set aside, toss out. **3.** *v.* To throw (cast the first stone). Launch, shoot, catapult, force, impel, radiate, eject, send, emit. **4.** *n.* The form in which a thing is constructed (metal cast). Shape, form, impression, model, mold, casing, pattern, stamp, replica, embodiment. See also configuration. **5.** *n.* Appearance (a dignified cast). Demeanor, mien, look, set, complexion, air, style, tone, guise, carriage, deportment, bearing. **6.** *n.* See copy (1).

Castaway, *adj., n.* See abandoned (1); tramp.

Caste, *n.* See class.

Castigate, *v.* To criticize severely (the judge castigated the tardy attorney). Rebuke, berate, scold, admonish, upbraid, discipline, punish, call to account, censure, flagellate, dress down, chastise, vituperate, excoriate, reprimand, chide, penalize, remonstrate, take to task, correct, smite, pummel, rail, baste, tongue-lash, drub, slap, flail, scourge, trounce, scathe. *Ant.* Compliment.

Castigation, *n.* See obloquy, correction (1), censure; castigate.

Castrate, *v.* To remove the testicles. Geld, emasculate, asexualize. See also disable, castigate.

Casual, *adj.* **1.** Unexpected (casual meeting). Accidental, random, fortuitous, haphazard, chance, unplanned, unintentional, unforeseen, spontaneous, offhand, serendipitous, hit-or-miss, unpremeditated, uncertain, unarranged, undesigned, extemporaneous, impromptu, impulsive. **2.** Irregular (casual employment). Temporary, occasional, impermanent, intermittent, erratic, periodic, infrequent. **3.** Indifferent (casual inspection). Superficial, informal, perfunctory, careless, negligent, aimless, blasé, half-hearted, lackadaisical, passing, apathetic, cursory, vague, aimless, purposeless, indiscriminate, unorganized, unexacting, unsystematic. *Ant.* Planned; permanent; directed.

Casualty, *n.* **1.** A serious or fatal accident; an accident that occurs by chance or without design (the insurance policy covered the casualty). Mishap, misfortune, disaster, loss, miscarriage, calamity, tragedy, fatality, emergency, catastrophe, cataclysm, bad fortune, setback. **2.** A person or thing lost, injured, or destroyed (he was the first casualty of the war). Injured, victim, prey, underdog, sufferer, wounded, missing. *Ant.* Intentional injury; beneficiary.

Casualty loss The complete or partial destruction of property resulting from an identifiable event of a sudden, unexpected, or unusual nature, e.g., flood, car accident.

Casus omissus An event or contingency for which no provision is made; a case omitted.

Cat, *n.* See animal (1).

Cataclysm, *n.* A sudden, large, violent change (the earthquake was a cataclysm). Catastrophe, disaster, eruption, debacle, calamity, upheaval, inundation, devastation, convulsion, ruination, collapse, tragedy, staggering blow. *Ant.* Good fortune.

Cataclysmic, *adj.* See adverse (2), bad (4), deleterious.

Catacomb, *n.* See cemetery.

Catalogue, *v., n.* See list; record (1, 2), codify (1), digest (3), organize.

Catalyst, *n.* That which precipitates action (she was a catalyst for reform). Stimulus, stimulation, impetus, motivation, goad, instigation, incitement, push, cause, provocation, motive, propellant, abettor, strategist, activator, prompter, leader, animator, incentive, inducement, sparkplug, accelerator, trigger, force, fuel, inspiration. *Ant.* Antagonist.

Catapult, *v.* See jettison (1), send, shoot.

Catastrophe, *n.* A disaster. Tragedy, calamity, casualty, mishap, ruin, hardship, misfortune, accident, cataclysm, devastation, mischance, miscarriage, crash, convulsion, upheaval, breakdown, collapse, emergency, scourge, debacle, distress, blow, reverse, destruction, ravage, decimation. *Ant.* Good fortune.

Catastrophic, *adj.* See deleterious, bad (4), adverse (2).

Catcall, *n.* See contempt (2).

Catch, *v.* See find (1), seize (1).

Catchall, *n.* A receptacle for odds and ends (catchall clause in a contract). Container, holder, depository, repository. See also vessel (2).

Catching, *adj.* See contagious; attractive.

Catch-22, *n.* See plight, contradiction.

Categorical, *adj.* **1.** Unconditional (categorical denial). Unqualified, absolute, definite, unreserved, unequivocal, emphatic, express, unlimited, total, utter, sheer, conclusive, definitive, dogmatic, flat, positive, unmitigated, decisive, convincing, clear-cut, authoritative, undeniable, ultimate, unmistakable, sure, pronounced, beyond all question, indisputable, forceful. **2.** Pertaining to a category (categorical assistance). Program, classification, grouping. *Ant.* Qualified; general.

Categorize, *v.* Classify, codify, organize (1), divide (1).

Category, *n.* See class (1), classification (2), kind (1), division, characterization.

Cater, *v.* See pander (2), furnish.

Cathedral, *n.* See church.

Catholic, *adj.* See comprehensive; religious, religion.

Cathouse, *n.* See brothel.

Cattle, *n.* See animal (1).

Caucasian, *n.* See race (1).

Caucus, *n.* A meeting of the members of a particular group (the gay rights caucus at the convention). Assembly, gathering, conference, session, council, conclave, summit, convocation, synod, parley, consultation, assemblage.

Causa, *n.* (*Lat.*) A cause, reason, occasion, motive, or inducement.

Causal, *adj.* Involving or indicating a cause (the storm was a causal factor in the resulting damage). Causative, originating, creative, formative, instrumental, germinal, generating, productive, determinative, primary, pivotal, producing, stimulative, influencing, decisive, active.

Causa mortis (*Lat.*) In contemplation of approaching death.

Causation, *n.* The fact of being the cause of something. The act by which an effect is produced. Origination, production, creation, manufacture, root, invention, formation, formulation, siring, fathering, mothering, spawning.

Cause 1. *n.* Something that precedes and brings about or helps to bring about an effect or result (the drug was the cause of death). Origin, source, agent, mover, parent, author, sire, reason, inducement, stimulus, but-for, provocation, occasion, genesis, instigation, stimulant, factor, derivation, beginning, ancestry, wellspring, fountainhead, inspiration, fount, foundation, nucleus, cradle, germ, embryo, basis, antecedent, mainspring, motive, incentive, determinant, generator, originator, producer, manufacturer. **2.** *v.* To be the cause or occasion of (he caused the injury). Bring into existence, author, create, produce, compel, effect, generate, institute, bring on, bring about, procreate, sire, father, spawn, found, develop, induce, give birth to, introduce, breed, cultivate, engineer, provoke, compel, effectuate, inspire, launch, motivate, evoke, raise, start, initiate, engender, inaugurate, precipitate. **3.** *n.* A lawsuit (the cause will be heard today). Suit, judicial proceeding, litigation, action, action at law, suit in equity, trial, case, legal proceeding. **4.** *n.* Issue or aim (the cause of grand jury reform). Question, problem, topic, principle, goal, ideal, object, purpose, side, conviction, motive, objective; cause célèbre, **5.** *n.* See campaign.

Cause in fact An actual cause of something. That without which an event would not have occurred.

Cause of action The facts that give a person a right to judicial relief. A legally acceptable reason for suing. Right of action, claim for relief, ground for relief.

Causeway, *n.* A raised road or path through low lands, wet ground, or water. Highway, thruway, access road, artery, expressway, parkway, turnpike, concourse, roadway, thoroughfare, speedway.

Caustic, *adj.* Sarcastic (the opening statement contained caustic remarks about the opposing counsel). Cynical, bitter, contemptuous, derisive, hateful, astringent, acid, stinging, corrosive, acrimonious, burning, biting, severe, scathing, sharp, gnawing, brusque, sardonic, abrasive, venomous, malicious, tormenting, cutting, terse, stringent, pungent, satiric, tart, ironic, slashing, vicious, malevolent, ill-tempered, hostile, abrupt, cruel, mocking, curt, unkind, excoriating, rude, austere, torturous, invidious, mordant. *Ant.* Gracious.

Caution 1. *v.* To give notice of danger (they were cautioned about the explosives before they entered the room). Warn, put on guard, forewarn, admonish, exhort, advise, counsel, enjoin, apprise, alert, guide, inform, notify, alarm, portend, forebode, "tip off," give notice, serve notice, make aware, dissuade, signal. **2.** *n.* Warning (great caution was clearly needed). Alarm, forewarning, exhortation, admonition, caveat, alert, omen. **3.** *n.* Prudence (caution must be used in operating the machine). Care, carefulness, discretion, circumspection, attentiveness, heed, regard, deliberation, thought, alertness, wariness, vigilance, providence, forethought, foresight, discrimination, precaution, watchfulness, attention, restraint, mindfulness, conscientiousness, heedfulness. *Ant.* Dare; ignorance; carelessness.

Cautionary instruction That part of a judge's charge in which he or she instructs the jury to consider certain evidence only for a specific purpose.

Cautious, *adj.* Careful (a cautious driver). Prudent, circumspect, discreet, wary, heedful, vigilant, chary, provident, guarded, calculating, safe, considerate, precautious, scrupulous, shrewd, gingerly, alert, judicious, canny, foresighted, attentive, watchful, awake, on the alert, apprehensive, observant, suspicious, regardful, wakeful, prescient, on the lookout, on guard, prepared, deliberate. *Ant.* Impetuous, careless.

Cavalier, *adj.* See arrogant, pompous, casual (3), indifferent (2).

Cavalry, *n.* See military, sailor.

Cave, *n.* Hollow space below the earth's surface. Hole, tunnel, pit, dugout, cellar, cavity, grotto, cavern, den, underground chamber, chasm, subway. See also cell.

Caveat, *n.* A formal notice or warning. "Let him beware." (He filed a caveat to be sure that he would be heard on the issue of probating the will.) Admonition, forewarning, alarm, monition, notification, advance notice, caution, advisement, communication, announcement, prewarning, "red flag."

Caveat actor Let the doer or actor beware.

Caveat emptor "Let the buyer beware." A buyer must examine and judge the product on his or her own. No warranties given, at your own risk, without guarantee.

Cavern, *n.* See cave.

Cavil, *v.* See complain (2), quibble, censor (2).

Cavity, *n.* See cave, abyss, cell.

Cease, *v.* To come to an end; to become extinct (cease operating the factory). Stop, suspend, desist, break off, refrain, terminate, intermit, quit, discontinue, fail, stay, conclude, finish, close, pause, rest, abate, halt, quell, drop, forbear, silence, abrogate, idle, relax, withdraw, vacate, arrest, interrupt, stem, relinquish, annul, void, cancel, expire, extinguish, bring to an end, wind up, run out, cut off, culminate, put an end to, bring to completion, lapse. *Ant.* Commence.

Cease-fire, *n.* See respite, cessation.

Ceaseless, *adj.* See constant (1), continual, continuous, perpetual.

Cede, *v.* To surrender or yield (the board ceded jurisdiction to the commission). Relinquish, abandon, deliver, assign, grant, transfer, convey, resign, give up, hand over, waive, forsake, abnegate, discard, forgo, sacrifice, abdicate, shed, lay aside, turn over, bequeath, donate, render, renounce, sign away, capitulate, make over, vouchsafe, concede, release, abjure, transmit, deed, demise, remise. *Ant.* Retain.

Ceiling. *n.* **1.** An upper limit (a ceiling on interest). Maximum, top limit, lid, limitation, restriction, control, restraint, check, highest degree, optimum, ultimate, farthest point, extremity, pinnacle, zenith. **2.** Roof (the ceiling collapsed). Topside, cover, overhead, surface, canopy, eaves, awning, dome, roofing. *Ant.* Minimum; floor.

Celebrate

Celebrate, *v.* See honor (2), proclaim, dedicate, perform, conduct (2); exult.

Celebrated, *adj.* See notorious (1), popular, great, conspicuous.

Celebration, *n.* **1.** Solemnization (celebration of marriage). Formalization, formalities, consecration, procedure, observance, dedication, ceremonial rite. See also ceremony. **2.** Festivity (holiday celebration). Jubilee, gala, event, festival, party, revelry, spectacle, pageant. See also spree. **3.** Praise (a celebration of excellence). Honor, laudation, commendation, trumpeting, eulogizing, applauding, exaltation, homage, veneration, accolade, glorification, worship.

Celebrity, *n.* See notoriety, reputation, note (4), honor (3).

Celestial, *adj.* See religious.

Celibacy, *n.* The condition of being unmarried; refraining from intercourse. Abstinence, bachelorhood, monasticism, virginity, chastity, spinsterhood, continence, single life. See also temperance, abstention; solitary.

Cell, *n.* A small confined area. Closet, hole, cage, solitary abode, cavity, cloister, recess, lockup, jail, prison, niche, compartment, stall, box, den, chamber, cubicle.

Cement, *v.* See cohere (1), connect (1), join (1), lock.

Cemetery, *n.* Burial ground. Graveyard, memorial park, necropolis, potter's field, ossuary, churchyard, catacomb.

Censor 1. *n.* A person who examines material in order to identify what is objectionable (the censor banned the book). Examiner, reviewer, inspector, critic, caviler, censurer, expurgator. **2.** *v.* To examine material in order to identify that which is objectionable (the film was censored). Examine, review, inspect, screen, criticize, cavil, control, police, judge, oversee. **3.** *v.* To remove objectionable material (the sex scene was censored). Delete, expurgate, veto, erase, excise, "blip," bowdlerize, edit, red-pencil, restrain, restrict, purge, cut, purify, clean up, amend, abridge, ban, suppress, disallow, quash, eliminate, prohibit, forbid, proscribe.

Censorship, *n.* Reviewing publications in order to identify and remove objectionable material (press censorship). Deletion, expurgation, veto, erasure, excision, editing, restriction, purification, abridgement, amendment, banning, suppression, disallowance, elimination, prohibition, proscription, quashing, abolition, stifling, blockage, blackout, impediment, bowdlerization, cancellation, bar, ban.

Censure 1. *n.* An official reprimand (she resigned after she received notice of the censure). Condemnation, denunciation, blame, rebuke, stricture, severe criticism, reprehension, reproof, disapproval, animadversion, scolding, castigation, accusation, vituperation, upbraiding, tirade, fulmination, disapprobation, admonition, invective, chiding, remonstrance, complaint, dressing down, tongue-lashing. **2.** *v.* To reprimand officially (the bar censured the attorney). Condemn, denounce, blame, criticize severely, disapprove, scold, castigate, upbraid, chide, admonish, reproach, find fault with, reprehend, reject, disdain, stigmatize, reprove, arraign, denunciate, proscribe, decry, deprecate, disparage, rail against, inveigh against, assail, recriminate, chastise, denigrate, rebuff, "chew out," impugn. *Ant.* Commendation; praise.

Census, *n.* An official counting of people (the 1990 census). Tabulation, computation, tally, statistics, demography, calculation, enumeration, registration, poll, measurement.

Center 1. *n.* Middle part (the center of the graph). Midpoint, middle point, dead center, central position, median, axis. **2.** *n.* A focal point or main part (the center of attention). Point of concentration, point of focus, point of convergence, core, nucleus, heart, crux, kernel, axis, interior, pivot, cornerstone, nerve center, essence, basis, substance, quintessence, sum and substance, gravamen, principal part, base, cardinal point. **3.** *v.* To place in the center; to concentrate on (the judge told the attorneys to center on the hearsay issue). Focus, centralize, converge, congregate, collect, unite, meet, direct, zero in on. *Ant.* Edge; subsidiary matter; scatter.

Central, *adj.* **1.** At or near the middle (the clerk's office is in a central location). Center, midpoint, middle position, halfway, centermost, focal, inner, midmost, intermediate, mid, median, interior, inner, internal. **2.** Dominant (the central issue in the case). Main, pivotal, critical, fundamental, essential, basic, substantial, quintessential, cardinal, principal, vital, causal, indispensable, chief, paramount, key, leading, predominant, crucial, primary, foremost, uppermost, requisite, supreme, prime, salient, important, all-absorbing, controlling. *Ant.* Outer; marginal.

Centralize, *v.* To concentrate power and authority in a central location or body; to unite (they centralized the administrative process). Consolidate, amalgamate, aggregate, systematize, streamline, converge, congregate, coalesce, combine, fuse, group, incorporate, delocalize, focalize, integrate, join, focus, come together, collect, ally, absorb, assemble, amass, merge, converge, fuse, organize, synthesize. *Ant.* Decentralize, scatter.

Century, *n.* One hundred years. See epic, cycle.

Cepit (*Lat.*) "He took."

Cerebral, *adj.* See academic (2), learned, literary (2), cultivated.

Ceremonial, *adj.* Pertaining to a ceremony (ceremonial occasion). Ritualistic, formal, solemn, liturgical, sacramental, conventional, stereotyped, pompous, routine.

Ceremonial marriage A marriage that follows all of the statutory requirements of blood tests, license, waiting period, and that has been solemnized by a person (religious or civil) authorized to preside at a marriage. See marriage, common-law marriage, marital, spouse.

Ceremony, *n.* A formal or conventional procedure (inaugural ceremony). Celebration, rite, formality, process, observance, protocol, etiquette, behavior, code, manners, regulations, proprieties, custom, amenities, civilities, testimonial, solemnization, form, ritual, occasion, commemoration, festivity. See also service (3), solemnity.

Certain, *adj.* **1.** Definite (the rental price must be certain). Specific, ascertained, clearly defined, well-defined, fixed, designated, stated, precise, expressed, clear-cut, concrete, exact, explicit, particular, marked, prescribed, settled, determinate, determined, constant, agreed upon, **2.** Confident (he is certain that there are no cases on point). Positive, sure, unwavering, secure, satisfied, unshaken, free from doubt, assured, self-assured, self-satisfied, sanguine, convinced, fully convinced. **3.** Beyond doubt (once the judge denied the motion, the defeat of his client was certain). Indisputable, inevitable, positive, doubtless, demonstrable, unquestionable, inescapable, irrefutable, conclusive, inexorable, indubitable, absolute, unequivocal, incontrovertible, clear, obvious, unqualified, infallible, unmistakable, plain, destined, fated, irrevocable, insured, ensured, guaranteed, dependable, warranted, well-grounded, certified, provable, sure, unerring, undeniable, patent, unfailing, prescribed, trustworthy, reliable, incontestable, beyond all question, real, past dispute, bound to happen, unalterable, unshakable, unchangeable, true, valid, satisfied, fixed, evident, cogent, authoritative, attested, verifiable, axiomatic, without doubt, without question, irrefragable, unimpeachable, concrete, tangible, established, self-evident, inflexible, inviolate, unassailable, capable of proof. *Ant.* Indefinite; dubious; inconclusive.

Certainty, *n.* **1.** Inevitability (it is a certainty that the case will be dismissed). Fact, reality, actuality, sure thing, foregone conclusion, truth, belief, conviction, datum, verity, presumption, guaranty, warranty, surety, valid conclusion. **2.** Confidence (the witness answered with certainty). Certitude, authoritativeness, assurance, assuredness, complete knowledge, unquestionableness, trust, conclusiveness, sureness, absence of doubt, accuracy, precision, conviction, credence, firmness, dogmatism, definiteness, positiveness, validity, incontrovertibility, unimpeachability, unequivocalness, absence of doubt, incontestability, reassurance, stability, inexorability. *Ant.* Uncertainty; equivocation, ambiguity.

Certificate, *n.* A written assurance or official representation that some act has or has not been done (the builder filed a certificate of compliance). Document, documentation, certification, affidavit, official statement, acknowledgment, recognition, written evidence, entitlement, attestation, credential, permit, instrument, testimonial, diploma, voucher, deed, validation, authorization, authority, license, declaration, contract, endorsement, testament, guarantee.

Certificate of occupancy A document certifying that the premises comply with zoning or building ordinances.

Certification, *n.* A formal assertion, usually in writing, of some fact (the union received certification from the NLRB). Confirmation, affirmation, substantiation, support, validation, attestation, endorsement, ratification, acknowledgment, testimony, authentication, documentary proof, verification, corroboration, assurance, declaration, credential, affidavit, recognition, authorization, documentation, ticket, permit, warrant, deposition, license, instrument, document.

Certification of a check See certified check.

Certification of record on appeal Formal acknowledgment of questions for appellate review, commonly signed by a lower court.

Certified, *adj.* Authorized, verified (certified representative). Warranted, guaranteed, possessing a certificate, licensed, proven, established, authenticated, corroborated, substantiated, acknowledged, documented, confirmed. *Ant.* Unauthorized.

Certified check A check whose payment will be guaranteed by the bank on which it is drawn. The acceptance of the check by the bank is a warranty that funds are available to cover it.

Certify, *v.* To state formally that something is true or genuine (the notary certified her signature). Authenticate, affirm, warrant, attest, verify, corroborate, aver, guaranty, guarantee, witness, vouch for, testify to, substantiate, prove, certificate, validate, assure, notarize, insure, ensure, stand behind, indemnify, acknowledge, document, proclaim, ratify, asseverate, bear witness, avouch, proclaim, sustain, reassure, countersign, assert, confirm, prove, manifest, establish. *Ant.* Repudiate.

Certiorari, *n.* "To be informed of." A higher court, in a case in which it has discretion to hear an appeal, asks a lower court to send up a certified copy of the record in the case so that the higher court can determine whether any irregularities have occurred in the proceedings. A writ of certiorari.

Certitude, *n.* Complete assurance (you can never achieve certitude in predicting what the court will do). Certainty, definitiveness, absoluteness, surety, assurance, infallibility, absolute certainty, inevitability, freedom from error. See also conviction (3). *Ant.* Doubt.

Cessation, *n.* Termination or interruption (cessation of hostilities). Ending, conclusion, close, halt, stoppage, desisting, discontinuing, discontinuance, cloture, closure, abandonment, breaking off, suspension, finish, surcease, intermission, pause, remission, expiration, delay, arrest, leaving off, adjournment, abeyance, lull, respite, windup, consummation, coda, armistice, hiatus, quietus, moratorium, letup, rest, ban, curb, discontinuity, severance, reprieve, interregnum, postponement, truce. *Ant.* Commencement.

Cession, *n.* A surrender (the land was acquired by cession). Yielding, relinquishment, giving up, ceding, assignment, transfer, award, resignation, grant, renunciation, conveyance, release, presentation, delivery, handing over, donation, renouncing claim to. *Ant.* Acquisition.

Cestui que trust, *n.* Beneficiary of a trust. See beneficiary.

Cf. Compare or confer. Refers to contrasted, analogous, or explanatory views or statements.

Chafe, *v.* See harass; wear (1).

Chagrin, *n.* See embarrassment.

Chain 1. *n.* A sequence (a chain of events). Series, train, string, succession, course, progression, line, unbroken line, continuity, link, cavalcade, cycle, concatenation, procession, row, order, cordon, array, connected series, congeries, column, sequel, suite, lace, catena, classification. **2.** *v.* To fasten or restrict (chain the gate). Secure, bind, fetter, moor, leash, enslave, enchain, cable, hitch, imprison, incarcerate, jail, tether, manacle, tie, hamper, handcuff, limit, cage, encumber, entomb. See also check (1), connect (1). *Ant.* Single incident; liberate.

Chain of command See hierarchy, bureaucracy.

Chain of title Successive conveyances or other transactions that affect a particular parcel of land, arranged consecutively from the original title holder to the present holder.

Chairman, *n.* The presiding officer (chairman of the board). Chair, chairperson, chairwoman, leader, speaker, conductor, moderator, administrator, supervisor, master of ceremonies, arbiter, mediator, executive, monitor, principal, overseer, facilitator, manager, governor, president, toastmaster. See also chief (1). *Ant.* Underling.

Chalet, *n.* See home (1).

Challenge 1. *v.* To put in question; to render doubtful (she challenged the credibility of the witness). Contradict, impeach, take exception, denounce, controvert, protest, resist, doubt, impute, defy, accost, dispute, question, dare, combat, brave, threaten, encounter, fight, oppose, mistrust, suspect, demur, retort, remonstrate, object, scorn, affront, query, argue, repudiate, negate, disapprove, impugn, malign, defame, assail, inveigh against, wrangle, hassle, pick holes in. **2.** *v.* To invite into competition; to call upon defiantly (she challenged him to produce the evidence). Summon, beckon, invite, goad, stimulate, animate, stir, spur, arouse, call to combat, requisition, dare, compel, oblige, solicit, order. **3.** *n.* Test (winning the case was the challenge of his life). Gage, trial, endeavor, venture, encounter, engagement, confrontation, contest, match, meet, stimulus, provocation, incentive, lure. **4.** *n.* Objection (challenge for cause). Exception, dissension, opposition, protestation, protest, demurrer, rejection, complaint, grievance, repudiation, negation, denunciation, charge. *Ant.* Concede (1); recoil (2).

Challenge for cause A request from a party that a certain prospective juror not be allowed to sit on the jury because of specified causes or reasons, e.g., bias.

Chamber, *n.* **1.** A room or office that is usually private (the attorneys discussed the case in the judge's chamber). Inner office, retreat, apartment, sanctum, study, recess, alcove, anteroom, hollow, cubicle, box, hall, parlor, stall, section, cell, partition; apartment, bedroom, boudoir, bedchamber. **2.** A legislative body (the lower chamber voted to repeal the statute). House, senate, assembly, congress, council, tribunal, legislature, parliament, diet, synod, court, committee; legislators, lawmakers.

Champagne, *n.* See liquor.

Champerty, *n.* An illegal bargain between one person (called a champertor) and a party to a lawsuit whereby the champertor carries on the litigation at his or her own expense and shares whatever is recovered. The bargain is called a champertous agreement. Barratry, maintenance, officious intermeddling, purchase of a lawsuit.

Champion 1. *n.* One who speaks, acts, or advocates for another (champion of the underdog). Advocate, defender, guardian, backer, protector, supporter, promoter, patron, vindicator, protagonist, friend, abettor, exponent, expounder, booster, partisan. **2.** *v.* To speak or advocate for (she championed the cause of the poor). Defend, support, fight for, battle for, contend, back, endorse, espouse, maintain, align with, protect, vindicate, assist, avenge, guard, plead for, justify, abet, aid. **3.** *n.* A winner (champion of the race). Victor, hero, heroine, vindicator, conqueror, paragon, subduer, number one. See also master. *Ant.* Opponent; oppose; loser.

Chance 1. *n.* A risk (to take a chance). Hazard, gamble, danger, speculation, jeopardy, peril, venture. **2.** *n.* Accident, fate (they met by chance). Fortuity, happenstance, luck, fortune, serendipity, coincidence, circumstance, hap, cast, providence, act of God, toss-up, vicissitude, destiny. **3.** *n.* The likelihood of something happening (the plaintiff wanted to know what chance he had of a favorable verdict). Possibility, probability, prospect, conceivability, realm of possibility, contingency, attainability, potential, potentiality. **4.** *n.* An opportunity (the employee was given another chance). Turn, attempt, try, occasion, "shot," opening, time, "break." **5.** *adj.* Unintended (a chance discovery). Accidental, unforeseen, unplanned, random, fortuitous, inadvertent, involuntary, arbitrary, unexpected, casual, unpremeditated, undesigned, lucky, incidental, off-hand, careless. **6.** *v.* See bet (2).

Chancellor, *n.* **1.** Judge in a court of equity. **2.** Prime minister. **3.** Chief executive officer.

Chancery, *n.* Equity; the system of jurisprudence administered in courts of equity (as opposed to courts of law).

Chance verdict A verdict determined by hazard or lot and not by careful deliberation.

Change 1. *n.* An alteration (a change in the terms of the will). Modification, substitution, addition, conversion, transformation, transmutation, deviation, variation, metamorphosis, variance, mutation, revolution, transition, exchange, remodeling, fluctuation, evolution. **2.** *v.* To alter or exchange (the judge changed the ruling). Modify, substitute, adapt, add, convert, deviate, transform, transmute, vary, mutilate, remodel, restyle, subrogate, displace, reorganize, recast, make different, turn, revolutionize, modulate, diversify, refashion, interchange, replace, remove, shift, diverge, reconstruct, permute, reform, revise. *Ant.* Permanence; preserve.

Changeable, *adj.* See variable, capricious, fluctuating, breakable.

Change of venue The removal of a suit begun in one court to another court, usually in a different county or district. See venue.

Channel, *n., v.* See river; trench, wrinkle (1); agency (4); instrument (3); convey (3), direct (3); passage (2), course (1), highway.

Chaos, *n.* See disorder, violence, riot, commotion, hysteria, confusion; catastrophe.

Chaotic, *adj.* See complex (1), disorderly (1), wild, emotional; confusion.

Chapel, *n.* See church.

Chaperon, *n.* See attendant (1), guardian.

Chaplain, *n.* See clergy.

Chapter, *n.* **1.** A division of an organization (a local chapter of the NAACP). Branch, subdivision, affiliate, group, department, bureau, local, office, component, associate. **2.** A division of a book (Prosser's chapter on duty). Section, portion, passage, article, paragraph, column, sector, part, segment. **3.** A period or episode (chapter in judicial history). Era, stage, time, event, age, phase.

Character, *n.* **1.** The aggregate of moral qualities that belong to and distinguish an individual (no one questioned the defendant's character). Integrity, honor, backbone, respectability, courage, sincerity, strength, rectitude, uprightness, status, reputation, standing, morality, truthfulness, conscientiousness. **2.** The personal qualities and pattern of behavior of an individual (we must all be judged by our own character). Traits, attributes, characteristics, features, constitution, tendencies, nature, mold, personality, dispositions, preferences, intellect, individuality, composition, temperament, mien, bearing, property, inclinations, proclivities, essence, fiber, leanings, mettle, manner, temper, makeup, habits. **3.** A person's reputation (character evidence). Estimation, position in society, status, respectability, notoriety, recognition, public esteem, standing, name, respect, account, place, fame, station, visibility, popularity, renown, repute. **4.** A person (a suspicious character). Individual, personality, specimen, mortal, human, party, someone, being, man, woman, personage, fellow, eccentric, oddity.

Characteristic 1. *n.* Trait (honesty was his main characteristic). Quality, character, identification, feature, peculiarity, mark, property, attribute, distinction, tendency, leaning, birthmark, point, badge, specialty, sign, mannerism, manner, style, penchant, bent, drift, mood, earmark, aspect, predilection, lineament, cachet, essence, nature, trademark, quirk, symptom. **2.** *adj.* Typical (the judge made the ruling with her characteristic promptness). Distinctive, distinguishing, representative, illustrative, unique, individualistic, idiosyncratic, emblematic, exclusive, special.

Characterization, *n.* Classification (a defamatory characterization). Portrayal, designation, specification, qualification, interpretation, representation, portrait, delineation, description.

Characterize, *v.* To describe or distinguish (he characterized the witness as an expert). Portray, designate, qualify, interpret, represent, classify, label, brand, specify, picture, construe, identify, stamp, denote, name, tag, depict, ascribe, attribute, differentiate, individualize, formalize, judge, render, define, delineate, translate, sketch, record, decode, decipher, term, exemplify, evaluate.

Charade, *n.* See pretense; conundrum.

Charge 1. *v.* To impose a burden or obligation (the board was charged with the task of reconciling the figures). Encumber, load, tax, oppress, afflict, freight, lade, saddle with, assign, entrust, delegate, nominate, appoint, levy. **2.** *v.* To instruct or command (the judge charged the jury on the law of libel). Direct, inform, counsel, enjoin, order, urge, require, bid, ascribe, dictate, decree, exact, requisition, adjure, ordain, summon, advise, guide, prepare, prescribe, recommend. **3.** *v.* To accuse (the police charged her with armed robbery). Blame, incriminate, impute, impeach, indict, reproach, arraign, implicate, allege, "book," call to account, involve, inform against, betray, inculpate, criminate, attack, cite, challenge, stigmatize, denounce, recriminate. **4.** *v.* To defer payment (he charged a new shirt). Take on credit, put on one's account, debit, incur a debit. **5.** *v.* To hold financially responsible (the store charged her for extra linen). Price, ask a price, fix a charge, levy, tax, appraise, request payment, assess, put a value on, fix as a price. **6.** *v.* To attack (the demonstrators charged the gate). Assault, set on, storm, rush, assail, besiege, beset, come at, close in on, strike, propel. **7.** *v.* To fill to capacity (the courtroom was charged with tension). Pack, stack, load, pervade, saturate, bathe, stuff, pile, choke, flood, swamp. **8.** *n.* A claim or encumbrance (any advancements made will constitute a charge against commissions that are due). Lien, burden, cost, expense, liability, debt, outlay, tax, expenditure, hold, obligation, pledge, assessment, toll, duty, indebtedness, commitment, tie. **9.** *n.* The price (the charge is $35). Cost, value, fee, toll, rate, rent, tap, tariff, assessment, expense, payment, debit, fare, quotation. **10.** *n.* An

Charge

accusation (the charge was murder). Indictment, imputation, allegation, crimination, incrimination, citation, presentation, information, arraignment, complaint, true bill, gravamen, condemnation, denunciation, summons, impeachment. **11.** *n.* Supervision (the infant was in the charge of the agency). Custody, protection, guardianship, safekeeping, patronage, jurisdiction, auspices, wardship, management, tutelage, administration, control, trust, keeping, chaperonage. See also client (2). **12.** *n.* An instruction or command (the charge to the jury). Direction, guidance, advice, address, exhortation, lecture, admonition, discourse, mandate, requirement, order, commission, bidding, enjoining, injunction, regulation, demand, precept, prescription, commandment, call, requirement. **13.** *n.* Duty (safety is the charge of the manager). Responsibility, task, mission, business, obligation, liability, assignment, trust, calling, burden, undertaking, promise, commitment, accountability.

Chargeable, *adj.* **1.** Subject to be charged (the offense was chargeable under state law). Punishable, accountable, liable, indictable, arraignable, answerable, imposable, responsible. **2.** Attributable (the tax was chargeable to the estate). Referable, assessable, traceable, imputable, imposable.

Chargé d'affaires, *n.* A diplomatic representative of an inferior rank. See delegate (2), agent.

Charge-sheet, *n.* A record kept at a police station in which you will find the names of the persons taken into custody, the nature of the accusation, and the name of the accuser in each case.

Charge to the jury A final address to the jury in which the judge instructs the jurors on the rules that they are to apply in reaching a verdict. See charge (12).

Charisma, *n.* See influence (1); attractive, intriguing.

Charitable, *adj.* **1.** Having the character or purpose of a charity (charitable deduction). Benevolent, eleemosynary, philanthropic, humanitarian, altruistic, almsgiving, giving, munificent, bountiful, benign, generous, lavish, good, humane, open-handed, magnanimous, unselfish. **2.** Lenient (to say that the new lawyer's brief was acceptable would be charitable). Gracious, kind, sympathetic, forgiving, warmhearted, indulgent, tolerant, helpful, obliging, considerate, broad-minded, mild, kindly, easy, soft, merciful, compassionate, tender, agreeable, liberal, thoughtful, accommodating, condoning, temperate, compliant, sensitive. *Ant.* Mercenary; rigid.

Charitable bequest A bequest or gift where the aim or accomplishment is religious, educational, political, or of general social interest to mankind, and the ultimate recipients are either the community as a whole or an indefinite and unascertainable portion thereof.

Charitable contribution A contribution made for tax purposes to a qualified, nonprofit charitable organization.

Charitable corporation A nonprofit corporation organized for charitable purposes, e.g., promoting the community's welfare.

Charitable immunity doctrine A charity is not liable for the torts it commits. The doctrine has been modified or abolished in many states.

Charitable trust A fiduciary relationship with respect to property arising as a result of a manifestation of an intent to create it, and subjecting the person by whom the property is held to equitable duties to deal with the property for charitable purposes.

Charitable use Uses of a religious, educational, political, or general social interest to mankind. Uses for the relief of poverty, advancement of education or religion, or beneficial to the general community.

Charity, *n.* **1.** A gift (she refused to accept charity). Alms, handout, dole, welfare, donation, aid, relief, help, philanthropy, grant, offering, assistance, gratui-

128

ty, present, succor, endowment, bequest, ration, subsidy, allowance, contribution. **2.** An institution engaged in public benevolent purposes (the Red Cross is a charity). Fund, charitable institution or organization, endowment, philanthropic or eleemosynary organization. **3.** The attempt to benefit and advance mankind in general, or those specifically in need, spiritually, socially, economically, physically, or intellectually without expectation of gain or profit to the donor (one of its corporate purposes is charity). Almsgiving, philanthropy, altruism, humanity, humanitarianism, magnanimity, liberality, benevolence, active goodness, generosity, self-sacrifice, Judeo-Christian love, assistance, patronage. **4.** Forgiveness (with malice toward none and charity for all). Clemency, kindness, tolerance, good will, grace, graciousness, hospitality, compassion, mercy, leniency, indulgence, consideration, thoughtfulness, understanding, benignity. *Ant.* Extraction; profitable corporation; parsimony; cruelty.

Charlatan, *n.* One who pretends to more knowledge and skill than he or she possesses (the lawyer turned out to be a charlatan). Fake, cheat, pretender, impostor, fraud, empiric, hypocrite, deceiver, defrauder, beguiler, trickster, cozener, mountebank, humbug, confidence man, sham, phony, shyster, mimic, pettifogger, bluff, hack. See also quack. *Ant.* Expert.

Charm, *n. v.* See appeal (3), beauty, affinity (2); entice, delight, entrap, interest (5), bait (3).

Charming, *adj.* See intriguing, attractive, debonair, convivial, friendly.

Chart, *n., v.* See map, plan (1, 2), record (2).

Charta, *n.* A charter, deed, or formal instrument, especially from the sovereign (e.g., Magna Charta).

Charter 1. *n.* A document from the state legislature or sovereign power that grants rights, liberties, or powers (corporate charter; city charter). Decree, certificate, license, promulgation, authority, constitution, patent, permission, covenant, agreement, compact, franchise, enfranchisement, contract, sanction, concession, deed, conveyance, pact, consent, privilege, delegation, acquiescence, entitlement, permit, liberty. **2.** *n.* A document created by an organization that states the fundamental purposes and powers of the organization. **3.** *v.* To rent for temporary use (charter a boat). Hire, lease, let, commission, employ, engage, sublease, subrent, sublet.

Chary, *adj.* See cautious, circumspect; bashful.

Chase, *v.* To pursue or follow rapidly with the intention of catching or driving away (the narcotic agent chased the defendant into the alley). Stalk, trail, run after, track down, shadow, hunt, hound, try to overtake, tail, search, "dog." See also pursue (2), ferret. *Ant.* Let go.

Chaser, *n.* See liquor.

Chasm, *n.* See cave, cell, crevice, abyss.

Chassis, *n.* See vessel (2).

Chaste, *adj.* **1.** Never having had unlawful sexual intercourse. **2.** Never having experienced any sexual intercourse. Virginal, continent, maiden, immaculate, abstinent, undefiled, celibate, unmarried. **3.** Virtuous (chaste character). Pure, modest, innocent, clean, self-restrained, simple, unaffected, refined, wholesome, decent, uncorrupted, righteous, unsullied, moral, elevated, subdued, elegant, simple, spotless, ethical, untainted, moderate, noble, saintly, decorous. *Ant.* Promiscuous; crude.

Chastise, *v.* See censure (3), beat (1), correct (3), amerce, fine (1).

Chastisement, *n.* See penalty, punishment, discipline (2), correction (1).

Chastity, *n.* The quality of being chaste. See chaste; innocence (2).

Chat, *v., n.* See communicate, converse (1), communication, conversation.

Chateau, *n.* See home (1); luxury.

Chattel, *n.* **1.** An article of personal property (e.g., car, rug, dog) as opposed to real property (e.g., land, house). Movable property. (A state tax on all chattels.) Personalty, article, effect, personal possessions, belongings, gear, paraphernalia, goods, personal estate, asset, things, tangibles, commodity, possession. **2.** See slave (1). *Ant.* Real property; free person.

Chattel lien A lien in personal property in favor of persons who have expended labor, services, or materials on the property at the request of the rightful owner or possessor.

Chattel mortgage A mortgage on personal property. A security interest is taken in the property.

Chattel paper A document or documents that evidence both a monetary obligation and a security interest in or a lease of personal property.

Chatter, *v.* See babble.

Chauffeur, *n.* A person employed to operate and attend to the motor vehicle of another. Driver, coachman, motorman. See also servant, employee.

Chauvinism, *n.* Superiority, nationalism. Partisanship, blind patriotism, machismo, jingoism, militarism, dominance, narrowness. See also patriot.

Cheap, *adj.* Low-priced, inexpensive. See economical; inferior (2), base (1, 2), obscene; gaudy; stingy, avaricious.

Cheapen, *v.* See disparage, adulterate.

Cheat 1. *v.* To deceive and defraud (the company cheated on its taxes). Swindle, dupe, purloin, trick, delude, beguile, victimize, cozen, mislead, fool, outwit, entrap, cajole, hoax, bamboozle, fleece, utter, overreach, "take," "con," "rip off," embezzle, betray, dissemble, circumvent, jockey, inveigle, act unfairly, commit a breach of faith, prevaricate. **2.** *n.* A swindler (she had a reputation as a cheat). Fraud, deceiver, cheater, con artist, thief, chiseler, charlatan, crook, confidence man, trickster, dodger, rogue, ensnarer, impostor, knave, montebank, artful dodger, pettifogger, rascal, embezzler, phony, quack, "shark," operator, scoundrel. *Ant.* Assist; person of integrity.

Check 1. *v.* To hold within bounds (the amendment is intended to check the power of the commissioner). Restrain, control, repress, restrict, chain, hinder, arrest, hobble, obstruct, block, stop, curb, hold back, brake, rein, choke, circumvent, muzzle, impede, stay, harness, inhibit, rebuff, abate, undermine, suppress, bar, abridge, reduce, decrease, estop, constrain, stem, countercheck, interrupt, diminish, detain, deter, encumber. **2.** *v.* To examine for accuracy (the witness was asked how often the gauge was checked for durability). Inspect, verify, audit, test, review, compare, assess, measure, scrutinize, look into, corroborate, peruse, validate, probe, authenticate, survey, confirm, canvass, watch, explore, oversee, question, supervise, monitor, scan, quiz, re-examine, sample, regulate, superintend. **3.** *v.* To conform (the computer figures check with his testimony). Correspond, fall in line with, harmonize, agree, accord, dovetail, fit, "jibe," tally, square, be uniform. **4.** *n.* A draft drawn upon a bank and payable on demand, signed by the maker or drawer, containing an unconditional promise to pay a sum certain in money to the order of the payee (paid by check). Note, bill of exchange, draft, commercial paper, banknote, instrument, negotiable instrument, money order, certificate. **5.** *n.* An obstruction (check on inflation). Restraint, bar, control, impediment, barrier, brake, stop, repression, arrest, suspension, curb, restriction, bridle, damper, interference, deterrent, checkmate, stopper, limit, prohibition, prevention, stay, limitation, barricade, proscription, cessation, obstacle, frustration, estoppel, delay, postponement, discontinuation, abeyance.

Check kiting The practice of writing a check against a bank account in which funds are insufficient to cover it, with the hope that before the check is deposited, the necessary funds will have been deposited.

Checkmate, *n., v.* See check (5), defeat, circumvent, clog.

Checkoff system A procedure whereby the employer deducts union dues directly from the pay of the employees and gives them to the union.

Cheer, *n.* See happiness, comfort; acclamation.

Cheerful, *adj.* See happy.

Cheerless, *adj.* See dismal, barren.

Chef, *n.* See servant, employee.

Chef-d'oeuvre, *n.* See masterpiece.

Chemistry, *n.* See science.

Cherish, *v.* See appreciate (3), adulate, enjoy (2).

Chew, *v.* See eat.

Chic, *adj.* Stylish. Sophisticated, elegant, modern, fashionable, in vogue, dapper, smart, current, sporty. See also aristocracy, debonair.

Chicanery, *n.* Trickery (the defendant's chicanery in obtaining the contract). Deception, intrigue, machination, subterfuge, fake, guile, fraud, cunning, dodge, sophistry, duplicity, beguilement, dishonesty, cajolery, treachery, knavery. See also connivance. *Ant.* Integrity.

Chide, *v.* See censure (2).

Chief 1. *n.* The leader (the chief of the division). Head, principal, boss, chairperson, supervisor, manager, superintendent, dean, superior, director, overseer, chieftain, commandant, master, ruler, lord, dictator, dominator, captain, general, commander, administrator, sovereign, monarch, overlord, senior, primate, employer, officer, foreman. **2.** *adj.* Dominant (the chief issue). Paramount, main, predominant, leading, foremost, premier, eminent, preeminent, primary, prime, outstanding, supreme, arch, essential, vital, master, great, cardinal, important, grand, first, highest, central, senior, superior, ranking, top, utmost, prevailing, key, governing. *Ant.* Follower; trivial.

Chieftain, *n.* See chief (1), master (1).

Child, children, *n.* Offspring of a human; a young person. Boy, girl, juvenile, adolescent, infant, youth, babe, junior, youngster, minor, issue, teen, teenager, mademoiselle, schoolgirl, schoolboy, maiden, kid, scion, lad, lass, toddler, newborn, descendant, heir, progeny, lineage, generation. *Ant.* Adult.

Childbirth, *n.* See birth (1).

Childish, *adj.* See juvenile (2).

Chilling, *adj.* Seriously discouraging (the rules had a chilling effect on free speech). Restricting, depressing, distressing, dampening, disheartening, withdrawing, inhibiting, restraining, curbing, constraining, interfering, arresting, impeding, retarding. *Ant.* Stimulative.

Chime, *n.* See noise.

Chip, *v.* See break (2).

Chiropractic(s), *n.* A system of therapeutic treatment that removes pressure on the nerves by the adjustment of the spinal vertebrae and other structures.

Chisel, *v.* See engrave, forge (2), inscribe, cut; cheat (1).

Chivalrous, *adj.* See courageous, civil (3), honest.

Choate, *adj.* Pertaining to that which has become perfected or ripened (choate lien). Whole, complete, full, ready, perfect.

Choate lien A lien that is perfected so that nothing more need be done to make it enforceable.

Choice 1. *n.* Decision (no one liked the choice that the judge made). Judgment, analysis, disposition, resolution, selection, order, settlement, assignment, conclusion, pick, preference, appointment, finding, verdict, evaluation, appraisal, pronouncement, outcome. **2.** *n.* The opportunity to choose (you have the choice). Option, discretion, election, alternative. **3.** *adj.* Preferable, excellent (a choice example of breeding). Select, valuable, superior, prime, fine, singular, unique, preeminent, consummate, extraordinary, exclusive, superlative, first-class, first-rate, elite, exquisite, uncommon, worthy, fine, precious. *Ant.* Indecision; coercion; inferior.

Choice of law The determination of what law should govern when a conflict of law issue is present in the case. See conflict of laws.

Choke, *v.* To strangle or obstruct. See suffocate, clog, constrict.

Choler, *n.* See wrath.

Cholera, *n.* See disease.

Choose, *v.* To select; to prefer (the judge chose to take the matter under advisement). Elect, resolve, pick, cull, make a choice of, single out, settle on, decide between, adopt, espouse, embrace, fancy, separate, isolate, appoint, exercise discretion, discriminate, commit oneself, will, support. See also select (1).

Chop, *v.* See cut (1), divide (1).

Chore, *n.* See duty (1), assignment (3), job (2).

Chorus, *n.* See music.

Chose, *n.* A thing; an article of personal property. See chattel (1).

Chose in action A right to recover something through a lawsuit.

Chose in possession A personal thing of which one has possession.

Christen, *v.* See initiate, call (4).

Chronic, *adj.* Of long duration (chronic illness). Obstinate, habitual, everlasting, constant, continuous, continuing, inveterate, confirmed, unending, perennial, sustained, lingering, eternal, persistent, deep-seated, hardened, rooted, unyielding, ceaseless, abiding, unmitigating, continual, periodic, intermittent, ingrained, incurable, protracted, long-lasting, enduring, unremitting, entrenched, unmitigated, incessant, tenacious, ever-present, unceasing, ongoing, recurrent, steadfast. *Ant.* Ephemeral.

Chronicle, *n., v.* See record (1, 2), account, description, recital.

Chronological, *adj.* See consecutive.

Chronometer, *n.* See clock.

Chubby, *adj.* See corpulent.

Chuck, *v.* See jettison (1).

Chum, *n.* See associate (2).

Church, *n.* A religious society following Christian doctrine and observing Christian ritual. Religion, congregation, house of worship or prayer, chapel, shrine, ecclesiastical body, temple, tabernacle, basilica, cathedral, mosque, pagoda, sanctum sanctorum, shul, sanctuary, synagogue, service, worship, devotions, cult, faith, sect, denomination, creed, belief, affiliation, persuasion.

Churl, *n.* See boor, idiot; wrongdoer.

Churlish, *adj.* See rude, caustic, arrogant.

Churning, *n.* An abuse of a customer's confidence by a broker by making excessive transactions for personal gain, e.g., increased commissions.

Chute, *n.* See vessel (2), conduit (2); watercourse.

Cigarette, *n.* Tobacco. Smoke, "weed," joint, menthol, filter, "butt," king-size, cigar, pipe, chewing tobacco, cigarello.

Cinder, *n., v.* See fire (1), burn.

Cinema, *n.* Theater, motion pictures. Movies, "flick," show, films, screen, cinematography, showcase, nickelodeon, drama.

Cipher, *n.* **1.** Secret writing unintelligible to someone without the key (the letter was written in cipher). Code, anagram, cryptograph, cryptogram, acrostic. **2.** Someone of no importance (she remained a cipher). Nonentity, obscurity, nobody, nullity, zero, lightweight, mediocrity.

Circa, *prep.* Approximately (he was born circa 1789). See about (1).

Circle 1. *n.* A ring. Disc, rink, wheel, band, orb, ball, circumference, loop, cordon, belt, corona, band, collar, crown. **2.** *n.* See coterie. **3.** *v.* See surround. **4.** *v.* See circumvent.

Circuit, *n.* A district or area traveled by a judge or minister (the judge rode circuit). Section, territory, division, jurisdiction, dominion, domain, zone, province.

Circuitous, *adj.* Roundabout and indirect (circuitous reasoning). Tortuous, twisting, devious, circular, meandering, complicated, winding, serpentine, labyrinthine, convoluted, zigzag, contorted, oblique, sinuous, roving, digressive, discursive, wandering. *Ant.* Straightforward.

Circuity of action A complex, indirect, or roundabout course of legal proceeding, making two or more lawsuits necessary when a more direct approach would have required only one lawsuit.

Circular 1. *adj.* Moving in a circle; roundabout (circular argument). Indirect, winding, circumlocutory, meandering, errant, vagrant, devious, serpentine, twisting, convoluted. See also circuitous. **2.** *n.* A handout (the circulars were distributed in the street). Announcement, handbill, advertisement, flyer, folder, release, pamphlet, notice, leaflet, petition, ad, throwaway, bulletin. **3.** *adj.* See round (2). *Ant.* Direct (1).

Circular note or letter of credit A writing that authorizes one person (or entity) to pay money or extend credit to another person (or entity) on the credit of the writer.

Circulate, *v.* To pass from place to place (the news circulated quickly). Disseminate, publish, publicize, make public, become public, spread, propagate, travel, revolve, flow, disperse, issue, scatter, announce, broadcast, divulge, transmit, voice, bandy, convey, distribute, promulgate, proclaim, advertise, enunciate, strew, trumpet, diffuse, radiate, reveal, acquire currency. *Ant.* Conceal.

Circulation, *n.* Transmission from person to person or from place to place (the defamatory remark received wide circulation). Dissemination, spreading, promulgation, transmigration, passage, movement, distribution, motion, rotation, publication, broadcasting, issuance, dispersion, ventilation, diffusion. *Ant.* Stagnation.

Circumference, *n.* See boundary, margin (1), verge; peripheral.

Circumlocution, *n.* See evasion, ambiguity; digress; pompous.

Circumscribe, *v.* **1.** To restrict (the parole board circumscribed the parolee's activities). Limit, proscribe, restrain, curb, bar, impede, bridle, hem, fix, constrain, check, hinder, contain, keep within bounds, fetter, trammel, delimit, narrow, contract, constrict. **2.** To surround by boundaries (the crime areas were circumscribed in pencil). Delineate, border, mark off, surround, encircle, circle, contour, belt, enclose, outline. *Ant.* Expand.

Circumspect, *adj.* Cautious (he was circumspect in approaching the mine). Prudent, careful, wary, vigilant, discreet, observant, attentive, heedful, on guard, apprehensive, judicious, provident, alert, watchful, mindful, conscientious, precautious, reflective, sensitive, chary, guarded, meticulous, scrupulous, discerning, perspicacious, intent, deliberate, contemplative, painstaking, thoughtful, prepared, thorough. *Ant.* Reckless.

Circumstances, *n.* Accompanying facts, events, or conditions (describe the circumstances of the firing). Surroundings, occurrences, happenings, incidentals, course of events, background, attendant facts. See also fact, factor (1), detail (2), particulars, contingency.

Circumstantial, *adj.* Indirect, inferential (circumstantial evidence). Deduced, conjectural, presumable, based on circumstances, suggestive, implicative, apparent, insubstantial, contingent, presumptive, ostensible, likely.

Circumstantial evidence Indirect evidence. The proof of certain facts in a case from which the jury may infer other connected facts that usually and reasonably follow according to common experience.

Circumvent, *v.* To evade; to go around (they tried to circumvent the statute). Escape, elude, avoid, eschew, bypass, detour, dodge, frustrate, thwart, shun, circle, skirt, circumnavigate, outwit, miss, outflank, entrap, defraud, trick, deceive, checkmate, beguile, dupe, inveigle, cheat, delude, cozen, mislead, confuse, disconcert, foil, defeat, abort, cloak, traverse, contravene, hoax, prevaricate, scheme, outmaneuver. *Ant.* Confront.

Circus, *n.* See amusement, celebration (2), cinema, auditorium; commotion, anarchy, confusion.

Cistern, *n.* See vessel (2).

Citadel, *n.* See protection, wall, building, home (1), asylum.

Citation, *n.* **1.** A notice or order to appear in court at a later date (the police issued the driver a citation). Summons, call, bidding, subpoena, injunction, charge, mandate, writ, notification, warrant, prescription. **2.** The reference to or quotation of authority (the citations in the brief were incomplete). Attribution, documentation, credit, mention, source, excerpt, cite, passage, allusion. **3.** Award (citation for bravery). Commendation, honor, praise, homage, decoration, recognition, eulogy, laurels.

Citator, *n.* A research book containing lists of references or cites (e.g., *Shepard's Citations*) that serve two main functions: first and foremost, to help you assess the current validity of a case, statute or other law; and secondarily, to provide you with leads to additional laws.

Cite 1. *v.* To notify someone to appear in a proceeding; to accuse (the lawyer was cited for contempt). Summon, name, implicate, blame, censure, impeach, complain, denounce, charge to appear, incriminate, inform, arraign, allege. **2.** *n.* A reference to or quotation of an authority (what is the cite of the Miranda case). Attribution, documentation, credit, mention, source, excerpt, citation, passage, reference, substantiation, data, footnote, allusion. **3.** *v.* To refer to (the witness was asked to cite an example). Provide, prove, state, adduce, allude to, indicate, elucidate, specify, document, advance, enumerate, present, substantiate, attest, make evident, exhibit, establish, certify, bring forward, mention, quote, advert, denominate. *Ant.* Disregard; conceal.

Citizen, *n.* A person born or naturalized in a country to which he or she owes allegiance and is entitled to full civil rights (U.S. citizen). Native, denizen, inhabitant, resident, domiciliary, subject, national, civilian, taxpayer, voter, compatriot, dependent, vassal, countryman, liege, servant, dweller. See also constituency (1). *Ant.* Foreigner.

Citizenry, *n.* See nation, people, country (1), constituency.

Citizen's arrest A private citizen making an arrest, usually for a crime that constitutes a breach of the peace.

City, *n.* A municipal corporation. Urban area, metropolis, municipality, megalopolis, metropolitan area, town, incorporated town, township, village, polity, county, political subdivision.

Civic, *adj.* Pertaining to a city or to citizenship (civic responsibility). Municipal, political, public, community, communal, metropolitan, social, neighborhood, governmental, civil, urban, local, moral.

Civil, *adj.* **1.** Relating to private rights and remedies sought by civil actions (civil proceeding). Noncriminal. **2.** Pertaining to the state or its citizenry (civil authorities). Civic, municipal, metropolitan, political, public, governmental, urban, social, civilian, societal, community, communal, state, secular, lay, temporal. **3.** Courteous (one must be civil in the courtroom). Polite, deferential, civilized, well-mannered, decorous, diplomatic, accommodating, gracious, cordial, courtly, well-bred, complaisant, refined, respectful, chivalrous, obliging, affable, urbane, cultivated, suave, mannerly, politic, gentlemanly, polished, genial, ingratiating, tactful, gentle, conciliatory, dignified, aristocratic, attentive, genteel. *Ant.* Criminal; religious, ecclesiastical, military; rude.

Civil action An action to enforce private rights. A lawsuit involving either (a) one private party suing another private party, or (b) a private party suing or being sued by the government, which does not directly involve criminal prosecution. See action (1), case (1).

Civil code The code containing the civil law of France. Code Civil, Code Napoleon.

Civil commitment Confinement, through a process other than criminal prosecution, of individuals who are insane, alcoholic, drug addicted, etc., who cannot care for themselves and/or who pose a danger to themselves or to society.

Civil conspiracy A combination of two or more persons who, by concerted action, seek to accomplish an unlawful purpose or to accomplish a lawful purpose by unlawful means.

Civil contempt A contempt of court that does not involve a serious affront to the authority of the court. A serious affront would be a criminal contempt. Example of civil contempt: failure to comply with an injunction.

Civil death All rights and privileges (e.g., the right to vote or to enter a contract) are forfeited once a person is convicted of a serious crime.

Civil disabilities Rights or privileges that are lost when a person is convicted of a serious crime (e.g., the right to vote, to hold public office, to obtain certain licenses).

Civil disobedience Breaking the law in order to demonstrate the injustice or unfairness of the law and to focus public attention on it.

Civilian, *adj.* Pertaining to private citizens (civilian task force). Nonmilitary, nonreligious, civil, lay, secular, mundane, temporal. *Ant.* Military, ecclesiastical, religious.

Civility, *n.* See comity (2); decorum, amenity (3).

Civilization, *n.* Progressive and improved conditions of a society under an organized government (western civilization). Development, education, culture, advancement, progression, progress, cultivation, enlightenment, edification, socialization, refinement, humanization, civilized society, evolution, acculturation, sophistication. *Ant.* Barbarism.

Civil law 1. Law that originated from ancient Rome rather than from the common law or from canon law. **2.** The law governing private rights and remedies as opposed to criminal law, military law, international law, natural law, etc.

Civil liberties Personal rights guaranteed by the Constitution (e.g., freedom of speech, press, religion). Natural rights or liberties.

Civil procedure The body of law concerning the methods, procedures, and practices in civil litigation. See procedure, procedural law, adjective law.

Civil rights See civil liberties.

Civil service Employment in federal, state, city, or town government often obtained through merit and competitive exams rather than through political connections. See bureaucracy, clerk.

Civil side Litigation on civil matters in a court that can hear both civil and criminal cases.

Civil war Armed conflict between opposing factions within the same country. See riot, revolt (1).

Claflin trust A type of trust in which the donor or settlor makes specific provisions for the termination of the trust. Courts respect these provisions by denying the beneficiary the right to terminate. An indestructible trust.

Claim 1. *v.* To demand as one's own or as one's right (the complaint claimed $750 in damages). Urge, insist, command, require, ask for, petition, sue for, lay claim to, challenge, call for, assert, deserve, clamor, merit, appeal, seek, compel, requisition, exact, warrant, plea, dun, press, seek as due, pick up. **2.** *n.* A cause of action (a negligence claim). Legal demand, action at law, basis for relief, legal assertion, right of action, right to relief, action, ground, plea, assertion, declaration, protestation, challenge, accusation. **3.** *n.* A right to something (his claim to the stock). Title, interest, ownership, stake, call, legacy, privilege, pretension, domain, share, franchise, inheritance, prerogative. **4.** *v.* To assert (she claimed that the room was wired). Contend, maintain, avow, asseverate, profess, allege, declare, charge, affirm, insist, put forward, state, argue, defend, avouch, emphasize, stress, advocate, certify, vow, attest, warrant. **5.** *n.* An assertion (the jury did not believe his claim of ignorance). Contention, asseveration, profession, allegation, declaration, affirmation, insistence, statement, defense, advocacy, attestation, certification, averment, proposition, postulation, avouchment.

Claimant, *n.* One who asserts a right, demand, or claim (Smith was the claimant in the action). Petitioner, plaintiff, challenger, applicant, prosecutor, asserter, accuser, complainant, litigant, party, appellant, pleader. *Ant.* Defendant, respondent.

Clairvoyance, *n.* **1.** See judgment (2), comprehension, ability (2). **2.** Extrasensory perception. Sixth sense, telepathy, prophecy, ESP, prescience. **3.** See foresight, prophecy.

Clairvoyant, *n.* See oracle; augur.

Clamor, *n.* See commotion, eruption, noise, opposition.

Clamorous, *adj.* See noisy.

Clamp, *n., v.* See lock, affix (1), attach (2).

Clan, *n.* See family, kindred.

Clandestine, *adj.* Concealed, often for an illegal or illicit purpose (clandestine meeting). Secret, hidden, surreptitious, underhanded, covert, furtive, stealthy, private, sly, undercover, conspiring, conspiratorial, disguised, veiled, masked, confidential, cloaked, secluded, secretive, unrevealed, feline, cunning, silent, shrouded, collusive, subterranean, camouflaged, obscure, ensconced, evasive, unknown, dishonorable, back-room. *Ant.* Public.

Clap, *n.* See gonorrhea.

Claptrap, *n.* See balderdash.

Clarification, *n.* Making something more clear (the judge asked the lawyer for a clarification of her position). Explanation, elucidation, description, illumination, interpretation, analysis, specification, enlightenment, explication, presentation, exposition, amplification, refinement, commentary, delineation, manifestation, simplification, deciphering, making lucid. See also annotation, definition (1), construction. *Ant.* Obfuscation.

Clarify, *v.* To make more clear (the court clarified its ruling in a later case). Explain, elucidate, describe, clear, illuminate, explicate, clear up, shed light on, unveil, articulate, unravel, untangle, simplify, decipher, disentangle, illustrate, annotate, analyze, break down, expound, spell out, make intelligible. See also interpret, construe, define. *Ant.* Confuse.

Clarity, *n.* The characteristic of being clear (the clarity of the argument in the brief). Lucidity, simplicity, unambiguity, intelligibility, comprehensibility, brilliance, radiance, perspicuity, distinctness, straightforwardness, transparency, definition, plainness, exactitude, luminosity, explicitness, directness, purity. *Ant.* Obscurity.

Clash, *v., n.* See collide, compete, conflict; collision (2).

Clasp, *v., n.* See affix.

Class, *n.* **1.** A group of persons, things, qualities, or activities having common characteristics or attributes (they are a protected class under the Constitution). Classification, type, denomination, category, kind, variety, genus, species, breed, genre, division, branch, sort, cast, mold, grouping, level, collection, brand, grade, pigeonhole, bracket, style, nature, assortment, caste, echelon, ilk, standing, rating, sect, family, subdivision, department, stripe, pedigree, estate, sphere, stratum, order. **2.** See school (1). *Ant.* Individual.

Class action A device by which a suit can be instituted by or against numerous persons whose interests are sufficiently common that the dispute involving all of them can be litigated in one action without joining everyone. One member of the class (the named representative) represents everyone. Before a class action is allowed, the court must be convinced that the class, although ascertainable, contains so many persons that it would be impracticable to bring them all before the court. It must also be clear that there is a well-defined commonality of interest among the group in the questions of law and fact involved in the dispute. Finally, the named representative must demonstrate that he or she will fairly and adequately represent everyone.

Class gift A gift of an aggregate sum to a body of persons whose number is uncertain at the time of the gift. The number of persons will be ascertained at a later time. Each is to receive a definite proportion or share of the gift in an amount that will be dependent on the ultimate number in the group.

Classic, *adj., n.* See outstanding (2), archetype, perpetual, traditional.

Classification, *n.* **1.** An arrangement into groups or categories on the basis of established criteria (classification began during orientation). Categorization, systemization, organization, codification, analysis, grouping, apportionment, assignment, placement, identification, cataloguing, assortment, ordering, distribution, allotment, specification, ordination, gradation, disposition, separation, taxonomy, allocation, hierarchy. **2.** The result of what is classified (he fell into the classification of disabled worker). Category, division, class, denomination, type, genus, species, genre, grade, bracket, pigeonhole, order, nature, subdivision, subtype, assortment, range, gradation, section, designation, family, standing, label, stripe, mold, description, breed, grouping, manner, style, ilk.

Classified information See confidence (2), secret.

Classify, *v.* To arrange in groups or categories on the basis of established criteria (the claims were classified by date). Systematize, organize, codify, group, assign, analyze, apportion, identify, catalogue, assort, distribute, separate, specify, allocate, order, tag, allot, type, divide, ticket, coordinate, departmentalize, index, brand, segregate, correlate, pigeonhole, number, methodize, stratify, screen, sort, distinguish, digest, name, file. *Ant.* Scatter.

Classroom, *n.* See school (1); education, learned.

Clatter, *n.* See noise.

Clause, *n.* A single sentence, paragraph, or other subdivision of a pleading, contract, will, statute, or other document (the refinancing clause was invalidated by the court). Division, section, term, article, provision, proviso, passage, phrase, stipulation, condition, particular, reservation, rider, detail, specification, qualification, exception, covenant, point.

Claustrophobia, *n.* Fear of confined places. See disease; insanity.

Clausum fregit "He broke the close." Relevant to a trespass action (e.g., stepping over a boundary line).

Claw, *v.* See cut (1), wound (1), tear.

Clay, *n.* See earth (1), dirt.

Clayton Act A 1914 statute dealing with antitrust regulations and unfair trade

Clayton Act

practices. It prohibited price discrimination, tying, exclusive dealing contracts, etc.

Clean 1. *adj.* Free from fraud or other wrongdoing (a clean record). Irreproachable, flawless, unsoiled, spotless, above suspicion, blameless, virtuous, fair, decent, upright, guileless, honorable, incorruptible, veracious, moral, unblemished, exemplary, innocent, equitable, unsullied, reputable, decorous, perfect, chaste, unimpaired, above reproach, uncorrupted, righteous, upstanding, inoffensive, angelic, high-principled, impeccable. **2.** *adj.* Unpolluted, clear (clean air). Uncontaminated, wholesome, pure, purified, uninfected, unadulterated, fresh, bright, sanitary, cleansed, hygienic, antiseptic, healthy. **3.** *adj.* Complete (a clean escape). Entire, thorough, total, final, decisive. **4.** *v.* See bathe, fumigate, disinfect. *Ant.* Dishonorable; impure; partial.

Clean bill Bill of exchange without documents attached.

Clean-cut, *adj.* See wholesome (1).

Clean hands doctrine Equity will not grant relief to a party who seeks to use the courts and obtain a remedy when that party has engaged in some prior unlawful or inequitable conduct in connection with the matter in litigation.

Cleanse, *v.* See clear (5); bathe, fumigate, disinfect.

Clear 1. *adj.* Obvious, plain (the clear intent of the legislature was not to allow this kind of takeover). Unhidden, manifest, well-defined, evident, express, unmistakable, patent, self-evident, apparent, unquestionable, visible, unambiguous, palpable, undeniable, conspicuous, unequivocal, indisputable, lucid, distinct, perceptible, perspicuous, understood, ascertained, categorical, unimpeachable, definitive, undisputed, comprehensible, orotund, limpid, intelligible, clear-cut, undeniable, positive, undisguised, straightforward, inescapable, unqualified, definite, lucent, free from ambiguity, luminous, exact, precise, conclusive, unassailable, emphatic, cogent, settled, transparent, uncomplicated, defined, incontrovertible, pronounced, authoritative, conclusive, visible, absolute, salient, blunt, perceivable, overt, observable, free from conjecture. **2.** *adj.* Free from encumbrance (clear title). Unencumbered, unburdened, unconstrained, unhampered, unobstructed, unchecked, unclouded, free from burden or encumbrance, unfettered, unrestrained, free from impediment, unlimited, unbridled, unentangled, open, uncurbed. **3.** *adj.* Radiant (a clear day). Shiny, shining, bright, brilliant, cloudless, luminous, glowing, lighted, lucent, incandescent, glistening, lit, serene, gleaming, aglow, resplendent, fine, lustrous, pellucid, crystalline, diaphanous. **4.** *adj.* Free from guilt (a clear conscience). Guiltless, exonerated, vindicated, acquitted, exculpated, freed, justified, free from criminal charges, purged, uncondemned, delivered, forgiven, condoned, discharged, immune, exempted, nonliable, innocent, immaculate, spotless, unsullied, moral, undefiled, virtuous. **5.** *v.* To vindicate (she was cleared of all charges). Free, exculpate, absolve, acquit, exonerate, forgive, purge, quash, discharge, amnesty, disentangle, reprieve, pardon, liberate, emancipate, unbind, disembroil, unchain, unfetter, deliver, excuse, let go, remit, wipe the slate clean, justify, loose, unloose. *Ant.* Unclear, doubtful; burdened; cloudy; guilty; convict.

Clearance, *n.* **1.** The act of a ship in clearing or leaving a port. **2.** In a contract for the exhibition of motion pictures, the interval of time between the conclusion of an exhibition in one theater and the commencement of one at another. **3.** Approval (security clearance). Permission, certification, substantiation, confirmation, verification, validation, corroboration, accreditation, documentation, authentication. See also concession. *Ant.* Disapproval.

Clear and convincing evidence That degree of evidence which will produce in the mind of the trier of fact a firm belief or conviction as to the truth of an allegation. Convincing clarity, highly likely, more than a preponderance but less than beyond all reasonable doubt, highly probable.

Clear and present danger Imminent danger. Danger that is approaching, forth-coming, close at hand, proximate, immediate, impending, threatening, looming, in the air, overhanging. *Ant.* Remote danger.

Clear-cut, *adj.* See clear (1).

Clearheaded, *adj.* See reasonable, logical, able, cautious, quiet (1, 2), rational.

Clearing account An account containing amounts to be transferred to another account(s) before the end of the accounting period.

Clearinghouse, *n.* An association or place where banks exchange checks and drafts drawn on each other and settle daily balances. Central location, central exchange, distribution center, information headquarters.

Clearly, *adv.* Unequivocally (clearly incorrect). Positively, assuredly, conclusive-ly, emphatically, distinctly, prominently, unambiguously, absolutely, totally, au-thoritatively, prima facie, obviously, recognizably, patently, explicitly, decisively, beyond doubt, beyond question, dogmatically, openly, verifiably, incontrovertibly, demonstrably, admittedly, plainly, indubitably, certainly, unmistakably, notice-ably, perceptibly, markedly, surely, understandably, wholly, entirely. *Ant.* Possi-bly.

Clearly erroneous Based on substantial error, a misapplication of law, the lack of substantial evidence; induced by an erroneous view of the law, or unsupported by substantial evidence.

Clear title Title that is free from any encumbrance, obstruction, burden, or limitation that presents a doubtful or even a reasonable question of law or fact. Good title, marketable title, a title free from palpable defects.

Clear view doctrine See plain view doctrine.

Cleave, *v.* See part (1), cut, divide.

Clemency, *n.* Mercy; treatment with less rigor than one's authority permits (the inmate received clemency when the governor commuted her sentence). Act of mercy, kindness, leniency, charity, sympathy, tolerance, indulgence, forgiveness, absolution, temperance, amnesty, reprieve, beneficence, pardon, compassion, mag-nanimity, consideration, liberality, humanity, grace, forbearance, mitigation, mol-lification, relief, alleviation, moderation, pity, soft-heartedness, tenderness, gentle-ness, extenuation, mildness, exemption, humanness. *Ant.* Harshness.

Clergy, *n.* Ministers of religion. Clergymen, ministry, pastors, clerics, the cloth, rabbis, priests, ecclesiastics, preachers, hierarchy, bishops, cardinals, archbishops, presbytery, episcopacy, the first estate, chaplains. *Ant.* Laity.

Clerical, *adj.* **1.** Pertaining to the clergy (clerical robes). Ecclesiastical, church-ly, religious, pastoral, ministerial, episcopal, monastic, rabbinical, apostolic, papal, hierarchic, priestly, pontifical, canonical, sacred, holy, sacredotal. **2.** Pertaining to the office or labor of a clerk (the sending out of the forms is a clerical function). Ministerial, routine, administrative, administrating, bookkeeping, record keeping, office, typing, filing, auxiliary, assisting, secretarial, stenographic. *Ant.* Lay; managerial.

Clerical error Generally, a mistake in writing or copying a document (e.g., an omission).

Clerk, *n.* **1.** An officer of the court who receives and files pleadings, motions, judgments, etc., issues process, and keeps records of court proceedings. Court official, judicial worker, prothonotary, court employee, recorder. See also official, officer. **2.** An office worker. Secretary, registrar, stenographer, clerical worker, civil servant, assistant, aide, filer, record keeper, scrivener, researcher, transcriber, scribe, teller, administrator. *Ant.* Superintendent.

Clerkship, *n.* **1.** The period that a law student spends in the office of a practicing attorney before being admitted to the bar. Apprenticeship. **2.** Employment of a law student or attorney with a judge. **3.** Employment of a law student at a law firm.

Clever, *adj.* See brilliant, able, competent, original (3), capable, apt (2, 3), cautious, deceptive, deceitful, facetious.

Cliché, *n.* A trite comment or idea. Stereotyped saying, worn out idea, hackneyed statement, chestnut, platitude, truism, bromide. See also commonplace (2), maxim.

Click, *n.* See noise.

Client, *n.* **1.** A person who employs or retains an attorney for advice and representation on legal matters. A client may also include someone who discloses confidential information to an attorney while seeking assistance, whether or not the attorney is actually hired. Person represented, advisee. **2.** A person who uses the services—often professional—of someone else; a customer. Patron, person served, buyer, emptor, purchaser, shopper, consumer, hirer, patronizer, dependent, minor, protégé, pensioner, charge, apprentice, pupil, underling.

Clientele, *n.* See customer, patron (1), client (2).

Cliff, *n.* See bluff (3), mountain.

Clifford trust A grantor trust whereby the grantor (i.e., creator) of the trust retains the right to possess again the property transferred in trust upon the occurrence of an event (e.g., the death of the beneficiary) or the expiration of a period of time. The grantor retains a reversionary interest.

Climate, *n.* **1.** The weather conditions (the climate in Boston). Weather pattern, weather zone, temperature, prevailing weather, meteorological conditions, environment, surroundings, clime, atmosphere. See also storm. **2.** Mood, attitude (the climate of opinion). Milieu, setting, tone, spirit, frame of mind, trend, drift, character, coloration, disposition, state, aura, ethos, feeling, influence, air, ambience, direction, sense, view, temper.

Climax, *n.* See crisis, milestone; altitude, apex.

Climb *n., v.* See ascent (2), ascend, advance (4, 5, 7).

Clinch, *v.* See settle (1), complete (1), culminate; affix (1), attach (2).

Cling, *v.* See affix (1), attach (2), cohere (1).

Clinic, *n.* See hospital, ward (3), home (2).

Clinical, *adj.* See objective (1, 2), analytic; medical.

Clinker, *n.* See mistake.

Clip, *v.* See cut (1), abridge (1).

Clipper, *n.* See vessel (1).

Clique, *n.* See coterie, club, family.

Cloak, *v.* To conceal; to disguise (the meeting was cloaked in secrecy). Mask, secrete, veil, camouflage, beguile, cover up, suppress, cloud, bury, falsify, seclude, mislead, muffle, hide, pretend, dissimulate, blanket, shroud, dissemble, dress up, shade, shelter, blind, distort, eclipse, dupe, masquerade, adumbrate, becloud, robe, befog, haze, ensconce, bluff, envelop, gloss over, feign. *Ant.* Display.

Clobber, *v.* See batter, attack (1).

Clock, *n.* Watch. Timepiece, dial, timer, horologe, speedometer, meter, chronometer.

Clod, *n.* See idiot, boor.

Clog, *v.* To obstruct (the accumulated pollution clogged the stream). Block, choke, dam up, encumber, impede, jam, occlude, trammel, restrict, retard, frustrate, fetter, restrain, interfere, delay, oppose, congest, close, burden, embarrass, hamper, hobble, bar, check, inconvenience, handicap, foil, saddle, countercheck, discontinue, checkmate, cram, congest, arrest, stymie, barricade, suppress, constrict, stifle, retard, stall, foreclose, detain, preclude, stultify. *Ant.* Clear.

Cloister, *v., n.* See confine (1); arcade; asylum; church.

Clone, *n.* See copy (1), imitation.

Close 1. *v.* To terminate; to wind up (he closed the account). Finish, end, bring to an end, complete, discontinue, halt, cease, suspend, shut down, dismiss, conclude, consummate, finalize, call a halt, expire, break off, prosecute to a conclusion, accomplish, achieve, satisfy, fulfill, surcease, adjourn, interrupt, recess, climax, clinch, culminate. **2.** *v.* To bar access to; to obstruct (after the license revocation, the store was closed). Shut up, estop, prevent entrance, confine, blockade, pen, secure, clog, occlude, jam, impede, barricade, bridle, shut down, block, enclose, lock, secure, turn off, plug, cork, coop, suspend, strike, bottle up. **3.** *n.* A portion of land enclosed by a hedge, fence, or other visible enclosure, or by an invisible boundary based on one's title (breaking the close). Enclosure, ground, confine, court, yard, area, pen, curtilage, garden, fold. **4.** *n.* The ending (the close of the trial). Finish, completion, suspension, discontinuation, consummation, finalization, expiration, culmination, windup, finale, adjournment, cessation, peroration, closure, stoppage. **5.** *adj.* Precise (the police provided close surveillance). Rigorous, vigilant, careful, thorough, fixed, attentive, taxing, uncompromising, assiduous, intense, meticulous, concentrated, minute, unremitting, intent, dogged, earnest, alert, tight, solid, keen, all-out, painstaking, harsh, punctilious, scrupulous, unsparing, stringent, faithful, relentless. **6.** *adj.* Near in time, space, or association (close associates; close confinement; close range). Imminent, impending, proximate, neighboring, bordering, adjacent, at hand, touching, approximate, approaching, immediate, contiguous, adjoining, nigh, forthcoming, strongly attached, intimate, confidential, brotherly, sisterly, fraternal, allied, familiar, inseparable, dear. **7.** *adj.* Confined, cramped (close quarters). Crowded, narrow, stuffed, dense, impenetrable, compact, solid, congested, compressed, packed, clotted, clogged, impermeable, restricted. *Ant.* Commence (1); open (2); beginning (4); sloppy (5); remote (6); spacious (7).

Close corporation A corporation whose shares (or at least whose voting shares) are held by a single shareholder or by a closely knit group of shareholders.

Closed-end borrowing A mortgage that does not permit additional borrowing.

Closed shop The practice whereby a worker must be a member of a union as a condition of employment.

Close-minded, *adj.* See narrow (2), inflexible, arbitrary.

Close-mouthed, *adj.* See mute, silent; hostile.

Closet, *n.* Room for storage. Cupboard, compartment, recess, cabinet, cubicle, wardrobe, pantry, cubby, stall, room. See also cell, alcove.

Closing, *n.* The final steps in a transaction for the sale of real estate (e.g., payment is made, mortgage is secured, taxes are allocated, etc).

Closing argument The final statements by the attorneys to the jury or to the court, summarizing the evidence that they think they have established and that the other side has failed to establish during the trial.

Closing costs Expenses in the sale of real estate in addition to the purchase price (e.g., fees for title examination, commission, insurance, appraisal, deed preparation, settlement statement, escrows for future payments of taxes or insurance, etc.).

Closure, *n.* See conclusion.

Clot, *v.* See cohere (1).

Cloth, *n.* See material (3), clothes.

Clothe, *v.* To cover or wrap (he tried to clothe his argument with authenticity). Envelop, invest, endow, cloak, drape, outfit, attire, appoint, furnish, encase, empower, array, cloud, sheathe, veil, screen, disguise, embroider, don, arm, garb, uniform, provide. *Ant.* Divest.

Clothes, *n.* Garments. Apparel, wear, costume, clothing, dress, garb, outfit,

141

uniform, vestments, wearing apparel, attire, habiliments, gear, outfit, duds; blouse, sweater, pants, shirt, coat, tunic, blue jeans, bodice, hat, cap, bonnet, footwear, boot, cape.

Cloture, *n.* A legislative procedure whereby extended and unreasonable debate is ended to allow a vote on the measure (cloture was invoked to end the filibuster).

Cloud 1. *n.* A claim or encumbrance (the mortgage constituted a cloud on the title). Debt, outstanding obligation, security interest, obstruction, flaw, imperfection, burden, hold, restraint, charge, indebtedness, taint, liability, prescription, hypothecation. **2.** *n.* Mistrust (following the arrest, his job was under a perpetual cloud). Suspicion, ill fortune, disgrace, blemish, stigma, stain, specter, apprehension, scandal, affliction, taint, gloom, darkness, haze, fog, shadow, blanket, curse, shroud, disbelief, contestability, distrust, lack of confidence or faith, skepticism, misgiving, incredulity, puzzlement. See also doubt (2). **3.** *v.* To obscure; to hide (the argument simply clouded the issue). Dim, darken, blunt, muddle, tarnish, eclipse, shroud, distort, veil, disturb, confuse, becloud, confound, complicate, disorganize, unsettle, overcast, overshadow, film, obfuscate, mar. *Ant.* Release; confidence; clarify.

Cloud on title An outstanding claim or encumbrance which, if valid, would affect or impair the title of the owner of a particular estate but which can be shown to be invalid or inapplicable to the estate in question.

Cloudy, *adj.* See indefinite; climate; mysterious.

"Clout," *n.,* *v.* See influence (1), authority (2), hold (6); attack (1), batter.

Clown, *n.* Comic, comedian, jester, joker, card, wag, wit, prankster, harlequin. See also boor, idiot.

Club 1. *n.* A voluntary, incorporated or unincorporated association of persons who have common purposes. Society, affiliation, community, league, federation, union, consortium, coterie, guild, lodge, sorority, fraternity, sisterhood, brotherhood, circle, set, fellowship, coalition, clique, gang, clan, band, alliance, company, sodality. **2.** *v.* See attack (1), batter.

Clubhouse, *n.* See building (1).

Clue, *n.* A suggestion or item of evidence that may or may not lead to a solution or answer. Guide, link, signal, lead, trace, suggestion, inkling, scent, cue, indication, indicator, insinuation, pointer, inference, direction, thread, key, glimmer, token.

Clumsy, *adj.* See awkward, gaudy.

Clunk, *n.* See boor, idiot; noise.

Cluster, *v., n.* See collect (1), coalesce, compile, group (2), accumulate; collection (2).

Clutch, *v.* See seize; handle (2), touch (1).

Clutter, *n., v.* See confusion; confuse.

Coach, *n., v.* See vessel (1); teacher; instruct (1), direct (2), manage (1), improve, nurture, discipline (4).

Coadjutant, *n.* See assistant.

Coadjutor, *n.* Helper or ally. See assistant, partner.

Coadventurer, *n.* One who takes part with others in an adventure, in a venture, or in a business undertaking containing risks.

Coalesce, *v.* To combine into one unit (the various factions coalesced on the issue of electoral reform). Unite, fuse, organize, band together, amalgamate, ally, merge, join forces, converge, confederate, league, cluster, mingle, herd, affiliate, assemble, centralize, unify, solidify, join, connect, consolidate, integrate, agglutinate, intermingle, fraternize, become one, incorporate. *Ant.* Disintegrate.

Coalition, *n.* An alliance for a special purpose (the Federation is a coalition of local paralegal associations). Cooperative, merger, league, consortium, partnership, amalgamation, union, confederacy, fusion, amalgam, binding, syndicate, convergence, compact, party, cartel, congress, fellowship, society, integration, mixture. *Ant.* Severance.

Coarse, *adj.* See awkward, rude, common (3), gaudy, base (1, 2) inferior (2).

Co-assignee, *n.* One of two or more assignees of the same subject matter.

Coast, *n.* See shore, border (1).

Coaster, *n.* See vessel (1).

Coast Guard, *n.* See military.

Coating, *n.* See protection.

Coax, *v.* See manipulate (1), entice, entrap, recommend, persuade.

Cocaine, *n.* See drug.

Cocky, *adj.* See arrogant, pompous, certain (2).

Co-conspirator, *n.* One who engages in an illegal alliance with others (President Nixon was named as an unindicted co-conspirator). Fellow conspirator, abettor, accessory, collaborator, partner in crime, associate, auxiliary, assistant, confederate, schemer, strategist, comrade. See also accomplice. *Ant.* Bystander.

Cocotte, *n.* See prostitute (1).

Coddle, *v.* See accommodate (1), yield (1), pander (2).

Code, *n.* A collection of laws, rules, or regulations organized by subject matter. (United States Code; dress code). Statutes, ordinances, legislation, canons, precepts, norms, standards, principles, enactments, bylaws, charter, codification, body of law, compilation, lex, guidelines, rubric, corpus juris, ethics, codex, maxim.

Code Civil The code that embodies the civil law of France. The name was later changed to Code Napoleon. It is the basis of some of the Louisiana Civil Code today.

Co-defendant, *n.* One of two or more defendants being sued in the same litigation or being charged with the same crime.

Codeine, *n.* See drug.

Code Napoleon See Code Civil.

Code of Federal Regulations (C.F.R.) An annual accumulation of some federal agency regulations.

Code of Military Justice The substantive and procedural law governing military justice and its administration in all of the armed forces of the United States.

Code of Professional Responsibility Rules of conduct governing the legal profession written by the American Bar Association and adopted by many states. Code of ethics, disciplinary rules.

Code pleading A system of pleading that replaced common-law pleading. In code pleading, the ultimate facts had to be stated as the basis for the cause of action or defense.

Codex, *n.* A code or collection of laws.

Codicil, *n.* **1.** A supplement or addition to a will (the state required the codicil to be executed with the same formality as the will itself). **2.** Something added. Addendum, explanation, extension, appendix, postscript, subscript, rider, accessory, epilogue, continuation, appurtenance, adjunct, complement, insertion, annex, accompaniment, attachment, sequel, additive. *Ant.* Main document.

Codification, *n.* The process of collecting and systematically arranging by subject matter, the laws, rules, or regulations of a particular geographic location (e.g., a state), or of a certain area of the law (e.g., criminal law statutes). Categorization, arrangement, systemization, classification, compilation, tabulation, preparation of a compendium.

Codify, *v.* To collect and arrange laws, rules, and regulations by subject matter (the statutes of the state were not codified until 1909). Categorize, arrange, systematize, compile, tabulate, assemble, divide, subdivide, classify, digest, consolidate, pigeonhole, standardize, index, rank, coordinate, catalogue, assort, rationalize, label, methodize, grade, group, order, formalize.

Coequal, *adj.* The same in rank, value, or degree (Congress is a coequal branch of the government with the executive and judicial branches). Equal, coordinate, uniform, equibalanced, on the same footing, of a kind, coextensive, commensurate, symmetrical, comparable, on a par, correlative, parallel, even, equivalent. *Ant.* Inferior, superior.

Coerce, *v.* To compel compliance (the spouse was coerced into signing the separation agreement). Force, intimidate, impel, constrain, overpower, oblige, dragoon, browbeat, threaten, bulldoze, exact, drive, bully, press, pressure, enjoin, command, demand, lure, railroad, extort, commandeer, threaten, abuse, dominate, conscript, harass, terrorize, dictate, subjugate, necessitate, harangue, bludgeon, interdict, foist, prod. *Ant.* Allow.

Coercion, *n.* Compelling something by force, arms, or threats (the confession was obtained by coercion). Force, intimidation, browbeating, compulsion, threats, constraint, violence, arm-twisting, pressure, menace, abuse, domination, undue influence, extortion, dictation, overpowering, bondage, control, blackmail, oppression, repression, tyranny, harassment, dictatorship, dominance. See also duress. *Ant.* Volition.

Coercive, *adj.* See involuntary, compulsory, forcible.

Co-executor, *n.* One who is a joint executor with one or more others.

Coexist, *v.* See accompany, coincide (2).

Coextensive, *adj.* Having the same boundaries or limits (your rights are coextensive under both contracts). Coequal, synonymous, comparable, parallel, analogous, congruent, matched, symmetrical, equivalent, even. *Ant.* Unequal.

Coffee break, *n.* See recess.

Coffee shop, *n.* See inn.

Coffer, *n.* The place where money or other valuables are stored. Strongbox, safe, treasury, bank, depository, vault, till.

Coffin, *n.* See burial.

Cog, *n.* See cipher (2), assistant, servant.

Cogent, *adj.* Convincing (the brief contained many cogent points). Persuasive, telling, weighty, conclusive, positive, authoritative, forceful, potent, irresistible, influential, meritorious, pertinent, sound, relevant, consistent, apropos, compelling, trenchant, rational, incontrovertible, inescapable, powerful, effective, germane, applicable, forcible, urgent, valid, puissant, well-grounded, substantiated, determinative, appealing, commanding, unequivocal, solid, logical, efficacious, undeniable. *Ant.* Ineffective.

Cogitate, *v.* See deliberate (1), consider (1), contemplate (1); debate (2).

Cognate, *adj.* Related; similar (cognate offenses). Kindred, generic, allied, parallel, coordinate, like, alike, connected, kin, analogous, affiliated, associated, collateral, close, matching, comparable, consanguine, interrelated, corresponding. *Ant.* Dissimilar, unrelated.

Cognates, *n.* Relations by the mother's side or by females.

Cognition, *n.* Perception; awareness. Intelligence, cognizance, understanding, insight, enlightenment, appreciation, familiarity, wisdom, knowledge, consciousness, sensibility, apprehension, illumination, conception, realization. See also comprehension. *Ant.* Ignorance.

Cognitive, *adj.* The mental process of comprehension, judgment, memory, and reasoning. (The child's cognitive functions were impaired). See cognition.

Cognizable, *adj.* **1.** Capable of being tried or examined before a designated tribunal; within the jurisdiction of the court to adjudicate (the offense was cognizable before the superior court). Triable, proper for examination, subject to the court's jurisdiction, justiciable, accountable. **2.** Capable of being known (the group was not a cognizable class for purposes of jury selection). Ascertainable, perceptible, clear, definite, explicit, discoverable, decipherable, recognizable, discernible, knowable, distinct, distinguishable.

Cognizance, *n.* **1.** The exercise of jurisdiction; the power to hear a case (the court shall have full cognizance over all maritime cases). Authority, decision-making power, dominion, legal power, capacity to decide. **2.** Judicial notice or knowledge (the court took cognizance of the general state of the economy). **3.** Awareness, understanding (the judge took cognizance of the objection). Consciousness, knowledge, observation, note, recognition, notice, comprehension, discovery, regard, grasp, sensibility, cognition, apprehension, sentience, intelligence, heed, consideration.

Cognizant, *adj.* Aware, informed (they were cognizant of their responsibility). Apprised, conscious, mindful, posted, enlightened, knowledgeable, versed in, educated, wise, instructed, perceptive, erudite, knowing, recognizing, intelligent, conversant, sentient, posted, familiar, discerning, acquainted, apprehensive, expert, sagacious, no stranger to, proficient, well-advised. *Ant.* Oblivious.

Cognomen, *n.* See name (1).

Cognovit note A written statement that the debtor owes money and "confesses judgment," or allows the creditor to obtain a judgment in court for the money whenever the creditor wishes or whenever a particular event takes place (such as a failure to make a payment).

Cohabit, *v.* To live together as husband and wife (the lawyer asked her whether she cohabited with her husband after they had the fight). Stay together, reside together, share bed and board, conjugate, dwell together continuously, live in sexual intimacy, copulate. *Ant.* Separate.

Cohabitation, *n.* The act of living together as husband and wife (there was no cohabitation in the state of Ohio). Mutual assumption of marital rights, residing together, union, alliance, matrimony, coverture, marital rights, wedlock, marriage, nuptial state. *Ant.* Separation, divorce.

Co-heir, *n.* One of several heirs to whom an inheritance passes or descends.

Cohere, *v.* **1.** To cling or stick together (the substance would not cohere). Glue, coalesce, stick, fasten, merge, blend, fuse, hold together, adhere, harden, unify, attach, combine, unite, associate, cement, solidify, cleave, condense, hold fast, consolidate, coagulate, affix, clot. **2.** To be logically consistent (the pieces of the testimony did not cohere). Make sense, agree, conform, be related, square, correspond, "hold water," follow, be logical, coincide, tally, be connected, be united, harmonize, hold together, match, concur. *Ant.* Detach; disagree.

Coherence, *n.* **1.** Logical consistency (the brief lacked organization and coherence). Logic, rationality, intelligibility, clarity, connection, unity, comprehensibility, understandability, congruity, harmony, agreement, cohesiveness, continuity, correspondence, meaning. **2.** Cohesion. Attachment, fusion, sticking, adherence, union, connection, adhesion, consolidation, blending, solidification, accretion, coalescence. *Ant.* Confusion; disintegration.

Coherent, *adj.* **1.** Logically sound (a coherent presentation of the options available). Rational, clear, intelligible, comprehensible, articulate, precise, lucid, cogent, consistent, orderly, easily understood, graphic, recognizable, understandable, systematic, organized, decipherable, forthright, meaningful, perceptive, harmonious, congruous, in agreement. **2.** Sticking together (a coherent substance). Cohesive, adhering, joined, tied, fused, connected, combined, united, composite, viscous, compressed, inescapable, holding together, solid, indivisible, impermeable, impenetrable, well-knit, consolidated. *Ant.* Confused; disjoined.

Cohesion, *n.* See coherence.

Cohesive, *adj.* Sticking together (a cohesive group of irate citizens). See coherent (2).

Cohort, *n.* **1.** A companion (her cohort was arrested 10 minutes later). Friend, collaborator, ally, partner, comrade, mate, helper, abettor, follower, colleague, peer, associate, accomplice, confederate, crony; following, retinue. **2.** A company or group. Band, detachment, troop, legion, wing, gang, squadron, detachment.

Coif, *n.* A hat or cap worn by sergeants at law. A title given to sergeants at law. See Order of the Coif.

Coin 1. *n.* Metal money; pieces of gold, silver, or other metal in a prescribed form authorized by the government to circulate as money. Coinage, currency, change, piece, capital, funds, wealth, cash, legal tender. See also money. **2.** *v.* To fashion pieces of metal into a prescribed form to circulate as money on the authority of the government. Issue, form, stamp, monetize, circulate. See also mint. **3.** *v.* To make up (to coin a phrase). Mold, devise, manufacture, originate, commence, launch, construct, produce, inaugurate, formulate, fabricate, concoct. See also create, invent, forge (2).

Coinage, *n.* **1.** The process or function of coining metallic money. **2.** The great mass of metallic money in circulation.

Coincide, *v.* **1.** To correspond (the two accounts of the accident did not coincide). Agree, square, harmonize, conform, tally, dovetail, accord, fit, equal, match, jibe, cohere, be of the same mind, be at one with. See also comport (1), correspond (1). **2.** To occupy the same position; to occur at the same time; to come together (the date of the hearing coincided with the date of the medical examination). Synchronize, unite, be simultaneous, occur simultaneously, converge, cross, coexist, accompany, be identical, fit exactly, be equal, be contemporaneous. *Ant.* Contradict; diverge.

Coincidence, *n.* A surprising occurrence; a seemingly accidental sequence of events (it was a coincidence that they arrived at the same time). Accident, fluke, chance, happenstance, serendipity, remarkable concurrence. *Ant.* Planned occurrence.

Coincidental, *adj.* See fortuitous; contingent.

Coinsurance, *n.* Insurance risks shared jointly, e.g., by two or more insurers, by the insurer and the insured.

Coitus, *n.* Sexual intercourse. Copulation, mating, coition, congress, consummation, fornication.

Coke, *n.* See drug.

Cold, *adj.* **1.** See apathetic, indifferent (2), callous, rude. **2.** Heatless. Arctic, polar, frigid, Siberian, crisp, cool, freezing, bitter, frosty, biting, nippy, chilly, penetrating. See also climate, storm.

Cold blood, *n.,* **cold-blooded,** *adj.* Something done willfully or deliberately (he acted in cold blood). With premeditation, calculation, malice, deliberation, without emotion, insensitive, hard-hearted, savage, barbarity, inhumanity, brutality, ruthlessness, merciless, detached, impervious, diabolical, evil, satanic, pitiless, villainous, heartless, unfeeling, uncaring, contemptuous. See also deadly, inhuman, malicious. *Ant.* Compassionate.

Cold turkey, *n.* Complete and immediate termination or withdrawal from that to which one is addicted.

Collaborate, *v.* See conspire, cooperate.

Collaboration, *n.* The act of working together in a joint project (the co-defendants worked in collaboration). Teamwork, alliance, cooperation, assistance, conspiracy, connivance, synergism, association, coaction, joining forces, cahoots, communion, working side by side. See also concert.

Collapse 1. *v.* To fall in (the building collapsed). Cave in, crumple, disintegrate, be demolished, drop, shatter, give out, give way, break apart, topple, tumble, buckle. **2.** *v.* To fail (the company collapsed when the claims were made). Fold, flounder, go under, abort, default, go up in smoke, fall through, succumb, falter, stumble, wash out, fizzle, be overthrown, keel over. **3.** *n.* See exhaustion, failure. *Ant.* Erect; succeed.

Collapsible corporation A corporation set up under a prearranged plan to fold or liquidate before it realizes substantial taxable income from its property.

Collate, *v.* See classify, compare (1), codify, check (3).

Collateral 1. *n.* Property that is pledged as security for the satisfaction of a debt (his house was the collateral for the loan). Insurance, pledge, guarantee, warranty, surety, endorsement, assurance, bond, deposit. **2.** *adj.* Subordinate (the judge told counsel to stay away from questions that were collateral to the central issue). Secondary, incidental, subsidiary, accessory, ancillary, unessential, immaterial, minor, unconnected, peripheral, trivial. **3.** *adj.* By the side; additional; confirming (collateral proceeding). Accompanying, parallel, attendant, supportive, supporting, corroborative, associated, corresponding, supplementary, sustaining, affiliated, concurrent, concomitant, related, kindred, supplemental, connected.

Collateral ancestor A phrase sometimes used to designate uncles, aunts, and other collateral "ancestors" who, strictly speaking, are not ancestors.

Collateral attack An attack against a judgment in an incidental proceeding. The attack is not brought in the original proceeding; it is brought in a proceeding other than the one that resulted in the judgment now being attacked. *Ant.* Direct attack.

Collateral consanguinity Persons are related collaterally when they have a common ancestor.

Collateral estoppel doctrine When an issue of law or fact has been litigated in one action (and when the determination of the issue was essential to the judgment), it cannot be relitigated in another action even if the two suits did not involve the same cause of action.

Collateral facts Facts that are not directly connected with the principal issue in the dispute.

Collateral heir An heir who is not of the direct line of the deceased, but comes from a collateral line—a brother, aunt, nephew, or cousin of the deceased.

Collateral issues Issues that are not directly involved in the case.

Collateral kinsmen Those who descend from the same common ancestor but not from one another.

Collateral line A line of descent connecting persons who are not directly related to each other as ascendants or descendants, but whose relationship consists in a common descent from the same ancestor.

Collateral mortgage A mortgage that is designed not directly to secure an existing debt, but to secure a mortgage note pledged as collateral security for a debt or succession of debts.

Collateral negligence The negligence attributable to a contractor employed by a principal for which the principal is not responsible. The principal would be responsible if his or her servant had committed the negligence.

Collateral relatives Next of kin (e.g., a cousin) who are not in the direct line of inheritance.

Collateral security A security given in addition to the direct security and subordinate to it. The creditor goes after the collateral security if the direct security fails.

Collateral source rule If an injured person receives compensation for his or her injuries from a source that is independent of the wrongdoer, the compensation is not deducted from the damages that the latter must pay.

Collateral warranty A warranty given by a third party (not the seller). This warranty does not run with the land; only the buyer (covenantee) can enforce it.

Collation, *n.* **1.** The comparison of a copy with its original to determine its correctness (a collation of corporate seals). Confirmation, examination, matching, pairing, checking, correlation, juxtaposition. **2.** Taking into account money or property already given to children (as an advance on an inheritance) by the deceased in order to equalize the shares when dividing the assets of the deceased. Hotchpot.

Colleague, *n.* An associate. Partner, fellow worker, mate, teammate, comrade, consort, companion, cohort, ally, co-worker, collaborator, accomplice, peer, adjunct, aide, abettor, confederate, confrere, coadjutor, helper, fellow, crony, backer. *Ant.* Competitor.

Collect, *v.* **1.** To bring scattered things into one mass or fund (the assets were collected). Accumulate, amass, gather, incorporate, unite, congregate, compile, concentrate, summon, aggregate, scrape together, muster, amalgamate, herd, convene. **2.** To obtain payment (the creditor came to collect on the debt). Receive payment, collect payment, settle accounts, redeem, execute, levy, realize, recoup, recover. *Ant.* Disburse; pay out.

Collectible, *n.* Obligations, debts, demands, and liabilities that one could be forced to pay by means of the legal process.

Collection, *n.* **1.** The act of bringing scattered things together into one mass (the collection of assets). Accumulation, amassment, gathering, congregation, compilation, aggregation, concentration, convening, mobilization, amalgamation, accretion, cumulation, conglomeration, stockpile, cluster, store. **2.** A group (collection of people). Audience, assembly, mob, assortment, miscellany, throng, cluster, convocation, assemblage, crowd, herd, flock. **3.** A form of endorsement on a note or check, which authorizes the transferee to collect the amount of it (for collection). **4.** The act of obtaining payment (collection of debts). Receiving payment, settling accounts, adjustment, remittance, restitution, indemnification, remuneration, clearance, reimbursement. **5.** Contribution (church collection). Alms, pledge, offering, gift. *Ant.* Disbursement; individual; payment.

Collective 1. *adj.* Relating to a group (collective bargaining). Common, representative, aggregate, mutual, whole, combined, unified, composite, cumulative, total, shared, joint, cooperative, concerted, consolidated, corporate, integrated, gathered, massed, comprehensive, broad. **2.** *n.* A group of people who comprise a work team or organization (farm collective). *Ant.* Individual.

Collective bargaining A procedure designed to achieve collective work agreements between employers and their accredited representative, the union.

Collective bargaining unit All of the employees of a single employer except for the employees of a particular department or division who have voted otherwise.

Collective mark A trademark or service mark used by members of a cooperative, an association, or other collective group.

College, *n.* See school (1).

Collide, *v.* **1.** To strike or dash against (the vehicles collided). Meet head on, strike against, crash, smash, converge, bump, knock into, hit, beat against, bang, impinge, slam, jolt, jar, run into, make contact. **2.** To conflict (their viewpoints collided). Meet in opposition, clash, differ, diverge, oppose, obstruct, be at variance, be antagonistic, be incompatible, counteract, contradict, wrangle, feud, quarrel, contend, run afoul of, confront. *Ant.* Evade; harmonize.

Colliery, *n.* See mine, cave.

Collision, *n.* **1.** Striking together of two objects, one of which may be stationary (a collision at the intersection). Crash, accident, impact, smashup, concussion, shock, wreck, demolition, destruction, blow, impingement, encounter, convergence, pileup, percussion, casualty, bump. **2.** Conflict (a collision of points of view). Confrontation, dispute, struggle, battle, engagement, challenge, disagreement, interference, opposition, friction, discord, dissension, clash, antagonism, skirmish, fracas, hostility, contention, altercation, embroilment, affray. *Ant.* Avoidance; agreement.

Colloquial, *adj.* See casual (3), informal.

Colloquium, *n.* **1.** That part of a complaint for defamation which alleges that the defamatory matter was published of and concerning the plaintiff. **2.** A conference. Group discussion, meeting, seminar, session, colloquy, round table.

Colloquy, *n.* See colloqium (2), conversation (1), communication (1), conference (1), intercourse (1).

Collude, *v.* See conspire, plot (3).

Collusion, *n.* **1.** An agreement between two or more persons to defraud someone of his or her rights by the forms of law, or to obtain an object forbidden by law (the police suspected collusion). Conspiracy, secret agreement, fraudulent agreement, complicity, intrigue, machination, scheme, scheming, trickery, plot, connivance, manipulation, engineering, covin, cabal, chicanery, treachery, collaboration, perfidy, secret understanding, contrivance, guile, deceit, hoax. **2.** An agreement between a husband and wife in a divorce proceeding that one of them will lie to the court in order to facilitate the obtaining of the divorce.

Collusive, *adj.* Pertaining to an agreement to defraud someone of his or her rights by the forms of the law, or to obtain an object forbidden by law (collusive suit). Conspiratorial, conspiring, plotting, dishonest, fraudulent, underhanded, deceitful, machinating, deceptive, beguiling, surreptitious, clandestine, treacherous, calculating, furtive, cunning. *Ant.* Honest.

Collusive action An action that is not founded on an actual controversy between the parties, but is brought for the purpose of securing a decision on a point of law out of curiosity or to settle the rights of third persons who are not parties.

Colonel, *n.* See military, officer, sailor.

Colonize, *v.* See occupy, reside (1), inhabit.

Colony, *n.* See mandate (2) area (1), zone, community.

Color 1. *n.* A deceptive appearance (the seizure was carried out under color of law). Guise, pretext, external appearance, semblance, show, facade, mask, front, masquerade, cloak, subterfuge, deception, device, fabrication, falsification, misrepresentation, pretense, false show, excuse, resemblance, distortion, exaggeration, representation, allegation. **2.** *n.* An apparent right. A prima facie right. **3.** *v.* To misrepresent (his prior involvement in the case colored his decision). Distort, pervert, taint, exaggerate, prejudice, falsify, embellish, garble, twist, embroider, stretch, understate, overstate, misconstrue, influence, adorn, affect, tilt, warp, doctor. **4.** *n.* Pigment. Dye, tint, paint, shade, coloring, hue, tone, complexion, tinge, glow. *Ant.* True picture; portray accurately.

Colorable, *adj.* **1.** Having only the appearance of truth (a colorable transaction). Deceptive, counterfeit, sham, pretended, fraudulent, deceitful, feigned, artful, spurious, ostensible, bogus, appearing. **2.** Plausible (colorable authority). Credible, supportable, presumable, seeming, tenable, believable, conceivable, apparent, convincing. *Ant.* True; implausible.

Colorful, *adj.* See compelling, beautiful, attractive, flamboyant, brilliant; wild; exaggerate.

Colorless, *adj.* See commonplace (2); neutral.

Color of authority The semblance or presumption of authority of a public officer derived from his or her apparent title to office or from a writ or other apparently valid process in his or her hands.

Color of law 1. The appearance of legal right but without the substance. **2.** The misuse of power possessed by virtue of state law and made possible only because the wrongdoer is clothed with the authority of the state.

Color of office The pretense of an official right to do an act by someone who has no such right.

Color of title Apparent title. The appearance or semblance of title but not the reality.

Colossal, *adj.* See big.

Colt, *n.* See animal (1).

Column, *n.* See post (4); article (4); array, succession (2), chain (1).

Comatose, *adj.* See oblivious, unconscious; stupor.

Comb, *v.* See investigate, ferret, trace.

Combat 1. *n.* A forcible encounter between two or more persons. Battle, duel, clash, conflict, fight, struggle, antagonism, war, contention, hostilities, siege, encounter, contest, polemic, debate, quarrel, argument, confrontation, wrangling, altercation, engagement. **2.** *v.* See compete. *Ant.* Accord; cooperate.

Combatant, *n., adj.* See sailor, adversary, competitor; hostile, offensive, assertive.

Combative, *adj.* See belligerent, hostile, contentious (1), litigious, competitive (1).

Combination, *n.* The union or association of two or more entities for the attainment of some common end (a combination in restraint of trade). Confederation, conspiracy, combining, joining, amalgamation, coalition, alliance, league, cabal, connection, fusion, grouping, guild, circle, consortium, trust, cartel, monopoly, merger, coalescence, federation, combine, club, syndicate, faction, ring, block, pool, coterie, affiliation, arrangement, aggregation. *Ant.* Dissolution.

Combination in restraint of trade An agreement or understanding between two or more persons, in the form of a contract, trust, pool, holding company, or other form of association, for the purpose of unduly restricting competition, monopolizing trade in a certain commodity, controlling its production, distribution, and price, or otherwise interfering with freedom of trade without statutory authority.

Combine, *v.,* **combine,** *n.* **1.** *v.* To merge (the two teams combined forces). Mix, associate, couple, amalgamate, league, synthesize, intermix, link, commingle, pool, incorporate, fuse, blend, consolidate, unify, connect, intertwine, unite, syndicate, collaborate, federate, affiliate, collude, conspire, band together. See also converge. **2.** *n.* See combination; vessel (1). *Ant.* Sever.

Combustion, *n.* See fire (1), burn.

Come, *v.* See approach (1), enter (2), appear (2).

Comedian, *n.* See clown, comic.

Comely, *adj.* See attractive, beautiful, proper.

Comeuppance, *n.* See retribution, punishment, retaliation.

Comfort, 1. *n.* Consolation or benefit (the comfort provided by a spouse). Contentment, relief, solace, encouragement, help, amenity, ease, succor, support, satisfaction, peace, convenience, sympathy, reassurance, serenity, calm, relaxation, well-being, gratification, luxury, pleasure, cheer, repose, rescue, security. **2.** *v.* See mitigate, assuage. *Ant.* Distress; aggravate.

Comfortable, *adj.* **1.** Agreeable or pleasant. Snug, pleasurable, relaxed, at ease, serene, habitable, cozy, quiet, contented, cheerful, ample, peaceful, enjoyable, genial, commodious, warm, luxuriant. **2.** See adequate.

Comic, *n.,* **comical,** *adj.* Amusing. Funny, witty, burlesque, absurd, jocular, facetious, entertaining, zany, droll, ridiculous, laughable, humorous. See also clown.

Coming, *adj., n.* See imminent; appearance (2).

Comity, *n.* **1.** The courts of one jurisdiction will give effect to the laws and judicial decisions of another state as a matter of deference and mutual respect even if no obligation exists to do so. **2.** A willingness to grant a privilege. Accommodation, courtesy, civility, harmony, affability, amenity, neighborliness, consideration, good-fellowship, goodwill. *Ant.* Hostility.

Command 1. *n.* An order (the command to proceed came from the chief). Instruction, commandment, proclamation, charge, warrant, injunction, decree, manifesto, directive, ultimatum, summons, edict, imperative, requirement, demand, prescript, assignment, fiat, behest, bidding, subpoena, mandate, requisition, dictum. **2.** *n.* Power to dominate and control (the superintendent assumed command). Authority, dominion, supremacy, reins, jurisdiction, leadership, charge, sovereignty, supervision, oversight, management, leadership, upper hand, domination, governorship. **3.** *v.* To direct (the judge commanded her to be present). Order, instruct, charge, require, mandate, adjure, rule, authorize, prescribe, decree, govern, impose, bid, enjoin, dictate, compel, coerce, obligate, exact, subpoena, ordain. *Ant.* Request; impotence; beg.

Commandeer, *v.* See seize, compel, appropriate (1).

Commander, *n.* See manager, master (1), officer; military, sailor.

Commanding, *adj.* See leading (1), dominant.

Commandment, *n.* See command (1).

Commemorate, *v.* See honor (2), dedicate, observe; memorial; solemnity.

Commence, *v.* To initiate by performing the first act (he commenced the suit by filing the complaint). Institute, start, begin, activate, instigate, inaugurate, originate, set in operation, open, enter upon, enter into, arise, come into existence, undertake, embark upon, venture into, introduce, install, take the initiative, pioneer. *Ant.* Terminate.

Commencement, *n.* The act of beginning (commencement of the action). Initiation, origination, opening, genesis, inauguration, onset, first step, emergence, conception, creation, establishment, actuation, infancy, birth, alpha, instigation, dawn. *Ant.* Conclusion.

Commend, *v.* See recommend, honor (2).

Commendable, *adj.* See meritorious (2).

Commendation, *n.* See approbation, approval, citation (3).

Commensurate, *adj.* Proportionate (she was not paid commensurate with her experience and ability). Corresponding, compatible, in accord, fitting, on a proper scale, commensurable, parallel, appropriate, equivalent, in keeping with, relative, analogous, synchronous, coordinate, coterminous, adequate, equal, on a scale suitable, coextensive, balanced, symmetrical, congruous, matching, in agreement, comparable, consistent, due. *Ant.* Incompatible.

Comment 1. *n.* A statement that explains, criticizes, illustrates, etc. (his comment clarified the matter). Explanation, illustration, criticism, annotation, elucidation, clarification, exposition, gloss, commentary, report, explication, reflection, remark, utterance, exemplification, note, opinion, animadversion, expansion, addendum, critique, review, judgment, assertion, notation, interpretation, exegesis. **2.** *v.* To make a comment (the senator was asked to comment on the amendment). Explain, illustrate, report, expand, critique, interpret, annotate, illuminate, shed light, discuss, opine, observe, footnote, amplify, exemplify, editorialize, make a statement on, construe, explicate, expound.

Commentary, *n.* See annotation, construction (1).

Commerce, *n.* Buying, selling, or exchanging property or services (commerce between the states). Trade, business, commercialism, marketing, traffic, bargaining, transportation of goods, commercial dealings, commercial intercourse, industry, trading, mercantilism, merchandising, barter, dealing, interchange, communion, fiscal dealings, enterprise, negotiation.

Commercial, *adj.* Related to trade, traffic, or commerce in general (commercial transaction). Profit-making, business, mercantile, entrepreneurial, monetary, material, salable, business, industrial, financial, fiscal, economic, marketing, wholesale, retail, pecuniary, crass, exploitative, profiteering.

Commercialize, *v.* See exploit (1).

Commercial paper Bills of exchange (drafts), promissory notes, bank checks, and other negotiable instruments for the payment of money, which, by their form and on their face, purport to be such instruments.

Commingle, *v.* To put together in one mass (the lawyer commingled the funds of his clients into one general account). Mingle, intermingle, blend, mix, amalgamate, unite, combine, intermix, scramble, confuse, incorporate, fuse, homogenize, admix, merge, coalesce, interlace, consolidate, compound. *Ant.* Separate.

Commiserate, *v.* To express sorrow. Pity, feel sympathy for, console, comfort, show compassion for, share grief, grieve, feel for. See also assuage.

Commiseration, *n.* See consolation.

Commissary, *n.* **1.** One who is sent or delegated to execute some office or duty as the representative of his or her superior (a commissary of the prime minister). Deputy, minister, surrogate, broker, factor, delegate, emissary, attorney in fact, steward, ambassador, lieutenant. **2.** An establishment that sells food (the workers in the commissary tried to unionize). Exchange, hall, mess, supply store, outlet, cafeteria, dining hall. See also inn.

Commission 1. *n.* The authority or instructions under which one person transacts business or negotiates for another (her commission was to seek the release of the hostages). Charge, authorization, mandate, duty, role, office, assignment, task, license, certification, accreditation, commitment, appointment, power, capacity, mission, warrant, deputation, entrustment. **2.** *n.* A group of persons appointed or elected to perform a function (the Civil Service Commission). Agency, department, bureau, body, board, committee, council, trustees, authority, embassy, mission, chamber, cabinet, entity. **3.** *n.* Compensation of fees, often based on a percentage of designated amounts involved in the transaction(s) (her commission was half of net sales). Earnings, payment, remuneration, stipend, honorarium, share, allowance, dividend, wage, bonus, allotment, profit, consideration, emolument, interest, reward, salary. **4.** *n.* The performance of something (commission of a crime). Carrying out, acting out, perpetration, act, conduct, achievement, operation, execution, completion, consummation, implementation. **5.** *v.* To empower (he was commissioned to set up the department). Authorize, charge, assign, accredit, command, endow, sanction, license, approve, deputize, obligate, engage, charter, enjoin, enfranchise, credit, delegate.

Commissioner, *n.* See administrator (1), manager, master, officer.

Commission merchant See factor (2).

Commit, *v.* **1.** To place into the custody of another (he was committed to the institution). Entrust, consign, deliver, institutionalize, incarcerate, intern, remand to custody, jail, impound, confine, transfer, deposit, immure, hospitalize, restrain, arrest. **2.** To perform an act (he did not commit the crime). Perpetrate, participate in, execute, consummate, carry out, effect, practice, enact, achieve, accomplish, "pull off," effectuate, produce, administer, bring about, carry through, transact, fulfill, realize, operate. **3.** To pledge (she agreed to commit her resources). Devote, obligate, dedicate, consign, assign, entrust, commission, bind, engage, make liable, allot, delegate, trust, invest in, turn over, relegate to, allocate, submit, deposit, place, covenant, undertake, warrant, promise. *Ant.* Release; omit; withhold.

Commitment, *n.* **1.** A warrant, order, or process by which a court directs an officer to institutionalize a person (civil commitment due to insanity). Institutionalization, confinement, imprisonment, incarceration, internment, detention, restraint, impoundment, constraint, sentencing, immuring, jailing, remanding to custody, committal. **2.** An agreement or pledge to do something (we had her commitment that she would be there). Word, assurance, guarantee, promise, decision, compact, warrant, certification, vow, undertaking, resolution, engagement, contract. **3.** An obligation (a commitment to pay the debt). Responsibility, liability, duty, bond, accountability, burden. **4.** An investment (a commitment of resources). Delivery, entrustment, consignment, giving over, dispatching, placement, delegation, transmission, commission, appointment, storing. *Ant.* Liberation; disavowal; withdrawal.

Committee, *n.* See group (1), body (3), board (1).

Commode, *n.* See bathroom.

Commodious, *adj.* See abundant, adequate, big, considerable (2).

Commodity, *n.* Something that is useful or serviceable as an article of merchandise (farm commodity). Good, stock, produce, article of commerce, ware, merchandise, product, staple, article of trade, capital, resource, holding, movable, personal property, property, line, advantage, raw material, necessity, essential, material, possession. *Ant.* Liability.

Commodity future A contract to purchase a fixed amount of a commodity at a future date for a fixed price.

Commodore, *n.* See officer, master (1), manager, sailor, military.

Common, *adj.* **1.** Familiar by reason of frequency (spraying is a common practice). Customary, routine, everyday, usual, commonplace, ordinary, unexceptional, accustomed, habitual, recurrent, normal, widespread, accepted, recognized, settled, stock, household, often met with, garden variety, oft-repeated, popular, conventional, established, repeated, traditional, standard, regular, prevalent, prevailing. **2.** Shared among several (a common passageway in the building). Communal, mutual, general, public, concerted, parallel, reciprocal, universal, collective, joint, societal, intermutual, belonging to many, pooled, participatory. **3.** Vulgar (common manners). Coarse, crude, crass, unrefined, vile, shabby, untutored, unseemly, depraved, base, pedestrian, inferior, mediocre, philistine. See also vulgar. *Ant.* Unusual; individual; refined.

Commonality, *n.* See mutuality.

Common carrier Any carrier required by law to transport passengers or freight without refusal if the approved fare or charge is paid. See vehicle (1), vessel (1). *Ant.* Private carrier, contract carrier.

Common disaster A case in which two people with shared interests appear to die simultaneously with no clear evidence of who died first. See disaster.

Common knowledge Information widely shared by a substantial number of people (the discriminatory practice was common knowledge). Public knowledge, widely known fact, general information. See also knowledge.

Common law 1. Judge-made law (based on ancient customs, mores, usages, and principles handed down through the ages) in the absence of controlling statutory or other enacted law. **2.** All the statutory and case law of England and the American colonies before the American Revolution.

Common-law action An action (litigation) governed by the common law rather than by statutory, equitable, or civil law.

Common-law marriage A nonceremonial marriage created by agreement and followed by cohabitation. Elements: (a) legal capacity to marry, (b) present agreement to be married, (c) living together as husband and wife, (d) openness—holding themselves out to the world as married.

Common-law trust A business trust in which trustees hold the property and manage the business; the shareholders are the trust beneficiaries. Massachusetts

153

trust.

Common nuisance See public nuisance.

Commonplace, *adj.* **1.** Ordinary (trespassing on the tracks was a commonplace occurrence). See common (1). **2.** Uninteresting (a commonplace argument). Dull, trite, worn, dry, stale, banal, unimaginative, stereotyped, hackneyed, mediocre, undistinguished, run-of-the-mill, routine, stock, boring, unfresh, insipid, tedious, inane, warmed-over, shopworn, overused, vapid, pedestrian, monotonous, conventional, corny, prosaic, worn-out, bourgeois, artless. *Ant.* Unusual; perceptive.

Common sense Sound practical judgment; that degree of intelligence and reason as exercised by the generality of the populace (common sense would dictate that the device is dangerous). Good sense, sound sense, practicality, intuition, sound perception, balanced judgment, practical knowledge, levelheadedness, native reasoning, "horse sense," normal intelligence, realistic or down-to-earth thinking, mother wit, clear thinking, natural sagacity, plain sense, reasonableness.

Common stock A class of corporate stock that represents the ownership of the corporation. The holders of this equity stock receive dividends after the holders of preferred stock.

Commonwealth, *n.* See people (1), nation, body politic, community (2).

Commotion, *n.* A condition of turmoil or civil unrest (the mob caused a commotion). Turbulence, upheaval, disruption, fracas, storm, agitation, brouhaha, explosion, tumult, perturbation, racket, ferment, tempest, affray, violence, brawl, skirmish, disorder, rampage, public disturbance, imbroglio, convulsion, insurgence, confusion, disquiet, clatter, fuss, excitement, bustle, mutiny, insurrection, riot, rebellion, uprising, revolution, revolt. See also eruption, noise, cataclysm. *Ant.* Tranquility.

Communal, *adj.* See public (2); commune.

Commune **1.** *n.* A small community of people (a religious commune). Collective, co-op, society, kibbutz. **2.** *n.* A self-governing town or village. **3.** *v.* To talk or communicate (commune with nature). Converse, dialogue, discuss, discourse, speak.

Communicable, *adj.* See contagious; poisonous.

Communicate, *v.* To make known (the memo fails to communicate the new theory of recovery). Notify, disclose, publish, inform, advise, declare, reveal, announce, share, transmit, convey, enlighten, impart, divulge, advertise, commune, converse, pass on, betray, report, recite, enact, discourse, delineate, voice, utter, reiterate, lecture, disseminate, broadcast, give, bestow, submit, instill, tell, relate, state, signify, exhibit, apprise, verbalize, articulate, specify, assert, set forth, mumble, pronounce, whisper, chat, exhort, harangue, sermonize, pour forth, propound, narrate, elucidate, recount, contend, cry, enumerate, mean, demonstrate, imply, symbolize, herald, promise, suggest, palaver, explain, murmur, expound, spread, telegraph, telegram, cable, wire, dispatch, connote, evince, manifest, represent, insinuate, portray, instruct, teach, caution, mention, render an account, engage in a dialogue, enunciate, proclaim, implant, link, connect, join, interchange, correspond. *Ant.* Suppress.

Communication, *n.* **1.** The sharing of knowledge by one with another (regular communication with a client tends to avoid problems). Transfer of information, exchange of information, dialogue, correspondence, conversation, interchange, intercourse, speaking, writing, publication, disclosure, dissemination, colloquy, discourse, intercommunication, enunciation, conveyance, transmission, parley, discussion, chat, conference, interlocution, transmittal, imparting, interface, commerce, consultation. **2.** A message (what time was the communication received). News, announcement, word, data, facts, notification, communiqué, dispatch, broadcast, intelligence, report, letter, call, cable, expression, bulletin, statement, utterance, account, advice, proposal, declaration, line, speech, address, vocalization, verbalization, oratory, articulation, gossip, revelation, proclamation. **3.** Rapport (there was little communication between the spouses). Harmony, liaison, fellowship, communion, accord, contact.

Communicative, *adj.* See direct (6).

Communion, *n.* See collaboration, cooperation, harmony, affinity, concord, conference (1).

Communiqué, *n.* See communication (2), report (1).

Communism, *n.* A system of social organization in which property is held in common—the opposite of the system of private property ownership. Marxism, Leninism, collectivism, Bolshevism, socialism. See also dogma, government. *Ant.* Capitalism.

Community, *n.* **1.** Locality (at the bail hearing she was asked how long she had lived in the community). Neighborhood, vicinity, district, area, quarter, environment, town, borough, city, hamlet, suburb, settlement, crossroads, village, township, parish, municipality. **2.** The citizenry (the community was outraged by the granting of parole). Public, society, group, people, body politic, population, general public, nation, populace, commonwealth, state. **3.** Identity; similar character (the parties shared a community of interests). Likeness, affinity, similarity, fellowship, concurrence, parallelism, uniformity, comparability, connection, harmony, kinship, agreement; sphere, realm, field, area, scope, range.

Community property Property owned in common by a husband and wife, with each having an undivided one-half interest in the property by reason of their marital status. For example, the earnings of one spouse during the marriage do not belong solely to that spouse; the earnings are community property.

Commutation, *n.* **1.** A change of punishment to one that is less severe. **2.** A substitution of one form of payment for another. **3.** A change or alteration. Adjustment, modification, abatement, exchange, replacement, reduction, mollification, curtailment, palliation, relaxation, amnesty, remission, abbreviation, alleviation, diminution, mitigation, relaxation.

Commute, *n.* See exchange (1), mitigate; commutation; travel.

Commuter, *n.* See traveler.

Compact, *n.*, **compact,** *adj.*, *v.* **1.** *n.* An agreement or contract between persons, states, or nations (an interstate compact on water rights). Covenant, treaty, concordat, protocol, compromise, understanding, pact, bargain, convention, stipulation, seal, bond, commitment, charter, pledge, accord, cartel, arrangement, engagement, coalition, alliance, league. **2.** *adj.* Closely or firmly united or packed (compact soil). Dense, crowded, close, tight, compressed, solid, pressed together, firm, concentrated, stuffed, thick, squeezed or bunched together, coherent, clustered, solidified. **3.** *adj.* Concise (a compact argument). Terse, succinct, condensed, abridged, abrupt, laconic, short, pithy, brief, pointed, sententious, abbreviated, crisp, straightforward, direct, to the point. **4.** *v.* To press together firmly (he had to compact the points onto one page). Cram, consolidate, contract, combine, merge, condense, concentrate, compress, stuff, squeeze, constrict, solidify. *Ant.* Discord; dispersed, sprawling; separate.

Companion, *n.* See associate (2), ally (1), partner; fellow; appendage.

Companionship, *n.* Friendship. Fellowship, camaraderie, comradeship, colleagueship, fraternity, esprit de corps. See also company (3), goodwill (2), community (3), association (2), consortium.

Company, *n.* **1.** A combination or association of persons to carry on a commercial or industrial enterprise (the company made steel). Business, establishment, firm, conglomerate, partnership, concern, venture, syndicate, house. See also corporation. **2.** A gathering (a small company of protesters gathered around the official). Crowd, group, assemblage, assembly, throng, body, aggregation, circle, congregation, party, set, concourse, troupe, battalion, garrison, corps, brigade, platoon, detachment, contingent, posse, mob, force, squad, legion, band. **3.** Companionship (the accident prevented her from enjoying the company of others). Fellowship, intimacy, intercourse, friendship, society, association, presence, camaraderie. *Ant.* Individual; isolation.

Company union A union under company domination.

Comparability, *n.* See correspondence (1), analogy.

Comparable, *adj.* Capable of being compared; equivalent (comparable terms). Similar, analogous, matching, parallel, resembling, on a par with, in the same class as, approximate, alike, related, akin, proportional, corresponding, close, synonymous, commensurable, tantamount, consonant, cognate, approaching, as good as, equal, relative, interchangeable, uniform, coordinate. *Ant.* Disparate.

Comparative, *adj.* Founded on or estimated by comparison (comparative hardship). By comparison, measured by comparison, comparable, estimated by comparison, relative, not absolute, contrasting with, matching, referring, qualified. *Ant.* Absolute.

Comparative negligence 1. The measurement of negligence by percentage. **2.** The damages allowed shall be diminished in proportion to the amount of negligence attributable to the victim. **3.** The victim's damages are reduced proportionately, provided his or her fault was less than that of the defendant.

Comparative rectitude In a divorce action, relief will be granted to the party least in fault when both have established grounds for the divorce.

Compare, *v.* **1.** To inspect in order to note similarities and differences (compare the two opinions). Contrast, differentiate, analogize, match, collate, examine, weigh, balance against, juxtapose, correlate, liken, estimate relatively, distinguish between, discriminate. **2.** To be considered as similar (your skill and his cannot compare). Compete, vie, parallel, be on a par with, approximate, match, equal, resemble, admit of comparison. *Ant.* Ignore; be unlike.

Comparison, *n.* **1.** The act of comparing (the judge drew a comparison between the two cases). Identification of similarities and differences, comparative estimate, relative estimate, distinction, matching, correlation, balance, crosscheck, analogy, measurement, judgment, association, estimation. **2.** Similarity (when the evidence was viewed, the comparison was striking). Likeness, alikeness, resemblance, equality, connection, comparability, parity, identity, affinity, agreement, correspondence, parallelism, kinship, uniformity, consonance, relationship. *Ant.* Divergence (2).

Compartment, *n.* See part (1); alcove, chamber, department.

Compartmentalize, *v.* See divide (1), classify.

Compass, *n.* See boundary, ambit.

Compassion, *n.* See mercy, charity (3, 4), benevolence, consideration (3), passion.

Compassionate, *adj.* See humanitarian, charitable (2), kind, benevolent.

Compatibility, *n.* Capable of functioning together in harmony (compatibility between the spouses). Rapport, congeniality, accord, affinity, concord, consistency, consonance, balance, congruence, like-mindedness, oneness, goodwill, fellowship, accommodation, comity, cooperation, amity, adjustment, coordination. *Ant.* Discord.

Compatible, *adj.* See concordant, concurrent (2), kindred (2), appropriate (3).

Compatriot, *n.* See colleague.

Compel, *v.* To urge forcefully; to oblige (he claims that he was compelled to confess). Coerce, pressure, overpower, control, overbear, impose, obligate, subject, bear down, dictate, insist, constrain, drive, necessitate, decree, limit, conscript, commandeer, force, "railroad," threaten, intimidate, browbeat, domineer, overwhelm, terrorize, oppress, impel, enforce, make, subdue, enjoin.

Compelling, *adj.* Powerful, strong (a compelling argument). Forceful, assertive, weighty, influential, great, potent, cogent, telling, conclusive, decisive, categorical, unavoidable, overpowering, dominant, irresistible, emphatic, pressing, valid, irrefutable, persuasive, binding, overriding, commanding. See also logical. *Ant.* Weak.

Compelling state interest The test used to uphold state action in the face of an Equal Protection or First Amendment attack. A substantial or serious need for the state to act. Also used to justify state action under the police power of the state.

Compendious, *adj.* See concise.

Compendium, *n.* A comprehensive summary (the editors prepared a compendium of the judge's rulings). Digest, syllabus, synopsis, abridgement, epitome, brief, abstract, condensation, survey, capsule, review, extract, outline, précis, compilation; analysis, treatise, study, tract.

Compensable, *adj.* Entitled to compensation (a compensable injury under the statute). Allowable, covered, coverable, payable, recompensable, reimbursable. *Ant.* Not covered.

Compensate, *v.* **1.** To make satisfactory payment (the witness was compensated for her time). Pay, recompense, reimburse, reward, repay, remunerate, indemnify, pay back, defray, settle accounts, remit, discharge a debt, requite. **2.** To counterbalance (the sincerity of the witness compensated for his nervousness). Offset, countervail, make up for, square, balance, cancel, redress, make amends, make good, counterweigh, nullify, cancel out, neutralize, equalize, atone, even, stabilize, level off, counterpoise. *Ant.* Renege; worsen.

Compensation, *n.* **1.** Remuneration for services rendered (her compensation was $300 a day). Payment, pay, consideration, wages, profit, earnings, retainer, commission, defrayal, emolument, salary, recompense, gratuity, price, "take," award, royalty, share, "cut," perks, perquisites, fringes, allowance, hire, bonus, fee, stipend, revenue, reimbursement, return, gain, honorarium, grant, percentage. **2.** Indemnification (compensation for injuries received). Payment of damages, making amends, making whole, restoration, satisfaction, restitution, recoupment, atonement, indemnity, recovery, reparation, reckoning, settlement. *Ant.* Loss; expenditure.

Compensatory, *adj.* Involving payment or reparation (compensatory damages). Remunerative, atoning, providing restitution, compensative, providing indemnity, making whole, providing reimbursement.

Compensatory damages Damages that will compensate the injured party for the injury sustained and nothing more. Damages that will make good or replace the loss caused by the wrong or injury. Includes out-of-pocket expenses, pain and suffering.

Compete, *v.* To strive for something that someone else is also seeking (the companies compete for the same market). Vie, combat, fight, contend, struggle, rival, contest, oppose, match strength, battle, wrestle, collide, spar, emulate, clash, challenge, duel. *Ant.* Yield.

Competence, *n.* **1.** Having sufficient skill (the inmate challenged the competence of her attorney). Ability, capability, competency, training, expertise, fitness, qualification, capacity, suitableness, mastery, eligibility, experience, facility, faculties, effectiveness, authority, aptitude, equipment, efficiency, talent, suitability, proficiency. **2.** Having a sound mind (her competence at the time of the act). Rationality, normality, sanity, mental balance, coherence. *Ant.* Incompetence; irrationality.

Competency, *n.* The presence of those characteristics or the absence of those disabilities that render a witness legally fit to give testimony in a court. See competence.

Competent, *adj.* **1.** Duly qualified; meeting all the requirements (a competent witness). Legally acceptable, eligible, capable, mentally capable, able, responsible, properly qualified. **2.** Skillful (a competent attorney). Trained, efficient, dependable, experienced, proficient, prepared, effective, knowledgeable, accomplished, resourceful, enterprising, apt, endowed; responsible, sane, compos mentis, sober, logical, lucid, rational, reasonable. **3.** Adequate (a competent presentation). Sufficient, fitting, suitable, credible. *Ant.* Unqualified; incompetent; unsuitable.

Competition, *n.* **1.** A contest between rivals. The efforts of two or more parties, acting independently, to secure the business of a third party by the offer of the most favorable terms (competition among auto manufacturers). Opposition, match, conflict, encounter, struggle, rivalry, scramble, combat, strife, trial, warfare, engagement, tournament, emulation. **2.** One's competitors (the conglomerate tried to buy out its competition). Rivals, challengers, opponents, antagonists, adversaries, contenders, contesters. *Ant.* Teamwork; allies.

Competitive, *adj.* **1.** Opposing, contending (competitive spirit). Adversary, vying, competing, combative, antagonistic, conflicting, adverse, contrary, rival, clashing. See also contentious (1), litigious. **2.** Unrestricted, open (competitive bids). Equal, free, accessible to all, public, common. *Ant.* Cooperative; closed.

Competitor, *n.* A rival (no competitors were in the market). Opponent, contender, contestant, antagonist, enemy, fighter, candidate, aspirant, foe, challenger, opposition. See also adversary. *Ant.* Ally.

Compilation, *n.* **1.** A bringing together of statutes that already exist and, in the process, removing repealed statutes, adding amendments, arranging the text in a convenient order, etc. (the legislature appropriated funds for the compilation). **2.** An organized collection (a compilation of data). Aggregation, gathering, classification, assembling, collating, codifying, marshaling. *Ant.* Dissipation.

Compile, *v.* To collect and arrange (the paralegal compiled all of the documents needed for trial). Draw together, systematize, order, assemble, marshal, muster, group, prepare, select, compose, arrange, aggregate, garner, accumulate, cluster, combine, amass, bring together. *Ant.* Scatter.

Complacent, *adj.* See arrogant, pompous, narrow (2); certain (2); quiet (1, 2).

Complain, *v.* **1.** To make a formal charge (complain to the authorities). Blame, accuse, denounce, incriminate, press charges, implicate, sue, prosecute, arraign, cite, challenge, prefer charges, state a grievance, file a claim, take action, inculpate. **2.** To find fault with (the union complained about the longer hours). Criticize, disapprove, reproach, protest, deplore, grumble, moan, bemoan, whine, carp, cavil, express dissatisfaction, decry, admonish, condemn, malign, berate, remonstrate, castigate, disparage, reprove, censure. See also mope. *Ant.* Accept; compliment.

Complainant, *n.* One who applies to the courts for legal redress by filing a complaint; one who instigates a criminal prosecution (she was the complainant in the tort action). Plaintiff, claimant, aggrieved party, prosecution, petitioner, complaining party, challenger, litigant, accuser, suitor. *Ant.* Defendant.

Complainer, *n.* See grouch, complainant, plaintiff.

Complaint, *n.* **1.** The original or initial pleading that sets forth the plaintiff's claim for relief (the complaint alleged fraud). Petition, charge, allegation, grievance, accusation, information, indictment. **2.** An expression of criticism (customer complaints). Dissatisfaction, "beef," objection, protest, lament, rebuke, censure, denunciation, remonstrance, disparagement, castigation, "bitch," outcry. **3.**

Sickness (a complaint of soreness). Malady, disability, illness, disorder, disease, ailment, affliction. *Ant.* Commendation; good health.

Complaisant, *adj.* See cooperative (2), accommodating, amenable, reasonable, flexible, friendly.

Complement, *v., n.* See complete (1), consummate; balance (1); correlate (2); aggregate.

Complementary, *adj.* See correlative, reciprocal, concurrent (2).

Complete, 1. *v.* To accomplish that which one starts out to do (she completed cross-examination at noon). Finish, conclude, end, terminate, perform, execute, consummate, fulfill, discharge, close, achieve, effect, effectuate, realize, carry through, perfect, ripen, settle, culminate, enact, bring to an end, clinch, finalize, determine, cap, complement, round out. **2.** *adj.* Entire; including all elements without omissions or deficiencies (a complete record of the trial was sent). Full, undiminished, unabridged, whole, unbroken, undivided, intact, comprehensive, all-inclusive, absolute, unqualified, inclusive, thorough, unreserved, total, universal, aggregate, uncut, all-out, exhaustive. **3.** *adj.* Perfect; not lacking in any element or particular (complete legal title). Consummate, flawless, unmarred, without defect, realized. *Ant.* Begin; incomplete.

Completion, *n.* Finishing or accomplishing something in full (completion of the trial). Finalization, consummation, conclusion, execution, fulfillment, performance, enactment, culmination, expiration, satisfaction, achievement, fruition, maturation, effectuation, windup. See also perfection (1). *Ant.* Commencement.

Complex, *adj.,* **complex,** *n.* **1.** *adj.* Complicated; difficult to understand (a complex document). Perplexing, tangled, elaborate, intricate, involved, knotty, labyrinthian, enigmatic, manifold, cryptic, tortuous, mosaic, entangled, obscure, abstruse, unorganized, circuitous, inextricable, muddled, convoluted, sinuous, chaotic, inscrutable, sophisticated, multifarious, bewildering, winding. **2.** *n.* A whole made up of various parts (an industrial complex). Conglomeration, network, aggregate, system, association, structure, totality, unit, composite, collective, compound, maze, web, setup, arrangement, labyrinth. *Ant.* Clear; fragment.

Complexion *n.* See appearance (3), countenance (2), condition (2), attribute (2), climate, characteristic (1).

Complexity, *n.* See complication, ordeal, confusion, affliction.

Compliance, *n.* **1.** Submission, obedience (compliance with the terms of the contract). Conformance, subservience, yielding, concession, adherence, observance, keeping. See also conformity. **2.** Assent (the attorney expected his compliance). Acquiescence, consent, acceptance, nonresistance, cooperation, accord, concurrence, accommodation, adaptability, pliancy, deference, malleability, capitulation. *Ant.* Noncompliance; rejection.

Compliant, *adj.* See flexible, passive (2), amenable.

Complicate, *v.* See obscure (3), confuse, compound (2).

Complicated, *adj.* See complex (1).

Complication, *n.* A factor that complicates a situation (the new evidence was an unexpected complication). Stumbling block, difficulty, complexity, entanglement, obstacle, snag, handicap, obstruction, intricacy, predicament, disadvantage, hitch, drawback, aggravation, quandary, barrier, impediment, development, hindrance. See also confusion (2). *Ant.* Advantage.

Complicity, *n.* The state of being an accomplice; participation in guilt (her complicity in the scheme was evident). Collusion, conspiracy, confederacy, implication, connivance, partnership, abetment, collaboration, intrigue. See also corruption. *Ant.* Innocence.

Compliment, *v., n.* See honor (2), appreciate (3); flattery, approbation, approval, citation (3).

159

Complimentary, *adj.* **1.** Laudatory. Flattering, praising, favorable, adulatory, commendatory, appreciative, eulogistic. **2.** See free (2).

Comply, *v.* To accept or yield (the inmates refused to comply). Obey, surrender, bend, succumb, acquiesce, observe, follow, bow, conform, respect, concur, defer, carry out, accede, heed, perform, adhere, acknowledge, give in, abide by, stoop, cooperate, fulfill, resign, relent. *Ant.* Spurn.

Component, *n.* Ingredient (undue delay is a main component of the defense's strategy). Piece, section, constituent, essential, item, segment, module, subdivision, fundamental, detail, particular, facet, aspect, portion, feature, division, installment, unit. See also factor, element, part (1). *Ant.* Whole.

Comport, *v.* **1.** To agree (her actions comport with her allegations). Correspond, harmonize, conform, parallel, match, coincide, be consonant with, square, reconcile. **2.** To behave in a certain manner (he comported himself with arrogance). Carry, deport, acquit, conduct, manage, discipline, represent. *Ant.* Conflict.

Comportment, *n.* See behavior, conduct (1).

Compose, *v.* **1.** To constitute or form (seven judges compose a full bench). Comprise, embody, make up, complete, be part of, belong to. **2.** To create (he plagiarized the poem she composed). Write, develop, assemble, fashion, devise, author, design, formulate, conceive, produce, make up, invent, contrive, imagine, fabricate, forge, arrange, achieve, bring into existence, originate, build, generate, draft, orchestrate. See also construct. **3.** To calm (he composed himself). Quiet, pacify, settle, placate, solace, soften, console, adjust, regulate, relax, modulate, soothe, still, tranquilize. *Ant.* Destroy; antagonize.

Composed, *adj.* See quiet (1, 2), moderate (1).

Composer, *n.* See author (1).

Composite, 1. *adj.* Made up of individual units (a composite arrangement). Combined, consolidated, synthesized, aggregate, incorporated, assembled, compound, united, fused, connected, amassed, integrated, mosaic. See also mixed. **2.** *n.* See compound (3), accumulation. *Ant.* Unmixed; fragment.

Composition, *n.* Formulation (the composition of the play took a year). Creation, manufacture, framing, devising, composing, organization, arrangement, formation, compilation, preparation, forging, origination, construction, establishment, production, assembly, collation, systematization, synthesis, innovation. *Ant.* Disintegration.

Composition deed An agreement embodying the terms of a composition between debtor and creditors.

Composition with creditors An agreement, founded on sufficient consideration, between a debtor and his or her creditors whereby the latter agree to accept a lesser payment, to be distributed pro rata among the creditors, in discharge of the entire debt. Satisfaction, release, compromise, concession, clearance.

Compos mentis, *adj.* See sane (1).

Compost, *n.* **1.** See compound (3). **2.** Fertilizer, organic mixture, manure.

Composure, *n.* Self-control (the witness responded with great composure). Calm, tranquillity, levelheadedness, quiet, serenity, dignity, aplomb, coolheadedness, equanimity, coolness, self-possession, balance, detachment, self-assurance, confidence, equilibrium, restraint, forebearance, reserve, fortitude, presence of mind, patience, poise. *Ant.* Impatience.

Compound, *v.,* **compound,** *n.* **1.** *v.* To form or make up a composite product by combining different elements (to compound several ingredients to produce the medicine). Unite, compose, consolidate, mix, mingle, concoct, intermingle, amalgamate, synthesize, fuse, blend, commingle, merge. **2.** *v.* To intensify (the lawyer compounded his error by trying to evade it). Exacerbate, widen, aggravate, multiply, magnify, heighten, augment, reinforce, worsen, complicate, increase, add to, expand, inflate, enhance, prolong. **3.** *n.* A combination of two or more elements or things, often as a result of human intervention (a compound of the three chemicals). Mixture, composite, amalgam, conglomeration, aggregation, incorporation, assimilation, congregation, embodiment, intermingling, merger, alloy, fusion, compost, blend, composition, melange, concoction, complex. *Ant.* Separate; ameliorate; individual.

Compounding crime Elements of this offense: (a) the agreement not to prosecute or not to inform against someone who has committed a crime, (b) the knowledge of the actual commission of a crime, and (c) the receipt of property or other consideration in exchange for the agreement.

Compound interest Interest on interest; the interest that is earned generates further interest on this earning.

Comprehend, *v.* **1.** To understand fully (the defendant did not comprehend the nature of the plea). Know, grasp, appreciate, absorb, realize, conceive, fathom, assimilate, discern, recognize, be cognizant of, apprehend, penetrate, digest, gather, glean, catch on, master, perceive, imagine, apperceive, discriminate. **2.** To include (the assignment comprehended a search in all the regional reporters). Embrace, take in, embody, encompass, involve, contain, comprise, constitute, be comprised of, encircle, span. *Ant.* Misunderstand; exclude.

Comprehensible, *adj.* Understandable (the insurance policy could hardly be described as comprehensible). Lucid, unobscure, logical, consistent, discernible, explicit, graphic, unambiguous, decipherable, legible, penetrable, self-explanatory, apprehensible, graspable, knowable, plain, obvious, distinct, articulate. See also intelligible, evident, clear, definite (1), direct (6). *Ant.* Obscure.

Comprehension, *n.* Understanding (the patient had limited powers of comprehension). Intelligence, recognition, discernment, perception, imagination, consciousness, insight, acumen, intuition, cognition, erudition, mental capacity, attentiveness, reason, sense, learning. *Ant.* Misconception.

Comprehensive, *adj.* Extensive (a comprehensive research assignment). Wide-reaching, thorough, expansive, complete, full, inclusive, unrestricted, broad, total, encyclopedic, universal, general, wide, large, sweeping, unqualified, capacious, voluminous, widespread, thoroughgoing, large-scale, wholesale, radical, exhaustive, far-reaching, extreme, omnibus, wall-to-wall, indiscriminate, pandemic, absolute, unconditional, panoramic, blanket, copious, pervasive, extended. *Ant.* Superficial.

Compress, *v.* See condense, compact (4).

Compressed, *adj.* See compact (2).

Comprise, *v.* To include (the brief is comprised of seven parts). Contain, embrace, cover, be composed of, embody, amount to, hold, incorporate, consist of, constitute, comprehend, subsume, envelop, total, make up, take in.

Compromise, 1. *n.* The settlement of a dispute through mutual concessions (the compromise avoided the litigation). Arrangement, composition, bargain, agreement, harmonization, coming to terms, reaching a middle ground, understanding, adjustment, truce, trade-off, arbitration, conciliation, negotiation, mediation, balance. **2.** *v.* To endanger (the lawyer's misrepresentation compromised the entire case). Jeopardize, expose, embarrass, imperil, risk, render vulnerable, undercut, discredit, implicate, prejudice, put at hazard. **3.** *v.* See arbitrate (3), negotiate. *Ant.* Disagreement; enhance.

Compromise and settlement An agreement by which a controversy is terminated. The consideration for the agreement is mutual concessions by the disputants.

Compromise verdict A verdict that is reached when one or more jurors surrender their conscientiously held positions on an issue in the case in exchange for the surrender of similarly held positions by other jurors on other issues.

Comptroller, *n.* See controller.

Compulsion, *n.* **1.** Forcible inducement to the commission of an act (he claimed that he signed under compulsion). Duress, coercion, obligation, urging, forcing, pressure, objective necessity, violence, domination, stress, oppression. See also constraint. **2.** An overpowering impulse (a compulsion to steal). Drive, urge, urgency, obsession, need, preoccupation, irresistible impulse, fetish, craze, addiction. *Ant.* Free choice.

Compulsive, *adj.* See irresistible, compelling; excess.

Compulsory, *adj.* Obligatory by agreement or law (compulsory vaccination). Required, mandated, binding, unavoidable, coerced, authoritative, enforced, without choice, compulsive, necessary, commanded, prescriptive, inescapable, exigent, mandatory, imperative, involuntary, not to be evaded. See also involuntary; coercion.

Compulsory counterclaim The counterclaim is logically related to the original claim and arises out of the same subject matter on which the original claim is based.

Compulsory nonsuit An involuntary termination of an action ordered by the court when the plaintiff totally fails to substantiate its claim by evidence.

Compulsory process Compelling the attendance of a person in court through subpoena, arrest warrant, attachment, etc.

Compunction, *n.* See guilt (2), contrition, disgrace, embarrassment.

Compurgation, *n.* Exoneration through the testimony of others on innocence. See vindicate.

Computation, *n.* The act of numbering or estimating (the computation of time to be served in jail). Calculation, reckoning, figuring, measurement, enumeration, appraisal, determination, assessment, estimation, tallying, scoring, arithmetic, valuation.

Compute, *v.* See measure (3), calculate, rate (3).

Computer, *n.* Data processor, word processor, calculator, electronic brain, microcomputer, PC, personal computer, portable computer, digital computer.

Comrade, *n.* See cohort, intimate, associate (2), ally, partner, fellow, member (1).

"Con," *v., n.* See deceive, cheat (1); convict (2).

"Con artist" See cheat (2), wrongdoer.

Conceal, *v.* To withhold from the knowledge of others (she tried to conceal the knife). Hide, secrete, withdraw from observation, cover up, camouflage, cloak, shelter, enshroud, keep quiet, disguise, screen, mask, keep out of sight, obfuscate, dissemble, bury, eclipse, veil, harbor, seclude, cache, stow, withhold, hoard, cover, curtain, stash, closet, shroud, sheathe, wrap, squirrel away, stockpile, envelop, shade, entomb. *Ant.* Reveal.

Concealed, *adj.* See hidden.

Concealment, *n.* **1.** A withholding of something that one knows and which, in duty, ought to be revealed. See conceal. **2.** Hiding (in concealment). Seclusion, retreat, disappearance, under cover, incognito, obscurity, privacy, silence. See also secrecy. *Ant.* Disclosure.

Concede, *v.* **1.** To admit as true (he conceded that little chance existed for a favorable judgment). Acknowledge, accede, be persuaded, vouchsafe, confess, grant, allow, agree, acquiesce, come to terms, recognize. **2.** To acknowledge defeat (he conceded the issue to his opponent). Relinquish, cede, abandon, deliver, surrender, succumb, yield, give up, resign, hand over. *Ant.* Contest; resist.

Conceit, *n.* See arrogance.

Conceited, *adj.* See arrogant, pompous.

Conceivable, *adj.* See possible, comprehensible.

Conceive, *v.* See think, comprehend (1); devise (3); beget; fantasize, dream (1), invent, create.

Concentrate, *v.* **1.** To focus (the defense team decided to concentrate on the damage issue). Consider closely, center, centralize, zero in on, coalesce, focalize, attend, study, scrutinize, examine carefully, converge, heed, cluster, close in, come together. **2.** To gather or collect (criminal law offices are concentrated on Fifth Street). Cluster, consolidate, crowd, unite, congregate, flock together, assemble, mass, meet, converge. **3.** See condense. *Ant.* Scatter.

Concentration, *n.* **1.** Focus. Application, study, absorption, deep thought, engrossment, regard, intensity, devotion, deliberation, scrutiny. **2.** See collection (1, 2). **3.** See center.

Concentration camp, *n.* See jail (1).

Concept, *n.* An idea or theory (the concept of the memo was sound). Conception, hypothesis, thought, opinion, notion, impression, belief, assumption, judgment, sentiment, inspiration, inclination, presumption, abstraction, conclusion, evaluation, deduction, mental picture, representation, surmise, view. See also conviction (2).

Conception, *n.* **1.** The beginning of pregnancy. The fecundation of the female ovum by the male spermatozoon, resulting in human life capable of survival under normal conditions. (The alleged father was out of town at the time of conception.) Fertilization, becoming pregnant, inception of pregnancy. **2.** An idea. See conviction (2), concept. **3.** The formulation of an idea (her conception of the plan was brilliant). Invention, launching, originating, imagination, visualization, speculation, genesis, development, drafting.

Concern 1. *v.* To have reference to (the meeting concerned settlement). Pertain to, relate to, belong to, be of interest to, be of importance to, have connection with, involve, affect, affect the interest of, touch, appertain, apply, be relevant to, implicate, regard, absorb, embrace, respect, be pertinent to, have a bearing on. **2.** *v.* To be troubled by; to be mindful of (the lawyer was concerned about the discrepancy). Worry, disturb, distress, make anxious, vex, bother, disquiet, make uneasy; be vigilant, pay attention to, watch, be mindful of, direct one's attention to, examine carefully, take note, look after. **3.** *n.* An interest (her main concern was legal education). Profession, occupation, preoccupation, involvement, affair, duty, matter, charge, responsibility, consideration, expertise, training, specialty, field, mission, subject, job. **4.** *n.* A business (a going concern). Company, establishment, house, corporation, organization, partnership, enterprise, store, undertaking, venture. **5.** *n.* Worry, care (concern over the danger). Anxiety, regard, distress, solicitude, trouble, thoughtfulness, vigilance, caution, conscientiousness, alertness, heed, watchfulness, consideration. *Ant.* Be irrelevant to; be unconcerned; disinterest; hobby; disregard.

Concerned, *adj.* Worried. Anxious, troubled, disturbed, on edge, distressed; involved, interested. *Ant.* Carefree.

Concerning, *prep.* Relating to. Pertaining to, affecting, involving, taking part in, substantially engaged in. See about (2), in re, concern (1).

Concert, *n.* Acting with another to bring about a preconceived result (they acted in concert). Agreement, conspiracy, collaboration, interaction, concordance, concord, unanimity, unison, alliance, joint action, confederation, complicity, teamwork, association, union, pool, merger. *Ant.* Opposition.

Concerted, *adj.* Planned or arranged by parties who have agreed to act together pursuant to a design or scheme (concerted action). Prearranged, preplanned, collaborative, collaborating, united, joint, premeditated, agreed upon, by consent, cooperative, synergetic, collusive, coactive, contrived, by mutual agreement, combined, conjoined, synchronized, leagued, abetting, aligned, colluding, concurring, conniving, in alliance. *Ant.* Individual.

Concerto, *n.* See music.

Concession, *n.* **1.** A grant or authorization (the state granted the company a concession in the park). License, franchise, right, permit, warrant, sanction, indulgence, boon, allowance, authority, endowment, clearance, privilege, permission, leave. **2.** A yielding to a claim or demand (concessions made at the bargaining table). Conceding, surrender, acknowledgment, compromise, adjustment, giving in, allowance, admission, acquiescence, cession, capitulation, compliance, modification, accord, relinquishment. *Ant.* Denial; intractability.

Concierge, *n.* See servant, employee.

Conciliate, *v.* See assuage, settle (1), mitigate.

Conciliatory, *adj.* Having an inclination to adjust and settle a dispute in an unantagonistic manner (his conciliatory attitude). Accommodating, pacifying, agreeable, congenial, affable, compromising, soothing, peacemaking, obliging, adaptable, deferential, bipartisan, harmonious, understanding, submissive, placatory, reconciling, mollifying, amicable, friendly, appeasing, reassuring, pacific, forbearing. *Ant.* Antagonistic.

Concise, *adj.* To the point and clear (a concise argument). Condensed, brief, terse, trenchant, sparing, pithy, succinct, epigrammatic, crisp, forceful, short, synoptic, summarized, laconic, compact, compendious, pregnant, pointed, compressed, curt, abridged, lean, to the point, gnomic, clipped, aphoristic, neat, summary, shortened, straightforward, cryptic, coded, brusque, curtailed, tight, clear-cut, abbreviated. *Ant.* Verbose.

Conclave, *n.* See meeting (1), conference (1).

Conclude, *v.* **1.** To finish (she concluded cross-examination). End, terminate, bring to an end, halt, close, discontinue, complete, suspend, expire, postpone indefinitely, abort, seal, fulfill, culminate, exhaust, finalize, consummate, execute, adjourn, discharge, dispose of, run its course, quit. **2.** To resolve or decide (the negotiations were concluded to everyone's satisfaction). Determine, accomplish, arrange, compromise, bargain, fix, establish, decree, judge, figure, rule, adjudge, engineer, arbitrate, attain, elect, prefer, deliver judgment; infer, deduce, assume, reason, surmise. *Ant.* Commence; leave hanging.

Conclusion, *n.* **1.** The termination (the conclusion of the cross-examination). End, close, finale, completion, stoppage, discontinuation, bringing to a close, phaseout, cessation, last stage, suspension, omega, terminus, quitting period, discontinuance, expiration, eradication, windup, closure, denouement, consummation, realization, culmination, last stage. **2.** The final decision (the conclusion of the court). Outcome, judgment, result, determination, resolution, settlement, finding, decree, opinion, verdict, thinking, reasoning, deduction, declaration, adjudication, upshot, arrangement, product, assessment, evaluation, pronouncement, final result, view, consequence, ruling. *Ant.* Commencement.

Conclusion of fact An inference drawn from subordinate or evidentiary facts.

Conclusion of law A statement by the court of the law that applies to the facts found by the jury or by the trial judge if no jury is present.

Conclusive, *adj.* Final; shutting out all further evidence (the document was conclusive evidence). Putting an end to the inquiry, irrefutable, decisive, beyond question, beyond dispute, manifest, plain, clear, obvious, visible, apparent, indubitable, palpable, definitive, determinative, unavoidable, incontestable, sure, self-evident, ascertained, decided, complete, ultimate, absolute, compelling, demonstrable, categorical, clinching, incontrovertible, last, final, unarguable, authoritative, unimpeachable. See also convincing. *Ant.* Contestable.

Conclusive presumption A presumption that requires the trier of fact to find a fact as it is conclusively presumed. Evidence to the contrary is inadmissible.

Irrebuttable presumption.

Concoct, *v.* See fabricate (1), contrive (2), combine (1).

Concomitant, *adj.* Occurring together (concomitant actions). Concurrent, simultaneous, accompanying, incident, collateral, coincident, connected, related, supplemental, conjoined, accessory, parallel, affiliated, merged, coupled, additional, attendant, side-by-side, synchronized, consolidated, united, correlative, corollary, adjunct, ancillary. *Ant.* Independent.

Concord, *n.* **1.** An agreement settling differences (the countries reached a concord concerning the border dispute). Settlement, contract, treaty, covenant, compact, armistice, concurrence, pact, convention, truce, consensus, concordat. **2.** Peace, harmony (live in concord). Tranquillity, communion, rapport, cooperation, neighborliness, oneness, friendship, goodwill, unity, amicability, fellowship, brotherhood, sisterhood, order. See also agreement (2). *Ant.* Disagreement; strife.

Concordance, *n.* **1.** See concord (1), agreement (1). **2.** An alphabetical index of key words in a book or set of books.

Concordant, *adj.* Agreeable (a concordant posture). Harmonious, agreeing, concurring, accommodating, consenting, compatible, uniting, sympathetic, congruous, at one, coexisting, in unison, congenial, conforming. See also kindred. *Ant.* At odds.

Concordat, *n.* A formal agreement or treaty. See concord (1), agreement (1).

Concourse, *n.* See assemblage (1), assembly (1); highway.

Concrete, *adj.* Particular, definite (concrete evidence). Demonstrable, physical, bodily, factual, discrete, material, explicit, substantial, real, specific, precise, firm, actual, determinate, substantive, sensible, bona fide, manifest, plain, graphic, genuine, unequivocal, tangible, distinct, solid, free from abstraction, palpable, certain, exact, obvious, authentic, reliable. *Ant.* Vague.

Concubinage, *n.* **1.** Living together without being legally married. See cohabitation. **2.** The state of being a concubine.

Concubine, *n.* A woman who cohabits with a man with whom she is not married (she was his concubine). Kept woman, mistress, paramour. See also prostitute.

Concupiscent, *adj.* See prurient.

Concur, *v.* To agree (Justice Holmes concurred in the result but not in the reasoning). Consent, accept, go along with, accord, act together, acquiesce, approve, harmonize, assent, allow, support, comply, yield, condone, come to terms, be in accord, correspond, join, cooperate, square, covenant, endorse, countenance, subscribe, sanction, ratify. *Ant.* Dispute.

Concurrence, *n.* **1.** A meeting of the minds (they achieved concurrence). Coming together, agreement in action, union in action, union in design, consent, mutual consent, alliance, approbation, cooperation, consolidation, unification, merger, unanimity, harmony, accord, concordance, correspondence, consensus, coexistence. See also conjunction. **2.** A simultaneous occurrence (the concurrence of the two discoveries). Coincidence, contemporaneity. *Ant.* Discord.

Concurrent, *adj.* **1.** Running together (concurrent sentences). Parallel, coexistent, contemporary, coupled, contemporaneous, simultaneous, bordering, coterminous, accompanying, coupled, coinciding, concomitant, coincident, conjoined, attendant, linked. **2.** In agreement (their views are concurrent). Compatible, harmonious, correspondent, united, merged, common, concurring, concordant, unanimous, cohesive, like-minded, consistent, allied, blended, complementary, consolidating, conforming, wedded, consonant. *Ant.* Independent; incompatible.

Concurrent causes Causes acting roughly contemporaneously and together causing an injury.

Concurrent jurisdiction The jurisdiction of several different tribunals, each authorized to adjudicate the same subject matter at the choice of the petitioner.

Concurrent negligence The negligence of two or more persons concurring in producing a single indivisible injury. The persons need not have acted at the same time.

Concurrent power The power of either Congress or the state legislatures, each acting independently of the other, to make laws on the same subject matter.

Concurrent sentences Two or more terms of imprisonment, all or a part of each to be served simultaneously. The prisoner is entitled to be discharged at the expiration of the longest term specified. *Ant.* Consecutive sentences.

Concurring opinion A separate opinion delivered by one or more judges on a case that agrees with the result of the majority opinion but provides separate reasons for reaching that result.

Concussion, *n.* See shock (1), injury.

Condemn, *v.* **1.** To find or adjudge guilty and impose a sentence (the defendant was condemned to a year in prison). Convict, pass sentence, pronounce guilty, execute justice, carry out a sentence, penalize, inflict punishment, exact retribution, exact a penalty, discipline, doom, damn, punish, incarcerate, imprison, adjudicate, ordain. **2.** To set apart or expropriate for public use in the exercise of the power of eminent domain (his property was condemned by the state). Seize, appropriate, expropriate, arrogate, dispossess, take possession, nationalize, confiscate, attach, divest, sequestrate, impound. **3.** To censure (it was premature to condemn the worker for the fire). Rebuke, denounce, blame, assail, impeach, reprehend, decry, scold, vilify, chastise, criticize, castigate, implicate, admonish, attack, disparage, belittle, disapprove, berate, charge, execrate, disdain, spurn, rebuff, ignore, repulse, scorn, despise, mock, detest, revile, ridicule, deride, taunt, deprecate, indict, reproach. *Ant.* Exonerate; liberate; praise.

Condemnation, *n.* **1.** The process of taking private property for public use through the power of eminent domain. See condemn (2). **2.** See censure, obloquy, correction (1).

Condense, *v.* To make more concise (the long brief had to be condensed). Abbreviate, capsule, digest, summarize, abridge, shorten, compress, synopsize, abstract, trim, cut, contract, boil down, reduce, concentrate, consolidate, curtail, epitomize, outline, truncate. *Ant.* Expand.

Condescend, *v.* To lower oneself. Vouchsafe, indulge, stoop, deign, humble oneself, descend, talk down to. See also patronize (2).

Condescending, *adj.* See arrogant, pompous, contemptuous.

Condescension, *n.* See reserve (4), contempt (2); condescend.

Condign, *adj.* See adequate, proper.

Condition 1. *n.* A future and uncertain event on which an obligation is dependent (he agreed on condition that he would be in control). Provision, proviso, qualification, term, stipulation, clause, prerequisite, sine qua non, consideration, reservation, limitation, contingency, requirement, necessity, antecedent, precondition, exception, assumption, demand, point, premise, hypothesis, article, postulate, specification, supposition. **2.** *n.* The state or manner of existence (the company's financial condition). Situation, affairs, standing, shape, predicament, circumstances, appearance, quality, grade, state of affairs, plight, case, phase, mode, status, tenor, complexion, health, class, aspect, position, disposition, mien, estate, state, constitution, posture, temper, frame, form, fettle. **3.** *v.* To prepare (clinical education conditioned her for court practice). Equip, teach, warm up, fit, accustom, adapt, mold, habituate. **4.** *v.* See maintain (1).

Conditional, *adj.* Pertaining to that which is dependent on a condition (conditional acceptance of the contract). Subject to a condition, provisional, qualified, stipulative, with reservations, indefinite, modified, limited, restricted, probationary, tentative, changeable, subject to change, indeterminate. See also contingent.

Ant. Absolute.

Conditional indorsement One by which the indorser annexes some condition (other than the failure of prior parties to pay) to his or her liability.

Conditional sales contract The seller reserves title until the buyer pays for the goods, at which time title passes to the buyer.

Conditioned, *adj.* See contingent, dependent (3); able-bodied.

Condition precedent A condition that must happen or be performed before some right dependent thereon accrues or some act dependent thereon is performed.

Condition subsequent A condition referring to a future event, upon the happening of which an obligation no longer becomes binding on the other party at the option of the latter. A condition subsequent divests liability that has already attached.

Condolence, *n.* See consolation; commiserate.

Condominium, *n.* A system of separate ownership of individual units in a multiple-unit building. See home (1).

Condonation, *n.* **1.** A voluntary forgiveness for an offense (he did not expect the condonation). Absolution, clemency, pardon, remission, overlooking, dispensation, remitting, acquittal, reprieve, expiation, discharge, exemption, magnanimity, mercy. **2.** Voluntary forgiveness by one spouse of the marital wrong of the other, barring the former from a divorce action on the basis of the wrong.

Condone, *v.* To overlook or accept without protest (the manager would not condone the violence). Forgive, forget, ignore, pardon, justify, let pass, disregard, remit, absolve, countenance, tolerate, permit, excuse, grant immunity, amnesty, waive. *Ant.* Punish.

Conduce, *v.* To contribute to as a result (the evidence may conduce to establish that result). Foster, advance, encourage, influence, promote, predispose. See also cooperate. *Ant.* Inhibit.

Conducive, *adj.* Tending to cause or assist (preparation is conducive to favorable results). Contributive, leading to, promotive, favorable, tending, productive, accessory, advantageous, instrumental, calculated, ancillary, subservient, salutary, contributory, beneficial. See also convenient. *Ant.* Counterproductive.

Conduct, *n.,* **conduct,** *v.* **1.** *n.* Personal behavior (unacceptable conduct). Mode of action, deportment, carriage, habit, custom, deeds, ways, demeanor, attitude, comportment, posture, mien, manner of life, bearing, air, style, morals, decorum, operation, fashion, performance, behavior. **2.** *v.* To manage (she conducts the affairs of the business). Administer, carry out, govern, transact, superintend, pilot, guide, supervise, lead, convoy, head, oversee, engineer, steer, order, rule, direct, command, handle, preside over. See also manage (1), execute (1). **3.** *v.* See convey (3).

Conductor, *n.* See manager; music.

Conduit, *n.* **1.** A go-between (she acted as a conduit between the rivals). Intermediary, agent, delegate, emissary, surrogate. **2.** A channel (the air passed through the conduit). Passageway, pipe, canal, avenue, medium, route, instrument, tube, duct, drain, artery. See also vessel (2), highway.

Confabulate, *v.* See communicate, converse (1), babble.

Confederacy, *n.* **1.** The association or banding together of two or more persons to commit an act or to further an enterprise that is forbidden by law, or which, though lawful in itself, becomes unlawful when carried out through the confederacy (evidence of a confederacy was uncovered). Conspiracy, plot, scheme, cabal, collusion, connivance, syndicate, ring. **2.** A union of persons or countries (the regions formed a trade confederacy). Confederation, league, alliance, organization, block, guild, affiliation, coalition, compact, federation, combine, partnership, trust, amalgamation, consolidation, merger, coterie, fellowship, entente, corporation.

Confederation, *n.* A league or compact for mutual support. See confederacy (2).

Confer, *v.* **1.** To consult (the judge asked the lawyers to confer with each other on a new date). Compare notes, discuss, deliberate, discourse, talk, talk over, consult, palaver, confide, parley, advise, counsel, negotiate. **2.** To bestow (the award was conferred at the ceremony). Grant, give, convey, present, accord, transfer, administer, endow, transmit, vouchsafe, donate. *Ant.* Ignore; withdraw.

Conference, *n.* **1.** A meeting of several persons for deliberation (a conference on bail reform). Interchange of opinion, parley, dialogue, symposium, convention, communion, caucus, council, consultation, conclave, colloquy, seminar, convocation, assembly, talks, negotiation. See also meeting. **2.** An association of groups (the Eastern League Conference). Alliance, confederation, synod, division, league.

Confess, *v.* To admit the truth of a charge or accusation (she confessed to the robbery). Acknowledge, concede, grant, inculpate, reveal, expose, "come clean," avow, bring to light, unbosom oneself, divulge, lay bare, make a clean breast, purge oneself, yield, disburden. *Ant.* Deny.

Confession, *n.* A voluntary statement acknowledging guilt or responsibility for the offense charged (written confession). Admission, acceptance of guilt, revelation, divulgence, avowal, exposé, declaration, acquiescence, self-condemnation, inculpatory or incriminating statement, self-incrimination. *Ant.* Denial.

Confession and avoidance A plea in which one admits (expressly or by implication) the truth of the allegations of fact in the complaint, but then proceeds to allege new matter that tends to neutralize or avoid the legal consequence of the allegations in the complaint.

Confession of judgment A written confession of the action by the defendant by virtue of which the plaintiff enters judgment. Allowing a judgment to be entered against someone without legal proceedings. See cognovit note.

Confessor, *n.* See intimate (5), minister (1).

Confidant, *n.* See intimate (5).

Confide, *v.* To place something in the confidence of another (he confided in his attorney). Trust, entrust, reveal, divulge, place reliance on, believe in, count on, unburden, impart, commit, commend, consign, place faith in, hold responsible for. *Ant.* Keep secret.

Confidence, *n.* **1.** Trust, reliance (she had confidence in her attorney). Credence, faith, belief, dependence, security, assurance. **2.** A secret (the attorney must not reveal the confidences of a client). Classified information, privileged matter, intimacy, private information, confidential communication. **3.** Self-assurance (the witness spoke with confidence). Certitude, self-confidence, self-reliance, spirit, aplomb, courage, poise, conviction, boldness, daring, intrepidity, firmness, calmness. *Ant.* Mistrust; public knowledge; timidity.

Confidence game Obtaining money or other property by trick. Elements: (a) intentional false representation to the victim concerning a present fact, (b) known to be false, (c) with the intent that the victim rely on the information, (d) the representation is made to obtain the victim's confidence and thereafter his or her money or other property, and (e) the defendant abuses this confidence.

Confidence man Swindler. See wrongdoer.

Confident, *adj.* See certain (2), assured (4), assertive; arrogant.

Confidential, *adj.* Pertaining to that which is done in confidence with the expectation of privacy (confidential report). Private, secret, eyes-only, not for publication, classified, undisclosed, privileged, inside, closet, discreet, hidden, restricted, concealed, sub rosa, off-the-record, unofficial, in camera, undercover. *Ant.* Public.

Confidential communication Privileged statements or communications between

168

designated individuals (e.g., attorney and client, doctor and patient, confessor and penitent). The speaker must have clearly intended the statement to be heard only by the person in whom confidence was placed. The latter cannot be forced to disclose the statement.

Confidentiality, *n.* The state or quality of being confidential.

Confidential relation A fiduciary relationship such as exists between attorney and client, husband and wife, principal and agent, etc. The relationship calls for the utmost degree of good faith in all transactions between the parties; they cannot deal with each other at arm's length.

Configuration, *n.* The arrangement or form of something (the configuration of the center). Border, framework, frontier, format, layout, skeleton, structure, outline, cast, contour, perimeter, delineation, figure, construction, character, composition, frame, profile, pattern, interrelationship, constitution.

Confine, *v.*, **confines,** *n.* **1.** *v.* To keep in (the inmate was confined in segregation). Enclose, imprison, incarcerate, fence in, impound, lock up, quarantine, jail, immure, bound, constrain, check, circumscribe, barricade, subjugate, hold captive, cage, intern, harness, enchain, remand, detain. **2.** *v.* To place within limits (confine your closing statement to the evidence). Restrict, govern, regulate, delimit, demarcate. See also control (2). **3.** *n.* Bounds, border (remain within the confines of the institution). Edge, boundaries, margin, frontier, perimeter, fringes, compound, enclosure, environs, compass, limits, precincts. *Ant.* Liberate; expand.

Confinement, *n.* **1.** State of being confined (solitary confinement). See detention, control (4); confine (1). **2.** Childbirth (she spent 10 hours in confinement). Labor, delivery, lying-in, parturition.

Confirm, *v.* **1.** To verify (he confirmed the testimony of the earlier witness). Corroborate, validate, affirm, authenticate, acknowledge, concur, fortify, endorse, second, substantiate, support, bear out, uphold, strengthen, avouch, justify, buttress, reinforce. **2.** To approve (she confirmed the contract). Accept, authorize, legalize, sanction, endorse, bind, warrant, underwrite, subscribe, charter, assent, license, ratify. *Ant.* Deny; annul.

Confirmation, *n.* **1.** The giving of formal approval (confirmation by the board is required). Authorization, acceptance, sanction, acknowledgment, consent, assent, acquiescence, affirmation, endorsement, stamp of approval, ratification, passage, enactment, validation. **2.** Substantiation (his testimony was confirmation of the contents of the report). Corroboration, verification, authentication, proof, testimony, evidence, assurance, warranty, attestation, support, witness, documentation, establishment, security. *Ant.* Rejection; repudiation.

Confirmed, *adj.* See accurate, official (2).

Confiscate, *v.* To seize or take private property for public use (the police confiscated the weapon). Appropriate, expropriate, usurp, arrogate, divest, dispossess, commandeer, impound, preempt, mulct, sequester, condemn, attach, annex, impress, assume, distrain, take summarily. *Ant.* Restore.

Confiscation, *n.* See seizure (1).

Confiscatory, *adj.* Characterized by confiscation. See confiscate.

Conflagration, *n.* A large fire (the explosion led to a conflagration). Devastating fire, bonfire, holocaust, blaze, inferno, wildfire.

Conflict, *n.*, **conflict,** *v.* **1.** *n.* Opposition, combat (the judgment did not end the conflict between the parties). Fight, antagonism, strife, battle, war, controversy, encounter, contest, collision, discord, fray, clash, disagreement, contention, variance, disunity, inconsistency, warfare, skirmish, scuffle, engagement, fracas, division, friction, bout, donnybrook, altercation, animosity, turmoil, antipathy, rivalry, argument, dispute, resistance, enmity, hostility, quarrel, feud, dissension, bad blood, tension, faction. **2.** *v.* To be at odds with (the holdings in the two cases conflict). Disagree, be inconsistent, be contradictory, clash, oppose, diverge, collide, differ, contrast, interfere with, run counter to, refute, counteract. *Ant.* Harmony; agree.

Conflicting, *adj.* See contradictory.

Conflict of interest A clash of loyalties (it would be a conflict of interest for the lawyer to represent both sides in the dispute). Serving two different masters, divided loyalties, conflicting loyalties, clash of interests, dilemma, compromising situation.

Conflict of laws A branch of jurisprudence based on an inconsistency or difference among the laws of different states or countries that are involved in a controversy between the parties, e.g., a contract dispute in which the contract was signed in Ohio for the delivery of goods in New York and the contract law of these two states is different. The conflict-of-law problem is to determine whether the contract law of Ohio or of New York applies to the case.

Conform, *v.* **1.** To comply with (conform to the regulations). Abide by, obey, fall in line with, observe, respect, yield, submit, adhere to, go along with, measure up to, follow. **2.** To agree with or correspond to (the structure must conform to the blueprint). Match, harmonize, square, tally, reconcile, accommodate, be in keeping, be similar to or like, observe, be reconciled with, synchronize, adjust, adapt, comport, bring into agreement, bring into correspondence, suit. *Ant.* Violate; differ.

Conformable, *adj.* See consonant, similar.

Conformed copy An exact copy of a document on which explanations of things have been written that could not be or were not copied.

Conforming, *adj.* In accordance with the contract or the law (conforming goods). See conform.

Conforming use The use of a structure that is in conformity with the uses permitted by zoning and land use planning laws.

Conformity, *n.* Correspondence in form, manner, or use (the plan must be executed in conformity with the code). Agreement, harmony, congruity, compliance, compatibility, accord, affinity, consonance, uniformity, fidelity, faithfulness, concord, consent, consistency, obedience, adherence, congruence, conjunction, likeness, aptness, submission, yielding, assent, similarity, accommodation, union, association. *Ant.* Opposition.

Confound, *v.* See obscure (3), confuse, amaze, surprise (1).

Confraternity, *n.* See association.

Confrere, *n.* See colleague.

Confront, *v.* To come face to face (confront your accuser). Encounter, challenge, dialogue, engage, interview, meet, stand facing, accost, brave, defy, oppose, resist, stand up to, attack, counterattack, oppugn, assail, dispute, strike back, rebuff, protest, pit against. *Ant.* Evade.

Confrontation, *n.* **1.** Allowing an accused a face-to-face opportunity to cross-examine adverse witnesses. See confront. **2.** A serious conflict (the meeting soon turned into a confrontation). Argument, altercation, fray, battle, threat, crisis, clash, brawl, struggle, combat, collision, row. See also fight (1), feud. *Ant.* Harmony.

Confuse, *v.* To puzzle (the argument confused the jury). Perplex, mystify, muddle, bewilder, frustrate, baffle, befuddle, mislead, fog, stupefy, obfuscate, unsettle, daze, nonplus, befog, embarrass, distract, fluster, stump, rattle, throw into disorder, clutter, entangle, snarl, disorganize, throw off balance, perturb, discountenance, mess, darken, disconcert, addle, mortify. *Ant.* Clarify.

Confusing, *adj.* See ambiguous, inconsistent, obscure (1).

Confusion, *n.* **1.** The state of disorder (the gunfire caused confusion in the room). Disarray, unrest, disturbance, chaos, disorientation, embarrassment, jumble, mess, bedlam, anarchy, turbulence, trouble, snarl, commotion, shambles, abashment, ferment, disquiet, rampage, havoc, pandemonium, madhouse, uproar, tumult, upset, derangement, agitation, furor, convulsion, melee, riot. **2.** Doubt, bewilderment (confusion in reasoning). Ambiguity, puzzlement, bafflement, perplexity, uncertainty, disorganization, disorientation, vagueness, complication, enigma, lack of clarity. *Ant.* Calm; clarity.

Confute, *v.* To prove to be false, defective, or invalid (to confute the defense's theory). Disprove, invalidate, demolish, rebut, contradict, negate, defeat, discredit, subvert, overthrow, gainsay, negative, silence. See also counter. *Ant.* Validate.

Congenial, *adj.* See concordant, kindred (2), amenable (2), cooperative (2), friendly.

Congenital, *adj.* A condition present at birth (congenital deformity). Inborn, inherited, inbred, ingrained, deep-rooted, innate, hereditary, connate, constitutional, in the blood. See also inherent, native (3). *Ant.* Acquired.

Congeries, *n.* See collection, accumulation (1).

Conglomerate 1. *n.* A corporation that has diversified its operations, usually by acquiring enterprises in widely varied industries (the conglomerate dominated the entire market). Firm, cartel, monopoly, giant, multinational holding company. See also corporation. **2.** *adj.* Massed together. Aggregate, clustered, mixed, grouped, merged, amassed, blended, mingled, united, heterogenous, miscellaneous. *Ant.* Individual.

Conglomeration, *n.* See conglomerate (1), compound (3), accumulation.

Congratulate, *v.* See honor (2), appreciate (3); acclamation.

Congratulation, *n.* Best wishes. Salute, blessing. See also approbation.

Congregate, *v.* To come together (the demonstrators congregated in the office). Assemble, meet, crowd, mobilize, convene, cluster, herd, swarm, mass, flock, muster, throng, accumulate, unite, bunch, converge, aggregate, forgather. *Ant.* Disperse.

Congregation, *n.* A gathering (a hostile congregation of demonstrators). Society, meeting, multitude, council, group, crowd, membership, audience, circle, association, mob, caucus, assemblage, session, convention, collection, mobilization, community, fold, flock. See also assemblage, assembly.

Congregationalism, *n.* Self-governing local church congregations.

Congress, *n.* **1.** The federal legislature (Congress enacted the budget). Council, parliament, House, Senate, diet, lawmakers, General Assembly, House of Delegates. **2.** A formal meeting of delegates or representatives (a congress of dentists). Assembly, conclave, conference, convention, gathering, congregation, convocation.

Congruence, *n.* See conformity, harmony.

Congruent, *adj.* See concordant, consonant, alike (1).

Congruity, *n.* See agreement (2), conformity.

Congruous, *adj.* See consonant, concordant, alike (1).

Conjectural, *adj.* See, speculative, hypothetical, abstract (4).

Conjecture, *n.* An idea or surmise inducing a slight degree of belief founded on some possible or perhaps probable fact as to which no positive evidence exists (without a hearing, his decision would be based on conjecture). Speculation, guess, suspicion, hypothesis, theory, estimate, supposition, deduction, inference, assumption, opinion, premise, forecast, notion, feeling, thought, surmise, impression, suggestion, soupçon, inkling. See also contemplation. *Ant.* Certainty.

Conjoin, *v.* See join (1), bind (2).

Conjoint, *adj.* Joined together; involving more than one in combination (conjoint robbery). United, combined, allied, coupled, associated, common, attached, connected, consolidated, coordinate, affiliated, cohesive, concerted, paired, federated, merged, linked. *Ant.* Individual.

Conjugal, *adj.* Of or belonging to marriage or to the married state (conjugal rights). Matrimonial, connubial, spousal, nuptial, paired, united, wedded, hymeneal, espoused. *Ant.* Single.

Conjugal rights The rights that wife and husband have to each other's society, support, and affection.

Conjunction, *n.* Combination (the investigation was carried out in conjunction with the police). Connection, union, agreement, harmony, alliance, league, concurrence, link, junction, collaboration, merger, consolidation, cooperation. *Ant.* Separation.

Conjure, *v.* To cause to appear (she claimed to be able to conjure up a spirit). Make appear, call forth, fabricate, visualize, invent, improvise, dream up, devise, bewitch, command.

Con man See cheat (2), wrongdoer.

Connect, *v.* **1.** To join or fasten together (the courtroom is connected to the judge's chambers). Tie, unite, merge, combine, link, chain, lock, fuse, abut, flank, consolidate, pair, annex, match, entwine, secure, affiliate, incorporate, neighbor, sew, attach, couple, cohere, interlock, cement, anchor. **2.** To associate or consider as related (the attorney connected the disappearance with the fire). Relate, draw a parallel, ascribe, attribute, correlate, bridge, match, interrelate, compare, hinge, identify, show a kinship, equate. *Ant.* Separate; disassociate.

Connection, *n.* **1.** The state of being joined or linked (the connection between the computer and the printer). Union, link, tie, juncture, blend, abutting, marriage, meeting, attachment, bond, conjunction, merger, junction. **2.** A logical interrelationship (there was a tenuous connection between the testimony and the incident). Nexus, correlation, coherence, alliance, association, affinity, dependence, bearing, common denominator, relevance, parallel. **3.** Someone with whom one is associated (a business connection). Associate, kin, relative, friend, acquaintance, ally, sponsor. *Ant.* Separation; independence; stranger.

Connective, *adj.* See link.

Conniption, *n.* See fit (2).

Connivance, *n.* A secret or indirect consent or permission to allow another to commit an unlawful act (his connivance consisted in allowing his wife to commit adultery). Intentional failure to discover, voluntary blindness, passive consent, overlooking, disregarding, condoning, implied consent, conspiracy, collaboration, corrupt consent, silent complicity, chicanery, contrivance, concert, collusion. *Ant.* Innocence.

Connive, *v.* To cooperate secretly with (the mayor connived with the contractor). Have a clandestine understanding with, have a secret deal, cooperate privately, aid, abet, provide passive assistance, look the other way, be an accessory to, shut one's eyes to, wink at, blink, condone, disregard, overlook, plot, conspire, be a party to, maneuver, collaborate, tolerate, countenance, pretend ignorance, gloss over.

Connoisseur, *n.* See expert (1), judge (1), epicure.

Connotation, *n.* An implied association or meaning (a derogatory connotation). Implication, insinuation, suggestion, allusion, undercurrent, coloration, significance, interpretation, inference, tone, import, essence, drift, intention, evocation, substance, nuance, impact, construction, gist, spirit, tenor. *Ant.* Obvious meaning.

Connote, *v.* See intimate (6).

Connubial, *adj.* See conjugal, marital; marriage.

Conquer, *v.* To win or take, usually by force (conquer one's enemies). Overcome, best, overpower, subdue, vanquish, seize, appropriate, expropriate, humble, master, annex, subjugate, surmount, defeat, triumph, prevail, crush, overthrow, route, overwhelm, beat, dominate, capture, enslave, subordinate, suppress, tame, domesticate, smash. *Ant.* Lose.

Conquering, *adj.* See dominant, predominant.

Conqueror, *n.* Winner. Champion, victor, vanquisher, lord, hero.

Conquest, *n.* Domination, victory. Triumph, defeat, subjection, invasion, vanquishment. See also dominion; plunder (2).

Consanguinity, *n.* The relation of persons descended from the same stock or common ancestor (a cousin in the second degree of consanguinity). Kinship, kindred, common stock, family tie, blood relationship, common lineage. *Ant.* Affinity, unrelated.

Conscience, *n.* The faculty of judging the moral quality of actions or of discriminating between right and wrong (her conscience would not allow her to participate). Moral sense, sense of right and wrong, standards, ethics, scruples, honesty, code of honor, voice within, moral faculty, rectitude, truth, fairness, uprightness.

Conscience-stricken, *adj.* See contrite.

Conscientious, *adj.* **1.** Guided by one's conscience (conscientious objector). Principled, ethical, upright, incorruptible, straightforward, honorable, just, moral, virtuous, righteous. **2.** Careful (a conscientius worker). Meticulous, exacting, cautious, scrupulous, fastidious, responsible, attentive, particular, diligent, reliable, thorough, strict, heedful, prudent, judicious, religious, faithful, stern, punctilious, undeviating, unswerving, ardent, zealous, creditable, self-assured, mature, dutiful, stable, assiduous, observant. See also circumspect. *Ant.* Irresponsible; neglectful.

Conscientiousness, *n.* See caution (3), care (1), concern (5); character; perfection.

Conscientious objector One who by reason of religious training and belief is sincerely opposed to war in any form.

Conscious, *adj.* **1.** Aware (he was not conscious after the collision). Perceiving, observant, awake, sentient, alive, living, apprehending, breathing, alert, aware, reasoning, sensible, apperceptive. See also cognizant. **2.** Deliberate (conscious misrepresentation). Premeditated, purposeful, rational, intentional, calculated, studied, on purpose, willful. *Ant.* Unconscious; accidental.

Consciousness, *n.* See cognizance (3), cognition, comprehension.

Conscript, *v.* To draft. Impress, induct, seize, commandeer, call up, recruit, enlist, register, press. See also levy (2), constrain (1); sailor, military.

Conscription, *n.* Compulsory enrollment and induction into military service (Congress enacted a conscription law). Draft. See conscript; military.

Consecrate, *v.* See anoint, devote (2), dedicate, honor (2).

Consecutive, *adj.* Succeeding one another in regular order (consecutive defeats). Successive, chronological, unbroken, continuous, continuing, serial, uninterrupted, seriatim, sequential, following regularly, regular, cumulative, recurrent. *Ant.* Random.

Consecutive sentences One sentence of imprisonment begins after another sentence of imprisonment ends. *Ant.* Concurrent sentences.

Consensual, *adj.* Coming into existence through consent (consensual intercourse). Voluntary, endorsed, approving, mutually agreeable, unopposed, acceptable, yielding, cooperating, confirming, uncontested, unchallenged. *Ant.* Involuntary.

Consensus, *n.* Collective agreement (a consensus among the group to adjourn). General agreement, common consent, unanimity, concord, harmony, majority opinion, concurrence, unison, affirmation, mutual point of view. *Ant.* Disagreement.

Consent

Consent 1. *v.* To agree or approve (the spouse consented to the terms of the separation agreement). Assent, endorse, accept, acquiesce, yield, sanction, authorize, subscribe, permit, accommodate, incline to, ratify, let, allow, concur, acknowledge, comply with, affirm, grant, tolerate, license, corroborate, accede, support. **2.** *n.* A voluntary agreement by a person, in the possession and exercise of sufficient mental capacity, to make an intelligent choice to do something proposed by another (consent to surgery). Approval, confirmation, ratification, acceptance, affirmation, permission, adoption, support, accord, harmony, acquiescence, approbation, endorsement, authorization, subscription, certification, willingness, compliance, permit, countenance, concurrence, consensus, cooperation, yielding, grant, empowering, toleration. *Ant.* Disagree; rejection.

Consent decree Agreement by the defendant to cease activities that the government asserts are illegal. When the court approves the agreement, the government's action against the defendant is dropped.

Consent judgment A judgment whose terms are settled and agreed to by the parties to the action.

Consequence, *n.* **1.** That which follows from an earlier occurrence (deformity was the consequence of taking the medication). Result, fruit, outcome, reaction, repercussion, upshot, issue, aftermath, response, development, culmination, conclusion, event, corollary, sequence, sequel, side effect, finale, derivation. See also effect (1). **2.** Significance (her appointment to the bench was an event of great consequence). Importance, noteworthiness, impressiveness, urgency, seriousness, magnitude, value, prominence, meaning, influence, weight, moment, distinction, interest, standing, concern, note, import, gravity, account, usefulness, substance, eminence, exigency. *Ant.* Cause; triviality.

Consequent, *adj.* See subsequent.

Consequential, *adj.* **1.** Following as a conclusion. **2.** Notable. See consequence.

Consequential damages Damages, losses, or injuries that do not directly and immediately flow from the act of the defendant. They result from special circumstances that are not ordinarily predictable.

Consequently, *adv.* As a result (consequently, he agreed to perform). Therefore, accordingly, wherefore, for this reason, in which case, it follows therefore, ergo, thus, on this account. See also a fortiori.

Conservation, *n.* The act of preserving or protecting (conservation of resources). Preservation, maintenance, husbandry, safekeeping, defense, upkeep, custody, care, salvation, managing, control, supervision, economy, safeguarding, guarding, storage, nursing. *Ant.* Waste.

Conservatism, *n.* An inclination to resist change. Orthodoxy, moderation, caution; the right.

Conservative, *adj.* Cautious (the trustee made only conservative investments). Safe, noncontroversial, sober, traditional, moderate, guarded, prudent, discreet, orthodox, unextreme, temperate, protecting, conventional. See also narrow (2), reactionary. *Ant.* Risky.

Conservator, *n.* Someone appointed by the court to manage the affairs of an incompetent person, to liquidate a business, etc. (the mentally ill person was under the control of a conservator). Protector, preserver, manager, steward, overseer, superintendent, caretaker.

Conservatory, *n.* See school (1).

Conserve, *v.* To save or protect from loss or damage (conserve the tapes). Guard, maintain, shield, secure, keep safe, preserve, safeguard, keep, spare, nurse, uphold, reserve, prolong, avoid wasting. *Ant.* Squander.

Consider, *v.* **1.** To fix the mind on something in order to examine it carefully (consider your options before you sign). Weigh, inspect, examine, study, contemplate, ponder, analyze, scrutinize, meditate, think about, ruminate, deliberate, heed, cogitate, judge, reflect on, appraise, mind, muse, scan, speculate, discuss, digest, investigate, probe, mark, observe, debate, confer. **2.** To believe (they considered the arbitrator to be biased). Judge, adjudge, regard, deem, think, opine, hold, imagine, infer, account, look upon, estimate, presume, assume, suspect, fancy, surmise, speculate, theorize, reckon, feel, expect, gather, divine, conjecture, postulate, intuit, hypothesize, guess, suppose. *Ant.* Disregard; disbelieve.

Considerable, *adj.* **1.** Worthy of consideration; required to be observed (the witness had a considerable reputation in her field). Substantial, noteworthy, notable, respectable, remarkable, significant, distinguished, illustrious, venerable, compelling, valuable, dominant, impressive, potent. **2.** Substantial (the nuisance caused considerable discomfort). Sizeable, extensive, not small, estimable, big, large, abundant, plentiful, goodly, a lot, a great deal, appreciable. See also extensive, comprehensive. *Ant.* Insignificant.

Considerate, *adj.* See kind (2), charitable.

Consideration, *n.* **1.** That which induces someone to enter a contract, e.g., a right, interest, benefit, or profit accruing to one party; or a forbearance, detriment, loss, or responsibility assumed by the other party (the consideration for the contract was their mutual promise to perform). Something given in exchange, something of value, that which is bargained for, incentive, inducement, return, reward, benefit, detriment, reason for contracting, value to be received; fee, pay, compensation, remuneration, payment. **2.** Thought or attention (cursory consideration to the offer). Inspection, reflection, study, deliberation, contemplation, judgment, meditation, review, regard, thinking, notice, heed, pondering, forethought. See also examination. **3.** Respect for others (an unfortunate lack of consideration shown by the attorney). Solicitude, thoughtfulness, tact, kindness, courtesy, sympathy, concern, forebearance, compassion, deference, understanding, manners, mercy. *Ant.* Irrelevance; inattention; thoughtlessness.

Considered, *adj.* See deliberate (2).

Consign, *v.* To entrust goods; to deliver goods to a merchant for sale (the cars were consigned to the dealership). Transfer, deposit, remit, entrust, leave with, forward, commit, delegate, convey, assign, hand over, charge, ship, transport, send. *Ant.* receive.

Consignee, *n.* One to whom a consignment is made. A person to whom goods are shipped for sale. A person named in a bill of lading to whom or to whose order the bill promises delivery. See bailee; donee. *Ant.* Consignor.

Consignment, *n.* The commitment of property for sale by the consignee for the consignor. A bailment for sale, the transportation of consigned goods, agency for sale. See consign.

Consignor, *n.* One who sends or makes a consignment. One who ships goods. The person named in a bill of lading as the person from whom the goods have been received for shipment. *Ant.* Consignee.

Consist, *v.* To be composed or made up of (the bench consists of five justices). Comprise, contain, include, incorporate, amount, embrace, embody, add up to, constitute, entail, hold, form.

Consistency, *n.* See constant (2), symmetry, coherence, harmony, agreement (2); consistent.

Consistent, *adj.* **1.** Being in agreement with itself or with something else (the document is internally consistent). Harmonious, compatible, accordant, not contradictory, congruous, consonant, agreeing, uniform, suitable, correspondent, congenial, homogeneous, sympathetic, conforming, coherent, equal. See also logical. **2.** Regular (a consistent winner). Steady, persistent, dependable,

Consistent

tenacious, faithful, expected, constant, undeviating, unwavering, assiduous. *Ant.* Contradictory; erratic.

Consolation, *n.* Comfort or ease (after the injury, her husband provided consolation). Satisfaction, contentment, pleasance, happiness, enjoyment, succor, support, encouragement, solace, reassurance, relief, condolence, pity, commiseration, compassion, assuagement, abatement, calm, alleviation, mitigation. *Ant.* Aggravation.

Console, *v.* See mitigate, assuage, comfort.

Consolidate, *v.* **1.** To unify into one mass or body (the two bills were consolidated by the Senate). Unite, pair, combine, fuse, incorporate, connect, federate, league, integrate, conjoin, join, centralize, organize, amass, add to, ally, amalgamate, conglomerate, synthesize, affiliate, link, merge, couple, intertwine, mobilize, herd, coalesce, piece together. **2.** To solidify (consolidate their gains by further documentation). Strengthen, fortify, harden, crystallize, make firm or solid, secure, reinforce. *Ant.* Sever; weaken.

Consolidation, *n.* The combination of two or more corporations into a newly created corporation. The old corporations are extinguished, and the new one takes over the assets and liabilities of the old. See association, consolidate.

Consolidation of actions Uniting several suits or actions into one trial where they all involve the same parties in the same court and have substantially similar subject matters, issues, and defenses.

Consonance, *n.* See accordance, correspondence (1).

Consonant, *adj.* In agreement (an admissible consonant statement). Consistent, concordant, in accord, corresponding, congruous, conformable, congruent, commensurate, uniform, logically related, parallel, harmonious, in harmony, compatible, suitable, concurring, coherent, at one. See also similar. *Ant.* Inconsistent.

Consonant statement A prior hearsay declaration of a witness whose credibility has been impeached, which the court will allow to be proved by the person to whom the declaration was made in order to support the credibility of the witness.

Consort, *n.*, **consort,** *v.* **1.** *n.* A partner or companion (his consort was also arrested). Ally, abettor, mate, comrade, associate, colleague, alter ego, crony, co-conspirator, fellow conspirator; spouse. **2.** *v.* To associate with (consort with criminals). Fraternize, keep company with, mingle, accompany. See also associate, befriend. *Ant.* Enemy; disassociate.

Consortium, *n.* **1.** The society, affection, assistance, conjugal fellowship, and sexual relations that one spouse has a right to expect from another (loss of consortium). Companionship, intimacy, association, help, services, understanding, comfort, friendship. **2.** A coalition of companies or groups (the oil consortium sought to control prices). Amalgamation, conglomeration, union, cartel, monopoly, trust, combine, syndicate, pool, consolidation. *Ant.* Hostility; individual.

Conspectus, *n.* See digest (1).

Conspicuous, *adj.* **1.** Obvious (a conspicuous notice). Blatant, easily seen, manifest, prominent, unequivocal, glaring, express, flagrant, clear, noticeable, reasonably noticeable, visible, discernible, plain, apparent, definite, marked, patent, recognizable, well-defined, graphic, explicit, unmistakable, discoverable, observable, well-marked, pronounced. **2.** Distinguished (a conspicuous accomplishment). Outstanding, celebrated, illustrious, eminent, brilliant, famous, great, glorious, preeminent, splendid, striking, notable, remarkable, memorable. *Ant.* Concealed; modest.

Conspiracy, *n.* A combination or confederacy between two or more persons formed for the purpose of joining efforts to commit some unlawful or criminal act (conspiracy to control prices). Intrigue, plot, collusion, machination, secret plan, cabal, contrivance, scheme, connivance, coalition, composition; treason, sedition.

Conspirator, *n.* See accomplice.

Conspire, *v.* To engage in a conspiracy (they conspired to commit murder). Plot, abet, scheme, collaborate, connive, collude, contrive, maneuver, machinate, devise, intrigue, concur, confederate, cabal, engineer, plan, band together, design, act in concert, league, unite, calculate.

Constable, *n.* An officer (often elected) of a municipality who has duties similar to that of a sheriff, e.g., preserve the peace, execute process, serve writs, maintain custody of juries. See police (1).

Constancy, *n.* See fidelity; continuance (2), continuity.

Constant 1. *adj.* Continually recurring (constant pain due to the accident). Regular, steady, continuous, chronic, persisting, uniform, ceaseless, unbroken, sustained, inveterate, persevering, obstinate, enduring, invariable, nonstop, unceasing, unending, incessant, unrelenting, interminable, perpetual, unremitting, recurrent, certain, endless, habitual, lasting, perennial, uninterrupted, permanent. **2.** *n.* That which does not change (music was the one constant in her life). Consistency, certainty, fixed point, standard, uniformity, stability, regularity, pattern, immutability. **3.** *adj.* Loyal (constant companion). Faithful, devoted, trusty, true, staunch, unflagging, dedicated, abiding, dependable, indefatigable, durable, steadfast, tenacious, unflinching, longstanding, resolute, undeviating, unruffled, determined, unfaltering, secure, immovable, unwavering. *Ant.* Infrequent; instability; wavering.

Constellation, *n.* See assemblage, collection (2).

Consternation, *n.* Amazement (the verdict of acquittal caused consternation). Dismay, horror, fright, apprehension, alarm, shock, trepidation, astonishment, indignation, panic, anxiety, agitation, sudden dismay or fear, dread, awe, bewilderment, paralysis, disillusionment, surprise. *Ant.* calm.

Constituency, *n.* **1.** The inhabitants of an electoral district (her constituency voted her out of office). Voters, membership, citizens, electors, electorate. **2.** Supporters (the union's liberal constituency). Followers, associates, community, backers, chapter, affiliates, constituents.

Constituent 1. *n.* A voter in a certain district. See constituency (1). **2.** *adj.* Component (constituent part). Integral, elemental, basic, intrinsic, fundamental, composing, forming; feature, installment, sector, ingredient, subdivision. **3.** *adj.* With the authority to make law (constituent assembly). Empowered, authorized, amending.

Constitute, *v.* **1.** To establish (the board was constituted to revise the rules). Set up, form, institute, name, commission, found, create, organize, appoint, induct, install, empower, charter, license, sanction, develop, incorporate, ordain, inaugurate, decree, enact, sanction, originate. **2.** To formulate or add up to (the facts alleged did not constitute a cause of action). State, amount to, consist of, classify as, embody, make up, produce, involve, embrace, include, comprise, compose. *Ant.* Dismantle.

Constituted authorities Properly appointed officers.

Constitution, *n.* **1.** The fundamental law of a nation or state that establishes the branches and powers of the government and the basic principles for the regulation of society to which officials, citizens, and all other laws must conform (United States Constitution; Ohio Constitution). Supreme law, fundamental principles, organic law, charter of government, paramount law. **2.** The physical structure of something (a healthy person with a strong constitution). Frame, makeup, composition, physique, formation, design, architecture, arrangement, shape, mold, cast, grain. See also essence, character (2).

Constitutional, *adj.* Consistent with the constitution (the statute was constitutional). Valid, legal, lawful, legitimate, not conflicting with, authorized, licit, enforceable. See also inherent, congenital. *Ant.* Unconstitutional.

Constitutional court A court expressly named or established by the U.S. Constitution. An Article III court. *Ant.* A legislatively created court.

Constitutional right A right guaranteed to the citizens by the Constitution, with which the legislature or others must not interfere.

Constitutional tort When a person subjects another to a deprivation of any rights, privileges, or immunities secured by the Constitution and laws while acting under color of any statute, ordinance, regulation, custom, or usage of a state or territory, that person shall be liable to the injured party in an action at law, suit in equity, or other proper proceeding for redress.

Constrain, *v.* **1.** To compel (she was constrained to file a grievance). Pressure, urge, coerce, oblige, necessitate, prevail upon, force, drive, provoke, require, press, command, charge, impel, enforce, order, obligate, conscript, arm-twist. **2.** To confine (they were constrained by the police). Quarantine, cage, isolate, imprison, incarcerate, jail, restrain, prevent, chain, subjugate, oppress, repress, keep down, tie down, enclose, impede, immure, check, circumscribe, arrest, detain, impound, commit, trammel, harness, block, prohibit, institutionalize, suppress, intern, bar, hinder, limit, proscribe.

Constraint, *n.* **1.** Coercion (constraint of law). Pressure, compulsion, restriction, prohibition, interdiction, duress, obligation, necessity, force, enforcement, limitation. See also blockade, obstruction. **2.** Confinement (kept in constraint). Imprisonment, captivity, incarceration, detention, subjugation, arrest, impoundment, quarantine, custody. **3.** Holding back one's feelings (the new lawyer spoke with constraint). Inhibition, modesty, reserve, diffidence, timidity, embarrassment, restraint. *Ant.* Freedom; liberation; arrogance.

Constrict, *v.* To make more narrow; to impede (constrict her opportunities). Compress, shorten, restrict, squeeze, tighten, strangulate, cramp, contract, abridge, telescope, abbreviate, condense, reduce, narrow, repress, crowd, shrink, block, stifle, interfere with, control, arrest, slow, choke, stymie, frustrate, retard. *Ant.* Release.

Constriction, *n.* See restraint (1), constraint.

Construct, *v.* To build or design (construct a passageway). Make, manufacture, mold, fashion, create, erect, invent, frame, engineer, sculpture, model, elevate, produce, compose, formulate, assemble, fabricate, arrange, raise, organize, institute, form, devise. *Ant.* Raze, destroy.

Construction, *n.* **1.** The process of determining the sense, real meaning, or proper explanation of obscure or ambiguous terms in a statute, contract, will, etc. (strict construction of the criminal law). Interpretation, clarification, commentary, expounding, inference, deduction, understanding, reading, exegesis, explication, rendering, delineation, illumination, translation, version, elucidation. **2.** See building (2); construct.

Construction contract A contract in which the plans and specifications for construction (e.g., of a building) are made a part of the contract itself. The contract is often secured by performance and payment bonds.

Constructive *adj.* **1.** True legally even if not factually (constructive eviction). Inferred, presumed from circumstances, just as if, implied, established by legal interpretation, tantamount to, indirect, inferential, implicit, legal, apparent, inferable, in essence. **2.** Helpful (constructive criticism). Beneficial, practical, valuable, useful, affirmative, productive, advantageous, efficient, instrumental, usable, applicable, favorable, worthy. *Ant.* Actual; destructive.

Constructive authority Authority inferred or assumed to have been given because of the grant of some other prior authority.

Constructive desertion Arises when one spouse, through misconduct, forces the other to abandon the marital abode. The former spouse is the deserting party in the eyes of the law.

Constructive eviction Occurs when the landlord makes the rented premises uninhabitable or unfit for the tenant. If the tenant leaves because of this condition, the landlord has evicted him or her.

Constructive knowledge Knowledge of a fact that the law presumes a person has if, in the exercise of reasonable care, he or she would have known it (e.g., knowledge of a matter of public record).

Constructive notice Notice that the law presumes a person has by reason of the obvious or notorious nature of the subject of the notice.

Constructive possession Possession that one has the power and the intent to control even though not actually possessing it. Hence, you can be in possession of your apartment even if you are not in it at a given time.

Constructive taking An act not amounting to an actual taking of personal property but which shows an intent to convert it to one's own use.

Constructive trust A trust created by operation of law against one who has improperly obtained possession of or legal rights to property through fraud, duress, abuse of confidence, or other unconscionable conduct.

Construe, *v.* To determine the meaning of language (the court construed the clause broadly). Interpret, explain, decipher, read, analyze, expound, elucidate, understand, comprehend, decode, ascertain the meaning, infer, opine, figure out, translate, characterize, illuminate, judge, unravel, explicate, deduce.

Consul, *n.* An officer appointed by a country to watch over commercial and tourist interests and its citizens in foreign countries. Consular agent, attaché, consul general, diplomatic minister, plenipotentiary, envoy.

Consulate, *n.* See delegate (2), consul.

Consult, *v.* **1.** To seek advice (consult a lawyer). Seek the opinion of, confer with, take counsel, call in, discuss, seek guidance, refer to. See also confer (1). **2.** To talk over (the two doctors consulted on the case over the phone). Deliberate together, compare notes, exchange views, meet, discuss.

Consultant, *n.* See expert, professional.

Consultation, *n.* **1.** Seeking advice. See consult. **2.** A conference (the lawyers had a 10-minute consultation during recess). Meeting, dialogue, communication, colloquy, argument, debate, caucus, huddle, interview, talk, session.

Consultative, *adj.* See advisory (1).

Consume, *v.* **1.** To use or use up (the trial consumed considerable energy). Waste, exhaust, expend, squander, devour, deplete, eat, dissipate, spend, employ, devote, invest, occupy, utilize, splurge, drain, impoverish, wear out, fritter, lavish, run through, wear away, gorge. **2.** To destroy (consumed by fire). Devastate, lay waste, annihilate, demolish, ruin, desolate, eradicate, level, prostrate, erase. *Ant.* Supply; create.

Consumer, *n.* A person who purchases, uses, keeps, and disposes of goods and services (suit by the consumer). Shopper, vendee, customer, patron, spender, purchaser, emptor. See also buyer, client. *Ant.* Seller.

Consumer credit sale Any sale in which consumer credit (loan) is extended to or arranged by the seller.

Consumer Price Index (CPI) A price index computed and printed monthly by the U.S. Bureau of Labor Statistics, which tracks the price level of a group of goods and services purchased by the average consumer.

Consummate, *v.,* **consummate,** *adj.* **1.** *v.* To complete (the deal was consummated in her office). Realize, close, fulfill, achieve, finish, terminate, execute, accomplish, effect, crown, finalize, effectuate, prosecute, carry to conclusion. See also commit (2), perfect (3). **2.** *adj.* Supreme (a consummate trial lawyer). Perfect, excellent, total, skilled, gifted, absolute, finished, accomplished, thorough. *Ant.* Begin; inferior.

Consummation, *n.* See conclusion (1), completion, perfection (1).

Consumption, *n.* **1.** Using up something (consumption of liquor). Consuming, depletion, assimilation, utilization, expenditure, exhaustion, waste, destruction, loss, wear, dissipation, ruin. **2.** Tuberculosis. TB, tabes, emaciation, wasting away. See also atrophy. *Ant.* Conservation.

Contact 1. *n.* Touching (offensive contact). Connection, junction, meeting, collision, union, abutment, impact, nexus, juxtaposition. **2.** *n.* A useful connection (business contact). Reference, association, alliance, fellowship, link, bond, tie, relation, relationship, lead, acquaintance, referral. **3.** *v.* To communicate with (contact your attorney). Reach, get in touch with, approach, seek out, call, signal, notify, establish communication. **4.** *v.* To touch (the two currents contact). Connect, meet, join, abut, collide, link, overlap, interconnect, unite, encounter, rub.

Contagion, *n.* See circulation, communication (1), transmission.

Contagious, *adj.* Capable of being communicated or transmitted by contact (contagious disease). Communicable, infectious, catching, epidemic, spreadable, transmittable.

Contain, *v.* See restrain, control (2), hold (4); comprise, comprehend (2).

Container, *n.* See vessel (2), package, wrapper.

Container ship See vessel (1).

Contaminant, *n.* That which contaminates. See contaminate; poison (1).

Contaminate, *v.* To make impure by mixture or contact with a foreign substance (they contaminated the food). Spoil, poison, infect, pollute, defile, dirty, tarnish, stain, pervert, foul; corrupt, vitiate, degrade, dishonor. See also adulterate. *Ant.* Purify.

Contaminated, *adj.* See rotten, foul.

Contamination, *n.* See corruption, pollution.

Contemn, *v.* See censure (2), mock (1).

Contemplate, *v.* **1.** To view or consider with continued attention (contemplate the consequences). Think about, regard thoroughly, ponder, study, plan, meditate, reflect, watch, deliberate, examine, survey, scan, ruminate, cogitate, gaze, peer, mull over, revolve. **2.** To anticipate (she did not contemplate using the witness). Envision, plan, conceive, project, intend, imagine, visualize, design, aim, foresee, expect. *Ant.* Ignore.

Contemplation, *n.* Consideration of an event or state of facts with the expectation that it will happen (contemplation of death). Anticipation, deliberation, meditation, rumination, thought, musing, speculation, study, pondering, conjecture, dream, vision, determination, aim, intention, purpose, review, weighing, reverie.

Contemplation of death The apprehension or expectation of approaching death due to present sickness or impending danger. See in contemplation of death.

Contemplative, *adj.* Introspective. Deliberative, reflective, thoughtful, musing, meditative, engrossed, ruminating, rapt, studious, speculative, lost. See also preoccupied.

Contemporaneous, *adj.* Occurring at the same time (contemporaneous interpretation). Contemporary, coincident, coexistent, concurrent. See also simultaneous.

Contemporary *adj., n.* See contemporaneous, simultaneous, concurrent (1); present (3); chic, avant-garde.

Contempt, *n.* **1.** A willful disregard or disobedience of a public authority (contempt of court). Defiance, insubordination, violation, resistance, disrespect, insolence, dereliction, impertinence, dissension, irreverence, noncooperation, failure to comply, obstinacy, rudeness, recalcitrance. **2.** Scorn or hatred (the victim described the accused with contempt). Loathing, disgust, revulsion, abhorrence, ridicule, condescension, malice, disdain, contumely, derision, aversion, antipathy, distaste, abomination, odium, disparagement, opprobrium, deprecation, mockery, scorn, sarcasm, haughtiness, insolence, catcall, disregard, scoffing, arrogance, humiliation, shame. *Ant.* Respect.

Contemptible, *adj.* Deserving scorn (contemptible conduct). Base, shabby, revolting, vile, loathsome, abhorrent, worthless, detestable, mean, low, shameful, ignominious, despicable, reprehensible, deplorable, disgraceful, paltry, cheap, inferior, abject, atrocious, perfidious, damnable, egregious, heinous, depraved. See also bad (2), awesome, appalling, cruel, odious, corrupt, repulsive, repugnant, offensive, malicious. *Ant.* Respectable.

Contempt of court An act that is calculated to embarrass, hinder, or obstruct the court in the administration of justice, or that is calculated to lessen the court's authority or dignity.

Contemptuous, *adj.* Displaying contempt (contemptuous of opposing counsel). Scornful, arrogant, insolent, supercilious, disdainful, insulting, haughty, pompous, abusive, spiteful, obnoxious, defamatory, derogatory, disparaging, condescending, sneering, mocking, derisive, cynical, uncivil, rude, impertinent. *Ant.* Respectful.

Contend, *v.* **1.** To compete or argue (they contended for the victory). Vie, contest, struggle, fight, wrangle, challenge, war, clash, engage, dispute, quarrel, spar, altercate. **2.** To assert (he contended that he was innocent). Maintain, allege, aver, claim, declare, affirm, advance, insist, propound, put forward, warrant, avow.

Content, *n.,* **content,** *adj.* **1.** *n.* Subject matter (the content of the memo). Topic, scope, part, drift, detail, theme, thesis, thought, substance, design, meaning, gist, object, intention, import, point, sense, essence, nature, text. **2.** *adj.* Satisfied (she was content with a partial judgment). Pleased, untroubled, unconcerned, delighted, thrilled. See also happy.

Contented, *adj.* Satisfied, pleased. See content (2), happy, comfortable (1).

Contention, *n.* **1.** A position taken in an argument (his contention was that the witness was lying). Viewpoint, allegation, claim, assertion, point of view, point, thesis. **2.** A quarrel (bitter contention). Struggle, hostility, contest, altercation, combat, debate, polemic, friction, wrangling, controversy, discord. See also feud, fight (1), conflict (1).

Contentious, *adj.* **1.** Quarrelsome (a contentious witness). Belligerent, aggressive, obstinate, bellicose, stubborn, petulant, wrangling, disputatious, perverse, carping, argumentative, litigious, bickering, competitive, hostile, cantankerous, recalcitrant, irascible, combative. See also controversial. **2.** Contested (contentious jurisdiction). In opposition, adversary, at issue, debated. *Ant.* Cooperative; ex parte.

Contentment, *n.* See satisfaction (2), happiness; content (2).

Conterminous, *adj.* Having a common boundary (conterminous land). Adjacent, adjoining, coterminous. See also immediate (2), coextensive, contiguous.

Contest, *v.,* **contest,** *n.* **1.** *v.* To raise a defense to an adverse claim (he contested the divorce). Oppose, dispute, litigate, call in question, defend, challenge, controvert, debate, counter, question, contradict, resist. See also compete. **2.** *n.* A competition (a bitterly fought contest). Battle, war, struggle, match, encounter, bout, engagement, altercation, test, meet, tournament, contention, controversy, confrontation, antagonism, disagreement, wrangle, dissent, variance, trial, game, race, dissension. *Ant.* Concede; peace.

Contestable, *adj.* At issue (contestable clause). In dispute, debatable, questionable. See also controversial. *Ant.* Stipulated.

Contestant, *n.* See competitor, adversary.

Contested

Contested, *adj.* See contentious (2); challenge.

Context, *n.* That which surrounds words or sentences and helps to determine their meaning (taking a passage out of context). Surroundings, environment, setting, background, circumstances, scope, connection, meaning, sense, qualifying circumstances, substance.

Contiguous, *adj.* In close proximity (contiguous territory). Adjoining, neighboring, in close contact, touching, coterminous, meeting, converging, verging, proximate, end-to-end, near, next to, juxtaposed. *Ant.* Remote.

Continence, *n.* See celibacy, abstention, balance (5), temperance, reserve (4), restraint (2).

Continent, *adj.* See chaste, moderate (1), balance (5); land.

Contingency, *n.* An event that may or may not occur (the gift was subject to a contingency). Unforeseen event, possibility, chance, circumstance, fortune, luck, likelihood, accident, uncertainty, event, conditional event, happening. *Ant.* Certainty.

Contingent 1. *adj.* Possible but not assured (contingent liability). Conditioned, conditional, uncertain, fortuitous, coincidental, provisional, dependent, incident to, relying upon, subordinate, subservient, hinging, unforeseeable, chance, serendipitous, unpredictable. **2.** *n.* See convoy. *Ant.* Certain.

Contingent beneficiary A person who may or will receive a benefit, but only if the primary beneficiary becomes disqualified for the benefit, e.g., by death.

Contingent estate, interest, or right An estate, interest, or right that depends for its effect on an event that may or may not happen.

Contingent fee A contractual arrangement whereby an attorney agrees to represent the client with the compensation to be a percentage of the amount recovered for the client.

Contingent remainder A remnant of an estate that is either (a) limited to a person not in being or not certain or ascertained, or (b) limited to a certain person when his or her right to the estate depends on some uncertain event in the future.

Continual, *adj.* Repeated often (continual interruptions by counsel). Frequent, endless, recurring, perpetual, everlasting, constant, steady, incessant, habitual, interminable, infinite, nonstop, uninterrupted, permanent, unremitting, persistent. See also indestructible. *Ant.* Occasional.

Continuance, *n.* **1.** The adjournment or postponement of a session, hearing, trial, or other proceeding to a later day or time (the judge granted the continuance until May 5. See interruption, cessation; adjourn, postpone. **2.** A prolongation (a continuance of hostility). Extension, protraction, permanence, endurance, lengthening, constancy, perseverance, repetition. *Ant.* Termination.

Continuation, *n.* **1.** A further extension (a continuation of the fraud). Addition, prolongation, sequel, furtherance, resumption, advancement, perpetuation, continuity, succession, protraction, augmentation, persistence, maintenance, sustaining. **2.** Resumption (a continuation of the relationship after the split). Restoration, reestablishment, reversion, reopening. *Ant.* Severance.

Continue, *v.* **1.** To persist (she continued to research the issue). Keep on, persevere, remain, perpetuate, endure, survive, outlive, outlast, abide, outwear, subsist, maintain course, extend, forge ahead, progress, press forward. **2.** To postpone (the case was continued). Adjourn, halt, delay, suspend, hold over, table. **3.** To remain (she will continue as chief judge). Survive, endure, abide, tolerate, suffer, maintain, last, weather, stay, extend, prolong, retain. **4.** To resume (after the bench conference, the case continued). Reopen, return, begin again, recommence, reestablish. See also renew. *Ant.* Give up; commence; leave; terminate.

Continuing, *adj.* Enduring, subsisting. See continue, continual, continuous.

Continuing jurisdiction A court that once acquired jurisdiction on a case continues to possess it in order to modify its orders.

Continuity, *n.* Continuous, coherence (continuity in the presentation). Connection, constancy, flow, chain, perpetuation, consistency, continuum, uninterruptedness, succession, sequence, constant flow, interrelationship. See also continuation. *Ant.* Interruption.

Continuous, *adj.* Uninterrupted (continuous adverse possession). Unbroken, not intermittent, persistent, connected, extended, prolonged, without cessation, consecutive, linked, incessant, perpetual, constant, continual, steady, progressive, whole, perennial, sustained, running. *Ant.* Sporadic,

Continuous offense A crime that is committed over a span of time. The last act of the offense controls for purposes of the beginning of the statute of limitations.

Continuum, *n.* See continuity, continuation.

Contort, *v.* To distort (a face contorted with rage). Twist, deform, misshape, pervert, warp, bend, convolute, disfigure. See also distort. *Ant.* Straighten.

Contour, *n.* See boundary, cast (4); form (1), composition, design (1).

Contra (*Lat.*) Against. Opposite to, confronting, on the contrary, on the other hand. See also insurgent.

Contraband, *n.* Property that is unlawful to produce, possess, transport, or import (arrested for possession of contraband). Smuggled goods, illegal goods, unlicensed property, illegal traffic, prohibited goods, banned goods, bootlegged goods, confiscated or seized articles, illegal trade.

Contraceptive, *n.* Birth control device. Prophylactic, pill, condom, diaphragm, foam, douche, IUD, rhythm, preventative, coil; family planning. See also prevention.

Contract, *n.*, **contract,** *v.* **1.** *n.* A legally binding agreement that creates an obligation to do or not to do a particular thing. There must be mutuality of agreement and obligation, legal consideration, and competent parties (a contract to sing). Bargain, commitment, obligation, accord, accordance, warranty, undertaking, pack, negotiated agreement, mutual promise, covenant, compact, treaty, convention, arrangement, bond. **2.** *v.* To make a bargain (they contracted for the delivery). Covenant, mutually promise, bargain, come to terms, agree, engage. **3.** *v.* See incur. **4.** *v.* See constrict, decline, diminish.

Contract clause U.S. Const., Art. I, Sec. 10, providing that no state shall pass a law impairing the obligation of contract.

Contract for deed An agreement by a seller to deliver the deed to the property when certain conditions have been met (e.g., completion of the payments by the buyer).

Contraction, *n.* See abridgement (1), abatement (2); condense, constrict.

Contractor, *n.* See architect, independent contractor, supplier, builder, entrepreneur.

Contradict, *v.* To deny; to prove the contrary (the witness contradicted her earlier testimony). Refute, disprove, disclaim, repudiate, deny, annul, negate, gainsay, traverse, run counter to, counter, disaffirm, rebut, cancel, abrogate, impugn, confute, controvert, challenge, take issue with, disagree, belie. *Ant.* Corroborate.

Contradiction, *n.* One statement that contradicts or is inconsistent with another (the testimony was full of contradictions). Discrepancy, clash, denial, opposition, negation, antithesis, conflict, variance, discord, disagreement, incongruity, rebuttal, dispute, refutation. *Ant.* Confirmation.

Contradictory, *adj.* Inconsistent (contradictory assertions). Opposing, opposite, at variance, conflicting, antithetical, negative, antagonistic, nullifying, negating, counteractive, at odds, adverse, clashing, diametrically opposed, dissenting, irreconcilable, countervailing, paradoxical, repugnant. *Ant.* Compatible.

Contraindicate

Contraindicate, *v.* To suggest or show that an approach or treatment is not recommended or warranted.

Contraption, *n.* See apparatus, device (1).

Contrary, *adj.* Opposed to or in conflict with (a contrary position). Against, in opposition to, at variance, antagonistic, conflicting, repugnant, disagreeing, contradictory, discordant, adverse, irreconcilable, refuting, opposite, inconsistent, antithetical, disparate, at cross purposes, clashing, contrasting, denying. *Ant.* Parallel.

Contrast, *n.*, **contrast,** *v.* **1.** *n.* The act of comparing or contrasting (a striking contrast). Comparison, difference, distinction, antithesis, disagreement, disparity, contradiction, differentiation, discrimination, polarity. **2.** *v.* See compare (1). *Ant.* Similarity (1).

Contravene, *v.* To violate or go against (the action contravened the judge's order). Oppose, frustrate, nullify, annul, infringe, act against, disobey, impugn, transgress, thwart, defeat, hinder, abort, obstruct, trespass, cross, foil. *Ant.* Observe.

Contravention, *n.* See violation.

Contretemps, *n.* See mistake, accident.

Contribute, *v.* **1.** To help produce (she contributed to her own injury). Participate, help bring about, have a hand in, influence, share responsibility for, be a contributing factor, help cause, bear a part, advance. See also cooperate. **2.** To lend assistance to or aid a common purpose (contribute to the fund). Donate, grant, furnish, volunteer, accommodate, assist, support, minister, succor, endow, provide, provide alms, offer a gratuity, offer charity, bequeath, benefit, provide sustenance or a subsidy, furnish, serve, augment, fortify, subsidize, promote, supply.

Contributing, *adj.* See contributory; contribute.

Contributing cause Any factor that contributes to a result.

Contribution, *n.* **1.** A tortfeasor against whom a judgment is rendered is entitled to recover proportional shares of the judgment from other joint tortfeasors whose negligence contributed to the injury and who are also liable to the plaintiff (the defendant sought contribution from the other drivers). **2.** A donation. See gift, charity, assistance (2), bounty (2); contribute. **3.** See part (2), function, assignment (3).

Contributor, *n.* See patron (2), champion (1), catalyst, party (2).

Contributory, *adj.* Lending assistance to or having a part in bringing about a given result (contributory negligence). Helpful, instrumental, assisting, lending assistance, auxiliary, aiding.

Contributory negligence An unreasonable act or omission on the part of the complaining party which, concurring with the defendant's negligence, is the proximate cause of the injury.

Contrite, *adj.* Remorseful (a contrite heart). Penitent, regretful, repentant, sorry, troubled, humble, guilty, apologetic, conscience-stricken. *Ant.* Arrogant.

Contrition, *n.* Repentance. Compunction, regret, sorrow, penitence, remorse, qualms of conscience, atonement, self-reproach, anguish, self-mortification, pangs, pain. See also guilt (2), embarrassment, disgrace.

Contrivance, *n.* Any device that has been arranged to deceive (the contrivance of the accountants was uncovered). Scheme, machination, deception, method, subterfuge, arrangement, plot, artifice, plan, intrigue, invention, stratagem, fabrication, collusion, connivance, wile, maneuver. See also conspiracy; apparatus, instrument (2), equipment.

Contrive, *v.* **1.** To scheme. See conspire; contrivance. **2.** To invent or organize (contrive a plan). Fashion, imagine, develop, concoct, manage, create, improvise, cause, sketch, shape, compose, draft, pattern.

Contrived, *adj.* See feigned, deceitful, deceptive, false.

Control 1. *v.* To exercise a directing influence over something (the company controlled its workers). Regulate, govern, steer, dominate, guide, supervise, discipline, direct, rule, superintend, dictate, manage, master, regiment, administer, engineer, command, operate, manipulate, pilot, oversee. **2.** *v.* To restrain (control the client's temper). Restrict, contain, deter, curb, limit, encumber, guard, arrest, suppress, confine, inhibit, constrain. **3.** *n.* Power to regulate (the director had full control). Authority, supervision, command, jurisdiction, management, regulation, government, domination, dominion, stewardship, oversight, mastery, sovereignty. **4.** *n.* Restraint (control over one's temper). Suppression, confinement, deterrence, moderation, inhibition, curb, brake.

Controller, *n.* An officer in charge of audits, accounting, bookkeeping, etc. (she was the bank's controller). Comptroller, financial officer, registrar, accountant, auditor, bookkeeper, examiner, inspector, treasurer, bursar.

Controlling, *adj.* See dominant, leading (1).

Controversial, *adj.* Producing controversy (a controversial ruling). Controvertible, debatable, arguable, provocative, polemical, litigious, widely discussed, at issue, doubtful, contestable, argumentative, dubious, suspect, in dispute, contentious. *Ant.* Innocuous.

Controversy, *n.* **1.** A concrete case admitting of an immediate and definitive determination of legal rights of parties in an adversary proceeding upon facts alleged. Claims based merely on assumed potential invasions of rights are not enough. (Case and controversy.) A litigated question, legal proceeding, action, an adversary proceeding in court. **2.** A dispute (a controversy over the school's grading policy). Debate, argument, strife, conflict, feud, disagreement, dissension, wrangle, altercation, clash, opposition, contention, brawl, disputation, discussion, war of words, discord, confrontation, rumpus, friction. *Ant.* Agreement.

Controvert, *v.* To take issue with (his theory was easy to controvert). Dispute, deny, oppose, contest, contradict, rebut, impugn, traverse, repudiate, answer, counter, oppugn, challenge. *Ant.* Accept.

Contumacious, *adj.* Rebellious, disobedient (contumacious conduct). Stubborn, obstinate, headstrong, intractable, perverse, willful, insolent, insubordinate, cantankerous, repulsive, contemptuous, refractory, mutinous, bullheaded, obdurate, fractious, rash. *Ant.* Complaisant.

Contumacy, *n.* The refusal or intentional failure to appear in court as required or to obey a court order (her contumacy led to a contempt citation). Insubordination, disobedience, resistance, rebellion, infraction, perversity, willfulness. *Ant.* Obedience.

Contumely, *n.* Rudeness compounded by haughtiness and contempt (a contumely that could not be tolerated). Derision, scurrility, abuse, arrogance, discourtesy, insult, indignity, contempt, pomposity, cynicism, dishonor, vulgarity, disdain, insolence, vituperation. *Ant.* Gentleness.

Contusion, *n.* Wound. Bruise, cut, abrasion, scrape, sore, swelling, blemish, bump, black-and-blue mark. See also hurt, injury, lesion, break (3).

Conundrum, *n.* An engima or puzzle. Problem, perplexity, sphinx, riddle, anagram, charade, paradox, secret. See also mystery, ambiguity.

Convalesce, *v.* See recover (2), heal; cure (2), remedy (2), correct (2).

Convalescence, *n.* See rehabilitation; invalid (2).

Convene, *v.* To call together (convene a special session of the court). Cause to assemble, convoke, summon, muster, collect, rally, congregate, assemble, round up, amass, mobilize, reunite, unite, consolidate, converge. *Ant.* Disband.

Convenience, *n.* Suitability. Utility, accessibility, usefulness, appropriateness, serviceability, fitness, benefit, handiness. See also comfort (1); convenient.

Convenient

Convenient, *adj.* Suitable; easy to use (the most convenient forum in which to sue). Proper, just, fit, adapted, easily accessible, available, serviceable, conducive, helpful, reachable, nearby, favorable, well-suited, advantageous, beneficial, useful, opportune. *Ant.* Unsuitable.

Convent, *n.* Nunnery, cloister, abbey. See asylum, church.

Convention, *n.* **1.** An agreement (Geneva Convention). Compact, treaty, pact, covenant, concordat, contract. **2.** A formal meeting (Democratic Convention). Session, assembly, council, caucus, gathering, congregation, congress, forum, diet, term, consultation, seminar, hearing, sitting, conclave, synod. **3.** A custom (wigs are not a U.S. court convention). Protocol, tradition, code. See also practice (1), formality (1), custom (1).

Conventional, *adj.* **1.** Conforming to generally accepted practices (the safety check was conventional in the trade). Orthodox, standard, normal, habitual, routine, commonplace, everyday, approved, stock, popular, prevalent, universal, set, typical, usual, widespread, regular, conforming, basic, accustomed, accepted, established, traditional, ordinary. See also customary. **2.** Arising from the mutual agreement of the parties (conventional lien). Contractual, bargained for. *Ant.* Abnormal; imposed.

Converge, *v.* To come together at a certain place (the demonstrators converged at the square). Unite, center, concentrate, combine, draw together, focus, approach, assemble, convene. *Ant.* Scatter.

Conversant, *adj.* Familiar (she was conversant with forensic science). Acquainted, up-to-date, skilled, comfortable with, learned, proficient or versed in. *Ant.* Ignorant of.

Conversation, *n.* **1.** Talk or discussion between people (political conversation). Discourse, dialogue, communication, palaver, chat, conference, colloquy, interchange of ideas, "rap." **2.** See criminal conversation.

Converse, *v.,* **converse,** *n.* **1.** *v.* To engage in conversation (they conversed during the recess). Talk, communicate, speak, chat, discourse, discuss, exchange ideas, dialogue, confer with, confabulate. **2.** *n.* The opposite (the jury believed the converse of the testimony). Reverse, antithesis, contrary. See also opposite, inverse; negative (1). *Ant.* Be silent; the same.

Conversion, *n.* **1.** The unauthorized exercise of dominion or control over someone's personal property (chattel). Elements: (a) a chattel; (b) the plaintiff is in possession of the chattel or is entitled to immediate possession of the chattel; (c) the defendant intends to exercise dominion or control over the chattel; (d) there is a serious interference with the plaintiff's possession; (e) that is caused by the defendant. (He sued for conversion of his car.) Misappropriation, appropriation, embezzlement, larceny, theft, expropriation, stealing, diversion, misuse, wrongful assumption. See also trover, trespass to chattels. **2.** A change (the judge's conversion was unexpected). Transformation, metamorphosis, changeover, alteration, modification, switch, shift.

Convert, *v.,* **convert,** *n.* **1.** *v.* To misappropriate (she converted the funds). Embezzle, steal, misuse, misapply, expropriate, divert, mismanage. See also rob. **2.** *v.* To change the character or function of something (converted into cash). Transform, alter, modify, reshape, amend, substitute, revise, refashion, turn, switch. **3.** *v.* To cause someone to change an opinion or belief (the judge was converted to our point of view). Convince, enlist, influence, reform, proselytize, win over, propagandize. **4.** *n.* A person who has been converted. New member, proselyte, disciple, neophyte, apprentice, follower, apostle. See also adherent.

Convertible, *adj.* Capable of being changed (convertible insurance). Adaptable, interchangeable, exchangeable, transposable, alterable, adjustable, reversible. *Ant.* Unalterable.

186

Convey, *v.* **1.** To transfer or deliver to another (he conveyed his full interest in the land to his wife). Grant, deed, cede, leave, bequeath, devise, alienate, will, pass, assign, donate, hand over, relinquish, contribute, shift, pass title. See also carry. **2.** To communicate (convey a message to the judge). Relate, confide, transmit, disclose, advise, tell, inform, announce, broadcast, make public, state, divulge, contact, educate, specify, describe, reveal, impart, remark, point out. **3.** To move or carry to a place (convey the goods). Transport, take, bear, conduct, guide, channel, bring, fetch. *Ant.* Keep; conceal; receive.

Conveyance, *n.* **1.** The transfer of an interest in land, e.g., title, mortgage, lease, assignment (involuntary conveyance). Transference, delivery, alienation, disposition, grant, deed, relinquishment. See assignment. **2.** The act of transportation (conveyance by rail). Movement, shipment, carriage, hauling, carrying, transmission. **3.** A vehicle of transportation (the conveyance broke down). Van, cart, bus, car, train, plane, truck, wagon. See also carriage, vehicle (1), vessel (1). *Ant.* Retention; receipt.

Conveyancer, *n.* One whose business is to prepare deeds and mortgages, examine title, and perform other functions relating to the transfer of real estate.

Conveyancing, *n.* Performing the various functions relating to the transfer of real property. See convey, conveyance, and conveyancer.

Conveyer, *n.* See carrier.

Convict, *v.*, **convict,** *n.* **1.** *v.* To find a person guilty of a criminal charge (the jury convicted her of assault). Declare guilty, punish, denounce, doom, prove guilty, adjudge responsible, hold responsible, find against. See also condemn (1). **2.** *n.* A person in prison serving a sentence (the convict escaped). Prisoner, inmate, "con," captive, intern, felon, "lifer," "jailbird," condemned man, repeater, recidivist, criminal. *Ant.* Exonerate; free person.

Conviction, *n.* **1.** A judgment of guilty following a verdict or finding of guilt, a plea of guilty, or a plea of nolo contendere (conviction for robbery). Finding of guilt, proof of guilt, adjudication of guilt, condemnation. See also censure. **2.** A firm belief (political convictions). Philosophy, view, opinion, faith, viewpoint, tenet, doctrine, concept, profession, conclusion, declaration of faith, dogma, judgment, position, conception, theory, predisposition, principle, teaching, creed, persuasion. **3.** The state of being convinced (the witness spoke with conviction). Certitude, certainty, assurance, positiveness, sureness, steadfastness, zeal, intensity, fervor, earnestness, ardor. *Ant.* Innocence; doubt; hesitation.

Convince, *v.* To persuade by argument (the jury was not convinced). Satisfy, impress, win over, prove, cause to believe, prevail upon, influence, bring around, sway, assure, enlist, motivate, actuate, coax, propagandize, lure, inspire, woo, talk into, seduce, incite, spur, affect, bring to reason, overcome resistance, entice, induce, convert, indoctrinate. *Ant.* Dissuade.

Convincing, *adj.* Persuasive (a convincing argument to the court). Believable, cogent, sound, effective, solid, telling, conclusive, self-evident, assured, well-founded, well-argued, coherent, powerful, substantial, compelling, plausible, valid, logical, incontrovertible, creditable, sustainable, decisive, strong, forceful, reliable, genuine, rational, influential, profound, irrefutable, prevailing, moving, positive. *Ant.* Dubious.

Convincing proof Proof that is sufficient to establish the proposition in question beyond hesitation, ambiguity, or reasonable doubt in an unprejudiced mind.

Convivial, *adj.* Sociable. Festive, cheerful, gay, cordial, joyous, lively, merry, genial, gregarious, amiable, affable. See also friendly, festive.

Convocation, *n.* See assembly (1), collection.

Convoke, *v.* See collect (1), convene.

Convoy, *n.* An escort for protection (Navy convoy). Guard, bodyguard, force,

187

security, screen, backup, caravan, contingent, fleet, group, cover, custody, column.

Convulse, *v.* See disturb.

Convulsion, *n.* See fit (2); disturbance, eruption.

Convulsive, *adj.* See demented; involuntary.

Cook, *v., n.* See bake; servant, employee.

Cool, *adj., v.* See cold (2), indifferent; self-confidence; hostile; mitigate.

Cool-headed, *adj.* See dispassionate, sane (1), rational, constant (3).

Cooling-off period A period of time in which no action of a particular sort may be taken by either side in a dispute.

Coolness, *n.* See reserve (4), indifference; hostility, animus.

Co-obligor, *n.* Someone bound jointly with another (or others) in a bond or obligation (co-obligor on the note). A joint obligor.

Co-op, *n.* See cooperative (1).

Cooperate, *v.* To act jointly or concurrently toward a common end (they cooperated in secret). Work together, collaborate, connive, collude, conspire, combine, pool, unite, join hands, contribute, lend assistance, act in concert, work as a team, ally, participate, associate, confederate, federate, lend support, conduce, take part, coact. *Ant.* Rival.

Cooperation, *n.* The association of persons for a common benefit (cooperation by the insured in the litigation). Concert, participation, collaboration, combination, teamwork, joint action, concurrence, unity, union, complicity, collusion, coordination, solidarity, unification, fellowship, mutual assistance, harmony, conspiracy, concerted action, reciprocity, pooling, interaction, logrolling, pulling together, agreement. *Ant.* Discord.

Cooperative, 1. *n.* A business owned by its customers. A corporation or association organized for the purpose of rendering economic services (without gain to itself) to shareholders or members who own and control it (consumer cooperative; housing cooperative). Collective, union, membership, enterprise, alliance, joint operation, federation, co-op, coalition, partnership. **2.** *adj.* Available to work together with others (cooperative witness). Helpful, assisting, accommodating, harmonious, collusive, synergetic, obliging, aiding, united. *Ant.* Sole proprietorship; hostile.

Cooperative apartment Dwelling units in a multi-dwelling complex in which each owner has an interest in the entire complex and a lease of his or her own apartment. Unlike a condominium, the owners do not own their individual apartments.

Cooperative federalism The distribution of power between (a) the national government and (b) the local or state governments, with each recognizing the powers of the other.

Co-opt, *v.* To preempt. Assume, usurp, monopolize, absorb.

Coordinate 1. *v.* To adjust or bring together for integrated action (she coordinated the activities of the investigating committee). Integrate, organize, arrange, methodize, systematize, harmonize, categorize, regulate, synchronize, marshal, equalize, regularize, combine, proportion, mesh, interrelate. **2.** *adj.* Of the same order, rank, degree, or importance (a coordinate branch of the government). Equal, not subordinate, coequal, parallel, on the same footing, synonymous, reciprocal, alike, analogous. *Ant.* Disorganize; unequal.

Coordinate jurisdiction Jurisdiction possessed by courts of equal rank or authority to deal with the matter in question. Concurrent jurisdiction.

Coordination, *n.* See harmony, concord (1), agreement (1), cooperation, unity.

Cop, *n., v.* See police; larceny.

Cop a plea To plead guilty. See Confess.

Coparcenary, *n.* An estate that arises when several persons inherit property (from the same ancestor) to share as if they were one person or one heir.

Copartner, *n.* A member of a partnership. See associate, partner.

Cope, *v.* See manage (2), deal (3), continue.

Copious, *adj.* Abundant (he took copious notes on what the witness said). Plentiful, large, extensive, ample, full, overflowing, lavish, excessive, many, thriving, fertile, considerable, prolific, liberal, profuse, innumerable, generous, well-stocked, rich. *Ant.* Meager.

Coprincipal, *n.* **1.** One of two or more participants in a crime who actually perpetrates the crime or who is present, aiding and abetting the persons who commit it. See accomplice. **2.** One of two or more persons who has appointed agents whom he or she has the right to control.

Copse, *n.* See woods, timber.

Copulate, *v.* To engage in sexual intercourse. See join; coitus, fornication.

Copulation, *n.* See coitus, fornication.

Copy 1. *n.* A reproduction of the original (a copy of the will). Double, transcript, facsimile, imitation, replica, representation, duplicate, carbon, image, likeness, print, counterfeit, forgery, fake, cast, offprint, replication, simulation. **2.** *v.* To reproduce or make a copy of something (he copies the figures on the account). Duplicate, simulate, imitate, mirror, forge, trace, print, photostat, ape, restate, counterfeit, parody, transcribe, follow, depict, impersonate, plagiarize. *Ant.* Original; originate.

Copyhold, *n.* An old form of holding land at the will of the lord. Records of this estate were often kept in court rolls according to local custom.

Copyright, *n.* The intangible right or privilege of an author (or other originator) to control for a limited period the copying, publication, and sale of books, articles, movies, records, or other original works of authorship fixed in any tangible medium of expression. Copyright is a limited monopoly or franchise granted by statute or by common law. Authority, authorization, license, right of literary property.

Coquet, *v.* See flirt.

Coquette, *n.* See prostitute.

Coram nobis In our presence; before us. A writ of coram nobis asks a court to reform its own judgment due to an error or mistake of fact that did not appear on the face of the record because of fraud, duress, or excusable neglect (e.g., the petitioner did not present certain facts during the trial, because the other side fraudulently prevented the petitioner from discovering them). If the facts had been known, the same judgment allegedly would not have been rendered.

Coram vobis Before you. A writ of error (to correct an error of fact) directed by a court of review to the court that tried the case.

Cord, *n.* See bond (4), connection; rope, thread (1).

Cordial, *adj.* See friendly, affectionate, cooperative (2).

Cordon, *v., n.* See enclose; quarantine; divide (1).

Core, *n.* See center (1, 2), essence (1), intent.

Co-respondent, *n.* A person summoned with another to answer a bill, petition, or libel (he was charged with adultery as the co-respondent in the divorce case). Co-defendant.

Cornball, *n.* See boor, idiot.

Corner, *n.* **1.** A combination among dealers in a specific commodity to buy up most of that commodity and hold it back from sale until the price rises. See monopoly. **2.** See intersection.

Cornerstone, *n.* See foundation (2), basis (1), base (3), center (2).

Cornucopia, *n.* See sufficiency.

Corny, *adj.* See commonplace (2), facetious, comic; joke.

Corollary, *n.* An obvious or easily drawn deduction or inference (the corollary to her argument). Conclusion, logical consequence, collateral consequence, secondary consequence, follow-up, result, resultant, fruit, upshot, product, outcome, effect.

Coroner, *n.* A public official who has the duty to make inquiry into the causes and circumstances of any death that occurs through violence or suddenly and with marks of suspicion (i.e., an unnatural death). A medical examiner. See medical examiner, autopsy.

Corporal, *adj.* Physical; relating to the human body (corporal punishment). Corporeal, material, carnal, tangible, incarnate, anatomical, temporal, somatic, animal, nonspiritual, sensual, fleshly. *Ant.* Mental.

Corporal punishment Punishment of or inflicted on the body. Physical punishment. Depending on the context, the phrase may or may not include imprisonment itself.

Corporate, *adj.* Pertaining to a corporation (corporate profits). Incorporated. See corporation.

Corporate charter A document issued by a state agency (e.g., secretary of state), granting a proposed corporation its legal existence and right to function as a corporation.

Corporate veil See piercing the corporate veil.

Corporation, *n.* **1.** An organization that is an artificial person or legal entity created by or under the authority of the government. The corporation has an existence that is distinct from its members (shareholders). Artificial entity, body corporate, corporate body. **2.** A business (sales corporation). Company, association, firm, conglomerate, multinational, concern, parent company, holding company, house, business association, establishment, syndicate, industry.

Corporeal, *adj.* Perceptible by the senses (corporeal property). Corporal, objective, tangible, actual, nonspiritual, existent, demonstrable, real, substantive, bodily, somatic, solid, embodied, animal, definite, concrete, temporal. See also material (2), physical. *Ant.* Spiritual.

Corps, *n.* See party (3); sailor; military.

Corpse, *n.* The dead body of a human being (examination of the corpse). Deceased, remains, carcass, cadaver, victim, corpus, "stiff."

Corpsman, *n.* An enlisted man or woman trained in hospital work. See sailor; military.

Corpulent, *adj.* Obese. Fat, overweight, rotund, portly, chubby, stout, plump, stocky, heavy.

Corpus, *n.* **1.** Body (corpus juris). Physical substance, aggregate, core, collection, bulk, sum total, collectivity, gross amount, quantity, structure, mass, res, whole, sum and substance. **2.** Principal sum as opposed to interest or income.

Corpus delicti The body of a crime. The material substance upon which a crime has been committed, e.g., the charred remains of a house that has been burned.

Corpus Juris 1. A body of law; collections of law. **2.** The first edition of a legal encyclopedia by West Publishing Company.

Corpus Juris Civilis The body of the civil law. The system of Roman jurisprudence compiled and codified under the direction of Emperor Justinian in A.D. 528–534, consisting of the Institutes, Digest (or Pandects), Code, and Novels.

Corpus Juris Secundum (C.J.S.) The second edition of a legal encyclopedia by West Publishing Company.

Corral, *n., v.* See enclose, collect, seize, apprehend, quarantine.

Correct 1. *adj.* Accurate (correct assessment). True, valid, precise, actual, faultless, literal, exact, perfect, unerring, errorless, factual, careful, proper, authorized, legal, without flaws, unimpeachable, strict, truthful. **2.** *v.* To remove errors (correct the transcript). Remedy, revise, rectify, cure, rehabilitate, better, adjust, amend, reform, redress, fix, set right. See also heal. **3.** *v.* To rebuke (correct deviant behavior). Punish, censure, chastise, reprimand, scold, lecture, discipline, blame. *Ant.* Invalid; impair; praise.

Correction, *n.* **1.** The act or system of imposing discipline and treatment on offenders (Board of Corrections). Censure, penalty, discipline, chastisement, castigation, admonishment, scolding, reprimand, criticism, fine, condemnation, retribution, lesson; improvement, reform, reformation, reparation, remediation, rehabilitation, cure. **2.** That which is presented as a substitute for an error (correction in the calculations). Alteration, redress, amendment, change, emendation, antidote, remedy, corrective, adjustment, renovation, rectification, revision, repair, modification. *Ant.* Award; error.

Corrective, *adj.* See remedial, correction (2); punitive, disciplinary.

Correlate 1. *v.* To show a relationship between things (the paralegal was asked to correlate the sets of figures). Connect, relate, contrast, compare, link, coordinate, bring together, correspond. **2.** *n.* One of two things that are mutually related (victory is the correlate of success). Counterpart, ally, supplement, match, analogue, associate, parallel, affiliate, complement. *Ant.* Disconnect; antithesis.

Correlation, *n.* A mutual relationship (no correlation existed between the incidents). Reciprocity, quid pro quo, correspondence, mutuality, interdependence, tie-in. See also connection (2), ratio, correspondence. *Ant.* Independence.

Correlative, *adj.* Having a mutual or reciprocal relation in the sense that the existence of one necessarily implies the existence of the other (correlative rights). Complementary, interconnected, analogous, interrelated, correspondent, similar, associated, akin, parallel, concurrent, linked, dependent, interdependent. *Ant.* Independent.

Correspond, *v.* **1.** To be in conformity (the testimony of the two witnesses does not correspond). Agree, parallel, relate, harmonize, concur, conform, square, equate, coincide, converge, suit, fit, compare, accord, cohere, equal, approximate, resemble, pertain, coordinate, bear a resemblance to. **2.** To communicate (they corresponded by telegram). Contact, reply, write, answer, stay in touch. *Ant.* Disagree.

Correspondence, *n.* **1.** The agreement of things with one another (a weak correspondence existed between the two theories). Similarity, resemblance, comparability, agreement, analogy, uniformity, harmony, conformity, congruity, parity, relation. See also ratio, correlation. **2.** An interchange of written communication (correspondence on settlement efforts). Letters, mail, dispatches, communiqués, bulletins. *Ant.* Disagreement.

Correspondence school See school (1), education.

Correspondent, *n., adj.* A securities firm, bank, or other financial organization that regularly performs services for another in a place or market to which the other does not have direct access (a correspondent on an exchange; correspondent bank). See also analogous, correlative.

Corresponding, *adj.* See consonant, analogous, correlative, proportionate.

Corridor, *n.* See highway, passage (2), course (1), entrance.

Corrigible, *adj* See amenable, malleable; salvageable.

Corroborate, *v.* To add weight or credibility to a thing by additional and confirming facts or evidence (her testimony was corroborated by the document). Strengthen, back up, substantiate, confirm, validate, certify, authenticate, support, document, reinforce, endorse, uphold, affirm, verify, ratify, fortify, attest, establish, vindicate, attest, give credence to, sanction, bear witness to, accredit, sustain. *Ant.* Contradict.

Corroborating

Corroborating, *adj.* See affirmative (1).

Corroborating evidence Evidence supplementary to that already given, which tends to strengthen or confirm it. Additional evidence of a different character to the same point.

Corroboration, *n.* See proof; corroborate.

Corroborative, *adj.* See affirmative (1).

Corrode, *v.* See consume (1), impair; corrupt (2).

Corrosion, *n.* See deterioration, wear and tear; destroy.

Corrosive, *adj.* See caustic, cruel.

Corrupt 1. *adj.* Spoiled; morally degenerate (a corrupt transaction). Tainted, vitiated, depraved, debased, shady, fraudulent, immoral, evil, unscrupulous, perverse, dishonest, deceitful, base, adulterated, mischievous, recreant, disloyal, disgraceful, dishonorable, villainous, faithless, reprobate, craven, guileful, scheming, traitorous, cowardly, dastardly, perfidious, wicked, malignant, horrid, venomous, dissolute, devious, crooked, scurvy, treacherous, double-dealing, mercenary, nefarious, insincere, debauched, venal, foul, odious, sinful, diabolical, scandalous, guilty, inimical, malign, malicious, unprincipled, cruel, marred, degraded, untrustworthy, underhanded, criminal. **2.** *v.* To change one's morals and principles from good to bad (money corrupted the lawyer). Prostitute, contaminate, pollute, defile, bribe, subvert, corrode, defraud, debase, adulterate, seduce, debauch, entice, lure, lead astray. *Ant.* Principled; reform.

Corruption, *n.* An act done with the intent to give some advantage that is inconsistent with an official or fiduciary duty and the rights of others (judicial corruption). Abuse of position, breach of trust, disloyalty, dishonesty, depravity, underhandedness, deception, fraud, bribery, evil, knavery, distortion, vice, shady dealings, graft, defilement, immorality, perversion, abandon, adulteration, lack of principle, degeneracy, mercenariness, taint, turpitude, decadence, complicity, villainy. *Ant.* Trustworthiness.

Cosign, *v.* To sign an instrument or document with another (she cosigned the note). Endorse, certify, vouch for, guarantee, insure, assure, underwrite, countersign, validate.

Cosignatory, *n.* One who cosigns.

Cosigner, *n.* See promoter; cosign.

Cosmetic, *adj.* Superficial. See peripheral, surface (1); ointment.

Cosmic, *adj.* See big, universal.

Cosmopolitan, *adj.* See metropolitan, universal, worldly; civil (3), aristocratic, cultivated, chic.

Cosmos, *n.* See world.

Cost, *n.* **1.** The sum (or equivalent) expended, paid or charged for something (actual cost of the shipment). Price, charge, bill, fee, valuation, value, outlay, expenditure, toll, demand, appraisement, market value, worth, payment, consideration, rate, tariff, price tag, quoted price. **2.** A loss or detriment (she exonerated the boss at the cost of her own job). Sacrifice, damage, penalty, injury, consequence, punishment, suffering, loss, pain.

Cost bond A bond given by a party to an action to secure the eventual payment of such costs as may be awarded against him or her.

Cost-effective, *adj.* Economical in light of what is spent and received.

Costly, *adj.* Expensive. Steep, dear, high-priced, extravagant, precious. See also exorbitant; deleterious; waste (1).

Cost of living clause A contract clause (often in union, pension, and retirement agreements) providing an automatic wage or benefit increase that is tied to cost-of-living rises in the economy as measured by indicators such as the Consumer Price Index (CPI).

Cost-plus contract A contract that fixes the amount to be paid to a contractor based on the cost of the material and labor plus an agreed percentage thereof as profit.

Costs A monetary allowance made to the successful party in litigation (and recoverable from the losing party) for the expenses incurred in bringing or defending the action (e.g., filing and service expenses). Attorney fees are usually not included. Costs are entirely separate from what is sought or won in the litigation itself.

Costume, *n.* See clothes, uniform (2), apparel.

Co-sureties, *n.* Two or more sureties to the same obligation. Joint sureties.

Cot, *n.* See bed (1).

Cotenancy, *n.* An interest in property whereby two or more persons have an undivided right to possession (e.g., tenancy in common, joint tenancy).

Coterie, *n.* An exclusive association of persons (corporate coterie). Clique, circle, club, clan, fraternity, sect, set, society, brotherhood, sisterhood, elite, aristocracy, group, faction, alliance, coalition, lodge.

Coterminous, *adj.* See conterminous, coextensive; immediate (2).

Cottage, *n.* See home (1).

Couch, *n.*, *v.* See bed (1); express (2), communicate.

Council, *n.* A group of people who convene to advise, assist, or legislate (city council). Assembly, board, advisors, cabinet, conference, convention, committee, panel, chamber, session, caucus, congress, synod.

Councilman, councilwoman, *n.* See legislator.

Counsel 1. *n.* An attorney (counsel of record). Lawyer, counselor, counselor at law, legal adviser, legal representative, member of the bar, advocate, barrister, solicitor, officer of the court. **2.** *n.* Advice and assistance given by one person to another (a lawyer's counsel). Consultation, guidance, opinion, recommendation, deliberation, instruction, warning, caution, teaching. See also advice, admonition, approbation. **3.** *v.* To provide advice (she counseled against suing at this time). Recommend, suggest, warn, caution, advocate, urge, dissuade, propose, consult, confer, admonish, instruct, advise, direct.

Counsel of record An attorney who has filed a notice of appearance for a party in court.

Counselor, *n.* See counsel (1).

Count 1. *n.* In pleading, a separate and independent claim or charge (Count I, Count II, etc.). Allegation, declaration, cause of action, averment, enumeration, listing, numbering. **2.** *v.* See calculate, measure (3), rate.

Countenance 1. *v.* To give approval or encouragement (the judge would not countenance such behavior). Condone, allow, endorse, recognize, go along with, license, further, sanction, back, promote, champion, abet, facilitate, assist, patronize, put up with, foster. **2.** *n.* Face, expression (a countenance of fear). Look, appearance, features, physiognomy, complexion, mien, visage, form, profile, aspect. *Ant.* Forbid; interior.

Counter, *v.* To oppose (he countered by offering $150). Offset, return, answer, contradict, retaliate, defy, countervail, repel, neutralize, check, contravene, thwart, match, confront, hit back, annul, deny, rebut, challenge, antagonize, fight, contend, resist, protest. *Ant.* Concede.

Counteract, *v.* To check or neutralize (she counteracted by suing). Negate, frustrate, annul, nullify, invalidate, equalize, go against, counterbalance, overpower, thwart, defeat, act against, traverse, countervail, resist, hinder, cross, clash, contend, defy, foil, squelch, rival, inhibit. *Ant.* Promote.

Counterbalance, *v.* See offset (2), compensate (2), balance (3).

Counterclaim, *n.* A cause of action or claim asserted by one or more defendants against one or more plaintiffs in the same action (a counterclaim for fraud). Assertion against the plaintiff, claim for relief by the defendant, countercharge.

Counterculture, *n.* See avant-garde; nonconformist.

Counterfeit 1. *v.* To copy without authority in order to deceive by passing off the copy as genuine (he counterfeited the note). Imitate, fabricate, forge, falsify, simulate, pass off, reproduce, plagiarize, feign, duplicate; profess, concoct, posture, dissemble, affect, practice chicanery, sham, claim. **2.** *adj.* Fake (counterfeit coin). Phony, spurious, false, fraudulent, sham, pseudo, imitation, not genuine, mock, synthetic, bogus, misleading, ersatz, simulated, affected, apocryphal, mock. *Ant.* Originate; genuine.

Countermand, *v.* To change or revoke instructions or authority previously issued (she countermanded the order). Cancel, annul, invalidate, counter, abolish, amend, ban, withdraw, repeal, reverse, nullify, recall, abrogate, set aside, disestablish, retract, overrule, vitiate, override, vacate, suppress. *Ant.* Reinstate.

Counteroffer, *n.* A statement by the offeree that has the legal effect of rejecting the offer and of proposing a new offer to the offeror (her new price proposal was a counteroffer). Counterproposal, different offer, counter terms.

Counterpart, *n.* In conveyancing, the corresponding part of an instrument; a duplicate or copy (the counterpart was mailed yesterday). Match, reproduction, parallel, double, twin, replica, likeness, facsimile; mate, fellow, complement, correlative, correlate. See also contrast.

Counterpoise, *n.* See offset (1), balance (4); compensate.

Counterproductive, *adj.* See harmful.

Countersign, *v.* **1.** To sign in addition to the signature of another in order to attest authenticity (the secretary countersigns all checks). **2.** To underwrite. See back (1), finance (1), vouch, promote.

Countervail, *v.* See counteract, offset (2), compensate (2); countervailing.

Countervailing, *adj.* Counterbalancing (countervailing equity). Balancing, contrary, opposed, compensating, substitute, acting against with equal force, weakening, countering, contradicting, negating, matching, thwarting, neutralizing, canceling. *Ant.* Supporting.

Countless, *adj.* See incalculable, many, big, great (1).

Country 1. *n.* The territory occupied by an independent nation or people (the country of Poland). State, commonwealth, realm, kingdom; people, citizens, inhabitants, public, citizenry, population, soil, fatherland, motherland, homeland. See also nation. **2.** *adj.* Pertaining to a rural or farm area (an accident on a country road). Secluded, wooded, remote, forest, provincial, rustic; countryside, farmland.

County, *n.* The largest territorial division of a local government in many states (the county board authorized new roads). District, parish, region, municipal corporation.

Coup, *n.* An achievement. Accomplishment, maneuver, feat, deed, victory, masterstroke. See exploit (2).

Coup de grâce, *n.* Mortal wound, knockout, decisive blow. See calamity, catastrophe; crisis.

Coup d'état, *n.* A political overthrow of the current government (a bloodless coup d'état). Revolution, uprising, mutiny, rebellion, revolt, insurgence, putsch.

Couple, *v., n.* See join, connect (1), consolidate (1), bind (2); two.

Coupled, *adj.* See conjoint.

Coupon, *n.* An interest or dividend certificate in detachable form (a matured coupon). Stub, voucher, ticket, token, credit, check.

Courage, *n.* See valor, resolution (4), spirit (2), self-confidence; courageous.

Courageous, *adj.* Fearless. Bold, daring, defiant, resolute, audacious, forward, strong, unafraid, lionhearted, stouthearted, dauntless, valiant, virile, gallant, staunch, heroic, intrepid, unflinching, game, unyielding, gutsy, chivalrous. See also adventurous, alive (2), ardent, ambitious; arrogant.

Courier, *n.* See messenger, emissary.

Course, *n.* **1.** The path or direction that something takes; the typical or normal manner of proceeding (in the course of business). Mode of action, customary passage, route, development, action, flow, procedure, progression, trail, program, method, activity, system, conduct, scheme, practice, endeavor, furtherance, channel, trend, itinerary, way, run, beat, round, orbit, tack, circuit, succession, arrangement, schedule, advance, track, order, line. **2.** In surveying, the direction of a line with reference to a meridian.

Course of dealing A sequence of previous acts and conduct between the parties to a particular transaction, which fairly establishes a common basis of understanding for interpreting their communications and other conduct.

Course of employment As a worker's compensation term: A worker is in the course of employment when, within the time covered by the employment, he or she is doing something at a proper place, which he or she might reasonably do while so employed. See scope of employment.

Court 1. *n.* A unit of the judicial branch of government that applies the law to disputes and administers justice (trial court). Court of law, court of justice, court of equity, judiciary, bench, judicial tribunal, forum, chamber, panel, bar. **2.** *v.* To attempt to gain (court disaster). Invite, seek, induce, provoke, solicit, attract, tempt, inspire, generate, elicit. **3.** *v.* See square (1). **4.** *v.* See flatter; suitor. *Ant.* Spurn (2).

Courteous, *adj.* See civil (3); courtesy (2).

Courtesan, *n.* See prostitute (1).

Courtesy, *n.* **1.** See curtesy. **2.** Polite behavior (the judge extended a courtesy to the lawyer). Consideration, respect, deference, indulgence, civility, amenity, hospitality, friendliness, thoughtfulness. See also favor (1). *Ant.* Rudeness (2).

Court-martial A military or naval court, operating under the Code of Military Justice, for trying and punishing offenses committed by members of the armed forces.

Court of Admiralty A court having jurisdiction of admiralty and maritime matters.

Court of Appeals for the Federal Circuit A federal court that reviews decisions of the United States Claims Court and the Court of International Trade.

Court of Chancery A court administering equity; a court that proceeds according to the forms and principles of equity; a court of equity as distinguished from a common-law court.

Court of Claims A court that hears designated claims of individuals against the government (e.g., breach-of-contract claims).

Court of Customs and Patent Appeals See Court of Appeals for the Federal Circuit.

Court of Equity See Court of Chancery.

Court of Error A court of last resort with the power to review the decisions of lower courts.

Court of first instance A court of original or primary jurisdiction (e.g., a trial court).

Court of General Sessions The name given in some states to a court of general original jurisdiction in criminal cases.

Court of Military Appeals An appellate tribunal that reviews court-martial convictions in the armed services.

Court of Nisi Prius A trial court with a jury and one presiding judge; any court of general, original jurisdiction in civil cases.

Court of Orphans A probate or surrogates court with general jurisdiction over matters of probate, estate administration, orphans, wards, and guardians.

Court of record A court that is required to keep a record of its proceedings and that may fine or imprison.

Court packing An attempt to restructure a court so that people who agree with the appointing chief executive's views are chosen.

Court reporter 1. A person who transcribes testimony by shorthand (or who takes it down stenographically) during court proceedings or during trial-related proceedings such as depositions. 2. The person responsible for the publication of the opinions of the court; the Reporter of Decisions.

Court rules Regulations with the force of law, governing practice and procedure in various courts (e.g., the Federal Rules of Civil Procedure).

Courtyard, *n.* See square (1).

Cousin, *n.* The male or female child of the brother or sister of one's father or mother; kindred in the fourth degree.

Cove, *n.* See harbor; sea (1); cave; alcove.

Covenant, *n.* An agreement, convention, or promise of two or more parties, by deed in writing, signed and delivered, by which one of the parties (a) pledges to the other that something is done, shall be done, or shall not be done, or (b) stipulates the truth of certain facts (a covenant to build an adjoining wall). Contract, vow, bond, treaty, oath, compact, obligation, arrangement, deal, understanding, warranty, commitment. See also agreement.

Covenant against incumbrances A covenant that there are no incumbrances on the land conveyed.

Covenantee, *n.* The party to whom a covenant is made.

Covenant for quiet enjoyment An assurance against the consequence of a defective title and of any disturbances by hostile claimants.

Covenantor, *n.* The party who makes a covenant.

Covenant running with the land A covenant that goes with the land and cannot be separated from it. The land cannot be transferred without the covenant. Hence, future buyers of the land are bound by it.

Cover 1. *v.* To protect by means of insurance (he is not covered for water damage). Insure, compensate, guard against, safeguard, provide for, replace, pay. 2. *v.* To conceal (he tried to cover up his involvement). Shroud, veil, obscure, mask, camouflage, screen, fog, darken, bury, secrete. See also disguise, hide, conceal, cloak. 3. *v.* To include (the opinion did not cover taxes). Embrace, take in, encompass, deal with, comprehend, involve, consider, report, incorporate, examine. 4. *n.* The right of a buyer, after breach by a seller, to purchase goods in substitution for those due from the seller if such purchase is made in good faith and without unreasonable delay (the costs of cover are included in the damages). Replacement, exchange, alternate. 5. *n.* See ceiling (2). 6. *n.* See convoy. 7. *n.* See package, wrapper, vessel (2), bandage; rug; awning. 8. *v.* See pave; submerge. *Ant.* Neglect (1); reveal (2); exclude (3).

Coverage, *n.* The amount and extent of risk covered by an insurer (immediate coverage). Undertaking, indemnity, reimbursement, assurance, protection, warranty, guarantee, surety.

Covering, *n.* See protection; wrapper, package, vessel (2); cover.

Covert, *adj.* Concealed (covert transaction). Covered, sheltered, protected, clandestine, insidious, surreptitious, clouded, disguised, furtive, veiled, hidden, unknown, secret, camouflaged, masked, stealthy, underhanded, sub rosa, screened, cryptic, latent, unsuspected, mysterious. *Ant.* Overt.

Coverture, *n.* The condition or state of a married woman (property acquired during coverture). Marriage, married state, matrimony, nuptial bond.

Cover up, *v.,* **coverup,** *n.* See conceal, cover (2); pretext, deception.

Covet, *v.* See desire (1).

Covetous, *adj.* See avaricious.

Cow, *n.* See animal (1); intimidate.

Coward, *n.* One who runs from pain or danger. Recreant, sissy, milquetoast, quitter, dastard, caitiff, milksop, craven. See also yellow (1).

Cowardice, *n.* Timidity. Weak knees, poltroonery, baseness, faint-heartedness. See also yellow (1).

Cower, *v.* See grovel, cringe.

Co-worker, *n.* See associate (2), fellow, colleague, partner.

Coy, *adj.* Sheepish, coquettish, playful. See bashful.

Cozen, *v.* See deceive.

Cozy, *adj.* See comfortable (1), safe.

Crab, *n.* See grouch.

Crabby, *adj.* Irritable. Grouchy, cross, testy, moody. See also contentious (1), litigious, rude, inflexible, particular (2), difficult (3).

Crack, *v., n.* See break (2, 3), cut (1), separation (2); defect.

Crackdown, *n.,* **Crack down,** *v.* See correction, discipline.

Crackpot, *n.* See ass, boor, idiot; insanity, lunatic.

Crackup, *n.* See collision (1); insanity; shock.

Cradle, *n.* See commencement; bed; nurture.

Craft, *n.* **1.** A trade or occupation requiring skill and training, particularly manual skill, combined with a knowledge of the principles of the art (the craft of welding). Business, vocation, calling, pursuit, job, employment, handicraft, profession, métier. **2.** Deception (she obtained the land by craft). Cunning, guile, ruse, intrigue, trickery, artifice, contrivance, duplicity, chicanery. *Ant.* Candor (2).

Craftsman, craftswoman, *n.* See artisan.

Crafty, *adj.* See deceitful; expert (2), prudent.

Cram, *v.* See pack, force (4).

Cramp, *n., v.* Spasm, contraction, pang, charley horse. See seizure (2); restrain.

Crank, *n.* See grouch.

Cranky, *adj.* See crabby, contentious (1), rude, inflexible, difficult (3).

Craps, *n.* A game using dice. See gambling.

Crash, *v., n.* See collide (1); collision (1), accident.

Crashworthy, *adj.* See safe (2).

Crass, *adj.* See rude, vulgar.

Crate, *n., v.* See vessel (2); convey (3), carry (1).

Crater, *n.* See mine, cave, cell.

Crave, *v.* See desire (1), petition (2), apply (1).

Craven, *adj.* See base (2), yellow (1); coward.

Craving, *adj.* See desire (4).

Crawl, *v.* See limp, walk, grovel, cringe.

Craze, *v., n.* See distract (2); caprice, style (3).

Crazed, *adj.* See violent, insane.

Crazy, *adj.* See distracted, demented, deranged, insane (2), lunatic; irrational, odd (1), anomalous, dumb, absurd, wild, extraordinary.

Cream, *adj., n.* See primary, main; food.

Crease, *n.* See wrinkle (1), trench.

Create, *v.* To bring into being (they created the crisis). Cause to exist, generate, originate, found, produce, initiate, inaugurate, shape, fashion, compose, beget, spawn, formulate, pattern, make, conceive, improvise, procreate, devise, install, launch, engineer. See also invent, coin (3). *Ant.* Demolish.

Creation, *n.* See birth (2); invention.

Creative, *adj.* See original (3), brilliant, able, competent, apt (2, 3), fertile.

Creator, *n.* See author (2); God.

Creature, *n.* See person, animal, character (4), object (3), entity.

Credence, *n.* Belief (he placed little credence in the evidence). Trust, faith, assurance, credit, credibility, trustworthiness, confidence, dependence, reliance. *Ant.* Disbelief.

Credentials, *n.* Documentary evidence of a person's authority or capacity (the credentials of the witness). Authorization, vouchers, recommendations, endorsements, certificates, degrees, diplomas, qualifications, references, accreditation, certification, testimonials.

Credibility, *n.* Worthiness of belief (the credibility of the witness). Reliability, believability, veracity, plausibility, integrity, trustworthiness, reasonableness. *Ant.* Implausibility.

Credible, *adj.* Worthy of belief (credible testimony). Believable, acceptable, trustworthy, reliable, persuasive, tenable, well-founded, well-grounded, inspiring confidence, worthy of belief, incorruptible, conceivable, sound, valid, not improbable, feasible, reputable, dependable, likely. *Ant.* Dubious.

Credit, *n.* **1.** The right to delay payment; the ability of a business or person to borrow money or to obtain goods on time, as a result of the favorable opinion that the lender has of the borrower's solvency and reliability (purchased on credit). Installment buying, time payments, loan, deferred payment plan. **2.** That which is due a person (he was given a credit on the account). **3.** Recognition (she was given credit for the brief). Acknowledgment, merit, commendation, standing, esteem, regard, praise, honor, acclaim, approval, notoriety. *Ant.* Cash; debit; dishonor.

Creditable, *adj.* See meritorious (2), good.

Credit bureau Establishments that make a business of collecting information relating to the credit, character, and reputation of businesses and individuals in order to furnish the information as credit reports to subscribers, e.g., merchants, banks.

Creditor, *n.* A person to whom a debt is owed by another; one who has the right to require the fulfillment of an obligation or contract (demand for payment by the creditor). See lender. *Ant.* Debtor.

Credit rating The evaluation of a person's or a business's ability and past performance in paying debts.

Credit union A cooperative association that uses money deposited by a defined group of persons (e.g., fellow employees) and lends it out again to persons within this group at favorable interest rates.

Creditworthy, *adj.* See solvent; safe.

Credo, *n.* See creed.

Credulity, *n.* Gullibility. Blind faith, naiveté. See also innocence (2).

Credulous, *adj.* Gullible. Overtrusting, unsuspicious, naive, believing, unwary, green. See also innocent.

Creed, *n.* One's formal beliefs, often religious beliefs (persecution for one's creed). Dogma, doctrine, principles, tenets, faith, canons, convictions, persuasion, credo, ethical beliefs.

Creek, *n.* See river, watercourse.

Cremate, *v.* See burn.

Crest, *n.* See apex, culmination.

Crestfallen, *adj.* See depressed, despondent.

Crevice, *n.* A narrow opening. Fissure, crack, split, hole, breach, gap, cleft, rupture, groove, scission. See also cave, cell, abyss.

Crew, *n.* See group (1), company (2); sailor.

Crib, *n.*, *v.* See bed; cheat (1).

Crick, *n.* See cramp.

Crier, *n.* An officer of the court who makes proclamations, e.g., announces the opening of the court, calls the names of jurors, witnesses, and parties.

Crime, *n.* A positive or negative act that violates the penal law of the state or federal government; any act done in violation of those duties which an individual owes to the community and for the breach of which the law has decided that the offender shall make satisfaction to the public (the crime of murder). Public wrong, misdemeanor, felony, offense, criminal act, misconduct, malefaction, transgression, unlawful act, violation of the law, infraction, wrong, wrongdoing, evil deed, vice, dereliction, delinquency, corruption, misfeasance, malfeasance, nonfeasance.

Crimen *Lat.* Crime (crimen furti—crime of theft).

Criminal 1. *n.* One who has been convicted of a crime (habitual criminal). Felon, malefactor, wrongdoer, culprit, fugitive, racketeer, bandit, swindler, habitual offender, underworld figure, hardened criminal, evildoer, violator, offender, transgressor, convict, prisoner, recreant, inmate, outlaw, recidivist, gangster, delinquent. **2.** *adj.* Pertaining to that which is connected with the law of crimes; pertaining to that which has the character of a crime (criminal justice; criminal intent). Unlawful, lawless, law-breaking, felonious, illegal, illicit, wrong, nefarious, iniquitous, guilty, culpable, blameworthy. *Ant.* Innocent person; legal.

Criminal contempt A crime involving the obstruction of judicial duty; conduct directed against the dignity and authority of the court, often in the presence of a judge. See contempt.

Criminal Conversation (Crim. Con.) A tort against the marriage bed: The defendant has sexual relations with the plaintiff's spouse. See adultery; coitus.

Criminal negligence The failure to use the degree of care required to avoid criminal consequences. Negligence for which the law imposes a criminal penalty. See neglect (2).

Criminal nonsupport The willful and unreasonable failure to support those whom one is legally obligated to support. See nonsupport.

Criminal syndicalism Any doctrine or precept advocating, teaching, or aiding the commission of the crime of sabotage or unlawful acts of violence or terrorism as a means of achieving industrial or political change. See racket, racketeer.

Criminal trespass An offense that is committed when one, without license or privilege, enters or surreptitiously remains in a building or on the property of another. The person does so knowingly, intentionally, or recklessly when he or she has notice that this conduct is not allowed.

Criminate, *v.* To charge one with a crime (the question tends to criminate him). Implicate, expose. See accuse, incriminate.

Criminology, *n.* The science that studies the causes, prevention, and punishment of crimes.

Cringe, *v.* To flinch. Recoil, shrink, draw back, shy, kneel, cower, start, crouch, dodge, quail, bend, bow; grovel, bootlick.

Cripple, *v.* See maim, impair, disable.

Crisis, *n.* A critical point or situation in the course of things (a crisis of confidence). Turning point, climax, tense moment, crucial time, exigency, predicament, quandary, emergency, critical stage, critical juncture, decisive turn of events, crossroad, pinch, zero hour.

Crisp, *adj.* See active (3), brilliant; breakable.

Criterion, *n.* The standard by which to judge something (biased criterion). Benchmark, norm, rule, guiding principle, yardstick, gauge, measure, guidepost, guide, model, example, barometer, paradigm, formula, archetype, test, parameter.

Critic, *n.* See judge (1), expert (1), authority (4), arbiter.

Critical, *adj.* **1.** Involving a crisis or crucial point (a critical stage in the proceeding when rights may be lost). Serious, urgent, perilous, sensitive, pivotal, overshadowing, decisive, telling, important, pressing, imperative, exigent, climactic, vital, determining, material, momentous, conclusive, weighty, precarious, dangerous, risky, hazardous; turning point. **2.** Disapproving (the report was critical of the jury system). Faultfinding, disapproving, abusive, denouncing, indicting, disparaging, carping, belittling, condemning, uncomplimentary, reproachful, censorious, accusing, scathing, chiding, rebuking, nagging, scolding, quibbling. *Ant.* Run-of-the-mill; laudatory.

Criticism, *n.* **1.** Finding fault. See censure, objection; critical (2). **2.** A critique or serious review (valuable criticism of the memo). Commentary, scrutiny, analysis, evaluation, assessment, reflection, appraisal, editorial, study, appreciation, notice. **3.** Objection. See exception (1).

Criticize, *v.* See assess (1); censure (2), defame.

Critique, *n.* See criticism (2), assessment.

Crony, *n.* See ally, intimate (5), associate (2), partner, fellow; gang.

Cronyism, *n.* See nepotism.

Crook, *n.* A person engaged in crooked or fraudulent practices (the crook was arrested). Swindler, sharper, thief, forger, professional rogue, bandit, thug, embezzler, felon, criminal, cheat, deceiver, miscreant, imp, scoundrel, villain, blackguard, charlatan, quack, fraud, knave. See also wrongdoer.

Crooked, *adj.* **1.** See dishonest. **2.** Bent. Wavy, zigzag, winding, twisted, curved, angular. See also tortuous (1).

Crop, *n., v.* See yield (2); cut.

Cross, *v., n., adj.* See travel, pass (4), sail, walk; burden (2), misfortune, onus; contradict; hybrid; delete; angry; intersection.

Cross-action, *n.* An independent suit brought by a defendant against a plaintiff or a co-defendant.

Cross appeal, *n.* An appeal by the appellee.

Crosscheck, *v.* See check (2), verify.

Cross-claim, *n.* A related claim by one party against a co-party.

Cross-complaint, *n.* A pleading filed by the defendant, stating any related cause of action the defendant has against a party who filed the complaint against the defendant, or against a person alleged to be liable thereon whether or not this person is currently a party.

Cross-demand, *n.* When a person against whom a demand is made by another in turn makes a demand against that other, these mutual demands are called cross-demands (e.g., a set-off).

Cross-examination, *n.* The examination of a witness (at a trial, hearing, or deposition) by the other side after the direct examination of the witness by the side that initially called the witness (the cross-examination was within the scope of the direct examination). Interrogation, probe, inquiry, challenge, grilling, inspection, investigation, inquest, questioning.

Cross-examine, *v.* To question. Scrutinize, grill, quiz, interrogate, inspect, probe. See also cross-examination; ask (1), investigate; question.

Crossing, *n.* See intersection.

Cross-remainder, *n.* Property that is given to several persons as a group. As each person dies, the others share that person's interest.

Crossroad, *n.* See intersection; crisis.

Cross section, *n.* A representative sample (a cross section of opinion within the bar). Typical of the whole, fair sample, profile, exemplification, average, norm, embodiment. *Ant.* Unique sample.

Crouch, *v.* See cringe, grovel.

Crowd, *n.*, *v.* See company (2), mob, congregation, assembly, coterie; push, congregate, collect (1), accumulate.

Crown, *n.* The sovereign power and position of a monarch.

Crucial, *adj.* Very important (a crucial decision of the court). Decisive, critical, far-reaching, determining, profound, conclusive, significant, momentous, pressing, urgent, vital, sensitive, pivotal, eventful, climactic, compelling, grave, serious, consequential, influential. *Ant.* Insignificant.

Crucible, *n.* See ordeal; vessel.

Crucify, *v.* To torment. Torture, persecute, rack, distress, trouble, harass, brutalize, mistreat. See also abuse (1).

Crude, *adj.* See backward (1), base (1, 2), rude, gross (1), common (3), inferior, awkward, gaudy, imperfect.

Cruel, *adj.* Causing suffering intentionally or recklessly; being indifferent to suffering (cruel treatment by a spouse). Inhuman, inhumane, heartless, severe, harsh, barbarous, vicious, satanic, brutal, merciless, unfeeling, stinging, hardhearted, sanguinary, heinous, savage, sadistic, mischievous, perverse, bloodthirsty, dangerous, fiendish, perverted, ferocious, villainous, venomous, horrid, evil, treacherous, malign, unprincipled, malignant, wicked, disgraceful, torturous, harrowing, tormenting, racking, relentless, outrageous, monstrous, pitiless, mean, implacable, hard, inexorable, diabolical, ill-natured, malicious. *Ant.* Compassionate.

Cruel and unusual punishment Such punishment that would amount to torture or barbarity; any degrading punishment not known to the common law; punishment that is so disproportionate to the offense as to shock the moral sense of the community; uncivilized and inhumane punishment.

Cruelty, *n.* The intentional and malicious infliction of physical or mental suffering on living creatures (the cruelty of allowing the dogfight to continue). Inhumanity, barbarity, viciousness, sadism, masochism, tyranny, atrocity, savagery, meanness, harshness, ruthlessness, cold-bloodedness, heartlessness, maliciousness, torture, violence. *Ant.* Sympathy.

Cruise, *v.*, *n.* See sail, wander; solicit (2); voyage, junket.

Cruiser, *n.* See vessel.

Crumble, *v.* See collapse (1).

Crusade, *n.*, *v.* See campaign.

Crush, *v.* See squeeze, stamp (2), defeat (1), crucify, push, break (2).

Crust, *n.* See surface, exterior.

Crutch, *n.* A support or aid. Brace, staff, arm.

Crux, *n.* See essence (1), gist.

Cry, *v.* 1. To weep. Lament, grieve, moan, groan, whine, sob, blubber, whimper. 2. See proclaim, utter, pronounce.

Crying, *adj.* See critical (1), crucial; cry (1); crabby, contentious, litigious.

Crypt, *n.* See grave (1).

Cryptic, *adj.* See ambiguous.

Crystallize, *v.* See consolidate (2), form (4).

Cubicle, *n.* See closet, alcove, chamber.

Cuckold, *n.* A man whose wife is unfaithful (John made a cuckold of Mr. Smith by seducing Mrs. Smith).

Cuddle, *v.* See caress, handle (2), touch.

Cudgel, *v.*, *n.* See beat (1); weapon.

Cue, *n.* See suggestion, manifestation.

Cul-de-sac, *n.* A blind alley; a street open at one end only; an impasse.

Cull, *v.* See select (1), glean.

Culminate, *v.* To reach the most important point (the long dispute culminated in litigation). Climax, result, terminate, ripen, cap, wind up, complete, consummate, accomplish, attain the zenith, execute, crown. *Ant.* Begin.

Culmination, *n.* The highest point (the victory was the culmination of her career). Zenith, apex, consummation, climax, summit, pinnacle, limit, cap, crest, maximum, extremity, apogee, top. See also conclusion, expiration, cessation, rescission. *Ant.* Bottom.

Culpability, *n.* Blameworthiness (criminal culpability). Guilt, blame, criminality, wrongdoing, misconduct, delinquency, fault, transgression, dereliction, responsibility, censurability. *Ant.* Innocence.

Culpable, *adj.* Pertaining to that which is deserving of moral blame (all of the defendants are culpable). Blamable, blameworthy, censurable, involving a breach of duty, criminal, at fault, peccable, chargeable, delinquent, impeachable, discreditable, lawless, improper, responsible, liable, indictable, punishable, dissolute, sinful, reprovable. *Ant.* Innocent.

Cult, *n.* See school (2), religion, group (1), denomination (2).

Cultivate, *v.* See nurture, foster, instruct (1); farm (2).

Cultivation, *n.* See growth.

Cultivated, *adj.* Refined. Educated, polished, cultured, advanced, civilized. See also civil (3), learned, literary (2).

Culture, *n.* See civilization; honor (3), character (1), worth (1), merit (1), dignity.

Cultured, *adj.* See cultivated, learned, civil (3).

Cum (*Lat.*) With (cum testamento annexo—with the will annexed).

Cumbersome, *adj.* See awkward, difficult (2).

Cumulate, *v.* See accumulate.

Cumulative, *adj.* Involving the addition of things together (the cumulative effect of the evidence was devastating). Increasing, heaping up, aggregate, amassed, additive, multiplying, snowballing, swelling, totaling, continually increasing, incremental, strengthening, widening, growing, advancing, conglomerate, chain. *Ant.* Individual.

Cumulative evidence Additional or corroborative evidence to the same point.

Cumulative legacies Legacies given in addition to a prior legacy.

Cumulative preferred dividend A dividend on preferred stock which, if declared at the end of a particular year, must be paid before any common stock dividend is paid.

Cumulative sentence A sentence that is to take effect after the expiration of a prior sentence. *Ant.* Concurrent sentence.

Cumulative voting A type of voting in which the number of members of the board of directors to be elected is multiplied by the total number of voting shares a shareholder has. The result equals the number of votes a shareholder has. This total can be cast for one or more nominees for director.

Cunnilingus, *n.* A sexual act in which the mouth or lips come into contact with the female sexual organs. See deviation; coitus.

Cunning, *adj.* See deceptive, deceitful; able, apt (3); artifice, ability (2).

Cupidity, *n.* See avarice.

Curable, *adj.* See salvageable, amenable, malleable.

Curate, *n.* See minister (1), assistant; clergy.

Curative, *adj.* Tending to cure; avoiding the ordinary legal consequences of defects or errors (a curative measure). Remedial, restorative, restoring, mending, corrective, healing, therapeutic.

Curator, *n.* **1.** A temporary guardian or conservator appointed by the court to care for the property or person of an incompetent, a spendthrift, or a minor. **See** guardian. **2.** The manager of a museum or collection. **See** manager.

Curb, *v., n.* See restrain; border (1).

Cure 1. *n.* Something that heals or restores to soundness after an injury (the cure for the disease). Remedy, curative, antidote, medicine, medication, tonic, prescription, drug, help, treatment, panacea, redress, balm, restorative. **2.** *v.* To correct or heal (the motion cured the defect). Restore, improve, doctor, fix, mend, repair, ameliorate, rehabilitate, revive, regenerate, relieve, rectify, make whole.

Curfew, *n.* A rule on when individuals must be off the streets. See prohibition (1), limitation (1).

Curia, *n.* A court of justice.

Curing title Removing those defects from the title to land which make it unmarketable; removing any clouds on the title.

Curiosity, *n.* See interest (3); curious.

Curious, *adj.* **1.** Inquisitive. Prying, nosy, questioning, searching, meddlesome, meddling, interested, scrutinizing, eavesdropping. **2.** See odd (1).

Curmudgeon, *n.* See grouch (1).

Currency, *n.* Authorized money (i.e., coin and paper money) that circulates from hand to hand as the medium of exchange (the currency of Italy). Legal tender, cash, bills, specie, notes; funds, capital.

Current 1. *adj.* Present existence (current assets). Running, now in transit, now in progress, now passing, immediate, going on, actual, contemporary, contemporaneous, existent, belonging to the present time. **2.** *adj.* Generally accepted (current practice). Prevalent, prevailing, general, widespread, orthodox, common, habitual, regular, predominant, customary, standard, average. **3.** *adj.* Fashionable (current style). Up-to-date, stylish, popular, in vogue, au courant, conversant, "hip," up-to-the-minute, topical. **4.** *n.* See flood, stream (2). *Ant.* Past; uncommon; out-of-date.

Current market value The present value of an asset that may be realized in an arm's length transaction between a willing buyer and a willing seller.

Curriculum, *n.* Courses offered for study at a school. See calendar (3), list.

Curriculum vitae, *n.* A résumé.

Curse, *n., v.* See censure (2), anathema, condemn.

Cursory, *adj.* Superficial (cursory examination). Hasty, not thorough, brief, surface, offhand, summary, loose, quick, casual, perfunctory, careless, hurried, haphazard, slight, passing, desultory, shallow. *Ant.* Meticulous.

Curt, *adj.* See rude; concise.

Curtail, *v.* To cut off or shorten (the illness of the witness forced us to curtail the questioning). Terminate, abbreviate, trim, diminish, halt, abridge, truncate, decrease, reduce, contract, constrict, pare down, clip. *Ant.* Expand.

Curtain, *n.* Drape, drapery. Covering, shade, screen, tapestry, cloak.

Curtesy, *n.* A husband's right to a life estate in the property left by his deceased wife.

Curtesy consummate The husband's curtesy interest in the estate of his wife after she dies if children were born of the marriage capable of inheriting.

Curtesy initiate The husband's curtesy interest in his wife's estate before she dies and after the birth of children capable of inheriting. An interest in expectancy.

Curtilage, *n.* The enclosed space of ground and buildings immediately surrounding a dwelling-house. See close (3).

Curve, *v.* See meander.

Cushion, 1. *n.* Pillow. Pad, padding, mat, buffer, shock absorber, bolster. **2.** *v.* To soften. Buttress, lessen. See also offset (2), mitigate.

Cuss, *v.* See censure (2).

Custodial interrogation Questioning initiated by law enforcement officers after a person has been taken into custody or otherwise deprived of his or her freedom in any significant way.

Custodian, *n.* Someone who has charge or custody of property, papers, etc. (custodian of the account). Caretaker, keeper, guard, steward, guardian, conservator, watchman, superintendent, warden, curator, watchdog, supervisor, protector, monitor; janitor. See also fiduciary (1).

Custody, *n.* **1.** The care and control of a thing or person (joint custody of a child). Protection, guardianship, care, safekeeping, direction, trusteeship, wardship, possession, keeping, custodianship, preservation, management, superintendence, administration, safety, jurisdiction. **2.** Physical confinement. See detention.

Custom, customs, *n.* **1.** An established practice or habit (local custom). Tradition, procedure, convention, fashion, usage, precedent, routine, wont, institution, manner, established way, ritual, form. See also practice (1), formality (1). **2.** A tax on the importation and exportation of commodities (collection of customs). Duty, levy, tariff, exaction, impost, toll, assessment.

Custom and usage A habitual or customary practice, more or less widespread, which prevails within a geographical or sociological area. By repetition and uninterrupted acquiescence, the practice acquires the force of a tacit and common consent.

Customary, *adj.* Founded on, growing out of, or dependent on a custom (the court clerk's customary procedure). Regular, normal, common, usual, typical, traditional, conventional, ordinary, well-known, accustomed, routine, general, characteristic, accepted, everyday, commonplace, uniform, standard, orthodox, established. *Ant.* Irregular.

Customer, *n.* One who makes purchases from or has other commercial dealings with a business (a cash customer). Shopper, consumer, purchaser, buyer, vendee, lessee, prospect. See also client (2), patron (1). *Ant.* Seller.

Customize, *v.* To adjust to the tastes of the customer. See adapt.

Cut 1. *v.* To penetrate, separate, or lacerate as with a sharp object (cut the victim). Gash, chop, dismember, divide, wound, injure, cleave, pierce, lance, slice, nick, ax, split, slash, lacerate. **2.** *v.* To shorten or reduce in content, time, or amount (cut the memo). Abbreviate, abridge, curtail, edit, delete, trim, pare, diminish, retrench. **3.** *n.* See earnings. **4.** *n.* See division (1), break (3), crevice. *Ant.* Make whole; enlarge; losses.

Cutback, *n.* See reduction; diminish.

Cute, *adj.* See attractive, beautiful; artificial.

Cutoff, *n.* See conclusion (1), cessation, cloture.

Cutthroat, *n., adj.* See wrongdoer; cruel.

Cutting, *adj.* Stinging. Harsh, sarcastic, pointed, mean, bitter, chilling, penetrating, raw, insulting. See also offensive, caustic, biting.

Cyanide, *n.* See poison.

Cycle, *n.* A period of time when something happens regularly (cycle of events). Progression, series, sequence, chain, course, succession, flow, rotation, run, recurrence, circuit, revolution. See also life (2).

Cyclic, *adj.* See periodic, intermittent.

Cyclone, *n.* See storm.

Cylinder, *n.* See vessel (2).

Cynic, *n.* Pessimist. Skeptic, defeatist, misanthrope, naysayer, detractor, critic, carper, faultfinder. See also cynical.

Cynical, *adj.* Skeptical, scornful (cynical disposition). Distrustful, disbelieving, pessimistic, sarcastic, arrogant, mocking, disdainful, suspicious, doubting, sardonic, sneering, scoffing, derisive, censorious, carping. See also contemptuous. *Ant.* Optimistic.

Cy-pres As near as possible. The intention of the author of an instrument (e.g., will, trust) will be carried out as near as can be, when giving the instrument its literal effect is impossible.

Czar, *n.* See tyrant, king.

D

ABC**D**EFGHIJKLMNOPQRSTUVWXYZ

Dad, *n.* See father, parent.
Daffy, daft, *adj.* See distracted, deranged, insane, demented, lunatic.
Dagger, *n.* See weapon.
Daily, *adj.* **1.** Every day in the week (daily publication). Everyday, per diem, day-to-day, diurnal, quotidian. **2.** Commonplace (a daily occurrence). Regular, established, customary, usual, ordinary, recurring, periodic, routine. See also habitual.
Dainty, *adj.* Delicate. Refined, petite, exquisite, graceful, precious, elegant, fastidious, fussy. See also squeamish, beautiful, attractive.
Dally, *v.* See loiter, loaf; flirt.
Dam, *n.* See blockade, obstruction, wall (1); bank (4).
Damage 1. *n.* An injury or loss to person, property, or rights (causing damage to the engine). Impairment, harm, destruction, ruin, misfortune, disaster, deterioration, erosion, defacement, marring, mischief, toll, detriment. **2.** *v.* To cause an injury or loss to person, property, or rights (she damaged her reputation). Harm, destroy, impair, mar, defile, cripple, ravage, abuse, wrong, lacerate, blemish, violate, deform, diminish, contaminate, pollute, cheapen, undermine, incapacitate, disparage, spot, defame. *Ant.* Benefit; improve.
Damages, *n.* Monetary compensation that may be recovered in court by someone who has suffered injury or loss to person, to property, or to rights through an unlawful act or omission of another ($10,000 in damages for slander). Restoration, restitution, fine, satisfaction, indemnity, indemnification, pecuniary compensation, reparation, repayment, expenses, recovery.
Dame, *n.* See woman.
Damn, *v.* See censure.
Damnable, *adj.* See offensive.
Damnation, *n.* See anathema, censure.
Damnum absque injuria A loss that does not give rise to an action for damages against the person causing it.
Damp, *adj.* See muggy.
Dampen, *v.* See water (2), inundate; mitigate; diminish.
Danger, *n.* Exposure to loss or injury (a danger to pedestrians). Jeopardy, peril, hazard, risk, menace, threat, insecurity, liability, exposure, uncertainty, vulnerability, crisis, precariousness; cloud, sword of Damocles, portent, omen, Cassandra. *Ant.* Safety.
Dangerous, *adj.* Hazardous (a dangerous structure). Attended with risk, perilous, risky, threatening, unsafe, precarious, shaky, vulnerable, harmful, untrustworthy, uncertain, chancy, unhealthy, serious, hit-or-miss, menacing, scary, crippling, incapacitating, dire, mortal, fearful, exposed, assailable, unsteady, alarming, unreliable, ominous, destructive, injurious, vicious, treacherous. *Ant.* Secure.
Dangerous instrumentality Anything that has the inherent capacity (by itself or through careless use) to place people in peril.
Dangle, *v.* To hang. Sway, wave, drop, oscillate. See also suspend; entice.

Dare, *n.* See challenge, venture (2).

Daredevil, *n.* Adventurer. Madcap, showoff, lunatic, fool.

Daring, *adj.* See valor; courageous; reckless; enterprise (2).

Dark, *adj.* Somber; lightless. Black, unlit, opaque, murky, shadowy, dingy, overcast. See also grave (3); mysterious.

Darken, *v.* See obscure (3).

Darling, *n., adj.* Beloved, pet. Dear, adorable, precious, favorite, honey, cherished. See also suitor (2).

Dart, *v.* See run (2).

Dash, *v.* See run (2); pound (1); frustrate.

Dastard, *n.* See coward; wrongdoer.

Data, *n.* Organized information often collected for a specific purpose, e.g., to make a decision (insufficient data). Facts, evidence, materials, conditions, statistics. See also documentation.

Date 1. *n.* A specific point in time—day, month, year (date of acceptance). Period, point of time, moment. **2.** *v.* To determine the time of something (date all memos). Fix the time of, assign a date to, time, calendar, affix the date. **3.** *n.* See meeting, appointment.

Dated, *adj.* See obsolete, old, ancient.

Date of issue An arbitrary date fixed or agreed upon as the beginning or effective date of a document, which may be later than the date the parties prepared the document.

Datum, *n.* See fact, data.

Daughter, *n.* See descendant, child.

Daunt, *v.* See intimidate.

Dauntless, *adj.* See courageous.

Dawdle, *v.* See loiter, loaf, trail (3).

Dawn, *n.* See birth (2), morning.

Day, *n.* See date; age (1); daily.

Daybreak, *n.* See morning.

Daydream, *n.* See hallucination, dream; preoccupied.

Day-to-day, *adj.* See customary, habitual, daily.

Daze, *v., n.* See amaze, animate, surprise (1), confuse; incite; agape; stupor, trance.

Dazzle, *v.* See amaze, animate, surprise (1), blind (3), incite, confuse; agape.

Dazzling, *adj.* See awesome, flamboyant.

Deacon, *n.* See minister (1), assistant; clergy.

Deactivate, *v.* See incapacitate, withdraw (1); rescind; death (2).

Dead 1. *adj.* Without life. See death. (He was pronounced dead.) Lifeless, expired, deceased, inanimate, defunct, passed away, departed, extinguished, breathless. **2.** *n.* See corpse. **3.** *Adj.* Useless (a dead issue). Insignificant, inoperative, stagnant, barren, squelched, obsolete, lapsed, fruitless, unfruitful, stale, infertile, worn out, inactive, paralyzed, sterile, unproductive, unprofitable, *Ant.* Alive; living; vital.

Deadbeat, *n.* See parasite.

Deadbolt, *n.* See lock (3).

Deaden, *v.* See mitigate; incapacitate.

Dead end, *n.* See deadlock.

Dead freight When a vessel is chartered, dead freight is the amount paid for the portion of the vessel that is contracted for but not used.

Dead heat, *n.* See tie (4).

Deadline, *n.* See limitation.

Deadlock, *n.* A standstill (a deadlock in the negotiations). Impasse, stand-off, stalemate, draw, paralysis, block, quandary, stoppage, checkmate, predicament, dilemma. *Ant.* Settlement.

Deadly, *adj.* Likely to cause or intended to cause death or serious bodily harm (deadly force). Lethal, mortal, savage, ferocious, destructive, murderous, poisonous, violent, barbarous, brutal, venomous, pernicious, grave, cataclysmic, unsafe, bloodthirsty, implacable, noxious, malignant, injurious, hazardous, dangerous, heartless, cold-blooded, unrelenting, toxic, virulent, vicious, inhuman, internecine, homicidal, perfidious. *Ant.* Innocuous.

Deadly force Force, whether reasonable or unreasonable, that is likely or intended to cause death or great bodily harm.

Dead man's statute An evidential disqualification that renders inadmissible oral promises or declarations of a dead person when offered in support of claims against the estate of the dead person.

Deaf, *adj.* Hard of hearing; insensitive. See indifferent, callous, narrow (2).

Deafen, *v.* To muffle. Drown out, stifle. See also quiet (2), mitigate.

Deafening, *adj.* See noisy, wild, blatant.

Deal 1. *n.* An arrangement to obtain a desired result by a combination of interested parties (grain deal with the Soviets). Bargain, contract, trade, dealings, pact, negotiation, agreement, transaction, compact, sale, purchase, scheme, understanding, "shake," compromise, settlement, pledge. **2.** *v.* To transact business (he dealt in futures). Traffic, exchange, market, export, merchandise, import, bargain, negotiate, haggle, barter, do business, buy and sell. **3.** *v.* To be concerned with (she dealt with the matter effectively). Conduct oneself, behave, administer, manage, treat, give attention to, control, act, dispense, oversee, cope with.

Dealer, *n.* One who buys goods for resale to final customers (a commodities dealer). Wholesaler, merchant, jobber, seller, broker, shopkeeper, agent, factor, shipper, consignor, hawker, intermediary, conduit, representative, vendor, middleman, tradesman, trafficker, businessman, trader, retailer, huckster, fence. *Ant.* Consumer.

Dealer's talk The puffing of goods to induce their sale. Seller's talk. See puffing (1).

Dealings, *n.* Transactions in the course of trade or business (fraudulent dealings). Commerce, traffic, trade, negotiation, conduct, arrangement, affairs, proceedings, concerns, activities, deals, undertakings, enterprises, intercourse, contracts, relations.

Dean, *n.* See head, principal (2).

Dear, *adj.,* *n.* See darling; costly.

Dearth, *n.* A scarcity (a dearth of supporting evidence). Paucity, want, absence, shortage, deficiency, need, lack, inadequacy, poverty, insufficiency, drought, deprivation, leanness, meagerness. *Ant.* Abundance.

Death, *n.* **1.** Permanent cessation of all vital functions and signs. See brain death. States have enacted laws that determine the moment of death for various purposes, e.g., discontinuation of life support systems. (Death by drug overdose —DOD.) Cessation of life, demise, termination of life, passing, expiration, rigor mortis, decease, dying, mortality. **2.** Annihilation (the death of the doctrine of immunity). Destruction, ruin, obliteration, extinction, end, finale, departure, downfall, undoing, dissolution. *Ant.* Life; resurrection.

Deathtrap, *n.* A structure or situation involving imminent risk of death or serious bodily harm; a place that is apparently safe but actually very dangerous to life.

Debacle, *n.* Sudden collapse (the negotiations turned into a debacle). Fiasco, breakdown, breakup, disruption, disaster, wreck, devastation, catastrophe, cataclysm, defeat, havoc, ruin, dissolution, tragedy, setback, upset, rout, reverse, misfortune. *Ant.* Success.

Debarment, *n.* See removal.

Debase, *v.* **1.** To reduce the value of something (debase the currency). Reduce the quality of, impair, downgrade, deteriorate, depreciate, damage, bastardize, devalue, injure, alloy, adulterate, pollute, lower, depress, weaken. **2.** To degrade or dishonor (the witness debased himself by lying). Disgrace, defile, desecrate, discredit, tarnish, contaminate, corrupt, poison, vitiate, stain, taint, pervert, humble, foul, soil, demean, prostitute, dehumanize, humiliate. *Ant.* Upgrade; enhance.

Debatable, *adj.* Open to debate; questionable (a debatable theory). Undecided, disputable, arguable, uncertain, problematic, open to discussion, borderline, doubtful, dubious, controversial, ambiguous, unsettled, contestable, at issue, in question, speculative, unresolved, conjectural. *Ant.* Resolved.

Debate 1. *v.* To argue over (the attorneys debated the issue). Contest, disagree, differ, dispute, discuss, wrangle, quarrel, contend, altercate, negotiate, controvert, refute. **2.** *v.* To consider (the attorney debated whether to file the motion). Ponder, reason, mediate, deliberate, contemplate, cogitate, reflect. **3.** *n.* An argument or dispute (the debate within the legislature). Discussion, controversy, altercation, disputation, contest, war of words, argumentation, contention, competition. *Ant.* Agree; ignore; harmony.

Debauch, *v.* See corrupt (2), defile.

Debauchery, *n.* Sexual immorality or excesses (the spendthrift was given to debauchery). Dissipation, self-indulgence, profligacy, self-gratification, lust, immoderation, excesses, depravity, corruption, lewdness, licentiousness, seduction, womanizing, revelry, intemperance, binge, bacchanalia, incontinence, fornication, vice, carnality, obscenity. *Ant.* Purity.

Debenture, *n.* A promissory note or bond backed by the general credit of a corporation and usually not secured by a mortgage or lien on any specific property.

Debilitate, *v.* To weaken (she was debilitated by the ordeal of the trial). Make feeble, enervate, wear out, devitalize, harm, exhaust, prostrate, enfeeble, fatigue, incapacitate, emasculate, deplete, tire out, cripple, undermine, diminish. *Ant.* Restore.

Debility, *n.* Weakness. Frailty, illness, infirmity, exhaustion, delicacy, decrepitude, senility. *Ant.* Strength.

Debit, *n.* A sum due or owing; an entry made on the asset (left) side of a ledger or account (it was recorded as a debit). Debt, indebtedness, amount due, obligation, arrears, liability. *Ant.* Credit.

Debonair, *adj.* Suave. Dapper, lighthearted, carefree, smooth, buoyant, well-bred, free, gay, sportive. See also casual (3), active (3), happy, attractive, indifferent, chic.

De bonis asportatis For taking away goods; for goods taken away (trespass de bonis asportatis).

De bonis non administratis Of the goods not administered. When an administrator is appointed to succeed another administrator who left the estate partially unsettled, the successor is granted administration de bonis non, that is, of the goods not already administered.

Debouch, *v.* See drain (1).

Debrief, *v.* See cross-examine.

Debris, *n.* See refuse (2).

Debt, *n.* An amount of money that is due (uncollectable debt). Obligation, debit, liability, bill, deferred payment, arrears, indebtedness, delinquency, outstanding charge, deficit, encumbrance, commitment, burden, claim, sum due, account

Debt

owing, nonpayment, balance owed, burden; in the red. *Ant.* Credit.

Debt adjusting Engaging in the business of entering contracts with the debtor, whereby the debtor agrees to pay a certain amount of money periodically to a person in the debt-adjusting business, who then distributes the money among certain creditors.

Debtee, *n.* A person to whom a debt is due. See creditor.

Debt financing Funds raised by issuing bonds or notes—unlike equity financing by issuing stocks.

Debtor, *n.* One who owes a debt. Borrower; deadbeat. See also buyer.

Debt pooling An arrangement by which the debtor adjusts many debts by distributing his or her assets among several creditors who may or may not agree to take less than what is owed. An arrangement by which the debtor agrees to pay a sum of money in regular installments to one creditor who agrees to discharge all his or her debts.

Debt service The interest and charges currently payable on a debt, including principal payments.

Debunk, *v.* See expose (1), clarify.

Debut, *n.* Coming out, introduction, premiere, launching, initiation, unveiling. See also commencement, inauguration.

Decadence, *n.* See corruption, delinquency (2), decline (3); decadent, corrupt.

Decadent, *adj.* Corrupt (the spendthrift's decadent lifestyle). Base, immoral, dissolute, decayed, wasted, wasting, degenerate, tainted, deteriorating, effete, hedonistic, corrosive, sinking, disintegrating, withering. See also corrupt, bad. *Ant.* Uplifting.

Decamp, *v.* See depart (1), flee.

Decanter, *n.* See vessel (2).

Decay, *n., v.* See corruption, decline (2, 3), die, dissolve, perish, decompose, lapse.

Decease, *v.* See die.

Deceased, *n.* A dead person (the deceased's will). See decedent.

Decedent, *n.* A dead person (the decedent's dying declaration). Deceased, demised, testate, intestate, departed, recently departed.

Decedent's estate Real and personal property that a person possesses at the time of death. See estate, property.

Deceit, *n.* See fraud.

Deceitful, *adj.* Dishonest (a deceitful defendant). Lying, untrustworthy, deceptive, cunning, collusive, misleading, hypocritical, artful, clandestine, illusory, insidious, fallacious, disingenuous, fraudulent, false, insincere, duplicitous, counterfeit, bogus, spurious, scheming, Machiavellian, Janus-faced. *Ant.* Honest.

Deceive, *v.* To mislead (he was deceived into turning over the stock). Defraud, trick, delude, decoy, cheat, take advantage of, fool, swindle, misinform, victimize, misguide, ensnare, lie, dupe, prevaricate, overcharge, fleece, exploit, beguile, overreach, "gyp", bilk, "rook," "con," entrap. *Ant.* Tell the truth.

Decelerate, *v.* See diminish; mitigate; impede.

Decency, *n.* Propriety of action, speech, manners, etc. (he had the decency to refrain). Good manners, decorum, goodness, modesty, civility, respectability, appropriateness, virtue, kindness, correctness, amenity, generosity, fitness. *Ant.* Rudeness.

Decennial, *adj.* Concerning a 10-year period.

Decent, *adj.* See proper, moral (2), fair.

Decentralize, *v.* To distribute the power or function of a central organization to smaller entities (the legislature decentralized the banking system). Divide, subdivide, separate, apportion, disperse, diffuse, delegate, section, fragment, disjoin. *Ant.* Concentrate.

Deception, *n.* Intentional misleading by spoken or acted falsehood (an undetected deception). Fraud, fraudulence, hoax, chicanery, dishonesty, ruse, stratagem, misrepresentation, sham, illusion, pretext, trick, artifice, subterfuge, deceit, duplicity, circumvention, treachery, trap, camouflage, counterfeit, cheat, guile, masquerade, ploy, concoction, dodge, perjury, evasion, invention, delusion, equivocation, deviation, artful contrivance, gimmick, plan, feint, plot, intrigue, wile, tactic, blind, maneuver, stall, snare, cabal, gambit, conspiracy, fabrication, machination. *Ant.* Honesty.

Deceptive, *adj.* Having the tendency to deceive (deceptive advertising). Misleading, specious, fraudulent, deceitful, artificial, underhanded, dishonest, false, disingenuous, fallacious, unreliable, delusive, confounding, camouflaged, insidious, prevaricating, unreal, hollow, mock, insincere, counterfeit, untrue, spurious, sham, pseudo, fictitious, illegitimate, apocryphal, bogus, faulty, pretended, not genuine, synthetic, simulated, contrived, forged, deceiving. *Ant.* Trustworthy.

Decide, *v.* To arrive at a determination (the court refused to decide the question). Resolve, determine, umpire, settle, arbitrate, adjudicate, judge, referee, arrange, award, pass judgment, conclude, rule, terminate, dispose of, finalize, ascertain, vote, adjudge, decree, choose. *Ant.* Waver.

Decided, *adj.* See definite, clear (1), blatant (1), categorical (1), certain (3).

Deciduous, *adj.* See temporary.

Decimate, *v.* See destroy.

Decipher, *v.* See clarify, interpret.

Decision, *n.* **1.** A determination arrived at after a consideration of relevant factors, e.g., the facts and the law (a majority decision of the court). Judgment, resolution, adjudication, decree, ruling, settlement, conclusion, order, finding, verdict, pronouncement, opinion, result, outcome, sentence, choice, selection. **2.** Resolve (a woman of decision). Determination, purpose, strength, conviction, tenacity, decisiveness, perseverance, purpose, firmness, will. *Ant.* Indecision (2).

Decisive, *adj.* **1.** Conclusive (a decisive victory). Clear, pronounced, definitive, fateful, final, emphatic, absolute, unqualified, significant, crucial, categorical, authoritative, deciding, compelling, irrevocable, critical, pivotal, unconditional, indisputable, consequential, far-reaching, determining, determinative. **2.** Self-confident (a decisive judge). Self-assured, masterful, steadfast, resolute, positive, firm. *Ant.* Inconclusive; vacillating.

Deck, *n., v.* See platform (2), floor (4); clothe.

Declamation, *n.* See address (3).

Declamatory, *adj.* See pompous, arrogant.

Declarant, *n.* A person who makes a declaration (it was hearsay because the declarant was not in the court). Speaker, affiant, one who affirms, affirmant, deponent, attester, informer. *Ant.* Listener.

Declaration, *n.* A formal statement (declaration of innocence). Pronouncement, testimony, affirmation, utterance, recital, recitation, assertion, attestation, avowal, acknowledgment, notice, announcement, protestation, proclamation, publication, revelation, asseveration, admission, comment, manifesto, account, affidavit, recapitulation, explanation, report, narrative, specification, reckoning, valuation, assessment, fiat, communication, verbalization, vocalization, articulation, remark, averment, observation, dictum, exclamation, speech, claim, communiqué, exposition, delineation, profession, presentation. *Ant.* Silence.

Declaration against interest A statement that at the time made (a) conflicts with the pecuniary or proprietary interest of the person making it, or (b) tends to subject him or her to civil or criminal liability, or (c) tends to render invalid his or her claim against someone else.

Declaration of state of mind A statement concerning a person's state of mind, e.g., "I'm furious".

Declarative, *adj.* See affirmative.

Declaratory, *adj.* Designed to fix or elucidate what has been uncertain or doubtful (declaratory judgment). Explanatory, elucidating, clarifying.

Declaratory judgment A binding adjudication of the rights and status of the litigants in a justiciable controversy without granting any coercive relief, e.g., no damages are awarded, no injunction is issued.

Declaratory statute A statute enacted for the purpose of removing doubts or of putting an end to conflicting decisions as to what the law is in relation to a particular matter.

Declare, *v.* To make known or to announce (the accused declared her innocence). Signify, assert, utter, publish, pronounce, proclaim, articulate, aver, confirm, swear, propose, profess, asseverate, contend, insist, certify, communicate, advance, hold, allege, maintain, claim, submit, inform, predicate, divulge, broadcast, assure, voice, say, specify, report, comment, account, delineate, expose, verbalize, protest, manifest. *Ant.* Suppress.

Déclassé, *adj.* See inferior.

Declassify, *v.* To make available; to remove security classification.

Declination, *n.* A document filed in court by a fiduciary who chooses not to serve in his or her named capacity.

Decline 1. *v.* To refuse or reject (the witness declined to answer). Turn down, forgo, avoid, spurn, deny, disapprove, repudiate, veto, eschew, dissent, abstain, renounce, resist. 2. *v.* To deteriorate (after she left, the quality of the firm declined). Fall, sink, descend, depress, decrease, weaken, diminish, regress, degenerate, dwindle, worsen, flag, lessen, ebb, recede, wane, decay, suffer, fall off, drop off, languish, become feeble. 3. *n.* A decrease; a falling off or downward tendency (a decline in her ability to work since the accident). Regression, sinking, diminution, deterioration, wane, depreciation, collapse, descent, downturn, subsidence, erosion, retrogression, impairment, recession, failing, decay, weakening. *Ant.* Accept; improve; increase.

Decode, *v.* See interpret.

Decompose, *v.* To decay. Disintegrate, rot, spoil, fall apart. See also dissolve, divide.

Decontrol, *v.* To remove or minimize regulatory restrictions. Deregulate. See liberate.

Décor, *n.* See decoration (1).

Decorate, *v.* See beautify, furnish, color (3).

Decoration, *n.* 1. Ornamentation. Embellishment, adornment, ornament, trimming, trappings, array, exaggeration, enrichment, frill, beautification. 2. See medal.

Decorum, *n.* Conformity to accepted standards of behavior (a lack of decorum in the courtroom). Good manners, protocol, civility, appropriateness, tact, dignity, delicacy, courtesy, social grace, decency, polish, formality, etiquette, taste, gentility, good form, deportment, comportment. See also propriety. *Ant.* Laxness.

Decoy, *v.,* **decoy,** *n.* 1. *v.* To lure (he was decoyed into accepting service of process). Entice, allure, ensnare, entrap, bait, attract, beguile, induce, tempt, inveigle, mislead. 2. *n.* Allurement (the call was a decoy to get her away from the window). Trick, diversion, inducement, stratagem, pretense, sham, camouflage, pitfall, deception, simulation, disguise, chicanery. *Ant.* Repulse; repellent.

Decrease, *v., n.* See diminish, decline, mitigate.

Decree 1. *n.* The judgment of a court of equity or chancery (consent decree). Decision, order, resolution, adjudication, opinion, ruling, mandate, direction, declaration, injunction, sanction, sentence. 2. *n.* An official law (by decree, the town was closed). Edict, regulation, ordinance, statute, act. **3.** *v.* To decide by decree (the court decreed an end to the practice). Order, adjudicate, ordain, proclaim, prescribe, direct, award, command, rule, oblige, dictate.

Decree nisi A provisional decree that upon motion will be made absolute unless cause is shown against it.

Decrement, *n.* The act of decreasing (a sharp decrement in value).

Decrepit, *adj.* **1.** Disabled; weakened by defects (he was in a decrepit condition). Infirm, aged, senile, doddering, incapacitated, feeble, wasted. See also weak, frail. **2.** Dilapidated (decrepit building). Broken-down, run-down, rickety, antiquated, superannuated, decayed. *Ant.* Healthy; strong.

Decrepitude, *n.* See dotage, infirmity, disease, debility; decrepit.

Decriminalization, *n.* Officially declaring (through a new law) that acts or omissions that were once criminal are no longer criminal (the decriminalization of the marijuana laws).

Decry, *v.* To criticize or belittle (the judge decried the lack of lawyer preparation). Condemn, belittle, censure, deprecate, disparage, fault, denounce, rail against, disapprove, discredit, depreciate, traduce, demean, damn, curse, admonish, berate, denigrate, malign, scorn, recriminate. *Ant.* Praise.

Dedicate, *v.* To appropriate and set apart one's private property to some public use (the will dedicated the alleyway for neighborhood use). Pledge, commit, devote, vest, endow, confer, offer, present, ordain, consecrate, convey, bestow, donate; enshrine, immortalize, celebrate, anoint, inscribe.

Dedication, *n.* **1.** The appropriation of land, or an easement therein, by the owner for the use of the public and accepted for such use by or on behalf of the public. See dedicate. **2.** The first publication of a work, without having secured a copyright, is a dedication of it to the public. See abandonment, cession. **3.** See fidelity, determination.

Deduce, *v.* To reach a conclusion based on facts or assumptions (from the testimony, I deduced that she was not present). Conclude, infer, reason, understand, surmise, calculate, guess, assume, judge, gather, opine, imagine, presume, glean, construe, conjecture.

Deduct, *v.* To subtract. Remove, take away, withdraw, decrease. See also diminish; deduction.

Deductible, *adj.* Capable of being taken away or subtracted (a tax deductible debt). Removable, allowable, discountable.

Deduction, *n.* **1.** The part taken away; that which is deducted (itemized deductions on the tax return). Subtraction, abatement, withdrawal, lowering, removal, curtailment, exemption, diminution, allowance, decrease, discount, recoupment, credit, write-off. **2.** Reasoning from the general to the particular (an unsupported deduction from the evidence). Conclusion, inference, analysis, rationalization, implication, assumption, corollary, understanding, speculation, consequence. *Ant.* Addition; induction.

Deductive, *adj.* See analytic, logical.

Deed, *n.* **1.** A conveyance of real property transferring title from the grantor to the grantee (the deed was improperly executed). Instrument, release, assignment. **2.** See act (3).

Deed in fee A deed conveying the title to land in fee simple with the usual covenants.

Deed of trust An instrument used in some states, taking the place and serving the functions of a mortgage, by which the legal title to real property is placed in trustee(s) to secure the repayment of money or the performance of other conditions. A security.

Deem, *v.* To consider (the lawyer was deemed incompetent). Believe, treat as if, determine, hold, regard, view, judge, surmise, reckon, estimate, calculate, opine, adjudge, conceive, perceive, suspect, look upon, account.

Deep, *adj.* See mysterious, ardent, emotional, strong (2).

Deep-felt, *adj.* See earnest (2), active (3).

Deep pocket The defendant who has resources with which to pay a judgment if rendered.

Deep-seated, *adj.* Ingrained, innate. See inherent, congenital, habitual.

Deep-six, *v.* See destroy.

De-escalate, *v.* See diminish.

Deface, *v.* To mar or destroy the physical appearance of something (he defaced the will). Deform, blot, blemish, injure, spoil, damage, disfigure, scratch, delete, soil, blur, wipe away, impair, efface, destroy, erase, mutilate, smear, tarnish, contort, expunge, eradicte. *Ant.* Preserve.

Defacement, *n.* See malicious mischief; deface, destroy.

De facto, *adv., adj., (Lat.)* In fáct (they were never legally married, but he was her husband de facto). Actually, as a matter of fact, in actuality, in deed, in reality, in existence, existing, real, in point of fact, in effect, present, demonstrable, in substance, bona fide. *Ant.* De jure.

De facto government A government that maintains itself by force against the will of the rightful legal government.

De facto officer An officer who is in actual possession of the office, but is not holding it in the manner prescribed by law.

De facto segregation Segregation that is inadvertent and without the active assistance of the government. It is caused by social, economic, and other factors rather than by state action.

Defalcate, *v.* See embezzle.

Defalcation, *n.* Misappropriation of funds (the treasurer's defalcation). Embezzlement, fraud, false pretenses, misuse of funds, violation of fiduciary duty.

Defamacast, *n.* Defamation by broadcast. See slander, defamation.

Defamation, *n.* Libel and slander, the two defamation torts. Generally, the elements of both torts are as follows: (a) a defamatory statement by the defendant, (b) of and concerning the plaintiff, (c) that is published, (d) causing, (e) damages. See defamatory statement, slander; defamatory.

Defamatory, *adj.* Injurious to reputation (a defamatory speech). Calumnious, abusive, casting aspersion, disparaging, vilifying, denigrating, shameful, slanderous, libelous, tainting, denunciatory, stigmatizing, insulting, vituperative, detracting, invidious, scandalous, pejorative, debasing, infamous, critical, scurrilous, maligning, humiliating. See also derogatory; slander. *Ant.* Laudatory.

Defamatory per quod Those words that require an allegation of facts, aside from the words themselves, to show how the words were used to libel the plaintiff.

Defamatory per se Words that by themselves injure the reputation of the plaintiff. No external proof is needed.

Defamatory statement A statement of fact that in the eyes of at least a substantial and respectable minority of people would tend to harm the reputation of another by lowering him or her in the estimation of those people or by deterring them from associating with him or her.

Defame, *v.* To injure someone's reputation (the book defamed the professor). Malign, accuse, denigrate, slander, libel, vilify, revile, assail, disparage, discredit, stigmatize, insult, misrepresent, asperse, smirch, blemish, ostracize, denounce, damn, scorn, scandalize, impugn, curse, belittle, dishonor, degrade, anathematize, defile, cast aspersions on, destroy one's good name, slur, sully, shame. *Ant.* Applaud.

Default, *n.* An omission of that which ought to be done; the failure to carry out a duty (the failure to pay rendered him in default). Nonperformance, breach, neglect, nonfulfillment, nonfeasance, delinquency, repudiation, deficiency, defect, being in arrears, evasion, negligence, failure, lapse, reneging. *Ant.* Compliance, performance.

Default judgment A judgment rendered against a party from whom affirmative relief was sought because the party failed to file an answer or otherwise defend the action.

Defeasance, *n.* See annulment (2).

Defeasance clause A provision in a mortgage that assures the revesting of title in the mortgagor when all of the terms and conditions of the mortgage have been met, e.g., making all the payments.

Defeasible, *adj.* Subject to being revoked or terminated upon the happening of specified conditions (defeasible title). Liable to be defeated, voidable, revocable, dissoluble, removable, subject to cancellation. *Ant.* Unalterable.

Defeat 1. *v.* To prevent or overcome (the scheme was designed to defeat creditors). Frustrate, circumvent, thwart, abort, conquer, overpower, rout, subdue, overwhelm, overturn, suppress, best, cancel, check, block, impede, repulse, silence, choke, muzzle, checkmate, vanquish, subjugate, squelch, upset, humble, terminate, bar. **2.** *n.* A failure or setback (the defeat of the cause of action). Overthrow, downfall, conquest, refutation, collapse, invalidation, loss, default, breakdown, debacle, frustration, impediment, hindrance, nonsuccess, misadventure, stumbling block, obstruction, misfortune, disappointment, undoing, checkmate, fall, relapse, regression, rebuff, upset, thwarting, adversity, mischance, subversion, reversal, demolition, annihilation, abolition, ruin, inversion, disestablishment, obliteration, abolishment, vanquishment. *Ant.* Support; success.

Defeatist, *n.* See cynic.

Defect, *n.* The lack of something required (a latent defect). Imperfection, delinquency, insufficiency, fault, shortcoming, deformity, weakness, impairment, error, stain, "bug," crack, omission, foible, drawback, scar, flaw, default, failing, frailty, deviation, infirmity, inadequacy, shortage. *Ant.* Perfection.

Defective, *adj.* Lacking in some particular that is essential to completeness, safety, or legal sufficiency (a defective design). Imperfect, impaired, flawed, deficient, inadequate, marred, substandard, poor, broken, subnormal, below standards, faulty, damaged, unhealthy, subpar, out of order, crippled, inoperative, unsound. *Ant.* Sufficient.

Defend, *v.* **1.** To protect (she was denied the opportunity to defend herself). Safeguard, guard, secure, vindicate, represent, justify, advocate, rally to, shield, make a stand for, champion, promote, argue for, sponsor, certify, befriend, indorse, endorse, support, guarantee, underwrite, shelter. **2.** To contest or oppose (a dismissal for failure to defend). Challenge, counter, take issue, battle, dispute. *Ant.* Attack; concede.

Defendable, *adj.* See defensible, justifiable, logical.

Defendant, *n.* The person defending or denying; the person against whom relief or recovery is sought (the defendant filed a motion to dismiss). Respondent, accused, the party charged, the party sued, responding litigant. *Ant.* Petitioner, plaintiff.

Defender, *n.* See advocate (1).

Defense, *n.* **1.** Allegations of fact or legal theories offered to offset or defeat claims or demands (the defense of the statute of limitations). Rebuttal, rationalization, justification, extenuation, excuse, rejoinder, vindication, explanation. **2.** Protection (the defense of freedom). Advocacy, preservation, safekeeping, security, assistance, bulwark, maintenance, armament. *Ant.* Offense; denigration.

Defenseless, *adj.* Helpless. Vulnerable, unarmed, unprotected, powerless, weak, imperiled, impotent, unguarded. See also destitute, insecure (1).

Defense of property The use of force that is reasonable under the circumstances to protect one's property. Such force can be a defense to a tort or criminal action, e.g., assault.

Defensible, *adj.* Capable of being defended (the alibi is a defensible position). Sound, justifiable, tenable, reasonable, defendable, believable. See also logical, justifiable. *Ant.* Indefensible.

Defensive, *adj.* See responsive; defend, defense.

Defer, *v.* 1. To delay or postpone (to defer payment). Put off, table, suspend, stall, procrastinate, hold up, remand, shelve, interrupt, hold in abeyance, set aside, adjourn. 2. To yield (the lawyer deferred to the doctor's judgment). Respect, submit, bow to, accede, capitulate, conform, accommodate, give deference to, give in, abide by, subscribe, honor, consent, accept. *Ant.* Hasten; resist.

Deference, *n.* See consideration (3), courtesy (2); regard (2), affection.

Deferential, *adj.* See kind, civil (3), judicious.

Deferment, *n.* See defer (1), delay (3).

Deferral, *n.* See defer (1), delay (3).

Deferred compensation Compensation that will be taxed when received or upon the removal of certain restrictions on its receipt. It will not be taxed when earned.

Defiance, *n.* A contemptuous opposition or open disregard of something (her defiance of the court's order). Challenge, rebellion, combativeness, scorn, insubordination, intransigence, disobedience, contempt, hostility, dare, resistance, affront, impudence, recalcitrance, noncooperation, noncompliance, revolt. *Ant.* Obedience.

Defiant, *adj.* See disobedient, contentious, hostile, contumacious, nonconforming.

Deficiency, *n.* A shortage or insufficiency (tax deficiency). Lack, inadequacy, defect, weakness, failing, absence, flaw, need, deficit, imperfection, foible, shortfall, default, arrears, incompleteness, shortcoming, loss, insufficiency, impairment, nonfulfillment, omission, dearth, scarcity. *Ant.* Adequacy.

Deficiency judgment A judgment for an unpaid balance after the creditor has used up all available secured property of the debtor.

Deficient, *adj.* Inadequate (the design of the product was deficient). Defective, flawed, inferior, unsatisfactory, weak, wanting, incomplete, imperfect, second-rate, faulty, malfunctioning, below par, marred, substandard, unsound, unsafe, incompetent, lacking. See also insufficient, inadequate, small, few, marginal, nugatory. *Ant.* Adequate.

Deficit, *n.* An excess of expenditures over revenues (the company borrowed to cover the deficit). See deficiency, arrearages. *Ant.* Surplus.

Defile, *v.* To corrupt or debase (publicly defile the flag). Dishonor, sully, dirty, stain, tarnish, blemish, taint, debauch, pollute, poison, contaminate, assault, foul, rape, adulterate, ravish, deflower, ruin, desecrate, denigrate, defame, disgrace, violate, shame, blacken, smear. *Ant.* Sanctify.

Define, *v.* 1. To explain or state the exact meaning of words or phrases (the court defined the damage clause). Interpret, construe, characterize, translate, elucidate, expound, clarify, exemplify, fix the meaning, illustrate. 2. To set the limits of something (the statute defines the role of the agency). Set out, delineate, specify, enumerate, spell out, delimit, detail, describe, determine, demarcate, establish, circumscribe, prescribe, represent, identify. *Ant.* Obscure; conceal.

Defined, *adj.* See definite (1).

Definite, *adj.* 1. Clearly defined (a definite responsibility). Unambiguous, precise, bounded, specific, delineated, circumscribed, narrow, restricted, established, manifest, ascertained, authoritative, beyond question, well-defined, categorical, unqualified, conclusive, decisive, unimpeachable, demonstrable, unequivocal, distinct, immutable, undeniable, inescapable, inevitable, settled, exact, determinate. **2.** Positive (how definite was she on the proposed sale?). Express, exact, absolute, forthright, complete, final, conclusive, sure, clear-cut, invariable, confident, true, guaranteed, convinced, resolute, evident. *Ant.* Ambiguous; indefinite.

Definite sentence A sentence of imprisonment for a specified number of years (a definite sentence of 3 years). Determinate sentence. *Ant.* Indeterminate sentence.

Definition, *n.* An explanation of the meaning of language (the definition of intent). Interpretation, construction, deciphering, translation, connotation, denotation, characterization, clarification, sense, decoding, elucidation, illumination, explication.

Definitive, *adj.* Complete, clear, final (the definitive ruling ended the controversy). Conclusive, unconditional, absolute, decisive, settling, categorical, ultimate, positive, perfect, reliable, thorough, consummate, authentic, unimpeachable, incontestable, authoritative, beyond doubt, beyond question, crowning, decided. See also explicit. *Ant.* Inconclusive.

Deflagrate, *v.* See burn.

Deflate, *v.* See diminish, depreciate.

Deflation, *n.* A decrease in price levels, currency, and available credit.

Deflect, *v.* See divert, ricochet, boomerang.

Defloration, *n.* Seduction of, debauching (the defloration of a minor). See debauchery.

Deflower, *v.* See defile, rape (1).

Deforce, *v.* See withhold.

Deform, *v.* See mar, mutilate (1).

Deformed, *adj.* Irregular, grotesque. Distorted, crippled, awry, misshapen, bent, warped, unnatural, unsightly. See also lame.

Deformity, *n.* A deformed or misshapen condition (the drug caused a deformity of the leg). Malformation, disfigurement, imperfection, deformation, distortion, contortion, irregularity, abnormality, damage, aberration, monstrosity. See also defect. *Ant.* Correction

Defraud, *v.* See deceive, cheat; fraud.

Defray, *v.* To pay (help defray the cost of litigation). Cover, bear, finance, discharge, contribute, indemnify, fund, reimburse.

Defrost, *v.* See thaw.

Deft, *adj.* See apt (3), expert (2), able.

Defunct, *adj.* Having ceased to exist (a defunct corporation). No longer operative, dead, deceased, extinct, nonexistent, obsolete, expired, canceled, void, demised, terminated, annulled, inactive, finished, ended, not in force. *Ant.* Functioning.

Defuse, *v.* See mitigate, remedy (2).

Defy, *v.* See challenge (1), resist, confront; defiance.

Degeneracy, *n.* See corruption, debauchery.

Degenerate, *v., adj.* See decline (2); corrupt, abandoned (2), immoral, obscene.

Degeneration, *n.* See deterioration, degradation.

Degradation, *n.* Moral or intellectual decadence (the degradation led to his dismissal). Degeneration, degeneracy, deterioration, disgrace, humiliation, debasement, decline, dishonor, corruption, perversity, opprobrium, mortification, disrepute, ignominy, odium, depravity, perversion, turpitude, baseness. *Ant.* Exaltation.

Degrade, *v.* See defile, debase, diminish, abase; embarrass, discredit, disparage.

Degraded, *adj.* See corrupt, abandoned (2).

Degrading, *adj.* Exposing someone to disgrace (a degrading attack). Reviling, humiliating, demeaning, disgraceful, contemptible, debasing, shameful. See also abandoned (2), corrupt. *Ant.* Uplifting.

Degree, *n.* **1.** The measure or scope of something (the degree of her culpability). Level, magnitude, extent, size, dimension, range, amount, intensity, scale, grade, order, rate, proportion, severity, ratio, strength, seriousness, volume, value, caliber. **2.** Formal recognition from a school (honorary degree). Certificate, academic title, diploma, credential, qualification, distinction, honor, rank. **3.** A step in the line of descent (the second degree of kindred). Blood relationship, blood tie, consanguinity, family connection. See also descent.

Degrees of kindred The relationship between a deceased and his or her survivors.

Dehors, *(Fr.)* Beyond (dehors the record). Out of, without, foreign to, unconnected with. See also extrinsic (1).

Dehumanize, *v.* See debase, defile.

Deify, *v.* See anoint, adulate.

Deign, *v.* See condescend.

Deinstitutionalize, *v.* To let out of an institution. See release (1).

Deity, *n.* See God.

Déjà vu, *n.* The feeling of having experienced something before. See repetition, illusory, dream.

Dejected, *adj.* See depressed.

De jure, *adv., adj.* Sanctioned by law; in compliance with the law (de jure corporation). Of right, authorized by law, lawful, within the law, by statute, in accordance with the law.

De jure segregation Segregation directly intended or mandated by the law.

Delay 1. *v.* To postpone (the judge delayed the start of the trial). Stay, put off, suspend, defer, shelve, prolong, recess, break, table, adjourn, intermit, hold in abeyance. **2.** *v.* To set up obstacles (to delay creditors). Hinder, block, curb, arrest, impede, inhibit, check, slow, hold up, encumber, retard, obstruct, halt, stymie, hamper, interfere, detain, clog, interrupt. **3.** *n.* A postponement (an unexpected delay). Adjournment, intermission, deferment, suspension, pause, moratorium, impediment, detention, reprieve, prolongation, tarrying, procrastination, laxity, retardation. *Ant.* Proceed; assist; progression.

Delectable, *adj.* Savory. Delicious, agreeable, luscious, juicy, creamy, scrumptious, rich, satisfying, tasty, exciting, gratifying, pleasurable, appealing, pleasant, inviting. See also attractive, enjoyable.

Delegate 1. *v.* To give a duty, responsibility, or power to another (the board delegated the task to the president). Assign, commission, license, entrust, appoint, designate, nominate, accredit, sanction, authorize, employ, charge, invest, empower, name, entitle, enable, deputize, ordain, consign, install, relegate, allot, charter, consign, commit, qualify, order, choose, depute. **2.** *n.* A person who is authorized or commissioned to act for another (her delegate made all the arrangements). Representative, agent, envoy, proxy, intermediary, surrogate, appointee, emissary, ambassador, go-between, substitute, vicar, alternate, deputy, factor, stand-in, mouthpiece, attaché, chargé d'affaires, spokesperson. *Ant.* Principal (2).

Delegation, *n.* See delegate, embassy.

Delete, *v.* To erase, remove, or strike out (the testator deleted the bequest). Cancel, blot out, expunge, eradicate, wipe out, obliterate, efface, cut out, eliminate, expurgate, censor, omit, exclude, dele. *Ant.* Insert.

Deleterious, *adj.* Morally or physically harmful (the fighting had a deleterious effect on the child). Injurious, unwholesome, poisonous, hurtful, malicious, damaging, detrimental, corrupting, ruinous, pernicious, destructive, fatal, adverse, unhealthy, unfavorable, lethal, deadly, baneful, menacing, toxic, mortal, corrosive, bad. *Ant.* Wholesome.

Deletion, *n.* See omission; delete.

Deliberate 1. *v.* To weigh or examine (the judge deliberated for a week before reaching a decision). Ponder, consider, reflect, meditate, think over, take under advisement, take under consideration, mull over, contemplate, cogitate, ruminate, reason, analyze, confer, debate, brood, consult, investigate, review, speculate, scrutinize, evaluate, discuss, cerebrate, study. **2.** *adj.* Carefully considered; willful (deliberate misrepresentation). Calculated, well-advised, dispassionate, volitional, considered, conscious, thought-out, designed, intended, planned, purposeful, studied, plotted, aforethought. See also premeditated, willful, voluntary, intentional. **3.** *adj.* Cautious (a deliberate pace). Steady, leisurely, painstaking, unhurried, careful, prudent, methodical, levelheaded, sober, moderate, circumspect, slow, scrupulous, laborious. *Ant.* Ignore; accidental; impulsive.

Deliberately, *adv.* Willfully; with premeditation; in cold blood. See deliberate (2), knowingly; intentional.

Deliberation, *n.* The act of weighing and examining the reasons for and against a contemplated act. See deliberate; examination, consideration (2).

Delicacy, *n.* Diplomacy. Skill, sensitivity, savoir-faire, finesse, discrimination, subtlety. *Ant.* Rudeness.

Delicate, *adj.* See breakable, weak, frail, ill (1); squeamish; subtle; dangerous.

Delicatessen, *n.* See merchant, retailer; market; restaurant, inn.

Delicious, *adj.* See delectable, attractive.

Delictum, *n.* A tort, wrong, injury, or offense.

Delight, *v.* To gratify or please. Excite, enchant, charm, fascinate, cheer. See also pander (2), exult, enjoy (2), enjoyment, happiness, satisfaction (2).

Delighted, *adj.* See happy, content (2).

Delightful, *adj.* See attractive, amicable, enjoyable.

Delimit, *v.* To mark or lay out the limits or boundaries (to delimit his authority). Demarcate, limit, bound, determine, measure, enclose, surround, encircle. See also define (2).

Delineate, *v.* To describe, sketch, or outline (the report failed to delineate the way the system operates). Portray, depict, trace, diagram, map, chart, blueprint, represent, illustrate, picture, illuminate, design, paint, evoke, draw, contour, specify. See also define.

Delineation, *n.* See definition, description, map; delineate.

Delinquency, *n.* **1.** A violation of duty (delinquency in payment). Dereliction, omission, failure, carelessness, negligence, remiss, default, breach, breach of duty, nonperformance, lapse, shortage, inadequacy, arrearage, insufficiency, deficiency, debt, nonfeasance, nonfulfillment, nonobservance, neglect. **2.** An offense or misconduct; unruly or immoral behavior (contributing to the delinquency of a minor). Illegality, decadence, corruption, malfeasance, wrongdoing, lawlessness, disobedience, truancy, trespass, sin, misbehavior, fault, transgression, criminality, turpitude, devilishness, impropriety, mischievousness, wickedness, profligacy, misdeed, lawbreaking, vice, degeneracy. *Ant.* Performance; obedience.

Delinquency charges Additional money assessed against the borrower solely because of the failure to make timely payments.

Delinquent 1. *adj.* Pertaining to that which is still due (delinquent payments). Overdue, outstanding, payable, owing, unsettled, missing, unpaid, tardy, late, in arrears, deficient, short. **2.** *adj.* Failing to abide by the law or to conform to moral standards (delinquent minor). Culpable, criminal, lawbreaking, neglectful, negligent, immoral, unseemly, unscrupulous, blameworthy, remiss, reprehensible, in the wrong, dishonest, at fault, disreputable, scandalous, incorrigible, profligate, corrupt, offending, unprincipled, worthless, guilty. **3.** *n.* Someone who has committed a crime, offense, violation of duty, or other misconduct (juvenile delinquent). Offender, culprit, troublemaker, wrongdoer, lawbreaker, miscreant, transgressor, criminal, felon, misdemeanant, ruffian, nuisance, undesirable, rascal, scofflaw, hooligan, imp, rogue. *Ant.* Paid; honest; innocent person.

Delinquent child A person below a designated age (e.g., 16) who has violated criminal laws or who engages in disobedient, indecent, or immoral conduct and who is in need of treatment, rehabilitation, and supervision. An infant who is beyond the control of parents or other guardian because of habitual truancy, defiance of other school rules, continuous lawbreaking, running away from home, etc.

Delirious, *adj.* See wild (3), hysterical.

Delirium, *n.* See insanity, hysteria.

Delirium tremens (DTs), *n.* Sickness or delirium caused by alcohol poisoning.

Deliver, *v.* **1.** To carry or convey (the sheriff delivered the summons). Hand over, transfer, bring, carry, surrender, distribute, forward, cede, relinquish, remit, entrust. **2.** To pronounce (deliver a speech). Proclaim, utter, recite, enunciate, articulate, announce, publish, voice, declare, communicate, impart, advance.

Deliverance, *n.* See release (3), rescue, emancipation; removal.

Delivery, *n.* The act by which something is placed within the possession or control of another (delivery of the gift). Relinquishment, conveyance, surrender, transfer, shipment, transferral, sending, passage, transportation, consignment, handing over, commitment.

Delude, *v.* See deceive, misrepresent; seduce.

Deluge, *n.* See flood, catastrophe; inundate, submerge.

Delusion, *n.* A belief that is contrary to fact but adhered to in spite of tangible evidence that it is false (delusions of persecution). Deception, self-deception, misconception, unreality, aberration, irrationality, hallucination, fallacy, misapprehension, myth, misbelief, misinformation, subterfuge, misrepresentation, counterfeit, figment, trick, ruse, phantasm, misinterpretation, mistake. *Ant.* Enlightenment.

Delusive, *adj.* See deceptive.

De luxe, *adj.* Luxurious. Grand, elegant, first-class, splendid, fine, sumptuous, rich, posh, exclusive.

Delve, *v* See investigate, search (1), audit (2).

Demagogue, *n.* See agitator.

Demand 1. *v.* To claim as one's right (demand for payment). Require, cry, press, sue, insist, clamor, order, call for, exact, necessitate, urge, assert, enjoin, request, direct, dun. **2.** *n.* The assertion of a legal right (payable on demand). Requirement, order, command, direction, ultimatum, bidding, exigency, suit, claim, request, requisition, exaction.

Demandant, *n.* See plaintiff.

Demanding, *adj.* See strict (2), extreme (1), compelling, difficult, draconian, exigent.

Demand note A note that expressly states it is payable on demand, on presentation, or on sight.

Demarcate, *v.* See define (2); demarcation.

Demarcation, *n.* A boundary line (they could not agree on the property demarcation). Border, frontier, zone, partition, line, division, periphery, margin, bound, distinction, separation, end, edge, segregation, delimitation, differentiation.

Demarkation, *n.* See demarcation.

Demean, *v.* See debase, defile, abase, diminish, slander; grovel.

Demeaning, *adj.* See derogatory, negative.

Demeanor, *n.* Physical appearance (the demeanor of the witness). Outward bearing, behavior, conduct, presence, countenance, comportment, manner, actions, expression, style, carriage, mien, air, physiognomy, posture, look, guise, attitude.

Demented, *adj.* Of unsound mind (his demented state was clear to all). Insane, distracted, crazy, psychotic, psychopathic, lunatic, mad, frenzied, hysterical, irrational, idiotic, daft, crazed, convulsive. See also deranged; insanity. *Ant.* Rational.

Dementia, *n.* A form of mental disorder in which cognitive and intellectual functions of the mind are affected (e.g., impairment of memory). See insanity, lunacy.

Dementia praecox, *n.* Schizophrenia. See insanity, lunacy.

Demerit, *n.* See fault (1).

Demesne, *n.* Domain (demesne lands used by the lord's family).

Demilitarize, *v.* To remove the influence or presence of the military. See depart (1), withdraw (1).

De minimis Very small; trifling (the court considered the error de minimis and therefore did nothing about it). Insignificant, petty, inconsequential, minor, meaningless, unimportant. *Ant.* Critical.

Demise 1. *n.* A conveyance of an estate to another for life, for years, or at will (a demise of the land). Lease, conveyance for a term, transfer, alienation. **2.** *v.* To convey or create an estate for years or for life (demised by the testator). Lease, bequeath by succession, bequeath by inheritance, transmit, confer, endow, leave, will, devise, deliver. **3.** *n.* Death (the demise of the immunity doctrine). Decease, ruin, passing, fall, collapse, expiration, annihilation, ending, extinction, downfall, finish, departure, cessation, extermination.

Demise charter The hiring of a vessel, transferring possession and control for a limited purpose; title does not pass.

Demised premises The property or portion of property that is leased to a tenant.

Demission, *n.* See abdication.

Democracy, *n.* Government through representatives elected by the people. See government, authority (1), republic.

Demography, *n.* The study of human vital statistics.

Demolish, *v.* To pull down or destroy (the test results demolished his theory). Raze, pull to pieces, take apart, devastate, crush, mutilate, level, ruin, break, undo, annihilate, exterminate, total, vanquish, devour, pulverize, desolate, destroy, finish, conquer, cancel, terminate, consume, erase, liquidate, stamp out. *Ant.* Construct.

Demolition, *n.* Wreckage, devastation, tearing down, gutting. See destroy.

Demon, *n.* Monster. Devil, fiend, animal, evil spirit. See also wrongdoer.

Demonic, *adj.* See animal (2), bad (2), inhuman, cruel, malicious.

Demonstrable, *adj.* **1.** Capable of being shown or proven (she called for demonstrable positions rather than pure abstractions). Establishable, verifiable. See also empirical, provable. **2.** Obvious (a demonstrable lie). Undeniable, clear, apparent, unimpeachable, evident, conclusive, definite, unequivocal, absolute, unqualified, positive, assured, unmistakable, established. *Ant.* Vague; subtle.

Demonstrate, *v.* **1.** To prove by reasoning or evidence (the attorney demonstrated that the car was defective). Substantiate, make evident, establish, fix, authenticate, certify, verify, affirm, document, support, corroborate, validate, confirm. **2.** To describe by illustrations or examples (the senior partner demonstrated the techniques of cross-examination to the associate). Illustrate, exhibit, clarify, elucidate, teach, exemplify, manifest, express, explain, display, reveal, illuminate, lay out, instruct. **3.** To participate in a public display over an issue or a person (they demonstrated against sexism in the office). Parade, march, protest, challenge, sit-in, strike, boycott, complain, clamor, object, dissent, resist. See also

Demonstrate

picket, walkout.

Demonstration, *n.* See proof; production, exposition (2), array (2); strike, demonstrate.

Demonstrative, *adj.* **1.** Serving to demonstrate (demonstrative evidence). Illustrative, clarifying, descriptive, illuminating, informative, enlightening, telling, supportive. **2.** Having a tendency to express feelings (a demonstrative witness). Expressive, revealing, passionate, communicative, fervent, effusive, open, emotional, affectionate, unrestrained, excitable, temperamental, histrionic. *Ant.* Vague; reserved.

Demonstrative bequest A testamentary gift that by its terms must be paid from a specific fund.

Demonstrative evidence Evidence addressed directly to the senses apart from the testimony of witnesses; real evidence (e.g., gun, map, photo).

Demonstrative legacy A bequest of a certain sum of money with the direction that it be paid out of a particular fund.

Demoralize, *v.* To dishearten. Discourage, depress, sadden, deject, cripple, enfeeble, dispirit, weaken. See also debilitate.

Demoralized, *adj.* See depressed.

Demote, *v.* To downgrade. Lower, dethrone, fire, displace, humble, reduce in rank, degrade, "bust," strip. See also demotion, punishment.

Demotion, *n.* A reduction to a lower rank, grade, or type of position (an unexpected demotion at work). Downgrading, lowering, penalty, decrease, humiliation, humbling, degrading, dispossession. See also punishment. *Ant.* Promotion.

Demur, *v.* **1.** To state a demurrer (after the complaint was filed, the defendant demurred). See demurrer. **2.** To take exception (the chairperson demurred). Challenge, protest, dissent, contradict, object, contest, refute, balk, remonstrate.

Demure, *adj.* See bashful; coy; prudent, cautious.

Demurrage, *n.* The money paid to the owner of a ship or railroad car by a person who holds or uses it beyond the contract time.

Demurrer, *n.* An admission, for the sake of argument, of the allegations of fact made by the other party in order to show that even if they are true, they are insufficient to entitle this party to relief, e.g., the facts do not state a cause of action.

Demystify, *v.* See interpret, clarify.

Den, *n.* See cave.

Denial, *n.* **1.** A declaration that something is not true (denial of the allegations in the complaint). Contradiction, challenge, disavowal, dissent, repudiation, renunciation, rebuttal, disclaimer, disowning, answer, traverse, objection. **2.** Refusing to do something (a denial of the motion to dismiss). Rejection, rebuff, turndown, prohibition, veto, disapproval, disallowance, nonacceptance. *Ant.* Acknowledgment; granting.

Deniable, *adj.* See debatable.

Denigrate, *v.* See decry, defile, slander.

Denigrating, *adj.* See defamatory.

Denigration, *n.* See slander, censure, denial.

Denizen, *n.* Inhabitant (denizen of the country). Dweller, citizen, occupant, tenant, addressee, resident, subject, national, native, frequenter, patron.

Denominate, *v.* See name (2).

Denomination, *n.* **1.** A designation (she refused to be classified under that denomination). Grouping, category, name, heading, specification, title, species, identification, nomenclature, appellation, type, classification, division, subdivision, characterization, terminology, section, subsection, genre, caption, description. **2.** A society of individuals (the denomination of the church). Order, sect, faction,

222

fellowship, clan, cult, affiliation, school, persuasion.

Denotation, *n.* See indication; denote.

Denotative, *adj.* See explicit; denote.

Denote, *v.* To be a sign of (the asterisk denotes an amendment). Indicate, depict, signal, portray, symbolize, mark, designate, mean, imply, stand for, equals, represent.

Dénouement, *n.* See outcome, resolution (1), answer.

Denounce, *v.* **1.** To condemn openly (the commission denounced the rejection). Assail, censure, disparage, blacklist, scold, castigate, chastise, rebuke, vilify, curse, upbraid, fulminate against, stigmatize, malign, defame, degrade, reprimand, denigrate, deprecate, excoriate, impugn, berate. **2.** To accuse (he denounced her as an embezzler). Inform against, blame, complain, name, involve, inculpate, arraign, report, charge, incriminate, impeach, implicate. *Ant.* Praise; exonerate.

Denouncement, *n.* See censure, correction (1); denounce.

De novo, *adv.* Anew (hearing de novo). Afresh, a second time, over again, another time.

De novo trial Trying a case again as if the first trial had not taken place.

Dense, *adj.* See coherent (2); blind (1); full.

Dent 1. *n.* A hollow. Pit, cavity, depression, relief, cell, niche. **2.** *v.* See cut (1).

Dental hygienist, *n.* See paraprofessional, assistant, aid (3).

Dentist, *n.* See doctor (1); medicine, medical.

Denude, *v.* See bare (2), strip (2); despoil.

Denunciation, *n.* See censure, obloquy.

Deny, *v.* **1.** To contradict (the witness denied signing the contract). Dispute, traverse, disagree, controvert, dissent, disavow, disclaim, repudiate, disaffirm, gainsay, negate, oppose, rebut, refute. **2.** To refuse to grant or accept (the court denied the motion). Veto, turn down, prohibit, reject, disallow, decline, withhold, forbid. *Ant.* Concede; grant.

Deodorize, *v.* To ventilate. Sanitize, air, disinfect, freshen, fumigate.

Depart, *v.* **1.** To go away from (when he departed, he did not intend to return). Leave, go, set out, set forth, withdraw, quit, recede, escape, exit, disappear, evacuate, vanish, disengage, backtrack, decamp, vacate, fall back, move back, recoil, abscond, take flight, resign, secede, retreat, absent oneself, make oneself scarce, desert, separate, sequestrate, surrender, flee, march off, retire. **2.** To deviate (she departed from her prepared remarks). Digress, diverge, veer, swerve, wander, bend. See also stray (1). *Ant.* Remain; conform.

Departed, *adj.* See decedent.

Department, *n.* A separate unit within the executive branch of the government or within another organization (Department of Defense). Bureau, branch, section, division, subdivision, office, agency, service, commission, chapter; jurisdiction, zone, area, sphere, region, district.

Departmentalize, *v.* See organize (1).

Department store, *n.* See merchant, market.

Departure, *n.* **1.** Deviation from a standard (a departure from his daily routine). Deviation, divergence, change, digression, variance, aberration. **2.** Leaving (a noon departure). Exit, retreat, exodus, retirement, secession, removal, bolting, breakaway, defection, schism, resignation, withdrawal, separation. *Ant.* Conformity; coming.

Depend, *v.* To hinge, rest, rely on, count on, bank on, lean on, be contingent on.

Dependable, *adj.* Trustworthy (a dependable witness). Reliable, faithful, true, principled, honest, responsible, reputable, steady, authoritative, sure, trusted, strong, stable, proven, loyal, upright. See also conscientious. *Ant.* Unreliable.

Dependence, *n.* The state of looking to another for support, care, maintenance,

Dependence

comfort, etc. (a dependence on public assistance). Reliance, attachment, dependency, trust, interdependence, subordination, helplessness, connection, need. *Ant.* Self-sufficiency.

Dependency, *n.* See dependence.

Dependent 1. *n.* One who derives his or her main support from another (she listed him as her dependent). Minor, charge, ward. **2.** *adj.* Deriving existence, support, or direction from another (dependent child). Helpless, minor, weak, immature, trusting, subordinate, parasitic, poor, vulnerable, defenseless, indigent. **3.** *adj.* Contingent (dependent claim). Conditional, qualified, ancillary, corollary, limited, subordinate, restricted, provisional. *Ant.* Principal; independent; unconditional.

Dependent relative revocation When a person revokes a will with the objective of creating a new one, some courts will assume that he or she intended the revocation of the old will to be dependent on the validity of the new will. If for any reason the later will fails, the court will presume that the person would not have revoked the earlier will, which can now be admitted to probate.

Depict, *v.* See describe, delineate.

Depiction, *n.* See description, map, definition.

Deplete, *v.* To reduce or lessen through use, exhaustion, waste, etc. (deplete the inventory). Drain, consume, decrease, exhaust, depreciate, empty, weaken, bleed, purge, evacuate, wear out, bankrupt, impoverish, undermine, "milk," diminish. See also expend (2). *Ant.* Augment.

Depletion, *n.* **1.** A emptying, exhausting, or wasting of assets. See reduction; deplete. **2.** A reduction during the taxable year of oil, gas, or other mineral deposits and reserves as a result of production. An allowance for this reduction through a tax deduction represents a return of capital. See reduction.

Deplorable, *adj.* Lamentable. Miserable, sorry, wretched, ill-fated, unfortunate, awful, reprehensible, distressing, heinous, despicable, outrageous, solemn. See also grievous.

Deplore, *v.* See censure, bemoan.

Deploy, *v.* See employ (2), place (2), array (3).

Depone, *v.* See attest; deposition.

Deponent, *n.* A person who gives testimony under oath, e.g., at a deposition (the deponent refused to answer). Witness, affiant, attester, informant.

Deport, *v.* See oust, expel, bar (4); deportation; exile.

Deportation, *n.* Banishment to a foreign country; the transfer of an alien out of the country (a hearing on the deportation). Exile, eviction, ejectment, expatriation, removal, displacement, purge. See also expulsion. *Ant.* Immigration.

Deportee, *n.* One who has been deported.

Deportment, *n.* See demeanor, behavior.

Depose, *v.* **1.** To make a deposition; to give sworn testimony; to take sworn testimony (they deposed the witness). **2.** To remove a head of state from office against his or her will (the king was deposed). Dethrone, dismiss, impeach, oust, evict, discharge, usurp, fire, unseat.

Deposit, 1. *v.* To place for safekeeping (he deposited his check at Interstate Federal Savings Bank). Entrust, save, commit, invest, store, hoard, secure, accumulate, consign, bank. **2.** *n.* Money given as security for the performance of a contract which is forfeited upon nonperformance (she gave a deposit on the house). Pledge, down payment, partial payment, collateral, installment, earnest money. *Ant.* Withdraw; withdrawal.

Depositary, *n.* The party or institution (e.g., bank) receiving a deposit for safekeeping (the depositary charged a fee). Trustee, fiduciary, guardian, stewart. See also bailee. *Ant.* Depositor.

Deposition, *n.* A pretrial discovery device by which one party questions the other party or a witness for the other party. It usually takes place in the office of one of the lawyers, in the presence of a stenographer or court reporter who transcribes what is said. For most depositions, questions are asked and answered orally. Occasionally, the questions are submitted in writing and answered orally. Sworn statement, testimony, testimony under oath, declaration under oath.

Depositor, *n.* Someone who makes a deposit. See customer, creditor, bailor.

Depository, *n.* The place where a deposit is placed and kept for safekeeping (the depository is insured). Repository, safe, vault, archives, warehouse, treasury. See also bank (2), bailment.

Depot, *n.* Terminal. Station, stop, bus station. See also warehouse.

Depraved, *adj.* Having an inherent deficiency of moral sense and rectitude (depraved mind). Corrupt, perverted, malicious, dissolute, debauched, contaminated, immoral, degenerate, lewd, wicked, vile, vicious, lecherous, base, disreputable, foul, evil, indecent, animal, vulgar, twisted, lascivious, unscrupulous. *Ant.* Wholesome.

Depravity, *n.* See degradation, corruption, cruelty.

Deprecate, *v.* See decry, denounce (1).

Depreciable life The time period over which the depreciable cost of an asset is to be allocated.

Depreciate, *v.* To lower or fall in value or worth (the house depreciated dramatically). Deflate, lessen in value, devalue, decline, deteriorate, cheapen, downgrade, depress, sink, drop, diminish, plunge, dilute, shrink. See also decry. *Ant.* Appreciate.

Depreciation, *n.* A decline in the value of property that is caused by wear or obsolescence. Depreciation is usually measured by a set formula that reflects these factors over a given period of the property's useful life. (He claimed a tax deduction for the depreciation of the building.) Devaluation, reduction, deflation, diminution. *Ant.* Appreciation.

Depredate, *v.* See plunder; depredation.

Depredation, *n.* Plundering or robbing (an act of violent depredation). Pillaging, raid, seizure, piracy, theft, looting, desolation.

Depress, *v.* See demoralize; debase.

Depressant, *n.* See drug.

Depressed, *adj.* Melancholy. Sad, crestfallen, morose, blue, unhappy, dispirited, downhearted, glum, sullen, dejected, despondent, discouraged. See also depressing.

Depressing, *adj.* Sad. Mournful, melancholy, bleak, cheerless, disappointing, discouraging, saddening. See also depressed.

Depression, *n.* **1.** Feelings of dejection, self-depreciation, inadequacy, guilt, etc. (the plaintiff experienced depression after the accident). Low spirits, sadness, hopelessness, despondency, blues, despair, discouragement, desolation, melancholy, gloom, ennui, pessimism. **2.** A period of severe economic stress, often accompanied by poor business conditions, high unemployment, etc. (the Great Depression). Economic decline, recession, decline, stagnation. **3.** See trench, wrinkle (1). *Ant.* Joy; recovery.

Deprivation, *n.* A taking away or confiscation (deprivation of property without due process of law). Seizure, removal, withholding, denial, stripping, loss, foreclosure, sequestration, dispossession, divesting, attachment, commandeering, impounding, usurpation, conversion, stealing, theft. *Ant.* Granting.

Deprive, *v.* See withhold, neglect (1), dispossess.

Deprived, *adj.* See needy.

Deprogram, *v.* To reorient. See counteract.

Depth, *n.* See measure (1); comprehension, ability (2), judgment (2).

Deputation, *n.* See appointment (1).

Depute, *v.* See appoint (1), delegate (1), deputize.

Deputize, *v.* To empower someone to act on behalf of another (the mayor deputized the clerk). Commission, authorize, license, nominate. See also delegate (1), appoint (1), name (2).

Deputy, *n.* A person duly authorized to act on behalf of another (county deputy). Agent, representative, delegate, minister, substitute, appointee, proctor, envoy, second, factor, broker, surrogate, vicar, apostle, intermediary. *Ant.* Principal.

Derail, *v.* See defeat (1), destroy, impede.

Derange, *v.* See disturb.

Deranged, *adj.* Mentally deficient (deranged patient). Mentally disordered, crazy, insane, mentally ill, mad, psychotic, irrational, incompetent, schizophrenic, demented, unbalanced, berserk, frenzied, hysterical, unrestrainable, uncontrollable, raving, disturbed, bizarre. *Ant.* Normal.

Deregulate, *v.* To remove or minimize regulatory restrictions. Decontrol. See liberate; freedom.

Derelict, 1. *adj.* Abandoned (derelict property). Forsaken, discarded, neglected, rejected, deserted, adrift, unwanted, repudiated, castaway, unclaimed, jettisoned, relinquished. **2.** *adj.* Delinquent (the welder was derelict in her duty). Negligent, lax, remiss, irresponsible, neglectful, untrustworthy, thoughtless, indifferent, inconsiderate. See also careless, heedless; neglect (2). **3.** *n.* A vagrant (the derelict was arrested). Outcast, tramp, wanderer, beggar, pariah, drifter, hobo, vagabond, rogue. *Ant.* Claimed; scrupulous; upstanding citizen.

Dereliction, *n.* **1.** Neglect (dereliction of duty). Failure, default, carelessness, evasion, delinquency, omission, laxity, disregard, abandonment, infraction, transgression, breach, nonfeasance, truancy, desertion, inattentiveness. **2.** The gaining of land from the water as a result of the sea's shrinking back below the usual watermark (the dereliction increased the value of her property). See alluvion.

Deride, *v.* See mock (1), disparage, censure (2), slander (2).

De rigueur, *adj.* Required by social custom or fashion. See necessary, mandatory, right (2).

Derision, *n.* See slander (1), censure.

Derisive, *adj.* See derogatory, defamatory, caustic.

Derivation, *n.* See cause (1).

Derivative, *adj.* Coming from another; secondary (derivative liability). Consequential, resulting, subordinate, derived, attributable, ensuing, subsidiary, unoriginal. *Ant.* Original, primary.

Derivative action A suit by a shareholder to enforce a corporate cause of action.

Derivative contraband Property not otherwise illegal but subject to forfeiture because of the use to which it is placed.

Derivative evidence Evidence that is inadmissible because it is derived or spawned from other evidence that was illegally obtained.

Derivative tort Tort liability imposed on one person (e.g., a principal) because of a wrong committed by someone else (e.g., an agent).

Derive, *v.* **1.** To receive from a specified source or origin (the income derived from the business). Originate, stem from, obtain, acquire, extract, secure, trace, harvest, bring forth, realize, cull, glean. See also ensue. **2.** To obtain through reasoning (she derived the theory by reading the cases). Infer, conclude, deduce, gather, develop, formulate, work out, opine, surmise.

Dermal, *adj.* Pertaining to the skin.

Dermatology, *n.* The study of the skin.

Derogate, *v.* See disparage, slander (2); deviate (1).

Derogation, *n.* A partial repeal or abolishing of a law, as by a subsequent act that limits its scope or impairs its ability and force (the statute is in derogation of the common law of libel).

Derogatory, *adj.* Belittling (a derogatory letter). Disparaging, injurious, humiliating, pejorative, unfavorable, demeaning, depreciative, slighting, calumnious, libelous, slanderous, harmful, damaging, vituperative, scurrilous, scandalous, maligning, detracting. See also defamatory. *Ant.* Favorable.

Derringer, *n.* See gun, weapon.

Descend, *v.* **1.** To pass by succession, as when an estate immediately vests by operation of law in the heirs upon the death of the ancestor (the land descended to the children). Pass by operation of law, pass by inheritance, inherit, hand down. **2.** To acquire by a will (the testator provided that the land should descend to his grandchildren). Go to, belong to, transfer, deed, transmit.

Descendant, *n.* Those persons who are in the bloodline of an ancestor, e.g., children, grandchildren, great-grandchildren (the descendants shared equally in her will). Offspring, progeny, posterity, issue, family, successor, heir, kin, lineage, offshoot, seed, scion. *Ant.* Ascendants.

Descent, *n.* **1.** Succession to the ownership of an estate by inheritance (title by descent). Inheritance from ancestors. **2.** Hereditary derivation (he was of Polish descent). Lineage, stock, origin, ancestry, roots, line, breed, birth, pedigree, genealogy, bloodline, forefathers, parentage, source, extraction, heritage.

Describe, *v.* To explain or portray (the court described the events). Narrate, express, set forth, relate, verbalize, recount, depict, delineate, report, chronicle, detail, sketch, communicate, characterize, represent, articulate, specify, annotate, set down, incorporate, elucidate, outline, identify, expound. See also define (2).

Description, *n.* An account of a particular subject (a description of the land in the deed). Portrayal, characterization, profile, definition, representation, version, report, specification, commentary, identification, illustration, delineation, verbalization.

Descriptive, *adj.* Serving or aiming to describe; graphic (a descriptive account of the accident). Clear, illustrative, representative, vivid, detailed, explanatory, imaginative, colorful, particularized, realistic, eloquent, photographic, specific, lifelike, revealing. *Ant.* Vague.

Descry, *v.* See discover (1), notice (2).

Desecrate, *v.* To violate the sanctity of something (desecrate a public monument). Profane, violate, dishonor, abuse, contaminate, cheapen, debase, defile, corrupt, ravage, blaspheme, misuse. See also attack (1). *Ant.* Honor.

Desecration, *n.* See blasphemy; desecrate, defile, debase.

Desegregate, *v.* To end segregation. See commingle, associate (1); desegregation.

Desegregation, *n.* The elimination of segregation on the basis of unacceptable classifications, e.g., race, sex (the court ordered the state to design a plan for the desegregation of its schools). Intermixing, elimination of discrimination. See also integration. *Ant.* Segregation.

Desensitize, *v.* See inure (2).

Desert, *v.,* **desert,** *n., adj.* **1.** *v.* To leave or quit with the intention to cause a permanent separation (he deserted his spouse). Abandon, forsake, withdraw, quit, vacate, flee, repudiate, relinquish, renounce, bail out, depart, abdicate. **2.** *adj.* See barren. **3.** *n.* A wasteland, barren wilderness, dust bowl, Sahara, tundra, prairie, marsh, heath, uncultivated land. *Ant.* Return; fruitful; farmland.

Deserter, *n.* See traitor.

Desertion, *n.* **1.** Abandonment (desertion of a spouse). Leaving, departure, forsaking, withdrawal, flight, defection, evacuation, escape, renunciation. **2.** A ground for divorce. Elements: (a) voluntary separation of the spouses; (b) for an uninterrupted statutory period of time; (c) with the intent not to return; (d) the separation was without the consent of the other spouse; and (e) there was no justification for the separation. **3.** Criminal desertion is the abandonment of a spouse or the willful failure without just cause to provide for the care, protection, or support of a spouse in need. **4.** Without authority, remaining absent from one's military unit or place of duty with the intent to remain away permanently. *Ant.* Reunion.

Deserve, *v.* See merit (2), warrant (2).

Deserved, *adj.* See due (2), fair, proper.

Deserving, *adj.* See meritorious (2).

Design 1. *v.* To form a plan of something (she designed a new computer program). Devise, conceive, fashion, originate, blueprint, invent, nurture, outline, prepare, structure, chart, diagram, map, create, scheme, draft, lay out, build, style, model, graph. **2.** *n.* Purpose or intention (premeditated design). Aim, goal, objective, resolution, target, end, ambition, strategy, resolve, bent, pursuit, determination, inclination, mission, course of action, motive, aspiration, destination, hope. **3.** *n.* See form (1), composition, pattern (1), plan (1), organization (2).

Designate, *v.* To appoint or select (she designated the officer for the command). Nominate, choose, pick, name, commission, license, indicate, point out, identify, mark, elect, assign, authorize, empower, fix, denote, ordain, pinpoint, induct.

Designation, *n.* **1.** A distinctive title or association added to one's name, e.g., Mary Jones, president-elect (do not include the party's designation in the citation). Label, trademark, appellation, pseudonym, alias, classification, token. **2.** An appointment (the designation of the chairperson). Nomination, selection, assignment, election, induction, delegation, authorization, commission, installation, ordination. **3.** Pointing out something (the designation of price and credit terms). Indication, specification, notation.

Designee, *n.* See appointee, nominee (1).

Designer, *n.* See inventor, author.

Designing, *adj.* See deceptive, deceitful.

Desirable, *adj.* See attractive, worthy, marketable.

Desire 1. *v.* To wish (England desired peace). Hope for, want, yearn for, prefer, hunger, need, aspire to, thirst, long for, pine, lust after, crave, fancy, ache, covet. See also intend. **2.** *v.* To request (the board desired additional proof). Solicit, urge, require, call for, appeal for, wish for, pursue, summon, petition. **3.** *v.* To command (if Tom predeceases Bill, I desire the estate to go to Fred). Insist, demand, order. **4.** *n.* A craving or wish (the desire for revenge). Appetite, yearning, ambition, preference, impulse, aspiration, fancy, lust, longing, hunger, affection, attraction, need, covetousness, thirst, passion, eagerness.

Desirous, *adj.* See ambitious, avaricious.

Desist, *v.* To stop (the court ordered the warden to desist from the practice). Stay, cease, refrain, halt, abstain, forbear, give up, renounce, terminate, discontinue, suspend, postpone, quit, curb, decline, abandon, resign, drop, leave off, interrupt, check, freeze. *Ant.* Continue.

Desk, *n.* See table (3); branch.

Desolate, *adj.*, *v.* See barren; depressed; destroy.

Desolation, *n.* See depression; demolition; destroy.

Despair, *n.*, *v.* See depression (1), distress (3), affliction, anguish, anxiety, pain; despond.

Desperado, *n.* See wrongdoer, revolutionary.

Desperate, *adj.* See wild (3), reckless; critical (1); dangerous; grave (2); destitute.

Desperation, *n.* See depression (1), anguish; reckless.

Despicable, *adj.* See deplorable, grievous, base (1, 2).

Despise, *v.* See abhor, disapprove (2); hostility.

Despite, *prep., n.* See although; malice.

Despoil, *v.* To plunder (they despoiled the market). Dispossess, ravage, attack, devour, loot, denude, ransack, pillage, rob, vandalize, damage, seize, confiscate, commandeer. *Ant.* Restore.

Despond, *v.* To lose hope. Despair, be depressed, give up, lose heart.

Despondency, *n.* See depression, anguish, anxiety, pain, affliction.

Despondent, *adj.* Depressed (she was despondent for weeks after the accident). Discouraged, dejected, broken, saddened, dispirited, wretched, unhappy, downcast, beaten, dismal, pessimistic, somber, melancholy, mournful, burdened, gloomy, disconsolate. *Ant.* Optimistic.

Despot, *n.* See tyrant.

Despotism, *n.* See tyranny, coercion, oppression.

Destabilize, *v.* To upset, disorganize, throw into disarray. See disable.

Destination, *n.* **1.** The purpose for which something is set up (the destination of the legacy). Goal, intention, aim, object, plan, motive, raison d'être, target, wish, design, aspiration. **2.** The place to which someone or something is going (the destination is South Boston). Terminal point, end of the line, resting place, finish, last stop, terminus, home.

Destination contract A contract between the buyer and seller according to which the risk of loss passes to the buyer upon the seller's tender of the goods at the destination.

Destine, *v.* See design (1), allot; predetermine.

Destiny, *n.* Fate. Inevitability, karma, lot, fortune, predetermination, kismet. See also ill-fated.

Destitute, *adj.* Not having the necessities of life (she left him destitute). In extreme want, bereft, impoverished, needy, broke, indigent, penniless, poor, defenseless, vulnerable, insolvent, bankrupt, drained, stripped, squalid, helpless. *Ant.* Affluent.

Destitution, *n.* See poverty, privation.

Destroy, *v.* To ruin, injure, or mutilate beyond possibility of use (he destroyed the effectiveness of the system). Extinguish, erase, crush, ravage, waste, annihilate, devastate, exterminate, cancel, demolish, decimate, eradicate, quash, collapse, undo, atomize, deface, incinerate, shatter, destruct, abolish, mangle, raze, consume, abort, liquidate, gut, disintegrate, frustrate, invalidate, desolate, kill, overturn, smash, despoil, plunder, vitiate, abrogate, annul, prevent, rescind, dismantle, nullify, void. *Ant.* Create.

Destroyer, *n.* See vessel.

Destructible, *adj.* Capable of being destroyed (destructible trust). Dissolvable, extinguishable. *Ant.* Indestructible.

Destruction, *n.* The condition of being destroyed (the destruction of taxable property). See mischief; abolition, rescission, elimination, reversal, neutralization, defeat (2), abjuration; destroy.

Destructive, *adj.* See deleterious, bad, violent, wild, gross (1), dangerous, harmful.

Desuetude, *n.* Discontinuation of use (the statute fell into desuetude). Disuse, inaction, dormancy, obsolescence.

Desultory, *adj.* See inconsistent (2).

Detach, *v.* See divide, withdraw, depart (1), sequester.

Detached, *adj.* See dispassionate, neutral, disinterested; divide.

Detachment, *n.* Objectivity. Fair-mindedness, indifference, justice. See also neutrality; division (2), separation; removal, departure.

Detail 1. *v.* To enumerate (the report detailed the deficiencies). List, itemize, specify, delineate, particularize, catalogue, recite, designate, stipulate, name, set forth, cite, mark out, differentiate, disclose, demarcate, circumscribe, characterize, outline, indicate, paint, clarify, illustrate, chronicle, recount, elucidate, picture, depict. See also define (2), develop (2). **2.** *n.* An item (the details of the crime). Particular, feature, fact, part, piece, aspect, factor, point, circumstance, component, respect, element, unit, datum. *Ant.* Generalize; whole.

Detailed, *adj.* See comprehensive, complex (1); intimate (1).

Detain, *v.* **1.** To restrain from proceeding (he was detained by the storm). Check, delay, hinder, retard, stay, stop, inhibit, obstruct, stall, constrain, fetter, suppress, circumscribe, contain. **2.** To hold in custody (the detective detained him in jail). Arrest, confine, jail, quarantine, incarcerate, secure, imprison, isolate. *Ant.* Facilitate; liberate.

Detainee, *n.* One who is detained or confined. See accused, inmate.

Detainer, *n.* **1.** Illegally withholding possession of land or goods from a person; restraint of a person's liberty against his or her will (forcible detainer). Impoundment, detention, sequestration, commandeering. **2.** A notification filed with an institution in which a prisoner is serving a sentence advising the institution that the prisoner is wanted in connection with criminal charges in another jurisdiction (when the sentence was fully served, the inmate was not released because of the detainer in his file).

Detect, *v.* See discover, bare (2); notice (2); note (6).

Detectable, *adj.* See palpable, appreciable.

Detection, *n.* The act of discovery (detection of crime). Ferreting out, exposing, exposure, unmasking, uncovering, observation, unraveling, perception, revelation, disclosure, ascertainment, recognition.

Detective, *n.* Someone whose business is to detect criminals and solve crimes (police detective). Investigator, inspector, officer, agent, sleuth.

Detention, *n.* Keeping back or withholding a person or thing (her detention lasted several hours). Confinement, detainment, custody, imprisonment, jailing, incarceration, captivity, restraint, quarantine, arrest, hindrance, commitment, internment, bondage. See also jail. *Ant.* Liberation.

Deter, *v.* To discourage or stop by fear (does capital punishment deter crime?). Prevent, stop, hinder, dissuade, impede, restrain, check, divert, undermine, disincline, obstruct, daunt, frustrate, stymie, block, avoid, hamstring, repress. *Ant.* Motivate.

Deteriorate, *v.* See decline (2), lapse (2); deterioration.

Deterioration, *n.* Degeneration in the substance of a thing (deterioration of the victim's condition). Decline, downturn, slump, regression, erosion, disintegration, decay, dilapidation, demoralization, debasement, adulteration, worsening, corrosion, aggravation, emaciation. *Ant.* Improvement.

Determinable, *adj.* **1.** Capable of coming to an end upon the happening of a certain contingency (determinable interest). Liable to come to an end, subject to termination, terminable. **2.** Susceptible of being determined or settled (determinable life expectancy). Ascertainable, computable, measurable, verifiable, discernible, knowable, discoverable. *Ant.* Indestructible; inscrutable.

Determinant, *n.* A decisive or determining factor. Cause, main influence, driving force, essential element, impetus.

Determinate, *adj.* Capable of being fixed or ascertained (determinate obligation). Specific, definite, established, confirmed, demonstrated, settled, decided. *Ant.* Indeterminate.

Determinate sentence A sentence to confinement for a fixed period as specified by statute. *Ant.* Indeterminate sentence.

Determination, *n.* **1.** A decision (the agency made an unwise determination). Judgment, conclusion, resolution, adjudication, opinion, appraisal, solution, finding, decree, arbitration, settlement, diagnosis, verdict, resolve, confirmation, verification, discovery, pronouncement, recommendation, declaration. **2.** Resoluteness (she is an attorney with determination). Strength, tenacity, willpower, firmness, motive, purpose, fortitude, perseverance, zeal.

Determine, *v.* See adjudge, decide, define (2), settle; determination (1).

Determined, *adj.* See constant (3), firm, fixed, earnest (2).

Determining, *adj.* See decisive (1).

Deterrent, *n.* Anything that impedes or has a tendency to prevent (the punishment is a deterrent to crime). Hindrance, impediment, barrier, discouragement, restraint, curb, obstruction, check, hurdle, deterrence, restriction, imposition, warning, admonition, inhibition. *Ant.* Encouragement.

Detest, *v.* See abhor, disapprove (2); hostility.

Detestable, *adj.* See repugnant (1), contemptible, deplorable, grievous.

Dethrone, *v.* See depose (2), oust, expel, bar (4).

Detinue, *n.* An action for the recovery of personal property from one who acquired it lawfully but has kept it without right. The plaintiff also seeks damages for the detention.

Detonate, *v.* To explode. Burst, fire. See also discharge (4), shoot.

Detonation, *n.* See eruption.

Detour, *n.* A temporary turning aside from the usual or regular route, course, task, or procedure (the accident occurred while on a detour). Deviation, indirect route, circumvention, digression, departure, bypass, alteration, diversion, drifting, meandering, skirting, straying, changed direction. See also meander.

Detoxify, *v.* To offset the toxic effects. See counteract, offset (2).

Detract, *v.* See diminish; disparage; divert.

Detraction, *n.* See abuse (2); removal.

Detriment, *n.* Any loss or harm suffered to person or property (not having access to the funds was a detriment to the offeree). Drawback, limitation, hindrance, adversity, weakness, damage, disadvantage, injury, misfortune, impairment, handicap, mishap, prejudice, mischief, spoiling, affliction, aggravation, privation, blemish, cost, inconvenience, decay, corrosion, hardship, disturbance, deterioration. *Ant.* Benefit.

Detrimental, *adj.* See deleterious.

Detrimental reliance A loss, disadvantage, or injury suffered by a promisee because of his or her reliance on the promise of the promisor.

Devaluate, *v.* See debilitate, depreciate.

Devaluation, *n.* A reduction in the value of a currency or of a standard monetary unit (the president's devaluation of the dollar).

Devastate, *v.* **1.** To waste or destroy (the storm devastated the area). Spoil, ruin, wreck, level, gut, obliterate, despoil, ravage, lay waste, plunder, strip, annihilate, sack. See also demolish. **2.** To overwhelm (the defeat devastated him). Confound, humiliate, discombobulate, disconcert, crush, conquer, undo, mortify, defeat, overcome. See also destroy. *Ant.* Develop; exhilarate.

Develop, *v.* **1.** To progress or improve (she developed into a fine attorney). Grow, expand, mature, advance, ripen, flower, germinate, improve, train, educate, bloom, flourish, burgeon, shape, blossom, maturate. **2.** To enlarge upon (the supervisor asked him to develop the theory). Amplify, augment, widen, unfold, broaden, expand, reinforce, build, cultivate, detail, elaborate, magnify, extend, promote, perfect, flesh out, strengthen, refine, supplement, add to, enrich, expound, exploit. **3.** To bring into being (she developed a new approach to the case). Institute, create, organize, build, stimulate, bring forth, generate, establish, form, invent, fashion, erect. *Ant.* Regress; stifle; destroy.

Developer, *n.* A planner (the developer of the project). Entrepreneur, promoter, builder, originator, designer, organizer.

Development, *n.* **1.** Advancement (the development of the theory). Progression, evolution, growth, expansion, strengthening, unfolding, improvement, history, flowering, advance, maturation, escalation, enlargement, furtherance, organization, transformation, betterment, increase, ripening. **2.** An event (an unexpected development in the case). Circumstance, phenomenon, upshot, aftermath, result, happening, episode, occurrence, item, incident. *Ant.* Stagnation (1).

Developing, *adj.* See formative, malleable, amenable (2).

Devest, *v.* To take away. See withdraw (1).

Deviant 1. *adj.* Not following accepted norms of society (deviant behavior). Abnormal, nonconforming, deviate, atypical, unnatural, eccentric, unorthodox, aberrant, stray, unconventional, wandering, idiosyncratic, anomalous. **2.** *n.* Someone who violates conventional social and moral standards, often in the area of sexuality (they rejected him because they believed he was a deviant). Pervert, deviate, degenerate, sadist, masochist, fiend, psychopath, maniac. *Ant.* Conventional.

Deviate 1. *v.* To wander or depart (she deviated from her regular duties). Part, veer, alter, diverge, bend, sidetrack, swerve, change direction, vary, clash, meander, drift, detour. See also wander, digress, stray, depart. **2.** *n.* See deviant (2). *Ant.* Adhere (1).

Deviating, *adj.* See nonconforming, irregular, deviant (1).

Deviation, *n.* Departure from established or usual conduct or ideology (a deviation from the trial strategy). Alteration, discrepancy, variance, switching, variation, change of direction, nonobservance, detour, diversion, nonconformity, disparity, aberration, shifting, digression, anomaly, separation. See also deviant; nonconforming. *Ant.* Conformity.

Deviation doctrine A doctrine that allows a variation in the terms of a will or trust where the purposes of the document would be defeated if the variation is not allowed.

Device, *n.* **1.** An invention or contrivance (gambling device). Apparatus, mechanism, instrument, tool, gadget, contraption, implement, equipment, agent, appliance, expedient, creation, invention, makeshift. **2.** A scheme to trick or deceive (a device to increase the damages). Artifice, ruse, strategem, conspiracy, gimmick, subterfuge, maneuver, setup, fraud, hoax, plot, angle, design.

Devil, *n.* See demon, wrongdoer.

Devilish, *adj.* See inhuman, cruel, animal (2), bad (2).

Devil's advocate, *n.* One who takes an opposing view in order to test the validity of a position. See advocate.

Deviltry, *n.* See mischief.

Devious, *adj.* Dishonest (devious behavior). Cunning, crafty, deceptive, deceitful, fraudulent, sly, indirect, calculating, Machiavellian, treacherous, insidious, circuitous, tortuous, evasive, covert, serpentine, not straightforward, plotting, disingenuous, surreptitious, roundabout. *Ant.* Frank.

Devisavit vel non An issue as to whether a document is the will of the testator.

Devise 1. *n.* The gift of land (and sometimes personal property) through a will (a devise of all my lands). Testamentary disposition, bequest, conveyance, transfer, legacy, inheritance. **2.** *v.* To dispose of land or personal property by will (he devised his property to his son). Confer, give, convey, bequeath, will, endow, hand down, assign, allot, leave. **3.** *v.* To invent (she devised a paralegal training program). Plan, create, formulate, organize, arrange, prepare, construct, contrive, compose, originate, design. See also frame (1).

Devisee, *n.* The person to whom real property is devised or given in a will.

Devisor, *n.* The person who devises or gives real property in a will.

Devitalize, *v.* See debilitate, destroy.

Devoid, *adj.* Lacking (the witness was devoid of feelings). Not possessing, without, empty, wanting, deficient, barren, free, missing, denuded, destitute, void, deprived, short, in default, divested, stripped. *Ant.* Full.

Devolution, *n.* The transfer or transition of a right, title, estate, or office from one person to another (devolution of the lease by operation of law). Delivery, succession, assignment, transference, transmission, delegation, conveyance, devise, bequest.

Devolve, *v.* To pass or be transferred from one person to another (her estate devolved to her only heir). Fall on, accrue to, deliver, grant, transfer, bequeath, descend, transmit, convey.

Devote, *v.* **1.** To set apart (she devoted her land to public use). Assign, give, dedicate, allot, consecrate, consign, set aside, allocate, apportion. **2.** To apply or give (he dedicated himself to the case). Direct, utilize, pledge, commit, concentrate, focus, invest, occupy, concern.

Devoted, *adj.* See faithful (1).

Devotee, *n.* See partisan, addict (1), adherent, champion (1).

Devotion, *n.* See worship, love, fidelity, affection, regard (2).

Devour, *v.* See consume (1); defeat (1).

Devout, *adj.* See religious (1), holy, conscientious (2).

Dexterity, *n.* See facility (3), competence, address (4), ability.

Dexterous, *adj.* See apt (3), expert (2), able, active (3).

Diabolic, *adj.* See base (2), bad (2), inhuman, cruel, malicious.

Diagnose, *v.* See assess (1), investigate, canvass (1); medical, doctor, diagnosis.

Diagnosis, *n.* The discovery of the nature of a patient's illness; the determination of the nature of a disease from a study of its symptoms (a negligent diagnosis). Categorization, analysis, problem identification, investigation, scrutiny, appraisal, study. See also assessment (1, 3), medicine, medical, doctor.

Diagram, *n., v.* See map; delineate, describe.

Dialect, *n.* See language.

Dialectic, *adj., n.* See analytic, logical; argument (1), reason (2).

Dialogue, *n.* See colloquium (2), conversation (1), communication (1), conference (1).

Diameter, *n.* See scope, measure (1).

Diametrical, *adj.* See contrary.

Diamond, *n.* See gem.

Diaphragm, *n.* See contraceptive.

Diary, *n.* See record (2); confession, biography.

Diatribe, *n.* See reprimand, censure, obloquy; speech (2), address (3).

Dibs, *n.* See money; claim.

Dice, *n.* See gambling, game.

Dicker, *v.* See negotiate (1), bargain (2), barter.

Dicta, *n.* See dictum, which is the singular form of dicta.

Dictate 1. *v.* To order or instruct what is to be said or done (the founding partner dictated the procedures of the firm). Ordain, prescribe, direct, decree, lay down, promulgate, impose, enjoin, rule, compel, charge, oblige, require. **2.** *n.* A principle or rule (a dictate of conscience). Bidding, mandate, exhortation, edict, code, norm, guideline, precept, commandment, imperative, requirement, stricture, prompting, injunction, inclination, fiat. *Ant.* Submit; suggestion.

Dictator, *n.* See tyrant.

Dictatorial, *adj.* See arbitrary (2), strict (2), absolute.

Dictatorship, *n.* See tyranny.

Diction, *n.* See language.

Dictum, *n.* An observation made by a judge in an opinion that is not essential to the determination of the case; comments that go beyond the facts before the court (you are relying on dictum rather than on the court's holding).

Didactic, *adj.* Educational, instructive, enlightening, pedagogic, teaching, informative, pedantic, edifying, moralizing, preachy.

Die, *v.* To cease to live (she died of the wounds). Expire, pass away, decease, succumb, demise, suffer death, perish, depart. *Ant.* Survive.

Dies, (*Lat.*) A day; days.

Diesel, *n.* See vehicle.

Diet, *n.* The name of the legislature in some countries. See legislature.

Differ, *v.* See contradict, counter.

Difference, *n.* **1.** A state of being unlike (there is a difference between privilege and immunity). Inconsistency, contradiction, dissimilarity, variety, antithesis, nonconformity, discrepancy, imbalance, incongruity, deviation, disparity, unlikeness, variation, disharmony, inequality, separateness, opposition, uniqueness, contrast, departure, divergence, diversity, differentiation, contradistinction. **2.** A dispute (a settlement of differences). Clash, argument, quarrel, controversy, disagreement, discord, dissension, misunderstanding, strife, altercation, contention, feud. *Ant.* Similarity; agreement.

Different, *adj.* Characterized by being unlike (different crimes). Divergent, contrasting, individual, antagonistic, unique, separate, antithetical, discordant, distinct, at variance, at odds, contrary, incompatible, alien, contradictory, disparate, incongruous, atypical, dissimilar, diverse, mismatched, novel, singular, distinctive, unconventional, peculiar. *Ant.* Identical.

Differential, *n.* See disparity, discrepancy.

Differentiate, *v.* See distinguish, discriminate (2), divide.

Difficult, *adj.* **1.** Hard to solve or grasp (a difficult case). Perplexing, involved, abstract, incomprehensible, labyrinthine, obscure, abstruse, convoluted, intricate, troublesome, unaccommodating, complicated, puzzling, unclear, Herculean, bewildering, baffling, problematical, impenetrable, thorny. **2.** Arduous (a difficult task). Demanding, onerous, formidable, exhausting, strenuous, grueling, tough, burdensome, awkward, fatiguing, obstinate, painful, trying, challenging. **3.** Hard to please (a difficult child). Stubborn, fastidious, fussy, unmanageable, wild, rambunctious, uncontrollable. *Ant.* Simple; easy; cooperative.

Difficulty, *n.* See ordeal, emergency, plight (1), affliction, complication, crisis, obstruction, blockade, embarrassment; impede.

Diffident, *adj.* See bashful, quiet (2), insecure (2).

Diffuse 1. *v.* To scatter or disseminate (the gas odor diffused throughout the area). Permeate, distribute, pervade, disperse, radiate, broadcast, circulate. **2.** *adj.* Scattered, rambling (a diffuse presentation). Unfocused, disjointed, wandering, loose, dispersed, broad, pervasive, garrulous, verbose, oblique, roundabout, wordy, endless, long, circuitous, ambiguous. *Ant.* Focus; concentrated.

Diffusion, *n.* See distribution (2), circulation; diffuse.

Dig, *v.*, *n.* See exhume; appreciate (2, 3); slander.

Digest, *n.*, **digest,** *v.* **1.** *n.* An organized summary or abridgement (a digest of the discovery documents). Abstract, capsule, condensation, syllabus, synopsis, outline, précis, restatement, brief, rephrasing, paraphrase, review, collection, consolidation. **2.** *n.* A set of volumes that contain small-paragraph summaries of court opinions, arranged by subject matter (Federal Practice Digest, 3d). **3.** *v.* To condense (the paralegal was asked to digest the documents). Summarize, codify, abstract, brief, catalogue, classify, outline. **4.** *v.* To grasp mentally (the jury digested very little of the testimony). Comprehend, understand, absorb, fathom, incorporate, register, assimilate, appreciate, consider.

Digit, *n.* See number.

Dignified, *adj.* See elevated, formal, grave (3).

Dignify, *v.* See honor (2).

Dignitary, *n.* See chief (1).

Dignity, *n.* Solemnity. Grandeur, stateliness, loftiness. See also honor (3), character (1), worth (1), merit (1); delicacy.

Digress, *v.* To depart from the topic (the memo digressed to a new issue). Deviate, wander, swerve, diverge, stray, go off on a tangent, sidestep, meander, ramble, drift, roam. *Ant.* Remain.

Digression, *n.* See deviation, detour.

Dike, *n.* See blockade, obstruction, wall (1); lesbian.

Dilapidate, *v.* See decompose, dissolve, decline, die; dilapidated.

Dilapidated, *adj.* The condition of ruin or decay (the dilapidated structure collapsed). Worn, damaged, impaired, shabby, decayed, decrepit, crumbling, deteriorated, weathered, battered, marred, run-down. *Ant.* Sturdy.

Dilapidation, *n.* See disrepair; dilapidated.

Dilate, *v.* See augment, extend (1); increase.

Dilatory, *adj.* Tending or intended to cause delay, to gain time, or to put off a decision (dilatory trial tactics). Procrastinating, loitering, stalling, forestalling, dawdling, tardy, deferring, slow, languid, lackadaisical, neglectful. *Ant.* Prompt.

Dilemma, *n.* A circumstance calling for a choice between evenly balanced alternatives (she tried to avoid the dilemma). Predicament, quandary, perplexity, troublesome choice, puzzle, bind, impasse, Hobson's choice, catch 22, knot. See also emergency, mystery, conundrum, plight, complication.

Dilettante, *n.* See amateur, beginner.

Diligence, *n.* **1.** Persistent activity (diligence in trying to locate the missing spouse). Resolution, effort, perseverance, tenacity, industry, determination, insistence, constancy, doggedness, zeal, application, vigor, intentness, steadfastness, exertion. **2.** Prudence, carefulness (due diligence). Heedfulness, attention, vigilance, alertness, watchfulness, caution, observation, inspection, study, foresight, meticulousness, circumspection, assiduity, care. *Ant.* Laziness; negligence.

Diligent, *adj.* Attentive and persistent in doing something (diligent inquiry). Untiring, relentless, active, sedulous, persevering, persistent, concerted, painstaking, zealous, conscientious, industrious, thorough, hardworking, assiduous, indefatigable, exact, steadfast, undaunted, resolute. *Ant.* Indifferent.

Dilute, *v.* To weaken (her comment diluted the intensity of her attack). Decrease, reduce, thin, subtract, minimize, adulterate, water down, temper, mitigate, moderate, alter, qualify, attenuate, cut, pollute. *Ant.* Strengthen.

Dim, *adj., v.* See ambiguous, indefinite, mysterious; obscure; dark; cloud (3).

Dimension, *n.* See spread (1), extent; measure (1).

Diminish, *v.* To lessen or reduce (the supply diminished). Shorten, narrow, decline, abate, wither, lower, contract, remit, moderate, soothe, relinquish, alleviate, relax, assuage, temper, quell, soften, slacken, extenuate, allay, palliate, subside, dwindle, condense, truncate, minimize, abridge, ebb, wane, recede, subtract, depreciate, mitigate, deplete, weaken, shrivel up, dampen, degrade, prune, retard, retrench. *Ant.* Augment.

Diminished capacity or responsibility The lack of capacity to achieve the state of mind needed for the commission of a crime; partial insanity.

Diminishing, *adj.* See dying.

Diminution, *n.* The act or process of taking away or diminishing (diminution in value). Reduction, decrease, alleviation, cutback, abridgement, abatement, curtailment, subsidence, contraction, attrition, weakening, shrinking, minimizing, recession. See also decline (3). *Ant.* Inflation.

Din, *n.* See noise, commotion; eruption.

Dine, *v.* See eat; restaurant, inn; entertain (2).

Diner, *n.* See restaurant, inn; merchant.

Dingbat, *n.* See boor, idiot.

Dinghy, *n.* A small boat. See vessel (1).

Dingy, *adj.* See dark, dismal, dilapidated; mysterious.

Dinner, *n.* See banquet.

Diocese, *n.* See district, jurisdiction (2); religion.

Dip, *v.* See water (2).

Diploma, *n.* See certificate.

Diplomacy, *n.* See discretion (3), prudence.

Diplomat, *n.* See delegate (2), intermediary.

Diplomatic, *adj.* See judicious, cautious, prudent, discreet, civil (3).

Diplomatic immunity, *n.* Exemption from legal process given to designated diplomats in foreign countries. See immunity.

Dipsomania, *n.* A mental disease characterized by an uncontrollable desire for intoxicating liquor.

Dire, *adj.* See grievous, appalling, awesome, bad, dismal.

Direct 1. *v.* To command (the court directed the practice to cease). Order, decree, enjoin, warrant, charge, prescribe, demand, dictate. **2.** *v.* To regulate or manage (the managing partner directed the firm's finances). Supervise, govern, superintend, regulate, engineer, administer, orchestrate, oversee, dominate, head, preside, rule, operate. **3.** *v.* To aim or cause to move in a certain direction (the lawyer directed the jury's attention to the chart). Point, show, indicate, steer, navigate, designate, escort, channel, guide. **4.** *adj.* Without interruption; immediate (direct cause). Unbroken, continuous, uninterrupted, proximate, straight, undeviating, unswerving, near, connected. See also immediate (2). **5.** *adj.* Personal (direct confrontation). Face-to-face, firsthand, head-on, unmediated. **6.** *adj.* Honest, straightforward (a direct response). Blunt, sincere, clear, candid, plain, explicit, aboveboard, outspoken, frank, unpretentious, pointed, unreserved, truthful, simple, precise, absolute, unqualified, forthright, categorical, ingenious, unambiguous. See also honest, open. *Ant.* Obey; follow; scatter; indirect; secondhand; vague.

Direct attack To seek to have a judgment or decree corrected, vacated, or enjoined in a proceeding instituted for this specific purpose, e.g., an appeal. *Ant.* Collateral attack.

Direct cause That which sets in motion a chain of events that brings about a result without the intervention of any actively operating force from a new or independent source; that without which the injury would not have happened. See cause.

Direct contempt A contempt committed in the presence of the court or so near the court as to interrupt its proceedings. See contempt.

Directed verdict In a case in which the party with the burden of proof has failed to present a prima facie case, the trial judge may order the entry of a verdict without allowing the jury to consider it. See verdict, judgment.

Direct estoppel A form of estoppel by judgment where the issue has actually been litigated and determined in an action between the same parties based on the same cause of action. See estoppel.

Direct evidence Evidence that, if believed, proves the existence of the fact in issue without using any inferences or presumptions; testimony from a witness who actually saw, heard, or touched the matter in question. See evidence. *Ant.* Circumstantial evidence.

Direct examination The first interrogation or questioning of a witness by the party who has called the witness. See examination.

Direction, *n.* **1.** An order or command (the court gave the jury detailed directions). Instruction, regulation, prescription, charge, injunction, demand, commandment, rule, directive, guideline, dictate, recipe, mandate, fiat, warrant, edict. **2.** Administration (legal matters were handled under the direction of the general counsel). Guidance, management, surveillance, supervision, auspices, jurisdiction, office, governorship, leadership, superintendence, oversight, eye, navigation, tutelage, protection. **3.** The line of development (the judge was irritated by the direction of the questioning). Course, aim, tendency, route, path, bent, track, tenor, approach, pattern, inclination, leaning, map, outline, blueprint, trend, scheme, fashion.

Directive, *n.* See direction (1), order (1).

Direct line A line of descent traced through those persons who are related to each other directly as descendants or ascendants. See descent.

Direct loss A loss resulting immediately and proximately from the occurrence and not remotely from some of the consequences or effects thereof. See loss, detriment.

Director, *n.* One who directs, regulates, guides, or orders (the director of the agency). Manager, superintendent, supervisor, boss, leader, chief administrative officer, executive, principal, governor, foreman, proctor, overseer, organizer, curator, chairperson, master, commander, marshal, regent, dean, president, ruler. *Ant.* Follower.

Directorate, *n.* See board (1).

Directory 1. *adj.* A provision in a statute that does not relate to the essence of the statute. Noncompliance with a directory provision does not invalidate a transaction or action if there is compliance with the other parts of the statute. (The 20-day filing period in the statute is directory.) **2.** *n.* A book containing names, addresses, occupations, organizations, phone numbers, etc. (phone directory). List, catalogue, schedule, docket, index, register, inventory, enumeration. See also record.

Direct tax A tax that is imposed directly on property (rather than on a right or privilege) according to its value. Property tax, ad valorem tax. See tax.

Dirge, *n.* A funeral song. Requiem, elegy, lament.

Dirigible, *n.* See aircraft, vehicle.

Dirk, *n.* See weapon.

Dirt, *n.* Grime. Filth, dust, stain, ashes, slime, mud, smut, garbage, muck, soot. See also pollution; pollute; obscene.

Dirty, *adj.* Unclean. Grimy, muddy, foul, polluted, begrimed, spotted. See also filthy, obscene; pollution.

Disability, *n.* **1.** The lack of legal capacity to perform an act (the disability prevented him from testifying). Disqualification, incapacity, unfitness, impediment, inability, powerlessness, lack of competence, disadvantage, impotence. **2.** A disabled condition (permanent disability in her right arm). Handicap, infirmity, affliction, defect, sickness, weakness, illness, paralysis, disorder, ailment, malady, incapacitation, impairment. *Ant.* Qualification, advantage; strength.

Disable, *v.* To render incapable of effective action (the court's order disabled the board). Cripple, incapacitate, impair, hinder, weaken, bar, sabotage, cancel, disqualify, injure, mutilate, paralyze, annul, neutralize, dismantle, invalidate, render powerless, nullify, emasculate, disenfranchise, debilitate, undermine, inactivate, destabilize, tax, disarm. *Ant.* Fortify.

Disabled, *adj.* See infirm, ill, frail, weak, senile; defective; disable.

Disabuse, *v.* See clarify.

Disadvantage 1. *n.* A drawback or infirmity (the loss of the contract option was a disadvantage). Hindrance, loss, injury, harm, prejudice, weakness, handicap,

Disadvantage

encumbrance, detriment, nuisance, deprivation, impediment, imposition, adversity, circumstance, obstacle, burden, embarrassment, trouble, flaw, imperfection, restriction, setback, barrier, fault, damage, inconvenience, stumbling block, liability. **2.** *v.* To subject to a burden (the ruling disadvantaged their case). Restrict, injure, thwart, interfere, weaken, cripple, encumber, impede, limit, prejudice, frustrate, inhibit, hamper. *Ant.* Asset; benefit.

Disadvantaged, *adj.* See destitute; disadvantage.

Disadvantageous, *adj.* See deleterious, difficult (2).

Disaffected, *adj.* Estranged. Dissatisfied, bitter, distant, unfriendly, discontented, torn, vindictive. See also angry, hostile; alienate (2).

Disaffirm, *v.* To repudiate; to revoke consent (the minor disaffirmed her contract). Disavow, reverse, recant, disclaim, negate, abnegate, disregard, overrule, vacate, retract, disown, withdraw, rescind, void, countermand, veto, forswear, renege, relinquish, nullify, renounce. See also abjure. *Ant.* Ratify.

Disaffirmance, *n.* The refusal to accept the legal consequences of one's acts (the minor's disaffirmance of his contract).

Disagree, *v.* See contradict, counter, argue, disapprove, rebut.

Disagreeable, *adj.* See offensive, odious.

Disagreement, *n.* **1.** The lack of uniformity of views (disagreement among the justices). Difference of opinion, conflict, variance, disharmony, dissension, incompatibility, diversity, discrepancy, split, dissimilarity, controversy, discord. **2.** A quarrel (the lawyers were having a disagreement). Argument, contention, altercation, misunderstanding, feud, debate, fight, polemic, strife. *Ant.* Harmony; agreement.

Disallow, *v.* To refuse to allow (the court disallowed the claim). Deny, reject, veto, set aside, forbid, abrogate, spurn, disaffirm, repudiate, disapprove, rebuff, negate, oppose, object. *Ant.* Grant.

Disappear, *v.* To fade away. Vanish, recede, evaporate, fade, dissolve, melt. See also depart, withdraw (1).

Disappearance, *n.* See departure (2); disappear.

Disappoint, *v.* See frustrate, fail.

Disappointment, *n.* See failure, defeat (2).

Disapproval, *n.* See censure, objection; disapprove, reprimand.

Disapprove, *v.* **1.** To pass unfavorable judgment upon (the motion was disapproved). Reject, disallow, refuse to confirm, refuse to ratify, deny, veto, negate, rebuff, resist, repel, turn down, withhold consent, repudiate, disclaim, oppose, take exception. **2.** To criticize (the court disapproved of the lawyer's tactic). Censure, castigate, disfavor, scold, condemn, dislike, denounce, discountenance, rebuke, impeach, object to, admonish, disparage, blame, decry, upbraid, revile, malign, protest, berate, chide. *Ant.* Allow; applaud.

Disarm, *v.* See incapacitate, disable, withdraw (1), dissolve.

Disarmament, *n.* Arms reduction. Demobilization, arms control, demilitarization.

Disarming, *adj.* See attractive, irresistible.

Disarrange, *v.* See disturb.

Disarray, *n.* See disorder (1).

Disassemble, *v.* See part (3), divide.

Disassociate, *v.* See disavow, divide (1).

Disaster, *n.* An event of considerable misfortune (the disaster caused by his negligence). Calamity, tragedy, fiasco, catastrophe, cataclysm, mishap, wreck, adversity, accident, blow, affliction, casualty, ravage, collapse, setback, misadventure, distress, failure, holocaust. *Ant.* Blessing.

Disastrous, *adj.* See bad (4), deleterious, adverse (2).

Disavow, *v.* To repudiate; to deny responsibility (she disavowed the actions of her agent). Reject, renounce, veto, disaffirm, deny, rescind, shun, relinquish, abjure, contradict, divorce oneself from, gainsay, disown, decline, invalidate, disassociate, refuse to accept, forswear. *Ant.* Acknowledge.

Disband, *v.* See dissolve, dismiss (3), divide (3), withdraw (1).

Disbar, *v.* To revoke an attorney's license to practice law (she was disbarred after her conviction for robbery). Divest, disqualify, expel, suspend, invalidate, void, rescind, remove. *Ant.* Swear in.

Disbarment, *n.* See expulsion, disbar.

Disbelief, *n.* See doubt (2).

Disbelieve, *v.* See doubt (1).

Disburden, *v.* See liberate, relieve (1).

Disburse, *v.* See expend, pay (2); disbursement.

Disbursement, *n.* The act of paying out money; expenditure (the treasurer did not authorize the disbursement). Payment, spending, costs, outlay, expense, money disbursed, money expended, remittance, issuance, fees. *Ant.* Receipt.

Discard, *v.* See abandon (1), reject (1), jettison.

Discern, *v.* See discover (1), notice (2), apprehend, recognize, comprehend (1).

Discernible, *adj.* See determinable (2); intelligible, comprehensible.

Discerning, *adj.* See acute (1), judicious, discreet, able.

Discernment, *n.* See apprehension (1), discovery (2).

Discharge, *v.*, **discharge,** *n.* **1.** *v.* To relieve of an obligation (discharge them of the debt). Cancel, extinguish, rescind, avoid, abolish, release, abrogate, negate, forgive, nullify, disencumber, invalidate, revoke, quash, excuse, absolve, exempt. **2.** *v.* To fulfill an obligation (she discharged her responsibilities under the contract). Accomplish, execute, effect, carry out, perform, observe, achieve, meet, enforce, implement, settle, effectuate, pay, defray, comply, go through with, honor, satisfy, redeem, amortize, liquidate, square, realize, consummate, complete, transact, conclude. **3.** *v.* To liberate (she was discharged from prison). Set free, release, allow out, emancipate, turn loose, extricate, absolve, acquit, clear, exonerate, exempt, reprieve, manumit, enfranchise, deliver, parole. **4.** *v.* To shoot (he discharged the gun). Detonate, fire, fulminate, ignite, explode, set off, activate, trigger, bombard, launch, burst. See also shoot. **5.** *v.* To release from employment or service (discharged for insubordination). Dismiss, oust, evict, displace, terminate, unseat, remove, "sack," lay off, give notice, give a pink slip, fire, "axe," "bounce," cashier, disbar, suspend, depose, retire, release, expel. **6.** *n.* See eruption. *Ant.* Charge; renege; imprison; deactivate; hire.

Discharge in bankruptcy The release of a bankrupt from all nonexcepted debts that are provable in a bankruptcy proceeding.

Dischargeable claim A claim against the bankrupt that, if properly scheduled, is barred when the latter receives an adjudication of bankruptcy.

Disciple, *n.* See partisan (1), champion (1), adherent.

Disciplinarian, *n.* Taskmaster. Sergeant, stickler, martinet; authoritarian. See also strict (2), arbitrary.

Disciplinary, *adj.* Involving discipline (disciplinary proceedings against the lawyer). Punitive, corrective, regulatory, penal. *Ant.* Honorary.

Discipline 1. *n.* Strict training (military discipline). Instruction, practice, exercise, preparation, schooling, conditioning, stoicism, devotion, fidelity, will power, self-denial, obedience, compliance, malleability, rehearsal, teaching, coaching, development, self-control, self-restraint, regimen, drills, habit, order, indoctrination, method, routine, submissiveness, procedure. **2.** *n.* Punishment (the imposition of discipline in prison). Penalty, correction, chastisement, castigation, penance, reprimand, infliction, reproof, crackdown, criticism, amercement, deprivation, retribution, forfeiture. **3.** *n.* Branch of knowledge (she entered the discipline of law). Field of study, doctrine, branch, area, curriculum, course, teaching, education. **4.** *v.* To train or develop (she disciplined herself to study for long hours). Educate, indoctrinate, nurture, accustom, condition, drill, coach, habituate, prepare, qualify, govern, harden, tutor, practice, break in, direct, guide, school, prime, enlighten, edify, inculcate, oversee, regulate, control, manage, supervise.

Disclaim, *v.* See disavow, disaffirm; disclaimer.

Disclaimer, *n.* The repudiation of a claim, power, or obligation (disclaimer of liability). Disavowal, revocation, relinquishment, abandonment, renunciation, denial, rejection, renouncement, refusal, refusal to accept, negation, disowning, retraction, discarding, abjuration. *Ant.* Acceptance.

Disclose, *v.* To bring into view by uncovering (he disclosed the evidence). Expose, make known, lay bare, reveal, free from secrecy, divulge, publish, communicate, unveil, utter, air, broadcast, unmask, exhibit, promulgate, disseminate, voice, circulate, report, announce, present, notify, apprise, bring to light, impart, tell, betray, inform. *Ant.* Conceal.

Disclosure, *n.* The act of revealing that which is secret or not fully understood (the disclosure of the fraud). Revelation, communication, exposure, uncovering, announcement, acknowledgment, discovery, confession, publication, presentation, declaration, assertion, report, exposé, divulgence, profession, recitation, bringing to light, admission, enlightenment, proclamation, testimony. *Ant.* Concealment.

Disco, *n.* See amusement, entertainment; music.

Discolor, *v.* See mar.

Discombobulate, *v.* See devastate (2), outrage (2), disturb.

Discomfort, *n.* See anxiety, anguish, pain, disease.

Discommode, *v.* See burden (3), disturb, harass, outrage (2).

Discompose, *v.* See disturb, confuse, outrage (2).

Disconcert, *v.* See confuse, disturb, harass, outrage (2).

Disconnect, *v.* See dislocate, divide.

Disconnected, *adj.* See incoherent, inconsistent, irrational.

Disconsolate, *adj.* See depressed, depressing, despondent, destitute.

Discontent, *n.* See dissatisfaction.

Discontented, *adj.* See despondent, depressed, angry.

Discontinuance, *n.* Ending; causing to cease (discontinuance of the action by the plaintiff). Giving up, ceasing to use, leaving off, termination, abandonment, cessation, discontinuation, phaseout, cancellation, defeasance, suspension, withdrawal, dismissal, interruption, remission. See also dissolution. *Ant.* Commencement.

Discontinuation, *n.* See cessation, conclusion (1), rescission, expiration, discontinuance.

Discontinue, *v.* See dissolve, end (2).

Discontinuity, *n.* See interruption, breach, separation (2).

Discord, *n.* See conflict (1), dissent, argument (2), disagreement.

Discordant, *adj.* See inconsistent, adverse (1), contentious.

Discotheque, *n.* See amusement, entertainment, music; inn; merchant.

Discount 1. *n.* An allowance or deduction from the original price or debt (a 30% discount). Reduction, break, abatement, concession, markdown, rebate, cutback. **2.** *v.* To disregard or minimize (we discounted the minor's exaggerated account of the accident). Discredit, gloss over, distrust, doubt, suspect, belittle, ignore, detract, deflate, scale down. *Ant.* Increase; heed.

Discount rate A percentage of the face amount of commercial paper (e.g., note) which a holder pays when he or she transfers the paper to a financial institution for cash or credit; the rate charged for discounting a loan.

Discourage, *v.* To dishearten. Depress, dispirit, blunt, dismay, deject. See also deter, dissuade.

Discouraged, *adj.* See depressed, despondent.

Discouragement, *n.* See depression; obstruction.

Discourse, *n.* See conversation, communication, speech (2).

Discourteous, *adj.* See rude, hostile.

Discourtesy, *n.* Insolence. Incivility, irreverence, affront, slight, indignity, neglect, disrespect, vulgarity. See arrogance; rude.

Discover, *v.* **1.** To uncover that which was hidden, concealed, or unknown (he discovered the fraud after the work was done). Detect, ascertain, locate, solve, unearth, recognize, reveal, discern, come upon, unravel, expose, deduce, understand, perceive, diagnose, determine. **2.** To invent (discover a cure). Design, pioneer, originate, innovate. *Ant.* Conceal (1).

Discovered peril doctrine An exception to the rule of contributory negligence. Elements: (a) an exposed condition brought about by the negligence of the plaintiff, (b) the actual discovery by the defendant of the plaintiff's perilous situation in time to have averted the injury by the use of means commensurate with the defendant's own safety, (c) the failure to use such means.

Discovery, *n.* **1.** Pretrial devices that can be used by a party to obtain information about a suit from the other side in order to assist in preparing for the trial, e.g., interrogatories, deposition (discovery lasted 3 months). **2.** The ascertainment of that which was previously unknown (discovery of the defect). Identification, exposure, disclosure, detection, unearthing, perception, revelation, uncovering, realization, inspection, investigation. **3.** An invention (discovery of a cure). Find, breakthrough, innovation; eureka.

Discovery rule A cause of action for medical malpractice will not accrue until the patient knows, or in the exercise of reasonable diligence should have known, of the alleged malpractice.

Discredit, *v.* To destroy or impair the credibility of a person (she tried to discredit the witness). Impeach, disparage, weaken, downgrade, tarnish, shame, malign, denigrate, cast aspersions, detract, disprove, censure, humiliate, puncture, demean, degrade, undermine, disgrace, challenge, mock, stigmatize, injure. See also defame. *Ant.* Support.

Discreditable, *adj.* See blameworthy, inexcusable, immoral, illicit, improper, grievous (1).

Discreet, *adj.* Prudent; careful judgment (a discreet inquiry into the circumstances of the death). Circumspect, cautious, diplomatic, polite, alert, discretionary, thoughtful, watchful, guarded, sensitive, intelligent, attentive, strategic. See also judicious, prudent. *Ant.* Precipitate.

Discrepancy, *n.* A difference between two things that ought to be identical (a discrepancy between the testimony of the two witnesses). Variance, nonconformity, inconsistency, dissimilarity, incongruity, gap, discordance, deviation, conflict, split, clash, disharmony, irreconcilability, contradiction, incompatibility, contrast, disparity, differential. *Ant.* Conformity.

Discrete, *adj.* Separate (discrete items of evidence). Distinct, unconnected, different, detached, segregated, individual, distinguished. *Ant.* Linked.

Discretion, *n.* **1.** The power or right to act according to the dictates of one's own judgment and conscience (the board has the discretion to make an exception). Right to choose, freedom, the power to make an independent decision. See also administrative discretion. **2.** Individual preference (the supervisor told her employee to use his discretion). Choice, will, desire, option, selection, decision, self-determination, predilection, inclination. **3.** Good judgment; diplomacy (unfortunately, poor discretion was used). Prudence, tact, maturity, caution, sagacity, moderation, restraint, judgment, discrimination, wisdom, sense, polish, savoir faire, suavity, finesse, delicacy, sensibility, urbanity, subtlety, circumspection, grace, acumen, expertness, cleverness, insight, presence of mind, reasoning, taste, competence, resourcefulness, refinement, common sense, responsibility.

Discretionary, *adj.* Resolved by one's discretion (discretionary review). Optional, volitional, elective, not imperative, nonobligatory, free, not compulsory. See also discreet. *Ant.* Mandatory.

Discriminate, *v.* **1.** To make decisions on the basis of prejudice (the company discriminated against minorities). Show preferences, demonstrate bias, show bias, show partiality, treat unfairly, disenfranchise, segregate, prejudge, display favoritism, be partial, predispose. **2.** To make distinctions (you must discriminate between the two doctrines). Differentiate, separate, compare, sift, assess, set apart, draw a distinction, distinguish, classify, individualize, label, contrast. *Ant.* Be impartial; unite.

Discriminating, *adj.* See acute (1), cultivated; particular (2), precise.

Discrimination, *n.* **1.** Unfair treatment or denial of privileges to persons because of their sex, age, race, nationality, or religion (employment discrimination). Bigotry, prejudice on the basis of class, favoritism, intolerance, racism, sexism, ageism, bias, inequality, chauvinism, injustice, partiality. **2.** See discretion (3). *Ant.* Impartiality; indiscretion.

Discuss, *v.* See converse (1), communicate.

Discussion, *n.* See conversation, communication.

Disdain, *n., v.* See contempt; disparage.

Disdainful, *adj.* See contemptuous.

Disease, *n.* Deviation from the healthy or normal condition of any of the functions or tissues of the body (occupational disease). Sickness, infirmity, disorder, illness, affliction, weakness, distemper, ill health, ailment, defect, handicap, disability, breakdown, malady, abnormality, plague, complaint, derangement, attack, discomfort, delicate constitution, delicate condition, debility, suffering, malaise, nausea, pathology, frailty, attack, cancer, cholera, virus, "bug," syndrome. *Ant.* Health.

Disembark, *v.* See alight.

Disenchanted, *adj.* See disillusioned.

Disencumber, *v.* See discharge (1), clear (5), facilitate.

Disenfranchise, *v.* See dispossess, disqualify, withhold; disinherit.

Disenfranchisement, *n.* See deprivation, slavery, bondage.

Disengage, *v.* See dissolve, divide (1), liberate.

Disentangle, *v.* See clarify; divide (1), liberate, clear (5).

Disestablish, *v.* See annul.

Disfavor, *n.* See disgrace.

Disfigure, *v.* See mar, mutilate, injure; disfigurement.

Disfigurement, *n.* Impairment of or injury to the beauty, symmetry, or appearance of a person or thing so as to render the external form unsightly, misshapen, or imperfect (the accident caused permanent disfigurement). Scar, damage, defacement, deformity, destruction, distortion. See also mar, mutilate, injure. *Ant.* Beautification.

Disfranchise, *v.* See dispossess, withhold.

Disgorge, *v.* To vomit, throw up, spit out, heave, "puke," discharge, "barf," expel, ejaculate. See also relinquish, return.

Disgrace, *n.* Shame, dishonor (damages for the disgrace caused by the libel). Embarrassment, humiliation, scandal, mortification, degradation, odium, discredit, condemnation, opprobrium, blemish, disfavor, disparagement, indignity, notoriety, stain, smear, disrepute, ignominy, onus, infamy, scar, reproach, abasement, culpability, defamation, disesteem, taint, aspersion, censure, vilification, baseness, demoralization, disapproval, ill repute, slur, revilement, invective, belittlement, downgrading, ridicule, stigma. *Ant.* Honor.

Disgraceful, *adj.* See repugnant (1), odious, contemptible, offensive, appalling, repulsive, bad (2).

Disguise 1. *v.* To change the appearance of something, usually for concealment (an attempt to disguise his real intent). Camouflage, cloak, mask, counterfeit, falsify, misrepresent, veil, garb, shroud, gloss over, cover, cover up, hide, dissemble, feign, screen, deceive, obscure, masquerade, distort, muffle. **2.** *n.* Something worn for the purpose of concealment (a poor disguise). Facade, screen, artifice, deception, camouflage, guise, veneer, ruse, subterfuge, illusion, pretense, smoke screen, masquerade, front, covering, pose, costume.

Disgust, *v., n.* See revolt (2), displease; contempt (2).

Disgusting, *adj.* See odious, offensive, repugnant, repulsive.

Disharmony, *n.* See discrepancy, conflict (1), disagreement, argument (2).

Dishearten, *v.* See discourage.

Disheveled, *adj.* Slovenly. Untidy, confused, dirty, unkept, disarranged, sloppy, disorderly. See also wild (3), ragged.

Dishonest, *adj.* Characterized by cheating and a lack of integrity (a dishonest answer). False, unscrupulous, corrupt, fraudulent, insidious, untruthful, untrustworthy, phony, illegal, shameless, deceitful, deceiving, deceptive, unprincipled, immoral, scheming, discreditable, perfidious, underhanded, unreliable, specious, spurious, conniving, cunning, disreputable, crooked, disingenuous, misleading, knavish, counterfeit, thievish, fallacious, meretricious, unethical, two-faced, devious, dishonorable, double-dealing, mendacious, hypocritical, surreptitious, perjured. *Ant.* Principled.

Dishonesty, *n.* See fraud, deception; dishonest.

Dishonor 1. *v.* To refuse to accept or pay a draft or to refuse to pay a promissory note when duly presented (the bank dishonored the check). **2.** *n.* Shame (the dishonor of the conviction for fraud). Disgrace, scorn, degredation, discredit, humiliation, downfall, aspersion, contumely, indignity, scandal, notoriety, stigma, reproach, mortification, odium, stain, insult, vilification, blemish, disrepute, opprobrium, derogation, obloquy, abasement, condemnation, disfavor, infamy, ridicule. **3.** *v.* To degrade (he dishonored his profession). Tarnish, smear, discredit, bring shame upon, shame, disgrace, debauch, defile, stigmatize, desecrate, malign, blacken, sully, stain, insult, injure, abuse, defame, libel, slander, denigrate. *Ant.* Honor; respect.

Dishonorable, *adj.* See corrupt, disloyal, dishonest, repugnant (1), odious.

Disillusioned, *adj.* Disenchanted. Disabused, undeceived, informed, enlightened, cynical. See also dissuade.

Disincentive, *n.* See deterrent.

Disinclination, *n.* See opposition, hostility.

Disinclined, *adj.* Reluctant. Unwilling, opposed. See hostile, adverse.

Disinfect, *v.* To sterilize. Sanitize, deodorize, clean. See also bathe, fumigate.

Disinformation, *n.* See fraud; misrepresent.

Disingenuous, *adj.* See deceptive, deceitful, lying, collusive, corrupt (1), false (2), artificial (2), feigned.

Disinherit, *v.* To deprive someone of the right to inherit something (the owner disinherited his nephew). Cut off, cut out, forsake, abandon, repudiate, renounce, deprive. *Ant.* Bestow.

Disintegrate, *v.* See dissolve.

Disintegration, *n.* See dissolution.

Disinter, *v.* To take a body out of the grave (the state ordered the body disinterred for an autopsy). Exhume, disinhume, unbury, untomb, disentomb, dig up, remove. *Ant.* Inter.

Disinterest, *n.* See indifference; ennui; disinterested.

Disinterested, *adj.* Having nothing to gain or lose as a result of the transaction or proceeding (disinterested witness). Impartial, fair, not biased, not prejudiced, detached, free from self-interest, evenhanded, open-minded, uninvolved, nonpartisan, neutral, equitable, impersonal, dispassionate, objective. *Ant.* Biased.

Disjoin, *v.* See divide (1).

Disjointed, *adj.* See incoherent; split (3).

Disjunctive, *adj.* Designating a conjunction (such as "or," "either," "neither," "nor," "but," "although") that denotes an alternative contrast or opposition between the ideas it connects (a disjunctive allegation that the defendant stole the car or caused it to be stolen).

Dislike, *v., n.* See disapprove (2), abhor, revolt (2); opposition, hostility.

Dislocate, *v.* **1.** To put out of proper place (dislocate her shoulder). Displace, disconnect, unhinge, separate, disjoin. **2.** To disorganize (the strike dislocated the functions of the firm). Confound, scatter, disturb, complicate, upset, derail. *Ant.* Join; order.

Dislodge, *v.* See oust.

Disloyal, *adj.* Not true to; unfaithful (a disloyal employee). False, untrustworthy, dishonorable, treacherous, deceitful, two-faced, perfidious, unpatriotic, treasonable, faithless, disaffected, apostate, untrue, traitorous, fickle, insincere, rebellious, subversive, inconstant, seditious, recreant, undutiful. See also corrupt. *Ant.* Constant.

Disloyalty, *n.* See betrayal, mutiny.

Dismal, *adj.* Dreary. Mournful, cheerless, gloomy, grim, discouraging, depressing, dull, miserable, flat, monotonous, destitute, melancholy, barren, sad, somber, morose, dark, austere, morbid. See also abandoned (1), depressed, despondent. *Ant.* Bright.

Dismantle, *v.* See destroy, part (3), divide.

Dismay, *v.* See discourage, intimidate, disturb, outrage (2).

Dismember, *v.* See mutilate, mar, divide (1), injure.

Dismiss, *v.* **1.** To dispose of an action, suit, or motion without a trial on the issues involved (the judge dismissed the case after the defendant failed to appear). Conclude, discontinue, terminate, quash. **2.** To discharge (the boss dismissed him for insubordination). Let go, fire, suspend, dispossess, oust, eject, unseat, ban, exile, force out, remove, expel, displace, purge, "bounce," cashier, banish. **3.** To send away (the delegates were dismissed). Disperse, excuse, dissolve, disband, adjourn, liberate, free, eject. **4.** To reject (the police dismissed the rumor). Disregard, brush aside, ignore, disavow, write off, pay no attention to, eliminate, discard. *Ant.* Hear; hire; convene; embrace.

Dismissal, *n.* **1.** An order or judgment disposing of an action, suit, or motion without a trial of the issues involved (the plaintiff sought a voluntary dismissal of her action). Termination, nonsuit, discontinuance, quashing, disposal. **2.** A discharge (a dismissal for alleged incompetence). Ouster, firing, expulsion, displacement, pink slip, "walking papers," laying off, release, severance, elimination.

Dismissal without prejudice A dismissal without prejudice to the right of the complainant to sue again on the same cause of action.

Dismissal with prejudice An adjudication on the merits; a final disposition barring the right to bring an action on the same cause of action.

Dismount, *v.* See alight.

Disobedience, *n.* See insubordination, betrayal, mutiny, defiance; disobedient.

Disobedient, *adj.* Insubordinate or ungovernable (disobedient child). Defiant, wayward, obstinate, rebellious, unmanageable, willful, recalcitrant, disorderly, mischievous, remiss, unruly, unsubmissive, mutinous, incorrigible, noncompliant, intractable, contrary, stubborn, refractory, obstreperous, headstrong, delinquent, wild, disrespectful, undisciplined, hostile, uncooperative, irresponsible, riotous, obdurate, neglectful. *Ant.* Submissive.

Disobey, *v.* See challenge (1), resist, confront, disregard; break (1), encroach, interfere, attack (1), assault (3); disobedient.

Disorder, *n.* **1.** Turbulent or riotous behavior (the disorder following the strike). Breach of the peace, commotion, chaos, confusion, unrest, disturbance, scramble, disruption, anarchy, brawl, riot, quarrel, turbulence, disarray, tumult, uproar, dissension, uprising, fracas, racket, pandemonium, storm, agitation, upheaval, bedlam, lawlessness. **2.** A physical or mental health impairment (mental disorder). Illness, condition, affliction, sickness, disease, malady, infirmity, derangement, complaint, indisposition. *Ant.* Order; good health.

Disordered, *adj.* See complex (1); disorder (1).

Disorderly, *adj.* **1.** Violative of the public peace, good order, or good behavior (disorderly conduct). Rowdy, unruly, riotous, agitated, disobedient, aberrant, wild, aggressive, tumultuous, bellicose, boisterous, misbehaving, defiant, incorrigible, recalcitrant, rude, uncontrolled, uncivil, undisciplined, lawbreaking, turbulent, rough, ungovernable, rebellious, unmanageable, improper, mutinous, violent, intractable. **2.** Messy (a disorderly desk). Chaotic, disordered, disorganized, irregular, topsy-turvy, unsystematic, careless, slipshod, random, helter-skelter, scrambled. *Ant.* Complaisant; organized.

Disorderly conduct Behavior that tends to disturb the public peace, to scandalize the community, or shock the public sense of morality. Engaging in the following activities with the purpose of causing (or recklessly causing) a public annoyance: fighting, threatening, making unreasonable noise, using abusive language, creating offensive displays, creating unnecessarily hazardous conditions.

Disorderly house A house or place where acts are performed that tend to corrupt the morals of the community, promote breaches of the peace, or become a nuisance to the neighborhood (e.g., house of prostitution, gambling house). See brothel.

Disorganization, *n.* See confusion.

Disorganize, *v.* See confuse.

Disorganized, *adj.* See disorderly (2), complex.

Disorient, *v.* See confuse, divert.

Disorientation, *n.* See confusion, disturbance.

Disown, *v.* See reject (1).

Disparage, *v.* To discredit one's person or property (the merchant disparaged her competitor's service). Smear, libel, vilify, belittle, criticize, denigrate, ridicule, slight, mock, undervalue, injure, damage, assail, malign, stigmatize, affront, condemn, downgrade, disgrace, humiliate, minimize, underrate, derogate, disdain, "badmouth," falsify, misrepresent, demean, decry, deride, lampoon. See also defame, slander. *Ant.* Acclaim.

Disparagement, *n.* A tort with the following elements: (a) false statements of fact, (b) disparaging the plaintiff's business, property, or title to property, (c) publication of the statements, (d) intent or malice, (e) causation, (f) special damages. Disparagement of title; disparagement of goods; injurious falsehood; conduct that adversely influences the public's dealings with the plaintiff, e.g., causes the public not to buy from the plaintiff. Trade libel. See also slander.

Disparaging, *adj.* See derogatory, defamatory.

Disparate, *adj.* See different.

Disparity, *n.* A marked difference in quantity or quality between two things or among many things (the disparity between the promised goods and the delivered goods). Inequality, distinction, dissimilarity, unevenness, divergence, disproportion, variance, inconsistency, contradiction, diversity, imbalance, gap, incongruity, contrast, discrepancy, deviation, gulf, nonconformity. See also difference (1). *Ant.* Similarity.

Dispassionate, *adj.* Impartial (a dispassionate mediator). Neutral, disinterested, uninvolved, detached, fair, calm, unshaken, self-controlled, composed, open-minded, evenhanded, objective, levelheaded, unbiased, without bias, without prejudice, just, impersonal, equitable, aloof, controlled, sober, temperate, even-tempered, subdued, tranquil. See also deliberate (2). *Ant.* Emotional, biased.

Dispatch 1. *v.* To send off with speed (she dispatched the brief to her opponent). Forward, transmit, direct, address, speed, ship, deliver, transfer, post, hasten, route, commit, launch, rush, freight. **2.** *v.* To deal with or complete something quickly (all of the remaining matters were dispatched without controversy). Dispose, execute, expedite, accomplish, achieve, finish, work out, carry out, fulfill, see through, settle, finalize, consummate, conclude. **3.** *n.* Speed in completing something (undertaken with dispatch). Promptness, urgency, haste, expeditiousness, rapidity, movement, quickness, alacrity. **4.** *n.* A message (a dispatch received at noon). Letter, communication, correspondence, notification, communiqué, telegram, mail; report, bulletin; news.

Dispel, *v.* To clear or drive away (the evidence dispelled all doubts). Scatter, remove, dismiss, banish, expel, repel, eliminate, oust, disintegrate, route, disseminate, cast off, break up, dissipate, release, shake off, disperse. *Ant.* Accumulate.

Dispensable, *adj.* See needless, gratuitous (2), frivolous, expendable (2), collateral (2), superfluous.

Dispensary, *n.* A place where medicine is prepared or distributed. See drug, hospital.

Dispensation, *n.* An exemption from a law (the legislature granted the veteran a dispensation from the licensing requirement). Allowance, permission, authorization, leave, approval, relaxation, clearance, exception, immunity, relinquishment, favor, reprieve, pardon, amnesty, release, variance, indulgence, warrant, grace, permit, license.

Dispense, *v.* **1.** To give, distribute, or administer (dispense justice). Allot, mete, parcel out, render, assign, dole, issue, apportion, disseminate, divide, bestow, confer, furnish, apply, prescribe, engineer, effectuate, allocate. See also distribute (2). **2.** To do without (the judge dispensed with the preliminaries). Do away with, abolish, reject, cancel, rescind, revoke, ignore. *Ant.* Withhold; observe.

Dispenser, *n.* See package, vessel (2); seller.

Dispersal, *n.* See distribution (2).

Disperse, *v.* See dispense (1), dissipate (2), circulate, communicate.

Dispirited, *adj.* See depressed, despondent.

Displace, *v.* **1.** To take the place of (the word processor displaced the typewriter). Crowd out, supplant, replace, supersede, substitute, interchange, trade, exchange, succeed. **2.** To remove (the board displaced the treasurer). Dislodge, move, expel, deport, evict, unseat, dismiss, force out, "bump," discharge, eject, discard, oust, purge. *Ant.* Remain.

Displaced person (DP) See emigrant, immigrant, exile, tramp (1).

Displacement, *n.* See dispossession, removal, replacement; displace.

Display 1. *v.* To exhibit (the witness displayed no understanding of the questions). Manifest, demonstrate, show, present, reveal, expose, publicize, evince, flaunt. **2.** *n.* See exposition (2), array (2), production. *Ant.* Conceal (1).

Displease, *v.* To dissatisfy. Disgust, offend, nauseate, irk, vex, harass, incense, exacerbate, annoy, aggravate, pique. See also angry, dissatisfied.

Displeased, *adj.* See dissatisfied; angry.

Displeasure, *n.* See dissatisfaction, annoyance.

Disposable, *adj.* **1.** Available for use (disposable income). Within reach, accessible, reachable, movable, spendable, exploitable, usable. **2.** Capable of being discarded or disposed of after use (disposable ribbon). Throwaway, nonreturnable. *Ant.* Frozen; permanent.

Disposal, *n.* **1.** The sale, consumption, or other disposition of a thing (the disposal of the property was within the discretion of the trustee). Transfer, conveyance, settlement, use, assignment. **2.** Throwing away (the disposal of the incriminating evidence). Discarding, dumping, scrapping, junking. **3.** The exercise of control over something (the assets at her disposal). Command, power, authority, supervision, direction, administration, management. *Ant.* Retention; collection; impotence.

Dispose, *v.* **1.** To transfer property (she disposed of her land in her will). Allocate, alienate, apportion, relinquish, sell, give, distribute, convey, bestow, allot, deal out. **2.** To finalize (the court disposed of the remaining issue). Settle, end, resolve, decide, determine, order, classify. See also dispatch (2). **3.** To discard (she disposed of the incriminating evidence). Part with, get rid of, put out of the way, dump, destroy, throw away. *Ant.* Maintain; postpone.

Disposition, *n.* **1.** The transferring of property (the gift of the land by the debtor was a fraudulent disposition). Conveyance, transfer, alienation, disposal, delivery, assignment, relinquishment. **2.** The final arrangement or decision (we awaited the court's disposition). Conclusion, settlement, determination, solution, resolution, outcome, dispensation, direction, regulation, upshot. **3.** An arrangement (the disposition of the signs). Organization, placement, grouping, adjustment. **4.** One's nature or way of thinking (the judge's condescending disposition). Attitude, temperament, mood, inclination, bent, spirit, idiosyncrasy, soul, character, propensity, makeup, predilection, streak, complexion, humor, personality.

Disposition hearing A judicial proceeding in which a criminal or juvenile defendant is sentenced or otherwise handled as a result of what has been adjudicated on the substance of the case.

Dispositive facts Those facts that are critical to the resolution of an issue.

Dispossess, *v.* To oust or eject from land (the landlord dispossessed the tenant). Expel, deprive of, depose, displace, divest, retake, dislodge, supplant, evict, disseise. *Ant.* Enter, install.

Dispossession, *n.* An ouster (an action for dispossession of the land owner). Eviction, displacement, deprivation, disseisin, usurpation, ejectment, exclusion, expulsion, exile, sequestration, foreclosure, abduction, confiscation, expropriation, impoundment, capture, retaking.

Disproportion, *n.* See disparity, difference; disproportionate.

Disproportionate, *adj.* Lopsided or unbalanced (a disproportionate sentence). Out of proportion, uneven, extreme, unequal, excessive, unwarranted, asymmetrical, incongruous, ill-suited, disparate, unjustifiable, discordant, undue, unsuitable, inappropriate, irrational, inconsistent. *Ant.* Balanced, proportionate.

Disprove, *v.* To prove to be false or erroneous (counsel has failed to disprove the allegation). Refute, contradict, discredit, negate, expose, rebut, confound, answer, defeat, contravene, overturn, belie, traverse, invalidate. *Ant.* Demonstrate.

Disputable, *adj.* Arguable (a disputable theory). Questionable, open to question, unresolved, subject to doubt, doubtful, dubious, uncertain, contestable, ambiguous, vague, hypothetical, controversial, at issue, in doubt, undemonstrated, indefinite, theoretical, problematic. See also debatable. *Ant.* Validated.

Disputants, *n.* Those involved in the dispute (the disputants refused to meet).

Disputants

Contestants, adversaries, opponents, antagonists, rivals, adverse parties, combatants, litigants, contenders, dissenters. *Ant.* Allies.

Disputatious, *adj.* See contentious (1), litigious (1).

Dispute 1. *n.* A conflict or controversy (a dispute over damages). Argument, debate, feud, altercation, battle, contention, clash, disagreement, wrangle, strife, brawl, discussion, challenge, polemic, contest, discord, variance, dissension. **2.** *v.* To doubt or question the accuracy of something (the witness disputed the allegation). Debate, contest, rebut, refute, challenge, take exception, take issue, object, resist, contradict, differ, deny, controvert. *Ant.* Agreement; accept.

Disqualification, *n.* See disability (1), removal; disqualify.

Disqualify, *v.* To render ineligible or unfit (her bias disqualified her). Deny participation, disable, disenfranchise, bar, expel, declare ineligible, eliminate, exclude, block, render unfit, preclude. See also disbar, incapacitate. *Ant.* Qualify.

Disquiet, *n., v.* See anxiety, disturbance; disrupt, disturb, harass, outrage (2).

Disquietude, *n.* See anxiety.

Disregard 1. *v.* To treat as unworthy of regard or notice (the judge instructed the jury to disregard the remark). Ignore, take no notice of, set aside, forget, overlook, de-emphasize, underplay, neglect, minimize, skip, disdain, dismiss, abandon, pretermit, gloss over, slight, shelve, pass over, not consider, leave out of consideration. **2.** *n.* Neglect or violation (his disregard of the law). Negligence, oversight, contempt, omission, disdain, affront, overlooking, indifference, default, oblivion, infraction, nonobservance, insensitivity, scorn, carelessness, lack of consideration, delinquency. *Ant.* Respect.

Disrepair, *n.* The state of being in need of repair or restoration as a result of decay or damage (the engine fell into disrepair). Deterioration, dilapidation, neglect, ruin, collapse, degeneration, impairment, corrosion. *Ant.* Repair.

Disreputable, *adj.* See base (2), corrupt (1), dishonest, delinquent (2), bad (2).

Disrepute, *n.* Disesteem (the doctrine of immunity had fallen into disrepute). Bad reputation, unpopularity, shame, ill repute, humiliation, ignominy, contempt, disfavor, disrespect, dishonor. *Ant.* Distinction.

Disrespect, *n.* See discourtesy, arrogance.

Disrespectful, *adj.* See rude, impertinent (2); derogatory, defamatory.

Disrobe, *v.* See strip (2); bare (2).

Disrupt, *v.* To create disorder (the outburst disrupted the courtroom). Upset, annoy, disorganize, disturb, dislocate, interrupt, disconcert, convulse, interfere with, cause chaos, obstruct, intercept, confuse, distract, hinder, intrude, disquiet, impede. *Ant.* Calm.

Disruption, *n.* See interruption; commotion.

Disruptive, *adj.* See disorderly, disobedient.

Dissatisfaction, *n.* Displeasure. Frustration, unhappiness, misery, pique, annoyance, anger, discontentment, sadness, uneasiness.

Dissatisfied, *adj.* Unhappy. Disappointed, frustrated, unfulfilled, discontent, displeased. See also depressed, despondent; angry; displease.

Dissatisfy, *v.* See displease; angry.

Dissect, *v.* See divide, cut; investigate, reason (3), canvass (1).

Dissection, *n.* See examination, inquiry (1).

Disseise, *v.* To deprive. See dispossess.

Disseisee, *n.* One who is wrongfully put out of possession of his or her lands.

Disseisin, *n.* Dispossession; a wrongful invasion of the possession of another.

Disseisor, *n.* One who wrongfully dispossesses another of his or her lands.

Dissemble, *v.* To conceal by assuming a false appearance (the witness could not dissemble her bias). Mask, camouflage, screen, feign, veil, falsify, counterfeit, shroud. See also disguise (1). *Ant.* Demonstrate.

Disseminate, *v.* See disclose, dispense (1), communicate, circulate, dissipate (2), distribute (2).

Dissemination, *n.* See publication (1), communication (1), circulation, distribution (2).

Dissension, *n.* See conflict (1), argument (2), disagreement, commotion.

Dissent 1. *n.* A disagreement (the judge filed a dissent to the court's holding). Difference of opinion, objection, challenge, nonagreement, nonassent, opposition, variance, noncompliance, disclaimer, repudiation, protest, resistance, nonconformity, disapproval. **2.** *v.* To disagree (the judge dissented). Withhold approval, withhold assent, differ, dispute, refute, repudiate, take exception to, protest, challenge, resist, argue, contradict, contest, reject, take issue with. *Ant.* Accord; concur.

Dissenter, *n.* One who dissents (Holmes was the lone dissenter). Objector, dissident, heretic, recusant, defector, renegade. See also nonconformist. *Ant.* Follower.

Dissertation, *n.* See speech (2), book (4).

Disservice, *n.* See injury, detriment, harm (1).

Dissidence, *n.* See dissent, dispute (1), conflict (1), disagreement (1); nonconformist

Dissident, *n.* See nonconformist.

Dissimilar, *adj.* See different.

Dissimilarity, *n.* See difference (1), disparity.

Dissimulate, *v.* See conceal, dissemble.

Dissipate, *v.* **1.** To destroy or waste (the trust was set up to prevent her from dissipating the estate). Squander, deplete, spend foolishly, abuse, misuse, consume, dissolve, exhaust, lavish, fritter; carouse, drink, revel, wassail, overindulge. See also expend (2). **2.** To scatter or dispel (dissipate the crowd). Disperse, break up, spread, disintegrate, disseminate, spread out, shatter, divide, disband, diverge, separate, diffuse, dissolve. *Ant.* Amass; concentrate.

Dissipated, *adj.* See dissolute, wanton (1); obscene.

Dissipation, *n.* See debauchery, intemperance, diversion (2), amusement.

Dissociate, *v.* See divide, dislocate, dissolve.

Dissoluble, *adj.* See defeasible.

Dissolute, *adj.* Loose in morals and conduct (dissolute life). Lawless, indifferent to moral restraint, reckless, abandoned, wanton, profligate, corrupt, unrestrained, immoral, depraved, dissipated, unprincipled, decadent, shameless, incorrigible, degenerate, unchecked, loose, wayward, wild, fast; lewd, debauched, licentious, obscene, impure, lustful, carnal, prurient, indecent. *Ant.* Restrained, chaste.

Dissolution, *n.* The act or process of dissolving (the dissolution of a marriage). Termination, winding up, cessation, suspension, finish, disbanding, rescission, nullification, demolition, eradication, discontinuance, death, end, revocation, annihilation, abolishment, obliteration, liquidation. *Ant.* Establishment.

Dissolve, *v.* To terminate (dissolve the corporation). Abrogate, release, cancel, annul, disintegrate, unloose, conclude, disband, free, destroy, break up, disperse, sever, untie, dismiss, prorogue, disjoin, quash, disengage, discontinue, wipe out, divorce, separate, divide, erase, revoke, disunite, abolish, dissipate, rescind, dismantle, detach, loosen. *Ant.* Unite.

Dissonance, *n.* See dissent (1), conflict (1), disagreement, disparity.

Dissonant, *adj.* See inconsistent, contradictory; nonconformist.

Dissuade, *v.* To advise and procure a person not to do an act (she improperly dissuaded the witness from testifying). Persuade against, talk out of, advise against, discourage, urge against, deter, turn aside from, divert, argue against, advocate against, disillusion, frighten away from, disincline, restrain. *Ant.* Inspire.

Distaff, *n.* See woman.

Distance, *n.* See range (2), area, measure.

Distant, *adj.* See remote (1), indifferent; hostile; alienate (2).

Distaste, *n.* See opposition, hostility, dissatisfaction, annoyance.

Distasteful, *adj.* See repugnant (1), indecent, improper, illicit.

Distemper, *n.* See disease, infirmity, disability.

Distill, *v.* **1.** To vaporize the more volatile parts of a substance and condense the vapor that is formed (the liquor is distilled locally). Extract, strain, brew, squeeze, separate, expel. **2.** To locate or take out the essence of something (distill the main portions from the transcript). Reduce to the essence, concentrate.

Distilled liquor All potable alcoholic liquors obtained by the process of distillation (e.g., whiskey, brandy, rum, gin). See liquor, intoxicating liquor.

Distinct, *adj.* **1.** Clear to the senses or mind (the blueprint showed distinct errors). Easily perceived, easily understood, plain, unmistakable, clear-cut, self-evident, apparent, manifest, unequivocal, conspicuous, vivid, evident, concrete, graphic, definite, well-defined, obvious, transparent, palpable, glaring, pronounced, noticeable. **2.** Observably or decidedly different (the two opinions are quite distinct). Distinguishable, individual, separate, unlike, dissimilar, unconnected, diverse, unique, not identical, peculiar, discrete, divergent, set apart. *Ant.* Vague; analogous.

Distinction, *n.* See difference; discriminate (2); merit, supremacy, superiority, eminence, dominion, reputation, notoriety, grandeur; eccentricity.

Distinctive, *adj.* See different, distinct (2), new, individual (1); acute (1), cultivated; peculiar, abnormal; outstanding (2), extraordinary.

Distingish, *v.* To point out an essential difference (she distinguished the cases to show that the one cited by her opponent was not applicable). Note the major differences, differentiate, separate, characterize, classify, divide, segregate, categorize, demarcate. See also discriminate (2).

Distinguishable, *adj.* See different; manifest (1).

Distinguished, *adj.* See elevated, conspicuous, outstanding (2).

Distort, *v.* To twist out of natural or regular shape (the account of the witness distorted what occurred). Fabricate, exaggerate, misconstrue, pervert, twist the meaning, deform, contort, misinterpret, misshape, alter, color, mangle, warp, invert, falsify, corrupt, misstate, change, inflate, mislead, transform. See also misrepresent, lie. *Ant.* Portray accurately.

Distortion, *n.* See fraud; deformity; distort.

Distract, *v.* **1.** To divert one's attention (she was distracted by the light). Draw away attention, turn aside, interrupt, sidetrack, change course. **2.** To confuse (the jury was distracted by all the legalisms). Perplex, trouble, bewilder, puzzle, mystify, annoy, confound, muddle, madden, disturb, complicate, unsettle, dement, unhinge, derange, agitate, alienate, befuddle.

Distracted, *adj.* Mentally ill (a distracted person). Deranged, delirious, mad, beside oneself, insane, distraught, irrational. See also demented; insanity.

Distraction, *n.* See confusion, insanity, hysteria; commotion; diversion, amusement.

Distrain, *v.* To take and hold the personal property of another until the latter performs an obligation (the landlord distrained the tenant's animals until the tenant paid all back rent). Appropriate, seize, impound, sequester, attach, levy, take possession.

Distrainee, *n.* A person who has been distrained.

Distraint, *n.* Seizure of personal property to enforce a right; the act of distraining or making a distress (distraint for rent). Expropriation, sequestration, appropriation, impoundment, confiscation, attachment.

Distraught, *adj.* See wild (3), irrational, insane, feverish, hysterical.

Distress 1. *n.* A common-law right of the landlord, now regulated by statute, to seize a tenant's goods and chattels in a nonjudicial proceeding to satisfy a debt for past rent (distress for rent). Confiscation, sequestration, attachment, impoundment, dispossession. **2.** *n.* The taking of goods and chattels out of the possession of a wrongdoer into the custody of the party injured, to procure the satisfaction of a wrong committed. **3.** *n.* Anxiety (damages for the distress he caused). Suffering, agony, torment, pain, worry, misery, despair, torture, trouble, woe, depression, concern, grief, sorrow, anguish, tribulation, despondency, oppression. **4.** *v.* See disturb, harass.

Distressed property Property that must be sold because of a mortgage foreclosure or on probate of an insolvent estate.

Distressing, *adj.* Troubling. Vexing, aggravating, distressful, irksome, troublesome, galling, annoying, nettlesome, unpleasant. See also offensive.

Distress warrant A writ authorizing an officer to make a distraint. See distraint.

Distribute, *v.* **1.** To deal or divide out in proportion or in shares (the will required the trustee to distribute all accumulated income to the three beneficiaries). Apportion, allot, organize, arrange, classify, group, parcel, dispense, assign, prorate, dole, ration, divide, partition. **2.** To hand out; to spread over an area (they distributed the petition to everyone on the street). Disseminate, circulate, broadcast, give out, deliver, pass around, convey, dispense; scatter, sprinkle, strew, diffuse. *Ant.* Accumulate, collect, retain.

Distributee, *n.* A person entitled to share in the distribution of an estate (the distributee under the will). Beneficiary, heir, donee, recipient, transferee.

Distribution, *n.* **1.** The apportionment and division of something (the distribution of assets). Allocation, parceling, assignment, allotment, arrangement, systematization, grouping, classification, partition, categorization, organization, tabulation, cataloging, codification. **2.** Dispersing something (the distribution of the chemical). Dissemination, circulation, shipment, scattering, delivery, transference. *Ant.* Accumulation; collection.

Distributive, *adj.* Pertaining to a distribution (distributive share).

Distributive share The share or portion that is given to a person upon the distribution of a fund (e.g., an estate, the assets of a dissolved partnership, the remaining assets of an insolvent).

Distributor, *n.* An individual or organization that stands between the manufacturer and the retail seller in purchases, consignments, or contracts for sale of consumer goods (distributor of computer equipment). Wholesaler, middleman. See also merchant.

District, *n.* One of the geographic or territorial areas into which an entire state, country, county, municipality, or other political subdivision is divided for judicial, political, electoral, or administrative purposes (Third Congressional District). Region, unit, neighborhood, precinct, zone, department, sphere, province, section, tract, canton, jurisdiction, realm, domain, community, parish, circuit, ward, sector, borough, quarter.

District attorney, *n.* The prosecutor for the government in criminal cases for a certain area or district (the district attorney decided not to prosecute the case). The prosecution, public prosecutor, state's attorney. See also prosecutor. *Ant.* Defense counsel.

Distrust, *v.* See doubt (1).

Distrustful, *adj.* See suspicious (2), cynical.

Disturb, *v.* To throw into disorder (the noise disturbed the neighbors). Interrupt, annoy, plague, vex, unnerve, arouse, exasperate, disrupt, inconvenience, trouble, confuse, enrage, irk, dismay, pique, baffle, pester, stir, discompose, distress, bother, distract, upset, alarm, convulse, disconcert. See also outrage (2), harass. *Ant.* Settle.

Disturbance, *n.* Any act causing annoyance to another (she sought an injunction against the disturbance). Disorder, disruption, uproar, commotion, tumult, disquiet, racket, turbulence, riot, nuisance, irritant, revolt, fracas, noise, agitation, unrest, altercation, fray, outbreak, convulsion, disorientation, annoyance, imposition.

Disturbance of the peace An interruption of the peace, quiet, and good order of a neighborhood or community; an affray or public disturbance. See commotion.

Disturbing, *adj.* See distressing, offensive.

Disunion, *n.* See division, commotion, interruption.

Disunity, *n.* See conflict (1), argument (2), disagreement, commotion.

Disuse, *n.* See neglect, discontinuance.

Ditch, *n., v.* See trench, conduit (2), river, watercourse; abandon (1).

Ditto, *n.* See copy.

Diurnal, *adj.* See daily (1).

Dive, *v., n.* See fall (2); restaurant, inn.

Diverge, *v.* See digress, deviate (1); counter, contradict.

Divergence, *n.* See deviation, detour, disparity, difference.

Divergent, *adj.* See different, separate.

Divers, *adj.* Various, several (divers proposals). Sundry, numerous, assorted, mixed, miscellaneous, differing; motley. See also many, multiple, multifarious.

Diverse, *adj.* See separate, different, individual, divers.

Diversified, *adj.* See multifarious, multiple, divers.

Diversify, *v.* See change (2), divide; diffuse.

Diversion, *n.* **1.** A turning aside or altering the natural course or route of a thing (diversion of the river; diversion of funds). Detour, digression, drawing away, deviation, turning aside, deflection. **2.** An amusement (boating was one of her diversions). Distraction, hobby, avocation, pastime, recreation, pleasure, refreshment, entertainment. **3.** See sport (2).

Diversion program An alternative to incarceration; the disposition of a criminal defendant (before or after a finding of guilt), in which the court directs the defendant to participate in a work or educational program in the community.

Diversity, *n.* The quality of being unlike (diversity of opinion). Variety, divergence, assortment, dissimilarity, variation, irregularity, multiplicity, contrast, distinctiveness. See also disparity. *Ant.* Unanimity.

Diversity of citizenship One of the ways a federal court acquires jurisdiction: the case is between citizens of different states and the controversy between them involves the minimum monetary requirement.

Divert, *v.* To alter the course of things (he diverted the funds to his own use). Sidetrack, deflect, turn aside, turn out of the way, withdraw, draw away, separate, misdirect, redirect, mislead. See also distract, deter. *Ant.* Preserve.

Divest, *v.* To deprive someone of rights, duties, or possessions (she divested herself of all interest in the company). Dispossess, strip, dislodge, forfeit, displace, purge, relieve, rid, oust, discharge, remove, free; confiscate, attach. *Ant.* Confer.

Divestiture, *n.* In antitrust law, the order of a court to a defendant to divest itself of property, securities, or other assets.

Divide 1. *v.* To cut into parts (the court divided the land). Separate, disunite, keep apart, sever, demarcate, categorize, classify, disjoin, disconnect, split, segment, divorce, cut, partition, subdivide, part, apportion, untie, splinter, truncate, amputate, saw, tear, shear off, quarter, halve, fracture, dichotomize, redivide, rend, type, single out, cordon off, disassociate, dissolve, unravel, dismember, rupture, intersect, section, disband, mark off, segregate, remove, isolate, branch out, diverge, bifurcate, detach, sunder, cleave, disengage, abstract, disentangle, uncouple, bisect, fragment, distinguish. **2.** *v.* To split and distribute (the court divided the estate among the heirs). Distribute, allocate, dole, assign, parcel, dispense, administer, mete, disperse, prorate, issue, allot, ration. **3.** *v.* To cause dissension (the proposal divided the committee). Split, break up, alienate, disunite, polarize, set at odds, pull apart, interlope, come between, disband, part company, estrange. **4.** *n.* See valley. *Ant.* Unify; retain.

Divided, *adj.* See separate (1); divide.

Dividend, *n.* The payment designated by the board of directors of a corporation to be distributed pro rata among the outstanding shares (the dividend was taxed as ordinary income). Distribution of earnings, profit, benefit, reward, allocation, share.

Divine, *adj., v.* See attractive, superior (2), worthy, beautiful; religious, religion, God, holy, minister, church; expect (1), foresee, augur.

Divinity, *n.* See God; religion, minister, church.

Divisible, *adj.* Capable of being divided (divisible assets). Severable, apportionable, detachable. *Ant.* Indivisible.

Divisible divorce A divorce decree is divisible when only part of it is enforceable in another state. The part that dissolves the divorce may be enforceable, but, due to a lack of personal jurisdiction, not the part that awards alimony, child support, and a property settlement.

Divisible offense An offense that includes one or more offenses of lower grade (e.g., murder includes assault with intent to kill, battery, etc.).

Division, *n.* **1.** The act of dividing among a number (the division of assets). Separation, allocation, splitting up, dissemination, distribution, departmentalization, schism, breach, disunion, rupture, split, break, subdivision, bisection, fission, partition, severance, apportionment, disconnection, breakup, divorce, detachment, dismemberment, segmentation, allotment. **2.** An operating or administrative unit of an organization (chief of the division). Unit, branch, chapter, district, department, wing, section, detachment, arm, sector. *Ant.* Unification; whole.

Divisive, *adj.* See contentious, hostile, offensive, adverse.

Divorce, *n.* The termination of a marital relationship by a court judgment or decree. The word divorce sometimes refers to a legal separation—a limited divorce, or a divorce from bed and board—which allows the parties to live separate and apart but does not dissolve the marriage. Dissolution of a marriage, divorce a vinculo matrimonii. See also dissolve, annul, dismiss, cease, rescind, conclude (1), expire.

Divorce a mensa et thoro A judicially approved separation; the spouses remain married but no longer cohabitate. A separation from bed and board, a limited divorce, a partial divorce, a qualified divorce, a legal separation. *Ant.* Absolute divorce.

Divorce a vinculo matrimonii An absolute divorce in which the marital relationship is dissolved. *Ant.* Legal separation.

Divulge, *v.* To make known (divulge classified data). Report, air, reveal, inform, communicate, expose, release, publicize, advertise, impart, tell, leak, declare, broadcast, publish, confide, spill, confess. See also disclose. *Ant.* Conceal.

Divvy, *v.* See divide (1).

Dizzy, *adj.* Bewildered. Lightheaded, swimming, reeling, flighty, giddy, vertiginous, unsteady, shaky, woozy. See also capricious; intoxicated; insane, lunatic.

Do, *v.* See perform, administer (1), complete, settle (1).

Doable, *adj.* See practicable, feasible, possible.

Docile, *adj.* See flexible, malleable, amenable (2), bashful, quiet (2).

Dock 1. *n.* The cage or enclosed space in a criminal court where prisoners stand when brought in for trial. **2.** *n.* A landing place for boats. Pier, marina, quay. See also landing; harbor, wharf. **3.** *v.* To curtail or diminish (dock her wages). Reduce, deduct, abridge, decrease, pare down, subtract.

Docket 1. *n.* A list or calendar of cases to be tried at a specified term of the court (criminal trial docket). Register, agenda, program. **2.** *n.* A minute, abstract, or brief entry; the book containing such entries; a formal record, entered in brief, of the proceedings in a court of justice. **3.** *v.* To make a brief entry of any proceedings in a court of justice (to docket the case). See record.

Doctor 1. *n.* A licensed practitioner of medicine (prescription from a doctor). Surgeon, physician, medical practitioner, resident, general practitioner, healer, M.D., medical examiner, "medico," intern, dentist, specialist. **2.** *n.* Someone who holds the highest degree in designated areas (Doctor of Divinity). **3.** *v.* To prescribe or treat medically (doctor a cold). Repair, minister, heal, cure, care for. **4.** *v.* To falsify (they doctored the records). Fabricate, misrepresent, tamper, distort, alter. See also interpolate, rig, manipulate.

Doctorate, *n.* See certificate; scholar, learned, school.

Doctor-patient privilege In the law of evidence, the right of the patient to exclude from evidence (by refusing to divulge or by preventing the doctor from divulging) confidential communications made by the patient to the doctor.

Doctrinaire, *adj.* See inflexible, strict (2), narrow (2), arbitrary, absolute (1); bias.

Doctrine, *n.* A rule or principle (the doctrine of merger). Tenet, theory, precept, thesis, dogma, canon, philosophy, teaching, school, science, belief, faith, conviction. See also rule (1).

Document 1. *n.* Any physical embodiment of information or ideas, e.g., letter, contract, map, X-ray plate, blueprint (the document was admitted into evidence). Instrument, report, archive, paper, writing, monument, publication, register, book. See also record. **2.** *v.* To support with documentary evidence or with authorities (he could not document his allegation of fraud). Substantiate, corroborate, buttress, authenticate, verify, demonstrate, back up, validate, detail, uphold. See also prove; documentation.

Documentary evidence Evidence that is furnished by written instruments, inscriptions, and documents of all kinds; tangible or material objects that are symbols of ideas. *Ant.* Oral evidence.

Documentary stamp A stamp required by some governments to be affixed to deeds and other documents of transfer before they may be recorded.

Documentation, *n.* The production of supporting documents, other evidence, or authorities (the lawyer provided impressive documentation). Substantiation, confirmation, backing, certification, authentication, proof, corroboration, sources, data, facts.

Document of title A document that is accepted in the trade as proof that the person possessing it has the right to receive and dispose of goods covered by the document, e.g., a bill of lading, a warehouse receipt.

Doddering, *adj.* See infirm, frail, weak, ill, defective, senile.

Dodge, *v., n.* See avoid (2), circumvent, divert; evasion; deceive.

Dodger, *n.* See malingerer.

Doer, *n.* See actor, partisan, advocate, nonconformist, entrepreneur.

Dog, *n.* See animal; wrongdoer.

Dogged, *adj.* See inflexible, arbitrary, unreasonable, firm (2); indefatigable, strong (2), diligent.

Dogma, *n.* Authoritative and formal principles or doctrines (church dogma). Tenet, conviction, belief, maxim, creed, canon, teaching, credo, precept, proposition. See also rule.

Dogmatic, *adj.* See inflexible, arbitrary, firm (2); bias.

Do-gooder, *n.* See good samaritan, champion, backer; humanitarian.

Doing business Carrying on, conducting, or managing a business; the exercise of the ordinary functions for which the business was organized.

Dolce vita, *n.* See debauchery, luxury.

Doldrums, *n.* See depression, boredom.

Dole, *n., v.* See allotment (1), charity (1), donation; distribute.

Doleful, *adj.* See depressed, depressing, despondent, dismal, abandoned (1), serious (5), dark.

Dollar, *n.* See money, asset (1).

Dolt, *n.* See boor, idiot.

Domain, *n.* **1.** Land that is owned; the complete and absolute ownership of land (a federal domain). Territory, estate, real property, demesne, acreage, real estate, kingdom, holding. **2.** Sphere of influence; field (the domain of science). Jurisdiction, area, discipline, bailiwick, orbit, specialty, assignment, circuit, capacity, business, function, occupation, scope, perimeter, field, region, department, realm, province.

Dome, *n.* See arc.

Domestic 1. *adj.* Pertaining, belonging, or related to a home, a domicile, the place of birth, or the place or origin (domestic tasks). Family, residential, household, local, indigenous, native, homemade, homegrown. **2.** *n.* A household servant (minimum wage for domestics). Help, attendant, housekeeper. See also servant, employee. *Ant.* Foreign; manager.

Domestic animals Tamed animals; those that are habituated to live in or around the habitations of humans (e.g., dogs, sheep, horses). *Ant.* Wild animals.

Domesticate, *v.* To adapt to human use; to convert to domestic use (domesticate a wild horse). Train, habituate, assimilate, tame, break in, discipline, harness, curb, subjugate, orient.

Domestic corporation When a corporation is organized and chartered in a particular state, it is considered a domestic corporation of that state; all others are foreign corporations.

Domestic relations Family law (e.g., the law governing marriage, divorce, adoption, custody).

Domicile 1. *n.* The place (a) where someone has physically been present (b) with the intention to make that place a permanent home; the place to which one would intend to return when away. The word "residence" is sometimes used interchangeably with "domicile," but there is a distinction. A residence is a temporary place of abode. A person can have many residences but only one domicile. (The court's jurisdiction to divorce the parties depended on the domicile of either spouse.) Permanent home, fixed home, principal establishment, abode, main address, legal residence. See also home. **2.** *v.* See inhabit.

Domicile of choice The domicile that an individual has the power to select through intent and physical presence. A child does not have this choice. A child automatically acquires the domicile of his or her parents, which is referred to as a domicile of origin or a domicile by operation of law.

Domiciliary, *n.* Someone who is physically present in a place with the intent to remain there indefinitely (jurisdiction over the domiciliary). Citizen, resident, native, inhabitant, dweller. See also domicile; domestic.

Domiciliary administration The administration of an estate in the state where the decedent was domiciled at the time of death. Principal administration, primary administration.

Dominance, *n.* See power, dominion, superiority, hold (6), control (3), sovereignty, authority (2), tyranny, coercion, duress (1).

Dominant, *adj.* Exerting the main influence, control, or authority (she was the dominant force in the company). Principal, commanding, primary, leading, cardinal, supreme, prevailing, conquering, winning, determining, triumphant, effective, successful, operative, overruling, superior, paramount, chief, predominant, governing, authoritative, preeminent, dominating, ruling, master, controlling, ascendant, sovereign, transcendent. *Ant.* Secondary.

Dominate, *v.* To master or control (the issue of damages dominated the negotiations). Rule, lead, monopolize, govern, tower over, direct, domineer, overpower, overbear, dictate, intimidate, terrorize, subordinate, permeate, tame, subdue, command. See also overcome, best (2), exceed, prevail. *Ant.* Follow.

Dominating, *adj.* See dominant, leading (1), ascendent (2), arbitrary (2), strict (2), absolute.

Domination, *n.* See power, dominion, authority (2), supremacy, control (3), coercion, duress (1), tyranny, sovereignty.

Domineer, *v.* See dominate, intimidate, coerce, compel.

Domineering, *adj.* See dominant, ascendent (2), leading (1), arbitrary (2), strict (2), absolute.

Dominion, *n.* The exercise of the right of ownership; control over the disposition of something (the exercise of dominion over someone else's property). Primacy, authority, supremacy, mastery, jurisdiction, power, domination, dominance, claim. See also government.

Don, *n., v.* See teacher; clothe.

Donate, *v.* To contribute or give (donate money to the hospital). Confer, allot, pledge, award, bequeath, present, bestow, subscribe, grant, aid, assist, help, furnish. See also charity. *Ant.* Receive.

Donation, *n.* A gift (tax deductible donation). Contribution, present, alms, gratuity, philanthropy, benefaction, handout, offering, munificence, bounty, assistance, bequest, dole, grant. See also charity.

Donative, *adj.* Pertaining to a gift (donative intent). Eleemosynary, gratuitous, philanthropic. See also charitable, benevolent.

Donative intent The intent of the donor that title to the subject matter of the gift be irrevocably and presently transferred.

Donator, *n.* See donor.

Done, *v.* See realize, perform, complete.

Donee, *n.* One to whom a gift is given; one who is invested with a power of appointment (the donee mentioned in the will). Beneficiary, transferee, grantee, heir, recipient, legatee. *Ant.* Donor.

Donee beneficiary In a third-party contract, the person who receives the benefit of the contract. He or she is not one of the contracting parties.

Donnybrook, *n.* See commotion, fight (1).

Donor, *n.* One who makes a gift, confers a power, or creates a trust (the donor revoked the gift). Grantor, donator, giver, benefactress, benefactor, contributor, transferor, philanthropist, bestower. *Ant.* Recipient.

Do-nothing, *n.* See malingerer.

Doodle, *v.* See loiter; draft (2), draw (1).

Doom, *v., n.* See condemn; destroy; destiny.

Door, *n.* See access (2), entrance.

Doorman, *n.* See servant, employee.

Doorway, *n.* See access (2), entrance; egress.

Dope, *n.* **1.** An opium derivative; any narcotic (possession of dope). Heroin, marijuana, opiate. See also drug. **2.** See idiot, boor.

Dorm, *n.* See home, inn, institution, school.

Dormant, *adj.* In abeyance; sleeping (a dormant disease). Inactive, idle, latent, resting, quiescent, hibernating, static, slumbering, inoperative, suspended, passive, unused, immobile, undeveloped, silent, unemployed, disengaged, inert. *Ant.* Active.

Dormant corporation An inactive but legal corporation that is capable of being activated.

Dormant judgment An unsatisfied judgment that has remained unexecuted for so long that it needs to be revived before execution can be issued on it.

Dormant partner One whose name is not known or whose name does not appear as a partner, but who nevertheless is a silent partner and shares in the profits.

Dormitory, *n.* See home, inn, institution, school.

Dosage, *n.* See amount (1, 2), portion, medicine (2).

Dose, *n.* See amount (1, 2), portion, medicine (2).

Dossier, *n.* A group of papers on a person or event (stolen dossier). Brief, file, portfolio, report, documentation. See also record.

Dot, *n.* See mark; iota; dowry.

Dotage, *n.* Feebleness of the mental faculties proceeding from old age (the testator was entering his dotage). Senility, decrepitude, second childhood. See also insanity, infirmity, disease, debility.

Dotal property Property that the wife brings to the husband to assist him in bearing the expenses of the marriage establishment (civil law concept).

Double, *adj.* Acting in two capacities or having two aspects (double recovery). Twofold, twin, multiplied by two, dual, two-part, twice, paired, duplicate. *Ant.* Single.

Double-check, *v.* See verify.

Double-cross, *v.* See deceive, betray.

Double-dealing, *n.* See bad faith, duplicity, machination, fraud, infidelity.

Double dipping, *n.* Receiving two incomes from the government (e.g., a military pension and a paycheck from a civilian government job).

Double-entendre, *n.* See ambiguity, vagueness.

Double entry, *n.* A system of bookkeeping in which the entries are posted twice in the ledger—once as a credit and once as a debit.

Double hearsay An out-of-court statement is introduced into evidence, and this statement contains another out-of-court-statement by someone else, e.g., an officer makes a report (statement # 1) of what a motorist says (statement # 2) at the scene of the accident.

Double indemnity Payment of twice the basic benefit in the event of loss resulting from specified causes or under specified circumstances, e.g., a life insurance policy provides twice the face amount of the policy in the event of death by accidental means.

Double jeopardy A second prosecution after the first trial for the same offense.

Double standard, *n.* See inconsistency; injustice.

Double talk, *n.* See ambiguity, deception; quibble.

Double taxation Taxing the same thing twice for the same purpose by the same taxing authority during identical taxing periods.

Doubt 1. *v.* To question or hold questionable (the jury doubted the testimony of the witness). Distrust, disbelieve, be skeptical, suspect, dispute, challenge, discredit, mistrust, debate, equivocate, fluctuate, wonder, lack confidence in, query, demur, entertain doubts, have misgivings, waver, be apprehensive of, feel unsure, have reservations, be unconvinced, be uncertain. **2.** *n.* The absence of a settled opinion or conviction (the jury had doubts about her version). Uncertainty of mind, skepticism, suspicion, apprehension, qualm, mistrust, scruple, disbelief, ambiguity, incredulity, hesitation, wariness, reluctance, indecision, hesitancy, vacillation, dubiety, problems, questions, anxiety, lack of faith, insecurity, confusion, ambivalence, lack of confidence. See also reservation (3). *Ant.* Believe; assurance.

Doubtful, *adj.* **1.** Experiencing doubt (the jury was doubtful about the accuracy of the testimony). Hesitant, indecisive, wavering, skeptical, dubious, unsettled, ambivalent, uncertain, undecided, suspicious, unconvinced. **2.** Obscure, debatable (doubtful validity). Questionable, ambiguous, puzzling, indefinite, arguable, speculative, open to question, unconvincing, vague, inconclusive, precarious, conjectural, incredible, untenable, problematic, disputable. *Ant.* Positive; conclusive.

Doubtful title A title that raises such doubts as to its validity that it could reasonably invite or expose the party holding it to litigation. *Ant.* Marketable title.

Doubtless, *adv., adj.* See absolutely (2), certain (3), clear (1).

Douche, *v.* See bathe, water (2).

Dour, *adj.* See inflexible, firm (2), extreme (1), strict (2), grave (3), depressed, depressing, dark, dismal, abandoned (1).

Douse, *v.* See water (2); extinguish.

Dovetail, *v.* See connect, conform, correspond; harmonize.

Dowager, *n.* A widow who holds property from her deceased husband. See woman.

Dower, *n.* The provision that the law makes for a widow out of the lands or tenements of her deceased husband. It has been abolished or replaced in most states. At common law, it consisted of a life estate in one-third of the lands of which the husband was seised in fee at any time during the marriage and which could have been inherited by their issue. (She waived her right of dower.) See interest, property.

Dow Jones average A stock market performance indicator that consists of the price movements in the top 30 industrial U.S. companies.

Downcast, *adj.* See depressed, dark; mope.

Downfall, *n.* See defeat (2), misfortune, abolition, rescission; collapse, destroy.

Downgrade, *v., n.* See demote, discredit; decline.

Down payment An amount of money paid by the buyer to the seller at the time of sale, which represents only a part of the total cost.

Downpour, *n.* See flood, storm, eruption.

Downtrodden, *adj.* Oppressed. Burdened, exploited, mistreated, powerless, miserable, beset, helpless, feeble, afflicted, sorry, overcome, haggard, plagued. See also defenseless, destitute.

Downturn, *n.* See decline, reversal.

Dowry, *n.* Property that a woman brings to her husband upon marriage (they agreed that no dowry was needed). Portion, dot, dos, marriage settlement.

Doze, *v.* See sleep; drowsy.

DP, *n.* Displaced person. See emigrant, immigrant, exile; tramp (1).

Drab, *adj., n.* See barren, dirty, homely, dilapidated; commonplace (2); prostitute.

Draconian, *adj.* Severe (draconian measures were taken by the warden). Harsh, strict, austere, ruthless, rigid, uncompromising, arduous, demanding, intense, merciless, inhuman, brutal, inflexible, puritanical, exacting, fanatical. *Ant.* Mild.

Draft 1. *n.* A written order by the first party (called the drawer) instructing a second party (called the drawee, e.g., a bank) to pay a third party (called the payee); an order to pay a sum certain in money, signed by the drawer, payable on demand or at a definite time to order or to bearer (the draft was not accepted).

Money order, check, bill of exchange, commercial paper, negotiable paper, negotiable instrument, promissory note, warrant, bank note. **2.** *v.* To write a document (she drafted the will). Frame, compose, draw, prepare, diagram, sketch. **3.** *v.* See conscript, constrain (1). **4.** *n.* See registration; inauguration.

Draftee, *n.* One who is drafted. See conscript.

Draftsman, draftswoman, *n.* See architect; employee.

Drag, *v.* See tow; trail (3).

Dragnet, *n.* See arrest, apprehension (2).

Dragnet clause A provision in a mortgage in which the mortgagor gives security for past and future advances as well as for present indebtedness.

Drain 1. *v.* To draw off liquid (they drained the river). Pump, remove, empty, extract, withdraw, siphon, discharge, debouch, pump out, divert. **2.** *n.* A trench or ditch to convey liquid from an area (the leak in the drain). Conduit, channel, pipe, tube, outlet, sewer. **3.** *v.* To use up (the funds were drained by wasteful spending). Exhaust, deplete, impoverish, consume, bleed, empty. See also expend (2). *Ant.* Supply (1, 3).

Drainage rights A landowner may not obstruct or divert the natural flow of a watercourse or natural drainage course to the injury of another.

Drama, *n.* **1.** Theater. Show, comedy, tragedy, stage, play, presentation, art. See also cinema, legend. **2.** See emotion, passion.

Dramatic, *adj.* See moving, compelling, touching, emotional, ardent, strong (2); pompous, flamboyant.

Dram Shop Act A civil liability act in many states, which imposes liability on the seller of intoxicating liquor (which may or may not include beer) when a third party is injured as a result of the intoxication of the buyer, where the sale has caused or contributed to the intoxication. In some states, the Act also applies to gifts of intoxicating liquor.

Drape, *v., n.* See cover (2); curtain.

Drastic, *adj.* See draconian, strict (2), extreme (1), serious (2).

Draw, *v.* **1.** To prepare a legal document (draw a bill of exchange). Draft, make out, prepare, compose, write out. **2.** To withdraw money (she drew from the account). Take out, extract, deplete, exhaust. **3.** To advance money periodically on a construction loan agreement. **4.** To select a jury.

Drawback, *n.* **1.** A refund of taxes or duties on imported goods when they are exported rather than sold here (a dispute over the amount of the drawback). **2.** A disadvantage (the main drawback was the excessive noise). Hindrance, obstacle, impediment, flaw, problem, stumbling block, damper, liability, handicap, deficiency, hitch, detriment, minus, difficulty. *Ant.* Benefit (2).

Drawee, *n.* The person on whom a bill or draft is drawn; the one who is requested to pay the amount mentioned in the bill of exchange or draft (the drawee of a check is the bank on which it is drawn).

Drawer, *n.* The person who draws a bill, draft, or order for the payment of money (the drawer of a check is the person who signs it).

Drawing, *n.* See description, map, definition.

Dread, *n., v.* See fear (1, 2), anxiety, anguish, apprehension (3).

Dreadful, *adj.* See awesome, bad (2), appalling, hazardous, dangerous.

Dream 1. *n.* Fantasy. Delusion, fancy, illusion, vision, phantom, nightmare, chimera, ghost, conceit, daydream, reverie, hallucination, specter. See also trance, stupor. **2.** *n.* See aim (3). **3.** *v.* See fantasize.

Dreaming, *adj.* See preoccupied; engage (2), dream.

Dreary, *adj.* See dismal, dark, commonplace, barren, dirty, dilapidated, serious (5), grievous, grave.

Dredge

Dredge, *v.* See disclose, betray (2), bare (2), discover.

Dred Scott Case The case that held the descendants of African slaves imported into this country were not "citizens" under the U.S. Constitution. Dred Scott v. Sandford, 60 U.S. (19 How.) 393, 15 L.Ed. 691 (1857).

Dregs, *n.* See refuse (2).

Drench, *v.* See water (2).

Dress, *n., v.* See clothes; clothe.

Dressing, *n.* See bandage.

Drift, *v., n.* See wander, loiter; migratory; accumulate; accumulation (1); gist (1).

Drill, *n., v.* See practice (3); discipline (4), nurture, instruct (1).

Drink, *n., v.* See beverage, liquor; consume (1).

Drinkable, *adj.* Potable. See fit (1).

Drive, *v., n.* See coerce, make (2), compel; operate; travel; advance (3, 4); incite; ambition, determination (2), diligence (1), enterprise (2).

Drive-in, *n.* See cinema, arena, merchant; restaurant, inn.

Drivel, *v., n.* See babble; refuse (2).

Driver, *n.* See chauffeur, operator, servant, employee; merchant.

Driveway, *n.* A private road. See highway.

Droit, *n.* (*Fr.*) A legal right; a body of law.

Droll, *adj.* See comic, odd (1).

Drone, *n.* See noise.

Drool, *v.* See babble.

Drop, *v., n.* See decline (3), oust, diminish; abandon (1); dismiss (2, 4); iota, scintilla.

Dropout, *n.* One who withdraws from school or society. See nonconformist; tramp.

Drought, *n.* Aridity, dryness, dehydration. See dearth, absence (2).

Drown, *v.* See inundate, submerge, suffocate; overcome (2).

Drowsy, *adj.* Lethargic, groggy. Sleepy, languid, listless, slow, dozy, yawning, sluggish, dull, lifeless. See also dormant, lazy.

Drub, *v.* See overcome (2), defeat (1), batter, attack (1).

Drudge, *v., n.* See labor (2), slave, work.

Drudgery, *n.* Hard work, travail, toil. See bondage, slavery, oppression.

Drug, *n.* **1.** An article intended for use in the diagnosis, treatment, or prevention of disease in humans and in animals; any substance used as a medicine (defective drug). Medication, remedy, prescription, compound. **2.** A narcotic (overdose of drugs). Opiate, "dope," sedative, stimulant, depressant, tranquilizer, "benny," "upper," "downer," caffeine, codeine, "pot," amphetamine, marijuana, alcohol, quinine, hallucinogen, acid, "coke," cocaine, nicotine, "weed," cannabis, peyote, LSD, "speed," "smack," hash, hashish.

Drug abuse A state of chronic or periodic intoxication detrimental to the individual and to society, produced by repeated consumption of a natural or synthetic drug. See intoxication, intoxicated.

Druggist, *n.* Pharmacist, apothecary. See merchant, business.

Drum, *n.* See noise; music; vessel (2).

Drummer, *n.* Traveling salesperson. See peddler, seller, jobber.

Drunk, *adj.* Intoxicated; so far under the influence of intoxicating liquor as to be impaired in judgment, sense perceptions, muscular coordination, continuity of thought, or speech (she was drunk when she fired the gun). Inebriated, "high." See also intoxicated; drunkard. *Ant.* Sober.

Drunkard, *n.* One who is habitually intoxicated (common drunkard). Alcoholic, drunk, problem drinker, imbiber, inebriate, sot, tippler, "souse," "lush," "boozer," "tipsy," "rummy," "sponge."

"Druthers," *n.* See option, preference, choice.

Dry, *adj.* **1.** Without imposing any duty or responsibility; without bringing any profit or advantage; nominal (dry trust). **2.** See arid, barren. **3.** Boring. See commonplace (2).

Dry run, *n.* A rehearsal or test. See appraisal, examination.

Dry trust A passive trust; a trust that requires no action on the part of the trustee beyond turning over money or property to the cestui que trust.

DT's See delirium tremens.

Dual, *adj.* Consisting of two (dual responsibility). Twofold, two-part, twin, binary, paired, duplicate, coupled. See also double. *Ant.* Single.

Dual citizenship Pertaining to persons who are citizens of the United States and of a particular state.

Dual-purpose doctrine If the work of an employee creates a necessity for travel, he or she is in the course of employment while doing that work even though at the same time he or she is serving a purpose of his or her own. An injury on a trip that serves both business and personal purposes is within the course of employment if the trip involves service for the employer that would have caused the trip to have been taken by someone even if it had not coincided with a personal purpose.

Dub, *v.* See name.

Dubiety, *n.* See doubt (2), confusion (2).

Dubious, *adj.* See doubtful, indefinite, disputable, debatable, suspicious (2); cynical; dangerous.

Duces tecum, Bring with you. See subpoena duces tecum.

Duck, *v.* See avoid (2), hedge, quibble; cringe.

Duct, *n.* See drain (2), vessel (2).

Ductile, *adj.* See flexible.

Dud, *n.* See failure (1).

Due, *adj.* **1.** Payable (the note is due). Collectable, owing, owed, outstanding, in arrears, unpaid, delinquent. **2.** Proper; just, regular, sufficient (due care). Reasonable, lawful, appropriate, rightful, proportionate, fitting, suitable, adequate, correct, satisfactory, commensurate, legitimate, allowable, authorized. **3.** Caused by (the fire was due to her carelessness). Resulting from, sustained by, sustained by means of, sustained in consequence of, sustained through, because of. *Ant.* Paid (1); improper, illegal (2).

Due care Just, proper, and sufficient care under the circumstances; that care which an ordinary prudent person would have exercised under the same or similar circumstances. Reasonable care, ordinary care. See also reasonable.

Due course holder See holder in due course.

Due diligence The prudence and effort that is ordinarily used by a reasonable person under the circumstances. See reasonable, diligence.

Duel, *n., v.* See fight, contest, war, argument (2), compete.

Due notice Notice that is reasonably intended to reach and that has the likelihood of reaching the particular target or public; sufficient, legally prescribed notice.

Due process of law Law in its regular course of administration through the courts of justice; fundamental fairness; substantial justice. See procedural due process, and substantive due process, fairness, justice, right (4).

Dues, *n.* See assessment (2), charge (8, 9).

Dull, *adj.* See commonplace (2), ordinary (2); limited (2); blind (1), dumb.

Dullard, *n.* See ass, boor, idiot; dumb.

Duly, *adv.* In due and proper form or manner (duly elected). Regularly, properly, fittingly, rightly, at the proper time, correctly, according to law.

Dumb

Dumb *adj.* **1.** Foolish. Stupid, foolhardy, unintelligent, obtuse, thick, dimwitted. See also lunatic, absurd; backward, reckless, rude, juvenile. **2.** See silent, mute.

Dumfound, *v.* See amaze, surprise (1), confuse; agape.

Dummy 1. *n.* One who purchases property and holds the legal title for someone else, usually to conceal the identity of the real owner (his role was to be the dummy in the transaction). Straw man, agent, double, stand-in. **2.** *adj.* Sham, imitation (dummy corporation). Make-believe, pretended, bogus, phony, false, spurious, hollow. *Ant.* Principal; operational.

Dummy corporation A corporation formed for sham purposes and not for the conduct of legitimate business, e.g., formed solely to avoid paying certain creditors.

Dump 1. *v.* See oust, abandon (1), discharge (5), dispose of (3). **2.** *n.* Junkyard. See refuse, merchant. **3.** *n.* See dumping.

Dumping, *n.* **1.** Selling in quantity at a very low price. **2.** Selling goods abroad at less than the market price at home—at less than its fair value (the country was accused of dumping its steel in the United States).

Dun, *v.* **1.** To make persistent demands (the creditor dunned the debtor for payment. Urge, besiege, solicit, press, importune, clamor, plague, insist. See also demand (1). **2.** *n.* A demand for payment.

Dunce, *n.* See ass, idiot, boor; dumb.

Dungeon, *n.* See cell, prison.

Dunk, *n.* See submerge, water.

Dupe, *v., n.* See deceive, betray, cheat; fraud; victim, pawn (3).

Duplex, *n.* See home.

Duplicate 1. *v.* To reproduce (it would be difficult to duplicate her performance). Match, replicate, copy, double, repeat, clone. **2.** *n.* A counterpart produced by the same impression as the original, or by photography, electric re-recording, etc.; that which exactly resembles or corresponds to something else (a duplicate of the will). Copy, twin, carbon, carbon copy, facsimile, reproduction, replica, parallel.

Duplication, *n.* See copy (1), duplicate (2); surplusage, excess, waste (1).

Duplicitous, *adj.* **1.** Characterized by deception. See deceptive, evasive; duplicity (1). **2.** Joining two or more distinct and separate offenses in a single count (a duplicitous indictment). See duplicity (3).

Duplicity, *n.* **1.** Deliberate deception or double-dealing (she suspected duplicity in the negotiations). Deceit, chicanery, dishonesty, cunning, hypocrisy, guile, betrayal, treachery. See also fraud. **2.** The technical fault in common-law pleading of uniting two or more causes of action in one count in a writ, or two or more grounds of defense in one plea. **3.** Charging several distinct, unrelated crimes in one indictment (rule of duplicity).

Durability, *n.* See endurance; durable.

Durable, *adj.* Resisting decay; stable; powerful (durable material). Lasting, substantial, hardy, enduring, dependable, sturdy, permanent, strong, tenacious, constant, surviving, firm, sound, persistent, long-wearing, tough, steadfast, herculean, stalwart, rugged, mighty, vigorous, forceful, athletic, healthy, energetic, potent, robust, muscular, puissant, unchanging. *Ant.* Weak.

Duration, *n.* The extent, limit, or time (the duration of the lease). Period, tenure, continuance, continuation, span, term, interval, era, season, epoch, interim, course, life, age.

Duress, *n.* **1.** Coercion; acting under the pressure of an unlawful act or threat (he signed under duress). Constraint, compulsion, extortion, force, oppression, demand, great pressure, subjection, undue influence, dominance, control. See also coercion, threat. **2.** Illegal confinement or imprisonment (duress of goods).

262

Quarantine, incarceration, detention, captivity, bondage, isolation. *Ant.* Free will; release.

Duress of goods A tortious seizure or detention of property from the person entitled to it and requiring some act before it is surrendered.

Durham rule The irresistible impulse test of criminal responsibility. Under the Durham Rule, to find a defendant not guilty by reason of insanity or mental irresponsibility, the jury must find (a) that the accused was suffering from a diseased or defective mental condition at the time of the commission of the act charged, and (b) that there was a causal relation between this disease or defective condition and the act. Durham v. United States, 214 F.2d 862 (D.C.Cir. 1954).

Dusk, *n.* See evening, sunset.

Dust, *n.* See dirt, earth (1).

Duties, *n.* A tax on imported or exported goods (the collection of duties). Impost, custom, tariff, fee, charge, levy, government imposition, excise, toll, burden, assessment, exaction, rate.

Dutiful, *Adj.* See loyal, amendable (2), cooperative (2), flexible, diligent, conscientious (2); kind, civil (3).

Duty, *n.* **1.** A legal or moral obligation (duty to support one's children). Mandatory act, responsibility, charge, requirement, trust, chore, function, commission, debt, liability, assignment, role, pledge, dictate, office, engagement. **2.** A tax on imports or exports. See duties.

Dwarf, *v.* **dwarfish,** *adj.* See overcome (2); small; dying.

Dwell, *v.* **1.** To live in a place (dwell in the community). Inhabit, live, sojourn, reside, stay, rest, quarter, occupy, room, domicile, settle, remain. **2.** To emphasize (the judge dwelt on the issue). Linger, stress, harp on, reiterate, impress, ponder, elaborate. *Ant.* Depart; ignore.

Dweller, *n.* See inhabitant, tenant.

Dwelling, *n.* The house or other structure in which persons live (breaking into a dwelling). Residence, abode, habitation, apartment, homestead, quarters, lodging, household, domicile. See also home.

Dwindle, *v.* See decline (2), diminish.

Dye, *n.* See color (4).

Dyed-in-the-wool, *adj.* See comprehensive, complete (2).

Dying, *adj.* **1.** Concerning death; approaching death (dying declaration). Expiring, moribund, passing, deteriorating, at death's door. **2.** Fading (a dying doctrine). Disappearing, declining, vanishing, waning, retiring, receding, diminishing. See also obsolete. *Ant.* Vigorous.

Dying declaration Statements made by a person who is lying at the point of death and, who is conscious of his or her approaching death, concerning the circumstances leading up to the injury or death (e.g., who caused it).

Dying without issue Dying without a child either before or after the decedent's death.

Dynamic, *adj.* See active (3), durable, ardent, strong (2), incendiary; life (3), vigor.

Dynamite, *adj., n.* See incendiary, outrageous; ammunition, arms, weapon.

Dynamite instruction See Allen charge.

Dynasty, *n.* See family.

E

Each, *adj., adv.* See all.

Eager, *adj.* See active (3), earnest (2).

Earlier, *adj.* See prior (1), previous.

Early, *adj.* See prompt (1), first; old, ancient.

Earmark, *v.* **1.** To place a mark on a thing to distinguish it from another (the property was earmarked by the clerk). Label, identify, designate, use a trademark, place a symbol on, insert an emblem, tag, name, stamp, brand. See also specialty. **2.** To set aside (money earmarked for research). Reserve, hold, store, cache, appropriate.

Earn, *v.* **1.** To acquire by labor, service, or performance (ability to earn). Gain, win, achieve, profit, realize, reap, garner, clear, draw, attain, secure. **2.** To merit or deserve (she earned the admiration of her colleagues). Deserve, rate, have a right to, qualify for, harvest. *Ant.* Spend; lose.

Earned income Income (e.g., wages, salary, fees) derived from labor, professional service, or entrepreneurship as opposed to income derived from invested capital (e.g., rents, dividends, interest).

Earned surplus The surplus that has been generated from profits as opposed to a paid-in surplus.

Earnest 1. *n.* Earnest money. The payment of a part of the price by the buyer at the time of entering the contract to indicate the intention and ability of the buyer to carry out the contract. (The real estate contract involved $5,000 in earnest money.) Deposit, down payment, installment, stake money, security, binder, pledge. **2.** *adj.* Sincere (an earnest effort to meet the deadline). Zealous, deep-felt, assiduous, diligent, serious, fervent, passionate, ardent, devoted, determined, eager, intent, industrious, spirited, urgent, committed, profound, thoughtful, firm, purposeful, hearty, decisive, enthusiastic. *Ant.* Principal; indifferent.

Earning capacity The capability of a worker to sell his or her labor or services in any reasonably accessible market, taking into consideration his or her age, prior earnings, education and training, prior work experience, physical health, mental health, and other responsibilities.

Earnings, *n.* That which is earned; money earned from the performance of labor, services, sale of goods (a tax on earnings). Wages, salary, commission, revenue, profit, proceeds, receipts, winnings, cut, return, stipend. See also income, compensation. *Ant.* Losses.

Earnings and profits A tax concept peculiar to corporate taxpayers, which measures economic capacity to make a distribution to shareholders that is not a return of capital.

Earth, *n.* **1.** Soil of all kinds (removal of the earth around the wall). Gravel, clay, loam, topsoil, turf, humus, dust, silt, terra, sod. See also dirt, shrubbery, woods. **2.** The world (orbit the earth). Globe, planet. See also world.

Earthly, *adj.* See secular, profane (2), material (2), physical.

Earthquake, *n.* See eruption, act of God, chance (1, 2).

Ease 1. *n.* Comfort, enjoyment (a life of ease). Consolation, contentment, happiness, pleasure, satisfaction, security, peace, peace of mind, facility, freedom, rest, relief, tranquility, prosperity, leisure. **2.** *v.* To lessen the burden (the medication eased the suffering). Alleviate, mitigate, lighten, help, abate, assuage, soothe, pacify, moderate, tranquilize, relax, mollify, ameliorate, quiet. *Ant.* Misery; aggravate.

Easement, *n.* A right to use the land of another for a special and limited purpose not inconsistent with a general property in the owner (the right of way was an easement). Privilege, liberty, advantage, servitude, dominant tenement, service way. See affirmative easement, negative easement.

Easement appurtenant As easement interest that attaches to the land and passes with it.

Easement by implication An easement that the law imposes by inferring that the parties to a transaction intended it even though they did not express it.

Easement by necessity An easement that arises by operation of law when land conveyed is completely shut off from access to any road by the land retained by the grantor or by the land of the grantor and that of a stranger.

Easement by prescription An easement created by the open, notorious, hostile, adverse, uninterrupted, exclusive, and continuous use of the land for a designated period of time.

Easement in gross An easement that is a purely personal right to use the land of another and usually ends with the death of the grantee.

Easement of access The right that an abutting owner has of ingress and egress to and from his or her premises and to have the premises accessible to patrons.

Easy, *adj.* See simple (1, 2), comfortable, quiet (1, 2), effortless.

Easygoing, *adj.* See quiet (1, 2), casual (3), happy, indifferent.

Eat, *v.* To take food into the mouth and swallow it. Chew, grind, masticate, ingest, gulp, devour, dine, consume, feed, bite, snack, break bread, feast, gobble, munch.

Eatable, *adj.* See edible.

Eavesdrop, *v.* Knowingly and without lawful authority or consent (a) to enter into a private place with the intent to listen surreptitiously to private conversations, or (b) to install or use outside a private place any device for hearing, recording, amplifying, or broadcasting sounds originating in such place when such sounds would not ordinarily be audible or comprehensible outside, or (c) to install or use any device or equipment for the interception of any telephone, telegraph, or other wire communication. Wiretap, spy, monitor, overhear, tap, intercept. See also "bug," inspection.

Ebb, *v.* See decline, withdraw, abate (2).

Ebullience, *n.* See passion, happiness, spirit (2).

Ebullient, *adj.* See emotional, happy, earnest (2), active (3), ardent, strong (2).

Eccentric, *n., adj.* See nonconformist, odd (1), anomalous, wild; eccentricity.

Eccentricity, *n.* Personal or individual peculiarities of mind and disposition which markedly distinguish the person from the ordinary, normal, or average, but do not amount to mental unsoundness or insanity (the eccentricities of the testator). Oddity, idiosyncrasy, mannerism, nonconformity, irregularity, individuality, abnormality, aberration, incongruity, quirk, deviation, uniqueness, capriciousness, caprice, whim. See also difference, discrepancy. *Ant.* Normalcy.

Ecclesiastical, *adj.* Pertaining to the church (ecclesiastical courts). Nonsecular, clerical, churchly, religious, spiritual, priestly, pastoral, episcopal, ministerial, hierarchical. *Ant.* Secular.

Echelon, *n.* See rank (1), hierarchy, office, authority.

Echo, *n., v.* See repetition, copy, repeat, return (2), duplicate, resemble; reverberate.

Eclectic

Eclectic, *adj.* See comprehensive, divers, multiple.

Eclipse, *v., n.* See block, obscure (3), obliterate, beat (2); abolition, rescission.

Ecological, *adj.* Pertaining to the study or science of the relationship between organisms and their environment (ecological impact statement). Environmental, pollution, conservation.

Ecology, *n.* See environment, science, conservation; pollution.

Economic, *adj.* Pertaining to the production, distribution, and management of the wealth, goods, and services within a unit, e.g., home, state, country (economic forecast). Fiscal, monetary, pecuniary, financial, budgetary, material, productive. *Ant.* Cultural.

Economical, *adj.* Thrifty in the management of resources (an economical administrator). Prudent, careful, frugal, modest, conservative, provident, cheap, niggardly, saving, parsimonious. *Ant.* Prodigal.

Economize, *v.* See save (2), conserve.

Economy, *n.* **1.** The economic status or structure of an area (inflationary economy). Wealth, regulation of fiscal resources, material well-being, financial management, economic system. **2.** Prudent expenditure of money or use of resources (the need for economy in the administration of the department). Frugality, providence, husbandry, thrift, conservation, economizing, supervision of resources, budgetary control, budgetary discipline.

Ecstasy, *n.* See happiness, heaven, passion, emotion, spirit (2), afterlife.

Ecstatic, *adj.* See happy, ardent, emotional, earnest (2), active (3), strong (2).

Ecumenical, *adj.* See universal, comprehensive, complete (2), broad (1).

Eddy, *n.* Countercurrent. Whirlpool, vortex.

Edge, *n., v.* See verge, border (1), boundary, extension; benefit (1), aid (2); sharpen.

Edgy, *adj.* See apprehensive, concerned; anxiety.

Edible, *adj.* Fit to eat. Comestible, eatable, digestible, nutritious. See also wholesome, delectable. *Ant.* Toxic.

Edict, *n.* A formal decree, command, or proclamation (the employees resented the edicts of the director). Pronouncement, order, regulation, ordinance, direction, fiat, mandate, law, manifesto, declaration, canon, enactment, dictate, bull, precept, injunction, ruling, ukase, prescript. *Ant.* Suggestion.

Edification, *n.* See education, information (2), judgment (2), discretion (3).

Edifice, *n.* See building (1), facility (2).

Edify, *v.* See educate, instruct, improve, nurture, discipline (4).

Edit, *v.* See censor, correct (2), revise.

Edition, *n.* See book (4), revision.

Editor, *n.* See censor.

Educable, *adj.* See flexible, amenable (2).

Educate, *v.* To give proper moral, intellectual, and physical instruction; to prepare oneself for a task or occupation (the parent had insufficient means to educate the child). Develop, teach, enlighten, train, guide, indoctrinate, brief, coach, cultivate, preach, school, explain, inform, civilize, rear, tutor, familiarize. See also instruct, improve, nurture, discipline (4), convey (2).

Educated, *adj.* See capable (2), brilliant, learned, able, apt (3, 4), cognizant, familiar (1); civil (3), debonair.

Education, *n.* The acquisition of knowledge (vocational, intellectual, moral, physical), tending to train and develop the individual (child support covering the expenses of education). Training, schooling, mental development, upbringing, knowledge, direction, guidance, scholarship, instruction, tutelage, cultivation, discipline, edification, acculturation, learning, erudition, culture, pedagogy, academics.

Educational, *adj.* See academic (2).

Educator, *n.* See teacher, scholar.

Eerie, *adj.* See odd, mysterious, odious, bad (2), repulsive.

Efface, *v.* See cancel (1), expungate, expunge, extinguish, kill, destroy.

Effect 1. *n.* That which is produced (the effect of the board's decision was insolvency). Result, outcome, consequence, aftermath, upshot, end product, sequel, development, repercussion, issue, impact, reaction, by-product, fallout. **2.** *v.* To bring about (the board tried to effect change). Execute, accomplish, do, produce, effectuate, cause, enforce, actuate, create, bring to pass, initiate, attain, realize. *Ant.* Cause; block.

Effective, *adj.* **1.** Having the desired effect (an effective oral argument to the jury). Successful, impressive, capable, skillful, practical, cogent, striking, powerful, efficacious, strong, competent, adequate, sufficient, telling, forceful, productive, moving, incisive, compelling, emphatic, effectual. **2.** In operation (the contract clause becomes effective at noon). Operational, valid, in effect, working, active, operative, activated, current, a reality, in force. *Ant.* Impotent; inactive.

Effects, *n.* The personal estate or property of someone (the gun was found among her effects). Goods, assets, belongings, movables, possessions, wealth, resources, chattels, holdings, personalty. See also estate, property.

Effectual, *adj.* See effective, efficient, adequate, competent, sufficient, legal, sound, valid, fit.

Effectuate, *v.* See cause (2), effect (2), enact, enforce, execute (1).

Effectuation, *n.* See enforcement.

Effeminate, *adj.* Emasculated, unmanly, sissyish. See weak.

Effervescent, *adj.* See happy, emotional, active (3), ardent, earnest (2), strong (2), life (3).

Effete, *adj.* See decadent, weak, barren, corrupt.

Efficacious, *adj.* See effective, sound, valid, able, efficient, apt (3), active, strong (3), fit.

Efficacy, *n.* Effectiveness. See power, competence, ability; effective.

Efficiency, *n.* See ability, power, facility (2), competence, fitness.

Efficiency apartment A small apartment. See home.

Efficient, *adj.* Properly producing a desired effect; adequate in performance (an efficient paralegal). Effective, competent, productive, potent, skillful, proficient, energetic, experienced, accomplished, timesaving, capable. See also fit, able, functional, practicable. *Ant.* Ineffective.

Efficient cause The cause that produces the effect or result; the procuring cause; the immediate agent in the production of an event. See cause.

Efficient intervening cause A new and independent force that breaks the causal connection between the original wrong and the injury; a new and independent force that so interrupts the chain of events as to become the proximate cause of the injury. See cause.

Effigy, *n.* An image, model, or representation of a person. See copy, model, sculpture.

Effort, *n.* A struggle directed to the accomplishment of an object (the effort to repeal the order). Attempt, endeavor, exertion, work, strain, toil, push, venture, discipline, essay, trial, industry, aim, energy. See also labor.

Effortless, *adj.* Painless. Easy, simple, uncomplicated, facile, smooth, not difficult. See also casual.

Effrontery, *n.* Audacity. Brazenness, impudence, nerve, indiscretion, impertinence, gall, cheek, presumption, temerity. See also arrogance, spirit (2), insolence.

Effusive, *adj.* See emotional, earnest (2), active (3), ardent; verbose.

267

Egalitarian

Egalitarian, *adj.* See equal.

Egghead, *n.* An intellectual. See teacher, scholar; brilliant.

Egg on, *v.* See encourage, entice, provoke (1).

Ego, *n.* See spirit (3), mind, life.

Egoistic, *adj.* See arrogant; boast; showoff.

Egregious, *adj.* See extreme (1), offensive, notorious (2), odious, repulsive, grievous (2), deplorable.

Egress, *n.* The means or act of going out (blocked egress). Exit, outlet, gate, departure, way out, doorway, escape, vent, passage out, exodus, window, opening. *Ant.* Entrance.

Eight ball, *n.* See disadvantage.

Ejaculate, *v.* See emit (2); proclaim.

Ejaculation, *n.* See declaration, communication; emission; discharge; precipitate (1).

Eject, *v.* To throw out (the manager ejected the trespasser). Oust, cast out, dispossess, expel, thrust out, dismiss, eliminate, remove, "bounce," exile, jettison, deport, discharge, banish, force out, evict. See also shoot. *Ant.* Invite.

Ejection, *n.* See removal, expulsion, emission, discharge (5).

Ejectment, *n.* An action for the recovery of the possession of land and for damages for its unlawful detention. The action was used as a method of establishing the title to the land.

Ejusdem generis Of the same kind, class, or nature. In a written document (e.g., statute, contract), general words sometimes follow a list of specific items (e.g., dogs, cats, *and other animals*). When the meaning of the general language at the end is in doubt, it is to be interpreted as being limited by the kind, class, or nature of the items in the specific list unless it is otherwise clear that the general language was intended to have a broader meaning.

Elaborate, *v., adj.* See develop (2), add (1, 2), augment, comment (2); complete (2), complex (1).

Elaboration, *n.* See development (1), clarification, attachment (3)

Elan, *n.* See spirit (2).

Elapse, *v.* See lapse (1), end (2).

Elastic, *adj.* See flexible, malleable, conciliatory, amenable; convertible.

Elated, *adj.* See happy, emotional, active (3), ardent, strong (2).

Elbowroom, *n.* See margin (2).

Elder, *adj.* Senior. See old; chief, veteran, superior.

Elect, *v.* See select (1), choose.

Election, *n.* The act of choosing or selecting one or more from a greater number of persons, things, courses, or rights (the election of a chairperson). Selection by vote, nomination, designation, poll, voting, balloting; choice, pick; contest, competition, politics. See also preference. *Ant.* Rejection.

Election against the will See election by spouse.

Election at large An election in which a public official is selected from a major election district, e.g., the entire city, rather than from a subdivision within the larger unit.

Election by spouse The right provided by statute allowing a surviving spouse to take what her husband provided for her in his will *or* to take the share of his estate designated by the statute even if it is more than the will provided. If she elects against the will, the statute often gives her what she would have received if her husband had died intestate.

Election of remedies A choice between two inconsistent remedies by a party. Today, most courts allow a party to plead inconsistent remedies. There was a time, however, when a choice had to be made and the party was bound by the choice.

Elective, *adj.* Dependent on choice (elective surgery). Voluntary, optional, picked, discretionary, chosen. *Ant.* Mandatory.

Elective share The statutory share selected by a widow against the will. See election by spouse.

Elector, *n.* A duly qualified voter. See voter.

Electoral College A body of electors from each state who are chosen to elect the president and vice-president. Each state legislature determines how the electors are appointed. The number of electors from a state is equal to the total number of representatives and senators of the state in Congress.

Electorate, *n.* See voter, people, constituency, country (1), citizen, nation.

Electric, *adj.* See moving (1).

Electrify, *v.* See surprise (1), animate, incite; amaze.

Electronic surveillance See eavesdrop, bug.

Eleemosynary, *adj.* Having to do with charity (eleemosynary motive). Philanthropic, humanitarian, nonprofit, altruistic, generous, munificent. See also charitable, benevolent. *Ant.* Commercial.

Eleemosynary corporation A private corporation created for charitable and benevolent purposes.

Elegance, *n.* See delicacy, dignity; honor (3), character (1), worth (1); wealth.

Elegant, *adj.* See formal, cultivated, beautiful, chic, current, debonair, attractive, aristocratic, civil (3); grave (3).

Elegit (*Lat.*) "He has chosen." A writ of execution chosen by the plaintiff by which the debtor's property was delivered to the plaintiff in satisfaction of the debt. The debtor's land was also held by the plaintiff if further satisfaction was needed. During this period, the plaintiff's interest in the debtor's land was called an "estate by elegit."

Element, *n.* A constituent part (an element of a crime). Segment, subdivision, ingredient, particular, member, detail, basic part, unit, essential portion. See also component, factor, part (1). *Ant.* Whole.

Elemental, elementary, *adj.* See fundamental, essential, intrinsic, primary; original, clear, simple.

Elements, *n.* The forces of nature (anticipate the impact of the elements). Weather, atmospheric conditions. See also environment, climate.

Elevate, *v.* See honor (2), advance (4), back, build, augment, lift (2), raise (2).

Elevated, *adj.* Dignified. Lofty, grand, stately, eminent, exalted, majestic, noble, illustrious, sublime, imposing, distinguished, preeminent, admirable. See also honest, meritorious.

Elevation, *n.* See altitude, ascent (2), extent.

Elevator, *n.* Lift. Conveyor, escalator.

Elicit, *v.* See extract (1), ferret, derive (2), deduce, extort, provoke, induce.

Eligible, *adj.* Fit and proper to be chosen (eligible for the directorship). Qualified, acceptable, suitable, worthy, desirable, satisfactory, appropriate, preferable. *Ant.* Ineligible.

Eliminate, *v.* See erase, rescind, annul, bar, ban, destroy, kill, oust; elimination.

Elimination, *n.* The act of rejection or eradication (the elimination of the inconsistency in the argument). Abolition, repudiation, exclusion, dissolution, eviction, cancellation, editing out, deletion, suppression, expulsion, excision, termination, exile, ouster, annihilation, destruction, extermination, liquidation, prohibition, nullification, evacuation, censoring, renouncement, dismissal. See also removal. *Ant.* Incorporation.

Elite, *n., adj.* See aristocracy, coterie, establishment (4); favored, dominant.

Elitist, *adj.* See arrogant, pompous; parochial (2), narrow (2), bias.

Elixir, *n.* See cure (1); essence.

Ellipsis, *n.* The omission or words or clauses from something that is quoted (use dots [...] or asterisks [* * *] to indicate ellipsis).

Elliptical, *adj.* See ambiguous; brief (3).

Eloign, *v.* To remove in order to conceal (his property was eloigned).

Elongate, *v.* See extend (1), prolong.

Elope, *v.* See flee, run (2); marriage.

Eloquent, *adj.* See articulate (2), cogent, effective, moving (1), concise, descriptive, demonstrative.

Elucidate, *v.* See clarify, define, develop (2), comment (2), add (1, 2), augment.

Elucidation, *n.* See clarification, definition, development (1).

Elude, *v.* See avoid (2), escape (1), flee; frustrate.

Elusive, *adj.* See evasive, intangible, mysterious, transitory (2), brief (4).

Eluvium, *n.* Deposits of soil and rock produced by the wind.

Emaciate, *v.* See consume (2), wear (1), decline (2), diminish; atrophy, consumption (2).

Emaciated, *adj.* See frail, infirm, weak, thin.

Emanate, *v.* See arise (1), emerge, emit (2), escape (3), discharge.

Emancipate, *v.* See discharge (3), release (1), liberate; emancipation, enfranchisement.

Emancipation, *n.* The express or implied consent of a parent to relinquish his or her control and authority over a child. The parent no longer supports the child, and the latter no longer must turn over his or her earnings to nor perform services for the parent (his emancipation took place when he was drafted). Liberation, unfettering, unbridling, suffrage, self-government, liberty, manumission, freedom. See also enfranchisement, release (3). *Ant.* Subjugation.

Emasculate, *v.* See debilitate, incapacitate.

Embalming, *n.* See preservation; burial, morgue.

Embankment, *n.* See bank (4).

Embargo, *n.* A proclamation or order of the government prohibiting the departure of ships or goods from some or all ports until further order; government order prohibiting commercial trade with individuals or businesses of other countries (the embargo led to war). Restriction, detention, prohibition, barrier, stoppage, proscription, interdiction.

Embark, *v.* See commence, begin, establish (1); board (3), enter (4).

Embarrass, *v.* To make ill at ease, (embarrassed by the libelous speech). Mortify, shame, annoy, abash, disconcert, upset, vex, faze, fluster, chagrin, humble, confuse, disturb, discomfort, perplex, bewilder, worry, nonplus, discountenance. See also discredit, disparage; ashamed.

Embarrassing, *adj.* See awkward; embarrass, embarrassment.

Embarrassment, *n.* Humiliation or mortification (embarrassment caused by the scandal). Shame, unease, bewilderment, awkwardness, discomfort, self-consciousness. See also anxiety, ordeal, distress (3), disgrace, constraint (3).

Embassy, *n.* The mission, headquarters, or official residence of an ambassador; the body of diplomatic representatives headed by the ambassador (hostages taken at the embassy). Consulate, delegation, legation. See also delegate (2).

Embed, *v.* See enclose, fix (2), attach (2), establish (3).

Embellish, *v.* See beautify, furnish, clothe, color (3), enhance; exaggerate, distort, lie, manufacture (3).

Embellishment, *n.* See decoration.

Ember, *n.* See fire (1).

Embezzle, *v.* To willfully take or convert to one's own use the money or property of another, which the wrongdoer initially acquired lawfully because of a position of trust (the employee embezzled the firm's funds). Misappropriate, swindle, steal, defalcate, misuse, peculate, pilfer, commit larceny. See also cheat, deceive, fraud.

Embezzlement, *n.* See embezzle, fraud, larceny.

Embitter, *v.* See harass, exacerbate, disturb; angry, hostile; aggravated.

Emblem, *n.* See manifestation, badge.

Emblements, *n.* The crops annually produced by the labor of the tenant to which the latter is entitled.

Embodiment, *n.* Incarnation. Image, expression, incorporation, personification, exemplification, concretization. See also manifestation.

Embody, *v.* See manifest (2), comprehend (2); prove; represent (2); embodiment.

Embrace, *v.* See caress; comprehend (2), include, fall (1), entail (3), cover (3); adopt (2).

Embracery, *n.* The crime of corruptly trying to influence a jury by promises, entertainments, etc. (the embracer was convicted of embracery).

Embroider, *v.* See color (3), distort, misrepresent, exaggerate, enhance, beautify.

Embroil, *v.* See disturb, confuse, implicate.

Embryo, *n.* See commencement; birth (1); root.

Embryonic, *adj.* See inchoate, initial.

Emend, *v.* See correct, improve.

Emerge, *v.* To arise; to come to light (the inconsistency in the documents emerged after the interview). Materialize, manifest, become evident, issue, emanate, become visible, derive from, develop, turn up, loom, surface, spring, proceed, arise, rise, become noticeable, crop up. See also escape (3). *Ant.* Disappear.

Emergence, *n.* See appearance (2), issue (2); emerge.

Emergency, *n.* A sudden unexpected happening (the driver was faced with an emergency). Unforeseen occurrence, perplexing contingency, sudden occasion for action, exigency, pressing necessity, imminent peril, urgency, accident, predicament, dilemma, quandary, crisis, extremity, "jam," difficulty, crucial time. See also plight.

Emergency doctrine When a person is confronted with a sudden peril requiring instinctive action, he or she is not held to the exercise of the same degree of care as when there is time for mature reflection. There may be no liability for negligence if this person injures someone while responding to the peril if he or she used due care to avoid getting into the emergency and responded as prudently as possible under these unusual circumstances.

Emergency room, *n.* See hospital, ward (3).

Emigrant, *n.* One who leaves his or her country with the intention to reside elsewhere and not return (she hired emigrants to work in Canada). Expatriate, émigré, alien. See also exile (2); immigrant.

Emigrate, *v.* See leave (2), move (2), depart; emigration.

Emigration, *n.* The act of moving from one country to another with the intention of not returning (restrictions on emigration). Migration, exodus, relocation, resettling. See also departure, immigration.

Émigré, *n.* See emigrant, exile (2); immigrant.

Eminence, *n.* Prominence, superiority (her eminence as an attorney). Greatness, distinction, majesty, standing, reputation, importance, noteworthiness, esteem, influence, celebrity, supremacy, prestige, exaltation. See also note (4), regard (2), notoriety. *Ant.* Disrepute.

Eminent, *adj.* See elevated, outstanding (2), great (2), reputable.

Eminent domain The power of government to take private property for public use upon the payment of just compensation (in order to build the road, the city acquired the land by eminent domain). Condemnation, expropriation, forced sale, compulsory acquisition. See also condemn (2).

Emissary, *n.* A person sent on a mission as the agent of another (an emissary from the king). Messenger, deputy, courier, representative, envoy, go-between, spy, informer. See also delegate.

Emission, *n.* The discharge of something (emission of pollution). Ejection, throwing out, expulsion, transmission, issuance, projection, ejaculation, drainage. *Ant.* Reception.

Emit, *v.* **1.** To place in circulation (no state shall emit bills of credit). Issue, circulate, distribute, publish. **2.** To put forth or send out (the engine emits poisonous gas). Discharge, throw off, transmit, exhale, expel, radiate, ejaculate, secrete, perspire, emanate, beam, exhaust, squirt, ooze. *Ant.* Withhold; absorb.

Emolument, *n.* Compensation for services or for an occupation (an investigation into secretly received emoluments). Wages, fringes, remuneration, benefits, gain, reward, stipend, earnings, allowance; kickback, graft, bribe. See also compensation, income.

Emotion, *n.* **1.** A subjective mental state such as hate, love, sorrow, etc. (the witness was asked to describe his emotions at the time). Sentiment, feeling, sensation, disposition attitude, temper, temperament, morale, humor, pulse, frame of mind, affection, constitution, proclivity, propensity, complexion, reaction, response. **2.** A state of mental agitation (she spoke with emotion). Disturbance, enthusiasm, eagerness, concern, despair, excitement, fervor. See also passion. *Ant.* Rationalization; indifference.

Emotional, *adj.* Easily stirred by emotion; pertaining to emotions (an emotional witness). Impetuous, excitable, fervent, nervous, hot-blooded, volatile, temperamental, tense, frantic, demonstrative, impassioned, zealous, fiery, impulsive, hypersensitive, ardent, vulnerable, high-strung, sentimental, enthusiastic, dramatic, melodramatic, pathetic, susceptible, thin-skinned, inflammable; sympathetic, affectionate, compassionate. *Ant.* Apathetic.

Emotionless, *adj.* See indifferent, callous, apathetic.

Empanel, *v.* See impanel.

Empathize, *v.* To identify with the situation or predicament of another. Sympathize, feel one with, relate to, understand. See also commiserate, appreciate (2).

Empathy, *n.* Commiseration. Identification, understanding. See also mercy, charity (3, 4), consideration (3).

Emperor, *n.* See king, tyrant, authority (3).

Emphasis, *n.* See emphasize; accent, weight.

Emphasize, *v.* To place a special significance or weight on something (the memo emphasized the damage issue). Underline, accentuate, call attention to, stress, highlight, underscore, note, dramatize, headline, belabor, intensify, dwell on, feature, punctuate, italicize, pinpoint, press, give prominence to, spotlight. See also accent. *Ant.* Ignore.

Emphatic, *adj.* See express (1), positive (1), assertive, explicit.

Empire, *n.* The territory ruled over by one country; supreme dominion (the director was accused of building an empire). Kingdom, realm, imperial power, sovereign command, sovereignty, vast area, power accumulation. See also domain.

Empirical, *adj.* Based on experience, experiment, or observation (empirical evidence). Sensed, heard, felt, observed, seen, concrete, experiential, verified, scientific, firsthand, practical, factual. *Ant.* Speculative. See also demonstrable.

Employ, *v.* **1.** To engage in one's service; to use as an agent or substitute in transacting business (she employed three accountants). Hire, commission, appoint, recruit, enroll, apprentice, place on the payroll, retain, place. See also engage. **2.** To make use of (the lawyer employed a variety of techniques).

Utilize, apply, operate, exercise, practice, manipulate, handle, ply, devote, capitalize on, avail oneself of, wield, exert, have recourse to, profit from, put to use, play, occupy, have the use of, resort to, press into service, drain, consume, bleed, dedicate, waste, take advantage of, exploit. *Ant.* Dismiss; reject.

Employee, *n.* A person in the service of another under an express or implied, oral or written contract of hire, in which the employer has the power and the right to control and direct the employee in the material details of how the work is to be performed (the employee acted within the scope of her employment). Servant, salaried worker, agent, wage earner, laborer, jobholder, staff member, hand, apprentice, journeyman, retainer, hireling, lackey, messenger, attendant, subordinate, workman, artisan, mechanic, craftsman, workaholic, breadwinner, helper, aide, henchman, valet, underling, domestic, retainer, white-collar worker, proletarian, hustler, flunky, man Friday, personnel. See also assistant. *Ant.* Employer.

Employer, *n.* One who employs the services of others for wages or other compensation, with the right and power to control and direct them in the material details of how the work is to be performed (the employer was liable for the tort of her employee). Master, proprietor, contractor, owner, principal, manager, director, boss, chief; company, business, organization. See also builder, entrepreneur, patron (2), backer. *Ant.* Employee.

Employment, *n.* The activity in which a person is engaged or is employed, usually on a day-to-day basis (employment as a paralegal). Occupation, job, profession, work, vocation, line, trade, activity, labor, craft, livelihood, service, business, calling, task, assignment, function, position, situation, industry, living, career, specialty, duty, post. See also domain (2), operation, application.

Empower, *v.* To grant authority (she empowered her agent to sign the contract). Authorize, commission, license, sanction, accredit, qualify, warrant, delegate, entitle, certify, entrust, charter, franchise, permit, equip, outfit, capacitate, vest, invest, grant, deputize, confer authority on, endow, grant permission. *Ant.* Enjoin.

Emptor, *n.* A buyer or purchaser. See caveat emptor.

Empty, *adj.* See void (3), null and void, vacant, unoccupied, barren, worthless, frivolous, nugatory.

Empty-headed, *adj.* See dumb, absurd, irrational, juvenile; idiot, boor.

Emulate, *v.* See copy (2), follow (1).

Enable, *v.* To give power to do something (the court order enabled the sheriff to seize the property). Empower, authorize, qualify, accredit, license, commission, sanction, facilitate, outfit, capacitate, aid, deputize, delegate, endow, permit, appoint, validate, arm, franchise, legalize. See also entitle, vest. *Ant.* Incapacitate.

Enabling clause That portion of a statute or constitution which gives to governmental officials the right to put it into effect and to enforce it.

Enact, *v.* To establish by law (be it enacted). Legislate, institute by law, put into effect, decree, command, codify, establish, dictate, sanction, effect, pass, prescribe, make, proclaim, effectuate, execute. *Ant.* Repeal.

Enacting clause A clause at the beginning of a statute, which states the authority by which it is made (e.g., "Be it enacted by the people of the state of Illinois represented in general assembly").

Enactment, *n.* The method or process by which a bill in the legislature becomes a law; the law itself that is enacted (the enactment was declared unconstitutional). Legislation, codification, measure, statute, law, act, rule, bill, regulation, ordinance, fiat.

Enamor, *v.* To captivate. Fascinate, charm, enchant, excite, bewitch, enthrall, infatuate. See also entice, absorb (2).

273

En banc A session of the court in which the full membership of the court, rather than a smaller grouping or panel of the judges, will participate in the decision (the court sitting en banc). Full bench, all together, collectively, as a whole, as a unit.

Encase, *v.* See enclose.

Enchain, *v.* See confine, bind, dominate, coerce, compel, intimidate, conquer.

Enchant, *v.* See enamor, absorb (2), entice, entrap, delight, interest (5), bait (3), inveigle.

Enchanting, *adj.* See attractive, intriguing, amicable, debonair, affectionate; compelling, enjoyable, beautiful.

Encircle, *v.* See confine, surround, enclose.

Enclose, *v.* **1.** To surround or fence (the owner enclosed the area to keep out trespassers). Bound, hem in, shut in, encircle, circle, wall in, circumscribe, encase, confine, engird, enwrap, blockade, ring, pen. **2.** To insert (payment is enclosed). Include, contain, send along, package. *Ant.* Open; remove.

Enclosure, *n.* Land surrounded by visible obstruction; that which is enclosed (trespass into the enclosure). Fence, confine, court, yard, close, pen, compound, cloister, camp, stockade, circle, boundary, fenced area, zone, perimeter; stall, booth, bay, cubicle, room.

Encompass, *v.* See surround, enclose; include, comprehend (2), cover (3), fall (1).

Encounter, *n., v.* See meeting, confrontation, argument, face (2), conflict, confront.

Encourage, *v.* **1.** To instigate (the defendant encouraged the co-defendant to commit the crime). Incite, aid, advocate, embolden, foment, lobby, induce, impel, sway, promote, prompt, stir up, "egg on," succor, foster, help, urge, goad, countenance, inflame, exhort. See also instigate, abet, influence. **2.** To raise someone's confidence to be able to do something (she was encouraged to attend law school). Inspire, support, hearten, boost, favor, inspirit, animate, reassure, stimulate, motivate. *Ant.* Deter; discourage.

Encouragement, *n.* See hope (2), help (1), assistance, approbation; encourage.

Encouraging, *adj.* See optimistic, certain (2), positive (1), auspicious; beneficial.

Encroach, *v.* To enter by gradual steps or stealth into the possessions or rights of another (the fence encroached on her property). Intrude, trespass, invade, infringe, interfere, arrogate, violate, transgress, infiltrate, presume upon, overstep, impinge, overrun, usurp, obtrude, interlope. *Ant.* Respect.

Encroachment, *n.* **1.** An act of encroaching. See intrusion, infringement, violation, invasion, wrong (1); encroach. **2.** An illegal intrusion on a street or navigable river, with or without obstruction.

Encumber, *v.* To burden, hinder, or obligate (he encumbered the land with the mortgage). Saddle, charge, impose, block, tax, limit, constrain, weigh down, handicap, disadvantage, shackle, make responsible, weaken, inconvenience, impede. *Ant.* Unburden.

Encumbrance, *n.* Any right to or interest in land that may subsist in another, resulting in a diminution in the value of the land; a claim, lien, charge, impediment, or liability attached to and binding real property, e.g., mortgage, mechanics' lien, judgment lien, tax lien, security interest, easement. See encumber, burden, liability.

Encyclopedic, *adj.* See comprehensive, big, universal, extensive, complete (2), erudite.

End 1. *n.* The object or intent (the end sought by the legislature in the statute). Result, impact, goal, objective, change, design, expectation, aim, target, raison d'être, motive, motivation, effect, consequence, idea, intention, cause, destination, guiding principle, mission. **2.** *v.* To terminate (the court ended its session). Conclude, finish, consummate, wind up, cease, extinguish, settle, quit, arrest, discontinue, accomplish, culminate, check, expire, adjourn, stop, surcease, bring to a close, desist, bring closure; die, decline, destroy, eliminate, abolish. **3.** *n.* See conclusion (1), expiration, rescission, cessation. *Ant.* Means; commence; commencement.

Endanger, *v.* To expose to danger (they endangered the lives of the passengers). Imperil, put in jeopardy, jeopardize, compromise, risk, hazard, threaten, render defenseless, leave unprotected, take a chance. See also expose (2). *Ant.* Safeguard.

Endear, *v.* See enamor, honor (2), delight, interest (5), absorb (2); entice, entrap, bait (3).

Endearing, *adj.* See attractive, amicable, affectionate.

Endearment, *n.* See affection (1).

Endeavor 1. *v.* To exert physical and intellectual strength toward the attainment of an object (they endeavored to overturn the decision). Attempt, undertake, exert oneself, venture, toil, strive, tackle, strain, aspire, struggle, apply oneself, assay, labor, pursue. **2.** *n.* A systematic or continuous effort (the endeavor had little support). Try, exertion, enterprise, quest, cause, work, campaign, scheme, exploit, pursuit, trial, deed, effort.

Endemic, *adj.* See native (2), local.

Ending, *n.* See conclusion (1), expiration, cessation, rescission.

Endless, *adj.* See perpetual, permanent, indestructible, incalculable; big, great.

Endorse, *v.* **1.** See back (1), finance (1), guarantee (1), recommend, approve, authorize, certify. **2.** See indorsement.

Endorsement, *n.* See indorsement, backing, certification, approval.

Endorsee, *n.* See indorsee, beneficiary.

Endorser, *n.* See indorser, guarantor, patron.

Endow, *v.* **1.** To bestow upon (the testator endowed her college with a large gift). Bequeath, grant, will, subsidize, present, contribute, award, provide, fund, donate, furnish, enrich, allot. **2.** To give a dower. **3.** To equip (she is endowed with excellent advocacy skills). Grace, bless, favor, qualify, adorn, clothe, furnish, crown with. See also enhance, imbue. *Ant.* Divest.

Endowment, *n.* A transfer, usually by gift, of property or money to an institution for a particular purpose (a research endowment for the college). Subsidy, contribution, gift, stipend, allotment, donation, fund, appropriation, legacy, bequest, benefaction, award, grant, inheritance, presentation, bestowal, provision, assistance, aid.

Endurable, *adj.* See bearable, perpetual, durable; endurance.

Endurance, *n.* The power of continuing under pain, stress, and hardship without being overcome (everyone admired the endurance of the jury). Durability, perseverance, stamina, tenacity, backbone, composure, forbearance, tolerance, hardihood, staying power, patience, stoicism, persistence, stick-to-itiveness, permanence. See also resolution (4), force (1), valor, vigor, character (1), quality (2), survival. *Ant.* Frailty.

Endure, *v.* See last (2), live (2), abide, continue, suffer (3), tolerate (2), bear (2), recognize (2).

Enduring, *adj.* See perpetual, durable; patient (2); compelling.

Enemy, *n.* An adversary (she considered him her enemy). Opponent, antagonist, rival, contender, competitor, foe, detractor, nemesis, invader, attacker. See also adversary, assailant. *Ant.* Collaborator.

Enemy alien, *n.* An alien residing or traveling in a country that is at war with the country of which he or she is a national.

Energetic, *adj.* See active (3), alive (2), ardent, indefatigable, diligent, strong (2), durable, prompt (1); spirit (2).

Energize, *v.* See initiate, revive, incite, animate, provoke (1), cause (2).

Energy, *n.* See spirit (2), power, force (1), emotion, ambition, determination (2), diligence (1), enterprise (2).

Enervate, *v.* See debilitate, debase, encumber, wear (1), attenuate, disable; infirm.

Enfeeble, *v.* See disable, attenuate, debilitate, wear (1), encumber, debase; infirm.

Enfeoff, *v.* To invest with an estate; to place someone in possession of an estate in fee (the grantor enfeoffed his nephew).

Enfold, *v.* See cover (3), surround, enclose.

Enforce, *v.* To make effective; to put into execution (the sheriff enforced the order). Carry out, carry through, press, implement, prosecute, accomplish, discharge, administer, realize, compel, put into effect, coerce, make effective, effectuate, exact, fulfill, supervise, manage, oversee, apply, oblige, perform. *Ant.* Disregard.

Enforceable, *adj.* See effective (2), binding, lawful; enforce, enforcement.

Enforcement, *n.* The act of putting something into effect (the enforcement of the judgment). Realization, implementation, administration, execution, effectuation, insistence, fulfillment, prosecution, management, obligation, compulsion, imposition. *Ant.* Waiver.

Enfranchise, *v.* See liberate, authorize (1), entitle.

Enfranchisement, *n.* The act of giving freedom or a franchise to someone (the enfranchisement of the slave). Freedom, emancipation, release, manumission, liberation, licensing, authorization, naturalization, charter, deliverance. See also license. *Ant.* Enslavement.

Engage, *v.* **1.** To employ (they engaged an investigator for the case). Hire, obtain, enlist, appoint, secure, retain, book, lease, rent, commission, sign, take on, enroll, choose, reserve, charter, contract for. **2.** To participate (he was engaged in another activity when the accident occurred). Occupy oneself, involve, undertake, engross, embark on, immerse, absorb, entertain, interest. **3.** To meet in battle (they engaged the enemy). Fight, combat, contest, encounter, war, tangle, interlock, compete, clash, battle, join. **4.** To pledge oneself (they were engaged to be married). Commit, promise, agree, contract, betroth, obligate, affiance. *Ant.* Dismiss; withdraw.

Engaged, *adj.* **1.** Absorbed. Busy, engrossed, occupied, preoccupied, wrapped up, diverted, rapt, involved, immersed. **2.** See bound (1).

Engagement, *n.* See meeting, appointment, enterprise (1), confrontation; duty (1).

Engaging, *adj.* See attractive, amicable, beautiful, irresistible, compelling, intriguing.

Engender, *v.* To bring about (the dismissal engendered considerable hostility). Excite, occasion, call forth, beget, yield, produce, generate, induce, instigate, incite, foment, originate, breed, give rise to, quicken, stimulate, arouse. See also cause (2), precipitate, produce (2). *Ant.* Repress.

Engine, *n.* See apparatus, instrument (2), equipment, device; automation; agency (2).

Engineer, *v., n.* See cause (2), provoke (1), execute (1), realize (2); operator; manipulate, plot (3).

Engineering, *n.* See science, knowledge; fraud, deception.

Engrave, *v.* To etch or carve. Cut, mark, print, imprint, blaze, stamp, brand, scratch, ingrain, embed, inscribe.

Engross, *v.* See engage (2), absorb (2), enamor.

Engrossed, *adj.* See engaged, preoccupied.

Engrossing, *adj.* See engaged, intriguing, attractive, compelling, irresistible; amicable, beautiful.

Engrossment, *n.* **1.** The drafting of a resolution or bill in the legislature just prior to the final vote (the delay was caused by an error in the engrossment). **2.** Buying up or securing enough of a commodity in order to obtain a monopoly. **3.** Preparing a deed for execution. **4.** See concentration (1), preoccupation.

Engulf, *v.* See inundate, submerge, devastate, overcome, overtake; flood.

Enhance, *v.* To make greater (the road enhanced the value of the land). Increase, inflate, strengthen, advance, intensify, embellish, augment, elevate, enlarge, improve, fortify, complement, magnify, perfect, reinforce, escalate, amplify, enrich, emphasize, maximize, boost, expand, appreciate, deepen, sharpen, extend. See also endow (3). *Ant.* Depreciate.

Enhancement, *n.* See increase, advancement (2), accretion; enhance.

Enigma, *n.* See conundrum, mystery, ambiguity.

Enigmatic, *adj.* See mysterious, ambiguous, obscure (1), incoherent, complex (1).

Enjoin, *v.* To require a person to perform or to abstain from some act (the court enjoined the company from making the payment). Command, require, direct, charge, decree, rule, oblige, dictate, ordain, impose, instruct, warn, order, prescribe; ban, suppress, forbid, proscribe, block, thwart, restrict, curb, interdict, impede, prohibit, preclude, retard, repress, hinder.

Enjoy, *v.* **1.** To have, possess, and use with satisfaction (the standard of living enjoyed before the divorce). Have the benefit of, occupy, benefit, reap the benefits of, own, retain, avail oneself of, partake, hold, utilize, keep, maintain, command. **2.** To experience pleasure (she enjoyed her first class). Delight in, appreciate, savor, relish, revel, fancy, adore, adulate, cherish, love, like. *Ant.* Deny; dislike.

Enjoyable, *adj.* Pleasurable. Satisfying, delightful, pleasant, agreeable, entertaining, appealing, gratifying, pleasing, nice, savory, lovely. See also attractive, delectable; enjoy, enjoyment.

Enjoyment, *n.* **1.** The exercise of a right or privilege (an interference with the enjoyment of her property). Use, employment, utilization, occupation, maintenance, possession. **2.** Comfort, pleasure (enjoyment of recreational activities). Happiness, consolation, ease, satisfaction, amusement, relaxation, delight, contentment, gratification, fun, diversion, relish, refreshment, ecstasy, bliss, gaiety. *Ant.* Handicap; loathing.

Enkindle, *v.* See provoke (1), incite; bum.

Enlarge, *v.* To make larger or extend (enlarge the photo). Magnify, add to, increase, inflate, supplement, amplify, widen, extend, lengthen, elongate, grow, escalate, dilate, spread, double, expand, bloat, accelerate, protrude, bulge, stretch, snowball, tumefy, appreciate, intensify, protract. See also augment. *Ant.* Diminish.

Enlargement, *n.* See increase, appreciation (1), growth; enlarge.

Enlighten, *v.* See educate, instruct, improve, nurture, discipline (4), apprise.

Enlightened, *adj.* See informed, judicious, learned, cultivated, open (7).

Enlightenment, *n.* See education, information, judgment (2), discretion (3), comprehension, clarity, common sense, competence.

Enlist, *v.* See enroll, levy (2), engage, employ, induce; enlistment.

Enlisted man, *n.* One who has enlisted in the military without an officer's commission. See military, sailor.

Enlistment, *n.* Voluntary entry into one of the armed services by one other than a commissioned officer (enlistments were down). Sign-up, registration, enrollment, recruitment. *Ant.* Withdrawal.

Enliven, *v.* See revive, incite, animate, provoke, initiate.

En masse, *adv.* In bulk; all together (the committee arrived en masse). In a mass, in a lump, in bulk, in a body, as a block, collectively, as one, as a group, as a unit. *Ant.* Individually.

Enmesh, *v.* See implicate, entrap, mire (2).

Enmity, *n.* See hostility, animus (2), malice, odium.

Ennui, *n.* Boredom. Indifference, tedium, languor, apathy, doldrums, malaise, weariness. See also apathetic, indifferent, casual (3).

Enoc Arden doctrine When a spouse leaves under such circumstances and for such a period of time as to allow the other spouse to believe that the missing spouse is dead, the law will presume that death has occurred. States differ, however, as to what happens if the spouse in fact returns.

Enormity, *n.* See amplitude; enormous; cruelty, degradation, corruption, atrocity.

Enormous, *adj.* Excessively large (an enormous windfall). Huge, mammoth, immense, colossal, prodigious, vast, elephantine, gargantuan, astronomic, gigantic, stupendous, titanic, tremendous. See also big. *Ant.* Minute.

Enough, *adj.* See adequate, abundant.

Enrage, *v.* See provoke, incite, harass; aggravated (2), angry.

Enrich, *v.* See endow (1), enhance, improve, advance (4), remedy (2), benefit (2).

Enrichment, *n.* See betterment (2), amelioration, appreciation (1), endowment; decoration.

Enroll, *v.* **1.** To become a member (enroll in law school). Enlist, matriculate, join, register, subscribe, recruit. See also, impanel, engage (1). **2.** To record (the ship was enrolled). Docket, inscribe, catalogue, chronicle, list, insert. See also record (1), enter (1, 3), inscribe.

Enrolled bill The final copy of a bill or joint resolution that has been passed by both houses of the legislature and is ready for signature; a bill that has gone through all the steps necessary to make it a law.

Enrollment, *n.* See registration; enroll.

En route *adv., adj.* In the course of a voyage or journey (the loss occurred while the goods were en route). On the way, in transit, in the course of transportation, along the way, on the road, while traveling.

Ensconce, *v.* See locate (2); conceal, cover (2), cloak.

Enseal, *v.* To affix a seal (enseal the deed).

Ensemble, *n.* See entirety; whole; uniform (2), apparel, clothes.

Enshrine, *v.* See dedicate, anoint, devote (2), honor (2).

Enshroud, *v.* See conceal, cover (2), cloak.

Ensign, *n.* A commissioned officer. See sailor, military.

Enslave, *v.* See confine, bind, dominate, coerce, compel, intimidate, conquer.

Enslavement, *n.* See bondage, slavery.

Ensnare, *v.* See entrap.

Ensue, *v.* To follow after (when the lawyers met, an argument ensued). Result, arise, develop, derive, happen, transpire, eventuate, follow as a consequence, come after, proceed. *Ant.* Precede.

Ensure, *v.* See insure, assure.

Entail 1. *v.* To impose a limitation on who can inherit real property (they cannot sell the land because it is entailed). **2.** *n.* A fee estate that is limited as to who can inherit it; it does not descend to all the heirs of the owner (the restrictions imposed by the entail). **3.** *v.* To require or impose as a necessity (the assignment entailed considerable legal research). Call for, demand, involve, obligate, necessitate, imply, embrace, contain, comprise, lead to, be incumbent.

Entangle, *v.* See implicate, entrap; mire (2), include; confuse, obscure, compound (2).

Entanglement, *n.* See ordeal, affliction, confusion, complication.

Entente, *n.* See compact (1), agreement, harmony (1).

Enter, *v.* **1.** To place anything before a court or on the court records in a formal way (enter a plea). Register, check in, inscribe, file, post, join, list, enroll, post, docket, document, tabulate, schedule, calendar, set down in writing, note. See also record (1). **2.** To cause to go into or be received into (he entered the land and took possession). Pass into, proceed into, board, come in, insert, set foot in, gain admittance, go upon, arrive, break in, penetrate, invade, trespass, intrude, pierce, wound, puncture, infiltrate, stab, perforate. **3.** To participate in (the lawyer entered the discussion). Join, share, sign up, commit oneself, affiliate, enroll, become a member of, take part in. **4.** To begin (the negotiations entered a new phase). Start, commence, launch, embark, undertake, depart, start off. *Ant.* Stand mute; exit; withdraw; terminate.

Enter a judgment To record the judgment formally on the rolls or records (e.g., the civil docket) of the court, which is necessary before bringing an appeal or an action on the judgment. In some states the judgment is entered merely by filing the judgment with the clerk.

Enterprise, *n.* **1.** A venture or undertaking often involving a financial commitment (the board had no jurisdiction to regulate this kind of enterprise). Engagement, pursuit, activity, plan, campaign, cause, project, endeavor, scheme, operation, gamble, job, task; business, syndicate, economic entity, concern, firm, company, establishment. **2.** Initiative (the secretary's enterprise). Energy, zeal, ambition, spirit, force, courage, boldness, ingenuity, determination, aggressiveness, daring, drive.

Enterprising, *adj.* See courageous, adventurous, ambitious, ardent, assertive.

Entertain, *v.* **1.** See amuse, enamor, interest (5); entertainment, amusement, game. **2.** To show hospitality to. Greet, welcome, dine, fête, regale, host, treat, lodge.

Entertaining, *adj.* See enjoyable, comic, attractive, beautiful; entertainment.

Entertainment, *n.* Amusement or recreation (expenses for entertainment). Diversion, party, pleasure, satisfaction, pastime, enjoyment, fun, sport, distraction, gaiety, show, escapade, merriment.

Enthrall, *v.* See entice, enamor, entertain, entrap, interest (5), bait (3); deceive.

Enthralling, *adj.* See attractive, enjoyable, beautiful.

Enthusiasm, *n.* See life (3), emotion, spirit (2), enterprise (2), determination (2), force (1), passion.

Enthusiast, *n.* See partisan, addict (1), adherent, champion (1), aficionado.

Enthusiastic, *adj.* See active (3), earnest (2), emotional, ardent, strong (2), alive (2).

Entice, *v.* To solicit wrongfully (he enticed the child to leave her home). Procure, allure, coax, lure, tempt, beckon, tantalize, importune, instigate, beguile, inveigle, bait, lead on, decoy. See also solicit (2), induce, incite, persuade. *Ant.* Dissuade.

Enticement, *n.* See invitation, solicitation; entice, entrap.

Enticement of a child A tort with the following elements: (a) an intent to interfere with the parent's custody over the child; (b) affirmative conduct to abduct, force, or encourage the child to leave its parents and/or to stay away; (c) the child in fact leaves the custody of the parent; (d) the defendant causes this.

Entire, *adj.* Whole; without division, separation, or diminution (the will gave her the entire estate). Complete, total, unimpaired, full, comprehensive, all-inclusive, undivided, unmixed, gross, absolute, indivisible, unabridged, unbroken, aggregate, perfect. *Ant.* Partial.

Entirely, *adv.* Wholly. Completely, full, comprehensively, thoroughly. See also exclusively, absolutely, en masse.

Entirety, *n.* The whole (tenants by the entirety). Completeness, totality, unity, entire amount, all of it, gross, undivided amount, aggregate, in all respects, accumulation, ensemble, collection, mass, indivisibility. See also integrity (2); indivisible. *Ant.* Part.

Entitle

Entitle, *v.* To give a right, claim or legal title to (the certificate entitles him to the benefits). Authorize, qualify, sanction, make eligible, license, warrant, permit, enfranchise, enable, empower, charter. *Ant.* Disqualify.

Entitlement, *n.* The right to benefits, income, or other property, which cannot be abridged without due process. See right (3), entitle.

Entity, *n.* A real and distinct being or organization (legal entity). Existence, article, substance, actuality, tangible thing, separate being, body, unit, individual, creature, structure, object. *Ant.* Illusion.

Entomb, *v.* See inter; burial.

Entourage, *n.* See coterie; associate (2).

Entrance, *n.* Opening or passage for entering (the entrance was blocked). Door, passageway, opening, reception, access, portal, gate, way in, corridor, approach, foyer, hallway, threshold, porch, vestibule, archway, waiting room, lobby. See also ingress. *Ant.* Exit.

Entrant, *n.* See applicant, candidate, competitor; adversary.

Entrap, *v.* To induce a person to commit a crime that he or she is not contemplating in order to arrest and prosecute him or her for that crime; to originate an idea for a crime and then induce someone to commit it when the latter is not already disposed to do so (her defense was that the police entrapped her). Catch by artifice, ensnare, entice, tempt, bait, trap, allure, "bag," inveigle, decoy, deceive, beguile, cajole, enmesh.

Entrapment, *n.* See deception, invitation, entrap.

Entreat, *v.* See petition (2), apply (1), appeal (4); entreaty.

Entreaty, *n.* An earnest plea (the defendant's entreaty for a dismissal). Supplication, appeal, solicitation, invocation, prayer, request, cry, adjuration, application, beseeching. See also petition.

Entrench, *v.* See establish (3), fix (2); attach (2), affix (1).

Entrepreneur, *n.* One who initiates and assumes the financial and management responsibility for a new enterprise (she is the entrepreneur who is backing the project). Executive, industrialist, tycoon, businessperson, contractor, owner, organizer, director, impressario, producer, employer, builder, capitalist, magnate. *Ant.* Employee.

Entrust, *v.* To give something to another after a relationship of trust has been established (he entrusted the bonds to the agent). Assign, deliver, place in charge of, authorize, delegate, appoint, give over for safekeeping, commit, invest, commend, confide, depute. See also give.

Entrusting, *n.* The transfer of possession of goods to a merchant who deals in goods of that type and who may in turn transfer such goods and all rights therein to a purchaser in the ordinary course of business.

Entry, *n.* **1.** The act of making and entering a record; placing something before the court in writing; the record itself (entry of judgment). Memorandum, document, statement, report, account, item, minute, notation, registration, description, bulletin, brief, chronicle, file. **2.** The act of entering a structure or place (entry onto the land). Admission, entrance, passage, access, ingress, admittance, approach, penetration, arrival, intrusion, entree. **3.** For purposes of burglary, the least entry with the whole or any part of the body or with any instrument or weapon introduced for the purpose of committing a felony is sufficient to complete the offense. **4.** A passageway. See entrance.

Entry in the regular course of business A record of a fact made by someone in the ordinary and regular course of one's business, employment, office, or profession when it is the duty of this person to make the record in such manner, or when the record is commonly or regularly made, or when it is convenient to make the record in the conduct of the business to which it pertains.

280

Entry of judgment See enter a judgment.

Entry, writ of See writ of entry.

Enumerate, *v.* See list, record (1), itemize, express (2), detail (1); enumerated.

Enumerated, *adj.* Mentioned specifically (the enumerated powers of Congress in the Constitution). Designated, listed, expressly granted or named, detailed, itemized, specified, cited, spelled out, recounted, indexed, catalogued, tabulated. *Ant.* Implied.

Enumeration, *n.* See record (2); enumerated.

Enunciate, *v.* See pronounce, declare, proclaim, assert, voice (2), express (2); clarify.

Enunciation, *n.* See communication, declaration, report (2).

Enure, *v.* See inure.

Envelop, *v.* See surround, enclose, include, comprehend (2), cover (3), fall (1); conceal; confine.

Envelope, *n.* See wrapper, package, vessel (2).

En ventre sa mere (*Fr.*) In its mother's womb; an unborn child (there was a child en ventre sa mere at the time of the testator's death).

Enviable, *adj.* See attractive, worthy.

Envious, *adj.* See avaricious, jealous.

Environment, *n.* The totality of physical, economic, cultural, and social circumstances or factors that surround and affect the quality of life and the value of property (the child's unhealthy home environment). Milieu, atmosphere, influences, background, surroundings, element, setting, situation, habitat, medium, aura, scene, environs, ambiance, context, vicinity, neighborhood, community, purlieu, conditions.

Environs, *n.* See neighborhood, vicinity, environment.

Envisage, *v.* See contemplate (2), comprehend (1), devise (3), regard (1).

Envision, *v.* See contemplate (2), think, foresee, regard (1), expect (1).

Envoy, *n.* A diplomat of the rank of minister or ambassador sent by a country to the government of a foreign country to execute a special mission or to serve as a permanent diplomatic representative. Consul, plenipotentiary, deputy, courier, attaché, legate, messenger, nuncio, chargé d'affaires, agent, emissary. See also delegate.

Envy, *n., v.* See desire (1, 4), avarice; jealous; malice.

Enwrap, *v.* See enclose, surround, confine; absorb (2), engage (2).

Eon, *n.* See age (1), epoch.

Ephemeral, *Adj.* See temporary, brief (4), evasive, intangible, weak, breakable, perishable.

Epic, *adj.* See great, elevated, historic.

Epicure, *n.* **epicurean,** *adj.* Connoisseur. Gourmet, aesthete, bon vivant; luxurious, hedonistic, lavish, self-indulgent.

Epidemic 1. *n.* A disease (or other phenomenon) that is widely spread or generally prevailing at a given place and time (the government had no plan to respond to the epidemic). Malady, infection, pest, contagion, plague, pestilence, outbreak, rash. **2.** *adj.* Widespread (the disease reached epidemic proportions). Extensive, general, rampant, far-reaching, wide-ranging, infectious, rife, pandemic, sweeping, pervasive. See also popular. *Ant.* Contained (2).

Epidermis, *n.* See skin.

Epigram, *n.* See maxim, moral (3).

Epigrammatic, *adj.* See concise, biting.

Epilepsy, *n.* An occasional, periodic, excessive, and disorderly discharge of nerve cells in the brain; a disruption of the normal rhythm of the brain, manifesting itself in seizures. See disease, infirmity.

Epilogue, *n.* See appendix.

Episcopacy, *n.* A form of church government by bishops; the office of a bishop. See church, religion, hierarchy; clerical (1).

Episode, *n.* See event, circumstances, fact, detail (2).

Episodic, *adj.* See intermittent, periodic, incidental (2), casual (2), accidental (1).

Epistle, *n.* See letter, communication (2).

Epithet, *n.* See name (1), alias, mark; censure, slander.

Epitomize, *v.* See manifest (2), comprehend (2); embodiment.

Epoch, *n.* A particular period of time; the time at which a new computation is begun (an epoch of violence). Era, age, season, interval, eon, generation, cycle, span.

Equal, *adj.* **1.** On the same plane or level with respect to efficiency, worth, value, amount, or rights (equal treatment). Alike, uniform, evenhanded, commensurate, proportionate, unbiased, impartial, just, egalitarian, balanced, even, equitable, comparable, on the same footing, harmonious. **2.** Identical (equal partners). Same, parallel, coequal, interchangeable, synonymous. *Ant.* Unequal.

Equal degree Persons are related to a decedent "in equal degree" when they are all removed by an equal number of steps or degrees from the common ancestor.

Equality, *n.* The condition of possessing substantially the same rights, privileges, and immunities, and being subject to substantially the same duties. See equal, parity, balance (4), harmony.

Equalization, *n.* The act or process of making equal or bringing about conformity to a common standard (the Board of Equalization had the role of making sure that assessments and taxes were equitably imposed). Regulation, standardization, balancing, regularization, making symmetrical, synchronization, accommodation, making level.

Equalize, *v.* See adjust, balance (3), harmonize; equalization.

Equal protection of the law A constitutional guarantee that no person or class of persons shall be denied the same protection of the laws concerning life, liberty, property, and pursuit of happiness that is enjoyed by other persons or other classes in like circumstances; all persons similarly situated shall be treated alike. *Ant.* Arbitrary legislation or its application.

Equal Rights Amendment Proposed constitutional amendment: "Equality of rights under the law shall not be denied or abridged by the United States or by any State on account of sex."

Equanimity, *n.* See composure, self-confidence, balance (5).

Equate, *v.* To match. Identify, even out, liken, draw a parallel, equalize. See also compare, balance (3).

Equation, *n.* See parity, balance (4), harmony.

Equidistant, *adj.* See middle, intermediate.

Equilibrium, *n.* See balance, harmony, parity; self-confidence, composure; discretion (3).

Equip, *v.* To supply whatever is necessary for the efficient operation of something (they equipped the law firm with the latest word processors). Furnish, outfit, provide, prepare, fit, gear, implement, accouter, array, arm, stock, adorn. See also strengthen, augment, defend (1), build. *Ant.* Divest.

Equipment, *n.* Furnishings or what is needed for the required purposes (defective equipment). Gear, supplies, fittings, accouterments, paraphernalia, provisions, apparatus, material.

Equitable, *adj.* **1.** Just; conformable to the principles of justice and right (an equitable decision by the agency). Evenhanded, fair, impartial, reasonable, proper, detached, unbiased, honest, dispassionate, objective, due, rightful, neutral, upright, fair-minded, merited, deserved, disinterested, justifiable, well-advised. **2.**

See proportionate. **3.** Existing under equity; available or sustainable in equity or under the principles of equity (an equitable doctrine). *Ant.* Biased; uneven; common law or statutory.

Equitable abstention doctrine A court may refrain from exercising jurisdiction that it possesses in the interests of comity between courts and between states. See abstention.

Equitable action An action seeking an equitable remedy of relief (e.g., an injunction). See action.

Equitable adjustment theory In the settlement of federal contract disputes, the contracting officer should make a fair adjustment within a reasonable time before the contractor is required to settle with its subcontractors, suppliers, and other creditors. See adjustment.

Equitable adoption For some purposes (e.g., determining heirship), a child will be considered the adopted child of a person who has made a contract to adopt the child even though the statutory adoption procedures were not followed if the contract was otherwise performed. See adoption.

Equitable assignment An assignment that, though invalid at law, will be recognized and enforced in equity. See assignment.

Equitable conversion An "equitable conversion" takes place when a contract for the sale of real property becomes binding on the parties. Thenceforth, the buyer is deemed the equitable owner of the land, and the seller is the owner of the purchase price. For a limited purpose, there is a constructive alteration in the nature of the property; the real estate is considered personalty and the personal estate is considered realty. See convert, conversion.

Equitable distribution Following a divorce, the equitable (but not necessarily equal) division between the former spouses of all property legally and beneficially acquired during the marriage by either party regardless of which party holds legal title. See distribution.

Equitable election The obligation imposed upon a party to choose between two inconsistent or alternative rights or claims in cases where there is a clear intention that this party should not enjoy both (e.g., a party cannot accept the benefits of a will and at the same time refuse to recognize the validity of the will in other respects). See election.

Equitable estoppel The voluntary conduct of a person will preclude him or her from asserting rights against another who has justifiably relied on the conduct and who would suffer damage or injury if the person is now allowed to repudiate the conduct. Such a repudiation would be against equity and good conscience. See estoppel.

Equitable interest The interest of a beneficiary under a trust is considered equitable as contrasted with the legal interest of the trustee who holds legal title to the trust property. See interest.

Equitable lien A right to have specific property applied in whole or in part to the payment of a particular debt or class of debts. See lien.

Equitable mortgage An agreement to post certain property as security before the security agreement is formalized. See mortgage.

Equitable owner The person who is recognized in equity as the owner of the property even though bare legal title to the property is in someone else. See owner.

Equitable recoupment A rule of law that diminishes the right of a party to recover a debt to the extent that the party holds money or property of the debtor to which the party has no moral right. See recoupment.

Equitable relief The kind of relief sought in a court with equity powers (e.g., injunction, specific performance of a contract). See relief, remedy.

Equitable restraint doctrine

Equitable restraint doctrine A federal court will not intervene to enjoin a pending state criminal prosecution absent a strong showing of bad faith and irreparable injury. See restraint.

Equitable servitude A restriction on the use of land, enforceable in a court of equity. See servitude.

Equity, *n.* **1.** Justice administered according to fairness in a particular case as contrasted with the strictly formalized rules of the old common-law courts. This kind of justice was available in Courts of Equity or Courts of Chancery. Since the merger of law and equity, however, equitable principles or doctrines are applied in most courts today. **2.** Fairness, justice, and right (they questioned the equity of the arrangement). Right dealing, fair play, propriety, morality, even-handedness, reasonableness, uprightness, impartiality, objectivity, fair-mindedness, legitimacy, ethics. **3.** The monetary value of the property in excess of what is owed on it (she borrowed on her equity in the house). *Ant.* Common law; injustice; liability.

Equity financing Raising capital by a corporation by issuing (i.e., selling) stock as opposed to debt financing, which is raising capital by issuing bonds or by borrowing money. See finance, back.

Equity jurisdiction Those cases that are proper subjects for the application of equitable principles. Before law and equity were merged in the same court, "equity jurisdiction" referred to the power of a separate Court of Equity to hear the case. See jurisdiction.

Equity of a statute A rule of statutory construction that includes within the scope of a statute those situations that are neither expressly included nor excluded but which are clearly within the spirit and general meaning of the statute. The statute is treated as a declaration of policy which serves as precedent in analogous situations not expressly covered by the statute itself. See statute, construction (1); interpret.

Equity of redemption The right of a mortgagor upon payment of the debt plus interest and costs to redeem mortgaged property after it has been forfeited by a breach of a condition of the mortgage. See redemption.

Equity shares Shares of any class of stock, whether or not preferred as to dividends or assets, having unlimited dividend rights. See share (3).

Equivalence, *n.* See parity, balance (4), harmony, correspondence, agreement; equal; equivalent.

Equivalent, *adj.* Equal in value, force, measure, volume, power, or effect (the list was substantially equivalent). Alike, identical, synonymous, on a par with, commensurate, coequal, corresponding, comparable, tantamount, equalized, parallel, matching, interchangeable, homogenous, on the same footing, same, like, exact, transposable, correlative, reciprocal. *Ant.* Dissimilar.

Equivocal, *adj.* Having more than one meaning or sense (an equivocal argument). Ambiguous, obscure, vague, debatable, puzzling, dubious, hazy, enigmatic, indeterminate, questionable, ambivalent, oblique, uncertain, indefinite, multileveled, circuitous, cryptic, incomprehensible, cloudy, perplexing, confusing, nebulous, deceptive, imprecise. *Ant.* Precise.

Equivocate, *v.* See hedge, quibble, avoid (2), deceive, disguise (1), dissemble.

Equivocation, *n.* See evasion, avoidance (2), quibble, falsehood.

Era, *n.* See age (1), epoch.

Eradicate, *v.* See destroy, abolish, rescind, annul.

Eradication, *n.* See abolition, rescission, elimination, removal.

Erase, *v.* To obliterate words or marks from a written instrument by rubbing, scraping, or scratching them out (the testator erased her signature). Blot out, expunge, wipe out, eliminate, annul, cancel, remove, strike out, efface, cross out, dissolve, delete. See also destroy. *Ant.* Insert.

Erect, *v.* See build, construct, collect, accumulate.

Erection, *n.* See building, establishment (2); construct.

Ergo, *adv.* Therefore (ergo, he lost). Hence, consequently, as a result, thus, accordingly, for that reason, so. See also therefore.

Erie v. Tompkins The landmark case holding that in an action in a federal court, the law to be applied is the law of the state in which the federal court is situated, except as to matters governed by the U.S. Constitution and acts of Congress. 304 U.S. 64, 58 S.Ct. 817, 82 L.Ed.2d 1188 (1938).

Eristic, *adj.* See contentious, litigious; argument, debate.

Erode, *v.* See consume, wear (1), decline (2), diminish; erosion.

Eros, *n.* See lust.

Erosion, *n.* Wearing away by the action of water, wind, or other elements (the insurance did not cover damage by erosion). Reduction, washing away, eroding, disintegration, deterioration, shrinkage, attrition, wear and tear, depreciation, corrosion, decay, destruction, dilapidation, impairment, crumbling, decrease, thinning, abrasion, devouring, gnawing. *Ant.* Repair.

Erotic, *adj.* See prurient, lascivious, obscene.

Err, *v.* To be in error (the lower court erred in denying the motion). Make a mistake, fall into error, miscalculate, be inaccurate, lapse into error, go astray, be incorrect, transgress, blunder, misjudge, misconstrue, misunderstand, misinterpret, be at fault, wander, stray, deceive oneself. *Ant.* Be accurate.

Errand, *n.* See assignment (3), job (2), duty (1).

Errant, *adj.* **1.** Wandering (an errant judge). Traveling, roaming, itinerant; nomadic, transient. **2.** See erroneous. *Ant.* Stationary; accurate.

Erratic, *adj.* See capricious, variable, fluctuating, inconsistent, anomalous, odd, wild.

Erratum, *n.* See error.

Erroneous, *adj.* Involving error; deviating from the law (an erroneous judgment). Incorrect, mistaken, wrong, inaccurate, fallacious, groundless, amiss, in error, faulty, fictitious, unsound, spurious, untrue, unsupportable, invalid, "off base," aberrant, unsustainable, unfounded, blundering, counterfeit, imprecise, amiss, flawed, bogus. See also false (1). *Ant.* Accurate.

Error, *n.* A mistaken judgment or incorrect belief as to the existence or the consequences of a fact; a false or mistaken conception or application of the law (errors in the record). Mistake, flaw, fallacy, misinterpretation, miscalculation, misunderstanding, misreading, misstatement, misconstruction, misapprehension, misconception, distortion, fault, delusion, oversight, wrongheadedness, untruth, erratum, defect, blunder, slip, fumble, aberration, blooper, faux pas, deviation. *Ant.* Accuracy.

Error coram nobis See coram nobis.

Error coram vobis See coram vobis.

Ersatz, *adj.* See bogus, counterfeit (2), deceptive.

Erstwhile, *adj.* See former.

Erudite, *adj.* See learned, brilliant, literary (2), cultivated, civil (3), able, capable (2), cognizant.

Erupt, *v.* See detonate, discharge (4), flare, attack (1), batter; eruption.

Eruption, *n.* Storm. Outburst, blaze, explosion, convulsion, deluge, spasm, fury, rush, blast, detonation, discharge, flash, blowup, torpedo, bomb, dynamite. See also brawl, calamity, catastrophe, commotion.

Escalate, *v.* See raise (2), augment, spread (3, 4), accumulate; aggravated (1), increase.

Escalation, *n.* See increase, appreciation, growth; aggravated (1).

Escalator

Escalator, *n.* Lift, conveyor, elevator.

Escalator clause In a union contract: A clause that wages will rise or fall depending on a standard such as the cost-of-living index. In a lease: A clause that the rent may be increased to reflect increases in operating costs or increases allowed by new rent-control regulations. In a construction contract: A clause authorizing the contractor to increase the contract price if the costs of labor and materials increase.

Escapade, *n.* See antic, mischief.

Escape 1. *v.* To flee from or avoid (he tried to escape responsibility for the damage). Evade, desert, get away, elude, flee, disappear, abscond, shun, eschew, avert, dodge, bolt, circumvent, decamp, vanish. **2.** *n.* The voluntary departure from lawful custody by a prisoner with the intent to evade the due course of justice (when recaptured, she was convicted of escape). Getaway, exodus, flight, evasion, avoidance, deliverance, release, breakout, freedom. **3.** *v.* To leak or flow from an enclosure (gas escaped). Emanate, issue, gush, pour out of, seep, leak, stream, emerge. *Ant.* Confront; capture; seal.

Escape clause A provision in a contract or other document allowing the parties to avoid liability or performance under certain conditions.

Escheat, *n.* A reversion of property to the state when no individual is available who qualifies to inherit it (the state claimed the bank account of the deceased by escheat). Forfeiture, appropriation, expropriation, seizure.

Eschew, *v.* See decline (1), abandon, abstain.

Escobedo rule An accused has been denied assistance of counsel when the following circumstances occur: A police investigation has begun to focus on a particular suspect, the suspect is in custody, the suspect requests and is denied counsel, and the police have not warned him or her of the right to remain silent. No statement elicited during such interrogation may be used in a criminal trial.

Escort, *n.,* **escort,** *v.* See attendant (1), guardian, coterie; accompany, assist.

Escrow, *n.* Property (e.g., money, stock, deed) delivered by one person (called the grantor, promisor, or obligor) into the hands of another person (e.g., bank, escrow agent) to be held by the latter until a designated condition or contingency occurs, at which time the property is delivered to the grantee, promisee, or obligee. See bailment.

Escrow account A bank account generally held in the name of the depositor and an escrow agent, which is returnable to the depositor or payable to a third person on the fulfillment of the escrow condition.

Esoteric, *adj.* See ambiguous, equivocal.

Especial, *adj.* See outstanding (2), important; odd.

Espionage, *n.* Gathering, transmitting, or losing information on national defense with the intent or with reason to believe that the information will be used to the injury of the United States or to the advantage of any foreign nation (she was convicted of espionage). Spying, subversive act, undercover work; treason. See also, betrayal, mutiny, spy, eavesdrop, bug.

Esplanade, *n.* See passage (2), highway, conduct (2).

Espousal, *n.* See advocacy, defense.

Espouse, *v.* See advocate (2), champion (2), defend.

Esprit de corps, *n.* See spirit (2), company (3), goodwill (2), affinity, community (3), companionship, confederacy, coalition, concord (2), cooperation.

Espy, *v.* See recognize (1), observe.

Esquire, *n.* The title given to an attorney (Mary Pike, Esquire). See attorney.

Essay, *v.* **essay,** *n.* See attempt (2, 3); article (4), book, communication, speech (2).

Essence, *n.* **1.** The gist or substance of something (the issue stated the essence of the case). Core, heart, quintessence, nature, soul, lifeblood, pith, crux, significance, kernel, sum, principle, gravamen, meat, quiddity, main point, marrow, reality, tenor, hypostasis, purport, backbone, meaning, force, burden, intent, sense. **2.** That which is indispensable (time is of the essence in the contract). A vital constituent, vital element, necessary part. *Ant.* Periphery; accessory.

Essential, *adj.* Required for the continued existence of a thing (an essential term of the contract). Necessary, indispensable, urgent, critical, primary, vital, cardinal, requisite, crucial, needed, principal, capital, important, mandatory, compulsory, chief, pressing, fundamental, basic, elemental, integral. *Ant.* Incidental.

Establish, *v.* **1.** To make or form (establish uniform paternity laws). Create, construct, build, introduce, start, initiate, begin, launch, organize, set in motion, found, institute, fabricate, structure, undertake, embark, commence, compose, bring about, inaugurate, open, empower, license, authorize, commission, accredit, sanction, enact. **2.** To place beyond doubt or dispute (the evidence established her innocence). Prove, convince, corroborate, demonstrate, show, certify, ratify, validate, authenticate, confirm, warrant, justify, substantiate, attest to, uphold, document. **3.** To make secure (she established herself as a securities attorney). Fix, settle, install, develop, root, entrench, consolidate, solidify, perpetuate, implant, stabilize, situate, sustain. *Ant.* Destroy; cast doubt upon; uproot.

Established, *adj.* See firm (2), fixed.

Establishment, *n.* **1.** A business or institution (the establishment went bankrupt). Company, corporation, concern, association, syndicate, enterprise, cartel, combine, office, firm, outfit, plant, industry, organization. **2.** The act of creating, building or establishing (an establishment of a trust fund). Formation, initiation, founding, organization, erection, commencement, construction, setting up. **3.** Providing governmental sponsorship, aid, or preference of one religion over another (Establishment Clause). **4.** The people or institutions that dominate a society (rebellion against the Establishment). System, elite, power structure, ruling class, intelligentsia, nobility, entrenched order, social order.

Estate, *n.* **1.** An interest in real or personal property; the extent of one's interest in real or personal property (an estate in land). See interest. **2.** The total property of whatever kind that is owned by a decedent prior to the distribution of that property according to the terms of a will or according to the laws of inheritance if the decedent dies intestate; all of the property of a bankrupt, incompetent person, insane person, ward, etc. (she was appointed administrator of the estate). Assets, wealth, effects, belongings, possessions, tangible property, intangible property, rights, valuables, equity, realty, personalty, chattels, holdings, interests, fortune, title, goods. See also property. **3.** A large amount of property on which someone lives (country estate). Manor, compound, abode, residence, acres, ranch, villa. See also home. **4.** The social, civil, or political condition or standing of a person (individuals of every estate). Rank, degree, status, class, situation, order, place, dignity, stratum, level, caste.

Estate at sufferance The interest that someone has in land when he or she comes into possession of it by permission of the owner, but who continues to occupy the land after the permission has ended.

Estate at will The interest that a person has in land that is held at the will of the lessor or of both parties.

Estate by elegit See elegit.

Estate by purchase An estate acquired by a method other than descent (e.g., through a sale).

Estate by the entirety See tenancy by the entirety.

Estate for life See life estate.

Estate for years An estate for a fixed and determinate period of time (e.g., a lease of land for 3 years).

Estate from year to year 1. An estate for which the parties have agreed to renewal for successive 1-year periods. **2.** An estate that arises after a tenant has been allowed to hold over after the expiration of his or her term; an estate that arises when no term has been set by the parties.

Estate in common See tenancy in common.

Estate in coparcenary See coparcenary.

Estate in expectancy An estate that is not yet in possession; the enjoyment of the estate will begin at a future time.

Estate in severalty An estate held by a person in his or her right only, without any other person being joined or connected in point of interest during his or her estate.

Estate in tail An estate of inheritance that, instead of descending to heirs generally, goes to the heirs of the donee's body—the donee's lawful issue, the donee's children, and through them to the donee's grandchildren and on in a direct line.

Estate of inheritance An estate that may descend to heirs.

Estate planning The branch of the law that arranges a person's property and estate, taking into account the law of wills, taxes, insurance, property, and trusts so as to gain maximum benefit of all laws and to carry out the person's wishes for the disposition of his or her property upon death.

Estate pur autre vie An estate that is held during the period of someone else's life (i.e., someone other than the holder).

Estate tax A tax imposed on the right to transfer property at death; the tax is imposed on the decedent's estate and not on the recipients of the property. The latter pay an inheritance tax. See tax.

Estate upon condition An estate in lands having a qualification annexed to it by which it may be created, enlarged, or destroyed upon the happening of a particular event.

Esteem, *v., n.* See honor (2, 3), approbation, affection (1), regard (2), affinity (2), attachment (4), eminence, note (4).

Esteemed, *adj.* See great (2), elevated, reputable.

Esthetic, *adj.* See aesthetic, beautiful.

Estimate 1. *n.* An attempt to value or rate something without actually measuring, weighing, etc. (an estimate of the distance). Guess, educated guess, "guesstimate," considered guess, rough calculation, rough approximation, assessment, judgment, speculation, estimation, valuation, surmise, belief, reckoning, opinion. **2.** *v.* To evaluate (she estimated the worth of the ring). Consider, appraise, rate, gauge, price, measure, compute approximately, weigh, assay, survey, adjudge, calculate.

Estimated tax A tax that is initially computed without fully accurate and complete information, filed as a preliminary matter to be followed by a final tax return.

Estimated useful life The period over which an asset will be used by a particular taxpayer.

Estimation, *n.* See estimate (1), assessment (1), opinion (2).

Estop, *v.* To stop or bar (the defendant was estopped from claiming that no marriage existed). Impede, restrict, prevent, preclude, hinder, thwart, block, restrain, interfere, handicap, forbid, cut off, interrupt, suspend, squelch, terminate, shut off, arrest, halt. *Ant.* Authorize.

Estoppel, *n.* Prevention of a party, due to his or her own conduct, from claiming a right to the detriment of another party when the latter was entitled to rely and did in fact rely on this conduct (adoption by estoppel). Prohibition, barrier, preclusion, impediment, restraint. See also bar, ban. *Ant.* Allowance.

Estoppel by deed A grantor in a warranty deed who did not have title at the time of the conveyance but who subsequently acquires title, is estopped from denying that he or she had title at the time of the transfer. Such after-acquired title inures to the benefit of the grantee and his or her successors.

Estoppel by election An estoppel that arises by a voluntary and intelligent choice between inconsistent positions; the party so choosing cannot afterward reverse his or her election and dispute the state of affairs or rights of others resulting from his or her original choice.

Estoppel by judgment When a fact has been agreed upon or decided in a court of record, neither party shall be allowed to call it into question or have it tried over again at any time thereafter so long as the judgment or decree stands unreversed; a final adjudication of a material issue by a court of competent jurisdiction binds the parties in any subsequent proceeding between or among them, irrespective of any difference in the forms or causes of action.

Estoppel by verdict Under the doctrine of estoppel by verdict or collateral estoppel, when a particular issue is actually or necessarily finally determined by a court of competent jurisdiction and then is put into issue in a subsequent suit on the same or on a different cause of action between the same parties or those in privity with them, the former adjudication of the issue is held to bind the parties or their privies in the subsequent suit.

Estoppel in pais A person may be precluded by his or her act, conduct, or silence (when there is a duty to speak) from asserting a right that he or she otherwise would have had. A prohibition imposed due to action or inaction on the part of one against whom estoppel is asserted, which induces reliance thereon by another to the detriment of the latter.

Estrange, *v.* See alienate (2), leave (2), divide (3).

Estranged, *adj.* Separated, parted, alienated, at odds, disaffected. See also solitary; separate; alienate (2).

Estuary, *n.* See river, sea (1).

Et al. And others (Jones v. Smith et al.).

Et cetera And others, and so on, and the rest, and so forth, etc.

Etch, *v.* See engrave, inscribe.

Eternal, *adj.* See permanent, perpetual, incalculable; God, holy, religious

Eternity, *n.* See perpetuity; perpetual, permanent.

Ethereal, *adj.* See intangible, temporary, brief (4), evasive, weak, perishable.

Ethical, *adj.* Conforming to standards of professional conduct (it is ethical to make the disclosure). Legitimate, proper, aboveboard, correct, unimpeachable, principled, honorable, decent, upright, acceptable, respectable. See also right (1), just, legal, honest, moral. *Ant.* Unethical.

Ethics, *n.* Standards of professional conduct (the ethics of lawyers). Principles, moral principles, code of conduct, right and wrong, values, conscience, moral philosophy, mores, criteria. See principle (2), right (4), code of professional responsibility, canon.

Ethnic, *adj.* See characteristic.

Ethos, *n.* See civilization, character.

Etiquette, *n.* See decorum, propriety, amenity (3).

Et seq. And following; and the material immediately following (28 U.S.C. 245 et seq.).

Et ux. And wife (the land was conveyed to John Smith et ux.).

Eugenics, *n.* See genetics.

Eulogize, *v.* See honor (2); promote; tribute (2).

Eulogy, *n.* See tribute (2), indorsement (2), speech (2), flattery.

Euphemism, *n.* A less harsh way of saying something. See mitigate, modify.

Euphoria, *n.* See happiness; spirit (2), passion, emotion.

Eureka, *interj.* See invention, discovery (2, 3), invent, discover.

Euthanasia, *n.* The act or practice of painlessly putting to death those persons who are suffering from incurable and distressing diseases. See kill; death; disease.

Evacuate, *v.* See depart (1), retire (1), abandon (1), leave (2), escape (1).

Evacuation, *n.* See removal, departure (2), abandonment, exit (2).

Evade, *v.* See avoid (2), escape (1); neglect (2); evasion; deceive.

Evaluate, *v.* See appraise, assess (1, 3), judge (3).

Evaluation, *n.* See appraisal, assessment (1, 3), opinion, judgment (1), criticism (2).

Evanescent, *adj.* See intangible, temporary, transitory, evasive, brief (4), weak, perishable, breakable.

Evangelical, *adj.* See religious, clerical (1); God; preach, emotional, ardent, diligent, earnest (2), strong (2).

Evaporate, *v.* See disappear, withdraw (1), diminish, decline, pass (6), perish, dissolve.

Evasion, *n.* The act of eluding or avoiding something by artifice (evasion of responsibility). Dodging, shunning, circumventing, escape, subterfuge, sidestepping, retreat, vacillation, fabrication. See also avoidance. *Ant.* Confrontation.

Evasive, *adj.* Tending or seeking to evade (evasive answer by the witness). Elusive, hedging, misleading, devious, indirect, equivocal, ambiguous, vacillating, equivocating, concealed, vague, surreptitious, clandestine, duplicitous, ambivalent, quibbling, covert. See also intangible, transitory, temporary. *Ant.* Forthright.

Even, *adj.* See equal, regular (1), constant (1), parallel, equitable (1), fair; flat; grade (1).

Evenhanded, *adj.* See equal (1), equitable (1), fair, impartial, objective (2), honest.

Evening, *n.* The closing part of the day and early night before bedtime (the accident occurred in the evening). Sundown, nightfall, dusk, twilight, close of day. See also sunset, nighttime. *Ant.* Dawn.

Event, *n.* Something that happens (fortuitous event). Occurrence, happening, happenstance, episode, occasion, development, deed, fact, outcome, incident, circumstance, transaction, affair, experience, matter, milestone, phenomenon.

Eventful, *adj.* See outstanding (2); active (1, 3), engaged.

Eventual, *adj.* See future, prospective, final (1).

Eventuality, *n.* See likelihood, possibility, probability.

Everlasting, *adj.* See permanent, perpetual.

Every, *adj.* See all, universal, comprehensive, aggregate, complete (2), whole, wholly.

Everybody, *pron.* See all, universal, comprehensive, aggregate, complete (2), whole; wholly.

Everyday, *adj.* See daily; commonplace, customary, regular, familiar (2).

Everyone, *pron.* See all, universal, comprehensive, aggregate, complete (2), whole; wholly.

Everything, *pron.* See all, universal, comprehensive, aggregate, complete (2), whole; wholly.

Evict, *v.* To dispossess (the landlord evicted the tenant). Eject, turn out, remove, disseise, kick out, dislodge, jettison. See also oust, expel. *Ant.* Install.

Eviction. *n.* The act of depriving a person of land or rental property that he or she has held or leased; dispossession by process of law (an injunction against the eviction). Dislodgement, expulsion, disseisin, deprivation of possession, ouster, throwing out, ejection, divestment. See also removal.

Evidence 1. *n.* Any kind of proof offered to establish the existence or nonexistence of a fact in dispute, e.g., testimony, writings, other material objects, demonstrations (admissible evidence). Documentation, records, verification, substantiation, confirmation, grounds, data, sign, signal, exemplification, authentication, certification, validation, corroboration, relevant facts, indication, testimony, trace, information. **2.** *v.* See exhibit (1).

Evident, *adj.* Clear to the understanding; apparent to observation (it was evident that the witness did not know). Noticeable, observable, obvious, transparent, apparent, visible, perceptible, patent, incontrovertible, unmistakable, express, lucid, conspicuous, palpable, exposed, recognizable, explicit, unequivocal, pronounced, tangible, unquestionable, axiomatic. See also blatant (1), certain (3), distinct (1), demonstrable, clear (1), categorical, manifest, cogent. *Ant.* Vague.

Evidentiary facts Those facts that are necessary for a determination of the ultimate facts; the premises upon which conclusions of ultimate facts are based. See premises (3).

Evidentiary harpoon Deliberately placing improper evidence by the prosecution before the jury, e.g., evidence of prior arrests where such evidence would not be admissible.

Evil, *adj., n.* See bad (2), malicious, base (2), cruel, obscene, filthy; corruption, fault (1), wrong (1), delinquency, debauchery, lapse (3).

Evil-minded, *adj.* See cruel, bad (2), corrupt, malicious.

Evince, *v.* See prove, manifest (2), establish, exhibit (1).

Evoke, *v.* See recall (3), provoke, extract (1), induce, cause.

Evolution, *n.* See development (1), process (1), advancement (2), growth, production, maturity (2).

Evolve, *v.* See develop, mature (1), advance (3, 4, 5), emerge, produce (2).

Exacerbate *v.* To aggravate or annoy. Intensify, worsen, sour, embitter, exaggerate, add insult to injury, fan the fire. See also harass, disturb; provoke.

Exact *adj., v.* See accurate, precise; same; careful, conscientious (2); extort, extract (1), compel; impose; exaction.

Exacting *adj.* See strict (2), draconian, severe, extreme (1), serious (2), difficult, compelling, exigent.

Exaction, *n.* Taking that which is not due; the wrongful act of an officer or other person in compelling payment of a fee or reward for his or her services under color of his or her official authority, where no payment is due (an exaction of $5,000). Extortion, demand, imposition, blackmail, "rip-off," extraction.

Exactitude, *n.* See veracity, conformity, verity, fact.

Exactly, *adv.* See accurate, precise.

Exaggerate, *v.* To overstate (the defendant exaggerated his damages). Embroider, overrate, magnify, embellish, stretch, hyperbolize, overdo, oversell, romance, overestimate, heighten, inflate, bloat, maximize. See also distort, falsify, lie, color (3); pompous; aggravated.

Exaggeration, *n.* See redundancy; flattery, puffing; falsehood, lie; caricature; increase; exaggerate.

Exalt, *v.* See honor (2), promote, recommend, appreciate (3).

Exaltation, *n.* See honor (3), approbation, affection (1), indorsement (2), tribute (2); exultation, grandeur.

Exalted, *adj.* See elevated, outstanding (2).

Exam, *n.* See assessment (3), appraisal, examination.

Examination, *n.* An inspection or interrogation (examination of the witness by counsel). Investigation, questioning, probing, probe, scrutiny, inquiry, inquest, study, checkup, survey, exploration, canvass, research, perusal, analysis, audit, test, biopsy, observation, trial, review, looking over. See also inspection, search.

Examine, *v.* See investigate, audit (2), ask (1), poll (1), canvass (1), review, cross-examine, examination.

Examined copy A copy of a record, public book, or register that has been compared with the original.

Examinee, *n.* The person being examined. See candidate, witness (3).

Examiner, *n.* An officer or other person authorized to conduct an examination or appointed by the court to take the testimony of witnesses (bank examiner). Investigator, questioner, inquisitor, researcher, reviewer, censor, auditor, inspector.

Example, *n.* See sample (1), model, archetype, instance.

Exasperate, *v.* See disturb, harass, exacerbate, frustrate.

Exasperation, *n.* See dissatisfaction, annoyance, nuisance.

Ex cathedra, *adj., adv.* From the authority of the office.

Excavate, *v.* To dig up. Unearth, scoop, burrow, gouge. See also extract (1), shovel, exhume.

Excavation, *n.* See mine, cave, cell, trench.

Exceed, *v.* To go beyond (exceed the speed limit). Surmount, transcend, outdo, go ahead, overshoot, better, outspace. See also beat (2), pass (3).

Excel, *v.* See beat (2), exceed, pass (3).

Excellence, *n.* See merit, quality (2), worth (1), perfection (2), ability, eminence, supremacy, superiority, dominion; grandeur.

Excellent, *adj.* See superior (2), worthy, outstanding (2), predominant, exceptional, best (1), beautiful, attractive, extraordinary.

Except 1. *v.* To leave out (the group was excepted from the order). Omit, exclude, eliminate, bar, pass over, reject, delete, subtract, excuse, remove, disallow, ignore, deduct, separate, discriminate against. **2.** *prep.* Other than (the court closed all the stores except yours). But for, not including, excluding, saving, with the exception of, apart from, exclusive of, barring. *Ant.* Incorporate; including.

Exception, *n.* **1.** An objection to an order or ruling of a hearing officer or judge (exception overruled). Nonagreement, disagreement, protest, criticism, outcry, complaint, rejection, nonacceptance, dissatisfaction, opposition, challenge, dissent. **2.** The act of excluding or separating something out; that which is not included (an exception was made in the statute). Exclusion, separation, noninclusion, exemption, segregation, severance, departure, omission. **3.** A deviation (an exception to the rule). Nonconformity, inconsistency, irregularity, oddity, anomaly, unusual case, peculiarity, departure, variance, deviation, aberration. *Ant.* Agreement; inclusion; conformity.

Exceptional, *adj.* Out of the ordinary (exceptional circumstances). Unusual, special, uncommon, irregular, abnormal, unconventional, rare, odd, unnatural, unique, freakish, singular, queer, unparalleled, high-class, incomparable, phenomenal, uncustomary, anomalous, aberrant; excellent. See also extraordinary, outstanding (2). *Ant.* Customary.

Excerpt, *v., n.* See extract (1, 2), passage (4), quotation (1), part (1).

Excess, *adj.* Pertaining to an act or amount that goes beyond what is usual, proper, or necessary (excess profits tax). Undue, extra, excessive, surplus, overflow, over and above, residue, spare, superfluous, inordinate, overflowing, remainder, unnecessary, extreme, immoderate. See also exorbitant. *Ant.* Scarce.

Excessive, *adj.* Greater than what is usual or proper; going beyond a just measure or amount (excessive assessment). See excess, irrational, disproportionate, extreme (1), extraordinary, exorbitant.

Excessive bail A sum that is more than will be reasonably sufficient to prevent evasion of the law by flight or concealment; bail that is per se unreasonably great and clearly disproportionate to the offense involved or shown to be so by the special circumstances of a particular case. See bail.

Excessive damages Damages awarded by a jury that are grossly in excess of the amount warranted by law on the facts and circumstances of the case; unreasonable or outrageous damages. See damages.

Excessive force That amount of force which is beyond the need and circumstances of the particular event or which is not justified in the light of all the circumstances (e.g., the use of deadly force to protect property when life or limb is not in jeopardy). See force.

Excess profits tax A tax levied on profits that are beyond the normal profits of a business; a tax on corporations that accumulate an unreasonable surplus of profits rather than paying them out as dividends.

Exchange 1. *v.* To barter, transfer, or give (they exchanged promises). Swap, trade, reciprocate, interchange, convert, replace, switch, supplant, put in place of, supersede, displace, transpose, invert, traffic, substitute. **2.** *n.* The act of giving or taking one thing for another; a transaction in which one piece of property is given in return for another piece of property (an unfair exchange). Trade, deal, bargain, transfer, reciprocity, substitution, replacement, supplanting, quid pro quo. **3.** *n.* An organization that provides a marketplace or facilities for bringing together buyers and sellers of securities (New York Stock Exchange). See market, securities.

Exchange broker One who negotiates bills of exchange drawn on foreign countries or on other places in the same country; one who makes and concludes bargains for others in matters of money or merchandise.

Exchange rate The value of one country's money in terms of the value of another country's currency (e.g., the dollar vs. the pound). See worth (1), currency.

Exchequer, *n.* The department in the government of England in charge of collecting national revenue; the Treasury Department.

Excise, *n.*, **excise,** *v.* **1.** *n.* A tax imposed on the performance of an act, engaging in an occupation, or the enjoyment of a privilege (collection of the excise on liquor). Levy, exaction, duty, impost, toll, tariff, fee, custom, assessment. See also tax. **2.** *v.* To remove or cut away (the testator excised the clause in the will). Extract, cut off, clip, tear out, expunge, delete, eradicate, strike out. See also censor (3).

Excitable, *adj.* High-strung. Volatile, temperamental, irritable, nervous, irascible, flappable, inflammable, moody, hotheaded. See also emotional, active (3), ardent, spirit (2), strong (2), violent, incendiary (2), dangerous, hysterical.

Excite, *v.* See incite, animate, provoke (1), cause, revive, amaze, surprise (1).

Excited, *adj.* See excitable, emotional, happy, active (3), ardent, strong (2), violent.

Excited utterance A statement relating to a startling event or condition, made while the declarant was under the stress of excitement caused by the event or condition. Such statements are exceptions to the hearsay rule.

Excitement, *n.* See emotion, spirit, power, force, passion, happiness, adventure; danger, disturbance, confusion.

Exciting, *adj.* Thrilling. See touching, moving (1), attractive, intriguing, enjoyable, irresistible, outstanding (2), ardent, active (3), adventurous, dangerous.

Exclaim, *v.* See proclaim, communicate, voice (2).

Exclamation, *n.* See proclamation, declaration, communication, eruption, noise, opposition.

Exclude, *v.* See bar, ban, oust, dispossess, except (1), prohibit; exclusion.

Exclusion, *n.* Denial of entry or admittance (the exclusion of evidence). Ban, rejection, dismissal, nonadmission, preclusion, prohibition, disallowance, elimination, omission, expulsion, purge, segregation, repudiation, boycott, bar, nonacceptance, banishment, blackball, eviction, prevention. See also exception (2), removal. *Ant.* Inclusion.

Exclusionary rule Where evidence has been obtained in violation of the U.S.

Exclusionary rule

Constitution (e.g., evidence obtained through an illegal search and seizure), the evidence will be excluded from the trial. Exceptions to this rule now exist.

Exclusionary zoning Any form of zoning ordinance that tends to exclude specific classes of persons or businesses from designated districts or areas.

Exclusive, *adj.* Not allowing others to participate; belonging to one person or group (exclusive possession). Restricted, closed, limited, selective, sole, private, personal, individual, shutting out, unique; complete, entire, whole, all, total. *Ant.* Unrestricted.

Exclusive agency A grant to an agent of the exclusive right to sell within a particular market or area.

Exclusive agency listing An agreement between a property owner and a real estate broker whereby the owner agrees to pay a fee or commission to the broker if the property is sold during the listing period, regardless of whether the broker is responsible for the sale.

Exclusive jurisdiction The power of a court or other tribunal over an action or person to the exclusion of all other courts or tribunals. See jurisdiction.

Exclusively, *adv.* Apart from all others (exclusively used for charitable purposes). Only, solely, substantially all, for the greater part, to the exclusion of all others, fully, entirely, completely.

Excommunicate, *v.* See bar, ban, oust, expel.

Excommunication, *n.* See bar, ban, ouster, exclusion, removal, exile (1).

Ex contractu From or out of a contract (an action arising ex contractu).

Excoriate, *v.* See denounce, censure, discipline.

Excrement, *n.* See refuse (2).

Excruciating, *adj.* See painful, acute.

Exculpate, *v.* To free from guilt or blame (she was exculpated of the crime). Exonerate, clear, vindicate, justify, pronounce innocent, absolve, free, emancipate, dismiss, excuse, pardon, condone. See also acquit. *Ant.* Convict.

Exculpation, *n.* See pardon, exoneration (1); exculpate.

Exculpatory, *adj.* Clearing or tending to clear from alleged fault or guilt (exculpatory evidence). See exculpate.

Exculpatory statement A statement that tends to justify, excuse, or clear the defendant from alleged fault or guilt.

Excursion, *n.* See voyage, junket.

Excusable, *adj.* Capable of being forgiven; implying the existence of a legal excuse (excusable neglect). Pardonable, forgivable, faultless. See also justifiable.

Excusable neglect The failure to take the proper steps at the proper time not because of carelessness, inattention, or recklessness but because of (a) some unexpected or unavoidable hindrance or accident, (b) reliance on the care and vigilance of one's attorney, or (c) reliance on promises made by an adverse party.

Excuse 1. *n.* A reason alleged for doing or not doing something; a reason for relief or exemption from some duty or obligation (he used the order as the excuse). Extenuation, explanation, defense, vindication, alibi, rationalization, pretext, mitigation, argument, apology. See also justification. **2.** *v.* To grant forgiveness to or for (she excused the infraction). Pardon, vindicate, exculpate, justify, acquit, clear, condone, mitigate, overlook, prove innocence, ignore, extenuate, forbear, absolve, reprieve, liberate. *Ant.* Accusation; condemn.

Ex delicto From a tort, fault, crime, malfeasance, or delict (an action that arose ex delicto; a suit ex delicto).

Exeat See ne exeat.

Execrate, *v.* See censure, abhor.

Execute, *v.* **1.** To complete or carry into full effect (the deed was executed according to law). Effectuate, accomplish, perform, fulfill, effect, consummate,

294

enforce, realize, exercise, finalize, administer, complete, prosecute, carry through, implement, perpetuate, transact, commit, discharge, enact, attain, engineer. See also manage (1), pursue. **2.** To put to death (the inmate was executed). Kill, purge, eliminate, assassinate, dispatch, condemn, sentence to death, murder.

Executed, *adj.* Carried out according to its terms (executed contract). Already done or performed, carried into full effect, taking effect immediately, now in existence, now in possession. *Ant.* Executory.

Executed remainder A remainder that vests a present interest in the tenant, though the enjoyment is postponed to the future. See remainder, interest.

Execution, *n.* **1.** Carrying out some act or course of conduct to its completion (judgment execution). Conclusion, accomplishment, performance, discharge, achievement, fulfillment, implementation, realization, administration, putting into force, effectuation. **2.** The process of carrying into effect the decisions in a decree or judgment; a court officer, e.g., sheriff, is commanded to take the property of the losing litigant in order to satisfy the judgment debt (writ of execution). **3.** Capital punishment. See kill, execute (2).

Execution creditor A creditor who has obtained a judgment against a debtor and has caused an execution to be issued on the judgment.

Execution lien A lien created when execution is levied. See execution (2).

Execution of an instrument The performance of all acts necessary to render an instrument (e.g., a will) complete, to make it valid, or to carry it into effect (e.g., signing it, delivering it).

Execution sale A sale of a debtor's property under the authority of a writ of execution by a sheriff or other ministerial officer.

Executive 1. *adj.* Pertaining to that branch of government which is charged with carrying the laws into effect (executive order). Administrative, managerial, supervisory, regulatory, presidential, gubernatorial, mayoral, official. **2.** *n.* A managing official (executive of the company). Supervisor, chief, principal, superintendent, president, administrator, boss, director, leader, chairperson. See also manager. *Ant.* Legislative, judicial; employee.

Executive agreement An agreement with another country, in which the president may bind the country without seeking the approval of the Senate. See concord, agreement.

Executive clemency The power of the president or a governor to pardon or commute a criminal sentence (e.g., reduce a death sentence to life imprisonment). See pardon.

Executive order An order or regulation issued by the president for the purpose of interpreting, implementing, or giving administrative effect to a constitutional provision, statute, or treaty. See order.

Executive privilege The privilege, based on the separation of powers, that exempts the chief executive from disclosing information and documents where the exemption is necessary to the discharge of highly important executive responsibilities and the frank expression necessary in intragovernmental advisory and deliberative communications. See privilege.

Executive session A meeting of a board or governmental unit that is closed to the public.

Executor, *n.* A person appointed by a testator to carry out the directions in his or her will, e.g., dispose of the testator's property as provided in the will (executor of the estate). Personal representative, legal representative, administrator, fiduciary, custodian. See also representative, agent.

Executory, *adj.* Yet to be executed or performed; remaining to be carried into operation or effect; dependent on a future performance or event (executory contract). Incomplete, unperformed, contingent, unfulfilled, potential. See also inchoate. *Ant.* Executed.

Executory accord An agreement for the future discharge of an existing claim by a substituted performance; a compromise agreement; an accord that has not been fully performed. See accord.

Executory bequest A bequest of a future, deferred, or contingent interest in personal property. See bequest.

Executory contract A contract that has not yet been fully completed or performed. See contract.

Executory devise The disposition of a future estate in a will. See devise.

Executory interest A future interest created in someone other than the grantor, which is not a remainder and vests upon the happening of a condition or event; an estate in futuro. See interest.

Executory process An extraordinary procedure, summary in nature, designed to expedite the satisfaction of delinquent negotiable paper and make it more acceptable in commerce. See procedure.

Executory remainder A contingent remainder; one that exists where the estate is limited to take effect either to a dubious and uncertain person or upon a dubious and uncertain event. See remainder.

Executory sale A sale whose terms have been agreed upon but which has not yet been carried into full effect in some of its terms or details. See sale.

Executory trust A trust in which a further conveyance or settlement is to be made by the trustee. See trust.

Executrix, *n.* A female executor; a woman appointed by a will to carry it out. See executor, representative, agent.

Exegesis, *n.* See annotation, comment (1), clarification.

Exemplar, *n.* See sample (1), model, archetype, instance, measure (1).

Exemplars, *n.* Nontestimonial identification evidence taken from the defendant, e.g., fingerprints, blood sample, lineup identification, voiceprints, handwriting sample (contested exemplar). See sample (1).

Exemplary, *adj.* **1.** Serving as a warning (exemplary punishment). Admonitory. **2.** Serving as a model (exemplary behavior). Meritorious, worthy, ideal, superior, praiseworthy, model, admirable, noteworthy, commendable, laudable, excellent. See also outstanding (2).

Exemplary damages Punitive damages; increased damages awarded to the plaintiff over and above what will compensate for his or her property loss, where the wrong was aggravated by circumstances of violence, oppression, malice, fraud, or wanton conduct of the defendant. See damages, punishment.

Exempiflication, *n.* An official transcript of a document from public records, made in a form to be used as evidence, authenticated or certified as a true copy. See evidence; sample (1).

Exemplified copy A copy of a document that has been authenticated.

Exemplify, *v.* See represent (3), mean (2), demonstrate (2), characterize, exhibit (1).

Exempt 1. *v.* To release from liability (she was exempted from military duty). Discharge, waive, excuse, set free, absolve, dispense, clear, exclude, spare. See also except. **2.** *adj.* Freed from a duty (the property is exempt from taxation). Immune, unrestrained, not liable for, privileged, not subject to, excluded from, discharged, unencumbered, not responsible for, shielded, freed, favored, pardoned. *Ant.* Obligate; accountable.

Exemption, *n.* **1.** Freedom from a general duty or service (exemption from jury duty). Immunity, release, allowance, liberty, freedom, special treatment, privilege, absolution, excuse, dispensation, impunity, license. See also exception (2). **2.** A privilege allowed by law to a judgment debtor by which he or she may hold designated property free from all liability to levy and sale on execution or attachment; property exempt in bankruptcy proceedings. **3.** An amount to be subtracted from gross income to determine taxable income (tax exemption for a dependent). *Ant.* Obligation.

Exercise, *v.* **1.** To make use of (she exercised her option to purchase stock). Avail oneself of, take advantage of, exploit, utilize, manipulate, put to use. See also employ (2). **2.** To fulfill or perform (she exercised her powers as governor). Carry out, discharge, wield, apply, pursue, prosecute, put into action or practice, transact, carry on, administer, officiate, effectuate. See also execute. **3.** See discipline (4); practice, athletics. *Ant.* Disregard; evade.

Exert, *v.* See exercise, employ (2), apply, attempt (3).

Exertion, *n.* See work (3), attempt (2), power, force, enterprise, spirit (2), determination.

Exhaust, *v.* To use up completely, to try all options (exhaust administrative remedies). Deplete, consume, run through, complete, wear out, spend, expend, finish, dissipate, tax, empty, strain, drain; waste, disable, impoverish, fatigue, enervate. *Ant.* Preserve.

Exhausted, *adj.* Fatigued. Weary, drawn, tired, worn-out, "bushed," spent, "burnt-out," run-down, pale, emaciated, "beat;" exhaustion, exhaust. See also frail, weak, thin.

Exhaustion, *n.* Fatigue. Tiredness, prostration, weariness, weakness, debility, enervation, collapse, feebleness, lethargy, draining. See also exhaust.

Exhaustion of administrative remedies A party must first seek relief by trying all available administrative remedies before going to a court to ask for judicial action.

Exhaustive, *adj.* See comprehensive, universal, extensive, complete (2), big.

Exhibit 1. *v.* To show; to offer for inspection (the witness exhibited little emotion). Display, reveal, unveil, air, disclose, uncover, illustrate, evidence, indicate, manifest, demonstrate, present, evince, unfurl, brandish, produce, exemplify, express, make public, lay bare, parade, expose, bring to light; teach, inform, coach, school, tutor, instruct, indoctrinate. **2.** *n.* A paper, document, chart, or other thing that is shown to a judge, jury, hearing officer, auditor, arbitrator, etc., and upon being received, is marked for identification and made a part of the case or proceeding. See array (2), exposition (2), production. *Ant.* Conceal (1).

Exhibition, *n.* See production, exposition (2), array (2), performance (3).

Exhibitionism, *n.* Indecent exposure of sexual organs. See deviant.

Exhibitionist, *n.* A showoff. Flasher, extrovert. See also deviant, showoff.

Exhilarate, *v.* See delight, enjoy (2), incite, animate, provoke, revive, amaze.

Exhilarating, *adj.* See attractive, enjoyable, outstanding (2), ardent, active (3), strong (2), happy, content (2), irresistible, moving.

Exhilaration, *n.* See enjoyment, happiness, spirit (2), emotion, passion, power, force, adventure, exultation.

Exhort, *v.* See press (1), encourage (1), provoke, entice, persuade, advocate; beseech, petition; preach.

Exhortation, *n.* See persuasion, entreaty, warning, counsel.

Exhume, *v.* To remove from the earth something that was buried (exhumed the body). Disinter, dig up, disentomb, unearth, resurrect. *Ant.* Bury.

Exigency (exigence), *n.* Something arising suddenly, calling for immediate action (a careless response to the exigency). Plight, difficulty, crisis, "jam," imperative, demand, need, necessity, urgency, imperativeness, command, pressure, circumstance, problem, contingency, requirement, constraint, need. See also emergency.

Exigent, *adj.* Pressing, requiring a prompt response (exigent circumstances). Urgent, demanding, crucial, necessary, compelling, vital, acute, exacting, imperative, stringent, menacing, threatening, critical, inescapable, serious.

Exigent circumstances The emergency-like demands of the occasion call for immediate police response, e.g., the presence of weapons in a car stopped on the road. Such circumstances may justify a warrantless search and seizure.

Exile 1. *n.* Banishment (she was in exile). Eviction, deportation, expatriation, expulsion, ostracism, quarantine, excommunication. **2.** *n.* A person who is banished (the exile protested). Outcast, émigré, pariah, displaced person, expatriate, expellee. **3.** *v.* See expel, oust, evict.

Exist, *v.* **1.** To live or have life; to be in present force, activity, or effect at a given time (the principle exists even today). Endure, survive, continue to be, subsist, breathe, persist, be viable, remain. See also last (2), abide. **2.** To occur (the event exists only in the imagination of the witness). Materialize, happen, result, ensue, arise, take place. *Ant.* Disappear.

Existence, *n.* See object (3), entity, presence, life.

Existent, *adj.* See live (3), present (3).

Existing, *adj.* See present (3), living (3), real, current.

Exit, *n.* **1.** A way out (they blocked the exit). Door, passageway, egress, passage out, outlet, doorway, gate, window, hatch, vent. **2.** Departure (a precipitous exit). Exodus, withdrawal, retreat, leaving, escape, evacuation, pullback, pullout, retirement, ebb, reversion, abandonment, flight. See also emigration, removal, departure. *Ant.* Entrance.

Exodus, *n.* See exit (2), removal, departure, emigration.

Ex officio, *adv., adj.* By virtue of the office; because of holding a particular office; implied by reason of the office (an ex officio member of the board of directors).

Exonerate, *v.* To free from guilt (the testimony exonerated the defendant). See exculpate, acquit, liberate; exoneration.

Exoneration, *n.* **1.** The removal of a burden, charge, responsibility, or duty (a complete exoneration following the hearing). Vindication, freedom, absolution, forgiveness, exculpation, clearance, release, acquittal, dismissal. See also pardon. **2.** The right to be reimbursed by reason of having paid that which another should be compelled to pay.

Exorbitant, *adj.* Deviating from the normal or customary course; going beyond the rule of established limits of right or propriety (an exorbitant demand). Excessive, outrageous, unconscionable, intemperate, gross, unreasonable, egregious, undue, immoderate, inflated, preposterous, extortionate, extreme, immense, extravagant, unwarranted, gouging, monstrous, immoderate. See also disproportionate, excess, prodigal. *Ant.* Equitable.

Exorcise, *v.* See expel, oust.

Exorcism, *n.* See expulsion; witchcraft.

Exoteric, *adj.* See common.

Exotic, *adj.* See different, anomalous, peculiar (2), odd, foreign (3), novel.

Expand, *v.* See augment, add, develop (1, 2), open, mature (1), advance, emerge, produce (2).

Expanse, *n.* See extent, range, scope, measure (1).

Expansion, *n.* See increase, appreciate, growth, accumulation, accretion, development (1), production.

Expansive, *adj.* See comprehensive, universal, extensive, broad (1), open (4, 6, 7), free (1).

Ex parte, *adv., adj.* In behalf of or on application of one party only (an ex parte hearing without the defendant present). With only one side present, unilateral, for one party alone.

Ex parte divorce A divorce proceeding in which only one spouse participates or in which the other spouse does not appear.

Ex parte hearing or proceeding A hearing in which the court or tribunal hears only one side of the controversy.

Expatriate, *v., n.* See exile, expel, oust, emigrant, immigrant; tramp (1); expatriation.

Expatriation, *n.* **1.** The voluntary act of abandoning one's country and becoming a citizen or subject of another (developing countries discourage expatriation by professionals). Emigration, migration, withdrawal, renouncement. **2.** Sending someone into exile (a decree of expatriation). Deportation, banishment, ejection, excommunication. See also exile, expulsion. *Ant.* Immigration.

Expect, *v.* **1.** To look forward to something intended, promised, or likely to happen (he expects to receive a bequest). Envision, foresee, anticipate, reckon on, assume, wait for, contemplate, prepare for, count on, apprehend, figure on, calculate on, divine, envisage, plan on. **2.** To require (the judge expects compliance). Demand, insist, rely on, intend, exact, bargain for.

Expectancy, *n.* That which is expected or hoped for; the condition of being deferred to a future time; the condition of being dependent on an expected event (an estate in expectancy). Contingency. See also likelihood, hope (2), chance (3), probability, presumption. *Ant.* Vested right.

Expectant, *adj.* Contingent as to possession or enjoyment (expectant heir). Prospective, awaiting, potential, ready, expecting, likely, future. See also concerned, apprehensive. *Ant.* Vested, present.

Expectant right A right that is contingent, not vested; one that is dependent on an event or condition that may not happen.

Expectation, *n.* See likelihood, hope (2), chance (3), probability, presumption.

Expediency, *n.* Opportunism. Practicality, utility, usefulness, appropriateness, profit, politics. See also expedient (1).

Expedient 1. *adj.* Whatever is suitable and appropriate to a particular end (an expedient measure). Advantageous, utilitarian, useful, practical, judicious, proper, reasonable, right, sensible, opportune, prudent, beneficial, worthwhile, seasonable, effective, wise, auspicious, politic, convenient. See also advisable. **2.** *n.* The means used to accomplish something (a necessary expedient). Procedure, vehicle, method, agency, device, maneuver, scheme, tool, measure, instrument, strategy, apparatus, technique, formula, plan, practice, tactic, process.

Expedite, *v.* To hasten; to make haste (expedite the shipment). Speed, facilitate, advance, stimulate, accelerate, dispatch, precipitate, quicken, aid, assist, forward, promote, push, hurry, rush. *Ant.* Retard.

Expediter, *n.* Someone who sees to it that materials are always available for production (a unionized expediter).

Expedition, *n.* **1.** An important journey or excursion (they were on a secret expedition). Mission, enterprise, pilgrimage, exploration. See also voyage, assignment, campaign. **2.** The persons making the important journey or excursion (the expedition arrived at noon). Travelers, explorers, troop, squad, company, crew. See also group.

Expeditious, *adj.* Performed with speed and efficiency (an expeditious adjustment of course). Rapid, fast, accelerated, prompt, timely, swift, alacritous, efficient, immediate, instant, alert, accomplished, efficacious, punctual. See also effective. *Ant.* Dilatory.

Expel, *v.* To drive out, often by the use of force (she was expelled from the store). Oust, eject, put out, banish, thrust out, discharge, evict, force out, eliminate, "bounce," dismiss, exile, cashier, dispel, dispossess, deport, isolate, reject, remove, ostracize, transfer, bar, proscribe, segregate, discard, transport, exclude, excommunicate. *Ant.* Invite.

Expend, *v.* **1.** To pay out (the company expended $3,000 in legal fees). Lay out, disburse, spend, apportion, render payment, distribute, contribute, give, "shell out," allocate. **2.** To consume (expend energy). Use up, exhaust, deplete, waste, dissipate, empty, drain, finish. *Ant.* Receive; conserve.

Expendable, *adj.* **1.** Consumed over a short period of time; available for use or consumption (expendable resources). Spendable, disposable, employable, at hand, consumable. **2.** Not essential or critical to preserve (she removed the expendable portions of the memo). Nonessential, accessory, superfluous, marginal, replaceable, auxiliary, unimportant, irrelevant, extraneous, surplus, unnecessary, peripheral, negligible, inconsequential, spare. *Ant.* Indispensable (2).

Expenditure, *n.* The act of spending or paying out money (unauthorized expenditure). Disbursement, outgo, outlay, expense, cost, remittance. *Ant.* Receipt.

Expense, *n.* An outlay, cost, or price (the expense of bringing the litigation). Charge, fee, expenditure, disbursement, consideration, appraisal, rate; drain, depletion, consumption, financial burden. *Ant.* Return.

Expensive, *adj.* See costly, high (1), exorbitant, excess; marketable, worthy.

Experience 1. *n.* The skill, facility, or practical wisdom gained by personal knowledge, feeling, and action (invaluable experience as a trial lawyer). Wisdom, know-how, judgment, sophistication, competence, training, understanding, proficiency, savoir-faire, expertise. **2.** *n.* An event or encounter (the experience of her first case). Incident, occasion, adventure, happening, ordeal, circumstance, episode, occurrence, vicissitude, situation. **3.** *v.* See apprehend (1), comprehend (1). *Ant.* Immaturity; theory.

Experienced, *adj.* See mature (2), expert (2), competent, qualified, effective, able, apt (3); learned, brilliant.

Experience rating A method of determining insurance rates by using the loss experience of the insured over a period of time.

Experiential, *adj.* See empirical, concrete.

Experiment 1. *n.* A special test or observation made to confirm or disprove something doubtful (the experiment to determine the durability of the substance). Trial, research, analysis, investigation, procedure, demonstration, assay, venture, operation, experimentation, tryout, assessment, verification. See also attempt. **2.** *v.* See investigate, assay.

Experimental, *adj.* See hypothetical, speculative, tentative (1); empirical; mathematical.

Expert 1. *n.* One who is knowledgeable, through experience or education, in a specialized field (an expert on accident reconstruction). Master, authority, professional, virtuoso, connoisseur, gourmet, critic, practitioner. See also teacher, scholar, specialist. **2.** *adj.* Skilled and knowledgeable (expert witness). Qualified, competent, proficient, able, trained, experienced, professional, "pro," polished, versed, accomplished, schooled, adroit, dexterous, capable, ace, adept, apt, efficient. *Ant.* Novice; amateurish.

Expertise, *n.* See experience, facility (3), skill (1), field (2).

Expert testimony The opinion evidence of a person who possesses special skill or knowledge in some science, profession, or business that is not common to the average person. See evidence, attestation, opinion.

Expert witness A person who by reason of education or specialized experience possesses superior knowledge on a subject about which persons of no particular training are incapable of forming an accurate opinion or deducting correct conclusions. See evidence, opinion.

Expiate, *v.* See satisfy (1), redress, amend, redeem (2), remedy (2).

Expiation, *n.* See contrition, satisfaction (1), amends, compensation, restitution.

Expiration, *n.* Coming to a close from the mere lapse of time (expiration of the lease). Termination, end, culmination, death, finish, discontinuance, windup, closure. See also cessation, conclusion (1). *Ant.* Commencement.

Expire, *v.* To come to an end from the mere lapse of time (the offer expires at noon). Terminate, conclude, vanish, stop, discontinue, die, lapse, perish, cease, decease, become void, disappear, fail, depart. See also end. *Ant.* Revive.

Explain, *v.* See develop (2), demonstrate, comment (2), define, clarify, exhibit, add (1, 2), augment, describe, communicate.

Explanation, *n.* See development (1), clarification, definition, description, communication.

Explanatory, *adj.* See descriptive, demonstrative (2), didactic.

Expletive, *n.* See profanity, censure (1), slander.

Explicable, *adj.* See ascertainable, intelligible.

Explicate, *v.* See clarify, describe, define.

Explication, *n.* See exposition (1).

Explicit, *adj.* Clear in understanding; not obscure or ambiguous (an explicit offer). Specific, straightforward, direct, candid, categorical, blatant, patent, unequivocal, express, definitive, exact, unconditional, absolute, lucid, comprehensible, sure, perspicuous, plain, positive, stated, unreserved, certain, pointed, forthright, evident, transparent. See also precise, concrete. *Ant.* Cryptic.

Explode, *v.* See detonate, discharge (4), attack (1), batter; eruption.

Exploit, *v.* **exploit,** *n.* **1.** *v.* To take unjust advantage of another for one's own advantage or profit (he exploited his elderly uncle). Misuse, victimize, trick, delude, "milk," "bleed," ill-treat, oppress, deceive; capitalize on, profit by; commercialize, utilize, employ, put into operation, promote, apply, consume, operate. See also manipulate, abuse. **2.** *n.* A noteworthy deed (the exploits of the president). Adventure, feat, achievement, accomplishment, act, success, stunt, performance, job, maneuver.

Exploration, *n.* Discovery efforts directed at the unknown; the examination and investigation of land, which may contain valuable minerals, by drilling, boring, sinking shafts, driving tunnels, etc. (oil exploration). Inspection, scrutinization, investigation, research, canvass, probe. See also search, discovery.

Explore, *v.* See investigate, audit (2), canvass (2), review, cross-examine.

Explosion, *n.* See eruption, collision (1), accident, noise.

Explosive, *n., adj.* See ammunition, arms, gun, weapon; incendiary (1, 2), outrageous, dangerous, bad.

Exponent, *n.* See advocate, champion, backer representative; judge.

Export *v.,* **export,** *n.* **1.** *v.* To carry or send abroad (we export steel). Sell abroad, market overseas, transport, ship. **2.** *n.* A thing or commodity that is exported (tax on exports). Goods and articles of foreign trade, trade goods, shipped wares. See also property. *Ant.* Import.

Export-Import Bank An independent agency of the federal government whose function is to aid in financing exports and imports.

Expose, *v.* **1.** To offer for public view (to exposes misconduct). Display, reveal, unveil, publish, uncover, exhibit, unearth, bring to light, strip, bare, unmask, divulge, broadcast, unfold, detect, make manifest, release, print, advertise, make known. **2.** To submit to danger or harm (the parent exposed the child to disease). Endanger, hazard, deprive, imperil, risk, jeopardize, lay open, put through, experience, endure, undergo, make liable to, make vulnerable, subject. **3.** See denounce. *Ant.* Conceal; protect.

Exposé, *n.* A statement or account of a discreditable matter concerning a person or organization (an exposé by the committee). Revelation, exposure, sensational report, explanation. See also, disclosure, communication, report.

Exposed, *adj.* See hazardous, dangerous, defenseless, dependent (2).

Exposition, *n.* **1.** An explanation or interpretation (an exposition of the judge's philosophy). Clarification, essay, explication, exegesis, overview, elucidation,

Exposition

commentary, account, critique, survey, treatise, annotation, discourse. **2.** An elaborate public display (annual exposition). Exhibit, show, fair, market, bazaar. See also production, array (2), exhibition (2).

Expository statute A statute enacted to explain the meaning of a previously enacted statute.

Ex post facto, *adv., adj.* After the fact (an ex post facto approval). At a later time, afterward, later in time, thereafter, at a subsequent time, by subsequent matter. *Ant.* Ab initio.

Ex post facto law A law passed after the occurrence of a fact or the commission of an act, which retroactively changes the legal consequences of this fact or act.

Expostulate, *v.* See protest (3).

Exposure, *n.* The act or state of exposing or being exposed (indecent exposure). See disclosure, publication (1), communication, report, exposé; expose; jeopardy, hazard, danger.

Expound, *v.* See describe, define, clarify, comment (2), develop (2), communicate.

Express 1. *adj.* Definite; unambiguous and not left to inference (express statement of purpose). Clear, plain, direct, unmistakable, not dubious, declared, set forth, distinct, explicit, purposeful, calculated, intentional, specified, deliberate, unequivocal, manifest, categorical, absolute, unconditional, lucid, forceful, particular, conscious, positive, outlined, fixed, exact, emphatic. **2.** *v.* To verbalize (the witness expressed her fear). State, specify, phrase, voice, say, pronounce, mention, describe, assert, demonstrate, represent, discuss, enumerate, mouth, formulate, enunciate, communicate, articulate, utter, couch, reveal, indicate, observe, herald, announce, breathe, define, expose, illustrate. **3.** *adj.* See prompt (1). *Ant.* Implied; conceal; slow.

Express active trust A trust where the will confers general authority upon the executor to manage the property of the estate and to pay over net income to devisees or legatees. See trust.

Express authority Authority delegated to an agent by words that expressly, plainly, and directly authorize him or her to perform a delegated act. See authority, agent, agency.

Express contract An actual oral or written agreement of the parties, the terms of which are openly uttered or declared at the time the agreement is made. See contract, agreement.

Expression, *n.* See communication, declaration, comment (1), report (1), manifestation, language; appearance (3), countenance (2); emotion.

Expressio unius est exclusio alterius A maxim or canon of statutory construction: When the legislature expressly mentioned one thing in a statute, we can assume that it intended to exclude other things (e.g., if the statute says "teachers" must register, the implication is that police officers do not have to register under this statute).

Expressive, *adj.* See demonstrative, descriptive, pregnant (2), articulate (2), cogent, effective, moving (1), concise, assertive, explicit, positive (1), express (1).

Expressly, *adv.* See absolutely.

Express malice Actual malice; malice in fact; ill will or wrongful motive; a deliberate intention to commit an injury; knowing falsehood or a reckless disregard for truth or falsity. See malice.

Express private passive trust A trust where land is conveyed to or held by one person in trust for another without any power being expressly or impliedly given to the trustee to take actual possession of the land or to exercise acts of ownership over it except by direction of the beneficiary. See trust.

Express trust A trust created or declared in express terms for specific purposes and usually in writing. See trust. *Ant.* Inferred trust, constructive trust,

302

resulting trust.

Express warranty An affirmation of fact or promise made by the seller to the buyer, which relates to the goods and becomes part of the basis of the bargain and creates an express warranty that the goods shall conform to the affirmation. Any description of the goods and any sample or model that is made part of the basis of the bargain creates an express warranty that all of the goods shall conform to the description, sample, or model. See warranty.

Expressway, *n.* See highway.

Expropriate, *v.* To take private property for public purposes (the state expropriated the land under eminent domain). Seize, dispossess, disseise, confiscate, deprive, evict, divest, eject, attach, dislodge, arrogate, usurp, impound, commandeer, appropriate, oust, remove, sequester, foreclose; pirate, purloin. See also condemn (2).

Expropriation, *n.* See nationalization, appropriation (1), eminent domain; expropriate.

Expulsion, *n.* A putting or driving out; a permanent cutting off from the privileges of an institution or society (expulsion from the land). Ejectment, banishment, eviction, deportation, ban, ostracism, excommunication, rejection, dislodgement, excision, suspension, disbarment, expatriation, elimination, isolation, repudiation, ejection, removal, discharge, exile, prohibition, dispossession, separation, eradication. *Ant.* Inclusion.

Expunge, *v.* To erase or eliminate (expunge the record). Destroy, blot out, obliterate, strike out, efface, annul, extinguish, cross out, remove, delete, censor, cancel, omit, drop, edit out, nullify. See also excise (2), erase. *Ant.* Insert.

Expungement, *n.* See expulsion, removal, elimination; expunge.

Expungement of record The process by which the record of (a) a criminal conviction, (b) an arrest, or (c) an adjudication of delinquency is destroyed or sealed after the expiration of a designated period of time.

Expurgate, *v.* To purge or cleanse (the obscenity was expurgated from the film). Remove, erase, weed out, cross out, take out, purify, expunge, purge, blue-pencil, censor, soften, emasculate, sanitize. See also delete, excise (2).

Expurgation, *n.* See removal, elimination, expulsion; expurgate.

Expurgator, *n.* A censor; someone who expurgates. See censor.

Exquisite, *adj.* See beautiful, attractive, superior (2), outstanding (2), extraordinary, exceptional, best (1), predominant, moving.

Ex rel. Upon relation or information (State ex rel. Doe v. Roe). Legal proceedings that are instituted by the attorney general, or other proper person, in the name of the state but on the information and at the instigation of an individual who has a private interest in the matter are said to be taken "on the relation" (ex rel.—the abbreviation for ex relatione) of such person, who is called the relator.

Ex relatione See ex rel.

Ex rights Without certain rights (stock sold ex rights).

Extant, *adj.* See alive (1), live (3), living (3), current (1), present (3), real.

Extemporaneous, *adj.* See spontaneous, sudden.

Extend, *v.* **1.** To enlarge; to carry or draw out further than the original limit (the judge extended the filing deadline). Expand, prolong, lengthen, widen, stretch out, add, supplement, continue, broaden, increase, amplify, protract, inflate, dilate, elongate, augment; postpone, suspend, recess, adjourn, stay, pause, defer. **2.** To give or offer (extend one's apologies). Tender, propose, introduce, proffer, impart, present, bestow, submit, advance, grant. *Ant.* Contract; withdraw.

Extended, *adj.* See comprehensive, extensive, long.

Extension, *n.* **1.** An increase in the length of time (extension of the lease). See continuation, increase; extend (1). **2.** An addition or enlargement to a structure (the extension of the hospital collapsed). Annex, wing, expansion, appendage, attachment, branch. See also addition.

Extensive, *adj.* Widely extended in space, time, or scope (extensive revision of the memo). Wide-reaching, expansive, voluminous, universal, lengthy, ample, wholesale, large-scale, considerable, vast, general, far-reaching, great, commodious, thorough, protracted, colossal, diffuse, exhaustive, unrestricted, massive, mass, sweeping, catholic, sizable, substantial, gargantuan. See also big, broad (1), comprehensive. *Ant.* Minor.

Extent, *n.* Amount, scope, range, or magnitude (the extent of his liability). Bounds, quantity, range, degree, intensity, volume, capacity, area, arena, term, dimension, proportion, domain, sweep, breadth, size, border, comprehensiveness, width, stretch, expanse, bulk, compass, amplitude.

Extenuating, *adj.* Tending to lessen or mitigate; making something less heinous or reprehensible than it would otherwise be (extenuating circumstances). Alleviating, palliative, qualifying, mitigating, diminishing, moderating, reducing, explanatory, tempering, lessening, softening, exculpating, justifying. *Ant.* Aggravating.

Extenuation, *n.* That which renders a crime or tort less heinous or offensive. See justification, excuse; mitigate; extenuating. *Ant.* Aggravation.

Exterior, *n.* The surface (the witness displayed a cold exterior). Appearance, facade, covering, face, skin, demeanor, shell, outside, mien, aspect. See also countenance. *Ant.* Interior.

Exterminate, *v.* See abolish, rescind, annul, destroy, kill, erase, extinguish, extirpate.

Extermination, *n.* See abolition, rescission, elimination.

External, *adj.* **1.** Outward (external appearance). Surface, outlying, outer, peripheral, outside, extrinsic, superficial, foreign. See also exterior. **2.** Acting from without (external cause). *Ant.* Internal.

Exterritoriality, *n.* An exemption from a foreign country's local laws, enjoyed by ambassadors and many subordinates when living in that country.

Extinct, *adj.* No longer in existence or use (an extinct mine). Defunct, extinguished, dead, dormant, inactive, nonexistent, finished, liquidated, obsolete, eradicated, disappeared, evaporated, quenched, archaic. *Ant.* Active, current.

Extinction, *n.* See death, rescission, cessation, expiration, conclusion (1); elimination, abolition; extinct.

Extinguish, *v.* To bring an end to (the verdict extinguished all hope). Squash, terminate, quench, cancel, eradicate, obliterate, liquidate, erase, delete, abort, wipe out, abolish, kill, murder, extirpate, annihilate, douse, eliminate, devastate, efface, suffocate, dismantle, ruin, stifle, nullify. *Ant.* Stimulate.

Extinguishment, *n.* The destruction or cancellation of a right, power, contract, or estate (extinguishment of a debt). See abolition, elimination, rescission; extinguish.

Extirpate, *v.* To destroy or waste (extirpate bigotry). Stamp out, liquidate, abolish, eliminate, quash, annul, void, eradicate, vanquish, demolish, terminate, cancel, efface, raze, level, dissolve, quell, consume, subvert, defeat, purge. *Ant.* Foster.

Extol, *v.* See honor (2), promote, recommend, appreciate (3), tribute (2).

Extort, *v.* To compel or coerce; to gain by wrongful methods (extort a confession). Extract, blackmail, wrench, squeeze, wrest, fleece, gouge, "bleed." See also force (4), coerce, compel, intimidate; extortion.

Extortion, *n.* Obtaining property from another through the wrongful use of actual or threatened force, violence, or fear. This includes a threat to cause public officials to take designated action (i.e., a threat that is made under color of official right). Shakedown, intimidation, blackmail, bullying, bleeding, threat, extraction, terrorization, squeeze. See also coercion.

Extortionate, *adj.* See costly, exorbitant; coercion; usury.

Extra 1. *adj.* Additional (extra pay). Further, other, reserve, subsidiary, more, auxiliary; redundant, superfluous, secondary, incidental. See also supplemental. **2.** *pref.* Beyond (extrajudicial proceedings). Outside of, except, without.

Extract, *v.,* **extract,** *n.* **1.** *v.* To draw out or forth; to pull out from a fixed position (to extract information). Dig out, withdraw, excavate, pry out, wrench, deduce, remove, extirpate, uproot, excise, pluck, force, tear out, draw forth, elicit, pick out, wrest, distill. **2.** *n.* A portion or segment of a writing (the judge read extracts from the testimony). Abstract, quotation, summary, selection, excerpt, clipping, fragment. *Ant.* Implant; full text.

Extraction, *n.* See removal; ancestry.

Extradition, *n.* The surrender by one state or country to another of an individual accused or convicted of an offense outside its own territory and within the territorial jurisdiction of the other, which, being competent to try and punish the individual, demands the surrender (Florida sought extradition from New Hampshire).

Extrahazardous, *adj.* Concerning conditions of special and unusual danger (an extrahazardous occupation). Ultrahazardous, precarious, treacherous, ominous, perilous, abnormally dangerous, destructive, highly vulnerable. *Ant.* Safe.

Extrajudicial, *adj.* Done, given, or effected outside the course of regular judicial proceedings; unconnected with an action in a court of law (extrajudicial oath). See private, separate, independent.

Extrajudicial confession A confession made out of court; one that is not made in the course of a judicial examination or investigation. See confession.

Extramural, *adj.* Occurring or exercised outside of designated boundaries (the extramural powers of the city). *Ant.* Intramural.

Extranational, *adj.* Beyond the territorial and governing limits of a country.

Extraneous, *adj.* **1.** Irrelevant (an extraneous argument). Immaterial, peripheral, inapplicable, not pertinent, nonessential, inadmissible, unrelated, inconsequential, superfluous, not germane, unnecessary, inapposite, redundant, dispensable, impertinent, incidental, accidental, adventitious. See also expendable, irrelevant. **2.** Foreign (an extraneous substance). Of external origin, coming from without, alien, strange, exotic. See also extrinsic. *Ant.* Relevant; internal.

Extraneous evidence As to a document (e.g., contract, will), extraneous evidence is evidence not furnished by the document itself but derived from outside sources.

Extraordinary, *adj.* Exceeding the usual, average, or normal measure or degree (extraordinary expenses). Remarkable, uncommon, irregular, rare, unusual, exceptional, amazing, notable, inconceivable, phenomenal, odd, incredible, fantastic, unprecedented, unique, unparalleled, enormous, outstanding, noteworthy, abnormal, unconventional, individual, strange, striking, outlandish, arresting, anomalous, matchless, peerless, surpassing, select, wonderful, atypical, conspicuous, eminent, of consequence, choice, superior, marvelous, unnatural, eccentric, noticeable, out of the ordinary, curious, unheard-of, monstrous, unbelievable, bizarre, singular, astonishing, unexpected. *Ant.* Customary.

Extraordinary dividend A dividend of a corporation that is nonrepetitive and generally paid at an irregular time because of some unusual corporate event. See dividend.

Extrapolate, *v.* **1.** To deduce one principle from another. See deduce, reason. **2.** To estimate an unknown number. See estimate (2).

Extrasensory, *adj.* Beyond the normal bounds of the senses. See intangible, religious.

Extraterritoriality, *n.* The operation of laws to persons who are physically beyond the limits of the enacting state or nation but still amenable to its authority. See jurisdiction.

Extraterritorial jurisdiction Judicial power that extends beyond the physical limits of a particular state or country.

Extravagance, *n.* See waste (1); excess, immoderate.

Extravagant, *adj.* See immoderate, improvident, prodigal, excess, irrational, disproportionate, high, extreme, exorbitant, absurd.

Extravaganza, *n.* A spectacle. Circus, pageant, show, panorama. See also array (2), exposition, production.

Extra vires Beyond powers. See ultra vires.

Extreme 1. *adj.* Intense, abnormal (extreme cruelty). Inordinate, extensive, great, extraordinary, immoderate, excessive, aggravated, violent, flagrant, intemperate, unwarranted, drastic, bizarre, exaggerated, unreasonable, harsh, amplified, magnified, unprecedented, grotesque, eccentric, egregious, unconventional, outrageous, severe. **2.** *adj.* Concerning the most remote in a direction (extreme left). Outermost, farthest, ultimate, outer, removed, most distant. **3.** *n.* The utmost edge (he went to extremes). Maximum, acme, pinnacle, extremity, ultimate, summit, height, end, depth, limit. *Ant.* Conservative; near, minimum.

Extreme case A case in which the facts, the law, or both reach the outer limits of probability; a desperate case.

Extremis, in See in extremis.

Extremist, *n.* See fanatic, nonconformist, partisan.

Extremity, *n.* **1.** A limb of the body (lower extremities). Member, part, arm, leg, finger, toe, hand. **2.** The farthest point, section, or part (the eastern extremity of the state). Frontier, edge, boundary, border, tip, brink, limit, periphery, termination, precipice. See also margin (1). **3.** See emergency, distress (3).

Extricate, *v.* See release (1), clear (5), liberate; ransom, rescue.

Extrinsic, *adj.* **1.** From outside sources (extrinsic cause). Foreign, dehors, alien, peripheral, exterior, coming from without, outward, external, environmental. **2.** Not essential (extrinsic argument). Extraneous, collateral, nonessential, irrelevant, unrelated, adventitious, unnecessary, accessory, subsidiary. *Ant.* Intrinsic; essential.

Extrinsic evidence External evidence; evidence that is not contained in the body of an agreement or other document; evidence outside of the writing. See evidence.

Extrinsic fraud Fraud that is collateral to the issues tried in the case where the judgment is rendered; the type of deceit that may form the basis for setting aside a judgment. See fraud.

Extrovert, *n.* An outgoing person. Sociable person, socializer. See also exhibitionist.

Exuberance, *n.* See life (3), emotion, spirit (2), passion, enterprise (2), determination (2), force (1), ambition.

Exuberant, *adj.* See active (3), emotional, ardent (3), strong (2), earnest (2), alive (2); abundant; juvenile (2).

Exude, *v.* See exhibit (1); emit.

Exult, *v.* To be jubilant. Rejoice, celebrate, cheer, glory, dance, revel, gloat, be elated.

Exultation, *n.* Jubilation. Delight, exaltation, joy, rejoicing.

Eye-catching, *adj.* See outstanding (2).

Eye for an eye See reprisal, retaliation, recrimination (1).

Eye opener, *n.* See shock (1); extraordinary.

Eyesight, *n.* See sight (1).

Eyesore, *n.* See slum; deformity.

Eyewitness, *n.* A person who saw the act, fact, or transaction to which he or she is

306

giving testimony (an eyewitness on the stand). Observer, spectator, viewer, identifier, corroborator, attestant, onlooker, beholder. See also witness (2), bystander.

F

Fable, *n.* See symbol, legend.

Fabric, *n.* See material (3); foundation, form, composition, design (1).

Fabricate, *v.* **1.** To invent or make up (the witness fabricated her account). Concoct, contrive, forge, prevaricate, trump up, hatch, formulate, feign, falsify, embroider, simulate, deceive, defraud, distort, counterfeit. See also fake (1). **2.** To manufacture (the company fabricated the parts on the premises). Construct, build, erect, structure, assemble, produce, frame, fashion, mold, shape, form, compose, cast.

Fabricated evidence Evidence manufactured or arranged after the fact; it is either wholly false or distorted by contrivance with an evil intent. See evidence, deception.

Fabrication, *n.* See lie, distortion, fraud, fake (2).

Fabulous, *adj.* See outstanding (2), attractive, beautiful, enjoyable, extraordinary; deceptive, false; absurd.

Facade, *n.* See disguise (2), deception, pretense; exterior, surface (1), face.

Face 1. *n.* That which is apparent to a spectator (the document is void on its face because of the wrong name). Surface, front, visage, appearance, upper part. See also exterior, countenance. **2.** *v.* To confront (he faced his accuser). Encounter, defy, meet, challenge, brave. See also confront. *Ant.* Implication; avoid.

Face amount The amount shown on the document or instrument, not including interest. See amount.

Face of the instrument That which is shown by the language used by the document without any explanation, modification, or addition from extrinsic facts or evidence. See instrument.

Facet, *n.* See attribute (2), component, characteristic (1), appearance (3).

Facetious, *adj.* Humorous (a facetious witness). Tongue-in-cheek, funny, witty, flippant, amusing, playful, jovial, whimsical, frivolous, merry, ironic, giddy, pungent. See also comic, happy.

Face value The value expressly stated in the security, policy, or other document.

Facile, *adj.* See simple; apt (3), expert (2), able; casual, cursory, effortless.

Facilitate, *v.* To free from difficulty or impediment (the clerk facilitated his admission to the bar). Alleviate, smooth, advance, ease, disencumber, assist, promote, further, simplify, foster, lighten, aid, speed, subsidize, make possible, abet, uncomplicate. See also expedite, precipitate, accelerate, favor (3). *Ant.* Hamper.

Facilitation, *n.* In criminal law, the act of making it easier for another to commit a crime. See help; abet; accessory, accomplice; facilitate.

Facility, *n.* **1.** That which promotes the ease of any action or course of conduct (defective navigation facilities). Instrumentality, agency, medium, tool, appliance, resource, aid, convenience, means, apparatus, device. **2.** Something built or installed to perform a particular function (sports facility). Structure, edifice, complex, network, system, accommodation, office, institution, bureau, arena, foundation. **3.** Aptitude or skill (a facility in conducting investigations). Proficiency, propensity, smoothness, fluency, talent, dexterity, flexibility, competence, expertise, adroitness, flair, efficiency, capability, ease, grace. See also gift (2), ability, power. *Ant.* Obstruction (1); incompetence (3).

Facsimile, *n.* An exact copy of the original (the court accepted a facsimile). Duplicate, reproduction, replica, reprint, photostat, likeness, image, simulation, carbon, representation. See also copy. *Ant.* Original.

Fact, *n.* That which is ascertained by the senses or by the testimony of witnesses describing what they perceived; an actual thing, event, action, circumstance, or occurrence (a determination of the facts). Happening, incident, experience, phenomenon, affair, episode, statistic, datum, specific, truth, reality, certainty, gospel, verifiable event, verity, actuality. See also detail (2), event, circumstances, particulars. *Ant.* Fabrication.

Faction, *n.* See group; dissent.

Factious, *adj.* See contentious, hostile, adverse, offensive, partisan.

Factor, *n.* **1.** A circumstance or influence that brings about or contributes to a result (the weather was a factor in the accident). Ingredient, consideration, constituent, cause, instrument, reason, means, determinant, aid. See also element, component, detail, fact, circumstances, contingency. **2.** A commercial agent employed by a principal to take custody of and sell merchandise consigned to him or her on behalf of the principal (the factor embezzled the funds). Deputy, broker, middleman, proxy, representative. See also agent.

Factorage, *n.* **1.** The wages, allowance, or commission paid to a factor. See compensation. **2.** The business of a factor. See factor (2), agent.

Factoring, *n.* The sale of a firm's accounts receivable to a factor at a discounted price. See sale.

Factory, *n.* See building, facility (2); manufacture, production, merchant, commerce.

Fact question See issue of fact.

Factual, *adj.* See empirical, accurate, credible, authentic, correct (1), faithful.

Factum, *n.* **1.** The fact; the existence; the doing. **2.** A statement of facts. **3.** The execution of a will.

Faculties, *n.* **1.** Abilities, powers, capabilities (in possession of her faculties). Talents, skills, intelligence, gifts, endowments, expertise, strengths, aptitudes, qualifications, genius, reason, instincts, qualities, propensities. See also ability. **2.** The capability of a husband to provide his wife with alimony. **3.** The teaching staff of a school (a unionized faculty). Teachers, professors, mentors, lecturers, tutors. See also teacher, education, school.

Fad, *n.* See style (3), caprice.

Fade, *v.* See decline (2), diminish, pass (6), disappear, withdraw (1), abate, wear (1).

"Faggot," *n.* Slang for homosexual. See gay.

Fail, *v.* **1.** To be unsuccessful (the business failed). Fold, miscarry, collapse, crash, come to naught, abort, slip, misfire, lose, flunk, botch, err, go wrong, be deficient, "bomb," sink, go bankrupt, perish, stop, fall short, disappoint; decline, dwindle, crumble, languish, deteriorate, weaken, lapse. **2.** To neglect to do something (fail to appear). Omit, miss, forsake, renounce, evade, avoid, abandon, forgo, ignore. *Ant.* Succeed; comply.

Failing, *n.* See defect, deficiency, error, fault (1).

Failure, *n.* **1.** The lack of success (the failure to obtain a majority). Defeat, fiasco, collapse, fall, overthrow, nonfulfillment, miscarriage, abortion, checkmate, washout, breakdown, ruin, error, debacle; bankruptcy, default, folding, insolvency. **2.** An omission (the failure to cure the defect). Neglect, nonperformance, oversight, lapse, delinquency, default, negligence, dereliction, slip, shortcoming, inability, mistake. See also deficiency, fault, defect. *Ant.* Fulfillment; compliance.

Failure of consideration The consideration, although originally existing and good, has since become worthless, has ceased to exist, or has been partially or entirely extinguished.

Failure of issue Dying without children.

Failure to state a cause of action The failure of the plaintiff to allege enough facts in the complaint to warrant the granting of relief even if the plaintiff could prove all of the facts alleged.

Faint, *adj.* See weak; dark, ambiguous, indefinite, obscure.

Faint-hearted, *adj.* See weak, infirm; bashful; yellow (1); coward, cowardice.

Fair, *adj.* Free from prejudice, favoritism, and self-interest (a fair panel). Detached, unbiased, evenhanded, just, square, disinterested, balanced, upright; appropriate, suitable, unobjectionable, acceptable, tolerable, sufficient, decent, satisfactory, adequate, bearable. See also dispassionate, equitable, impartial, objective (2), honest, reasonable. *Ant.* Biased.

Fair comment Statements made on a matter of public concern in the honest belief of their truth. See comment.

Fair hearing A hearing that is conducted according to fundamental principles of justice; a hearing that provides procedural due process of law (e.g., the right to an impartial decision maker, the right to present evidence, the right to have the decision based on the evidence presented). See hearing.

Fair Labor Standards Act A federal statute that sets the minimum standard wage (periodically increased by later statutes) and a maximum work week for industries engaged in interstate commerce. The statute also regulates child labor and established the Wage and Hour Division in the Department of Labor.

Fairly, *adv.* **1.** Equitably, honestly (the jury acted fairly). Impartially, impersonally, objectively, evenly, properly, squarely, morally, justly, evenhandedly, righteously, without bias or prejudice, honorably, dispassionately, candidly, lawfully. **2.** Somewhat (a fairly large settlement). Moderately, modestly, tolerably, adequately, sufficiently, mildly, passably, rather, reasonably. *Ant.* Unjustly; extensively.

Fair market value The amount at which property would change hands between a willing buyer and a willing seller, neither being under any compulsion to buy or sell and both having reasonable knowledge of the relevant facts.

Fair-minded, *adj.* See fair, objective, impartial, liberal (2), equitable, reasonable, dispassionate, honest.

Fairness, *n.* Justice, balance (fairness in the distribution of assets). Equity, impartiality, good faith, objectivity, scrupulousness, detachment, honesty, rectitude, conscientiousness, uprightness, equality, evenhandedness, veracity. See also justice, right (4). *Ant.* Bias.

Fairness doctrine The affirmative responsibility of a broadcaster to provide coverage of issues of public importance that is adequate and that fairly reflects differing viewpoints. Major advocates of both sides of political and public issues should be given fair or equal opportunity to broadcast their viewpoints.

Fair preponderance of the evidence Evidence that outweighs that which is offered to oppose it; the more convincing evidence. See evidence, preponderance.

Fair trade laws Statutes that permitted manufacturers or distributors of brand goods to fix minimum retail prices.

Fair use doctrine The privilege of someone other than the owner of copyrighted material to use the latter in a reasonable manner without consent.

Fair value The present market value; the price at which a seller, willing but not compelled to sell, would take, and a buyer, willing but not compelled to buy, would pay.

Fairy-tale, *adj.* See false (2).

Fait accompli, *n.* That which is done and cannot be changed (the termination is a fait accompli). Executed fact, accomplished fact, reality, certainty, fulfillment. See also fact.

Faith, *n.* **1.** Confidence, reliance, trust (faith in the jury's integrity). Optimism, belief, hope, security, credulity, assurance, reassurance, trustworthiness, surety, credence, dependence, stock, conviction, expectation, certitude. **2.** One's religious beliefs (the practice of his faith). Denomination, principles, persuasion, tenet. See also religion, God, church, creed. **3.** Loyalty (keeping faith). Fidelity, acceptance, pledge, constancy, allegiance, faithfulness. See also loyalty. *Ant.* Mistrust (1); disloyalty (3).

Faithful, *adj.* **1.** Honest, conscientious (faithful employee). Dependable, reliable, obedient, duteous, patriotic, incorruptible, resolute, unwavering, steadfast, tied, steady, sincere, devout, trustworthy; diligent, careful, assiduous, persistent, indefatigable, persevering, meticulous, industrious, methodical, demanding, thorough. See also loyal, constant, certain. **2.** Accurate (a faithful representation). True, exact, corresponding, realistic, truthful, verifiable, close, strict, on target, factual, correct. See also accurate, precise. *Ant.* Wavering; false.

Faithfully, *adv.* Diligently (faithfully performing). Religiously, completely, truthfully, conscientiously, scrupulously, precisely, obediently, carefully, without unnecessary delay, sincerely, meticulously, in good faith, closely, strictly, consistently, reliably, steadfastly, devotedly, exactly. See also absolutely. *Ant.* Carelessly.

Faithless, *adj.* See disloyal, false, cynical, suspicious (2), deceptive, dishonest.

Fake 1. *v.* To falsify (the witness faked a response). Fabricate, manufacture, act, imitate, contrive, feign, simulate, pretend, forge, invent, concoct, cheat, mislead, deceive, trick, delude, hatch, doctor, affect, dissemble, alter, disguise, misrepresent. **2.** *n.* A counterfeit (the will is a fake). Forgery, fraud, hoax, fabrication, ruse, fiction, lie, sham, phony, falsification, imitation; charlatan, impostor, quack. **3.** *adj.* Spurious (a fake response). Bogus, contrived, assumed, simulated, fictitious, artificial, pseudo, fraudulent. *Ant.* Correct; original; genuine.

Faker, *n.* See charlatan, fraud.

Fall, *v.* **1.** To come within (the case falls within the court's jurisdiction). Envelop, embrace, encompass, include, incorporate. **2.** Decrease (the price of the stock fell). Depreciate, recede, decline, abate, slide, diminish, wane, deteriorate, drop, plunge, crash, lower, collapse, cascade, succumb, sink, capitulate, die. *Ant.* Eliminate; accelerate.

Fallacious, *adj.* Logically inconsistent (fallacious reasoning). Misleading, wrong, invalid, unfounded, untenable, faulty, distorted, groundless, illusory, incorrect, sophistical; deceptive, fraudulent, delusive, guileful. See also baseless, false (1), erroneous, doubtful, deceitful. *Ant.* Factual.

Fallacy, *n.* See error, fault (1), deficiency, failure, defect, falsehood.

Fallible, *adj.* See weak, infirm, erroneous, imperfect.

Falling-out, *n.* See quarrel, disagreement.

Fallopian tube An essential part of the female reproductive system consisting of a narrow conduit, about 4 inches in length, which extends on each side of a woman's body from the base of the womb to the ovary upon that side; the tubes carry the egg cells to the uterus.

Fallout, *n.* See effect (1), consequence (1), result (1).

Fallow, *adj.* Barren (fallow land). Unproductive, impoverished, idle, neglected, uncultivated, unseeded, inactive, fruitless, dormant, exhausted, depleted. See also barren, dead (3). *Ant.* Productive.

False, *adj.* **1.** Knowingly, negligently, or innocently untrue (a false accusation). Erroneous, incorrect, unveracious, faulty, mistaken, wrong, inaccurate, fictitious, amiss, flawed, unreal, fallacious, inexact, ersatz, theatrical, improper, illogical,

False

apocryphal. **2.** Deceptive (a false impression). Spurious, artificial, misleading, untruthful, delusive, hypocritical, treacherous, fraudulent, fake, mock, circuitous, duplicitous, disingenuous, fictitious, pseudo, artificial, synthetic, feigned, pretended, trumped-up, phony, fairy-tale, copied, ungenuine, forged, perfidious, insincere, inconstant, counterfeit, beguiling, assumed, lying, recreant, unprincipled, knavish, dishonorable. See also dishonest, disloyal, corrupt, base (2), bogus. *Ant.* Accurate; honest, steadfast.

False arrest An unlawful restraint of an individual's personal liberty or freedom of locomotion; an arrest without proper legal authority. See false imprisonment, arrest.

Falsehood, *n.* A statement or assertion known to be untrue and intended to deceive (a patent falsehood). Misrepresentation, distortion, fabrication, perversion, lie, falsification, prevarication, perjury, canard, equivocation, pretense, misstatement, fallacy, falsity, untruth, fiction, deceit, duplicity, evasion, dissimulation, pretext, invention, sham, stratagem, hoax, wile, forgery, chicanery, trick, exaggeration, guile, concealment, artifice. See also fraud, error, defect, deficiency. *Ant.* Truth.

False imprisonment A tort with the following elements: (a) An act that completely confines the plaintiff within fixed boundaries set by the defendant; (b) intent to confine the plaintiff or a third person; (c) causation of the confinement; (d) the plaintiff either was conscious of the confinement or was harmed by it. See also false arrest, arrest, confine.

False light See invasion of privacy.

False pretenses A statutory crime. The elements are often as follows: (a) A false representation of a material present or past fact, (b) which causes the victim to pass title to his or her property to the wrongdoer, (c) who knows the representation is false and intends thereby to defraud the victim. See fraud, larceny.

False representation Elements: (a) A statement of fact that is untrue; (b) the defendant knew it was false or made it without knowledge as a positive statement of known fact; (c) the plaintiff believed the statement to be true; (d) relied and acted on it; (e) and was injured thereby. See fraud, falsehood.

False swearing Knowingly making a false statement under oath or affirmation.

False token A false document or sign of the existence of a fact, used for the purpose of fraud.

Falsification, *n.* See falsehood, lie (1).

Falsify, *v.* To give a false appearance to something (falsify the security instrument). Forge, counterfeit, feign, prevaricate, misstate, misuse, tamper, misquote, "doctor," gloss, adulterate, twist, exaggerate, pervert, camouflage, alter. See also fabricate, distort, misrepresent. *Ant.* Portray accurately.

Falsity, *n.* See falsehood, error.

Falter, *v.* See flounder, fall (2); fluctuating.

Fame, *n.* See reputation, notoriety, eminence, grandeur, superiority, honor (3), forefront.

Famed, *adj.* See notorious, popular, reputable, conspicuous, great, elevated, outstanding (2).

Familiar, *adj.* **1.** A fair or reasonable knowledge of something (the witness was familiar with the facts). Aware, acquainted, versed, educated, knowledgeable, apprised, cognizant, briefed, conscious, conversant, informed, abreast of, counseled, competent, intimate, experienced, privy to, enlightened. **2.** Commonplace (a familiar occurrence). Typical, customary, usual, general, ordinary, often encountered, proverbial, conventional, standard, natural, normal, everyday, widespread, habitual, accepted, regular, common, household, routine. *Ant.* Ignorant; rare.

Familiarity, *n.* See knowledge, comprehension, cognizance (3), acquaintance (2).

Familiarize, *v.* See educate, instruct, convey (2), introduce.

Family, *n.* Parents and children; a group of blood relatives; a collective body of persons who live in one house and under one head or management (income of the family). Clan, issue, progeny, relations, kin, descendants, stock, ancestral line, ancestry, folk, race, genealogy, forebears, dynasty, stirps, kinship, lineage, offspring, extraction, household, network.

Family planning, *n.* See contraceptive.

Family purpose (automobile) doctrine When a car is maintained by its owner for the general use and convenience of his or her family, the owner is liable for the negligence of a member of the family (who has general authority to drive the car) while the car is being used for the pleasure or convenience of a member of the family.

Family tree, *n.* See ancestry.

Famine, *n.* See dearth, absence (2), privation, want (1); hungry.

Famous, *adj.* See notorious, popular, conspicuous, great, elevated, outstanding (2).

Fan, *n.* See partisan, adherent, addict, aficionado.

Fanatic, *n.* A religious or political enthusiast; someone entertaining extravagant notions (he was a fanatic about computers). Zealot, radical, bigot, extremist, visionary, fiend, addict, partisan, freak. See also nonconformist.

Fanatical, *adj.* See draconian, cruel, gross, rude, extraordinary, extreme (1), ardent, emotional, wild, irrational.

Fanciful, *adj.* See, frivolous, capricious, irrational, odd, fictitious.

Fancy, *n., v.* See caprice; dream; desire (4); enjoy (2), appreciate (3), prefer (2).

Fanfare, *n.* Fuss. Build-up, publicity, show, demonstration, puffery, ballyhoo, trumpet, hullabaloo, blast, hoopla.

Fannie Mae See Federal National Mortgage Association.

Fantasize, *v.* To imagine. Speculate, daydream, hallucinate, gaze. See also dream (1).

Fantastic, *adj.* See extraordinary, outstanding (2), attractive, exceptional, beautiful; capricious, irrational, fictitious, absurd, odd (1), wild, anomalous.

Fantasy, *n.* See dream (1), hallucination, caprice, legend, fiction.

Far, *adj.* See remote (1), far-off.

Farce, *n.* See caricature; fraud; clown; comic.

Farcical, *adj.* See comic, facetious, enjoyable; absurd, odd (1), irrational, anomalous, capricious, wild; clown; amusement.

Fare, *n.* **1.** The transportation charge paid by a passenger (the commission regulates fares). Fee, ticket, toll, cost, expense, price, car fare, rate of charge. **2.** See food.

Farewell, *interj.* See adieu; departure (2).

Far-fetched, *adj.* See absurd, irrational, odd (1), wild, anomalous, doubtful, extraordinary, outrageous.

Far-flung, *adj.* See extensive, comprehensive, broad (1).

Farm 1. *n.* A track of land devoted to agriculture, stock raising, and the like (management of the farm). Ranch, range, tract, plantation, manor. See also home. **2.** *v.* To engage in the business of farming (she farms with her family). Cultivate, till, harvest, practice husbandry, plant.

Farm Credit Administration An independent agency that supervises and coordinates the activities of the cooperative Farm Credit System, which is comprised of federal land banks, federal land bank associations, federal intermediate credit banks and production credit associations, and banks for cooperatives.

Farmer, *n.* One engaged in agricultural pursuits as a livelihood or business (wheat farmer). Husbandman, agronomist, grower, tiller, agrarian, agriculturist, granger, planter, ranger, raiser, harvester. See also entrepreneur, merchant, employer.

Farm hand, *n.* See employee, servant.

Farmhouse, *n.* See home, farm (1).

Far-off, *adj.* Distant. Faraway, a long way off, afar, removed. See also remote (1).

Far-out, *adj., interj.:* See extraordinary, anomalous, beautiful, wild, odd (1).

Far-reaching, *adj.* See crucial, decisive, important; extensive, broad (1), comprehensive.

Far-sighted, *adj.* See acute (1), prudent.

Farthest, *adj.* See extreme (2).

FAS Free alongside. The sales price quotation includes all costs of transportation and delivery of the goods alongside the ship.

Fascinate, *v.* See entice, interest (5), enamor, inveigle, bait (3), delight, enjoy (2).

Fascinating, *adj.* See intriguing, attractive, beautiful, enjoyable.

Fascination, *n.* See appeal (3), bait (1).

Fascism, *n.* See tyranny; government; coercion, oppression.

Fascist, *n.* See tyrant.

Fashion, *n.* See style (3), manner (1), habit, mode, method, caprice; manufacture, make (1).

Fashionable, *adj.* See chic, current, cultivated, beautiful, attractive, aristocratic.

Fast, *adj.* See prompt (1), expeditious, immediate (1); speed (1).

Fasten, *v.* See affix (1), attach (2), connect (1), fix (2).

Fastidious, *adj.* See critical (2), precise (2), particular (2), difficult (3), squeamish, formal (3), inflexible.

Fast-talk, *v.* See deceive, persuade, manipulate (1), entice, entrap.

Fat, *adj.* See corpulent.

Fatal, *adj.* Causing death (fatal injury). Deadly, lethal, devastating, disastrous, destructive, terminal, catastrophic, cataclysmic, mortal, malignant, calamitous, fateful, poisonous, ruinous, injurious. *Ant.* Harmless.

Fatal error Errors that may reasonably be held to have worked substantial injury or prejudice to the complaining party; harmful error, reversible error.

Fatality, *n.* See death, casualty.

Fatal variance A variance between the pleading and the proof, which misleads the defendant in making a defense.

"Fat cat," *n.* See entrepreneur, chief, employer, owner, manager, promoter.

Fate, *n.* See chance (2), destiny; accident; fortuitous.

Fated, *adj.* See inevitable, certain (1); crucial, decisive, important; future.

Fateful, *adj.* See crucial, decisive, important; disastrous, fatal.

"Fathead," *n.* See ass, boor.

Father 1. *n.* A male parent (putative father). Forefather, procreator, sire. See also ancestor. **2.** *n.* The prime mover (the father of the computer age). Procreator, author, forerunner, inventor, originator, founder, designer. **3.** *v.* See beget, fabricate (2).

Fatherland, *n.* See nation, country (1).

Fathom, *v.* See digest (4), know, comprehend (1), construe, discover.

Fathomless, *adj.* Incomprehensible. See incoherent, mysterious, ambiguous, obscure.

Fatigue, *n.* See exhaustion, boredom, ennui; exhausted, frail, weak, thin.

Fatuous, *adj.* See absurd, irrational, juvenile (2), dumb, frivolous.

Fault 1. *n.* An error or defect of judgment or conduct to which blame and culpability attaches (she was at fault). Negligence, neglect, wrong, wrongdoing, aberration, flaw, failing, delinquency, misfeasance, misconduct, incapacity, dereliction, failure, imperfection, shortcoming, bad faith, mismanagement, miscalculation, omission, gaffe, blunder, inaccuracy, misstep, slip, misdeed, deficiency,

blemish, oversight, offense, transgression, peccadillo, infirmity, foible, lapse. **2.**
v. To blame (the judge faulted the director). Censure, hold responsible, deem
liable, criticize, impeach, accuse, rebuke, reprove, berate, chastise, upbraid, condemn, hold accountable, brand, assail. *Ant.* Perfection; exonerate.

Faultfinding, *adj.* See critical (2), querulous, difficult (3), particular (2), contentious; grouch.

Faultless, *adj.* See blameless, innocent (1).

Faulty, *adj.* See weak, infirm, imperfect, defective, erroneous, deficient, inferior
(2).

Faux pas, *n.* See error, mistake, fault (1), lapse (3), oversight.

Favor 1. *n.* An act of kindness and generosity (granting a favor). Courtesy,
indulgence, benefit, accommodation, service, charity, benefaction, good turn. **2.**
n. Partiality (the board showed favor to the contributor). Bias, prejudice,
leniency, favoritism, preference, disposition, sympathy, advocacy, special treatment, cooperation, encouragement, approbation, partisanship, leaning. **3.** *v.* To
show impartiality or unfair bias toward; to support (the judge favored the
plaintiff). Prefer, patronize, indulge, advocate, endorse, approve, guard, befriend,
sanction, select, advance, abet, cover, protect, oblige, aid, champion, promote,
benefit, facilitate, ease, bolster. *Ant.* Harm; impartiality; oppose.

Favorable, *adj.* See beneficial, auspicious, optimistic, positive, intriguing, attractive.

Favored, *adj.* Privileged. Well-off, preferred, advantaged. See also dominant,
preferential.

Favored nation See most favored nation clause.

Favorite, *adj.* Preferred. Chosen, choice, ideal; pet, darling. See also favored;
popular; prefer; best (1), superior (2), attractive.

Favoritism, *n.* Invidious preference and selection based on friendship and factors
other than merit (favoritism in the firm's promotion practices). Patronage,
nepotism, partiality, discrimination, prejudice, inequality, partisanship, injustice,
one-sidedness. See also favor (2). *Ant.* Impartiality.

Fawn, *v.* See pander (2), flatter; grovel; cringe; obedience.

Fawning, *adj.* See servile.

Faze, *v.* See intimidate.

FCA Federal Credit Administration.

FCC See Federal Communications Commission.

FCIC Federal Crop Insurance Corporation, which sponsors insurance coverage
against financial loss due to destruction of agricultural products resulting from the
elements of nature.

FDIC See Federal Deposit Insurance Corporation.

Fealty, *n.* Fidelity; allegiance to the feudal law of the manor (an oath of fealty).
Obedience, support, duty, service, homage, devotion. See also loyalty.

Fear 1. *n.* Apprehension of harm; consciousness of approaching danger (fear of
reprisals). Dread, dismay, trepidation, qualm, worry, fright, anxiety, disquietude,
awe, consternation, panic, alarm, horror, uneasiness, misgiving, specter, terror,
perturbation, disquiet, immobilization, shock, intimidation, concern, cowardice,
solicitude, suspicion, phobia, hesitation, agitation, foreboding. **2.** *v.* To dread
(the defendant feared the jury's decision). Be afraid, apprehend, mistrust, tremble
at, suspect, worry, distrust, anticipate with alarm. *Ant.* Indifference; ignore.

Fearful, *adj.* See afraid, apprehensive; appalling, awesome.

Fearless, *adj.* See courageous, adventurous, ardent, ambitious, assertive, certain
(2), assured (4); reckless.

Fearsome, *adj.* See awesome, appalling; afraid, apprehensive.

Feasance, *n.* A performance; the doing of an act. See malfeasance, misfeasance, nonfeasance.

Feasible, *adj.* Capable of being accomplished (a feasible plan). Practical, doable, workable, attainable, realistic, reachable, probable, appropriate, advisable, possible, viable, conceivable, expedient, achievable, manageable, realizable, likely, useful. See also practicable. *Ant.* Impractical.

Feast, *n., v.* See celebration (2), ceremony, extravaganza, banquet; eat.

Feat, *n.* See act (3).

Featherbedding, *n.* An employee practice designed to create or spread employment by unnecessarily maintaining or increasing the number of employees used or the amount of time consumed to work on a particular job, e.g., encouraging make-work and minimum crew regulations.

Feature, *n., v.* See characteristic (1), essence, property (2), quality (1), face (1), exterior, landmark; emphasize, display.

Featured, *adj.* See conspicuous, outstanding (2), elevated, notorious, popular, great, extraordinary.

FECA See Federal Employees' Compensation Act.

Feces, *n.* See refuse (2).

Feckless, *adj.* See irresponsible, careless.

Fecund, *adj.* See fertile, abundant, arable.

Federacy, *n.* See confederacy, alliance.

Federal, *adj.* Pertaining to the national government of the United States (federal jurisdiction). United States, central. See also national.

Federal Aviation Administration (FAA) The FAA, within the Department of Transportation, regulates air traffic to foster safety, operates a common system of air traffic control, etc.

Federal Communications Commission (FCC) The FCC regulates interstate and foreign communications by radio and television broadcasting; telephone, telegraph, and cable operations; two-way radio operators; and satellite communication.

Federal Deposit Insurance Corporation (FDIC) An independent federal agency that insures a designated amount of deposits in national banks and in state banks that meet prescribed qualifications.

Federal Employees' Compensation Act (FECA) A type of workers' compensation plan for federal employees by which payments are made for death or disability sustained in performance of employment duties.

Federal Employer's Liability Act (FELA) A federal workers' compensation law that protects employees of railroads engaged in interstate and foreign commerce, who are injured in the performance of employment duties.

Federal Home Loan Bank Board The board that charters and regulates federal savings and loan associations, and controls the system of Federal Home Loan Banks.

Federal Home Loan Banks Banks created for the purpose of keeping a permanent supply of money available for home financing. Savings and loans associations, insurance companies, and similar companies making long-term mortgage loans may become members of the Federal Home Loan Bank System and thus may borrow from one of the twelve regional banks throughout the country.

Federal Home Loan Mortgage Corporation (Freddie Mac) A federal agency that purchases first mortgages (both conventional and federally insured) from members of the Federal Reserve System and the Federal Home Loan Bank System.

Federal Housing Administration (FHA) A federal agency that insures mortgage loans made by FHA-approved lenders on homes that meet FHA standards in order to make mortgages more desirable investments for lenders.

Federal Insurance Contributions Act (FICA) A federal statute imposing social security taxes on employers, employees, and the self-employed.

Federalism, *n.* The interrelations between the states and the federal government and among the states.

Federalist Papers A series of essays by Alexander Hamilton, James Madison, and John Jay, expounding and advocating the adoption of the Constitution of the United States.

Federal jurisdiction The powers of the federal courts based on Article III of the U.S. Constitution and specific acts of Congress.

Federal Land Banks Regional banks established by Congress to provide mortgage loans to farmers.

Federal Maritime Commission The federal agency that regulates waterborne foreign and domestic offshore commerce of the United States, assures that U.S. international trade is open to all nations on fair and equitable terms, and guards against unauthorized monopoly in the waterborne commerce of the United States.

Federal Mediation and Conciliation Service A federal agency that helps prevent disruptions in the flow of interstate commerce caused by labor-management disputes by providing mediators to assist disputing parties in the resolution of their differences.

Federal National Mortgage Association (Fannie Mae) A federal agency that provides a secondary market for the purchase and sale of mortgages guaranteed by the Veterans Administration and those insured under the Federal Housing Administration.

Federal Power Commission (FPC) A federal agency that issues permits and licenses for nonfederal hydroelectric power projects, regulates interstate wholesale transactions in electric and natural gas, issues certificates for interstate gas sales and the construction of interstate pipeline facilities, conducts investigations of power industries, etc.

Federal pre-emption See pre-emption.

Federal question A legal issue in a case arising under and involving the interpretation and application of the U.S. Constitution, acts of Congress, or treaties; a case within the jurisdiction of the federal courts.

Federal Register A daily publication for making available to the public federal agency regulations and other legal documents of the executive branch. It includes proposed changes in rules, regulations, and standards on which the public is invited to submit commentary before final adoption.

Federal regulations See Code of Federal Regulations.

Federal Reporter (F., F.2d) A reporter that publishes opinions of designated federal courts, primarily the U.S. Courts of Appeals.

Federal Reserve Act The federal statute that created the Federal Reserve Banks, which act as agents in maintaining money reserves, issuing money in the form of bank notes, lending money to banks, and supervising banks.

Federal Reserve Board of Governors The seven-member board appointed by the president and confirmed by the Senate, which sets reserve requirements for member banks, reviews and approves the discount-rate actions of regional Federal Reserve Banks, sets ceilings on the rate of interest that banks can pay on time and savings deposits, and issues regulations.

Federal reserve notes A form of currency issued by Federal Reserve Banks in the likeness of noninterest-bearing promissory notes payable to bearer on demand (e.g., the one-dollar bill).

Federal reserve system A network of twelve central banks to which most national banks belong and to which state-chartered banks may also belong. Membership rules require investment of stock and minimum reserves. The system was designed to give the country an elastic currency, provide facilities for discounting commercial paper, and improve the supervision of banking.

Federal Rules Decisions (F.R.D.) A reporter that publishes some federal court decisions that construe or apply the Federal Rules of Civil, Criminal, and Appellate Procedure as well as the Federal Rules of Evidence.

Federal Rules of Appellate Procedure The rules governing procedure in appeals to United States courts of appeals from lower federal courts, and procedure in proceedings in the courts of appeals involving the review or enforcement of orders of federal agencies, boards, or commissions.

Federal Rules of Civil Procedure Procedural rules that govern civil actions in United States district courts.

Federal Rules of Criminal Procedure Procedural rules that govern criminal cases in United States district courts and before United States magistrates.

Federal Rules of Evidence Rules that govern the admissibility of evidence at trials in federal courts and before United States magistrates.

Federal Supplement (F.Supp.) A reporter that publishes some opinions of designated federal courts, primarily the United States district courts.

Federal Torts Claims Act The federal statute that gave the government's consent to be sued in tort in designated kinds of cases (e.g., a negligence action arising out of acts or omissions of a federal employee at the ministerial level where no discretion at the planning level is involved).

Federal Trade Commission (FTC) A federal agency that promotes free and fair competition in interstate commerce through prevention of general trade restraints such as price-fixing agreements, false advertising, boycotts, illegal combinations of competitors, and other unfair methods of competition.

Federate, *v.* See affiliate (2), combine.

Federation, *n.* A joining together of states or nations in a league or association; the league itself (Federation of Insurance Associations). Union, alliance, coalition, confederation, confederacy, syndicate, combine, sisterhood, brotherhood, society, pool, centralization, sorority, fraternity, combination. See also amalgamation.

Fee, *n.* **1.** Payment for a service (consultation fee). Price, compensation, charge, consideration, bill, admission, tariff, remuneration, recompense, stipend, honorarium, commission, emolument, reward, wage, exaction, toll, due tax, royalty. **2.** An estate of inheritance without condition; an estate in which the owner has full powers of disposition (the land was granted to her in fee). Absolute interest in property, unconditional estate.

Feeble, *adj.* See weak, infirm, frail, decrepit, defenseless.

Feeble-minded, *adj.* See backward, weak, infirm, senile, insane, demented, lunatic, deranged.

Feed, *v.* To lend additional support; to strengthen after the fact (to feed the mortgage through a subsequently acquired title). See nurture, foster, eat.

Feedback, *n.* See reply, appraisal, criticism (2).

Feel, *v., n.* See apprehend (1), comprehend (1), notice (2); touch (1), handle (2), caress; facility (3), ability.

Feeling, *n.* See emotion, passion; love, affection (1); perception (1), intuition, impression, apprehension, comprehension; opinion.

Fee simple absolute An estate in which the owner is entitled to the entire property with unconditional power of disposition during his or her life; if the owner dies intestate, the property descends to his or her heirs and legal representatives.

Fee simple conditional A fee that is limited or restrained to particular heirs exclusive of others.

Fee simple defeasible A fee estate that may end upon the happening of a specified event.

Fee splitting, *n.* Receiving part of the fee as a result of making a referral of the client.

Fee tail An estate of inheritance that, instead of descending to heirs generally, goes to the heirs of the body of the grantee or devisee and through them, to his or her grandchildren in a direct line.

Feign, *v.* See affect (2), dissemble, disguise (1); feigned.

Feigned, *adj.* Pretended (feigned response). Fictitious, supposititious, simulated, spurious, specious, assumed, fabricated, mock, play, fake, camouflaged, insincere, affected, pseudo, fraudulent, synthetic, sham, distorted, bogus, false, falsified, deceptive, counterfeit, concocted, misleading, contrived. *Ant.* Genuine.

Feint, *n.* See pretense, artifice.

Feisty, *adj.* See contentious, excited, emotional, incendiary (2), ardent, violent.

FELA See Federal Employers' Liability Act.

Felicitation, *n.* See congratulation; approbation.

Felicitous, *adj.* See appropriate (3), pertinent.

Felicity, *n.* See happiness, passion, emotion, harmony.

Fellatio, *n.* A sexual act in which the mouth or lips come into contact with the penis. See deviation; coitus.

Fellow, *adj., n.* Concerning a companion (fellow worker). Associated, affiliated, connected, joined; partner, counterpart, comrade, co-worker, colleague, mate, confrere, helpmate, equal.

Fellow servant, *n.* See associate (2), colleague, fellow.

Fellow servant rule At common law, in an action for damages brought against an employer by an injured employee, the employer may reduce or extinguish its liability by proving that the negligence of another employee was partly or wholly responsible for the accident resulting in the injury.

Fellowships, *n.* See community (3), companionship, cooperation, company (3), coalition, concord, confederacy, goodwill (2), affinity.

Felon, *n.* A person who has committed a felony (a three-time felon). See wrongdoer, offender, criminal.

Felonious, *adj.* Done with the intent to commit a crime (felonious assault). Treacherous, villainous, iniquitous, illegitimate, malignant, with evil heart or purpose, heinous, base, wrongful, criminal, illegal, cruel, perfidious, wicked, vicious, corrupt, noxious, pernicious, infamous. See also immoral, malicious. *Ant.* Legal.

Felonious assault A criminal assault that amounts to a felony; aggravated assault. See also assault, felony.

Felonious entry A type of statutory burglary. See also entry, felony.

Felonious intent An act of the will in which one forms a desire to commit a felony.

Feloniously, *adv.* Proceeding from an evil heart or purpose; done with the deliberate intent to commit a crime; pertaining to a felony. See felonious, malicious, immoral; felony.

Felonious taking Taking with the intent to steal. See larceny, seizure, felony.

Felony, *n.* Any offense punishable by death or imprisonment for a term exceeding a year; a crime more serious than a misdemeanor (she was convicted of the felony of armed robbery). Gross offense, heinous crime, capital offense, serious offense, wrongdoing, transgression. See also wrong (1), crime.

Felony murder rule At common law, one whose conduct brought about an unintended death in the commission or attempted commission of a felony was guilty of murder.

Female, *adj.* See woman.

Feme covert A married woman. *Ant.* Feme sole.

Feminine, *adj.* Delicate. Tender, soft, dainty. See also woman.

Feminism, *n.*. A movement in support of equal rights for women. See campaign.

Fence, *n.* **1.** An enclosure about a field or other space (a fence in disrepair). Railing, barrier, stockade, boundary, hedge. See also wall, landmark. **2.** A receiver of stolen property (alleged to be a fence).

Fencing, *n.* See athletics, sport, game (1).

Fend, *v.* See prevent, avoid (2); manage, provide.

Feoffee, *n.* One to whom a fee is conveyed.

Feoffment, *n.* The grant of a fee (i.e., full ownership of an estate); the grant of a corporal hereditament where seisin is passed by investiture or by livery of seisin.

Feoffor, *n.* The person making a feoffment.

Feral, *adj.* Pertaining to wild animals. See wild (1); cruel.

Ferine, *adj.* Untamed. See wild.

Ferment, *n.; ***ferment,** *v.* See commotion, disturbance, confusion; emotion, passion; disrupt, provoke.

Ferocious, *adj.* See wild, cruel, gross, base (2), bad, offensive, repulsive, odious, demonstrative, emotional.

Ferocity, *n.* See cruelty, bestiality; odium.

Ferret, *v.* To track down or discover (the investigator ferreted out the secret). Search out, trail, elicit, pursue, hunt, bring to light, unearth, root out, smoke out, exhume, pry into.

Ferry, *v.* To transport people or property cross a body of water commercially. Shuttle, taxi, pilot, chauffeur, convey.

Ferryboat, *n.* See vessel (1).

Fertile, *adj.* Productive. Rich, yielding, fruitful, potent, virile, prolific, spawning, lush. See also pregnant (2), abundant.

Fertilizer, *n.* Compost, manure, dung.

Fervent, *adj.* See demonstrative (2), emotional, ardent, earnest (2), active (3), strong (2), diligent, violent.

Fervid, *adj.* See fervent.

Fervor, *n.* See passion, emotion, spirit (2), force (1), enterprise (2), determination (2).

Fester, *v.* See disturb, harass; dissolve.

Festival, *n.* See celebration (2), ceremony, extravaganza, banquet; amusement, entertainment, game, sport; happiness.

Festive, *adj.* Joyous. Playful, merry, gay, holiday, hearty, jubilant. See also happy, social, convivial; community.

Festivity, *n.* See festival, game (1).

Fetal, *adj.* Pertaining to an unborn child (fetal death). See fetus.

Fetch, *v.* See get (1), convey, carry (1).

Fete, *n.* See festival.

Feticide, *n.* The destruction of a fetus. See kill.

Fetid, *adj.* See foul, rotten.

Fetish, *n.* Fixation. See compulsion (2); witchcraft.

Fetishism, *n.* See witchcraft, deviation.

Fetter, *n.* Chain or shackle (fetters were placed on the inmate). Iron, manacle, bond, handcuff, leash, yoke, hindrance, bridle, encumbrance, strap, restraint, inhibition, lock, confinement, deterrent, obstruction, detention, constraint, handicap, trammel, prohibition, paralysis, restriction, impediment, cage.

Fetus, *n.* Unborn offspring. In humans, the unborn offspring in the postembryonic period after major structures have been outlined—from 7 or 8 weeks after fertilization until birth (operation on the fetus). See abortion; person.

Feud 1. *n.* Bitter strife between individuals or groups (the feud between the associations). War, battle, controversy, altercation, dissension, quarrel, schism, vendetta, hostility, wrangle, conflict, disagreement, rupture, argument, breach, animosity, tension, animus, split, rivalry, enmity, clash, faction, ill will, dispute, estrangement. See also fight (1), contention (2). **2.** *n.* An inheritable right to the use and occupation of land, held on condition of rendering services to the lord or proprietor who retained the property in the land. **3.** *v.* See fight (2), argue.

Feudal, *adj.* Pertaining to a feud or fee; growing out of feudalism based on the relationship between the vassal and the lord. See feud (2).

Fever, *n.* See emotion, spirit, power, force, passion; confusion, hysteria, insanity.

Feverish, *adj.* **1.** Hetic. Frantic, frenzied, uncontrolled, restless, agitated, highstrung, zealous, impatient, driven, overwrought. See also emotional, ardent, earnest (2), active (3), strong (2), violent. **2.** Hot. Flushed, glowing, burning, sweating. See also dizzy.

Few, *adj.* An indefinite expression for a small or limited number (the doctrine had few adherents). Not many, small number, hardly any, one or two, several, divers, some, sundry, handful; limited, meager, sparse, infrequent, sporadic. See also seldom, intermittent, periodic, incidental (2). *Ant.* Numerous.

FHA See Federal Housing Administration.

FHLB See Federal Home Loan Banks.

FHLBB See Federal Home Loan Bank Board.

FHLMC See Federal Home Loan Mortgage Corporation.

Fiancé, fiancée, *n.* See betrothal; engage (4); marriage.

Fiasco, *n.* See failure, catastrophe, cataclysm, casualty, abortion (2), disaster.

Fiat, *n.* An authoritative order or decree; "let it be done" (he managed by fiat). Command, mandate, dictate, rule, prescript, sanction, edict, directive, injunction, regulation, ordinance, commandment, manifesto, admonition, pronouncement. See also order (1), direction (1). *Ant.* Suggestion.

Fiat money Paper currency not backed by gold or silver; also called "flat money." See currency.

FICA See Federal Insurance Contributions Act.

Fickle, *adj.* See capricious, variable, fluctuating, inconsistent, odd, wild.

Fiction, *n.* Something imagined or invented (the court relied on a fiction to reach its result). Invention, product of the imagination, myth, fabrication, fable, concoction, figment, fantasy, coinage, improvisation, tale, canard. *Ant.* Actuality.

Fictional, *adj.* See fictitious, feigned, false (2) deceptive, illusory.

Fictionalize, *v.* See fabricate, fake.

Fiction of law An assumption or supposition of law that a state of facts exists that has never really taken place. An assumption, for purposes of achieving justice, that a fact is true even though it may not be true (e.g., an assumption that you are in possession of your home even though you may not be actually in it all the time). See constructive.

Fictitious, *adj.* Based on a fiction (fictitious name). Pretended, counterfeit, misrepresented, unreal, not genuine, nonexistent, imaginary, apocryphal, untrue, spurious, specious, simulated, mythical, fictional, synthetic, bogus, fanciful, sham, unfounded, artificial, forged, pseudo, concocted, fake, misleading. See also false (1, 2), feigned, erroneous, deceptive, baseless, fallacious, illusory. *Ant.* Genuine.

Fiddle, *v., n.* See dissipate (1); music.

Fidelity, *n.* Integrity and loyalty (fidelity to the nation). Trustworthiness, honesty, allegiance, devotion, dedication, fealty, reliability, honor, conscientiousness, dependability, constancy, adherence, good faith, responsibility, permanence, patriotism. *Ant.* Infidelity.

Fidelity bond or insurance A contract whereby the insurer agrees to indemnify the insured against loss resulting from the dishonesty or default of a designated person. See insurance.

Fides, *n.* Faith, honesty, veracity. See bona fide; mala fides, bad faith.

Fidgety, *adj.* See feverish, apprehensive, concerned.

Fiducial, *adj.* See fiduciary (2) (fiducial office).

Fiduciary 1. *n.* A person or institution that manages money or property for another; someone in whom another has a right to place great trust and to expect great loyalty (the fiduciary of the estate was sued for fraud). Trustee, guardian, agent, executor. See also caretaker, custodian. **2.** *adj.* Pertaining to someone who manages money or property for another and who owes the latter considerable loyalty (fiduciary relationship). Fiducial, trusted, worthy of confidence, trustee. See also confidential.

Fiduciary bond A type of surety bond that the court requires of persons who serve as trustees, administrators, executors, guardians, and conservators to insure proper performance of their duties. See bond, surety.

Fiduciary capacity Acting on behalf of another in a relationship that necessitates great confidence, trust, and good faith.

Fiduciary or confidential relation A relationship founded on trust, reliance, dependence, or confidence, reposed by one person in the integrity and fidelity of another who is in a position of relative dominance and influence (e.g., the attorney-client relationship). See also confidential, confidence (1).

Fief, *n.* An estate in fee; feud; land held by a vassal.

Field, *n.* **1.** An open area of land commonly used for cultivation or pasturage (an unenclosed field). Grounds, lawn, meadow, clearing, common, arena, region. **2.** A domain or area of interest (her field was physics). Specialty, specialization, sphere, forte, domain, expertise, training, bailiwick, calling, line, department, province, profession, vocation, occupation, business, pursuit, job.

Field audit An audit conducted on the business premises of the taxpayer. See audit.

Field book A description of the courses and distances of the lines, and of the corners of the lots of the town as they were surveyed, and as they appear by number and division on the town plan. See description, map, record.

Field Code The original New York Code created by David Dudley Field in 1848, calling for the simplification of civil procedure. See code.

Field warehousing An arrangement whereby a wholesaler, manufacturer, or merchant finances its business through a pledge of goods remaining on its premises. See pledge, goods.

Fiend, *n.* See wrongdoer, deviant (2), demon.

Fiendish, *adj.* See cruel, gross (1), inhuman, wild, base (2), bad, violent, emotional, deleterious, extreme, malicious; obscene; angry.

Fierce, *adj.* See wild, cruel, gross (1), base (2), bad, violent, emotional, deleterious, extreme, malicious; angry.

Fiery, *adj.* See emotional, excited, incendiary (2), violent, ardent, outrageous, feverish, demonstrative, angry.

FIFO First in, first out; an inventory flow assumption by which ending inventory cost is determined from the most recent purchases, and the cost of goods sold is determined from the oldest purchases including the beginning inventory.

Fifth degree of kinship The degree of kinship between a deceased intestate and the children of the deceased's first cousin.

Fight 1. *n.* A hostile encounter (a fight ensued). Fracas, row, skirmish, affray, war, combat, assault, exchange of blows, brawl, battle, strife, feud, riot, melee, clash, struggle, dissension, engagement, quarrel, duel, altercation, contention, set-to, campaign, conflict, imbroglio, confrontation, dispute, outbreak, schism, wrangle, disagreement. **2.** *v.* To oppose; to engage in battle (they will fight the relocation plan). Resist, protest, thwart, stand up to, contest, dispute, repulse, argue, dissent, challenge, attack, assail, defy, deviate, contradict, oppugn, harass, confound, traverse, reject, frustrate, take issue with. *Ant.* Reconciliation; concede.

Fighter, *n.* See adversary, competitor; sailor.

Fighting words Words that would have a tendency to cause acts of violence by the person to whom they are addressed.

Figment, *n.* See fiction, hallucination, falsehood, delusion.

Figuration, *n.* See form (1).

Figurative, *adj.* See symbolic, descriptive, demonstrative (2).

Figure, *n., v.* See form (1), composition, design (1), manifestation, embodiment, sample (1), model; number; calculate, assess.

Figurehead, *n.* Someone who can function in name only. Puppet, straw, instrument, cipher, nonentity, front man, dummy, token.

Filch, *v.* To steal something, usually of small value (filch an apple). Shoplift, purloin, embezzle, swipe, take, loot, misappropriate, pilfer, convert, pirate, defraud. See also rob; larceny.

File 1. *n.* A record; the place where records are kept (the file on the Smith case). Document, folder, archives, register, docket, portfolio, drawer, roll, arrangement, envelope, compartment, receptacle, registry, dossier, stacks, notebook. **2.** *v.* To deposit in the custody or among the records of another (the plaintiff filed a motion for summary judgment with the court). Deliver, give, hand over, enter, transfer, docket, formally submit, register, make application, turn in. **3.** *v.* To arrange something in a particular order (he filed the correspondence). Pigeonhole, organize, collate, systematize, classify, rank, categorize, codify, alphabetize.

File clerk, *n.* See clerk (2), assistant, employee.

File wrapper estoppel If, to obtain a patent, an inventor restricts what is claimed, he or she is thereafter bound by that surrender, which may readily be ascertained by an examination of the file wrapper. The latter is the written record of the preliminary negotiations between the applicant and the Patent Office for a patent monopoly. One cannot recapture in an infringement action the breadth of a patent previously abandoned in the patent office.

Filial, *adj.* Relating to or befitting a child (filial obligation). See child.

Filiate, *v.* To assign or determine paternity. See filiation proceeding; paternity.

Filiation, *n.* A judicial determination of paternity. Fatherhood, parentage, blood relationship, blood tie.

Filiation proceeding A statutory proceeding, criminal in form but in the nature of a civil action, to establish paternity and to enforce the duty to support the child.

Filibuster, *n.* A tactic designed to obstruct and delay legislation by prolonged and often irrelevant speeches on the floor of the legislature (the senator's filibuster against the tax bill). Interference, retardation, impediment, stalling. See also prolong.

Filius nullius The son or child of nobody; an illegitimate child. See bastard; illegitimate, child.

Fill, *v.* To satisfy or complete (fill the need). Make full, fulfill, perform, outfit, supply, provide, stock, store, satiate, execute, saturate, carry out, function, discharge. *Ant.* Spurn.

Filler, *n.* See attachment (3), increase, accessory (2).

Fill-in, *n.* See replacement (2), agent (1), representative (1).

Film, *n.* See cinema.

Filter, *v.* To filtrate. Screen, strain, sift, purify, percolate, pass through, refine, clarify. See also drain.

Filth, *n.* See dirt, pollution, refuse; obscene, filthy.

Filthy, *adj.* Morally depraving; vulgar (a filthy display). Sordid, indecent, obscene, lewd, offensive, debasing, squalid, polluted, vile, foul, putrefied, corrupt, slimy, shameless, unclean, objectionable, ribald, coarse, stained, fecal, sleazy, base. See also dirty, pornographic. *Ant.* Wholesome.

Filtrate, *v.* See filter, drain (1).

Finagle, *v.* See manipulate, deceive, cheat.

Final, *adj.* **1.** Conclusive (the final resolution of the dispute). Decisive, unchangeable, definitive, ultimate, irrevocable, determinative, incontrovertible, fixed, extreme, complete, unappealable, exhaustive, eventual, resulting, crowning, culminating, finished. **2.** Last (the final assignment). Closing, terminable, ending, endmost, rearmost, latest. *Ant.* Inconclusive; initial.

Finale, *n.* See conclusion (1).

Finality, *n.* Conclusiveness. Definitiveness, decisiveness, completion.

Finalize, *v.* See end (2), settle (1), finish (1), consummate (1), perfect (3).

Final judgment A judgment is final when it determines the rights of the parties and disposes of all the issues involved so that no future action by the court will be necessary in order to settle and determine the entire controversy.

Finance 1. *v.* To supply with funds through the issuance of stocks, notes, etc.; to provide with capital or loan money for a business (his brother financed it). Capitalize, subsidize, underwrite, pay for, supply, lend, sponsor, back, subscribe, endow, invest, vouch for, guarantee, set up, promote, stake, fund, assure, indorse, champion, advocate, uphold, act as surety for, insure, warrant, assist. **2.** *n.* The management of money, credit, investments, etc.; the acquisition and valuation of financial resources (the Department of Finance). Income, economics, fiscal matters, counseling, accounts, treasury, purse strings, revenue, budget.

Finance charge The extra cost imposed for the privilege of deferring payment of the purchase price.

Financial, *adj.* Relating to finances (financial officer of the company). Fiscal, budgetary, economic, monetary, pecuniary.

Financial Responsibility Acts State statutes that require owners of motor vehicles to produce proof of financial accountability (through personal assets or insurance) as a condition of acquiring a license and registration so that judgments rendered against them arising out of the operation of the vehicles may be satisfied. See insurance.

Financier, *n.* A person or institution that financially backs business ventures; a person or institution skilled in investments and money matters (they were unable to locate a financier for the project). Capitalist, backer, sponsor, broker, investor, tycoon, underwriter.

Find, *v.* **1.** To come upon by effort or by chance (he found the watch). Discover, detect, identify, uncover, happen upon, encounter, notice, ascertain, decipher, unveil, ferret out, stumble upon, unearth, expose, retrieve, catch, espy, meet, observe, experience. See also locate. **2.** To make a determination (we find for the plaintiff). Decree, rule, award, decide, judge, pronounce, adjudge, conclude, resolve, establish. See also adjudicate. *Ant.* Lose; defer.

Finder, *n.* Someone who finds or locates something for another, e.g., someone who secures mortgage financing for a borrower (the finder charged a fee). Locater, go-between, intermediary, contact, dealer. See also agent, broker.

Finding, *n.* The result of the deliberations of a jury, referee, arbitrator, court, agency, or other entity conducting an inquiry (a finding of neglect). Judgment, conclusion, pronouncement, ruling, verdict, decree, order, deduction, resolution, outcome, inference, decision, report. See also opinion.

Fine 1. *v.* To sentence a person convicted of an offense to pay a penalty in money (she was fined $5,000). Assess, charge, impose, mulct, punish, amerce, confiscate. **2.** *n.* A monetary punishment imposed on someone convicted of an offense (she paid a fine of $5,000). Penalty, pecuniary penalty, liability, forfeiture, amercement, assessment. **3.** *adj.* See outstanding (2), superior (2), extraordinary.

Finesse, *n.* See delicacy, discretion (3); ability, facility; deception.

Finger, *n., v.* See member (2); handle (2), touch.

Fingerprint, *n.* An impression from the inner surface of the tip of the fingers, often used for identification purposes (fingerprints left on the weapon). Prints, marks, anthropometry.

Finicky, *adj.* See particular (2), precise (2), critical (2), difficult (3), squeamish.

Finis, *n.* See conclusion (1), cessation, expiration.

Finish 1. *v.* To bring to a close or end (she finished drafting the legislation). Complete, accomplish, culminate, discontinue, fulfill, carry through, perfect, wind up, terminate, stop, draw to a close, realize, finalize. See also end. **2.** *n.* See conclusion (1), expiration, cessation. *Ant.* Commence; commencement.

Finished, *adj.* See finish (1); absolute, complete, entire, perfect.

Finishing school, *n.* See school.

Finite, *adj.* See imperfect, limited (1), temporary.

Fink, *n.* See informer; boor.

Fire 1. *n.* The effect of combustion (negligently set fire). Ignition, burning, flame, conflagration, inferno, flare, holocaust, blaze, incandescence, searing, glare; ember, coal, cinders; bonfire, campfire. **2.** *v.* To dismiss from a position or employment (he was fired for insubordination). Terminate, oust, let go, evict, eject, dispose, "bounce," cashier, remove, dispose, drop, "sack," riff. See also discharge. **3.** *v.* See shoot.

Firearm, *n.* An instrument used in the propulsion of shot, shell, or bullets by the action of gunpowder exploded within it (registration of firearms). Gun, pistol, revolver, rifle, shotgun. See also weapon, ammunition.

Firebrand, *n.* See revolutionary, partisan, incendiary (3), nonconformist.

Firebug, *n.* An arsonist, or pyromaniac. See incendiary.

Firecracker, *n.* See ammunition; weapon.

Fire engine, *n.* See vehicle.

Firefighter, *n.* See employee.

Fireproof, *adj.* Flame resistant. See safe (2).

Firm 1. *n.* A business or professional entity (law firm). Enterprise, company, association, partnership, house, institution, corporation, sole proprietorship, establishment, trust, concern, organization, conglomerate. See also merchant, business. **2.** *adj.* Fixed, binding (firm offer). Secured, anchored, unyielding, rigid, stationary, established, irrevocable, constant, irreversible, indissolvable; inert, immovable, motionless, moored, entrenched, sturdy, unalterable, settled, decided, abiding, lasting, sure, deep-rooted. See also final, definite (2).

Firm bid or offer An offer that by its terms will remain open and binding until accepted or rejected.

First, *adj.* Preceding all others; entitled to preference or priority above others (first mortgage). Initial, senior, foremost, main, superior, paramount, principal, key, outstanding, cardinal, primary, uppermost, premiere, premier, major, prime, chief, head, ranking, inaugural, leading, dominant, sovereign. *Ant.* Secondary.

First aid, *n.* See treatment; medicine; doctor.

First-class, *adj.* See superior (2), outstanding (2), primary (1), extraordinary, best (1).

First-degree murder Killing someone (a) with malice aforethought—premeditation—or (b) with extreme cruelty or atrocity, or (c) in the commission or

325

attempted commission of a crime punishable by death or life imprisonment. See murder.

Firsthand, *adj.* From the original source (firsthand account). Primary, direct, proximate, next. See also immediate, eyewitness. *Ant.* Hearsay.

First impression, case of A case that presents the court with an entirely new or novel question of law. See case.

First in, first out See FIFO.

First lien A lien that takes priority and must be satisfied before all other charges or encumbrances upon the same property. See lien.

First mortgage A senior mortgage that has a priority right of payment on default over all junior encumbrances. See mortgage.

First place, *n.* See forefront, dominion, superiority.

First-rate, *adj.* See superior (2), outstanding (2), extraordinary, best (1).

Fisc, *n.* The treasury of a governmental body.

Fiscal, *adj.* Having to do with financial matters, e.g., revenue, taxes (fiscal responsibility). Budgetary, monetary, pecuniary, capital, treasury. See also economic, financial.

Fiscal year A period of 12 consecutive months chosen by a business as the accounting period for annual reports (e.g., 7/1 to 6/30, or 1/1 to 12/31).

Fish, *v.* See investigate, audit; search.

Fishing expedition A loose, vague, or unfocused questioning or investigation; an overly broad use of the discovery process. See exploration, examination.

Fishy, *adj.* See suspicious, odd, anomalous; devious.

Fission, fissure, *n.* See division (1), break (3), crevice.

Fistfight, *n.* See fight, feud, commotion, battery.

Fisticuffs, *n.* See athletics, sport, game; battery, attack.

Fit 1. *adj.* Suitable (the drug was not fit for humans). Appropriate, legitimate, adapted, conformable, designed, prepared, accommodated, compatible, congruous, applicable, efficient, adequate, harmonious, right, consonant, relevant, fitting, eligible, acceptable, worthy, seaworthy, apposite, ready, germane, pertinent, befitting, tolerable, advantageous, seasonable, marketable, salable, merchantable, qualified, sturdy, intact, well-built, safe, firm, solvent, well-constructed, unmarred, healthy, reliable, trustworthy, responsible, durable, tough, efficacious, effective, competent. **2.** *n.* A sudden attack or illness (a fit of coughing). Seizure, spasm, convulsion, stroke, outbreak, paroxysm, frenzy; conniption, outburst, explosion, snit, fury, tantrum. **3.** *adj.* See healthy, able-bodied.

Fitful, *adj.* See intermittent, irregular.

Fitness, *n.* **1.** Suitability (the fitness of the product). Qualification, appropriateness, usefulness, aptness, propriety, applicability, serviceability, value, utility, worth. **2.** See health. *Ant.* Inappropriateness.

Fitness for a particular purpose, warranty of Where the seller at the time of contracting has reason to know any particular purpose for which the goods are required and that the buyer is relying on the seller's skill or judgment to select or furnish goods that are suitable, there is, unless excluded or modified, an implied warranty that the goods shall be good for that purpose. See warranty.

Fitting, *adj.* See fit (1), appropriate, relevant, apt (1).

Fix 1. *v.* To determine (fix a date for the hearing). Settle, arrive at, work out, specify, agree, stabilize, define, establish, prescribe, designate, conclude, seal, arrange, set, choose, place, nail down, stipulate, name. **2.** *v.* To fasten (fix the warning sign to the fence). Attach firmly, secure, lock, stabilize, connect, tie, hitch, bolt, link, brace, bind, affix, implant, anchor, moor, focus, rivet, cement, position, immobilize. **3.** *v.* To repair (fix the lock). Mend, correct, straighten, patch, redress, renovate, restore, remedy, overhaul, ameliorate, purify, improve, refurbish, recondition, adjust, rectify; regulate, systematize, order, prepare, classify, sort, catalogue, organize. **4.** *v.* To assign (fix the blame). Impose, place, fasten, affix, put. **5.** *v.* To prearrange something dishonestly (fix an election). Tamper, bribe, corrupt. **6.** *n.* See ordeal, affliction, plight (1), emergency.

Fixation, *n.* See compulsion (2), desire; irresistible.

Fixed, *adj.* **1.** Not subject to change (fixed price). Set, stable, definite, established, unchangeable, settled, entrenched, not fluctuating, inflexible, unwavering. See also firm (2), permanent; liquidated. **2.** Stationary (fixed income). Anchored, securely placed, secured, rigid, stable, bound, constant, still, rooted, persistent, steadfast. *Ant.* Flexible.

Fixed assets Plant assets (e.g., machinery, land, buildings). See goods, property. *Ant.* Liquid assets.

Fixed capital The amount of money that is permanently invested in the business. See capital.

Fixed charges Expenses that must be borne regardless of the condition of the business (e.g., interest and tax payments). See charge (9), fee (1).

Fixed income Income that does not fluctuate over a period of time (e.g., interest on a bond). See income, compensation.

Fixed opinion A bias or prejudgment as to guilt or liability. See bias, prejudice.

Fixture, *n.* Something so attached to land as to be deemed a part of it; something attached to land by roots, embedded in it, permanently resting on it, or connected by cement, plaster, bolts, etc. (as a fixture, the furnace was sold along with the house). Attachment, permanent addition, installation, immovable equipment. See also appurtenance.

Fizzle, *v., n.* See collapse, abort (2); noise.

Flabbergast, *v.* See amaze, surprise (1); agape, lost (3).

Flabby, *adj.* See corpulent; weak, frail; flaccid.

Flaccid, *adj.* Limp. Flabby, sagging, soft, slack, baggy. See also weak, frail, exhausted.

Flag, *n., v.* See symbol, badge, manifestation; signal (3).

Flagellate, *v.* See beat (1), batter, pound (1); castigate, censure.

Flagellation, *n.* See flogging, whipping, battery, attack, beat, punishment; censure.

Flagrant, *adj.* Notorious (flagrant violation of the law). Scandalous, shocking, monstrous, conspicuous, egregious, glaring, outrageous, brazen, shameless, heinous, arrogant, gross, ostentatious, obtrusive, coarse, audacious, indecent, infamous, impudent, wanton, flaming, immodest, enormous, nefarious, iniquitous, obvious, manifest, open, evident. See also extreme (1). *Ant.* Concealed.

Flagrant necessity A case of urgency, rendering lawful an otherwise illegal act.

Flagship, *n.* See vessel (1); chief.

Flail, *v.* See beat, batter, pound (1).

Flair, *n.* See gift (2), ability (2), facility (3).

Flak, *n.* See censure, objection.

Flamboyant, *adj.* Ostentatious. Ornate, colorful, flashy, vulgar, tinsel, overdone, theatrical, garish, dazzling, tawdry, tasteless, brilliant, showy, gay, vivid, loud. See also gaudy, wild (2), awesome; exaggerate.

Flame, *n., v.* See fire, passion, emotion; beau; burn.

Flaming, *adj.* See flagrant; ardent, emotional, incendiary; fire, burn.

Flammable, *adj.* Inflammable. Combustible, incendiary.

Flap, *n.* See crisis, emergency, commotion, eruption.

Flare, *v.* To erupt. Explode, blow up, rage, thunder, breakout. See also burn; fire, extend (1), augment.

Flash, *n.* See eruption; minute, interval; fire, burn.

Flashback, *n.* See retrospect.

Flashy, *adj.* See flamboyant; wild (2).

Flask, *n.* See vessel (2).

Flat, *adj.* **1.** Level. Smooth, horizontal, plane, even, flush, straight, unbroken, uniform, regular, equal. **2.** See definite, plain. **3.** See commonplace, barren, pedestrian (2).

Flatboat, *n.* See vessel (1).

Flat bond A bond that includes accrued interest in the price. See bond.

Flat money See fiat money.

Flatten, *v.* See grade (1).

Flatter, *v.* To compliment; to fawn over. Laud, extol, praise, cajole, court, disarm, inflate, wheedle, ingratiate, curry favor, toady to, "butter up." See also honor (2), promote; tribute (2); deceive; parasite; flattery.

Flattery, *n.* False or excessive praise (obnoxious flattery toward the judge). Fawning, cajolery, obsequiousness, toadyism, blarney, sycophancy, laudation, compliment, adulation, blandishment, eulogy. See also parasite. *Ant.* Condemnation.

Flatulence, *n.* See babble.

Flatulent, *adj.* See pompous, arrogant, verbose.

Flaunt, *v.* See brandish; manifest (2), exhibit (1), publish; flamboyant.

Flavor, *n.* **1.** See essence, characteristic (1), quality (1). **2.** Taste. Savor, spice, seasoning, relish, tang.

Flavorful, *adj.* See delectable, attractive, wholesome.

Flaw, *n.* See defect, deficiency, failure, error, fault (1), eccentricity.

Flawless, *adj.* See perfect (2), sound, valid, cogent, complete.

Flay, *v.* See censure, abuse, castigate; cheat, deceive.

Flea market, *n.* See market; merchant; commerce.

Fledgling, *n.* See amateur, beginner, assistant, intern, juvenile (1).

Flee, *v.* To run away (flee from custody). Escape, take flight, abscond, exit, elope, desert, retreat, disappear, evade, withdraw, abandon, decamp, vanish, shun, dodge, bolt. *Ant.* Return.

Fleece, *v.* See cheat, embezzle, deceive; fraud; plunder, rape, larceny.

Fleet, *n.* An organized group of boats, ships, cars, or other vehicles (the fleet was attacked). Squadron, division, force, number, band, flotilla, armada. See also vessel (1); military.

Fleeting, *adj.* See temporary, brief (4), intangible, perishable, weak.

Fleet policy A blanket insurance policy that covers a number of vehicles owned by the same insured. See insurance, vehicle.

Flexible, *adj.* Capable of change and adaptation (flexible approach). Pliant, adaptable, elastic, yielding, adjustable, conformable, amenable, receptive, malleable, supple, ductile, moldable, lithe, plastic, resilient, tractable, manageable, complaisant, versatile, docile, indulgent, compliant, limber. *Ant.* Rigid.

Flight, *n.* See flee, departure, escape.

Flighty, *adj.* See capricious, erratic, irregular, reckless, wild, lunatic; frivolous.

Flimflam, *n.* A form of confidence game in which the victim is tricked into turning over money. See deception, fraud, confidence game.

Flimsy, *adj.* See frail, weak, inferior, perishable, breakable, inadequate, temporary, transient, petty, frivolous.

Flinch, *v.* See cringe.

Fling, *v., n.* See jettison (1), shoot; spree.

Flint, *n.* See rock.

Flip, *v.* See jettison (1).

Flip-flop, *n.* See reversal.

Flippant, *adj.* See arrogant, pompous, rude, indifferent, cursory, casual (3).

Flipping, *n.* Refinancing consumer loans. See refinance.

Flirt, *v.* To tease. Play, lead on, toy with, beguile, coquet, tantalize, trifle, dally. See also entice, entertain, solicit; invitation.

Float, *n., v.* **floating,** *adj.* **1.** *n.* The time between the deposit of a check in one bank and its subtraction from an account in another bank; checks and other items in the process of collection. **2.** *v.* To allow a given currency to freely establish its own value as against other currencies by the law of supply and demand. **3.** *adj.* See fluctuating.

Floater policy An insurance policy that is issued to cover items that have no fixed location (e.g., jewelry that is worn). See insurance.

Floating debt Liabilities, other than bonds, that are payable on demand or at an early date (e.g., accounts payable). See debt, liability.

Floating easement An easement for a right-of-way that is not limited to any specific area on the land to which the easement attaches. See easement.

Floating interest rate A rate of interest that is not fixed but which varies depending on the existing rate in the money market. See interest (2).

Floating lien A security interest under which the borrower pledges security for present and future advances. Such security is not only in inventory or accounts of the debtor in existence at the time of the original loan but also in its after-acquired inventory or accounts. See lien, interest (1), security interest, pledge, inventory, account, advance.

Floating stock The process by which stock is issued and sold. See share (3), stock (1).

Floating zone A special detailed use district of undetermined location in which the proposed kind, size, and form of structures must be preapproved. See zone.

Flock, *n., v.* See mob, company (2), congregation, assemblage, assembly; collect (1), congregate, accumulate.

Flogging, *n.* Thrashing or beating with a whip or lash (flogging was barred). Horsewhipping, flagellation, lashing, flailing. See also whipping, beat.

Flood, *n.* An inundation of water over land (flood insurance). Torrent, overflow, deluge, rush, surge, outpouring, downpour, cascade.

Floor 1. *n.* The lower limit (a floor on prices). Minimum, base, bottom. **2.** *n.* The part of the legislature in which members sit and cast their votes (debate on the floor of the Senate). **3.** *n.* The right of someone to address the assembly (she has the floor). **4.** *n.* The lower surface of a room or structure (fell on the floor). Ground, flooring, planking, bed, deck, groundwork. See also platform (2). **5.** *v.* See devastate (2).

Floor plan financing A loan to a retail seller that is secured by the items to be sold and that is paid off as each item sells.

Floozy, *n.* See prostitute.

Flop, *n., v.* See disaster, casualty, catastrophe, failure; fail (1), collapse.

Flotsam, *n.* Goods that float on the sea when cast overboard for the safety of the ship or when the ship is sunk.

Flounder, *v.* To struggle, stagger, hesitate. Stumble, toss, swing, careen, lurch, pitch, wobble, totter, wallow, falter, squirm, twist, jerk, shift, writhe, fidget, turn, flinch, fumble, stammer, shuffle, waver. See also wander, collapse, blunder, err.

Flourish, *v.* See develop, mature (1), advance (3, 4, 5), produce (2).

Flout, *v.* See disparage, defame, slander.

Flow, *v., n.* See drain, discharge, emerge, emit (2), arise, circulate; flood, stream (2).

Flower, *v., n.* See advance (3, 4, 5), develop, mature; prime (3), apex, culmination, ceiling (1).

FLSA See Fair Labor Standards Act.

Flub, *v.* See blunder, err.

Fluctuate, *v.* See fluctuating; alternate (1), stray (1).

Fluctuating, *adj.* Moving irregularly (fluctuating prices). Vacillating, altering, rising and falling, shifting, wavering, equivocating, undulating, oscillating, swaying, veering, varying, changing, alternating. *Ant.* Fixed.

Fluctuating clause A type of escalator clause that is inserted in some long-term contracts to allow for an increase in costs during the contract period.

Fluency, *n.* See facility (3).

Fluent, *adj.* See articulate (2), concise, cogent, descriptive, effective.

Fluid, *adj., n.* See fluctuating, flexible, indefinite; beverage, liquor, water.

Fluke, *n.* See chance (2), destiny, accident, windfall.

Flunky, *n.* See servant, slave, employee, parasite; grovel, flatter.

Flurry, *n.* See storm; commotion.

Flush, *adj., v.* See flat, water; commotion; abundant, copious.

Flux, *n.* See change (1), action (2), activity; fluctuating.

Fly, *v.* See flee, run (2), speed (2).

Fly-by-night, *adj.* See temporary, transitory; frivolous; dishonest, deceptive, vagabond (2).

Flyer, *n.* See circular (2), placard (1), report (1), journal.

FMC See Federal Maritime Commission.

FMCS See Federal Mediation and Conciliation Service.

FNMA See Federal National Mortgage Association.

FOB Free on board. Generally, as used in a sales price quotation, FOB means that the seller assumes all responsibilities and costs up to the point of delivery, including insurance, transportation, etc.

Focus, *v., n.* See center (2, 3), concentrate (2), emphasize, accent; essence (1), concentration, intent.

Foe, *n.* See enemy, adversary, competitor, disputant, litigant, assailant.

Fog 1. *n.* Haze, smog. Vapor, overcast, mist, veil. **2.** *n.* See confusion. **3.** *v.* See obscure, cloud (3), cover (2).

FOIA See Freedom of Information Act.

Foible, *n.* See defect, deficiency, fault (1).

Foil, *v., n.* See hinder, restrain, counter, overcome, beat (2); contrast, opposite.

Foist, *v.* See impose, cheat, deceive; palming off, fraud.

Fold, *v., n.* See fail (1), collapse (2); cover (3), enclose; community, congregation, assembly, assemblage.

Folio, *n.* A sheet of paper folded to form two leaves resulting in four pages of a book or manuscript; a page number.

Folk, *n., adj.* See family; nation, public; native, local; backward.

Folklore, *n.* See legend; fiction; record (2); communication.

Follow, *v.* **1.** To accept as authority (the court followed the Smith opinion). Adopt, use, rely on, accept as precedent, comply with, conform to, yield to, echo, obey, heed, copy, emulate, reflect, be guided by, imitate, model after. **2.** To go or come after (Burger followed Warren on the Court). Succeed, replace, supplant, result, ensue, trail, come next. **3.** See pursue (2), chase, trace (2), ferret. *Ant.* Reject; precede.

Follower, *n.* See partisan (1), constituency, adherent, student.

Following, *n., adj.* See coterie, partisan (1), public (1); subsequent.

Folly, *n.* See balderdash, mistake, error, fault.

Foment, *v.* See abet, provoke, incite, bait (3), exacerbate.

Fond, *adj.* See affectionate; enamor.

Fondle, *v.* See caress, touch (1), handle (2).

Fondness, *n.* See affection (1), love, desire.

Food, *n.* Nourishment, fare, nutriment, sustenance, victuals, groceries, mainte-nance, bread. See also necessaries, provision (2).

Food and Drug Administration A federal agency within the Department of Health and Human Services, established to set safety and quality standards for foods, drugs, cosmetics, and other consumer products.

Fool, *n.* See ass, idiot, boor.

Foolhardy, *adj.* See reckless, careless, impetuous, dumb, irrational, juvenile, frivo-lous.

Foolish, *adj.* See dumb, absurd, lunatic, irrational, juvenile, frivolous, heedless, careless, reckless.

Foolproof, *adj.* See safe, effective.

Foot acre One acre of coal 1 foot thick.

Football, *n.* See athletics, game, sport, amusement.

Foot-dragging, *n.* See delay; dilatory.

Foothold, *n.* See foundation (2).

Footing, *n.* See foundation (2), base (3).

Footloose, *adj.* See carefree, free, indifferent.

Foray, *n.* See attack, assault, invasion.

Forbear, forebear, *v.* See abstain, desist, abandon, resist; tolerate (2); forbear-ance.

Forbearance, *n.* The act by which a creditor waits for payment of a debt after it becomes due from the debtor; refraining from taking action, especially to enforce one's rights (the creditor sought an additional 2% for his forbearance). Indul-gence, patience, delay, abstinence, restraint, self-restraint, clemency, endurance, mercy, inaction, moderation, refraining, withholding, holding back. See also pardon, amnesty, temperance. *Ant.* Enforcement.

Forbid, *v.* See prohibit, proscribe, ban (2), outlaw.

Forbidding, *adj.* See hostile, dangerous, hazardous, odious, distressing, imminent.

For cause A reason that is relevant to ability and fitness to perform one's duty (the commissioner was dismissed for cause).

Force 1. *n.* Strength directed to an end (the force of arms). Power, energy, stamina, animation, violence, drive, puissance, might, pressure, potency, clout, momentum, vigor, endurance, intensity, velocity, impetus, magnetism, charisma, discipline, urgency, speed, tension. **2.** *n.* Physical coercion (taken out of the room by force). Duress, subjugation, compulsion, exaction, domination, dicta-tion, command, influence, oppression, control, restraint, enforcement, authority, necessity. See also violence. **3.** *n.* Legal validity (the regulation in force). Efficacy, legal efficacy, operation, potency, potential, effectiveness. **4.** *v.* To coerce (he was forced to sign). Compel, drive, order, extort, constrain, enforce, impel, pressure, push, overpower, exact, enjoin, require, induce, thrust, drag, coax, obligate, necessitate. **5.** *n.* See group (1). *Ant.* Weakness; freedom; dorman-cy; allow.

Force and arms Done with violence.

Forced, *adj.* See involuntary, compulsory; feigned, false (2), artificial; violent.

Forced heir Persons whom the testator or donor cannot deprive of the portion of his or her estate reserved for them by law unless a just cause exists to disinherit them.

Forced sale A sale of property pursuant to an execution of a judgment (e.g., to satisfy a mortgage or tax debt).

Forceful, *adj.* See positive (1), assertive, express (1), explicit, effective, efficient, cogent.

Force majeure An unexpected event; an irresistible and superior force. See act of

God.

Force of habit, *n.* See custom; habitual, mechanical, spontaneous.

Forcible, *adj.* Obtained by compulsion or violence; effected by force against resistance (forcible entry). Aggressive, oppressive, dominant, coercive, compelling, armed, forceful. See also compulsory, violent, onerous, unconscionable. *Ant.* Amicable.

Forcible detainer A summary, speedy, and adequate statutory remedy to obtain possession of premises to which one is entitled. The remedy exists against a person who originally had rightful possession of the realty but who refused to surrender it when his or her right ended.

Forcible entry Taking possession of lands or tenements with force and arms, against the will of those entitled to possession, and without lawful authority.

Forcible trespass Taking or seizing the personal property of another by force, violence, or intimidation, or by forcibly damaging it.

Forebear, forbear, *n.* See ancestor; family, author (2).

Forebode, *v.* See augur; expect (1), foresee.

Foreboding, *adj.* See apprehension (3), harbinger, warning; peril, danger, hazard.

Forecast, *v.* See anticipate, augur, foresee, expect (1).

Foreclose, *v.* **1.** To initiate a procedure by which mortgaged property is sold in satisfaction of the mortgage debt upon default of the mortgagor; to destroy an equity of redemption (the bank foreclosed). **2.** To exclude (his attitude foreclosed any possibility of settlement). Block, destroy, deter, prevent, shut out, hinder, remove, evict, rule out, omit, confiscate, dispossess, forfeit, extinguish, dislodge, banish, prohibit, forbid. See also bar, ban.

Foreclosure, *n.* See foreclose; obstruction, prohibition, blockage (1), check (5), prevention.

Forefather, *n.* See ancestor, antecedent (2, 3), author (2).

Forefront, *n.* Lead. Vanguard, first place, fore, helm, fame, acceptance.

Forego, *v.* To precede. See antedate (2); forgo.

Foregone, *adj.* See former.

Foreign, *adj.* **1.** Belonging to another nation or country (foreign currency). International, nonresident. See also alien. **2.** Relating to or rendered in another state (the Texan obtained a foreign divorce in Ohio). **3.** Unfamiliar (resignation is foreign to her nature). Strange, extrinsic, unrelated, inapt, inconsistent, removed, outside, extraneous, uncharacteristic, inapplicable, incongruous, unnatural, unaffiliated, remote, antipathetic, incompatible. See also odd, peculiar, anomalous, different, alien (2), irregular, exceptional, deviate (1). *Ant.* Domestic; forum; characteristic.

Foreign agent A person who acts as a lobbyist representing the interests (e.g., trade, foreign aid) of a foreign nation or corporation. See agent, lobbying.

Foreign corporation A corporation doing business in one state but chartered or incorporated in another state or in another country. See corporation, business, commerce.

Foreigner, *n.* A person who is not a citizen of the state or country in which he or she is present (hostility toward foreigners). Stranger, immigrant, alien, outsider, newcomer, non-native. *Ant.* Native.

Foreign exchange Conversion of the money of one country into its equal of another country. The process by which the money of one country is used to pay balances due in another. See currency.

Foreign judgment A judgment of a sister state or of a foreign nation. See judgment, jurisdiction.

Foreign jurisdiction The jurisdiction of a sister state or of a foreign nation. The exercise by a state or nation of jurisdiction beyond its own territory. See jurisdiction.

Foreign substance A substance in any part of the body or organism where it is not normally found, usually introduced from without.

Foreknowledge, *n.* See foresight, clairvoyance (2).

Foreman, *n.* **1.** The presiding member and spokesperson of a jury (the foreman announced the verdict). Chairperson. **2.** A superintendent (an unfair labor practice was filed against the foreman). Boss, crew leader, overseer, coordinator. See also manager, director, master.

Foremost, *adj.* See first, primary (1).

Forensic, *adj.* **1.** Belonging to courts of justice (forensic matter). Judicial, legal, jurisprudential. **2.** Concerning argumentation (forensic skills of the advocate). Debating, argumentative, polemical, rhetorical, dialectical; litigious, disputable, arguable.

Forensic medicine The science of applying medical knowledge to the purposes of the law.

Foreordained, *adj.* See inevitable; destiny.

Forerunner, *n.* See antecedent (2), harbinger, ancestor, author (2).

Foresee, *v.* To see or know in advance (the company should have foreseen that children would enter the yard). Forecast, predict, prognosticate, foretell, visualize, envision, prophesy, divine, foreknow, surmise, apprehend, see, contemplate. See also anticipate, expect (1), augur.

Foreseeability, *n.* The ability to see or know in advance; the extent to which something can be known in advance; reasonable anticipation of something (the foreseeability of danger). See foresee.

Foreseeable, *adj.* See forthcoming, prospective, imminent, foresee.

Foreshadow, *v.* See augur, anticipate, foresee, expect (1).

Foresight, *n.* Reasonable anticipation of the consequences of certain acts or omissions; prudence (foresight is needed in planning the strategy). Prevision, clairvoyance, prophecy, prescience; wisdom, preparation, heed, discretion, presence of mind, judgment, discrimination, shrewdness, farsightedness. See also caution (3), care (1), prudence, precaution, vigilance. *Ant.* Neglect.

Forest, *n.* See woods, timber, shrubbery.

Forestall, *v.* To intercept or obstruct (they tried to forestall a walkout). Prevent, thwart, anticipate, ward off, cancel, divert, sidetrack, counteract, stymie, arrest, prohibit, avert, deter, circumvent, veto, preclude, obstruct, estop, avoid, stifle, impede. See also frustrate. *Ant.* Facilitate.

Foretell, *v.* See foresee, anticipate, augur.

Forethought, *n.* See foresight, prudence, precaution, caution; consideration (2), vigilance.

Forever, *adv.* See always; perpetual.

Forewarn, *v.* See admonish (1).

Forewarning, *n.* See warning, admonition (1).

Foreword, *n.* See preamble.

Forfeit, *v.* To lose the right or privilege to something because of error, default, or crime (he forfeited the money by not appearing). Give up, give away, relinquish, renounce, sacrifice, squander, miss, concede, surrender, forgo, repudiate. See also lapse (1), foreclose, abandon, waive. *Ant.* Claim.

Forfeiture, *n.* A deprivation or destruction of a right or privilege due to neglect, crime, nonperformance of a condition, etc.; that which is forfeited. Divestiture, dispossession, punishment, confiscation, penalty, disenfranchisement, seizure, foreclosure, amercement. See also forfeit; waiver; obstruction, blockage, prohibition.

Forge, *v.* **1.** To fabricate by false imitation (forge his signature). Counterfeit, falsify, imitate fraudulently, simulate, reproduce, feign; utter. **2.** To give shape to (forge a compromise). Construct, manufacture, fashion, build, originate, model, invent, compose, hammer out, chisel, devise. See also form (4), coin (3). **3.** To make progress (the task force forged ahead). Press on, drive, push on, proceed, advance, progress.

Forgery, *n.* **1.** Making a false document or altering a real one with the intent to commit a fraud (engaged in the forgery of bank notes). Fraudulent simulation, counterfeiting, falsification, misrepresentation, artful manipulation, fabrication. See also deception, fraud. **2.** The document or thing that is forged (the forgery was confiscated). Sham, fraud, hoax, imitation, reproduction.

Forget, *v.* To fail to remember. See oblivious, oblivion; fail (2), ignore, disregard, waive; forgive, excuse (2).

Forgetful, *adj.* See oblivious, careless, remiss, absent (2), negligent, reckless.

Forgetfulness, *n.* See oblivion.

Forgive, *v.* **1.** To cancel (to forgive the debt). Forget, absolve from payment, nullify, erase, release, delete, pass over, discharge. See also waive. **2.** To stop feeling resentment (forgive the assailant). Pardon, release, clear, excuse, grant amnesty, condone, reprieve, exculpate, reinstate, exonerate, exempt, acquit, overlook. *Ant.* Enforce; condemn.

Forgiveness, *n.* See pardon, forbearance, amnesty.

Forgo, *v.* See relinquish, abstain, desist, forfeit, abandon, resist; forbearance.

Forlorn, *adj.* See abandoned (1), dismal, depressed, depressing, despondent.

Form 1. *n.* Technical matters of style and format not involving the merits or substance of something (an objection to the form of the pleading). Formation, arrangement, exterior, shape, pattern, design, configuration, manner, appearance, mode, outline, contour, structure, formula, frame, feature, profile, scheme. **2.** *n.* A document, usually preprinted, to be filled in and adapted to one's needs (standard form). Questionnaire, blank. **3.** *n.* Kind or type (the separation agreement is a form of contract). Species, class, breed, denomination, variety. **4.** *v.* To make or give shape to something (they formed a partnership). Create, organize, assemble, manufacture, chisel, model, structure, fabricate, devise, establish, erect, sketch, crystallize, constitute, cast, contour. See also forge (2).

Formal, *adj.* **1.** Following accepted procedures or regulations (formal requirement). Conventional, customary, standard, proper, orthodox, prescribed, pro forma, regulated, systematic, methodical, correct, prescriptive, authoritative, perfunctory, settled, lawful, fixed, legal, solemn. See also official (2), precise. **2.** Pertaining to matters of form (formal characteristics). External, apparent, superficial, formalistic. **3.** Requiring elaborate ceremony (formal reception). Ceremonial, rigid, pretentious, decorous, unbending, reserved, prim, distant, academic. See also inflexible, pompous. *Ant.* Unorthodox; substantive; informal.

Formality, *n.* **1.** The conditions required by the law to use a legal proceeding (e.g., civil action) or to make an instrument (e.g., contract, conveyance) in order to ensure the regularity and validity of the proceeding or instrument (the formality of two witnesses to the signing of the will). Form, steps, method, technicality, right, motion, convention, ritual, custom, necessity. **2.** The condition of being formal. See formal.

Formalize, *v.* See settle (1), perfect (3); form (4).

Forma pauperis See in forma pauperis.

Format, *n.* See form (1), formula (1), composition, design (1), organization (2), pattern (1), plan (1).

Formation, *n.* See form (1), composition, design (1); development (1), organization (2), pattern (1), plan (1).

Formative, *adj.* Shaping. Developing, early, susceptible, plastic, impressionable, vulnerable. See also malleable, amenable (2), original (2).

Former, *adj.* Taking place earlier in time (the former chief justice). Prior, previous, preceding, past, first-mentioned, aforementioned, preliminary, foregone, preexistent, erstwhile, late, quondam. See also antecedent (1). *Ant.* Latter.

Former adjudication A final determination of questions of fact or rights in a former action. See res judicata.

Former jeopardy Double jeopardy: A person cannot be tried for the same offense more than once. See double jeopardy.

Formidable, *adj.* See awesome, difficult, acute (2), irresistible, compelling, onerous, predominant; appalling, repulsive.

Formless, *adj.* See indeterminate, indefinite, abstract, intangible (3), obscure (1), ambiguous, irregular.

Forms of action The procedural devices or remedies (e.g., trespass on the case) that were used to take advantage of common-law theories of liability.

Formula, *n.* **1.** A fixed way of doing something (no formula exists for effective discovery). Ritual, incantation, equation, prescription, protocol, format, guide, code, usage, recipe, commonplace, schedule, dictate, rule. See also expedient (2), form (1), formality. **2.** A set form of words used in judicial proceedings at common law.

Formula instruction An instruction that advises the jury that under certain facts hypothesized in the instruction, the jury should reach a verdict for one of the parties: "If you find that ..., then your verdict should be for ...."

Formulate, *v.* See devise (3), frame (1), design (1), define, describe, delineate.

Fornication, *n.* Unlawful sexual intercourse between two unmarried persons (an allegation of fornication). Illicit sexual intercourse, congress, carnal knowledge, seduction, copulation, liaison, coition. See also intercourse (2), coitus; prostitute.

Forsake, *v.* See abandon, desert, flee, neglect, jettison, forswear.

Forsaken, *adj.* See isolated, abandoned.

Forswear, *v.* **1.** To give up something completely (forswear smoking). Abjure, renounce, abandon, spurn, eschew, recant, withdraw, cede, surrender, disavow, desert, abhor, shun, waive, decline, quit, drop, refrain, discontinue, abnegate, yield, discard, sacrifice. **2.** To make an oath on what one knows to be untrue (he forswore that he was not there). Perjure, deceive, lie, prevaricate, equivocate. *Ant.* Embrace.

Fort, *n.* See wall, building, protection, asylum.

Forte, *n.* See ability, facility (3), gift (2), power.

Forthcoming, *adj.* **1.** About to happen (forthcoming verdict). Approaching, eventual, foreseeable, imminent, on hand, impending, inevitable, advancing, upcoming, awaited, anticipated, looming, expected, in the works, in the offing, coming, near, fated, destined. **2.** Outgoing (a forthcoming witness). Affable. *Ant.* Remote.

Forthright, *adj.* See outright, explicit, direct (6), honest, open (4), free (1); abrasive, rude.

Forthwith, *adv.* Without delay (the court ordered the school to desegregate forthwith). Immediately, directly, now, at once, right away, straightaway, presently, without delay, instantly, promptly. See also summarily.

Fortification, *n.* See wall, trench, building, protection, asylum.

Fortified, *adj.* See armed.

Fortify, *v.* See strengthen, equip, augment; defend (1), confirm; build.

Fortiori See a fortiori.

Fortitude, *n.* See valor, resolution (4), spirit, self-confidence, endurance, character (1), quality (2); courageous.

Fortnight, *n.* Two weeks.

Fortress, *n.* See wall, building, protection, asylum.

Fortuitous, *adj.* Happening by chance or accident (fortuitous collision). Accidental, unexpected, without known cause, undesigned, unavoidable, unforeseen, adventitious, unrehearsed, spontaneous, inadvertent, involuntary, haphazard, unintentional, random, incidental, surprising. *Ant.* Planned.

Fortuity, *n.* See chance (2), accident, destiny.

Fortunate, *adj.* Lucky. Blessed, endowed, favored, bequeathed, graced, felicitous, prosperous, successful. See also auspicious, happy, seasonable, expedient (1), convenient.

Fortune, *n.* See chance (2), destiny, accident; wealth, luxury, property (1); excess.

Forum, *n.* **1.** The court; the court where the litigation is brought (the forum state). Tribunal, judiciary, bench. See also court. **2.** A setting or place for public discussion (the forum for expressing disagreement). Means, method, mode, instrument, assembly, arena, platform, outlet, rostrum, panel, seminar, hearing, gathering.

Forum non conveniens The discretionary power of a court to decline the exercise of the jurisdiction that it has when the convenience of the parties and the ends of justice would be better served if the action were brought and tried in another forum. See convenience, justice, jurisdiction.

Forum shopping An attempt by a party to find a particular court or jurisdiction to try the case, where he or she believes the chances are greatest for a favorable decision—assuming more than one jurisdiction is available to take the case. See jurisdiction, court.

Forward 1. *v.* To send to a destination (the document was forwarded to the lawyer). Ship, transmit, deliver, mail, relay. **2.** *adj.* See rude, offensive. **3.** *adj.* See progressive. **4.** *v.* See foster, back, champion.

Forwarder, *n.* A person or firm in the business of receiving goods for further handling by way of warehousing, packing, carload shipping, delivery, etc.

Foster, *v.* To encourage or support (the victories fostered a feeling of self-confidence). Shelter, uphold, accommodate, promote, favor, champion, nurse, harbor, oblige, advocate, train, stimulate, forward, cultivate, further, boost, succor, facilitate, maintain, rear, protect, befriend, mother, feed, help, indulge. See also nurture, instruct (1), assist, back. *Ant.* Inhibit.

Foster home A home where substitute family care can be provided for a child when its own family cannot care for it for a temporary or extended period and adoption is neither desirable nor possible at the present time. See home, institution, charity.

Foul 1. *adj.* Rancid, musty. Putrid, rank, fetid, stinking. See also dirty. **2.** *adj.* See base, obscene, filthy, offensive, bad, corrupt (1). **3.** *v.* See corrupt (2), contaminate.

Found, *v.* See find (1); institute (1), initiate, begin, create, introduce (2).

Foundation, *n.* **1.** A permanent fund established and maintained for charitable, educational, religious, or other benevolent purpose (gifts to the foundation are tax-deductible). Philanthropy, eleemosynary institution, endowment, charity, charitable organization. **2.** Basis or support (the theory was the foundation of her argument). Underpinning, principle, foothold, rationale, purpose, footing, groundwork, cornerstone, rock, justification, premise, root, bed, skeleton. See also base (3).

Founder, *n.* An originator or supplier of funds (founder of the hospital center). Creator, organizer, financier, builder, planner, strategist. See also developer, cause (1), father, inventor, architect, author (2), producer.

Foundling, *n.* A deserted or abandoned child (the foundling was declared a ward of the state). Waif, outcast. See also orphan.

Fountain, *n.* See cause (1), root, author (2), birth; river, water, stream.

Four corners The face of a written document (the four corners of the statute).

Fourth estate See press (1).

Foyer, *n.* See entrance.

Foxy, *adj.* See deceptive, deceitful; original (3).

FPC See Federal Power Commission.

FPR Federal Procurement Regulations.

Fracas, *n.* See brawl, fight, commotion.

Fraction, *n.* See division, portion, part; iota, scintilla.

Fractious, *adj.* See disorderly (1), disobedient, contentious, difficult (3), wild, rude.

Fracture, *v., n.* See break (2, 3), breach, division; cut, contusion, injury, wound.

Fragile, *adj.* See frail, weak, tender (6), breakable, infirm, decrepit.

Fragment, *n.* See part, division; iota; sample.

Fragmentary, *adj.* See partial, separate; imperfect; intermittent, fluctuating.

Fragrance, *n.* See aroma; fragrant.

Fragrant, *adj.* Aromatic. Sweet, balmy, redolent, perfumed, odorous, scented, mild. See also attractive, beautiful.

Frail, *adj.* Weak, emaciated. Gaunt, thin, ill, undernourished, haggard, skeletal, lean, feeble, tender, puny, fragile, flimsy, unsound, impotent, debilitated, infirm. See also breakable, weak, decrepit, defenseless.

Frailty, *n.* See defect, fault, imperfect, disease.

Frame 1. *v.* To draft or formulate (frame a response). Prepare, create, sketch, conceive, plan, institute, imagine, establish, compose, organize, draw up, concoct, contrive, fashion, embody, shape, articulate, incorporate, devise, systematize, outline, erect, project, manufacture, cast, forge, map, coin, elevate, carve, originate, mold, write, compose, produce. **2.** *n.* To incriminate a person on false evidence (they framed the manager). Falsely accuse, charge falsely, conspire against, use fabricated evidence, impeach fraudulently, falsely blame, lie, "set up," bear false witness against, falsify evidence, use counterfeit evidence, trap someone, plot against. **3.** *n.* See form (1), composition, design (1).

Frame of mind See emotion, disposition (4), manner.

Framework, *n.* See foundation, form (1), composition, design, plan.

Franchise, *n.* **1.** A privilege that is granted or sold (a hamburger franchise). License, authorization, freedom, immunity, right, consent, assent, concession, sanction, grace, warrant, prerogative, permission, permit. See also charter (1). **2.** The right to vote (the board's action limited the franchise). Suffrage, ballot, enfranchisement, voting power, voice. **3.** See market, business.

Franchise tax A tax on the right and privilege of a company to engage in business. See tax.

Frank, *adj.* See direct (6), bona fide, explicit, definite (1), outright, open (4, 5), free, honest; abrasive, rude.

Franking privilege The privilege of sending certain matter through the mail without paying postage.

Frankness, *n.* See candor.

Frantic, *adj.* See feverish (1), hysterical, irrational, wild, insane.

Fraternal, *adj.* See loyal, social, kindred.

Fraternal benefit association or society A nonprofit association of persons of similar calling or background who aid and assist one another and promote worthy causes. The organization has a representative form of self-government, a lodge system, and ritualistic practices. See charity, benevolent.

Fraternity, *n.* See club (1), assembly, community, companionship, goodwill (2), affinity; school.

Fraternize, *v.* See befriend, consort (2), associate (2), commingle.

Fratricide, *n.* The killing of one's brother or sister. See murder, kill.

Fraud

Fraud, *n.* A harmfully false and deceptive statement of fact. Elements of this tort (also called deceit): (a) a statement of past or present fact, or a concealment of past or present fact, or a nondisclosure of past or present fact where there is a duty to disclose; (b) the statement is false; (c) scienter, the intent to deceive—in some states this element is met by negligently misleading the victim; (d) the defendant intends to have the victim rely on the statement or has reason to believe that the victim will rely on it; (e) the victim actually relies on it; (f) the victim's reliance is justifiable; (g) the victim suffers actual damages (an allegation of fraud committed through the financial statement). Misrepresentation, dishonesty, trickery, trick, deceit, duplicity, underhandedness, counterfeit, deception, hypocrisy, guile, artifice, machination, dissimulation, cozenage, covin, chicanery, double-dealing, stratagem, imposture, overreaching, collusion, hoax, sham, prevarication, falsification, lying, beguilement, pretense, cunning, cheating, treachery, subterfuge, swindle, masquerade, imposter, imitation, reproduction, copy, ersatz, artificiality, pretention, insincerity, airs, speciousness, tinsel, simulation. *Ant.* Honesty.

Fraud in law Constructive or presumed fraud.

Fraud in the factum Fraud that goes to the nature of the document itself.

Fraud in the inducement Fraud that induces the transaction by misrepresenting motivating factors such as value and usefulness.

Frauds, Statute of See Statute of Frauds.

Fraudulent, *adj.* Performed with the purpose of carrying out a fraud (fraudulent scheme). Deceitful, unscrupulous, criminal, bogus, false, sham, underhanded, deceptive, dishonorable, insidious, scheming, unprincipled, knavish, guileful, collusive, beguiling, unethical, immoral, counterfeit, spurious, illegal, cunning, conniving, untrue, meretricious, phony, feigned, discreditable, fallacious, perfidious, fake. *Ant.* Trustworthy.

Fraudulent concealment The hiding or suppressing of a material fact or circumstance that one is legally or morally bound to disclose.

Fraudulent conveyance or transfer A conveyance or transfer of property made with the goal of defrauding, hindering, or delaying a creditor by placing the property beyond the reach of the creditor.

Fraught, *adj.* See full.

Fray, *n., v.,* See brawl, commotion, fight, affray; wear.

Frazzle, *n.* See exhaustion; collapse.

F.R.C.P. See Federal Rules of Civil Procedure.

F.R.D. See Federal Rules Decisions.

Freak, *n.* See aberration, eccentricity.

Freakish, *adj.* See exceptional, odd, anomalous, peculiar, irregular, extraordinary; repulsive, odious.

Freddie Mac See Federal Home Loan Mortgage Corporation.

Free 1. *adj.* Not subject to the legal constraint of another (free will). Unconstrained, liberated, not coerced, under no duress, unchained, unimpeded, untrammeled, unbound, voluntary, unregulated, at liberty, emancipated, at large, delivered, unencumbered, untied, decontrolled, enfranchised, released, unmuzzled. **2.** *adj.* Available without charge (free pens). Gratis, complimentary, gratuitous, costing nothing, "on the house," costless. **3.** *adj.* Exempt from a burden or condition (free from fault). Exonerated, relieved, discharged, excused, extricated, vindicated, delivered, forgiven, purged, pardoned, disengaged, immune, absolved, spared, devoid of, saved, cleared. **4.** *adj.* With political independence (a free country). Self-governing, independent, sovereign, self-ruling, autonomous. **5.** *v.* See discharge (3), liberate. *Ant.* Coerced; expensive; burdened; subjugated; incarcerate.

Freedom, *n.* The state of being free (freedom of choice). Liberty, self-determination, absence of restraint, autonomy, self-government, deregulation, self-rule, license, independence, self-direction, emancipation, discharge, noncoercion, franchise, immunity, free will, liberation, choice, authorization, exemption, latitude, privilege, range, leave, sweep, scope, carte blanche. See also sovereignty; independent. *Ant.* Bondage.

Freedom of Information Act (FOIA) A federal statute making information held by federal agencies available to the public unless it falls within categories that are exempt from public disclosure.

Free-for-all, *n.* See brawl, commotion; confusion.

Freehold, *n.* An estate for life or in fee; an estate in real property of uncertain duration (freehold estate).

Freeload, *v.* To take advantage of another's generosity. See abuse (1), exploit (1), manipulate; parasite.

Free on Board See FOB.

Freethinker, *n.* See nonconformist.

Freeway, *n.* See highway.

Freewheeling, *adj.* See careless, free (1).

Free will, *n.* See freedom, discretion; voluntary.

Freeze, *v.* See clog, incapacitate; cold; frozen.

Freight, *n.* Goods transported by carrier. The price paid for transported goods. The transportation itself. Cargo, load, merchandise, article of commerce, shipment, consignment, tonnage, haul, burden. See also baggage.

Freighter, *n.* See vehicle.

Frenetic, *adj.* See wild, irrational, distracted, insane, feverish, hysterical.

Frenzied, *adj.* See ardent, emotional, violent, feverish, angry, excited, demonstrative, irrational, wild.

Frenzy, *n.* See fit (2), hysteria, insanity, passion, emotion; compulsion.

Frequent, *adj.*, **frequent,** *v.* **1.** *adj.* Occurring often (frequent phone calls from the creditor). Habitual, repetitive, repeated, recurrent, recurring, constant, numerous, continual, continuous, incessant, customary, oft-repeated, common, everyday, regular, usual, many. **2.** *v.* To resort to often or habitually (she frequents the establishment). Visit often, go frequently, visit repeatedly, revisit, resort, habituate, repair, patronize, haunt. *Ant.* Occasional; avoid.

Frequenter, *n.* A person, who is neither an employee of the owner of the premises nor a trespasser, who may go in or be in a place of employment or a public building (a duty of care owed to a frequenter). See guest, invitee.

Fresh, *adj.* Following without any material interval (fresh pursuit). Immediate, continuous, recent, uninterrupted. See also hot (1), new, prompt; current; novel; further; active (3), ardent, alive (2); wholesome, delectable, lush (2).

Freshman, *n.* See student, amateur, beginner.

Fresh pursuit Hot pursuit. The common-law right of a police officer, engaged in a continuous and uninterrupted pursuit, to cross geographic or jurisdictional lines to arrest a felon.

Fret, *v.* See suffer; mope, bemoan, complain (2); harass; wear.

Fretful, *adj.* See afraid, concerned, apprehensive; crabby, inflexible, difficult (3).

Friction, *n.* See opposition, hostility, animus (2), conflict (1); traction.

Friend, *n.* See cohort, intimate, suitor, associate (2).

Friendly, *adj.* Pertaining to someone who is favorably disposed (friendly witness). Predisposed, agreeable, cooperative, propitious, advantageous, helpful, sympathetic, affable, congenial, obliging, civil, courteous, affectionate, accessible, hospitable. See also amenable. *Ant.* Disinterested.

Friendly fire A fire burning in a place where it is intended to burn. See fire; burn.

Friendly suit A suit instituted by agreement between the plaintiff and the defendant in order to obtain the opinion of the court on a question in which both are interested.

Friend of the court See amicus curiae.

Friendship, *n.* See attachment (4), companionship, harmony (1) peace.

Frigate, *n.* See vessel (1).

Fright, *n.* See apprehension (3), fear, consternation; anxiety, distress (3).

Frighten, *v.* See intimidate, disturb, harass, outrage (2); yellow (1).

Frightful, *adj.* See grievous, appalling, grave (2), awesome, dismal; dangerous; repulsive, odious, bad.

Frigid, *adj.* See cold; strict (2); extreme (1); indifferent; climate, elements.

Frill, *n.* See pretense; decoration.

Fringe, *adj.* Secondary (fringe benefits). Accompanying, peripheral, extra, bonus, supplemental, marginal. See also border (1); frontier. *Ant.* Main.

Fringe benefits Side benefits that accompany or are in addition to a person's regular compensation (e.g., paid insurance, paid holidays and vacations).

Frisk, *v.* To conduct a pat-down search of a suspect in order to discover weapons (the police frisked the defendant in the store). Examine, check, scrutinize, inspect, scan, study, scour, rummage, explore, investigate, search, hunt for.

Frisky, *adj.* See active (3).

Fritter, *v.* See dissipate, waste (3), loiter, loaf; malingerer.

Frivolity, *n.* Levity. Triviality, folly, superficiality, silliness. See also sport (2); frivolous.

Frivolous, *adj.* Clearly insufficient on its face; of little weight or importance (a frivolous attack). Insignificant, minor, petty, foolish, flippant, worthless, pointless, flighty, trifling, senseless, unworthy, paltry, flimsy, empty, silly, piddling, superficial, shallow, airy, fatuous. *Ant.* Meritorious.

Frivolous appeal An appeal raising no justiciable issue and devoid of merit in that the prospect of its success is very small. See also appeal.

Frolic, *n.* See antic, spree, sport (2), amusement, entertainment, game, diversion; junket, journey; mischief, caprice.

Front, *n., adj.* See face (1), exterior; pretense, disguise (2); first.

Frontage, *n.* The front part of property between the building and the street; the line of property on a public street (frontage assessment).

Frontier, *n.* That portion of the territory of any country which lies close along the border line of another country and hence "fronts" or faces it (grazing in the frontier). Outskirts, borderland, outlying district, marsh, new terrain, outpost, backcountry, bush, hinterland, fringes, sticks; edge, boundary, perimeter, line, border, limit, rim.

Front wages or pay Prospective payments made to a victim of job discrimination who cannot yet be given the job to which he or she is entitled. These payments, given until the job comes through, make up the difference between money earned now and money that would be made now if the new position were immediately available.

Frost, *n.* See cold; elements, climate; frozen.

Frosty, *adj.* See cold, arrogant, formal.

Frown, *v.* To scowl. Look askance, grimace, fret, glower, mope, glare, sulk. See also disapprove.

Frozen, *adj.* Immobilized (frozen account). Obstructed, stalemated, clogged, stymied, inhibited, restricted, unavailable, inaccessible. *Ant.* Available.

Frozen account An account in which no activity is permitted until a court order is lifted.

Frugal, *adj.* See economical, cautious, prudent; ascetic, stingy.

Fruit, *n.* The effect or consequence of an act or operation (fruits of crime). Result, product, outcome, outgrowth, harvest, effect, profit, upshot, advantage, award, return, benefit, issue, production, produce, reward.

Fruitful, *adj.* See fertile, abundant, pregnant (2), effective, dominant, active, efficient, strong (3).

Fruition, *n.* See completion, perfection (1), satisfaction (2).

Fruitless, *adj.* See worthless (1), barren (2), fallow, dead (3).

Fruit of the poisonous tree doctrine An unlawful search taints not only the evidence obtained at the search but also facts discovered by the process initiated by the unlawful search.

Frustrate, *v.* To prevent or thwart (their efforts were frustrated). Obstruct, undo, foil, abort, check, cancel, neutralize, stymie, nullify, cripple, annul, stultify, circumvent, forestall, defeat, incapacitate, stop, impede, counter, baffle, undermine, checkmate, interrupt, counteract, short-circuit, spoil, confound, disappoint, balk, confuse, disconcert, mar. *Ant.* Facilitate.

Frustration, *n.* See defeat (2), failure, dissatisfaction, annoyance, nuisance, neutralization.

Frustration of contract The duty to perform a promise in a contract is discharged in the following circumstances: The parties expressly agree or impliedly understand that a specific thing is necessary for the performance of the promise and the thing is no longer in existence at the time for performance.

Frustration of purpose A promisor is excused from performance when the objectives of the contract have been utterly defeated by circumstances arising after the formation of the agreement even if performance is still technically possible.

Fry, *v.* See bake, burn; fire.

F. Supp. See Federal Supplement.

FTC See Federal Trade Commission.

"Fudge," *v., n.* See hedge, quibble, avoid (2); deceive; balderdash.

Fuel, *n., v.* See ammunition; incite, provoke.

Fugitive, *n.* One who flees; someone who escapes from the law (the fugitive was captured). Escapee, deserter, runaway, outlaw, vagabond, outcast, pariah, renegade, refugee.

Fulfill, *v.* See realize (2), fill, consummate (1), satisfy, attain, perfect (3), conclude, keep (6).

Fulfillment, *n.* See completion; satisfaction, happiness; perfection (1), performance (1); enforcement.

Full, *adj.* Sufficient in quantity or degree; not wanting in any essential quality (full disclosure). Abundantly provided, complete, entire, detailed, perfect, mature, ample, comprehensive, whole, plenary, abundant, swollen, crowded, populous, teeming, jammed, thickly settled, swarming, packed, concentrated, replete, brimming, saturated, glutted, maximum, all-inclusive, laden, satisfied, intact, undivided, highest, uncut, exhaustive, unabridged, satiated, rich, flowing, all-encompassing. *Ant.* Incomplete.

Full blood Children of the full blood, whole blood, or entire blood have the same mother and father.

Full court A court en banc; a bench with all the judges present.

Full faith and credit The states must recognize (give full faith and credit to) the legislative acts, public records, and judicial decisions of sister states. U.S. Const., Art. IV, Sec. 1.

Full-fledged, *adj.* See full, entire; expert (2), professional (1).

Fully, *adv.* See wholly.

Fulminate, *v.* See denounce (1), curse, attack, detonate; explosion.

Fulsome, *adj.* See excess, disproportionate, extreme (1), exorbitant, odious, offensive, rude.

Fumble, v. See flounder, blunder, err.

Fume 1. v. To explode. Boil, rant, flare up, storm, rage, rave, seethe, fuss, boil. **2.** v. See emit (2). **3.** n. See aroma.

Fumigate, v. To sanitize. Disinfect, cleanse, clean, decontaminate, sterilize, vaporize. See also bathe.

Fun, n. See diversion (2), amusement, happiness, enjoyment (2).

Function 1. v. To perform (the court functioned without the seventh judge). Administer, execute, act, work, carry on, operate, practice, behave, serve, go, run. **2.** n. The nature and proper action of anything (the function of the commission). Purpose, duty, task, range, mission, office, employment, role, charge, vocation, assignment, line, profession, responsibility, business, niche, power, raison d'être, pursuit, sphere, realm, station, position.

Functional, adj. Capable of operating (a functional plan). Practical, adequate, workable, functioning, usable, operational, suitable, fitted, serviceable, operable, pragmatic, efficient, profitable, sensible, handy, utilitarian, applied. See also practicable, possible, feasible, running. Ant. Inoperable.

Functionary, n. Someone who serves a special function; a public officer or employee (a functionary within the company). Public servant, administrator, representative, civil servant, bureaucrat, deputy, minister, delegate. See also official.

Fund 1. v. To provide money to pay interest or principal (to fund a debt). Endow, finance, subsidize, capitalize, grant, underwrite, deposit, patronize, support, donate, furnish, invest, stake, contribute, back, bestow. **2.** n. An asset or a group of assets set aside for a specific purpose (education fund). Money, resources, capital, reserve, endowment, investment, savings, stock, nest egg, reservoir, accumulation, purse, means, revenue, stake, treasury, coffer, cash, wherewithal, pool, bankroll, hoard, portfolio.

Fundamental, adj. Basic, essential (fundamental right). Central, necessary, principal, vital, indispensable, rudimentary, inherent, critical, cardinal, elementary, integral, structural, constitutional, main, key, chief, foremost, requisite, bottom, prime, substantive, constituent, elemental, underlying; sine qua non, core, cornerstone. See also essential, intrinsic, primary, organic (1). Ant. Incidental.

Fundamental error An error that goes to the merits of the plaintiff's cause of action; error of such character as to render the judgment void.

Funded debt A debt that has resources earmarked for the payment of interest and principal as they become due (e.g., a special fund, future taxation).

Funeral, n. See burial, morgue.

Funereal, adj. See dismal, depressed, depressing, barren, despondent, serious (5), grievous (1), grave, dark.

Fungibles, n. Goods consisting of identical and interchangeable particles or components (e.g., grain, storage).

Funnel, n., v. See vessel (2); filter, convey (3).

Funny, adj. See comic, enjoyable; absurd, anomalous; amusement.

Furbish, v. See repair (1), fix (3); equip.

Furious, adj. See angry, aggravated (2); wild, violent, reckless.

Furlough, n. A leave of absence (injured while on furlough). Time off, holiday, liberty, R and R, rest and relaxation, respite. See also leave (5), vacation. Ant. Assignment.

Furnish, v. To supply for a particular purpose (furnish the new law office). Provide, outfit, stock, endow, arm, accommodate, dress, give, prepare, render, accouter, clothe, array, gear, lavish, enable, drape, invest, cater, rig. See also equip, nurture, foster, beautify. Ant. Remove.

Furnishing, *n.* See decoration (1), paraphernalia.

Furniture, *n.* See property, effects, movables.

Furor, *n.* See wrath, animus (2), annoyance, eruption, commotion, passion, fit (2), hysteria, confusion, spirit, insanity; feverish.

Furrow, *n.* See trench, wrinkle (1).

Further 1. *adj.* Additional (further instructions). Wider, fuller, new, more extended, extra, supplemental, auxiliary, accessory, fresh, more, contributory. **2.** *v.* To promote (to further their interests). Advance, assist, aid, favor, nourish, patronize, accelerate, accommodate. See also strengthen, foster, back, champion. *Ant.* Less; impede.

Furtherance, *n.* An act of helping forward (in furtherance of the objective). Assistance, support, advancement, boost, advocacy, patronage, backing, elevation, succor, lift. *Ant.* Hindrance.

Furthermore, *adv.* See moreover.

Furtive, *adj.* By secret or stealth (furtive operation). Veiled, masked, shrouded, clandestine, undercover, covert, evasive, surreptitious, cloaked, conspiratorial, secretive, back-door, wily, unseen, private, elusive, secluded, collusive, subtle, confidential, concealed. *Ant.* Public.

Fury, *n.* See fit (2), hysteria, eruption, commotion, wrath, animus (2), annoyance, insanity, confusion, passion; feverish.

Fuse, *v.* See adhere (1).

Fusillade, *n.* See eruption, violence; discharge (4).

Fusion, *n.* See alliance (2), connection.

Fuss, *n.* See commotion, disturbance, confusion; emotion, passion; opposition.

Fussy, *adj.* See precise (2), particular (2), squeamish, difficult (3), critical (2); concerned, apprehensive; feverish.

Futile, *adj.* See worthless (1), barren (2), fallow, dead (3), abortive.

Futility, *n.* See failure, impossibility, impotence (2).

Future, *adj.* Pertaining to what is still to come or to a later time (future damages). Anticipated, upcoming, impending, looming, approaching, prospective, scheduled, planned, destined, hereafter, tomorrow, imminent, in the offing, at hand, next, probable, eventual, unborn, subsequent, ultimate, succeeding, fated. *Ant.* Prior.

Future advances Money lent after a security interest has attached, and secured by the original security agreement.

Future interests Interests in land or in other things in which the privilege of possession or other enjoyment is future and not present.

Futures, *n.* Items sold or bought to be delivered in the future. See commodity, commodity future, stock.

Futures contract A present right to receive at a future date a specific quantity of a given commodity for a fixed price.

"Fuzz", *n.* See police.

Fuzzy, *adj.* See ambiguous, indefinite, obscure.

G

ABCDEF**G**HIJKLMNOPQRSTUVWXYZ

Gab, *v.* See babble, communicate.

Gadfly, *n.* A pest, critic. See nuisance; nonconformist, arbiter.

Gadget, *n.* See apparatus, implement (1), novelty, instrument (2), equipment, device; automation.

Gaffe, *n.* See mistake, error.

Gag 1. *v.* To silence (gag the participants). Stifle, block, still, quiet, muffle, clog, plug, suppress, muzzle, stop, choke, smother, squelch, censor, obstruct, contain. **2.** *n.* See joke.

Gag order An order by the court (a) to bound and gag an unruly defendant to prevent further interruptions of the trial, or (b) to stop attorneys and witnesses from discussing the case with the media, or (c) to stop the media from reporting aspects of the trial.

Gaiety, *n.* See happiness, spirit (2), emotion, amusement.

Gain 1. *n.* Profits; winnings; increments of value; differences between receipts and expenditures (taxable gain). Benefit, advantage, interest, return, proceeds, earnings, accumulation, bonus, yield, augmentation, appreciation, enhancement, assets, pay, remuneration, emolument, black ink, increase. **2.** *v.* To secure or obtain (gain acceptance at the firm). Accomplish, win, collect, acquire, harvest, enlist, achieve, net, assume, derive, avail, reach, attain, gather, procure, succeed, glean, capture, realize, master, extract profit. **3.** *n.* See advancement (2), development (1), growth, production. *Ant.* Losses; lose; setback.

Gainful, *adj.* Advantageous, profitable (gainful employment). Lucrative, beneficial, desirable, remunerative, rewarding, fertile, worthwhile, money-making, fruitful, productive. *Ant.* Futile.

Gainsay, *v.* See deny (1), disavow, oppose.

Gala, *n.* See banquet, celebration (2).

Galaxy, *n.* See world.

Gall, *n., v.* See effrontery; hostility, animus (2); harass, disturb, outrage (2).

Gallant, *adj.* See courageous; civil (3); firm (2).

Gallantry, *n.* See resolution (4), spirit, honor, self-confidence, character (1), quality (2); courtesy (2); civil (3), courageous.

Galling, *adj.* See distressing, offensive, vexatious.

Gallop, *v.* See run (2), flee.

Gallows, *n.* Scaffold. Rope, noose, gibbet.

Galore, *adj.* See abundant, excess; luxury.

Galvanize, *v.* See move (3), initiate, incite, animate, cause (2), muster, organize.

Gambit, *n.* See artifice, device, plan.

Gamble, *v., n.* See gambling, bet (2), venture (2); hazard (2), risk, danger.

Gambler, *n.* One who practices games of chance or skill with the expectation of winning something (a compulsive gambler). Speculator, oddsmaker, "crapshooter," bettor, player, gamester, "bookie," "sport," wagerer.

Gambling, *n.* The dealing, operating, carrying on, or maintaining any game for pay involving chance and the possibility of a reward (illegal gambling). Betting, wagering, risk taking, bookmaking, stake, venture, hazard, jackpot, pool, bingo, playing a game of chance. See also bet (1), speculation.

Gambling device An apparatus or device used and employed for gambling where money is staked, wagered, lost, or won as a direct result of its employment or operation. See apparatus, equipment.

Gambol, *n.* See antic, game, diversion, enterprise (1).

Game 1. *n.* A sport, pastime, or contest (game of chance). Match, competition, tourney, tournament, meet, duel, event, bout, scheme, device, encounter, rivalry, conflict, race, engagement; amusement, recreation, festivity, diversion, play. **2.** *n.* Wild birds and beasts (preservation of game). Wild animals, prey. **3.** *Adj.* See lame.

Gamekeeper *n.* See guardian, manager, overseer.

Game laws Laws for the preservation of wild birds and beasts.

Game of chance A game in which success or failure depends less on skill and experience than on purely fortuitous or accidental circumstances not under the control of the player. See gambling.

Gaming, *n.* Playing games of chance. An agreement between two or more persons to play together at a game of chance for a stake or wager, which becomes the property of the winner and to which all contribute. See gambling, wager, bet (1).

Gamut, *n.* See range (2), scope, measure (1), extent.

Gang, *n.* Persons who act in concert, usually for criminal purposes (street gang). Pack, coterie, band, alliance, brotherhood, mob, circle, clique, associates, rink, troop, cronies, co-workers, detachment, team, force, club, order, bunch, crew, group, troupe, junta, outfit, federation, bloc, faction, society, affiliation, association, fraternity, family, party, organization, league, cabal.

Gangster, *n.* See racketeer, wrongdoer, criminal (1), fugitive, malefactor.

Gangway, *n.* See passage (2).

GAO See General Accounting Office.

Gaol, *n.* See jail.

Gap, *n.* See interval, lapse (4); disparity; break (3); vacancy; valley, abyss.

Gape, *v.* See observe (3), watch, spy (2), notice (2).

Garage, *n.* See building, warehouse; merchant.

Garb, *n.* See clothes, uniform (2), apparel.

Garbage, *n.* See refuse; balderdash.

Garble, *v.* See falsify, misrepresent, corrupt.

Garden, *n.* See square (1), close (3), farm; shrubbery, woods.

Garden-variety, *adj.* See simple (1), commonplace.

Gargantuan, *adj.* See big.

Garish, *adj.* See gaudy, flamboyant, awkward, common (3), worthless.

Garment, *n.* See clothes, uniform (2), apparel.

Garner, *v.* See collect, accumulate.

Garnish, *v., n.* See beautify, furnish, exaggerate, color (3), enhance, equip, array (3); decoration.

Garnishee, *n.* A person against whom the process of garnishment is issued; a person who has property of the judgment debtor that is being reached or attached (garnished) by another.

Garnishment, *n.* A statutory proceeding whereby a person's property or credits in the possession or under the control of another are applied to the former's debt to a third person; the satisfaction of an indebtedness out of property or credits of the debtor in the possession of or owed by another (garnishment of the debtor's wages by the creditor). Attachment, seizure, impoundment, levy, appropriation, execution, dispossession, annexation, enforcement, collection, confiscation, sequestration, taking, reaching.

Garret, *n.* See attic.

Garrison, *n.* See division (1); military; sailor; patrol.

Garrulous, *adj.* Talkative. Verbose, loquacious, "gabby," prattling, windy, glib, chatty, long-winded, voluble. See also babble; prolixity.

Gash, *v., n.* See cut, hurt, injure; injury, contusion, lesion.

Gate, gateway, *n.* See entrance, passage, exit; proceeds.

Gather, *v.* See collect, marshal (2), accumulate, muster; conclude (2), judge (2, 3).

Gathering, *n.* See congregation, assemblage, assembly.

GATT General Agreement on Tariffs and Trade. A multilateral international agreement that requires foreign products to be accorded no less favorable treatment under the law than that accorded domestic products.

Gauche, *adj.* See backward; gaudy, gross (1); arrogant.

Gaudy, *adj.* Loud, flashy. Cheap, tawdry, showy, tasteless, ostentatious, tinsel. See also vulgar, blatant (2), flamboyant, awkward, common (3), gross (1), worthless.

Gauge 1. *v.* To measure (the witness was asked to gauge the distance). Calculate, evaluate, determine, weigh, guess, assess, appraise, judge, adjudge, compute, count, figure, ascertain, rate, surmise, rank, deduce, infer, value, demarcate, estimate. **2.** *n.* See measure (1).

Gaunt, *adj.* See frail, weak, thin.

Gauntlet, *n.* See challenge.

Gawk, *v., n.* See observe (3), watch, spy (2), notice (2); boor, ass.

Gawky, *adj.* See awkward.

Gay, *adj.* **1.** Attracted to the same sex, homosexual, homophile, lesbian. **2.** See festive, happy; attractive; spirit, active; flamboyant; friendly, convivial, amicable.

Gaze, *v.* See observe (3), watch, spy (2), notice (2).

Gazette, *n.* See press.

Gear, *n., v.* See equipment, paraphernalia; clothes, uniform (2), apparel; furnish, equip, provide, prepare (1), fill.

Gem, *n.* A precious stone. Bijou, pearl, ornament, trinket, jewel; treasure, prize, marvel, masterpiece, flower, find.

Gendarme, *n.* See police.

Gender, *n.* See sex.

Genealogy, *n.* The summary history or table of a family, showing how the persons listed are related to each other; an examination of descent from an ancestor. Pedigree, breed, heritage, roots, ancestry, family descent, line, lineage, bloodline, background, birth, extraction, parentage, derivation, house, filiation, heredity.

General, *adj.* Pertaining to all or most; not limited in scope (general principle). Extensive, not particular, prevailing, blanket, common, representative, habitual, broad, widespread, regular, usual, wide, unrestricted, sweeping, not exclusive, universal, catholic, categorical, generic, inclusive, characteristic, prevalent, public, popular, customary, frequent, vague, not specific, imprecise. See also comprehensive, complete (2); indefinite, abstract, indeterminate; obscure, ambiguous. *Ant.* Particular.

General Accounting Office (GAO) An independent nonpolitical agency in the legislative branch of the federal government. The GAO assists Congress in carrying out its legislative and oversight functions (e.g., by conducting audits and other accountability investigations of federal programs). See audit.

General administration An unrestricted grant of authority to administer the entire estate of the decedent. See administration, estate, agency.

General appearance The defendant submits his or her person to the jurisdiction of the court by coming to the court in person or through a duly authorized representative; a consent to the jurisdiction of the court. See appearance, jurisdiction. *Ant.* Special appearance to contest jurisdiction.

General assignment for the benefit of creditors A transfer of legal and equitable title to all of the debtor's property to a trustee, who will have the authority to liquidate the debtor's affairs and distribute the proceeds to creditors. See bankruptcy, creditor, assignment.

General bequest A gift payable out of the general assets of the estate, not a gift of a particular item. See bequest, estate.

General contractor One who contracts to construct an entire building or project rather than a portion of it; a prime contractor who hires subcontractors, coordinates the work, etc. See entrepreneur, builder.

General Court The name of the legislature in Massachusetts and in New Hampshire. See legislature.

General denial A response by a party that controverts all of the allegations in the preceding pleading. See denial (1), pleading, reply.

General Digest One of the units of the American Digest System. The General Digest gives small paragraph summaries of published opinions for every court during the period of time since the last Decennial Digest was published.

General indorsement An indorsement without mentioning the name of an indorsee. See indorsement.

Generality *n.* A broad, vague statement. See communication; ambiguous, indefinite.

Generalization, *n.* See inference, deduction (2), assumption, conclusion (2).

Generalize, *v.* To make a broad statement or conclusion. See deduce, reason, assume (2); classify.

General jurisdiction Jurisdiction that extends to all controversies that may be brought before a court. See jurisdiction.

General partner One of two or more persons who associate to carry on a business as co-owners for profit and who are personally liable for all the debts of the partnership. See associate, partner; merchant, business. *Ant.* Limited partner.

General power of appointment One exercisable in favor of any person the donee may select. See appointment, trust, will, gift.

General practitioner See attorney, doctor.

General Services Administration (GSA) The federal agency that manages government property and records. The GSA supervises building construction and operation, supply procurement, communication systems, etc.

General welfare The government's concern for the health, peace, morals, and safety of its citizens. See also welfare.

Generate, *v.* See produce (2), manufacture (1), cause (2), occasion (1).

Generation, *n.* **1.** A single succession of living beings in natural descent; a degree of removal in computing descents; individuals born around the same time period; the average span of time between the birth of parents and that of their offspring (first generation Americans). Progeny, issue, lineage, kin, stock, race, tribe, seed. See also family, offspring. **2.** The production of something (the generation of electricity). Creation, evolution, procreation, invention, formation, origination, development, genesis, growth, reproduction, begetting, effectuation, causation, manufacture, institution, inception.

Generic, *adj.* Relating to or characteristic of an entire group or class (generic drug). General, common, universal, not specific, blanket, all-inclusive, nonspecific.

Generosity, *n.* See benevolence, charity (3), gift.

Generous, *adj.* See benevolent, liberal, charitable; abundant.

Genesis, *n.* See cause (1), root, author (2), ancestry, birth (2); commencement.

Genetics, *n.* The study of heredity. Breeding, eugenics, genetic engineering. See also heredity; hereditary.

Geneva Convention An 1864 international agreement for the conduct of nations at war, providing that a belligerent shall give proper care to enemy sick or wounded, that Red Cross personnel shall be respected, etc.

Genial, *adj.* See friendly, convivial, amicable, accessible, civil (3), conciliatory; amenable, flexible; happy; attractive.

Genitals, *n.* Reproductive organ. Phallus, penis, testis, sex organs, private parts, scrotum, genitalia.

Genius, *n.* Great intelligence. See brilliant; judgment (2), capacity (2), faculties, perception (2), gift (2); author, architect, inventor.

Genocide, *n.* See murder, homicide; kill.

Genoese lottery The numerical lottery. Out of ninety consecutive numbers, five are to be selected or drawn by lot; the players wager that one, two, or more of their selected numbers will be drawn among the five or that they will appear in a certain order. See lottery, gambling.

Genre, *n.* See class (1), classification (2), kind (1).

Genteel, *adj.* See civil (3), aristocratic, elevated, cultivated, chic, debonair, formal, beautiful, attractive.

Gentle, *adj.* See kind (2); friendly; amenable, flexible; quiet; moderate.

Gentlemanly, *adj.* See civil (3), cultivated, elevated, debonair, chic, formal, attractive; aristocracy.

Gentleman's agreement An agreement reached without formalities; an agreement based on honor. See agreement, contract.

Gentrification, *n.* The process by which deteriorated or slum neighborhoods are renovated by those with financial resources. See restoration; repair.

Gentry, *n.* See aristocracy, establishment (4).

Genuine, *adj.* The document or other item is genuine when it is what it purports to be (the signature is genuine). Authentic, correct, true, not forged, valid, original, attested, factual, verified, pure, unquestionable, authenticated, "kosher," legitimate, veritable, licit, certified, warranted, honest, unadulterated, proven, unalloyed, demonstrable, guaranteed. See also bona fide, accurate, precise. *Ant.* Fraudulent.

Genuine issue An issue that can be sustained by substantial evidence; a real issue; a triable issue where sufficient evidence exists to warrant a jury determination. See issue.

Genus, *n.* See class (1), classification (2), kind (1).

Geography, *n.* See map; bound (4), boundary; science.

Geology, *n.* See science.

Geometry, *n.* See mathematical; science.

Geopolitics, *n.* The relationship between politics and geography. See politics; political.

Geriatrics, *n.* The study of old age. See age; old, ancient; senile; medicine, science.

Germ, *n.* **1.** Bug, virus. Microorganism, microbe, infection, bacterium, bacillus. **2.** See commencement, root, birth, cause (1).

Germane, *adj.* Pertinent (the question was not germane to the issue). Connected, relevant, related, on point, applicable, analogous, material, suitable, apropos, native, relative, congruent. See also pertinent, appropriate (3). *Ant.* Extraneous.

Germ-free, *adj.* See sanitary, healthy, wholesome.

Germinate, *v.* See begin, develop, mature (1), advance.

Gerrymander, *n.* Dividing a geographic area into voting districts or divisions in order to provide an unfair advantage to one political party. See rig, manipulate; politics, apportionment.

Gestalt, *n.* See entirety; entire, whole.

Gestate, *v.* To carry in the uterus following conception. See pregnant; gestation.

Gestation, *n.* The time during which a woman carries a fetus in her womb from conception to birth (period of gestation). Pregnancy, incubation, propagation, development, gravidity.

Gesture, *n.* A motion of the body calculated to express a thought or used for emphasis (spontaneous gesture). Gesticulation, wave, nod, indication, body language, nudge, pantomime. See also motion (2), move (4), manifestation; signal (3).

Get 1. *v.* To receive (the testator wanted her to get the land). Gain possession, obtain, "pocket," acquire, achieve, clear, realize, inherit, procure, net, earn, win. **2.** *n.* Under Hebraic law, evidence of the granting of a divorce.

Ghastly, *adj.* See appalling, repulsive, odious, dismal; extraordinary.

Ghetto, *n.* See slum; neighborhood, zone.

Ghost, *n.* Phantom. Apparition, spirit, specter, spook, shadow, phantasm. See also demon; legend; intangible.

GI, *n.* See enlisted man; military; sailor.

Giant, *n.* See big.

Gibberish, *n.* See balderdash; blabber; prolixity; ambiguity.

Gibbet, *n.* See gallows.

Gibe, *v., n.* See mock (1), censure, disparage, slander.

Giddy, *adj.* See frivolous, facetious, dizzy, impetuous, careless, reckless.

Gift, *n.* **1.** A gratuitous transfer of property to another. Elements: (a) There must be a delivery of the property; (b) the transfer must be voluntary; (c) the donor must have legal capacity to make a gift; (d) the donor must intend to divest him or herself of title and control of what is given; (e) the donor must intend that the gift take effect immediately; (f) there must be no consideration (e.g., payment) from the donee; (g) the donee must accept the gift. Donation, benefaction, present, endowment, legacy, offering, contribution, bequest, allowance, dispensation, boon, subsidy, gratuity, grant. **2.** A talent or ability (a gift for advocacy). Skill, aptitude, ability, capacity, turn, qualification, proficiency, forte, knack, flair, genius, bent, faculty, expertise, competency, mastery, intelligence, cleverness. *Ant.* Sale; deficiency.

Gift causa mortis A gift of personal property made in the expectation of the donor's death and on condition that the donor die as anticipated.

Gifted, *adj.* See capable (2), brilliant, able, apt (3, 4), cognizant, erudite.

Gift inter vivos A gift between the living; a gift that is perfected during the lifetime of the donor and the donee.

Gifts to Minors Act A Uniform Act adopted by most states to provide a method of transferring property to a minor. An adult custodian receives the property, invests it, and makes the income available for the support of the minor.

Gift tax A tax imposed on the transfer of property by gift, which is paid by the donor.

Gigantic, *adj.* See big.

Giggle, *v.* See laugh.

Gigolo, *n.* See paramour, prostitute, suitor, parasite.

Gild, *v., n.* See exaggerate, color, deceive; guild.

Gill, *n.* One-fourth of a pint.

Guilt-edged, *adj.* See superior (2).

Gimmick, *n.* See contrivance, deception, fraud; plan; novelty.

Gin, *n.* See liquor.

Gingerly, *adv.* Guardedly. See careful, cautious.

Ginnie Mae See Government National Mortgage Association.

Gird, *v.* See surround; strengthen.

Girl, *n.* See juvenile, child; woman; servant, employee.

Girlfriend, *n.* See suitor, intimate, cohort.

Gismo, gizmo, *n.* See apparatus, instrument (2), device.

Gist, *n.* **1.** The essential point (the gist of the argument). Substance, principle, heart, lifeblood, backbone, sine qua non, theme, spirit, significance, crux, drift, sum and substance, basis, import, quintessence, pith, soul, meaning, core, sense, effect, center, main idea. See also essence (1). **2.** The essential ground or object in point of law, without which no cause of action would exist. See gravamen.

Give, *v.* To make a gratuitous transfer of property to another (she gave each child $5,000). Grant, turn over, donate, endow, assign, bestow, vouchsafe, allot, confer, contribute, entrust, offer, commit, leave, deliver, supply, apportion, award, will, indulge, hand out, distribute, bequeath, transmit, hand down, surrender. See also gift. *Ant.* Retain.

Give and take, *n.* See mediation; arbitrate, negotiate, bargain.

Glacial, *adj.* See cold; hostile.

Glad, *adj.* See happy.

Glamorize, *v.* See exaggerate; falsify; beautify; honor (2); tribute (2).

Glamorous, *adj.* See attractive, beautiful, enjoyable; gaudy; entice.

Glamour, *n.* See beauty; adventure; emotion, passion, spirit; danger; grandeur, appeal (3).

Glance, *v.* Glimpse. Look, peek, view, scan, peep, squint. See also observe (3), notice (2).

Glare, *n.* Gleam, flash. Blaze, luster, radiance, brilliance, blinding light, glow, splendor, incandescence, illumination, beam, ray, spark, flame. See also light.

Glaring, *adj.* See gross (1), conspicuous; gaudy; strong (2), explicit, blatant (2).

Glean, *v.* To gather or collect slowly (the investigator gleaned the figures from the reports.) Cull, learn, accumulate, procure, amass, reap, discover, extract, assemble, harvest, deduce, garner, conclude, sift, pick up.

Glee, *n.* See happiness; emotion, passion.

Glib, *adj.* See articulate (2); facetious; artificial (2), deceptive, deceitful; pompous.

Glimpse, *v.* See glance, observe (3).

Glitch, *n.* See accident.

Gloat, *v.* See boast.

Globe, *n.* See world.

Gloom, *n.* See depression (1), distress (3), anguish.

Gloomy, *adj.* See dismal, abandoned (1), despondent, depressed, depressing, dark, barren.

Glorify, *v.* See honor (2); worship; tribute (2).

Glorious, *adj.* See beautiful, attractive, extraordinary, primary (1), predominant, exceptional.

Glory, *n.* See honor (3), eminence, notoriety, superiority, grandeur.

Gloss 1. *v.* An interpretation of a text (the gloss provided by the expert on the statute). Commentary, construction, critique, explanation, explication, reading, footnote, scholium, exegesis, translation, annotation. **2.** *v.* See cover (2), hide, conceal. **3.** *n.* See justification, excuse.

Glow, *n.* See glare.

Glue, *v., n.* See affix (1); lock; drug.

Glum, *adj.* See dismal, abandoned (1), despondent, depressed.

Glut, *v.* See inundate, fill; excess.

Glutted, *adj.* See full; excess.

Gluttonous, *adj.* See prodigal, improvident; predatory.

Gluttony, *n.* See intemperance, debauchery.

Gnaw, *v.* See wear (1), diminish; erosion.

GNMA See Government National Mortgage Association.

GNP See gross national product.

Goad, *v.* See encourage (2), incite, provoke.

Go-ahead, *n.* See permission.

Goal, *n.* See objective (3), purpose (1), object (2), intent (1), end (1), aim (3), cause (4), motive, pursuit (2).

Gobble, *v.* See eat; consume (1).

Gobbledygook, *n.* See balderdash; prolixity; ambiguity; term of art; language; babble.

Go-between, *n.* See intermediary, agent, referee, judge (1).

God, *n.* The Supreme Being who created the universe and rules over it (belief in God). Almighty, Lord, Father, the Omniscient, Creator, the Omnipotent, Divine Being, Jehovah, Providence, Allah, Yahweh, the Prime Mover; divinity, deity, spirit, power.

Godforsaken, *adj.* See barren, abandoned (1), dismal, unoccupied.

God-given, *adj.* See natural (3).

Godlessness, *n.* See atheism, blasphemy, profanity; irreverent.

Godsend, *n.* See windfall, benefit, gift, help.

"Gofer," *n.* One who runs errands. See servant, employee.

Going, *n., adj.* See departure, removal, exit; alive, operative (1), running (1), active (1).

Going and coming rule While an employee is going to or coming from work, he or she is generally not considered to be within the scope of employment for purposes of workers' compensation benefits and respondeat superior. See workers' compensation, agency, respondeat superior, scope of employment.

Going concern An existing solvent business operating in its ordinary and regular manner.

Going private Delisting a class of equity securities from a national securities exchange; removing the authorization to quote a class of equity securities in an interdealer quotation system of a registered national securities exchange.

Going public Issuing stock for public purchase for the first time; becoming a public corporation.

Goings-on, *n.* See behavior, conduct (1), circumstances, fact, detail (2).

Gold, *n.* See wealth, luxury, property (1).

Goldbrick, *n.* See fraud, imitation, copy; malingerer.

Golden, *adj.* See extraordinary, outstanding (2), auspicious, gainful.

Golden rule 1. A canon of statutory interpretation in which we presume that the legislature did not intend an interpretation that would lead to absurd or ridiculous consequences. **2.** In the golden rule argument, the jurors are urged by counsel to place themselves in the position of the injured party or victim.

Golf, *n.* See athletics, game, sport, amusement, diversion.

Gondola, *n.* See vessel (1).

Gonorrhea, *n.* See venereal disease, infirmity, disease.

Good, *adj.* **1.** Sufficient in law (good cause). Unobjectionable, valid, effectual, licit, sound, responsible, satisfactory, appropriate, functional, efficient, passable, worthy, solid, legitimate, competent, complete, proper, qualified, fitting, timely, lawful, true. See also adequate. **2.** Orderly; conformable to law (good behavior). Honorable, unsullied, moral, innocent, virtuous, untainted, obedient, dutiful, well-behaved, reliable. See also faithful, amenable, cooperative, loyal. **3.** Collectible (the check is good). Solvent, valuable, certifiable, authentic, confirmed. See also genuine. *Ant.* Invalid; corrupt; worthless.

Good-by, *interj.* See adieu.

351

Good cause A cause that affords a legal excuse; sufficient reason; legally sufficient ground or reason. See ground.

Good faith A state of mind characterized by honest belief, absence of malice or intent to defraud, absence of a design to seek an unconscionable advantage or of knowledge that such an advantage is likely to occur (the employer acted in good faith). Bona fides, faithfulness, honesty, sincerity, morality. See also candor, integrity. *Ant.* Bad faith.

Good faith purchaser Someone who buys without notice of circumstances that would place a person of ordinary prudence on inquiry as to whether the seller has title to what he or she is trying to sell. See buyer.

Good-for-nothing, *adj.* See worthless.

Goodhearted, *adj.* See kind, friendly, benevolent, charitable, liberal.

Good-looking, *adj.* See attractive, beautiful.

Good-natured, *adj.* See kind, friendly, amendable, benevolent, charitable, liberal.

Goodness, *n.* See integrity, justice, right, fairness.

Goods, *n.* Movable things other than money, securities, or intangible rights (goods covered by the policy). Merchandise, furnishings, belongings, assets, stock, materials, commodities, staples, possessions, chattels, products, sundries, artifacts, things, appurtenances, wares, gear. See also effects, paraphernalia, property, movables, inventory.

Good Samaritan Someone who unselfishly comes to the assistance of another. Rescuer, humanitarian, helper, aider. See also patron, backer, volunteer.

Goodtime allowance A credit for good conduct that reduces the time a prisoner must spend in prison. See reduction.

Good title A title that is free from reasonable doubt; one that is valid in fact and could be sold to a reasonable purchaser or mortgaged to a person of reasonable prudence. See title, marketable title.

Goodwill, *n.* **1.** The reputation of a company that generates additional customers; the ability of a business to generate income in excess of what is normal because of superior management skills, market position, new product technology; the custom or patronage of any established trade or business (the purchase price of the business included $25,000 for goodwill). Customer approval, competitive advantage, established reputation, commercial advantage, sponsorship, patronage. **2.** Kindness (a settlement was reached in an atmosphere of goodwill). Friendliness, brotherhood, tolerance, helpfulness, benevolence, consideration, concern, mutual support, cordiality, humanity.

Goof, *n.* See mistake, blunder.

"Goof-off," *n.* See loiter, loaf; malingerer.

Goofy, *adj.* See absurd, anomalous, odd (1); comic.

Goon, *n.* See wrongdoer; idiot, ass.

Gore, *v., n.* See pierce, enter (2); murder.

Gorge, *n., v.* See abyss, crevice; inundate.

Gorgeous, *adj.* See attractive, beautiful, outstanding (2), enjoyable, intriguing.

Gory, *adj.* Bloody, sanguinary. See repulsive, appalling, cruel, violent, odious, gross (1), wild (3), base (2).

Gospel, *n.* See bible; authority (5); creed; religion.

Gossip, *n., v.* See rumor, hearsay; babble, report, communicate.

Gouge, *v.* See extort, extract (1).

Gourmet, *n.* See epicure; expert (1), judge (1).

Govern, *v.* **1.** To direct or control by authority (she has governed the country for 5 years). Rule, pilot, administer, supervise, lead, manage, head, dictate, command, reign, dominate, wield power, regulate, guide, steer, superintend. **2.** To be a guiding principle (the holding in the *Smith v. Smith* opinion governs our case).

Be a precedent, influence, sway, incline.

Governance, *n.* See government, regulation (2).

Governess, *n.* See teacher.

Government, *n.* The process of governing; the framework of political institutions by which the executive, legislative, and judicial functions of the state are carried on (representative government). Administration, political structure, governance, polity, authority, dominion, management, superintendence, supervision, order, reign, rule, guidance, regulation, oversight; regime, political community, sovereign, representatives, presidency, leadership, legislature, council, cabinet; incumbency, republic.

Governmental functions The functions of a municipality that are essential to its existence; functions that can be performed adequately only by the government, e.g., operation of the courts. *Ant.* Proprietary functions of a government (e.g., operation of a government-owned liquor store).

Governmental immunity A government cannot be sued in tort except for those categories of cases where it has consented to be sued. See immunity.

Governmental instrumentality A government agency created by the constitution or by the legislature. See agency.

Government de facto A government not established according to its constitution but nevertheless operating in fact as the government. See de facto.

Government de jure A government of right established according to its constitution. See de jure.

Government instrumentality doctrine The doctrine that governmental instrumentalities are tax exempt. See exemption, taxation.

Government National Mortgage Association (Ginnie Mae) The federal agency within the Department of Housing and Urban Development that makes a market for higher risk loans by acquiring the loans from lenders who otherwise would not make such mortgage loans.

Government Printing Office (GPO) The federal office that prints and publishes laws, regulations, forms, and other documents.

Government survey system A type of legal description whereby the United States is generally divided into checks or tracts of ground, which are further broken down by smaller descriptions such as metes and bounds. See survey, map.

Governor, *n.* A chief executive official (the governor of Ohio). Director, administrator, overseer, chairperson, head, official, dean, magistrate, leader. See also manager.

Gown, *n.* See apparel, clothes, uniform.

GPO See Government Printing Office.

Grab, *v.* See seize, extort, plunder (1), appropriate (1).

Grace, *n.* **1.** A favor or indulgence (2-week period of grace). Benefit, mercy, leniency, compassion, reprieve, forgiveness, exemption, pardon, stay, respite, forbearance. **2.** See honor (3), character (1), balance (5), merit (1).

Graceful, *adj.* See articulate (2), cultivated, formal, beautiful, attractive, debonair, aristocratic, civil (3); casual.

Grace period A designated period beyond the due date of a premium on an insurance policy, during which the insurance is continued in force. If the premium is paid during this period, the policy will be kept in good standing.

Gracious, *adj.* See kind, friendly; charitable, benevolent; cultivated, debonair; amenable.

Gradation, *n.* See chain (1), series, succession (2), development (1); hierarchy.

Grade 1. *v.* To bring property to the level of an abutting highway; to establish a level by mathematical points and lines and then bring the surface of a street or highway to the level by the elevation or depression of the natural surface to the line fixed (negligence in grading the area). Flatten, level, make horizontal, even, smooth, roll. **2.** *n.* The line of the street's inclination from the horizontal; a part of a street inclined from the horizontal (street grade). Slant, pitch, slope, ramp, gradient, hill, angle, rise, acclivity, incline, bank, ascent, adit, approach, declivity. **3.** *n.* A unit or degree in a scale (grades of crime). Rank, step, stage, mark, notch, standing, class, classification, value, relative position, lot, rating.

Grade crossing A place where a railroad is crossed at grade by a public or private road, or by another railroad, or where one highway crosses another.

Grade school, *n.* See school.

Gradient, *n.* See grade (2).

Gradual, *adj.* Step-by-step. Slowly, piecemeal, imperceptible, deliberate, even, measured, little-by-little. See also progressive, successive, continuous.

Graduate, *v.* See adjust (1), grade (1); complete (1), finish (1); student.

Graduated, *adj.* Marked with or divided into degrees (graduated tax). Arranged in grades, divided into steps or successive levels, measured by steps.

Graduated lease A lease arrangement that provides that the rent will vary depending on future contingencies such as the amount of gross income produced.

Graduated tax A tax that is structured so that the rate increases as the amount of income of the taxpayer increases.

Graduation, *n.* See commencement, advancement (2), certification.

Graft, *n.* Money, advantage, or personal gain unlawfully received because of one's position of public trust (an allegation of graft in city hall). Corruption, bribery, spoils, kickback, unlawful gain, profiteering, illicit gain, hush money, payoff, racket, plunder, blackmail, extortion. See also gratuity (2), bribe (1).

Grain, *n.* **1.** In Troy weight, the twenty-fourth part of a pennyweight. **2.** Any kind of corn sown in the ground. **3.** See iota.

Grain alcohol, *n.* See liquor, intoxicating liquor.

Grammar school, *n.* See school.

Grand, *adj.* See elevated, great, outstanding (2), big, extraordinary, notorious, predominant; pompous, arrogant, formal; comprehensive; enjoyable, attractive.

Grandchild, *n.* Descendant of the second degree; the child of one's child. See descendant.

Grandeur, *n.* Pomp and majesty. Glory, glamour, magnificence, stateliness, fame, luster, splendor, exaltation, excellence, nobility, impressiveness. See also supremacy, superiority, eminence, solemnity.

Grandfather clause An exception to a restriction that allows all those already doing something to continue doing it in spite of the restriction; a special exemption for those already doing that which is now prohibited.

Grandiloquent, *adj.* See pompous, arrogant, exorbitant.

Grandiose, *adj.* See pompous, arrogant, flamboyant; outstanding (2), elevated; solemnity.

Grand Jury A jury of inquiry that receives complaints and accusations in criminal cases, hears the evidence of the prosecutor, and issues indictments in those cases in which the jury is satisfied that a trial should be held.

Grand larceny Taking and carrying away personal property of another valued in excess of a statutorily set amount (e.g., $100) with the intent to feloniously deprive the owner or possessor of it permanently. See larceny, petty larceny.

Grange, *n.* A farm furnished with barns, granaries, stables, and all conveniences for husbandry. See farm, business, merchant.

Granite, *n.* See rock.

Grant 1. *v.* To bestow or confer on another with or without compensation (the will granted him the estate). Donate, award, give, transfer, bequeath, demise, transmit, impart, pass on, furnish, accord, apportion, assign, allot, cede, convey, devise, entrust, offer, lease, dispense. **2.** *n.* A transfer of title to real or personal property by deed or other instrument (a fee simple grant of land). Conveyance, devise, assignment, disposition, transmission, transfer, alienation, bounty, subsidy, donation, present, allotment, bestowal, legacy, bequest, largess, indulgence, award, endowment. **3.** *v.* To concede (he refused to grant that he made the error). Admit, allow, vouchsafe, yield, consent, cede, agree, acknowledge, recognize. *Ant.* Accept; retention; refute.

Grantee, *n.* The person to whom a grant is made.

Grant-in-aid A sum of money given by a governmental agency to a person or institution for a specific purpose such as education or research.

Granting clause That portion of a deed or instrument of conveyance which contains the words of transfer of a present interest.

Grantor, *n.* The person who makes the grant; the transferor.

Grantor-Grantee Index A master index to all recorded instruments, containing the volume and page number where the specific instrument can be located in the record books.

Grapevine, *n.* See informant, rumor, hearsay.

Graph, *n.* See map, outline.

Graphic, *adj.* See demonstrative, descriptive, clear, explicit, blatant.

Grapple, *v.* See deal (3), manage (2), confront; seize.

Grasp, *v.* See digest (4), know, comprehend (1); construe, discover; seize, capture; handle (2), touch (1).

Grasping, *adj.* See predatory, avaricious; jealous.

Grass, *n.* The street name for marijuana. See drug.

Grassroots, *n.* See people (1), constituency, nation, country (1); foundation, root.

Grate, *v., n.* See disturb, harass, provoke, exacerbate; rock (1).

Grateful, *adj.* See appreciative; benevolent; happy; amicable; enjoyable.

Gratification, *n.* See enjoyment, happiness, amusement, diversion (1), satisfaction (2).

Gratify, *v.* See satisfy (2), delight, pander (2), amuse, interest (5).

Gratis, *adv., adj.* Without reward or consideration (the lawyer provided the service gratis). Gratuitously, without charge, complimentary. See also free (2), gratuitous (1).

Gratitude, *n.* Appreciation, thankfulness, thanks, acknowledgment, obligation, recognition. See also indebtedness.

Gratuitous, *adj.* **1.** Given or granted free, without consideration (gratuitous transfer). Gratis, without charge, charitable, donated, complimentary, for nothing, courtesy, uncompensated. **2.** Unwarranted (a gratuitous attack). Uncalled-for, senseless, unprovoked, wanton, without foundation, baseless, superfluous, unnecessary, impertinent, irrational, excessive, unrequired, dispensable, extraneous, expendable, supplementary, overmuch, supererogatory, inappropriate, undue. See also needless. *Ant.* Expensive; appropriate.

Gratuitous bailee A person to whom possession of personal property is transferred and who furnishes no consideration for such transfer. See bailment.

Gratuitous guest or passenger A person riding in an automobile at the invitation of the owner or authorized agent but without paying any consideration or fare. See guest, passenger.

Gratuitous licensee A person who has permission (though not an invitation) to come on the property of another and who has furnished no consideration for such permission. See license, permission, guest.

Gratuitous promise A promise made by one who has received no consideration for it. See promise, gift.

Gratuity, *n.* **1.** Something acquired without bargain or inducement (a gratuity to the porter). Tip, award, present, contribution, favor, bonus, offering, honorarium, handout, dividend, extra. **2.** A bribe (the mayor was charged with accepting gratuities). Kickback, illegal payment, corrupt payment. See also bribe (1), graft.

Gravamen, *n.* The material part of a grievance; the gist of a charge (the gravamen of his allegation is fraud). Core, nucleus, focus, cornerstone, thrust, substance, crux, heart, soul, theme, lifeblood, underpinning, foundation, pith. See also essence (1), gist (1).

Grave 1. *n.* The place where a dead body is buried or the place of interment for a corpse (memorial service at the grave). Excavation, tomb, crypt, burial place, mausoleum, sepulcher, catacomb, receptacle, vault. **2.** *adj.* Important (the grave implications of the decision). Monumental, serious, consequential, imperative, severe, urgent, weighty, vital, dangerous, momentous, life-and-death, substantial, crucial, acute, critical, awe-inspiring, major, grievous, frightening. **3.** *adj.* Solemn (the grave expression on the face of the victim's parent). Dignified, somber, sedate, pensive, grim, dour, subdued, distant, gloomy, august, thoughtful, frowning, earnest, preoccupied. See also despondent, dismal, dark. *Ant.* Insignificant (2); frivolous (3).

Gravel, *n.* See earth (1), rock.

Gravitate, *v.* To be drawn to. Lean toward, incline to, have a proclivity for, zero in on. See also tend.

Gravity, *n.* See affinity (2); solemnity, dignity; worth; importance, import (2).

Gray, *adj.* See dark, dismal.

Graze, *v.*, *n.* See injure, hurt; touch; contusion, injury.

Grease, *v.* See bribe, corrupt.

Great, *adj.* **1.** Considerable in magnitude, power, importance, intensity, or degree (great bodily injury). Immense, gross, extraordinary, huge, colossal, manifold, voluminous, large, prodigious, countless, inexhaustible, extensive, abundant, protracted, unlimited, extreme, inordinate, unreasonable, multitudinous, gargantuan, spacious, ample, gigantic, outrageous, pronounced, extravagant, remarkable. See also big, many. **2.** Influential (the group said it was a great decision). Outstanding, important, noteworthy, remarkable, eminent, sensational, leading, tremendous, major, incomparable, thundering, esteemed, prominent, first-rate, magnificent, famous, marvelous, celebrated, good, superior. *Ant.* Minor.

Greed, *n.* See avarice.

Greedy, *adj.* See avaricious; jealous.

Green, *adj.* See raw (1), amateur, beginner; innocent (2).

Greenback, *n.* United States paper currency. See currency, money.

Green Beret, *n.* See military; sailor.

Greenery, *n.* See shrubbery, woods.

Greenhorn, *n.* See amateur, beginner; immigrant; innocent, credulous.

Green light See approval, license, permission.

Greet, *v.* See address (2), entertain (2), face (2); confront.

Gregarious, *adj.* See friendly, amicable, convivial.

Grenade, *n.* See ammunition, arms, gun, weapon; military; war.

Grief, *n.* See anguish, anxiety, pain, apprehension, affliction, depression; disaster; hardship, loss.

Grievance. *n.* **1.** An injury or wrong that gives ground for a complaint (redress of grievances). Injustice, violation, outrage, indignity, unfairness, hardship, affliction, iniquity, problem, oppression, vexation, damage, affront, cruelty, aggression, offense, abuse, inflammation, insult, slur, atrocity, annoyance, aggravation, disturbance, wound, sting, hurt. See also wrong. **2.** A charge (a grievance filed by the union against management). "Beef," allegation, accusation, "gripe," objection, protest.

Grieve, *v.* See bemoan, suffer, cry (1); anguish, pain; mope.

Grievous, *adj.* **1.** Causing grief or sorrow (a grievous loss). Painful, afflictive, hard to bear, harmful, agonizing, lamentable, burdensome, unbearable, heart-breaking, distressful, sorrowful, tragic, onerous, crushing. **2.** Outrageous (a grievous insult). Flagrant, gross, heavy, offensive, heinous, intolerable, severe, shocking, appalling, iniquitous, egregious, destructive, nefarious, critical, harsh. See also deplorable. *Ant.* Entertaining; inconsequential.

Grill, *v.* See ask (1), cross-examine, abuse (1); bake.

Grimace, *n.* See frown.

Grime, *n.* See dirt, pollution.

Grimy, *adj.* See dirty.

Grin, *n.* See smile, laugh; frown.

Grind, *n., v.* See oppression, bondage, slavery; oppress, abuse, break (2); sharpen.

Grip, *n.* See seizure, capture; comprehension.

Gripe, *n.* See grievance (2), complaint.

Gripping, *adj.* See touching, moving (1), compelling, emotional, intriguing, great, extraordinary.

Groan, *v., n.* See bemoan, suffer, cry, complain; anxiety, anguish, pain, affliction, depression.

Grocery, *n.* See food; merchant, commerce.

Groom, *n., v.* See marriage, nuptial; man, suitor, spouse; prepare (1), discipline (4), educate, nurture, maintain (1).

Groove, *n., v..* See crevice, trench, wrinkle (1), abyss; appreciate (3), enjoy (2).

Grope, *adj.* See flounder; search, investigate.

Gross, *adj.* **1.** Glaring, reprehensible (gross neglect). Great, culpable, flagrant, odious, obnoxious, aggravated, extreme, shocking, grievous, exorbitant, egregious, dreadful, unmitigated, deplorable, heinous, utter, glaring, manifest, uncivilized, wild, unrefined, undisciplined, profligate, corrupt, licentious, debauched, primitive, barbaric, rude, savage, barbarian, ferocious, ignorant, brutish, unpolished, gauche, immoderate, inordinate, absolute, obvious, considerable, enormous, disgusting, massive, unqualified, blatant, shameful, vulgar, raw. See also offensive, filthy, obscene. **2.** Total; before or without diminution or deduction (gross income). Whole, complete, aggregate, entire, inclusive, all-inclusive, undivided, uncut, comprehensive, outright, full, exhaustive. *Ant.* Minor; net.

Gross alimony See alimony in gross.

Gross earnings The total receipts of a person or business before deductions and expenses. See income.

Gross estate The property owned or previously transferred by a decedent that will be subject to the federal death tax. See estate, tax.

Gross income All income from whatever source derived (e.g., compensation, fees, commissions; gains from dealings in property; business income; interest, rents, royalties, dividends, annuities; alimony received, etc.). See income, compensation.

Gross lease A lease in which the lessee pays a flat sum for rent, out of which the lessor is required to pay all expenses such as taxes, water, utilities, insurance, etc. See rent, lease.

Gross national product (GNP) The market value within a nation of all goods and services produced, as measured by final sales of goods and services to individuals, businesses, and governments, plus the excess of exports over imports. See worth (1), appraisal.

Gross neglect Serious failure to attend to one's duties; substantial nonfeasance. See neglect.

Gross negligence The intentional failure to perform a manifest duty in reckless disregard of the consequences to the life or property of another; aggravated carelessness; conduct that is highly culpable although less serious than willful and intentional conduct. See negligence, neglect.

Gross receipts The total amount of money or the value of other consideration received from selling property or from performing services. See income, compensation, receipt.

Gross up To add back to the value of the property or income received the amount of the tax that has been deducted. See tax.

Grotesque, *adj.* See repulsive, odious, repugnant (1), offensive, abject (2), anomalous, odd (1), abnormal.

Grouch 1. *n.* A complainer. Grumbler, crab, crank, bear, "bitch," curmudgeon, faultfinder; complaint, grievance. **2.** *v.* See complain.

Grouchy, *adj.* See crabby, contentious (1), litigious, difficult (3), rude, inflexible.

Ground 1. *n.* Foundation; points relied on (reasonable ground to believe). Basis, premise, footing, cause, rationale, excuse, reason, motive, qualification, purpose, assumption, occasion, argument, object, base, support, evidence. **2.** *n.* The earth's surface (fell to the ground). Soil, earth, terra firma, dirt, terrain, loam, dust; acres, territory, arena, yard. **3.** *v.* See establish (3), fix (2), attach (2).

Groundless, *adj.* See baseless, frivolous, illusory, fictitious, fallacious, erroneous.

Ground rent Rent paid to the owner for the use of the land, usually to construct a building on it. See rent, lease.

Ground rule See rule (1), procedure.

Groundwork, *n.* See preparation.

Group 1. *n.* Several persons or things that are considered a unit (group of demonstrators). Herd, collection, assembly, family, pack, class, body, mass, company, tribe, clique, sect, persuasion, camp, school, order, faction, creed, coterie, cabal, club, suit, team, army, cadre, convoy, committee, corps, party, section, conglomeration, force, squad, gathering, aggregation, gang, lot, troupe, congregation, subdivision. **2.** *v.* To form into a unit (he grouped together the evidence on damages). Classify, arrange, categorize, tabulate, align, index, organize, rank, segregate, marshal, alphabetize, cluster, associate, sort, catalog. *Ant.* Individual; disperse.

Group legal services Legal advice and representation given to members of an organization, who pay for the services in advance in a manner similar to group health insurance programs. See attorney.

Group libel The holding up of a group to ridicule, scorn, or contempt to a respectable and considerable part of the community. See slander.

Grouse, *v., n.* See complain; grouch; grievance (2), complaint.

Grovel, *v.* To demean oneself. Crawl, toady, fawn, cower, bow before, kowtow, crouch, bend, lower oneself, stoop. See also cringe, pander.

Grow, *v.* See develop, mature (1), advance (3, 4, 5), produce (2); augment; growth.

Growl, *v.* See complain, grouch.

Growth, *n.* **1.** Development, increase (the growth of law office management as a specialty). Evolution, advancement, progress, improvement, maturation, blossoming, advance, prime, unfolding, expansion, augmentation, ascent, surge, rise, multiplication, enlargement, ripening, escalation, increment, addition, cultivation, success, spread, prospering. See also development (1). **2.** See shrubbery, woods. *Ant.* Decline; desert.

Grubby, *adj.* See dirty, foul.

Grudge, *n.* Resentment, spite. See animus (2), malice.

Grueling, *adj.* Exhausting, backbreaking. See difficult, severe, extreme, draconian.

Gruesome, *adj.* See repugnant, repulsive, odious, offensive, gross (1), appalling, cruel, violent, deadly.

Gruff, *adj.* See rude, caustic, impetuous.

Grumble, *v.* See complain; grouch.

Grumpy, *adj.* See difficult (3), crabby, contentious (1), litigious.

GSA See General Services Administration.

Guarantee 1. *n.* An assurance that a particular outcome will occur; a contract of guaranty; the obligation of a guarantor (a guarantee that the machine will handle the weight). Guaranty, warranty, promise, word, commitment, certification, agreement, pledge, insurance, endorsement, avowal, bond, affirmation, token, oath. **2.** *v.* To assume the obligations of a guarantor (the doctor did not guarantee success). Insure, warrant, certify, underwrite, pledge, safeguard, promise, contract, vouch for, stake, assume responsibility for, become a surety for, secure, obligate, sponsor, stand behind, assure, mortgage, engage, vow.

Guarantor, *n.* One who makes a guaranty; one who becomes secondarily liable for another's debt or performance (the deal failed for want of a guarantor). Sponsor, warrantor, endorser, voucher, underwriter, bondsman. See also backer, patron, surety.

Guaranty 1. *n.* A collateral agreement by a guarantor for the performance of another's undertaking or promise—the principal obligor; if the latter fails to perform, the guarantor will do so (she provided a guaranty that her brother would pay the note). Warranty, assurance, engagement, pledge, surety, promise, covenant, voucher, commitment, contract, indemnity, warrant; security, deposit, collateral, bond. **2.** *v.* To undertake collaterally to answer for the payment of another's debt or performance. See guarantee (2).

Guard, *n., v.* See attendant (1), foreman, caretaker, manager; patrol, police, oversee, watch (1).

Guarded, *adj.* See cautious, circumspect; suspicious (1).

Guardian, *n..* A person who lawfully has the power and duty to care for the person, property, or rights of another who is incapable of managing his or her own affairs, e.g., a minor, an insane person (his guardian invested the child's money). Caretaker, supervisor, conservator, advocate, watchdog, safekeeper, trustee, champion, steward, keeper, bodyguard, protector, defender, custodian. See also manager, curator, watchman. *Ant.* Adversary.

Guardian ad litem A special guardian appointed by the court to defend or bring a suit on behalf of an infant or incompetent.

Guardianship, *n..* The office, duty, or authority of a guardian; the relationship that exists between guardian and ward.

Guerrilla, *n.* See revolutionary, insurgent, anarchist.

Guess, *n., v.* See estimate, speculation, conjecture, hypothesis.

Guest, *n.* **1.** One who receives lodging for payment at an inn, hotel, or motel (the guest was assaulted in his room). Patron, invitee, client, transient, roomer, boarder, lodger. See also customer; tenant (1). **2.** One who is received and entertained at another's home, club, etc., other than a regular member; one who takes a ride in an automobile driven by another without providing any funds or benefits for the driver (an injury suffered by the guest). Caller, company. See also visitor. *Ant.* Trespasser.

Guest statute Operators of automobiles shall be liable for injuries to guests only if caused by gross or willful negligence. A guest is a recipient of voluntary and gratuitous hospitality of the driver or owner of the car.

Guidance, *n.* See education, information (2), judgment (2), discretion (3); regulation (2), administration, direction, advice, counsel; auspices, charge (11), patronage.

Guide, *v., n.* See educate instruct, improve, nurture, discipline (4); accompany, assist, navigate; regulate, administer; attendant (1), guardian, patron, watchman, manager, director.

Guideline, *n.* See policy (1), maxim, measure (1).

Guild, *n.* A voluntary association of persons pursuing the same trade, art, profession, or business (a guild of masons). League, alliance, organization, fraternity, order, brotherhood. See also union (1), federation.

Guile, *n.* See fraud, deception, artifice.

Guilt, *n.* **1.** Criminal responsibility for an offense (evidence of guilt). Criminality, blameworthiness, misconduct, dereliction, misfeasance, nonfeasance, malfeasance, delinquency, wrongdoing, culpability, turpitude, lawlessness, blame, dishonesty, transgression, immorality, reprehensibility, vice, misbehavior, misdemeanor, felony, violation, sin. See also fault, corruption. **2.** A feeling of remorse for wrongdoing (her own sense of guilt was evident). Shame, stigma, humiliation, regret, sorrow, self-reproach, self-disgust, infamy, compunction, contrition, unease, penitence, disgrace; apologetic. *Ant.* Innocence; arrogance.

Guiltless, *adj.* See blameless, innocent.

Guilty, *adj.* **1.** Having committed a crime or tort (the court found him guilty of trespass). Responsible, culpable, at fault, accountable. See also blameworthy. **2.** Fraudulent, corrupt (guilty knowledge). Criminal, offensive, errant, deceitful, iniquitous, felonious, willful, illegal, censurable, reprehensible. *Ant.* Innocent.

Guinea pig Someone used for experimental purposes. See victim, volunteer.

Guise, *n.* See appearance (3), exterior, countenance; pretense, disguise (2), deception; clothes, uniform (2), apparel.

Gulf, *n.* See abyss; interval (2); disparity; vacancy; valley.

Gullible, *adj.* See superstitious; susceptible, innocent, credulous; amateur.

Gully, *n.* See valley, abyss; watercourse.

Gumption, *n.* See initiative (3), ambition, enterprise, spirit (2), resolution (4), self-confidence; judgment (2).

Gun, *n.* Portable firearm (registration of guns). Rifle, pistol, revolver, shotgun, carbine, automatic, iron, rod, repeater, enforcer. See also weapon, arms.

Gunpowder, *n.* See ammunition; weapon, arms, gun.

Guru, *n.* See teacher, scholar, authority (3, 4), master (1), oracle; augur, clairvoyance (2).

Gush, *n., v.* See eruption; emit; babble.

Gusto, *n.* See spirit (2), life (3), vigor, passion, enterprise (2), determination (2).

Gut, *v., adj.* See devastate, destroy; spontaneous.

"Guts," *n.* See character (1), endurance, spirit (2), resolution (4), valor.

Gutter, *n.* See course (1), conduit (2), vessel (2).

Guy, *n.* See man, person.

Guzzle, *v.* See consume (1), eat.

Gymnasium, *n.* See arena; athletics; school.

Gynecology, *n.* See medicine; doctor, woman.

Gypsy, *n.* See migratory; tramp (1).

Habeas corpus "You have the body." A writ designed to bring a party before a court in order to test the legality of his or her detention or imprisonment (e.g., a prisoner in the custody of a warden, a child in the custody of a relative).

Habendum clause The portion of a deed beginning with the words, "to have and to hold," which describes the ownership rights being transferred (i.e., the estate or interest being granted).

Habit, *n.* A disposition or condition of the body or mind, acquired by custom or repetition of the same act or function (the company's habit of allowing children to play in its yard). Practice, convention, usage, customary conduct, course of behavior, manner, bent, wont, praxis, mode, routine, fashion, style, pattern, tendency, rule, mannerism, inclination, fixed practice, proclivity, predilection, disposition, leaning, peculiarity, tradition, recurrence, second nature, ways, nature, characteristic, trait, temperament, idiosyncrasy, property, quirk, personality, form, technique, beaten path.

Habitability, *n.* The condition of the premises that permits an inhabitant to live free of serious defects that endanger health and safety. See warranty of habitability.

Habitable, *adj.* Suitable for living (habitable structure). Livable, occupiable, acceptable, tenantable, fit for habitation. See also comfortable, adequate. *Ant.* Uninhabitable.

Habitancy, *n.* A fixed place of abode to which one intends to return when away; a fixed and permanent residence. See domicile.

Habitation, *n.* Place of abode; occupancy (unsuitable for habitation). Residence, settlement, housing, tenancy, shelter, habitat, lodging, house, domicile, accommodation, dwelling, quarters, tenement, address, homestead. See also home.

Habitual, *adj.* Customary (habitual truant). Usual, regular, common, ordinary, chronic, typical, hardened, routine, commonplace, set, normal, traditional, continual, accustomed, daily, persistent, inveterate, constant, periodic, standard, automatic, deep-seated, recurrent, frequent, confirmed, established, faithful, dedicated, perpetual. *Ant.* Occasional.

Habitual criminal Someone who can be subjected to more severe punishment after having been convicted of crimes a designated number of times (e.g., three); repeat offenders on whom greater sentences can be imposed. See wrongdoer.

Habitual drunkenness or intoxication Repeated and excessive indulgence in intoxicating liquor so as to acquire a fixed habit and an involuntary tendency to become inebriated as often as the temptation is presented.

Habituate, *v.* See addict (2), domesticate, adapt, inure (2), accommodate (2); accustomed.

Hack, *v., n.* See cut, mutilate, amputate; charlatan; vehicle.

Hackneyed, *adj.* See commonplace (2), ordinary (2).

Haggard, *adj.* See exhausted; frail, weak, thin.

Haggle, *v.* See bargain (2), barter, negotiate (1).

Hail, *v.* See summon (1), call (1, 2); address (2); honor (2).

Hairdresser, *n.* See barber, merchant; business.

"Hairy," *adj.* See precarious, difficult, dangerous.

Hale, *adj.* See healthy.

Half blood (half brother, half sister) The degree of relationship that exists between persons who have the same father or the same mother but not both.

Halfhearted, *adj.* See indifferent, passive, apathetic, casual (3).

Halfway house A house in the community that helps individuals make the adjustment from prison or other institutionalization to normal life.

Half-wit, *n.* See ass, idiot.

Hall, *n.* See entrance; arena.

Hallmark, *n.* See badge, manifestation.

Hallowed, *adj.* See holy, religious.

Hallucinate, *v.* See fantasize; dream (1); hallucination.

Hallucination, *n.* An apparently real sensory perception, auditory or visual, without any real external stimuli to cause it (the accident caused her to have hallucinations). False perception, illusion, nightmare, mirage, aberration, phantom, apparition, specter, fantasy, delusion, figment, chimera, misapprehension, confusion, image, daydream.

Hallucinogenic drug A drug that induces hallucinations (e.g., mescaline, LSD). See drug.

Halt, *v., n.* See ban, bar, prevent, prohibit, obstruct, arrest, cessation.

Halve, *v.* See divide, cut.

Hammer, *v.* See batter, beat (1).

Hammurabi, Code of One of the oldest compilations of law in history, prepared by the Babylonian king 1792–1750 B.C. (circa).

Hamper, *v.* See hinder, interfere, impair, disrupt, bar (5), delay (2), deter, block, prejudice (2), frustrate, limit (1).

Hamstring, *v.* See impair, hinder, disable, maim, injure, frustrate, obstruct, limit (1).

Hand, *n.* See assistance; employee; assistant; part (2); member (2).

Handbill, *n.* A written or printed notice displayed, handed out, or posted to provide information (handbills distributed on the picket line). Flyer, circular, poster, announcement, placard, notice, handout, release, bulletin, leaflet. See also report, communication.

Handcuff 1. *n.* Chains to secure the wrists (handcuffs placed on the accused). Restraint, shackles, irons, bonds, manacle, harness. See also fetter. **2.** *v.* To restrain by the use of handcuffs (the police handcuffed the accused). Chain, leash, manacle; strap, bind, fasten, secure, tether, rope, enchain, tie, bridle. See also obstruct, frustrate.

Handful, *n.* See few.

Handgun, *n.* See gun, weapon.

Handicap, *v., n.* See hinder, interfere, obstruct, frustrate, deter, ban, bar; obstruction, blockade, disadvantage, liability.

Handicraft, *n.* See craft (1), skill (1), facility (3).

Handle, *v.* **1.** To manage or operate (the witness was asked if she handled the account). Take care of, supervise, command, treat, control, officiate, regulate, oversee, preside over, govern, pilot, superintend, steer, direct, maneuver, work, represent, train, utilize, execute, employ, have authority over. See also manage, administer. **2.** To touch (handle it with care). Finger, feel, manipulate, fondle, press, pick up, clutch, wield, grasp, massage, lift. **3.** To trade in (the firm handles the product). Market, deal in, barter, merchandise, sell, traffic in, conduct business, vend, exchange.

Handout, *n.* See handbill; donation, charity (1).

Hand over See yield (1).

Handsel, *n.* First installment or down payment. See earnest (1).

Handsome, *adj.* See attractive, beautiful; liberal (3).

Handwriting, *n.* The cast or form of writing peculiar to a person—the size, shape, and style of letters, etc. (handwriting expert). Chirography, penmanship, script, scrawl, jottings, calligraphy.

Handwriting exemplars Samples of one's handwriting for purposes of comparison. See exemplars, sample (1).

Handy, *adj.* See convenient, accessible; able, apt (3), expert (2).

Hang, *v.* See dangle, suspend (4); execute (2), kill.

Hanging, *adj.* See pending.

"Hang-up," *n.* See complication, obstruction.

Haphazard, *adj.* See inconsistent (2), fluctuating, casual, capricious, arbitrary, accidental; fortuitous.

Hapless, *adj.* See ill-fated, abject.

Happen, *v.* See occur (1), arise (1), result (2), emerge.

Happening, *n.* See event, occurrence, development (2), experience (2), incident (2), occasion (3), circumstances, coincidence, accident (1).

Happenstance, *n.* See coincidence, accident, chance (2), destiny.

Happiness, *n.* Satisfaction, enjoyment (the pursuit of happiness). Consolation, contentment, pleasure, gaiety, joyfulness, joy, ecstasy, jubilation, elation, high spirits, comfort, gratification, cheer, bliss, felicity, delight, good fortune, gladness, beatitude, glee, exhilaration. See also ease (1), satisfaction; happy. *Ant.* Misery.

Happy, *adj.* Joyful. Blessed, cheerful, pleased, contended, joyous, blissful, felicitous, buoyant, elated, sunny, gay, blithe, jocund, merry, spirited, animated, jovial, jubilant, enthusiastic, playful, jolly, ebullient, frolicking, glad, carefree. See also fortunate, gainful, beneficial; happiness.

Hara-kiri, *n.* See suicide.

Harangue, *n., v.* See address (3), speech (2); reprimand; bludgeon (3), intimidate.

Harass, *v.* To annoy or abuse (the creditor harassed the debtor). Vex, bedevil, hound, molest, torture, beleaguer, oppress, nag, harry, distress, infuriate, heckle, malign, bother, browbeat, intimidate, plague, persecute, disturb, threaten, worry, badger, agitate, outrage, strain, coerce, pester, bait, "hassle," "bug," torment, taunt, provoke, afflict, wear down, infuriate, confound, disquiet, rankle, anger, incense, pique, aggravate, excerbate, gall, embitter, grieve, upset, miff, exasperate, push, discommode, bully. *Ant.* Accommodate.

Harassment, *n.* See annoyance, assault (2); harass.

Harbinger, *n.* Something that indicates what is to come (a harbinger of danger). Messenger, forerunner, precursor, announcer, courier, omen, indication, sign, symbol, warning, premonition, auspice, prediction. See also herald, predecessor.

Harbor 1. *v.* To shelter or protect; to receive clandestinely and without lawful authority (they harbored the escapee). Aid, stow away, quarter, house, shield, safeguard, guard, secure, give refuge to, take in, care for, secrete, foster, nurture, embrace, hide, accommodate, give asylum to, provide sanctuary for. **2.** *n.* A place of retreat or shelter (a harbor from the battle). Refuge, sanctuary, haven, hiding place, cover, protection. **3.** *n.* A port for ships (harbor privileges). Dock, basin, bay, inlet, cove. See also mooring, anchor.

Hard, *adj.* See difficult, severe, extreme (1), strict (2), serious (2), draconian; firm (2); complex; cruel; unconscionable, onerous.

Hard-core, *adj.* See explicit, blatant, demonstrative; incorrigible.

Harden, *v.* See strengthen, inure (2), augment.

Hardened, *adj.* See habitual, inflexible, incorrigible.

Hard hat, *n.* See laborer, employee.

Hardheaded, *adj.* See inflexible, arbitrary, unreasonable, firm (2), difficult; objective, reasonable, rational.

Hardhearted, *adj.* See cruel, callous, malicious, inflexible, willful, arbitrary.

Hard labor, *n.* See servitude, bondage; labor (2).

Hardly, *adv.* Barely. Only, almost, scarcely, rarely, just, not often, infrequently.

Hardship, *n.* Privation, suffering (hardship resulting from the regulation). Ordeal, adversity, oppression, woe, grief, unhappiness, agony, misery, difficulty, travail, misfortune, tribulation, burden, encumbrance, trial, torment, stress, cross, peril, blow, severity, desolation, harm, damage, casualty, deprivation, grievance, bane, destitution, suffering, pain. See also privation. *Ant.* Fortune.

Hardware, *n.* See equipment, paraphernalia; arms, ammunition, weapon.

Hard-working, *adj.* See diligent, strong (2), indefatigable, constant (3).

Hardy, *adj.* See able-bodied, fit (1), durable; reckless, impetuous.

Harebrained, *adj.* See frivolous, lunatic, reckless, dumb, irrational, juvenile.

Harem, *n.* See brothel.

Harlequin, *n.* See clown; ass, idiot, boor.

Harlot, *n.* See prostitute.

Harm 1. *n.* Loss or detriment to a person (harm suffered because of the intrusion). Misfortune, damage, injury, destruction, mischief, trauma, havoc, agony, desolation, abuse, devastation, suffering, waste, defilement, impairment, disservice, pain, adversity, deterioration, calamity, marring. **2.** *v.* To injure (the report harmed his reputation). Damage, wrong, mar, debase, spoil, wound, ruin, pollute, adulterate, worsen, demolish, bruise, aggravate, subvert, stab, do violence to, destroy, sabotage, impair, abuse, molest, undermine, mistreat, maltreat, maim, batter, defile, degrade, ill-use, aggrieve, cripple, attack, rape, blemish, corrode, exacerbate. *Ant.* Benefit.

Harmful, *adj.* Likely to cause damage or illness (harmful ingredient). Noxious, damaging, hurtful, pernicious, injurious, detrimental, unhealthy, baneful, prejudicial, insidious, cataclysmic, vicious, toxic, counterproductive, inimical, malicious, unsafe, corrosive, disadvantageous, unwholesome, evil, septic, crippling, foul, disastrous, unpropitious, subversive, virulent, malign, undermining, dire, bad. See also deleterious, dangerous, defective. *Ant.* Beneficial.

Harmless, *adj.* Not causing any damage (a harmless investigation). Innocuous, impotent, bland, inoffensive, ineffective, mild, benign, safe, insignificant, trivial, minute, well-meaning. See also innocent (2). *Ant.* Prejudicial.

Harmless error An error committed that was trivial, formal, and not prejudicial to the substantial rights of the party alleging it. See error.

Harmonious, *adj.* See cooperative (2), kindred (2), amicable; concordant, consistent (1), concurrent (2) appropriate (3); quiet.

Harmonize, *v.* To bring into accord or agreement (the two theories could not be harmonized). Reconcile, attune, accommodate, balance, conciliate, dovetail, adjust, moderate, orchestrate, adapt, match, conform, integrate, mesh, unify, arbitrate, placate, restore harmony, synthesize. See also coordinate (1), correspond (1). *Ant.* Sever.

Harmony, *n.* **1.** Agreement, conformity (the absence of harmony in the household). Unity, fellowship, consensus, tranquility, brotherhood, unanimity, amity, understanding, sympathy, congeniality, communion, friendship, rapport, comradeship, peace, affinity, love, rapprochement, compatibility. **2.** Consistency (the cases could not be brought into harmony). Symmetry, parallelism, concurrence, conformity, coordination, synthesis, accord, correspondence, proportion. See also balance (4). *Ant.* Disagreement.

Harness, *v.* See control, restrain.

Harp, *v.* See dwell (2); badger, harass.

Harrowing, *adj.* See distressing, dangerous, hazardous.

Harsh, *adj.* See draconian, difficult, extreme (1), serious (2), strict (2), cruel, grievous (2), onerous, violent.

Harum-scarum, *adj.* See reckless, irresponsible.

Harvest, *v., n.* See produce, yield; glean.

Hashish, *n.* A drug that is formed of resin scraped from the flowering top of the cannabis plant. See drug.

Hassle, *v., n.* See harass, disturb; annoyance, argument, difficulty.

Haste, *n.* See speed (1), dispatch.

Hasten, *v.* See accelerate, expedite; dispatch, speed.

Hasty, *adj.* See reckless, impetuous, careless; prompt, brief.

Hatch, *v.* See invent (1), create, coin (3).

Hatch Act A federal statute that prohibits federal, state, and local employees from partaking in certain types of political activities.

Hatchet, *n.* See weapon.

Hate, *v., n.* See abhor, disapprove (2); odium, malice, hostility, degradation, dishonor, animus (2).

Hateful, *adj.* See odious, repugnant, gross (1), offensive, contemptible.

Hatred, *n.* See contempt (2), odium, malice, hostility, degradation, dishonor, animus (2).

Haughty, *adj.* See arrogant, pompous; indifferent.

Haul, *v.* See import (1), carry (1), transfer (1), send.

Haunt, *v.* See frequent (2); hover (1).

Haven, *n.* A place of safety; a place where ships can ride and anchor safely (a haven for drug dealers). Refuge, shelter, sanctuary, port, hideaway, citadel, retreat, anchorage, cover, preserve, protection, immunity, quarantine, cache, haunt, dock, bay, pier; shrine, temple, sanctum, chapel, church, mosque, synagogue, holy place. See also asylum.

Have, *v.* See possess, hold.

Have-not, *n.* See indigent, destitute.

Havoc, *n.* See confusion, catastrophe, cataclysm, disaster.

Hawker, *n.* A traveling salesperson who carries goods in order to sell or "hawk" them (an unlicensed hawker). See peddler, seller; sell.

Haywire, *adj.* See wild, disorderly (1), complex (1); confusion.

Hazard 1. *n.* A risk or danger lurking in a situation which by chance or fortuity could become an active agent of harm (the display was a hazard because of the weak material used). Peril, jeopardy, threat, crisis, insecurity, endangerment, pitfall, menace, uncertainty, chance, precariousness, gamble. **2.** *v.* To speculate (hazard a guess). Venture, dare, wager, attempt, risk, volunteer, hypothesize, theorize, chance, gamble. **3.** *v.* See endanger, expose (2).

Hazardous, *adj.* Exposed to or involving danger (hazardous to health). Perilous, threatening, insecure, unsafe, precarious, menacing, ominous, risky, inauspicious, exposed, fraught with peril, disquieting, chancy, alarming, unreliable, unstable. See also dangerous, deadly, deficient, harmful. *Ant.* Secure.

Hazardous employment High-risk and extra-perilous work.

Haze, *v., n.* See initiate; harass; climate (1).

H.B. House Bill. A proposed statute being considered by the House of Representatives. See legislation, statute.

Head 1. *n.* The principal person or chief (head of the household). Leader, authority, manager, master, director, administrator, boss, chairman, foreman, captain, ruler, president, executive, commander, ringleader, secretary, speaker, dean, governor. **2.** *v.* See rule (3), manage. *Ant.* Subordinate; follow.

Headache

Headache, *n.* See pain; plight, affliction, ordeal.

Heading, *n.* See caption.

Headmaster, *n.* See principal (2), head; school.

Headnote, *n.* A small paragraph summary of a portion of a court opinion. The headnotes are placed before the beginning of the opinion.

Head of household An individual in one household who actually supports and maintains one or more individuals who are closely connected with him or her by blood, marriage, or adoption, and whose right to exercise family control and provide for dependent members is based on some moral or legal obligation. See head, manager.

Headquarters, *n.* See seat; department.

Headstrong, *adj.* See inflexible, arbitrary; reckless, incorrigible, wild (3), heedless; litigious, contentious, hostile.

Head tax A tax of a flat amount per person. See tax.

Headway, *n.* See advancement (2), growth, development.

Heal, *v.* To restore to health (the doctor was not able to heal him). Rehabilitate, resuscitate, treat, ameliorate, regenerate, mend, recuperate, alleviate, soothe, make whole, cleanse, purify, improve, convalesce, repair; reconcile, pacify, mitigate. See also recover, cure (2), remedy (2), correct (2). *Ant.* Injure.

Health, *n.* Freedom from pain or sickness; being whole in body and mind (restored to health). Well-being, fitness, strength, vitality, robustness, power, energy, stamina, wholesomeness, soundness. *Ant.* Feebleness.

Healthy, *adj.* Freedom from or not being peculiarly susceptible to disease, injury, or ailment (she was healthy prior to her employment). In good condition, fit, strong, vigorous, sturdy, well, robust, lusty, hearty, uninjured, unharmed, undiminished, hale, recovered, healed, sound, whole, in good shape; muscular, herculean, wiry, sinewy, husky, tough, virile, strapping, athletic, well-built, stalwart, potent, powerful, burly, brawny. See also able-bodied, durable. *Ant.* Infirm.

Heap, *v., n.* See litter, jettison; collection.

Hear, *v.* See apprehend (1), eavesdrop; adjudicate, judge (2, 3).

Hearing, *n.* A proceeding with definite issues of fact or law to be resolved in which witnesses are heard, the parties confront each other, and an impartial officer presides (administrative hearing). Inquiry, examination, litigation, conference, probe, adjudication, trial, inquest, review, inquisition, confrontation, interrogation. See also action (1), contest (2).

Hearing de novo A second hearing; trying the matter anew as if it had not previously been heard. See de novo, trial do novo.

Hearing examiner or officer See administrative law judge, judge.

Hearsay, *n.* Testimony in court of a statement made by another out of court when the statement is being offered to assert the truth of the matter in the statement. The value of such a statement depends on the credibility of the out-of-court asserter. (The hearsay was ruled inadmissible.) Secondhand information, that which one has heard; report, grapevine, gossip. See also rumor.

Heart, *n.* See emotion, passion; disposition (4); mercy, charity (3, 4), consideration (3); spirit, self-confidence, resolution (4), endurance, character (1); essence, center (2), foundation (2), basis (1), base (3).

Heartache, heartbreak, *n.* See anguish, anxiety, depression, affliction, pain.

Heart Balm Statute A law abolishing the right to sue for breach of promise to marry, alienation of affections, criminal conversation, and the seduction of a nonminor.

Heartbreaking, *adj.* See grievous (1).

Hearten, *v.* See encourage, strengthen.

Heartfelt, *adj.* See emotional, ardent, strong (2), genuine.

Heartless, *adj.* See cruel, callous, malicious, indifferent.

Heartbroken, *adj.* See despondent, abandoned (1), depressed, dismal.

Hearty, *adj.* See earnest (2); able-bodied, healthy; friendly, convivial; emotional, genuine, ardent.

Heat, *n.* See passion, emotion, vigor, determination (2), spirit (2), force (1); fire, burn.

Heated, *adj.* See hot (2), emotional, angry, ardent, strong (2), violent.

Heath, *n.* See desert (3); park (1).

Heat of passion A state of violent and uncontrollable rage engendered by provocation; an emotional state of mind that is so intense that reason is overcome to the extent that the person could not form a deliberate purpose and fully control his or her actions. See passion, emotion; insanity.

Heaven, *n.* Paradise. Nirvana, bliss, infinity, Zion, Kingdom of God, life beyond, City of God, Mecca, perfection, glory. See also afterlife, happiness.

Heavy, *adj.* See onerous, difficult (2), serious, awkward, grievous (1); big, corpulent; bulk (2).

Heavy-handed, *adj.* See awkward; onerous, cruel, severe, arbitrary (2); coercion.

Heckle, *v.* See harass, provoke, disturb.

Hectic, *adj.* See disorderly, emotional, ardent, blatant, wild; noisy, confusion.

Hedge, *v.* To avoid committing oneself (the witness hedged). Evade, be evasive, avoid a direct answer, dodge, equivocate, weasel, prevaricate, shield, be defensive, "fudge," conceal, screen, sidestep, temporize, hesitate, duck. See also quibble. *Ant.* Confront.

Hedges, *n.* See shrubbery, woods.

Hedging, *n.* Safeguarding oneself from loss on a bet, bargain, or speculation by making compensatory arrangements on the other side.

Hedonistic, *adj.* See decadent; debauchery, epicure; luxury.

Heed, *v.* See observe (1), abide (1), comply, accede (1), conform (1), keep (6).

Heedless, *adj.* Disregard for the rights or safety of other (heedless workers). Thoughtless, impetuous, rash, neglectful, mindless, foolish, inconsiderate, negligent, headstrong, blind, irresponsible, impulsive, precipitate, unobservant, lax, frivolous, imprudent, inattentive, hasty, deaf. See also careless, reckless, derelict (2). *Ant.* Vigilant.

Hegemony, *n.* The leadership or predominant influence of one independent state over others (a policy to combat the country's hegemony over its neighbors). Domination, sway, ascendancy, superiority, command, supremacy, dominion, control.

Height, *n.* See altitude, extent, extreme (3); apex.

Heighten, *v.* See exacerbate; exaggerate; strengthen, augment, advance, lift (2), raise (2).

Heinous, *adj.* See cruel, repulsive, odious, offensive, malicious, bad.

Heir, *n.* One whom the state designates to receive the estate of a person who has died without leaving a valid will (heir by adoption). Successor, devisee, inheritor, recipient, donee. See also beneficiary, descendant, offspring.

Heir apparent One who will receive the inheritance if he or she survives the ancestor; one next in line of succession. See descendant, offspring.

Heir at law Lineal descendant; one who has the right to inherit the estate of his or her ancestor if the latter dies without leaving a valid will; one who has a right to the real property of his or her intestate ancestor. See descendant, offspring.

Heir collateral One who is not lineally related to the decedent but is of collateral kin (e.g., uncle, cousin, brother, nephew). See descendant, offspring.

Heir general An heir at law. See descendant, offspring.

Heir of the blood One who inherits because of consanguinity (relationship by blood) with the decedent in the ascending or descending line, including illegitimate children, but excluding husbands, wives, and adopted children. See descendant, offspring.

Heir of the body An heir begotten or borne by the person referred to, or a child of such heir; any lineal descendant of the decedent, excluding a surviving spouse, adopted children, and collateral relations. See descendant; offspring.

"Heist," *n.* See larceny, robbery, seizure; hijack.

Held, *v.* Decided (the court held the statute unconstitutional). See hold (3).

Helicopter, *n.* See aircraft, vehicle.

Hell, *n.* See abyss; censure (1); chaos; ordeal, anguish, anxiety, affliction, pain, depression.

Helm, *n.* See forefront; seat.

Helmet, *n.* See protection; shield (1).

Help 1. *n.* Assistance (their effort was of no help). Relief, support, aid, encouragement, advancement, contribution, succor, backing, benefit, use, remedy, gift, cure, utility, cooperation, lift, kindness, protection, favor, advantage, resource, advocacy, accommodation, rescue, guidance, avail, facilitation, good turn, boost, championship, promotion, sustenance, charity, collaboration. **2.** *v.* To provide assistance (the computer helped a great deal). Assist, support, cooperate, cure, alleviate, abet, save, liberate, contribute, endorse, redeem, facilitate, serve, better, patronize, strengthen, improve, lend a hand, champion, befriend, minister to, back, intercede for, avail, extricate, remedy, relieve, stand behind, ease, allay, expedite, reassure, sustain, fortify, second, further, benefit. *Ant.* Hindrance; aggravate.

Helper, *n.* See assistant, aid (3), employee.

Helpful, *adj.* See beneficial, benevolent, humanitarian, practicable, friendly, gainful, cooperative (2), flexible, amenable.

Helpless, *adj.* See dependent (2), abject, defenseless, frail, weak, destitute, lost (3); impotence (2).

Helpmate, *n.* See aid (3), attendant, assistant, employee; spouse.

Helter-skelter, *adj.* See disorderly (3), careless, reckless; confusion, commotion.

Hem, *v., n.* See surround, circumscribe; border (1), bound (4).

Hemisphere, *n.* See world; domain; border (1), bound (4), boundary.

Hence, *adv.* See therefore.

Henchman, *n.* See attendant, guardian; aid (3), assistant, employee, wrongdoer; accomplice; coterie.

Henpeck, *v.* See badger, harass.

Herald 1. *v.* To indicate or announce (the appointments to the bench heralded a new alignment). Foreshadow, forecast, advertise, presage, harbinger, signify, augur, apprise, prognosticate, trumpet, publicize, inform, circulate, reveal, report, usher in. **2.** *n.* See messenger.

Herculean, *adj.* See acute (2), irresistible, onerous; big; healthy.

Herd, *n.* See group (1), assembly.

Hereafter 1. *adv.* A future time excluding both the present and the past (the land is to be used hereafter for farming). Afterwards, subsequently, from this time forth, henceforth, ultimately, later. See also future. **2.** *n.* The afterlife (the testator constantly talked of the hereafter). Next world, life beyond, paradise, after world; immortality, eternity. See also heaven, afterlife.

Hereditament, *n.* Anything that can be inherited (conveyance of hereditaments). Land, real property, personal property, chattel, tangible property, intangible property, inheritance. See also property.

Hereditary, *adj.* **1.** Capable of being inherited (hereditary estate). Passed down, ancestral, transferred, lineal, passed through, devised. **2.** Genetically transmitted or transmittable from parent to offspring (hereditary disease). Genetic, inbred, transmissible, cognate, innate, inbred. See also inherent, native (3), congenital.

Heredity, *n.* The transmission of characteristics from parent to child through genes (the mannerism was attributed to heredity). Inheritance, genetics, blood, ancestral tie.

Hereinafter, *adv.* In a later part of this document or text (hereinafter referred to as the Board). From now on, subsequently.

Heresy, *n.* An opinion contrary to church dogma; an opinion contrary to orthodox views (her views were considered heresy). Unorthodoxy, fallacy, nonconformity, dissent, dissension, infidelity, iconoclasm. See also apostasy, error. *Ant.* Conformity.

Heretical, *adj.* See profane (1), irreverent; heresy, blasphemy, profanity.

Heretofore, *adv.* Until this time (heretofore the clerk initialed the pleading). Previously, until now, formerly, hitherto.

Hereunder, *adv.* Mentioned elsewhere in this document (discussed hereunder).

Heritable, *adj.* Capable of being inherited (heritable property). Inheritable, hereditary, transferable, alienable.

Heritage, *n.* Property that can be or has been inherited; that which can be passed down to future generations (the common law is part of our heritage). Tradition, birthright, inheritance, ancestry, legacy, endowment, history, share, estate, heirloom, patrimony, descent, derivation. See also archives (2), record (2), geneology.

Hermeneutics, legal The science or art of interpreting or construing legal documents.

Hermit, *n.* Recluse. Eremite, cave dweller, anchorite. See also isolated; hide; solitary.

Hero, heroine, *n.* See champion (3); master, sailor; courageous.

Heroic, *adj.* See adventurous, courageous; elevated; enterprise (2); able-bodied; reckless.

Heroin, *n.* A narcotic drug that is a derivative of opium; diacetyl-morphine. See drug.

Hesitant, *adj.* See doubtful (1), dilatory, suspicious; fluctuating, variable, inconsistent, capricious.

Hesitate, *v.* See doubt (1), delay (1), defer (1); hedge; alternate (1), stray (1); fluctuating.

Hesitation, *n.* See doubt (2), delay (3); confusion (2); fluctuating.

Heterogeneous, *adj.* See mixed, multifarious, divers, odd (2), different; conglomerate (2).

Heterosexual, *adj.* Attracted to the opposite sex.

HEW Department of Health, Education, and Welfare. Now two separate agencies: the Department of Health and Human Services, and the Department of Education.

Hiatus, *n.* See interruption, delay, respite, break (3); disparity.

Hibernate, *v.* See sleep; retire (3); hide; depart (1).

Hick, *n.* See backward; boor.

Hidden, *adj.* Concealed (hidden assets). Not easily seen, out of view, veiled, shrouded, latent, cryptic, obscure, mysterious, buried, lurking, masked, occult, covered, undisclosed, secluded, camouflaged, screened, undetected, unseen, puzzling, clandestine, dark, suppressed, clouded, invisible, unknown, secluded, unpublished, secret, invisible, undercover, hush-hush, unacknowledged, esoteric, abstruse, unrevealed, undivulged, sly, closed-mouthed, sheltered, retired, submerged, subterranean, ulterior, underground, surreptitious. *Ant.* Obvious.

Hidden defect A deficiency in property that is not discoverable by reasonable inspection and for which a lessor or seller is generally liable if such defect causes harm to a user. See defect.

Hide, *v.* To place or keep out of view (she hid in order to avoid service of process). Seclude, bury, veil, cover up, disguise, withhold, store away, secrete, suppress, mask, cache, shelter, ensconce, obscure, cloak, closet, hibernate. See also conceal. *Ant.* Come forward.

Hideaway, *n.* See asylum (2); haven.

Hideous, *adj.* See odious, repugnant, offensive, repulsive, base, gross (1), obscene, filthy.

Hierarchy, *n.* An institution organized into ranks or degrees of position, power and authority (church hierarchy). Grouping, categorization, stratification, chain of command, gradation. See also institution, organization, bureaucracy; clerical (1).

High, *adj.* **1.** Extreme (high speed). Great, excessive, unreasonable, uncurbed, inordinate, costly, extravagant, unbridled, immoderate, violent, vigorous. **2.** Superior (High Court). Elevated, noble, prime, chief, principal, leading, primary, major. **3.** See intoxicated. *Ant.* Moderate; minor; dry.

Highbrow, *n.* See, aristocracy; cultivated, debonair, erudite; pompous, arrogant.

Highest, *adj.* See major, primary, extraordinary; great, big, high (1).

Highhanded, *adj.* See arbitrary (2), onerous, strict (2), absolute (1), arrogant.

Highlight, *v., n.* See emphasize; essence.

High-rise, *n.* See building; home.

High school, *n.* See school.

High seas That portion of the ocean which is beyond the territorial jurisdiction of any country. See sea.

High-strung, *adj.* See hot (2), emotional, feverish, excitable.

High-water line or mark The line on the shore to which high tide rises under normal weather conditions.

Highway, *n.* A public roadway that everyone has the right to use (an emergency on the highway). Street, avenue, boulevard, freeway, expressway, thoroughfare, thruway, interstate, toll road, turnpike, artery, drive, parkway, causeway, route, path, lane, roadway, concourse, strip, channel, exit, byway, trail, detour, bypass, corridor, via, mews, block, way, drag, alley, passage.

Hijack, *v.* To rob goods or vehicles while they are in transit; to seize a vehicle and force it to go in another direction (the plane was hijacked to Havana). Pirate, commandeer, kidnap, skyjack, plunder, dispossess, capture, expropriate, take prisoner, coerce, heist, dragoon. See also abduct; kidnapping.

Hilarious, *adj.* See comic, enjoyable, attractive; absurd, anomalous, wild; amusement.

Hill, *n.* See grade (2), mountain.

Hinder, *v.* To impede (the inadequate facilities hindered his research). Obstruct, thwart, frustrate, hamper, handicap, block, cripple, detain, stay, foil, encumber, arrest, restrain, inconvenience, discourage, retard, cramp, muzzle, stalemate, interrupt, delay, bar, clog, hamstring, slow down, hobble, inhibit, stymie, fetter. *Ant.* Facilitate.

Hindrance, *n.* See blockade, obstruction, drawback (2), bar, limit (2), limitation (1).

Hint, *v., n.* See intimate (6), suggest; suggestion, innuendo (2).

Hinterland, *n.* See inland.

Hip, *adj.* See cognizant, current (3), chic.

Hire 1. *v.* To purchase the temporary use of a thing; to engage the labor of another for a fee (they refused to hire ex-felons). Employ, enlist, retain, take on,

370

place, appoint, install, add, fill, recruit, commission, staff. **2.** *v.* To purchase the temporary use of a thing (hire a car). Lease, charter, rent, secure, sublease, procure. **3.** *n.* Compensation for labor, services, or the use of a thing (the firm could not afford her hire). Payment, stipend, fee, emolument, charge, profit, pay, remuneration, salary, earning, reward, honorarium. See also compensation.

Hiring at will Employment that can be ended at any time by either side; a general and indefinite hiring.

Hiring hall An agency or office operated by a union (or by both union and management) to place applicants for work.

Historian, *n.* See recorder.

Historic, *adj.* Of major importance (historic decision). Momentous, celebrated, remarkable, famed, famous, well-known, ground-breaking, significant, crucial. See also landmark (2), important, outstanding (2).

History, *n.* See heritage, legend, archives (2), record (2), genealogy, lineage.

Histrionic, *adj.* See flamboyant, emotional; artificial, feigned.

Hit, *v., n.* See batter, beat, assault; collide; coup.

Hitch, *n., v.* See complication, obstruction, cloud (1); attach (2).

Hitchhike, *v.* See travel.

Hitherto, *adv.* Referring to a time already passed (hitherto the court allowed the practice). Until now, up to this time, previously, formerly, thus far, before now, in the past, heretofore, once, until this time.

H.L. House of Lords.

Hoard, *v.* To acquire and hold goods in short supply beyond one's reasonable needs (during the crisis they were hoarding gas). Collect, set aside, accumulate, aggregate, amass, congregate, stockpile, buy up, cache, save, lay away, accrue, store, cluster, husband, preserve, squirrel away, reserve, lump, gather, group, stash, garner, bank. *Ant.* Share.

Hoary, *adj.* See ancient, old.

Hoax, *n.* See artifice, fraud, deception.

Hobble, *v.* See hinder, fetter; limp.

Hobby, *n.* An activity not engaged in for profit (the IRS called it a hobby and refused the deduction). Interest, avocation, relaxation, enjoyment, play, toy, diversion, pastime, entertainment, sideline, recreation. See also amusement, sport, game. *Ant.* Business.

Hobo, *n.* See tramp.

Hobson's choice See dilemma, mystery, conundrum; illusory.

Hoc This (hoc nomine—in this name).

Hock, *v.* See pawn (1).

Hockey, *n.* See athletics, sport, game.

Hocus-pocus, *n.* See artifice, deception, fraud; witchcraft.

Hodgepodge, *n.* See mixture, compound (3); composite; confusion, disorder.

Hoist, *v.* See lift (2).

Hold 1. *v.* To possess something by virtue of a lawful title (the deed gave the land to John "to have and to hold"). Occupy, enjoy, retain, control, own, inherit, receive, take over, keep, have, secure. **2.** *v.* To occupy a position (she held office for two years). Be incumbent, command, keep, maintain, direct, be in charge of. **3.** *v.* To adjudge or decide (the court did not hold the statute invalid). Decree, settle, determine, adjudicate, find, rule, resolve, announce, pronounce. **4.** *v.* To restrain or control (the police will hold the suspect until noon). Detain, incarcerate, maintain custody over, lock up, confine, sequester, impound, contain, repress, suppress, hinder, check, halt, bar, delay, retard, thwart, block, coerce, compel, squelch, seize. **5.** *v.* To consider or declare (they hold you responsible). Regard, affirm, deem, surmise, conclude, maintain, bind, believe, assume, presume, view, judge, reckon, suspect, see, conceive. **6.** *n.* Influence (she exerted a strong hold over the testator). Domination, power, sway, control, clout, dominance, mastery, ascendancy.

Holder, *n.* The person who has possession of something; the person who has legally acquired possession of an instrument (e.g., a check, a promissory note) and who is entitled to receive payment of the instrument (holder in due course). Possessor, keeper, recipient, payee, bearer, owner, proprietor.

Holder for value Someone who has given valuable consideration for the document of title, instrument, or investment security in his or her possession. See consideration; instrument.

Holder in due course A holder who takes an instrument for value, in good faith, and without notice that it is overdue, that it has been dishonored, or that there is any defense against it or claim to it by any person. See buyer; instrument.

Hold harmless To assume any liability in a situation or transaction and thereby relieve from responsibility the party who is being held harmless. See indemnify, insurance.

Holding, *n.* **1.** A court's answer to or resolution of the legal issue before it (the holding cannot be extended to cover these facts). Decision, conclusion, adjudication, resolution, order, legal principle, finding. **2.** Property owned by a person or an organization (extensive holdings). Realty, personalty, chattel, asset, goods, investment, belongings, estate, possessions, land, capital, wealth, means. See also property, effects.

Holding company A company that confines its activities to owning stock in and supervising the management of other companies. See corporation, conglomerate.

Holdover tenant A tenant who retains possession after the expiration of a lease or after a tenancy at will has been terminated. See tenant; lease.

Holdup, *n.* See interruption, delay (3); larceny, robbery.

Hole, *n.* See interval (2); break (3), crevice; defect; plight, emergency.

Holiday, *n.* A day set apart for commemorating an important event in history; a day of exemption from labor (the union bargained for an additional holiday). Celebration, commemoration, day off, holy day, observance, ritual, ceremony, anniversary, occasion. See also vacation, leave (5), furlough.

Hollow, *adj., n.* See worthless, frivolous, barren; vacant, void (3); token (2); trench, wrinkle (1).

Holocaust, *n.* See murder, homicide; kill.

Holographic, *adj.* Pertaining to a will or deed written entirely by the testator or grantor in his or her own handwriting and not witnessed or attested (holographic will). In longhand, scribbled, cursive, handwritten.

Holy, *adj.* Hallowed. Consecrated, sacrosanct, blessed, sacred, venerated, adored, worshiped, sanctified, divine, godly, pious, venerable, angelic, immaculate, revered. See also inviolate, religious; church; God.

Homage, *n.* **1.** In feudal law, the service that a tenant was bound to perform for his lord; the ceremony for rendering such service. Allegiance, obeisance, submission, fidelity, faithfulness, subservience, vassalage, bondage. **2.** The showing of respect or honor (homage to the late jurist). Tribute, esteem, worship, adulation, deference, reverence, veneration.

Home, *n.* **1.** One's dwelling place (she had no intention to return to his home). Residence, domicile, abode, habitation, refuge, apartment, tenement, household, quarters, condominium, hearth, roof, manor, ranch, domain, lodging, room, shelter, flat, accommodations, address, cabin, flophouse, studio, penthouse, duplex, bungalow, bunker, camp, chalet, chateau, castle, cottage, habitat, sanctuary; headquarters, birthplace, motherland, fatherland, native land. **2.** An institution for the special care of individuals in need (home for the elderly). Hospital, asylum, orphanage, sanatorium, poorhouse, eleemosynary institution.

Homeless, *adj.* See abandoned (1), itinerant, migratory; tramp.

Home Loan Bank See Federal Home Loan Banks.

Homely, *adj.* Unattractive. Ugly, plain, unsightly, drab, uncomely, graceless. See also backward (2), commonplace; innocent (2).

Homemade, *adj.* See domestic (1).

Homemaker, *n.* See head, head of household, man, woman, spouse.

Homeowner policy A multiperil insurance policy covering fire, burglary, water, and liability. See insurance.

Home owners warranty (HOW) A warranty and insurance protection program offered by many home builders, providing protection for 10 years against major structural defects. See insurance.

Home port doctrine A vessel engaged in interstate and foreign commerce is taxable only at its home port (e.g., where it is registered or enrolled). See tax.

Home rule A designated amount of self-government exercised by local cities and towns. Limited sovereignty, autonomy, political independence, self-determination. See also government.

Homestead, *n.* The dwelling house and adjoining land where the head of the family dwells; the home farm. See dwelling, domicile, home, residence.

Homestead exemption laws Laws that allow a householder or head of a family to designate a house and land as his or her homestead, which is exempted from execution or attachment for his or her general debts.

Homework, *n.* See preparation; school.

Homicide, *n.* The killing of one human being by the act, procurement, or omission of another. It is a crime only if done knowingly, purposefully, recklessly, or negligently and without justification (criminal homicide). Termination of life, slaying, murder, manslaughter, assassination, destruction of life, fratricide, infanticide, feticide, matricide, bloodshed, slaughter, euthanasia.

Homily, *n.* See speech (2), address (3); moral (3); religious.

Homogeneous, *adj.* See alike (1), equivalent, consistent (1), constant (1); mixed.

Homologous, *adj.* See analogous, akin (2), like.

Homophile, *adj.* See gay (1).

Homophobic, *adj.* Fearful of homosexuality. See fear.

Homo sapiens, *n.* See mankind, people, person, man, woman.

Homosexual, *adj.* See gay (1).

"Honcho," *n.* See head, manager, director, entrepreneur.

Hone, *v.* See sharpen.

Honest, *adj.* Trustworthy, truthful (an honest appraisal). Principled, unbiased, aboveboard, genuine, ethical, unadulterated, forthright, open, authentic, fair, sound, conscientious, creditable, valid, honorable, undistorted, accurate, moral, objective, staunch, faithful, unjaundiced, uncolored, respectable, factual, candid, impartial, frank, evenhanded, just, straightforward, undiluted, incorruptible, guileless, disinterested, righteous, reasonable, equitable, impeccable, reliable, legitimate, veracious, responsible, dependable, worthy, loyal, dispassionate, licit, simple, blunt, exact, reputable, stainless, unvarnished, unreserved, bona fide, believable, sincere, scrupulous, square, plainspoken, solid, ingenuous. *Ant.* Unscrupulous.

Honesty, *n.* See integrity, candor, justice, right (4), fairness, honor (3), equity (2).

Honeymoon, *n.* See vacation; marriage; happiness.

"Honky," *n.* A white person.

Honky-tonk *n.* See inn; merchant.

Honor 1. *v.* To pay or to accept and pay (the bank honored the check). Credit, acknowledge, cash, make good, redeem. **2.** *v.* To give respect or esteem (the committee honored its president). Applaud, venerate, laud, congratulate, pay homage to, commend, celebrate, extol, consecrate, revere, praise, give deference to, approve, regard, exalt, appreciate, respect, salute, dignify, recognize, adore, commemorate, cite, lionize. **3.** *n.* Integrity (a woman of honor). Rectitude, principle, morality, innocence, virtue, truthfulness, conscientiousness, constancy, decency, trustworthiness, justice, equity, veracity, credibility, dignity, self-respect, acclaim, good name, high regard, standing, repute, character, status, reliability, nobility, righteousness. See also integrity. *Ant.* Dishonor; censure; duplicity.

Honorable, *adj.* Characterized by integrity (honorable intentions). See honest, good (2), moral (2), right (1), meritorious (2), loyal, outstanding (2).

Honorable discharge An authoritative declaration by the government that a soldier has left the service in a status of honor.

Honorarium, *n.* A fee for services or a special reward (an honorarium given to the speaker). Emolument, commission, payment, gratuity, consideration, remuneration, stipend, salary. See also compensation.

Honorary, *adj.* Referring to a title or office given as a mark of honor and esteem without duties or compensation (honorary national chairperson). In name only, honorific, titular, complimentary. See also nominal.

Hood, hoodlum, *n.* See wrongdoer, offender, criminal (1), racketeer, delinquent (3).

Hoodwink, *v.* See deceive, cheat, entice.

Hook, *v.* See entrap, seize; affix (1), attach (2), connect.

Hooker, *n.* See prostitute.

Hook Up, *v.* See install (2).

"Hooky," *n.* See absence (1); delinquency.

"Hoopla," *n.* See commotion, confusion, emotion; noise.

Hope 1. *v.* To desire or expect (the testator hoped that the land would be used for a hospital). Trust, contemplate, count on, reckon on, anticipate, feel sure, look forward to, desire, foresee, rely, believe, assume. **2.** *n.* A desire or expectation (he lost all hope when the witness made the accusation). Confidence, ambition, faith, expectation, prospect, optimism, reliance, aspiration, encouragement, assurance, conviction. *Ant.* Despair.

Hopeful, *adj.* See optimistic, auspicious, gainful, fortunate, certain (2), positive, happy.

Hopeless, *adj.* See abject, despondent, abandoned (1), depressed, distressing; barren (2), odious; imminent; dangerous; impossible; incorrigible, incurable, irreconcilable.

"Hophead," *n.* See addict (1).

Hopper, *n.* See vessel (2).

Horde, *n.* See group (1), mob, assembly.

Horizon, *n.* See view (5), range (2), scope.

Horizontal merger The acquisition of one company by another company producing the same or a similar product and selling it in the same geographic market. See merger, monopoly.

Horizontal price fixing Agreements between producers, wholesalers, or retailers as to sale or retail prices. See price fixing, monopoly, agreement.

Horizontal restraint An agreement between competitors at the same level of market structure. See monopoly, agreement.

Horn, *n.* See music; noise.

Hornbook, *n.* A book explaining the basics or fundamentals of a topic (hornbook on criminal law). Digest, manual, text, treatise, study guide, condensation, abstract, capsule, outline, review. See also book (4).

"Horny", *adj.* See animate, incite, provoke; obscene.

Horrendous, *adj.* See bad (2), awesome, appalling, odious, repulsive, repugnant, offensive, contemptible, corrupt, cruel, base; odd (1) anomalous.

Horrible, *adj.* See horrendous.

Horrid, *adj.* See horrendous.

Horrified, *adj.* See agape.

Horrify, *v.* See outrage (2), intimidate, disturb, disrupt; harass.

Horror, *n.* See fear (1), consternation, shock (1), outrage (1), apprehension (3), indignity, scandal.

Horse, *n.* See animal.

Horseplay, *n.* Buffoonery. Rowdy play, pranks. See also antic.

"Horse sense," *n.* See common sense.

Hospice, *n.* See inn, hotel; hospital.

Hospitable, *adj.* See friendly, convivial, amicable, cooperative, benevolent, kind (2).

Hospital, *n.* An institution for the treatment and care of sick, wounded, infirm, or aged persons (negligence in the emergency room of the hospital). Clinic, medical center, infirmary, home, polyclinic, hospice, sanitarium, sanatorium.

Hospitality, *n.* Benevolence.

Host, *n.* See group (1), mob, lot (2), multitude, multiplicity, assembly.

Hostage, *n.* An innocent person held captive by one who threatens to kill or harm the person if certain demands are not met by others (hostages taken by the terrorists). Prisoner, pawn, guaranty, gage. See also victim.

Hostel, *n.* See inn, home; merchant.

Hostile, *adj.* Having the character of an enemy (hostile witness). Opposing, unfriendly, aggressive, adverse, contrary, abusive, dissenting, uncooperative, militant, antagonistic, clashing, rancorous, inimical, repugnant, contentious, warlike, challenging, argumentative, oppugning, contesting, disputatious, averse, quarreling, competitive, bellicose, pugnacious, fighting, acrimonious, antisocial, cold, battling, testy, at war, incompatible, bitter, mean, at odds. See also disaffected, disobedient, malicious. *Ant.* Sympathetic.

Hostile fire A fire that breaks out or spreads to an unexpected area. See accident; fire, burn.

Hostile or adverse witness A witness who manifests so much hostility or prejudice under examination that he or she can be treated as though called by the other side (i.e., the witness can be cross-examined by the side that called him or her). See witness; cross-examination.

Hostile possession The person in possession asserts that all other claims to possession are invalid. See adverse possession, possession.

Hostility, *n.* A state of enmity between individuals or nations (hostilities broke out). Antagonism, fighting, war, conflict, feud, aggression, hatred, fracas, altercation, bickering, ill will, opposition, contempt, animosity, vindictiveness, defiance, malice, viciousness, rancor, malevolence, estrangement, bad blood, antipathy, alienation, loathing. See also animus, odium. *Ant.* Comity.

Hot, *adj.* **1.** Close behind (hot pursuit). Recent, fresh, new, very close, near, latest. **2.** Excited (hot temper). Animated, passionate, intense, violent, furious, ardent, impetuous, seething, wrathful, raging, fervent, irascible, burning, boiling, torrid, zealous, live, sensitive, fiery, frenzied, tempestuous, earnest, enthusiastic, blistering, sizzling, rash, aggressive, desperate, excessive, heated, high-strung, irrepressible, savage, piquant, turbulent, feverish, ungovernable, wanton, inflamed, choleric, fuming. **3.** See muggy, climate. *Ant.* Interrupted; dispassionate.

"Hot air" *n.* See balderdash, prolixity; ambiguity; babble.

Hot blood The condition of one whose passions have been aroused to an uncontrollable degree, causing the charge of homicide to be reduced from murder to manslaughter. See manslaughter, homicide; irresistible.

Hot-blooded, *adj.* See emotional, hot (2), ardent, wild, violent, contentious, litigious.

Hot cargo 1. Goods produced or handled by an employer with whom a union has a dispute. **2.** Stolen goods.

Hotchpot, *n.* The blending and mixing of property belonging to different persons in order to divide it equally.

Hotel, *n.* A place where all transient persons can pay a fee to be guests for lodging and related services (inadequate security in the hotel). Motel, lodging, hospice, boarding house, public house, pension. See also inn, merchant.

Hotheaded, *adj.* See hot (2), emotional, excitable, contentious, litigious, belligerent, ardent, wild, violent, reckless.

Hot pursuit See fresh pursuit.

"Hot rod," *n.* A rebuilt automobile. See vehicle.

Hound, *v.* See pursue (2), chase, ferret, trace (2); badger, harass, provoke.

Hour, *n.* See interval (1), period.

House, *n.* **1.** A structure that serves as the living quarters for one or more persons or families. See domicile, habitation, home, residence. **2.** A business firm (securities house). Establishment, shop, company, stock, enterprise, partnership, corporation, concern, store. See also business, commerce.

House arrest, *n.* The confinement of an individual in his or her home rather than in an institution. See arrest, confinement.

Houseboat, *n.* See vessel (1), vehicle; home.

Housebreaking, *n.* Breaking and entering a dwelling-house with the intent to commit any felony therein. Burglary, raiding, forcible entry, stealing, appropriation, looting, thievery, plundering. See also larceny.

House counsel A lawyer who is an attorney-employee of a business or organization. He or she works for a salary, unlike an independent attorney who works for a fee. See attorney.

Household 1. *adj.* Belonging or pertaining to the house and family (household expenses). Housekeeping, domestic, residential; everyday, common, conventional, ordinary, routine, garden-variety, habitual, standard, repeated, average. **2.** *n.* A family living together. See family, home (1).

Housekeeper, *n.* See servant, employee.

House of Commons One of the constituent houses of the British parliament, composed of representatives of the counties, cities, and boroughs.

House of Delegates The lower branch of the legislative assembly of several states (e.g., Maryland, Virginia).

House of ill fame See bawdyhouse, brothel.

House of Lords The upper chamber of the British parliament. It is the court of final appeals in most civil cases and has jurisdiction over impeachment.

House of prostitution See bawdyhouse, brothel.

House of Representatives The lower house of the U.S. Congress, consisting of 435 members elected to 2-year terms.

Housewife, househusband, *n.* See head, head of household, spouse, woman, man; servant.

Housework, *n.* See labor; household (1).

Housing, *n.* See home, habitation.

Housing Code Laws concerning fitness for habitation, setting forth standards and requirements for construction, maintenance, operation, use, or appearance of buildings, premises, and dwelling units. See habitable, warranty of habitability.

Hover, *v.* **1.** To hang around. Linger, pervade, attend, haunt, loom. **2.** To waver. Oscillate, seesaw. See also fluctuating.

HOW See Home Owners Warranty

However, *adv.* See although; nevertheless; difference, contrast, compare.

Howitzer, *n.* See weapon, arms; war.

Howl, *v., n.* See yell; proclaim; bemoan; noise.

H.R. See House of Representatives

H.R. 10 plans See Keogh Plan.

Hub, *n.* See center.

Hubris, *n.* See arrogance; pompous.

Huckster, *n.* **1.** A peddler (a huckster of fruit). Dealer, hawker, vendor, haggler. See also peddler, merchant. **2.** A petty merchant (the book portrayed him as a huckster). Scrooge, money grabber, niggard, miser.

HUD Department of Housing and Urban Development.

Huddle, *n., v.* See mob, company (2), congregation, group, assembly; meeting (1), conference; congregate, collect (1).

Huff, *n.* See wrath, hostility.

Hug, *v.* See caress, touch (1).

Huge, *adj.* See big, great (1).

Hullabaloo, *n.* See commotion, disturbance, eruption, confusion, emotion, passion.

Human, *adj., n.* See imperfect, temporary; mankind, man, person.

Humane, *adj.* Demonstrating compassion. See humanitarian, charitable, benevolent, kind (2), friendly.

Humanitarian, *adj.* Concerned with social welfare and social reform (humanitarian gesture). Humane, eleemosynary, philanthropic, generous, charitable, understanding, altruistic, helpful, merciful, good, magnanimous, unselfish, compassionate, forbearing, clement, lenient, tender, decent, fraternal, bounteous, forgiving, accommodating, benign, human. See also benevolent, kind. *Ant.* Mercenary.

Humanitarian doctrine See last clear chance.

Humanity, *n.* See mankind, people, person, man, woman; world, universe; charity, benevolence.

Humble, *adj., v.* See quiet (2), bashful; amenable (2), flexible; awkward (2); embarrass, discredit, disparage; ashamed.

Humbug, *n.* See balderdash, prolixity.

Humdrum, *adj., n.* See commonplace, routine, household; boredom; depression.

Humid, *adj.* See muggy, climate.

Humiliate, *v.* See discredit, disparage, patronize (2), embarrass, slander, decry, defy; ashamed.

Humiliation, *n.* See ignominy, disgrace, embarrassment, guilt (2), depression, contrition, obloquy, censure; ashamed.

Humility, *n.* Modesty. Shyness, docility, meekness, bashfulness, timidity, subservience, diffidence; reverence, tolerance. See also contrition.

Humor, *n., v.* See disposition (4), emotion, manner; pander (2), satisfy (2), accommodate, delight, yield (1); patronize (2); antic; comic, joke, clown, laugh.

Humorous, *adj.* See comic, enjoyable, facetious, attractive; absurd, anomalous; amusement; laugh.

Hunch, *n.* See clue, intuition.

Hunger, *n.* See dearth, absence (2), privation, want (1); desire.

Hung jury A jury so irreconcilably divided in opinion that a verdict cannot be agreed upon. See jury.

Hungry, *adj.* Famished. Starved, undernourished, malnourished. See also frail, weak, barren; avaricious; ambitious.

Hunt, *v., n.* See chase, pursue (2), ferret, trace (2), search (1); athletics, sport, game.

Huntley hearing A separate proceeding in a criminal case wherein the admissibility of the accused's extrajudicial statements is determined. See evidence; admissible.

Hurdle, *n.* See blockade, obstruction, drawback (2), limit (2), liability, disadvantage (1), bar (3), block (1), complication; nuisance.

Hurl, *v.* See jettison, launch.

Hurricane, *n.* See storm, eruption, cataclysm, act of God; climate.

Hurry, *v.* See accelerate, expedite; speed; summary, summarily.

Hurt, *v.* To damage or injure (the libel hurt his chances for promotion). Wound, spoil, waste, offend, impede, retard, disable, fragment, pervert, minimize, diminish, frustrate, hamper, thwart, reduce, narrow, mutilate, plague, preclude, devastate, cripple, stab, abuse, lame, mar, maim, bruise, deface, hold back, obstruct, lessen. *Ant.* Benefit.

Hurtful, *adj.* See harmful, deleterious, injurious.

Husband 1. *n.* A married man (her husband initiated divorce proceedings). Spouse, mate, consort. See also man. **2.** *v.* To supervise carefully (husband one's assets). Manage, store, conserve, maintain, preserve. *Ant.* Wife; squander.

Husbandry, *n.* Operating land to raise crops and livestock (implements of husbandry). Agriculture, farming, agribusiness, agronomy, gardening.

Husband-wife privilege See marital communications privilege.

Hush, *v.*, *n.* See quiet (2), accommodate, pander (2); silence (1); mute.

Hush money Payment to secure silence; a bribe to hinder information. See bribe, fraud.

Husky, *adj.* See able-bodied, healthy.

Hussy, *n.* See prostitute; woman.

Hustle, *v.*, *n.* See run (2), accelerate, expedite; manipulate; activity, commotion, confusion, speed; deceive; solicit; industry (2), initiative (2).

Hut, *n.* See building, home.

Hybrid, *adj.* Concerning something of mixed composition (hybrid service). Intermingled, commingled, amalgamated, half-breed, conglomerate, compound; impure. See also mixed.

Hybrid security A security in the form of a debenture containing elements of indebtedness and elements of equity stock.

Hydrofoil, *n.* See vessel (1), vehicle.

Hydroplane, *n.* See aircraft, vehicle.

Hygiene, *n.* See sanitation; health.

Hygienic, *adj.* See sanitary, wholesome; preventive; healthy.

Hymen, *n.* The membrane covering the vaginal opening.

Hymeneal, *adj.* See marital; marriage.

Hymn, *n.* See music; honor, tribute; religious.

"Hype," *n.*, *v.* See puffing, deception; fanfare; exaggerate, exhibit, augment.

Hyperactive, *adj.* See excitable, emotional; violent, wild.

Hyperbole, *n.* See puffing, decoration; increase; exaggerate.

Hypercritical, *adj.* See contentious, critical (2), difficult.

Hypnotism, *n.* Artificially inducing a state of sleep or trance by verbal suggestion or by concentration on an object.

Hypochondria, *n.* Excessive concern over one's health. See disease, compulsion.

Hypocrisy, *n.* See pretense, pretext, deception.

Hypocritical, *adj.* See false (2), fake, deceptive, dishonest, feigned, artificial.

Hypothecate, *v.* To pledge property as security or collateral for a debt; the pledged property is usually not physically transferred to the lender (authority to hypothecate the farm). See mortgage, pledge.

Hypothesis, *n.* An assumption or theory to be proven or disproved (the evidence contradicted the hypothesis). Supposition, speculation, postulate, premise, inference, guess, starting point, deduction, surmise, conclusion, conception, conjecture, presumption, suspicion, thesis, predication, opinion, axiom, theorem, presupposition, proposition, concept, plan, idea, formula, proposal.

Hypothesize, *v.* See presume, assume.

Hypothetical, *adj.* Based on conjecture (hypothetical case). Theoretical, possible, assumed, presumptive, supposed, imaginary, pretended, speculative, contingent, unreal, conditional, postulated; dubious, questionable, debatable, uncertain. *Ant.* Confirmed.

Hypothetical question A form of question calling for an opinion from an expert based on stated fact assumptions; the expert is asked to give an opinion on the assumption that the facts are true. See question.

Hysteria, *n.* Frenzy. Delirium, madness, rage, fury, intoxication, fever, incoherence. See also insanity.

Hysterical, *adj.* Characterized by extreme emotionalism (he became hysterical when he heard the news). Beside oneself, distraught, crazy, overcome, uncontrollable, mad, possessed, berserk, irrational, explosive, raging, delirious, convulsive. *Ant.* Somber.

Ibid. In the same place; in the work previously cited or mentioned; in the same book.

ICC See Interstate Commerce Commission.

Iconoclastic, *adj.* See profane (1), irreverent; profanity, blasphemy; anarchist, nihilist.

Id. The same; used to indicate a reference previously made.

Idea, *n.* See concept, proposal, conviction (2), belief (1), opinion (2).

Ideal, *adj., n.* See exemplary (2), perfect (2), perfection (2), outstanding; abstract (4); model, measure (1), principle, archetype; objective, aim (3), end (1), design.

Idealistic, *adj.* See ideal; honest, good (2), moral (2), right (1); hypothetical.

Identical, *adj.* Exactly the same for all practical purposes (an identical offense). Matching, comparable, alike, indistinguishable, selfsame, synonymous, interchangeable, duplicate, without distinction, tantamount, twin, uniform, substitute, approximate. See also equal (2), equivalent. *Ant.* Distinct.

Identification, *n.* The act of identifying something; proof of identity; the proving that a person, subject, or article before the court is as it is alleged to be (a positive identification). Verification, corroboration, recognition, revelation, disclosure, detection, ascertainment, authentication, indication, pinpointing. See also mark, manifestation.

Identify, *v.* See recognize (1), detail (1), verify, notice (2), distinguish; equate; identification.

Identity, *n.* **1.** Individuality (the identity of the victim could not be established). Distinguishing features, name, personality, peculiarities, uniqueness, self, selfness, mannerisms, nature, person, idiosyncrasies, difference, originality, personal characteristics. **2.** Sameness (an identity of interests). Duplication, similarity, likeness, uniformity, homogeneity, agreement, oneness, unity, harmony, indistinguishability, equality, correspondence, accord, interchangeability, resemblance, equivalence. *Ant.* Universality; dissimilarity.

Identity of interests Closely related in business operations or in other activities. See interest.

Idiocy, *n.* **1.** Mental retardation; subnormal intellectual ability (congenital idiocy). Feeble-mindedness, mongolism, insanity. **2.** Stupidity (the idiocy of the fight). Recklessness, absurdity, foolhardiness, fatuity, madness, senselessness, lunacy, asininity, irrationality, insipience, immaturity.

Idiom, *n.* See language.

Idiosyncrasy, *n.* See eccentricity, disposition (4), character (4), property (2); notoriety, reputation; deviation, deviant.

Idiot, *n.* A stupid person. Blockhead, dunce, moron, numskull, fool, imbecile, pinhead, dullard, ignoramus, sap, lightweight, dope, jerk, schmuck, half-wit, bonehead, boob, bungler, buffoon, fumbler, klutz, clod. See also boor.

Idiotic, *adj.* See dumb, absurd, lunatic, irrational.

Idle, *v., adj.* See loiter; lazy, dilatory, apathetic, indifferent; dormant, vacant, barren, worthless, frivolous.

Idolize, *v.* See adulate, honor (2).

Idyllic, *adj.* Pastoral. Romantic, rustic, peaceful, simple, bucolic, unspoiled.

i.e. That is; that is to say.

Ignite, *v.* See burn, detonate, discharge (4); incite, provoke, exacerbate, harass.

Ignominious, *adj.* See contemptible, repulsive, repugnant, odious, offensive, bad (2), base, malicious.

Ignominy, *n.* Public disgrace (the ignominy suffered as a result of the defamation). Reproach, dishonor, abasement, ostracism, degradation, disparagement, humiliation, disfavor, chagrin, shame, blot, disrepute, stigma, abjection, embarrassment, contempt, mortification, scorn. See also infamy. *Ant.* Esteem.

Ignoramus, *n.* See idiot, boor, ass.

Ignorance, *n.* The absence of knowledge (ignorance of the law). Lack of knowledge, want of knowledge, unconsciousness, unfamiliarity, blindness, unawareness, confusion, unenlightenment, perplexity, incomprehension; stupidity, innocence, lack of learning, illiteracy, obtuseness, lack of perception, naiveté; uninformed. *Ant.* Comprehension.

Ignorant, *adj.* See dumb, illiterate, backward, blind; innocent, credulous; lunatic, absurd; rude, reckless, juvenile.

Ignorantia legis neminem excusat Ignorance of the law excuses no one.

Ignore, *v.* To disregard willfully (he ignored the danger). Refuse to recognize, decline to take notice of, be ignorant of, be unacquainted with, eschew, scorn, neglect, be blind to, overlook, dodge, discard, brush aside, be oblivious to, shut one's eyes to, turn one's back on, slight, omit, evade, avoid, repudiate. *Ant.* Confront.

Ilk, *n.* See class (1), classification, kind (1).

Ill, *adj.* **1.** Sick (the report made him ill). Unhealthy, infirm, ailing, invalid, sickly, indisposed, impaired, diseased, nauseated, feeble, sore, confined, afflicted, feverish, debilitated, unwell, laid up. See also weak; illness, disease. **2.** Cruel (ill treatment). Wrong, corrupt, hostile, evil, immoral, adverse, unfavorable, foul, malicious, pernicious, irascible, nocuous, harmful, vengeful, sinful, degenerate, mean, nefarious, belligerent, unfriendly, injurious, damaging. See also cruel. *Ant.* Healthy; beneficial.

Ill-advised, *adj.* See improvident, careless, impetuous, reckless, dumb, lunatic.

Illegal, *adj.* Against the law; not authorized by the law (an illegal purchase). Forbidden, improper, under the table, unlawful, banned, unwarranted, unauthorized, unallowed, unsanctioned, outside the law, wrongful, illegitimate, prohibited, immoral, felonious, proscribed, outlawed, unconstitutional, impermissible, unjustified, invalid, actionable. See also criminal, wrong; baseless, illicit. *Ant.* Lawful.

Illegal entry Unauthorized entry; an alien is guilty of illegal entry if he or she (a) enters at the wrong time or place in the country, or (b) eludes an examination by the immigration officers, or (c) obtains entry by fraud.

Illegality, *n.* That which is contrary to the principles of the law (the trustee was accused of investment illegalities). Wrongdoing, malfeasance, nonfeasance, criminality, impropriety, illegitimacy, infraction, unlawfulness, transgression. See also offense, corruption, violation, delinquency. *Ant.* Legitimacy.

Illegal per se Illegal in and of itself.

Illegible, *adj.* Indecipherable. Unreadable, unintelligible, obscured. See also incoherent, ambiguous.

Illegitimate, *adj.* **1.** Born out of wedlock (illegitimate child). Bastard, misbegotten, natural, baseborn, adulterine. **2.** Contrary to law (illegitimate transaction). See illegal, wrong, criminal, baseless, irregular, corrupt, fraudulent, illicit, delinquent (2), deceptive, dishonest.

Ill fame Evil repute; notorious bad character (prostitutes in the house of ill fame). See notorious.

Ill-fated, *adj.* Unlucky. Unfortunate, doomed, luckless, ill-starred, hapless, jinxed. See also destiny; calamity.

Ill-founded, *adj.* See baseless, invalid (1).

Illiberal, *adj.* See narrow (2), arbitrary; arrogant, pompous.

Illicit, *adj.* Not permitted (illicit trade). Not allowed, prohibited, unlawful, forbidden, proscribed, tortious, actionable, immoral, impermissible, felonious, illegitimate, clandestine, improper, banned, wrongful, censored, unprincipled, furtive, underhanded, under the counter, unseemly, iniquitous. See also illegal, criminal, wrong, delinquent (2), corrupt (1), fraudulent, dishonest, deceptive. *Ant.* Authorized.

Illicit cohabitation Two unmarried persons living together as man and wife. See fornication; cohabitation; adultery.

Illiterate, *adj.* Characterized by an inability to read or write (illiterate transient). Unschooled, uneducated, ignorant, untutored, unenlightened, unversed, unlettered. See also blind.

Ill-mannered, *adj.* See rude, gross (1), base (1, 2), gaudy, awkward, backward (1), caustic, crabby.

Ill-natured, *adj.* See malicious, hostile, contentious, difficult (3), biting, caustic, crabby.

Illness, *n.* Sickness, disease, or disorder of the body or mind (the illness began after the accident). Affliction, malady, ailment, disorder, wound, neurosis, psychosis, infection, indisposition, complaint, disability, delicate constitution, delicate condition, invalidism, infirmity, unhealthiness, debility, suffering, malaise, nausea, pathology, handicap, frailty, infection, derangement, abnormality, attack, burnout, exhaustion, ill health, pain. See also disease. *Ant.* Health.

Illogical, *adj.* See baseless, fallacious, false, invalid (1), absurd, incoherent, inconsistent, irrational.

Ill-tempered, *adj.* See angry, contentious, caustic, rude, crabby, difficult (3).

Illuminate, *v.* See demonstrate (2), clarify, describe; instruct, improve, convey.

Illuminating, *adj.* See informative, demonstrative (1), descriptive.

Illumination, *n.* See light, glare; knowledge, clarity, education, discovery; judgment (2), discretion (3).

Ill-use, *v.* See harm, injure, abuse (1), manipulate, exploit (1).

Illusion, *n.* See falsehood, error; dream (1), hallucination, fiction; illusory.

Illusive, *adj.* See illusory.

Illusory, *adj.* Deceiving by false appearances (illusory benefit). Unreal, distorted, misinterpreted, perverted, misleading, dreamlike, chimerical, illusive, untrue, nonexistent, mythic, fallacious, delusive, counterfeit, hallucinatory, spurious, apparent, sham, seeming, ostensible, tenuous, fanciful, unsubstantial, sophistic, tricky, beguiling. See also fictitious, deceptive, erroneous. *Ant.* Real.

Illusory appointment A nominal, overly restrictive, or conditional transfer of property under a power of appointment; lacking in substantial existence. See power of appointment.

Illusory promise A supposed promise that leaves the promisor's performance optional or entirely within the discretion of the promisor. See promise, contract; optional, discretionary, voluntary.

Illusory trust A "trust" where the creator (settlor) has retained so much control over the "trust" property that he or she clearly did not intend to relinquish any rights in the "trust" property; an invalid trust. See hoax, fraud; trust.

Illustrate, *v.* See demonstrate (2), exhibit (1), express (2), describe, clarify, develop (2).

Illustration, *n.* See case (3), sample (1), instance; representation, description; model, archetype.

Illustrative, *adj.* See demonstrative (2), descriptive, informative.

Illustrious, *adj.* See elevated, notorious, great, outstanding, brilliant, extraordinary.

Ill will, *n.* See malice, hostility, animus.

Image, *n.* See manifestation, appearance; copy, model; concept, conviction (2), belief, opinion (2), impression (1).

Imaginable, *adj.* See possible, comprehensible.

Imaginary, *adj.* See hypothetical, fictitious, illusory, deceptive, feigned.

Imagination, *n.* See ability (2), judgment (2), capacity (2), gift (2), faculties, clarity, comprehension; enterprise, initiative; hallucination, dream (1), fiction, caprice.

Imaginative, *adj.* See original (3), brilliant, able, competent, apt (2, 3), fertile.

Imagine, *v.* See fantasize, dream (1); realize (3), invent, create, think, comprehend (1); fabricate.

Imbalance, *n.* See disparity, difference; disproportionate.

Imbecile, *n.* See idiot, ass, boor.

Imbecility, *n.* A condition of mental deficiency or feeble-mindedness. See disease, illness, insanity; infirm, demented, deranged.

Imbibe, *v.* See consume; eat.

Imbroglio, *n.* See complication, obstruction, blockade, ordeal; confusion, commotion; conflict, opposition.

Imbue, *v.* **1.** To inspire. Inculcate, ingrain, endow, instill, infuse, indoctrinate, propogandize, color. See also impress, animate, incite, cause (2), provoke (1). **2.** To permeate. Saturate, bathe, pervade, drown. See also fill, inundate.

Imitate, *v.* See copy (2); imitation.

Imitation, *n.* The making of one thing in the likeness of another (imitation of a trademark). Fabrication, duplication, mimicry, simulation, forgery, fraud, replica, parody, travesty, plagiarism, impersonation, facsimile, reproduction, representation, burlesque, adaptation, caricature, spoof, lampoon, drawing, resemblance. See also copy. *Ant.* Original.

Immaculate, *adj.* See clean, clear, perfect; innocent, blameless, honest.

Immanent, *adj.* See inherent, congenital, native (3).

Immaterial, *adj.* Not material, essential, or necessary (the lack of a certificate is immaterial). Unimportant, not pertinent, not decisive, unnecessary, of no substantial consequence, of no material significance, insignificant, inconsequential, a matter of indifference, without substance, irrelevant, nonessential, trifling, petty, airy, inconsiderable, minor, worthless, unrelated, groundless, of little account, of little moment, without any bearing. See also extraneous, excess, baseless, frivolous, illusory. *Ant.* Germane.

Immaterial evidence Evidence offered to prove a proposition that is not in issue. See evidence.

Immaterial variance A discrepancy between the pleading and the proof that is so slight that a party cannot claim to have been misled thereby. See discrepancy.

Immature, *adj.* See juvenile (2); inchoate, imperfect, partial; amateur, beginner; crabby, difficult (3).

Immeasurable, *adj.* See incalculable, perpetual, permanent; big, great.

Immediate, *adj.* **1.** At once; not deferred by any interval of time (the allegation called for an immediate response). Prompt, without delay, speedy, instant, instantaneous, sudden, simultaneous, early, abrupt, punctual, swift, timely, present, quick, fast, rapid. **2.** Not separated by the intervention of any intermediate object, cause, or relation (immediate result). Direct, nearest, proximate, now, current, not distant, adjacent, close, contiguous, verging, close at hand, on hand, actual, existing, coterminous. *Ant.* Postponed; remote.

Immediate cause The last of a series or chain of causes tending to a given result, and which, of itself and without the intervention of any further cause, directly produces the result or event. See cause.

Immediately, *adv.* Without any delay or lapse of time (the court ordered him to return the car immediately). Forthwith, straightaway, instantly, tout de suite, at once, directly, right away, instantaneously, speedily, this instant, suddenly. See also summarily, now. *Ant.* Later.

Immemorial, *adj.* Beyond human memory (immemorial usage). Ancient, beyond recorded history, ancestral, dateless, archaic, long-standing, unchanging, customary, habitual. See also incalculable, perpetual, permanent, old. *Ant.* Recent.

Immense, *adj.* See big, great; incalculable.

Immerse, *v.* See submerge, inundate, imbue, fill, water.

Immersion, *n.* See concentration (1), preoccupation; absorption.

Immigrant, *n.* A foreigner who comes into a country with the intention to live there permanently (illegal immigrant). Non-native, expatriate, outsider, migrant; emigrant. See also alien (3).

Immigrate, *v.* See immigration; enter, move (2), depart, leave (2); emigration.

Immigration, *n.* The entry of foreigners into a country for purposes of permanent residence (immigration quotas). Migration, admission, expatriation, alien entry, transmigration, ingress.

Immigration and Naturalization Service (INS) A federal agency responsible for administering the immigration and naturalization laws relating to the admission, exclusion, deportation, and naturalization of aliens.

Imminent, *adj.* Near at hand; threatening (imminent death). Close, probable, gathering, overhanging, ominous, looming, forthcoming, in the wind, momentary, alarming, expected, next, in view, impending, mediate, on the point of happening, menacing, perilous, approaching, proximate, inescapable, brewing, coming, unavoidable, upcoming, inevitable, likely, forecasted, foreseeable. See also prospective. *Ant.* Remote, contingent.

Imminently dangerous article An article that is reasonably certain to place life or limb in peril. See dangerous.

Imminent peril Such position of danger to the plaintiff that if existing circumstances remain unchanged, injury to the plaintiff is reasonably certain. See danger, peril.

Immobile, *adj.* See inflexible, stationary, firm, dormant.

Immobilize, *v.* See impede, hinder, obstruct (1), abort (2), check (1, 5), gag, frustrate, arrest (3), clog, bar (5), deter.

Immoderate, *adj.* Not within reasonable limits (immoderate consumption of liquor). Excessive, undue, self-indulgent, inordinate, unconscionable, extravagant, gargantuan, intemperate, prodigious, unreasonable, unrestrained, exorbitant, unwarranted, exaggerated, squandering, unlimited. See also decadent, excess. *Ant.* Restrained.

Immodest, *adj.* See repulsive, odious, repugnant, offensive, bad (2); obscene, indecent, filthy; wanton, reckless; arrogant, rude.

Immoral, *adj.* Contrary to good morals; inimical to public welfare according to the standards of a given community as expressed through laws and otherwise (immoral contract for prostitution). Unprincipled, impure, evil, dissolute, vicious, depraved, polluted, iniquitous, unscrupulous, heinous, unethical, reprobate, blameworthy, culpable, flagrant, unconscionable, irredeemable, debased, irreverent, incorrigible, scandalous, licentious, dissipated, wicked, self-indulgent, sinful, loose, infamous, lewd, debauched, amoral, unwholesome, dishonorable, pernicious, vile, shameless, hardened, profligate, nefarious, perverted, foul, libertine, prurient, disreputable, promiscuous, ignoble, unlawful, exploitative, objectionable. *Ant.* Virtuous. See also illicit, base (2), corrupt (1), cruel, wrong, obscene, bad, illegal.

Immorality, *n.* See debauchery, wrong (1), corruption, fault, delinquency, lapse (3).

Immortal, *adj.* See perpetual, permanent, indestructible, incalculable; God; holy; religious.

Immortalize, *v.* See honor (2); conserve.

Immovable, *adj.* See stationary, firm; inflexible, dormant; permanent, perpetual; indifferent, callous; irreconcilable.

Immovables, *n.* Land and those things so firmly attached to it as to be regarded as part of it; property that cannot be moved (immovables transferred in her will). Fixed assets, fixtures, real estate, property affixed to the land, realty. See also property, land.

Immune, *adj.* Protected or exempt (immune from liability). Free, not susceptible to, privileged, inoculated, invulnerable, safe, resistant, absolved, unaffected, impregnable, released, inaccessible, excused, sheltered, unthreatened, inviolable. *Ant.* Susceptible.

Immunity, *n.* Exemption or freedom from a duty, penalty, or liability (immunity from prosecution; tort immunity). Special privilege or treatment, release, safety, license, prerogative, insusceptibility, absolution, indemnity, liberty, charter. See also protection, insurance. *Ant.* Responsibility, vulnerability.

Immunization, *n.* The condition of being or the act of rendering one immune or protected, especially from communicable disease (flu immunization program).

Immunize, *v.* See inoculate, defend, preserve, conserve, oversee, shelter, fortify, guard; treatment, medicine.

Immure, *v.* See confine (1), incarcerate.

Immutable, *adj.* See permanent, perpetual, certain (3), inflexible, firm, inevitable.

Imp, *n.* See delinquent (3); juvenile.

Impact, *n.* **1.** Effect or influence (the impact of the decision). Repercussion, consequence, implication, thrust, burden, brunt, bearing, impression. **2.** Collision (death upon impact). Clash, crash, shock, encounter, blow, contact, concussion, stroke, meeting, touch, percussion, force, impression, slam, striking, thump, impingement.

Impacted area An area whose school district has been burdened because of attendance by the children of a large number of federal employees and which may be losing tax revenues because of the U.S. government's immunity from land taxes.

Impair, *v.* To weaken or otherwise affect in an injurious manner (the injunction impaired the effectiveness of the protest). Make worse, lessen in power, diminish, relax, damage, worsen, contaminate, pollute, paralyze, hinder, undermine, demolish, debilitate, adulterate, water down, deteriorate, sap, stifle, devalue, vitiate, obstruct, mar, depreciate, pervert, spoil, debase, corrupt, stain, vulgarize, dilute, tarnish, deplete, rob, reduce, afflict, exhaust, enervate, devitalize, impoverish, prostrate, milk, sabotage, blight, destroy, subvert, cripple, undercut, enfeeble, deplete, taint, erode, blemish, shatter, deface, attenuate. *Ant.* Strengthen.

Impaired capital Condition of a business when the surplus account shows a negative balance, and hence the capital is reduced below its value from when the stock was issued. See capital.

Impairment, *n.* See defect, error, blockade, obstruction, bar (3), liability (2), inconvenience, constraint (1), block (1), limitation (1), cloud (1), restraint (1).

Impair the obligation of contracts To render the contract less valuable or less enforceable by changing its terms or the availability of remedies for its enforcement; to nullify or materially change existing contract obligations.

Impalpable, *adj.* See intangible; ambiguous; hypothetical.

Impanel, *v.* To make a list of jurors who have been selected for the trial of a particular case (impanel a jury). Enroll, enter, register, sign, calendar, docket, schedule, list.

Impart, *v.* See communicate, report, disclose; dispense, grant (1).

Impartial, *adj.* Favoring neither side; not prejudging the merits of the case (impartial tribunal). Fair, disinterested, unbiased, treating all alike, just, equitable, judicious, nonpartisan, open-minded, unswayed, reasonable, detached, uncolored, honorable, neutral, unprejudiced, evenhanded, dispassionate, objective, independent. *Ant.* Discriminatory.

Impasse, *n.* See dilemma, deadlock, blockade, block (1), bar (3), obstruction, complication, prevention, limit (2).

Impassioned, *adj.* See ardent, emotional, hot (2), feverish.

Impassive, *adj.* See indifferent, quiet (1, 2); reserve (4), composure; dispassionate.

Impatience, *n.* Restlessness. See anxiety, anguish.

Impatient, *adj.* Uneasy. Restless, nervous, tense, high-strung, edgy, jittery, jumpy, anxious. See also feverish, excitable; crabby, difficult (3), rude.

Impeach, *v.* To attack; to accuse; to challenge the credibility of (impeach the witness). Dispute, contradict, disparage, sue, charge, malign, denounce, indict, upbraid, stigmatize, vituperate, reprimand, implicate, decry, impugn, call to account, blame, ridicule, admonish, rebuff, allege, discredit, deprecate, criticize, recriminate, incriminate, brand, denigrate, fault. See also censure. *Ant.* Extol.

Impeachment, *n.* **1.** An attack because of impropriety or lack of veracity (impeachment of verdict; impeachment of witness). See attack (2), impeach. **2.** A procedure against a public officer before a quasi-political court (e.g., a legislative body), instituted by a written accusation called articles of impeachment. See impeach; indictment, complaint, charge.

Impeccable, *adj.* See blameless, perfect, clear, clean, correct (1).

Impecunious, *adj.* See indigent, destitute, bankrupt.

Impede, *v.* To obstruct or delay (the stockholder's attempt to impede the sale). Block, check, hinder, clog, inhibit, thwart, embargo, discourage, oppose, make difficult, bottleneck, drag down, counteract, limit, resist, shackle, use red tape against, frustrate, slow down, hamper, disrupt, stymie, retard, arrest, mar, decelerate, annul, invalidate, inconvenience, restrain, quash, estop, burden, suppress, place a barrier, postpone, slacken, fetter, detain, foreclose, circumscribe, suffocate, barricade, encumber, deadlock, blockade, paralyze, embarrass, deter, contravene, confound, bar, sabotage, handicap, repress, intercept, checkmate, neutralize. *Ant.* Facilitate.

Impediment, *n.* Disability or hindrance to the making of a contract (the impediment of infancy). See blockade, obstruction, defect, limitation (1), inconvenience, complication, block (1), blockage (1), cloud (1), deterrent; disease, illness; impede.

Impediment to marriage A legal obstacle to contracting a valid marriage (e.g., being under age). See annulment, divorce.

Impel, *v.* See induce, incite; force (4), constrain.

Impending, *adj.* See imminent, future, prospective; final.

Impenetrable, *adj.* See invulnerable, immune; callous; ambiguous, mysterious, complex, equivocal.

Imperative, *adj.* Urgent, mandatory (it is imperative that the complaint be filed within 2 years). Obligatory, crucial, pressing, necessary, unavoidable, vital, requisite, critical, essential, binding, demanded, insistent, decisive, required, demanding, needful, indispensable, exigent. See also inescapable, compulsory, compelling, important. *Ant.* Optional.

Imperceptible, *adj.* See intangible; gradual; small (1), minor (2), minimal; hidden; indefinite, ambiguous.

Imperceptive, *adj.* See blind (1), latent, dumb, juvenile (2), absurd, irrational.

Imperfect, *adj.* Defective or incomplete (imperfect description). Deficient, faulty, flawed, inoperative, deformed, ruined, inferior, crude, deteriorated, hurt, lame, tainted, unsatisfactory, unacceptable, unsuitable, injured, decrepit, warped, mediocre, inexact, sloppy, feeble, damaged, marred, unsound, unfinished, partial, immature, undeveloped, limited. See also inadequate, corrupt, weak; inchoate. *Ant.* Flawless.

Imperfection, *n.* See defect, deficiency, failure, error, fault (1); imperfect.

Imperial, *adj.* See arbitrary (2); pompous, arrogant; sovereign.

Imperil, *v.* See endanger, expose (2).

Imperious, *adj.* See peremptory (3), pompous, arrogant, dominant, arbitrary.

Impermanent, *adj.* See temporary, transitory, weak, frail, perishable, brief (4).

Impermeable, *adj.* See invulnerable, immune; remote (1); compact.

Impermissible, *adj.* See illicit, illegal, immoral, criminal, wrong, inadmissible.

Impersonal, *adj.* See indifferent, callous, formal, remote; dispassionate, neutral, objective (2).

Impersonate, *v.* To pretend or represent oneself to be another (the crime of impersonating an officer). Simulate, imitate, parody, assume the guise of, personate, mirror, monkey, echo, mimic, caricature, pose, masquerade, pass oneself off as, ape, mime, assume the role of, parrot, portray, act, burlesque.

Impersonation, *n.* See imitation, copy; fraud.

Impertinence, *n.* See effrontery, insolence.

Impertinent, *adj.* **1.** Irrelevant (strike impertinent material from the pleading). Inapposite, outside the issues, beyond the mark, not germane, inapplicable, unrelated, beside the point, off the subject, incidental, disconnected, unimportant, not pertinent, inappropriate; surplusage. See also alien (2), extraneous, extrinsic (2), foreign (3), immaterial. **2.** Rude (impertinent behavior). Rash, insolent, crude, vulgar, impudent, disrespectful, audacious, brazen, presumptuous, uncivil, abusive, discourteous, insulting, bellicose, unrefined, irreverent, surly, coarse, scoffing, provocative, defiant, insubordinate. See also rude, arrogant, contemptuous. *Ant.* Germane; deferential.

Impervious, *adj.* See immune, invulnerable; remote; callous; permanent, perpetual.

Impetuous, *adj.* Hasty, impulsive. Brash, precipitate, offhand, fickle, abrupt, swift, unrestrainable, headstrong, obstinate, hot-blooded, headlong. See also careless, reckless, emotional, capricious, violent.

Impetus, *n.* See motivation, motive, impulse, cause (1), catalyst.

Impinge, *v.* See encroach, interfere, break (1), hinder, impede; attack (1), assault (3); collide; affect (1).

Impious, *adj.* See irreverent, profane (1); rude; blasphemy.

Impish, *adj.* See juvenile; vexatious; antic.

Implacable, *adj.* See irreconcilable, firm, inflexible; close (5); inhuman.

Implausible, *adj.* See doubtful (2), improbable, absurd, anomalous, extraordinary, irrational, wild, outrageous.

Implead, *v.* To bring a new party into the action on the ground that the new party is or may be liable for all or part of the current claim to the party bringing him or her in. See pleading.

Impleader, *n.* The procedure by which a new party is impleaded. See implead.

Implement 1. *n.* A tool used for trade or farming (obsolete implements for rescue operations). Tool, utensil, material, contrivance, gadget, mechanism, machine, gear, appliance, means, agent, wherewithal, resources. See also apparatus, instrument (2), equipment, device. **2.** *v.* To carry out (the agency must implement the statute). Execute, carry through, actualize, realize, accomplish, enforce, start, complete, expedite, bring about, fulfill, begin, enact, set in motion, consummate, discharge, effectuate. See also perform.

Implicate, *v.* To connect a person with something; to accuse (the report implicated the mayor). Involve, incriminate, embroil, inculpate, associate, catch, net, ensnare, criminate, enmesh, link, draw in, entangle. See also charge, accuse. *Ant.* Dissociate.

Implication, *n.* **1.** An inference of something not directly said but arising from what is admitted or expressed (an implication of guilt). Suggestion, connotation, innuendo, allusion, indication, insinuation, ramification, significance, intimation, import, drift, meaning, assumption, purport, hint, reference, interpretation. See also intent. **2.** The act of implicating. See indictment, accusation; implicate.

Implicit, *adj.* See implied; constructive (1); deduce; inherent; latent; complete (2), perfect, full.

Implied, *adj.* Gathered by implication or deduction from the circumstances (implied rejection). Implicit, suggested, inferred, tacit, assumed, understood, insinuated, deduced, unexpressed, unvoiced, unstated, acknowledged, taken-for-granted, symbolized, unspoken, intimated. See also constructive (1); deduce, reason; silent (2). *Ant.* Express.

Implied authority Actual power given by a principal to his or her agent, which necessarily follows from the express authority that is given; authority that is necessary, usual, and proper to accomplish the main authority that is expressly conferred. See authority; agency; agent.

Implied consent Signs, actions, facts, inaction, or silence that raise a presumption that consent has been given. See consent, approval.

Implied contract A contract not created or evidenced by the explicit agreement of the parties but inferred as a matter of reason and justice from their conduct and the surrounding circumstances; a contract that exists by the tacit understanding of the parties. See contract.

Implied promise A fiction that the law creates to render one liable on a contract theory in order to avoid fraud or unjust enrichment. See contract; fraud.

Implied reservation An easement created by a grantor for the benefit of land retained by him or her and not included in the conveyance. See easement.

Implied warranty A warranty imposed by operation of law regardless of the intent of the parties; a warranty that is based on the apparent intentions of the parties. See warranty of fitness for a particular purpose, warranty of habitability, warranty of merchantability.

Implore, *v.* See apply (1), petition (2), beseech, solicit, press (2).

Imply, *v.* See suggest, intimate (6); intend, mean (2); express (2); reason (3), argue, deduce.

Impolite, *adj.* See rude, impertinent (2).

Impolitic, *adj.* See improper, dumb, improvident, careless, rude.

Imponderable, *adj.* See incoherent, ambiguous; intangible; big; extraordinary.

Import, *v.*, **import,** *n.* **1.** *v.* To bring goods into a country from a foreign country (they import the equipment). Introduce, carry, transport, haul, convey, ship, cart, freight, truck, move. **2.** *n.* Importance, significance (everyone pondered the import of the decision). Meaning, seriousness, point, substance, core, heart, moment, gravity, ramification, thrust, connotation, value, intent, weight, emphasis, force, repercussion. See also essence, gist, implication, importance. *Ant.* Export; insignificance.

Importance, *n.* The condition of being important (the importance of the decision cannot be overestimated). Significance, influence, moment, seriousness, distinction, import, relevance, worth, weight, urgency, value, gravity, consequence, substance, primacy, noteworthiness, magnitude, concern, eminence, prominence, merit, precedence. *Ant.* Triviality.

Important, *adj.* Having special influence or meaning (the court made an important contribution to tort law). Valuable, leading, material, far-reaching, considerable, serious, crucial, large, chief, original, well-known, formidable, consequential, major, prime, commanding, essential, distinguished, sizable, seminal, critical, heavy, superior, authoritative, respected, grand, esteemed, illustrative, preeminent, salient, creative, remarkable, substantive, notable, substantial, capital, famous, imposing, supreme. See also outstanding, effective, primary (1). *Ant.* Negligible.

Importune, *v.* To make an urgent request (they importuned the judge to waive the defect). Beg earnestly, implore, cajole, solicit, sue, pray, urge, plague, beset, appeal, imprecate, plead, supplicate, hound, pester. See also press (2), apply (1), petition (2), beseech; solicit; harass, entice.

Impose, *v.* To inflict, thrust, or levy (impose a tax; impose yourself). Burden, encumber, demand, require, charge, necessitate, command, prescribe, exact, institute, dictate, apply, exert, enact, lay on, place on, place, saddle, force, extort, enforce, direct, execute, order, oblige, press, constrain, subjugate, subject, overcome, compel, intrude, invade, trespass, exploit, interfere, trouble, inconvenience, foist, bother. *Ant.* Withdraw.

Imposing, *adj.* See elevated; important, outstanding (2); big.

Imposition, *n.* An unreasonable request or burden; a tax or impost; the act of imposing. See burden (1); impose; impediment, duties.

Impossibility, *n.* That which no person in the course of nature or the law can do or perform; that which can be done only at an excessive and unreasonable cost (the impossibility of making the delivery on time). Futility, insurmountability, hopelessness, impracticality, infeasibility, unattainability, unworkability, inconceivability. See also impotence (2).

Impossibility of performance Strict impossibility or impracticality because of extreme and unreasonable difficulty, expense, or loss.

Impossible, *adj.* Not capable of being done (impossible demands). Unachievable, absurd, illogical, hopeless, inconceivable, unworkable, incredible, unbelievable, out of the question, unfeasible, beyond reason, intolerable, unattainable, intransigent, impractical, untenable, beyond reach, ridiculous, contradictory, preposterous, unobtainable, unimaginable, unreasonable, unthinkable, unreal. See also extraordinary, fallacious, exorbitant. *Ant.* Feasible.

Impostor, *n.* See wrongdoer, cheat (2); impersonate.

Imposts, *n.* Taxes, duties, or impositions that are levied. See duties, levy, tax.

Impotence, *n.* **1.** The organic, mental, or functional inability to perform the act of sexual intercourse (impotence was alleged as one of the grounds for the annulment). **2.** Powerlessness (the impotence of the commission). Weakness, ineffectiveness, incapacity, helplessness, senility, futility, paralysis, fruitlessness, sterility, fallowness, debility, ineptitude, effeteness, feebleness, barrenness, frailty, debilitation. See also impossibility. *Ant.* Virility; potency.

Impotent, *adj.* See barren (2), worthless (1), unable, fallow, invalid (1), abortive, weak, frail, dead (3); impotence; ill-fated.

Impound, *v.* To seize and take into custody of the law (the police impounded the car). Sequester, take possession of, attach, appropriate, expropriate, fence, secure, confiscate, confine, incarcerate, distrain, imprison, encage. See also seize. *Ant.* Release.

Impoverish, *v.* See exhaust.

Impoverished, *adj.* See indigent, destitute, bankrupt; barren; exhausted.

Impracticable, *adj.* Not capable of being accomplished (an impracticable court order). Unattainable, useless, hopeless, far-fetched, unfeasible, unrealizable, unsuitable, unachievable, unworkable, impractical, impossible, inoperable, unmanageable, rash, inexpedient, quixotic, theoretical, romantic. *Ant.* Feasible.

Impractical, *adj.* See impracticable, impossible, improbable, speculative, difficult, absurd, insane (2).

Imprecate, *v.* See condemn, slander.

Imprecise, *adj.* See approximate (3); wrong (3), false; error.

Impregnable, *adj.* See invulnerable, safe, inviolate, immune.

Impregnate, *v.* **1.** To make pregnant. Inseminate, fertilize, fecundate. See also beget. **2.** See inundate, imbue, fill.

Impresario, *n.* See manager.

Impress, *v.* **1.** To influence greatly (the judge was not impressed by the argument). Sway, arouse, inspire, move, electrify, stimulate, provoke, thrill, amaze, pierce, touch, affect, excite, stir, awe, rouse, galvanize, overwhelm. See also influence (2), persuade. **2.** To seize persons or property for some government purpose (e.g., military needs). See conscript, conscription.

Impression, *n.* **1.** See first impression, case of. **2.** A feeling about something (an initial impression of the witness). Belief, notion, intuition, consciousness, thought, understanding, conviction, conception, opinion, hunch, sensation, image, reaction, response. **3.** Influence (the demonstration made an impression on the jury). Effect, imprint, sensation, mark. See also impact. **4.** See mark, manifestation.

Impressionable, *adj.* See susceptible, malleable, amenable (2), formative, flexible; innocent.

Impressive, *adj.* See outstanding (2), elevated, important, effective, attractive, beautiful, intriguing.

Imprimatur, *n.* Let it be printed; authorization, license, or sanction. See indorsement (2), ratification, approval, license (1), mark.

Imprint, *n.*, **imprint,** *v.* See manifestation; engrave, label.

Imprison, *v.* To place in confinement (the defendant was imprisoned following the sentence). Restrain, immure, jail, detain, lock up, hold in captivity, commit, impound, impress, intern, entomb, fence in, shackle, circumscribe, deprive of liberty. See also confine (1), incarcerate; surround. *Ant.* Release.

Imprisonment, *n.* See detention; jail (1); imprison.

Improbable, *adj.* Unlikely to be true or to occur; not to be readily believed (a favorable verdict was improbable). Doubtful, unforeseeable, implausible, inconceivable, dubious, unthinkable, ridiculous, questionable, unreasonable, impractical, absurd, a long shot, highly uncertain, unexpected, chancy. See also impossible. *Ant.* Likely.

Impromptu, *adj.* See spontaneous, fortuitous, sudden.

Improper, *adj.* Not in accordance with fact, truth, procedure, or good taste (improper expenditure). Wrong, false, untrue, incorrect, unlawful, unsuitable, unfit, inappropriate, unseemly, inapt, unbecoming, irregular, indecent, out of place, erroneous, faulty, untimely, inconvenient, unseasonable, inapplicable, unsound, mistaken, undesirable, irrelevant, discordant, impolitic, underhanded, inopportune, inadvisable, unwarranted, fraudulent, unprincipled, untrustworthy, deceitful, devious, insincere, treacherous, unreliable, awkward, unreasonable, objectionable, inadmissible, forbidden, indelicate, unallowed, undue. See also illicit, illegal, corrupt, dishonest, deceptive, immoral, offensive. *Ant.* Fitting.

Impropriety, *n.* See blunder (1), error, omission, neglect (2), mistake, fault (1), nonfeasance, lapse (3).

Improve, *v.* To make better; to increase the value of something (the reforms failed to improve the system). Redress, correct, ameliorate, meliorate, upgrade, enhance, fix, help, repair, refresh, overhaul, rectify, humanize, civilize, rewrite, revamp, progress, further, advance, promote, polish, enrich, elevate, recondition, rearrange, reorganize, regenerate, remodel, revive, remedy, redeem, edify, educate, modernize, refurbish, clean, refine, purge, purify, amend, perfect, develop, revise, cultivate, make productive, right, mend, illuminate. See also rehabilitate, heal, cure, strengthen. *Ant.* Damage.

Improved land Real estate whose value has been increased by the addition of sewers, roads, utilities, etc. See appreciation (1).

Improvement, *n.* A valuable addition made to property or an amelioration of its condition, costing labor and capital and intended to enhance its value, utility, or beauty, or to adapt it for new or further purposes; permanent addition to or betterment of property that enhances its capital value beyond mere repairs or replacement. See correction (2), betterment (2), amelioration, appreciation (1), endowment; decoration; increase; improve.

Improvident, *adj.* Lacking in care and foresight (the improvident administrator of the estate was dismissed). Careless, unwise, spendthrift, reckless, negligent, extravagant, unthinking, heedless, imprudent, profligate, remiss, wasteful, shortsighted, thriftless, lavish, lax, inattentive, uneconomical, shiftless, feckless, indiscreet, lackadaisical, impulsive, headstrong, dissipated. See also precipitate (2), prodigal. *Ant.* Prudent.

Improvise, *v.* See create; spontaneous.

Imprudent, *adj.* See careless, impetuous, dumb, lunatic, improvident, improper, neglect (2).

Impudence, *n.* See effrontery, insolence, insubordination.

Impudent, *adj.* See rude, offensive, impertinent (2), odious.

Impugn, *v.* See slander, decry, attack, disparage, defame, impute, challenge, confront, counter.

Impulse, *n.* A sudden urge or thrusting force within a person (the impulse to steal). Inclination, emotion, bent, appetite, force, motive, impelling force, encouragement, propensity, desire, drive, impetus, mania, itch, boost, incentive, stimulus, lust, passion, spur, need, penchant, instinct. *Ant.* Deliberation.

Impulsive, *adj.* See impetuous, sudden, improvident, spontaneous, careless, reckless, emotional, excitable, capricious.

Impunity, *n.* Exemption or protection from penalty or punishment (the money was taken with impunity). Privilege, freedom, absolution, license, immunity, release, pardon, nonliability, amnesty, clearance, prerogative. *Ant.* Sanction.

Impure, *adj.* See immoral, corrupt, bad, base, wrong, obscene, filthy, dirty.

Impurity, *n.* See corruption, pollution, debauchery; obscene, pornographic.

Imputation, *n.* See attribution; accusation; impute.

Impute, *v.* To charge or attribute (she denied responsibility for the crimes imputed to her). Blame, accuse, credit, associate, fix, implicate, arrogate, connect, assign, refer, ascribe, lay at the door of, allege, brand, cite, drag, saddle, defame, misrepresent, impugn. See also charge. *Ant.* Exonerate.

Imputed, *adj.* Attributed vicariously; making one person responsible for the actions, omissions, or knowledge of another because of that person's relationship with the other. See impute, attribute, assign; attribution.

Imputed income A value or monetary worth that is assigned to certain property, transactions, or situations for tax purposes, e.g., the value of a home provided by an employer for an employee. See income, tax.

Imputed knowledge Implied notice; knowledge attributed or charged to a person because the facts in question were open to his or her inspection, and his or her duty was to be aware of them. See knowledge.

Imputed negligence One person responsible for the negligence of another because of the relationship between them, e.g., the negligence of an employee within the scope of employment is imputed to the employer. See negligence.

Inability, *n.* See incapacity, impotence, impossibility, defect, incompetence.

Inaccessible, *adj.* See remote (1), frozen; barren.

Inaccurate, *adj.* See wrong (3), false, erroneous.

Inactive, *adj.* See dormant, silent (2), latent, lazy; abeyance.

Inadequate, *adj.* Lacking in effectiveness; nonconformity to a prescribed standard or measure (inadequate warning). Incomplete, slight, wanting, unsatisfactory, mediocre, incompetent, scant, short, sparse, scarce, low, slender, failing, substandard, defective, disappointing, inept, inefficient, flawed, below par, powerless, unqualified, meager, ineffective, disabled, feeble, undeveloped, impotent, ineffectual, poor. See also weak, frail, deficient, imperfect, insufficient, inferior (2). *Ant.* Sufficient.

Inadequate remedy at law An ineffective legal remedy; the remedy in its nature and character is unfitted or not adapted to the end sought (e.g., collecting damages would be an inadequate remedy to get the defendant to stop poisoning the plaintiff's prize dogs; only an injunction will be adequate). See remedy.

Inadmissible, *adj.* Pertaining to evidence that cannot be received and considered (inadmissible hearsay). Objectionable, banned, unallowable, excludable, disallowed, not allowed, unacceptable, unwelcome, barred, incompetent, inappropriate. See also improper, illegal, imperfect. *Ant.* Admissible.

Inadvertent, *adj.* Careless, accidental (inadvertent failure to file). Unpremeditated, neglectful, heedless, unmeant, thoughtless, unintentional, chance, unplanned, unthinking, unwary, fortuitous, unmindful, inattentive, absent-minded, unreflecting. See also involuntary; lapse (3). *Ant.* Deliberate.

Inadvisable, *adj.* See improvident, irrational, dumb, impracticable.

Inalienable, *adj.* Incapable of being bought, sold, or transferred (inalienable right to believe). Nontransferable, absolute, inviolate, indefeasible, permanent, unforfeitable, inviolable, inherent, sacrosanct, unassailable.

Inane, *adj.* See worthless, barren, dumb, lunatic, irrational, backward, dead (2).

Inanimate, *adj.* See dead; dormant, stationary.

Inapplicable, *adj.* See extraneous, irrelevant, immaterial; inconsistent, improper.

Inapposite, *adj.* See irrelevant, extraneous, immaterial; disproportionate, impracticable.

Inappropriate, *adj.* See improper, impracticable, inconvenient, ineligible, inconsistent, incompatible, disproportionate; dumb, wild, irrational, invalid (1).

Inarticulate, *adj.* See incoherent, inconsistent; ambiguous, silent (1), mute.

Inattentive, *adj.* See negligent, careless, heedless; impertinent, rude.

Inaudible, *adj.* See silent (3).

Inaugural, *adj.* See maiden (1), first.

Inaugurate, *v.* See launch, institute, initiate, install, commence; provoke; inauguration.

Inauguration, *n.* The act and ceremony of installing or inducting into office (the inauguration of the governor). Induction, consecration, initiation, installation, investiture, swearing in, ushering in, launching, institution, origination, activation, commencement, introduction, breaking ground.

Inauspicious, *adj.* See ill-fated; adverse (2), deleterious, bad (4).

In banc See en banc.

In being In existence.

In-between, *adj.* See intermediate, middle.

Inborn, *adj.* See congenital, inherent, intrinsic, native (3); mechanical, involuntary.

In bulk Without division or separation into packages or parcels (sold in bulk). As an entirety, as a whole. See also whole, bulk (1).

Inc. Incorporated. See corporation; incorporate.

Incalculable, *adj.* Inestimable. Boundless, unfathomable, measureless, limitless, immeasurable, inexhaustible, endless, interminable, countless, infinite, vast. See also perpetual, permanent; many; big, great. *Ant.* Finite.

In camera In private with the judge; in chambers; without spectators (hearing held in camera). See secret.

Incandescent, *adj.* See clear (3); burn, fire, light.

Incapable, *adj.* See incompetent, weak, decrepit, frail, inferior (2), deficient, imperfect, inadequate, insufficient.

Incapacitate, *v.* To deprive of power or strength (the accident incapacitated the defendant). Paralyze, sideline, cripple, handicap, weaken, debilitate, undermine, inactivate, prostrate, sterilize, impair, neutralize, emasculate, deactivate, mar, enervate, immobilize, freeze, halt, destroy, disarm. See also disqualify, disable, maim, mutilate. *Ant.* Strengthen.

Incapacitated person A person who is impaired by reason of mental illness, mental deficiency, physical illness or disability, advanced age, or drug or alcohol addiction, to the extent of lacking sufficient understanding or capacity to make or communicate responsible decisions concerning his or her affairs. See insanity.

Incapacity, *n.* The absence of legal power or ability to act; the existence of an impediment preventing action (incapacity resulting from the injury). Inability, incapability, weakness, helplessness, inefficiency, lameness, immobilization, feebleness, powerlessness, dotage, incapacitation, impotence, unfitness, ineptitude, incompetence, infirmity. See also disability (1). *Ant.* Capacity.

Incarcerate, *v.* To imprison or confine (the defendant was incarcerated after the sentence). Jail, commit, intern, impound, impress, cage, immure, hold, restrain, pen, check, place under lock and key, enclose, restrict, hold captive, bind, corral. See also imprison. *Ant.* Liberate.

Incarceration, *n.* See detention; incarcerate, imprison, jail.

Incendiary 1. *adj.* Causing fire (incendiary device). Flammable, inflammable, ignitable, combustible. **2.** *adj.* Tending to inflame (incendiary remarks). Provocative, inflammatory, inciting, instigating, infuriating, seditious, rabble-rousing, subversive, fiery, stirring. See also outrageous. **3.** *n.* One who maliciously and willfully sets fire to the buildings of others. Arsonist, house burner, pyromaniac, inciter, agitator, firebrand. See also partisan (1), revolutionary.

Incense, *v.*, **incense,** *n.* See provoke, incite, harass; aggravated (2), angry; aroma, fragrant.

Incensed, *adj.* See angry, hot, emotional, hysterical, wild.

Incentive, *n.* See motivation, motive, catalyst, impulse, cause (1).

Inception, *n.* Commencement (the terms of the contract have not been met since its inception). Opening, initiation, beginning, start, source, genesis, birth, inauguration, debut, starting point, outset, installation, conception, onset, arrival. *Ant.* Termination.

Incessant, *adj.* See constant (1), perpetual, permanent, habitual, continuous, continual.

Incest, *n.* Sexual intercourse between a man and woman who are related to each other within prohibited degrees (e.g., brother and sister). See coitus.

In chief Principal; directly obtained; a term applied to the evidence obtained from a witness upon his or her examination by the party that called the witness, i.e., the direct examination of the witness (examination in chief). See primary.

Inchoate, *adj.* Begun but not completed; partial (inchoate instrument). Preliminary, incomplete, incipient, embryonic, developing, unfinished, fragmentary, accruing, undeveloped, rudimentary, unexecuted, nascent. See also primary, imperfect, dormant, inadequate. *Ant.* Perfected.

Inchoate crime A crime in its early stage, which generally leads to another crime (e.g., assault is an inchoate battery). See crime.

Inchoate dower A wife's interest in the land of her husband's during his life; a possibility of acquiring dower. See dower, expectancy, probability, chance (3).

Inchoate instrument If an instrument must be registered, it is inchoate prior to its registration. See instrument (1), record.

Inchoate interest An interest in land that is not a present interest but which can ripen into a vested interest if not barred, extinguished, or divested. See interest; expectancy.

Inchoate lien The lien of a judgment. See lien.

Incident 1. *adj.* Connected with or inherent in something else (a search incident to an arrest). Arising out of, in connection with, relating to, allied to, following upon, subsidiary to, associated with, linked with, dependent on, subordinate to, happening in the course of, naturally growing out of. **2.** *n.* An occurrence (testimony on the incident). Action, affair, occasion, happening, scene, event, phenomenon, transaction, episode, chapter, case, proceeding, experience, adventure, story, encounter, matter. See also fact, circumstances.

Incidental, *adj.* **1.** Depending upon and secondary to something else (incidental expenses). Subordinate, minor, accessory, extraneous, allied, dependent, circumstantial, nonessential, contingent, supplemental, parenthetic, additional, minor. **2.** Random (incidental comment). Unexpected, casual, indiscriminate, occasional, circumstantial, accidental. See also fortuitous, irregular. *Ant.* Principal; planned.

Incidental beneficiary Someone who benefits from the performance of a contract though not a party thereto. See beneficiary.

Incidental powers Such powers as are directly and immediately appropriate to the execution of the powers expressly granted. See power, authority.

Incidental use In zoning, the use of premises that is dependent on or affiliated with the principal use of such premises. See use, zoning.

Incident of ownership Ownership rights; a measure of control.

Incinerate, *v.* See burn, fire; incendiary (1).

Incipience, *n.* See infancy (2).

Incipient, *adj.* See inchoate, initial.

Incision, *n.* See cut; injury, medicine, surgery, doctor.

Incisive, *adj.* See acute (1), brilliant, able, capable (2); intimate (1); caustic; explicit, precise, concrete.

Incite, *v.* To urge; to instigate another to commit a crime (incite a riot). Arouse, encourage, spur on, goad, stir up, set in motion, persuade, motivate, further, abet, stimulate, foment, prod, activate, prompt, inflame, rouse, thrust, fire up, influence, force, animate, invigorate, coax, prevail upon, impel, rally, counsel, initiate, excite, egg on, exhort, forward, solicit, trigger, advocate, recommend, advise, inspire, press. See also induce, provoke, launch. *Ant.* Inhibit.

Incivility, *n.* See indignity; rude.

Inclement, *adj.* See violent, extreme (1), serious (2); storm; climate.

Inclination, *n.* See disposition (4), preference, manner, character, eccentricity, bias.

Incline, *n.*, incline, *v.* See grade (2); gravitate, tip (3).

Inclose, *v.* See enclose.

Inclosure, *n.* See enclosure.

Include, *v.* To contain; to place within (picketing is not included within the injunction). Encompass, take in, cover, involve, subsume, entail, incorporate, comprehend, embrace, enclose, comprise, enfold, place, envelop, make up, classify, group, count, categorize, register. *Ant.* Eliminate.

Included offense A crime that is part of another crime (e.g., an assault and battery is included within murder).

Inclusive, *adj.* **1.** Including the two extremes as well as what falls in between (twelve to fifteen inclusive). Without exception, taking in, comprehending, enclosing, containing, embracing from start to finish. **2.** Comprehensive (an inclusive list). Broad, sweeping, exhaustive, wide, encyclopedic, general, catch-all, all-embracing. See also comprehensive. *Ant.* Exclusive; incomplete.

Incognito, *adj.* See hidden, anonymous.

Incoherent, *adj.* Disconnected. Confused, unintelligible, jumbled, disorganized, incomprehensible, muddled, puzzling, indistinct, muffled. See also inconsistent, irrational, illegible, ambiguous, indefinite, absurd.

Income, *n.* The financial return or gain derived from one's business, labor, or invested capital (royalty income). Profit, wages, salary, earning, emolument, revenue, allowance, subsidy, payment, remuneration, proceeds, wealth, annuity, stipend, honorarium, fringes, winnings, pension, receipts, return, livelihood, means. See also compensation, yield. *Ant.* Losses.

Income averaging A method of computing income taxes by an individual who has unusually large income in the current taxable year as compared with the four prior years, whereby the taxpayer elects to have the excess taxed as if it had been received ratably over a 5-year period.

Income basis A method of computing the rate of return on a security based on the dividend or interest and on the price paid rather than on its face or par value.

Income tax A tax on the yearly profits arising from property, business pursuits, professions, trades, etc. See tax.

Incommensurate, *adj.* See disproportionate; insufficient, inadequate.

Incommodious, *adj.* See inconvenient.

Incommunicado, *adj., adv.* Without a way of communicating with others (she was held incommunicado). Isolated, cut off, separate, exiled, sequestered, segregated.

Incomparable, *adj.* See great (2), outstanding (2), extraordinary, superior (2).

Incompatible, *adj.* **1.** Disagreeing; characterized by deep and irreconcilable conflicts in personalities or temperaments so that it is impossible to live together normally (incompatible spouses). Antagonistic, inharmonious, unaccommodating, at odds, unsuitable, discordant, unsympathetic, jarring, uncongenial, hostile, clashing, mismatched, quarreling. **2.** Mutually exclusive (incompatible arguments). Contradictory, inconsistent, opposite, adverse, divergent, conflicting, counter, antithetical, unadaptable. *Ant.* Compatible.

Incompetence, *n.* See incapacity, neglect (2); inadequate, incompetent.

Incompetent, *adj.* **1.** Without ability, legal qualification, or fitness (mentally incompetent). Incapacitated, unable, deficient, disqualified, incapable, unsuitable, untrained, ineligible, inadequate. **2.** Inefficient (incompetent worker). Bungling, inept, ineffective, gauche, ignorant, maladroit, ineffectual, amateurish,

Incompetent

unskilled, inexperienced, useless, stupid, awkward, floundering. See also negligent, inadequate, insufficient, deficient, imperfect, inferior (2). *Ant.* Competent; skilled.

Incompetent evidence Evidence that is not admissible under the rules of evidence. See inadmissible, evidence.

Incomplete, *adj.* See partial, separate; imperfect, inadequate, insufficient, deficient, incompetent; inchoate.

Incomprehensible, *adj.* See incoherent, ambiguous, mysterious, obscure, illegible; complex (1); irrational, inconsistent.

Inconceivable, *adj.* See doubtful, improbable, impossible, irrational, absurd, wild, anomalous, extraordinary, outrageous.

Inconclusive, *adj.* Not final; capable of being disproved or rebutted (inconclusive presentation). Unproven, undemonstrated, unpersuasive, hollow, indecisive, indefinite, weak, unsettled, unsubstantiated, undetermined, tenuous, unconvincing, flimsy, open, uncorroborated, unestablished, eluding, vague, fallible, unconfirmed. See also disputable, doubtful (1), ambiguous. *Ant.* Decisive.

Incongruous, *adj.* See improper, impracticable, inconsistent, incompatible, odd, anomalous, irrational, wild.

Inconsequential, *adj.* See petty (2), nugatory, frivolous.

Inconsiderate, *adj.* See rude; caustic; heedless, careless.

Inconsistent, *adj.* **1.** Mutually repugnant in the sense that acceptance of one implies the abandonment of the other (inconsistent defenses). Contradictory, contrary, illogical, conflicting, irreconcilable, incompatible, at odds, at variance, incongruous, antagonistic, discordant, inimical, clashing, adverse, uncongenial, antipathetic, dissonant, inconsonant, inharmonious, averse, opposing, opposed, jarring. See also hostile, alien. **2.** Erratic (the discipline was inconsistent). Fickle, unsteady, changeable, incoherent, vacillating, volatile, unbalanced, haphazard, mutable, flighty. See also capricious, fluctuating. *Ant.* Consistent.

Inconspicuous, *adj.* See small, minimal, minor (2); hidden.

In contemplation of death With a view toward death. A transfer made within 3 years of the decedent's death is deemed to be made in contemplation of death for federal estate tax purposes, resulting in the inclusion of the value of the property in the decedent's estate. See contemplation; death; tax.

Incontestability clause A clause in an insurance policy providing that after the policy has been in effect a certain length of time (e.g., 2 years), the insurer cannot contest it as to statements made in the application. See noncontestable, incontestable; insurance.

Incontestable, *adj.* Incapable of being disputed (incontestable assertion). Irrefutable, unimpeachable, clear, beyond question, indisputable, unassailable, absolute, unquestionable, undeniable, final, unequivocal, impregnable, peremptory. See also noncontestable, definitive, conclusive, certain (3); irrevocable, indestructible, perpetual, permanent. *Ant.* Questionable.

Incontinent, *adj.* **1.** Lacking moderation; unchaste (incontinent personality). Uncontrolled, unrestrained, lacking self-restraint, wanton; immoral, licentious, bestial, libertine, promiscuous, lecherous, lewd. See also disorderly (1), obscene, dissolute, immoderate; intemperance. **2.** Not being able to control urination or defecation.

Incontrovertible, *adj.* See incontestable, noncontestable, definitive, conclusive, certain (3).

Inconvenience, *n.* An annoyance or difficulty (a mere inconvenience). Nuisance, hardship, trouble, awkwardness, bother, burden, pain, drawback, hindrance, disadvantage, impediment, encumbrance, disturbance, untimeliness, imposition, irritation, vexation, obstruction. See also annoyance, limit (2). *Ant.* Advantage.

Inconvenient, *adj.* Annoying. Burdensome, untimely, troublesome, distressing, inopportune, bothersome, ill-timed, inappropriate, distracting. See also improper, awkward, difficult, onerous.

Incorporate, *v.* **1.** To create a corporation (Jones Chemical, Inc. was incorporated in Delaware). Form, organize, charter, establish, start, file, affiliate. See also launch, initiate. **2.** To unite or fuse (the new allegation was incorporated in the report). Encompass, embody, blend, weave, absorb, coalesce, take in, merge, consolidate, assimilate, introduce into, comprise, couple, compound, compact, express, personify, amalgamate. See also include, combine.

Incorporation, *n.* See merger, amalgamation; include, incorporate (2).

Incorporation by reference The method of making one document a part of another separate document by referring to the former in the latter and declaring that the former shall be considered part of the latter.

Incorporator, *n.* A person who joins with others to form a corporation. See entrepreneur, producer, developer.

Incorporeal, *adj.* Not of a material nature; intangible (incorporeal rights). Bodiless, nonphysical, discarnate, spiritual, immaterial, ethereal, phantom, airy, disembodied. See also intangible. *Ant.* Corporeal.

Incorporeal hereditament A right growing out of or concerning a corporeal thing (e.g., the right to dispose of water onto the property of another). See hereditament, property.

Incorporeal right Rights to intangibles such as legal actions rather than rights to property. See right (3), interest.

Incorrect, *adj.* See erroneous, wrong (3), false; improper, impracticable, inconvenient, incompatible, disproportionate; irrational.

Incorrigible, *adj.* Incapable of being corrected (an incorrigible delinquent). Unmanageable, unreformable, hopeless, intractable, uncontrollable, beyond saving, unruly, hard-core, ungovernable, hardened, irremediable, depraved, inveterate, lost cause, chronic, obstinate, reprobate, unsalvageable, wicked, obdurate, iniquitous. See also disobedient, bad (2), disorderly; incurable, irreparable; inflexible, difficult (3); hysterical. *Ant.* Amenable.

Incorruptibility, *n.* See integrity.

Incorruptible, *adj.* Not capable of being influenced by dishonesty or other immorality (an incorruptible judge). Above reproach, unimpeachable, faultless, righteous, trustworthy, reliable, impeccable, conscientious, honorable, stainless, constant, unblemished, dependable, untarnished, irreproachable, moral, ethical, scrupulous, virtuous, upright, reputable. See also blameless, innocent, just. *Ant.* Venal.

Increase, *n.,* **increase,** *v.* **1.** *n.* Growth, enlargement (increase of hostility). Addition, increment, development, accession, extension, augmentation, elevation, escalation, aggravation, amplification, accrual, maximization, magnification, inflation, expansion, upsurge, surge, boost, improvement, advancement, broadening, heightening, supplement, reinforcement, rise, gain, benefit, proliferation, lengthening, swelling, exaggeration, acceleration, annexation, appreciation, multiplication, progression. **2.** *v.* See augment.

Incredible, *adj.* See doubtful, improbable, extraordinary, impossible, irrational, absurd, wild; anomalous, outrageous.

Increment, *n.* An increase in quantity or value. See appreciation (1), attachment (3), increase.

Incriminate, *v.* To charge with a crime; to involve oneself in the possibility of criminal prosecution (answering the question would tend to incriminate her).

Incriminate

Implicate, entangle, connect, involve, enmesh, impute, impeach, inculpate, denounce, reproach, stigmatize, indict. See also accuse, blame, condemn. *Ant.* Exonerate.

Incriminating evidence Evidence that tends to establish guilt or from which an inference of guilt can be drawn.

Incrimination, *n.* See incriminate, self-incrimination.

Incriminatory, *adj.* Having a tendency to incriminate (incriminatory evidence). Damning, condemning, disparaging, damaging, implicating. See also inculpatory.

Incriminatory statement A statement that tends to establish the guilt of the accused or from which guilt can be inferred; a statement that tends to disprove a defense to a crime. See evidence.

Inculcate, *v.* See imbue; educate, prepare (1); impregnate; initiate.

Inculpate, *v.* To impute blame or guilt; to involve in guilt or crime. See accuse, charge (3), incriminate.

Inculpatory, *adj.* Tending or intending to establish guilt (inculpatory evidence). Incriminating, damning, damaging, blaming, exposing, disparaging, accusatory, convincing, denunciatory, revealing, imputing. *Ant.* Exonerating.

Incumbent 1. *n.* A person who is presently in possession of an office (a campaign against the incumbent). Occupant, officeholder, holdover. See also official. **2.** *adj.* Obligatory (it is incumbent on the director to act). Imperative, binding, compelling, prescribed. See also mandatory, necessary, compulsory.

Incumbrance, *n.* See encumbrance, burden (1).

Incur, *v.* To become liable or subject to; to bring down upon oneself (to incur a debt). Undertake, assume, invite, enter into, induce, acquire, expose oneself to, arouse, bring about, become responsible, bring on, bargain for. See also commit (3), contract, provoke. *Ant.* Evade.

Incurable, *adj.* Not capable of being cured or corrected (incurable disease). Beyond hope, hopeless, terminal, beyond cure, inoperable, without remedy, uncorrectable; relentless, stubborn. See also incorrigible. *Ant.* Remediable.

Incursion, *n.* See invasion, assault, attack; violation, infringement.

Indebted, *adj.* See bound (1), appreciative, benevolent.

Indebtedness, *n.* The state of being in debt; an obligation (excessive indebtedness). Liability, responsibility, debts; appreciation, gratitude, thankfulness. See also arrearage, encumbrance.

Indecent, *adj.* Obscene, vulgar (indecent language broadcast over the air). Lewd, immodest, immoral, carnal, depraved, salacious, dirty, libidinous, licentious, coarse, prurient, blue, lascivious, distasteful, unseemly, indiscreet, uncivil, in bad taste, profane, shameless, promiscuous, perverted, abusive, repulsive, rank, disgusting, scurrilous, suggestive, scandalous, wanton, unsuitable, inappropriate, degenerate. See also obscene, filthy, pornographic; rude, improper, illicit. *Ant.* Modest.

Indecent exposure Exposing the private parts of the body in a lewd or indecent manner in a public place where he or she knows or should know that the act will be open to the observation of others.

Indecision, *n.* See doubt (2).

Indecisive, *adj.* See doubtful (1), capricious, variable, fluctuating, inconsistent; weak; bashful, quiet; inconclusive, disputable.

Indecorous, *adj.* See rude, impertinent (2), gross, illicit, improper, indecent, offensive.

Indeed, *adv.* In fact. In reality, truly, precisely, really, without question, undeniably. See also absolutely (2).

Indefatigable, *adj.* Tireless. Unyielding, vigorous, unflagging, staunch, inexhaustible, energetic, unfaltering, dogged, tenacious, hard-working, persistent, unwavering. See also diligent, strong (2), constant (3).

Indefeasible, *adj.* Not capable of being defeated, revoked, or made void (indefeasible right). Immutable, inalienable, indissoluble, entrenched, irreversible, unalterable, incontestable, inviolable, incontrovertible. See also irrevocable, permanent, perpetual, indestructible. *Ant.* Vulnerable.

Indefensible, *adj.* See inexcusable, wrong, illicit, invalid (1), illegal; defenseless, destitute, dependent (2).

Indefinite, *adj.* Not definite; no fixed boundaries (the answer of the witness was indefinite and evasive). Vague, imprecise, inexact, cryptic, unclear, unspecified, tentative, amorphous, ill-defined, dubious, inexplicit, wide, unintelligible, cloudy, opaque, indistinct, nondescript, enigmatic, doubtful, unlimited, blurred, equivocal, wavering, veiled, loose, abstruse, dim, lax, uncertain, confused, general, unrestrained, boundless, formless. See also indeterminate, ambiguous, obscure (1), intangible (3), abstract; inconclusive. *Ant.* Specific.

Indefinite failure of issue A failure of issue whenever it shall happen, sooner or later.

Indefinite legacy A legacy that passes property by a general or collective term without enumeration of number or quantity (e.g., a bequest of all the decedent's goods or of the bank account). See legacy.

Indelible, *adj.* See permanent, perpetual, indestructible, durable, outstanding (2).

Indelicate, *adj.* See awkward, offensive, improper, illicit, rude; indecent, obscene.

Indemnification, *n.* See amends, indemnity (2), restitution, compensation, insurance.

Indemnify, *v.* To secure someone against loss or damage; to restore the victim of a loss by payment, repair, or replacement (indemnify against liability). Compensate, hold harmless, restore, secure, refund, make good, atone, insure, provide restitution, guarantee, guard, return, make amends, answer for, reimburse, stand behind. See also satisfy (1), pay.

Indemnitee, *n.* A person who is protected by another through a contract of indemnity.

Indemnitor, *n.* A person who is bound by an indemnity contract to indemnify or protect another. See surety, guarantor.

Indemnity, *n.* **1.** A right to receive compensation (or the compensation itself) to make one person whole from a loss that has already been sustained but which in justice ought to be sustained by the person from whom indemnity is sought; the obligation or duty resting on one person to make good 100% of the loss or damage another has incurred while the latter was acting at the request or for the benefit of the former (one tortfeasor sought indemnity from the other tortfeasor). **2.** An agreement to protect another against loss suffered by the latter (indemnity insurance). Indemnification, remuneration, repayment, security, restitution, vindication, assurance, satisfaction, restoration, refund, recoupment, guarantee, reimbursement. See also insurance.

Indenture, *n.* **1.** A written agreement under which bonds and debentures are issued; the agreement sets forth terms such as the maturity date and the interest rate. **2.** A mortgage, deed of trust, or similar instrument in which there is a lien or other security interest. See instrument. **3.** An apprenticeship agreement. See artisan, assistant; articled.

Independence, *n.* See freedom, liberty, sovereignty, autonomy; authority, license, privilege; emancipation, enfranchisement, release (3); confidence (3), self-confidence.

Independent, *adj.* Not subject to control, restriction, modification, or limitation from a given outside source (independent advice). Unrestricted, uncoerced, self-directed, disinterested, unencumbered, unbridled, separate, unprejudiced, unrestrained, detached, spontaneous, unaffiliated, unchecked; self-governing, sovereign, autonomous. See also free, voluntary; impartial, proud. *Ant.* Controlled.

Independent contractor A contractor who carries on an independent business and contracts to do a piece of work according to his or her own methods without being subject to the control of the employer except as to the product or result of the work. See builder, entrepreneur.

In-depth, *adj.* See comprehensive, extensive, complete (2).

Indescribable, *adj.* See extraordinary, great (2), outstanding (2); odd, anomalous, wild.

Indestructible, *adj.* Not capable of being destroyed (indestructible trust). Inextinguishable, indissoluble, undying, perennial, endless, indefeasible, invulnerable, unbreakable, constant, enduring, immortal, unalterable, everlasting, imperishable, irrevocable, invincible, persevering, durable. See also incorruptible; permanent, perpetual. *Ant.* Transient.

Indeterminate, *adj.* Uncertain or not designated with particularity (an indeterminate length). Open, undefined, unfixed, undecided, ill-defined, not ascertained, uncategorized, unknown, unmeasured, unspecified, unresolved, undetermined, imprecise; vague, unclear, blurred, amorphous, shapeless, formless, nebulous, confused, cryptic. See also irregular, ambiguous, obscure (1), intangible (3), abstract, indefinite, inconclusive, general. *Ant.* Defined.

Indeterminate sentence A sentence to imprisonment for the maximum period defined by law, subject to termination by the parole board or other agency after the service of a minimum designated period. See punishment, adjudication.

Index, *v., n.* See classify, codify (1), list, inventory; manifestation.

Indexing, *n.* Linking the level of payments on bonds, pensions, or benefits to an index such as the Consumer Price Index. See link.

Indian, *n.* See native; aboriginal.

Indian Claims Commission An agency that hears and determines claims against the United States by American Indians.

Indicate, *v.* See express (2), intimate (6), describe, communicate, comment (2), develop (2), clarify.

Indication, *n.* A fact pointing to some inference or conclusion (an indication that the company is insolvent). Sign, omen, suggestion, token, trace, link, designation, evidence, clue, presage, warning, guide, reference, intimation, mark, augury, foreboding, demonstration, illustration, allusion, signpost, showing, expression, index, symptom. See also manifestation, notice (1).

Indicative, *adj.* See characteristic; important.

Indicator, *n.* See measure (1), gauge.

Indicia, *n.* Circumstances that point to the existence of a given fact as probable but not certain (indicia of fraud). Signs, indications, tokens, marks, expressions, circumstantial evidence, symbols. See also manifestation, characteristic, evidence.

Indicia of ownership Evidence of control or title.

Indict, *v.* To accuse formally of a crime through an indictment (she was indicted for robbery). See accuse, blame (3), censure, arraign; indictment.

Indictable, *adj.* Subject to being indicted (indictable offense).

Indicted, *adj.* Charged in an indictment with a criminal offense.

Indictment, *n.* A sworn accusation of crime against one or more persons, made by a grand jury; a true bill (indictment for murder). Complaint, denunciation, allegation, incrimination, charge, impeachment, presentment. See also blame (2).

Indifference, *n.* Unconcern. Disinterest, lack of interest, impassiveness, callousness, coolness, nonchalance, insouciance, insensitivity, aloofness; insignificance. See also ennui.

Indifferent, *adj.* **1.** Impartial (an indifferent tribunal). Unbiased, evenhanded, disinterested, neutral, unprejudiced, detached, fair-minded. See also objective, fair, impartial, dispassionate, equitable (1). **2.** Not displaying any concern (an indifferent observer). Unemotional, removed, emotionless, stoical, aloof, insensitive, impervious, nonchalant, cool. See also apathetic, callous, blind. **3.** See routine, commonplace, average (2). *Ant.* Biased; compassionate.

Indigenous, *adj.* See native (2), local; inherent.

Indigent, *adj.* Being needy and poor. In need, without resources, impoverished, penurious, distressed, poverty-stricken, deprived, penniless, insolvent, helpless, wanting. See also bankrupt, destitute. *Ant.* Affluent.

Indignant, *adj.* See angry, aggravated (2), hot (2).

Indignation, *n.* See wrath, animus, annoyance.

Indignity, *n.* Cruelty (he sued for a divorce on the ground of indignity). Mistreatment, outrage, affront, humiliation, ignominy, contemptuous behavior, insult, disrespect, vulgarity, habitual contumely, intentional incivility, unmerited reproach. See also notoriety (2), abuse, cruelty. *Ant.* Courtesy.

Indirect, *adj.* Not direct; depending on some intervening factor; not having immediate application (indirect cause). Roundabout, winding, collateral, digressive, zigzag, circuitous, remote, secondary, serpentine, deviating, sinuous, meandering, oblique, collateral, backhanded, circumlocutory, devious, inferential, implicit, circumstantial, ancillary, incidental, contingent. See also implied; ambiguous. *Ant.* Direct.

Indirect tax A tax upon some right, privilege, or franchise rather than a tax directly on property according to its value. See tax.

Indiscreet, *adj.* See improper, blatant (2), careless, juvenile (2), dumb, impetuous, rude, common (3), improvident.

Indiscretion, *n.* See effrontery; error, mistake, fault (1).

Indispensable, *adj.* Not capable of being spared, omitted, or dispensed with (indispensable evidence). Essential, mandatory, vital, obligatory, pivotal, crucial, required, unavoidable, requisite, needed, key, basic, cardinal, exigent, pressing, elementary, binding. See also imperative, compulsory, compelling, necessary; inherent, intrinsic, native (3), congenital. *Ant.* Expendable.

Indispensable party A necessary party whose absence should force the court to dismiss the action. A party is indispensable if a case cannot be decided on its merits without prejudicing the rights of that party.

Indisposed, *adj.* See ill (1), sick; feeble, weak.

Indisputable, *adj.* See incontestable, noncontestable, definitive, conclusive, certain (3), clear (1), definite.

Indissoluble, *adj.* See indestructible, irrevocable, permanent, perpetual, indefeasible, inalienable.

Indistinct, *adj.* See indefinite, ambiguous, illegible, abstract, obscure (1), inconclusive.

Indistinguishable, *adj.* See identical, equal (2), equivalent.

Individual 1. *adj.* Pertaining to or characteristic of one person or thing (individual assets). Discrete, unassociated, unique, peculiar, isolated, detached, single, solitary, exclusive, personal, specific, special, private, unattached, singular, unassimilated, unconventional, original, personalized, uncommon, restricted, unallied, extraordinary. See also independent, different, separate, particular (1). **2.** *n.* A single person as opposed to a group or class (he appeared as an individual). Distinct personal entity, human, personality, body, party, autonomous entity, being, personage, distinct person, soul, character, creature. *Ant.* Collective; group.

Individualist, *n.* See nonconformist.

Individuality, *n.* See identity (1), eccentricity; speciality (1); property (2), essence; individual.

Individual proprietorship See sole proprietorship, business; merchant.

Individual Retirement Account (IRA) An individual retirement trust account in which qualified persons can set aside a certain amount of income each year. The amount can be deducted, and will be subject to income tax only upon withdrawal as specified in the regulations of the account.

Indivisible, *adj.* Not susceptible of division or apportionment (indivisible asset). Inseparable, entire, undividable, inseverable, not severable, united, unbreakable, indissolvable, indissoluble. See also indestructible. *Ant.* Divisible.

Indoctrinate, *v.* See discipline (4), imbue, instruct, educate, persuade, initiate.

Indoctrination, *n.* See discipline (1), education; inauguration.

Indolent, *adj.* See lazy, dilatory, indifferent, apathetic.

Indomitable, *adj.* See indestructible, invulnerable, inviolate; courageous, adventurous, assertive, certain (2), assured (4); inflexible.

Indorse, *v.* **1.** To support. See back (1), finance (1), guarantee (2), recommend, approve, authorize, certify. **2.** See indorsement.

Indorsee, *n.* The person to whom a negotiable instrument, promissory note, bill of lading, etc., is assigned by indorsement.

Indorsement, *n.* **1.** The act of a payee, drawee, accommodation indorser, or holder of a negotiable instrument (e.g., note, bill, check) in writing his or her name on the back of the instrument, with or without further words, whereby the ownership or property in the instrument is assigned and transferred to another (indorsement for collection). **2.** The giving of approval (indorsement of the plan). Sanction, acceptance, assent, ratification, recommendation, affirmation, subscription, approval, authorization, stamp, imprimatur, championship, certification, approbation, commendation, support, backing, advocacy, concurrence, sponsorship, permission, consent, encouragement, guarantee, testimonial, validation, voucher, attestation, underwriting. *Ant.* Rejection.

Indorser, *n.* One who indorses; the payee or holder who writes his or her name on the back of a negotiable instrument.

Indubitable, *adj.* Beyond doubt (indubitable evidence). Unquestionable, sure, beyond dispute, unimpeachable, undeniable, positive, absolute, incontrovertible. See also certain (3), incontestable, clear (1), conclusive, definite (1), definitive, categorical (1). *Ant.* Uncertain.

Induce, *v.* To bring on, cause, or influence (induced to sign). Prevail on, persuade, effectuate, convince, generate, talk into, pressure, motivate, inspire, coax, sway, stimulate, create, procure, abet, precipitate, cajole, goad, trigger, impel, instigate, entice, activate, produce, kindle, lure, occasion, effect. See also incite, provoke. *Ant.* Hinder.

Inducement, *n.* **1.** In contracts, the benefit or advantage that the promisor is to receive from a contract is the inducement for making it. **2.** The act of inducing. See motivation, motive, impulse, catalyst, cause (1); induce.

Induct, *v.* To place in possession or enjoyment; to enter formally (induct into the military). Introduce, swear in, inaugurate, invest, usher in, commission, name, delegate, process. See also initiate, launch, install.

Induction, *n.* See inauguration, registration.

Inductive, *adj.* Obtaining the general from the particular. See analytic, logical; deduce.

Indulge, *v.* See delight, pander (2), satisfy (2), accommodate, yield (1), condescend, patronize (2).

Indulgence, *n.* See luxury, debauchery, intoxication; charity, mercy, accommodation (1), toleration; leave (4), permission.

Indulgent, *adj.* See permissive, flexible, cooperative (2), liberal, amenable; charitable, benevolent, kind; immoderate, improvident, excess, wild, intoxicated.

Industrial, *adj.* Pertaining to industry (industrial development). Commercial, trade, manufactured, technological, mercantile, factory-produced. See also business; merchant.

Industrial disease A physical disorder that is caused by or is incident to a particular occupation. See disease, illness.

Industrial relations The relationship between employer and employee (e.g., collective bargaining, safety on the job).

Industrious, *adj.* See diligent, strong (2), indefatigable, constant (3).

Industry, *n.* **1.** An art, occupation, or business conducted as a means of livelihood or for profit, especially one that is a distinct branch of trade (the milk industry). Pursuit, line, field, business, enterprise, commerce, trade, manufacture, traffic, production **2.** Diligence (her industry was impressive). Energy, hard work, attention, determination, zeal, drive, constancy, activity, application, enthusiasm, assiduity, hustle, labor, persistence, effort, endurance, steadfastness, tenacity.

Inebriated, *adj.* See intoxicated.

Inedible, *adj.* Not fit for human consumption. See foul, deleterious, harmful.

Ineffective, *adj.* See inadequate, weak, frail, incompetent, imperfect, deficient, inferior (2), worthless, invalid (1).

Inefficiency, *n.* See incapacity, defect, deficiency, failure, fault (1).

Inefficient, *adj.* See inadequate, incompetent, insufficient, deficient, imperfect, inferior (2), dumb, weak; careless.

Inelegant, *adj.* See common (3), vulgar, pompous, rude.

Ineligible, *adj.* Disqualified; having a legal incapacity (he is ineligible for benefits). Unacceptable, unsuitable, disallowed, inappropriate, eliminated, inapplicable, improper, unentitled, unqualified, inept, unequipped, disapproved. See also inadmissible, incompetent, inadequate. *Ant.* Eligible.

Inept, *adj.* See dumb, incompetent, inferior (2), negligent, deficient, imperfect, inadequate, weak; careless.

Inequality, *n.* See disparity, difference (1); prejudice (1), bias (1).

Inequitable, *adj.* See partisan (2), arbitrary (2), unequal (1), wrong (2), corrupt (1).

Inert, *adj.* See dormant, stationary, quiet, lazy; loiter.

Inescapable, *adj.* Being helpless to avoid a consequence by oneself; inevitable (inescapable peril). Inexorable, certain, unavoidable, uncontrollable, predestined, fated, sure, ineluctable, unpreventable, unyielding. See also inevitable. *Ant.* Preventable.

Inestimable, *adj.* See great (2), outstanding (2), exclusive, extraordinary, incalculable, perpetual, permanent; big; costly, exorbitant.

Inevitable, *adj.* Incapable of being avoided; transcending human power to prevent (inevitable delay). Unalterable, predestined, guaranteed, unpreventable, fated, immutable, inexorable, ineluctable, sure, destined, irrevocable, conclusive, involuntary, unquestionable, ineludible, automatic, imminent, foreordained, compelling, coercive, at hand, unfailing, definite. See also certain (3), inescapable. *Ant.* Uncertain.

Inevitable accident An unavoidable accident; one produced by an irresistible physical cause; one that cannot be prevented by human skill or care. See act of God, accident.

Inexact

Inexact, *adj.* See erroneous, wrong (3), false; indefinite; careless.

Inexcusable, *adj.* Pertaining to what could not or should not be excused or justified (inexcusable behavior). Unjustifiable, unacceptable, unforgivable, indefensible, unpardonable, unallowable, unwarranted, without excuse, shameful, outrageous, unbearable, intolerable, reprehensible, discreditable, wicked, disreputable, iniquitous, atrocious, heinous, vicious, monstrous. See also immoral, illicit, improper, frivolous, baseless, grievous (1). *Ant.* Defensible.

Inexcusable neglect Such neglect that will preclude setting aside a default judgment; neglect that is due to more than unintentional inadvertence or common frailty. See neglect.

Inexhaustible, *adj.* See great (1), outstanding (2), extraordinary; incalculable, perpetual, permanent; big.

Inexorable, *adj.* See inescapable, inevitable, irreconcilable, irrevocable; inflexible, strong (2), severe, strict (2), cruel.

Inexpedient, *adj.* See impracticable, dumb, wrong.

Inexpensive, *adj.* Low-priced. See economical; reasonable.

Inexperienced, *adj.* See backward (1), new, innocent; amateur, beginner.

Inexplicable, *adj.* See mysterious, ambiguous, obscure (1).

In extremis In the last illness (declaration in extremis). At the point of death, dying, near death, approaching death, expiring, terminally ill, beyond hope of recovery, deathly ill, impending death.

Inextricable, *adj.* See complex (1).

Infallible, *adj.* See perfect, blameless; certain, sound, incontestable.

Infamous, *adj.* Having a notorious reputation; shameful (infamous deed). Disgraceful, sordid, profligate, scandalous, disreputable, scurrilous, villainous, ignoble, iniquitous, perfidious, abominable, foul, detestable, heinous, nefarious, outrageous, ignominious, loathsome, obnoxious, flagrant, dishonorable, contemptible, vile, atrocious, despicable, revolting. See also immoral, odious, corrupt, base, bad, offensive. *Ant.* Reputable.

Infamous crime A crime punishable by death or by imprisonment in a prison or penitentiary; a crime that brings shame and disgrace on the person who commits it. See crime.

Infamy, *n.* The condition of being infamous, shameful, and notorious (a crime of infamy). Dishonor, villany, abomination, scandal, opprobrium, evil, stigma, perfidy, notoriety, turpitude, depravity, infidelity, abasement, reproach, obloquy, baseness, contempt, derision, disgrace. See also corruption, ignominy, wrong (1), debauchery, delinquency, odium. *Ant.* Integrity.

Infancy, *n.* **1.** Under the age of legal majority; at common law, under 21; today, usually under 18 (the disability of infancy). See minority (1). **2.** The early stages of something (the new procedure is in its infancy). Commencement, conception, nascence, dawn, genesis, cradle, incipience, start, inception. *Ant.* Adulthood; termination.

Infant, *n.* See child, infancy (1), minor (1); juvenile.

Infanticide, *n.* The murder or killing of an infant soon after its birth. See murder, homicide.

Infantile, *adj.* See juvenile (2); inchoate, initial.

Infantry, *n.* See military; division (2); sailor.

Infatuate, *v.* See enamor, entice, absorb (2), occupy (3).

Infeasible, *adj.* See impracticable, doubtful.

Infect, *v.* See contaminate, corrupt (2), pollute; imbue, impress, animate.

Infection, *n.* See disease, infirmity, illness; germ.

Infectious, *adj.* See contagious, poisonous.

Infeoffment, *n.* The act or instrument of feoffment. See feoffment.

Infer, *v.* See deduce, assume (2), reason (3), conclude (2), construe, clarify; inference.

Inference, *n.* A process of reasoning by which a fact or proposition sought to be established is deduced from other facts; the deductions or conclusions reached by this process (the jury drew a favorable inference). Assumption, surmise, supposition, speculation, belief, corollary, conjecture, presumption, hypothesis, judgment, sequitur, construction, observation, thesis, theory, intuition. See also opinion, conclusion (2).

Inferior, *adj.* **1.** Having less authority and power in relationship to others (inferior officer). Subordinate, secondary, lower rank, ancillary, junior, subservient, lesser, minor, menial, side, accessory, collateral, subsidiary, alternative, derived, vicarious, nonessential, dependent, supplementary, indirect, contingent, derivative, utility, provisional, reserve, parenthetical, extraneous, negligible, extrinsic, inconsequential, tangential, subaltern, under, auxiliary. **2.** Poor quality (inferior goods). Second-rate, shoddy, damaged, low-grade, bad, cheap, mediocre, unsatisfactory, adulterated, polluted, indifferent, substandard, unacceptable, defective, paltry, subnormal, marginal, wanting, pedestrian. See also inadequate, incompetent, insufficient, deficient, imperfect. *Ant.* Superior.

Inferior court Any court that is subordinate to the highest court within its judicial system; a special court whose judgments are not given presumptive jurisdictional validity.

Infernal, *adj.* See infamous, odious, corrupt, malicious.

Inferno, *n.* See abyss, chaos.

Infertile, *adj.* See barren, fallow, worthless; impotence.

Infest, *v.* See inundate, overcome (2), encroach, spread; communicate.

Infidel, *n.* See anarchist, nihilist, insurgent, atheist, nonconformist; irreverent, profane (1); profanity, blasphemy.

Infidelity, *n.* Unfaithfulness in marriage, usually involving adultery (he charged her with infidelity). Betrayal, violation of the marriage bed, disloyalty, deceit, perfidy, treachery, bad faith, breach of trust, double-dealing, unchastity, cheating, having an affair, defection, falsity, inconstancy, rebellion, perfidiousness, falseheartedness, cuckoldry. See also adultery, duplicity. *Ant.* Fidelity.

Infighting, *n.* See contention (2), feud (1), fight (1).

Infiltrate, *v.* See enter, pierce, encroach, interfere; imbue; attack (1); invasion, intrusion.

Infinite, *adj.* See incalculable, perpetual, permanent; big, great; perfect, whole; ubiquitous; God.

Infinitesimal, *adj.* See small (1), minimal, minor (2); hidden; iota.

Infinity, *n.* See perfection; God; perpetuity; universal; incalculable.

Infirm, *adj.* Lacking health or moral character (too infirm to testify). Feeble, fragile, emaciated, faltering, unsound, decrepid, unstable, worn, impotent, insecure, enervated, powerless, weakened, doddering, disabled, exhausted, confined, shaky, enfeebled. See also weak, ill, frail, defective, senile. *Ant.* Robust.

Infirmary, *n.* See hospital, ward (3); institution.

Infirmative, *adj.* Having the tendency to weaken or to render infirm (infirmative evidence). Exculpatory. See exculpate; evidence.

Infirmity, *n.* Disability, feebleness (insurance coverage for the infirmity). Impairment, incapacity, sickness, ailment, malady, infection, decline, debility, debilitation, fragility, frailty, handicap, decrepitude, malaise, indisposition, disorder, deficiency, vulnerability, failing, decay, collapse, defect, deterioration, fault, weakness. See also disease, illness, affliction. *Ant.* Vitality.

Inflame

Inflame, *v.* See provoke, incite, abet, animate; harass; aggravated (2), angry; fire, burn.

Inflammable, *adj.* See incendiary, flammable; emotional, excitable; feverish; outrageous.

Inflammatory, *adj.* See incendiary (2), violent, outrageous, excitable, feverish.

Inflate, *v.* See exaggerate, flatter; extend (1), augment; distort, spread.

Inflation, *n.* See increase, appreciation, growth; pompous.

Inflexible, *adj.* Adamant, unyielding (an inflexible position). Stubborn, willful, bullheaded, obdurate, pigheaded, adamant, unrelenting, headstrong, immutable, tenacious, cantankerous, mulish, unrelenting, unruly, intractable, obstinate, resolute, determined, unmanageable, ungovernable, intransigent, opinionated, unpliable, hardened, indocile, refractory, unalterable, tenacious, uncompromising, perverse, contrary, steadfast, unbending, rigid, immovable, ironclad, indomitable, unsympathetic, intolerant, unmalleable, merciless. See also firm, strict. *Ant.* Compromising.

Inflict, *v.* See impose, perform, cause, administer.

Infliction, *n.* See perpetration, performance.

Influence 1. *n.* Power exerted over others (an undue influence over the testator). Sway, strength, ascendancy, hold, command, authority, inspiration, control, sovereignty, pressure, domination, dominance, magnetism, manipulation, weight, dominion, reign, instigation, force, mastery, predominance, effect, potency, leverage, leadership, importance, charisma, "clout," direction, rule, guidance. **2.** *v.* To affect, act upon, or modify by physical, mental, or moral power (an attempt to influence the jury). Manipulate, control, sway, arouse, incite, convince, dominate, move, compel, activate, bias, impel, regulate, manage, incline, wield, guide, brainwash, urge, prompt, stimulate, inveigle, cajole, pressure, bend, induce, predispose, exercise influence on, prejudice, impress, form. See also persuade, instigate.

Influential, *adj.* See strong, great (2), elevated, important, decisive, crucial, effective, dominant, outstanding (2).

Inform, *v.* See advise, notify, report; educate, instruct, improve, nurture, discipline (4); communicate; information.

Informal, *adj.* Not observing formal regulations; deficient in legal form; casual (informal understanding). Offhand, unofficial, unstrict, unceremonial, common, relaxed, familiar, simple, unstudied, unconstrained, unconventional, unorthodox, cavalier, nonconforming, ordinary, nonchalant, extemporaneous, natural, unauthorized. See also spontaneous, irregular, deviant. *Ant.* Official.

Informal proceedings Proceedings that are less formal (usually considerably so) than a normal court trial (e.g., an agency hearing in which the technical rules of evidence do not apply). See process, procedure, proceeding.

Informant, *n.* See informer.

In forma pauperis In the character or manner of a pauper; permission given to a poor person to proceed without having to pay court fees or costs. See bankrupt.

Information, *n.* **1.** A formal accusation for a criminal offense other than through an indictment; a written accusation from a prosecutor rather than from a grand jury (a hearing upon an information filed by the district attorney). See accusation. **2.** Knowledge or facts that have been acquired (the information in the report). Data, news, background, revelation, intelligence, account, notes, wisdom, statistics, figures, enlightenment, understanding, communication, story, message, material, briefing, notification, learning, tidings, announcement, word, proclamation, lore, bulletin, communiqué. See also notice, circumstances, fact, evidence, education, knowledge, comprehension.

Information and belief Good faith belief as to the truth of an allegation, not based on firsthand knowledge.

Informative, *adj.* Instructive. Revealing, illuminating, edifying, enlightening, educational, helpful; detailed. See also advisory.

Informed, *adj.* Based on knowledge or understanding (informed judgment). Enlightened, knowledgeable, advised, notified, apprised, expert, learned, familiarized, undeceived, forewarned, well-grounded, prepared, familiar, conscious, mindful, aware, abreast. *Ant.* Blind.

Informed consent A person's agreement to allow something to happen based on a full disclosure of the facts needed to make the decision intelligently. See consent.

Informer, *n.* A person who informs or brings an accusation against another on the basis of a suspicion that the latter has committed a crime; the identity of the informer is usually undisclosed, and he or she volunteers the information confidentially (an anonymous call from an informer). Informant, reporter, tipster, "stool pigeon," spy, announcer, source, witness, divulger, messenger, whistle blower, "deep throat" intelligencer, rat, denouncer, tattler, betrayer. See also accuser.

Infra, *adv.* Below; later in the text (Smith v. Jones, infra). *Ant.* Supra, above, earlier in the text.

Infraction, *n.* A breach, violation, or infringement of a law, agreement, right, or duty (contract infraction). Transgression, intrusion, break, nonobservance, default, trespass, overstepping, error, encroachment, dereliction, faux pas, omission, disobedience, delinquency, lawbreaking, sin, insubordination. See also violation, wrong, offense, lapse. *Ant.* Compliance.

Infrastructure, *n.* See composition, form (1), design (1), organization (2), pattern (1), plan (1).

Infrequent, *adj.* See seldom, few, periodic, intermittent.

Infringe, *v.* See encroach, interfere, break (1), wrong (4), attack (1), assault (3); infringement.

Infringement, *n.* An invasion of a right; a violation of a law or duty (patent infringement). Encroachment, transgression, interference, intrusion, nonobservance, misfeasance, malfeasance, usurpation, breach, noncompliance, inroad, raid, incursion, evasion, seizure, misappropriation, expropriation, dispossession, trespass. See also wrong, abuse, violation, infraction, intervention (2).

Infringement of copyright The unauthorized use of copyrighted material. See copyright.

Infringement of patent The unauthorized making, using, or selling (for practical use or profit) of an invention covered by a valid claim of patent during the life of the patent. See patent.

Infringement of trademark The unauthorized use or colorable imitation of a mark already appropriated by another on goods of a similar class. See trademark.

Infuriate, *v.* See provoke, incite, harass; aggravated (2), angry.

Infuriated, *adj.* See angry, aggravated (2), hot, hysterical, wild.

Infuse, *v.* See inundate, fill, imbue, impress, influence, educate, impregnate.

In futuro At a future time (the estate will vest in futuro). Later, in the future. See also future, expectancy. *Ant.* In praesenti.

Ingenious, *adj.* See brilliant, able, original (3), competent, capable, apt (2, 3); deceptive, deceitful, facetious.

Ingenuity, *n.* See initiative (3), address (4), ability, competence, facility (3).

Ingenuous, *adj.* See direct (6), honest, open (5).

Ingrained, *adj.* See congenital, inherent, native (3).

Ingrate, *n.* An opportunist or self-seeker.

Ingratiate, *v.* See flatter; flattery; grovel; servile.

Ingratiating, *adj.* See friendly, attractive, convivial, amicable; flattery; flatter; servile.

Ingratitude, *n.* Being ungrateful (the ingratitude of the donee). Unappreciativeness, unthankfulness, thanklessness. *Ant.* Appreciation.

Ingredient, *n.* See component, factor, element, part (1).

Ingress, *n.* The act or right of entering (the landlord retained control over ingress to the building). Passage, access, way in, entryway, door, coming, ingoing, incoming, opening, route, pathway, gate, approach, admission, admittance. See also entrance. *Ant.* Egress.

In-group, *n.* See coterie, group (1).

In gross In a large sum or quantity; without deduction or division. See gross (2), whole.

Ingrossing, *n.* See engrossment.

Inhabit, *v.* To dwell or live (the area was inhabited by squatters). Stay, sojourn, rest, occupy, domicile, remain, rent, locate, settle, abide, people, tenant, populate, nest, camp. See also reside (1).

Inhabitant, *n.* One who actually and permanently resides in a given place and has his or her domicile there (inhabitants of the region). Citizen, native, settler, tenant, dweller, incumbent, renter, denizen, occupier, squatter, homesteader, pioneer, immigrant, frontiersman, founder, colonist, indweller, addressee, lessee, aborigine. See also occupant, resident, lodger.

Inhalation, *n.* See breath.

Inhere, *v.* To be innate. See exist, pertain, appertain; inherent.

Inherent, *adj.* Existing as a permanent or essential component (inherent powers). Intrinsic, innate, constitutional, basic, deep-rooted, inveterate, inalienable, characteristic, indigenous, inborn, inseparable, instinctive, natural, hereditary, implicit, integral, subsistent, ingrained, immanent, ineradicable, deep-seated, intimate, internal, normal, distinctive, integral. See also native (3), congenital. *Ant.* Incidental.

Inherently dangerous A danger inhering in the instrumentality or condition itself at all times so as to require special precautions to prevent injury; dangerous per se without requiring human intervention to produce the harmful effects. See dangerous, hazardous.

Inherent power An authority possessed without its being derived from another; a power in the nature of the organization or person. See power, authority.

Inherit, *v.* To take by inheritance on the death of an ancestor (he inherited the fund). Take by succession, be left, be the heir of, gain, take by descent, succeed to. See also obtain, acquire, receive.

Inheritance, *n.* Property that descends to an heir when an ancestor dies without leaving a valid will, i.e., intestate (her inheritance was challenged by the administrator). Property received by descent, endowment, legacy, bestowal, devise, bequest, donation, share; patrimony, heritage, birthright. See also gift, property.

Inheritance tax A tax imposed on the privilege of receiving property from a decedent at death; a tax on the right to acquire property gratuitously by descent or will. Succession duty or tax. See tax.

Inhibit, *v.* To restrain or hold back (the threat of a suit inhibited further action). Obstruct, suppress, check, impede, muzzle, repress, arrest, cramp, smother, constrain, forbid, curb, frustrate, veto, paralyze, choke, strangle, estop, control, bridle, interfere, proscribe, suspend, delay. See also hinder, bar, prohibit. *Ant.* Facilitate.

Inhibition, *n.* See restraint (1), obstruction, limitation (1), deterrent.

In hoc In this; in respect to this.

Inhospitable, *adj.* See hostile, rude.

Inhuman, *adj.* Lacking compassion; cruel (inhuman living environment). Barbarous, cold, merciless, unsympathetic, barbaric, murderous, relentless, malignant, brutal, unfeeling, fiendish, savage, satanic, inhumane, vicious, implacable, diabolical, unrelenting, ruthless, monstrous, pitiless, cold-blooded, venomous, cold-hearted, heartless, devilish, malign, remorseless. See also cruel, callous, malicious. *Ant.* Benevolent.

Inhumane, *adj.* See inhuman, cruel, callous, malicious.

Inhuman treatment As a ground for divorce: Such mental or physical cruelty as to endanger the life or health of the party to whom it is addressed, or as to create a well-founded apprehension of such danger. See divorce, ground.

Inimical, *adj.* See dangerous, deleterious, injurious; hostile, malicious, inhuman, cruel.

Inimitable, *adj.* See perfect, extraordinary, superior (2), great (2).

Iniquitous, *adj.* See inexcusable, infamous, immoral, corrupt, offensive.

Iniquity, *n.* See injustice, crime, corruption, wrong, debauchery, delinquency.

Initial, *adj.* Beginning (initial filing). First, original, premier, formative, commencing, introductory, prime, inaugural, incipient, germinal, opening, primal, early, rudimentary, inchoate, fundamental, maiden, embryonic, prefatory, leading. *Ant.* Terminal.

Initiate, *v.* To commence or originate (she initiated negotiations). Start, begin, launch, establish, prompt, undertake, institute, usher in, trigger, pioneer, create, install, get going, kick off, inaugurate, found, lay the foundation for, broach, inculcate, prepare, activate, baptize, actuate, organize, set up. See also introduce, instigate. *Ant.* Terminate

Initiation, *n.* See inauguration, commencement, admission (3); ceremony.

Initiative, *n.* **1.** An electoral process whereby designated percentages of the electorate may initiate legislative or constitutional changes through the filing of formal petitions to be acted on by the legislature or by the total electorate; the power of the people to propose laws and to enact or reject them at the polls independent of the legislative assembly (an initiative on gun control). **2.** The first step (she took the initiative). First move, opening move. **3.** Determination; the ability to carry through (her initiative was rewarded). Enterprise, aggressiveness, drive, creativity, dynamism, independence, ambition, leadership, forcefulness, energy, hustle, originality. See also industry (2), determination (2).

Inject, *v.* See introduce (1), imbue, interpolate, fill.

Injection, *n.* See treatment; medicine.

Injudicious, *adj.* See improvident, dumb, juvenile (2), careless, impetuous.

Injunction, *n.* A prohibitive, equitable remedy issued by a court to forbid someone to do an act that he or she is threatening to do or to restrain him or her from continuing the act; a court order requiring a person to do or to refrain from doing a particular thing (an injunction against the strike). Ban, stay order, interdiction, proscription, mandate, admonition, imperative, direction, ruling, dictate, prescription. See also prohibition, restraint (1), obstruction, limitation (1).

Injure, *v.* To violate the legal right of another or to inflict an actionable wrong; to impair the soundness of (the report injured his reputation). Damage, mistreat, trespass, aggrieve, violate, offend, wound, disfigure, mar, blemish, mutilate, hurt, debase, lacerate, misuse, bruise, mangle, ruin, tarnish, vitiate, incapacitate, prejudice, deform, contort, waste, ill-treat, demoralize, oppress, cripple, slander, libel,

Injure

defame, invade, malign, pain, molest, spoil. See also wrong (2), abuse, harm. *Ant.* Restore.

Injuria absque damno A wrong done, but from which no loss or damage results, will not sustain an action.

Injurious, *adj.* Causing harm or injury (injurious consequences). Destructive, unhealthy, unfavorable, damaging, corruptive, hurtful, adverse, corrosive, calamitous, noxious, detrimental, pernicious, offensive, disadvantageous, ruinous, abusive, inimical, disastrous, unwholesome, disparaging, scandalous, insulting, scurrilous, malign, malignant, derogatory, virulent, inequitable. See also harmful, deleterious; dangerous, immoral, illicit. *Ant.* Salutary.

Injurious falsehood A tort with the following elements: (a) a false statement of fact; (b) publication of the statement; (c) intent; (d) the statement is harmful to the interests of the plaintiff—special damages; (e) causation. See prima facie tort, disparagement, slander, fraud, tort.

Injury, *n.* Any wrong or damage done to another; an invasion of a legally protected interest of another (injury resulting from the publication). Harm, violence, loss, depravation, impairment, misdeed, destruction, disservice, wound, affront, aspersion, blow, indignity, vilification, evil, outrage; bruise, gash, laceration, scrape, trauma, mutilation, puncture, disfigurement, contusion. See also grievance, abuse, injustice, wrong, violation, detriment; cut. *Ant.* Benefit.

Injustice, *n.* The denial of justice; the act, fault, or omission of a court in a particular case (the injustice of the dismissal). Wrong, transgression, offense, abuse, inequity, discrimination, prejudice, infringement, unlawfulness, persecution, unfairness, partiality, inequality, malpractice, infraction, partisanship, wrongdoing, imposition, encroachment, mistreatment, favoritism, disservice, maltreatment, bigotry, tyranny, illegality, disparity, violence. See also grievance (1), bias, injury, violation, delinquency, neglect. *Ant.* Fairness.

In kind Of the same species or category. See kind (1).

Inkling, *n.* See suggestion, indication, innuendo (2); intimate (6).

Inland, *adj.* Pertaining to the interior part of a land mass; within a country, state, or territory (inland trade). Upriver, internal, heartland, midland, backwoods, hinterland.

Inlet, *n.* See entrance, ingress; harbor; sea (1).

In lieu of In place of (he took a check in lieu of cash). Instead of, in substitution, as a substitute for, rather than, as an alternative. See also replacement.

In limine On or at the threshold (motion in limine). At the very beginning, preliminarily. See also commencement.

In loco parentis In the place of a parent; assuming the duties of a parent without adoption (a stepparent in loco parentis). See authority, parent, replacement, discipline.

Inmate, *n.* **1.** A person confined in a jail, prison, state hospital, etc., convict, captive. See also prisoner, accused; wrongdoer. **2.** A person who dwells in the same house with another, occupying different rooms but using the same door for passing in and out of the house. Roomer, dweller, inhabitant, resident, denizen, occupier. See also occupant.

Inn, *n.* A public lodging establishment; a restaurant or bar (inadequate security at the inn). Hotel, motel, hostel, roadhouse, pension, hospice, rooming house; public house, tavern, bar and grill, saloon, bistro, lodge, cafeteria, commissary, café, cabaret.

Innate, *adj.* See congenital, inherent, native (3), natural (3).

Inner, *adj.* See interior; intangible; private, confidential; intrinsic, inherent.

Innkeeper, *n.* See merchant; inn.

Innocence, *n.* **1.** The absence of guilt (he asserted her innocence). Blamelessness, clean hands, sinlessness, inculpability, impeccability. See also innocent, blameless. **2.** Simplicity (the child's innocence). Naiveté, purity, inexperience, artlessness, chastity, virtue, guilelessness, honesty, truthfulness, modesty, sincerity, candor. See also ignorance. *Ant.* Guilt; cunning.

Innocent, *adj.* **1.** Free from guilt (innocent bystander). Faultless, unoffending, unblameworthy, irreproachable, above suspicion, clean-handed, exculpatory, free from guilt, not guilty, unblemished, not responsible, uninvolved, sinless, inculpable, upright, unimpeachable. See also blameless, incorruptible. **2.** Harmless (an innocent inquiry). Innocuous, inoffensive, honest, simple, naive, pure, unsophisticated, trusting, inexperienced, rustic, sincere, homey, unpretentious, down to earth, common, humble, green, artless, childlike, ingenuous, virtuous, impeccable, open, unworldly, unadulterated, simple-minded; stupid, dumb, foolish, slow, obtuse. *Ant.* Guilty; mischievous.

Innocent trespasser One who enters another's land unlawfully but inadvertently and unintentionally, or in the honest and reasonable belief in his or her right to do so.

Innocuous, *adj.* See innocent (2), harmless.

Innovate, *v.* See create, invent, coin (3).

Innovation, *n.* See invention, novelty, change (1).

Innovative, *adj.* See original (3), brilliant, able (2, 3), competent.

Innovator, *n.* See avant-garde.

Inns of Court Private associations or societies in London (e.g., Gray's Inn, the Middle Temple) that have the exclusive privilege of calling men and women to the bar (i.e., conferring on them the rank or degree of barrister—a trial attorney).

Innuendo, *n.* **1.** In a defamation action, the innuendo is that portion of a complaint which seeks to explain the derogatory meaning of language (or its application to the plaintiff) that otherwise might be considered innocuous or so ambiguous that the defamatory sense is not revealed. See slander, defamation. **2.** An indirect derogatory comment or suggestion (she objected to the innuendo of fraud in the report). Insinuation, allusion, whisper, accusation, overtone, implication, aspersion, hint, reflection, intimation, indication, aside, inkling, animadversion, imputation, inference, reference.

Innumerable, *adj.* See many, incalculable; big.

Inobtrusive, *adj.* See quiet; bashful; hidden.

Inoculate, *v.* To vaccinate. Protect, immunize, safeguard, shield, inject, shoot, mitigate. See also prevent; treatment; cure (1); medicine; safe, sanitation.

Inoffensive, *adj.* See innocuous, harmless, innocent.

Inoperable, *adj.* See incurable.

Inoperative, *adj.* See barren, worthless, invalid (1); weak, frail, deficient, inadequate, inferior (2), imperfect.

Inopportune, *adj.* See inconvenient, improper, precipitate (2), improvident, careless, dumb.

Inordinate, *adj.* See excess, immoderate, disproportionate, extreme, exorbitant; irregular, odd, anomalous.

In pais Done informally or without legal proceedings; not arising from a deed, record, or written contract. See estoppel in pais.

In pari delicto In equal fault; equally culpable or criminal.

In pari materia Upon the same matter or subject. Statutes in pari materia are to be construed together; even though they may have been enacted at different times, a court will attempt to interpret such statutes as consistent with each other if possible.

Inpatient, *n.* A patient receiving care in an institution. See patient (1); hospital.

In perpetuity See perpetuity.

In personam Against the person. In personam jurisdiction is the power that a court has over the defendant himself or herself as distinguished from the more limited power a court has over his or her interest in property (quasi in rem) or over the property itself (in rem). See jurisdiction.

In praesenti At the present time. See now. *Ant.* In futuro.

Input, *n.* See part (2), assignment (3), function.

Inquest, *n.* An inquiry by a coroner or medical examiner, sometimes with the aid of a jury, to determine the cause of death of a person who appears to have died suddenly or by violence. See inquiry (1), search (1).

Inquire, *v.* See ask, cross-examine, investigate, search, audit, canvass; inquiry.

Inquiry, *n.* **1.** A careful examination of a matter (an inquiry into the death of the victim). Inquest, investigation, hearing, quest, questioning, exploration, canvassing, trial, analysis, survey, hunt, scrutiny, probe, research, interrogation, pursuit, delving, check, study, inspection, reconnaissance, autopsy, biopsy, test. See also audit, search, examination. **2.** A question (an inquiry from the judge). Query, interrogatory, request for information, inquisition, quiz. See also question.

Inquisition, *n.* See inquiry, inquest, investigation, examination.

Inquisitive, *adj.* See curious (1); prying.

Inquisitor, *n.* A person (e.g., coroner, sheriff) who has the power to inquire into certain matters. See investigator, coroner.

In re In the matter of; a way of designating a court case in which there are no adversary parties in the traditional sense but merely some "res" concerning which a judicial determination must be made, e.g., a bankrupt's estate, an estate in probate court, a proposed public highway (In re Estate of Smith). In the affair of; regarding, pertaining, in regard to, in respect of, with respect to. See also concerning, about (2); pertain.

In rem Designating a proceeding or action binding the whole world which determines rights in specific property or the status of a specific subject matter. In a sense, the "defendant" in such a case is the property, status, or subject matter itself.

Inroad, *n.* See intrusion, infringement, invasion, violation, attack, assault, injury.

Inroll, *v.* See enroll.

INS See Immigration and Naturalization Service.

Insane, *adj.* **1.** Characterized by insanity. See deranged, demented; insanity. **2.** Absurd (an insane proposal). Foolish, ridiculous, outrageous, stupid, crazy, silly, ludicrous, impractical, immature, unreasonable, bizarre, mad, extravagant, queer, incoherent, childish, fatuous, asinine, nonsensical, eccentric, idiotic, scatterbrained, unsound, moronic, fanatic, senseless, imbecilic, laughable, fantastic, unrealistic, visionary. See also juvenile, lunatic, dumb, absurd, irrational, irregular, odd (1), anomalous, impracticable; comic. *Ant.* Rational.

Insane delusion The conception of a disordered mind that imagines facts to exist for which there is no evidence. See insanity, hallucination.

Insanity, *n.* **1.** That degree of mental illness which negates the individual's legal responsibility or capacity. **2.** Restatement test: A person is not responsible for criminal conduct if, at the time of such conduct as a result of mental disease or defect, he or she lacks substantial capacity either to appreciate the criminality (wrongfulness) of his or her conduct or to conform his or her conduct to the requirements of the law. **3.** Durham test: An accused is not criminally responsible if his or her unlawful act was the product of mental disease or mental defect. **4.** M'Naghton test: At the time of committing the act, the accused was laboring under such a defect of reason, from disease of the mind, as not to know the nature and quality of the act the accused was doing, or if the accused did know it, he or she did not know that it was wrong. Lunacy, derangement, madness, mental deficiency, mental illness, mental incompetence, dementia, psychopathy, psychosis, aberration, delirium, idiocy, schizophrenia, imbalance, dotage, alienation, distraction, acromania, imbecility, disorientation, neurosis, dementia praecox, frenzy, delirium tremens, senility, craziness, mania. See also hallucination, disease, illness, delusion, hysteria, eccentricity. *Ant.* Sanity.

Insatiable, *adj.* See avaricious; jealous; excess, extreme (1); intemperance.

Inscribe, *v.* To enter on a list; to write in or mark on (her name was inscribed on the watch). Register, etch, pen, impress, autograph, chisel, imprint, post, insert, enscroll. See also engrave, record, enter (1), enroll.

Inscription, *n.* **1.** Anything written or engraved on a solid substance intended for great durability (the inscription on the ring). Legend, engraving, epigraph, dedication, memo, notation, message, calligraphy. See also inscribe. **2.** The entry of a mortgage, lien, or other document in a book of public records. See registration, recording.

Inscrutable, *adj.* See ambiguous, obscure (1), mysterious, incoherent, illegible, complex (1).

Insecure, *adj.* **1.** Not secure or safe (insecure lock). Hazardous, perilous, risky, at risk, undependable, vulnerable, unbalanced, precarious, tottering, exposed, infirm, in jeopardy, fallible, unprotected, unreliable, untrustworthy, susceptible, dubious, treacherous, unsteady, borderline, rickety, adrift. See also dangerous, weak, defenseless, frail. **2.** Uncertain (insecure future). Unsure, fragile, dubious, uneasy, adrift, changeable, fickle, anxious, diffident, open, doubtful, nervous, hesitant. See also apprehensive, impatient, feverish, excitable, concerned, fluctuating, tentative. *Ant.* Trustworthy; confident.

Insecurity, *n.* **1.** The state of being insecure. See doubt (2), jeopardy (2); insecure; danger, risk. **2.** The lack of self-confidence (the insecurity of the witness). Self-doubt, apprehensiveness, hesitation, instability, lack of assurance, absence of self-reliance, diffidence, bashfulness, embarrassment, uncertainty, shyness, self-consciousness, timidity, reluctance. *Ant.* Confidence.

Inseminate, *v.* See impregnate; beget.

Insensate, *adj.* See oblivious.

Insensitive, *adj.* See callous, blind (1), indifferent (2), blatant (2), careless, dumb, impetuous, rude, oblivious.

Inseparable, *adj.* See inherent, indivisible.

Insert, *v.* See introduce, imbue, fill, inscribe, enter (1), record, add, interpolate.

Insertion, *n.* See interlineation, addendum, attachment (3), intervention (2).

Inside, *n., adj.* See interior; coterie; confidential, private; intangible.

Insider, *n.* **1.** Someone who has knowledge of facts not available to the general public (securities violations by the insider). **2.** A member of a select group (one of the insiders making the decisions). See official (1), associate (2).

Insider trading Buying and selling corporate shares by officers, directors, and shareholders who own more than 10% of the stock of a corporation listed on a national exchange.

Insidious, *adj.* See infamous, illicit, corrupt, odious, deceitful, deceptive.

Insight, *n.* See comprehension, perception, apprehension (1), information, knowledge.

Insightful, *adj.* See acute (1).

Insignia, *n.* Distinctive mark (the company's insignia). Badge, trademark, trait, label, stripe, symbol, sign, patch, decoration, regalia, emblem, star, stamp, token, identification, characteristic.

Insignificant, *adj.* See petty (2), nugatory, frivolous, de minimus, expendable; iota.

Insincere, *adj.* See false (2), fake, cynical, deceptive, dishonest, feigned, artificial; evasive; arrogant, pompous.

Insinuate, *v.* See intimate (6), suggest; mean (2), intend; insinuation.

Insinuation, *n.* An indirect comment or suggestion (the insinuation of guilt). Whisper, allusion, indication, hint, aspersion, veiled comment, reference, inference, intimation, slur, implication, animadversion, ascription. See also innuendo.

Insipid, *adj.* See commonplace, barren, indifferent.

Insist, *n.* See press (2), demand (1), instigate, assert.

Insistent, *adj.* See assertive, firm (2), inflexible, compelling, diligent, constant (3).

Insolent, *adj.* See impertinent (2), rude.

Insolence, *n.* Presumption, rudeness. Boldness, sauciness, audacity, impudence, chutzpah, incivility. See also effrontery, arrogance; spirit (2), neglect (2).

Insolvency, *n.* The condition of being unable to pay one's debts as they fall due or in the usual course of trade and business (the judgment pushed her into insolvency). Failure, bankruptcy, destitution, impoverishment, default, ruin, impecuniousness, pauperism, indebtedness, nonpayment, penury, mendicancy, mendicity. See also poverty; bankrupt. *Ant.* Financial stability.

Insolvency, act of See act of insolvency.

Insolvent, *adj.* See bankrupt, indigent, destitute.

Insomnia, *n.* Sleeplessness. See disease, illness.

Insouciant, *adj.* See debonair, indifferent, casual, frivolous.

Inspect, *v.* See investigate, audit, search, watch, observe (3); inspection.

Inspection, *n.* An examination to determine the quality, quantity, authenticity, or condition of something (inspection of the records). Investigation, scrutiny, checking, probe, appraisal, audit, surveillance, inventory, study, search, consideration, inquisition, research, evaluation, supervision, assessment, exploration, survey, ascertainment, perusal, trial, test, experiment, observation, scanning, contemplation, review, attention, vigil, lookout, superintendence, vigilance, visitation, view, reconnaissance, trailing, bugging, eavesdropping, spying, oversight. See also examination, inquest, inquiry.

Inspector, *n.* Officers whose duty is to inspect things over which they have jurisdiction (safety inspector). Investigator, observer, examiner, watchman, evaluator; detective, auditor, engineer, appraiser, assessor. See also spy.

Inspiration, *n.* See motivation, motive, cause (1), impulse, influence; passion, emotion.

Inspire, *v.* See incite, animate, provoke (1), cause (2); imbue, influence, prompt (2).

Instability, *n.* See insecurity, jeopardy (2), doubt (2), infirmity; weak, dangerous.

Install, *v.* **1.** To place in an office (installed as governor). Induct, instate, inaugurate, invest, ordain, set up, seat, admit, introduce, coronate, usher in, receive, consecrate, chair. See also initiate, launch, institute. **2.** To place in position or fix for use (install the computer). Position, service, make operative, connect, hook up, establish, situate, station, locate, plant. *Ant.* Remove.

Installation, *n.* See inauguration; division (2); install.

Installment, *n.* **1.** Partial payment of a debt; a portion of a debt payable at successive periods; a part of something coming out or issued in stages (the alimony was payable in installments). Segment, division, periodic payment, advance payment, unit, allotment, fragment, section, portion, earnest, deposit; chapter. **2.** Installation. See install.

Installment credit A commercial arrangement in which the buyer undertakes to pay in more than one payment, and the seller agrees to sell on this basis, for which a finance charge may be imposed. See credit; periodic.

Installment loan A loan to be repaid in specified, and often equal, amounts over a designated number of months. See loan; periodic.

Installment method A method of accounting enabling a taxpayer to spread the recognition of gain on the sale of property over the payout period. See sale; periodic.

Installment sale A commercial arrangement by which a buyer makes an initial down payment and signs a contract for the payment of the balance in installments over a period of time. See sale; periodic.

Instance, *n.* An illustration (the witness could not recall one instance of harassment). Example, case in point, citation, situation, specific, demonstration, paradigm, prototype, circumstance, exemplification, antecedent, specimen. See also sample (1), precedent, case (3).

Instant, 1. *adj.* Now under consideration (the instant case). Present, current, pending, at hand, existing, existent, prevailing, contemporary, imminent, forthcoming, near at hand, upcoming, approaching. **2.** *adj.* Prompt (the judge wanted an instant response). Immediate, on the spot, quick, early, at once, forthwith, sudden, direct, speedy, expeditious, simultaneous, instantaneous, unhesitating, split-second, fast, momentary, abrupt, without delay, punctual, hasty. See also summary. **3.** *n.* A moment (visible for an instant). Flash, trice, minute, split second, fraction of a second. **4.** *adj.* Capable of being prepared easily (instant coffee). Precooked, ready-to-use, packaged. *Ant.* Prior; delayed; forever.

Instantaneous, *adj.* Occurring without delay. See immediate (1), summary, prompt, instant (2).

Instead, *adv.* See replacement.

Instigate, *v.* To stimulate or goad to an action (she instigated the robbery). Stir up, foment, press, predispose, rouse, start, generate, kindle, impel, entice, prevail upon, induce, agitate, exhort, prompt, "egg on," initiate, set in motion, invigorate, coax, cajole, cause, excite, provide an impetus, give incentive, insist, inspire, jolt, actuate, embolden, support, urge, taunt, solicit, suborn, motivate, lobby, inflame, animate, tempt, incline, entrap. See also introduce, provoke, incite, abet, influence, encourage. *Ant.* Hamper.

Instill, *v.* See imbue, introduce; educate, instruct.

Instinct, *n.* See impulse, intuition; ability, facility (3), gift (2), power.

Instinctive, *adj.* Arising from impulse. See spontaneous; mechanical, habitual, involuntary; impetuous; inherent, congenital, native (3).

In stirps See per stirps, stirps.

Institute 1. *v.* To inaugurate; to commence (institute a lawsuit). Establish, originate, develop, launch, begin, start, undertake, introduce, erect, effectuate, enact, get under way, beget, actuate, lay the foundation for, organize, pioneer, engender, usher in, install, set up, prescribe, found, constitute. See also commence, initiate, instigate. **2.** *n.* An organization that studies or promotes a particular area (American Law Institute). Foundation, academy, college, league, body, fellowship, center, institution, establishment. See also association, school. **3.** *n.* Textbooks containing elementary principles of jurisprudence (Institutes of Justinian).

Institution, *n.* **1.** An organized society (charitable institution). Organization, foundation, alliance, league, corporation, fellowship, academy, fraternity, center, institute, sodality, conglomerate, firm. See also association, school, establishment.

Institution

2. An established custom, practice, or principle (the institution of slavery). Law, code, tradition, rule, fixture, habit, ritual, rite. See also convention (3), custom (1). **3.** The act of instituting something (the institution of a lawsuit). See institute (1), establishment (2), commencement.

Instruct, *v.* **1.** To give information; to teach (the lawyer instructed her secretary). Guide, tell, recommend, advise, advocate, apprise, enlighten, inform, tutor, explain, demonstrate, lecture, indoctrinate, school, impart, conduct classes, exercise, prepare, prime, implant, profess, propound, illuminate, groom, cultivate, instill, infuse, warn, moralize, point out, coach, notify, familiarize, initiate, ground, announce, counsel, admonish, drill, edify. See also educate, discipline (4), nurture, clarify, preach. **2.** To give an order (she was instructed to return at noon). Command, mandate, decree, order, impose, require, ordain, tell, enjoin, direct, prescribe, charge.

Instruction, *n.* See education, knowledge, clarity, information (2), direction, advice; order (1), mandate; instruct; charge (12).

Instruction to the jury A statement given by a judge to the members of the jury informing them of the law applicable to the case (counsel's request for an instruction on the point was denied). See charge (12).

Instructive, *adj.* See demonstrative (1), descriptive, informative; academic (2).

Instructor, *n.* See teacher; school.

Instrument, *n.* **1.** A written document (negotiable instrument). Record, paper, writing, legal document, deed, contract, grant, charter, will, lease. **2.** A tool or utensil (surgical instrument). Machine, gadget, article, equipment, mechanism, appliance, invention, gear, machinery, contrivance, aid, wherewithal. See also apparatus, device, implement (1). **3.** A means for accomplishing something (the court is an instrument of justice). Medium, power, force, vehicle, intermediary, facility. See also agency, agent, instrumentality.

Instrumental, *adj.* Helpful to achieve an end (the report was instrumental). Useful, essential, indispensable, advantageous, contributory, conducive, vital, valuable, supportive, crucial, active, decisive, significant. See also important, effective, beneficial, gainful. *Ant.* Useless.

Instrumentality, *n.* A means or agency (dangerous instrumentality). Operation, machine, vehicle, device, tool, channel, force, power, manner, equipment, technique, resource, wherewithal, mechanism, system, mode. See also agency, method, process, procedure; apparatus.

Instrumentality rule The corporate existence of a subsidiary will be disregarded when it is so organized and controlled in its affairs by its parent corporation that it is really an adjunct and instrument of the latter. The corporate veil will be pierced, making the parent liable for the obligations of the subsidiary. See alter ego (2), piercing the corporate veil.

Insubordinate, *adj.* See disobedient, contentious, hostile, incorrigible, disorderly; insubordination.

Insubordination, *n.* Disobedience to constituted authority; a willful or intentional disregard of the lawful and reasonable instructions of an employer (terminated for insubordination). Noncompliance, impudence, insurgence, unruliness, insurgency, protest, disruption, disorderliness, disloyalty, obstinacy, transgression, infraction, dissension, treachery, infringement, contumacy. See also defiance, rebellion. *Ant.* Submissiveness.

Insubstantial, *adj.* See petty (2), nugatory, frivolous, de minimus, expendable; intangible (3); iota.

Insufferable, *adj.* See inexcusable, grievous (1), painful, cruel, severe, extreme, difficult.

Insufficient, *adj.* Inadequate to meet a need, purpose, or use (insufficient funds to cover the check). Lacking, incomplete, wanting, meager, sparse, incommensurate, unsatisfactory, depleted, absent, exhausted, short, uneven, poor, incompetent, not enough, impotent, scarce, impoverished, lacking, unqualified, minus, small, limited, piddling, nominal, scant, tight, in short supply; paucity, dearth. See also inadequate, deficient, imperfect, inferior (2), few. *Ant.* Sufficient.

Insular, *adj.* **1.** Pertaining to an island or its inhabitants (insular possessions of the United States). See island. **2.** Isolated or narrow (insular ideas). Narrow-minded, provincial, limited, restricted, regional, illiberal, bigoted, circumscribed, apart, confined. See also parochial.

Insulate, *v.* See cover; divide, group (2), sequester.

Insult, *v.*, **insult,** *n.* See slander, affront, abuse, decry, condemn, harass, offense, wrong, indignity.

Insuperable, *adj.* See onerous, difficult (2), serious, acute (2), irresistible; indestructible, invulnerable; impossible.

Insurable, *adj.* Capable of being insured against loss, damage, death, etc. (insurable interest). Affording a sufficient ground for insurance; proper to be insured.

Insurable interest A relationship to the subject of the insurance that will necessarily entail pecuniary loss in case of its injury or destruction; an interest that furnishes a reasonable expectation of pecuniary benefit from the continued existence of the subject of the insurance.

Insurance, *n.* A contract to provide compensation for a loss on a specified subject by specified perils (liability insurance). Indemnification, assurance, coverage, policy, warranty, pledge, covenant, security, guarantee, indemnity against contingencies, bond, precaution, safeguard. See also guaranty, surety.

Insurance agent Someone who represents a particular insurance company in dealing with the public on insurance matters. See agent, broker.

Insurance broker An intermediary or middleman between the public and an insurer on insurance matters. A broker, unlike an agent, is not tied to a particular insurance company. See broker, agent.

Insurance policy An instrument in writing by which one party (insurer) engages for the consideration of a premium to indemnify another (insured) against a contingent loss by providing compensation if a designated event occurs, resulting in the loss. See indemnity (2); compensation; indemnify.

Insurance premium The consideration paid by an insured to an insurer for insurance protection. See cost, payment (1).

Insurance rating The process by which the premium for a policy is set after considering the risks involved. See rate.

Insurance trust An agreement between an insured and a trustee, whereby the proceeds of a policy are paid directly to the trustee for investment and distribution to designated beneficiaries as provided in the trust agreement. See trust.

Insure, *v.* To engage to indemnify a person against pecuniary loss from specified perils or possible liability (the company insured its inventory). Obtain insurance, secure against loss, underwrite; guard, safeguard, shield, back, check, warrant, arrange, provide, assure, reassure. See also cover (1), guarantee.

Insured, *n.* The person covered by insurance.

Insurer, *n.* The underwriter or insurance company with whom a contract of insurance is made (the insurer claimed the loss was not covered by the policy). Indemnitor, indemnifier, guarantor, assurer. See also surety.

Insurgence, *n.* See mutiny, defiance, rebellion, insurrection, insubordination; insurgent.

Insurgent 1. *n.* One who participates in an insurrection (the insurgents were captured). Rebel, rioter, revolutionary, agitator, mutineer, traitor, insurrectionist, reformer, dissident, guerrilla, resister, extremist, adversary, iconoclast, enemy. See also anarchist, nonconformist, nihilist, wrongdoer. **2.** *adj.* Rebellious (insurgent forces). Lawless, disobedient, seditious, out of control, treasonable, unmanageable, subversive, insubordinate. See also mutinous. *Ant.* Loyalist; obedient.

Insurmountable, *adj.* See impossible, onerous, difficult, unconscionable; invulnerable.

Insurrection, *n.* A rising of citizens or subjects in revolt against their government (damage caused by the insurrection). Uprising, riot, coup d'état, insurgence, revolution, subversion, putsch, coup, anarchy, sedition, outbreak, disturbance, overthrow, political violence, takeover, civil disorder. See also mutiny, defiance, rebellion, insubordination.

Intact, *adj.* See whole, complete (2), entire, full; integrity (2).

Intangible 1. *adj.* Not capable of being perceived by the senses (intangible property). Nonphysical, without physical substance, abstract, imperceptible, impalpable, unworldly, transcendental, metaphysical, disembodied, soulful, intellectual, philosophical, theoretical, psychic, intuitive, ghostly, supernatural, phantom, spectral, psychological, inner, moral, incorporeal, bodiless, immaterial, nonmaterial, invisible. **2.** *n.* Property that is a "right" rather than a physical object even though the right may be evidenced by a physical piece of paper (e.g., patent, stock, trademark, copyright, goodwill, chose in action). **3.** *adj.* Incapable of being readily defined (an intangible fear). Amorphous, uncertain, inconspicuous, vague, evanescent, indefinite, imaginary, fleeting, insubstantial, occult, mystic, imponderable, obscure, esoteric, mysterious. *Ant.* Tangible.

Integral, *adj.* See inherent, native (3), congenital, intrinsic, dispensable; whole, complete (2), entire, full.

Integrate, *v.* See commingle, associate (1), group (2); desegregation; integrated (1); integration.

Integrated, *adj.* **1.** Open to different groups without restriction (an integrated school). Desegregated, mixed, racially balanced, available, assimilated. **2.** Unified into a whole (an integrated presentation). Coordinated, harmonized, harmonious, cohesive, smooth, consolidated, complete, blended, organized, synthesized, systematized. See also associated. *Ant.* Segregated; scattered.

Integrated bar A bar association to which all lawyers must belong if they want to practice law in the geographic area covered by the association. The highest court in this area has supervisory control over the association. See bar.

Integrated contract A contract that contains within its four corners the entire agreement of the parties and is the final expression of their agreement. See contract.

Integration, *n.* **1.** Bringing together different groups as equals (racial integration). Desegregation, assimilation, union, harmonization, coexistence, See also cooperation, harmony. Mix, solidarity. **2.** The act or process of making whole or entire (the integration of all the factions). Unification, consolidation, synthesis, alliance, incorporation, combination, blending, amalgamation, affiliation, coalition, federation, fusion, mixture. See also association, merger. *Ant.* Separation.

Integrity, *n.* **1.** Soundness; having moral principle and character (questions about the integrity of the trustee). Rectitude, honesty, reliability, incorruptibility, virtue, fairness, uprightness, backbone, trustworthiness, sincerity, responsibility, fidelity, truthfulness, purity, justness, probity, fair-mindedness, decency, straightforwardness, moral fiber, moral stature, forthrightness. See also honor (3). **2.** Wholeness (territorial integrity). Completeness, oneness, entirety, unity, strength, totality, intactness. *Ant.* Corruption; disintegration.

Intellect, *n.* See mind (1), ability, judgment (2), reason (2), comprehension, capacity (2), character (2), competence, common sense.

Intellectual, *adj., n.* See brilliant, able, capable (2), learned, literary (2), rational, reasonable; academic; scholar, teacher, student.

Intelligence, *n.* See judgment (2), capacity (2), knowledge, education, literacy, clarity, cognition, gift (2), cognizance (3), common sense, competence; bulletin, communication (2), information (2).

Intelligencer, *n.* See informer, spy, agent.

Intelligent, *adj.* See capable (2), brilliant, able, apt (3, 4), cognizant, discreet, learned, acute (1), prudent, careful.

Intelligentsia, *n.* See aristocracy, coterie, establishment (4); nonconformist.

Intelligible, *adj.* Comprehensible (the lawyer failed to make the case intelligible to the jury). Understood, understandable, obvious, luminous, precise, well-defined, decipherable, unambiguous, cognizable, lucid, perceptible, translucent, apparent, knowable, discernible, manifest, unmistakable. See also comprehensible, definite (1), clear (1), direct (6), evident. *Ant.* Confused.

Intemperance, *n.* The lack of restraint (intemperance in the use of alcohol). Excess, self-indulgence, abandon, extravagance, exaggeration, insatiability, unreasonableness, self-gratification, gluttony, dissipation, incontinence, profligacy, promiscuity, insobriety, drunkenness, alcoholism. See also debauchery, intoxication. *Ant.* Restraint.

Intemperate, *adj.* See immoderate, extreme (1), excess, aggravated; intoxicated; wanton, wild, violent; lascivious, lewd, obscene.

Intend, *v.* To plan for, design, or expect a certain result (he did not intend the contact). Propose, mean, calculate, scheme, aspire, determine, reckon, resolve, contemplate, try, strive, dream of, presume, incline, wish, destine, labor for, essay, designate, plot. See also intent; desire, plan (3), aim.

Intendant, *n.* See manager.

Intended, *adj.* See premeditated, willful, intentional, deliberate (2), voluntary.

Intendment, *n.* The true meaning of something (intendment of the law). See intent, meaning, understanding.

Intense, *adj.* See emotional, ardent, strong (2), explicit; blatant, conspicuous, grievous, acute; harmful, injurious.

Intensify, *v.* See exacerbate, exaggerate, strengthen, augment, advance, raise (2), lift (2).

Intensity, *n.* See measure (1); passion, emotion, power, spirit (2), force (1), vigor, diligence (1), industry (2).

Intensive, *adj.* See comprehensive, complete, extensive, intense.

Intent, intention, *n.* **1.** The design or aim of a person in acting; the desire to cause the consequences of one's acts or the knowledge with substantial certainty that the consequences will follow from what one does (intent to publish the derogatory statement). Determination, scheme, plan, resolve, view, goal, contemplation, will, leaning, premeditation, end, mark, resolution, target, ambition, destination, fixed purpose, proposal, undertaking, decision, direction, inclination, plot, object, objective, idea, purport, import, drift, choice. **2.** The meaning or sense of something (intent of Congress). Drift, implication, connotation, intendment, tenor, effect, denotation, sum and substance, essence, indication, signification, core, message, significance, cast, direction, character, nature, sense, gist, mood, tendency, vein, course, proclivity, flow, path, quality, route, propensity, penchant, bias, leaning, impetus, current.

Intentional, *adj.* Done on purpose; planned (intentional interference). Pre-

Intentional

planned, calculated, plotted, intended, considered, contemplated, resolved, purposeful, schemed, designed, conscious, thought out, purposive, contrived, willed, witting, aimed, thoughtful, prearranged, voluntary. See also premeditated, voluntary, deliberate (2). *Ant.* Fortuitous.

Inter, *v.* To bury. Entomb, inurn, inhume, sepulcher; burial.

Interact, *v.* See affect, relate (1), connect.

Interactive, *adj.* See mutual.

Inter alia Among other things.

Intercede, *v.* See arbitrate (3), represent (1), assist.

Intercept, *v.* To interfere; to seize; to acquire the contents of a wire or oral communication through the use of any electronic, mechanical, or other device (she intercepted the call). Detain, reroute, foil, abort, obstruct, commandeer, block, impound, cut off, stop, expropriate, catch, thwart, dispossess, interpose, impede, deflect, nab, get hold of, confiscate, stay, arrest, repress, frustrate, grab. See also eavesdrop, bug; inhibit, hinder. *Ant.* Expedite.

Intercession, *n.* See petition, entreaty, suit.

Interchange, *v.,* **interchange,** *n.* See exchange (1); reciprocity.

Interchangeable, *adj.* See identical, mutual, same, equivalent, equal (2), analogous; variable.

Interchangeably, *adv.* Capable of switching one for the other (the two terms are used interchangeably by the legislature). Mutually, reciprocally, synonymously, equally, equivalently, in exchange. *Ant.* Differently.

Interconnection, *n.* See relation (1), connection; relative (2).

Intercourse, *n.* **1.** Communication, exchange (commercial intercourse). Dialogue, trade, correspondence, dealings, traffic, business, connection, communion, speech, dealing, colloquy, talking, congress, contact, intercommunication, flow, parley, liaison. See also communication, commerce, conversation (1), colloquium, conference. **2.** Sexual intercourse (his defense was that the intercourse was voluntary). Sexual relations, copulation, coupling, carnal knowledge, intimacy, mating. See also coitus, fornication.

Interdependent, *adj.* See mutual, reciprocal, related; mutuality.

Interdict, *v.,* **interdict,** *n.* **1.** *v.* To forbid, prevent, restrict (interdict the flow of drugs). See bar, ban, prohibit. **2.** *n.* An ecclesiastical censure.

Interest 1. *n.* A right, claim, title, or legal share in something; a right to have the advantage accruing from something (a financial interest in the company). Stake, holding, portion, property, part, ownership, possession, investment, stock, percentage, slice, equity, piece, estate, privilege. See also power, right, claim. **2.** *n.* A charge that is paid to borrow or use money (the bank charged high interest). Premium, profit, gain, return, increase, accrual, dividend; benefit, enrichment, boon, advantage. See also cost, payment; compensation. **3.** *n.* A feeling of curiosity or concern (an interest in the child's welfare). Solicitude, absorption, attention, study, heed, notice, regard, anxiety, conscientiousness, worry, thoughtfulness, preoccupation, enthusiasm, mindfulness. See also consideration (2), concern (5). **4.** *n.* Participation in something (diverse interests). Pursuit, avocation, engrossment, pastime, care, affair, regard, attraction. See also diversion, amusement. **5.** *v.* To cause someone to become involved or curious (efforts to interest the workers in the union). Engage, attract, absorb, excite, captivate, induce, tempt, engross, infect, grip, occupy, influence, lure, incline, sway, divert, affect, entertain, arouse, rouse, stir, beguile, titillate, entangle. See also entice, provoke.

Interested, *adj.* Involved, nonobjective (interested witness). Influenced, biased, concerned, prejudiced, undetached, jaundiced, affected, connected, engaged, implicated. See also partisan, partial, one-sided. *Ant.* Detached.

Interest equalization tax A tax imposed on each acquisition by a U.S. person of the stock of a foreign issuer or of a debt obligation of a foreign obligor if such obligation has a period remaining to maturity of a year or more. See tax.

Interesting, *adj.* See attractive, intriguing, compelling, enjoyable, outstanding (2), exceptional.

Interest rate The percentage of an amount of money that is paid for its use for a specified time. See also cost, rate.

Interfere, *v.* To hamper or meddle (he interfered with the performance of the contract). Inhibit, check, hinder, infringe, encroach, trespass, disturb, intervene, interpose, conflict, intercede, oppose, handicap, interrupt, restrain, counter, be a hindrance, frustrate, jar, "butt in," block, collide, impede, inconvenience, foil, thwart, encumber, cripple, contravene, intrude, cramp, sabotage, arrest, retard, countervail, intercept, deter. See also obstruct. *Ant.* Facilitate.

Interference, *n.* See obstruction, opposition, prohibition, blockage (1), intervention (2), inconvenience, constraint, prevention; interfere.

Interim 1. *n.* Intervening time (in the interim, he filed the motion). Meanwhile, intermission, recess, pause, interlude, meantime, interregnum, break. **2.** *adj.* Temporary (an interim appointment). Provisional, intermediate, transient, substitutional, pro tempore, stopgap, makeshift. See also temporary, acting. *Ant.* Future; permanent.

Interim financing A short-term loan usually obtained to pay for the construction costs of a building or house, with the final financing to be covered by a mortgage. See loan; back, finance.

Interior, *adj.* Dealing with the inner part of something (interior design). Internal, inward, inmost, innermost, enclosed, inland, inside, center. *Ant.* Exterior.

Interior Department A federal agency overseeing Indian affairs, mining, fish and wildlife, geologic research, land management, national parks and monuments, flood control, conservation, etc.

Interject, *v.* See interpolate, introduce, add.

Interlineation, *n.* The act of writing between the lines of an instrument; that which is written between the lines (interlineations in the will). Insertion, interjection, placement, sliding in, infusion, interpolation, supplement, addition, inset. See also interpolate.

Interlining, *n.* The practice whereby a carrier, whose certified routes do not reach a particular shipment destination, transfers the shipment to another carrier for delivery.

Interlock, *v.* See lock (2), connect (1), converge, cooperate; interlocking.

Interlocking, *adj.* Closely joined or fitted together (interlocking companies). Interlinked, united, dovetailed, linked, interwoven, interlaced. *Ant.* Independent.

Interlocking directorate A board of directors of one corporation linked with the board of another corporation, with some of the same people serving on both boards so that the businesses of the two companies are to some degree under one control. See board, corporation.

Interloctory, *adj.* Not final; interim (interlocutory order). Provisional, tentative, intermediary, transient, intervening. See also interim (2), temporary, acting. *Ant.* Permanent.

Interlocutory appeal An appeal of an issue or matter that is taken before the trial court reaches its final judgment. See appeal.

Interloper, *n.* A person who meddles in the affairs of others, to which he or she has no right or responsibility (the interloper was not allowed to speak or vote). Intermeddler, trespasser, busybody, infiltrator, encroacher, raider, stowaway, crasher. See also intruder, wrongdoer.

Interlude, *n.* See interim (1).

Intermarriage, *n.* The marriage between people from different races, religions, or other groups. See miscegenation.

Intermeddle, *v.* To interfere wrongly with the property or affairs of another (an injunction against one who intermeddles). Invade, trespass, intrude, infringe, interrupt, intercept, hinder, inhibit, thwart, "butt in." See also interfere, encroach, impede, interloper, prying; intervention (2). *Ant.* Ignore.

Intermediary, *n.* One who tries to resolve a matter or problem between two or more persons or groups (the intermediary attempted to settle the strike). Mediator, arbitrator, broker, middleman, go-between, contact, vehicle, moderator, medium, emissary, representative, means, umpire, intercessor, factor, attorney, negotiator, proxy, link, intervener. See also agent, referee, messenger.

Intermediary bank Any bank to which an item is transferred in the course of collection except the depositary or payor bank. See bank.

Intermediate, *adj.* Occurring or lying between the beginning and end (intermediate stop). Halfway, in-between, median, intermediary, central, mid, equidistant, intervening, transitional, interposed. See also middle. *Ant.* Terminal.

Intermediate courts Courts with general jurisdiction (trial, appellate, or both) that are below the court of last resort in the jurisdiction. See court.

Intermediate order A nonappealable order made between the commencement of an action and its final determination on an incidental or ancillary matter that does not finally resolve the case. See order; interlocutory.

Interminable, *adj.* See incalculable, permanent, continuous, continual, perpetual; big, great; diffuse (2).

Intermingle, *v.* See commingle, consort (2), associate (1); mixture, compound (3).

Intermission, *v.* See interim (1), delay (3), interruption; adjourn.

Intermittent, *adj.* Starting and stopping at intervals (intermittent pain). Off-and-on, spasmodic, interrupted, cyclical, alternate, recurring, recurrent, not continuous, occasional, fitful, infrequent, discontinuous, broken, seasonal, punctuated, random. See also inconsistent, irregular, fluctuating, periodic. *Ant.* Uniform.

Intermix, *v.* See commingle, consort (2), associate (1).

Intern, *v.,* **intern,** *n.* **1.** *v.* To restrict or confine a person or group (they were interned during the war). See confine (1), imprison, jail. **2.** *n.* A graduate student obtaining practical experience and training outside the classroom; an assistant resident doctor (a heavily supervised intern). Journeyman, novice, "greenhorn," apprentice, trainee, neophyte. See also student; doctor; amateur, beginner, assistant, employee.

Internal, *adj.* **1.** Relating to the interior or the inside (internal medicine). Inner, innermost, inmost. See also interior. **2.** Relating to the domestic affairs of a country (internal security). Home, in-house, civil, municipal, state, national. **3.** Relating to the nature of a thing (internal evidence). Inborn, innate, infixed, implanted. See also inherent, intrinsic, congenital, native (3).

Internal revenue Government tax revenue from internal sources as contrasted with revenue from customs and foreign sources. See tax, revenue, income.

Internal Revenue Code (I.R.C.) The federal statute in title 26 of the U.S. Code that codifies federal tax laws including income, estate, stamp, gift, excise, and other taxes. See tax, revenue.

Internal Revenue Service (I.R.S.) The federal agency responsible for enforcing the internal revenue laws except those relating to alcohol, tobacco, firearms, explosives, and wagering. See tax, revenue, enforcement.

Internal security Laws and government activity dealing with measures to protect the country from subversive activities. See protection, security (2).

International, *adj.* Concerning two or more countries (international commerce). Foreign, worldwide, global; universal, cosmopolitan. See also world. *Ant.* Domestic.

International Court of Justice The judicial arm of the United Nations with jurisdiction to give advisory opinions on matters of law and treaty construction, and to settle legal disputes voluntarily submitted to it by the parties. See court.

International Monetary Fund (IMF) An agency of the United Nations established to stabilize international exchange and to promote balanced international trade.

Internecine, *adj.* See deadly, violent, deleterious; internal, domestic.

Internee, *n.* See inmate.

Internist, *n.* A specialist in internal medicine. See doctor, specialist.

Internment, *n.* The detainment or confinement of enemy aliens or persons suspected of disloyalty (internment in the labor camps). See detention; confine.

Interplay, *v., n.* See connect, relate; connection, reciprocity.

Interpleader, *n.* A procedure to determine the rights of rival claimants to property held by a third party (called the stakeholder) when the latter has no interest in the property. For example, an insurance company is willing to pay out on a policy, but is faced with several persons who say they are separately entitled to the funds. To avoid possible multiple liability, the stakeholder uses interpleader to force the rivals to resolve their dispute in one action. See pleading, party.

Interpol, *n.* International Criminal Police Organization; a coordinating group for international law enforcement.

Interpolate, *v.* To insert additional or false words in a complete instrument or document, and thus alter its meaning (the son interpolated a new provision into his father's will). Inject, introduce, amend, edit "doctor," annex, change, append, interline, rewrite; footnote, annotate; insinuate. See also interlineation.

Interpose, *n.* See introduce, add, enter (1), interpolate.

Interposition, *n.* The doctrine that a state in the exercise of its sovereignty can reject a law or mandate of the federal government that the state deems to be unconstitutional or beyond the powers delegated to the federal government in the U.S. Constitution.

Interpret, *v.* To seek out the meaning of language (the court interpreted the statute). Translate, delineate, explain, unscramble, untangle, decipher, explicate, elucidate, paraphrase, decode, annotate, expound, illustrate, gloss, restate, demonstrate, illuminate, deduce, unravel, make clear, throw light on, figure out, solve, infer, read, understand. See also clarify, define, construe.

Interpretation, *n.* See construction (1), definition, clarification, annotation.

Interregnum, *n.* An interval or vacancy between reigns or governments. See interim.

Interrelate, *n.* See connect, relate; organic (3); related.

Interrogate, *n.* See cross-examine, ask (1), investigate; question; interrogation.

Interrogation, *n.* A methodical process of questioning (interrogation by the police). Grilling, inquisition, catechizing, cross-examination, scrutiny, testing, pumping, third degree. See also investigation, examination, inquiry, inquest, audit.

Interrogatories, *n.* A discovery device consisting of written questions about the case submitted by one side of a lawsuit to the other. See discovery (1).

In terrorem clause A provision in a document such as a lease or will that is a warning designed to frighten a beneficiary or lessee into doing or not doing something (e.g., a clause in a will stating that a gift will be forfeited if a beneficiary contests the validity of the will).

Interrupt, *v.* See delay; end (2); dissolve; disturb, interfere, obstruct; interruption.

Interruption, *n.* A break in continuity or uniformity (an interruption of service). Interference, severance, suspension, stoppage, intermission, disturbance, disruption, pause, hiatus, hindrance, lull, standstill, abeyance, impediment, armistice, discontinuance, disconnection, cessation, recess, interlude, cancellation, division, punctuation, lacuna, stay, truce, disjunction, moratorium, reprieve, deferment, gap. See also delay, break (3), interval. *Ant.* Continuation.

Intersect, *v.* See cut (1), divide; connect, contact (4); intersection.

Intersection, *n.* A space occupied by more than one street, road, track, etc., at the point where they cross each other (a collision at the intersection). Junction, juncture, nexus, convergence, meeting point, crossing, corner, interchange.

Intersperse, *v.* See sprinkle; distribute; interpolate, add, introduce, enter (1).

Interspousal, *adj.* Relating to husband and wife (interspousal communication). Marital, conjugal, matrimonial, connubial, nuptial, paired, hymeneal, wedded, uxorial.

Interspousal immunity A prohibition against tort actions between husband and wife. The immunity has been abolished or limited by most states (e.g., allowing property tort actions such as conversion). See immunity, litigation.

Interstate, *adj.* Between or affecting two or more states; between places or persons in different states (interstate agreement). See national. *Ant.* Intrastate.

Interstate commerce Traffic, intercourse, commercial trading, or transportation of persons or property between or among the states of the United States. See commerce, intercourse.

Interstate Commerce Commission (ICC) A federal regulatory agency with jurisdiction over carriers (railroads, trucks, buses, etc.) engaged in transportation in interstate commerce and in foreign commerce to the extent that it takes place within the United States. The ICC assures that the carriers it regulates will provide the public with rates and services that are fair and reasonable. See vehicle, regulate.

Interstate compact An agreement between two or more states that is designed to meet common problems (e.g., flood control, boundary disputes). See compact (1).

Intertwine, *v.* See lock (2), join, connect (1), converge, cooperate; twist.

Interval, *n.* **1.** Time between two events (payments made at regular intervals). Gap, halt, recess, lull, break, lapse, opening, intermission, pause, interim, hiatus, spell, distance, respite, stretch, stop, discontinuance, interlude, stoppage. See also interruption, cessation. **2.** A gap of space (seeds planted at 3-foot intervals). Opening, lacuna, separation, gulf, hole, stop, aperture, interstice.

Interval ownership Ownership of property for a portion of a year (e.g., 2 weeks).

Intervene, *v.* See arbitrate; represent (1); interfere, encroach; delay; impede, hinder; intervening.

Intervening, *adj.* Coming or occurring between two times or events (intervening cause). Between, intruding, interfering, obtrusive, parenthetical, infringing, interrupting, breaking in, intercepting. See also superseding; intermediate, middle; among.

Intervening cause A cause that comes between an antecedent and a consequence; a new force that breaks the causal connection between the original conduct and the injury; an independent cause that intervenes between the original act or omission and the injury, turning aside the natural sequence of events and producing a result that would not otherwise have followed and which could not have been reasonably anticipated. See cause, superseding cause.

Intervenor, *n.* One who voluntarily enters (becomes a party in) a lawsuit between other persons. See party.

Intervention, *n.* **1.** The procedure by which a third person, not originally a party but claiming an interest in the subject matter of the suit, is allowed to come into the case to protect his or her own interests (the court refused to allow intervention by the trustee). **2.** Intrusion (intervention by the ex-president). Interference, intermeddling, encroachment, interruption, obstruction, overstepping, incursion, insertion, interjection. See also intrusion, infringement. **3.** Mediation (intervention by the referee). Arbitration, ministry, intercession, negotiation.

Interview, *v., n.* See ask (1), canvass (1), poll (1), cross-examine, investigate, search; converse (1); conference, meeting, conversation, communication.

Inter vivos From one living person to another (a gift inter vivos). Between the living. See also alive (1), living (3). *Ant.* Testamentary.

Inter vivos gift A gift that is made and that takes effect when the donor is living. See gift, charity.

Intestacy, *n.* Dying without a valid will (a distant cousin inherited everything under the laws of intestacy). See estate, administration of estate.

Intestate, *adj. n.* Without making a valid will; the person who dies without making a valid will (she died intestate; property of the intestate). See estate, administration of estate.

Intestate succession The transfer of property to the relatives of a decedent who has died without leaving a valid will. In most states, a statute will specify which relatives receive intestate shares and in what amount. See succession, descent; descend.

In testimonium In witness; in evidence whereof.

Intimacy, *n.* See affection (1), love, intimate (2, 4).

Intimate 1. *adj.* Close in familiarity (the witness had an intimate knowledge of the system). Detailed, experienced, thorough, incisive, penetrating, sound, solid, profound. **2.** *adj.* Well-acquainted (an intimate friendship). Close, dear, bosom, amicable, brotherly, sisterly, familiar, trusted, faithful, warm, fraternal. **3.** *adj.* Personal and private (one's intimate thoughts). Secret, confidential, guarded, exclusive, privy. **4.** *adj.* Involving sex (intimate relations). Erotic, sexual, carnal, adulterous, physical, fornicative, passionate, immoral, fleshly. **5.** *n.* A close friend (the witness was an intimate of the decedent). Confidant, comrade, associate, mate, crony, buddy, companion, alter ego; inseparable. **6.** *v.* To communicate indirectly (the witness intimated that more damaging evidence was available). Hint, suggest, imply, connote, indicate, insinuate, infer, provide an inkling, state through innuendo, signal, allude, rumor. *Ant.* Superficial (1–3); spiritual (4); enemy (5); proclaim (6).

Intimation, *n.* See suggestion, indication, innuendo (2); intimate (6).

Intimidate, *v.* To coerce unlawfully (intimidated into signing the contract). Threaten, extort, subdue, compel, pressure, bully, overawe, tyrannize, browbeat, petrify, shock, terrorize, make timid, "buffalo," menace, imperil, frighten, admonish, hector, unnerve, strong-arm; duress. See also coerce, harass.

Intimidation, *n.* See coercion, duress, threat, blackmail; cruelty; intimidate.

Intolerable, *adj.* See inexcusable, grievous (1), painful, extreme, severe, difficult, offensive, odious, repulsive.

Intolerance, *n.* See bias, prejudice (1), discrimination.

Intolerant, *adj.* See inflexible, narrow (2), strict (2), unfair, one-sided; arbitrary; bias, prejudice.

In toto, *adv.* Completely (the contract is void in toto). In the whole, wholly, entirely, utterly, fully, collectively, in all respects, comprehensively, altogether, thoroughly, undividedly, absolutely. *Ant.* Partially.

Intoxicant, *n.* See liquor; beverage.

Intoxicated, *adj.* Under the influence of intoxicating liquor (the intoxicated driver was arrested). Drunk, drunken, inebriated, "plastered," "loaded," "high," dazed, befuddled, bibulous, "on the sauce," stupefied; alcoholic, imbiber, "souse," "lush," "boozer," drunkard, *Ant.* Sober.

Intoxicating liquor Any liquor containing alcohol that can produce intoxication when used as a beverage in sufficient quantities. See liquor, beverage.

Intoxication, *n.* A condition of an individual who does not have the normal use of his or her physical or mental faculties as a result of drinking intoxicants; a greatly lessened ability to function normally, caused by alcohol or drugs (arrested for public intoxication). Inebriation, drunkenness, intemperance, insobriety, alcoholism. *Ant.* Sobriety.

Intra, *pref.* Within. See intrastate commerce.

Intractable, *adj.* See irreconcilable, firm, inflexible, incorrigible, willful, disobedient, strict (2).

Intramural, *adj.* Existing within (the intramural powers of the city). Within its bounds or walls, carried on or exercised within. *Ant.* Extramural.

Intransigent, *adj.* See strict (2), narrow (2), inflexible, firm, willful, arbitrary, irreconcilable.

In transitu In transit (goods damaged in transitu). On the way, in passage, in the course of transportation, while passing from one person or place to another.

Intrastate commerce Commerce that occurs within a state; business carried on entirely in one state.

Intra vires Within the power; within lawful authority. See legal.

Intrepid, *adj.* See courageous, adventurous, alive (2), ardent, assertive, assured (4), certain (2); reckless.

Intricacy, *n.* See complication, confusion, mystery.

Intricate, *adj.* See complex (1), circuitous; mysterious, ambiguous, obscure; devious.

Intrigue, *n.,* **intrigue,** *v.* See duplicity, machination, plot (2, 3); conspiracy, conspire, plan.

Intriguing, *adj.* Fascinating. Engrossing, charming, alluring, appealing, engaging, provocative, enchanting, tantalizing, titillating, amusing, inviting, interesting, gripping, absorbing. *Ant.* Boring.

Intrinsic, *adj.* Pertaining to the essential nature of a thing (intrinsic worth). Internal, fundamental, natural, indwelling, permanent, authentic, real, inner, basic, indigenous, innate, inbred, per se, inseparable, organic, constitutional, substantial, underlying. See also inherent, native (3), congenital. *Ant.* Incidental.

Intrinsic fraud Fraud that occurs within the framework of the actual conduct of a trial and affects the determination of issues therein (e.g., perjured testimony, forged documents, concealment or misrepresentation of evidence). See fraud.

Intrinsic value The true, inherent, and essential value of a thing, not depending upon accident, place, or person, but being the same everywhere and to everyone. See worth (1), appraisal.

Introduce, *v.* **1.** To bring forward or present (the gun was introduced into evidence). Offer, proffer, tender, place before, insert, put forward, submit, make known, propose, recommend, bring into notice, inject, interweave, infuse, enter, interpose, surrender, admit, implant. See also present (5). **2.** To institute (the judicial committee introduced a new hearing procedure). Originate, create, recommend, sponsor, advance, announce, inaugurate, induct, instigate, pioneer, establish, start, launch, father, actuate, conceive. See also initiate. *Ant.* With-

426

draw.

Introduction, *n.* See preamble; inauguration.

Introspection, *n.* See consideration (2), examination; deliberate (1).

Introvert, *n.* A loner. Private person. See also bashful, quiet, private.

Intrude, *v.* See encroach, break (1), intermeddle, interfere; delay; attack (1), assault (3); impede, hinder; intrusion, invasion, violation.

Intruder, *n.* One who enters upon land without either the right to possession or color of title (the intruder was arrested). Trespasser, aggressor, invader, infiltrator, raider, encroacher, unlawful entrant. See also interloper, wrongdoer. *Ant.* Guest.

Intrusion, *n.* **1.** The act of wrongfully entering upon or taking possession of the property of another (an intrusion into the building). Invasion, encroachment, inroad, infiltration, trespass, meddling, obtrusion, imposition, incursion, aggression, impingement, overstepping. See also intervention, infringement, violation. **2.** See invasion of privacy. *Ant.* Invitation.

Intrusive, *adj.* See officious, prying, vexatious.

Intrust, *v.* See entrust.

Intuition, *n.* A hunch or feeling. Instinctive reaction, premonition, suspicion, sensation, inkling, clue. See also impulse, perception.

Intuitive, *adj.* See acute (1); spontaneous, inherent, natural (3), native (3); involuntary.

Inundate, *v.* To flood or swamp (inundated with requests). Fill, overflow, overwhelm, bury, engulf, saturate, deluge, overcome, immerse, glut, submerge, overburden, soak, overrun, steep, waterlog, swallow up, beset, envelop, tax, gorge, overdose, extend, overload, prostrate, oppress, drown.

Inure, *v.* **1.** To come to the benefit of a person; to take effect (the policy inured to the benefit of the stockholders). Accrue, vest, mature, ripen, yield, result; accumulate, profit, promote, assist, advance, bolster. **2.** To cause to withstand or endure (the preparation inured her to the pressures of the trial). Accustom, harden, toughen, adapt, acclimatize, familiarize, season, condition, temper, habituate, strengthen, desensitize, discipline.

Invade, *v.* See break (1), encroach, interfere, wrong (4), attack (1), assault (3); invasion.

Invalid, *adj.*, **invalid,** *n.* **1.** *adj.* Not of binding force or legal efficacy (an invalid order). Unfounded, faulty, inoperative, ineffective, illegal, improper, inadequate, insufficient, unacceptable, nugatory, void, baseless, futile, indefensible, fallacious, useless, defective, false, null, illogical, impotent, weak, erroneous, vitiated, vacated, irrational, ill-founded, abrogated, untrue, canceled, unbinding, vulnerable, unenforceable, impaired, ineffectual, unscientific, absurd, unjustifiable, untenable, rescinded, disavowed, spurious, irrelevant, fabricated, diluted, worthless, lame, inappropriate, dead, unsupportable, unreasonable, groundless, vain. **2.** *n.* A disabled person (the accident rendered him an invalid). Shut-in, convalescent, cripple, amputee, victim, patient, stricken person, paraplegic, valetudinarian. *Ant.* Valid; healthy person.

Invalidate, *v.* See overrule, cancel (1), annul, reverse (1), rescind, abolish, quash, countermand, override.

Invaluable, *adj.* See great (2), outstanding (2), extraordinary; incalculable, exclusive, costly, exorbitant.

Invariable, *adj.* See constant (1), consistent, uniform.

Invasion *n.* An encroachment on the rights of others (invasion into the affairs of the company). Intrusion, incursion, interference, trespass, overstepping, intermeddling, inroad, breach, aggression, raid, hostility, foray, penetration, assault,

Invasion

usurpation, infraction. See also infringement, assault, attack, violation. *Ant.* Respect.

Invasion of corpus principle Making payments from the principal rather than from the income.

Invasion of privacy Four separate torts. (a) Appropriation: The unauthorized use of a person's name, likeness, or personality for the benefit of another. (b) False light: Unreasonably offensive publicity placing the plaintiff in a false light. (c) Intrusion: An unreasonably offensive intrusion into someone's private affairs or concerns. (d) Public disclosure of a private fact: Unreasonably offensive publicity concerning the private life of a person.

Invective, *n.* See reprimand, censure, obloquy, abuse, slander.

Inveigh, *v.* See decry, protest (3), censure, abuse, slander.

Inveigle, *v.* To lead astray by deceitful means (he was inveigled into signing the contract). Entice, lure, beguile, seduce, decoy, mislead, bamboozle, allure, defraud, trick, delude, bait, deceive, ensnare, coax, persuade, cajole, tantalize, invite, snare, enchant, fascinate, importune, maneuver, tempt. See also influence (2), entrap.

Invent, *v.* **1.** To produce something not previously known or in existence by the exercise of independent investigation and experiment (she invented a new transmission). Father, author, fashion, originate, devise, design, discover, compose, improvise, find, formulate, develop, conceive, hatch, imagine, produce, patent, envisage, dream up. See also create, coin (3). **2.** To make up or falsify (he invented the story). Fabricate, prevaricate, concoct, trump up, feign, distort, misrepresent, pervert, pollute, exaggerate, misstate, counterfeit, simulate, manufacture.

Invention, *n.* See invent (1). Finding, discovery, creation, contrivance, improvisation, concoction, composition, innovation, fabrication, origination, production, device, contraption, mechanism, coup, gadget, stratagem, design, implement, instrument. See also novelty.

Inventive, *adj.* See original (3), brilliant, able (2, 3), acute, competent.

Inventor, *n.* One who invents (the inventor of the computer). Author, father, creator, deviser, pioneer, improviser, planner, producer, artist, generator, architect, builder, framer. See also originator.

Inventory, *n.* **1.** A detailed list of property (discrepancies on the inventory). Itemized list, menu, checklist, stock list, catalog, index, accounting, roster, register, account, enumeration, statement, tally, descriptive list. See also record. **2.** The property or goods themselves (inventory available for shipment). Merchandise, stock, stock in trade, vendibles, contents, line, backlog, accumulation, staples, supply, provisions, wares, commodities. See also movables, property.

Inverse, *adj.* Reversed in order; upside down (an inverse ratio). Opposite, backward, contrary, transposed, inverted, right to left, bottom to top, back to front, converse.

Inverse condemnation A cause of action for the taking of private property for public use without formal condemnation proceedings and without just compensation.

Invert, *v.* See turn (1), reverse; inverse, opposite.

Invest, *v.* **1.** To use money to acquire property or other assets in order to produce revenue (they invested in the new company). Speculate, lay out, put out capital, sink money into, support, venture. **2.** To furnish (under the rules, the director is invested with the power to terminate workers). Endow, vest, license, confer, appoint, commission, entrust, mandate, delegate, ordain, authorize, sanction, grant, enable.

Investigate, *v.* To search into (the office is investigating the matter). Inspect, look into, search for facts, seek evidence, track, inquire into, probe, observe, examine, analyze, scrutinize, dissect, explore, research, survey, sift, query, study, comb, delve, hunt, trail, seek, pry into, ransack, frisk, rummage, traverse, test, appraise, check, grope, reconnoiter, scour, audit. See also trace (2), pursue (2), chase, ferret.

Investigation, *n.* See experiment; search (1), inquiry (1), examination.

Investigator, *n.* One who investigates (an investigator on the case). Researcher, detective, fact-finder, inspector, inquirer, agent, auditor. See also examiner; spy.

Investiture, *n.* The ceremony by which land is transferred, authority is conferred, or an office is entered. See inauguration.

Investment, *n.* An expenditure to acquire property or other assets in order to produce revenue (investment in the company). Financing, venture, capital, speculation, stock purchase, portfolio, holding, securities, futures, risk, loan, plunge, stake.

Investment contract A contract, transaction, or scheme whereby one invests money in a common enterprise and is led to expect profits solely from the efforts of the promoter or a third party.

Investment tax credit A credit against taxes, consisting of a percentage of the purchase price of capital goods and equipment.

Inveterate, *adj.* See habitual, constant (1), continual.

Invidious, *adj.* See hostile, malicious, odious, offensive.

Invigorate, *v.* See strengthen, augment, incite, provoke.

Invincible, *adj.* See indestructible, permanent, perpetual, invulnerable; inflexible; safe.

Inviolability, *n.* The condition of being safe from trespass, assault, or violation (the inviolability of contract). Sacredness, invulnerability, indestructibility, unassailability, inalienability, sanctity, invincibility.

Inviolable, *adj.* See inviolate, immune, invulnerable; holy.

Inviolate, *adj.* Free from substantial impairment (the oath was kept inviolate). Not broken, not profaned, intact, unbroken, complete, not violated, whole, entire, untouched, secure, unblemished, pure, holy, sacrosanct, flawless, invulnerable, hallowed, indomitable, undamaged, sound, undefiled. *Ant.* Desecrated.

Invisible, *adj.* See intangible (1), hidden; mysterious, small (1).

Invitation, *n.* An express or implied request for someone to be present or involved; the act of one who solicits or entices others to enter upon, remain in, or make use of his or her property; the act of inducing others to believe that they should enter upon, remain in, or use the property (an invitation to participate). Enticement, attraction, allurement, petition, solicitation, overture, summons, urging, bidding, inducement, provocation, stimulus, open door, challenge, temptation, lure, magnetism, supplication, entreaty, bait, call, plea, proposal, teasing, appeal, instigation, flirtation, incitement. *Ant.* Rejection.

Invite, *v.* See entice, entrap, bait (5), encourage; flirt; petition, appeal (4), apply (1); invitation.

Invitee, *n.* Someone who is present on land with the express or implied invitation of the occupier of the land, and uses it for a purpose for which it is open to the public or to pursue the business of the occupier (the duty of care owed to an invitee). See guest.

Inviting, *adj.* See intriguing, attractive, irresistible, auspicious, beneficial.

Invocation, *n.* See entreaty, solicitation (2), petition; appeal.

Invoice, *n.* A document itemizing the details of a sale or purchase transaction (misrepresentation in the invoice). Written account, statement, reckoning, schedule, checklist, itemization, tab, inventory, bill, description, tally, specification, note, charges. See also list, record.

Invoke, *v.* See appeal (4), apply (1), petition, beseech; conjure; employ (2).

Involuntary, *adj.* Without will or power of choice; performed under duress, force, or coercion (involuntary payment). Forced, unwilling, coercive, obligatory, mandatory, imperative, reluctant; instinctive, conditioned, unintentional, automatic, reflex, uncontrolled, unconscious, convulsive. See also inevitable, spontaneous, inadvertent, fortuitous, compulsory, mechanical. *Ant.* Voluntary.

Involuntary confession A confession that is not the product of an essentially free and unrestrained choice of its maker; a confession that is extracted by a threat of violence, or obtained by improper promises or other influences. See confession; coercion.

Involuntary conversion The loss or destruction of property through theft, casualty, or condemnation. See conversion, larceny, casualty; condemn (2).

Involuntary manslaughter The unlawful killing of a human being without malice, without premeditation and deliberation, and without the intention to kill or to inflict serious bodily injury; the unlawful killing of a human being during the commission of an unlawful act not amounting to felony; death from negligence that is gross, wanton, willful, or criminal, indicating a culpable indifference to the safety of others. See manslaughter, homicide, neglect (2).

Involuntary nonsuit The dismissal of an action when the plaintiff is called but neglects to appear, or gives no evidence on which a jury could find a verdict, or is put out of court by some adverse ruling precluding a recovery. See dismissal, nonsuit.

Involuntary servitude The condition of a person who is compelled to labor for another by force, coercion, imprisonment, and against his or her will, whether or not payment is made for the labor. See bondage, slavery; labor.

Involuntary trust An implied trust imposed by law. See trust, constructive trust, resulting trust.

Involve, *v.* See include, comprehend (2), incorporate (2), entail, concern (1); implicate, entrap, mire (2).

Involvement, *n.* See part (2), function, assignment (3), cooperation, responsibility.

Invulnerable, *adj.* Unassailable. Formidable, indestructible, invincible, inviolable, unbeatable, insurmountable, undefeatable, powerful, impenetrable, secure. See also safe, inviolate, immune, strong.

Iota, *n.* The minutest quantity possible (not an iota of evidence available). Jot, fragment, hair, scintilla, faint, speck, whit, bit, shred, atom, shadow, trifle, trace, morsel, particle, tinge, molecule, sliver, glimmer, grain.

IOU, *n.* "I owe you." A memorandum of debt, containing the amount owed and the debtor's signature. See debt, note (1).

Ipse dixit He himself said it; a bare assertion resting on the authority of the individual.

Ipso facto By the mere fact; by the fact itself.

IRA See Individual Retirement Account.

Irascible, *adj.* See excitable, difficult (3), querulous, crabby, inflexible, feverish, hot (2), litigious, contentious.

Irate, *adj.* See angry, hot (2), aggravated (2).

I.R.C. See Internal Revenue Code.

Ire, *n.* See wrath, shock, outrage (1).

Irk, *v.* See disturb, harass, outrage (2), accost (1), exacerbate.

Irksome, *adj.* See distressing, offensive; annoyance.

Ironclad, *adj.* See firm, final, definite (2), inflexible, indestructible, certain (3).

Ironic, *adj.* See irrational facetious, contradictory, inconsistent, fortuitous; caustic, cruel, malicious.

Irony, *n.* See surprise, contradiction, chance (2), destiny; ambiguity, conundrum, mystery; contempt.

Irrational, *adj.* Illogical, lacking reason (irrational conduct). Unreasonable, foolish, stupid, unthinking, ridiculous, childish, thoughtless, unsound, ill-advised, bizarre, outrageous, weird, nonsensical, extravagant, unintelligent, demented, insane, emotional, crazy, incredible, ludicrous, unscientific, moronic, unthinkable, asinine, inane, vacuous. See also baseless, absurd, capricious, exorbitant, impossible, invalid (1), immoderate, illogical. *Ant.* Logical.

Irreconcilable, *adj.* Not capable of being harmonized or compromised (an irreconcilable relationship). Unsolvable, unadjustable, beyond reconciliation, unsalvageable, incompatible, implacable, estranged, alienated, immovable, intransigent, irreparable, irredeemable, unyielding, rigid, unalterable, unappeasable, uncompromising, hopeless, dissipated, irrecoverable, lost, inexorable. See also irrational, incorrigible, inflexible, hostile, inevitable, final. *Ant.* Reconcilable.

Irreconcilable differences A no-fault ground of divorce: Discord or conflict of personalities that destroys the legitimate ends of the marriage and prevents any reasonable expectation of reconciliation. Irretrievable breakdown. See also divorce, ground.

Irrecoverable, *adj.* See irreparable, irreconcilable.

Irrecusable, *adj.* Pertaining to a contract obligation imposed on a person without his or her consent or own act; not subject to challenge, refusal, or rejection (irrecusable duty).

Irredeemable, *adj.* See lost, irreparable.

Irrefutable, *adj.* See incontestable, noncontestable, definitive, conclusive, certain (3), manifest, evident.

Irregular, *adj.* Not according to rule; departing from the norm (a highly irregular proceeding). Deviate, abnormal, out of order, nonconforming, eccentric, extraordinary, singular, asymmetric, tortuous, erratic, inconsistent, variable, improper, flawed, unconventional, unusual, atypical, unwarranted, exceptional, disordered, insufficient, inadequate, blemished, uneven, devious, jagged, unnatural, disorderly, unsymmetrical, capricious, rare, strange, unruly, crooked, disarranged, confused, aberrant, lawless, off-key, queer, unique, unreliable, unequal, circuitous, unmethodical, straying, perverted, peculiar, changeable, distorted, idiosyncratic, malfunctioning, unorthodox, intermittent, indecorous, haphazard, unfitting, uncharacteristic, desultory, uncommon, loose. See also anomalous, odd, defective, immoral, illicit. *Ant.* Customary, proper.

Irregularity, *n.* See caprice, fluctuating, deviation, eccentricity; irregular.

Irrelevant, *adj.* Not relating or applicable to the matter in issue; not tending to prove or disprove any issue of fact involved in the case (an irrelevant question). Not relevant, impertinent, unconnected, extraneous, unrelated, inapplicable, beside the point, foreign, not germane, inappropriate, off-target, gratuitous, malapropos, inapposite, remote, inconsequential. See also immaterial, collateral (2), alien (2). *Ant.* Pertinent.

Irreligious, *adj.* See profane (1), irreverent; blasphemy, profanity.

Irremediable, *adj.* See irreparable, irreconcilable, incorrigible, lost.

Irreparable, *adj.* Not capable of being repaired or restored (irreparable harm). Irreversible, beyond repair, irremediable, beyond cure, irrevocable, beyond correction, hopeless, lost, remediless, incurable, beyond redress, unfixable, unsalvageable, finished, beyond recall, irrecoverable. See also incorrigible, irreconcilable, permanent, perpetual. *Ant.* Salvageable.

Irreparable harm or injury As a standard for granting injunctive relief: An injury that cannot be adequately redressed by an award of monetary damages; a wrong of a repeated and continuing nature. See injury, harm; continual, continuous.

Irrepressible, *adj.* See irresistible, free.

Irreproachable, *adj.* See innocent, blameless, moral (2).

Irresistible, *adj.* Not capable of being opposed or resisted (an irresistible offer). Overwhelming, irrepressible, unavoidable, compelling, overpowering, inexorable, formidable, omnipotent, indomitable, vigorous, invincible, imperative, unpreventable, powerful, inescapable, overriding, certain, overmastering; tantalizing, enticing, cogent, obsessive, alluring. See also attractive, amicable, intriguing, beautiful; invulnerable, indestructible; permanent. *Ant.* Resistible.

Irresistible impulse An urge to commit an act that cannot be resisted or overcome because mental disease or derangement has destroyed the freedom of will, the power of self-control, and the ability to choose. See insanity, will.

Irresponsible, *adj.* Untrustworthy. Unreliable, undependable, immature, lawless, unrestrained, volatile, unpredictable, thoughtless, harum-scarum, foolish, injudicious, unstable, rash, vacillating, uncommitted. See also frivolous, capricious, fluctuating, juvenile, heedless, careless, reckless, dumb.

Irretrievable, *adj.* See irreconcilable, irreparable, lost.

Irretrievable breakdown See irreconcilable differences.

Irreverent, *adj.* Impious. Sacrilegious, blasphemous, unholy, scandalous, irreligious, godless, heretical, iconoclastic, evil, wicked; infidel; disrespectful, uncivil. See also profane (1); blasphemy; rude.

Irreversible, *adj.* See permanent, perpetual, irrevocable, indestructible, inalienable, indefeasible, irreparable, lost, final.

Irrevocable, *adj.* Not capable of being revoked or recalled (irrevocable offer). Irreversible, final, unmodifiable, inextinguishable, unalterable, immovable, indissoluble, changeless, inflexible, conclusive, unrepealable, immutable, fixed, beyond recall, indelible. See also indestructible. indefeasible, permanent, perpetual, inalienable. *Ant.* Revocable.

Irrigate, *v.* See water (2); Inundate; bathe, wash, fumigate, disinfect, clean (5).

Irrigation, *n.* The supply of water by pipes, channels, streams, etc. (irrigation district).

Irritable, *adj.* See crabby, contentious (1), difficult (3), particular (2), rude, inflexible, impatient, feverish, hot.

Irritant, *n.* See disturbance, nuisance, annoyance.

Irritate, *v.* See harass, disturb, accost (1), outrage (2), exacerbate, provoke, assault, attack.

Irritated, *adj.* See angry, aggravated (2).

Irritating, *adj.* See distressing, offensive.

Irritation, *n.* See annoyance, animus (2), wrath.

I.R.S. See Internal Revenue Service.

Island, *n.* Land surrounded by water (offshore island). Isle, islet; oasis, sanctuary, archipelago, enclave.

Isolate, *v.* See abandon, expel, divide, withdraw, depart (1), sequester, circumscribe, bar (4); protect; alone; isolated.

Isolated, *adj.* Detached, separate (isolated transaction). Independent, solitary, unique, secluded, single, remote, private, segregated, sequestered, severed, disconnected, disengaged, exiled, disunited, forsaken, out-of-the-way, cut off, confined, insulated, withdrawn, stranded. See also abandoned (1). *Ant.* Connected.

Isolated sale A sale that occurs only once or very infrequently within the ordinary course of business.

Isolation, *n.* See expulsion, quarantine (1), separation, division; departure, removal, concealment; alone.

Issuable, *adj.* Capable of producing an issue for debate or for litigation (issuable plea).

Issue 1. *v.* To send forth or promulgate (the court issued its order). Print, disseminate, publish, announce, distribute, reveal, enunciate, circulate, release, state, assert, pronounce, broadcast, propound, declare, proclaim, herald, put out, utter, discharge, allot, proceed, emerge, notify, air, expose, manifest, transmit, flow, emanate, exit, originate. See also communicate. **2.** *n.* Sending forth, promulgation (date of issue). Issuance, appearance, dissemination, publication, presentation, exhibition, emergence, disclosure, dispensation, granting, giving out, broadcasting. **3.** *n.* A matter in controversy. Question, cause, problem, dispute, contention, topic, subject, affair, theme, debatable matter, disputed matter, proposition, agenda, argument, bone of contention. See also issue of fact, issue of law. **4.** *n.* All persons who have descended from a common ancestor (she died without issue). Heirs, progeny, children, grandchildren, descendants, posterity, family, lineage, stirps, scions, seed, line, young. See also offspring.

Issue of fact A question at a trial or hearing that concerns facts or events, whether such occurred, and how they occurred, as contrasted with the law governing these facts or events; the controversy that exists when one party asserts a fact that is disputed by the other side. See issue (3).

Issue of law The question that arises in litigation when the facts are not in dispute either because the evidence is undisputed or because the facts are assumed upon a demurrer; a question that involves the application or interpretation of a law. See issue (3).

Issue preclusion No relitigation of an issue. See collateral estoppel doctrine, res judicata.

Itch, *n.* See impulse.

Item, *n.* A unit in a series or collection (missing items). Entry, piece, particular, object, feature, aspect, circumstance, thing, subject, point, detail, sample, example, ingredient, member, artifact, consideration, asset, merchandise. See also component, factor, element, part (1); list.

Itemize, *v.* To set down or list by item (she itemized her deductions). Individualize, specify individually, catalog, particularize, rank, inventory, tabulate, designate, register one by one, enumerate, document, number, spell out. See also detail (1), list, record.

Itinerant, *adj.* Wandering or traveling from place to place (itinerant vendor). Migrant, nomadic, journeying, transient, roving, wayfaring, peripatetic, roaming, unsettled, pilgrim, drummer, circuit rider. See also migratory. *Ant.* Resident.

Itinerary, *n.* See agenda, schedule (1).

Ivory tower, *n.* See impracticable, dream (1), hallucination; remote (1); scholar.

J

ABCDEFGHIJKLMNOPQRSTUVWXYZ

J. The abbreviation for justice or judge (Smith, J., presiding).

Jab, *v.* See batter, assault; pierce.

Jackass, *n.* See idiot, boor, ass.

Jackknife, *n.* See weapon.

Jackpot, *n.* See purse, prize; gambling.

Jactitation, *n.* False boasting; false claims.

Jaded, *adj.* See exhausted; indifferent.

Jail 1. *n.* A place of confinement, usually for persons awaiting trial or serving sentences for minor crimes (a 6-month term in jail). House of detention, gaol, correctional institution, lockup, brig, prison, pen, penitentiary, stockade, penal institution, reformatory, reform school, cell, workhouse. **2.** *v.* To confine (she was jailed by the police). Imprison, lock up, take into custody, place behind bars, incarcerate, commit, immure, seize, apprehend, intern, impound, restrict. See also detain.

Jailer, *n.* See keeper, watchman, manager.

Jailhouse lawyer A prisoner who studies law on his or her own in prison and provides legal assistance and advice to other prisoners. See paralegal.

Jam, *n., v.* See complication, ordeal, emergency; obstruct, hinder, clog, block (2).

Jamboree, *n.* See festival, celebration (2), ceremony, extravaganza, amusement; crowd.

Janitor, *n.* See keeper, custodian, servant, employee.

Janus-faced, *adj.* Two-faced; used to describe an argument that looks in both directions at the same time. See deceptive.

Jar *n., v.* See vessel; surprise, disturb, disrupt.

Jargon, *n.* See term of art, language, balderdash; prolixity; babble; communication.

Jaundiced, *adj.* See bias, narrow (2); prejudice; hostile; suspicious (2), cynical; jealous, avaricious.

Jaunt, *n.* See voyage.

Jazz, *n.* See music; balderdash.

J.D. The law degree: Juris Doctor or Doctor of Jurisprudence.

Jealous, *adj.* Envious. Grasping, possessive, grudging, resentful, green, itching. See also avaricious, suspicious.

Jealousy, *n.* See avarice, desire, animus (2), malice; jealous.

Jeer, *v.* See mock, harass, censure (2).

Jehovah's Witnesses, *n.* A Christian sect that is opposed to war and government interference in matters of conscience. It also believes in the imminent end of the world. See religion, church, God, creed.

Jejune, *adj.* See commonplace, thin; juvenile

Jencks rule A criminal defendant in federal court is entitled to access to government documents for use in the cross-examination of witnesses.

Jeopardize, *v.* See expose (2), endanger, risk (2), hazard (2); venture (2); jeopardy.

Jeopardy, *n.* **1.** Legal jeopardy: The danger of conviction and punishment once a criminal defendant has been placed on trial before the trier of fact in a court of competent jurisdiction acting on an indictment or information that is sufficient in form and substance to sustain a conviction (placed in jeopardy). **2.** Vulnerability (the project is in jeopardy). Exposure, threat, peril, insecurity, precariousness, venture, uncertainty, endangerment, instability, chance, liability. See also risk (1), danger, hazard.

Jeopardy assessment If the collection of a tax appears to be in question, the IRS may assess and collect the tax immediately without going through the usual formalities.

Jerk, *n.* See ass, idiot, boor.

Jest, *n.* See joke; facetious, comic.

Jet, *n.* See aircraft; vehicle.

Jetsam, *n.* Goods that the owner voluntarily throws overboard in an emergency in order to lighten the ship. See jettison.

Jettison 1. *v.* To discard, to throw overboard (the board jettisoned the proposal). Throw away, cast, cast aside, discharge, expel, dismiss, eject, eliminate, drop, reject, dump, scrap, unload, dispose, chuck, abandon, toss, fling, hurl, heave, project, launch, impel, junk, catapult, send, evacuate. **2.** *n.* The thing or things cast out. See jetsam.

Jetty, *n.* A projection of stone or other material, serving as a protection against the waves (the boat crashed into the jetty). Breakwater, pier, barrier, wharf, bulkhead. See also landing, harbor.

Jewel, *n.* See gem; decoration.

"Jim Crow", *n.* Discrimination against blacks. See segregation.

Jingoism, *n.* See chauvinism; patriot; military.

Jinx, *n.* See fate; ill-fated; witchcraft, anathema.

Jittery, *adj.* See impatient, feverish, excitable.

JNOV See judgment notwithstanding the verdict.

Job, *n.* **1.** An employment position (discrimination on the job). Profession, vocation, living, field, livelihood, calling, position, career, métier, appointment, niche, slot, work, engagement, opening, trade, pursuit, post, station, berth, capacity, situation, business. See also occupation. **2.** A specific task (the job of reforming the rules). Assignment, chore, duty, mission, charge, undertaking, responsibility, commission, activity, errand, concern. See also function.

Job action, *n.* See strike (1).

Jobber, *n.* One who buys and sells goods for others; a dealer in securities (an unlicensed jobber). Middleman, supplier, representative, salesperson, broker, wholesaler, consignor, itinerant, operator. See also agent.

"Jock", *n.* See athlete; able-bodied, healthy.

Jockey, *v.* See manipulate.

Jocular, *adj.* See comic, facetious, happy; joke.

Jog, *v.* See run (2).

Join, *v.* **1.** To come together; to combine or unite in time, effort, or action (join forces). Merge, connect, associate, consolidate, ally, wed, marry, fuse, cooperate, bind, bridge, mix, link, attach, federate, confederate, fasten, couple, coalesce, knit, enlist, meld, glue, cement, entwine, commingle, amalgamate, pool, fraternize, unify, assemble, conglomerate, converge, affix, collaborate, affiliate, interlink, band together, act in concert, league, amass, group, relate, weave, splice. **2.** To controvert formally (issue was joined when the defendant filed her answer). Engage, contest, take on, contend against, interlock.

Joinder, *n.* Uniting two or more into a single transaction or proceeding. See merger; join.

Joinder of issue The assertion of a fact by a party in a pleading and its denial by the opposing party; the filing of an answer. See join (2); issue.

Joinder of offenses Charging an accused with two or more crimes as multiple counts in a single indictment or information. See offense, indictment.

Joinder of parties The act of joining parties to an action as co-plaintiffs or as co-defendants. See party.

Joint, *adj.* Shared by or between two or more; coupled together in interest or liability (joint authorship). Mutual, collaborative, combined, concerted, common, acting in common, allied, united, merged, collective, unified, community, coalitional, consolidated, communal, corporate, synergetic, undivided, conjoined, in association, leagued, inseparable, mixed, federated. See also associated, integrated, complete (2), entire, full. *Ant.* Individual.

Joint adventure See joint venture.

Joint and several liability The liability that exists when a creditor has the option of suing one liable party separately or all liable parties together. Each wrongdoer is individually responsible for the entire judgment, and the person who has been wronged can collect from one wrongdoer or from all of them together until the judgment is satisfied. See liability.

Joint bank account An account in the names of two or more persons who have equal right to it, generally with the right of survivorship. See account, survivorship.

Joint enterprise An express or implied agreement among members of a group to carry out a common purpose, in which the members have a community of pecuniary interest and an equal right to a voice in the control and direction of the enterprise. See enterprise (1).

Jointly, *adv.* Combined or joined together in unity of interest or liability (jointly acquired property). Unitedly, in concert, in conjunction, in combination, collectively, in common, mutually, conjointly, in unison, communally, in collaboration, concurrently. *Ant.* Individually.

Joint tax return A federal, state, or local tax return filed by a husband and wife together. See tax.

Joint tenancy Property (an estate) held by two or more persons jointly (called cotenants or joint tenants) in undivided equal shares with the right of survivorship (when a cotenant dies, his or her share automatically passes to the surviving cotenants). The joint tenants have one and the same interest; accruing by one and the same conveyance, instrument, or act; commencing at one and the same time; with one and the same undivided possession. See ownership, survivorship.

Joint tort-feasors Two or more persons who are jointly and severally liable in tort for the same injury to person or property; persons who have acted in concert in committing a tort. See wrongdoer, tort.

Joint venture An association of persons who jointly undertake some commercial enterprise. There must be a community of interest in the performance of the enterprise, an equal right to direct and govern policy in connection with the enterprise, and a sharing in the resulting profits and losses. See enterprise (1).

Joint will A single testamentary instrument that contains the will of and is executed by more than one person. See will.

Joke, *n.* A wisecrack. Jest, pun, quip, facetious remark, one-liner, comedy, witticism, prank, tease, gibe, laugh. See also facetious, comic, happy.

Jolly, *adj.* See happy, festive, convivial, facetious.

Jolt, *v.* See surprise, amaze; push, collide, beat, batter.

Jostle, *v.* See push, collide; mill (2); beat, batter.

Journal, *n.* A book in which entries are made, often on a regular basis (Senate Journal). Chronicle, register, log, registry, ledger, notebook, diary, periodical, calendar, minutes, bulletin, organ, chronology, yearbook, gazette, magazine, album, memorandum, paper, scrapbook, account, serial, narrative. See also record.

Journalism, *n.* See press, newspaper; draw (1), draft (2).

Journey, *n., v.* See voyage, junket; travel, navigate.

Journeyman, *n.* A person who has progressed through an apprenticeship in a craft or trade and is now qualified to work for another. See employee, assistant, artisan; amateur, beginner.

Jovial, *adj.* See facetious, happy, festive, comic, friendly, convivial, optimistic; enjoyable, emotional.

Joy, *n.* See happiness, enjoyment (2), satisfaction (2), exultation, passion, emotion.

Joyful, *adj.* See jovial.

Joyriding, *n.* Temporarily taking an automobile without authorization but without the intent to deprive the owner of it permanently.

Jubilant, *adj.* See happy, ardent, emotional, earnest (2), active (3).

Jubilation, *n.* See exultation, happiness; festival, celebration (2), extravaganza, amusement.

Judex, *n.* A judge.

Judge 1. *n.* A public officer appointed or elected to preside over and to administer the law in a court of justice or similar tribunal (the judge denied the motion). Justice, adjudicator, surrogate, magistrate, arbitrator, chancellor, jurist, umpire, moderator, intermediary, decider, arbiter, go-between, mediator. See also official, referee. **2.** *v.* To resolve a dispute authoritatively (judge between the contestants). Pass judgment, try, review, hold, arbitrate, negotiate, mediate, rule, umpire, decree, sentence. See also adjudge, adjudicate, settle (1). **3.** *v.* To evaluate something (judge for yourself). Weigh, examine, conjecture, regard, deduce, interpret, gauge, analyze value, ascertain, criticize, appreciate, esteem, rate, rank, consider, perceive, infer, distinguish. See also assess, appraise.

Judge Advocate A legal officer on the staff of a military commander. See attorney.

Judgment, *n.* **1.** The official decision of a court in a case brought before it; a judicial determination of the rights and duties of parties growing out of litigation before a court (the judgment was reversed). Decree, holding, ruling, conclusion, opinion, award, sentence, finding, adjudication, verdict, arbitration. See also resolution (1). **2.** The ability to make wise and perceptive decisions (a woman of judgment). Understanding, perception, acumen, insight, reasoning, discrimination, discernment, conviction, wisdom, analysis, sagacity, clear-headedness, perspicacity, acuteness, awareness, incisiveness, intellect, intelligence, faculties, rationality, shrewdness, good sense, taste. See also discretion (3), prudence, common sense.

Judgment book The book in which the clerk enters the judgments that are rendered; a judgment docket; a civil or criminal docket. See docket, record.

Judgment creditor A person in whose favor a money judgment is entered or who becomes entitled to enforce it. See creditor.

Judgment debtor A person who has yet to satisfy a judgment that has been rendered against him or her.

Judgment execution The formal or written evidence of the judgment that commands an officer to seize the property of the judgment debtor in order to satisfy the judgment. See execution.

Judgment in personam See in personam.

Judgment in rem See in rem.

Judgment lien A lien binding the real estate of a judgment debtor in favor of the judgment creditor, giving the latter the right to levy on the real estate to satisfy the judgment. See lien, execution.

Judgment notwithstanding the verdict (JNOV) A judgment of the court that is opposite to the verdict reached by the jury; a ruling by the judge that the jury was not reasonable in reaching its verdict because there was not sufficient evidence of all the essential elements on which to base the verdict.

Judgment on the merits A judgment, rendered after evidentiary inquiry and argument, determining which party is in the right, as opposed to a judgment based solely on a matter of form, a technical point, or a procedural error. See meritorious (1), substantial (1).

Judgment proof A person who has no available resources out of which a judgment can be satisfied. See bankrupt.

Judgment quasi in rem See quasi in rem.

Judgment roll The papers filed by the clerk on a case after entry of the judgment (e.g., summons, pleadings, admissions, jury instructions, verdict, findings, orders, the judgment). See record.

Judicare, *n.* Publicly funded legal services delivered by private practitioners (rather than by full-time "poverty lawyers") to low-income persons.

Judicature, *n.* The judiciary; the administration of justice; a court of justice; the jurisdiction of a court.

Judicial, *adj.* **1.** Pertaining to the office of a judge (judicial authority). Juristic, legal, judiciary. **2.** Judgelike; inclined to make judgments; judicious (acting in a judicial manner). Discriminating, wise, sagacious, equitable, prudent, just, fair, magisterial, keen, critical, perceptive, perspicacious.

Judicial immunity The absolute protection of all judges from civil liability arising out of the discharge of judicial functions. See immunity.

Judicial notice The recognition of certain facts (usually matters of common knowledge) that a court may take into consideration without requiring evidence to be introduced to establish the facts. See notice.

Judicial review 1. The power of a court to interpret statutes and to declare them unconstitutional when they violate the constitution. **2.** A form of appeal from an administrative body to the courts for a review of the agency's findings of fact or law. See appeal, supervision, control (3), direction (2).

Judicial sale A sale based on a decree of a court directing the sale. See execution.

Judiciary, *n.* The branch of government vested with the judicial power; the system of courts in a country; the body of judges; the bench. See court, judge.

Judicious, *adj.* Using good judgment (a judicious trustee). Wise, prudent, careful, shrewd, thorough, cautious, discerning, rational, enlightened, circumspect, tactful, sane, politic, levelheaded, perspicacious, diplomatic, well-advised, just, astute, percipient, reflective, logical, practical, calculating, expedient, knowledgeable, clever, intelligent, considerate, prudential, temperate. See also cultivated, brilliant, able, capable (2), discreet. *Ant.* Rash.

Judo, *n.* See athletics, game, sport.

Juggle, *v.* See alter, change; manipulate; deceive, cheat (1).

Jumble, *v., n.* See commingle, sprinkle, confuse; mixture, confusion; mixed.

Jump, *v.* **1.** To leap. Vault, spring, bounce, skip, hop. **2.** See neglect, avoid, escape. **3.** See attack, assail, assault. **4.** See anticipate.

Jumpy, *adj.* See uneasy, feverish, excitable, emotional.

Junction, *n.* See intersection, conjunction, line, link, association, merger, combination.

Juncture, *n.* See crisis; period, interval; junction.

Jungle, *n.* See confusion, complication; woods; wild.

Junior, *adj.* Lower in age, position, or preference (junior lien). Younger, subordinate, second, secondary, lesser, underling, early, immature. See also juvenile, inferior. *Ant.* Senior.

Junior mortgage A mortgage that is subordinate to the priority or prior mortgage. See mortgage.

Junk, *n.* See refuse (2).

Junket, *n.* A trip or tour taken at public expense; an arrangement to go to a gambling casino hotel, in which the hotel pays part of the expenses (the senator took another junket). Frolic, journey, cruise, excursion, expedition, trek, picnic. See also voyage.

Junkie, *n.* See addict; drug.

Junta, *n.* See gang; government.

Jural, *adj.* Pertaining to law, rights, and obligations (jural relations).

Jurat, *n.* A certificate of a person before whom a writing was sworn; the clause on an affidavit as to where, when, and before whom it was sworn. See attestation.

Jure By the law; by right.

Juridical, *adj.* Relating to the administration of justice or to the office of a judge. See judicial, judicious, equity, legal; judge, court.

Juris Of law; of right (Corpus Juris Secundum).

Jurisdiction, *n.* **1.** The power of a court to decide a matter in controversy (a challenge to the jurisdiction of the court). Capacity, authority, authorization, right, charter, judicature, license, sovereignty. See also power. **2.** The geographic area over which a particular court has authority (the matter has not been decided in this jurisdiction). Territory, region, domain, district, circuit, state, quarter, field, province, bounds, sphere, reach. See also zone.

Jurisdictional amount The amount involved in the particular case; the value of the object sought to be attained in the litigation.

Jurisdictional dispute The competing claims made to an employer by different unions that their respective members are entitled to perform certain work. See union; dispute.

Jurisdictional facts Those facts that must exist before the court can properly take jurisdiction of the particular case (e.g., the amount in controversy, service of process).

Jurisdiction in personam See in personam.

Jurisdiction in rem See in rem.

Jurisdiction of the subject matter See subject matter jurisdiction.

Jurisdiction quasi in rem See quasi in rem jurisdiction.

Juris Doctor (J.D.) Doctor of laws. The degree received by lawyers, replacing the LL.B. degree.

Jurisprudence, *n.* The philosophy of law; the science that seeks to ascertain the principles on which legal rules are based; the science of positive law and legal relations. See justice, law, science.

Juris publici Of common right; of common or public use (e.g., highways).

Jurist, *n.* A legal scholar (judges, lawyers, and other jurists on the panel). Learned counsel, law professor, legal authority, legal expert. See also attorney (1), judge (1), scholar, teacher.

Juror, *n.* **1.** A member of a jury (each juror was polled). Fact-finder, trier of fact. **2.** See judge (1), expert (1), authority (4), arbiter.

Jury, *n.* **1.** A group of men and women selected and sworn to inquire into matters of fact and to declare the truth on the basis of the evidence to be presented before it (selection of the jury). Fact-finder, trier of fact, reviewers, panel of peers, venireman. **2.** See juror (2).

Jury instructions A direction given by the trial judge to the jury, concerning the law of the case that they will need to know in order to reach a verdict. See charge (12).

Jury panel A group of prospective jurors who are summoned to appear on a stated day and from which a grand jury or a petit jury is chosen.

Jury trial The trial of a matter before a judge and jury as opposed to a trial solely before a judge. See hearing, action (1).

Jury wheel A physical device or electronic system for the storage and random selection of the names or identifying numbers of prospective jurors.

Jus Law; system of law; right; power; privilege; authority.

Jus civile The system of law peculiar to one state or people; civil law.

Jus civitatus The right of citizenship.

Jus gentium The law of nations.

Jus publicum Public law; the law relating to the constitution and functions of government and its officers.

Just, *adj.* Conforming to or consonant with what is legal or lawful (a just resolution). Rightful, equitable, principled, honest, merited, due, fair, reasonable, rational, virtuous, unbiased, worthy, evenhanded, righteous, noble, unimpeachable, licit, precise, fitting, appropriate, authentic, justifiable, detached, logical, constitutional, judicious, flawless, uncorrupt, upstanding, truthful, objective, dispassionate, requisite, sensible, proper, impartial, conscientious, ethical, disinterested, moral, aboveboard, trustworthy, tolerant, accurate, upright, unprejudiced, condign, suitable, balanced, acceptable, bona fide, factual. See also blameless, incorruptible. *Ant.* Inequitable.

Just cause Such reasons as will suffice in law to justify the action taken (revocation of the license for just cause). Legitimate cause, legal ground, legal cause. See also ground, cause (3).

Just compensation Compensation that is fair to both the owner and the public when property is taken for public use through eminent domain; adequate compensation; fair market value at the time of taking. See damages, compensation; condemn (2).

Jus tertii The right of a third person; defending what one has done or proposes to do on the basis of rights (e.g., ownership) in third persons. See defense.

Justice, *n.* **1.** A judge, usually of a higher court. See judge (1). **2.** The proper administration of the law; the resolution of legal matters or disputes so that all receive their due (she claimed that there had been a denial of justice). Fairness, equity, evenhandedness, fair play, legality, impartiality, uprightness, integrity, evenness, objectivity, neutrality, right, truthfulness, truth, fair-mindedness, probity, rectitude, goodness, legitimacy, morality, validity, dispassionateness, merit, correctness.

Justice Department A federal agency headed by the attorney general. The agency enforces federal laws, gives legal advice to other agencies, represents the government in court cases, etc.

Justice of the Peace A judicial magistrate of inferior rank with very limited jurisdiction. See magistrate, judge, official.

Justiciable, *adj.* Referring to a matter appropriate for court review (justiciable controversy). Litigable, proper for court action, actionable, ready, suitable for judicial examination. See also ripe, appropriate; seasonable. *Ant.* Premature, moot.

Justifiable, *adj.* Warranted or sanctioned by law (justifiable refusal). Rightful, defensible, acceptable, reasonable, understandable, rational, allowable, vindicable, valid, proper, fit, sensible, legitimate, forgivable, condonable, pardonable, defendable, merited, excusable, plausible, well-grounded, tenable, warrantable, lawful, sane, credible. See also meritorious, sound, correct (1), blameless. *Ant.* Unwarranted.

Justifiable homicide Killing another when permitted by law (e.g., in self-defense when faced with the danger of death or with serious bodily injury). See homicide.

Justification, *n.* A just or lawful reason to act or to fail to act (justification for temporary detention). Extenuation, acceptable explanation, rationalization, vindication, apology, basis, alibi, warrant, ground, explanation, mitigation, authorization, story, legitimation, clearance, redemption, palliation. See also excuse, defense; extenuating.

Justified, *adj.* See legitimate, authentic.

Justify, *v.* **1.** To prove to be correct or valid (she was justified in bringing the action). Sustain, prove right, confirm, uphold, establish, warrant, endorse, legitimate, support, sanction, defend, advocate, speak for, substantiate, vindicate, maintain, champion, strengthen, bolster, explain. See also corroborate. **2.** To absolve (she tried to justify the killing). Exonerate, redeem, clear, free from blame, excuse, pardon, remove guilt, dismiss. See also exculpate, acquit, forgive.

Justness, *n.* Conformity to truth, propriety, or accuracy (the justness of his claim). Justice, correctness, lawfulness, equity, exactitude, fidelity, accuracy, justifiability, rightness. *Ant.* Injustice.

Juvenile 1. *n.* A young person who has not yet reached the age at which he or she should be treated as an adult for purposes of the criminal law; in some states, a person under 18 (as a juvenile, he should not be detained with adults). Infant, youth, youngster, teenager, stirpling, kid, ward, teen, adolescent, innocent, beginner, urchin, fledgling, junior, schoolchild, mademoiselle, lad. See also child, minor (1). **2.** *adj.* Immature (juvenile behavior). Childish, inexperienced, puerile, sophomoric, callow, green, asinine, jejune, naive, silly, inane, irresponsible, simple-minded, infantile, shallow, unwise, nonsensical, adolescent, tender, indiscreet, injudicious, frivolous, rash, foolish, imprudent, exuberant, unsettled, pubescent, unsophisticated. *Ant.* Adult.

Juvenile delinquent See delinquent child, delinquent; wrongdoer.

Juxtapose, *v.* To place side by side for comparison (juxtapose the two pictures). Position together, border, connect, parallel, compare, associate, neighbor, abut, bring near, match.

K

Kaleidoscopic, *adj.* See fluctuating, divers; odd.

Karate, *n.* See athletics, sport, game, diversion, defense.

Karma, *n.* See destiny, chance (2); fortuitous.

K.B. See King's Bench.

Keel, *v., n.* See capsize; vessel.

Keen, *adj.* See acute (1), cogent, brilliant, capable (2), judicious, erudite, able; caustic.

Keep 1. *v.* To continue (keep watch over the defendant). Persevere, remain, persist, stick, maintain, be constant, perpetuate, sustain, endure, be steadfast, secure, uphold, survive, lengthen, extend. **2.** *v.* To have or retain in one's power or possession (she decided to keep the ring). Hold, retain, dominate, grasp, embrace, shelter, preserve, have, possess, bank, treasure, look after, safeguard, amass, nurture, withhold, clench. **3.** *v.* To detain (keep the accused for questioning). Hold up, restrain, subjugate, deter, chain, confine, retard, delay, hold back, hinder, thwart, bar, check, encumber, stall, shackle, arrest, obstruct, frustrate, enclose, impede, tie up, block, clog, hamstring, hobble. **4.** *v.* To carry on or maintain (keep a bawdy house). Conduct, manage, operate, stock, run, foster, nourish, subsidize, keep alive, trade in, deal in, tend, harbor, pursue. **5.** *v.* To refrain from disclosing (the attorney tried to keep the facts from the jury). Conceal, silence, camouflage, withhold, screen, cloud, disguise, shelter, veil, suppress, muffle, hide, mask. **6.** *v.* To adhere to (keep your word). Fulfill, discharge, observe, follow, satisfy, honor, carry out, heed, acknowledge, celebrate, perform, commemorate, comply with, consummate, execute, accomplish, mind, complete. **7.** *n.* Means of sustenance (she earned her keep). Nourishment, livelihood, means, food and lodging, maintenance, upkeep, room and board, necessities. *Ant.* Abandon, release.

Keeper, *n.* One who has the care, custody, or management of something (keeper of a gambling house). Custodian, superintendent, warden, guard, caretaker, curator, preserver, bodyguard, retainer, jailer, executor, escort, nurse, protector, sentry, doorkeeper, proprietor, director, shepherd, supervisor, sentinel, housekeeper, administrator, janitor. See also attendant, manager, guardian.

Keeping, *n.* See custody, protection, care (3); agreement, harmony.

Keepsake, *n.* See memento; memory, recollection.

Keg, *n.* See vessel (2); liquor, beverage.

Keogh plan A retirement plan for self-employed taxpayers—the contributions to which are tax deductible up to a certain amount each year; an H.R. 10 plan.

Kernel, *n.* See gist, essence, center.

Key, *adj., n.* See important, historic, landmark (2), fundamental, indispensable, necessary, essential, material; resolution (1), outcome; clarification, definition, description.

Key number; key topic and number Part of the subject-matter classification system for the digests of West Publishing Company (e.g., under the key topic of "Libel & Slander," key number 8 (☞8) summarizes court opinions on an aspect of this area of the law).

Kibbutz, *n.* See commune, cooperative (1).

Kick, *v.* See batter, attack, assault.

Kickback, *n.* A payment back by the seller of a portion of the purchase price to the buyer or to a public official in order to induce the purchase or to influence future business transactions (the mayor was indicted for accepting a kickback from the contractor). Payoff, payola, cut, illegal compensation, illegal fee. See also bribe, graft, gratuity (2), corruption.

"Kid," *n.*, *v.* See child, juvenile, minor; joke; deceive.

Kidnap, *v.* See kidnapping; abduct, hijack, seize.

Kidnapping, *n.* The taking and carrying away of a human being by force, fraud, threats, or intimidation against the victim's will and without lawful authority (kidnapping for ransom). Seizure, abduction, impressment, commandeering, capture, hijacking, shanghaiing, making off with, waylaying.

Kill, *v.* **1.** To destroy the life of a person or animal (kill in self-defense). Slay, execute, slaughter, assassinate, murder, fatally injure, exterminate, liquidate, cut down, butcher, dispatch, massacre, dispose of, victimize, put to death. **2.** To put an end to something (the committee killed the proposal). Terminate, obliterate, cancel, vanquish, quash, crush, stifle, ruin, arrest, contravene, smother, counteract, stop, silence, dispatch, defeat, squelch, stay, break, annul, void, invalidate, abolish, repress, suppress, thwart, excise, delete, omit, extirpate, overthrow, veto, discontinue, prohibit, disallow, remove, table, exhaust, overpower, annihilate, squander, muffle, efface, butcher. *Ant.* Nurture; revive.

Kilogram, *n.* 2.2046 pounds or 1,000 grams.

Kilometer, *n.* .62137 mile.

Kilowatt, *n.* 1,000 watts.

Kin, *n.* See family, kindred.

Kind 1. *n.* Generic class; type (she was not the kind to waste resources). Sort, genus, description, variety, breed, ilk, designation, nature, mold, brand, cast, genre, character, categorization, manner, denomination, style, sort, selection, order, make, grouping, fashion, brand, category, classification, stripe, habit, form, species, strain, persuasion, color, inclination, temperament. **2.** *adj.* Goodhearted (kind disposition). Gentle, considerate, charitable, tender, sympathetic, gracious, affectionate, obliging, understanding, civil, cordial, amiable, accommodating, humane, benign, benevolent, humanitarian, tactful, philanthropic, decent, loving, merciful, neighborly. See also friendly, convivial, humanitarian; affection, love. *Ant.* Individual; cruel.

Kindness, *n.* See love, affection (1), benevolence, charity; kind (2).

Kindred 1. *n.* Family, relatives (a desire to provide for her kindred). Clan, next of kin, ancestors, stock, blood relations, tribe, children, heirs, kinship, household, progeny, issue, lineage, flesh, strain, consanguinity. **2.** *adj.* Of the same kind (kindred spirits). Related, like, agreeing, cognate, congenial, analogous, allied, similar, parallel, paired, collateral, matching, simpatico, harmonious. See also concordant. *Ant.* Stranger; alien.

King, *n.* A male sovereign or ruler with complete or limited power over a nation. Autocrat, czar, monarch, potentate, lord, master, governor; tycoon, magnate, chief, patriarch, boss, dean. See also tyrant, manager.

Kingdom, *n.* See country, land, domain, zone.

King's Bench (K.B.) One of the superior courts of common law in England.

"Kink," *n.* See defect, deficiency, failure, fault (1), eccentricity.

"Kinky," *adj.* See depraved, deviant (2); odd, anomalous.

Kinship, *n.* See family, ancestry, kindred (1); correspondence.

Kismet, *n.* See destiny, chance (2); fortuity.

Kiss, *v.* See caress, handle (2), touch.

Kiting, *n.* Writing checks against a bank account in which the funds are insufficient to cover them, with the hope that the necessary funds will be deposited before the checks are presented.

Kitty, *n.* See purse, prize.

Klan, *n.* See Ku Klux Klan.

Kleptomania, *n.* An irresistible propensity to steal. See larceny; compulsion (2), illness, disease, insanity.

Klutz, *n.* See idiot, ass, boor.

Knack, *n.* See gift (2), ability, facility (3).

Knave, *n.* A false, deceitful person. See crook, wrongdoer.

Knee-jerk, *adj.* See spontaneous, sudden, involuntary, mechanical.

Knife, *n. v.* See weapon; cut, pierce, mutilate, maim.

Knock, *adj.* See batter, attack, assault, push; collide.

Knot, *n.* See mystery, conundrum.

Knotty, *adj.* See difficult (1), obscure (1), complex (1), mysterious, distressing.

Know, *v.* To have knowledge or understanding (the witness knew the defendant). Recognize, perceive, possess information, be acquainted with, identify, discern, distinguish, be conscious of, fathom, realize, differentiate, comprehend, grasp, experience, penetrate, be cognizant of, appreciate, have dealings with, be informed. See also apprehend.

Know-how, *n.* See experience, facility (3), gift (2), ability, competence.

Knowingly, *adj.* With knowledge; intentionally (knowingly transport a drug). Consciously, willfully, intelligently, deliberately, mindfully, calculatedly, by design, wittingly.

Knowledge, *n.* Acquaintance with fact, truth, or understanding (knowledge of the defect). Familiarity, perception, realization, instruction, experience, cognizance, consciousness, intelligence, discernment, education, recognition, appreciation, grasp, enlightenment, cognition, apperception; wisdom, learning, erudition, scholarship, data, information. See also apprehension. *Ant.* Ignorance.

Knowledgeable, *adj.* See informed, cognizant, learned, competent, capable, able, apt.

Known, *adj.* Understood (a known danger). Perceived, recognized, discovered, acknowledged, sensed, discerned, estimated, noted, comprehended, appreciated, learned, experienced, fathomed, seen, apprehended, familiar, revealed; exposed, patent, obvious; avowed, plain, evident, published, publicised, self-evident, vented, admitted, notorious, transparent. See also manifest. *Ant.* Unrecognized.

"Kook," *n.* See idiot, ass, boor.

Koran, *n.* See Bible; God; religious.

Kosher, *adj.* See genuine, official (2), accurate, precise (2), proper, regular (1), conventional (1), conservative, religious.

Kowtow, *v.* See grovel, cringe, pander (2), flatter.

Kudos, *n.* See acclamation, indorsement (2), honor (2).

Ku Klux Klan, *n.* An organization that supports segregation and white supremacy. See discrimination, bias (1), prejudice (1); fear, outrage (1); intimidate; wrongdoer.

Label, *v.* To provide identifying information (they labeled the medicine deceptively). Classify, brand, identify, name, stamp, characterize, denominate, earmark, title, entitle, describe, ticket, call, demarcate, term, set apart, imprint, portray, style, stereotype, docket, mark, provide an emblem or insignia.

Labor 1. *n.* Mental or physical exertion (compensation for her labor). Work, occupation, profession, line, trade, calling, livelihood, commission, drudgery, toil, service, job, enterprise, pursuit, task, discipline, undertaking, effort, industry, struggle, plodding, responsibility, assignment, travail, sweat, pains. **2.** *v.* To perform work (they labored for hours in the library). Struggle, toil, strive, drudge, exert oneself, apply oneself, occupy oneself, slave, suffer, agonize oneself. *Ant.* Relaxation; rest.

Laborer, *n.* One who performs work for another for a living (the laborers were unionized). Worker, white-collar worker, blue-collar worker, help, hard hat, toiler, proletarian, workman. See also employee. *Ant.* Employer.

Laborious, *adj.* See difficult (2), onerous, severe, extreme, draconian, inconvenient; careful, precise.

Labor union, *n.* See union, association, federation.

Labyrinth, *n.* See confusion, complication, conundrum, mystery.

Labyrinthine, *adj.* See circuitous, indirect, indefinite, complex (1), diffuse (2), equivocal, fluctuating.

Lacerate, *v.* See cut (1), break (2), mutilate, attack, assault.

Laceration, *n.* See injury, contusion, lesion, wound, hurt; cut (1), break (2).

Laches, *n.* An equitable defense arising when there has been an unexplained delay in asserting a right of such duration and character as to render the enforcement of the right inequitable; such neglect or omission to assert a right over a period of time which, when taken with other circumstances causing prejudice to the party asserting the defense, operates to bar relief in equity (the action was dismissed because of laches). Prejudicial delay, unconscionable delay, inexcusable delay, unreasonable delay, procrastination, laxity, nonfeasance, failure to act, undue inaction, sitting on one's rights. See also neglect.

Lack, *n.* See deficiency, arrears, dearth, absence (2), privation, want.

Lackadaisical, *adj.* See apathetic, indifferent (2), casual (3), lazy, callous, dilatory, frivolous; loiter.

Lackey, *n.* See attendant, parasite, servant, employee, slave, assistant.

Lacking, *adj.* See void (3), deficient, insufficient, inadequate.

Laconic, *adj.* See concise, compact (2, 3), brief, summary; abrasive, caustic.

Lacrosse, *n.* See athletics, sport, game, diversion.

Lad, *n.* See child, minor, juvenile, man.

Ladder, *n.* See ascent, hierarchy.

Lady, *n.* See woman; debonair; aristocracy.

Lag, *v., n.* See loaf, loiter, delay; diminish; interval, interruption.

Lagoon, *n.* See lake, sea (1), harbor.

Laissez-faire, *n.* A political-economic philosophy of government that allows the marketplace to operate relatively free of restrictions and intervention. Nonintervention, noninterference, hands-off doctrine; indifference, let-alone policy. See also liberty; neglect (2).

Laity, *n.* People not part of the clergy. See people, constituency, country, nation.

Lake, *n.* A considerable body of standing water in a depression of land or in an expanded part of a river. Lagoon, pond, bayou, pool, mere, reservoir, basin, catchment, tarn.

Lambaste, *v.* See censure (2), reprimand, condemn, batter, beat, attack, assault.

Lame, *adj.* Disabled, weak (lame from the accident). Infirm, feeble, hamstrung, injured, ineffective, deficient, hobbled, impaired, crippled, handicapped, faltering, deformed, unsound, imperfect, game, clumsy, ineffectual, incapacitated, damaged. See also frail, weak. *Ant.* Vigorous.

Lamebrain, *n.* See idiot, ass, boor; absurd, irrational, dumb.

Lame duck An elected official during the time when he or she is waiting to be succeeded by a replacement.

Lame duck session A legislative session conducted after the election of new members but before they are installed.

Lament, *v., n.* See bemoan, suffer, cry (1); grievance, complaint.

Lamentable, *adj.* See deplorable, grievous (1), distressing, abject.

Lamentation, *n.* See contrition, guilt (2); lament.

Lamp, *n.* See light.

Lampoon, *n., v.* See caricature, mock, slander.

Lance, *n., v.* See weapon; cut, pierce, mutilate.

Land, *n.* **1.** Any ground, soil, or surface of the planet (surrounding land). Earth, real estate, real property, terrain, terra firma, tract, turf, plain, acres, plot, loam, realty. **2.** Region (the land of his ancestry). State, country, district, nation, kingdom, zone, dominion, native soil, domain, region, republic, continent, county, precinct.

Landed, *adj.* Owning land; having an estate in land; consisting of real estate or land.

Landed securities Mortgages or other encumbrances affecting land. See mortgage, encumbrance, securities.

Land grant A donation of public land to an individual, corporation, or subordinate government.

Landing, *n.* **1.** A place on a river or other navigable water for loading and unloading goods or passengers (structurally unsound landing). Stage, dock, port, pier, jetty, wharf, runway, harbor. **2.** The act of coming back to land after a voyage or flight (crash upon landing). Docking, arrival, debarkation, disembarkation, alighting, mooring, unloading, touchdown, deplaning, berthing. See also alight.

Landlady, *n.* See landlord, owner.

Landlocked, *adj.* Referring to land belonging to one person that is surrounded by land belonging to other persons so that it cannot be approached except over their land.

Landlord, *n.* The owner who leases land, buildings, or apartments to another (the landlord evicted the tenant). Landowner, landholder, possessor. See also owner, proprietor, lessor, holder. *Ant.* Lessee.

Landmark 1. *n.* A feature of the land, a monument, or other marker set up on the boundary line of two adjoining estates to fix such boundary (landmarks noted in the deed). Stake, marker, feature, post, waymark, peg. See also wall, fence. **2.** *adj.* Historically important (the landmark case). Benchmark, precedent-setting, decisive, key, significant, monumental, pivotal; milestone, turning point. See also historic, important.

Landowner, *n.* See landlord, owner, proprietor, holder, possessor.

Land patent A document or instrument conveying a grant of public land; the land so conveyed.

Landscape, *n.* See view (5), environment, neighborhood.

Lane, *n.* See highway, passage (2), course (1), entrance.

Language, *n.* Any means of conveying or communicating ideas (vague language in the statute). Speech, dialect, expression, tongue, vocabulary, verbalization, terminology, rhetoric, idiom, jargon, verbal intercourse, speaking, discourse, talk, diction, phraseology, words, "lingo," locution, parlance, gobbledygook, vernacular, slang, text, legalese, colloquy, colloquialism.

Languid, *adj.* See frail, thin, anemic, weak, drowsy, exhausted, ill (1); lazy, apathetic, indifferent (2).

Languish, *v.* See diminish, decline, lapse (2), wear (1); idle; fail; deserve (1).

Lanky, *adj.* See tall; thin; big, able-bodied, healthy.

Lantern, *n.* See light.

Lapse 1. *v.* To end because of a failure to use or a failure to fulfill a condition; to fail to vest because of the death of the prospective beneficiary before the death of the donor (the offer lapsed after 2 days; the bequest lapsed). Terminate, cease, become obsolete, expire, stop, abate, run out, revoke, discontinue, cancel, default, revert, nullify, conclude, elapse, fail. See also forfeit, waive. **2.** *v.* To deteriorate (lapse into a coma). Collapse, recede, sink, regress, fade, degenerate, decline, subside, return, pass into, languish, lower, decay, wane, worsen, fall. See also wear (1). **3.** *n.* A mistake or error (lapse of memory). Delinquency, neglect, backslide, fall, deviation, transgression, regression, inadvertence, blunder, negligence, nonfeasance, breach, omission, shortcoming, forfeiture, laxity, flaw, peccadillo, faux pas, oversight, retrogression. **4.** *n.* A period of time (after a lapse of 2 years). Interval, intermission, hiatus, lull, break, pause, interim, interruption, gap, stay, elapse. *Ant.* Vest; revive; correction.

Lapsed, *adj.* Expired (lapsed insurance policy). Terminated, elapsed, outdated, abrogated, invalidated, out-of-date, dead, superseded. See also lost; lapse. *Ant.* Effective.

Larcenous, *adj.* Having the character of or contemplating larceny (larcenous purpose). Thieving, predatory, rapacious, plundering, ravaging. See also felonious, immoral, malicious; avaricious.

Larceny, *n.* The unlawful stealing, taking and carrying, or driving away another's personal property with the intent to convert it to one's own use, to deprive the owner of it, or otherwise to deal with it in a manner inconsistent with the owner's rights (larceny of an automobile). Misappropriation, appropriation, embezzlement, shoplifting, theft, peculation, fleecing, robbery, pilferage, rustling, stealing, filching, breaking and entering, plagiarism, expropriation, commandeering, burglary, feloniously taking, looting, thievery, swindling, purloining, palming, banditry, purse snatching, hijacking, piracy, "copping," petnapping, abaction, false pretenses.

Large, *adj.* See big, great, massive.

Largess, *n.* See charity, benevolence, gift (1), bounty (1); asset (1).

Largest, *adj.* See major, primary, extraordinary.

Lark, *n.* See antic, sport, game, mischief, caprice; gambling.

Lascivious, *adj.* Tending to incite lust (lascivious scenes in the movie). Lewd, dirty, licentious, indecent, erotic, wanton, debauched, corrupt, immoral, lurid, vulgar, bawdy, lecherous, immodest, shameless, dissolute, blue, satyric, profligate, depraved, unclean, salacious, carnal, gross, lustful, goatish, ribald, coarse. See also obscene, pornographic, filthy, prurient. *Ant.* Modest.

Lash, *v.* See batter, beat, assault, attack; censure (2), condemn, reprimand.

Lass, *n.* See child, minor, juvenile, woman.

Last 1. *adj.* Final (her last act was to sign the will). Concluding, ultimate, finishing, rearmost, terminating, terminal, furthest, extreme, latest, most recent, eventual, climactic, endmost, ending; previous, earlier, former; settling, decisive, definitive. **2.** *v.* To continue (the demonstration lasted a minute). Go on, endure, persist, hold on, remain, persevere, stay, extend, outlive, keep, survive, carry on, withstand, live. See also abide, exist. *Ant.* Initial; cease.

Last antecedent rule A canon of statutory construction that qualifying words are to be applied only to the immediately preceding words unless the qualifying words were clearly intended to apply to other language in the statute as well. See construction (1).

Last clear chance doctrine Even though a plaintiff has been contributorily negligent in placing himself or herself in a position of peril, he or she can still recover if the negligent defendant had the last clear chance to avoid the accident and failed to do so. Supervening negligence doctrine, discovered peril doctrine. See also defense.

Last in, first out (LIFO) A method of identifying and valuing inventories which assumes that the last goods purchased are the first ones sold and therefore the goods left in inventory at the end of the year are assumed to be those first purchased.

Lasting, *adj.* See perpetual, permanent, durable, continual, continuous, indestructible.

Last resort Refers to a court from which there is no further appeal (court of last resort). See court, appeal.

Latch, *v.* See lock, affix (1), attach (2), connect (1).

Late, *adj.* **1.** Recently existing or alive, but now dead (the late chief justice). Deceased, demised, defunct; former, one-time, ex. **2.** Recent (a late addition to the bench). New, fresh, current, newborn. **3.** Not being on time (late for the trial). Tardy, overdue, dilatory, procrastinating, unpunctual, detained, belated, remiss, slow, postponed, adjourned, deferred. See also delinquent.

Latent, *adj.* Concealed, dormant (latent defect). Hidden, unseen, camouflaged, unexposed, undetected, submerged, unsuspected, covered, veiled, invisible, lurking, covert, inconspicuous, covered up, deceptive, screened, imperceptible; potential, undeveloped, passive, quiescent, inactive, hibernating, slumbering. *Ant.* Manifest.

Later, *adj.* See subsequent; last.

Lateral, *adj.* Relating to the side (lateral support). Sideways, sidelong, edge, flanked, marginal.

Latitude, *n.* See margin (2), freedom, liberty, license; range (2), scope, measure (1), extent.

Latrine, *n.* See bathroom.

Latter, *adj.* See subsequent, last.

Latter-day Saint, *n.* See Mormon.

Laud, *v.* See honor (2), worship; tribute (2).

Laudable, *adj.* Commendable, meritorious, exemplary, model, worthy.

Laugh, *v.* To chuckle. Giggle, cackle, roar, snicker, crow, titter, twitter. See also smile, yell, noise, mock, entertainment, amusement.

Laughable, *adj.* See comic, enjoyable, facetious, frivolous, absurd, insane (2), anomalous; amusement; laugh.

Launch, *v.* To push into motion (launch the proposal). Establish, propose, activate, trigger, start, embark, premier, broach, usher in, found, engender, undertake, catapult, venture upon, inaugurate, begin; eject, propel, set afloat, thrust, impel, fire off, push, prod, hurl. See also institute, initiate, commence, provoke. *Ant.*

Quash.

Launder, *v.* See bathe; pass (4, 5); fraud, deception.

Laurel, *n.* See award, citation (3), approbation, tribute, honor.

Lavatory, *n.* See bathroom.

Lavish, *adj.* See abundant, liberal (3); excess, wild, extreme, exorbitant.

Law, *n.* A rule of action or conduct prescribed by a controlling authority and having binding force; that which must be obeyed (the law of products liability). Code, regulation, statute, constitution, charter, decree, rule, ordinance, prescript, prescription, mandate, dictate, command, standard, tenet, act, controlling principle, holding, canon, proclamation, edict, commandment, precept, formula, axiom, absolute, enactment, precedent, prohibition, ukase, injunction. *Ant.* Suggestion.

Lawbreaker, *n.* See wrongdoer, offender.

Lawful, *adj.* Legal, authorized (lawful arrest). Warranted, sanctioned, allowed, valid, legitimate, constitutional, permitted, due, rightful, conformable, licit, prescribed, proper, legalized, statutory, legislated, accepted, complying, suitable, sound, chartered, ordered. See also legal, just, bona fide, appropriate. *Ant.* Illegal.

Lawless, *adj.* **1.** Not observing the rules and forms of the law (lawless transaction). Illegal, unauthorized, wrongful, unwarranted, forbidden, criminal, illegitimate, disobedient, felonious, ultra vires, lawbreaking. See also delinquent, illicit, wrong. **2.** Uncontrolled (lawless society). Rebellious, unruly, anarchic, uncivilized, savage, untamed, recalcitrant, riotous, degenerate, disreputable, wayward, unbridled, nihilistic, unchecked, seditious, defiant, disorganized, wanton, terrorist, insubordinate, insidious, mutinous, unaccountable. See also incorrigible, violent, dissolute, immoral, odious, infamous, corrupt. *Ant.* Legal; tame.

Law list A publication containing the names and addresses of practicing attorneys and information of interest to the legal profession (e.g., court calendars, attorneys practicing in certain specialties). See list, Martindale-Hubbell.

Law merchant Commercial law; mercantile law; the law applicable to the rights and relations of persons engaged in commerce, trade, or mercantile pursuits. See commerce.

Lawn, *n.* See field, ground (2); close (3).

Law of the case doctrine Once a court has decided a point in a case, that point becomes and remains settled unless and until it is reversed or modified; the law applied on the first appeal of a case is binding on the second appeal; the initial determination of an issue governs the case throughout subsequent stages unless compelling circumstances call for a redetermination.

Law reports; law reporters Volumes containing decisions and opinions of state and federal courts.

Law review A student-edited journal published by a law school, containing articles, notes, studies, book reviews, etc.

Laws, *n.* **1.** See law, regulation, statute. **2.** The statutes or session laws of the legislature.

Lawsuit, *n.* See action (1), cause (3).

Lawyer, *n.* See attorney.

Lax, *adj.* See careless, heedless, negligent; casual; permissive, flexible.

Laxity, *n.* See lapse (3), oversight, neglect; license (2).

Lay 1. *adj.* Nonprofessional; nonecclesiastical (lay judge). See paralegal, paraprofessional; secular, profane (2). **2.** *adj.* Pertaining to a person with no particular expertise (lay witness). Nonspecialist, ordinary citizen, nonexpert. See also amateur, beginner. **3.** *v.* To state or allege in a pleading (lay damages; laying venue). See allege, plead.

Lay advocate See paralegal.

Layaway, *adj.* Pertaining to an agreement by a retail seller with a consumer to hold consumer goods for sale to the consumer at a later date at a specified price.

Layman, *n.* See paraprofessional, citizen; paralegal.

Layoff, *n.* A temporary or permanent termination of employment at the will of the employer (retaliatory layoff). Suspension, firing, discharge, sacking, displacement, forced retirement, elimination, removal, idling, lockout; unemployment. See also ouster, dismissal (2), purge (2); union. *Ant.* Hiring.

Lazy, *adj.* Sluggard. Idle, inactive, indolent, slothful, slack, supine, remiss, loafing, lackadaisical, lethargic, inert, shiftless, laggard, dallying, neglectful, torpid, tired, procrastinating. See also apathetic, indifferent, drowsy; loiter, loaf, malingerer.

LEAA Law Enforcement Assistance Administration.

Lead, *v.* See direct (2), manage, control (1), patrol, preside; influence, affect (1); exceed, beat (2), pass; pursue (3); flirt; precedence.

Lead counsel The attorney who is managing and directing the litigation for a party represented by more than one attorney.

Leader, *n.* See catalyst, manager, foreman, master, chairman, administrator, director, head; avant-garde.

Leadership, *n.* See administration, management, supervision; supremacy; ability.

Leading, *adj.* **1.** Chief, predominant (the leading authority on trusts). Foremost, top, central, prime, principal, greatest, dominant, head, stellar, nonpareil, main, unsurpassed, prevailing, unparalleled, notable, first, matchless, supreme, capital, governing, ruling, front. See also primary (1), outstanding (2), best (1). **2.** Directing, controlling (leading question). Manipulative, suggestive, guiding, tricky, steering, managing. See also manipulate. *Ant.* Minor; perfunctory.

Leading case An opinion that has had an important influence in the development of the law on a particular point.

Leading question A question that suggests the answer because of the way that it is asked (e.g., "You were speeding, isn't that correct?").

Lead on, *v.* See flirt, manipulate.

Leaflet, *n.* See circular (2), report.

League 1. *n.* An association of people, groups, or countries for a common purpose (antidefamation league). See alliance, association (1), federation. **2.** *v.* See join (1), connect (1).

Leak, *v., n.* See divulge, disclose; emit (2); trickle; break (2, 3).

Lean, *v.* To incline toward something (the court leans toward expansion of the doctrine). Prefer, favor, gravitate, tend, trend, verge, aim, be partial toward, have a propensity for, be attracted to, be disposed toward; tilt, career, slope, swerve, veer, deviate, totter, stumble, lurch, shift, diverge.

Leap, *v.* See jump (1), run; advance; growth.

Learn, *v.* To gain knowledge or skill; to acquire by investigation and study (learn to draft pleadings). Master, comprehend, pick up, ascertain, unearth, become informed, memorize, detect, find out, determine, assimilate, exhume, perceive, chance upon, hear, read, become apprised. See also glean, discover (1), ferret, apprehend (1). *Ant.* Forget.

Learned, *adj.* Well-informed (learned in the law). Erudite, knowledgeable, educated, sophisticated, accomplished, wise, professional, scholarly, experienced, enlightened, informed, cultured, profound, intellectual, well-read, deep, pedantic, lettered, versed, proficient, studious. See also literary (2), judicious, cultivated, brilliant, able, capable (2), qualified. *Ant.* Ignorant.

Learning, *n.* The acquisition of knowledge or skill; knowledge or skill that is acquired (learning to use the computer). Study, scholarship, culture, research, schooling, wisdom, investigation, inquiry, edification, search, exploration, lore, science, literacy. See also knowledge, education, information. *Ant.* Ignorance.

Lease 1. *n.* A contract for the exclusive possession of lands or tenements for a determinate period; a contract by which the lessor grants the lessee the exclusive right to possess and use personal property of the lessor for a specified period. Landlord-tenant agreement, lessor-lessee agreement. See also contract, agreement. **2.** *v.* To let, rent, demise, engage, sublease, sublet, subrent, convey, grant.

Leaseback, *n.* A transaction whereby a party sells property and later leases it back.

Leasehold, *n.* An estate in real property held under a lease; property held by a lease.

Leash, *v.* See limit (1), restrain, control.

Least, *adj.* See minimal, small (1), minor (2).

Leave 1. *v.* To give (she decided to leave her estate to charity). Will, transmit, convey, bequeath, demise, award, give, impart, assign, endow, commit, consign, allot, present, entrust. **2.** *v.* To withdraw (the boss ordered him to leave). Depart, retreat, quit, go, resign, exit, move on, separate, embark, split, abandon, vanish, disappear, escape, flee, vacate, migrate, emigrate, drop out, remove, ship out, surrender, desert, yield, forsake, abdicate, cease, let go. **3.** *v.* To allow or cause to remain or stay the same (leave the issue in the brief). Maintain, keep, retain, sustain, let continue. **4.** *n.* Permission to do something (the court granted her leave to amend the complaint). Warrant, authorization, sufferance, allowance, grace, favor, indulgence, license, tolerance, sanction, endorsement, consent, approval, concession, assent, liberty, acquiescence, certification, approbation. **5.** *n.* Authorization to be absent (on leave). Liberty, retreat, break, recess, absence, holiday, sabbatical, respite, rest. See also vacation, furlough. *Ant.* Retain; enter; remove; denial; work.

Leave of absence Temporary absence from employment or duty with the intention to return. See leave (5), furlough, vacation.

Leave of court Permission of the court to take some action. See permission.

Lecherous, *adj.* See lascivious, lewd, obscene.

Lecture, *v., n.* See address (2, 3), speech (2); preach, reprimand, censure; school, teacher.

Ledge, *n.* See border (1), boundary.

Ledger, *n.* A book of account in which a record of transactions is made (inconsistencies in the ledger). Register, logbook, accounts, file, registry, diary, journal. See also record, account.

Leech, *n.* See parasite.

Leer, *v.* See spy (2), observe (3), watch; obscene, lewd.

Leery, *adj.* See suspicious, doubtful, cautious, careful.

Leeway, *n.* See margin (2), freedom, liberty, license.

Left, *adj.* See liberal (4).

Leftover, *n.* See remainder, residue; refuse.

Legacy, *n.* **1.** A disposition of personal property by a will (the legacy lapsed when the beneficiary died before the testator). Bequest, testamentary disposition, inheritance, grant, patrimony, present, donation, endowment, estate. See also gift, charity. **2.** Something handed down (a legacy of freedom). Tradition, heirloom, background, history, birthright. See also heritage; genealogy.

Legal, *adj.* Required, permitted, or involving the law (it is legal to demonstrate). Authorized, permissible, within the law, licit, proper, allowable, ordered, decreed, approved, within bounds, commissioned, constitutional, prescribed, sanctioned, mandated, valid, ordained, rightful; juridical, judicial, jurisprudential, forensic. See also lawful, legitimate. *Ant.* Unlawful.

Legal age The age at which a person acquires the capacity to make contracts or to enter legal relations. The age may differ depending on what the person wants to do (e.g., vote, buy liquor, marry). For most situations, however, the legal age is

18. Age of consent, age of majority. See also majority (1), emancipation.

Legal aid A system of providing legal services to people who cannot afford private counsel. See attorney.

Legal capital The par or stated value of issued capital stock; the amount of contributed capital that must be kept in the firm as protection for creditors; property sufficient to balance capital stock liability. See capital, capital stock.

Legal cause Proximate cause; substantial factor in bringing about the harm; the causal sequence by which a person's tortious conduct resulted in an invasion of a legally protected interest of another, so that the law holds the person responsible for the harm. See cause, proximate cause.

Legal conclusion A statement of a legal duty without stating the facts from which the duty arises. See conclusion (2), result (1).

Legal death See death, brain death, civil death.

Legal description A description of real property by government survey, metes and bounds, or lot numbers of a recorded plat, including a description of portions subject to any easements or other restrictions. See map, record (2), metes and bounds, bound, boundary.

Legal detriment The giving up or the doing of something that the promisee, immediately prior thereto, was privileged to retain or to refrain from doing; a change of position or an assumption of a duty or liability that did not exist earlier. See detriment, consideration, contract.

Legal entity Legal existence; an entity other than a natural person (e.g., a corporation) which can function legally, sue, be sued, act through agents, etc. See entity; person.

Legalese, *n.* See term of art, language; balderdash.

Legal ethics Usages, customs, and rules among members of the legal profession involving their moral and professional duties toward one another, toward clients, and toward the courts (e.g., client confidentiality). See ethics, principle (2), right (4), canon, code of professional responsibility.

Legal fiction See fiction of law, constructive.

Legal impossibility 1. The defendant's intended acts, even if completed, would not amount to a crime. See defense, excuse, justification. **2.** See impossibility of performance, impossibility.

Legal investments Those investments, sometimes called legal lists, in which banks and other financial institutions may invest. See also investment, securities.

Legal issue 1. A legal question (framing a legal issue). See issue of law, question. **2.** Descendants (legal issue of the decedent). See issue (4), descendant, offspring.

Legality, *n.* Lawfulness; the state of being legal (the legality of the transaction was in doubt). Constitutionality, rightfulness, accordance with law, licitness, permissibility. See also validity, legitimacy.

Legalization, *n.* The act of making something legal or lawful (the legalization of the drug). Approval, sanction, authorization, validation, confirmation, legitimization, entitlement, accreditation, making acceptable, formally ratifying, certification. *Ant.* Criminalization.

Legalize, *v.* See approve, authorize, legitimate (3).

Legal jeopardy See jeopardy (1), risk (1), danger, hazard.

Legal list See legal investments.

Legal malpractice The failure of a lawyer to use such skill, prudence, and diligence as lawyers of ordinary skill and capacity commonly possess and exercise. See malpractice, neglect (2), negligence.

Legal newspaper A newspaper containing summaries of important decisions, notices of local court proceedings, and news of general interest to the legal profession. See press.

Legal representative One who stands in the place of and represents another; one who oversees the legal affairs of another. See personal representative, administrator (2), executor, attorney, overseer.

Legal residence The place of domicile or permanent abode as opposed to a temporary residence. See domicile, home.

Legal separation A court order allowing a married couple to live separately and establishing their rights and duties while separated. Judicial separation, separation from bed and board, limited divorce, divorce a mensa et thoro. See also separation; divorce.

Legal Service Corporation (LSC) A federal government agency that provides funds for legal services to the poor in noncriminal cases.

Legal tender All coins and currencies of the United States that can be used to pay debts. See currency, coin, money.

Legal title A title that is recognizable and enforceable in a court of law; a title that provides the right of ownership but no beneficial interest in the property, which exists in another. See title (1), right (3).

Legate, *n.* See delegate (2), agent.

Legatee, *n.* The person to whom personal property (and sometimes real property) is given by will (the legatee could not be found). Recipient, transferee, devisee, inheritor, donee, distributee. See also beneficiary. *Ant.* Testator.

Legation, *n.* A diplomatic mission below the rank of an embassy; the staff and premises of such a mission. Consulate, envoy, delegation, foreign office, ministry, chancery. See also embassy; delegate (2).

Legem; leges Law; laws.

Legend, *n.* Fable. Saga, story, myth, lore, allegory, tale, drama, history, adventure, yarn, epic, old wives' tale, parable, romance, ballad. See also fiction.

Legendary, *adj.* See fictitious; popular, notorious; historic, landmark (2).

Legible, *adj.* See clear (1), precise.

Legion, *n.* See company (2); military; sailor; mob, group (1), assembly.

Legislate, *v.* To enact laws or pass resolutions through legislation (the attempt to legislate in a crisis atmosphere). Formulate laws, make laws, codify, ordain, draft, pass, put through, prescribe, fix. See also enact, regulate. *Ant.* Adjudicate.

Legislation, *n.* 1. The enactment of laws by the legislature (legislation through committees). Lawmaking, making laws, preparation of laws, establishment of laws. See also codify, codification. 2. Law or laws passed by the legislature (social legislation). Statute, session law, measure, charter, bill, canon, ordinance, edict, regulation, enactment, body of law, provision, precept. See also act (2), law.

Legislative, *adj.* Pertaining to the enactment of laws by the legislature (legislative intent). Statutory, congressional, lawmaking, parliamentary, senatorial.

Legislative apportionment See apportionment; gerrymander.

Legislative counsel The person or office that assists legislators in tasks of research, drafting, etc. See attorney.

Legislative court A court created by the legislature as opposed to one created by the Constitution. See court.

Legislative divorce A divorce granted to a couple by an act of the legislature rather than by a court decree. See divorce.

Legislative history The background of events leading up to the enactment of a law (e.g., the text of the proposed law, amendments considered, committee reports, committee hearings, floor debate).

Legislative immunity An immunity from civil suit enjoyed by a member of Congress while engaged in legislative functions (e.g., voting, giving a speech on legislation, making reports, engaging in debates). See immunity.

Legislative veto A statutory provision under which Congress, or a unit of Congress, is purportedly authorized to adopt a resolution that will impose on the executive branch of government a specific requirement to take or to refrain from taking an action. The provision contemplates a procedure under which one or both houses of Congress, or a committee of one house, may overrule, reverse, revise, modify, suspend, prevent, or delay an action by the president or by some other part of the executive branch.

Legislator, *n.* A member of a legislative body (the legislator abstained). Senator, representative, congressman, lawmaker, assemblyman, delegate, alderman, selectman, council member, parliamentarian, member of parliament; politician, statesman.

Legislature, *n.* The assembly or body of persons that makes statutory laws for a state or nation (the legislature repealed the tax). Congress, legislative branch of government, parliament, diet, Senate, House, chamber. See also counsel.

Legitimacy, *n.* **1.** The condition of being born in wedlock (the legitimacy of the child). Lawful birth. **2.** The condition of being in compliance with the law or with established standards (the legitimacy of the claim). Rightfulness, lawfulness, authenticity, genuineness, soundness, appropriateness. See also validity, legality. *Ant.* Illegitimacy.

Legitimate 1. *adj.* Lawful, valid, or genuine (legitimate excuse). Licit, sanctioned, legal, authorized, official, allowed, well-grounded, constitutional, sound, rightful, within the law, empowered, permissible, real, mandated, justified, proper, well-founded, plausible, tenable, warranted, authoritative, reliable, recognized, statutory, cogent, acknowledged, ordained, decreed, trustworthy, pure, de jure, licensed. See also authentic, credible, reasonable, accurate. **2.** *adj.* Born to married parents (legitimate child). **3.** *v.* To make lawful; to confer legitimacy (the evidence legitimated her claim). Certify, validate, vindicate, sanction, justify, legalize, pronounce lawful, license, condone, support, charter, warrant. See also authorize, approve, acknowledge, ratify, adopt. *Ant.* Invalid; illegitimate; pollute.

Legitimation, *n.* Making legitimate or lawful that which was not originally so; the statutory procedure for legitimating the status of an illegitimate child.

Legitimize, *v.* See acknowledge (1), ratify, adopt, legitimate (3), authorize, approve.

Legwork, *n.* See labor.

Leisure, *n.* See freedom, liberty, ease (1), amusement, avocation.

Leitmotif, *n.* See matter (1), issue (3).

"Lemon," *n.* See defect, defective, deficiency.

Lend, *v.* To provide money to another for a period of time, usually for an interest charge; to give something of value to another for a fixed or indefinite time, with or without compensation, with the expectation that it will be returned (lend him $1,000). Accommodate, give credit, supply, place at one's disposal, furnish, lease, let, grant, allow, oblige. See also advance (2), entrust, give; loan. *Ant.* Borrow.

Lender, *n.* One from whom money or some other thing is borrowed (unregulated lender). Creditor, bank, loaner, mortgagee, seller, pawnbroker, usurer. *Ant.* Borrower.

Length, *n.* See extent, range, scope, measure.

Lengthy, *adj.* See long.

Leniency, *n.* See clemency; charity.

Lenient, *adj.* See permissive, flexible; kind, charitable, humanitarian, benevolent.

Lesbian, *n.* A female who is sexually attracted to other females. "Butch," "dyke," sapphist. See also gay (1).

Lesion, *n.* A wound (suffered lesions to the head). Trauma, bruise, damage, detriment, blemish, disfigurement, impairment, mutilation, disorder, harm, sore, laceration, swelling, abnormality, contusion, cut, injury, wound, gash, fracture.

Less, *adj.* See lesser, small (1), minimal, minor (2); inferior.

Lessee, *n.* A person who rents property from another (the lessee failed to return the property on time). Renter, possessor, holder; boarder, roomer. See also tenant. *Ant.* Lessor.

Lessen, *v.* See abate, mitigate, diminish; decline.

Lesser, *adj.* Smaller in degree, amount, or value (lesser of two evils). Subordinate, secondary, slighter, less important, junior. See also minor (2), inferior. *Ant.* Principal.

Lesser included offense Another offense that is necessarily established by proof of the greater offense in that it is impossible to commit the greater offense without having committed the lesser offense; an uncharged offense that does not require the proof of any additional elements beyond those required by the greater offense that was charged (e.g., larceny is a lesser included offense within the offense of robbery). All of the elements of the lesser crime are also elements of the greater crime, but not vice versa. See offense.

Lesson, *n.* See assignment (3), plan (1); school, teacher, education; warning, correction (1).

Lessor, *n.* A person who rents property to another (the lessor increased the rent). Landlord, lender, loaner, creditor. See also owner. *Ant.* Lessee.

Let, *v.* 1. To authorize (the judge let him use the diagram). Permit, sanction, license, warrant, allow, commission, suffer, enfranchise, empower, indulge, tolerate, approve, endorse, consent, assent, vouchsafe, grant leave, accede, enable. 2. To rent (let the house). Lease, sublease, sublet, convey, lend, assign, loan, demise, hire out. 3. To award to one of several applicants (let the contract to the highest bidder). See award (3). *Ant.* Refuse; borrow; deny.

Letdown, *n.* See depression (1); dissatisfaction, failure, defeat (2); affliction.

Lethal, *adj.* Deadly (lethal weapon). Mortal, fatal, destructive, malign, baneful, devastating, malignant, killing, toxic, virulent, venomous, suicidal, internecine, pernicious, injurious, murderous, dangerous, noxious, slaughterous, detrimental, infectious. See also harmful, poisonous. *Ant.* Innocuous.

Lethargic, *adj.* See lazy, apathetic, indifferent, drowsy, exhausted; oblivious; ill (1); trance.

Letter, *n.* 1. A message sent from one person to another usually in a sealed envelope (the letter arrived too late). Missive, dispatch, epistle, message, note, memo, communiqué, billet, acknowledgment. See also communication. 2. A commission, patent, or written instrument containing or attesting the grant of some power, authority, or grant (letters of administration).

Lettered, *adj.* See learned, literary (2), cultured.

Letter of credit A written instrument addressed by one person to another requesting the latter to give credit to the person in whose favor it is drawn. The drafter of the letter promises to repay the person making the advance.

Letters of administration A formal document issued by the probate court, appointing an administrator of an estate. On the kinds of administrators that can be appointed, see *administration* and the entries that follow it.

Letters patent A document issued by the government to a patentee, which grants or confirms the right to the exclusive possession and enjoyment of land or of a new invention or discovery. See patent.

Letters rogatory A request by one court to a court in another jurisdiction to take the testimony of a witness residing in the latter jurisdiction or to otherwise assist the requesting court in a pending case.

Letters testamentary A formal document issued by a court which empowers a person to act as an executor of a will.

Letup, *n.* See abatement, interruption, delay (3).

Levee, *n.* See bank (4); dock (1); ceremony.

Level, *adj.*, *v.* See flat; equal; grade (1); point (6).

Levelheaded, *adj.* See deliberate (3), reasonable, lucid, cautious, prudent.

Leverage, *n.* **1.** Added power or influence (the leverage of her inside contacts). Weight, pull, clout, strength, advantage, edge. See also influence (1), authority (2). **2.** The ability to control an investment by a small outlay such as a down payment; the use of a smaller investment to generate a larger rate of return through borrowing; the effect on common stockholders of the requirement to pay bond interest and preferred stock dividends before the payment of common stock dividends.

Levy 1. *v.* To assess or impose (levy a fine). Exact, collect, inflict, tax, affix, require, place, demand, charge, lay on, toll, subject. **2.** *v.* To conscript (levy an army). Enlist, draft, call up, raise, convene, activate, impress, mobilize, muster, induct. **3.** *v.* To seize in order to satisfy a claim (levy the goods). Confiscate, execute, wrest, attach. **4.** *v.* To wage or carry on (levy war). Launch, declare, instigate, originate, pursue, prosecute, start. **5.** *n.* A tax or charge (a levy of 5%). Toll, duty, fee, fine, money, exaction, assessment, excise, tariff, custom, surcharge, dues, impost. See also tax. **6.** *n.* The obtaining of money by legal process through the seizure and sale of the property (notice of levy). Confiscation, attachment, execution, appropriation, sequestration, condemnation, annexation, arrogation, expropriation.

Lewd, *adj.* See indecent, lascivious, obscene, filthy, pornographic, prurient, carnal, suggestive.

Lewdness, *n.* Gross and wanton indecency in sexual matters. See debauchery, obscene.

Lex, *n.* Law or a collection of laws.

Lex contractus The law of the place where the contract was formed.

Lex domicilii The law of the domicile.

Lex fori The law of the forum where the suit is brought.

Lexis A computerized legal research system.

Lex loci actus The law of the place where the act was done.

Lex loci delictus The law of the place where the wrong or crime took place.

Lex situs The law of the place where the property is situated.

Liability, *n.* **1.** The condition of being responsible for a possible or actual loss, penalty, evil, expense, or burden; a legal obligation (liability for breach of contract). Debt, accountability, amenability, encumbrance, answerability, duty, indebtedness, pledge, exposure, vulnerability, obligation, culpability, arrears, debit. See also responsibility. **2.** A disadvantage (shyness is a liability in a lawyer). Handicap, impediment, minus, obstacle, cross, shortcoming, hindrance, barrier, nuisance, weight, onus. See also burden, obstruction.

Liability in solido Either of the debtors may be required to discharge the obligation in full at the creditor's election. See joint and several liability.

Liability insurance The insurer pays those covered damages which the insured is obligated to pay to a third person. The insurer agrees to indemnify the insured against loss from specified causes. See insurance.

Liable, *adj.* **1.** Bound or obligated in law or equity (he was found liable). Chargeable, answerable, compellable to make satisfaction or restitution, obligated, guilty, blameworthy, tied, censurable, amenable. See also responsible. **2.** Susceptible (liable to be burned). Exposed, likely to happen, prone, tending, in danger of, ripe for, vulnerable, open, at the mercy of, subjugated, enslaved, captive, subordinate, affected by, governed by, sensitive, subject, apt, disposed, predisposed. See also susceptible, likely. *Ant.* Immune.

Liaison, *n.* See link (1), contact (1), connection; middleman, mediator; affairs.

Libation, *n.* See beverage, liquor; offering.

Libel, *n.*, *v.* A defamatory statement expressed by print, writing, pictures, or signs. See defamation, defamatory, defamatory statement, defame, libelous, slander.

Libelant, *n.* The complainant in an admiralty action. See plaintiff.

Libelee, *n.* The defendant in an admiralty action. See defendant.

Libelous, *adj.* Constituting or involving libel (a libelous report). Defamatory, derogatory, insulting, damaging, discreditable, scurrilous, denigrating, calumnious, abusive, traducing, vilifying, notorious, humiliating, vitriolic, acrimonious, scandalous, detracting, injurious, maligning, slanderous, backbiting, invidious, perjorative, debasing, disfavorable, stigmatizing, scurrile, shameful, caustic. See also offensive, malicious. *Ant.* Laudatory.

Libelous per quod Extrinsic proof is needed to show the defamatory nature of the statement; the statement is not obviously defamatory or defamatory on its face.

Libelous per se The statement is defamatory on its face without the need of extrinsic proof; the statement is so obviously and naturally hurtful to the aggrieved person that proof of its character is unnecessary.

Liberal, *adj.* **1.** Not literal; not restricted or restrained (liberal interpretation). Extended, open, broad, loose, unrigorous. See also flexible, general. **2.** Tolerant (liberal handling of the proceeding). Broad-minded, fair, unprejudiced, impartial, unbiased, neutral, dispassionate, nonpartisan, fair-minded, receptive, unbigoted, disinterested. **3.** Generous (liberal giving). Bounteous, philanthropic, lavish, magnanimous, abundant, ample, handsome, extravagant, plenteous, munificent, full, unsparing, unstinting, humanitarian, bountiful, unselfish, extensive, altruistic, ungrudging, profuse, charitable. **4.** Pertaining to a political philosophy that tends to favor the use of government to promote social reforms, civil liberties, and economic regulation (liberal candidate). Progressive, civil libertarian, advanced, reformist, radical, left-wing, latitudinarian. **5.** See permissive, flexible. *Ant.* Conservative (1, 3, 4).

Liberal construction An expansive interpretation of the meaning of a statute or other law to include facts or cases that are within the spirit and reason of the law, or are within the mischief that the law was designed to remedy. Reasonable doubts are resolved in favor of the applicability of the law unless an intent to the contrary is clear. See construction (1).

Liberalize, *v.* See extend (1), widen, augment.

Liberate, *v.* To release (liberate the hostages). Free, rescue, emancipate, deliver, extricate, redeem, disengage, unshackle, untie, separate, acquit, manumit, let out, untangle, enfranchise, unchain, detach, ransom, unfetter, extract, loose, dislodge, disburden, parole, dismiss. See also release, discharge (3), clear (5). *Ant.* Subjugate.

Liberation, *n.* See emancipation, freedom, liberty, enfranchisement, release (3).

Libertine, *adj.* See dissolute, base (2), corrupt, immoral, carnal, prurient, prodigal, epicure.

Liberty, *n.* Exemption from extraneous control; freedom regulated by law; the enjoyment of personal rights (deprivation of liberty). Self-determination, independence, enfranchisement, freedom to choose, right to choose, license, franchise, emancipation, privilege, liberation, self-direction, decontrol, release, laissez-faire, nonintervention, latitude, option. See also freedom, sovereignty, autonomy. *Ant.* Compulsion.

Libidinous, *adj.* See prurient, lascivious, obscene.

Library, *n.* See archives, depository.

License 1. *n.* Permission to do that which otherwise would be illegal, a trespass, or a tort (a license to practice law). Authorization, leave, sanction, franchise, liberty, warrant, grant, allowance, dispensation, consent, assent, authority, charter, title, imprimatur, passport, permit, ticket, right, sufferance, privilege, credential, patent, commission, certificate, certification, bestowal, entitlement, clearance, power, endorsement, accreditation, countenance. **2.** *n.* Misused liberty (license taken by the occupying troops). Lack of self-restraint, irresponsible use of freedom, excessive freedom, excess, laxity, recklessness, arrogance, debauchery, disorder, abandon, lack of control, excuse. **3.** *v.* See legitimate (3), authorize, approve. *Ant.* Restriction; restraint.

Licensee, *n.* A person acting for his or her own purposes who has a privilege to enter or remain on land due to the express or implied consent of the possessor of the land (e.g., someone soliciting money for charity). See guest.

Licensor, *n.* The person who gives or grants a license. See owner.

Licentious, *adj.* **1.** See lascivious, prurient, obscene. **2.** Acting with disregard for ethics, law, or the rights of others. See lawless, reckless, wanton.

Licit, *adj.* See legal, lawful, legitimate, admissible.

Lid, *n.* See maximum, ceiling (2); package, wrapper, vessel (2).

Lie 1. *n.* The uttering or acting of that which is false for the purpose of deceiving (the statement is a lie). Deliberate untruth, intentional misstatement, perjury, deception, mendacity, deceit, falsification, prevarication, distortion, perversion, misrepresentation, invention, coloring, slanting, calumny, fiction, equivocation, story, exaggeration, enlargement, inaccuracy, corruption. See also fraud. **2.** *v.* To make a false statement intentionally (the witness lied). Falsify, fool, prevaricate, deceive, defraud, misrepresent, pervert, fabricate, embroider, forswear, perjure, fib, misstate, equivocate, invent, counterfeit, dissemble, twist, magnify, embellish, distort, evade, strain, romance, concoct, misinform, misguide, overstate, mince. **3.** *v.* To exist; to be sustainable (an action lies). Is maintainable, subsist, is available, is warranted, is permissible, is appropriate, stand, is supportable. **4.** *v.* To recline (to lie on the couch). Rest, extend, sit, stretch, repose, lounge, sprawl, relax.

Lie detector A machine that records (by a needle on a graph) the varying emotional disturbances that occur when answering questions truthfully or falsely, due to fluctuating blood pressure, respiration, perspiration, etc. Polygraph, pathometer. See also examination, inspection, search.

Liege, *n., adj.* A feudal lord; bound by feudal tenure and allegiance.

Lien, *n.* A charge, security, or encumbrance on property; a claim or charge on property for the payment of a debt, obligation, or duty (mechanic's lien). Hold, pledge, mortgage, stake, liability. See also charge (8), encumbrance.

Lien creditor One whose debt or claim is secured by a lien on particular property. *Ant.* General creditor.

Lienee, *n.* One whose property is subject to a lien.

Lienor, *n.* One who has a lien on the property of another.

Lieu, *n.* See in lieu of, replacement.

Lieutenant, *n.* See officer, manager; military, sailor.

Life, *n.* **1.** The state of humans, plants, animals, and insects in which the natural functions and motions are performing or are capable of performing; the sum of the forces by which death is resisted (reckless disregard for life and limb). Endurance, survival, being, animation, animate being, from birth to death, living thing, subsistence, living organism; human, person, individual. See also mind (1), spirit (3). **2.** The duration of existence (the car has a useful life of 4 years). Cycle, span, duration, lifetime, longevity, survival, life expectancy, path, term, career, days, generation. **3.** Energy, spirit (full of life). Vitality, animation, vivacity, dash, exuberance, buoyancy, vim, soul, liveliness, zest, fire, verve, enthusiasm, dynamism, joviality, ardor, effervescence. see also vigor.

Lifeblood, *n.* See animus (1), design (2), destination (1), motivation, impulse, passion, emotion.

Life estate An estate or interest in property whose duration is limited to the life of the party holding the estate or of some other person. See estate.

Life in being The remaining length of time in the life of a person who is in existence at the time that a deed or will takes effect.

Life insurance A contract for the payment of a specified amount to a designated beneficiary upon the death of the insured. See insurance.

Lifeless, *adj.* See barren, fallow, abortive, dead, arid, dormant.

Lifelike, *adj.* See natural, authentic.

Lifer, *n.* Someone serving a life sentence. See inmate, prisoner.

Lifesaver, *n.* See windfall, benefit, gift, help.

Lifestyle, *n.* See manner (1).

LIFO See last in, first out.

Lift, *v.* **1.** To remove (lift the prohibition). Cancel, eliminate, terminate, withdraw, end, revoke, rescind, countermand, stop, annul, desist. **2.** To raise (lift the chair). Elevate, hoist, put up, stand, boost, heighten, heave. See also raise (2). *Ant.* Impose; lower.

Ligament, *n.* Tissue that connects bones or cartilages. Tissue that supports organs. See anatomy, link.

Ligature, *n.* See bandage.

Light 1. *n.* Illumination. Shining, incandescence, brilliance, day, gleam, brightness, luster, blaze, fire, glimmer, flash, glow, star, streak, glare, conflagration, beam, radiation, fluorescence. See also sunshine; clear (3). **2.** *n.* See comprehension, knowledge. **3.** *adj.* See happy; casual, cursory; simple.

Lighten, *v.* See facilitate, mitigate, assuage, assist, help.

Lighthearted, *adj.* See happy, convivial, friendly.

Lightning, *n.* See storm, climate.

Lightweight, *adj., n.* See petty (2), frivolous, nugatory, worthless; nonentity, cipher (2).

Likable, *adj.* See attractive, convivial, friendly, happy, amicable, cooperative (2).

Like, *adj.* Similar (like benefits). Parallel, identical, equal, comparable, matched, resembling, allied, cognate, homologous, corresponding, approximating, not unlike, same, equivalent. See also analogous, akin (2). *Ant.* Diverse.

Likelihood, *n.* Probability (the likelihood of injuring someone). Fair prospect, potentiality, strong possibility, reasonable prospect, good chance, eventuality, well-grounded prospect, certainty, expectancy. See also probability, chance (3), hope (2).

Likely, *adj.* Probable; in all probability (likely to cause harm). Apt, expected, inclined, destined, anticipated, conceivable, possible, reasonably expected. See also liable (2). *Ant.* Doubtful.

Likeness, *n.* See copy, imitation, analogy, affinity (3), correspondence.

Limb, *n.* See member (2).

Limber, *adj.* See flexible, malleable, active (3).

Limbo, *n.* See detention, exile, oblivion.

Limelight, *n.* See notoriety, reputation, eminence, superiority, honor (3), note (4), fanfare.

Limestone, *n.* See rock, earth.

Limine See motion in limine, commencement.

Limit 1. *v.* To confine or abridge (to limit access). Restrict, circumscribe, suppress, bridle, fence in, bound, hinder, thwart, prohibit, constrict, deter, enjoin, leash, demarcate, ration, inhibit, curb, prescribe, proscribe, assign, bar, specify, fix, trammel, appoint, impede, narrow. See also obstruct, qualify, define, restrain, check (1). **2.** *n.* A restriction (limits imposed by the court). Restraint, check, hindrance, blockade, encumbrance, inhibition, obstacle, deterrent, embargo, inconvenience, interruption, discouragement, drawback, circumscription, limitation, ceiling, quota. See also obstruction. **3.** *n.* Boundary (taken to the limit). Extreme, edge, line, frontier, demarcation, verge, perimeter, ambit, outline, rim, periphery, fringe, furthest point, terminus, confines, enclosure. *Ant.* Open; facilitation; middle.

Limitation, *n.* **1.** Restriction (the limitations of time). Circumscription, impediment, drawback, embargo, hindrance, catch, check, proscription, disadvantage, roadblock, prohibition, qualification, block, handicap, encumbrance, reservation, chain, stricture, control, brake, condition, curtailment, barrier, liability, deterrent. See also obstruction. **2.** A certain time allowed by statute for bringing an action at the risk of losing it. See statute of limitation. *Ant.* Expansion.

Limited, *adj.* **1.** Restricted in duration, extent, or scope (limited power). Confined, bounded, prescribed, curbed, restrained, enclosed, controlled, diminished, checked, reduced, circumscribed, cramped, minimal, impeded, prevented, finite, hemmed in, demarcated, delimited. See also narrow (1). **2.** Lacking imagination (limited personality). Dull, vacuous, unimaginative, narrow, simple, slow. **3.** "Ltd." a designation indicating that a business is a corporation with limited liability (Times Chemical Co. Ltd.). **4.** See imperfect, temporary.

Limited divorce See legal separation, separation, divorce.

Limited partnership A type of partnership comprised of one or more general partners who manage the business and who are personally liable for partnership debts, and one or more limited partners who take no part in running the business and who incur no liability for partnership obligations beyond the contribution they invested in the partnership.

Limiting, *adj.* See restrictive.

Limitless, *adj.* See incalculable, perpetual, permanent; big, great.

Limousine, *n.* See vehicle; luxury.

Limp 1. *v.* To hobble. Crawl, stagger, totter, falter, jerk, halt, skulk. See also walk, grovel, cringe. **2.** *adj.* See flaccid, weak, frail, exhausted.

Limpid, *adj.* See clear (1), comprehensible, definite (1), intelligible; reasonable, coherent, rational.

Linchpin, *n.* See basis (1), base (3), foundation.

Line, *n.* **1.** A demarcation, border, or limit (property line). Rim, edge, periphery, boundary, frontier, perimeter, division, subdivision, margin, brim, verge, compass. **2.** A person's livelihood (securities is not my line). Job, employment, trade, craft, business, profession, vocation, calling, pursuit, métier, department, domain, forte, walk, field, venture, specialty, specialization, interest, game. **3.** Ancestry; a chronological succession of related persons or things. See lineage, succession. **4.** A sequence. See chain (1).

Lineage, *n.* Line of descent from an ancestor (tracing her lineage). Family, progeny, race, stock, genealogy, breed, strain, derivation, heredity, antecedents, blood, bloodline, pedigree, stirps, tribe, dynasty, tree, descendants, house, extraction, succession, filiation, heritage, patrimony, background, roots, history, ancestry, parentage, forebears, clan.

Lineal, *adj.* Proceeding in a direct or unbroken line (lineal descendants). Hereditary, ancestral, uninterrupted, continuous, undeviating, unswerving, linear.

Lineal descendant A person in the direct line of descent, such as a child or grandchild, as contrasted with a collateral descendant such as a niece. See descendant.

Lineal descent Descent in a direct or right line as from father or grandfather to son or grandson. See descent, succession.

Lineal heir One who inherits in a line either ascending or descending from a common source, as distinguished from a collateral heir. See heir.

Linear, *adj.* See straight (2), direct (4).

Line of credit The maximum borrowing power (credit limit) of one person from another or from a financial institution.

Line-up, *n.* A police identification procedure by which the suspect in a crime is exhibited before the victim or a witness to determine whether the suspect can be identified as the one who committed the crime (he picked her out of the line-up as the robber). Group, grouping, array, arrangement, formation, alignment, inspection, queue, row, list.

Linger, *v.* See loiter, dwell (2), hover (1), delay (1).

"Lingo", *n.* See language, term of art, balderdash.

Link 1. *n.* Anything that serves to connect or bind together the things that precede and follow it; a unit in a connected series (a link in the chain of evidence). Tie, bond, association, element, connective, knot, clip, joint, hinge, relationship, attachment, liaison, member, coupling, pivot, joiner, dovetail, bridge. See also connection. **2.** *v.* See lock (2), connect (1), converge, cooperate.

Linkage, *n.* See connection, alliance, association.

Linked, *adj.* See interlocking.

Lionize, *v.* See worship, honor (2); tribute (2).

Lion's share See majority (2), mass (2), most, preponderance.

Lip, *n.* See effrontery, insolence, insubordination.

Liqueur, *n.* See liquor, beverage.

Liquid, *adj.* Consisting of cash or capable of being easily converted into cash (liquid assets). Convertible, changeable, interchangeable, exchangeable; currency, legal tender, money. See also beverage. *Ant.* Frozen.

Liquidate, *v.* **1.** To pay and settle (liquidate all obligations). Discharge, clear, cancel, retire, dispose, adjust, satisfy, extinguish, erase, account for, ascertain and pay, apportion, identify, redeem, honor, square, defray, amortize, wipe out. **2.** To wind up the affairs of a business by identifying assets, converting them into cash, and paying off liabilities (liquidate the company). Terminate, finish, sell, conclude, break up, dissolve, disband. **3.** To put to death or murder. See kill. *Ant.* Incur; create.

Liquidated, *adj.* Made clear or manifest (liquidated claim). Ascertained, determined, settled, adjusted, certain, declared, discharged. See also fixed.

Liquidated claim A claim whose amount has been agreed upon by the parties, has been fixed by operation of law, or is capable of ascertainment by mathematical computation.

Liquidated damages The amount of the damages has been stipulated by the parties or has been ascertained by a judgment. See damages.

Liquidation, *n.* See elimination, abolition, rescission.

Liquid debt A debt immediately and unconditionally due. See debt.

Liquidity, *n.* The condition of a person or business in terms of an ability to convert assets into cash. See liquid.

Liquify, *v.* See thaw.

Liquor, *n.* Alcoholic beverage made by distillation as opposed to wine, which is made by fermentation. Intoxicating beverage, hard liquor, spirits, distilled spirits, inebriant, drink, "booze," aqua vitae, beer, ale, malt, whiskey, bourbon, brandy, burgundy, champagne, chaser, alcohol. See also beverage.

Lis pendens A pending suit; notice of the pendency of an action affecting title to real property; confirmation of the power or jurisdiction of the court over property pending the outcome of legal proceedings.

List 1. *v.* To register; to place on a calendar; to enter in a directory (list the assets). Itemize, docket, enumerate, book, enroll, tabulate, number, file, inventory, schedule, post, particularize, spell out, address, delineate, narrate, portray, set down, count, document, arrange, catalogue, cite, mention, recite, specify. See also classify, record, codify. **2.** *n.* See agenda, schedule (1).

Listen, *v.* See apprehend (1), notice (2), eavesdrop; observe (1), abide (1), comply.

Listing, *n.* **1.** An agreement between an owner of real property and a real estate agent, whereby the latter agrees to secure a buyer or tenant under specified terms in return for a fee or commission. **2.** A contract between a firm and a stock exchange, covering the trading of that firm's securities on the stock exchange. **3.** Making a schedule or inventory. See list, record (2).

Listless, *adj.* See drowsy, exhausted; frail, weak, thin; lazy, apathetic, indifferent (2).

List price The published or advertised price of goods.

Litany, *n.* See agenda, schedule (1); petition; account.

Liter, *n.* Approximately 1.05668 liquid quarts. See amount, portion.

Literacy, *n.* The ability to read and write (literacy test). Intelligence, learning, education, enlightenment; basics, fundamentals. See also capacity, competence. *Ant.* Illiteracy.

Literal, *adj.* **1.** According to the exact language; adhering closely to the words (literal interpretation). Strict, verbatim, scrupulous, undeviating, textual, word-for-word; correct, faithful, factual, reliable, authoritative, real, dependable, meticulous, credible, clear, objective, unvarnished, unadulterated, unexaggerated, unimpeachable, trustworthy, truthful. See also bona fide, authentic, conscientious, honest, genuine, precise, natural. **2.** Unimaginative (a literal mind). Prosaic, mechanical, dull, matter-of-fact, boring, simple-minded, tedious, slow, colorless, obtuse, vapid. See also commonplace (2), limited (2). *Ant.* Loose; creative.

Literal construction The interpretation of a document according to its words alone without any consideration of the intent of the drafter(s). See construction.

Literary, *adj.* **1.** Pertaining to literature; connected with authors, books, and writings (literary work). Published, poetic, artistic, bookish, printed. **2.** Fond of learning (literary person). Lettered, literate, well-informed, versed, erudite, scholarly, pedantic, cerebral, cultured, proficient, intellectual, accomplished, aware, sapient, disciplined, skilled, informed, studious, conversant, polished, well-read, qualified, knowledgeable, formal, refined. See also cultivated, learned, academic (2).

Literary property The exclusive right that entitles an author and his or her assigns to the use and profit of his or her composition. See right, property, copyright.

Literary work Under the copyright law: Any work (except audiovisual works) expressed in words, numbers, or symbols regardless of its physical form. See copyright, art, article, book, manifestation.

Literate, *adj.* Able to read and write; knowledgeable and educated. See literary, learned, cultured, literacy.

Literati, *n.* See aristocracy, establishment, coterie; scholar, teacher, student, author.

Literature, *n.* See book (4), language, communication.

Litigant, *n.* A party in litigation (each litigant was served notice). Litigator, opponent, adversary, disputant, contender, challenger, pleader, contestant. See also accused, accuser, appellant, appellee, claimant, complainant, defendant, intervenor, petitioner, plaintiff, respondent.

Litigate, *v.* To settle a dispute or seek relief in a court of law (when negotiation failed, they litigated). Press or pursue in court, dispute, carry on a suit, contest at law, file, take to court, initiate proceedings, sue, prosecute, apply for relief, commence a suit, prefer a claim, summon, start a lawsuit, bring suit. *Ant.* Settle.

Litigation, *n.* A legal action including all the proceedings therein (tort litigation). Lawsuit, contest in a court of law, judicial contest, judicial controversy, suit at law legal proceedings, prosecution. See also action (1), cause (3).

Litigious, *adj.* **1.** Prone to engage in disputes and litigation (litigious personality). Argumentative, combative, pugnacious, militant, belligerent, disputatious, legalistic, bellicose, controversial, polemical, fiery, hotheaded, discordant, offensive, quarrelsome, warlike, hostile, aggressive, contrary, eristic. See also contentious. **2.** Used to describe the subject of a lawsuit or action.

Litmus test, *n.* See qualification, criterion, assessment, examination.

Litter 1. *v.* To dump, throw, place, deposit, or leave refuse or objects that tend to pollute, mar, or deface public or private roads, alleys, parks, etc. (littered the street). Strew, clutter, scatter, mess, pile, heap, dishevel, throw debris. See also pollute. **2.** *n.* See refuse (2). **3.** *n.* See mixture. *Ant.* Clean (1).

Little, *adj.* See small, short (2), minimal, minor (2), petty; hidden.

Littoral, *adj.* Concerning or belonging to the shore (littoral rights). Coastal, waterfront, beach.

Liturgy, *n.* See worship, ceremony; God, holy, religious.

Livable, *adj.* See habitable, comfortable, adequate.

Live 1. *v.* To reside in a place (live in South Boston). Dwell, room, be in residence, settle, abide, bunk, take root, lodge, occupy. **2.** *v.* To have life (testimony indicated that he would not live much longer). Survive, endure, cling to life, persist, continue, breathe, prevail, subsist, remain alive, persevere, sustain, thrive, maintain. See also last (2). **3.** *adj.* Having life (a live animal). Living, breathing, animate, extant, viable, existent, mortal, growing, vital, quick. See also alive (1). **4.** *adj.* Timely (a live issue). Relevant, current, pertinent, up-to-date, active.

Livelihood, *n.* Means of support or subsistence. See business, calling, career, employment, line (2).

Lively, *adj.* See alive (2), active, ardent, indefatigable, emotional.

Livery of seisin A ceremony for transferring possession of land (e.g., the parties went on the land where a twig as a symbol of the whole land was delivered by the grantor to the grantee).

Livestock, *n.* Domestic animals used or raised on a farm, especially those kept for profit; all domestic animals (sale of livestock). Herd, farm animals, cattle, pigs, horses. See also animal. *Ant.* Wild animals.

Livid, *adj.* See angry, hot (2), aggravated (2), feverish, wild; contusion, wound, lesion.

Living 1. *n.* Existing (cost of living). Surviving, continuing in operation, being, activity, animation, life, breathing. **2.** *n.* The financial means for maintaining life (make a living by painting). Livelihood, support, subsistence, upkeep, sustenance, income. See also calling, career, employment, line (2). **3.** *adj.* Having life (living authors). Alive, live, possessing life, existing, extant, quick, animate, here, organic, corporeal, in the flesh, vital, active, operative, ongoing, enduring, continuing, current, prevailing, remaining. *Ant.* Death; poverty; defunct.

Living separate and apart A ground for divorce: Spouses live separately for a statutorily designated period, with no present intention of resuming marital relations. See incompatible, irreconcilable differences, ground, divorce, separation.

Living trust An inter vivos trust; a trust that is active during the life of the creator of the trust—the settlor. See trust. *Ant.* Testamentary trust.

Living will A will specifying the conditions under which a person suffering from a terminal illness does not wish to be kept alive by life-support instruments. See brain death.

L.J. Law Journal.

LL.B.; LL.M.; LL.D. Law degrees: bachelor (LL.B.), master (LL.M.), doctor (LL.D.) See also J.D.

Load, *n., v.* See burden (1), onus, obligation; freight, baggage; fill; loading.

Loading, *n.* **1.** That portion of the insurance premium used for meeting selling and administrative expenses beyond the portion required to meet the liability reserve. **2.** Filling; placing in or on a structure (injury sustained during the loading of the bus). Stacking, putting, inserting, packing, heaping, stuffing, burdening.

Loaf, *v.* To spend time in idleness. Lounge, fritter, dally, malinger, "goof off," vegetate, waste time, kill time, lie or lounge around. See also loiter; malingerer. *Ant.* Toil.

Loan, *n.* Anything furnished for temporary use with or without compensation on the condition that it or its equivalent in kind be returned (a $3,000 loan). Financing, advance, credit, accommodation, allowance, lending; mortgage. See also lend.

Loaned servant doctrine When an employer lends its employee to another for the performance of some special service, the employee becomes the employee of the party to whom he or she has been loaned with respect to that special service. See respondeat superior, agency.

Loan ratio The ratio, expressed as a percentage, of the amount of a loan to the value or selling price of the real property. See ratio.

Loansharking, *n.* Lending money at excessive and usurious rates with the threat or actual use of force to obtain repayment. See usury, extortion, coercion; intimidate.

Loathe, *n., v.* See abhor, disapprove (2).

Loathing, *n.* See contempt (2), odium, hostility, animus (2), malice.

Loathsome, *adj.* See odious, repulsive, offensive.

Lobby, *n.* See lobbying, advocacy; entrance.

Lobbying, *n.* All attempts, including personal solicitation, to induce legislators to vote in a certain way or to introduce legislation (lobbying to repeal the tax). Influence, pressure, persuasion, promotion, urging, encouragement, espousing, advancing, pushing, instigation, request, representing, pulling strings. See also advocacy.

Lobotomy, *n.* A surgical operation in which designated nerve connections in the brain are cut. See surgery, medicine, medical, doctor, cut, lesion, contusion, sterilization.

Local, *adj.* Belonging or confined to a particular place (local customs). Localized, native, home, indigenous, district, sectional, regional, provincial, near, territorial, citywide, hometown; narrow, restricted, delimited, circumscribed, insular. See also parochial, neighborhood, domestic. *Ant.* National, general.

Local action An action or lawsuit wherein all the principal facts on which it is founded are of a local nature; an action that must be brought in the jurisdiction where the act occurred or where the subject matter is located. See action (1). *Ant.* Transitory action.

Local agent A person who takes care of a company's business in a particular area; an agent at a given place or within a definite district. See agent, representative (1).

Locale, *n.* See neighborhood, zone, locality.

Local government City, county, or other governing body at a level smaller than a state. See government, home rule.

Locality, *n.* A definite region in any part of space; geographical position (operating in the locality). Site, scene, district, area, province, situs, precinct, sector, locale, spot, vicinity, quarter, tract, domain, bailiwick, point, ward, township, range, city, environment, terrain, county, setting. See also zone, neighborhood, place (1).

Localize, *v.* To focus on a certain area; to restrict to a local area (the company localized its operations in Belmont). Confine, limit, delimit, situate, concentrate, pinpoint, quarantine, narrow, encircle, fix, individualize, particularize, restrain. *Ant.* Broaden.

Locate, *v.* **1.** To find (they located the defect). Ascertain, define, reveal, detect, unearth, bring to light, pinpoint, uncover, happen upon, determine, track down, search out, stumble upon, delineate. See also find (1), ferret, expose (1), discover (1). **2.** To settle (the company located in Santa Monica). Establish, move to, reside, camp, plant, situate, take up residence, stay, take root, station, occupy, anchor, dock, place, house, lodge, ensconce, deposit, nest, build, construct, post, position, park, squat, install. *Ant.* Lose; leave.

Location, *n.* The site or place where something is or may be located (the location of the mine). Spot, area, territory, point, whereabouts, locale, station, district, position, residence, domicile, region, locus, quarter, vicinity, precinct, base, field, environment, range, section, tract, province. See also locality, neighborhood, place (1), zone.

Locative calls The description of land in a deed or other document by using landmarks, natural objects, and the like, by which the land is located and identified. See metes and bounds, map.

Lock 1. *v.* To confine (locked in the room). Cage, shut in, incarcerate, jail, imprison, immure, bolt, barricade, latch, encircle, intern, pen, enclose, impound, padlock, handcuff, block, fence, bar, secure, clamp. **2.** *v.* To join together tightly (the pieces were locked in place). Unite, hold, clamp, interlink, entwine, fasten, bolt, seize, embrace, intertwine, cement, latch, connect, entangle, marry, league, fuse, jam, couple, bond, glue. **3.** *n.* A device used to hold, secure, or close something (a lock on the door). Latch, catch, clamp, padlock, bar, safety catch, hook, deadbolt. *Ant.* Unlock, release.

Locker, *n.* See cabinet, alcove, vessel, warehouse; protection.

Lockout, *n.* Withholding work from employees; temporarily closing down a business during a labor dispute; employer work stoppage. See union.

Lockup, *n.* A place of detention in a police station, court, or other facility used for persons awaiting trial or court appearance. See jail, detention.

Locomotive, *n.* See vehicle; carriage.

Loco parentis See in loco parentis, authority, parent, replacement, discipline.

Locus, *n.* A place; a place where a thing is done (locus delicti—the place where the wrong or offense was committed). See locality, location, place (1).

Lodge 1. *v.* To present formally (lodge a complaint). File, register, record, place, call, charge, prosecute, bring. **2.** *v.* To stay in a place temporarily (they lodged at the airport inn). Reside, room, quarter, live, abide, settle, berth, situate, camp, sleep, locate, station, put up, sojourn, anchor, encamp, house, accommodate, shelter, stay, dwell, park. **3.** *n.* A place where one stays temporarily (security problems at the lodge). Motel, hotel, cabin, hut, resort, cottage, camp.

Lodger, *n.* An occupant who has the use of property without exclusive possession (ouster of the lodger). Roomer, guest, boarder, tenant, resident, occupier, inmate, transient, possessor, dweller, lessee. See also occupant.

Lodging, *n.* See lodge (3), home.

Loft, *n.* See attic.

Lofty, *adj.* See elevated, high (2), great, notorious.

Loggerheads, at See contention, feud, fight, argument (2).

465

Logic, *n.* See reason (2), common sense, deduction (2); logical.

Logical, *adj.* Internally consistent; concerning logic (logical argument). Reasonable, sound, coherent, equitable, wise, organized, pertinent, intelligent, plausible, clear, judicious, sensible, relevant, valid, viable, analytical, lucid, convincing, reasoned, germane; deductive, inductive, syllogistic. See also cogent, consistent (1), rational, compelling. *Ant.* Irrational.

Logistics, *n.* See plan, agenda, schedule; supervision; cooperation.

Logo, *n.* See badge, manifestation, slogan, symbol.

Logrolling, *n.* A strategy of obtaining approval of a proposal, which the voters (or legislators) would probably not accept if voted upon independently, by combining it with one or more other proposals on different topics that they are more likely to accept; trading political favors. See politics.

Loiter, *v.* To stand idly around (arrested for loitering). Linger, wander, ramble, laze, lurk, tarry, dally, dawdle, procrastinate, delay, idle, hang around, stroll, lag, saunter, slouch, kill time, fritter, vegetate. See also loaf, trail (3). *Ant.* Hustle.

Lone, *adj.* See alone (1), solitary.

Lonely, *adj.* See alone (2), solitary, barren, separate, remote (1), depressed, depressing.

Lonesome, *adj.* See lonely.

Long 1. *adj.* Outstretched, lengthy (long session). Protracted, extended, unending, widespread, elongated, sustained, extensive, reaching out, expanded, far-reaching, considerable. See also constant, continual, big. **2.** *v.* See desire (1). *Ant.* Confined; short.

Long arm statute A statutory method of obtaining personal jurisdiction by substituted service of process over a nonresident defendant who has sufficient purposeful contact with a state so that it is fair and reasonable for the state to adjudicate the dispute involving the defendant. See jurisdiction, service of process, substituted service, notice (1).

Longevity, *n.* Long life (advancement because of longevity). Durability, seniority, endurance, old age, survival, persistence, tenure, life span, survivorship, prolongation.

Longing, *n.* See wish (4), hope (2).

Long-lived, *adj.* See old, ancient, durable, permanent, perpetual.

Long-range, *adj.* See long, continuous, extensive, comprehensive.

Longshoreman, *n.* A maritime laborer who works about the wharves of a port; one who loads and unloads ships (longshoreman's union). Stevedore, loader, dockworker. See also employee, merchant.

Long-standing, *adj.* See long, durable, old, ancient, fixed, firm (2).

Long-term, *adj.* See long, continuous, continual.

Long-term capital gain The gain (profit) realized on the sale or exchange of a capital asset held for more than 12 months.

Long ton A measure of weight equivalent to 2,240 pounds. See amount, portion.

Look, *v., n.* See observe (3), watch, spy, notice (2), investigate, witness (2); appearance (3), demeanor.

Lookout, *n.* Keeping watch; one who keeps watch (drivers on the lookout for holes in the road). Guard, vigilance, alertness, heed, attention, prudence, circumspection, readiness, awareness, surveillance; sentry, observer, patrol, monitor, watchdog.

Loom, *v.* See appear (2), hover (1); menace (2).

Looming, *adj.* See future; imminent, prospective.

Loony, *adj.* See lunatic (2).

Loophole, *n.* See ambiguity, vagueness, omission, windfall.

Loose, *adj.* See indefinite; free (1); careless; immoral, obscene.

Loose-leaf service Texts with pages that are easily removable, often through three-ringed binders.

Loosen, *v.* See mitigate, assuage; release.

"Loot," *n.* See prize (1), plunder (2).

Lop, *v.* See cut, amputate, mutilate.

Lopsided, *adj.* See disproportionate, irregular.

Loquacious, *adj.* See garrulous, babble, prolixity; convivial, friendly.

Lord, *n.* See master, manager; God.

Lord Campbell Act A statutory remedy for wrongful death; a statute that creates a new cause of action for wrongful death in favor of the decedent's personal representative for the benefit of designated persons. See wrongful death; action (1).

Lord Mansfield's Rule The testimony of either spouse is inadmissible on the question of whether the husband had access to the wife at the time of conception, since such evidence would tend to "bastardize" the child. See bastardize (1); evidence, legitimacy, illegitimacy.

Lore, *n.* See legend, heritage; education, belief.

Lose, *v.* **1.** To suffer the loss of (lose a ring). Fail, incur the loss of, squander, misplace, misdirect, let slip, miss, be deprived of, forget, waste, mislay, vanish, lose sight of, drain, deplete, exhaust, consume. **2.** To be defeated (lose a case). Forfeit, flunk, fail, miscarry, abort, capitulate, be foiled, fall short, be outdistanced, succumb, default, fall, give up. *Ant.* Find; succeed.

Loser, *n.* See bankrupt, failure, victim.

Loss, *n.* The act of losing; the thing lost (loss of memory). Damage, deprivation, disaster, misfortune, deficit, disadvantage, privation, debt, calamity, sacrifice, ruin, debit, bereavement, depletion, forfeiture, trouble, wreck, undoing, extermination, destruction, prejudice, incapacitation, wreckage, injury, hurt, lapse, regression, dissolution. See also anguish, anxiety, pain, affliction; detriment, harm, failure, defeat. *Ant.* Gain.

Loss leader An item sold by a merchant at a very low price (perhaps even below cost) in order to attract people to come into the store. See merchant, merchandise.

Loss of consortium See consortium (1); tort, cause of action, cause (3).

Lost, *adj.* **1.** Not capable of being located (lost ring). Misplaced, missing, stray, astray, misdirected, gone, mislaid, absent, disappeared, adrift. See also abandoned (1). **2.** Destroyed (lost in battle). Ruined, perished, obliterated, wasted, dissipated, defeated, annihilated, squandered, killed, abolished, wrecked, extirpated, forfeited, undone, eradicated, wiped out, murdered, demolished, confiscated, sacrificed, taken, abandoned. See also exhausted. **3.** Confused (the witness was lost). At a loss, puzzled, bewildered, mystified, helpless, dazed, befuddled, baffled, perplexed, confounded, disoriented. See also aback, agape; surprise. *Ant.* Located; restored; in control.

Lost property Property that the owner has involuntarily parted with and does not know where to find or recover. Lost property is distinguishable from mislaid property, which has deliberately been placed somewhere and forgotten. See abandonment, abandoned (1).

Lot, *n.* **1.** One of several parcels into which real property is divided (lot and block number). Portion, share, plot, plat, block, division, patch, subdivision, tract, acreage, piece, field, square, ground, clearing, frontage. **2.** A number of associated persons or things taken collectively (the entire lot). Group, crew, body, company, crowd, host, contingent, pack, army, shipment, package, batch, load. See also collection (2). **3.** See chance (1), destiny.

Lotion, *n.* See ointment; medicine.

Lottery, *n.* A chance for a prize, for which a price is paid; a device whereby anything of value is, for a consideration, allotted by lot or by chance (unauthorized lottery). Game of chance, bet, gamble, scheme, draw, drawing, policy, raffle, wager, stake, sweepstakes, pool, risk, toss-up. See also gambling.

Loud, *adj.* See noisy, vociferous, flamboyant, wild (3), gaudy; noise, sound (5).

Loudmouth, *n.* See informer; boast; ass, idiot, boor.

Lounge, *n., v.* See inn; lie (4); loiter, loaf; lazy.

"Louse," *n.* See ass, parasite; wrongdoer.

Lousy, *adj.* See inferior, worthless, odious, offensive, base.

Lout, *n.* See boor, ass, idiot, parasite.

Loutish, *adj.* See backward, awkward, dumb, common (3), base, rude.

Lovable, *adj.* See attractive, amicable, friendly, convivial, happy.

Love, *n.* Affection (love of music). Attachment, devotion, passion, adoration, sentiment, longing, flame, liking, cordiality, enthusiasm, warmth, attraction, predilection, craving, worship, inclination, tenderness, affinity, esteem, solicitude, rapture, fidelity, zeal, compatibility, geniality, regard, allegiance, intimacy, caring. See also affection (1), charity, benevolence. *Ant.* Antipathy.

Love affair, *n.* See adultery, affairs, infidelity, coitus.

Love child, *n.* See bastard.

Lovely, *adj.* See enjoyable, comfortable, beautiful, intriguing.

Lovemaking, *n.* See coitus, fornication, intercourse; lust.

Lover, *n.* See suitor, paramour, prostitute.

Loving, *adj.* See affectionate, friendly, convivial, cooperative.

Low, *adj.* See inferior, inadequate, incompetent; depressed, depressing; base, malicious, disloyal; abject.

Lower, *v.* See demote, demoralize, defame, debase; decline, diminish, mitigate.

Lower class See proletariat, people, constituency; class (1).

Lower oneself See grovel, cringe.

Low-key, *adj.* See quiet (2), passive, bashful.

Lowly, *adj.* See average (2), inferior, ordinary, obscure, abject; bashful, quiet (2).

Loyal, *adj.* Faithful support to a cause, office, or person (loyal servant). Dutiful, reliable, trustworthy, steadfast, unwavering, staunch, true, resolute, dependable, committed, obedient, pledged, unswerving, dedicated, honest, veracious, earnest, reputable, scrupulous, conscientious, honorable, steady, unimpeachable, patriotic, fraternal, devoted, solid. See also faithful, constant, blameless, incorruptible, innocent. *Ant.* Perfidious.

Loyalty, *n.* Faithfulness (loyalty to the state). Allegiance, fealty, devotion, steadfastness, single-mindedness, obedience, dependability, zeal, patriotism, dedication, firmness, incorruptibility, constancy, reliability. See also faith (3), fidelity. *Ant.* Inconstancy.

LSAT Law School Admission Test: A standardized test on reasoning, general academic ability, and command of written English. Law schools consider performance on the test in making a decision on admission.

Ltd. See limited (3).

Lucid, *adj.* **1.** Sane (lucid interval). Rational, normal, competent, mentally capable, responsible, sensible, responsive, sober, levelheaded, oriented, balanced, sound. **2.** Easily understood (lucid presentation). Articulate, obvious, explicit, understandable, manifest, transparent, certain, perceptive, unequivocal, categorical, graphic, acute, plain, straightforward, pellucid. See also clear (1), intelligible, comprehensible, precise. *Ant.* Incompetent; cloudy.

Lucid interval A temporary restoration to sanity; a period during which an insane person has sufficient intelligence, judgment, and will to enter contractual relationships.

Luck, *n.* See chance, destiny, accident; windfall; coincidence; fortuitous.

Lucky, *adj.* See fortunate; auspicious, expedient, happy.

Lucrative, *adj.* Yielding gain or profit (lucrative career). Profitable, worthwhile, remunerative, money-making, fruitful, productive, fertile, rewarding, paying, successful, well-paying, yielding, advantageous, prosperous. See also beneficial, gainful. *Ant.* Marginal.

Lucre, *n.* Gain in money or goods. See income.

Ludicrous, *adj.* See absurd, odd (1), irrational, wild, anomalous; clown, joke.

Lug, *v.* See carry (1), transfer (1).

Luggage, *n.* See baggage, freight, cargo.

Lukewarm, *adj.* See indifferent, casual, passive, apathetic.

Lull, *n., v.* See interruption, break (3), delay, respite; abatement; mitigate, assuage.

Lumber, *n.* See timber, woods.

Luminary, *n.* See light; chief (1), champion (3); notoriety.

Luminous, *adj.* See notorious (1), popular, great, conspicuous.

Lump, *n., v.* See bulk (1), mass (1), lot (3), collection (2); pack, collect (1).

Lump-sum payment A single amount instead of in installments.

Lunacy, *n.* A major mental disorder; an impairment of one or more faculties of the mind (lunacy proceeding). Abnormality, madness, dementia, imbecility, craziness, instability, disorientation, imbalance, delusion, derangement, irrationality, psychosis, idiocy. See also insanity. *Ant.* Sanity.

Lunatic, *adj.* **1.** Pertaining to insanity. See deranged, insanity. **2.** Senseless (lunatic rescue proposal). Reckless, stupid, crazy, nonsensical, maniacal, mad, insane, demented, foolish, foolhardy, imprudent, unsound, unbalanced, frenzied, eccentric, hysterical, inane, illogical, asinine, ludicrous, imbecile, ridiculous, incoherent, childish, impractical, irresponsible. See also irrational, wild. *Ant.* Rational.

Lunch, *n.* See eat, food.

Luncheonette, *n.* See inn, merchant.

Lunge, *v.* See attack, assault (3); pierce, cut.

Lurch, *v.* See flounder; attack.

Lure, *v., n.* See entice, entrap, seduce, bait (2, 3), induce, provoke; invitation.

Lurid, *adj.* See violent, bad, appalling, odious, abandoned (2), repulsive, repugnant, offensive, obscene.

Lurk, *v.* See ambush.

Lurking, *adj.* See hidden.

Luscious, *adj.* See delectable, attractive, enjoyable, beautiful.

Lush, 1. *n.* See intoxicated. **2.** *adj.* Fresh, moist. Succulent, luxurious, verdant, green, flourishing, ripe, prolific. See also abundant.

Lust, *n.* Eros. Sexual desire, libido, sex, sexuality, eroticism, prurience, bestiality, sex appetite, licentiousness, lechery, wantonness, craving, carnal desire, fleshly desire. See also impulse, desire, passion, debauchery; obscene.

Luster, *n.* See grandeur; light; merit, honor.

Lustful, *adj.* See carnal, prurient, lascivious.

Lusty, *adj.* See able-bodied, healthy, durable, strong (2), indefatigable.

Luxuriant, *adj.* See luxurious; luxury.

Luxurious, *adj.* See deluxe, prodigal, costly, exorbitant, excess; fertile, abundant; comfortable, enjoyable, attractive, lush (2), epicure; gaudy, flamboyant; decadent; debauchery; luxury.

Luxury, *n.* **1.** An expensive item that is not a necessity but that gives comfort or pleasure (tax on luxuries). Indulgence, frill, finery, amenity, extravagance, delicacy. **2.** Lavishness (living in luxury). Opulence, excessiveness, elegance, riches, self-indulgence, comfort, bliss, self-gratification, paradise, splendor, exorbitance, hedonism, prodigality. See also wealth. *Ant.* Basics; poverty.

Lying, *adj.* Deceitful (lying tongue). Deceptive, cunning, perfidious, perjured, fabricating, mandacious, hypocritical, evasive, insincere, two-faced, dissembling, fake, treacherous, disingenuous, fraudulent, misleading, untruthful, delusory, wrong, fictitious, spurious, delusive. See also false (2), dishonest. *Ant.* Honest.

Lynch, *v.* See kill, execute (2), murder.

Lynch law The action of unofficial persons, bands, or mobs who seize persons suspected of crimes and summarily punish them without legal trial or authority. Lawlessness, mob rule, terrorism, anarchy, mobocracy.

Lyric, *adj.* Melodious. Warm, rhapsodic, mellifluous, poetic. See also beautiful, attractive, enjoyable; music.

Macabre, *adj.* See repugnant, repulsive, odious, gross (1), violent, deadly.

Mace, *n.* **1.** A chemical liquid which, when sprayed in the face of a person, causes dizziness and immobilization. **2.** A war club. **3.** An ornamented staff used as an emblem of authority.

Machiavellian, *adj.* See deceitful, devious, corrupt, depraved, arbitrary, clandestine; manipulate, conspire; machination.

Machinate, *v.* See conspire, manipulate, plot, plan; machination.

Machination, *n.* The act of planning or contriving a scheme to execute a purpose that is often evil (through machinations, she destroyed the company). Plot, manipulation, intrigue, design, wile, conspiracy, maneuver, artifice, engineering, device, stratagem, move, tactic, ruse, covin, cabal, trick, complicity. See also contrivance, deception, fraud, duplicity.

Machine, machinery, *n.* See apparatus, instrument (2), equipment, device (1), implement (1); automation; agent (2).

Machismo, *n.* Male superiority. See chauvinism, arrogance; vigor; pompous, man.

Macrocosm, *n.* See world; universal.

Mad, *adj.* See angry, aggravated (2), hot (2), feverish, wild, irrational, reckless, insane, deranged, demented.

Madam, *n.* See prostitute; woman; aristocracy.

Madcap, *adj.* See wild, impetuous, emotional, excitable, improvident, careless, reckless.

Madden, *v.* See disturb, outrage (2).

Maddening, *adj.* See offensive, obnoxious, odious, blatant (2).

Made 1. *adj.* Produced or manufactured. Constructed, formed, designed, assembled, fabricated, created, built. See also fake. **2.** *v.* Entered into or executed (contract made in New York). See execute (1), file (2), record.

Mademoiselle, *n.* See woman, maiden (2); minor, child, juvenile.

Madman, *n.* See maniac, insanity, lunacy; nonconformist, fanatic.

Maestro, *n.* See master (1), expert (1), judge (1), professional (2).

Mafia, *n.* See racket (1), racketeering; malefactor, wrongdoer; crime, gang, coterie.

Magazine, *n.* See press (1), newspaper, journal.

Magic, *n.* See witchcraft, hallucination, dream (1), beauty, fiction; appeal (3), illusory; entice, bait.

Magisterial, *adj.* See grandeur; important, formal, elevated, pompous, arrogant, prodigal.

Magistrate, *n.* **1.** A federal judicial officer appointed by judges of federal district courts, having some but not all the powers of a judge. Justice of the peace, surrogate. See also judge. **2.** A public civic officer with executive or judicial power. Mayor, prefect, municipal official. See also official.

Magna Charta The great charter, considered the foundation of English constitutional liberty. In 1215, King John granted the charter to the barons at Runnymade. Its provisions regulated the administration of justice, defined ecclesiastical jurisdiction, secured personal liberty and rights of property, defined limits on taxation, etc.

Magnanimous, *adj.* See charitable, benevolent, kind, liberal, flexible, elevated; forgive, pardon.

Magnate, *n.* See entrepreneur, owner, manager, employer, master, chief (1).

Magnet, *n.* See appeal (3), bait, interest (4, 5), invitation.

Magnetic, *adj.* See attractive, intriguing, compelling, outstanding.

Magnify, *v.* See exacerbate, exaggerate, strengthen, augment, advance, overrate; puffing.

Magnitude, *n.* See measure (1), extent, amount; power, spirit (2), force (1), vigor, diligence (1), industry (2); abundant.

Maid, *n.* See servant, employee; woman, maiden.

Maiden 1. *adj.* First (maiden voyage). Initial, virgin, beginning, introductory, original, leading, untried, fresh, untested, inaugural. See also first. **2.** *n.* A young unmarried woman (innocent maiden). Girl, damsel, ingenue, mademoiselle, lass, maid. See also woman; chaste. *Ant.* Final; matron.

Maidenhead, *n.* See hymen; celibacy, abstention; chaste.

Mail 1. *n.* That which is sent through the postal system (mail fraud). Letters, communication, packages, messages. **2.** *v.* To send through the postal system (mail a letter). Post, dispatch, address, forward, ship, direct, expedite. See also send.

Mailed, *adj.* Something is mailed when it is properly addressed, stamped with the correct amount of postage, and deposited in a proper place for the receipt of mail.

Maim *v.* To inflict an injury upon a person, which deprives him or her of the use of any limb or member of the body, or renders him or her lame or defective in bodily vigor (she maimed her opponent in the fight). Cripple, maul, incapacitate, disfigure, gash, deface, stab, amputate, slash, rupture, rip, mangle, lame, paralyze, massacre, dismember, hamstring, fracture, emasculate, lacerate. See also disable, mutilate, cut, batter, attack, assault. *Ant.* Heal.

Main, *adj.* Most important in size, extent, rank, strength, or utility (the main issue in the case). Principal, leading, chief, cardinal, banner, vital, foremost, top, major, dominant, premier, star, ranking, first, capital, central, predominant, preeminent, supreme, creme, critical, key, head, prevailing, crowning. See also primary, fundamental. *Ant.* Subordinate.

"Mainline" *v.* To take drugs directly into a vein. See drug.

Main purpose doctrine The Statute of Frauds requires contracts to answer for the debt, default, or misdoing of another to be in writing unless the main purpose of the promisor's undertaking is his or her own benefit or protection. See statute of frauds.

Mainspring, *n.* See root, cause (1), author, agent, impulse.

Mainstay, *n.* See base (3), foundation (2), security (2).

Maintain, *v.* **1.** To make repairs or perform other acts to prevent a decline from the present state or condition (maintain the premises). Preserve, conserve, uphold, cultivate, service, save, husband, guard, overhaul, remedy, retain, prolong, bolster, keep intact, groom, restore, oversee, condition, secure, keep up, manage, protect. **2.** To bear the expenses for the support of (maintain a household). Sustain, care for, finance, nourish, feed, shelter, nurture, supply, cater, accouter, minister, take care of, subsidize, provide for, keep. **3.** To declare or affirm (he maintained his innocence). Assert, state, stress, allege, emphasize, avow, profess, aver, contend, testify, defend, champion, represent, stand by, swear, insist, believe, vouch, broadcast, claim, announce, substantiate, vindicate, circulate, publish, warrant, certify, acknowledge, utter. **4.** To carry forward; to institute (maintain an action). Prosecute, pursue, persevere, carry on, hold out, keep on course, adhere, keep, extend, prolong, protract, keep alive, perpetuate, persist; launch, undertake, begin, introduce, set in motion, embark upon. *Ant.* Damage; abandon; deny; discontinue.

Maintenance, *n.* **1.** Support or assistance (the spouse's action for maintenance). Help, aid, finances, alimony, subsistence, livelihood, upkeep, financial aid, sustenance, backing, provisions, necessities, room and board, living, income, revenue, funds, allowance. See also assistance, necessaries. **2.** Keeping something in working order (maintenance of the hall). Upkeep, conservation, preservation, care, repair, safeguarding, protection, custodianship, continuation.

Majestic, *adj.* See elevated, important, great, extraordinary; grandeur.

Majesty, *n.* See grandeur; sovereignty, supremacy.

Major 1. *adj.* Greater or larger (the major portion of her time). Largest, main, bigger, capital, highest. **2.** *adj.* Of considerable importance (a major decision). Leading, principal, key, paramount, vital, significant, telling, far-reaching, weighty, formidable, pressing, capital, great, chief, memorable, serious unparalleled, fateful, remarkable, urgent, foremost, preeminent, consequential, indispensable, prime, superior, supreme, unrivaled, solemn, matchless. See also primary, outstanding (2), extraordinary, exceptional, best (1). **3.** *adj.* Concerning a person of full age. See majority (1). **4.** *n.* The officer next in rank above a captain. See military; sailor; officer. *Ant.* Minor.

Major general An officer next in rank above a brigadier general and next below a lieutenant general. See officer; military; sailor.

Majority, *n.* **1.** The age at which a person is entitled to the management of his or her own affairs and to the enjoyment of civil rights, e.g., voting (having reached majority). Legal age, full age, age of responsibility, maturity, manhood, womanhood, adulthood. **2.** The greater number (the majority voted to cancel). More than half, plurality, bulk, greater part, mass, lion's share, gross, main part, the weight of those present, preponderance. See also most. *Ant.* Minority.

Majority opinion The opinion of an appellate court in which a majority of its members joined. See opinion.

Make 1. *v.* To cause to exist (the company makes tires). Fabricate, create, originate, manufacture, produce, fashion, invent, sculpture, mold, assemble, shape, beget, cast, model, draft, erect, construct, build, form, forge, breed, effect, accomplish, actualize, compose, develop, execute, improvise, formulate, enact, frame, establish, bring to pass, foment, generate, coin, institute, complete, pattern, mint, imprint, contrive, frame, devise, elevate, put together, evolve, achieve, synthesize, author, constitute. **2.** *v.* To compel (make him retire). Force, constrain, induce, oblige, require, impel, press, necessitate, drive, obligate, pressure, prevail upon, railroad. **3.** *n.* See kind (1), model. *Ant.* Destroy; allow.

Make-believe, *adj.* See fictitious, false (1, 2), feigned, deceptive, illusory, baseless, dummy (2), bogus.

Maker, *n.* One who makes or executes; one who signs a note to borrow; one who signs a check (maker of a promissory note). See author, producer.

Makeshift, *adj.* See temporary, transitory, replacement, artificial; expedient.

Make-work, *n.* Busywork. See labor, assignment (3), function, job.

Maladjusted, *adj.* See estranged, abnormal; disproportionate; alienate (2), confuse.

Maladminister, *v.* See blunder, neglect; err, flounder; maladministration, incompetent.

Maladministration, *n.* Improper or wrong administration (blame for the maladministration). Inefficiency, mismanagement, bungling, dereliction of duty. See also misconduct, malfeasance, misfeasance, misdirection, neglect (2), bad faith; negligent.

Maladroit, *adj.* See incompetent, imperfect, inadequate, deficient, careless, negligent.

Malady, *n.* See disease, infirmity, illness, affliction, disorder (2).

Mala fides See bad faith.

Mala in se Wrongs in themselves; morally wrong acts; offenses against conscience. See offense, wrong.

Malaise, *n.* See ennui, boredom; apathetic, casual (3), indifferent.

Malapportionment, *n.* An improper or unconstitutional apportionment of legislative districts. See disparity, difference; injustice, grievance; gerrymander; disproportionate; apportionment.

Mala prohibita Acts that are made offenses by positive laws that prohibit them—they are not wrongs in themselves. See offense, wrong.

Malaria, *n.* See disease, illness; contagious.

"Malarkey," *n.* See balderdash.

Malcontent, *n., adj.* See nonconformist, insurgent (1, 2); depressed, despondent; crabby, contentious, litigious.

Male, *n.* See man.

Malediction, *n.* A curse. See censure (2), anathema, slander; defamatory, denounce, condemn.

Malefactor, *n.* One who is guilty or has been convicted of a crime or offense (the malefactors were brought to justice). Criminal, offender, felon, villain, outlaw, perpetrator, transgressor, delinquent, culprit, rascal, convict, trespasser, lawbreaker, gangster, malfeasant, troublemaker, scoundrel, hoodlum, reprobate, blackguard, miscreant, sinner, knave. See also wrongdoer. *Ant.* Innocent.

Malevolent, *adj.* See malicious, hostile, immoral, bad (2), base, harmful, injurious, deleterious, dangerous.

Malfeasance, *n.* Doing an act that a person ought not do at all (malfeasance in office). Compare with misfeasance—the improper performance of an act that a person has a right to do; and nonfeasance—the failure to do an act that a person ought to do. Dereliction, wrongful conduct, mismanagement, maladministration, misdeed, malpractice, negligence, carelessness, infringement, transgression, error, abuse, overstepping. See also violation, wrong.

Malfunction, *n.* See defect, failure, deficiency, error, fault, blunder.

Malice, *n.* The intentional doing of a wrongful act without just cause or excuse, with an intent to inflict injury or under circumstances that the law will imply an evil intent (published with malice). Willfulness, animosity, callousness, hate, ill will, venom, bitterness, wantonness, enmity, recklessness, hostility, maliciousness, aversion, antipathy, viciousness, harmful intent, desire to injure, acrimony, contempt, antagonism, malevolence, ill feeling, abhorrence, grudge, brutality, pique, bad blood, vindictiveness, gall, malignity, odium, spleen, envy, jealousy, rancor. See also actual malice, cruelty, animus, wrath, resentment, spite. *Ant.* Benevolence.

Malice aforethought The intentional doing of an unlawful act that was determined upon before it was executed; a predetermination to commit an act without justification or excuse. See premeditated, deliberate (2), intentional, willful, voluntary.

Malice in fact Express or actual malice; the desire or intent to injure.

Malice in law Implied, inferred, or legal malice; malice that is presumed from tortious acts that are deliberately done without just cause and that are reasonably calculated to injure others.

Malicious, *adj.* Performed with wicked or mischievous intentions or motives; doing a wrongful act intentionally and without just cause or excuse (malicious lie). Spiteful, hateful, vicious, acrimonious, wanton, reckless, invidious, vindictive, antagonistic, harmful, treacherous, destructive, viperous, diabolic, obnoxious, bitter, Vandalic, harsh, brutal, truculent, inimical, malignant, wicked, ruthless, evil-minded, baleful, pernicious, malevolent, savage, revengeful, rancorous, poisonous, satanic, pitiless, merciless, unfeeling, abusive. See also cruel, hostile, offensive, rude, callous, inhuman. *Ant.* Benign.

Malicious abuse of process Willfully misapplying a court process to obtain an object not intended by the law; the malicious perversion of a regularly issued process to obtain an end that the process was not designed to accomplish. See abuse of process, malicious prosecution, tort, wrong.

Maliciously, *adv.* Involving a wish to vex, annoy, or injure another; involving an intent to do a wrongful act; involving a direct intention to injure or a reckless disregard of another's rights (maliciously causing the building to burn). Deliberately, with ill will, viciously, cruelly, brutally, hatefully. See also malice, malicious. *Ant.* Benevolently.

Malicious mischief Willful destruction of personal property from wantonness, ill will, or resentment toward its owner or possessor. See mischief; destroy.

Malicious prosecution A tort with the following elements: (a) To initiate or procure the initiation of legal proceedings—civil or criminal; (b) without probable cause; (c) with malice; (d) the proceedings terminate in favor of the person against whom the proceedings were brought. See abuse of process, malicious abuse of process.

Malicious use of process The use of process for its ostensible purpose but maliciously and without probable cause; the wrongful initiation of a meritless suit with a malicious motive.

Malign, *v., adj.* See slander, decry, attack, disparage, defame, challenge, confront, counter; harmful, bad.

Malignant, *adj.* See malicious, hostile, odious; deadly.

Malingerer, *n.* One who pretends sickness or other disablement, especially for the purpose of escaping work (the malingerer was fired). Loafer, shirker, goldbrick, do-nothing, evader, dodger, slacker, truant, quitter. See also parasite.

Mall, *n.* See market, merchant, commerce; park (1).

Malleable, *adj.* Capable of being hammered into shape; flexible (a malleable temperament). Docile, yielding, accommodating, conforming, tractable, compliant, manageable, governable, pliable, plastic, adaptable, deferential, adjustable, willing, formable, impressionable, susceptible, responsive, ready, moldable, elastic, corrigible, trainable. See also formative, amenable (2). *Ant.* Intractable.

Mallory rule A confession is inadmissible if it is given by one who has been detained an unreasonable time before being brought before a magistrate. See confession.

Malnourished, *adj.* See frail, weak, infirm, thin, exhausted.

Malpractice, *n.* Professional misconduct or unreasonable lack of skill; the failure to exercise that degree of skill and learning commonly applied under the circumstances in the community by an ordinary, prudent, and reputable member of the profession in good standing (sued for malpractice). Misconduct, incompetence, breach of fiduciary duty, carelessness, negligence, dereliction, malfeasance, mismanagement, abuse, wrongdoing, neglect, unprofessional conduct, misdeed, unethical practice, misbehavior, fault, corruption, transgression, immorality. See also legal malpractice, medical malpractice.

Maltreat, *v.* See abuse, neglect, hurt, injure.

Maltreatment, *n.* Mistreatment. See abuse, malpractice, neglect, misfeasance, bad faith.

Malum in se A wrong in itself; an act that is inherently and essentially evil and immoral in its nature. See crime, wrong.

Malum prohibitum A prohibited wrong; an act that is wrong because it is expressly prohibited—the act is not inherently wrong, evil, or immoral. See wrong.

Malversation, *n.* See misconduct, misfeasance.

Mammoth, *adj.* See big, massive, great, extraordinary.

Man, *n.* Male. Boy, gentleman, sir, homemaker, head, head of the household, chap, beau, lad, valet; masculine. See also people, person, individual, mankind; vigor, courageous, strong, able-bodied.

Manacles, *n.* Chains for the hands (the defendant was in manacles). Handcuffs, shackles, restraints, bonds, irons, trammels.

Manage, *v.* **1.** To control and direct (she managed the firm). Operate, govern, administer, take charge of, conduct, carry on, execute, pilot, run, dominate, supervise, be at the helm, take care of, engineer, superintend, guide, oversee, regulate, mastermind, head, steer, propel, maintain, navigate, command, lead, coordinate, officiate, boss, shepherd, exercise charge over, preside over, rule, watch over, quarterback; manipulate, wrangle, work, handle. **2.** To survive (they managed without him). Function, make do, cope, succeed. *Ant.* Follow; fail.

Manageable, *adj.* See malleable, amenable, flexible.

Management, *n.* **1.** The act of managing by direction, regulation, or administration (case management). Government, control, superintendence, handling, guidance, stewardship, command, leadership, care, wardship, oversight, charge, governance, organization, transaction, surveillance, supervision, running, generalship, planning, government, manipulation, treatment, conduct, disposal. **2.** The individuals or entities that manage an organization (grievances presented to management). Leaders, directors, administrators, board of directors, officials, president, executives, bureau, committee, regime, headquarters, chairmen, supervisors, powers, managers, custodians, central office, directorate, bosses, controllers. See also establishment, authority. *Ant.* Neglect; servants.

Manager, *n.* One who is in charge of and controls something (law office manager). Administrator, director, supervisor, helmsman, superintendent, steward, foreman, chief, intendant, organizer, governor, leader, conductor, overseer, impresario, manipulator, head, executive, producer, master, guide, skipper; proctor, procurator, delegate, warden, guardian, keeper, custodian, curator, gamekeeper, protector, ranger, sentry, advisor. *Ant.* Follower.

Mandamus, *n.* "We command." An order to a public official from a court to compel the performance of a ministerial act or a mandatory duty where there is a clear legal right in the plaintiff. See order, official, officer.

Mandate, *n.* **1.** A judicial command; the order issued upon a court decision (the issuance of mandate). Direction, edict, authoritative order, decree, bidding, dictate, behest, charge, precept, requirement, imperative, license, commandment, ultimatum, ruling, commission, instruction, directive, authorization, warrant, prescription, dictation, proscription. See also order (1). **2.** A territory administered under a commission of the United Nations until the territory is ready for self-government (the mandate under its jurisdiction). Protectorate, colony, dependency.

Mandatory, *adj.* Compulsory (mandatory attendance). Obligatory, imperative, required, involuntary, commanding, decreed, incumbent on, compelled, binding, requisite, not optional, peremptory, exigent, decreed, indispensable, de rigueur, needful. See also necessary, essential. *Ant.* Elective.

Mandatory injunction That which requires a person to do some positive act. See injunction.

Mandatory instruction An instruction to the jury that sets up a factual situation: If the jurors find that a certain set of facts exist, then they must find for one party and against the other. See charge (12).

Mandatory sentence A person convicted of a certain crime must be sent to a penal institution—the statute gives the sentencing judge no discretion. See sentence.

Mandatory statute A provision in a statute on an essential matter that requires a course of action; the failure to comply renders the proceeding void to which it relates. See legislation (2), law. *Ant.* Directory provision.

Maneuver, *n., v.* See machination, plan, procedure, artifice, duplicity, conspiracy; manipulate, conspire.

Mangle, *v.* See maim, mutilate, cut, mar, disable, injure, batter, attack, assault.

Manhandle, *v.* See batter, attack, assault, coerce, abuse.

Manhood, *n.* See majority (1).

Manhunt, *n.* See search (1), investigation, inquest; audit.

Mania, *n.* Abnormal behavior; wild, excessive enthusiasm; insanity; manic-depressive psychosis. See impulse, insanity, compulsion (2).

Maniac, *n.* Madman. Psychopath, lunatic, "nut," psychotic, deranged person. See also deviant (2), insanity; nonconformist, fanatic; ass, idiot, boor.

Manic, *adj.* A phase of manic-depressive psychosis in which the mood of the patient is overactive and expansive; characterized by excessive ego valuation. See insanity.

Manifest 1. *adj.* Evident to the senses, especially to sight (manifest danger). Open, obvious, not hidden, not obscure, visible, unmistakable, indubitable, indisputable, self-evident, notorious, apparent, well-defined, flagrant, overt, marked, unclouded, striking, clear-cut, public, straightforward, avowed, displayed, express, tangible, defined, glaring, perceivable, observable, conspicuous, noticeable, patent, undeniable, plain, incontrovertible, palpable, lucid, revealed, visible, undisguised, transparent, naked, comprehensible, unambiguous, pronounced, gross, frank. See also clear (1), distinct (1), evident, blatant. **2.** *v.* To reveal or prove (the witness manifested his bias). Show, demonstrate, display, expose, disclose, air, lay bare, unveil, illustrate, parade, corroborate, evidence, advertise, broadcast, signify, certify, express, hold up to view, bring to light, divulge, publish, flaunt, announce. **3.** *n.* A list of cargo or passengers. See record. *Ant.* Latent (1); conceal (2).

Manifestation, *n.* A demonstration or sign (manifestation of intent). Display, symbol, representation, disclosure, revelation, evidence, exhibition, signal, show, expression, example, proof, presentation, indication, emergence, illustration, token, announcement, certification, declaration, unveiling, badge, emblem, publication, substantiation, clue, testimony, indicator, mark, figure, forecast, portent, index, omen, trademark, presage, forewarning, symptom, characteristic, augury, brand, motion, nod, harbinger, hallmark, device, letter, name, cue, footprint, scar, warning, stamp, gesture, tip, intimation, vestige, aroma, foreboding, premonition.

Manifest necessity As a ground for a mistrial: A sudden, unforeseeable, and overwhelming emergency beyond the control of the court (e.g., illness of the judge). The accused can be retried without violating double jeopardy rules. See emergency, ground, mistrial.

Manifesto, *n.* A formal written declaration that is made public (the union's manifesto). Announcement, proclamation, broadcast, credo, pronouncement, affirmation, annunciation, formal notification, poster, statement, edict.

Manifold, *adj.* See many, divers; incalculable; big.

Manipulate, *v.* **1.** To influence to one's advantage; to tamper (manipulate the accounts). Exploit, misuse, falsify, defraud, wrangle, finesse, machinate, trick, maneuver, circumvent, scheme, plot, overreach, beguile, angle, take advantage of, "doctor," fix, misrepresent, jockey, influence deviously, stack, deceive. See also conspire, influence, rig. **2.** To operate with the hands; to handle with skill (manipulate the connecting lines). Guide, pilot, drive, steer, engineer, direct, conduct, govern, treat, work, command, regulate, use, employ, utilize, apply, ply, run, wield. See also manage.

Manipulation, *n.* **1.** See manipulate. **2.** A series of transactions involving the buying or selling of a security for the purpose of creating a false or misleading appearance of active trading, or to raise or depress the price to induce the purchase or sale by others. See fraud, deception; securities.

Mankind, *n.* The race or species of human beings (charitable organization benefiting mankind). Humanity, multitude, humankind, society, homo sapiens. See also person, man, woman, world, people.

Mann Act The White Slave Traffic Act: A federal statute making it a crime to transport a woman or girl in interstate or foreign commerce for the purpose of prostitution, debauchery, or any other immoral purpose. 18 U.S.C. § 2421. See debauchery, prostitute; carry (1).

Mannequin, *n.* See model.

Manner, *n.* **1.** A mode of proceeding in any case or situation (offensive manner). Approach, procedure, method, style, practice, way, character, custom, routine, fashion, habit, comportment, tone, mien, action, tactic, operation, appearance, conduct, pattern, methodology, technique, system, aspect, posture, bearing, demeanor, presence, tenor, attitude, decorum, presence. **2.** Classification. See kind (1).

Mannerism, *n.* See manner, gesture, manifestation, eccentricity, character (4); pretense.

Manners, *n.* See decorum, amenity (3), comity, manner.

Man-of-war, *n.* See vessel.

Manor, *n.* See home, dwelling, residence.

Manpower, *n.* See labor, assistant, associate (2), employee, coterie.

Mansion, *n.* See home, estate (3); luxury.

Manslaughter, *n.* The unlawful killing of another without express or implied malice; criminal homicide committed recklessly or under the influence of extreme mental or emotional disturbance for which there is a reasonable explanation or excuse from the perspective of the defendant. See involuntary manslaughter, voluntary manslaughter, criminal negligence, homicide, murder; kill.

Manual 1. *adj.* Made or performed with the hands (manual labor). Hand-operated; physical, menial, arduous. See also manufacture (1). **2.** *n.* A book with basic practical information or procedures (discovery manual). Primer, guidebook, handbook, directory, workbook, text, how-to-do-it book. See also book (4), manuscript. *Ant.* Automatic; scholarly treatise.

Manual labor Work done with the hands or by the exercise of physical force, with or without the use of tools or equipment; work whose effectiveness depends chiefly on personal muscular exertion rather than on skill, intelligence, or adroitness. See labor, employee.

Manufacture 1. *v.* To make products by hand or machinery, especially on a large scale (they manufacture computer equipment). Build, assemble, fashion, form, fabricate, put together, mass-produce, frame, mold, chisel, turn out, construct, forge, develop; originate, engineer, create, devise. See also produce. **2.** *n.* The process or operation of making goods produced by hand, machinery, or other agency (the manufacture of supplies). Construction, assembling, creation. See also production. **3.** *v.* To fabricate (the witness manufactured the account). Concoct, embellish, make up, prevaricate, misstate, misrepresent, fictionalize, equivocate, embroider, color, hatch, falsify; deceive, defraud. See also lie.

Manufacturer, *n.* One who by labor, art, or skill transforms raw material into a finished product or an article of trade (the liability of the manufacturer).

Industrialist, maker, capitalist, builder. See also producer, financier, owner, employer, backer.

Manumission, *n.* The act of liberating a slave from bondage. See enfranchisement.

Manuscript, *n.* An author's handwritten or typed work product (transmittal of the manuscript to the publisher). Document, text, original, draft, script. See also book (4), manual (2).

Many, *adj.* Numerous (many errors). Considerable, countless, extensive, multitudinous, myriad, innumerable, manifold, multiple, copious; several, sundry, plural, various, varied. See also incalculable, divers, abundant. *Ant.* Few.

Map, *n.* A representation of the earth's surface or a portion of it showing the relative position of the parts represented (plat map). Chart, guide, survey, representation, graph, diagram, projection. See also blueprint, outline; bound (4), boundary.

Mar, *v.* To impair or damage (the explosion marred the painting). Disfigure, deface, ruin, wreck, blemish, blight, taint, spoil, scar, upset, harm, spot, defile, lame, warp, scratch, bruise, vitiate, wound, adulterate, befoul, mangle, diminish, subvert, deform, distort. See also maim, mutilate, injure, attack, assault, cut. *Ant.* Restore.

Marathon, *n.* See contest (2), race (2); effort; endurance.

Marauding, *n.* See piracy, plunder, hijack.

March, *v.* See walk, run, advance.

Margin, *n.* **1.** The edge or border (the testator wrote on the margin of the will). Rim, fringe, confine, skirt, ledge, side, flange, curb, outskirt, periphery, circumference, outline, verge. See also boundary, extremity (2). **2.** An amount available beyond what is needed (a margin of error). Safety, spare, leeway, surplus, extra, reserve, allowance, latitude, space, room, range, safeguard, contingency, supplement, premium, elbowroom, play, clearance, rein.

Margin account A method that the securities industry uses to extend credit to customers: A broker lends the customer money to purchase securities; the customer advances only a portion of the purchase price and pays interest on the balance. See securities, account, credit.

Marginal, *adj.* Minimal, barely acceptable (marginal performance). Borderline, passable, tenuous, minimum, so-so, fair, trifling, barely useful, moderate, meager, slight, wanting, undistinguished, negligible, average, weak, poor, replaceable, insignificant. See also minimal, minor (2), nugatory, frivolous.

Marijuana, marihuana, *n.* A drug prepared from cannabis sativa; any part of the hemp plant or extracts therefrom that induce somatic and psychic changes in a person (possession of marijuana). Weed, reefer, grass, pot, hashish, joint. See also drug, addict.

Marina, *n.* See harbor (3).

Marine, *adj.* Pertaining to the sea (marine life). Aquatic, oceanic, naval, seafaring, oceanographic, pelagic, fleet, shipping. See also maritime, nautical, sea; sailor. *Ant.* Terrestrial.

Marine insurance A contract whereby one party indemnifies another against designated perils or sea-risks to a ship, freight, or cargo during a certain voyage or for a fixed period of time. See insurance, indemnity (2).

Mariner, *n.* One engaged in navigating vessels upon the sea (workers compensation for the mariner). Seaman, pilot, seafarer, helmsman, jack, tar, bluejacket. See also sailor; marine; sea.

Marital, *adj.* Relating to the status of marriage (marital rights). Spousal, matrimonial, conjugal, uxorial, married, bridal, connubial, wedded, nuptial, hymeneal.

Marital communications privilege A spouse has a privilege to refuse to disclose and to prevent others from disclosing private or confidential communications between the spouses during the marriage. The privilege does not apply to prosecutions for crimes committed by one spouse against the other or against the children. See privilege, evidence, admissible, communication, private, confidential.

Marital deduction A deduction allowed upon the transfer of property from one spouse to another: Under the federal gift tax for lifetime—inter vivos—transfers, and under the federal estate tax for testamentary transfers. See deduction (1), tax.

Maritime, *adj.* Pertaining to navigable waters and the commerce thereon (maritime contract). Naval, oceanic, aquatic, seafaring, riparian, pelagic, seagoing. See also nautical, marine; sea; sailor. *Ant.* Terrestrial.

Maritime Administration An agency within the Department of Commerce that promotes and regulates the activities of the U.S. merchant marine, establishes specifications for shipbuilding and design, determines routes, etc.

Mark, *n.* A token, evidence, proof (a mark of fraud). Indication, signal, trademark, scent, footprint, omen, hallmark, signature, identification, hint, label, measure, emblem, symptom, signpost, trait, title, imprimatur, monogram, symbol, initials, escutcheon, representation, mold, mint, die, property, autograph, impression, marking. See also badge, manifestation.

Market, *n.* **1.** A place of commercial activity in which tangible or intangible property is bought and sold (purchases at the market). Trade center, exchange, marketplace, forum, fair, square, plaza, mart, store, firm, emporium, bazaar, place of business, booth, outlet, branch, stall, boutique, establishment, concession, franchise, department, arcade, house. **2.** Trade and commerce (stock market). Dealings, trade, commercial intercourse, marketing, speculation, barter, negotiation, mercantilism, brokerage. See also commerce, intercourse, business, enterprise. **3.** The geographical or economic extent of commercial demand (there was no market for the invention). Consumer demand, want, vogue, call, need, interest. See also appeal (3).

Marketability, *n.* The probability of selling property at a specific time and price. See marketable.

Marketable, *adj.* Capable of attracting buyers (marketable product). Salable, merchantable, commercial, in vogue, vendible, tradable, exchangeable, in demand, wanted, desirable. See also attractive, worthy, fit (1). *Ant.* Unmarketable.

Marketable title A title free from encumbrances and any reasonable doubt as to its validity; one that an informed business person would be willing to accept in the exercise of ordinary business prudence; one that would not expose the person who holds it to the hazards of litigation as to its validity. See cloud, encumbrance, title.

Market price The price at which a seller is ready and willing to sell, and a buyer is ready and willing to buy in the ordinary course of trade; the price actually given in current market dealings. See price, arm's length, fair market value.

Market value The price that would be fixed by negotiation and agreement between a willing buyer (who is not forced to buy) and a willing seller (who is not forced to sell) in the ordinary course of business. See worth (1), cost.

Marking up The process by which a legislative committee goes through a bill section by section, revising its language and amending it as desired.

Maroon, *v.* See abandon; isolated.

Marquee, *n.* See arena, sign (3).

Marriage, *n.* The legal union of one man and one woman as husband and wife; the status of a couple united as husband and wife (marriage ceremony). Matrimony, wedlock, nuptial state, nuptials, conjugality, coupling, linking. See also agreement, contract, marital, spouse, ceremonial marriage, common-law marriage.

Ant. Divorce.

Marriage settlement An agreement before the parties marry in which they release or modify property rights that would otherwise arise from the marriage. See antenuptial, agreement, contract.

Marrow, *n.* See center, essence (1), intent; power, force, vigor, life (3).

Marry, *v.* See marriage; contract, join (1).

Marsh, *n.* See frontier, swamp.

Marshal 1. *n.* A federal court officer who executes all lawful writs, process, and orders. An officer similar to the sheriff or constable at the state and local level. Peace officer, deputy, chief, bailiff. See also officer, official, police. **2.** *v.* To arrange or organize (marshal all arguments). Gather, shepherd, allocate, regiment, array, mobilize, systematize, order, apportion, rank, allot, coordinate, line up, rally, usher, distribute, compose, space, activate, assign, manage. See also muster, group (2).

Marshaling, *n.* Arranging, ranking, or disposing in order; an equitable doctrine that allows a court to arrange assets or claims so as to secure the proper application of the assets to the various claims and to allow all parties having interests therein to receive their due proportion. If claimant # 1 has two available funds of the debtor from which to satisfy a debt, and claimant # 2 can reach only one of these funds to satisfy its debt, then claimant # 2 can force claimant # 1 to use the fund that is not available to claimant # 2 in order to preserve the only fund available to the latter.

Mart, *n.* A place of public traffic or sale. See market (1); merchant, commerce, business.

Martial, *adj.* Characteristic of the military or of war (martial disposition). Soldierly, militant, combative, warlike, Spartan, bellicose, pugnacious, inimical. See also hostile, belligerent, military, contention, litigious, sailor.

Martial law The military authorities carry on the government or exercise varying degrees of control over civilian matters. See military, government, control.

Martindale-Hubbell Law Directory A set of books that contain a state-by-state list of attorneys.

Martini, *n.* See liquor, beverage.

Martyr, *n., v.* See victim, heroic, champion; harass, abuse (1); suffer.

Marvel 1. *n.* Spectacle. Phenomenon, sensation, curiosity, miracle, prodigy, rarity. See also grandeur, performance (3). **2.** *v.* See observe (3).

Marvelous, *adj.* See great (2), outstanding (2), extraordinary, intriguing, beautiful, attractive, enjoyable, comfortable.

Marxism, *n.* See communism, dogma, government.

Mary Carter agreement An agreement between the plaintiff and some, but less than all the defendants, whereby limitations are placed on the financial responsibility of the agreeing defendants, the amount of which is usually in inverse ratio to the amount of recovery that the plaintiff is able to make against the nonagreeing defendant(s).

Mascot, *n.* Good luck charm. Talisman.

Masculine, *adj.* See man.

Mash, *v.* See break (2), cut.

Mask, *n., v.* See disguise, hide, conceal, cloak, obscure.

Masked, *adj.* See hidden, obscure.

Masochism, *n.* Deriving increased sexual pleasure by being beaten and maltreated by someone else. See cruelty, insanity, maniac.

Masochist, *n.* See deviate (2), maniac.

Masquerade, *n., v.* See pretense, artifice, disguise, impersonate.

Mass, *n.* **1.** A collection of things (a mass of demonstrators). Carload, bundle, block, cluster, accumulation, aggregation, cumulation, horde, pile, concentration, assortment, miscellany, mountain, pack, load, congregation, throng, conglomeration, host, bunch, quantity. See also group (1), gang, collection (2), multitude, aggregate, whole, gross (2). **2.** A significant quantity (the mass of confusion). Abundance, preponderance, plurality, lion's share, ocean, considerable amount, bulk, almost all, world, profusion. See also majority, most. **3.** See extent, spread (1), amount.

Massachusetts Trust See business trust.

Massacre, *v., n.* See kill, murder, execute; homicide; assassination, defeat.

Massage, *n.* Rubdown. Chiropractic, stretching, manipulation, stroking, rubbing, kneading.

Massive, *adj.* See big, great, extraordinary, exceptional.

Mastectomy, *n.* Removal of a breast. See surgery, doctor, medicine, removal.

Master 1. *n.* A principal who hires others and who controls or has the right to control their physical conduct in the performance of their service (the master was liable for the negligence of her employee). Employer, boss, director, leader, chief, governor, industrialist, capitalist, lord, commander, supervisor, proprietor, captain, landlord, administrator. See also manager, owner, overseer. **2.** *n.* An officer appointed by the court to assist it in specific judicial duties (e.g., take testimony). See officer, official. **3.** *n.* One who has reached the summit of his or her trade, and who has the right to hire apprentices and journeymen. See artisan, expert (1), professional (2). **4.** *adj.* Main or central (the master plan for the city). First, paramount, supreme, ranking, best, controlling, leading, directing, ruling, arch, crowning, eminent, dominant, cardinal, predominant, choice, key; prototype, original, source. See also primary. **5.** *v.* To triumph over (she mastered her fear). Subdue, conquer, dominate, check, regulate, defeat, govern, curb, control, bridle, manage. **6.** *v.* To become proficient in (she mastered the technique). Learn, become skilled at, excel at. *Ant.* Servant (1); apprentice (3); minor (4); succumb (5); fail (6).

Masterful, *adj.* See able, competent, apt (3); dominant, arbitrary, arrogant.

Master in Chancery An officer of a court of chancery who acts as an assistant to the judge or chancellor (e.g., takes testimony, computes damages). See chancery, equity, officer, official.

Mastermind, *v., n.* See manage, design (1), invent, create; inventor, father, architect, author (2); brilliant, learned.

Masterpiece, *n.* Chef-d'oeuvre. Major work, greatest work, art, magnum opus, classic, treasure, brainchild, jewel. See also opus.

Mastery, *n.* See ability, address (4), competence, dominion, superiority, control (3), authority (2), coercion.

Match, *v., n.* See compare, equate; copy, duplicate; competition, contest (2); accommodate (2), adapt.

Matchless, *adj.* See best, exceptional, extraordinary, perfect.

Mate, *n., v.* See associate (2), ally (1), partner, cohort, intimate; spouse; copy, duplicate; join, consolidate (1), connect (1).

Material 1. *adj.* Having influence or effect (material fact). Convincing, decisive, relevant, influential, consequential, going to the merits, pivotal, significant, momentous, of concern, vital, pressing, essential, weighty, basic, salient, cardinal, principal, paramount, central, substantial, serious, germane, striking, direct. See also important, indispensable, compelling, intrinsic. **2.** *adj.* Pertaining to concrete matter (material substance). Physical, bodily, tangible, real, tactile, somatic, solid, organic, palpable. See also corporeal. **3.** *n.* A substance out of which something is made (building material). Supplies, fabric, goods, cloth, stock, mortar, medium, staple, cement; element, unit, component, factor, item, ingredient, constituent, feature. *Ant.* Insignificant; incorporeal; whole.

Material evidence Evidence that tends to influence the trier of fact because of its logical connection with the issue; evidence pertinent to the issue in dispute. See evidence, influence, relevant.

Material fact An influential fact; a fact that induced the action or inaction; an essential fact; a fact likely to affect the result. See fact, detail (2), event, essential.

Materialize, *v.* See emerge, occur (1), arise (1), result (2); produce, realize; appear (2).

Materialman, *n.* One who furnishes materials and supplies for construction or repair work. See independent contractor, supplier.

Material witness A person who can give testimony that no one else or few others can. See witness.

Materiel, *n.* See material (3), equipment, inventory (2), commodity (1).

Maternal, *adj.* Pertaining to, belonging to, or coming from the mother (maternal care). Motherly; protective, sheltering, caring, guarding, nourishing, warm, tender, doting. See also woman, parent.

Maternal line A line of descent or relationship between two persons, which is traced through the mother of the younger. See line, descent, family.

Maternity, *n.* The character or status of a mother; concerning pregnancy (maternity leave). Motherhood, childbirth, labor, pregnancy, parenthood.

Mathematical, *adj.* Concerning mathematics; precise (mathematical calculation). Accurate, meticulous, scientific, demonstrable, rigid, positive, clear-cut, exact, absolute, particular, certain, statistical, careful, punctilious, unerring. See also precise, empircal.

Matriarch, *n.* See manager, head, chief; woman.

Matricide, *n.* The murder of a mother. See homicide; kill, murder.

Matriculate, *v.* To enroll in or be admitted to an organization, e.g., a college (the university refused to matriculate her). See enroll, enter (1); school.

Matrimony, *n.* The relation and status of marriage (enter matrimony). Wedlock, nuptial bond, union, connubial state, match, conjugality, partnership, conjugal bond; cohabitation. See also marriage, spouse. *Ant.* Divorce.

Matrix, *n.* A substance within which something begins, develops, or is contained (the matrix of culture). Mold, stencil, stamp, form, mint, prototype, format, pattern, die, model, original, stone. See also cast (4).

Matron, *n.* **1.** Married woman; elderly woman. Lady, middle-aged woman, mature woman, dame, dowager, madam, stately woman. **2.** Female superintendent of an institution (matron of the prison). Director, directress, head mistress, warden, overseer, principal, supervisor.

Matter 1. *n.* The subject or concern (matter in controversy). Issue, topic, question, problem, case, proposition, affair, proceeding, transaction, situation, thing, action, episode, event, focus, thesis, adventure, occurrence, business, point, agenda, claim, dispute, substance, composition, circumstance, complication, content, inquiry, investigation, probe, grievance, predicament, element, material, cause, explanation, factor. **2.** *v.* To be of importance (it matters to him). Concern, affect, signify, weigh, make a difference.

Matter-of-fact, *adj.* See literal (2), commonplace, limited (2), routine, casual.

Maturate, *v.* See mature.

Mature 1. *v.* To be developed, complete, ripe for payment (the bond matured). Ripen, come of age, perfect, age, maturate, evolve, bloom, progress, season, flower, advance, finish, consummate, reach term, accrue, fall due. **2.** *adj.* Having attained full development (mature witness). Wise, seasoned, of age, experienced, ripe, dependable, independent, developed, self-sufficient, capable, complete, sophisticated, advanced, in one's prime, older, worldly, responsible, sensible. See also reliable.

Matured claim A claim that is unconditionally due and owing. See due (1), claim.

Maturity, *n.* **1.** The date on which an obligation becomes due (the principal of the bond will be paid at maturity). **2.** The state of being mature (surprised by the child's maturity). Development, responsibleness, reliability, dependability, refinement, perfection, readiness, wisdom, evolution, maturation, judgment, composure, experience, adulthood, manhood, womanhood, competence, sophistication, seasoning.

Maudlin, *adj.* See sentimental, emotional.

Maul, *v.* See bludgeon (2), mutilate, maim, disable, batter, attack, assault.

Mausoleum, *n.* See grave (1).

Maverick, *n.* See nonconformist; insurgent; eccentricity; author, architect.

Maxim, *n.* A principle; a general statement of a rule or a truth (maxim of statutory interpretation). Precept, canon, teaching, guideline, saying, proverb, adage, motto, tenet, axiom, moral, belief, truism, dogma, aphorism, postulate.

Maximize, *v.* See augment, strengthen; exploit, manipulate.

Maximum, *adj.* The highest or greatest amount, quality, value, or degree (maximum security prison). Most, utmost, climactic, extreme, paramount, supreme, top, maximal, predominant, biggest, superlative, unsurpassed, culminating, optimum. See also primary, best. *Ant.* Minimum.

Mayhem, *n.* Crime: depriving someone of a limb or member of the body; maliciously disabling, dismembering, or disfiguring. See maul, maim, mutilate.

Mayor, *n.* See official, officer, administrator, executive (1).

Mayoralty, *n.* The office, term, or dignity of a mayor.

Maze, *n.* See confusion, complication, conundrum, mystery.

McNabb-Mallory rule See Mallory rule.

McNaghten rule See M'Naghten rule, insanity.

M.D. Middle District (e.g., U.S. District Court for the Middle District of Ohio).

Meadow, *n.* See park (1); desert (3).

Meager, *adj.* See inadequate, insufficient, small (1), few, minimal, marginal, nugatory, minor (2); deficient; hidden.

Meal, *n.* See food, eat, inn.

Mean 1. *n.* A middle between two extremes (the national mean). Average, midpoint, medium, center point, par, norm; compromise, moderation, balance. **2.** *v.* To intend (what did the court mean). Have in mind, expect, aim at, propose, wish, contemplate, design, intimate, denote, signify, connote, typify, represent, stand for, suggest, import, symbolize, imply, convey. See also intend. **3.** *adj.* Vicious. See cruel, malicious.

Meander 1. *v.* To follow a winding course. Twist, snake, wander, zigzag, circle, spiral, stray, curve, bend, change, stroll; ramble, digress. **2.** *n.* A winding course (the meander of the river). Curvings, zigzags, turnings, detour.

Meaning, *n.* That which is intended to be, signified, or denoted by language or acts (the meaning of the statute). Intention, sense, import, idea, object, force, gist, denotation, sum and substance, upshot, meat, scheme, design, core, connotation, implication, pith, message, tenor, significance, inference, purport, signification, drift, substance, aim, point, suggestion, intimation, nature, purpose, quintessence, reality, embodiment. See also intent, essence.

Meaningful, *adj.* See pregnant (2), important, decisive, crucial, outstanding (2).

Meaningless, *adj.* See absurd, worthless, frivolous, nugatory, barren, irrelevant.

Meanness, *n.* See cruelty, malice, animus (2).

Means, *n.* That which is used to attain an end (the means available to finance the project). Wherewithal, resources, funds, capital, property, affluence, money, income, wealth; way, instrument, factor, measure, process, expedient, modus operandi, method, system, procedure. See also asset; agency.

Measurable, *adj.* See determinable (2); important, significant; moderate.

Measure 1. *n.* That by which length, breadth, thickness, capacity, or amount is ascertained (measure of success). Criterion, standard, gauge, yardstick, model, mold, scale; quota, allotment, degree, share, amount, unit, ideal, principle, norm, par, minor, test, basis of comparison, touchstone, mark, guideline, canon, rule, specification, pattern, archetype, exemplar, paradigm, prototype, benchmark, range. **2.** *n.* A statute or legislative proposal (sponsor of the measure). Legislation, bill, law, regulation, rule, enactment, scheme, proposition. **3.** *v.* To ascertain the dimensions of something (the court measured damages). Determine, appraise, survey, evaluate, compute, value, judge, calculate, compare, weigh, quantify, grade, rank, figure, enumerate, calibrate, tally, check, balance, contrast, delimit, probe. See also gauge, assess.

Measurement, *n.* See extent, scope, range, measure, estimate, assessment.

Measure up to See conform.

Mecca, *n.* See heaven, holy, God, religion.

Mechanic, *n.* A person skilled in the operation of machinery. See laborer, artisan, employee.

Mechanical, *adj.* **1.** Involving machines or tools (mechanical operation). Power-driven, automated, automatic, self-operating. See also technical. **2.** Perfunctory; lacking spontaneity (mechanical response). Routine, unthinking, impersonal, involuntary, unfeeling, habitual, reflex, lifeless, emotionless, programmatic, vapid, businesslike, uncaring, instinctive, reflexive. See also callous, indifferent, inadvertent. *Ant.* Manual; spirited.

Mechanic's lien A security interest (in the nature of a mortgage) created by law on real property and the improvements thereon to secure those persons who have furnished labor or materials for the erection of structures or for the making of improvements on the real property. See lien, security interest, laborer.

Mechanism, *n.* See apparatus, implement (1), instrument (2), equipment, device, agency, vehicle; automation.

Medal, *n.* Badge. Medallion, ribbon, star, laurel, citation, wreath, emblem, insignia, decoration. See also prize (1).

Meddle, *v.* See intermeddle, interfere, encroach, impose; interloper, intruder.

Meddlesome, *adj.* See officious, prying, vexatious; interloper, intermeddle.

Media, *n.* See press (1), newspaper, journal.

Median, *adj.* See mean, intermediate, middle.

Mediate, *v.* See arbitrate (3), negotiate, settle, judge (2), adjudge, mitigate, adapt, accommodate; mediation.

Mediation, *n.* The process by which a neutral third person assists and encourages parties in conflict to reach a settlement of the dispute that will be satisfactory to them all (mediation clause in the separation agreement). Intervention, conciliation, adjustment of difficulties, negotiation, refereeship, peacemaking, settlement, adjustment, instrumentality, give-and-take, intercession, pacification, reconciliation. *Ant.* Confrontation, adjudication.

Mediation and Conciliation Service An agency of the federal government that tries to settle labor disputes through mediation.

Mediator, *n.* One who tries to help disputing parties to reconcile or settle their differences (the mediator suggested a cooling-off period). Go-between, intermediary, liaison, peacemaker, moderator, umpire, referee, reconciler, arbitrator, conciliator. See also arbiter. *Ant.* Antagonist.

Medic, *n.* See doctor, intern (2); medicine.

Medicaid, *n.* A form of public assistance sponsored jointly by the federal and state governments, providing medical aid for people whose income falls below a certain level. See medicine, surgery, assistance.

Medical, *adj.* Involving the practice or study of medicine (medical care). Therapeutic, medicinal, healing, curative, clinical, remedial, diagnostic, salutary, restorative, surgical, patient, nursing, dental. *Ant.* Toxic.

Medical examiner A public officer with the responsibility of investigating all sudden, unexplained, unnatural, or suspicious deaths that are reported. See coroner, autopsy.

Medical malpractice Negligence by a doctor; injury caused by a doctor's failure to have and use the skill and learning commonly possessed by members of the profession in good standing. See malpractice, neglect (2).

Medicare, *n.* A federal program that provides hospital and medical insurance for the aged under the Social Security Act. See medicine, surgery, assistance.

Medication, *n.* See medicine, drug, treatment; doctor.

Medicine, *n.* **1.** The science and art dealing with the prevention, alleviation, and cure of diseases (the study of medicine). Healing art, practice, medical profession, therapeutics, hygiene. See also doctor, cure, health, medical, disease, injury. **2.** Substances used to treat a disease or injury (medicine taken at noon). Medication, remedy, prescription, restorative, pill, balm, vaccine, antidote, capsule, injection, dose. See also drug, ointment, bandage.

Medicolegal, *adj.* Medical questions that involve the law. See forensic medicine.

Medieval, *adj.* See old, ancient, obsolete.

Mediocre, *adj.* See average (2), marginal, pedestrian, commonplace (2), ordinary, household.

Meditate, *v.* See think, contemplate, consider (1), deliberate (1).

Medium, *n.* **1.** The means or agency through which something is done (medium of exchange). Instrumentality, vehicle, route, channel, tool, broker, machinery, intermediary, mechanism, mode, avenue, wherewithal, expedient, link, go-between, envoy, environment, manner, course, measure, apparatus, organ. See also agency (4), instruct (3). **2.** Middle ground. See mean (1), middle, intermediate.

Medley, *n.* See mixture, compound (3); music.

Meek, *adj.* See bashful, passive, awkward (2), quiet (2); flexible, amenable (2); kind.

Meet, *v., n.* See address (2), confront, face (2), contest; converge, convene, collide; meeting.

Meeting, *n.* **1.** A coming together of persons (meeting of the board). Assembly, convocation, get-together, caucus, congress, conclave, convention, concourse, gathering, huddle, council, powwow, parley, committee, assemblage. See also conference. **2.** Junction (meeting of the roads). Union, convergence, confluence, intersection, association, contact, merger. **3.** A rendezvous (negotiation meeting). Encounter, engagement, confrontation, clash, contest, collision, struggle, tryst, gathering point, date, tête-à-tête, focal point, assignation. *Ant.* Separation.

Megalopolis, *n.* See city.

Melancholia, *n.* Mental unsoundness characterized by extreme depression of spirits, ill-grounded fears, delusions, and brooding; the depressed phase of manic-depressive psychosis. See depression, insanity.

Melancholy, *adj., n.* See depressed, depressing, despondent; depression, melancholia.

Mélange, *n.* See mixture, compound (3), accumulation; aggregate, composite.

Melee, *n.* See brawl, fight, disturbance, commotion, confusion.

Meliorate, *v.* To make better. See mitigate, cure (2), improve, correct (2), amelioration, betterment (2), mitigation.

Mellow, *adj.* See quiet, moderate, kind, amenable, flexible, friendly, passive.

Melodious, *adj.* See lyric; music; harmony.

Melodramatic, *adj.* See emotional, sentimental, ardent, flamboyant, yellow (2).

Melody, *n.* See music, harmony; lyric.

Melt, *v.* See disappear, thaw, dissolve, pass (6), diminish.

Meltdown, *n.* The dissolving of a nuclear reactor core. See cataclysm, catastrophe.

Member, *n.* **1.** One of the persons constituting an organization (member of the Senate). Teammate, adherent, enrollee, initiate, associate, comrade, fellow. **2.** A part of the body (injury to a member of the body). Limb, organ, arm, leg, appendage, extremity, ear, nose, hand. **3.** A component part (member of the set). Element, constituent part, branch, section, division, subdivision, unit, segment, piece, factor, fragment, ingredient, portion.

Membership, *n.* See admission (3); club, association, constituency.

Memento, *n.* Keepsake, souvenir, memorabilia, relic, antique, reminder, remainder, remembrance, emblem, vestige, record. See also memorial, memory, trophy, recollection.

Memoir, *n.* See biography, confession, record.

Memorabilia, *n.* See memento.

Memorable, *adj.* See outstanding (2), important, great, attractive, beautiful, intriguing, popular, conspicuous.

Memorandum, *n.* A written statement or note that is often brief and informal (she sent a memorandum summarizing the phone call). Memo, notation, interoffice communication, recap, reminder, record, agenda, draft, jotting, minute. See also communication, report.

Memorandum decision The decision or ruling of a court with little or no statement of the reasons for it. See opinion, decision.

Memorial 1. *n.* A petition or statement of facts presented to the legislature or to the executive (the memorial was printed in the House record). **2.** *adj.* Commemorative (memorial plaque). Testimonial, memento, monumental, ceremonial, dedicatory, enshrining.

Memorialize, *v.* See honor (2), dedicate, observe (4); conserve.

Memorize, *v.* See retain (2).

Memory, *n.* The mental power to review and recollect the successive states of consciousness in their consecutive order; the ability to recollect past events; the recollection of past events (the selective memory of the witness). Remembrance, recall, recreation, reminiscence, recognition, reminder, memorial, retention, retrospection, awareness. *Ant.* Amnesia.

Menace 1. *n.* Showing or threatening a determination to inflict harm on another (a menace to the community). Danger, peril, warning, hazard, intimidation, cause for alarm, pitfall, quicksand, specter. **2.** *v.* To threaten or pose a threat (they menaced the community). Startle, intimidate, alarm, endanger, terrorize, loom, jeopardize, browbeat, risk, scare, compromise, expose, imperil, disconcert, unnerve, portend, disquiet. See also harass, disturb. *Ant.* Benefit; shelter.

Menacing, *adj.* See imminent, dangerous; exigent, menace.

Mend, *v.* See cure, fix (3).

Mendacious, *adj.* See fraudulent, illusory, deceptive, erroneous, invalid, feigned, fictitious.

Mendacity, *n.* See lie, fraud, pretense, deception.

Menial, *adj.* See senile, abject, inferior; servant; flatter, flattery; grovel.

Mens rea A guilty mind (evidence of mens rea). Guilty purpose, wrongful purpose, criminal intent, guilty knowledge, willfulness. See also malice, bad faith, felonious.

Mental, *adj.* **1.** Relating to or existing in the mind (mental anguish). Psychic, rational, thinking, perceptual, intellectual, psychological, cerebral, emotional, meditative, conscious, reasoning; subjective, inner, spiritual, ideological. **2.** Involving a mental illness (mental hospital). Neurotic, psychotic, lunatic, disturbed, deranged, demented, insane, disordered, abnormal, crazy, unbalanced, mad, deluded, eccentric. *Ant.* Physical; lucid.

Mental anguish or suffering The mental sensation of pain and the accompanying feelings of distress, fright, and anxiety. See anguish, anxiety, pain, affliction, depression.

Mental capacity or competence The ability to understand the nature and effect of the act in which the person is engaged and the business he or she is transacting. See ability, competence; rational.

Mental cruelty A ground for divorce: A course of conduct that can endanger the mental and physical health and efficiency of another to the extent of rendering a continuation of the relationship intolerable. See cruelty, danger, ground, divorce; health.

Mental disease or defect A condition that results in a lack of substantial capacity either to appreciate the criminality (wrongfulness) of one's conduct or to conform his or her conduct to the requirements of the law. See insanity, capacity.

Mentality, *n.* See mind, reason (2); disposition (4), manner.

Mental reservation An unexpressed exception to the general words of a promise or agreement, often with the aim of having a dishonest excuse to evade the promise or agreement. See reservation (3), deception, fraud.

Mention, *v.* See express (2), declare, comment (2), communicate, refer, intimate (6).

Mentor, *n.* See teacher, expert.

Menu, *n.* See agenda, schedule, list; food, eat.

Mercantile, *adj.* Involving the business of merchants, trade, commerce, trading, industry, finances, marketing, merchandising. See commerce, business, merchant.

Mercantile paper See commercial paper, negotiable instrument.

Mercenary, *adj.* See avaricious, corrupt.

Merchandise 1. *n.* Goods that merchants usually buy and sell at wholesale or retail (discount merchandise). Wares, commodities, stock, movables, chattel, products, specialty, durables, consumer products, effects, produce, articles, line, freight, cargo, vendibles, belongings, possessions. See also property. **2.** *v.* To engage in commerce (the product was merchandised in one area). Trade, sell, market, traffic, handle, advertise, distribute, publicize.

Merchant, *n.* A person who deals in the purchase and sale of goods (a licensed merchant). Dealer, seller, buyer, trader, retailer, trafficker, tradesman, jobber, wholesaler, shopkeeper, industrialist, capitalist, chandler, vendor, huckster, middleman, salesman, saleswoman, hawker, financier, purchaser, peddler. See also backer, entrepreneur.

Merchantability, *n.* The article sold is of the general kind described and is reasonably fit for the general purpose for which it is sold. See fit (1), fitness.

Merchantable, *adj.* Fit for the ordinary purposes for which the goods are used; acceptable without objection in the trade under the contract description; conformable to ordinary standards of care; of average grade, quality, and value of similar goods sold under similar circumstances (the goods were not merchantable). See fit (1), marketable, salable.

Merchantable title A good and marketable title that is acceptable to a knowledgeable buyer not under duress to purchase; a title that would be free from litigation, palpable defects, and grave doubts; a title that will enable the owner to hold it in peace and to sell it to a person of reasonable prudence; a readily transferable title in the market. See title, cloud, arm's length, market value.

Merchant seaman One employed on a private vessel. See sailor; employee.

Merciful, *adj.* See benevolent, charitable, kind; forgive, pardon.

Merciless, *adj.* See cruel, callous, inflexible, draconian, rude.

Mercurial, *adj.* See capricious, irregular, inconsistent, active (3), ardent, feverish, excited, incendiary.

Mercy, *n.* Forbearance, leniency (mercy shown by the court). Compassion, clemency, benevolence, forgiveness, generosity, liberality, indulgence, humanity, mildness, sympathy, understanding, lenity, grace, kindness, magnanimity, patience. See also charity (3, 4), consideration (3), pardon. *Ant.* Vindictiveness.

Mercy killing See euthanasia, homicide.

Mere, *adj.* Nothing more or less than what is stated (a mere trespasser). Pure, simple, bald, unmitigated, absolute, utter, whole, sole, complete, unadulterated, unadorned, stark, nothing but, sheer, only, plain. See also bare (1).

Mere licensee One who enters upon the land or property of another without objection or by the mere permission, sufferance, or acquiescence of the owner or occupier. See licensee, guest, permission, acquiescence.

Meretricious, *adj.* Involving vulgarity, insincerity, or unlawful sexual relations (meretricious relationship). Tawdry, cheap, tasteless, flashy, specious, tinsel, ornate, sham, hollow, licentious, plastic, garish, theatrical; fake, bogus, lewd, deceitful, deceptive, misleading. See also immoral, obscene, illicit, gaudy, artificial. *Ant.* Respectable.

Merge, *v.* See join (1), affiliate, connect (1), converge; amalgamation, merger.

Merged, *adj.* See joint, associated, integrated.

Merger, *n.* The fusion or absorption of one thing or right into another; the absorption of one company by another, with the latter retaining its own identity and name. The absorbed company ceases to exist as a separate business entity (corporate merger). Federation, union, consolidation, confederation, syndication, incorporation, affiliation, integration, combination, conglomeration, coalition, alignment; monopoly, pool, cartel. See also amalgamation, association. *Ant.* Disbanding.

Meridians, *n.* Imaginary north and south lines used in the Government Survey System which intersect the base line to form the starting point for the measurement of land.

Merit 1. *n.* The worth or quality of something; strict legal right (decided on the merits). Value, ability, excellence, stature, righteousness, goodness, superiority, worthiness, distinction. See also worth (1), appraisal. **2.** *v.* To earn or be deserving (the action did not merit that response). Rate, invite, qualify for, be worthy of, prompt. See also warrant (2).

Meritorious, *adj.* **1.** Characterized by merit; deserving serious judicial inquiry; going to the heart or essence of the case (meritorious defense). Not dilatory, not procedural, not technical, creditable, substantive, substantial, of substance. **2.** Deserving reward (meritorious conduct). Sound, praiseworthy, commendable, noteworthy, estimable, first-rate, creditable, invaluable, satisfying, reputable, sterling, honorable, heroic, irreproachable, chivalrous, incorrupt, noble, tested, decent, distinctive, righteous, idealistic, blameless, worthy, reliable, laudable, honest, admirable, worthwhile, preeminent, desirable, approved, impeccable, virtuous, eminent, choice, superlative, conscientious, exemplary. See also good (2), moral (2), right (1), loyal, ethical. *Ant.* Frivolous.

Merit system The system used for hiring and promoting government employees to civil service positions on the basis of competence rather than patronage. See civil service, competence.

Merriment, *n.* See happiness, diversion (2), amusement, enjoyment (2), emotion, passion.

Merry, *adj.* See happy, comic, enjoyable, friendly, convivial.

Mescaline, *n.* See drug; hallucination.

489

Mesh, *v.* See harmonize, connect.

Mesmerize, *v.* See entice, bait (3), amaze, surprise; agape.

Mesne, *adj.* Intermediate; intervening; occurring between two periods or ranks (mesne profits while the wrongdoer held the land). See intermediate.

Mess, *n.* See dirt, pollution, disorder, confusion, dilemma, emergency; litter.

Message, *n.* A communication sent from one person to another (an intercepted message). Note, word, memo, dispatch, letter, communiqué, epistle, notification, statement, bulletin, transmittal, wire, card, missive, line, cable, answer, speech, announcement, address, response, information, declaration, tidings. See also communication, report.

Messenger, *n.* One who bears messages or performs errands. Carrier, envoy, bearer, deliverer, emissary, courier, go-between, runner, nuncio, rider. See also middleman, delegate, intermediary, agent.

Messuage, *n.* Dwelling-house with the adjacent buildings and curtilage.

Messy, *adj.* See dirty; disorder, confusion, pollution; awkward.

Metabolism, *n.* The sum total of all processes of the human body by which food is transformed into chemicals, which are absorbed into the bloodstream and lymphatic system to nourish the body so that it can continue to function.

Metamorphosis, *n.* See change (1).

Metaphor, *n.* See symbol, comparison, language.

Metaphysical, *adj.* See abstract (4), intangible, incorporeal, hypothetical.

Mete 1. *v.* To apportion or distribute (mete out punishment). Administer, deliver, ration, assign, dole, measure, dispense, allot, parcel, give, divide. **2.** *n.* See boundary.

Meter, *n.* **1.** An instrument of measurement (gas meter). See measure (1), gauge. **2.** A metric unit of length equal to 3.28 feet.

Metes and bounds The boundary lines of land with their terminal points and angles; a way of describing land by listing the compass directions and distances of the boundaries. See map, bound, boundary.

Methadone, *n.* A synthetic opiate of approximately the same strength as morphine, used in treating drug addiction. See drug, addict, treatment.

Methamphetamine, *n.* A synthetic drug closely related to amphetamines, producing prominent central stimulant reactions without peripheral effects. See drug, addict.

Method, *n.* A mode of operation or means of attaining a result (a method of cross-examination). Manner, technique, system, program, discipline, process, way, fashion, style, design, sequence, procedure, scheme, course of action, operation, methodology, routine, formula, approach, tact, organization, blueprint, logistics, usage, custom, arrangement, structure, form. See also instrumentality, agency, means, modus operandi.

Methodical, *adj.* See coherent (1), regular, precise, efficient, complete (2), careful, deliberate.

Methodology, *n.* See method, plan (1), process, organization.

Meticulous, *adj.* See precise (2), careful, deliberate, critical, particular (2), difficult (3).

Métier, *n.* See craft, career.

Metric system A decimal system of weights and measures, based on the meter as the unit length and the kilogram as the unit mass. See measure, amount.

Metropolis, *n.* See city, environment, neighborhood.

Metropolitan, *adj.* Pertaining to a city and the surrounding towns (metropolitan planning). Municipal, urban; urbanized, populated; sophisticated, cosmopolitan. See also civic. *Ant.* Rural.

Mettle, *n.* See disposition, character, spirit (2), resolution (4), self-confidence.

Mezzanine, *n.* See balcony.

Miasma, *n.* See pollution.

Microbe, *n.* See life (1); germ.

Microcosm, *n.* The universe in miniature. See model, sample, archetype, manifestation; world.

Microfiche, *n.* A photographic film (microfilm) containing a large amount of material in reduced form. Ultrafiche contains an even greater amount.

Microscopic, *adj.* See small, minimal; hidden.

Middle, *adj.* Occurring halfway (middle ground). Center, central, equidistant, mid, midway, mean, median; nucleus, heart. See also intermediate. *Ant.* Outer.

Middle class, *n.* **middle-class,** *adj.* See people, public (1, 2); common, commonplace, class.

Middleman, *n.* One who brings parties together (the middleman's commission). Go-between, intermediary, broker, liaison, connection, factor, mediator, medium, interceder, attorney, envoy, interagent, jobber, moderator, umpire, contact. See also agent, messenger.

Middle-of-the-road, *adj.* See moderate.

Midget, *n.* See small.

Midpoint, *n.* See middle, center (1); intermediate.

Midst, *n.* See center, interior.

Midwife, *n.* A woman who assists at childbirth. See assistant, medical, birth (1).

Mien, *n.* See demeanor, disposition (4), manner, carriage (3).

Might 1. *v.* Past tense of may (might have been brought). Was possible, had power, had the physical or moral opportunity to be contingently possible. **2.** *n.* Considerable force (the might of the nation). Strength, power, influence, energy, muscle, prowess, intensity, vigor, durability, puissance, brawn, toughness, sturdiness, sinew, fortitude, stamina, clout, weight, invincibility, endurance. *Ant.* Feebleness (2).

Mighty, *adj.* See strong, awesome, predominant, durable, able-bodied, great, big, outstanding, dominant, invulnerable; might (2).

Migraine, *n.* See pain, anguish; suffer.

Migrant, *n., adj.* See immigrant, emigrant; itinerant, tramp (1); exile (2), migratory.

Migrate, *v.* See move (2), enter, depart, leave (2), flee; immigration, emigration.

Migration, *n.* Movement from one place to another; movement from one region or country to another (migration from Europe). Resettlement, relocation, emigration, immigration, expedition, journey, wandering, departure, roaming, passage, vagabondage, pilgrimage, trek, nomadism; escaping, fleeing. See also voyage, travel.

Migratory, *adj.* Involving travel or migration (migratory birds). Transient, roaming, moving, nomadic, vagabond, mobile, uprooted, floating, footloose, displaced, drifting, gypsy, touring, transitory, peripatetic, wayfaring. See also itinerant. *Ant* Stationary.

Migratory divorce A divorce obtained by a spouse who travels (migrates) to another state or country for a temporary period in order to obtain the divorce, which is often procedurally easier to obtain than in the state of original domicile. See jurisdiction, divorce.

Mil, *n.* One-thousandth of an inch.

Mild, *adj.* See kind, civil (3), amicable, charitable, convivial, friendly, moderate, innocent (2), harmless.

Mile, *n.* A measure of length or distance: 5,280 feet. See measure, range (2), area.

Mileage, *n.* **1.** Money for traveling expenses at a certain rate per mile (allowance for mileage). Reimbursement, payment, allotment, compensation; levy, rate, charge, fee. **2.** Usefulness (the opponent obtained a lot of mileage out of the mistake). Gain, profit, service, benefit, wear, advantage.

Milestone, *n.* **1.** An important event (the opinion was a milestone in the development of the law). Turning point, achievement, climax, anniversary, decisive occasion, memorable event. See also crisis. **2.** Stones set up to mark the miles on a road or railway. Pointer, signpost, milepost.

Milieu, *n.* See environment, neighborhood, climate (2).

Militant, *adj.* See belligerent, hostile, contentious, litigious, military, martial.

Military 1. *adj.* Pertaining to the armed forces, war, or defense (military appropriations). Service, soldierly, Spartan, warlike, combative, militaristic, armed, regulated, defensive, fighting, aggressive, militant, contentious, militarist; regimented, strict, organized, systematized. See also martial, belligerent. **2.** *n.* The armed forces (funding for the military). Troop, legion, division, army, navy, soldiers, marines, militia, air force. See also sailor.

Military law A system of laws governing the armed forces. See Code of Military Justice, Court of Military Appeals.

Militia, *n.* Citizen army; a citizen military force used in emergencies (mobilization of the militia). Volunteers, minutemen, reserves, standbys. See also posse comitatus. *Ant.* Professional army.

Milksop, *n.* See coward; boor; wrongdoer.

Mill 1. *n.* One-tenth of one cent. **2.** *v.* To move aimlessly (mill around the area). Wander, meander, roam, teem, swarm, converge, jostle.

Millennium, *n.* See heaven.

Millimeter, *n.* One-thousandth of a meter or .0394 inch.

Millionaire, *n.* See entrepreneur, owner; luxury, wealth.

Millstone, *n.* See burden (2), onus.

Milquetoast, *n.* See coward; boor; wrongdoer.

Mimic, *v.* See copy (2); slander, disparage.

Mince, *v.* See break (2); mitigate.

Mind 1. *n.* The totality of brain processes (the mind of a child). Intelligence, faculties, judgment, reasoning, psyche, thinking, intellect, rationality, mentality, senses, awareness, reason, comprehension, perception, mental balance, thought, understanding, wits, gray matter, cognitive function, ego, brain power, logic, cerebrum, soul, contemplation, memory, recollection, concentration, reflection, apprehension, conscious, unconscious, insight, "marbles," opinion, persuasion, retrospection, sanity. **2.** *v.* To look after (mind the store). Attend to, take care of, heed, protect, watch, observe, nurse, notice, guard, keep an eye on, baby-sit. **3.** *v.* To resent (she does not mind). Object to, resist, eschew, hate, abhor, detest, disapprove of, shrink from, loathe. *Ant.* Body; ignore; favor.

Mind-boggling, *adj.* See awesome, appalling, extraordinary, outstanding (2); repulsive; agape.

Mindful, *adj.* See cautious, careful; cognizant, informed.

Mindless, *adj.* See heedless, careless, reckless; dumb, absurd, lunatic, irrational, juvenile, frivolous.

Mindset, *n.* See bias.

Mine, *n.* An excavation in the earth from which ores, coal, or other mineral substances are removed (safety in the mine). Quarry, pit, crater, shaft, excavation, tunnel, colliery. See also excavate.

Mineral, *n.* A lifeless substance formed or deposited through natural processes and found either in or upon the soil or in the rocks beneath the soil; a natural constituent of the crust of the earth, inorganic or fossil, homogeneous in structure, having a definite chemical composition and known crystallization.

Mingle, *v.* See consort (2), commingle, associate, befriend.

Miniature, *adj., n.* See small; model.

Minimal, *adj.* Smallest amount (minimal effort). Minimum, minor, insufficient, diminished, slight, scant, fragmentary, least possible, token, nominal, least acceptable, diminutive, meager, infinitesimal, slender, abbreviated, thin, modest, deficient, paltry, moderate, slightest, very small. See also small. *Ant.* Maximum.

Minimize, *v.* See diminish, condense, abridge; color (3), discredit, demote.

Minimum, *n.* The least quantity possible or acceptable (conflict was kept to a minimum). Margin, bottom line, smallest amount, modicum, fragment, base, morsel, trace, lowest quantity, smidgen, particle; quorum. See also iota, scintilla. *Ant.* Profusion.

Minimum fee schedules A bar association suggested list of fees to be charged by lawyers. See fee, compensation, bar.

Minimum or minimal contacts A standard used to determine when a state can acquire personal jurisdiction over a nonresident defendant who is not served in the state: There must be a sufficient connection between the defendant and the state to make it fair to force him or her to defend the action in the state. See jurisdiction.

Minimum sentence The least severe sentence that a court may impose on a convicted defendant. See sentence, punishment.

Minimum wage The amount set by federal statute that employees must be paid by employers engaged in businesses that affect interstate commerce. See compensation, Fair Labor Standards Act.

Mining, *n.* The process or business of extracting from the earth precious or valuable metals in their native state or in their ores. See excavate, extract (1).

Minion, *n.* See servant, slave, employee, parasite; grovel, flatter.

Minister, 1. *n.* A person ordained by a Christian church to preach and perform other religious functions (the minister solemnized the marriage). Pastor, clergyman, cleric, father, priest, preacher, man of the cloth, chaplain, parson, vicar, ecclesiastic, evangelist, shepherd, rector, curate, missionary. **2.** *n.* An administrator or person in charge of a department (foreign minister). Secretary, commissioner, chief, manager, cabinet member, officer, executive, ambassador, consul, emissary, delegate, representative. **3.** *v.* To give attention or assistance to another (minister to his needs). Cater to, wait on, accommodate, nurse, comfort, succor, assist, relieve, support, tend, help, console, pander to, nourish, abet. See also nurture.

Ministerial, *adj.* Involving obedience to instructions and no special discretion, judgment, or skill (ministerial act). Implemental, administrative, auxiliary, attending, subsidiary, subservient, ancillary, operative; uncomplicated, clear, fixed, simple, definite. *Ant.* Discretionary.

Ministry, *n.* Religious ministers; the duties or functions of a religious minister (enter the ministry). Holy orders, clergy, service, priesthood, presbytery, religious vocation, pulpit.

Minor 1. *n.* A person under the legal age, usually under 18 (the minor disaffirmed her contract). Infant, young person, adolescent, junior, teenager, youth, youngster, boy, girl, juvenile, ward, baby. See also child. **2.** *adj.* Lesser in importance, seriousness, or size (a minor offense). Inferior, trivial, insignificant, secondary, slight, inconsequential, subsidiary, mediocre, lightweight, inconsiderate, amateurish, moderate, underlying, picayune, dependent, second-rate, unimportant, accessory, superficial, peripheral, minimal, dispensable, insufficient, wanting, imperceptible, negligible, tiny, modest, infinitesimal, immaterial. See also small, nugatory, petty. *Ant.* Adult; major.

Minority, *n.* **1.** The status of being under the legal age—under the age of majority (still in his minority). Nonage, childhood, infancy, juvenility, youth, legal incompetence, adolescence; immaturity. **2.** The smaller number (the minority asked for a recount). Outvoted number, less than half, secondary group, lesser proportion, handful. *Ant.* Majority.

Minority opinion An opinion in a case written by less than a majority of the court. It can be a dissenting opinion (disagreeing with the result and with the reasoning of the majority) or a concurring opinion (agreeing with the result but disagreeing with the reasoning of the majority). See opinion, decision.

Mint 1. *n.* The place where bullion is coined into money under the authority of the government. **2.** *v.* To coin money. Cast, monetize, issue, stamp, print, forge, counterfeit. See also coin.

Minus, *adj., n.* See inferior, petty; deficiency; arrearages.

Minuscule, *adj.* See small, petty, minor (2).

Minute, *n.,* **minute,** *adj.* **1.** *n.* Moment. Short time, brief moment, flash, jiffy, second, wink. See also interval, period. **2.** *adj.* See small, petty, minor (2).

Minutes, *n.* A record of what occurred at a meeting; an account of the actions formally taken (the minutes of the meeting). Notes, summary, outline, transcript, log, memorandum. See also record.

Minutiae, *n.* See trivia, red tape, detail, fact.

Miracle, *n.* See windfall, mystery, marvel.

Miraculous, *adj.* See mysterious, extraordinary; shock, agape.

Mirage, *n.* See hallucination, dream (1), fiction, falsehood, error; illusory.

Miranda warnings Prior to any custodial interrogation, a person must be warned: (a) that he or she has a right to remain silent, (b) that any statement made can be used as evidence against him or her, (c) that he or she has the right to the presence of an attorney, and (d) that if he or she cannot afford an attorney, one will be appointed at government expense if desired.

Mire 1. *n.* See swamp, morass, dirt. **2.** *v.* To involve or wallow. Enmesh, entangle, bog down; soil, tarnish, smudge.

Mirror, *n.* See copy; model.

Mirth, *n.* See amusement, diversion (2), happiness, enjoyment (2); antic, ceremony.

Misadventure, *n.* An accident or misfortune (homicide by misadventure). Setback, mishap, hardship, mischance, reverse, adversity, catastrophe, bad break, casualty, miscarriage, woe, fiasco, checkmate, contretemps, disaster, slip, error, tragedy, infelicity, cross, reversal, failure. *Ant.* Windfall.

Misanthropic, *adj.* See cynical, contemptuous, crabby, rude.

Misapplication, *n.* The wrongful use of funds or other property (the misapplication of negotiable notes). Misuse, abuse, misappropriation, corrupt use, mismanagement, squandering, improper allocation, illegal handling, fraudulent use, dishonest use, mishandling. See also corruption.

Misappropriate, *v.* To take wrongfully; to use someone else's property to one's own advantage (misappropriate bank deposits). Misuse, defraud, mulct, misapply, defalcate, squander, pervert, misemploy, peculate, arrogate, waste, swindle, embezzle, rob, steal, rifle, usurp, desecrate. See also abuse, cheat.

Misbegotten, *adj.* See illegitimate; illegal, illicit.

Misbehaving, *adj.* See disobedient, contentious, incorrgible, disorderly; insubordination, misbehavior.

Misbehavior, *n.* Improper or unlawful behavior (a record of misbehavior). Indiscretion, disorderly conduct, misconduct, immorality, impropriety, unmanageableness, indiscretion, impertinence, bad manners, disrespect, obstreperousness, dereliction, horseplay. See also insubordination, delinquency, mischief. *Ant.* Discretion.

Miscalculate, *v.* See err, blunder (2), misrepresent, distort.

Miscalculation, *n.* See error, blunder (1), mistake, failure, deficiency.

Miscarriage, *n.* **1.** Poor management or administration (miscarriage of justice). Fiasco, failing, failure, nonperformance, frustration, misadventure, collapse, nonfulfillment, defeat, fizzle, debacle, downfall, loss, default, repulse, botch, stoppage, slip, casualty, crash, error, accident, unrealization, shipwreck, mischance, washout, disappointment, misfire. **2.** Premature expulsion of a nonviable fetus (a miscarriage suffered in the first month of pregnancy). Stillbirth, spontaneous abortion. *Ant.* Fruition (1).

Miscegenation, *n.* Mixture of races; marriage between persons of different races. See race, marriage.

Miscellaneous, *adj.* See multifarious, multiple, sundry, divers, odd (3), many, mixed, conglomerate (2), different; commingle; mixture.

Mischance, *n.* See accident, misfortune, casualty; mistake, blunder, error.

Mischief, *n.* Conduct that causes harm intentionally, recklessly, negligently, or accidentally. Wrongfulness, wrongdoing, annoyance, misbehavior, nuisance, roguery, vexation, devilment, naughtiness, rascality, scheming, depravity, destruction, maltreatment, nuisance, wickedness, criminality, transgression, fault, detriment, disservice, agitation, impishness, capriciousness, disruption, delinquency, weakening, meanness, playfulness, trouble, shenanigans, molestation, damage, vandalism, malice, disadvantage, hardship, discord; ornery. See also malicious mischief. *Ant.* Benefit.

Mischievous, *adj.* See harmful, injurious, deleterious, malicious; juvenile; antic; mischief.

Misconceive, *v.* See err, blunder (2); misrepresent, distort.

Misconception, *n.* See error, blunder (1), mistake, failure, deficiency.

Misconduct, *n.* A transgression of an established rule; willful impropriety (misconduct in office). Dereliction, misdeed, offense, misdemeanor, mismanagement, dishonesty, malpractice, crime, wrongdoing, delinquency, malfeasance, nonfeasance, misfeasance, misprision, negligence, impropriety, misbehavior, wickedness, maladversion, deviation, turpitude, error, peccadillo, failing. *Ant.* Lawfulness.

Misconstrue, *v.* See misrepresent, distort, err, blunder (2).

Miscreant, *n., adj.* See wrongdoer; corrupt.

Misdeed, *n.* See offense, wrong, violation, crime, error, mistake.

Misdelivery, *n.* Delivery of mail or goods to someone other than the specified or authorized recipient. See blunder, error, neglect (2).

Misdemeanant, *n.* A person convicted of a misdemeanor. See wrongdoer.

Misdemeanor, *n.* A crime other than a felony; a crime punishable by fine or by detention of less than a year in a jail or in an institution other than a penitentiary (petty larceny is a misdemeanor in this state). Offense, transgression, infringement, misconduct, wrong, dereliction, misdeed, delinquency, violation, illegality, lawbreaking, misbehavior, trespass.

Misdiagnose, *v.* See err, blunder; mistake; neglect (1, 2).

Misdirect, *v.* See err, blunder, flounder, misrepresent, distort, mistake; neglect (1, 2); misdirection.

Misdirection, *n.* An error made by the judge in the instruction given to the jury. Misinformation, misguidance. See also mistake; misleading.

Miser, *n.* See stingy, avaricious.

Miserable, *adj.* See depressed, despondent; abject; depression; inferior; indigent, destitute, sick.

Miserly, *adj.* See stingy, avaricious.

Misery, *n.* See affliction, anxiety, anguish, pain, depression, burden, hardship, ordeal (1), onus.

Misfeasance, *n.* The improper performance of an act that is otherwise proper (misfeasance in driving the car recklessly). Dereliction, negligence, transgression, wrongfulness, peccadillo, infringement, breach, misconduct, mismanagement. See also violation, wrong, malfeasance, nonfeasance.

Misfit, *n.* See nonconformist, tramp, insurgent; idiot.

Misfortune, *n.* An unforeseeable calamity arising by accident (the storm was a misfortune for the planners). Setback, catastrophe, misadventure, tragedy, casualty, disaster, ill fortune, bad luck, mishap, adversity, reverse, evil, mischief, ruin, blow, fortuity, cataclysm, woe, trouble, bale, affliction, disappointment, visitation, cross, hazard, hardship, tribulation, mischance, defeat, upset, contretemps, reversal, calamity, undoing, accident, loss, ordeal, infliction, failure, downfall, suffering. *Ant.* Good fortune.

Misgiving, *n.* See doubt (2), cloud (2); apprehension, anxiety, reservation (3).

Misguide, *v.* See deceive, misrepresent, distort, err, blunder (2), flounder.

Misguided, *adj.* See erroneous, false (1), misleading, improvident, careless, ill-fated.

Mishap, *n.* See accident, casualty, misfortune.

Mishmash, *n.* See confusion, disorder.

Misinform, *v.* See misrepresent, distort, err, blunder (2).

Misinterpret, *v.* See misrepresent, distort, err, blunder (2).

Misjoinder, *n.* The improper joining together of parties; the improper joining together of causes of action.

Misjudge, *v.* See err, blunder (2), misrepresent, distort; mistake.

Mislabel, *v.* See misrepresent, distort, err, blunder (2).

Mislay, *v.* To forget where one placed something. See lose; missing; mistake, oblivion.

Mislead, *v.* See deceive, betray, misrepresent, cheat, err, blunder, flounder; misleading.

Misleading, *adj.* Capable of leading one astray or into error (misleading advertisement). Deceptive, fraudulent, delusive, seductive, evasive, illusory, ambiguous, slippery, fallacious, hollow, deceitful, spurious, enticing, beguiling, bewildering, perplexing, distracting, confounding, deluding, sophistical, tricky, disingenuous, misguided, demagogic, victimizing, misrepresenting, false, casuistical. *Ant.* Honest.

Mismanage, *v.* See blunder, neglect, err, flounder; maladministration, incompetent.

Mismanagement, *n.* See maladministration, malpractice, misconduct, misfeasance, misdirection, neglect (2); negligent.

Mismatched, *adj.* See incompatible, inconsistent.

Misnomer, *n.* Incorrectly using a name or designation (the misnomer in the deed). Slip, misusage, misnaming, malapropism.

Misplace, *v.* See lose.

Misprint, *n.* See error, blunder (1), mistake.

Misprision, *n.* Maladministration of public office; contempt against the courts or the state; failure to prevent or disclose a crime (misprision of felony). See contempt (1), maladministration, malfeasance, misconduct, misfeasance.

Misprision of felony Concealing a felony committed by another, without prior concert with or subsequent assistance to the felon.

Misquote, *v.* See misrepresent, falsify, distort, err, blunder.

Misread, *v.* See falsify, misrepresent, distort, err, blunder (2).

Misrepresent, *v.* To portray something inaccurately (they misrepresented the quality of the car). Misstate, distort, fabricate, falsify, misguide, pervert, camouflage, prevaricate, lie, deceive, confuse, misquote, warp, exaggerate, embroider, simulate, dupe, dissemble, contort, beguile, overstate, understate, ridicule, defraud, minimize, parody, mock, belie, delude, feign, mislead, slant, color, miscolor, twist, doctor, disguise, alter, adulterate.

Misrepresentation, *n.* **1.** Any untrue statement of fact. See falsehood, error. **2.**

An intentionally false statement of fact. See fraud, deception; misrepresent.

Miss, *v., n.* See err, blunder, neglect, fail; failure, catastrophe, casualty, abortion; woman.

Missile, *n.* See weapon, arms.

Missing, *adj.* Not present; lost (missing person). Absent, displaced, wanting, gone, mislaid, minus, astray, lacking, forgotten, omitted.

Mission, *n.* See assignment (3), job (2), duty (1); embassy.

Missionary, *n.* See minister, religion, church, God, holy; champion, advocate.

Missive, *n.* See letter (1), communication.

Misstate, *v.* See falsify, misrepresent, distort, err, blunder.

Misstep, *v., n.* See err, blunder, mistake, error, lapse (3), fault (1), oversight.

Mist, *n.* See fog.

Mistake 1. *n.* An unintentional act, omission, or error arising from ignorance, surprise, imposition, or misplaced confidence (mutual mistake). Misconception, inaccuracy, lapse, aberration, slip, blunder, oversight, fallacy, faux pas, misunderstanding, erratum, fault, gaffe, indiscretion, misreading, transgression, dereliction, miscalculation, slipup, failure, confusion, deception, flaw, misjudgment, peccadillo, misidentification. **2.** *v.* See err, blunder (2).

Mistaken, *adj.* See erroneous, wrong (3), false, fallacious, baseless.

Mistreat, *v.* See abuse (1), harm (2), harass, wrong (4).

Mistreatment, *n.* See abuse (2), mischief.

Mistress, *n.* See prostitute; woman.

Mistrial, *n.* An erroneous, invalid, or nugatory trial (a mistrial was declared when the juror made an unauthorized visit to the scene of the accident). Termination, revocation, collapse, cancellation, abrogation. See also error, mistake.

Mistrust, *n., v.* See doubt (2), cloud (2); accuse.

Misunderstand, *v.* See err, blunder (2), misrepresent, falsify, distort.

Misunderstanding, *n.* See mistake, error, blunder (1); disagreement, argument (2).

Misuse, *v.* See exploit (1), manipulate, abuse (1), harm, wrong (4).

Mitigate, *v.* To render less painful or severe (mitigate the effect of the defeat). Moderate, relieve, diminish, decrease, meliorate, lighten, soften, temper, ameliorate, alleviate, weaken, restrain, allay, cushion, ease, reduce, tame, qualify, tranquilize, deaden, extenuate, let up, placate, mollify, soothe, assuage, abate, slacken, relax, appease, calm, succor, curb, blunt, regulate, pacify, mute, repress, decelerate, modify, subdue, cool, settle, stabilize, regulate, straighten out, order, palliate. *Ant.* Aggravate.

Mitigating, *adj.* Qualifying or extenuating (mitigating factors). Exonerative, modifying, cushioning, softening, alleviating, relieving, limiting, vindicating, tempering, abating, reducing. *Ant.* Enhancing.

Mitigating circumstances Circumstances surrounding the commission of an act, which in fairness can be considered as extenuating or reducing the severity or degree of moral culpability of the act, but do not serve to excuse or justify it. See excuse (1); extenuating.

Mitigation, *n.* See reduction; mitigate, mitigating, extenuating.

Mitigation of damages, doctrine of A rule of avoidable consequences: An injured party has a duty to use reasonable diligence and ordinary care in attempting to minimize his or her damages after an injury has been inflicted. See avoidable, damages, preventive, prevent.

Mittimus, *n.* An order commanding that a person be conveyed to a prison and held there.

Mix, *v., n.* See commingle, associate (1), consort (2); adulterate; mixture, compound (3), accumulation; mixed.

Mixed, *adj.* Formed by compounding or commingling (mixed blood). Blended, merged, composite, mingled, admixed, homogenized, incorporated, united, mongrel, amalgamated, fused, coalesced, adulterated, joined, heterogeneous, motley, conglomerate, assorted, half-and-half, combined, diversified, miscellaneous. See also hybrid. *Ant.* Isolated.

Mixed-up, *adj.* See composite (1), conglomerate (2); irrational; confusion.

Mixture, *n.* Hodgepodge. Jumble, composite, mélange, mosaic, potpourri, litter, patchwork, miscellany, conglomeration, medley, mix. See also compound (3), accumulation.

M'Naghten rule A test of insanity: An accused is not criminally responsible if, at the time of committing the act, he or she was laboring under such a defect of reason from a disease of the mind as not to know the nature and quality of the act, or if he or she did know this, he or she did not know that the act was wrong. The defendant must know and understand the nature and quality of the act and must be able to distinguish between right and wrong at the time of committing it. See insanity.

Moan, *v.* See bemoan, suffer, cry (1); anguish, pain.

Moat, *n.* See trench.

Mob 1. *n.* A group of many people acting in a violent or disorderly manner (an inability to control the mob). Throng, horde, mass, multitude, legion, collection, body, pact, gathering, posse, swarm, band, school, company, assembly, array, flock, accumulation, rabble. See also gang. **2.** *v.* See accumulate, collect (1).

Mobile, *adj.* See migratory, portable, ambulatory (2); movables.

Mobile home, *n.* See home; vehicle.

Mobilize, *v.* See muster, marshal (2), summon (1), organize, initiate, activate, animate, cause (2).

Mock 1. *v.* To treat with scorn or contempt (the speech mocked the mayor). Ridicule, deride, laugh at, satirize, disparage, taunt, lampoon, sneer, insult, make fun of, be contemptuous of, caricature, ape, assail, burlesque, tease, disdain, taunt, slander, libel, defame, scoff, flout, treat with derision, hold up to ridicule, parody, gibe, personate, imitate, mimic, feign, counterfeit. **2.** *adj.* Pretended (mock trial in school). Imitated, not real, make-believe, simulated, fake, forged, pseudo, sham, spurious, artificial, ersatz. *Ant.* Commend; genuine.

Mockery, *n.* See caricature, imitation, slander, contempt, fraud.

Mod, *adj.* See chic, current (3).

Mode, *n.* The manner in which a thing is done (mode of proceeding). Course, technique, fashion, system, style, procedure, practice, approach, process, outline, convention, formula, scheme, plan, trend. See also modus operandi, method.

Model, *n.* A representation or pattern of something to be made or of something already made (a model of the shopping center). Plan, archetype, mold, representation, prototype, facsimile, image, design, pattern, copy, standard, exemplar, type, paradigm, precedent, paragon, ideal, blueprint, sketch, scale, replica, mockup, miniature, example, criterion, mannequin, analogue. See also kind (1).

Model act A statute proposed to legislatures for adoption (e.g., the Model Probate Code proposed by the National Conference of Commissioners of Uniform State Laws).

Modem, *n.* An instrument that converts data from one form into another. See apparatus, device; change.

Moderate 1. *adj.* Within reasonable limits; not extreme (moderate dissent). Mild, dispassionate, calm, temperate, judicious, restrained, composed, sober, disciplined, modest, light, sporadic, average, rational, ordinary, measured, peaceful, steady, conservative, middle-of-the-road, pedestrian, fair. **2.** *v.* To preside over (she was chosen to moderate the session). Regulate, officiate, police, direct, pilot, emcee, mediate, govern, organize, manage, coordinate, chair. **3.** *v.* See arbitrate (3), negotiate. **4.** *v.* To make less severe or extreme (they moderated their demands). See mitigate, abate.

Moderation, *n.* See temperance; moderate.

Moderator, *n.* A person who presides over a meeting (moderator of the debate). Chair, chairperson, referee, master of ceremonies, umpire, presiding officer, president, arbitrator, mediator, negotiator, facilitator, discussion leader, ombudsman, anchor person.

Modern, *adj.* See current, chic, new, present (3).

Modernize, *v.* See reconstruct, repair (1), reform, improve, modify, change.

Modest, *adj.* See moderate, bashful, quiet (2), awkward, flexible, amenable (2), innocent (2); proper; small, minimal.

Modesty, *n.* See innocence (2), decorum, insecurity (2).

Modicum, *n.* See scintilla, iota, minimum.

Modification, *n.* An alteration that does not change the general purpose and effect of that which is modified (modification of the agreement). Qualification, deviation, limitation, inflection, reservation, variation, refinement, adaptation, adjustment, moderation. See also accommodation (2), amendment.

Modify, *v.* **1.** To make a slight change (they agreed to modify the contract). Amend, adjust, readjust, rework, vary, reorganize, transmute, reduce, lessen, increase, temper, restrain, qualify, reconstruct, revamp, adapt, make corrections, reform, edit, reshape, revise, ameliorate, vary, refine, modernize, recast, accommodate, overhaul, rearrange. **2.** To moderate. See mitigate.

Modulate, *v.* See adjust, regulate, mitigate, change (2), coordinate.

Modulation, *n.* See adjustment, regulation (2), change (1), correction (2).

Module, *n.* See component, element, part (1).

Modus Manner, means, way.

Modus operandi (MO) A method of doing things (the criminal's modus operandi). Methodology, system, routine, pattern, technique, tactic, process, usual procedure, repeated approach, style. See also means, method, mode.

Modus vivendi A way of living. See manner, method, mode.

Moiety, *n.* **1.** One-half (joint tenants hold by moieties). **2.** Portion. See part (1), allotment (1).

Moisten, *v.* See water (2); muggy.

Mold, *n., v.* See cast (4), archetype, model; create, forge (2), invent.

Molder, *v.* See perish, dissolve, decompose.

Moldering, *adj.* See rotten, foul.

Moldy, *adj.* See foul (1), old, rotten; state (1).

Molest, *v.* See abuse (1), harass, accost, batter, intimidate, rape.

Molestation, *n.* See abuse (2), mischief, annoyance, malice, affliction.

Mollify, *v.* See mitigate, assuage, quiet (2).

Molotov cocktail, *n.* See weapon, arms.

Moment, *n.* See minute, interval, period; iota; importance.

Momentary, *adj.* See temporary, transitory, intangible; immediate, instant (2); brief.

Momentous, *adj.* See outstanding (2), important, great, critical.

Momentum, *n.* See motivation, impulse, action (2).

Monarch, *n.* See king, tyrant, manager.

Monarchy, *n.* A government in which the supreme power is vested in a single person.

Monastic, *adj.* See isolated, extreme, strict (2); hermit, church, religious, celibacy.

Monetary, *adj.* Having to do with coinage or currency—money (monetary policy). Pecuniary, financial, fiscal, budgetary, numismatic. See also money, coin, currency.

Money, *n.* Coins and paper currency used as the circulating medium of exchange (money needed for current expenses). Cash, revenue, greenback, assets, wealth, specie, legal tender, wherewithal, funds, capital, collateral, affluence, wealth, bankroll, treasure, fortune, sum, resources.

Moneylender, *n.* See bank, lender; interest, usury.

Money order A type of negotiable draft used by the purchaser as a substitute for a check; a form of credit instrument calling for the payment of money to a named payee. See draft.

Monger, *n.* See dealer.

Mongrel, *n.* See mixed, hybrid.

Monition, *n.* **1.** A summons to appear in an admiralty case. **2.** A warning of danger. See admonition (1), warning.

Monitor, *v.* See oversee, watch (1), check (2), preside, police.

Monk, *n.* See hermit, minister; church, God, holy.

"Monkey business," *n.* See mischief, misconduct, antic.

"Monkey wrench," *n.* See block (1), complication, bar (3), nuisance, obstruction.

Monogamy, *n.* Being married to one person at a time. *Ant.* Polygamy, bigamy.

Monogram, *n.* See badge, manifestation, design.

Monograph, *n.* See book (4).

Monolith, *n.* See conglomerate.

Monolithic, *adj.* See big, indivisible, indestructible.

Monologue, *n.* See address (3), speech (2); joke.

Monopolize, *v.* See dominate, control; monopoly.

Monopoly, *n.* A form of market structure in which one or only a few firms dominate the total sales of a product; the power to fix prices, exclude competition, and control the market in a geographical area, coupled with policies designed to preserve that power (grain monopoly). Domination, corner, oligopoly; cartel, trust, amalgamation. See also merger, consortium.

Monotonous, *adj.* See commonplace, household, ordinary, customary, pedestrian (2).

Monotony, *n.* See boredom, ennui.

Monsignor, *n.* See minister; church, religion, hierarchy.

Monsoon, *n.* See storm; climate.

Monster, *n.* See aberration, demon, animal, wrongdoer.

Monstrous, *adj.* See wild, base (2), cruel, gross (1), blatant, immoral, depraved, deviant (1), absurd, anomalous.

Montage, *n.* See mixture; composition.

Month, *n.* Calendar month. The period from any day in a month of the calendar to the corresponding day of the next month. See interval, period.

Monument, *n.* **1.** Anything by which the memory of a person, thing, idea, art, science, or event is preserved or perpetuated (a monument to the struggle for freedom). Memorial, reminder, pillar, shrine, commemoration, remembrance, token, testimonial, landmark. **2.** Visible marks or indications left on natural or other objects (posts, stone markers, blazed trees, watercourse), indicating the lines and boundaries of a property survey. See metes and bounds, map. **3.** See sculpture (2).

Monumental, *adj.* See big, great, extraordinary, conspicuous, awesome; agape.

Mooch, *v.* See filch, rob; larceny.

Mood, *n.* See climate (2), disposition (4), emotion, manner; depression, anxiety.

Moody, *adj.* See depressed, despondent, abandoned (1); difficult (3), crabby, capricious, contentious.

Moonshine, *n.* Intoxicating liquor illicitly produced or smuggled into a community for beverage purposes; spirituous liquor, illegally distilled or manufactured. See liquor, beverage.

Moor, *v., n.* See attach (2), connect (1), fix (2); park (1), desert (3).

Mooring, *n.* Anchoring or securing a vessel to a shore or dock. Binding, fastening, hitching, tying up, chaining, fixing. See also anchor, harbor.

Moot, *adj.* **1.** Pertaining to a nonexistent controversy where the issues have ceased to exist from a practical point of view (the question is moot because the plaintiff received what he wanted before the trial began). Academic, theoretical, abstract, speculative, of no practical importance. See also hypothetical. **2.** A subject for argument (the moot question of whether the U.N. serves a useful purpose). Debatable, controversial, undecided, unsettled, arguable, contentious, disputable, problematical, disputed, eristic, undetermined, open, contestable, doubtful. *Ant.* Real; settled.

Moot court A simulated court in a law school where a hypothetical case is argued for learning purposes.

Mope, *v.* To sulk. Brood, pout, ache, grump, fret, grouse, whine, gloom, lament, pine, be downcast. See also complain (2), bemoan, cry (1), suffer; depressed, depression.

Moral 1. *adj.* Pertaining to conscience or to the general principles of right conduct (moral judgment). Ethical, religious, right-and-wrong. **2.** *adj.* Demonstrating correct character or behavior (moral person). Honorable, aboveboard, principled, appropriate, proper, noble, conscientious, worthy, upstanding, righteous, scrupulous, virtuous, chaste, right-minded, dutiful, incorruptible, praiseworthy, uncorrupt, wholesome, uplifting, ethical, virtuous, respectable, decent, square, trustworthy, pure, meritorious, correct, seemly, exemplary, commendable, innocent, responsible. See also honest, good (2), right. **3.** *n.* A lesson or principle (the moral of the story). Homily, significance, point, teaching, proverb, adage, canon, precept, truism, epigram, saying, motto. See also maxim.

Moral certainty That degree of assurance which induces a person of sound mind to act without doubt upon the conclusions to which it leads; a very high degree of probability although not demonstrable to a certainty. See likelihood, probability, chance (3).

Morale, *n.* See spirit, emotion, disposition (4); climate (2); confidence.

Moral hazard In fire insurance: The risk or danger of the destruction of the insured property by fire. See risk, insurance.

Morality, *n.* See virtue, integrity (1), honor (3).

Moralize, *v.* See preach; reprimand, discipline (4), advocate.

Moral obligation A duty that rests on moral considerations alone and is not imposed or enforced by positive law; a duty binding in conscience but not in law. See duty.

Moral turpitude Acts or behavior that gravely violates accepted moral standards of the community; baseness or depravity in private or social duties that one person owes another or owes society in general. See debauchery, corruption, ignominy.

Morass, *n.* A quagmire. Wallow, mess, mire, slough; predicament, dilemma. See also swamp; confusion, disorder, commotion.

Moratorium, *n.* Temporary suspension of the obligations of a debtor and the right to use remedies against him or her; a period of permissive or obligatory delay (court-approved moratorium). Postponement, pause, discontinuance, stoppage, abeyance, stay, cessation, respite, halt, deferral, recess, standstill. *Ant.* Continuation.

Morbid, *adj.* See odious, repugnant, repulsive, gross (1); violent, deadly; abnormal; grave (3), dark, depressed, depressing, abandoned (1), dismal.

Mordant, *adj.* See caustic, cutting, malicious, cynical, offensive; painful.

More, *adj.* See supplemental, extra.

More or less Approximately (more or less defeated). Mostly, substantially, chiefly, generally, principally, predominately, for the most part, primarily, mainly, somewhat, nearly. See also about (1).

Moreover, *adv.* Furthermore (moreover, the plan is fair). Likewise, beyond this, besides, also, in addition thereto, further, what is more, additionally, more than this.

Mores, *n.* See practice (1), convention (3), custom (1), formality (1).

Morgue, *n.* A place where dead persons are kept for a limited time for identification purposes. See burial.

Moribund, *adj.* See dying; obsolete, obsolescent; ancient, old.

Mormon, *n.* A member of the Church of the Latter-day Saints, organized by Joseph Smith in 1830 and headquartered in Salt Lake City, Utah. See church, religion, holy, minister.

Morning, *n.* Dawn. Daybreak, a.m., sunrise, morn, sunup, break of day, aurora, cockcrow, forenoon, morningtide.

Moron, *n.* A mentally defective person usually having a mental age of 8 to 12 years and an IQ of 50 to 70. See insanity; idiot, boor, ass.

Morose, *adj.* See depressing, depressed, dark, despondent, grave (3), dismal, extreme (1), ascetic, strict (2), formal (3), plain; caustic.

Morphine, *n.* See drug, addict, treatment, medicine; medical.

Morsel, *n.* See iota, scintilla, portion, part (1).

Mortal, *adj.* **1.** Exposing to death; destructive of life (mortal wound). Deadly, fatal, suicidal, life-and-death, disastrous, murderous. **2.** Relentless (a mortal enemy). Implacable, unremitting, remorseless, savage, inexorable, grave, bloodthirsty, bitter, unrelenting, severe, intense. **3.** See imperfect, temporary, limited (1). *Ant.* Innocuous.

Mortality, *n.* **1.** The death rate; the relative incidence of death (mortality table). **2.** The quality of being subject to death; humanity (thinking about his own mortality). Human race, humanity, vulnerability, mankind, mortals, homo sapiens. **3.** The number of deaths (heavy mortality). Death toll, fatality, carnage, human loss.

Mortality tables A means of ascertaining the probable number of years a male or female of a given age will live, assuming ordinary health. See probability, chance (3); insurance.

Mortgage 1. *n.* An interest in land created by a written instrument providing security for the performance of a duty or the payment of a debt (amortization of the mortgage). Collateral security, warranty. See also encumbrance, burden; indemnity. **2.** *v.* To make subject to a pledge (they mortgaged the farm). Hypothecate, obligate, encumber, stake, post, hock. See also pawn.

Mortgage bond A bond for which real estate or personal property is pledged as security that the bond will be paid as stated in its terms. See bond, pledge, security.

Mortgage company A firm engaged in the business of originating and closing mortgages, which are then assigned or sold to investors.

Mortgagee, *n.* The person who takes, receives, and holds a mortgage; the person to whom property is mortgaged.

Mortgage insurance Insurance from which the benefits are used to pay off the balance of a mortgage upon the death or disability of the insured; insurance against loss to the mortgagees in the event of default and a failure of the mortgaged property to satisfy the balance owing plus the costs of foreclosure. See insurance, indemnity (2).

Mortgage lien A lien on the property of the mortgagor, which secures the debt obligation. See lien, security.

Mortgagor, *n.* The person who mortgages his or her property; the person who pledges property; the person who gives legal title or a lien to the mortgagee to secure the mortgage loan.

Mortician, *n.* See merchant, business; burial, autopsy, mortuary.

Mortification, *n.* See ignominy, embarrassment, guilt (2), depression, contrition, disgrace, obloquy, censure.

Mortify, *v.* See discredit, disparage, embarrass, slander, decry, defy, debase.

Mortis causa By reason of death. See in contemplation of death.

Mortmain acts Statutes that are designed to prevent lands from permanently getting into the possession or control of institutions such as churches, which could not transfer them.

Mortuary, *n.* An undertaking and embalming establishment; a funeral home. See burial.

Mosaic, *n.* See mixture, compound (3).

Mosque, *n.* See church; religion, God, holy.

Most, *adj.* The largest in quantity or degree (most ability). Greatest, utmost, optimal, maximum, ultra, furthest, unsurpassed, unequaled, top, optimum. See also majority (2), plurality; best, exceptional, leading (1). *Ant.* Minimal.

Most favored nation clause A clause found in a treaty, providing that each side grants to the other the broadest rights and privileges that it accords to any other nation (any third nation) in treaties it has made or will make.

Motel, *n.* See inn; merchant, commerce.

Mother 1. *n.* A woman who has borne a child. Female parent, matriarch, mom, mater. See also woman. **2.** *v.* To protect (the aunt mothered her niece). Nourish, indulge, rear, shelter, watch over, smother, nurse, raise, care for. See also nurture. *Ant.* Father; neglect.

Motherland, *n.* See nation, country.

Motif, *n.* See proposition (2), matter (1), question (2), issue (3).

Motion, *n.* **1.** An application made to a court or other decision-making body in order to obtain a favorable action or decision (motion to dismiss). Request, petition, proposition, plan, demand, offering, recommendation, proposal, measure, claim. **2.** A gesture (a motion of the hand). Sign, wave, signal, demonstration, movement, action, nod, show. **3.** See action (2), activity; fluctuating.

Motion for a directed verdict A request that the court order a verdict in favor of the moving party, on the ground that the other side has failed to produce sufficient evidence of facts that support its theory of the case as to which it had the burden of proof. See prima facie, adequate.

Motion for a judgment notwithstanding the verdict (J.N.O.V.) A request that the judge enter a verdict contrary to that reached by the jury, on the ground that the evidence is insufficient to support the jury's verdict. See insufficient.

Motion for a judgment on the pleadings A request that the judge make a decision on the basis of the pleadings alone without a trial, on the ground that the material facts are not in dispute and only questions of law remain. See summary, summary judgment.

Motion for a more definite statement A request that the court order the other side to make its pleading more definite, since it is so vague or ambiguous that one cannot reasonably frame a responsive pleading. See ambiguous, definite (1).

Motion for a new trial A request that the trial judge set aside the judgment and order a new trial, on the ground that the trial was improper or unfair due to specified prejudicial errors that occurred (e.g., jury misconduct). See prejudice, injustice.

Motion in limine A motion made before or after the beginning of a jury trial for a protective order against the potential use of prejudicial statements or questions by the other side. See commencement, prejudice.

Motionless, *adj.* See stationary, fixed (2); quiet.

Motion picture, *n.* See cinema.

Motion to dismiss A request, usually made before the trial begins, that the judge dismiss the case because of an insufficiency in the pleadings of the other side. See dismiss, insufficient.

Motion to strike A request that the court order removed from a pleading any insufficient defense or any redundant, immaterial, or scandalous matter. See removal, immaterial, redundancy.

Motion to suppress A request that the court eliminate from the trial any illegally secured evidence. See illegal, exclusionary rule.

Motivate, *v.* See encourage (2), incite, induce, influence, provoke; motive.

Motivation, *n.* Impetus, incentive. Drive, stimulant, provocation, spur, push, propulsion, momentum, spark, thrust, inspiration, reason. See also motive, influence, cause, impulse, help (1).

Motive, *n.* The cause or reason that moves the will and induces action or inaction (the motives of the legislators). Inducement, rationale, stimulus, incentive, purpose, aim, enticement, end, prompting, persuasion, goal, occasion, design, intent, basis, objective, inspiration, stimulant, spur, compulsion, provocation, incitement. See also motivation, impulse, influence.

Motley, *adj.* See multifarious, multiple, divers, different, individual; irregular, mixed; mixture.

Motor, *n.* See apparatus, instrument (2), equipment, device; automation; vehicle.

Motorbike, motorcycle, *n.* See vehicle.

Motorist, *n.* See operator, chauffeur.

Motor lodge, *n.* See inn.

Motor vehicle, *n.* See vehicle.

Motto, *n.* See maxim, moral (3).

Mound, *n.* See mountain; collection (2), bulk (1), pack, lot.

Mount, *v.* See ascend, advance, accumulate.

Mountain, *n.* Large hill. Peak, butte, alp, ridge, cliff, elevation, promontory, range, crest, pinnacle. See also bluff (3); mass, multitude; aim (3); obstruction.

Mountebank, *n.* See charlatan, quack, cheat.

Mourn, *v.* See bemoan, suffer, cry (1), mope.

Mourning, *n.* See anguish, anxiety, pain, depression, loss.

Mouth, *n.* See entrance.

"Mouthpiece," *n.* See attorney, agent.

Movables, *n.* Things that can be carried from one place to another (an inventory of all movables). Chattels, personal property, personalty, goods, portable goods, transferable property, unattached property, possessions. See also property, effects. *Ant.* Fixture.

Movant, *n.* One who makes a motion or applies for a ruling or order. See petitioner, applicant.

Move 1. *v.* To make an application for a certain action or decision (the plaintiff moved for a new trial). Petition, demand, request, propose, propound, urge, advocate, recommend, suggest, ask for, apply, submit, introduce, exhort, plead, put forth, offer. **2.** *v.* To make a change in position (they moved the records). Transfer, alter, shift, proceed, switch, convey, transpose, advance, turn, budge, carry, transmit, transplant, relocate. **3.** *v.* To arouse (moved to action). Stir, prompt, instigate, encourage, activate, incite, arouse, stimulate, provoke, impel, set in motion, goad, impassion, galvanize, inspire, prick, pique. **4.** *n.* A step taken; a change in position (an unexpected move). Movement, alteration, activity, ploy, maneuver, endeavor, gesture, strategy, tactic.

Movement, *n.* See campaign, move (4), activity, gesture, signal (3).

Movie, *n.* See cinema; drama; merchant, business.

Moving, *adj.* **1.** Stirring (a moving presentation). Telling, persuasive, absorbing, exciting, rousing, provoking, stimulating, breathtaking, glowing, sensational, impressive, poignant, inspiring, pathetic, affecting, captivating, dramatic, eloquent, breathless, significant, gripping, arresting. See also compelling, emotional, intriguing, touching, extraordinary. **2.** Pertaining to that which moves (moving parts). Migratory, mobile, peripatetic, operating, running, interacting, locomotive, ambulatory, nomadic, traveling, wavering, itinerant. *Ant.* Dull; stationary.

Moving papers Papers or documents submitted in support of a motion. See document, pleading.

Moving party The party making the motion. See petitioner, applicant.

"Moxie," *n.* See spirit (2), determination (2), valor, ambition.

Much, *adj.* See great, big.

Muck, *n.* See refuse (2), dirt; slander.

Muckrake, *v.* See expose; corruption; yellow (2).

Mud, *n.* See dirt, refuse (2), morass, disorder, confusion.

Muddle, *v.* See confuse; adulterate; blunder; disorder.

Muddy, *adj.* See complex (1), mixed.

Mudslinging, *n.* See slander, censure, aspersion.

Muff, *v.* See blunder, flounder, err; mistake.

Muffle, *v.* See silence (2); hide, conceal.

Mug, *v., n.* See accost, attack, rob; mugshot; vessel (2).

Mugging, *n.* See attack, aggravated assault; larceny.

Muggy, *adj.* Humid. Warm, hot, sticky, moist, damp, clammy, steamy, sultry, sweaty, tropical, torrid.

Mugshot, *n.* A picture taken of an accused when he or she is arrested and booked.

Mulatto, *n.* A person of mixed Caucasian and Negro blood, or of Indian and Negro blood. See mixed, hybrid, race (1).

Mulct 1. *n.* A penalty or punishment imposed on a person guilty of some offense or tort. See fine, damages. **2.** *v.* To defraud a person of something (she tried to mulct him of his inheritance). See cheat (1).

Mull, *v.* See deliberate (1), consider (1), contemplate (1), assess, appraise.

Multidistrict litigation Civil actions involving one or more common questions of fact pending in several different federal district courts (e.g., antitrust cases, air crash cases). Such cases can be transferred to one district for coordinated and consolidated trial under a single judge. See jurisdiction, complex.

Multifarious, *adj.* Diverse (multifarious responsibilities). Varied, diversified, sundry, motley, heterogeneous, variegated, multiform, numerous, miscellaneous, multitudinous, many, several, eclectic. See also divers, mixed, hybrid, multiple. *Ant.* Uniform.

Multifarious issue An issue that inquires about several different facts, when each fact should be inquired about in a separate issue. See issue, confusion.

Multifariousness, *n.* In equity pleading, the misjoinder of causes of action in a bill. See misjoinder.

Multilateral, *adj.* Involving many sides, persons, firms, or nations (multilateral agreement). See multifarious, multiple, divers.

Multinational, *adj.* Having centers of operation in many countries (multinational corporation). See international, world.

Multipartite, *adj.* Divided into many or several parts. See multiple, part.

Multiple, *adj.* Involving more than one (multiple claims). Several, plural, divergent, sundry, myriad, diverse, various, assorted, mixed, diversified, miscellaneous.

Multiple

See also multifarious, many. *Ant.* Single.

Multiple access The defense of several men in a paternity case that more than one lover had access to the mother during the time of conception. See access, conception.

Multiple listing An arrangement between a number of real estate brokers in a given area whereby any member broker is authorized to sell the property listed with one broker. The latter shares the fee or commission with the broker who made the sale. See broker, listing.

Multiplicity, *n.* **1.** A large number or variety of matters or particulars (multiplicity of actions). Volume, host, bunch, array, multifariousness, diversity, mass. See also multitude. **2.** The charging of a single offense in several counts (multiplicity in the indictment).

Multiplicity of actions or suits Numerous and unnecessary attempts to litigate the same right against the same defendant. See harass.

Multiply, *v.* See beget, augment; double; increase.

Multitude, *n.* An assemblage of many people (the multitude listened attentively). Throng, herd, congregation, flock, pack, host, legion, horde, troop, sea, army, myriad, drove, swarm, tribe, body, assortment, array, aggregation, shipload, multiplicity, squad, gang, crush, conflux. See also mass. *Ant.* Individual.

Multitudinous, *adj.* See multifarious, divers.

Mum, *adj.* See mute, silent (1), quiet.

Mumble, *v.* To speak incoherently. See communicate, whisper.

Mumbo jumbo, *n.* See balderdash; witchcraft.

Mundane, *adj.* See commonplace, household, customary, ordinary; secular.

Municipal, *adj.* **1.** Pertaining to a city, town, or other local unit of government (municipal water system). Urban, community, neighborhood. See also city, civic, metropolitan. **2.** Pertaining to a self-governing or independent state or nation.

Municipal corporation A body corporate created by the legislature for the purpose of local government, with a corporate name and continuous succession, consisting of the inhabitants of a designated area or portion of the state. See political subdivision, division (1), city, corporation.

Municipality, *n.* A legally incorporated or duly authorized association of inhabitants of a limited area of the state for local government or other public purposes (the corporate responsibilities of the municipality). Metropolis, town, county, village, metropolitan area, township, parish, borough, hamlet, settlement, municipal corporation, burgh, community, district. See also city, metropolitan.

Munificent, *adj.* See charitable, benevolent, liberal, kind, humanitarian, abundant.

Muniments, *n.* Documentary evidence of title; documents the owner can use to defend his or her title to land.

Munition, *n.* See weapon, arms.

Murder 1. *n.* The unlawful killing of a human being, or fetus, with malice aforethought (the murder of the officer). Criminal homicide, liquidation, slaughter, obliteration, destruction, extermination, massacre, slaying, carnage, blood bath, butchery, genocide, pogrom, holocaust, savagery, intentional killing, execution, annihilation. See also assassination, homicide, manslaughter. **2.** See kill, execute.

Murderous, *adj.* See deadly.

Murky, *adj.* See ambiguous, mysterious, obscure; dismal.

Murmur, *v., n.* See whisper, mope; bemoan, cry (1); noise.

Muscle, *n.* See might (2), power, vigor.

Muscular, *adj.* See durable, able-bodied, healthy.

Muse, *v.* See deliberate, consider (1), contemplate (1).

Museum, *n.* See collection, archives, institution.

Mushroom, *v.* See develop, mature (1), advance.

Music, *n.* Organized tones. Harmony, melody, chord, rhythm, chorus, song, singing, composition, hymn, tune, verse, ballad, glee club, canticle, chant, concert, band, orchestra, ensemble, carol, voice, counterpoint, dance, opera, jazz, instrument, concerto, conductor, musician. See also poem.

Musing, *adj.* See preoccupied; engage (2).

Must, *v.* See compulsory, mandatory; obligation.

Muster, *v.* To assemble together (muster troops; muster arguments). Collect, summon, convene, mobilize, rally, invoke, generate, activate, cluster, congregate. See also marshal (2), organize, group (2). *Ant.* Disperse.

Mutable, *adj.* See variable; capricious, fluctuating.

Mutation, *n.* See change (1).

Mutatis mutandis With the necessary changes in any of the details.

Mute, *adj.* Speechless; concerning one who cannot or will not speak (she stood mute). Silent, quiet, dumb, taciturn, voiceless, wordless, mum, tongue-tied, inarticulate, noncommittal, reticent, tightlipped, close-mouthed, uncommunicative, still, aphonic, hush. See also mitigate. *Ant.* Glib.

Mutilate, *v.* **1.** To maim (an attempt to mutilate the victim). Dismember, disfigure, lame, amputate, cripple, deform, bruise, incapacitate, wound, butcher, gash, injure, hack, debilitate, lacerate, mangle, impair, disable, knife, commit mayhem, spoil, mar, distort, atomize, scar, blemish. See also maim. **2.** To alter or deface a document by cutting, tearing, burning, or erasing, without totally destroying it (mutilate the will).

Mutilation, *n.* See break (3); contusion, injury, hurt; mutilate, maim.

Mutinous, *adj.* Tending to incite or encourage mutiny (mutinous crew). Insubordinate, defiant, ungovernable, revolutionary, insurgent, unruly, insurrectionary, subversive, hostile, traitorous, malcontent, resistant, rebellious, factious, disaffected, contumacious, recalcitrant, refractory, noncompliant, anarchistic. *Ant.* Obedient.

Mutiny, *n.* An insurrection of soldiers or seamen against the authority of their commanders (prosecution for mutiny). Revolt, insurgency, takeover, coup, uprising, overthrow, strike, sedition, anarchy, treason, disloyalty, opposition, disobedience, boycott. See also defiance, rebellion, insubordination, resistance. *Ant.* Submission.

Mutter, *v.* See whisper, mope, communicate.

Mutual, *adj.* Common to both parties (mutual agreement). Reciprocal, interchangeable, interchanged, complementary, correlative, returned, joint, coincident, interactive, reciprocating, reciprocated, leagued, collaborative, parallel, shared, cooperative, related, conjoint, associated, bilateral, two-way, concurrent, interdependent, communal, participated, connected. See also identical, equivalent, analogous. *Ant.* Private.

Mutual combat A fight that both parties willingly enter. Two persons, upon a sudden quarrel and in hot blood, mutually fight on equal terms. See combat, hot.

Mutual company A company in which the customers are also the owners and receive the profits in proportion to the business they do with the company. See business, company.

Mutual fund An investment company that raises money by selling its own stock to the public and investing the proceeds in other securities. See fund, investment, securities, business, company.

Mutual insurance company An insurance company that has no capital stock and in which the policyholders are the owners. See insurance, business, company, owner.

Mutuality, *n.* An action by each of two parties; reciprocation; both sides being bound (mutuality of consent). Reciprocity, interchange, correspondence, mutual dependence, interdependence, interrelation, correlation, commonality, equivalence, exchange, coequality, community.

Mutuality of obligation Unless both sides are bound by the contract, neither is bound. See reciprocal, bound (1).

Mutual mistake A mistake common to both contracting parties, where each is laboring under the same misconception as to a past or existing material fact. The agreement entered into by the parties does not in its written form express what the parties actually intended. See mistake, error, reciprocal.

Mutual savings bank A banking institution that has no capital stock and in which the depositors are the owners. See bank, owner.

Mutual wills 1. Separate wills made by two persons, which are reciprocal in their provisions. **2.** Wills executed pursuant to an agreement between two persons to dispose of their property in a particular manner, each in consideration of the other. See will, reciprocal wills.

Muzzle, *v.* See restrain, confine, defeat (1), silence (2); mute.

Myopic, *adj.* Nearsighted, insensitive. See narrow (2), parochial (2), arbitrary.

Myriad, *adj.* See many, multiple, multifarious, multitude, divers; incalculable; big.

Mysterious, *adj.* Concerning a mystery or that which is difficult to comprehend (mysterious disappearance). Baffling, esoteric, puzzling, weird, enigmatic, mystifying, cryptic, nebulous, impenetrable, mystic, inexplicable, hidden, unfathomable, uncanny, occult, arcane, unexplained, strange, indecipherable, cloudy, magical, obscure, abstruse, numinous, recondite, surreptitious, coded, ineffable, preternatural, unknown, hermetic, veiled, screened, nebulous, sphinxlike, unaccountable, bizarre, insidious, profound, incomprehensible, mystical, unintelligible, cabalistic. See also clandestine, indefinite, ambiguous, irrational, dark. *Ant.* Straightforward.

Mystery, *n.* An event or thing that cannot be explained (her disappearance was a mystery). Puzzle, enigma, riddle, obscurity, dilemma, problem, secret, inscrutability, concealment, predicament, tangle, knot, cabalism, esoteric happening, quandary, perplexity, question mark, unfathomability. See also conundrum, ambiguity.

Mystic, *adj.* See mysterious, irrational, obscure, hidden; witchcraft.

Mystify, *v.* See distract (2), confuse, amaze, surprise (1).

Mystique, *n.* See aura, environment, influence.

Myth, *n.* See legend, dream (1), fiction, delusion, falsehood; balderdash, pretense.

Mythical, *adj.* See fictitious, illusory, fallacious, absurd, irrational; mysterious.

N.A. Not allowed; nonacquiescing; not available; not applicable.

Nag, *v.* See complain (2), censure (2), mope.

Nail, *v., n.* See affix (1), fix (2), attach (2), connect (1); spike.

Naive, *adj.* See innocent, credulous; illiterate, blind, juvenile (2), backward (1), shy, open.

Naiveté, *n.* See innocence, candor.

Naked, *adj.* **1.** Bare; incomplete; wanting in necessary conditions (the naked promise was unenforceable). **2.** Without covering or disguise (naked facts). Unadorned, plain, visible, sheer, overt, unexaggerated, stripped, undressed, exposed, frank, unqualified, nude, perceptible, austere, unadulterated, essential, fundamental, core, patent, defenseless, flagrant, undraped, pure, bald, unembellished, noticeable, stark, unmistakable, self-evident, conspicuous, explicit, unmixed, discoverable, recognizable, unvarnished, bald-faced. See also bare (1), mere, manifest, clear (1), blatant, evident, certain (3), obvious. *Ant.* Complete; veiled.

Name 1. *n.* The designation of an individual, firm, or corporation (registered corporate name). Appellation, tag, epithet, cognomen. See also badge, manifestation, alias, label. **2.** *v.* To designate (name a successor). Select, specify, define, identify, pick, commission, choose, delegate, ordain, deputize, assign, nominate, employ, indicate, entitle, elect, engage, empower; style, call, address, label, dub, term, christen, baptize, tag, title.

Named insured The person specifically mentioned in an insurance policy as the one protected. See insurance.

Nameless, *adj.* See anonymous, obscure.

Nap, *n.* See sleep; drowsy, bed.

Napalm, *n., v.* See weapon, arms; attack; incendiary.

"Narc," *n.* A law enforcement officer assigned to enforce the drug laws. See police, officer, drug.

Narcissistic, *adj.* See arrogant, pompous; boast.

Narcotic, *n.* Any drug that dulls the senses or induces sleep and which often becomes addictive after prolonged use (possession of narcotics). Opiate, sedative, painkiller, morphine, relaxant, barbiturate, depressant, antidepressant, soporific, palliative, dope, medication, anodyne, anesthetic, tranquilizer. See also drug.

Narrate, *v.* See communicate, report (4), describe.

Narration, *n.* See report (1), communication, recital, account (2), description; legend; narrative evidence.

Narrative evidence A descriptive account of a sequence of events. Anecdotes, episodic presentation, flowing account, recitation, narration, portrayal, discourse, restatement, summarization, rendition, depiction, sketch, recapitulation, recounting, continuing account, event-by-event account, chronicle. See also report (1).

Narrow 1. *adj.* Restricted in scope or area (a narrow interpretation). Thin, cramped, compressed, rigid, attenuated, tight, confined, constricted, circumscribed, literal, pinched, contracted, reduced, weakened, close, strict. See also limited. **2.** *adj.* Intolerant (a narrow point of view). Narrow-minded, illiberal, shallow, conservative, jaundiced, partisan, mean, rigorous, small, uncharitable, doctrinaire, intransigent, complacent, fundamentalist, authoritarian, provincial, prejudiced, opinionated, blind, bigoted, sexist, racist, elitist, closed-minded, one-sided, shortsighted, deaf, small-minded, biased, petty. See also parochial (2), arbitrary. **3.** *v.* See qualify (2), define, limit (1). *Ant.* Broad; progressive.

Narrow-minded, *adj.* See narrow (2), parochial (2), arbitrary, petty (3), partisan, blind.

NASA National Aeronautics and Space Administration.

Nascent, *adj.* See inchoate, initial.

NASD National Association of Securities Dealers, Inc., an association of brokers and dealers in the over-the-counter securities business.

Nasty, *adj.* See base, rude, common (3), odious, immoral, obscene, foul, dirty.

Natal, *adj.* See birth.

Nation, *n.* An aggregation of people united under one political system in a distinct portion of the globe, often with common traditions, customs, and history (the nation at war). Country, state, commonwealth, land, realm, community, polity, empire, republic, union, body politic, sovereign entity, principality, kingdom, dominion, confederation; race, tribe, population, citizenry, people, stock, clan, ethnic group.

National 1. *adj.* Pertaining to the nation as a whole (national applicability). Nationwide, coast-to-coast, central, federal, United States, general, interstate, overall, cross-country; internal, domestic. **2.** *n.* A citizen of a particular nation (a national of France). See citizen. *Ant.* Local; foreigner.

National bank A bank incorporated and doing business under the laws of the United States. See bank, business, commerce. *Ant.* State bank.

National Guard An organization that serves as a reserve of the Army and Air Force. Members of the Guard, serving on a statewide basis, are subject to being activated for federal service as well as for state emergencies. See military, martial; sailor.

Nationalism, *n.* See chauvinism, arrogance; spirit; nation; patriot, military.

Nationality, *n.* The status that arises as a result of a person's belonging to a nation because of birth or naturalization (her nationality was unknown). Citizenship, fatherland, motherland, origin, homeland, national status.

Nationalization, *n.* The acquisition and control of privately owned businesses by the government (nationalization of the oil refinery). Expropriation, seizure, socialization, taking. See also appropriation (1).

Nationalize, *v.* See expropriate, seize, appropriate (1); nationalization.

National Labor Relations Board (NLRB) An independent federal agency that seeks to prevent and remedy unfair labor practices, conducts employee elections in appropriate collective bargaining units, etc. See union, labor, business.

National Mediation Board An agency that mediates disputes between rail and air carriers, and the unions of their employees. See union, mediation, mediator.

National origin The country where a person was born or from which his or her ancestors came. See country.

Nationwide, *adj.* See national; interstate; broad (1).

Native 1. *n.* A citizen by birth (a native of Poland). Natural-born subject, settler, aborigine, primitive, inhabitant, Indian, countryman. **2.** *adj.* Peculiar to a certain place (native custom). Indigenous, homegrown, domestic, autochthonous, local, aboriginal, endemic, vernacular, rooted. **3.** *adj.* Innate (native intelligence). Ingrained, hereditary, intuitive, natural, inherent, genetic, intrinsic, basic, natal, congenital, inbred, inherited, indwelling, in the blood, organic. *Ant.* Foreigner; foreign.

Native American, *n.* See native; aboriginal.

Nativity, *n.* See birth (1).

Natty, *adj.* See chic, current, cultivated, beautiful, aristrocratic.

Natural, *adj.* **1.** Based on moral considerations; proceeding from or determined by physical conditions as opposed to positive enactments of the law; attributed to the nature of humankind (natural law). **2.** Not artificial or manmade (a natural condition of the land). Made by nature, unchanged, earthly, native, unaltered, pure, raw, ordinary, untouched, wild, original. **3.** Innate (natural talent). Ingrained, hereditary, inherited, intuitive, inherent, primitive, genetic, intrinsic, fundamental, basic, involuntary, natal, congenital, inbred, constitutional, indwelling, in the blood, organic, God-given, instinctive, inborn, normal, automatic, connate, indigenous, original. **4.** Normal (died of natural causes). Unexceptional, ordinary, routine, expected, usual, established, regular, customary, standard. **5.** Without artificiality (a natural gesture). Spontaneous, unaffected, artless, genuine, unpretentious, candid, open, unconscious, automatic, guileless, unstudied, authentic, unadulterated, realistic. *Ant.* Legal; manufactured; acquired; extraordinary; unnatural.

Natural affection The affection that naturally exists between near relatives. See affection (1), natural (5), family.

Natural and probable consequences Those consequences that a person using prudent human foresight should be able to anticipate as likely to result from an act because they result so frequently from this act in the experience of humanity. See foresee, consequence (1), probability, chance (3).

Naturalization, *n.* The process by which a person acquires citizenship after birth (petition for naturalization). Conferral, acceptance, admission, endowment. See also enfranchisement.

Naturalize, *v.* See entitle, endow.

Natural law A system of rules and principles (not created by human authority or enacted law) that can be discovered by the rational intelligence of a person as growing out of and conforming to the nature of men and women. See maxim, measure (1), law.

Natural resource See woods, mineral, land, resource.

Nature, *n.* See essence, character (2), disposition (4); kind (1); earth, world.

Naught, *n.* See nil, nullity; cipher (2).

Naughty, *adj.* See bad (2), incorrigible, disobedient; juvenile; offensive, immoral, corrupt; obscene.

Nausea, *n.* See contempt (2), odium; illness, disease.

Nauseate, *v.* See revolt (2), displease, disturb, outrage (2), disrupt.

Nauseous, *adj.* See offensive, odious, repulsive, repugnant.

Nautical, *adj.* Pertaining to ships, navigation, or the sea carriage business (nautical skills). Naval, yachting, navigational, seagoing, oceanic, seafaring, sailing. See also marine, maritime, sea, sailor.

Nautical mile About 6,076 feet. Geographical mile. See measure (1), range (2), area. *Ant.* Statute mile.

Naval, *adj.* Pertaining to the navy. See maritime, nautical, navy, sea, sailor.

Navigable, *adj.* Capable of being navigated or passed over by ships or vessels; affording a channel for useful commerce (navigable waters). Traversable, passable, negotiable.

Navigable waters Any body of water that, by itself or by uniting with other waters, forms a continuous highway over which commerce can be carried on with other states or countries. See sea, highway, commerce.

Navigate, *v.* To direct one's course (navigate by the stars). Steer, guide, chart, control, pilot, fly, sail, conduct, travel, boat, circumnavigate, aviate, journey, manage, convey, maneuver, cruise, ride, traverse, cross.

Navigation, *n.* The art, science, or business of traveling the sea or other navigable waters in ships or vessels. See navigate.

Navy, *n.* A fleet of ships; naval forces. Armada, submarines, destroyers, carriers, flotilla, convoy, task force, battleships. See also vessel (1), sailor, maritime, marine, nautical.

N.B. Note well; observe.

N.D. Northern District, e.g., U.S. District Court for the Northern District of New York (N.D.N.Y.).

Near, *adv.* Close by or adjacent (drawing near). Contiguous, abutting, close, touching, proximate, joining, nigh, within view, next door, in propinquity, at hand, bordering, at close quarters. See also adjacent; vicinity. *Ant.* Apart.

Neat, *adj.* See clean (2), precise, coherent (1), regular, efficient, competent.

Nebulous, *adj.* See ambiguous, obscure.

Necessaries, *n.* Those things that are indispensable or proper and useful for the sustenance of human life; those things that are suitable for the individual according to his or her circumstances and condition in life (an allowance for necessaries). Necessities, essentials, fundamentals, needs, requirements, vitals, qualifications, requisites, prerequisites, room and board, nurture, nourishment, accommodation, rations, maintenance, survival, sustenance, upkeep, basics, goods required for subsistence and support.

Necessary, *adj.* Essential, convenient, or suitable (do what is necessary to complete the project). Requisite, imperative, indispensable, required, needed, proper, useful, basic, key, called-for, important, substantive, obligatory, incumbent, prescribed, cardinal, needful, integral, vital, certain, fixed, ordained, demanded, strategic, urgent, rudimentary, fundamental, dictated, mandatory, unavoidable, designated, irresistible, wanted, fitting, prescriptive, ineluctable, expected, unpreventable, destined, sine qua non, prerequisite, crucial. See also unescapable, inevitable, compulsory. *Ant.* Optional.

Necessary and proper Appropriate and adapted to carrying a given object into effect. See appropriate (3).

Necessary party A party that must be joined in an action (as plaintiff or defendant) because complete relief cannot otherwise be obtained by the present parties; those persons who have such an interest in the controversy that a final judgment or decree cannot be made without either affecting their interests or leaving the controversy in such a condition that its final adjudication may be inconsistent with equity and good conscience. See party.

Necessitate, *v.* See require (1), demand (1), compel, force (4), obligate.

Necessities, *n.* See necessaries.

Necessitous, *adj.* Poverty-stricken (necessitous circumstances). Indigent, disadvantaged, impoverished, impecunious, destitute, "broke," distressed, penniless. See also needy. *Ant.* Wealthy.

Necessity, *n.* **1.** A power or impulse so great that it admits no choice of conduct (driven by necessity). Controlling force, irresistible impulse, compulsory factor, inevitability, unavoidability, fate, coercion, constraint, irresistibility, pressure, destiny. See also exigency, emergency. **2.** That which is indispensable (economic necessity). Precondition, requisite, prerequisite, sine qua non, essential, demand, exigency, requirement, basic ingredient, urgent component, integral element, mandatory factor, must-have, urgency, condition, crucial component, imperative, rudiment, fundamental detail. See also need (1).

"Neck," *v.* See caress, handle (2), touch.

Necropsy, *n.* See autopsy.

Need 1. *n.* The lack of something that is necessary or desired (a need for reform). Requirement, necessity, requisite, prerequisite, urgency, mandate, exigency, longing, deficiency, wish, shortcoming, precondition, scarcity, poverty, privation, dearth, indigence, absence, vacuum, insufficiency. **2.** *v.* To want or require (the plaintiff needs an extension). Desire, clamor for, have use for, demand, lack, yearn, necessitate, crave for, lust for, call for, hunger for, covet, hope for. *Ant.* Excess; reject.

Needful, *adj.* Requisite. See essential, indispensable, necessary.

Needle, *v.* See harass; incite, provoke; mock.

Needless, *adj.* Unnecessary; without any useful motive (needless expenditure). Silly, uncalled-for, excessive, redundant, useless, repetitious, nonessential, unneeded, pleonastic, dispensable, expendable, verbose, tautological, avoidable, wasteful, surplus, prodigal, extraneous, exorbitant, worthless, overabundant, inordinate, extra, unavailing, lavish, supererogatory. See also gratuitous (2), baseless, frivolous, superfluous. *Ant.* Essential.

Needy, *adj.* Very poor (needy family). Necessitous, poverty-stricken, destitute, impoverished, in want, strapped, bankrupt, penniless, impecunious, penurious, embarrassed, insolvent, pauperized, deprived, wanting, down and out, reduced. See also indigent. *Ant.* Prosperous.

Ne exeat A writ that forbids a person from leaving the country, state, or jurisdiction of the court.

Nefarious, *adj.* See bad (2), base (2), immoral, corrupt, malicious.

Negate, *v.* See cancel, annul; deny, contradict.

Negation, *n.* See nullification, cancellation, nullity, denial.

Negative, *adj.* **1.** Expressing or containing a denial or refusal (the court's answer was negative). Disapproving, dissenting, declining, canceling, prohibiting, disavowing, forbidding, vacating, converse, reverse, contradictory, opposed, objecting. See also opposite, inverse. **2.** Expressing an antagonistic or nonpositive perspective (negative attitude). Pessimistic, glum, uncooperative, unfriendly, bellicose, inimical, contrary, at odds, acrimonious, spurning, averse, adverse, factious, clashing, antipathetic, repugnant, argumentative, rancorous, belligerent, quarrelsome, cynical, recalcitrant, morose, complaining. See also litigious, contentious, hostile, incompatible. *Ant.* Approving; positive.

Negative averment An allegation of some substantive fact that is really affirmative in substance although negative in form. See averment, allegation.

Negative covenant A clause in an employment agreement or contract for the sale of a business, which prohibits the employee or seller from competing in the same area or market. See covenant, agreement.

Negative easement An easement that restrains a landowner from making a certain use of his or her land that would otherwise be lawful; the right of the owner of the dominant tenement to restrict the owner of the servient tenement in the exercise of certain property rights. See easement.

Negative income tax Money given by the government to individuals with income below a designated level.

Negative pregnant A negative statement that also implies an affirmative statement; a denial that admits important facts; a denial that is pregnant with an admission (e.g., "I deny that I owe $500" may be an admission that at least some amount is owed).

Negativism, *n.* See resistance, insubordination, depression; negative.

Neglect 1. *v.* To fail to do that which can be done and is required to be done (he neglected to secure the safety latch). Overlook, disregard, disdain, forget, skip, ignore, abandon, take no notice of, omit, gloss over, shirk, skimp, let ride, pretermit, renounce, be remiss, discount, lose sight of, scorn, make light of, forbear, forgo, reject, be lax, procrastinate. **2.** *n.* The failure to do what can be done and what is required to be done (neglect in caring for the child). Derelic-

Neglect

tion, default, omission, carelessness, laxity, disregard, oversight, inattention, heedlessness, negligence, unconcern, delinquency, nonfeasance, malfeasance, misfeasance, neglectfulness, inaction, indifference, procrastination, evasion, laziness, slovenliness, insolence, forgetfulness, abandonment, improvidence, irresponsibility, breach of duty, inattentiveness, thoughtlessness, noncompliance, nonperformance, nonpreparation, passivity, fecklessness, laissez-faire, recklessness, imprudence, remissness, slackness, sloth, laches, idleness, absentmindedness, inadvertence, lack of diligence. *Ant.* Complete; fulfillment.

Neglected child A child who is abandoned by its parent, who lacks proper parental care by reason of the fault or habits of the parent, or whose parent neglects or refuses to provide proper or necessary subsistence, education, or other care necessary for the health, morals, and well-being of the child. See abandonment.

Neglectful, *adj.* See careless, heedless, derelict (2), improvident.

Negligence, *n.* The failure to do what a reasonable person would have done under the same circumstances. A departure of the conduct that would be expected of a reasonably prudent person under like circumstances. A tort with the following elements: (a) a duty of reasonable care owed to the injured person, (b) a breach of this duty, (c) proximate cause, (d) actual damages. See neglect (2).

Negligence per se Negligence as a matter of law; acts or omissions that can be declared negligent without any argument or proof as to the particular surrounding circumstances either because (a) they are in violation of a statute or ordinance, or (b) they are so palpably opposed to the dictates of common prudence that it can be said without hesitation or doubt that no careful person would have acted or failed to act in the same way.

Negligent, *adj.* See neglect (2), negligence. Remiss, thoughtless, slack, indifferent, delinquent, unwary, irresponsible, forgetful, slovenly, inconsiderate, stupid, mindless, inattentive, unwatchful, neglectful, lax, loose, unobservant, oblivious, disregardful, inadvertent, unthinking, slipshod, rash, ill-considered, unheeding, injudicious, dilatory, indolent, sloppy, evasive. See also careless, heedless, reckless, derelict (2), improvident. *Ant.* Careful.

Negligent homicide A criminal offense committed by one whose negligence is the proximate result of another's death; the death of a human being through the instrumentality of a motor vehicle operated on a highway in a negligent manner. See homicide, manslaughter, crime, offense, vehicle.

Negligent misrepresentation A false statement made by someone who has no reasonable grounds for believing it to be true, although he or she does not know it is untrue, but does know that another is expected to rely on the statement and that the latter would be damaged if it is false. See fraud, deception; misrepresent.

Negligible, *adj.* See marginal, minimal, minor (2), nugatory, frivolous.

Negotiability, *n.* The legal character of being negotiable.

Negotiable, *adj.* **1.** Legally capable of being transferred by endorsement or delivery, e.g., checks, notes (negotiable bond). Transferable, assignable, marketable, alienable. **2.** Open to discussion (the wage demand was negotiable). Open to compromise, not final, subject to give and take, to be resolved, on the table. See also, arguable, debatable, controversial, moot; malleable. *Ant.* Non-negotiable.

Negotiable instrument An instrument, e.g., check, note, bill of exchange, that (a) is a writing signed by the maker or drawer, (b) contains an unconditional promise or order, (c) to pay a sum certain in money, (d) is payable on demand or at a definite time, (e) is payable to the bearer or to order, and (f) does not contain any other promise, order, obligation, or power given by the maker or drawer except as authorized by statute. See instrument, draft.

Negotiate, *v.* **1.** To bargain with another concerning a sale, settlement, or matter in contention (negotiate the terms of the contract). Come to terms, haggle, confer, adjust differences, arrange, dicker, compromise, deal, offer and counteroffer, debate, compose, agree, covenant, discuss; mediate, referee. See also bargain, arbitrate. **2.** To accomplish something; to pass through (negotiate the narrow roads). Surmount, succeed, engineer, manage, fulfill, orchestrate, perform, execute, cope, handle, cross, clear.

Negotiated plea The result of plea bargaining in which the accused agrees to plead guilty to the charge or to a reduced charge in return for a recommendation from the prosecutor for a less severe sentence. See sentence, bargain, punishment.

Negotiation, *n.* **1.** The transfer of an instrument through delivery (if the instrument is payable to bearer), or through endorsement and delivery (if it is payable to order) in such form that the transferee becomes a holder. See negotiable (1), negotiable instrument. **2.** The process of submitting and considering offers until a satisfactory offer is made and accepted. See negotiate (1), bargain.

Neighbor, *n.* One who lives in close proximity to another. Nearby dweller, borderer, abutter, adjoining property owner.

Neighborhood, *n.* The immediate vicinity (blight in the neighborhood). District, community, precinct, surroundings, surrounding area, domain, province, bailiwick, sphere, quarter, parish, confines, environs, environment, locale, region, locality, belt, territory, sector, ward. See also zone.

Neighborly, *adj.* See friendly, convivial, amicable, flexible.

Nemesis, *n.* See retribution, retaliation, punishment; defeat (2); nuisance.

Nemo No one; no man.

Neophyte, *n.* See amateur, beginner.

Nephew, *n.* See family, kindred; man.

Nepotism, *n.* Granting privileges, appointments, or other patronage to one's relatives by blood or marriage (blatant nepotism by the mayor). Cronyism, preferential treatment, partiality, partisanship, unfairness, injustice, leaning. See also favoritism, bias.

"Nerd," *n.* See boor, ass, idiot.

Nerve, *n.* See effrontery, animus (2), hostility; spirit (2), resolution (4), self-confidence; courageous.

Nervous, *adj.* See feverish, excitable, apprehensive, concerned, impatient, crabby, difficult (3); anxiety.

Nescience, *n.* See ignorance; innocence.

Nescient, *adj.* See blind (1), dumb, illiterate; innocent.

Nest, *n.* See asylum.

Nest egg, *n.* See fund (2).

Nestle, *v.* See lie (4); caress, touch (1), handle (2); inhabit, occupy, reside (1).

Net, *adj.* Pertaining to the amount that remains after all allowable deductions, e.g., charges, expenses, discounts, commissions, taxes (net return). Bottom-line, clear, realize in profit, winnings, earn. See also yield (2), gain (1), profit, return (5). *Ant.* Gross.

Net assets A bookkeeping balance obtained by subtracting a company's liabilities from its gross assets. See asset, gross (2), profit.

Net earnings The excess of the gross earnings over the expenditures incurred in producing them. See yield (2), gain (1), profit, return (5).

Net estate The gross estate less deductions for funeral expenses, claims against the estate, unpaid mortgages or indebtedness on property that is included in the gross estate, etc. See estate, yield (2), deduction (1).

Net income Income subject to taxation after allowable deductions and exemptions have been subtracted from gross or total income; what remains out of gross income after subtracting ordinary and necessary expenses incurred in efforts to

515

obtain or keep it. See income, yield (2), profit, deduction.

Net lease A lease in which the lessee pays not only rent, but also taxes, insurance, and maintenance charges. See lease, expense.

Net operating loss Loss before interest and income taxes but after depreciation produced by operating assets; the excess of the deductions allowed over the gross income. See loss, deduction.

Net proceeds Gross receipts less charges that can be deducted. See proceeds, income, profit, gross, deduction.

Net profits Profits after deductions of all expenses. See profit.

Nettle, *v.* See harass, disturb, provoke, outrage (2), exacerbate; nuisance.

Nettlesome, *adj.* See distressing, offensive.

Network, *n.* See organization; connection, contact; complication, confusion, mystery.

Net worth The total assets of a person or business less the total liabilities. See estate, effects, asset, worth.

Net worth method A method used by the IRS to reconstruct the income of a taxpayer who fails to keep adequate records: The gross income for the year is the increase in net worth of the taxpayer (i.e., assets in excess of liabilities) with appropriate adjustment for nontaxable receipts and nondeductible expenditures.

Neurology, *n.* The branch of medicine dealing with the nervous system and its disorders. See medicine, medical, treatment, doctor.

Neurosis, *n.* See illness, disease, insanity.

Neurotic, *adj.* See excitable, feverish; ill, sick; insanity.

Neuter, *adj.* See barren (2); impotence.

Neutral, *adj.* Not taking an active part with either of the contending sides (a neutral observer). Disinterested, unbiased, disengaged, nonpartisan, uninvolved, independent, withdrawn, unprejudiced, impersonal, detached, evenhanded, objective, nonaligned, remote, unaffected, nonfighting, aloof, open-minded; peaceful, pacifist, nonbelligerent, noncombatant. See also impartial, fair, dispassionate, indifferent, just. *Ant.* Participating.

Neutrality, *n.* The status of a nation that takes no part in a war between other nations (a movement away from neutrality). Nonalignment, impartiality, nonparticipation, nonbelligerence, abstinence.

Neutralization, *n.* Erasure or cancellation (neutralization of the testimony by contrary evidence). Undoing, counteraction, nullification, countervailing, counterbalancing, offsetting, normalization, balancing, incapacitation, frustration, checking, negation, invalidation. *Ant.* Corroboration.

Neutralize, *v.* See, offset, balance (3); counter, counteract, disable, frustrate, destroy, devastate.

Never, *adv.* Under no circumstances. Not at all, absolutely not, not ever.

Nevertheless, *adv.* Anyway, however. Nonetheless, regardless, notwithstanding, on the other hand, still, despite the fact.

New, *adj.* Recent; original; experienced for the first time (new ruling). Modern, late, novel, fashionable, up-to-the-minute, virgin, untried, green, topical, young, imaginative, unusual, unexpected, uncharted. See also maiden (1), current, fresh. *Ant.* Hackneyed.

Newborn, *n.* See child, minor (1); infancy (1).

Newcomer, *n.* See stranger, alien (3); amateur, beginner.

Newly discovered evidence Evidence discovered after the trial and not discoverable before the trial by the exercise of due diligence. See evidence, diligence, discover, discovery.

News, *n.* See information (2), notice (1), communication (2).

Newsboy, *n.* See seller, merchant.

Newsletter, *n.* See journal, circular (2), report (1).

Newsman, *n.* See press, newspaper.

Newspaper, *n.* A publication, usually in sheet form, intended for general circulation and published regularly at short intervals, containing information and editorials on current events and news of general interest. Tabloid, weekly, daily, gazette, organ, sheet. See also press (1), journal, circular (2).

Newspeak, *n.* See ambiguity.

Newsworthy, *adj.* See important, intriguing, interest (5), note (4).

New Testament, *n.* See bible, holy, religion, God.

New trial See motion for a new trial.

New York Stock Exchange An unincorporated association of member firms that handle the purchase and sale of securities for themselves and for customers. See exchange (3), securities.

Next, *adj.* **1.** Immediately following (the next case). Following, latter, ensuing, consequent. See also after, subsequent. **2.** Nearest (next door). Closest, adjacent, abutting, proximate, contiguous, bordering, nearby, neighboring. *Ant.* Prior; distant.

Next friend Someone specially appointed by the court to look after the interests of a person who cannot act on his or her own (e.g., a minor). See guardian, amicus curiae.

Next of kin 1. The nearest blood relatives of the decedent. **2.** Those who would inherit from the decedent if he or she died intestate, whether or not they are blood relatives. See blood (1), collateral line, consanguinity, family, heir, kindred (1).

Nexus, *n.* See link (1), connection, contact.

Nibble, *v.* See eat; food; iota.

Nice, *adj.* See amicable, cooperative (2), friendly, kind, attractive, enjoyable, intriguing, careful, precise.

Nicety, *n.* See difference, detail.

Niche, *n.* See alcove; occupation; place, zone.

Nick, *v.* See cut, maim, mar, injure.

"Nickel-and-dime," *adj., v.* See minor, petty; diminish.

Nickname, *n.* See name; alias.

Nicotine, *n.* See poison; cigarette; addict, drug.

Niece, *n.* See family, kindred; woman.

"Nifty," *adj.* See outstanding (2), exceptional, best, beautiful, attractive.

Niggardly, *adj.* See stingy; avaricious; economical, small, petty.

Niggling, *adj.* See petty; difficult (3), precise (2), critical (2).

Night, *n.* See evening, sunset, nighttime.

Nightclub, *n.* See inn; merchant; entertainment.

Nightlife, *n.* See amusement, entertainment; debauchery.

Nightly, *adj.* See daily, habitual.

Nightmare, *n.* See dream, hallucination.

Nighttime, *n.* The period between sunset and sunrise when there is not enough daylight to discern a person's face; 30 minutes after sunset to 30 minutes before sunrise (service during nighttime is prohibited). Twilight, dusk, dark, bedtime, nightfall. See also evening, sunset.

Nihilist, *n.* One who advocates the destruction of present political, religious, and social institutions. Revolutionary, agitator, iconoclast, syndicalist, reactionary, insurrectionist, firebrand, extremist. See also anarchist, wrongdoer. *Ant.* Conformist.

Nihil obstat, *n.* See approval.

Nil, *n.* Nothing (his contribution was nil). Zero, naught, "goose egg," cipher, wind. See also nullity.

Nimble, *adj.* See active (3), speedy.

Nip, *v.* See cut; check.

Nippy, *adj.* See cold, climate.

Nirvana, *n.* See heaven, happiness, afterlife; oblivion.

Nisi, *adj.* Unless.

Nisi decree See rule nisi.

Nit-pick, *v.* See hedge, quibble, complain (2); stickler.

Nitroglycerin, *n.* See weapon, arms, incendiary.

Nitroglycerine charge See Allen charge.

NLRB See National Labor Relations Board.

No, *n.* See rejection.

No bill In the opinion of the grand jury, the evidence is insufficient to justify a formal charge or indictment. See evidence, indictment.

Nobility, *n.* See aristocracy.

Noble, *adj.* See elevated, just, moral, good (2), honest, best, extraordinary.

Nobody, *n.* See nonentity; nullity; nil.

Nocturnal, *adj.* See nighttime.

Nocuous, *adj.* See harmful, injurious, deleterious, bad.

Nod, *n.* See motion (2), signal (3), gesture; approval, assent.

No fault 1. A type of automobile insurance in which each person's own insurance company pays for injury or damage up to a certain limit regardless of whether its insured was actually at fault. See insurance. **2.** No fault also refers to a divorce granted on a ground other than the marital fault of either side. See ground, incompatible (1), irreconcilable differences, living separate and apart.

Noise, *n.* Sound. Blast, roar, trumpet, honk, clamor, din, screech, clang, toot, bellow, scream, pop, explosion, wail, peal, cry, bleep, buzz, boom, clap, shot, detonation, cackle, chime, chirp, chug, clatter, click, clink, cluck, drone, hum, murmur, hiss, whir. See also racket (1), nuisance.

Noisy, *adj.* Clamorous. Boisterous, rackety, hectic, deafening, blaring, thundering, tumultuous, uproarious, strident. See also vociferous, wild, blatant, flamboyant, incorrigible, disorderly.

Nolle prosequi (nol-pros), *n.* A formal entry in the record by the prosecuting officer that he or she will not prosecute the case further. The entry is also used to indicate that civil cases will not be pursued further. See dismissal, cessation, quash.

No-load, *adj.* Sold without a commission—at net asset value.

Nolo contendere, *n.* "I will not contest it." A type of plea in a criminal case in which the defendant does not admit or deny the charges. The effect of the plea, however, is similar to a plea of guilty in that the defendant can be sentenced to prison, fined, etc. The trial judge must consent to the defendant's use of the plea of nolo contendere. See plea, punishment.

Nol-pros, *v.* See nolle prosequi.

Nomad, *n.* See alien; tramp.

Nomadic, *adj.* See migratory; voyage, travel, tramp.

Nom de plume, *n.* See alias, name.

Nomenclature, *n.* See language, term of art.

Nominal, *adj.* **1.** In name only; not real or substantial (nominal officer of the company). Titular, pretended, token, pseudo, so-called, self-styled, alleged, honorary, ostensible, theoretical, puppet, formal, supposed, would-be. See also symbolic. **2.** Trifling (nominal amount). Insignificant, trivial, very small, inconsequential, slight, insignificant, picayune, negligible, cheap; inexpensive, moderate. See also petty. *Ant.* Actual; excessive.

Nominal consideration Consideration bearing no relation to the real value of the contract or article. See consideration, worth (1).

Nominal damages A trifling sum awarded to the plaintiff because there was no substantial loss or injury to be compensated, although a technical invasion of rights did occur. See damages.

Nominate, *v.* To name or propose for an election or appointment (the governor nominated her for the bench). Suggest, recommend, submit, offer, present, designate, appoint, empower, commission, choose, assign, select, ordain, tag, vote, install, invest, deputize, elevate, authorize. *Ant.* Withdraw.

Nomination, *n.* See appointment; appoint, nominate.

Nominee, *n.* **1.** One who has been nominated or proposed for an office or appointment (nominee for the chief judgeship). Aspirant, candidate, competitor, entrant, runner, bidder. See also appointee. **2.** One designated to act for another as a representative in a limited sense. See agent (1).

Non-access, *n.* A defense in a paternity case in which the alleged father asserts the absence of opportunities for sexual intercourse with the mother. See evidence, remote, coitus.

Nonacquiescence (non acqu.; NA), *n.* A disagreement by the IRS on the result reached by the U.S. Tax Court. See rejection, disagreement.

Nonage, *n.* The status of being under legal age (annulment on the ground of nonage). See infancy, minor (1), minority (1).

Nonappearance, *n.* The failure to appear within the designated time limit (dismissal for nonappearance). Default, truancy, "no-show," nonattendance, absenteeism. See also absence.

Nonchalant, *adj.* See informal, casual, indifferent.

Noncombatant, *n.* A person connected with the armed forces for a purpose other than fighting (e.g., chaplain, surgeon; conscientious objector, CO).

Noncommissioned officer An officer of the armed forces (e.g., sergeant) who holds his or her rank by appointment by a superior officer rather than by commission. See military, martial, sailor.

Noncommittal, *adj.* See circumspect, suspicious (1), cautious; silent, mum.

Noncompliance, *n.* See nonperformance, dissent (1), insubordination; nonconforming.

Non compos mentis, *adj.* Not sound of mind (she was non compos mentis at the time she signed). Insane, mentally deranged, crazy, psychotic, demented, abnormal, mad, moronic, simple-minded, distraught, disoriented, lunatic, crazed, mentally incompetent, of unsound mind, mentally ill. See also insanity. *Ant.* Sane.

Nonconforming, *adj.* Not consistent or conforming with accepted customs, practices, or standards (nonconforming structure). Out of line, contrary, discordant, at odds, conflicting, deviating, unorthodox, noncompliant, dissenting, alien, unique, differing, unconventional, defiant, incongruous. See also irregular, inconsistent, different, deviant (1), anomalous, extreme, extraordinary. *Ant.* Conforming.

Nonconforming use A use that does not comply with present zoning provisions but which existed lawfully and was created in good faith prior to the enactment of the zoning provisions; a use permitted by zoning statutes or ordinances even though similar uses are not permitted in the same area. See zoning, use (2).

Nonconformist, *n.* One who refuses to join in the established forms of custom, belief, styles, rules, etc. (a nonconformist in investment practices). Loner, rebel, individualist, original, dissenter, maverick, heretic, free spirit, eccentric, radical, revolutionary, peculiarity, protester, renegade, iconoclast, rarity, bohemian, oddity, freethinker, abnormality, dissident, nonbeliever, deviator, secessionist. *Ant.* Follower.

Nonconformity, *n.* See conflict (1), dissent (1), insubordination; nonperformance.

Noncontestability clause

Noncontestability clause See incontestability clause.

Noncontestable, *adj.* Pertaining to that which cannot be disputed (noncontestable clause). Incontrovertible, undeniable, nonrefutable, nonchallengeable, undisputed, uncontested, nondebatable. See also incontestable, noncontestable, indubitable, certain (3), clear (1), definite. *Ant.* Disputable.

Noncooperative, *adj.* See incorrigible, disobedient, hostile, negative (2).

Noncumulative dividends If dividends are not paid in a given year or period, they are gone forever or lost; there is no obligation to pay them when the next dividend is paid. See dividend, cumulative, cumulative preferred dividend.

Nondeductible, *adj.* See payable, taxable.

Nondenominational, *adj.* See general; religious, God, holy; secular.

Nondescript, *adj.* See ordinary, indefinite, ambiguous, obscure.

Nondisclosure, *n.* The failure to reveal facts without necessarily concealing them. See conceal, concealment, silence, mum.

None, *pron.* See void (3), vacant, barren.

Nonentity, *n.* A nobody, lightweight, zero, "schlep," milquetoast. See also, nullity, cipher (2), boor, idiot.

Nonessential, *adj.* See extraneous, expendable, irrelevant, frivolous, petty, minor.

Nonetheless, *adv.* See nevertheless.

Nonexistent, *adj.* See absent, void (3), null and void, vacant, illusory, fictitious.

Nonfeasance, *n.* Nonperformance of an act that should be performed; neglect of duty (nonfeasance in office). Nonfulfillment, disregard, omission, negligence, dereliction, delinquency, laxity, oversight, failure, exclusion, passing over, ignoring, avoidance, slip, pretermission. See also neglect (2), default, deficiency, wrong, violation. *Ant.* Execution.

Nonfulfillment, *n.* See default, nonperformance, deficiency, nonfeasance, neglect (2).

Nonjoinder, *n.* The failure to join a person to a suit as plaintiff or defendant who ought to have been joined. See joinder.

Nonjudgmental, *adj.* See objective (2), dispassionate, disinterested, neutral, impartial.

Nonmailable, *adj.* Pertaining to letters and parcels that by law are excluded from transportation in the U.S. mail because of size, obscene content, etc. See improper, offensive, obscene.

Nonmerchantable title See merchantable title.

Non-negotiable, *adj.* Not capable of passing title or property by indorsement and delivery. See negotiable.

Non obstante veredicto Notwithstanding the verdict. See judgment notwithstanding the verdict.

Nonpartisan, *adj.* See neutral, objective, fair.

Nonpayment, *n.* The neglect, failure, or refusal to pay a debt (suit for nonpayment). Delinquency, evasion, default, dishonor, repudiation, oversight, breach, omission, being in arrears, arrearage, nonfeasance, nonfulfillment, remiss, dereliction, nonobservance, lapse, reneging. *Ant.* Satisfaction.

Nonperformance, *n.* The neglect, failure, or refusal to perform an act stipulated to be done (nonperformance of the contract). Dereliction, delinquency, nonfeasance, neglect, omission, nonfulfillment, nonobservance, evasion, noncompliance, disregard, infringement, repudiation, transgression, infraction, contravention, encroachment, nonadherence, distortion, laxity, abandonment, desertion. See also default, breach. *Ant.* Compliance.

Nonplus, *v.* See confuse, amaze, surprise.

Nonproductive, *adj.* See barren, worthless, fallow; impotence.

Nonprofessional, *adj.* See amateur, beginner, paralegal, paraprofessional.

Nonprofit, *adj.* Not run for profit (nonprofit venture). Eleemosynary, public service, humanitarian, philanthropic, altruistic, almsgiving, munificent, religious, educational, scientific, humane, unselfish, benign, magnanimous, fraternal, generous. See also charitable, benevolent. *Ant.* Commercial.

Nonprofit corporation A corporation that does not distribute any of its income to its members, directors, or officers; a corporation organized and operated exclusively for one or more of the following purposes: religious, charitable, scientific, testing for public safety, literary, educational, prevention of cruelty to children or animals, or fostering national or international sports. See corporation, charity.

Non prosequitur, *n.* A judgment against a plaintiff who fails to appear. See involuntary nonsuit, dismissal, nonsuit.

Nonrecourse, *n.* The status of a person who holds an instrument, which gives him or her no legal right against prior endorsers or the drawer to compel payment if the instrument is dishonored.

Nonresident, *n.* One who does not reside in the jurisdiction; one who is not an inhabitant of the state of the forum (service of process on the nonresident). Nonoccupant, nondomiciliary, noncitizen.

Nonresistance, *n.* See obedience, acceptance, compliance.

Nonsectarian, *adj.* See general, religious, God, holy, secular.

Nonsense, *n.* See balderdash, non sequitur; absurd.

Nonsensical, *adj.* See absurd, irrational, illogical, impossible, baseless, capricious.

Non sequitur, *n.* A statement or conclusion that does not logically follow (it is a non sequitur to say that she is a drug addict because she is a Republican). Faulty reasoning, false logic, fallacious argument, sophistry, specious argument, circular reasoning, fallacy, contradiction, flawed deduction, unwarranted conclusion, loose reasoning. See also illogical, irrational.

Nonsexist, *adj.* See neutral, objective (2), fair.

Nonstop, *adv., adj.* See habitual, daily, chronic, constant (1).

Nonsuit, *n.* A termination or dismissal of an action when the plaintiff is unable to prove his or her case, defaults, fails to prosecute, etc. (suffer a nonsuit). See involuntary nonsuit, voluntary nonsuit, dismissal.

Nonsupport, *n.* The unreasonable failure or neglect to support those to whom an obligation of support is owed (nonsupport of children). Failure to maintain, failure to nourish and nurture, noncontribution, omission, default, failure to provide sustenance, nonfeasance, irresponsibility. See also neglect (2), abandonment.

Nonuse, *n.* The failure to use (nonuse of the premises). Forbearance, abstinence, disuse, nonutilization. See also abstention.

Nonverbal, *adj.* See body language, gesture, manifestation, communication.

Nonviable, *adj.* See impracticable, absurd, impossible, barren.

Nonviolent, *adj.* See peaceable, amicable.

Nonworking, *adj.* See dormant; broken; loiter.

Nook, *n.* See alcove.

No-par, *adj.* Without par value. See par value.

Norm, *n.* See maxim, measure (1); mean (1).

Normal, *adj.* **1.** Conforming to a standard; not deviating from an established norm (normal procedures). Standardized, routine, regular, ordinary, average, typical, representative, orthodox, expected, customary, accepted, natural, conventional, common, familiar, traditional, prevailing, usual, habitual, commonplace, universal, accustomed, general, par. **2.** Average (normal for her age). Median, mean, center, reasonable, consistent, middling, even. **3.** Without mental problems (normal condition). Sane, sound, in shape, healthy, well-adjusted, lucid, sensible, responsible, rational. *Ant.* Abnormal.

Normality, *n.* See sanity (1), health.

Normalization, *n.* See reconciliation, harmony, agreement.

Normalize, *v.* See conform, regulate, stabilize, mitigate.

Normal school, *n.* A school that trains teachers. See school.

Normative, *adj.* See measure (1).

Norris-La Guardia Act A federal statute restricting the use of injunctions by federal courts in labor disputes. See union.

Noscitur a sociis "It is known by its associates." A guide to interpreting written language: The meaning of questionable words or phrases may be determined by the context of the words or phrases associated with them in the text.

Nostalgia, *n.* See memory.

"Nosy," *adj.* See prying, officious; eavesdrop.

Notable, *adj.* See conspicuous, outstanding (2), notorious, important, great, popular, historic, blatant.

Notarial, *adj.* Performed or taken by a notary (notarial acts).

Notarize, *v.* See certify, attest.

Notary public, *n.* One whose function is to administer oaths, certify documents, take affidavits, attest to the authenticity of signatures, etc.

Notate, *v.* See note (6), record (4).

Notation, *n.* See note (2), record (1), communication.

Notch, *n.* See degree (1).

Note 1. *n.* A two-party instrument made by the maker and payable to the payee, which is negotiable if signed by the maker containing an unconditional promise to pay a sum certain in money on demand at a definite time, to order or bearer (a $1,000 note). Check, negotiable instrument, money order, negotiable paper, bank note, bill, draft, promissory note, voucher, IOU. **2.** *n.* An informal statement in writing (he sent a note asking for payment). Letter, memo, memorandum, notification, declaration, announcement, dispatch, message, reminder, notation, record, missive, card, communiqué, acknowledgment, correspondence, epistle, warning, inscription, proclamation, admonishment. See also communication. **3.** *n.* A formal commentary (she wrote a note on the case for the law review). Commentary, comment, explanation, criticism, brief, annotation, footnote, exegesis, gloss, critique, scholium, explication, assessment, abstract. **4.** *n.* Distinction (a person of note). Importance, significance, prominence, renown, esteem, celebrity, power, influence, merit, fame, repute, name, sway, nobility, notability, reputation, consequence. See also eminence. **5.** *n.* Attention (take note of the discrepancy). Heed, notice, regard, care, guard, thought, vigilance, observation, cognizance, recognition, perception, awareness. **6.** *v.* To put down in writing; to indicate (note the distinction). Register, chronicle, acknowledge, mark, witness, recognize, mention, denote, refer to, be aware of, comment on, appreciate, jot down, document, take cognizance of, be conscious of, docket, hearken to, catalogue, insert, pencil, allude to, reveal, explain, inspect, glance at, observe, contemplate, monitor, review, study, visualize, illustrate, regard, infer, express, examine. See also record (4).

Notebook, *n.* See record (1), biography.

Noted, *adj.* See conspicuous, outstanding (2), elevated, great, popular, notorious; important, historic; blatant; novel.

Noteworthy, *adj.* See noted.

Not guilty A jury verdict acquitting the accused; a plea entered by the accused to a criminal charge. See innocent (1), adjudication; acquit.

Nothing, *n.* See nullity, nil; void (3), vacant, barren, oblivion.

Notice 1. *n.* Knowledge of facts that would naturally lead an honest and prudent person to make inquiry—this does not necessarily mean knowledge of all the facts (the wrapping put him on notice that the product was not new). Information, news, intelligence, discovery, cognizance, advice, announcement, notification, mention, disclosure, revelation, report, message, facts, tiding, inkling, publicity, specification, warning, forewarning, caution, hint, communication, intercommunication, promulgation, transmission of information, release, clue, annunciation, communiqué, enlightenment, apprising, word, indication, recognition, circumspection, admonishment, implication, caveat, enunciation, reminder, tip-off, bulletin, dispatch, allusion, broadcast, publication, citation, bulletin, observation, discernment, thought, surveillance, pamphlet, poster, attention, guard, vigil, perception, referral. **2.** *v.* To become aware of (notice the inconsistency in the testimony). Observe, see, sense, identify, mark, note, pay attention to, take cognizance of, heed, listen, discriminate, discover, bear in mind, acknowledge, examine, scrutinize, perceive, decipher, detect, glance at, allude to, refer to, appreciate, witness, inspect, assess, watch, take into account, realize, become conscious of, make out, remark, elucidate, distinguish, understand, regard. *Ant.* Ignorance; ignore.

Noticeable, *adj.* See appreciable, palpable, conspicuous, manifest, clear.

Notice of appeal A document filed with the appellate court and served on the opposing party, giving notice of an intention to appeal. See appeal, file.

Notice of appearance A written notice filed by a party or by its attorney that it is making an appearance in an action. See appearance, attorney, file.

Notice recording statute An unrecorded conveyance or other instrument is invalid as against a subsequent bona fide purchaser for value and without notice. See race-notice recording statutes, race recording statutes, recording statutes.

Notice to quit A written notice given by a landlord to the tenant stating that the landlord wishes to repossess the leased premises and that the tenant should leave at the end of the term or immediately if the tenancy is at will or by sufferance. See quit, dispossess.

Notification, *n.* See notice (1).

Notify, *v.* To inform by words or writing, in person, by message, or by any signs that are understood (notify the debtor of the default). Give notice to, enlighten, warn, apprise, make known to, advise, serve notice, acquaint, instruct, forewarn, counsel, send word, call attention to, tell, remind, broadcast, publicize, alert, voice, communicate, promulgate, contact, divulge, announce, relate, brief, mention, caution, convey, telephone, declare, transmit, post. See also publish.

Notion, *n.* See belief, opinion (2), conviction (2), concept; caprice, whim, impulse.

Notoriety, *n.* **1.** The state of being universally well known (gain notoriety). Publicity, renown, celebrity, popularity, fame, public notice, significance, distinction, prominence, conspicuousness, eminence, flagrancy, recognition. **2.** Bad reputation (the notoriety following the conviction). Shame, reproach, infamy, stain, dishonor, disrepute, bad odor, degradation, scandal, censure, stigma, discredit, opprobrium, disfavor, indignity, ill repute, odium. *Ant.* Inconspicuousness; esteem.

Notorious, *adj.* **1.** Well-known or widely known (notorious delinquency). Preeminent, generally known, conspicuous, on everyone's mind, notable, open, illustrious, famous, celebrated, recognized, glaring, blatant, flagrant, popular, arrant, outstanding. **2.** Infamous (notorious behavior). Ignoble, contemptible, scandalous, shameful, discreditable, ignominious, outrageous, villainous, degraded, odious, shocking, opprobrious, bizarre, disgraceful, stigmatized, egregious, outcast, unseemly. *Ant.* Inconspicuous; respected.

Notorious cohabitation Two persons openly living together while not being married to each other. See cohabitation.

Notwithstanding, *adv., prep.* See although, nevertheless.

Nourish, *v.* See nurture, maintain (2), minister, foster, back.

Nourishment, *n.* See food, necessaries.

NOV See judgment notwithstanding the verdict.

Novation, *n.* The substitution by mutual agreement of one debtor for another or of one creditor for another, whereby the old debt is extinguished; the substitution of a new contract, debt, or obligation for an existing one between the same or different parties. See replacement.

Novel, *adj.* New (novel question). Unique, unconventional, different, innovative, singular, unprecedented, unfamiliar, distinctive, unusual, foreign, eccentric, odd, untested, creative, irregular, modern, pristine, untried, peculiar, remarkable, startling, anomalous, uncommon, surprising, advanced, arresting, exotic, noteworthy, experimental, uncharacteristic, regenerated, recent, strange. See also avant-garde, original, extraordinary, exceptional; book (4). *Ant.* Conventional.

Novelist, *n.* See author; book (4).

Novelty, *n.* That which has not been known before (no patent was issued for want of novelty). Distinctiveness, uniqueness, innovation, originality, invention, peculiarity, newness, unfamiliarity, rarity, variety, specialty, unorthodoxy, departure; gadget, gimmick, contrivance, fad.

Novena, *n.* See prayer (2), worship; religious, holy, God, church.

Novice, *n.* See beginner, amateur, intern, assistant.

Now, *adv.* At the present time; at a time contemporaneous with something done (the director wanted it now). At this time, at present, presently, at once, without delay, straightaway, this moment. See also immediately, summarily.

N.O.W. account Negotiable Order of Withdrawal: an interest-bearing checking account. See account.

Noxious, *adj.* See harmful, deleterious, injurious, poisonous.

N.R. New Reports.

N.S. New Series.

NTSB National Traffic Safety Board.

Nuance, *n.* See connotation, suggestion, innuendo; intimate (6); degree.

Nub, *n.* See essence, center, gist (1).

Nucleus, *n.* See commencement, birth (1); gravamen, foundation, essence (1), gist (1); center.

Nude, *adj.* Naked; lacking an essential (nude contract). See naked; bare.

Nude pact A pact without consideration; an executory contract without consideration; a naked promise.

Nudge, *v.* See touch; push; signal (3).

Nudum pactum A promise or undertaking made without any consideration for it; a voluntary promise without consideration other than mere goodwill or natural affection.

Nugatory, *adj.* Without force, validity, or vitality (nugatory agreement). Worthless, invalid, trifling, futile, unenforceable, useless, frivolous, inconsequential, insignificant, ineffective, fatuous, void, irrelevant, superficial, null, inadequate, inane, slight, jejune, unavailing, incompetent, valueless, inoperative, meritless, picayune, idle, superfluous, groundless, slim, inappreciable, incidental, piddling, flimsy, unimportant, trite, banal, meaningless, nit-picking, empty, mediocre, shallow, abortive, meager. See also petty, barren. *Ant.* Effective.

Nugget, *n.* See mass (1), bulk (1).

Nuisance, *n.* An unreasonable interference with the use and enjoyment of land (see private nuisance); an unreasonable interference with a right that is common to the public (see public nuisance). Annoyance, vexation, affliction, pest, aggravation, distress, burden, tribulation, handicap, intrusion, pestilence, irritant, load, bore, plague, trouble, provocation, blight, headache, devilment, curse, scourge, molestation, trespass, hindrance, disturbance, trial, grievance, exasperation, displeasure, problem, salt in the wound, pique, hounding, nettling, pestering, bothering, taunting, inconvenience, misfortune. See also obstacle. *Ant.* Benefit.

Nuisance per se An act, occurrence, or structure that is a nuisance at all times and under all circumstances regardless of location or surroundings.

Null and void Pertaining to that which binds no one (the contract was null and void). Empty, without significance, pointless, valueless, ineffectual, unimportant, invalid, of no account, sterile, abortive, vain, trivial, hollow, dead, rescinded, defunct, revoked, annulled, quashed, abrogated, vacated, overruled, defeated, negated, powerless, extinguished, suspended, set aside, abolished, obliterated, extinct, omitted, without force, deleted, erased, superseded, nonexistent, inconsequential, superficial, useless, impotent, inane, negligible, inoperative. See also worthless, nugatory, frivolous, barren, baseless. *Ant.* Effective.

Nullification, *n.* The state or condition of being without legal effect or status; the process of rendering something void (nullification of the board's authority). Cancellation, voidance, revocation, repeal, retraction, abrogation, annulment, suspension, cessation, disestablishment, vitiation, defeasance, quashing, reversal, withdrawal, recall, disavowal, discontinuance, repudiation, neutralization, termination, elimination, expunging, annihilation, extermination, renouncement, extirpation, invalidation, rescinding, rescission, discharge, veto, frustration, destruction. *Ant.* Implementation.

Nullify, *v.* See cancel, annul, rescind.

Nullity, *n.* That which can be treated as having absolutely no legal force or effect, as though it never took place (nullity of the marriage). Erasure, naught, nothingness, nihilism, void, blank, nonexistence, inoperativeness, negation, null and void, nonreality, vacuum, futility, invalidity, nonentity.

Nullius filius The son of no one; an illegitimate child. See bastard (1).

Numb, *adj.* See oblivious, dead.

Number, *n.* **1.** Digit. Figure, integer, numeral, cipher. **2.** See amount, aggregate; extent, portion.

Numbers game, *n.* The player wages that on a given day, a certain series of digits will appear or "come out." The winning number is determined by a set process (e.g., the last three digits of the pari-mutuel payoff totals of particular races at a designated racetrack). See gambling.

Numerical, *adj.* Pertaining to numbers (numerical symbols). Arithmetical, statistical. See also mathematical.

Numerous, *adj.* See many, divers, incalculable; big.

Numismatic, *adj.* See coin, currency.

Nun, *n.* A woman in a religious order. See religion, church, holy, woman.

Nunc pro tunc Now for then; although a thing is done now, it will have the same force and effect as though it had been done when it should have been done; with retroactive effect. See retroactive.

Nuncupative will An oral will declared or dictated by the testator before witnesses; a will by verbal declaration. See will, oral.

Nuptial, *adj.* Pertaining to marriage (nuptial vows). Marital, spousal, matrimonial, coupled, wedding, hymeneal, conjugal, bridal, wedded, connubial, married.

Nurse, *v., n.* See minister (3), nurture; medicine, medical, treatment.

Nursery, *n.* See school.

Nurture, *v.* To bring up or train (nurtured the child). Give nourishment, feed, educate, raise, protect, aid, nurse, tutor, foster, cultivate, instruct, school, direct, succor, sponsor, support, maintain, assist, improve, provide for, acculturate, mother, strengthen, abet, discipline, mold, parent, advocate, cherish, enrich, promote, rear, further, sustain, harbor, prepare. See also minister (3). *Ant.* Abandon.

"Nut"

"Nut," *n.* See maniac; ass, idiot, boor.

Nutrition, *n.* See food, health, necessaries.

Nymphomania, *n.* Excessive sexual desires of a woman. See prostitute, prurient.

NYSE See New York Stock Exchange.

Oaf *n.* See ass, boor, idiot.

Oasis, *n.* See island; asylum.

Oath, *n.* An affirmation of the truth of a statement (loyalty oath). Solemn declaration, attestation, word, avowal, averment, vow, asseveration, pronouncement, deposition. See also warranty, guarantee, pledge (1), obligation, covenant, assurance (1), adjuration, promise (1), profession.

Obdurate, *adj.* See contumacious, wild (3), incorrigible, inflexible, callous, disobedient.

Obedience, *n.* The performance of what is required or abstinence from what is prohibited by authority (obedience to the court's decree). Yielding, subservience, fidelity, deference, subjection, observance, submissiveness, respect, adaptability, docility, obeisance, self-effacement, dutifulness, tractability, conformance, meekness, passiveness, malleability, prostration, fawning, ingratiation, reverence, giving in, capitulation, tameness, compliance, subjugation, abandonment, servitude, slavery, captivity, complaisance, resignation, passivity, pliancy. See also compliance (1), conformity, servitude (1), discipline (1), loyalty, acquiescence, fealty, allegiance. *Ant.* Defiance.

Obedient, *adj.* See amenable (2), flexible, cooperative (2), faithful (1), good (2), passive (2), loyal.

Obeisance, *n.* See obedience, homage (1).

Obese, *adj.* See corpulent.

Obey, *v.* See accede (1), comply, conform (1), observe (1), perform, abide (1), follow (1).

Obfuscate, *v.* See cloud (3), confuse, conceal, obscure (3).

Obfuscation, *n.* See vagueness, pretext, mystery, concealment; fraud.

Obiter dictum, *n.* Language in an opinion that is not necessary for the decision of the case; a remark of the court that does not directly bear on the issue before it and therefore is not binding as precedent.

Obituary, *n.* See list, death.

Object, *v.,* **object,** *n.* **1.** *v.* To express disapproval; to consider something improper or illegal and ask the court to take action accordingly (counsel objected to the question). Oppose, call in question, take exception, resist, be adverse, quarrel, complain, dissent, remonstrate, disagree, attack, except, controvert, condemn, find fault with, criticize, "knock," argue against, rebut, negate, expostulate, contravene, eschew, inveigh, balk. See also disallow, reprimand, demonstrate (3), challenge (1), demur, dispute (2), protest (3), refuse (1), disapprove (2), mind (3). **2.** *n.* The end aimed at; the thing sought to be accomplished (the object of the legislation). Goal, target, design, objective, intention, motive, aspiration, scheme, prize, desire, import, mark. See also meaning, intent (1), cause (4), destination (1), ground (1), purpose (1), reason (1), aim (3), end (1), point (4), pursuit (2). **3.** *n.* A material thing (the object was closely examined). Body, substance, it, phenomenon, artifact, element, stuff, contrivance, reality, manifestation, form, device, gadget. See also item, res, content (1), entity, article (2). **4.** *n.* See

527

victim. *Ant.* Acquiesce (1).

Objection, *n.* That which is presented in opposition; the act of objecting (she registered her objection). Disapproval, disagreement, dissatisfaction, criticism, complaint, dissension, contradiction, demurrer, remonstrance, rebuttal, defense, expostulation, dispute, dislike, refutation, reply. See also exception (1), reservation (3), denial (1), grievance (2), challenge (4), dissent (1), protest (1), refusal, rejection, question (3). *Ant.* Endorsement.

Objectionable, *adj.* See filthy, repugnant (1), repulsive, bad (1), odious, obscene, obnoxious, offensive, inadmissible, improper, immoral.

Objective 1. *adj.* Real; observable by the senses; existing outside the mind (objective symptom). Concrete, factual, tangible, physical, outward, material, external, phenomenal, perceptible. See also literal (1), actual (1, 2), corporeal, real (2), substantial (1). **2.** *adj.* Unbiased (an objective opinion). Detached, uncolored, unprejudiced, open-minded, impersonal, unswayed, judicial, fair-minded. See also dispassionate, just, fair, disinterested, rational, reasonable, equitable (1), neutral, honest, indifferent (1), impartial; fairly. **3.** *n.* Goal (the objective of the commission). Target, intention, scheme, destination, ambition, mission, mark, termination, desire, prize, plan, dream, wish, aspiration, hope. See also purpose (1), pursuit (2), purport (1), object (2), intent (1), motive, design (2), cause (4), reason (1), aim (3), end (1), resolution (3), policy (1), point (4), platform (1). *Ant.* Subjective (1); prejudiced (2).

Objectivity, *n.* See justice (2), fairness, right (4), equity (2); fairly.

Objector, *n.* See dissenter; nonconformist.

Oblation, *n.* See worship, prayer (2), offering (2).

Obligate, *v.* To bind or place under an obligation (the executor obligated the estate to make the payment). See force (4), require (1), commit (3), command (3), make (2), bind (1), commission (5), entail (3), engage (4), burden (3), mortgage, pledge (2), compel, pawn (1), constrain (1), guarantee (2), promise (2), prescribe.

Obligated, *adj.* See responsible (1), answer (4), liable (1), bound (1), articled, accountable (1).

Obligation, *n.* **1.** Any duty imposed by law, contract, morals, or social relations (an obligation to refrain from deceptive advertising). Responsibility, necessity, indebtedness, trust, task. See also onus, requirement, liability (1), compulsion (1), complaint (2), enforcement, burden (1), charge (8, 13), cloud (1), duty (1), constraint (1), allegiance, arrearages. **2.** A formal and binding agreement or acknowledgment of a liability to pay a certain sum or do a specific thing (interest paid on an obligation). Arrangement, compact, pledge, stipulation, assurance, security, surety, avowal, oath. See also debit, debt, guarantee (1), warranty, commitment (3), assignment (3), covenant, bond, agreement (1), contract (1), provision (3), promise, proviso; accountable (1).

Obligation of contract The duty of performance including the means of enforcement.

Obligatory, *adj.* Compulsory (attendance was obligatory). Required, mandated, unavoidable, coerced, categorical, commanded, necessitated, prerequisite, inescapable, requisite, enforced, unqualified, de rigueur, compelling, prescriptive, essential. See also involuntary, necessary, binding, compulsory, peremptory (1), mandatory, incumbent (2), indispensable, imperative. *Ant.* Optional.

Obligatory writing The technical name by which a bond is described in pleading. See bond, description.

Oblige, *v.* See order (2), impose, bind (1), decree (3), make (2), compel, enjoin, enforce, challenge (2), coerce, require (1), dictate (1), obligate; accommodate (1), permit, assist (1), foster, pander (2), lend, patronize (2), aid (1), favor (3).

Obliged, *adj.* See bound (1), obligatory.

Obligee, *n.* The person to whom an obligation is owed; the party to whom a bond is given; a promisee.

Obliging, *adj.* See kind (2), charitable (2), amenable (2), cooperative (2), accessible, civil (3), benevolent, beneficial, amicable, conciliatory; passive (2).

Obligor, *n.* The person obligated under a contract or bond; a promisor.

Oblique, *adj.* See equivocal, diffuse (2), circuitous, indirect, ambiguous.

Obliterate, *v.* To destroy or wipe out (obliterate the clause). Rub out, scratch, efface, gut, liquidate, raze, annihilate, exterminate, suppress, eradicate, decimate, extirpate, pulverize, remove, do away with, strike over, ruin, dissolve, annul, despoil, ravage, disintegrate, level, wreck, nullify, invalidate, void. See also kill (2), delete, extinguish, rescind, devastate (1), expunge, erase, abrogate, cancel (1), abate (1). *Ant.* Preserve.

Obliterated, *adj.* See null and void; obliterate.

Obliteration, *n.* See defeat (2), oblivion (1), death (2), abatement (1), abolition, murder, repeal, removal (3), annulment, dissolution; obliterate.

Oblivion, *n.* **1.** The state of being forgotten (rescued from oblivion). Forgetfulness, extinction, nirvana, obscurity, limbo, nonexistence, insignificance, eclipse, obliteration, invisibility, unconsciousness, darkness, abeyance, dormancy. See also disregard (2). **2.** A pardon or general amnesty (act of oblivion). See amnesty.

Oblivious, *adj.* Forgetful; not conscious of (oblivious of the warning). Preoccupied, unconscious, unaware, unobservant, absent-minded, pensive, inattentive, disregardful, heedless, blocked-out, blacked-out, senseless, insensate, comatose, incognizant, unmindful, unsuspecting, lethargic, asleep, numb, "stoned," indifferent, neglectful, insensible. See also careless, remiss, absent (2), negligent, reckless. *Ant.* Alert.

Obloquy, *n.* Censure and reproach (casting obloquy on her character). Reprehension, disgrace, castigation, vilification, defamation, discredit, shame, ignominy, criticism, humiliation, condemnation, insult, degradation, disparagement, opprobrium, derogation, mortification, denunciation, stigma, calumny, dressing down. See also dishonor (2), blame (2), slander, abuse (2), odium, aspersion, infamy. *Ant.* Praise.

Obnoxious, *adj.* Highly objectionable (obnoxious behavior). Reprehensible, disagreeable, displeasing, distasteful, abhorrent, detestable, hateful, disgusting, deplorable, rank, pernicious, intolerable, objectionable, repellent, loathsome, insufferable, vile, fulsome, unpleasant, unendurable, nauseous, blameworthy, heinous, nasty, unpalatable, vulgar, antagonizing, despicable, censurable, faulty, foul, abominable, nauseating, invidious, revolting, noxious, unsavory, annoying, contemptible, horrid, wretched, poisonous. See also gross (1), malicious, contemptuous, repulsive, repugnant (1), base (2), bad (2), odious, offensive, infamous, profane (1). *Ant.* Agreeable.

Obscene, *adj.* Objectionable or offensive to accepted standards of decency. Test: whether, taken as a whole, the predominant appeal of the material is to prurient interest, that is, a shameful or morbid interest in nudity, sex, or excretion, and whether it goes substantially beyond customary limits of candor in describing or representing such matters (obscene movie). Pornographic, vile, bawdy, lecherous, foul, immodest, lewd, blue, ribald, lurid, vulgar, shameless, sensational, sensual, libidinous, lubricous, indelicate, erotic, wanton, perverted, improper, smutty, loose, libertine, abusive, rakish, unchaste, coarse, licentious, promiscuous, bestial, suggestive, off-color, sexy, seductive, graphic, salacious, dirty, debauched, reckless, impure, profligate, unwholesome, lustful, risqué, scurrilous, scatological, depraved. See also profane (1), immoral, incontinent (1), indecent, rude, repugnant (1), repulsive, animal (2), lascivious, dissolute, carnal, base (2) filthy, unclean, prurient, gross (1). *Ant.* Respectable.

Obscenity, *n.* The character of being obscene; conduct tending to corrupt the public morals by its indecency or lewdness. See debauchery; obscene.

Obscure 1. *adj.* Not clearly expressed (obscure language). Hard to understand, vague, cryptic, puzzling, incomprehensible, confusing, uncertain, abstruse, esoteric, fuzzy, intricate, unintelligible, recondite, enigmatic, occult, murky, indefinable, perplexing, dim, imperceptible, subtle, blurred, veiled, indistinct, unfathomable, nebulous, faint, impenetrable. See also abstract (5), intangible (3), ambiguous, doubtful (2), indefinite, indeterminate, equivocal, difficult (1), mysterious, complex (1). **2.** *adj.* Not well known (an obscure case). Unheard of, unnoticed, inconspicuous, distant, apart, secluded, isolated, strange, alien, insignificant, unnoted, out-of-the-way, undistinguished, removed. See also clandestine, private (1), outside (4), hidden, blind (2). **3.** *v.* To conceal (the bushes obscured his view). Block, mask, fog, befog, eclipse, shroud, blur, cloak, adumbrate, obfuscate, veil, darken, overshadow, blind, mislead, bedim, camouflage. See also cover (2), disguise (1), cloud (3), hide, obstruct (2). *Ant.* Evident; celebrated; expose.

Obscurity, *n.* See concealment, oblivion (1), mystery, vagueness, privacy (2); cipher.

Obsequious, *adj.* See servile, amenable (2), passive (2); flatter, flattery.

Observable, *adj.* See open (5), manifest (1), conspicuous (1), patent (1), overt, palpable, objective (1), evident, clear (1).

Observance, *n.* See practice (1), service (3), ceremony, celebration (1), vigilance; obedience, compliance (1); responsibility.

Observant, *adj.* See acute (1), cautious, conscientious (2), conscious (1), circumspect, careful.

Observation, *n.* See declaration, note (5), notice (1), perception, cognizance (3), inference, apprehension, detection, search (1), examination, inspection, experiment, diligence (2).

Observe, *v.* **1.** To adhere to or abide by (observe the regulations). Follow, obey, fulfill, heed, carry out, execute, respect, submit to, attend to, acknowledge, acquiesce in, be submissive to, honor, cling to, yield to, maintain, be guided by, accede, satisfy. See also perform, discharge (2), comply, conform, abide (1), keep (6). **2.** To comment on (the judge observed that the lawyer was not prepared). Remark, voice, announce, assert, proclaim, profess, enunciate, utter, say, mention, opine, allude to, reflect, theorize, suggest, breathe, verbalize, interject, exclaim, state, declare, vocalize, articulate, tell, phrase. See also comment (2), express (2), note (6), consider (1), communicate. **3.** To watch carefully (the jury observed the demeanor of the witness). Behold, see, detect, perceive, study, scrutinize, discern, be conscious of, examine, review, scan, survey, attend to, peruse, analyze, weigh, evaluate, reconnoiter, contemplate, take in, trace, track, gape, gawk, goggle, stare, wonder, espy, descry, view, inspect, peer at, take stock of, note, heed, regard, mark. See also investigate, watch, police (2), spy (2), witness (2), notice (2), recognize (1), mind (2), find (1). **4.** To celebrate (observe the holiday). Commemorate, recognize, honor, solemnize, remember. *Ant.* Disobey; ignore.

Observed, *adj.* See empirical.

Observer, *n.* See inspector, witness (3), eyewitness, bystander, lookout.

Obsess, *v.* See occupy (3); harass, disturb; dominate.

Obsession, *n.* See compulsion, desire; irresistible.

Obsessive, *adj.* See irresistible, compulsory, compelling; compulsion, desire, addict; superstitious.

Obsolescence, *n.* Diminution in value caused by changes in taste or new technology, rendering the property less desirable on the market; the condition or process of falling into disuse (the anticipated obsolescence of the product). See desuetude, obsolescent, obsolete.

Obsolescent, *adj.* Gradually going out of use (an obsolescent practice). Dying, disappearing, fading, declining, on the way out, becoming out-of-date; vestigial, useless, purposeless, nonfunctional. See also obsolete, old, ancient, extinct, defunct, lapse (1). *Ant.* In vouge.

Obsolete, *adj.* Pertaining to that which is no longer used (obsolete product). Disused, neglected, not observed, unfashionable, dead, outdated, out-of-date, antiquated, archaic, old-fashioned, rejected, inoperative, passé, antique, anachronistic, dated, stale, outmoded, primitive, abandoned, extinct, retired, superannuated, aged, expired, discontinued, obsolescent. See also ancient, old. *Ant.* Modern.

Obstacle, *n.* See blockade, prevention, disadvantage (1), limit (2), liability (2), drawback (2), bar (3), block (1), complication, obstruction; nuisance.

Obstetrician, *n.* A doctor specializing in the treatment of women during pregnancy, birth, and recovery. See doctor, medicine, surgery, medical.

Obstinacy, *n.* See insubordination, resistance, contempt (1).

Obstinate, *adj.* See inflexible, arbitrary, firm (2), particular (2), querulous, incorrigible, chronic, contumacious, constant (1), difficult (3), disobedient.

Obstreperous, *adj.* See bad (2), blatant (2), contentious, litigious, disobedient, wild; misbehavior.

Obstruct, *v.* **1.** To hinder or prevent progress (the picketing obstructed construction). Curb, encumber, suppress, interrupt, thwart, slow, fetter, circumscribe, stymie, disable, retard, choke, barricade, stop, bridle, terminate, estop, eclipse, limit, hobble, baffle, manacle, burden, choke off, stay, hamstring, countervail, trap, cripple, stall, shut off, plug up. See also interfere, abort (2), preclude, check (1, 5), prejudice (2), prevent, gag, prohibit, impair, arrest (3), impede, inhibit, hurt, close (2), hinder, disrupt, collide, clog, bar (5), delay (2), deter, intercept, detain, forestall, resist, block (2), restrain, frustrate, contravene, keep (3). **2.** To screen (the truck obstructed his view). Cut off from sight, hide, shield. See also obscure (3). *Ant.* Facilitate; display.

Obstructed, *adj.* See blind (2); frozen.

Obstructing justice The act by which a person prevents or attempts to prevent the execution of lawful process; impeding the administration of justice (e.g., hindering witnesses from appearing). See interfere, prevention.

Obstruction, *n.* A hindrance or barrier (an obstruction of justice). Obstacle, blockade, snag, impediment, hurdle, embargo, restriction, stoppage, hitch, bottleneck, mountain, roadblock, veto, injunction, trammel, interdiction, interruption, fence, barrier, wall, barricade, congestion, interference, encumbrance, handicap, proscription, clog. See also opposition, prevention, prohibition, inconvenience, check (5), restraint (1), constraint (1), limitation (1), liability (2), deterrent, cloud (1), bar (3), blockage (1), complication, filibuster, fetter, defeat (2), intervention (2), block (1), sabotage, strike (1). *Ant.* Facilitation.

Obstructionist, *n.* See nihilist; assailant, enemy; obstruction.

Obstructive, *adj.* See adverse (2); resist, block (1); obstruction.

Obtain, *v.* **1.** To get possession of (the evidence was obtained illegally). Get hold of, accumulate, secure, gain, gather, pick up, capture, come by, seize, pocket, appropriate, expropriate, attain, grab, win, earn. See also recover (1), get (1), derive (1) realize (1), acquire, gain (2), buy, receive (1, 2), inherit, possess, procure, collect (2), profit (2); engage; acquisition, procurement. **2.** To be customary (the procedure still obtains in the jurisdiction). Persist, continue, exist, stand. See also prevail (1). *Ant.* Release; discontinue.

Obtainable, *adj.* See available, accessible.

Obtrude, *v.* See encroach; intrusion.

Obtrusive

Obtrusive, *adj.* See officious, intervening, blatant, flagrant.

Obtuse, *adj.* See blind (1), dumb, absurd, juvenile (2), irrational; innocent (2); literal (2).

Obviate, *v.* See prevent, preclude.

Obvious, *adj.* Easily discovered (an obvious risk). Easily perceived, manifest, well-defined, prominent, explicit, transparent, discernible, unconcealed, perceivable, glaring, unmistakable, pronounced, self-evident, plain, noticeable, revealed, undisguised, undeniable, boldfaced, in plain sight, striking. See also open (5), known, flagrant, clear (1), intelligible, gross (1), overt, broad (2), simple (2), naked (2), palpable, conclusive, evident, concrete, distinct (1), demonstrable (2), patent (1), apparent (1, 2), certain (3), lucid (2), blatant (1), conspicuous (1), comprehensible, public (3), appreciable, visible. *Ant.* Concealed.

Obviously, *adv.* See clearly; obvious.

Occasion 1. *v.* To cause or bring about by furnishing the condition or opportunity (the speech occasioned a demonstration). Generate, elicit, motivate, beget, inspire, give rise to, create, effect, induce, lead to, bring on, demand, produce, entail. See also provoke (1), prompt (2), include, engender, raise (1), bring about, operate, cause (2). **2.** *n.* That which produces an opportunity for a causal agency to act (the lack of training was an occasion for injury). Provocation, basis, motivation, justification, rationale, stimulus, inducement, determinant, explanation, excuse, incitement. See also reason (1), root, ground (1), motive, cause (1). **3.** *n.* An event or happening (they were prepared for the occasion). Instance, episode, affair, setting, contingency, time, juncture, adventure, circumstance, condition, venture; celebration, festivity, service. See also incident (2), occurrence, event, experience (2), milestone, case (3), chance (4); holiday, ceremony, party (4).

Occasional, *adj.* See casual (2), incidental (2), intermittent, odd (3), periodic, seldom.

Occlude, *v.* See close (2), clog.

Occult, *adj.* See mysterious, hidden, intangible, obscure; witchcraft.

Occupancy, *n.* Taking possession of property and using it; the period during which someone holds or uses property (occupancy of the land for 6 months). Enjoyment, control, tenure, habitancy, inhabitancy, residency, living, lodging, proprietorship, occupation. See also habitation, possession (1), tenancy (1). *Ant.* Relinquishment.

Occupant, *n.* A person in possession (the current occupant). Tenant, user, dweller, renter, lessee, occupier, boarder, guest, roomer, settler, addressee, inmate, householder, owner. See also inhabitant, denizen, possessor, incumbent (1), resident, lodger. *Ant.* Absentee.

Occupation, *n.* **1.** One's regular business or employment (the occupation of accounting). Livelihood, trade, line, vocation, sphere, specialty, walk of life, avocation, métier, undertaking, mission, specialization, activity. See also profession (1), industry (1), office, calling, field (2), appointment (2), business (1), craft (1), career, tenure, work (3), employment, job (1), labor (1), pursuit (2), concern (3), enjoyment (1), capacity; occupancy. **2.** Seizure (military occupation). Possession, control, subjugation, subjection, rule, bondage, authority, power, mastery. See also preemption, capture (1).

Occupational, *adj.* Pertaining to one's work or workplace (occupational hazard). See technical; occupation (1).

Occupational disease A disease resulting from exposure during employment to conditions or substances detrimental to health. See disease, illness, health, danger, workmen's compensation.

Occupational Safety and Health Administration (OSHA) A federal agency that develops occupational and health safety standards, and conducts investigations to determine compliance with the standards. See health, danger.

Occupation tax A form of excise tax imposed upon persons for the privilege of carrying on a business, trade, or occupation. See tax.

Occupiable, *adj.* See habitable.

Occupied, *adj.* See active (1); occupy (3); diversion, distract.

Occupier, *n.* See possessor, inhabitant, inmate, tenant (1), occupant, lodger.

Occupy, *v.* **1.** To take or hold possession for use (occupy the apartment). House, settle, take up residence, move in. See also inhabit, possess, live (1), dwell (1), reside (1), hold (1), locate (2), exist (3). **2.** To seize by force (the troops occupied the factory). Expropriate, conquer, subjugate, dominate, rule, annex, colonize, invade, capture, take over, garrison. **3.** To engage one's attention (occupy his mind). Fill, absorb, attract attention, entertain, fascinate, busy, engross, permeate, obsess, amuse, monopolize, captivate, direct the mind's attention, enthrall, immerse, excite, preoccupy, take up, mold, saturate, overrun. See also devote (2), employ (2), interest (5), engage (2), labor (2), enjoy (1), consume, hold (2), pass (6). *Ant.* Release; liberate; ignore.

Occur, *v.* **1.** To take place (the injury occurred at work). Transpire, come about, happen, come off, eventuate, ensue, befall, follow, become a fact, materialize, take effect, present itself, proceed. See also arise (1), result (2), accompany. **2.** To suggest itself (it never occurred to him). Come to mind, cross one's mind, come to, become aware, reveal, present itself, manifest itself, strike, enter one's mind, offer, meet the eye.

Occurrence, *n.* An incident or event (unexpected occurrence). Happening, episode, transaction, situation, phenomenon, predicament, fact, happenstance, deed, contingency, condition. See also development (2), incident (2) appearance, coincidence, adventure (2), experience (2), emergency, proceeding, affairs, occasion (3), matter (1), event, case (2), record (3), circumstances, particulars; accident (1).

Ocean, *n.* The main or open sea that is not subject to the territorial jurisdiction or control of any country; the high sea. See sea (1), water (1); mass; maritime, aquatic, marine, nautical.

Oculist, *n.* A doctor specializing in diseases of the eye. See doctor, treatment, medicine, surgery.

Odd, *adj.* **1.** Peculiar (an odd reaction). Uncommon, unconventional, unorthodox, singular, unique, strange, rare, bizzare, weird, curious, eccentric, uncanny, unparalleled, anomalous, deviant, freakish, burlesque, ludicrous, ridiculous, exaggerated, farcical, incongruous, erratic. See also novel, extraordinary, exceptional, peculiar (2), abnormal, irregular, special (1), suspicious (1), at odds. **2.** A remainder or part of an incomplete set (an odd player). Surplus, remaining, uneven, different, mateless, not matching, single. See also irregular. **3.** Miscellaneous (odd jobs). Varied, sundry, occasional, sporadic, casual, intermittent, fortuitous, stray, indeterminate.

Oddity, *n.* See eccentricity, specialty (1), character (4), nonconformist, exception (3); mystery, marvel.

Odd lot doctrine A finding of total disability is possible where the claimant is not altogether incapacitated for any kind of work but is nevertheless so handicapped that he or she will not be able to obtain regular employment in any well-known branch of the competitive labor market, absent superhuman efforts, sympathetic employers or friends, a business boom, or temporary good luck.

Odds, *n.* See probability, possibility; venture (2), chance (3).

Oddsmaker, *n.* See gambler.

Odious, *adj.* Hateful, repugnant (an odious scheme). Abominable, unbearable,

Odious

heinous, hideous, sickening, vile, nauseating, ugly, despicable, invidious, forbidding, evil, detestable, sinister, nasty, fulsome, rotten, grotesque, unpalatable, obnoxious, disgraceful, lurid, reprehensible, vulgar, abhorrent, ignominious, shameful, monstrous, loathsome, contemptible, repellent, execrable, dirty, shocking, nauseous, frightening, objectionable, coarse, horrible. See also abject (2), gross (1), blameworthy, corrupt (1), repulsive, repugnant (1), notorious (2), wrong (2), bad (2), offensive, infamous; disgrace. *Ant.* Agreeable.

Odium, *n.* Being subject to hatred and dislike (exposed to odium). Alienation, disgust, repugnance, abhorrence, displeasure, animus, ill will, venom, antipathy, hatred, offensiveness, enmity, repulsiveness, acrimony, rancor, derision, detestation, debasement, ignominy, scandal, avoidance, disapproval, resentment, loathing, dislike, discredit, opprobrium. See also disgrace, degradation, infamy, malice, slander (1), notoriety (2), outrage (1), dishonor (2), obloquy, contempt (2), hostility. *Ant.* Respect.

Odometer, *n.* Speedometer. See measure, gauge.

Odor, *n.* See aroma; fragrant; environment, air.

Odyssey, *n.* See adventure (1), endeavor (2), voyage.

Of age See adult, majority.

Of counsel An attorney who is assisting the attorney of record on a case; an associate. See attorney.

Off and on See intermittent.

"Off-base," *adj.* See wrong (3), erroneous.

"Offbeat," *adj.* See peculiar, irregular, odd.

Off-color, *adj.* See obscene.

Offend, *v.* See provoke (2), injure, hurt, revolt (2), patronize (2), affront (2), accost (1), wound (1), outrage (2).

Offended, *adj.* See aggravated (2), aggrieved.

Offender, *n.* One who has committed a crime or offense (apprehension of the offender). Transgressor, scofflaw, aggressor, violator, trespasser, culprit, sinner, reprobate, villain, degenerate, derelict, knave, scoundrel, misdemeanant, miscreant, lawbreaker, felon. See also wrongdoer, criminal (1), delinquent (3), racketeer, malefactor, perpetrator.

Offending, *adj.* See repugnant (1), repulsive, delinquent (2), odious, offensive.

Offense, *n.* A violation of the criminal law (sentenced for the offense). Battery, transgression, sin, attack, aggression, misfeasance, nonfeasance, malfeasance, negligence, peccadillo, breach, misprision, malefaction, disobedience, misdeed, wickedness, lapse, atrocity, insult, indignity, scandal, wrongdoing, unethical conduct, vice, debauchery, turpitude, insolence, impropriety, siege. See also infraction, injustice, illegality, fault (1), assault (2), misdemeanor, wrong (1), delinquency (2), violation, affront (1), crime, felony, misconduct, grievance (1), outrage (1), corruption.

Offensive, *adj.* Causing disagreeable sensations (offensive contact). Noxious, objectionable, displeasing, distasteful, affronting, disgusting, disturbing, gross, insulting, intolerable, hostile, rancid, insolent, insufferable, impertinent, distressing, nauseating, disrespectful, bellicose, irritating, combative, rank, appalling, beastly, unappetizing, dreadful, vexatious, aggravating, fulsome, antagonistic, provocative, exasperating, irksome, unsavory, contentious, annoying, hateful, opprobrious, unpalatable, execrable, invading, revolting, abominable, repellent, loathsome, abhorrent, detestable, indecent, outrageous, embarrassing, ugly, low, vile, biting, sarcastic, harsh, heinous, malignant, disruptive, bothersome, pestering, harassing, hounding, provoking, unbearable, disquieting, maddening, infuriating, troubling, nagging, inflammatory, sickening. See also improper, injurious, obscene, obnoxious, odious, libelous, litigious, grievous (2), filthy, guilty, repulsive, repugnant (1), rude, base (2), blatant (2); onset (2), attack (2). *Ant.* Innocuous.

Offer 1. *v.* To present for acceptance or rejection (she offered to withdraw the plan). Suggest, tender, proffer, submit, propose, put forward, hold out, pose, refer, lay before, yield, recommend, make a motion, sacrifice, place at one's disposal, be willing, put forth, urge, display, show, propound. See also present (5), profess (1), bid, approach, advance (6), move (1), extend (2), give, nominate, introduce (1), volunteer (2), sell, advise (1), assert, exhibit (1), negotiate (1), carry (3), protest (4), adduce. **2.** *n.* A proposal to do a thing or to pay an amount (an offer to cover the costs). Invitation, suggestion, submission, proffer, presentation, recommendation, approach, offering. See also proposal, bid, proposition, overture. **3.** *v.* See grant (1), dedicate, administer (2), contribute (2), bear (1).

Offeree, *n.* The person to whom an offer is made. *Ant.* Offeror.

Offering, *n.* **1.** An issue of securities offered for sale to the public or to a private group. **2.** A sacrifice, contribution, oblation, alms, bequest, subsidy, benefaction, grant. See also gratuity (1), charity (1), collection (5), donation, gift (1), present (1), benefit (1); submission (2), administration (3), offer (2), motion (1).

Offer of proof Telling the court what evidence a party proposes to present in order to obtain a ruling on admissibility. See evidence, admissible.

Offeror, *n.* The party who makes an offer. *Ant.* Offeree.

Off guard See surprise (1).

Offhand, *adj.* See informal, cursory; casual (1); spontaneous, fortuitous, chance (5).

Office, *n.* A position of trust; a right and correspondent duty to exercise a public trust (elective office). Position, post, job, service, task, charge, province, incumbency, role, station, assignment, mission. See also profession, business (3), calling, duty (1), occupation (1), appointment (2), function (2), career, commission (1), work (3); building (1), bureau, establishment (1), seat, agency (2), shop (1), department, facility (2), branch (1), chapter (1), affiliate (1); chamber (1); direction (2), management (2); capacity (3); clerical (2).

Office boy, *n.* See clerk (2), employee, servant.

Officeholder, *n.* See official (1), officer, incumbent (1); administration (2); nominee, appointee.

Officer, *n.* A person holding a position of trust, command, or authority in organizations (the officer in charge of billing). Head, bureaucrat, officeholder, appointee, dignitary, commander, leader, manager, deputy, secretary, commissioner, superintendent. See also treasurer, police (1), inspector, consul, bailiff (2), recorder (1), clerk (1), marshal (1), master (2), judge (1), director, counsel (1), attorney (1), minister (2), magistrate, functionary, moderator, chairman, official (1), chief (1), administrator (1), agent.

Officer of the court See counsel (1), attorney (1).

Office seeker See candidate.

Office worker See clerk (2), employee.

Official 1. *n.* An officer (the official denied the request). Insider, manager, director, minister, chief, superintendent, supervisor, officeholder, overseer, dignitary, chair, appointee, agent, commissioner; civil servant, bureaucrat, rubber stamp, politician, clerk, public servant. See also executive (1), governor, judge (1), clerk (1) functionary, officer, administrator, incumbent (1); cabinet, authorities, management (2), bureaucracy. **2.** *adj.* Concerning that which is authorized; proceeding from, sanctioned by, or pertaining to an officer (official report). Verified, approved, certified, accredited, valid, licensed, warranted, correct, dependable, allowed, authenticated, solemn, proper, "kosher," bona fide, conclusive, unimpeachable, guaranteed, documented, administrative, veritable, real, cleared, endorsed, proven, trustworthy, appointed, ceremonial, recognized, authoritative, validated, attested, ordained. See also formal (1), actual (1), stated, legitimate (1), political. *Ant.* Underling; unofficial.

Official immunity doctrine Government officials of suitable rank enjoy an absolute privilege from civil liability for activity falling within the scope of their authority. See immunity, immune, jurisdiction, authority.

Official record A record kept pursuant to the official duty of a particular officer whether or not required by statute. See record (2), report (1).

Official reports or reporters A collection of court opinions whose printing is authorized by the government (e.g., by statute). See report.

Official statement See certificate, record.

Officiate, *v.* See handle (1), moderate (2), rule (3), preside, administer (1), exercise (2), oversee, manage (1), sit.

Officio, ex See ex officio.

Officious, *adj.* Meddlesome (officious manager). Domineering, interfering, patronizing, meddling, intrusive, annoying, gratuitous, obtrusive, persistent, impertinent, snooping, forward, direct, inquisitive, "pushy," overzealous. See also prying; eavesdrop; offensive; champerty. *Ant.* Reserved.

Officious will A will in which everything is left to the decedent's family. See will.

Off-key, *adj.* See irregular, awkward.

Offset 1. *n.* A contrary claim or demand by which a given claim may be lessened or canceled; a deduction (pleaded by way of offset). Counterclaim, counterbalance, counterweight, antidote, counterblast, compensation, equivalent, recoupment, counterpart, equalizer, indemnity. See also neutralization, quid pro quo. **2.** *v.* To balance something (the losses offset the gains). Equalize, neutralize, countervail, adjust, trade off, counterweigh, nullify, cushion, make up for, handicap, contrast, juxtapose. See also cancel (2), counter, compensate (2), recover (1), balance, remedy, repay (1).

Offshoot, *n.* See offspring, descendant; branch (1).

Offshore, *adj.* See foreign, international; ocean, sea.

Offspring, *n.* Children (offspring of the testator). Heir, lineage, successors, young, progeny, offshoot, seed, progenitor, scion. See also issue (4), generation (1), descendant, family, child, posterity; product. *Ant.* Ancestor.

Off target See irregular, stray, lost.

Off-the-cuff, *adj.* See spontaneous.

Off-the-record, *adj.* See confidential, private (1).

Off-the-wall, *adj.* See absurd, irregular, wild.

Off-track betting, *n.* See gambling.

Of no account See null and void, worthless.

Of record Entered on the records; recorded (it is a matter of record). See record (2).

Of right As a matter of legal right (an appeal of right). See de jure, right.

Often, *adv.* See common (1), frequent (1); familiar (2); accustomed (1).

Oft-repeated, *adj.* See frequent (1), common (1).

Ogle, *v.* See observe, notice (2).

Ogre, *n.* See tyrant, demon, wrongdoer; animal.

Oil, *n.* Petroleum, mineral oil, motor oil, grease. See also ointment.

Ointment, *n.* Salve. Balm, balsam, unguent, cream, jelly, moisturizer, nard, conditioner, liniment, emollient, pomade. See also medicine; aroma.

O.K., OK, okay, *adv., adj.* Correct, approved. Accepted, satisfactory, assented to, all right, acceptable, accurate, agreeable, endorsed, permitted, encouraged, good. See also adequate, perfect (2); assent (1); pass (2). *Ant.* Unacceptable.

Old, *adj.* Not recent (old ways). Aged, advanced, remote, obsolescent, outdated, antiquated, experienced, enduring, veteran, venerable, timeworn, antique, mature, dateless, primeval, decayed, rusty, disintegrated, antediluvian, past, passé, lapsed, extinct, outmoded, anterior, infirm, traditional, weather-beaten, bygone, used. See also ancient, obsolete, senior (1), senile, weak, frail. *Ant.* Modern.

Old age See longevity, age (2); senile, old.

Oldest, *adj.* See primary (2).

Old Age, Survivors', and Disability Insurance A Social Security program, providing for retirement, disability, and benefits for widows, widowers, and dependents.

Older, *adj.* See mature (2).

Old-fashioned, *adj.* See ancient, obsolete, old.

Old hand, *n.* See professional (2), specialist, veteran (2).

Old hat, *adj.* See obsolete, old, ancient; commonplace, familiar (2).

Old maid, *n.* See woman.

Old Testament, *n.* See bible; holy, church, religion.

Old wives' tale, *n.* See legend, fiction, maxim.

Olfactory, *adj.* See aroma; fragrant.

Oligarchy, *n.* Government power in the hands of a few persons. See monopoly.

Oligopoly, *n.* A market climate dominated by a few sellers.

Olive branch, *n.* See overture; peace.

Olympian, *adj.* See big, elevated, superior; pompous; God.

Olympics, *n.* See game, competition.

Ombudsman, *n.* One who investigates grievances that people have against an organization. See intermediary, referee, agent, moderator; representative (1).

Omega, *n.* See conclusion (1), end.

Omen, *n.* See promise (3), indication, danger, caution (2), harbinger, manifestation, mark, warning, apprehension (3).

Ominous, *adj.* See extrahazardous, hazardous, imminent, dangerous, odious, distressing.

Omission, *n.* The intentional or unintentional failure to act (the omission of a signature). Noninclusion, deletion, avoidance, oversight, blank, elimination, hole, nonfulfillment, gap, slip, laxity, hiatus, inadvertence. See also infraction, injustice, rejection, neglect (2), fault (1), disregard (2), wrong (1), delinquency (1), failure (2), deficiency, blunder (1), dereliction (1), default, defect, nonfeasance, nonpayment, nonperformance, nonsupport, lapse (3), exception (2), exclusion, laches; absence (2). *Ant.* Inclusion.

Omit, *v.* See except (1), foreclose (2), delete, expunge; kill (2), fail (2), neglect (1), ignore.

Omitted, *adj.* See missing; null and void.

Omnibus, *adj., n.* See comprehensive; vehicle.

Omnibus bill 1. A legislative bill that includes a number of different subjects in one measure. **2.** In equity pleading, a bill that embraces the whole of a complex subject by uniting all parties in interest having adverse or conflicting claims.

Omnibus clause 1. A clause in a will passing all property not specifically mentioned or known at the time. **2.** A clause extending liability insurance coverage to persons using the car with the express or implied permission of the named insured.

Omnipotent, *adj.* See predominant, irresistible, strong, awesome, ubiquitous; perpetual, permanent; God; supremacy.

Omnipresent, *adj.* See ubiquitous, universal; present (4).

Omniscient, *adj.* See predominant; perpetual, permanent; God; supremacy.

On account In part payment; in partial satisfaction. See part, partial.

On account of See virtue (2), through.

On all fours The facts and issues in a client's case are the same as or substantially similar to the facts and issues covered in a particular court opinion. See analogous, like, akin.

On a par with See comparable, equivalent.

On call See available, accessible.

Oncoming, *adj.* See imminent, near, adjacent; approach.

On demand Payable on request; when demanded. See now.

On duty See present (4), active (1), accessible, available.

One, *adj.* See single (1); individual; person; sole; paramount.

One by one See seriatim; separate.

One more See another.

Oneness, *n.* See concord (2), unity, compatibility, integrity, identity (2).

One of a kind See outstanding (2), exceptional, extraordinary; different, distinct (2), isolated.

One or two See few.

One person See individual.

Onerous, *adj.* Unreasonably burdensome or one-sided (onerous responsibility). Crushing, unwieldy, heavy, oppressive, destructive, taxing, harrowing, exhausting, distressing, laborious, arduous, weighty, overbearing, grueling, hard to endure, wearisome, fatiguing, unendurable, injurious, harsh, overwhelming, formidable, exacting, cumbersome, toilsome, intolerable, corroding, overpowerful, rigorous. See also difficult (2), severe, serious, grievous (1), extreme, draconian, obnoxious. *Ant.* Trifling.

One-sided, *adj.* Unequal, partial (one-sided bargain). Warped, slanted, uneven, lopsided, disproportionate, unbalanced, unjust, mismatched, biased, prejudiced, colored, weighted. See also partisan (2), partial (2), interested, unequal (1), unilateral, unfair, narrow (2), unconscionable; favoritism, prejudice; political. *Ant.* Balanced.

One-track, *adj.* See inflexible.

Ongoing, *adj.* See living (3); current; chronic. On guard. See cautious, circumspect; admonish (1).

On hand See immediate (2), accessible, available, forthcoming.

On ice See suspended.

Onlooker, *n.* See witness (3), bystander, eyewitness.

Only 1. *adj.* Without others (the only remedy available). Solitary, individual, unique, lone, exclusive, alone, distinct, single. See also sole; mere. **2.** *adv.* Exclusively (she saw him only once). Solely, merely, no more than, purely, at most, in no otherwise, for no other purpose, without anything more, singly. See also exclusively; mere.

Onomastic, *adj.* Concerning names; referring to the signature of an instrument, the body of which is in a different handwriting from that of the signature.

On pins and needles See apprehension (3).

On point See germane, relevant.

On purpose See conscious (2), intentional; purposely; voluntary.

Onset, *n.* **1.** The beginning (the onset of the disability). Origin, start, embryo, inauguration, genesis, outset, opening, dawn, threshold, establishment, forging, infancy, incipience, entrance, debut. See also birth (2), commencement, inception. **2.** An attack (no one was prepared for the onset). Assault, strike, onslaught, aggression, invasion, raid, offensive, blitz, incursion, foray, intrusion. See also attack (2).

On short notice See summarily.

Onslaught, *n.* See violence, onset (2), assault (2), attack (2).

On tap See ready (1).

On target See right (2), relevant; faithful (2).

On that account See therefore.

On the alert See cautious, careful.

On the basis of See virtue (2); foundation.

On the grounds of See virtue (2); ground.

On the house See free.

On the lookout See cautious, careful.

On the other hand See contra; vice versa.

On the same footing See equivalent, coequal, equal (1).

On the spot See summarily, instant.

On the spur of the moment See summarily, instant.

On the table See negotiable.

On the verge See ready (1).

On the way See in transitu.

Onus, *n.* **1.** A burden or load (the onus was on her to produce the document). Weight, load, duty, cross, task, charge, albatross, tax, encumbrance, strain, impediment. See also liability (2), burden (1), obligation (1), care (2), blame (1), responsibility, requirement. **2.** Stigma. See disgrace.

Ooze, *v.* See emit (2); swamp (1).

Opaque, *adj.* See indefinite; ambiguous, obscure; vagueness.

OPEC Organization of Petroleum Exporting Countries.

Open 1. *v.* To give access to (open a road). Unclose, unlock, unblock, make passable, unclog, make accessible or visible, unbar, unfold. **2.** *v.* To start (the court opened with an announcement). Initiate, embark, inaugurate, usher in, launch, originate. See also begin, commence, establish (1), spread (3). **3.** *adj.* Not covered (an open tank). Unclosed, topless, agape, unfastened, ajar, unlocked, unsealed. **4.** *adj.* Approachable (an open administration). Available, accessible, unscreened, reachable, at hand, free, unrestricted, unbarred, within reach, susceptible, unfenced, unguarded. See also public (2), unlimited, broad (2), competitive (2), plenary, demonstrative (2); capable (1). **5.** *adj.* Manifest (open defiance). Exposed, within sight, blatant, obvious, published, perceptible, transparent, discernible, unhidden, apparent, glaring, noticeable, advertised, plain, conspicuous, broadcast, observable, marked, striking, prominent. See also visible, outright, clear (2), manifest (1), overt, patent (1), flagrant, public (3), notorious (1), honest, direct (6). **6.** *adj.* Receptive (open to suggestions). Reachable, flexible, sensitive, hospitable, sympathetic, impressionable, malleable, amenable, agreeable. See also responsive, susceptible. **7.** *adj.* Unprejudiced (an open mind). Unbiased, fair-minded, disinterested, unbigoted, just, tolerant, open-minded, impersonal. See also liberal (1), integrated, fair, impartial, neutral. **8.** *adj.* See natural (5), honest, bona fide, innocent (2). **9.** *adj.* See moot (2), indeterminate, inconclusive, precarious, debatable, outstanding (1), insecure (2). **10.** *adj.* See liable (2). **11.** *adj.* See optional. **12.** *adj.* See running (1).

Open account An account that has not been finalized, settled, or closed, but is still running or open to future adjustment or liquidation; a type of credit extended by a seller, which permits a buyer to make purchases without a note or security. See account, credit.

Open door See invitation; accessible, available.

Open-end credit Credit cards and "revolving charges," where one can pay a part of what is owed each month on several different purchases, with each new purchase representing an additional extension of credit. See credit, installment, periodic.

Open-ended, *adj.* Not restricted by definite limits (open-ended negotiation). Wide-open, unlimited, unbounded, unrestricted, undetermined, loose, continuing, unsettled, liberal, inexact, undefined, expansive, unending, indefinite, boundless, limit-

Open-ended

less, unconfined. See also general, comprehensive. *Ant.* Limited.

Open-hearted, *adj.* See benevolent, charitable, kind.

Opening, *n.* See crevice, valley, breach (2), break (3), window, ingress, egress, pass (8), access (2), admission (3), entrance, passage (2); overture, preliminary, preamble, initial, inception, birth (2), commencement, onset (1); vacancy, job (1), interval; chance (4); primary (2).

Openly, *adv.* See clearly.

Open-minded, *adj.* See open (7), dispassionate, disinterested, objective (2), neutral, impartial, progressive, amenable (2); toleration.

Open shop, *n.* A business in which union and nonunion workers are employed indiscriminately; a business in which union membership is not a condition of employment. See union.

Open to debate See debatable, moot, controversial, arguable.

Open to question See doubtful, disputable, arguable, suspicious (1).

Opera, *n.* See music, drama.

Operable, *adj.* See functional, practicable.

Operant, *adj.* See active (1), effective.

Operate, *v.* To perform a function or produce an effect (trained to operate the system). Run, conduct, govern, command, steer, carry on, guide, oversee, maneuver, be in charge of, superintend, engineer, take charge of, engage, preside, supervise, execute, use, minister, occasion, cause. See also work (1, 2), handle (1), keep (4), manipulate (2), employ (2), control (1), function (1), direct (2), regulate, commit (2), manage (1), exploit (1), act (5), administer (1), transact, pursue (3), apply (4).

Operating, *adj.* See moving (2), working, running (1), functional; operate; operation.

Operating expenses Expenses required to keep a business running (e.g., rent, utilities). See carrying charge, overhead.

Operation, *n.* **1.** The exertion of power; the process of performing or being at work (operation of the new alarm). Manipulation, employment, handling, management, running, working, transaction, activation, utilization, movement, thrust, exercise, execution, enactment, discharge, exploit, proceeding. See also force (3), manner, performance, commission (4), enterprise (1), method, agency (4), conduct (1), campaign, experiment, application (2), activity, action (2), act (3), instrumentality, use (2), practice (1, 2), procedure, affairs. **2.** Act(s) performed on the body of a patient for relief or restoration to normal conditions by the use of surgical instruments, as distinguished from therapeutic treatment (kidney operation). See surgery, treatment, doctor.

Operational, *adj.* See operative (1), functional, effective (2), running (1), active (1).

Operative 1. *adj.* Producing effects; functioning effectively (operative language in the deed). Operational, functional, working, applicable, instrumental, efficacious, powerful, helpful, fruitful, in effect, potent, performing, advantageous, vital, serviceable, in force, adequate. See also running (1), effective (2), living (3), active (1); dominant. **2.** *n.* A working person, especially in factories. See artisan, employee, artificer (1), laborer. **3.** *n.* A private or secret agent or detective. See investigator, spy (1). **4.** *adj.* See ministerial.

Operative words In a deed or lease, the words that carry into effect the transaction intended to be consummated by the instrument.

Operator, *n.* Driver, engineer. Conductor, pilot, executor, performer, manipulator, handler, practitioner, worker. See also employee, actor (2), agent (2), artisan; cheat (2); jobber.

Ophthalmologist, *n.* One who specializes in the treatment of diseases and disorders of the eye. See doctor, treatment, medicine.

Opiate, *n.* A narcotic containing opium or its derivatives, having an addiction-forming or addiction-sustaining liability similar to morphine or being capable of conversion into a drug with this characteristic. See also drug (2), dope, cannabis, narcotic, methadone.

Opine, *v.* See think, comment (2), deduce, deem, observe (2), consider (2), derive (2), construe, assume (2), advise (1).

Opinion, *n.* **1.** A statement by an individual judge or by a court of its decision in a case and the reasons for it (the opinions in the reporter). Report, pronouncement, determination. See also judgment, decision, finding, decree (1), ruling (1), adjudication. **2.** A belief or conclusion not proven by complete or positive knowledge but appearing to the witness to be true, based on his or her own ideas and thinking (in his opinion the car was speeding). Surmise, view, persuasion, notion, estimation, assumption, sentiment, theory, suspicion, fancy, slant, conception, feeling, position, stance, assessment, supposition, premise, deduction, thinking, valuation, vantage, thought, angle, facet, version, twist, standpoint, stand, evaluation, outlook, attitude, viewpoint, point of view, thesis, guess, perspective, posture; doctrine, creed, precept, dogma. See also judgment, puffing (1), determination, voice (1), appraisal, mind (1), conjecture, conclusion (2), concept, counsel (2), estimate (1), conviction (2), comment (1), advice (1), belief (1), speculation (2), result (1), regard (2), inference, hypothesis, impression (2), principle (1).

Opinionated, *adj.* See partisan (2), argumentative, litigious, contentious, inflexible, narrow (2), peremptory (3).

Opinion evidence or testimony Evidence of what the witness thinks, believes, or infers in regard to facts in dispute as distinguished from his or her personal knowledge of the facts themselves. See evidence, declaration, statement.

Opinion letter A document prepared by an attorney for a client, containing the attorney's understanding of the law as applicable to a state of facts submitted for this purpose. See advice, communication, report (1), memorandum.

Opium, *n.* A drug consisting of the inspissated juice of the opium poppy. See drug, dope.

Opponent, *n.* One who competes with or fights another. See adversary, enemy, assailant, disputant, litigant, competitor, competition (2), plaintiff.

Opportune, *adj.* See expedient (1), advisable, seasonable (1), appropriate (3), convenient, ripe, right (2), primary (1).

Opportunist, *n.* A self-seeker; opportunist. See expediency; expedient; parasite.

Opportunity, *n.* See option (2), chance (4), possibility, choice (2), access (1); vacancy.

Oppose, *v.* See interfere, disallow, disapprove (1), break (1), defend (2), object (1), contravene, conflict (2), fight (2), compete, resist, confront, deny (1), challenge (1), clog, collide (2), controvert, contest (1), counter, protest (3), rebut, argue, reject (1), impede, prevent, preclude.

Opposed, *adj.* See countervailing, alien (2), against (1), negative (1), inconsistent.

Opposite, *adj.* Counter (an opposite point of view). Conflicting, contrasting, polar, countervailing, discordant, inverted, resisting, countering, antithetical, clashing, oppugnant, inimical, antipodal, diametric, differing, opposing, facing, fronting. See also contra, contrary, adverse (1), contradictory, hostile, inconsistent (2), inverse, reverse (2), incompatible (2), unequal, converse (2), against (1), adversary; other; across. *Ant.* Identical.

Opposition, *n.* Being against or opposed (opposition to the reforms). Antagonism, obstruction, frustration, counteraction, confrontation, struggle against, refutation, animosity, repulsion, aversion, contention against, enmity, disapproval, negativism, barricade, impediment, hindrance, combating, bar, restriction. See also

Opposition

hostility, rejection, protest (1), animus (2), revolt (1), mutiny, defiance, competition (1), collision (2), challenge (4) adversary, violation, revolutionary, resistance, conflict (1), war, question (3), contradiction, dissent (1), controversy (2), competitor, party (1), adverse (1), difference (1), exception (1). *Ant.* Concurrence.

Oppress, *v.* See charge (1), harass, compel, burden (3), inundate, wrong (4), overload, constrain (2), abuse (1), exploit (1), injure.

Oppressed, *adj.* See captive (1), aggrieved; victim.

Oppression, *n.* An act of cruelty or excessive use of authority (measures to combat oppression). Suppression, persecution, cruelty, tyranny, injury, injustice, despotism, maltreatment, subjection, brutality, harshness, abuse, autocracy, suffering, enslavement, harassment, torment, despair, severity, fascism, hounding, ruthlessness, vexation, albatross, reign of terror, brute force, inhumanity, repression, agony, depression. See also affliction, ordeal (2), force (2), hardship, compulsion (1), distress (3), grievance (1), burden (2), servitude (1), slavery, coercion, duress (1). *Ant.* Compassion.

Oppressive, *adj.* See onerous, forcible, unconscionable, severe, extreme, draconian.

Oppressor, *n.* A person who oppresses another. Dictator, tormentor, autocrat, bully, browbeater, totalitarian. See also tyrant.

Opprobrious, *adj.* See notorious (2), wrong (2), offensive, calumnious.

Opprobrium, *n.* Contempt or dishonor. See disgrace, dishonor (2), notoriety (2), abuse (2), obloquy, contempt (2), odium, infamy.

Oppugn, *v.* See confront, controvert, fight (2); opposite, adverse (1), resistance, hostile.

Opt, *v.* See select (1), prefer (2); option.

Optical, *adj.* See sight.

Optimal, *adj.* See most, primary (1).

Optimism, *n.* See faith (1), hope (2), confidence (3), happiness; light.

Optimistic, *adj.* Positive. Hopeful, encouraging, upbeat, sanguine, confident, cheerful, enthusiastic, self-assured. See also certain (2), active (2), happy.

Optimum, *n., adj.* See maximum, ceiling (1); most, first, primary, exceptional, perfect, extraordinary.

Option, *n.* **1.** An agreement that gives the person to whom the option is granted (i.e., the optionee) the right and power within a limited time to accept an offer (a stock option). Continuing offer. **2.** An opportunity to choose (after the fire, her options were limited). Freedom, alternate, selection, preference, selectivity, "druthers," will, election, pick, power to select, possibility, liking, opportunity. See also discretion, resort (3), vote, voice (1), recourse, liberty, choice (2), alternative.

Optional, *adj.* Pertaining to that which is not required (an optional procedure). Volitional, nonobligatory, conditional, allowable, open, independent, a matter of personal or individual preference. See also discretionary, voluntary, elective. *Ant.* Compulsory.

Option to purchase A bilateral contract in which one party is given the right to buy the property within a period of time for a consideration paid to the seller. See contract.

Optometry, *n.* Treatment of eye problems that do not require the attention of a doctor. See treatment.

Opulence, *n.* See wealth, property (1), luxury; excess.

Opulent, *adj.* See abundant, affluent; luxury, wealth.

Opus, *n.* The product of work or labor; a work or composition (plagiarized opus). Product, creation, piece, volume, invention, production, tome, brainchild. See also publication (2), book (4), masterpiece.

Oracle, *n.* A prophet or sage. Soothsayer, sibyl, diviner, seer, high priest, clairvoyant, savant, guru, astrologer, spirit. See also augur, clairvoyance (2).

Oral, *adj.* Spoken, not written (oral promise). Voiced, said, uttered, word-of-mouth, expressed verbally, verbalized; unrecorded. See also parol, verbal.

Oral argument A verbal presentation before an appellate court of the reasons why the lower court's decision should be affirmed, modified, or reversed. See argument (1), case (4).

Oral will See nuncupative will.

Oration, *n.* See address (3).

Orator, *n.* See speaker (2).

Oratory, *n.* See communication (2); articulate (2), moving.

Orbit, *n.* See zone, purview (1), ambit, scope, domain (2), bailiwick, spread (1), area (2), course (1), bound (4).

Orchestra, *n.* See music; organization (1).

Orchestrate, *v.* See compose (2), direct (2), negotiate (2), plan (2), harmonize, oversee; manipulate.

Ordain, *v.* **1.** To institute or establish. See induct, install (1), instruct (2), allot, constitute (1), name (2), designate, command (3), appoint (2), charge (2), decree (3), dedicate, enjoin, pass (2), nominate, invest (1), delegate, dictate (1), require (1), order (2); condemn (1). **2.** To enact a law. See enact, legislate.

Ordained, *adj.* See necessary, positive (2), official (2), right (1), legitimate, stated.

Ordeal, *n.* **1.** An ancient form of trial in which the innocence of an accused person was determined by his or her ability to come away from an endurance test unharmed (e.g., hold a heavy, red-hot iron in the hand, plunge a bare arm in boiling water). **2.** A difficult or painful experience (the ordeal of the investigation). Strain, tribulation, nightmare, tragedy, torment, agony, curse, torture, grief, misery, hell, adversity, trial, oppression, trying experience, horror, vexation, wretchedness, suffering, calamity. See also experience (2), burden (2), pain, misfortune, hardship, affliction.

Order 1. *n.* An authoritative command (court order). Mandate, decree, direction, dictate, fiat, ukase, instruction, prescription, injunction, pronouncement, demand, rule, commandment, directive, edict, regulation, ultimatum, behest, manifesto, declaration, imperative, ordinance. **2.** *v.* To command (the court ordered her to remove the sign). Decree, require, insist on, instruct, dictate, adjure, direct, charge, enjoin, determine, compel, warn, oblige, constrain, coerce, force, bid, prescribe, impose, ordain, warrant, proscribe, assign. **3.** *n.* The designation of the person to whom a bill of exchange or negotiable promissory note is to be paid (payable to order). **4.** *n.* The arrangement of something (placed in order). Organization, systemization, classification, grouping, apportionment, formation, allotment, designation, categorization, tabulation, codification, adjustment, composition, cataloguing, alphabetization, progression, gradation. **5.** *n.* A scheme or logical system (a lower order). Plan, class, division, rank, species, character, station, stock, family, grade, standing, status, breed, temper, genus, caliber, degree, kind, sort. See also succession (2), symmetry, pattern. **6.** *n.* Harmony (maintain order). Peace, tranquillity, discipline, management, control, silence, lawfulness, concord, calm. **7.** *n.* Functioning properly (out of order). Working, shape, repair. **8.** *n.* A structured organization (religious order). See cabal (1), commune (1), community (2), confederacy (2).

Ordering, *n.* See classification (1), preparation, reconciliation; symmetry.

Orderly, *adj.* See coherent (1), regular, right (2), good (2), peace; symmetry.

Order nisi A provisional or conditional order that will not be made final if a designated act is performed.

Order of the Coif An honorary organization of law students and lawyers, whose membership is based on excellence.

Order to show cause

Order to show cause See show cause order.

Ordinance, *n.* The enactment of the legislative body of a municipality, e.g., city council; a rule established by authority (traffic ordinance). Charter, prescription, measure, restriction. See also law, proclamation, act (2), enactment, regulation (1), code, canon (1), bylaws, edict, rule (1), fiat, decree (2), legislation (2), order (1).

Ordinarily, *adv.* See regularly.

Ordinary, *adj.* **1.** Regular; according to established order (expenses in the ordinary course of business). Usual, common, recurring, settled, accepted, frequent, prevailing, routine, standard, traditional, established, expected, stock, prevalent, characteristic, widespread, representative, recognized, ritual, approved, acknowledged, understood, household, orthodox, typical. See also accustomed (1), normal (1), daily (2), natural, conventional (1), customary, regular, habitual, familiar. **2.** Average, unimpressive (ordinary ability). Unexceptional, mediocre, undistinguished, uninteresting, mean, banal, hackneyed, predictable, modest, unassuming, uninspired, inferior, drab, stereotyped, unpretentious, dull, prosaic. See also household (1), average (2), simple (1), moderate (1), commonplace, common, pedestrian, regular, vulgar (1); informal. *Ant.* Extraordinary.

Ordinary care The degree of care that an ordinarily prudent and competent person would exercise in similar circumstances; reasonable care. See due care; negligence.

Ordinary course of business That which transpires as a matter of daily custom in business; the transaction of business according to the usages and customs of the commercial world generally, of a particular community, or of a particular individual. See business, custom, practice (1).

Ordinary income Income taxed at ordinary rates; reportable income not qualifying as capital gain. See income.

Ordinary negligence The failure to use that degree of care which the ordinary or reasonable person would have used under similar circumstances. See negligence, neglect (2).

Ordinary repairs Repairs needed as a result of usual wear and tear in order to keep the property in good condition. See maintenance (2), repair; improvement.

Ordination, *n.* See appointment (1), designation (2), classification.

Ordnance, *n.* See weapon; military, martial, sailor.

Ore, *n.* See mining, mine.

Organ, *n.* See part (1), member (2); medium, journal, newspaper; pawn (3); music.

Organic, *adj.* **1.** Inherent, fundamental (organic law). Constitutional, elemental, structural, innate, primal, indigenous, rudimentary, underlying, instinctive. See also intrinsic, material, born (2), natural (3), native (3), fundamental. **2.** Pertaining to living things (organic substance). Animate, biological, corporeal, bodily, breathing, alive. See also living (3), born. **3.** Interrelated (organic whole). Ordered, designed, organized, uniform, arranged, classified, systematic, planned, developed. *Ant.* Superficial; inanimate; chaotic.

Organic law The fundamental law or constitution of a state or nation; the system of laws or principles that establish and define the organization of government. See law, constitution, charter.

Organism, *n.* See life (1), animal (1).

Organization, *n.* **1.** Two or more persons joined in a common purpose (the president of the organization). Group, alliance, coalition, company, society, league, order, federation, affiliation, corps, clique, club, syndicate, consortium, fraternity, sorority, partnership, school, establishment, bloc, consolidation, circle. See also guild, union, institution, concern (4), institute (2), association, campaign, bureau, entity, bureaucracy, confederacy (2) agency (2), party (3), gang, corporation (1), firm (1), foundation (1). **2.** The act of arranging things in an orderly way (the organization of the files). Systematization, arrangement, categorization, methodology, collection, structure, formation, grouping, consolidation, division, standardization, plan, chemistry, assortment, placement, unification, integration, gradation, figuration, construction, incorporation, coordination, structuring, scheme. See also array (2), composition, order, management (1), disposition (3), regulation (2), building (2), establishment, distribution (1), development (1), classification (1), method. *Ant.* Individual; chaos.

Organizational, *adj.* See administrative.

Organize, *v.* **1.** To arrange in some order (organize the files). Catalogue, systematize, plan, sequence, adjust, straighten, methodize, categorize, classify, coordinate, sort, regularize, standardize, align, marshal, index, pigeonhole, rank, schedule, enroll, assign, book, earmark, dedicate, order, rate, neaten, assort, regiment, correlate, group, structure, tabulate. See also codify. **2.** To bring together for concerted activity (organize the workers). Unionize, assemble, affiliate, federate, band together, unify, league, consolidate, fuse, ally. *Ant.* Scramble; disband.

Organized, *adj.* See coherent (1), logical, integrated (2), organic (3). Organized crime. See racket (1), racketeering. Organized labor. See union (1).

Organizer, *n.* See promoter, manager, architect, director, entrepreneur, developer, founder.

Orgy, *n.* See debauchery; lust; spree; obscene, carnal.

Orient, *v.* See domesticate, adjust, accommodate, direct, introduce.

Orientation, *n.* See adjustment, accommodation (2), direction, inauguration.

Origin, *n.* See ancestry, nationality, author (2), birth (2), root, descent (2), cause (1), onset; principle, paternal, impulse.

Original 1. *n.* The first form, from which copies are made (the original was kept in the safe). Master, model, mold, archetype, source, ancestor, pattern, prototype, precedent, exemplar, basis, first copy. **2.** *adj.* First in order (the original manuscript). Archetypal, initial, primitive, introductory, earliest, seminal, formative, aboriginal, primal, elementary, primeval, fundamental, basic, essential, underlying, inborn, germinal, maiden, infant, inaugural, beginning, commencing, incipient, rudimentary, nascent, embryonic, native. See also inchoate, primary (2). **3.** *adj.* Unusual or creative (an original strategy). Innovative, fresh, not copied, refreshing, clever, unique, novel, imaginative, unorthodox, atypical, daring, visionary, different, productive, unconventional, inspired, ingenious, eccentric, unexpected, unprecedented, unknown, virgin, resourceful, gifted, fertile, singular, fecund, inventive, extraordinary, strange. *Ant.* Imitation; copied; sterile.

Original document rule The best evidence of the contents of a document is the original of that document; the party with the burden of proving the contents of a document is required to produce the original unless it is unavailable. See evidence, best evidence.

Originality, *n.* See initiative (3), novelty; identity (1); original (3).

Original jurisdiction Jurisdiction in the first instance; the power of a court to hear a case at its inception. See jurisdiction. *Ant.* Appellate jurisdiction.

Original package Unbroken and undivided; a package remaining in the same condition as when it left the shipper. See package.

Originate, *v.* See fabricate (2), initiate, manufacture (1), make (1), institute (1), forge (2), arise (1), compose (2), begin, coin (3), devise (3), author (3), build (2), engender, create, constitute (1), derive (1), frame (1), issue (1), open (2), design (1), bring about, invent (1), introduce (2).

Originating, *adj.* See causal, building (2); conception (3).

Origination, *n.* See birth (2), causation, invention, generation (2), production, inauguration, commencement.

Originator, *n.* See developer, cause (1), father, inventor, architect, ancestor, author (2), artificer (2), producer.

Ornament, *n.* See gem, decoration.

Ornamental, *adj.* See ornate.

Ornate, *adj.* See gaudy, flamboyant, meretricious.

Orneriness, *n.* See mischief; antic.

Ornery, *adj.* See crabby, contentious, litigious, difficult (3), rude, inflexible; antic, juvenile; mischief.

Orotund, *adj.* See pompous, arrogant; clear (1).

Orphan, *n.* A minor who has lost both, or sometimes one, of his or her parents (benefits on behalf of orphans). Ward, homeless child, abandoned child, waif, castaway. See also foundling; survivor, victim, abandon.

Orphanage, *n.* See home (2), institution.

Orphan's Court A special court that handles probate, guardianship of minors and incompetents, etc.

Orthodox, *adj.* See customary, traditional, popular, proper, precise (2), normal (1), regular (1), current (2), conservative, ordinary (1), formal (1), conventional (1), religious, sectarian; belief (2), religion, church.

Orthopedics, *n.* Treatment of disorders of the bones, muscles, joints, etc. See medicine, doctor, treatment, health, disease.

Oscillate, *v.* See dangle, suspend (4).

Oscillating, *adj.* See fluctuating, capricious, inconsistent.

OSHA See Occupational Safety and Health Administration.

Osmosis, *n.* See absorption (1); absorb (1), incorporate.

Ossuary, *n.* See cemetery.

Ostensible, *adj.* Seeming, pretended (the ostensible purpose of the motion). Surface, assumed, visible, professed, presumable, plausible, specious, titular, feigned, declared, alleged, external, superficial, deceiving, supposed, declared, so-called, express, outward, claimed, avowed, superficial, purported, represented. See also putative, probable, illusory, apparent (2), colorable (1), patent (1), circumstantial, nominal, reputed.

Ostensible agency An agency based on estoppel; an implied or presumptive agency that exists where a person intentionally or negligently induces another to believe that a third person is his or her agent, though in fact the latter has not been hired as an agent. See agency, agent, estoppel, deception.

Ostensible authority Such authority as a principal intentionally or negligently causes or allows a third person to believe that an agent possesses. See authority, agent.

Ostentatious, *adj.* See flamboyant, emotional; artificial; pompous; wild (2) flagrant; exaggerate; pretense, pretext.

Osteopathy, *n.* A complete system of medical practice based on the maintenance of proper relationships among the various parts of the body. Osteopathic physicians emphasize manipulative therapy but also use other accepted therapeutic methods. See doctor, treatment.

Ostracism, *n.* See exile (1), banishment, expulsion, removal (2), boycott (1), segregation; ignominy.

Ostracize, *v.* See expel, proscribe, bar (4), block (2), boycott (2); defame.

Other, *adj.* Additional; different or distinct from that already mentioned (the other factors). Further, supplemental, augmented, more, auxiliary, remaining, alternate, disparate, contrary, differing, alternative, contrasting, reverse, separate, unlike. See also second (1), opposite, extra (1); adversary. *Ant.* Same.

Other than See except (2).

Otherwise, *adv.* **1.** In another manner (unless otherwise authorized by law). In a different manner, in other ways, differently, in disagreement, inversely, contrarily, in defiance, contrariwise. **2.** On the other hand (otherwise, you receive nothing). If not, under other circumstances, or else.

Ounce, *n.* The twelfth pound troy; the sixteenth pound avoirdupois. See iota, scintilla; extent, portion.

Oust, *v.* To remove; to deprive of possession (she was ousted from the land). Throw out, banish, drive out, unseat, exile, discard, "bounce", "sack," purge, turn out, repudiate, exclude, suspend, outlaw, expatriate, maroon, overthrow, remove, cast out, blackball. See also expel, dispossess, displace (2), eject, reject (1), bar (5), depose (2), cashier, discharge (5), dispel, fire (2), dismiss (2), expropriate, evict, divest. *Ant.* Install.

Ouster, *n.* A putting out (ouster of the squatters). Discharge, deportation, sacking, expulsion, dislodgment, deprivation, evacuation, banishment, excommunication, ejection, firing, exile, overthrow. See also dispossession, elimination, removal (2), eviction, dismissal (2), layoff, purge (2). *Ant.* Admission.

Out, *adv., adj.* See exit (1), egress; absent (1).

Outbreak, *n.* See fit (2), insurrection, fight (1), epidemic (1), disturbance.

Outbuilding, *n.* A small building used in connection with the main building and usually separated from it (e.g., outhouse, storage shed). See accessory building.

Outburst, *n.* See violence, eruption, discharge (4), commotion, disturbance, emotion, storm.

Outcast, *n.* See tramp (1), exile, emigrant, foundling, derelict (3), fugitive, reject (2), alien (3), abandoned, exile (2), solitary; notorious (2).

Outclass, *v.* See best (2), beat (2), defeat (1).

Outcome, *n.* The result (the outcome of the case). Issue, judgment, solution, dénouement, end, aftermath, yield, outgrowth, fruition, achievement, wake, answer, fulfillment, completion, "payoff," impact, upshot, side effect, harvest. See also decision (1), finding, effect (1), conclusion (2), ruling (1), fruit, consequence (1), corollary, disposition (2), choice (1), resolution (1); amount (3), product, proceeds, sum (1); event; purpose (1). *Ant.* Commencement.

Outcry, *n.* See acclamation, complaint (2), scandal (4), protest (1); sound (5), noise; exception (1).

Outdated, *adj.* See old, obsolete, lapsed.

Outdistance, *v.* See overtake, overcome (2), best (2).

Outdo, *v.* See beat (2), overtake, overcome (2), best (2), defeat (1).

Outdoor, *adj.* See outside (2).

Outer, *adj.* Removed from the center (outer reaches). Remote, exterior, outlying, outward, peripheral, outermost, surface, extramural, fringe. See also outside (2), external, extreme (2). *Ant.* Inside.

Outfit, *v., n.* See furnish, equip, clothe, provide, prepare (1), fill, enable, empower; party (3), paraphernalia, establishment (1), gang; uniform (2), clothes, apparel.

Outfitted, *adj.* See armed; apparel, clothes, uniform; equip, furnish.

Outflank, *v.* See circumvent, beat (2), overtake, overcome, defeat (1).

Outgo, *n.* See expenditure.

Outgoing, *adj.* See friendly, convivial, festive.

Outgrow, *v.* See relinquish; obsolete, obsolescent.

Outgrowth, *n.* See produce (1), fruit, result (1), outcome.

Outhouse, *n.* A smaller or subordinate building connected with and usually detached from a dwelling, used as a convenience or necessity for the latter and not to live in (e.g., shed, barn, privy, toolhouse, stable). See outbuilding, bathroom.

Outing, *n.* See voyage, junket; celebration, spree.

Outlandish, *adj.* See exorbitant, excess, extraordinary, peculiar (2), anomalous, irregular.

Outlast, *v.* See continue (1), last (2); defeat (1).

Outlaw 1. *v.* To prohibit or make illegal (the court outlawed the practice). Disallow, exclude, embargo, banish, forbid, quash, quarantine, suppress, check, repress, eradicate, constrain, deny, interdict, disallow, limit, expel, repudiate, debar, circumscribe, disallow, stop. See also oust, ban (2), reject (1), prohibit, boycott (2), proscribe. **2.** *n.* See criminal (1), fugitive, malefactor, racketeer, wrongdoer.

Outlay, *n.* See disbursement, cost (1), pay, charge (8), expenditure, expense, price (1).

Outlet, *n.* See market (1), commissary (2), forum (2); exit (1), egress; drain (2).

Outline, *n.* **1.** A summary or abstract (an outline of the argument). Sketch, synopsis, syllabus, table of contents, diagram, profile, précis, draft, resumé, overview, epitome, abbreviation, skeleton, fragment, agenda, condensation, core, review, recapitulation, thumbnail sketch, scenario, graph. See also plan (2), map, frame, form (1), direction, digest, design, configuration, mode, blueprint, abridgment (2), pattern (2), compendium, prospectus, schedule (1), trace (1), abstract (3), represent (2), delineate, condense, describe, brief (2), circumscribe, detail (1). **2.** The line that marks the outer limits of an object or figure. See boundary, margin (1), limit.

Outlive, *v.* See continue (1), last (2); defeat (1).

Outlook, *n.* See opinion (2), view (5), manner, disposition (4); probability, chance (3).

Outlying, *adj.* See outer, peripheral, remote (1), external; frontier.

Outmaneuver, *v.* See circumvent, beat (2), defeat (1), overcome (2).

Outmatch, *v.* See overcome (2), best (2), beat (2), defeat (1).

Outmoded, *adj.* See ancient, old, obsolete.

Out of control See insurgent (2); wild.

Out-of-date, *adj.* See obsolete, obsolescent, lapsed, ancient, old.

Out of line See nonconforming.

Out of order See defective, broken (3), irregular.

Out of place See improper.

Out-of-pocket expenses Expenditures usually paid for with cash; expenses incurred, paid, or disbursed. See expenditure, cost.

Out-of-pocket rule The determination of damages for fraudulent misrepresentation, which permits recovery of the difference between the price paid and the actual value of the property acquired. See damages.

Out of proportion See disproportionate.

Out of sight See hidden.

Out of the blue See unforeseeable.

Out of the question See impossible, absurd.

Out-of-the-way, *adj.* See obscure (2), isolated.

Out of view See hidden, isolated.

Outpatient, *n.* See patient (1); medicine, doctor.

Outpost, *n.* See frontier.

Outpouring, *n.* See flood, stream (2).

Output, *n.* That which is taken out or produced (a remarkable output). Productivity, accomplishment, harvest, earning, growth, profit, benefit, turnout, gain, crop, produce, take, achievement, fruit, result, reaping, show. See also product, yield (2); work (5).

Output contract A contract in which one party agrees to sell his or her entire output and the other agrees to buy it. See contract.

Outrage 1. *n.* A serious wrong to a person (the report was an outrage). Insult, grave injustice, violation, breach, monstrosity, brutality, evil, abomination, mistreatment, dereliction, delinquency, barbarity, slap, inhumanity, violence, abuse, transgression, savagery, insolence, humiliation, havoc, harm, cruelty, odium, wrongdoing, sacrilege, misdeed, infringement, wound, battery, persecution, mistreatment, excess, fiendishness, effrontery, contumely, desecration, discourtesy, ill treatment, rape, prostitution. See also grievance (1), affront, wrong, shock, atrocity, indignity, offense, revolt, scandal, assault, injury, profanity, blasphemy. **2.** *v.* To enrage (the lawyer's behavior outraged the court). Exasperate, shock, disgust, gall, incense, insult, make the blood boil, offend, nauseate, provoke, infuriate, distress, pique, repulse, astound, anger, affront, madden, vex, scandalize, make indignant, disquiet, arouse, discompose, irritate, stagger, electrify, paralyze, astonish, unsettle, perturb, revolt, immobilize, flabbergast, jar, jolt, shake, bewilder, discombobulate, stun, overwhelm, appall, dumfound, repel, horrify, upset, displease, excite. See also harass, accost (1), beat (2), disturb. *Ant.* Benefit; pacify.

Outrageous, *adj.* See offensive, notorious (2); odious, repulsive, exorbitant, excess, extreme (1), flagrant, wanton (1), grievous, irrational, cruel, bad (3), calumnious, inexcusable, infamous, insane (2), gross (2); great (1), doubtful.

Outright, *adj.* Complete (an outright lie). Direct, open, entire, without restraint, total, thorough, absolute, unconditional, straightforward, unequivocal, comprehensive, flagrant, downright, unreserved, utter, sweeping, consummate, full, perfect, out-and-out, distinct, undeniable, palpable, manifest, wholesale, rank, unqualified, undivided, undiminished, unmistakable, conspicuous, flat, incontestable. See also overt, blatant (1). *Ant.* Partial.

Outset, *n.* See onset (1), inception.

Outside 1. *n.* The exterior (the outside had deteriorated). Facade, outer side, skin, shell, coating, face, covering, front, appearance, externals. See also surface. **2.** *adj.* Outer (outside fence). Outdoor, exterior, visible. See also external, outer. **3.** *adj.* Not originating from within (outside influences). Non-native, unfamiliar, strange, exotic, extraneous, independent, unconnected, extrinsic, remote, imported, exported. See also alien (2), foreign (3). **4.** *adj.* Remote (outside chance). Obscure, distant, faint, small, improbable, marginal, unlikely. *Ant.* Interior; internal; native; likely.

Outsider, *n.* See stranger, foreigner, immigrant, alien (3).

Outskirt, *n.* See margin (1), border (1), bound (4), frontier.

Outsmart, *v.* See best (2), beat (2), defeat (2).

Outspoken, *adj.* See direct (6), explicit, free, honest; abrasive, rude.

Outstanding, *adj.* **1.** Uncollected (outstanding debts). Unpaid, undischarged, unsatisfied, unresolved, existing, owing, in arrears, unsettled, undissolved, open, remaining, unfinished, unconcluded, mature, receivable, pending. See also payable, residuary, delinquent (1), due (1), overdue; debt, arrearages, balance (1). **2.** Distinctive (outstanding presentation). Excellent, superior, prominent, striking, eminent, unforgettable, memorable, foremost, phenomenal, famed, notable, great, exceptional, terrific, special, extraordinary, splendid, conspicuous, renowned, celebrated, stunning, unmistakable, famous, bold, distinguished, magnificent, august, salient, signal, exemplary, noteworthy, sensational, classic, chief, impressive, venerable, majestic, luminous, consequential, well-known, obtrusive, principal, eye-catching, distinctive, incomparable, transcendent, important, paramount, illustrious, sublime, glaring, visible, supreme, significant, unparalleled, arresting, honored, amazing, astonishing, breathtaking, unique, one of a kind, nonpareil, unheard of, grand, stupendous, atypical, imposing; standout. *Ant.* Satisfied; mundane.

Outstrip

Outstrip, *v.* See overtake, best (2), defeat (1).

Outward, *adj.* See outer, extrinsic (1), external, objective (1), public (3), apparent (2); ostensible; demeanor.

Outweigh, *v.* See override, exceed, overcome; balance.

Outweighing, *adj.* See superseding.

Outwit, *v.* See circumvent, cheat (1), defeat (1), best (2), beat (2).

Oval, *adj.* See round.

Ovation, *n.* See acclamation.

Over, *prep.* In excess of (over the limit). More than, higher than, exceeding, on top of, greater than, transcending, surpassing. See also above (3); across.

Overabundant, *adj.* See needless; redundancy, rank (2), over.

Over again See de novo, anew.

Overage, *n.* See remainder (2).

Overall, *adj.* See comprehensive, entire; national.

Over and above See excess.

Overawe, *v.* See intimidate.

Overbearing, *adj.* See unconscionable, onerous, arbitrary; peremptory; compel, dominate.

Overbreadth doctrine A law is invalid if it does not aim specifically at evils within the allowable area of government control, but sweeps within its ambit other activities that constitute an exercise of protected expression or association rights.

Overburden, *v.* See inundate, overload, wear (1).

Overcast, *adj.* See fog; climate.

Overcharge, *v.* To charge more than is permitted by law (they were overcharged). Fleece, "rip off," "burn." See also deceive, cheat; unconscionable.

Overcome, *v.* **1.** To counterbalance; to outweigh (to overcome the presumption). See override, exceed; balance. **2.** To defeat or overwhelm (overcome the obstacles). Shatter, break down, vanquish, subdue, overpower, discomfit, best, transcend, suppress, quell, overrun, survive, surmount, get the better of, weather, submerge, triumph over, subjugate, master, crush, checkmate, dominate, outmaneuver, outdo, overwhelm, swallow, overshadow, command, outmatch, confound. See also beat (2), override (1), restrain, impose, inundate, defeat (1), conquer, devastate (2), prevail (2); convince; hysterical. *Ant.* Submit.

Overconfident, *adj.* See assured (4).

Overdo, *v.* See overload.

Overdone, *adj.* See artificial (2), flamboyant, gaudy.

Overdose, *n.,* **overdose,** *v.* See mistake, blunder, medicine, treatment; overload, inundate.

Overdraft, *n.* A check written on an account containing less funds than the amount of the check. See draft, mistake, fraud.

Overdraw, *v.* To draw upon a person or a bank in an amount in excess of the funds remaining to the drawer's credit with the drawee, or to an amount greater than what is due. Overextend, deplete, exhaust.

Overdue, *adj.* Pertaining to that which should have already been paid or done (overdue account). Unpaid, delayed, tardy, unsettled, in arrears, mature, owing, payable, dilatory, slow, unpunctual, untimely, remiss, past due, belated. See also back (2), delinquent (1), due (1), late (2), outstanding (1); arrearages. *Ant.* Premature.

Overestimate, *v.* See overrate; puffing, flattery; boast.

Overextend, *v.* See overdraw, overload.

Overflow, *v.,* **overflow,** *n.* See inundate; overload; excess, rank (2), flood, remainder (2), residue.

Overflowing, *adj.* See abundant, excess, copious.

Overgrow, *v.* See spread (4); rank (2).

Overhanging, *adj.* See imminent, prospective; menace (2), hover (1).

Overhaul, *v.* **1.** To investigate thoroughly with a view to repairs (overhaul the engine). Scrutinize, check into, audit, take inventory, renovate, reconstruct, recondition, service, restore. See also maintain (1), renew, revise, fix (3), repair (1), modify, improve; reorganization. **2.** To catch up with and pass. See overtake.

Overhead, *n.* **1.** All administrative costs incident to the management of a business or other operation that cannot be precisely attributed to any one department or product, e.g., taxes, utilities (10% overhead on all contracts goes to the central office). Continuous expenses, indirect costs, burden, oncosts, fixed costs, operating costs, upkeep, general expenses. See also carrying charge, expenditure, cost. **2.** See ceiling (2).

Overhear, *v.* See eavesdrop.

Overheat, *v.* See burn, overload.

Overindulgent, *adj.* See permissive (2); spree.

Overissue, *v.* To issue in excessive quantity; to issue in excess of the amount limited and prescribed by the charter (the stock was overissued). See excess.

Overkill, *n.* See surplusage; excess, waste (1).

Overlap, *v.,* **overlap,** *n.* See contact (4); waste (1); intersection.

Overload, *v.* To cause to bear too heavy a burden (overload the system). Load too heavily, overdo, overburden, encumber, weigh down, handicap, choke, saddle, overtax, strain, overwhelm, hamper, tie, saturate, oppress, impede, drag, hinder, deluge, pack, congest, overweigh. See also inundate, burden (3). *Ant.* Lighten.

Overlook, *v.* See excuse (2), ignore, condone, forgive (2), neglect (1), connive, disregard, waive; oversee; err, blunder (2).

Overlying right The right of an owner of land to take water from the ground underneath the land for use on the land.

Overmuch, *adj.* See excess, gratuitous (2).

Overpaid, *adj.* See excess, exorbitant; waste (1).

Overpass, *n.* See intersection; highway.

Overplus, *n.* The surplus or excess; what is left beyond a certain amount. See balance (1), remainder.

Overpower, *v.* See devastate (2), kill (2), force (4), defeat (1), conquer, coerce, beat (2), restrain, dominate, compel, overcome, counteract.

Overpowering, *adj.* See onerous, predominant, compelling, acute (2), irresistible; compulsion, coercion.

Overpraise, *v.* See overrate, flatter; flattery, puffing (1).

Overpriced, *adj.* See excess, exorbitant, costly.

Overrate, *v.* To rate too highly (he overrated the importance of the case). Overvalue, overestimate, oversell, misrepresent, overprize, exaggerate, overassess, overesteem, attach too much importance to. See also puffing, flattery. *Ant.* Underestimate.

Overreach, *v.* See betray, cheat (1), deceive, manipulate; overreaching, fraud.

Overreaching, *n.* Going too far; outsmarting by deception (prosecutorial overreaching). Misconduct, bad faith, harassment, undue advantage, prejudice, cheating, trickery, circumvention, misleading, undermining, excess. See also fraud, cheat. *Ant.* Fair play.

Overreact *v.* See exaggerate, color (3), distort.

Override, *v.,* **override,** *n.* **1.** *v.* To set aside (the senator voted to override the governor's veto). Nullify, upset, counteract, void, supersede, prevail over, take precedence over, negate, disregard, crush, defy, thwart, defeat, destroy, ignore, surmount, subdue, vanquish, conquer. See also abolish, rescind, overrule, reverse

Override

(1), countermand, annul, abrogate, overcome (2), cancel (1); prevail (2). **2.** *n.* A commission paid to managers on sales made by subordinates; a commission paid to a real estate agent when a landowner makes a sale on his or her own to a purchaser who was found by the agent.

Overriding, *adj.* See predominant, primary (1), cardinal, superseding, compelling, irresistible; rescission, override (1).

Overrule, *v.* To reject by subsequent action or decision; to deprive an earlier opinion of authority as precedent by rendering an opposite decision on the same question of law (the court was asked to overrule its earlier opinion). Supersede, void, abrogate, overturn, renounce, invalidate, disallow, nullify, retract, undo, vacate, veto, repudiate, thwart, recall, repeal. See also cancel (1), annul, revoke, reverse (1), countermand, rescind, disaffirm, override, reject (1), abolish, quash. *Ant.* Reaffirm.

Overrun, *v.* See encroach, overcome (2), inundate, occupy (3); remainder (2).

Oversee, *v.* To direct and watch over (oversee the estate). Supervise, superintend, guide, run, head, orchestrate, navigate, lead, manipulate, counsel, quarterback, dictate, officiate, look after, pilot, overlook, keep an eye on, attend to, take charge, mind, take care of, shelter, nurse, minister, shepherd, safeguard, defend, harbor, guard, steer. See also maintain (1), control (1), rule (3), direct (2), conduct (2), enforce, shield (1), regulate, manage, patrol, check (2), administer (1), preside, police (2), watch (1), audit (2), discipline (4), handle (1), operate; censor (2); deal (3).

Overseer, *n.* See manager, foreman, official (1), matron (2), master, caretaker, conservator, chairman, bailiff (2), administrator (1), proprietor, director; receiver; boatswain.

Oversell, *v.* See overrate; puffing; boast.

Oversensitive, *adj.* See feverish, emotional, hot; violent, squeamish.

Overshadow, *v.* See obscure (3), cloud (3), overcome (2).

Oversight, *n.* See supervision, direction (2), control (3), care (3), auspices, management (1), administration, protection, inspection, government; omission, neglect (2), lapse (3), mistake, error, failure, fault (1), blunder (1), nonfeasance, accident (2), nonpayment; disregard.

Oversimplify, *v.* See distort, color (3); exaggerate.

Overstate, *v.* See color (3), misrepresent, exaggerate, lie (2); encroach.

Overstatement, *n.* See puffing; exaggerate.

Overstepping, *n.* See intrusion, intervention (2), invasion, malfeasance, infraction.

Oversubscription, *n.* The existence of more orders or subscriptions for corporate stock than can be issued.

Oversuspicious, *adj.* See suspicious; paranoid.

Overt, *adj.* Open or manifest (overt antagonism). Visible, plain, revealed, unconcealed, exposed, undisguised, direct, outright, straightforward, observable, notorious, perceptible, unshrouded, flagrant, conspicuous, definite, seen, distinct, noticeable. See also manifest (1), obvious, naked (2), palpable, clear (1), patent (1), apparent (1), blatant (1), public (3), open (5). *Ant.* Latent.

Overt act An open, manifest act done in pursuance and manifestation of an intent or design; an outward act from which criminality may be implied. See conduct (1), evidence, manifestation.

Overtake, *v.* To catch up with and pass (overtake her competitor). Reach, outstrip, overhaul, outdistance, run down, outdo, overwhelm, surprise, gain on, leave behind. *Ant.* Fall behind.

Overtax, *v.* See overload, burden (3); onerous.

Over-the-counter, *adj.* Sold or exchanged independent of an exchange or without the need of a prescription (over-the-counter market). See medicine.

Overthrow, *v.*, **overthrow,** *n.* See defeat (2), confute, conquer, quash, reverse (1), restrain, rebut, tip (3), kill (2), oust; revolution, mutiny, ouster, abolition, revolt, failure (1), rebuttal, collapse, rescission, insurrection, coup d'état.

Overtime, *n.* After regular working hours; beyond the regular fixed hours (payment for overtime). See labor.

Overtone, *n.* See innuendo (2), undercurrent.

Overture, *n.* An opening or proposal (settlement overture). Plan, presentation, advance, tender, motion, proffer, prelude, preliminary, initiation, beginning, bid, signal, forward, introduction, recommendation, initiative, tender, appeal. See also request, invitation, offer (2), proposition (1), proposal; approach (3). *Ant.* Stalemate.

Overturn, *v.* See defeat (1), overrule, destroy, block (2), disprove, rebut, turn (1), tip (3), abolish; capsize.

Overused, *adj.* See commonplace (2).

Overvalue, *v.* See overrate.

Overview, *n.* See outline, exposition.

Overweight, *adj.* See corpulent.

Overwhelm, *v.* See devastate (2), surprise (1), defeat (1), conquer, inundate, compel, beat (2), overtake, overload, overcome (2), submerge, impress (1), outrage (2).

Overwhelming, *adj.* See acute (2), irresistible, onerous, difficult, serious; invulnerable, indestructible; extraordinary, outstanding (2), beautiful, attractive.

Overwork, *v.* See labor (2), burden (3).

Overwrought, *adj.* See feverish; exhausted; emotional, angry; weak, frail.

Overzealous, *adj.* See hot (2), emotional, active, ardent, officious.

Owe, *v.* To be bound to do or omit something (he owed $40). Be obligated to, be indebted to, be beholden to, be under an obligation to, be in debt to, be under contract for, be liable for.

Owing, *adj.* Unpaid. See outstanding (1), overdue, due (1), delinquent (1), balance, payable.

Own, *v.* **1.** To have a legal or rightful title to (he owns the suitcase). Control, keep, maintain, retain; belong. See also possess, hold (1), enjoy; personal, separate. **2.** See admit (1), recognize (2), acknowledge (1).

Owner, *n.* The person in whom title, ownership, or dominion is vested (the owner of the land). Landlady, lord, partner. See also possessor, holder, proprietor, occupant, entrepreneur, landlord, lessor, stockholder, employer, master (1).

Ownership, *n.* The complete dominion, title, or proprietary right in something; a collection of rights to use and enjoy property, including the right to transmit it to others (disputed ownership). Mastery, proprietorship, seisin, tenancy, freehold, control, holding. See also possession (1), domain (1), claim (3), dominion, right (3), interest (1).

Oyer and terminer A commission to a judge to inquire into and hear criminal cases.

Oyez, *interj.* Hear ye; a call announcing the beginning of a court proceeding or a proclamation.

P

Pace, *v., n.* See walk; rate (1).

Pacific, *adj.* See quiet (1, 2), passive; cautious; composure; harmony.

Pacification, *n.* The act of bringing peace or of calming a situation (fruitless pacification efforts). Quieting, alleviation, placation, mediation, tranquilization, conciliation, modulation, intervention, truce, mitigation, accommodation, consoling, appeasement, relaxation, assuagement, settlement, lessening, reconciliation, moratorium, adjustment, palliation, remission, negotiation, solacing, peace, restoration, détente, reduction, tempering; suppression; blunting, dulling. *Ant.* Aggravation.

Pacifist, *n.* One who refuses to bear arms for any purpose because of conscientious considerations; a conscientious objector; one who seeks to maintain peace and abolish war. See nonconformist.

Pacify, *v.* See mitigate, assuage, quiet (2, 3).

Pack 1. *v.* To assemble with an improper purpose (pack the jury). Tie, load, bunch, crowd, swarm, jam, compress, choke, constrict, weigh down, cram, ram. See also burden (3). **2.** *n.* See lot (3), collection (2); mass; package.

Package, *n.* A parcel; a bundle that is ready for transportation or for commercial handling; that which is wrapped, bound, tied up, or boxed; a shipping package (in its original package). Container, carton, unit, crate, case, pack, kit, packet, bundle, receptacle, composite, box. See also vessel (2).

Packing list A document that contains the contents, weight, and other information concerning a package to be shipped.

Pact, *n.* A bargain; an agreement between two or more nations or states (nonaggression pact). Compact, contract, treaty, reconciliation, concordat, stipulation, covenant, bond, alliance, collusion, convention, understanding, alliance, concordance, mutual promise, charter, deal, league, consortium, protocol, arrangement, cooperation, coming together.

Pad, *n.* See home; rug.

Padlock, *n.* See lock (3).

Pagan, *n.* See atheist; anarchist, nihilist; irreverent, profane (1).

Page, *n., v.* See servant, employee, attendant; summon (1).

Pageant, *n.* See extravaganza, ceremony, celebration (2), banquet, amusement, entertainment.

Paid, *v.* See satisfy (1), pay.

Paid-in capital Money or property paid to a corporation by its owners for its capital stock. See capital, corporation, pay.

Paid-in surplus That portion of the surplus of a corporation not generated by profits but contributed by the stockholders. See pay, back, contribute, corporation.

Paid-up stock Shares of stock for which full payment has been received by the corporation. See securities, share (3).

Pain, *n.* Physical discomfort and distress (pain from the injury). Agony, hurt, aching, soreness, throb, smarting, suffering, torment, twinge, tenderness, pang, distress, affliction, heartache, travail, tribulation, misery, nuisance, torture, displeasing sensation, inconvenience, woe, unhappiness, cross, trouble, bitterness, hell, ordeal, displeasure, wretchedness, sickness, vexation, aggravation, despondency; acute. See also anguish, annoyance, burden, disease. *Ant.* Relief.

Pain and suffering Physical discomfort and distress; mental and emotional trauma. See pain, suffer.

Painful, *adj.* Agonizing. Torturous, searing, burning, unbearable, grueling, tormenting, racking, insufferable, aching, unpleasant, throbbing, raw, stinging. See also tender (6), pain, suffer; distressing, obnoxious.

Painless, *adj.* See harmless, innocent (2); summary (1).

Painstaking, *adj.* See precise (2), critical, careful, particular (2); comprehensive.

Paint, *v.* See delineate, define, describe; distort, color.

Painting, *n.* See description; masterpiece; opus.

Pair, *n., v.* See two; connect (1), join, bind (2).

Pairing-off Two voting members of an organization agree to be absent on the day a vote is to be taken on an issue on which they would have voted differently if they had been present.

Pal, *n.* See cohort, intimate, associate (2), ally.

Palace, *n.* See home; luxury, wealth.

Palatable, *adj.* See delectable, enjoyable, attractive; admissible, adequate.

Palaver, *n., v.* See colloquium (2), conversation (1), conference; babble.

Pale, *adj., n.* See anemic, exhausted, frail, weak, thin; zone.

Palimony, *n.* The word "palimony" is the creation of the media to describe payments sought by one nonmarital party from another after they cease living together. The word is intended to describe the rough equivalent of alimony following the breakup of a marital relationship. In fact, it is not the legal equivalent of alimony. Nonmarital parties do not have to make support or other payments to each other after their relationship is over unless the following conditions are met: (a) They entered an express or implied contract for such payments, (b) the contract does not involve payment for sexual services, and (c) they live in a state that will recognize the contract as enforceable or that is willing to fashion other remedies to prevent an injustice. See cohabit, cohabitation.

Palliate, *v.* See mitigate, assuage; pacification.

Palliative, *n., adj.* See narcotic, drug; pacification; remedial, extenuating; mitigate, assuage.

Pallid, *adj.* See anemic, weak, frail, exhausted, thin.

Palming off Deception in selling or passing off goods of one manufacturer as those of another. See deception, fraud.

Palmistry, *n.* The practice of telling fortunes by an interpretation of the lines and marks on the hand; a trick with the hand. See oracle, augur, clairvoyance (2); fraud, deception.

Palpable, *adj.* Readily noticeable (a palpable lie). Manifest, apparent, obvious, easily perceivable, plain, readily visible, patent, distinct, tangible, touchable, unmistakable, discernible, evident, recognizable, perceptible, unveiled, bold, conspicuous, explicit, marked, self-evident, sensible, tactile, prominent, uncovered, discoverable, bald, ascertainable, flagrant, blatant, unambiguous, striking, exposed, egregious, physical, salient, clear-cut, overt, arresting, positive, substantial, solid, glaring, identifiable, observable. *Ant.* Imperceptible.

Paltry, *adj.* See petty (2), nugatory, frivolous, inferior, worthless.

Pamper, *v.* See delight, satisfy, accommodate, pander (2); caress.

Panacea, *n.* See cure (1), relief (1); resolution (1), answer (3); witchcraft.

Panache, *n.* See style (2).

Pandemic, *adj.* See extensive, general, broad (1); contagious.

Pandemonium, *n.* See commotion, hysteria, eruption, disorder, confusion; wild.

Pander 1. *n.* One who caters to the lust of others (he was little more than a pander). Panderer, pimp, go-between, procurer, runner, madam, whoremonger, procuress, "hustler," purveyor, supplier. **2.** *v.* To cater to the gratification of the lust of another; to cater to the base desires of others (the magazine pandered to the reader's interest in violence). Gratify, trade, purvey, indulge, exploit, satisfy, stoop, crawl, please, furnish, service, subserve, gratiate, tend, humor, court, provide, fawn, oblige, minister. See also flatter, grovel.

Panel, *n.* A group selected or summoned (panel of jurors). Forum, body, select group, committee, assembly, tribunal, council, round table, advisory group, board, conference.

Pang, *n.* See pain, anguish.

Panhandle, *v.* See beseech, petition (2); tramp, pauper; parasite.

Panic, *n.* See hysteria, confusion, insanity, anxiety, commotion, disorder, emotion, passion.

Panic-stricken, *adj.* See agape, paranoid, hysterical; fear (1), consternation.

Panorama, *n.* See view (5), environment, neighborhood.

Pantomime, *v., n.* See impersonate, mock; imitation, copy.

Paper, *n.* **1.** A written or printed document; written or printed evidence of a debt (commercial paper). Certificate, instrument, memorandum, record, notation, order, testament, note, chronicle, composition. **2.** A product made by a general process of matting fibers. **3.** A small bundle or package of narcotics.

Paper patent A discovery or invention that has never been put to commercial use nor recognized in the trade. See invention; dormant.

Paper profit An unrealized profit on a security or other investment that is still held. See profit; inchoate.

Par, *n.* **1.** Equal; an equality between the actual selling value and the nominal or face value of a bill of exchange, share of stock, etc. (the share is at par). Equivalence, agreement, symmetry, correspondence, unity, identity, equilibrium, equal footing, level, balance. See also parity, par value. **2.** An acceptable standard (up to par). Grade, scale, value, normal, average, mean, norm, guide, caliber, mark, usual, measure.

Parade, *v., n.* See exhibit (1), publish; extravaganza, ceremony, celebration (2).

Paradigm, *n.* See criterion, sample (1), model, instance, archetype.

Paradise, *n.* See heaven, luxury, happiness; afterlife; oblivion; religion, holy.

Paradox, *n.* See mystery, conundrum; ambiguity.

Paragon, *n.* See criterion, model, archetype, sample (1).

Paragraph, *n.* See clause; extract (2), passage (4).

Paralegal, *n.* A person with legal skills who works under the supervision of a lawyer or who is otherwise authorized by law to use his or her skills; a person engaged in the delivery of legal services beyond the secretarial level who is not licensed to practice law in the state in which he or she works (the paralegal represented the client at the Social Security hearing). Legal assistant, legal paraprofessional, legal technician, legal aide, litigation assistant, probate specialist, welfare specialist, paralegal specialist, lay assistant, legal service assistant, case aide, lawyer's assistant, attorney assistant, lay advocate, copyright paralegal, community worker, EEO specialist.

Parallel, *adj.* Corresponding or matching (parallel development). Coextensive, abreast, twin, complementary, concurrent, matched, comparable, equivalent, aligned, similar, comparative, duplicate, counterpart; analogue. See also analogous. *Ant.* Separate.

Parallel citation A reference to another set of books or reporters in which the same case—word for word—can be located. See citation (2).

Paralysis, *n.* See impotence (2), impossibility; disease, illness.

Paralyze, *v.* See incapacitate, disqualify, obstruct (1), arrest (3); maim.

Paramedic, *n.* A trained assistant to a doctor. See assistant.

Parameter, *n.* See constant (2), boundary.

Paramilitary, *adj.* Pertaining to a group that is organized similar to the armed forces. See military, martial.

Paramount, *adj.* Of the highest rank or nature (the paramount consideration). Superior, principal, chief, unsurpassed, higher, main, transcendent, foremost, incomparable, dominant, predominant, preeminent, supreme, premier, cardinal, without parallel, salient, leading, crowning, overruling, distinguished, master, superlative, reigning, head, sterling, prize, number-one, sovereign, outstanding, model, first, capital. See also extraordinary, exceptional. *Ant.* Minor.

Paramour, *n.* A lover, often in an adulterous alliance (the divorce complaint named his paramour). Mistress, gallant, concubine, playboy, gigolo, courtesan. See also prostitute, suitor.

Paranoid, *adj.* Concerning someone afflicted with paranoia—delusions of grandeur or persecution; excessive feelings of distrust or of self-importance (he became paranoid over the losses). Oversuspicious, paranoiac, fearful, apprehensive, insane, frightened, nervous, alarmed, crazed, unbalanced, panic-stricken, uneasy.

Paraphernalia, *n.* **1.** Miscellaneous articles, equipment, or personal belongings (drug paraphernalia). Gear, tools, accessories, effects, supplies, utensils, things, appliances, property, accouterments, trappings, apparatus, regalia, furnishings, appointments, rig, implements, instruments, fixtures, wherewithal, conveniences, contrivances, outfit, movables, chattels, resources, goods, personal property, assets. **2.** The separate property of a married woman, other than her dowry.

Paraphrase, *v.* To rephrase. Restate, summarize, reword, recapitulate, recap, rehash, repeat. See also abridge, condense; outline.

Paraprofessional, *n.* One who assists a professional person though not a member of the profession himself or herself. See assistant, paralegal.

Parasite, *n.* A freeloader or leech. Sponge, toady, bloodsucker, hanger-on, flatterer, barnacle, slacker, deadbeat, freeloader, lackey, courtier. See also malingerer, pimp; predatory, avaricious.

Paratrooper, *n.* A member of the army who parachutes. See military, martial, aircraft; sailor.

Parcel 1. *v.* To divide into portions (the court parceled the estate). Apportion, partition, carve up, distribute, allot, mete out, allocate, fragment, deal out, subdivide, measure, prorate, split up, segment, part. **2.** *n.* A small package or bundle (damaged parcel). Packet, box, bale, crate, carton, case, receptacle, container. See also vessel (2). **3.** *n.* A part or portion of land; a contiguous quantity of land (the parcel was sold). Lot, tract, acreage, plot, patch, square, division, subdivision, sector, plat, enclosure. **4.** *n.* A collection or group. See allotment (1), collection (1, 2), group (1). *Ant.* Unify; contents; whole; individual.

Parcener, *n.* A joint heir; one who, with another, holds an estate in coparcenary. See coparcenary, estate.

Parchment, *n.* The skin of a lamb, goat, young calf, or other animal prepared for writing on; stationery. See paper.

Pardon 1. *n.* An act of grace from the governing power, which exempts an individual from punishment for crime and from all civil disabilities that result therefrom (the governor granted a pardon to the inmate). Release, remission, absolution, forgiveness, exoneration, amnesty, commutation, relinquishment, forbearance, exculpation, dismissal, clemency, vindication, lenience, indulgence, mercy, indemnity, acquittal, reprieve, dispensation, justification, excuse, cancellation, purging, removal, expunging, emancipation, suspension, overlooking, deliverance. **2.** *v.* See forgive. *Ant.* Condemnation; condemn.

Pare, *v.* See diminish, dock (3), cut.

Parens patriae The state's power to act as a guardian of persons who suffer disabilities (e.g., minors, insane persons). See guardian, parent.

Parent, *n.* The lawful mother or father of a person (responsibility of the parent). Procreator, begetter, sire, ancestor, matriarch, patriarch, precursor, progenitor, generator, antecedent, forebear, predecessor; source, cause, fountainhead, nucleus, root, prime mover, agent, author, forerunner, producer. *Ant.* Child.

Parentage, *n.* The condition of being a parent; kindred in the direct ascending line. See lineage; beget, paternity.

Parental, *adj.* Pertaining to a parent (parental neglect). Maternal, paternal, motherly, fatherly. See also authority, protection, guardian.

Parent-child immunity In some states, a child cannot sue its parents for designated personal torts (e.g., battery). See immune, immunity.

Parent company A company owning more than 50% of the voting shares of another company; a corporation that controls its subsidiary corporations through stock ownership. See company, conglomerate.

Parenthetical, *adj.* See incidental; comment (2), clarification.

Par excellence, *adj.*, *adv.* See outstanding (2), extraordinary, exceptional.

Pariah, *n.* See exile, emigrant, tramp (1).

Pari delicto See in pari delicto.

Pari materia See in pari materia.

Pari-mutuel betting A betting pool; a mutual stake or wager in which those that bet on the winner share the total stakes less a percentage for management. See gambling.

Parish, *n.* **1.** A territorial government division in Louisiana. See county, zone. **2.** An ecclesiastical division of a city or town under the ministry of one pastor. See church, religion, division.

Par items Items that a drawee bank will remit to another bank without charge.

Parity, *n.* Equality in amount or value; equivalence in the prices of goods or services in two different markets (parity in armaments). Uniformity, balance, equilibrium, parallelism, closeness, semblance, congruity, comparability, correlation, likeness, proportion, symmetry, approximation, equation, par, harmony, analogy, nearness. See also identity (2), conformity, correspondence (1). *Ant.* Disparity.

Park 1. *n.* An enclosed pleasure ground in or near a city set apart for public recreation (renovation of the park). Meadow, green, grove, grassland, common, plaza, lawn, field, sanctuary, garden, woodland, preserve, range, forest, reservation. **2.** *v.* To stop a vehicle with the intent to remain standing for an appreciable length of time (park the car). Pull in, situate.

Parkway, *n.* See highway.

Parlay, *v.*, *n.* See augment; manipulate; bet, gambling.

Parley, *n.* See meeting, conference, mediation.

Parliament, *n.* The supreme legislative assembly of Great Britain, consisting of the House of Lords and the House of Commons. See legislature, Congress.

Parliamentary, *adj.* Pertaining to the legislature (parliamentary maneuver). Legislative, deliberative, lawmaking, congressional.

Parlor, *n.* See chamber (1).

Parochial, *adj.* **1.** Relating to a parish (parochial schools). Church, religious, sectarian. **2.** Narrow in scope (parochial considerations). Provincial, insular, sectional, regional, narrow-minded, confined, shortsighted, dogmatic, illiberal, backward, local, small, countrified, partisan, biased, jaundiced, limited, bigoted, prejudiced, myopic, uncatholic, uncultivated, petty, vapid, intolerant, self-righteous, conventional, traditional, unsophisticated, circumscribed, restricted. *Ant.* Secular; cosmopolitan.

Parody, *n., v.* See caricature; mock (1), slander; copy, imitation.

Parol, *adj.* Oral (parol contract). Unwritten, nuncupative, voiced, expressed by speech, uttered. See also oral, verbal, parol evidence rule. *Ant.* Written.

Parole, *n.* Release from confinement after serving part of the sentence; conditional release from prison under the supervision of a parole officer, who has the authority to recommend a return to prison if the conditions of parole (e.g., not leaving the state without permission) are violated. See release.

Parole Board The administrative body with the power (a) to determine whether a prisoner shall be conditionally released from prison before the expiration of his or her sentence, (b) to establish and modify the conditions of parole, and (c) to revoke parole after making a determination that the parolee has violated the conditions of parole. See agency (2).

Parolee, *n.* An ex-prisoner who has been placed on parole.

Parol evidence rule When parties put their agreement in writing, all previous oral agreements merge in the writing, and the contract as written cannot be altered or changed by oral or verbal evidence in the absence of mistake, duress, or fraud in the preparation of the writing. See evidence, contract.

Paroxysm, *n.* See fit (2), eruption, storm, disturbance, commotion, hysteria, passion.

Parricide, *n.* Killing one's father or other close relative. See homicide, murder.

Parrot, *v.* See repeat, mock (1), copy (2).

Parsimonious, *adj.* See economical, stingy, avaricious; petty.

Parsimony, *n.* See economy; stingy, avaricious; petty.

Parson, *n.* See minister (1); clergy, clerical (1).

Part 1. *n.* A portion of the whole (a part of the system). Segment, unit, subdivision, division, component, element, parcel, section, piece, moiety, constituent, fraction, ingredient, share, bit, particle, scrap, limb, member, department, detail, module, branch, sector, ratio, ration, lot, allowance, quota, cut, helping, apportionment, excerpt, complement, amount, organ, percentage, interest, morsel, region, snippet, item, joint, arm, allotment, proportion, contingent, appendage, chapter, clause, article, paragraph, measure, slice, quarter, shred, subgroup, detachment. **2.** *n.* Function (evidence of her part in the crime). Role, job, responsibility, undertaking, chore, participation, say, interest, duty, scope, task, concern, place, side, line, capacity, character. See also assignment (3), function. **3.** *v.* To separate (animosity when the spouses parted). Sever, split, disconnect, undo, detach, bifurcate, divide, partition, tear away, break off, cleave, diverge, branch off, dismantle, divorce, disjoin, rupture, sunder, uncouple, disengage, halve, estrange, dissect; isolate, go away, take leave, withdraw, retire, quit, evacuate, remove, scatter, escape. *Ant.* Whole (1); merge (3).

Partake, *v.* See enjoy (1), participate.

Partial, *adj.* **1.** Not complete (partial incapacity). Not entire, not universal, not general, not total, fractional, part, limited, incomplete, abridged, unfinished, imperfect, fragmentary, segmental, deficient, slight, inchoate, local, inconclusive, undeveloped, confined, wanting, sketchy, halfway, immature. **2.** Favoring one side; prejudiced (the judge was charged with being partial). Predisposed, one-sided, influenced, discriminatory, affected, biased, bigoted, inclined, unfair, prone, involved, unbalanced, jaundiced, prepossessed. See also partisan (2), interested. **3.** See affectionate. *Ant.* Complete; disinterested.

Partiality, *n.* See bias, favor (2), favoritism.

Particeps criminis A participant in a crime. See accomplice.

Participant

Participant, *n.* See party (2), accessory (1), accomplice, actor.

Participate, *v.* To experience in common with others (participate in the cover-up). Share, join, take part in, receive a share of, divide, partake, engage in, act in concert, work with, have something to do with, help, contribute, affiliate with, cooperate with, join forces with, merge with, encourage, agree with, involve oneself, be in on, be a party to. *Ant.* Withdraw.

Participation, *n.* See part (2), cooperation, responsibility, function; participate.

Particular 1. *adj.* Pertaining to a single person, class, or thing (a particular document). Individual, fixed, definite, specific, special, distinct, peculiar, distinctive, explicit, select, distinguished, personal, singular, strange, well-defined, sole, detailed, original, especial, exact, express, separate, precise, pronounced, certain, marked, concrete, itemized, characteristic, uncommon, unique, absolute, notable, chosen, exclusive. See also outstanding (2), extraordinary, exceptional. **2.** *adj.* Concerned with details (he was particular about his accounts). Precise, careful, detailed, scrupulous, fastidious, minute, discriminating, accurate, unyielding, attentive, meticulous, punctilious, demanding, difficult, exacting, conscientious, painstaking, finicky, selective, inflexible, uncompromising, critical, overcritical, rigorous, stringent, fussy, stern. **3.** *n.* A detail. See fact, particulars. *Ant.* General; casual.

Particularity, *n.* Precision in providing details; carefulness. See particular (2), careful.

Particularization, *n.* See specification.

Particularize, *v.* See detail (1), distinguish, discriminate (2), divide.

Particulars, *n.* The details (the testimony provided few of the particulars). Events, cases, specifications, points, features, items, aspects, specifics, niceties, articles, experiences, occurrences, pieces, information, incidents. See also circumstances, detail (2), fact, factor.

Particulars, bill of See bill of particulars.

Parties, *n.* See party.

Parting, *n.* See departure (2), exit, removal.

Partisan 1. *n.* An adherent to a particular cause or party (a partisan in the fight for reform). Champion, leader, advocate, fighter, believer, devotee, stalwart, disciple, supporter, adherent, sympathizer, zealot, booster, fan, partner, votary, comrade, ally, enthusiast, sponsor, henchman, patron. **2.** *adj.* One-sided (a partisan committee). Biased, predisposed, committed, prejudiced, devoted, jaundiced, subjective, bigoted, myopic, slanted, clannish, leaning, factional, unbalanced, opinionated. See also interested, partial. *Ant.* Critic; dispassionate.

Partisanship, *n.* See favor (2), favoritism, nepotism, bias.

Partition 1. *n.* The dividing of land held by joint tenants, tenants in common, or coparceners into distinct portions, resulting in individual ownership (judicial partition). Subdivision, division, splitting, apportionment, demarcation, segregation, assignment, disunion, allotment, segmentation, severance, split, cleavage, allocation, parting, detachment. See also wall. **2.** *v.* See part (3), divide. *Ant.* Merging; join.

Partner, *n.* One who has united with others to form a partnership (senior partner at the firm). Participant, copartner, associate, ally, co-worker, confrere, mate, collaborator, confederate, sharer, colleague, accomplice, accessory, aider, teammate, assistant, counterpart, conspirator, deputy, coadjutor, companion, abettor, cohort, sidekick, fellow.

Partnership, *n.* A voluntary contract between two or more competent persons to place their resources or services, or both, in a business or enterprise, with the understanding that there shall be a proportional sharing of the profits and losses (law partnership). Federation, alliance, league, combination, society, association, syndicate, affiliation, collaboration, pool, entity, consortium, union, trust, coalition, confederation, company, firm, guild, body, fraternity, fellowship, coterie, congress, sisterhood, brotherhood.

Part-time, *adj.* See temporary, partial; labor.

Parturition, *n.* See birth.

Party, *n.* **1.** A person whose name is designated on record as bringing a legal action or as being litigated against in the action (service on the parties). Plaintiff, defendant, litigant, respondent, opposition, claimant, pleader, supplicant, seeker, petitioner, appellant, appellee, intervenor, complainant, libelee, libelant, accused, contestant, suitor, adversary; side, faction, clique, federation, coalition, team, squad, wing, caucus, camp. **2.** One who is concerned with, has an interest in, or takes part in the performance of an act (she refused to be a party to the scheme). Participant, actor, member, participator, partner, conspirator, partisan, partaker, collaborator, sharer. See also accomplice, accessory. **3.** A voluntary association of persons sponsoring certain ideas of government or maintaining certain political principles in public policies of government; a group organized for a common purpose (rescue party). Organization, unit, body, team, assembly, faction, contingent, congregation, league, federation, circle, lobby, machine, combine, association, division, camp, corps, bureaucracy, coalition, outfit, brotherhood, sisterhood, sector, squadron, gang. **4.** A social function (retirement party). Festivity, occasion, fete. See also celebration (2), ceremony, banquet, extravaganza, amusement, entertainment, sport, game.

Party wall A wall on a property boundary as a common support to structures on both sides, which have different owners. See wall, joint.

Par value The face value of a share of stock; the value of a mortgage based on the balance owing without discount. See assessment, appraisal.

Parvenu, *n.* See upstart.

Pass 1. *v.* To utter or pronounce (the court passes sentence). Announce, declare, render, deliver, enunciate, impose, present, decide, express, circulate, publish, divulge, promulgate, broadcast, make known, disseminate. **2.** *v.* To accept (the amendment passed unanimously). Ratify, approve, vote upon favorably, validate, sanction, endorse, authorize, put through, succeed, legislate, enact, okay, affirm, ordain, decree, adopt, establish, license, legitimate, charter, acquiesce in, affirm, assent to, uphold, consent to, legitimize, put into force. **3.** *v.* To be successful (pass the bar exam). Succeed, get through, finish, qualify, satisfy, accomplish, graduate, achieve, endure, transcend, excel, surmount. **4.** *v.* To proceed (forbidden to pass). Go by, go through, permeate, move past, go ahead, progress, advance, flow, traverse, penetrate, travel through, gain access to. **5.** *v.* To change hands (title passed). Transfer, exchange, convey, deliver, grant, deed, cross, remise, change ownership, flow, devolve, transmit, bequeath, hand over, present, send, render, turn over, move, sell, trade, convert, ripen, transform, purchase. **6.** *v.* To terminate (time passes). End, die, disappear, leave, expire, consume, lapse, evaporate, melt, elapse, cease, fade, succumb, expend, take up, employ, occupy. **7.** *n.* Permission to come or go (he was denied a pass). License, authorization, ticket, visa, passport, warrant, privilege, waiver, clearance, leave, approval, carte blanche, sanction. **8.** *n.* An opening or passageway (a pass through the mountain). Route, way, road, tunnel, channel, canal, pathway, conduit, ingress, alley. *Ant.* Abstain; reject; fail; retreat; retain; commence; injunction; blockage.

Passable, *adj.* See navigable; average (2); adequate.

Passage, *n.* **1.** The act of approving (passage of the bill). Authorization, acceptance, enactment, certification, adoption, sanction, endorsement, approbation, affirmation, confirmation, legalization, establishment, validation. **2.** Route (passage

561

through the terrain). Channel, way, corridor, egress, exit, course, conduit, opening, entrance, entrée, hall, passageway, avenue, lane, street, arcade, artery, aisle, canal, corridor, tunnel, path, byway, thoroughfare, trail, access, track. **3.** Travel (passage was blocked). Movement, transit, voyage, emigration, progress, transition, passing, advance, flow, itinerary, trip, journey. **4.** An excerpt (the judge read a passage from the report). Portion, segment, paragraph, piece, clause, verse, selection, line. See also extract.

Passageway, *n.* See pass (8), passage (2), highway.

Passbook, *n.* A bankbook; a document issued by a bank, in which a customer's transactions are recorded (e.g., withdrawals). See record (2).

Passé, *adj.* See obsolete, obsolescent, old, ancient.

Passenger, *n.* One who is being carried by another for hire; any occupant of a vehicle other than the operator (the passenger was injured in the crash). Traveler, commuter, rider, hiker, itinerant. See also guest, client (2), patron (1).

Passing, *adj.* See temporary, brief (4), intangible; capricious, fluctuating; passage (3).

Passion, *n.* Any emotion that interferes with cool reflection of the mind (heat of passion). Anger, rage, fury, wrath, fire, intoxication, fervor, impulse, grief, rapture, hot blood, zeal, mania, excitement, agitation, storm, eruption, tempest, convulsion, temper, fear, love, perturbation, frenzy, lust, vehemence, paroxysm, animation, rampage, compulsion, worship, concupiscence, fanaticism, resentment, furor, indignation, attachment, exhilaration, desire, urge, delirium, idolatry, dedication, ecstasy, gusto, feeling, hunger, infatuation, craving, craze, flare-up, irritation, ardor, enthusiasm, transport, pique. *Ant.* Calm.

Passionate, *adj.* See emotional, earnest (2), feverish, hot; prurient, lascivious.

Passive, *adj.* **1.** Inactive (passive trust). Dormant, lifeless, inert, stagnating, still, static, abeyant, idle, indolent, quiescent. **2.** Submissive (during the sentencing the defendant remained passive). Docile, unresisting, unresponsive, patient, unmoved, lethargic, acquiescent, obedient, dutiful, yielding, malleable, listless, resigned, enduring, nonresistant, spiritless, apathetic, deferential, compliant, suffering, amenable, unassertive, pliant, undemonstrative, obliging, obsequious, motionless, indifferent, neutral, unperturbed, pacific, static, dispassionate, phlegmatic, meek. *Ant.* Active; assertive.

Passive negligence The failure to do something that should have been done; permitting defects, obstacles, or pitfalls to exist on premises. See neglect (2).

Passive restraint A safety device that provides protection automatically. See protection; vehicle.

Passive trust A trust as to which the trustee has no responsibilities or discretionary duties to perform. See trust.

Passport, *n.* A document that (a) identifies a citizen, (b) acts as evidence of permission from a sovereign to its citizen to travel to foreign countries, (c) acts as a request to foreign powers that the citizen be allowed to pass freely and safely (application for a passport). Credentials, license, clearance, means of access, travel papers, admission, permit.

Past, *adj.* See old, ancient, obsolete; previous, former.

Paste, *n., v.* See adhesive; affix.

Pastime, *n.* See avocation, entertainment, amusement.

Pastor, *n.* See minister (1); church, clerical (1), hierarchy, manager.

Pastoral, *adj.* See idyllic, country (2), innocent, happy; clerical (1).

Past recollection recorded A memorandum or record concerning a matter about which a witness once had knowledge but now has insufficient recollection to enable him or her to testify fully and accurately, shown to have been made or adopted by the witness when the matter was fresh in his or her memory and to reflect that knowledge correctly, is not excluded by the hearsay rule. See hearsay, evidence, memory.

Pasture, *n.* See park (1), land; farm.

Pat, *v.*, *adj.* See caress; appropriate, precise, apt.

Patch, *v.*, *n.* See fix (3), settle (1); parcel (3).

Patent 1. *adj.* Open, unsealed (a patent defect). Evident, manifest, obvious, apparent, visible, notorious, glaring, blatant, noticeable, prominent, unmasked, palpable, express, bald, conspicuous, self-evident, observable, perceivable, public, incontrovertible, explicit, undeniable, plain, transparent, pronounced, perceptible, unmistakable, tangible, crystal-clear, definite, indubitable, ostensible, overt. **2.** *n.* A grant of a privilege, property, or authority to an individual by the government; a grant made by the government to an inventor, securing to him or her the exclusive right to make, use, and sell the invention for a term of years (application for a patent). License, certificate, permit, trademark, letters patent, franchise, charter. *Ant.* Latent (1).

Patentable, *adj.* Suitable to be patented because the device embodies a new idea or principle not known before and constitutes a discovery as distinguished from mere technical skill or knowledge. See original, invention.

Patent and Trademark Office A federal agency in the Department of Commerce, which examines patent and trademark applications, issues patents, registers trademarks, etc.

Patentee, *n.* A person to whom a patent is granted.

Paterfamilias, *n.* The father of a family.

Paternal, *adj.* Concerning, belonging to, or coming from the father (paternal care). Patriarchal, paterfamilias, fatherly, fatherlike; tender, watchful, solicitous, devoted, parental, loving. See also kind (2), protective; protection.

Paternal line A line of descent or relationship between two persons, which is traced through the father.

Paternalistic, *adj.* See protective; arbitrary, strict.

Paternity, *n.* The state or condition of being a father (a determination of the paternity of the child). Fatherhood, male parentage; ancestry, lineage, bloodline, stock, origin, extraction, breed, descent, derivation. See also genealogy, father.

Paternity suit A civil action to prove that a person is the father of a child and to enforce the duty to support the child.

Path, *n.* See highway, passage (2), pass (8), course (1), entrance; life (2).

Pathetic, *adj.* See grievous, deplorable, distressing, touching (1), abject; bemoan.

Pathological, *adj.* See demented, abject; disease.

Pathology, *n.* That part of medicine which examines the nature, causes, and symptoms of diseases. See disease.

Pathos, *n.* See consolation, passion, emotion; commiserate.

Patience, *n.* See composure, temperance, endurance, accommodation, toleration, charity, mercy; patient (2, 3).

Patient 1. *n.* A person under medical or psychiatric treatment and care (the patient suffered a relapse). Sick person, case, victim, convalescent, shut-in, outpatient, sufferer. See also invalid (2). **2.** *adj.* Persistent (be patient). Untiring, persevering, diligent, resolute, dogged, determined, unflagging, tireless, indefatigable, resolved, unfaltering sedulous, industrious, enduring, unceasing, dutiful, relentless, steadfast, indomitable, tenacious, firm, inexorable, uncompromising, assiduous. **3.** *adj.* Sympathetic, calm (she was patient with her class). Forbearing, unperturbed, composed, unexcited, serene, unruffled, unflappable, relaxed, understanding, agreeable, docile, balanced, resigned, self-controlled, dispassionate, stoic, indulgent, passive, generous, permissive, acquiescent, levelheaded, mild, pliant, restrained, tranquil. *Ant.* Doctor; impatient; inflexible.

Patient-physician privilege See doctor-patient privilege.

Patriarch, *n.* See father, ancestor, head, teacher.

Patrician, *n.* See aristocracy.

Patricide, *n.* Killing one's father; a person who has killed his or her father. See homicide, murder.

Patrimony, *n.* That which is inherited from a father or from the father's side; an estate that has descended in the same family.

Patriot, *n.* One who is devoted to and supports his or her country. Chauvinist, flag waver, nationalist, loyalist, jingoist, militarist.

Patriotic, *adj.* See loyal; chauvinism; spirit.

Patrol, *v.* To go around in order to guard or inspect (the officer patrolled the area). Protect, watch over, oversee, shelter, shield, attend, walk, safeguard, monitor, maintain a vigil, defend, scout, preserve, make the rounds, police, escort, cover.

Patrolman, *n.* See watchman, police, guardian; patrol.

Patron, *n.* **1.** Customer (the store's patrons). Buyer, shopper, purchaser, dealer, vendee, frequenter, prospect, regular, visitor, habitué, subscriber, audience. See also customer, client (2). **2.** One who provides material assistance (patron of the arts). Promoter, benefactor, benefactress, helper, champion, backer, philanthropist, financier, patroness, exponent, advocate, booster, saint, angel, guardian, partisan, mainstay, supporter, protagonist, upholder, friend. See also patronage (3); back.

Patronage, *n.* **1.** The practice of a public official in making appointments to non-civil service jobs and in conferring awards (the central committee of the party controlled patronage). Spoils, politics, connections, favors, "pork barrel." **2.** The customers of a business. See patron (1). **3.** The assistance or encouragement received from a patron (they were dependent on her patronage). Help, support, finances, backing, favor, sponsorship, advocacy, championship, sustenance, guardianship, guidance, defense, ministration, aid, interest, care, protection, promotion, auspices, abetment, advancement, tutelage, friendship.

Patronize, *v.* **1.** To be a customer or patron (he patronized the store). Do business with, trade with, have an account with, shop at, frequent, be a client of, buy from, transact business with, support, deal with. **2.** To treat in a condescending way (he resented the way the boss patronized him). Look down upon, indulge, insult, offend, derogate, act disdainfully, humiliate, presume, underestimate, detract from, stoop, disparage, vouchsafe, arrogate, oblige, descend, tolerate, humor. See also condescend; arrogant.

"Patsy," *n.* See slave, pawn (3), attendant, servant, assistant; parasite, victim, ass, idiot.

Pattern, *n.* **1.** A reliable sample of traits, acts, or other observable features characterizing an individual (a pattern of dangerous conduct). Classification, type, format, theme, image, scheme, kind, genre, method, order, consistency, repetition, style, plan, system. **2.** A guide or model (pattern jury instructions). Standard, prototype, criterion, archetype, yardstick, measure, paradigm, design, outline, motif, precedent, exemplar, example, mold, cast, ideal, stamp, matrix, sample, original, gauge, blueprint, frame, format, test, norm.

Paucity, *n.* See dearth, absence (2); privation, want (1), need (1), deficiency, arrears.

Pauper, *n.* A person so poor that he or she must be supported at public expense (reduced to the status of a pauper). Indigent, beggar, bankrupt, insolvent, debtor, mendicant, poor person, panhandler, cadger; parasite. See also tramp (1). *Ant.* Tycoon.

Pause, *v., n.* See delay (1), adjourn, doubt (1), defer (1); hedge; interim (1), delay (3), interruption.

Pave, *v.* To cover. Blacktop, lay over, surface, macadamize, spread, level, asphalt, tar.

Pavilion, *n.* See arena; facility (2), building (1).

Paw, *v.* See touch (1), contact (4); caress; manipulate.

Pawn 1. *v.* To deliver property to another in pledge or as security for a debt (she pawned her silver). Mortgage, stake, obligate, hypothecate, post, borrow on. **2.** *n.* A pledge of chattels as security for a debt. See collateral (1). **3.** *n.* Someone exploited or manipulated by another (the hostage was a pawn in the struggle). Puppet, instrument, organ, vehicle, medium, robot, dupe, underling, tool, slave, lackey. See also victim, servant, attendant.

Pawnbroker, *n.* A person in the business of lending money on the security of property deposited with him or her. See merchant, business.

Pawnee, *n.* The person receiving a pawn or to whom goods are delivered by another in pledge.

Pawnor, *n.* The person pawning goods or delivering goods to another in pledge.

Pay 1. *n.* Compensation (inadequate pay). Wage, remuneration, salary, commission, fee, allowance, earnings, recompense, payment, consideration, stipend, emolument, return, gain, bonus, honorarium, paycheck, perk, gratuity, fringe, settlement. See also compensation, income. **2.** *v.* To discharge a debt by tender of payment due; to compensate for goods, services, or labor (she paid the lawyer). Expend, remit, honor, settle, liquidate, repay, recompense, square accounts, compromise, acquit oneself of, make good, defray, disburse, meet, satisfy, adjust, clear. See also indemnify, compensate (1). **3.** *v.* To be useful (it does not pay to delay). Profit, yield, benefit, be advantageous, compensate, capitalize, serve.

Payable, *adj.* Justly or legally due (payable immediately). Mature, owed, ripe, collectable, in arrears, redeemable. See also outstanding (1).

Payee, *n.* The person to whom or to whose order a check, bill of exchange, or promissory note is made payable. See beneficiary.

Payer or payor, *n.* The person who makes or should make payment, particularly on a check, bill of exchange, or promissory note.

Payment, *n.* **1.** The performance of a duty, promise, or obligation, or the discharge of a debt or liability by the tender and acceptance of money or some other valuable thing (a letter seeking payment). Satisfaction, defrayal, liquidation, reimbursement, disbursement, remittance, amortization, spending, contribution, acquittal, recompense, discharge, advance, amends, clearance, reckoning, indemnity, restitution, allotment, deposit; retribution, retaliation, reprisal. See also expenditure. **2.** See compensation, pay (1).

Payoff, *n.* See bribe (1), graft, kickback, gratuity, corruption.

Payola, *n.* See payoff.

Payor, *n.* See payer.

Payroll tax A tax based on and deducted from wages and salaries paid to employees. See tax, income.

P.C. Professional Corporation; Penal Code; Patent Cases; Pleas of the Crown.

Peace, *n.* Quiet, orderly behavior of individuals toward each other and the government (breach of the peace). Good order, tranquillity, fellowship, absence of conflict, harmony, amity, concord, conciliation, security, calmness, inactivity, repose, reconciliation, cooperation, brotherhood, sisterhood, unity, orderliness, truce, accord, respite. *Ant.* Hostility.

Peaceable, *adj.* **1.** Without force or violence (peaceable entry on the land). Nonviolent, unbellicose. **2.** Gentle, calm. See amicable, friendly, moderate (1); consent.

Peace bond A type of surety bond that must be provided by someone who has threatened to breach the peace. See bond.

Peaceful

Peaceful, *adj.* See patient (3), quiet, passive; harmony.
Peace officer, *n.* See police, watchman, guardian, officer; patrol.
Peak, *n., v.* See apex; culminate.
Pearl, *n.* See gem.
Peasant, *n.* See farmer, laborer, slave, proletariat, employee, attendant, servant; pawn (3); nonentity.
Peccadillo, *n.* See fault (1), error, blunder.
Pecking order, *n.* See hierarchy; dominate; harass.
Peculate, *v.* See embezzle, cheat (1); betray; larceny.
Peculation, *n.* The misappropriation of money or goods entrusted to one's care. See appropriation (1), cheat (1), deception, embezzle, false pretenses, misappropriate.
Peculiar, *adj.* **1.** Distinctive (peculiar knowledge of the facts). Special, particular, unique, singular, specific, select, exclusive, exceptional, distinct, private, solitary, especial, outstanding, innate, rare, sui generis, notable, significant, secret, individual, characteristic, representative, confidential, original, different, unequal, distinguishing. **2.** Unusual (peculiar behavior). Bizarre, weird, unconventional, unorthodox, curious, idiosyncratic, odd, incredible, nondescript, queer, absurd, grotesque, ludicrous, deviant, ridiculous, incongruous, comical, strange, whimsical, outlandish, capricious, extravagant, abnormal, funny, erratic, quaint, uncouth, atypical, unnatural, eccentric, perplexing, freakish, irregular, foreign, mysterious, unfamiliar, inexplicable, fanciful, anomalistic, remarkable, offbeat. *Ant.* Ordinary; predictable.
Peculiarity, *n.* See eccentricity, exception (3), specialty (3), character (4); nonconformist; peculiar; marvel.
Pecuniary, *adj.* Relating to money or that which can be valued in money (pecuniary bequest). Monetary, financial, fiscal, budgetary; nummular. See also economic.
Pecuniary damages Any loss, deprivation, or injury that can be estimated in and compensated by money. See injury, damages.
Pecuniary injury in wrongful death The deprivation of a reasonable expectation of a monetary advantage that would have resulted from a continuation of the life of the deceased. See damages, wrongful death.
Pedagogue, *n.* See teacher, student.
Pedantic, *adj.* See academic (2), learned, literary (2), cultivated; pompous, arrogant; pretense.
Peddle, *v.* See sell; circulate, communicate; peddler.
Peddler, *n.* A person who sells wares carried from place to place (unlicensed peddler). Itinerant trader, salesperson, huckster, entrepreneur, merchant, hawker, dealer. See also seller.
Pedestal, *n.* See base (3), platform (2).
Pedestrian 1. *n.* A person traveling on foot (the crash injured a pedestrian on the sidewalk). Stroller, walker, bystander, roamer, foot traveler, hiker, nonmotorist. **2.** *adj.* Unimaginative (pedestrian performance). Commonplace, dull, usual, banal, tedious, average, insignificant, prosaic, unexceptional, run-of-the-mill, flat, vapid, uninteresting, inconsequential, wearisome, meaningless, mediocre, ordinary, mundane, humdrum, so-so, spiritless, colorless, barren, dreary, plodding, drab, insipid, hackneyed, trite, dead, lifeless, boring, predictable, platitudinous, inferior, jejune, uncreative, uninspiring. *Ant.* Motorist; engaging.
Pediatrician, *n.* A doctor specializing in the care of children. See doctor, medicine, treatment.
Pedigree, *n.* The line of ancestors from which a person descends (he traced his pedigree). Lineage, descent, succession, ancestral line, house, roots, heritage,

birth, stock, parentage, derivation, tree, stirps, dynasty, extraction. See also genealogy.

Peek, *v.* See peep.

Peep, *v.* See observe (3), notice (2), sight, witness (2); eavesdrop, bug.

Peeping Tom, *n.* One who sneaks up to a window for the purpose of spying on or invading the privacy of the inhabitants, particularly women in the bedroom. See voyeur, wrongdoer, eavesdrop.

Peer, *n., v.* See associate, colleague; equal, equivalent; observe (3), notice (2).

Peerless, *adj.* See extraordinary, outstanding (2), best (1).

Peeve, *v.* See harass.

Peevish, *adj.* See crabby, litigious, contentious, difficult (3), particular (2).

Peg 1. *v.* To set or fix (the government decided to peg the price of gold to an established index). Control, limit, pigeonhole, freeze, nail, connect, tag, mark, join, attach. **2.** *n.* An excuse (a peg to justify the firing). Reason, pretext, basis, alibi, pretense, justification, motive, rationale, rationalization, cause, explanation.

Pejorative, *adj.* See derogatory, negative.

Pell-mell, *adv., adj., n.* See disorderly (3), careless, reckless; confusion, commotion.

Pellucid, *adj.* See clear (1).

Pelt, *v.* See beat (1), attack, batter, assault.

Pen, *n., v.* See prison; confine (1, 2), enclose.

Penal, *adj.* Concerning or containing a penalty (penal statute). Punitive, disciplinary, castigatory, of punishment, retributive, criminal, correctional, corrective, punishing.

Penal institution A place for the confinement for those convicted of crimes. See prison.

Penalize, *v.* See amerce, fine (1), correct (3).

Penalty, *n.* Punishment imposed by law (the penalty of imprisonment). Sanction, sentence, loss, forfeiture, disciplinary action, castigation, handicap, retribution, suffering, amercement, reprisal, deprivation, penance, retaliation, chastisement, condemnation, pain; consequence, fruit, result, cost, payment. See also punishment, discipline (2). *Ant.* Commendation.

Penalty clause A provision in a clause or law that calls for the imposition of a penalty instead of actual damages.

Penance, *n.* See penalty, punishment, correction (1), damages.

Penchant, *n.* See disposition (4), preference, affinity, bias.

Pendency, *n.* After something has begun but before its final disposition; while undecided (the pendency of litigation). See duration, continuance, interval; indeterminate, debatable, inconclusive.

Pendent, *adj.* **1.** Pertaining to matters that are additional, supplementary or complementary (pendent claims). Supplemental, adjunct, companion, connecting, allied, corresponding, appurtenant, subsidiary, auxiliary. **2.** See pending.

Pendente lite During the actual progress of the suit; pending the suit; during litigation.

Pendent jurisdiction doctrine A federal district court, in the exercise of jurisdiction over a federal law claim properly before it, has the discretion to extend its jurisdiction over a related state law claim where both claims arise from a common nucleus of operative facts.

Pending, *adj.* Begun but not yet completed; in the process of settlement or adjustment (a pending case). Undecided, undetermined, unresolved, up in the air, looming, approaching, dormant, prospective, forthcoming, awaiting, hanging, unfinished, imminent, in the offing, near, expectant, latent. See also inchoate. *Ant.* Consummated.

Penetrate, *v.* See enter (2), pierce, encroach, interfere, attack (1), assault (3);

comprehend.

Penetrating, *adj.* See acute (1), brilliant, able, capable (2), cogent; caustic; explicit, precise, concrete.

Penetration, *n.* **1.** The insertion of the penis, however slight, into the vagina. **2.** See perception.

Penitence, *n.* See guilt (2), contrition, disgrace, embarrassment.

Penitent, *adj.* See contrite; contrition; abject (1).

Penitentiary, *n.* A place of confinement for convicted felons (sentenced to the penitentiary). House of detention, detention center, jail, correctional institution, penal institution, lockup, reformatory, "slammer," "clinker," brig, cage, cell, workhouse. See also prison.

Penniless, *adj.* See needy, indigent, bankrupt.

Penny-pinching, *adj.* See stingy, avaricious.

Penology, *n.* The science of prison management, punishment, and the rehabilitation of criminals. See crime.

Pen register A device that records the numbers dialed on a telephone without overhearing the calls or determining whether they were actually completed.

Pension, *n.* Regularly paid retirement benefits, often based on a person's length of employment and salary level (drawing on a pension). Subsidy, annuity, old age income, allowance, benefits, fixed income, Social Security, remuneration, subsistence. See also compensation, fringe, fringe benefits.

Pension Benefit Guaranty Corporation An agency that guarantees the payment of insured benefits if a covered employee retirement plan terminates without sufficient assets to pay the benefits.

Pensioner, *n.* A recipient or beneficiary of a pension plan. See beneficiary.

Pension plan A plan established and maintained by an employer, primarily to pay determinable benefits to its employees or their beneficiaries over a period of years after retirement.

Pensive, *adj.* See preoccupied, engaged.

Pentagon, *n.* See military, martial, sailor, weapon, arms.

Penthouse, *n.* See home; luxury.

Pent-up, *adj.* See isolated; hidden; apprehensive, concerned; excitable, feverish.

Penumbra, *n.* The periphery. Margin, brink, fringe, shadow, shade. See also border (1), boundary.

Penumbra doctrine The implied powers of the federal government predicated on the Necessary and Proper Clause of the U.S. Constitution permit one implied power to be engrafted on another implied power.

Penurious, *adj.* See needy, bankrupt, indigent; stingy, avaricious.

Penury, *n.* See poverty, dearth, bankruptcy, privation.

Peon, *n.* See laborer, proletariat, slave, attendant, servant, nonentity.

Peonage, *n.* The condition of servitude compelling persons to perform labor in order to pay off a debt. See servitude (1).

People, *n.* **1.** The entire body of citizens of a state or nation (support of the people). Citizenry, population, commonwealth, inhabitants, community, countrymen, populace, nationals, public, society, natives, electorate, commonality, John Q. Public, working class, voters, residents, multitude, proletariat, general public, rank and file. **2.** Human beings (designed for people). Homo sapiens, humanity, humankind, mortals, persons, mankind, individuals.

Pep, *n., v.* See spirit (2); animate, incite.

"Pep pill," *n.* See drug.

Perambulate, *v.* See walk, wander.

Perambulation, *n.* To walk over the boundaries of land for the purpose of inspection or surveying. See patrol.

Per annum, *adv.* Yearly (9% per annum). See annual (1).

Per autre vie For or during another's life.

Per capita, *adv., adj.* According to the number of individuals (per capita tax). For each person, by each person, per person, per unit of population. See also individual.

Perceivable, *adj.* See palpable, appreciable, apparent, clear.

Per cent *n.* **1.** One part in every hundred; so many hundredths (8 per cent). **2.** See percentage.

Percentage, *n.* A proportion or share (the agent received a percentage). Fraction, piece, commission, ratio, per cent, cut, measure, quota, allotment, dividend, royalty, discount.

Percentage lease A lease using a percentage of the gross or net sales to determine the rent. See lease.

Perceptible, *adj.* See appreciable, palpable, apparent, clear.

Perception, *n.* **1.** The act of becoming aware of something through the senses (perception of trouble). Viewpoint, apprehension, sight, recognition, cognition, knowledge, realization, discovery, observation, estimate, attention, notice, impression, appreciation, appraisal, vision, comprehension, detection, revelation, grasp, notion, inkling, image, perceiving, sensation, eyesight, consciousness, awareness. **2.** Acumen (enviable perception). Penetration, intelligence, cleverness, judgment, sensitivity, wisdom, discernment, discrimination, experience, sagacity, foresight, sharpness.

Perceptive, *adj.* See acute (1), cogent, brilliant, capable (2), judicious, able; alive (2).

Percolate, *v.* See filter, drain.

Percolating water Water that passes through the ground beneath the surface of the earth without any definite channel and which does not form a part of the body or flow of any watercourse; water that oozes, seeps, or filters through the soil beneath the surface.

Per curiam By the court; an opinion of the whole court; an opinion written by the chief judge; a brief announcement of a decision without a written opinion.

Percussion, *n.* See collision; music.

Per diem, *adv. adj., n.* By the day; an allowance or amount of so much per day ($100 per diem while on the road). See daily, expense.

Perdition, *n.* See censure (1).

Peregrinate, *v.* See voyage, travel, walk, wander.

Peremptory, *adj.* **1.** Absolute (peremptory rule). Unconditional, irrevocable, unequivocal, total, definite, categorical, unalterable, irreversible, obligatory, unavoidable, unquestionable, incontrovertible, undeniable, decisive, flat, implicit, uncircumscribed, unreserved, assured, automatic, unqualified, unrestricted, conclusive, indisputable, binding, final. **2.** Imperative (peremptory command). Commanding, pressing, crucial, important, necessary, compulsory, compelling, exigent. **3.** Dogmatic (peremptory manner). Dictatorial, highhanded, arbitrary, autocratic, opinionated, domineering, obstinate, arrogant, authoritative, assertive, pompous, imperious, biased, close-minded, overbearing, despotic, insistent, supercilious, tyrannical, pontifical. *Ant.* Conditional; minor; accommodating.

Peremptory challenge The right to challenge and remove a prospective juror without giving any reasons. See challenge, removal, juror.

Peremptory rule An absolute rule; a ruling without conditions. See rule.

Perennial, *adj.* See habitual, daily, chronic, constant (1), permanent.

Perfect, *adj., perfect, v.* **1.** *adj.* Complete, executed (perfect title). Finished, whole, full, consummate, entire, exhaustive, comprehensive, absolute, confirmed, certain, real, demonstrable, categorical, positive, thorough, realized, plenary,

569

recorded, registered, filed, enforceable. **2.** *adj.* Without defect (perfect working condition). Faultless, excellent, unblemished, ideal, immaculate, inviolate, meticulous, okay, skilled, masterful, efficient, untainted, right, spotless, model, superb, flawless, well-equipped, correct, strict, unimpaired, letter-perfect, exact, precise, good, merchantable, marketable. **3.** *v.* To finish, complete, or put in final form (the notice was sufficient to perfect the claim; the security interest is perfected by filing). Consummate, execute, accomplish, bring to completion, finalize, achieve, cap, mature, realize, perform, fulfill, conclude, effectuate, culminate, close, develop. *Ant.* Incomplete; defective; unravel.

Perfected, *adj.* Completed; brought to a state of perfection. See perfect (1, 3).

Perfection, *n.* **1.** The act or process of making something complete. Consummation, effectuation, realization, accomplishment, fulfillment, attainment, ripening, development; acme, peak, apex, summit, nirvana, paragon. See also completion; perfect (1, 3). **2.** Flawlessness (a work of perfection). Impeccability, precision, ideal, exactitude, soundness, accuracy, authenticity, excellence, mastery, thoroughness, completeness, maturity, ripeness, correctness.

Perfectionist, *adj., n.* See precise, conscientious, careful; nonconformist.

Perfection of a security interest Taking the steps legally required to protect the secured party against other creditors of the debtor (e.g., filing with the secretary of state, taking possession of the collateral).

Perfidious, *adj.* See disloyal, corrupt.

Perfidy, *n.* Violation of a promise, vow, or trust. See betrayal.

Perforate, *v.* See pierce, cut, enter (2); inundate, fill.

Perforation, *n.* See break (3).

Perform, *v.* To fulfill an obligation according to its terms (perform the contract). Execute, accomplish, discharge, be faithful to, effectuate, consummate, abide by, satisfy, carry out, transact, perfect, observe, heed, realize, redeem, obey, solemnize, practice, respect, work, meet, do, enact, dispatch, conclude, follow through, conduct, manage, achieve, comply with, effect, perpetrate.

Performance, *n.* **1.** The fulfillment of an obligation according to its terms (incomplete performance of the agreement). Accomplishment, execution, satisfaction, completion, discharge, realization, consummation, conclusion, implementation, doing, attainment, dispatch, effectuation, culmination, achievement, operation. **2.** The manner in which something functions (performance rating). Running, action, handling, work, procedure, aptitude, composition, manufacture, conduct, capability, formation, caliber, quality, technique. **3.** A public presentation (the audience appreciated the performance). Showing, display, spectacle, entertainment, characterization, presentation, exhibit, exhibition, concert, ceremony, recital.

Performance bond A completion bond; a bond that guarantees that the contractor will perform the contract as awarded. See bond.

Perfume, *n.* See aroma; fragrant; ointment.

Perfunctory, *adj.* See apathetic, casual (3), cursory, pedestrian (2); summary, brief.

Peril, *n.* That which may cause damage or injury (discovered peril). Risk, dangerous contingency, vulnerability, jeopardy, insecurity, imperilment, menace, unsteadiness, pitfall, unsafety, threat, exposure, liability, crisis, uncertainty, emergency, foreboding, weak link, weakness, susceptibility, unpredictability. See also danger, hazard, doubt. *Ant.* Safety.

Perilous, *adj.* See dangerous, hazardous, harmful, deadly.

Perils of the sea Natural accidents peculiar to the sea that do not happen by the intervention of humans and cannot be prevented by human prudence. See act of God, accident.

Perimeter, *n.* See boundary, bound (4), margin (1).

Period, *n.* Any point, space, or division of time (a period of a year). Span, stretch, duration, spell, era, interval, age, cycle, course, extent, interlude, season, term, epoch, generation, continuance, day, while, chronology, interregnum, stage.

Periodic, *adj.* Recurring at fixed intervals; now and then (periodic reports). Recurrent, intermittent, repeated, systematic, regular, episodic, cyclic, alternate, routine, sporadic, predictable, rhythmic, frequent, circular, seasonal, fluctuating, returning, variable, occasional, serial.

Periodical, *adj., n.* See periodic; journal, newspaper, press (1).

Periodic payment of alimony An alimony payment of either (a) a fixed amount (e.g., $50 a week) for an indefinite period (e.g., for life); or (b) an indefinite amount (e.g., 10% of yearly income) for either a fixed period or an indefinite period. See alimony.

Periodic tenancy A tenancy that continues for successive periods (e.g., week to week) unless terminated at the end of a period by notice. See tenancy.

Peripatetic, *adj.* See migratory, itinerant.

Peripheral, *adj.* Pertaining to the outside edge; fringe (the judge did not consider the peripheral issues). Marginal, borderline, tangential, collateral, secondary, outlying, superficial, unnecessary, nonessential, dispensable, incidental, irrelevant, external. See also extraneous (1), immaterial, gratuitous (2). *Ant.* Central.

Periphery, *n.* See extremity (2), boundary, bound (4), margin (1), face (1).

Perish, *v.* To come to an end; to cease to be (perish in the fire). Die, destroy, decease, terminate, corrode, vanish, expire, disappear, eradicate, wither, evaporate, surrender, become extinct, crumble, rot, depart, burn, demolish, succumb, molder, disintegrate, dissolve, shrivel. *Ant.* Endure.

Perishable, *adj.* Subject to decay or material depreciation (perishable commodity). Decayable, decomposable, fleeting, biodegradable, short-lived, fragile, ephemeral, destructible, temporary, unstable, evanescent, transitory, momentary, fading. See also breakable. *Ant.* Permanent.

Perishable goods Goods that quickly decay if they are not put to their intended use within a short period of time.

Perjure, *v.* See lie (2), misrepresent; perjury.

Perjury, *n.* A crime committed by a person if, in an official proceeding, he or she makes a false statement under oath or equivalent affirmation when the statement is material and he or she does not believe it to be true (perjury committed while testifying before a legislative committee). Lying, misrepresentation, deceit, misstatement, falsehood, distortion, willful false statement, bearing false witness, falsification, forswearing, dishonesty, perversion of the truth, prevarication, equivocation, mendacity, fabrication, false swearing. See also fraud.

Perks, *n.* See perquisites

Permanence, *n.* See endurance, perpetuity; indestructible, perpetual, permanent.

Permanent, *adj.* Continuing in the same status without fundamental change; not temporary or transient (permanent residence). Fixed, lasting, abiding, inextinguishable, remaining, unwavering, ageless, perpetual, unending, persisting, unchanging, immutable, surviving, perdurable, unaltered, stable, everlasting, constant, invariable, unfailing, eternal, anchored, immortal, entrenched, incessant, indestructible, ingrained, sustained, incorruptible, durable, solid, infinite, unfading, forever, unyielding, deathless, perennial, continuous, inveterate, stationary, chronic, tenacious, irrevocable, deep-seated, indefatigable, invulnerable, dependable, steadfast, protracted, established, persevering, rooted, unbroken, uninterrupted. *Ant.* Transient.

Permanent disability A disability that will remain substantially the same during the remainder of the worker's life; a disability that causes impairment of earning capacity, impairment of the normal use of a member, or a competitive handicap in the open labor market. See disability, disease.

Permanent employment Employment that will continue indefinitely until either party wishes to sever the relationship. See employment.

Permanent injury An injury that will last during the lifetime of the injured person; permanent disability. See injury.

Permeate, *v.* See imbue, fill, inundate.

Permissible, *adj.* See admissible, legal, adequate; permission.

Permission, *n.* The authority to do something that would be unlawful without the authority (permission to open the safety deposit box). License, authorization, assent, go-ahead, visa, franchise, grant, warrant, consent, approval, sanction, allowance, indulgence, passport, acquiescence, tolerance, leave, concurrence, sufferance, permit, compliance, enfranchisement, liberty, countenance, freedom, concession, endorsement, agreement, dispensation, approbation, resignation, carte blanche. *Ant.* Prohibition.

Permissive, *adj.* **1.** Allowable (permissive counterclaim). Agreeing, consenting, allowed, granting, acquiescent. **2.** Lenient (permissive mother). Tolerant, indulgent, liberal, lax, accommodating, broad-minded, patient, forbearing, overindulgent, latitudinarian, easy, benevolent, unstrict, complaisant, yielding, soft, easygoing. See also flexible. *Ant.* Prohibitive; strict.

Permissive counterclaim A counterclaim that does not arise out of the same transaction or occurrence that is the subject matter of the plaintiff's claim. See counterclaim.

Permit, *v.*, **permit,** *n.* **1.** *v.* To expressly agree to the doing of an act; to acquiesce by failing to prevent (permit her to enter). Consent, allow, let, license, authorize, sanction, franchise, suffer, tolerate, countenance, enable, clear, warrant, empower, charter, endure, assent, endorse, commission, grant, vouchsafe, be resigned to, oblige, indulge, concede, humor, close one's eyes to, condone, support. **2.** *n.* A document that grants a person the right to do something (work permit). License, authorization, permission, consent, authority, sanction, certification, franchise, patent, commission, approbation, endorsement, carte blanche, leave, ticket, privilege. *Ant.* Deny; prohibition.

Permit card A document given by a union to a nonunion member, allowing the employer to hire him or her when not enough union members are available. See union, employment, permission.

Permutation, *n.* **1.** An exchange of goods. See barter, exchange. **2.** A transformation. See change (1), alter.

Per my et per tout By the half and by the whole; a phrase descriptive of the mode in which joint tenants hold the joint estate.

Pernicious, *adj.* See deleterious, bad, harmful, dangerous.

Peroration, *n.* See conclusion, close (4); address (3).

Perpetrate, *v.* See commit (2), impose, perform, administer, cause.

Perpetration, *n.* The commission of an act, often criminal in nature (the perpetration of a fraud). Infliction, implementation, carrying out, execution, doing, transaction, performance, maneuvering, effectuation, activation, practice, enactment, pursuance, exercise, production, enterprise. *Ant.* Avoidance.

Perpetrator, *n.* The person who commits wrongdoing or by whose immediate agency it occurs (the perpetrator was arrested). Offender, criminal, felon, trespasser, transgressor, scofflaw, malefactor, delinquent, accused, villain, lawbreaker, rogue, knave, scoundrel, rapscallion. See also wrongdoer. *Ant.* Bystander.

Perpetual, *adj.* Continuing without intermission (perpetual easement). Everlasting, eternal, continuous, never-ceasing, enduring, lasting, unlimited, constant, indestructible, immortal, inexhaustible, endless, incessant, perennial, infinite, permanent, abiding, repeated, sustained, unremitting, ceaseless, chronic, imperishable, sempitneral, nonstop, immutable, interminable, inviolate, deathless, indelible, persistent, inveterate, bottomless, boundless, deep, immeasurable, unfathomable. *Ant.* Temporary.

Perpetuate, *v.* To take steps to ensure that something will last and be available (perpetuate testimony). Preserve, conserve, retain, secure, maintain, memorialize, save, hold, protect, keep alive, prolong.

Perpetuity, *n.* Continuing forever (rule against perpetuities). Endless duration, eternity, infinity, perpetuation, continuation, interminability, continued existence, indefiniteness, forever, permanence.

Perplex, *v.* See confuse, distract, disturb, amaze.

Perplexed, *adj.* See agape.

Perplexity, *n.* See confusion, complication, mystery, conundrum.

Perplexing, *adj.* See difficult (1), obscure (1), complex (1), mysterious, intriguing, distressing.

Perquisites, *n.* Incidental profits or benefits attaching to an office or position (the car was one of her perquisites as president). Fringe benefits, emoluments, privileges, prerogatives, entitlements, extras, gratuities, dividends, gifts, "perks," allowances, rewards, advantages, donations, fees, tokens, stipend, return, compensation, pay, wage, gain. See also bonus, premium (1). *Ant.* Burden.

Per quod, *adv.* Whereby; by means of which. See libelous per quod.

Per se, *adv.* In itself; referring to activities or omissions that are so blatant that there is no need to look into underlying reasonableness or propriety (her conduct constitutes negligence per se). By itself, taken alone, without more, inherently, unconnected with other matters, as such, in isolation. See also intrinsic, inherent.

Persecute, *v.* See intimidate, harass, abuse (1), accost, hurt, menace, outrage (2).

Persecution, *n.* See oppression, affliction, cruelty, coercion, abuse (2), malice.

Persecutor, *n.* See tyrant, wrongdoer.

Perseverance, *n.* See endurance, diligence, industry (2), conviction (3), determination (2), spirit (2), passion, vigor, resolution (4).

Persevere, *v.* See last (2), abide, continue, bear (2), live (2), press (2).

Persist, *v.* See persevere.

Persistence, *n.* See perseverance.

Persistent, *adj.* See firm (2), diligent, durable; indefatigable, constant (3), compelling; inflexible, arbitrary.

Persnickety, *adj.* See particular (2), difficult (3), inflexible, petty, critical (2), precise (2).

Person, *n.* A natural person or human being, plus legal entities such as corporations, partnerships, unions, associations, firms, trustees, receivers, legal representatives, etc. (the person aggrieved). Party, being, life, soul, body, character, fellow, one, personage, individual, mortal, organization. See also mankind, people, man, woman.

Personable, *adj.* See friendly, convivial, amicable, attractive.

Person aggrieved The victim; the one who has actually suffered the injury. See victim.

Personal, *adj.* Pertaining or belonging to a particular individual (personal papers). Special, inward, exclusive, internal, inherent, intimate, subjective, peculiar, own, idiosyncratic, inner, characteristic, specific, distinct, privy, undisclosed. See also confidential, private, particular. *Ant.* Public.

Personal effects Articles associated with the person; movable or chattel property (e.g., clothing, car). See effects.

Personality, *n.* See individual (2), character; influence (1); attractive, intriguing.

Personal jurisdiction See in personam, jurisdiction.

Personal liability The kind of responsibility for the performance of an obligation that exposes the personal (not just business) assets of the person to the payment of the obligation. See liability.

Personal property Everything, other than real estate, that is the subject of ownership; any right or interest that one has in things movable; personalty. See chattel (1), property.

Personal property tax A state or local tax on items of personal property such as household furniture, jewelry. See tax.

Personal recognizance Pretrial release without posting a bond, based on the defendant's promise that he or she will appear at all future court proceedings in the case and remain amenable to the orders and processes of the court. Release on recognizance (ROR). See also release; bail.

Personalty *n.* Movable property. See asset, chattel (1), effects, holding (2), personal property.

Persona non grata, *n.* An undesirable person. See nonentity, fugitive, tramp (1).

Personate, *v.* To pass oneself off as another in order to deceive others. See impersonate.

Personification, *n.* See embodiment, manifestation, representation, symbol.

Personify, *v.* See manifest (2), exhibit (1), express (2).

Person in loco parentis See in loco parentis.

Personnel, *n.* See laborer, employee, coterie, associate.

Perspective, *n.* See view (5), sight, range (2), scope; environment; disposition (4), opinion, belief.

Perspicacious, *adj.* See acute (1), judicial (2), judicious; explicit.

Perspicacity, *n.* See judgment (2), discretion, prudence, common sense.

Per stirpes Taking by class or representation; together the class takes the share to which their deceased ancestor would have been entitled. *Ant.* Per capita.

Persuade, *v.* To induce someone to do or believe something by arguments, pleas, or other methods (she persuaded the judge to grant the motion). Convince, motivate, influence, impress, indoctrinate, rouse, lure, woo, incline, bribe, sway, inveigle, cajole, coax, inspire, seduce, wean, intimidate, wear down, entice, impel, win over, incite, bring around, convert, enlist, actuate, prompt, stir, proselytize, exhort, urge.

Persuasion, *n.* **1.** An act that persuades (powers of persuasion). Argument, advocacy, proselytizing, influence, argumentation, cajolery, solicitation, pleading, guidance, inducement, seduction, coaxing, blandishment, exhortation. **2.** Religious belief. See creed.

Persuasive, *adj.* See convincing, cogent, compelling, logical, irresistible, effective.

Pert, *adj.* See rude, impertinent (2), arrogant; active (3).

Pertain, *v.* To belong or relate to (the evidence pertained to the firing). Bear on, concern, touch, focus on, is pertinent to, is appropriate for, connect, involve, belong, associate, join. See also appertain, refer.

Pertaining, *adv., v.* See about, in re; pertain, appertain, pertinent.

Pertinent, *adj.* Relevant to the issue in dispute (pertinent argument). Applicable, related, material, apt, to the point, on the mark, apropos, pertaining, analogous, fitting, corresponding, connected, associated, suitable, apposite. See also appropriate (3), germane. *Ant.* Extraneous.

Perturb, *v.* See harass, disturb, exacerbate, outrage (2).

Perusal, *n.* See examination, inspection, search.

Peruse, *v.* See investigate, audit (2).

Pervade, *v.* See hover (1), imbue, fill, inundate.

Pervasive, *adj.* See extensive, comprehensive, ubiquitous, predominant.

Perverse, *adj.* See peculiar (2), irregular, odd, anomalous; inflexible, contentious, litigious; corrupt, immoral, bad, false, wrong.

Perversion, *n.* See deviation, debauchery, deviant, abuse, cruelty, corruption, degradation.

Pervert, *v.,* **pervert,** *n.* See debase, distort, corrupt, abuse; deviant, wrongdoer.

Perverted, *adj.* See depraved; perverse.

Pessimism, *n.* See depression, doubt.

Pessimist, *n.* See cynic; cynical; nihilist.

Pessimistic, *adj.* See cynical, suspicious (2), depressed, depressing, despondent, negative (2).

Pest, *n.* See nuisance, inconvenience, obstacle.

Pester, *v.* See harass, disturb, provoke; annoyance.

Pesticide, *n.* See poison.

Pestilence, *n.* See epidemic.

Pet, *n., adj., v.* See animal; favorite; caress, touch (1).

Petition 1. *n.* A formal written request (a petition for a rehearing). Plea, pleading, prayer, application, requisition, solicitation, adjuration, supplication, entreaty, orison, motion, demand, round robin, appeal, suit, beseechment, proposal. **2.** *v.* To make a formal request (she petitioned for an extension). Plead, advocate, seek, demand, solicit, move, apply, pray, entreat, ask, invoke, appeal, press, urge, beg, supplicate, sue, beseech, imprecate, adjure, implore.

Petitioner. *n.* One who presents a petition to a court or other body (the petitioner moved for a directed verdict). Pleader, applicant, litigant, supplicant, asker, suitor, solicitor, aspirant, party, bidder, complainant, plaintiff, appellant. *Ant.* Respondent.

Petition in bankruptcy A paper filed in a court of bankruptcy by a debtor seeking the benefits of the bankruptcy act, or by creditors alleging the commission of an act of bankruptcy by the debtor and seeking an adjudication of bankruptcy against the debtor. See bankruptcy.

Petit jury An ordinary jury for the trial of a civil or criminal action. See jury, grand jury.

Petrify, *v.* See intimidate, outrage (2), disturb, harass, disrupt.

Pettifogger, *n.* A small-time lawyer; a dishonest lawyer. Shyster, mouthpiece. See also charlatan, wrongdoer.

Pettifoggery, *n.* Quibbling over trivia; duplicity. See artifice, cheat, chicanery, corruption; dishonest.

Petty, *adj.* **1.** Of less importance (petty cash). Small, minor, little, petit, junior, lower, secondary, ancillary, subordinate. **2.** Of little merit (petty quarrel). Unimportant, worthless, nonessential, dispensable, paltry, inconsequential, picayune, niggling, inane, trivial, negligible, insignificant, trifling, flimsy, slight, piddling, meager, sparse, minute, foolish. See also nugatory, frivolous, marginal, minimal, minor (2). **3.** Spiteful (petty response). Narrow-minded, mean, prejudiced, shabby, twisted, bigoted, partial, myopic, ungenerous, cheap, ignoble, illiberal, unreasonable. See also parochial. *Ant.* Major; substantial; tolerant.

Petty cash, *n.* See fund (2).

Petty larceny, *n.* The larceny of goods with a value below a statutorily set amount (e.g., $100). Pilferage. See also larceny, grand larceny.

Petty officer, *n.* A noncommissioned naval officer. See military, officer, sailor.

Petulant, *adj.* See querulous, difficult (3), crabby, contentious, litigious, rude, inflexible, impatient, particular (2).

Peyote, *n.* A type of cactus called mescal, containing button-like tubercles that are dried and chewed as a hallucinatory drug. Mescaline is an alkaloid of it. See drug, hallucination.

Phantom, *n.* See hallucination, dream (1), fiction; illusory.

Pharmacy, *n.* Apothecary, drugstore. See merchant, business.

Phase, *n.* See interval, period; appearance (3); crisis.

Phaseout, *n.* See completion, conclusion (1), cessation; end, diminish.

Phencyclidine, *n.* See angel dust.

Phenomenal, *adj.* See exceptional, extraordinary, great, outstanding (2), attractive, intriguing.

Phenomenon, *n.* See mystery, marvel; event, occurrence.

Philanthropy, *n.* See charity, benevolence.

Philistine, *adj., n.* See rude, petty (3), pompous, arrogant; boor, ass.

Philosopher, *n.* See scholar, student, teacher, authority (3, 4), master (1), oracle; augur, clairvoyance.

Philosophical, *adj.* See learned, literary (2), cultivated, judicious, mature (2), rational, brilliant, able, capable (2), logical; abstract, preoccupied, engaged.

Phlegmatic, *adj.* See indifferent, apathetic, passive (2), lazy; loiter, loaf, malingerer.

Phobia, *n.* See fear, anxiety, odium.

Phone, *v.* See contact (3), communicate.

Phony, *adj.* See false, deceptive, illusory, fictitious.

Photocopy, *v.* See copy.

Photograph, *n.* See representation; description, copy.

Phrase, *n., v.* See language; communication, declaration; describe.

P.H.V. See pro hac vice.

Physical, *adj.* Pertaining to the body or other material things (physical disability). Corporeal, tangible, bodily, substantial, temporal, corporal, actual, somatic, palpable, external, solid, animal, real, sensible, unspiritual, surface, concrete, living, phenomenal, incarnate, carnal. *Ant.* Mental.

Physical force Actual violence; force applied to a body. See violence, force (2), coercion.

Physician, *n.* A person licensed to practice medicine. See doctor, medicine, treatment, medical.

Physician-patient privilege See doctor-patient privilege.

Physics, *n.* The study of matter and energy. See science.

Physiognomy, *n.* See demeanor, appearance, face, exterior.

Physiotherapy, *n.* The treatment of disease by physical remedies other than drugs; physical therapy. See medicine, doctor, treatment.

Physique, *n.* See body (5), constitution (2); able-bodied.

Picayune, *adj.* See minor (2), small, nugatory, frivolous, petty.

Pick, *v., n.* See select (1), prefer; choice (1), option.

Picket, *v.* To patrol the entrance of a business in order to inform other employees and the public of a strike and to deter them from entering (picket the supermarket). Boycott, protest, march, sit down, sit in, walk out, enclose, blockade, dissent, rally. See also demonstrate (3), strike (1), union, walkout, walk.

Pickpocket, *n.* A thief who secretly steals money or other property from the person of another. See thief, wrongdoer, larceny.

Pickup truck, *n.* See vehicle.

Picture, *n.* See description, map, definition, representation, copy; cinema.

Picturesque, *adj.* See beautiful, attractive, enjoyable, intriguing.

Piddle, *v.* See loiter, loaf, wander.

Piddling, *adj.* See petty, minor (2), small, nugatory, frivolous.

Piece, *n.* See part (1), portion; iota, scintilla.

Piecemeal, *adj.* See gradual, progressive; inconsistent, fluctuating.

Pier, *n.* See dock (1), jetty.

Pierce, *v.* To cut through (pierce the corporate veil). Penetrate, go through, lance, stab, gash, drive into, drill, insert, prick, perforate, gore, spike, make a hole in, force through; uncover. See also enter (2).

Piercing, *adj.* See caustic, biting, cutting, offensive, malicious; acute; noisy.

Piercing the corporate veil In certain cases (e.g., fraud) a court will disregard the principle of limited liability inherent in the corporate structure and impose personal liability on stockholders, officers, and directors. See also alter ego (2), instrumentality rule.

Piety, *n.* See religion, worship, fidelity; holy.

Pigeonhole, *v.* See peg (1), classify, organize, place (2).

Pigheaded, *adj.* See inflexible, contumacious, incorrigible, callous.

Pike, *n.* See highway.

Pile, *n., v.* See bulk (1), lot (3), collection (2); pack, collect (1); wealth.

Pilfer, *v.* To steal (pilfer the watch). Convert, take, rob, purloin, appropriate, snatch, misappropriate, thieve, pirate, usurp, pick, crib, filch, palm, make off with, deprive one of. See also embezzle, larceny. *Ant.* Restore.

Pilferage, *n.* Stealing small items; petty larceny. See larceny.

Pilgrimage, *n.* See voyage.

Pill, *n.* See drug, medicine, contraceptive.

Pillage, *n.* The forcible taking of private property, usually in times of war (the pillage of the town by the army). See appropriation (1), piracy, plunder, mischief, larceny.

Pillory, *n.* A frame with holes and movable boards, through which the head and hands of an offender were placed.

Pilot, *v., n.* See navigate, regulate, manage, administer; operator.

Pimp, *n.* One who obtains customers for a whore or prostitute (territory of the pimp). Go-between, panderer, whoremonger, "flesh peddler," purveyor, procurer, madam, runner. See also parasite, prostitute.

Pinch, *v., n.* See squeeze; arrest (2); crisis, emergency.

Pine, *v.* See mope, bemoan, suffer, cry (1), desire; wear (1), decline, diminish.

Pinhead, *n.* See boor, ass, idiot.

Pin money, *n.* Funds for incidental purchases; a small allowance set apart by a husband for the personal expenses of his wife. See fund.

Pinnacle, *n.* See apex.

Pinpoint, *v.* See define; identification.

Pioneer, *n.* See developer, producer, ancestor, inventor; harbinger.

Pious, *adj.* See holy, religious; worship.

Pipe dream, *n.* See dream (1), hallucination, legend, fiction; illusory.

Pique, *v.* See disturb, harass, outrage (2), provoke.

Piracy, *n.* Robbery and depredation on the high seas; stealing (piracy of the film). Pillage, plundering, theft, banditry, privateering, larceny, embezzlement, infringement, appropriation, misappropriation, expropriation, cribbing, vandalism, raid, deprivation, conversion, commandeering, plagiarism, devastation, copying, arrogation, usurpation. See also plunder; hijack. *Ant.* Restoration.

Pirate, *n.* See thief, wrongdoer.

Pistol, *n.* See gun, weapon.

Pit, *n.* See abyss, cave, cell.

Pitch, *v., n.* See jettison; build, establish; grade (2).

Pitfall, *n.* See danger, peril, ambush.

Pith, *n.* See gravamen, essence (1), gist (1).

Pithy, *adj.* See concise, effective, cogent.

Pitiful, *adj.* See abject, deplorable, distressing, grievous, worthless.

Pittance, *n.* See scintilla, iota, minimum.

Pity, *v., n.* See commiserate; assuage; consolation, benevolence.

Pivot, *v.* See turn (1).

P.J. Presiding Judge or Justice.

P.L. See public law.

Placard, *n.* **1.** A sign, advertisement, or public announcement (an injunction against the use of placards). Poster, notice, billboard, bulletin, flyer, broadside, handbill. **2.** A declaration. See edict, mandate (1), manifesto.

Placate, *v.* See accommodate, quiet, assuage, mitigate.

Place 1. *n.* Site; a locality limited by boundaries (the place where they met). Location, district, station, vicinity, field, area, territory, state, locale, venue, sector, neighborhood, spot, region, quarter, precinct, locus, mall, scene, setting, post, point, lot, environment, milieu, environs, situs, longitude, lane, square, space. See also zone. **2.** *v.* To arrange for something (place an order). Assign, commission, appoint, dispose, categorize, hire, entrust, fix, delegate, enlist, situate, organize, induct, group, determine, position, install, ensconce, locate, settle, attach.

Placement, *n.* **1.** Arranging or placing (placement in a home for delinquents). Installation, arrangement, seating, establishment, disposition, disposal, deployment, appointment, grouping, investiture, positioning, pigeonholing. **2.** Selling a new issue of securities. **3.** Arranging a loan or mortgage. **4.** Locating employment for someone.

Place of abode See abode, domicile, residence, home.

Placer, *n.* A superficial deposit of sand, gravel, or disintegrated rock, carrying precious metals along the shore of the sea, along the course of a watercourse, or under the bed of a watercourse; ground, including valuable deposits that are in a loose state.

Placid, *adj.* See quiet, patient (3); passive; composure.

Plagiarism, *n.* Appropriating part or all of the composition or ideas of another and passing them off as the product of one's own mind (plagiarism of the theories in a law review article). Theft, copying, unauthorized use, forgery, simulation, pilferage, arrogation, usurpation, reproduction, deceit, duplicity, piracy, infringement, counterfeiting, misappropriation. See also imitation, appropriation, larceny, fraud, palming off, deception.

Plagiarize, *v.* See copy, pilfer; fraud.

Plague, *v., n.* See epidemic, affliction, nuisance; harass, outrage (2), menace (2).

Plain *adj.* **1.** Clearly seen or understood (plain view). Manifest, patent, blatant, visible, lucid, bare, naked, recognizable, clear-cut, conspicuous, unmistakable, unambiguous, evident, distinct, unequivocal, apparent, intelligible, perspicuous, transparent, certain, palpable, glaring, notorious, explicit, legible, well-marked, prominent, avowed, cognizable, translucent, notable, graphic, pronounced, vivid, outstanding, discernible, openhanded, straightforward, self-explanatory, tangible, precise, unobscured, appreciable. **2.** See homely. **3.** See commonplace, pedestrian (2). *Ant.* Cryptic; beautiful; fresh.

Plainclothes man, *n.* A police officer who wears civilian clothes. See police, officer; clandestine, hidden.

Plain error rule Even though a party did not object to an error during the trial, an appellate court can still review the error if it is obvious, prejudicial, affects substantial rights, relates to the fundamental fairness of the trial, and which, if uncorrected, would be an affront to the integrity and reputation of the court.

Plainspoken, *adj.* See direct (6), explicit, honest; abrasive, rude, caustic.

Plaintiff, *n.* The person who complains and brings an action (the plaintiff moved for a directed verdict). Complainant, accuser, claimant, suitor, opponent, litigant, antagonist, challenger, asserter, pleader, appellant, adversary. See also petitioner, party. *Ant.* Defendant.

Plaintive, *adj.* See dismal, depressed, despondent, grievous.

Plain view doctrine If an incriminating object falls within the plain view of an officer who has the right to be present, the object can be seized without a warrant and introduced into evidence. See evidence, admissible, seize, observe.

Plan 1. *n.* An arrangement for the accomplishment of a particular act or object (a plan to change the rules). Procedure, scheme, program, course, strategy, proposal, blueprint, outline, map, agenda, prospectus, project, order, device, setup, formula, tactics, techniques, schedule, pattern, system, orchestration, plot, design, drawing, chart, delineation, draft, form, representation, layout, syllabus, method, process, formation, campaign, stratagem, suggestion, conception, idea, approach, methodology; conspiracy, machination, contrivance, ploy, intrigue, collusion, game, maneuver, connivance, subterfuge. **2.** *v.* To prepare a program (she planned a new approach). Outline, scheme, orchestrate, blueprint, schedule, chart, map, arrange, strategize, mold, project, concoct, formulate, organize, diagram, plot, design, invent, itemize, devise, frame, contrive, conspire, work out, collude, machinate, hatch, intrigue, study, calculate, manipulate, predetermine, cabal, weave, premeditate, visualize, block out, engineer, manage. **3.** *v.* To intend an act (he planned to sue). Resolve, consider, contemplate, premeditate, aspire, propose, hope, desire, aim, calculate, predetermine, envisage, mean, strive, figure on, designate.

Plane, *n.* See grade, class, flat; aircraft.

Planet, *n.* See world.

Plank, *n.* See platform.

Planned Unit Development (PUD) An area with a specified minimum contiguous acreage to be developed as a single entity according to a plan, containing one or more residential clusters or planned unit residential developments, and one or more public, quasi-public, commercial, or industrial areas. A device that has as its goal a self-contained mini-community built within a zoning district under density and use rules as to buildings and open space.

Plant, *n.* See building, facility (2); manufacture, production; merchant, commerce.

Plantation, *n.* See farm.

Plaster, *v.* See fix (3); cohere (1), pave.

Plastic, *adj.* See malleable, susceptible, amenable (2), formative; artificial.

Plat or plot, *n.* **1.** A map of a town, section, or subdivision showing the location and boundaries of individual parcels of land subdivided into lots, with streets, alleys, easements, etc., usually drawn to scale (an examination of the plat). Plan, sketch, chart, delineation, diagram. See also outline. **2.** A piece of ground. See lot (1), parcel (3).

Plateau, *n.* See grade; prairie; interim.

Platform, *n.* **1.** A statement of principles and policies (the party's platform). Program, positions, promises, creed, plank, plan, doctrine, tenets, scheme, course of action, stance, objectives, intentions, goals, beliefs, line. **2.** A raised structure (the platform collapsed). Stage, dais, pulpit, rostrum, scaffold, podium, deck, soapbox, landing, stand.

Platitude, *n.* See cliché; maxim; commonplace, pedestrian (2).

Platonic, *adj.* See abstract (4), incorporeal, dispassionate, objective, rational.

Platoon, *n.* See division (2), group; military, martial, sailor.

Plaudit, *n.* See approval, approbation, acclamation.

Plausible, *adj.* See believable, credible, cogent, convincing, rational.

Play, *n., v.* See game (1), sport (2), diversion (2), antic, horseplay; joke; gambling; drama; flirt; pretend.

Playboy, playgirl, *n.* See suitor, paramour, spendthrift; debauchery.

Player, *n.* See actor, party; accomplice, competitor.

Playful, *adj.* See happy, active (3); juvenile; antic.

Playground, *n.* See park (1).

Plaza, *n.* See park (1); market.

Plea, *n.* The first pleading of the defendant (a plea of not guilty). Answer, response, refutation, rebuttal, assertion, defense, extenuation, explanation, pretext, alibi, reason, retort, counterargument, justification, apology, claim, prayer, petition, suit, request, entreaty, argument, supplication, allegation.

Plea bargaining The process whereby the accused and the prosecutor work out a mutually satisfactory disposition of the case, subject to court approval (e.g., the defendant agrees to plead guilty to a lesser included offense or to one of the counts in a multicount indictment in exchange for a lighter sentence). See bargain, punishment, adjudication.

Plead, *v.* To file a pleading or to argue a case in court (the court ordered the party to plead over). Prosecute, defend, present, entreat, allege, maintain, advance, urge, petition, clamor, press, exhort, beseech, move, pray, solicit, implore, supplicate, appeal, beg, adjure, sue, affirm, contend, swear, stress, charge, recommend, profess, admit, concede, challenge.

Pleadings, *n.* Formal allegations by the parties of their claims and defenses (amendment of the pleadings). Answer, averment, rebuttal, plea, complaint, reply, denial, assertion, petition.

Plea in abatement A plea that, without disputing the justice of the plaintiff's claim, objects to the place, mode, or time of asserting it.

Plea of privilege A method of objecting to venue by which the pleader seeks to be sued in the county of the pleader's residence. See venue.

Pleasant, *adj.* See pleasing.

Pleasantry, *n.* A kind word. Greeting, polite comment. See also joke.

Please, *v.* See satisfy (2), delight, pander (2), amuse, interest (5).

Pleasing, *adj.* See enjoyable, attractive, beautiful, intriguing, delectable, kind, friendly, convivial, civil (3), happy.

Pleasure, *n.* See diversion (2), amusement, welfare, happiness, enjoyment (2), satisfaction (2); lust, desire.

Plebeian, *adj.* See base, rude, gross (1), common (3), backward (1), inferior.

Plebiscite, *n.* A vote of the people on a proposed law or policy submitted to them (a plebiscite on the raising of the debt ceiling in the state). Poll, election, direct vote, ballot, vox populi, referendum.

Pledge 1. *n.* The bailment or delivery of property as security for a debt, an engagement, or the performance of an act; a security interest in a chattel; a promise or agreement to do or forbear something (a pledge of the firm's inventory). Commitment, guarantee, assurance, covenant, contract, undertaking, vow, word, endorsement, warranty, adjuration, pact, avowal, oath; collateral, token, surety, bond, pawn, stake, deposit, earnest. **2.** *v.* To deposit something as security; to give a solemn promise (she pledged her assets). Post, stake, mortgage, guarantee, engage, obligate, bind, hypothecate, put up, present as collateral, warrant; promise, assure, covenant, give one's word, undertake, affirm.

Pledgee, *n.* The person to whom something is delivered in pledge; the one to whom a pledge is given.

Pledger or pledgor, *n.* The person who pledges; the one who delivers goods in pledge.

Plenary, *adj.* Complete; fully attended (plenary session of the legislature). Entire, unqualified, open, total, unrestricted, thorough, ample, unlimited, whole, absolute, comprehensive, unconfined, exhaustive. See also full. *Ant.* Restricted.

Plenary powers Authority and power as broad as is required in a given case. See authority.

Plenary session A meeting of all the members of a deliberative body. See meeting.

Plenipotentiary, *n.* One who has full power to do a thing; a diplomatic minister. See agent (1), consul, delegate (2).

Plentiful, *adj.* See copious, abundant, many, great, big, excess, plenary, incalculable; affluent; luxury.

Plenty, *n.* See plentiful.

Plethora, *n.* See sufficiency; sea (2); abundant.

Pliable, *adj.* See flexible malleable, formative, susceptible, amenable (2).

Pliant, *adj.* See pliable.

Plight 1. *n.* A dangerous condition or predicament (responding to the plight of the swimmer). Crisis, quandary, mess, trial, delicate situation, emergency, complication, jam, difficulty, embarrassment, imbroglio, spot, setback, misfortune, reverse, hardship, catch-22, tangle, stalemate, test, squeeze, exigency, "pickle," distress, impasse, vicissitude, tribulation, box, corner, quagmire; case, shape, posture, category, juncture, circumstances, state. **2.** *v.* To bind oneself. See pledge (2).

Plod, *v.* See walk; labor.

Plot 1. *n.* A parcel of land. See lot (1), plat, parcel (3), field (1). **2.** *n.* A secret and unscrupulous plan (a plot to take over). Stratagem, conspiracy, collusion, scheme, intrigue, maneuver, racket, deception, trick, ruse, strategy, cabal, machination, tactic, design, blueprint, manipulation, covin, contrivance, artifice. **3.** *v.* To design a devious plan (she plotted a takeover). Conspire, map, calculate, diagram, outline, mastermind, formulate, chart, determine, sketch, organize, cabal, prepare, engineer, connive, concoct, maneuver, premeditate, hatch, compute, draft, conceive, prearrange, brew, fabricate, structure, set up a strategy, envisage.

Plottage, *n.* The additional value of city lots because they are contiguous. Vacant and unimproved parcels held in one ownership are more valuable because of their greater use adaptability as a single unit.

Plow, *v.* See farm (2).

Pluck, *v.* See extract (1); seize.

Plug, *v.* See close (2); promote.

Plum, *n.* See bonus, prize.

Plumber, *n.* See laborer, merchant; business

Plummet, *v.* See fall (2), collapse.

Plump, *adj.* See corpulent.

Plunder 1. *v.* To take property from persons or places by open force; to take without right (the soldiers plundered the town). Pillage, loot, waste, seize, rape, sack, rob, despoil, strip, rifle, depredate, pilfer, ruin, raze, carry away, devastate, fleece, pirate, capture, ransack, divest, denude, lay bare, forage, exhaust, milk, bleed, foray, maraud, impoverish. **2.** *n.* That which is forcibly taken (the police confiscated their plunder). Booty, spoils, prize, loot, take, treasure, winnings, graft, pillage, gains, pickings, haul, grab, goods. **3.** *n.* The act of taking property by open force (the plunder of the town). Robbery, thievery, raid, appropriation, confiscation, seizure, rapine, despoilment, desolation, commandeering, pillage, depredation. See also piracy.

Plunge, *v.* See fall (2), collapse.

Plural, *adj.* Containing more than one. See many.

Plurality, *n.* In an appellate case with more than one opinion, if no opinion commands a majority of the court, the decision is by plurality; in a case in which there are not enough agreeing justices to form a majority of the court, a plurality is the opinion in which more justices join than in any concurring opinion; the side that receives the greatest number of votes without receiving a majority; the excess of the votes cast for one side over those of any other; a large number or quantity. See many, majority.

Plus, *n.*   See benefit, aid (2), mileage, fringe.

Plush, *adj.*   See deluxe, exorbitant, costly, flamboyant, decadent; luxury.

Plutocracy, *n.*   A government controlled by the wealthy.   See government, wealth.

Ply, *v.*   See employ (2), manipulate; nurture; navigate.

Pneumoconiosis, *n.*   Lung diseases caused by dust particles.   See disease, illness.

Poach, *v.*   To steal or destroy game on another's land; to hunt illegally.   See piracy, plunder (1), appropriation (1).

Pocket, *v., n.*   See pilfer, appropriate (1); cave; vessel (2); mass; bag.

Pocketknife, *n.*   See weapon.

Pocket veto, *n.*   Inaction on the part of the President when sent a bill just passed by Congress, which has the effect of vetoing it.   While Presidential inaction for ten days normally results in the bill becoming law as if signed, inaction by the Presidnet results in nonapproval through a "pocket veto" if Congress adjourns, thereby preventing the bill's return within the ten-day period.   At the state level, indirect vetoes of this kind are also possible in many states.   See veto, legislation.

P.O.D. account Payable on death.   An account payable to one person during life, and when he or she dies, payable to someone else who is designated.

Podium, *n.*   See platform.

Poem, *n.*   Verse.   Song, metrics, stanza, sonnet, couplet, jingle, ballad, rhyme, art.

Poet, *n.*   See author.

Poetic, *adj.*   See lyric, symbolic, beautiful, attractive, enjoyable.

Pogrom, *n.*   See murder, homicide; kill.

Poignant, *adj.*   See cogent, moving (1), intriguing, compelling, emotional; grievous, acute, painful, distressing; relevant.

Point 1. *n.*   A distinct proposition or question of law arising or propounded in a case (counsel argued the point).   Matter, item, detail, instance, thought, aspect, part, step, article, subject.   **2.** *n.*   A fee or charge equal to 1 percent of the principal amount of the loan, collected by the lender at the time the loan is made (two points paid).   **3.** *n.*   For shares of stock, a point is $1; for bonds, a point is $10.   **4.** *n.*   The essence or meaning (the point of the regulation).   Object, intent, design, gist, idea, substance, concept, core, root, nucleus, heart, central feature, quintessence, purpose, aim, target, crux, reason, value, objective, significance, purport, theme, motive, stance, motif, thrust, connotation, goal, use, end.   **5.** *n.*   A particular time or place.   See instant (5), location.   **6.** *v.*   To aim (point the rifle).   Direct, target, level, train, focus, beam, guide, face, slant, turn, bend, steer.

Pointed, *adj.*   See concise, brief; acute, caustic; apt, appropriated.

Pointless, *adj.*   See absurd, worthless, frivolous, barren, irrelevant.

Point of view, *n.*   See opinion, belief, disposition (4).

Poise, *n.*   See composure, self-confidence.

Poison 1. *n.*   A substance with inherent characteristics that are dangerous to life or bodily functions (killed by poison).   Venom, bane, toxin, toxicant, arsenic, virus, dangerous chemical, miasma, bacillus, hemlock, pathogen, cyanide, belladonna; cancer, malignancy, contamination, contaminant, corruption, plague, abomination.   **2.** *v.*   To corrupt; to kill with poison (poisoned the atmosphere).   See contaminate, pollute, corrupt (2).   *Ant.*   Antidote; purify.

Poisonous, *adj.*   Having a harmful impact; contaminated (poisonous influence).   Dangerous, unhealthy, malign, infectious, noxious, diabolic, invidious, venomous, toxic, baneful, virulent, deadly, leprous, unsanitary, pernicious, malicious, hazardous, demonic, injurious, septic, ruinous, nocuous, detrimental.   See also contagious, lethal, harmful.   *Ant.*   Innocuous.

Poisonous tree doctrine See fruit of the poisonous tree.

Poke, *v.* See push, beat (1); interfere, impose, intermeddle.

Polar, *adj.* See opposite, contradictory, hostile.

Polarization, *n.* See separation (2).

Polarize, *v.* See divide (3), alienate (2).

Pole, *n.* A measure of length equal to 5½ yards.

Polemic, *n.* See argument, debate; contentious, litigious.

Police 1. *n.* The branch of the government with the responsibility for the preservation of public order and tranquility, the promotion of public safety and morals, and the prevention and investigation of crime (the police kept order). Law enforcement agency, policemen, police officers, peace officers, constabulary, authorities, patrol, guard, sheriff, gendarme, trooper, police force; law and order, the law. See also marshal, officer, official. **2.** *v.* To guard or patrol (police the area). Watch, keep vigil, secure, protect, control, keep the peace, oversee, maintain order, superintend, preserve, safeguard, supervise, observe, prevent disorder, rule.

Police Court An inferior court in some states with jurisdiction over minor offenses, city ordinances, etc. See court, jurisdiction.

Police jury The governing body of Louisiana parishes. Parishes are comparable to counties in other states.

Police power The power of government to place restraints on the personal freedom and property rights of persons for the protection and promotion of public safety, health, morals, convenience, and prosperity. An authority conferred by the Tenth Amendment of the U.S. Constitution on individual states, which in turn is delegated to local governments, under which police departments can be established and laws enacted to prevent crime and secure the comfort, safety, morals, health, and prosperity of the citizens. See welfare, power.

Policy, *n.* **1.** The general principles by which an organization is guided and managed (public policy). Guidelines, goals, objectives, system, code, custom, plan of action, course of action, methodology, platform, approach, tenets, creed, beliefs, directions, scheme, habit, tactic, style, management, design, strategy, line, polity, proposal, protocol. **2.** An insurance contract. See insurance. **3.** A kind of lottery or game of chance in which bettors select numbers to bet on. See lottery, gambling.

Policyholder, *n.* The person who owns the policy of insurance whether or not he or she is the insured.

Polish, *v.* See perfect (3), correct (2); bathe.

Polished, *adj.* See clean (2); cultivated, learned, literary (2), brilliant, civil (3).

Polite, *adj.* See civil (3), cultivated, judicious, cautious, discreet.

Politic, *adj.* See expedient (2), prudent, judicious.

Political, *adj.* Pertaining to the policy or administration of government; pertaining to the organization of people, parties, and interests that seek to control the management of government (political considerations). Civic, public, official, governmental, bureaucratic; adversary, factional, one-sided. See also administrative, hierarchy, bureaucracy; clerical (1); partisan (2).

Political offenses Crimes that are incidental to and form a part of political disturbances; offenses committed in attacking the political order of things; offenses committed to obtain any political object. See crime.

Political party See party(3).

Political question A question of a purely political character; a question whose determination would involve the judiciary in an encroachment upon executive or legislative powers. See question, justiciable.

Political rights Rights established or recognized by constitutions, which give citizens the power to participate directly or indirectly in the establishment or administration of government. See right (3), civil liberties.

Political subdivision A division of the state, established by the constitutional authority of the state to carry out designated public functions. See division (1), government.

Politician, *n.* See administrator, official, officer, incumbent (1); candidate, applicant.

Politics, *n.* The science of government; the art or practice of administering public affairs; the attempts by a party or faction to obtain or retain political power. Political science, civics, statecraft, diplomacy, negotiation and compromise, accommodation, polity; political maneuvers. See also compromise; negotiate (1), bargain (2).

Polity, *n.* The system or form of government, state or organized society, body politic, civil constitution. See government, body politic.

Poll 1. *v.* To single out one by one; to question each juror after a verdict to determine whether he or she assents to the verdict (poll the membership). Question, survey, ballot, tabulate, interview, inquire, analyze, count, interrogate, register, compute, record, list. See also canvass. **2.** *n.* An individual person; a list or register of persons who may vote in an election. See record (2).

Poll tax A tax of a specific sum, levied upon everyone or upon each person within a certain class without reference to the amount of property owned by the person. See tax.

Pollutant, *n.* See dirt, poison.

Pollute, *v.* To contaminate the soil, air, water or environment in general by noxious substances or noises; to corrupt (the by-products polluted the stream). Foul, befoul, adulterate, defile, dirty, mar, blight, violate, scar, desecrate, degrade, infect, taint, putrefy, stain, smear, spot, blacken, muddy, begrime, besmear, besmirch, pervert, tarnish, soil, make filthy, alloy, undermine, abuse, poison, devalue, destroy, sully, deprave, debauch, dishonor, misuse, vitiate, mire, impair, litter, maculate, rot. See also corrupt (2). *Ant.* Cleanse.

Pollution, *n.* The process of contaminating (pollution control). Fouling, soiling, poisoning, defilement, adulteration, impairment, violation, dirtying, corruption, vitiation, debauchment, desecration, befoulment, contagion, degradation, perversion, prostitution, infection, deterioration, waste, disgrace, rape, ravishment, defiling, destruction, devaluation, depreciation. *Ant.* Purification.

Polyandry, *n.* A system permitting a woman to have more than one husband at the same time; a form of polygamy permitting a plurality of husbands. See bigamy. *Ant.* Monogamy.

Polygamy, *n.* The offense of having more than one spouse at the same time (religious practice of polygamy). Multiple spouses, multiple marriages, plural marriage. See also crime, bigamy. *Ant.* Monogamy.

Polygraph, *n.* Lie detector apparatus and test: an electromechanical instrument that simultaneously measures and records certain physiological changes in the human body that are believed to be involuntarily caused by an examinee's conscious attempt to deceive the questioner. See examination, inspection.

Pommel, *v.* See beat, batter.

Pomp, *n.* See grandeur, solemnity, ceremony, celebration, performance (3).

Pompous, *adj.* Arrogant (pompous presentation). Bombastic, empty, pretentious, verbose, vain, vainglorious, boastful, exaggerated, braggadocio, inflated, haughty, grandiose, ostentatious, swollen, flashy, showy, ornate, flowery, turgid, magniloquent, magisterial, supercilious, self-important, uppity, grandiloquent, conceited, egoistic, affected, dramatic, pedantic. *Ant.* Meek.

Pond, *n.* A body of stagnant water without an outlet, usually smaller than a lake. Basin, lagoon, reservoir, pool, tarn, hole.

Ponder, *v.* See fantasize, think, contemplate, consider, deliberate (1).

Ponderous, *adj.* See big, awkward, commonplace, pedestrian (2).

Pool 1. *v.* To combine for a common purpose (pool their resources). Unite, merge, blend, federate, amalgamate, unify, league, consolidate, share, ally, connect, mix, band together, associate. **2.** *n.* A combination or agreement by persons or companies, which has the effect of eliminating competition, establishing a monopoly, or controlling prices (an illegal pool). Cartel, trust, collaboration, combine, union, association, collective, alliance, coalition, syndicate. See also merger, amalgamation, consortium (2). **3.** *n.* A sum of money made up of stakes contributed by bettors (she won the pool). Purse, pot, kitty, reserve, ante, jackpot. See also fund (2). **4.** *n.* See pond.

Poor, *adj.* See indigent, destitute, bankrupt; inferior, worthless; dismal, abject.

Poorhouse, *n.* See asylum (1), home (2), institution.

Pope, *n.* See minister, clergy, church, hierarchy, clerical, head.

Poppycock, *n.* See balderdash; babble.

Populace, *n.* See people, constituency, citizen; country (1), nation.

Popular, *adj.* Prevalent or widespread (popular meaning). Prevailing, approved, conventional, orthodox, well-known, accustomed, normal, habitual, stock, current, standard, dominant, established, familiar, accepted, epidemic, general, public, rampant, extensive, customary, stylish, fashionable, garden-variety, in vogue, notorious, celebrated, famous. *Ant.* Unconventional.

Popularity, *n.* See approval, approbation, affection, acceptance.

Popularize, *v.* See circulate, publish, promote, back.

Populate, *v.* See inhabit, reside (1).

Population, *n.* See people, citizen, constituency, country (1), nation.

Populous, *adj.* See full.

Porch, *n.* See balcony, entrance.

Pore, *v.* See review, contemplate, consider, deliberate (1).

Pornographic, *adj.* Pertaining to material that the average person, applying contemporary community standards, would find appeals to the prurient interest; pertaining to material that depicts sexual conduct in a patently offensive way and that taken as a whole, lacks serious literary, artistic, political, or scientific value (pornographic literature). See obscene, prurient, carnal, lascivious. *Ant.* Innocuous.

Pornography, *n.* See pornographic, obscene; debauchery, lust.

Port, *n.* A place for the loading and unloading of vessels and for the collection of duties and customs on imports and exports (port of destination). Harbor, seaport, dock, haven, anchorage, landing, shelter.

Portable, *adj.* Mobile, moving, traveling, transportable, locomotive. See also ambulatory, migratory; movables.

Portal, *n.* See entrance.

Port authority A government agency that regulates and plans traffic through a port, encourages businesses to use the area served by the port, etc.

Portend, *v.* See augur, foresee, anticipate, expect (1); warning, harbinger, oracle.

Portentous, *adj.* See imminent, distressing, dangerous, crucial.

Porter, *n.* See servant, attendant, employee.

Portfolio, *n.* **1.** All the securities held by one person or institution. See investment, fund (2). **2.** The office of a government minister.

Portion, *n.* A part or share (portion of the estate). Division, percentage, cut, measure, segment, fragment, proportion, quota, sector, assignment, fraction, slice, allotment, dividend, ration, section, lot, quantity, allocation, serving, apportionment.

Portly, *adj.* See corpulent.

Portrait, *n.* See description, map, definition, representation, copy, outline.

Portray, *v.* See represent (2), describe, label.

Portrayal, *n.* See representation (2), description, map, definition.

Pose, *n.* See pretense; manner, disposition (4), carriage (3).

Posh, *adj.* See de luxe, exorbitant, costly, flamboyant, decadent, luxury.

Posit, *v.* See presume (1), assert, claim, place (2).

Position, *n., v.* See rank (1), hierarchy; job, occupation, office, carriage (3), disposition (4); opinion, belief, bias; order (4), plan (1), condition (2), composition, place; organize, establish, settle.

Positive, *adj.* **1.** Express, affirmative, or reliable (positive identification by the witness). Direct, absolute, explicit, conclusive, definite, unqualified, categorical, resolute, authentic, decisive, beyond doubt, unimpeachable, self-assured, emphatic, flat, indisputable, substantial, trusting, forceful, credulous, graphic, reliable, insistent, plain, unequivocal, trustworthy, sound, unambiguous, evident, incontestable, undisputed, clear, final, precise, corroborative, inescapable, factual, genuine. **2.** Actually enacted (positive law). Ordained, adopted, decreed, prescribed, instituted, commanded, legislated, established. **3.** See optimistic; happy. *Ant.* Qualified; contemplated; pessimistic.

Positive evidence Evidence that, if believed, establishes the truth or falsity of a fact in issue without the need of a presumption; direct proof or evidence. See evidence.

Positive law Law actually and specifically enacted or adopted by proper authority. See law.

Posse, *n.* See mob (1), gang, police.

Posse comitatus The power or force of the county; the entire population of a county, over the age of 15, which a sheriff could summon for assistance as an aid in keeping the peace, in apprehending felons, etc. Search party, detachment, civilian force, contingent. See also militia.

Possess, *v.* To have in one's actual and physical control; to own or be entitled to (possess the asset). Occupy, enjoy, maintain, take over, have, acquire, gain, assume, retain, receive, exercise control over, own, inherit, obtain, seize, dominate.

Possessed, *adj.* See demented, deranged; preoccupied, engaged; witchcraft.

Possession, *n.* **1.** The control or custody of property for one's use or enjoyment; the condition of being able to exercise control over a corporeal thing, to the exclusion of others (in possession). Dominion, right, seisin, proprietorship, interest, ownership, occupancy, authority, habitancy, guardianship, tenure, retention, keeping, grasp, title, monopoly. **2.** That which one holds or owns (her possessions). Goods, assets, belongings, movables, immovables, wealth, resources, holdings, personalty, valuables, equity, res, realty, items, things, money, capital, treasure, stock. See also property, chattel, estate, effects.

Possessive, *adj.* See avaricious, stingy, petty, suspicious.

Possessor, *n.* One who has possession (possessor of the land). Occupier, inhabitant, tenant, resident, inmate, dweller, addressee, owner. See also occupant.

Possessory, *adj.* Relating to, founded on, or claiming possession.

Possessory action An action that has for its immediate objective the actual possession of the subject matter. See action.

Possessory interest The right to exert control over specific property to the exclusion of others; the right to possess land whether or not based on title. See right, interest, control.

Possessory lien The creditor has a right to hold possession of the specific property until the debt or obligation is satisfied. See lien.

Possibility, *n.* An uncertain thing that may happen; a contingent interest in property (remote possibility). Potentiality, hope, expectation, prospect, conceivability, gamble, feasibility, odds, risk, anticipation, expectancy, opportunity, plausibility, eventuality, contingency. See also chance (3), likelihood, probability;

expectant. *Ant.* Certainty.

Possible, *adj.* Capable of existing, happening, or being (possible breakthrough). Feasible, likely, chance, probable, anticipated, potential, workable, attainable, realizable, conceivable, plausible, achievable, imaginable, doable, viable, credible, performable, within range, thinkable, procurable, tenable, promising, available. See also practicable, reasonable, logical. *Ant.* Futile.

Post 1. *prefix:* Later, coming after (postbellum). **2.** *n.* A military establishment (guarding the post). Camp, encampment, garrison, base, headquarters. See also division (2); military. **3.** *n.* A position to which one is assigned (strategic post). Place, station, lookout, beat, duty, assignment, appointment, seat, chore, mission, job, capacity, situation, charge, undertaking, commission. **4.** *n.* A solid material used as a marker or as support (the post collapsed). Stake, pole, column, cylinder, picket, stud, brace, pile. **5.** *v.* To publish (post the announcement). Announce, broadcast, display, enlighten, report, advertise, proclaim, acquaint, inform, apprise, advise, communicate, convey, deliver, circulate, spread, distribute, herald, disseminate, placard, propagate. **6.** *n.* The system of delivering mail; the mail delivered. See mail.

Postconviction remedies Remedies sought by a prisoner to challenge the legality of his or her conviction or sentence. See habeas corpus, coram nobis, remedy.

Postdate, *v.* To date an instrument at a time later than it was actually made (postdate a check).

Poster, *n.* See placard (1), circular (2).

Posterior, *adj.* See after, subsequent.

Posterity, *n.* All the descendants of a person in a direct line to the remotest generation (provisions made for posterity). Successors, issue, line, progeny, children, seed, succession, scions, heirs, lineage, future generations. See also family, offspring, child, genealogy. *Ant.* Ancestry.

Post facto After the fact. See ex post facto.

Posthaste, *adv.* See summarily, forthwith.

Posthumous, *adj.* Referring to events done after the death of a person (posthumous publication). Postmortem, after-death, following death, delayed, late, post-obit. See also after, subsequent. *Ant.* Contemporary.

Posthumous child A child born after the death of its father. See child.

Posting, *n.* **1.** A form of service of process in which process is displayed in a prominent place (posting on the front door of the defendant's residence). See service of process, notice (1). **2.** The act of transferring an original entry to a ledger. See record. **3.** The act of mailing a document. See mail.

Postmark, *n.* The official mark placed on mailable matter received at a post office for transmission through the mails; the mark which usually cancels the stamp and indicates the time and place of mailing. See mail, manifestation, badge.

Postmortem 1. *adj.* Pertaining to matters occurring after death (postmortem examination). Post-obit, posthumous, after-death, later, following. See also subsequent, after, death. **2.** *n.* An autopsy or review of what occurred (the postmortem revealed nothing new). Retrospective analysis, ex post facto examination, reconsideration. See also audit, examination.

Postnuptial agreement An agreement after marriage between spouses who may or may not be contemplating divorce (e.g., separation agreement, property settlement, property division). See agreement, nuptial, marriage, spouse, separation, agreement.

Post-obit, *n.* An agreement to borrow money to be repaid at a high interest upon the death of a person from whom the borrower hopes to inherit.

Postpone, *v.* **1.** To delay (postpone the trial). Put off, defer, continue, interrupt, suspend, put aside, hold up, shelve, table, pigeonhole, lay over, reserve, stay,

Postpone

remand, procrastinate, hold in abeyance, arrest, discontinue, intermit, prorogue, bring to a standstill, break, sideline, lay aside, recess. See also adjourn. **2.** To set below something else (the lien is postponed to a later lien). Subordinate, downgrade, set below.

Postponement, *n.* See delay (3), abeyance, interruption, cessation.

Postscript, *n.* See addendum, attachment, accessory (2).

Post-trial, *adj.* Pertaining to that which takes place after the trial (post-trial discovery).

Postulate, *v., n.* See presume (1), assert, claim, assume (2); hypothesis, assumption (2), premises (3).

Posture, *n.* See demeanor, disposition (4), condition (2), place; bias, pretense.

Pot, *n.* See marijuana, drug; prize.

Potable, *adj.* Suitable for drinking (potable water). Drinkable, uncontaminated. See also clean (2).

Potency, *n.* See might (2), power, influence, dominion, vigor.

Potent, *adj.* See strong, dominant, invulnerable, irresistible; effective, important, convincing, compelling; able-bodied, durable, healthy.

Potentate, *n.* A person with great power or sway (allegiance to a foreign potentate). Sovereign, prince, magnate, monarch, lord, master, chief executive, despot, dictator, king, tyrant.

Potential 1. *adj.* Naturally and probably expected to come into existence at some future time (potential danger). Anticipated, expected, likely, probable, realizable, promising, latent, embryonic, apparent, implicit, prospective, imaginable, dormant, lurking, undisclosed, waiting, conceivable, quiescent, budding, plausible. See also possible, imminent. **2.** *n.* Inherent abilities that can be developed (the potential for excellence). Capacity, capability, aptitude, potentiality, endowment, hope, competence, qualifications, talent, faculty, flair, expectation, gift, prospect, possibilities, promise, knack. *Ant.* Unlikely; deficiency.

"Pothead," *n.* See addict; drug.

Potion, *n.* See beverage, medicine, portion, amount, compound (3), mixture.

Potpourri, *n.* See compound (3), mixture, conglomerate; multifarious, multiple, divers.

Pouch, *n.* See vessel (2), bag.

Pounce, *v.* See beat (1), batter, attack, assault.

Pound 1. *v.* To beat or strike (pound the pavement). Hammer, pulverize, pommel, drum, smack, fustigate, pelt, maul, flail, storm, push, stab, pierce, collide, butt, assail, lunge at, smack, besiege, whack, trounce, rap, smite, contact, charge, slug, clap, whip, box, cudgel, flagellate, aggress, club, smash, "clobber," lambaste. See also beat, batter, assault, attack. **2.** *n.* A measure of weight equal to 16 ounces avoirdupois or 12 ounces troy. **3.** *n.* A place for the detention of stray animals. Doghouse, kennel, coop, shelter, pen.

Pour, *v.* See inundate, sprinkle, water (2).

Pour-over trust A provision in a will that directs the residue of the estate into a trust. See trust, residue.

Pout, *v.* See mope, bemoan.

Poverty, *n.* The state or condition of being poor (affidavit of poverty). Indigence, destitution, insolvency, scarcity, dire circumstances, penury, shortage, deficiency, privation, need, mendicity, impoverishment, meagerness, pennilessness, impecuniousness, exigency, necessity, starvation, pauperism, subsistence. See also bankruptcy, dearth; needy, indigent. *Ant.* Prosperity.

Powder keg, *n.* See vessel (2); danger.

Power, *n.* The right, ability, authority, or faculty of doing something; the ability of a person to produce a change in a given legal relation by doing or not doing a given act (implied power). Potency, prerogative, privilege, competency, potential, liberty, freedom, control, sovereignty, weight, authorization, puissance, ascendancy, rank, hegemony, warrant, carte blanche, capability, capacity; might, strength, force, intelligence, talent, attribute, property, endowment. See also dominion, ability, right, authority, jurisdiction, supremacy. *Ant.* Impotence.

Power coupled with an interest A right or power to do some act, together with an interest in the subject matter on which the power is to be executed. See interest. *Ant.* Naked power.

Powerful, *adj.* See strong, able, important, dominant, invulnerable, effective, compelling, convincing, irresistible, able-bodied, healthy, durable.

Powerless, *adj.* See dependent (2), defenseless, weak, frail, infirm, fallow, barren (2), dead (3), abject, lost; impotence.

Power of alienation The power to sell, transfer, assign, or otherwise dispose of property. See exchange, sell.

Power of appointment The power conferred on another (called the donee) to select the persons who are to receive a fund, an estate, or the income therefrom at a designated time. See appointment.

Power of attorney A document that authorizes another to act as one's agent or attorney. See attorney in fact, authority.

Powwow, *n.* See meeting (1), conference.

Practicable, *adj.* Pertaining to that which may be done, practiced, or accomplished (as soon as reasonably practicable). Practical, within reach, workable, achievable, doable, within the realm of possibility, operable, attainable, realizable, performable, accomplishable, acceptable, conceivable, usable, plausible, efficacious, sensible, potential, promising, logical, useful, likely, viable, expedient. See also feasible, possible, believable, functional. *Ant.* Unfeasible.

Practical, *adj.* See feasible, practicable, functional, possible, reasonable, rational, logical, efficient, expedient.

Practicality, *n.* See expediency; practicable, practical.

Practical nurse See assistant, associate; medicine, medical.

Practice, *n.* **1.** A repeated or customary action; habitual performance (the practice of retailers is to inspect the product before sale). Custom, usage, praxis, use, convention, wont, course of operation, manner of operation, mode of operation, routine, pattern, habit, modus operandi, protocol, approach, established procedure, system, policy, scheme, form, format, plan, tactic, rule, principle, ritual, fashion, tendency, process, procedure, observance. **2.** The act of carrying something out (we wanted to know how the theory worked in practice). Execution, actuality, realization, performance, action, process, operation, use, reality, the real world, application, discharge, commission, play. **3.** Training (more practice was needed). Exercise, drill, rehearsal, discipline, seasoning, repetition, preparation, conditioning, familiarization, schooling, perfecting, work, application, study, workout. **4.** The exercise of a profession or occupation (practice of law). Calling, undertaking, line, work, business, trade, pursuit, vocation, employment, engagement, labor, specialization, specialty, field, career, conduct. **5.** A scheme (questionable practices). Plot, device, stratagem, maneuver, ruse, chicanery, intrigue, trick.

Practitioner, *n.* **1.** One engaged in the exercise or employment of an art or profession (the professor yearned to become a practitioner). Worker, doer, performer, artisan, technician, craftsman. See also employer, laborer, actor. **2.** See attorney.

Praecipe, *n.* **1.** A formal request that a court clerk take some action. **2.** A writ ordering an action or a statement of the reasons why the action has not been taken.

Pragmatic, *adj.* See functional, practicable, feasible, rational, reasonable, efficient.

Prairie, *n.* An extensive tract of level or rolling land, usually with deep, fertile soil and no trees. Meadowland, grassland, range, pasture, country, plain, lea, tundra, moor.

Praise, *v., n.* See honor (2), indorsement (2), tribute (2), promote; approbation, approval, citation (3); flattery.

Praiseworthy, *adj.* See meritorious, good (2), moral (2), right (1), worthy, superior.

Prance, *v.* See run, walk, swagger.

Prank, *n.* See antic, joke, mischief.

Praxis, *n.* See practice (1), habit, process (1).

Pray, *v.* See petition (2), beseech; worship, holy, religious.

Prayer, *n.* **1.** A request that the court do something (prayer for relief). Petition, application, entreaty, plea, motion, solicitation, calling upon, imploration, call, demand, supplication, requisition, suit, appeal, beseechment. **2.** A method of worship (school prayer). Devotion, service, religious practice, orison, adoration, benediction, thanksgiving, meditation, glorification, veneration. See also worship.

Prayer for relief The demand for relief; the portion of the complaint that sets forth the requested relief or damages that the pleader seeks in the civil action.

Prayerful, *adj.* See precatory; holy, religious, conscientious (2).

Preach, *v.* To moralize. Give a sermon, sermonize, harangue, exhort, lecture, evangelize. See also reprimand, discipline; press (1), encourage, advocate.

Preacher, *n.* See minister, teacher.

Preamble, *n.* A clause at the beginning of a statute or constitution, explaining the reasons for its enactment and the objects sought to be accomplished (the court used the preamble of the statute to help explain an ambiguous clause). Preface, introduction, prologue, opening, preliminary, exordium, proem.

Prearrange, *v.* See plan, prepare, organize, establish; premeditated.

Precarious, *adj.* Uncertain; retained only by sufferance; dangerous (precarious situation). Vulnerable, weak, chancy, liable to terminate, unpredictable, dubious, exposed, questionable, unrealiable, shaky, capricious, controversial, unprotected, alarming, touch-and-go, unstable, perilous, undependable, open, fraught with uncertainty, treacherous, unsure, dependent, contingent, suspect, changeable, delicate, slippery, infirm, untenable, unfounded, ticklish, unsettled. See also insecure (1), hazardous, dangerous, helpless, irresponsible, doubtful, suspicious, imminent. *Ant.* Secure.

Precatory, *adj.* Embodying a recommendation or advice rather than a positive command or direction (precatory language). Suggestive, beseeching, prayerful, pleading, advisory, appealing, asking, begging. *Ant.* Ordering.

Precatory words Words of wish, recommendation, or desire in a will, which are ineffective to dispose of property. See language, desire.

Precaution, *n.* Care taken to prevent mischief or to secure the desired result (precaution against accident). Safeguard, insurance, preventive measure, foresight, security, preparation, wariness, providence, guarantee, safety measure, heedfulness, defense, escape valve, vigilance, circumspection, provision, mindfulness, discretion. See also forethought, prudence. *Ant.* Carelessness.

Precautionary, *adj.* See preventive, cautious, careful.

Precede, *v.* See antedate (2).

Precedence, *n.* The right of being placed first in order (her lien takes precedence over yours). Priority, coming before, seniority, supremacy, preference, lead, predominance, superiority, ascendancy, status, rank, primacy, importance, prevalence, pre-eminence, antecedence, dominance, advantage, transcendence.

Precedent, *n.*, **precedent,** *adj.* **1.** *n.* A prior decision that serves as an example or authority for resolving an identical or similar case; a prior court opinion that interpreted and applied a rule to a set of facts that is similar to the rule and facts currently before the court (the court followed the precedent of Smith v. Jones). Analogous case, guide, guidance, yardstick, model, frame of reference, starting point, archetype, standard, foundation, model, prototype, exemplar, pattern, criterion. See also measure (1). **2.** *adj.* Preceding (precedent condition). Prior, earlier, antecedent, previous, former, preliminary, anterior, aforementioned, precursory, pre-existent. See also primary (2).

Precedent condition See condition precedent.

Preceding, *adj.* See prior (1), previous, preliminary.

Precept, *n.* **1.** A rule imposing a standard of conduct or action (moral precept). Code, principle, motto, axiom, canon, dictate, commandment, rubric, doctrine, prescript, dogma, byword, commonplace, proverb, cliché, truism, adage, teaching, saw, tenet, law. See also maxim, moral (3). **2.** A warrant, writ, or order. See direction (1), mandate (1).

Precinct, *n.* A geographical unit of government; an election district (she carried the precinct). Ward, borough, section, subdivision, section, province, parish, barrio, neighborhood, area, community, territory. See also zone.

Precious, *adj.* See costly, exorbitant; darling; particular (2), difficult (3).

Precipice, *n.* See extremity (2), bluff (3), border, boundary, mountain.

Precipitate 1. *v.* To hasten the occurrence of something (he precipitated the foreclosure). Provoke, incite, cause, spur, speed, quicken, instigate, excite, rush, further, arouse, trigger, stimulate, push, jog, inspire, hurry, advance, catapult, launch, drive, propel, expel, heave, ejaculate, project, shoot. See also accelerate, expedite, facilitate. **2.** *adj.* Acting without careful deliberation (precipitate action). Headstrong, wild, rash, reckless, impulsive, hasty, impetuous, foolhardy, immediate, instantaneous, thoughtless, uncalculating, injudicious, unrestrained, adventurous, impassioned, frivolous, irresponsible, volatile, rampant, indiscreet. See also improvident, careless. **3.** *adj.* Unexpected (precipitate development). Spontaneous, unforeseeable, abrupt, sudden, unpremeditated, surprise, freakish. See also fortuitous. *Ant.* Retard; calculated; predicted.

Precipitous, *adj.* See impetuous, precipitate; bluff (3).

Précis, *n.* See abstract (3), prospectus.

Precise, *adj.* **1.** To the point; having determinate limitations (precise measurements). Specific, express, particular, rigid, unambiguous, unconditional, plain, distinct, thorough, unequivocal, mathematical, minute, detailed, clearly expressed. See also clear (1), explicit, definite (1), direct (6), categorical, outright. **2.** Accurate (the precise amount). Correct, true, literal, exact, errorless, factual, strict, valid, faithful, flawless, right, scrupulous, literal, scientific, proper, just, meticulous, fastidious, uncompromising, undeviating, authoritarian, rigorous, exacting, authentic, careful, conscientious, unyielding, orthodox, inexorable, religious, fastidious, firm, austere, veracious. See also accurate, perfect, absolute, mathematical, empirical. *Ant.* Vague; wrong.

Precision, *n.* See veracity, fact, validity; accurate, precise.

Preclude, *v.* To prohibit from doing something (the defendant was precluded from using the defense). Estop, prevent, obstruct, bar, preempt, ban, stay, impede, forbid, hinder, foreclose, defeat, forestall, constrain, oppose, deter, check, intercept, thwart, inhibit, obviate, avert, frustrate, encumber, choke, handicap, override, foil, discourage, veto, arrest, eliminate, clog, abort, restrain. *Ant.* Facilitate.

Preclusion, *n.* Making something impossible (preclusion order). See preclude.

Precocious, *adj.* Advanced. Premature, early. See also brilliant, learned, mature.

Preconception, *n.* See prejudice, bias; foresight; presumption.

Precondition, *n.* See requirement, necessity (2).

Precontract, *n.* A contract that precludes a person from entering into another contract of the same nature.

Precursor, *n.* See harbinger, herald, predecessor.

Predate, *v.* See antedate.

Predator, *n.* See wrongdoer; parasite; plunder; predatory.

Predatory, *adj.* Larcenous or preying (predatory design). Savage, plundering, exploitative, bestial, voracious, hunting, thievish, thieving, greedy, bloodthirsty, devouring, covetous, piratical, marauding, fierce, usurious, grasping, carnivorous, cannibalistic, pillaging, despoiling, plunderous. *Ant.* Benevolent.

Predecessor, *n.* One who goes or who has gone before (her predecessor on the bench). Forerunner, ancestor, former occupant, forefather. See also antecedent (2).

Predestination, *n.* See destiny, chance (2).

Predetermine, *v.* To preordain, foreordain, pre-establish, predestine, destine.

Predetermined, *adj.* Foreordained. Calculated, preplanned, decided in advance, prearranged.

Predicament, *n.* See emergency, plight, complication, dilemma, conundrum.

Predicate, *v.* See affirm, declare; base (4); presume (1).

Predict, *v.* See foresee, augur, anticipate (1), promise (3).

Prediction, *n.* See prophecy.

Predilection, *n.* See affinity, desire; bias, prejudice, preference, disposition (4).

Predispose, *v.* See gravitate, lean, tend, prepare.

Predisposition, *n.* See preference, disposition (4), affinity, bias, prejudice.

Predominance, *n.* See dominion, superiority, sovereignty, power, control, authority (2); predominant.

Predominant, *adj.* Something greater or superior in power and influence to others (the predominant factor in the decision). Overriding, dominant, controlling, ascendant, governing, paramount, principal, overruling, sovereign, chief, main, ruling, decisive, authoritative, preponderant, overpowering, major, prime, reigning, supreme, front-ranking, consummate, peerless, nonpareil, all-powerful, ruling, absolute, foremost, crowning, par excellence, uppermost, second-to-none, omnipotent, first-rate, capital, matchless, boundless, maximum, leading, potent, weighty, strong, cogent, telling, convincing, forceful, powerful, prevalent, pre-eminent. See also primary. *Ant.* Secondary.

Predominate, *v.* See overcome, exceed, prevail, dominate.

Pre-eminent, *adj.* See elevated, predominant, outstanding (2), extraordinary, exceptional, great (2).

Pre-empt, *v.* See foreclose, appropriate, seize, displace, manipulate; pre-emption.

Pre-emption, *n.* **1.** A judicially created doctrine based on the Supremacy Clause of the U.S. Constitution, providing that federal laws take precedence over state laws on a matter that is national in character when Congress has completely taken over the matter or has otherwise explicitly or implicitly excluded state regulation in the area; a legislative intent to regulate an entire area. Taking over, appropriation, substitution, displacement, assumption, usurpation, occupation, replacement, arrogation, seizure, capture, annexation. **2.** The right of first purchase.

Pre-emptive right The right of a stockholder to maintain a proportionate share of ownership by purchasing a proportionate share of any new stock issues. See right.

Pre-exist, *v.* See antedate.

Pre-existent, *adj.* See prior (1).

Prefabricate, *v.* See fabricate (2), build (2), prepare.

Preface, *n. v.* See preamble; begin.

Prefect, *n.* A public official in charge of administrating the law in France and in other countries. See official, officer.

Prefer, *v.* **1.** To prosecute or try (prefer an indictment). Proceed with, present, charge, file, lodge, place, advance, proffer, bring before. **2.** To give advantage, priority, or privilege (prefer one creditor over another). Embrace, select, choose, single out, prize, approve, further, elect, opt for, fancy, adopt, desire, espouse, like better. *Ant.* Nolle prosequi; reject.

Preferable, *adj.* See superior (2), best (1), favorite, attractive.

Preference, *n.* Making a payment or a transfer by an insolvent debtor to one of the creditors, to the detriment of the other creditors; the choice of one over another; the choice made (an impermissible preference). Election, partiality, selection, advantage, leaning, priority, precedence, predisposition, proclivity, fancy, prejudice. See also bias, favoritism. *Ant.* Evenhandedness.

Preferential, *adj.* Indicating or giving a preference (preferential treatment). Favored, choice, priority, partial, select, advantageous, special, partisan, capital, paramount, distinctive, unusual, prominent, first-rate, exceptional. See also outstanding (2), superior (2). *Ant.* Inferior.

Preferential debts In bankruptcy, those debts that are payable in preference to all others (e.g., employee wages, administrative costs). See bankruptcy, debt.

Preferred, *adj.* Having a priority, advantage, or privilege; having a prior or superior claim or right of payment as against another thing of the same kind or class (preferred security interest). See preferential, superior, prior; preference, prefer (2).

Preferred creditor A creditor with a prior right to payment over junior creditors, e.g., a creditor with a perfected security interest. See prior, superior.

Preferred stock Capital stock with a claim to income (dividends) or assets before common stock but after bondholders. See share, securities.

Pregnancy, *n.* See gestation; maternity, birth (1); pregnant.

Pregnant, *adj.* **1.** Having a developing fetus in the uterus (she was pregnant at the time of the injury). With child, carrying, gravid, expecting, gestating, parturient. **2.** Having significance (a pregnant comment). Momentous, creative, fruitful, telling, important, provocative, fertile, decisive, crucial, suggestive, forceful, stimulating, imaginative, original, consequential, productive.

Pregnant negative See negative pregnant.

Prejudge, *v.* See bias (2), presume; prejudice.

Prejudice **1.** *n.* A leaning toward one side of a cause for a reason other than the merits of the case (the judge's prejudice was evident). Bias, favoritism, slant, preconception, predisposition, jaundiced eye, partiality, warp, prepossession, prejudgment, bigotry, partisanship, forejudgment, colored point of view, blind spot, discrimination, predilection, one-sidedness, chauvinism, racism, sexism, subjectivity, intolerance. **2.** *v.* To injure (the move prejudiced his chances). Harm, damage, impair, hinder, bias, poison, contaminate, block, destroy, obstruct, warp, twist, distort, pollute, vitiate, infect, spoil, tarnish, pervert, adulterate, prostitute, undermine, subvert, incapacitate, disable, dash, wreck, sabotage, weaken, paralyze, mar, devalue, cripple, blemish, shatter, deplete, wrong, impose a loss, water down, undercut, diminish, demolish, disadvantage, cause detriment, inflict injury, impose a detriment. *Ant.* Impartiality; assist.

Prejudicial, *adj.* Causing prejudice (prejudicial remarks). Damaging, detrimental, injurious, deleterious, hurtful, biased, disadvantageous, pernicious, unfavorable, impairing, undermining, inimical, antagonistic, nocuous, malign, mischievous, ill, bad, destructive, incapacitating, eroding, marring. See also hostile. *Ant.* Beneficial.

Prejudicial error An error that substantially affects a litigant's rights; an error that affects or presumptively affects the final result of the trial. See error.

Prelate, *n.* See minister; church, religion, clerical.

Preliminary, *adj.* Preceding, introductory (preliminary considerations). Preparatory, inaugural, prefatory, anterior, opening, initiatory, beginning, early, precursive, former, foregoing. See also prior, previous, antecedent. *Ant.* Concluding.

Preliminary hearing A pretrial proceeding in which the court determines whether there is probable cause to believe that the accused committed the crime(s) charged and should be held for trial. See hearing, probable cause.

Preliminary injunction A temporary order designed to preserve the status quo pending a trial on the merits of the case. See injunction, temporary.

Premarital, *adj.* See antenuptial; nuptial.

Premature, *adj.* See precipitate (2), inconvenient, improper, careless, dumb.

Premeditated, *adj.* Pertaining to that which is deliberated in advance or thought of beforehand for any length of time (premeditated homicide is murder). Prearranged, thought-out, calculated, worked-out, planned, preplanned, contrived, studied, in cold blood, conscious, purposeful, predevised, schemed, knowing, plotted, aforethought. See also willful, deliberate (2), voluntary, intentional. *Ant.* Spontaneous.

Premeditation, *n.* See consideration (2); premeditated.

Premier, *adj.* See primary, first, original, chief (2), predominant, outstanding (2), best.

Premise, *n.* See premises (3).

Premises, *n.* **1.** The foregoing statements (in consideration of the premises). Matters stated earlier, matters hereinbefore stated, previously mentioned matters. **2..** Lands and buildings (removed from the premises). Grounds, property, dwelling, estate, boundaries, site, environs, vicinity. **3.** Prior statements asserted or accepted as true, from which conclusions are drawn (a faulty premise). Axiom, hypothesis, assumption, thesis, postulate, proposition, assertion, presumption, argument, theorem, proposal, surmise.

Premium, *n.* **1.** A prize or bonus for an act done (a premium of her choice). Reward, gift, gratuity, payment, return, benefit, compensation, incentive, bounty, extra, present, consideration, fringe, perquisite, gain, reparation, encouragement. **2.** Payment to an insurer as consideration for the insurance (nonpayment of premium). See cost, payment (1). **3.** Part of the rent that is capitalized and paid in a lump sum at the time the lease is granted. **4.** In high demand (at a premium). Difficult to obtain, in short supply, scarcity. See also popular. **5.** Above the normal value (pay a premium). Above par, excessive value, unreasonably high price. See also unconscionable.

Premium loan A loan made for the purpose of paying an insurance premium and secured by the policy. See loan, insurance, security.

Premonition, *n.* See intuition, harbinger, manifestation, warning; oracle, clairvoyance, augur.

Prenatal, *adj.* Pertaining to the time before birth (prenatal injuries). Unborn, during pregnancy, while carrying, while expecting. See also gestation, pregnant, prior; birth.

Prenuptial agreement See antenuptial.

Preoccupation, *n.* Engrossment. Obsession, intensity, musing, fixation. See also concentration (1), compulsion (2).

Preoccupied, *adj.* Pensive. Absorbed, thoughtful, musing, dreaming, fascinated, daydreaming, rapt, reflective, brooding, engrossed. See also contemplative, engaged; depressed, despondent.

Preoccupy, *v.* See absorb (2), engage (2); submerge.

Prepaid, *adj.* Paid beforehand. See pay (2), payment (1).

Prepaid legal services A plan by which people pay premiums to cover future legal services either from an attorney of his or her choice (open-ended plan) or from a designated list of attorneys (closed-ended plan). See attorney, plan, performance, service.

Preparation, *n.* Taking preliminary steps for a particular purpose (inadequate preparation). Groundwork, provision, homework, planning, studying, plotting, training, arrangement, development, precaution, foresight, apprenticeship, rehearsal, making ready, formation, education, grooming, alertness, readying, expectation, prescription, diagram, familiarization, setting up, practice, outfitting, arming, ordering.

Preparatory, *adj.* See preliminary, prior, first; preparation, prepare.

Preparatory school, *n.* See school; education.

Prepare, *v.* **1.** To make ready (prepare for trial). Provide with necessary means, do what is needed in anticipation of, arrange, outfit, compose, anticipate, equip, supply, construct, fix, train, adapt, clear the way, rehearse, accouter, coach, groom, prime, lay the groundwork, practice. See also plan, organize, educate, discipline (4). **2.** To put together or construct (prepare an outline). Manufacture, devise, concoct, invent, sculpture, hatch, fabricate, compound, brew, erect. *Ant.* Neglect; dismantle.

Prepayment, *n.* Making payment in advance or before maturity. See pay (2), payment (1).

Prepayment penalty A penalty or extra payment that is imposed when a promissory note, mortgage, or deed of trust is paid before it is due.

Prepense, *adj.* See aforethought, premeditated.

Preplan, *v.* See plan, organize, prepare; premeditated.

Preponderance, *n.* A greater weight, quantity, or importance (a preponderance of the claims were incomplete). Plurality, prevalence, predominance, bulk, more than otherwise, lion's share, profusion, greater number, dominance, surplus. See also weight; majority (2), most, many, mass (2). *Ant.* Minority.

Preponderance of evidence Evidence that is of greater weight or more convincing than the evidence offered in opposition to it; more probable than not; outweighing evidence. See evidence, weight.

Preponderant, *adj.* See superseding, predominant.

Prepossession, *n.* See prejudice, bias, preference; preoccupied.

Preposterous, *adj.* See absurd, insane, irrational, illogical, impossible, anomalous, odd, peculiar.

Prerequisite, *n., adj.* See requirement, necessity (2), need (1).

Prerogative, *n.* An exclusive or peculiar right or privilege (the prerogatives of the directorship). Perquisite, preference, benefit, authority, power, franchise, license, authorization, fringe, permission, carte blanche, immunity, warrant, status, rank, consent, title, precedence, freedom, liberty, due, advantage, claim, exemption, birthright, interest, influence, sanction, entitlement, priority, charter. See also right (3), privilege. *Ant.* Liability.

Pres Near. See cy pres.

Presage, *v.,* **presage,** *n.* See augur, foresee, anticipate, promise (3), expect (1); harbinger, oracle, warning.

Presbyterianism, *n.* A system of church administration or government through teaching or ruling elders. See ministry, religion, church; clerical.

Preschool, *n., adj.* See school; education.

Prescience, *n.* See foresight, clairvoyance; oracle, augur.

Prescribe, *v.* To lay down as a guide or rule; to recommend or mandate as a treatment (the committee prescribed standards; prescribed by law). Mark out,

Prescribe

define, direct, dictate, instruct, require, order, impose, administer, enjoin, institute, decree, assign, establish, designate, steer, exact, enact, oblige, advocate, authorize, necessitate, requisition, stipulate, specify, legislate, urge, appoint, rule.

Prescription, *n.* **1.** A method of acquiring the right to use a way, water, light, or air by reason of continuous usage (easement by prescription). Claim, interest, right, license, authorization, liberty, warrant, franchise, permit, privilege, title, entitlement, sufferance, clearance, leave, power. **2.** A bar to bringing an action or using a remedy as to claims that have been unasserted for an extended period of time. **3.** A direction or a formula for the preparation and use of a medicine. See prescribe, treatment, medicine, drug, doctor. **4.** A direction or order. See direction (1), command (1), law.

Prescriptive, *adj.* Arising or sanctioned by continuous usage (prescriptive easement). Long-standing, settled, rooted, long-established, fixed. See also customary, immemorial.

Prescriptive easement A right to use another's property, which is acquired by usage that is open, notorious, exclusive, adverse, under claim of right, and continuous for the statutory period of time. See easement, adverse (1), notorious.

Presence, *n.* **1.** The act, fact, or state of being in a certain place (offense committed in the presence of an officer). Nearness, within sight, within view, immediately reachable, at hand, here, attendance, appearance, existence, company, proximity, neighborhood, closeness, residence. See also vicinity; near. **2.** A person's bearing. See appearance (3). **3.** Self-assurance. See confidence (3), composure.

Present, *n., adj.,* **present,** *v.* **1.** *n.* A gift (wedding present). Gratuity, benefaction, tip, contribution, prize, allowance, largess, allotment, award, offering, donation, grant, bequest, endowment, legacy, boon. See also charity, benevolence, gift. **2.** *n.* Here and now (at present). Right now, this minute, today, nowadays, the moment, the time being. **3.** *adj.* Relating to the current time (present condition). Contemporary, recent, instant, immediate, existing, living, contemporaneous, existent, up-to-the-minute, at the moment, modern, present-day, coeval, prevalent, topical, latest, here, extant. See also current. **4.** *adj.* At hand (they were present when the crime was committed). Nearby, there, in the vicinity, omnipresent, in attendance, on duty, accessible, in view, visible, within reach, handy, close, attending, ubiquitous, nigh, ensconced, proximate. See also near, available. **5.** *v.* To submit or demonstrate (she presented her case). Display, argue, expose, proffer, produce, exhibit, declare, profess, unveil, provide, render, raise, represent, aim, contribute, put forward, tender, show, make known, uncover, summon, impart, convey, expound, advance, prosecute, allege, call up, state, apprise, recite. See also communicate, assert, offer, introduce. *Ant.* Sale; later; prior; absent; withhold.

Presentable, *adj.* See marketable, attractive, worthy, fit (1), adequate, civil (3).

Presentation, *n.* See gift, charity, present (1); performance (3), production, exposition (2), array (2), appearance; overture; speech (2).

Present danger See clear and present danger, imminent, danger.

Present-day, *adj.* See present (3), current, chic, new.

Pre-sentence report A report, often prepared by a social worker or probation officer, based on an investigation of the background of a convicted offender designed to assist the judge in imposing a sentence. See report (2), inquiry (1), examination.

Presenting bank Any bank presenting an item, except a payor bank. See bank.

Present interest An interest that entitles the owner to the immediate possession of the property. See interest.

Presentment, *n.* **1.** An accusation of crime initiated by a grand jury based on its

596

own knowledge. See accusation. **2.** Giving or producing a negotiable instrument to the drawee for its acceptance, or to the drawer or acceptor for payment; a demand for acceptance or payment made by or on behalf of the holder upon the maker, acceptor, drawee, or other payor. **3.** See presentation, present.

Present recollection recorded The use of a document that helps a witness revive or jog his or her memory of a past event. The evidence is the testimony of the witness, not the document itself. See memory, recollection.

Present recollection revived The use by a witness of some writing or other object to refresh his or her recollection so that testimony can be given about past events from present recollection. See memory, recollection.

Presents, *n.* This document; the present instrument (these presents).

Preservation, *n.* Keeping safe from harm or decay (preservation of the document). Maintenance, safekeeping, storage, upkeep, continuation, care, security, salvation, defense, perpetuation, guarding, support, sheltering, guardianship, nourishment, conservation, reservation; embalming, safeguarding, shield, saving, keeping, retention. *Ant.* Destruction.

Preserve, *v., n.* See conserve, save (1), maintain (1); asylum, harbor (2).

Preside, *v.* To exercise authority; to direct the proceedings (preside over the meeting). Control, superintend, oversee, chair, supervise, command, administer, moderate, guide, pilot, engineer, head, lead, govern, officiate, regulate, rule, watch, conduct, boss. See also manage. *Ant.* Follow.

President, *n.* The chief executive officer. See director, officer, official.

Presidential elector See electoral college.

President pro tempore, *n.* A senator who presides over the U.S. Senate in the absence of the vice-president. See pro tempore, officer, official.

Press 1. *n.* The print media (freedom of the press). Reporters, commentators, journalists, correspondents, writers, authors, editors, publishers, columnists, newsmen, newswomen, photographers, wire service, fourth estate, newspapers, magazines, periodicals; broadcasting industry. **2.** *v.* To solicit (he pressed for an adjournment). Plea, appeal, entreat, beseech, beg, implore, sue, petition, request, hound, urge, importune, imprecate, pressure, exhort, invoke, plead, pray, supplicate, nag, tax, dun, insist on, exact, prod, egg on, demand, requisition. **3.** *v.* See harass, badger.

Pressing, *adj.* See critical (1), crucial, important.

Press release, *n.* See information (2), notice (1), communication (2).

Pressure, *n., v.* See coercion, duress, compulsion, necessity (1); press (2), coerce.

Prestige, *n.* See eminence, note (4), grandeur, honor (3), reputation, notoriety.

Prestigious, *adj.* See great (2), elevated, reputable, popular, outstanding (2), exceptional.

Presumably, *adv.* By reasonable supposition or inference (presumably dead). Credibly deduced, fair to suppose, in all probability, seemingly, in all likelihood, surely, apparently, undoubtedly.

Presume, *v.* **1.** To assume beforehand; to believe or accept upon probable evidence (presume she is innocent). Assume, suppose, take for granted, posit, deem, infer, deduce, predicate, postulate, surmise, premise, believe, divine, conjecture, prejudge, understand, gather, speculate, suspect, conclude, presuppose, theorize, hypothesize. **2.** To dare (he presumed to instruct the judge). Make bold, impose, venture, arrogate, take the liberty, encroach, infringe, intrude, trespass.

Presumed intent A person is presumed to intend the natural and probable consequences of his or her voluntary acts. See intent, intend, consequence.

Presumption, *n.* **1.** An assumption of fact that a rule of law requires to be assumed from another fact or group of facts that have been established (a

Presumption

presumption that the child is legitimate). Inference, hypothesis, supposition, presupposition, premise, probability, deduction, speculation, preconception, conjecture, surmise, belief, expectation, anticipation, postulate, prejudgment, guess.
2. See arrogance, effrontery.

Presumption of innocence The government has the burden of proving every element of the crime beyond a reasonable doubt. The defendant does not have the burden of proving his or her innocence. See burden of proof, evidence, crime, innocence, innocent.

Presumption of legitimacy When it is established that a child was born to a woman while she was married to a specified man, the party asserting the illegitimacy of the child has the burden of proving that the man was not the father of the child. See burden of proof, evidence, paternity, illegitimate; bastard.

Presumptive, *adj.* Created by or arising out of a presumption (presumptive notice). Inferred, assumed, supposed, imagined, hypothetical, conjectured, postulated, presumed, logical, reasonable, well-founded, feasible, believable.

Presumptive death Death that is presumed from a long absence (e.g., 7 years) during which the person is not heard from and the absence is unexplained. See death, Enoc Arden doctrine.

Presumptive evidence Prima facie evidence; evidence sufficient to establish a given fact and which, if not rebutted or contradicted, will remain sufficient. See evidence, prima facie, adequate.

Presumptive trust A trust raised by implication of law and presumed always to have been contemplated by the parties because of the nature of the transaction. See trust, implied.

Presumptuous, *adj.* See arrogant, pompous, assertive, peremptory (2), rude; certain (2), assured (4).

Presuppose, *v.* See assume, presume; presumption, hypothesis.

Pretend, *v.* To hold out as real that which is false or baseless (pretend to be ill). Feign, simulate, counterfeit, lie, defraud, deceive, prevaricate, malinger, dissimulate, fabricate, cheat, pass off, delude, beguile, affect, assume, fake, impersonate, dissemble, play, imitate, masquerade, mimic, sham, fancy, make believe, imagine, misrepresent, disguise, mislead, cozen, put on, copy, play-act, ape, pose, mirror, mock, parody, caricature, bluff.

Pretense, *n.* A false appearance (they saw through the pretense). Sham, pretext, deception, fabrication, hypocrisy, trick, fraud, concoction, masquerade, ruse, subterfuge, misrepresentation, artifice, front, fiction, veneer, hoax, deceit, guile, bombast, ostentation, mendacity, camouflage, swindle, duplicity, forgery, pomposity, glare, effect, feint, trickery, boast, invention, imposture, disguise, acting, act, cover, wile, posturing, stratagem, charade, pose, show, affectation, mockery, display, bravado, artificiality, braggadocio, inflation. *Ant.* Sincerity.

Pretension, *n.* See pretense, pretext, arrogance; claim, ambition.

Pretentious, *adj.* See pompous, arrogant, peremptory (2), gaudy, flamboyant, vulgar.

Pretermission statute A law that makes provision for children and heirs who have been omitted from the will of the father or ancestor so that they will still be able to share in the estate. See will, heir, mistake.

Pretermit, *v.* To pass by, omit, or disregard. See disregard (1).

Pretext, *n.* A false appearance or excuse (a pretext for the mismanagement). False reason, deception, cover-up, pretense, prevarication, rationalization, reason, basis, front, ostensible motive, justification, explanation, story, vindication, guise, red herring, alibi, invention, subterfuge, misrepresentation, feint, ground, stall, ploy, hoax, dodge, professed purpose, evasion, apology, plea, pretension, ruse, charade, show, illusion, ostentation, mask, impression, pose, copy, reproduction, affectation, sham, appearance, obfuscation.

Pretrial conference A meeting of the lawyers and the judge before the trial to attempt to narrow the issues to be tried, to secure stipulations, and to make a final effort to settle the case without a trial. See conference, negotiate.

Pretrial discovery Devices that can be used by parties to help them prepare for trial (e.g., depositions, interrogatories, requests for admissions). See discovery.

Pretrial diversion The referral of a defendant in a criminal case to a community agency prior to trial, where he or she receives counseling, therapy, training, etc. If progress is made in this diversion program, the criminal charges are often dismissed.

Pretty, *adj.* See attractive, beautiful, enjoyable, intriguing.

Prevail, *v.* **1.** To be in general use or practice (the conditions that prevailed at the time). Govern, be in force, rule, obtain, hold sway, predominate, control, persist, abide, continue, exist, abound, be current, reign. **2.** To succeed (the defendant prevailed). Win, prove superior, overcome, triumph, be victorious, checkmate, conquer, be effective, transcend, exceed, surmount, withstand, override, endure. **3.** To persuade successfully (prevail upon the judge). See convince.

Prevailing, *adj.* **1.** Widespread, common, or current (the prevailing point of view at the meeting). Universal, controlling, fashionable, supreme, prevalent, in force, ruling, chief, rampant, widely accepted, characteristic, typical, contemporary, normal, natural. See also predominant, popular, commonplace, general. **2.** Victorious (prevailing side). See dominant.

Prevailing party The party in whose favor the decision or verdict is rendered and judgment is entered. See party.

Prevalent, *adj.* See prevailing, epidemic (2), popular, general, extensive, comprehensive.

Prevaricate, *v.* See lie (2), deceive, cheat.

Prevarication, *n.* The willful concealment or misrepresentation of the truth. See lie (1), deception.

Prevent, *v.* To keep from occurring (an action to prevent further trespassing). Prohibit, impede, obstruct, intercept, arrest, ward off, counteract, avert, bar, veto, hamper, interrupt, forestall, obviate, thwart, intervene, preclude, delay, neutralize, foil, abort, circumvent, muzzle, paralyze, checkmate, hinder, frustrate, sidetrack, deflect, anticipate, oppose, cramp, stop, inhibit, repel, turn back, block, hold at arm's length, stave off, scotch, repulse, disperse, rout, nonplus, spurn, stifle, quell, mute, suppress, avoid, contest, limit, retard. *Ant.* Facilitate.

Prevention, *n.* The act of preventing (crime prevention). Elimination, avoidance, inhibition, deterrence, veto, arrest, obstruction, embargo, impediment, injunction, restriction, defeat, thwarting, forestalling, interruption, prohibition, interdiction, ban, abortion, frustration, stoppage, hindrance, checkmate, obstacle, interception, safeguard, precaution, vaccine, remedy, medicine, prophylactic. *Ant.* Incitement.

Preventive, *adj.* Intended to prevent something (preventive medicine). Precautionary, watchful, deterrent, prophylactic, counteractive, antiseptic, forestalling, checking, blocking, hygienic, restraining, cautious, averting, neutralizing, shielding. See also protective. *Ant.* Provocative.

Preventive detention Detaining accused persons to prevent them from engaging in future antisocial behavior; confinement imposed on a defendant in a criminal case who threatens to violate the law while awaiting trial or disposition; confinement of a mentally ill person who poses a danger to self or to others. See detention.

Preventive law Steps taken in anticipation of and in an effort to avoid legal problems; policies and practices designed to maximize advantages within the law before any legal disputes have arisen.

Previous, *adj.* Prior (previous tenant). Before, next prior to, next preceding, above-mentioned, former, preceding, anterior, erstwhile, foregoing, aforementioned, pre-existent, foregone, aforesaid, earlier, precedent, recent, ex, said, latter, last, initial. See also prior (1), antecedent. *Ant.* Subsequent.

Prey, *n., v.* See victim; game (2); plunder, consume.

Price, *n.* **1.** The consideration given for the purchase of something (an agreed-upon price). Value, rate, toll, compensation, fare, worth, expenditure, quotation, estimation, valuation, appraisal, fee, figure, amount, assessment, tab, outlay. See also cost, charge (8). **2.** Penalty (the price of delay). Fine, pain, damages, punishment, consequence, sacrifice, dues.

Price-earnings ratio, *n.* The market value of a company's common stock per share divided by the earnings per common share for the past year. See ratio.

Price fixing, *n.* Agreements by competing firms on the setting of price levels or ranges; an agreement for the purpose of and with the effect of raising, depressing, fixing, pegging, or stabilizing the price of a commodity. See monopoly.

Priceless, *adj.* See costly, great (2), exclusive, outstanding (2), extraordinary; incalculable.

Price supports A device for keeping prices from falling below a predesignated level (e.g., loans, subsidies, government purchases, etc.).

Prick, *v.* See pierce, cut; provoke (1).

Pride, *n.* See proud; arrogance, pretense; pompous; spirit, dignity, character (1), honor (3); satisfaction, enjoyment, happiness.

Priest, *n.* A minister of a church, in between a bishop and deacon. See minister (1), church, religion, clergy; clerical.

Priest-penitent privilege A person can bar testimony as to the contents of a communication with his or her confessor. See privilege, evidence, prevention.

Priggish, *adj.* See squeamish, particular (2).

Prim, *adj.* See formal (3), inflexible, particular (2), squeamish.

Prima facie, *adv., adj.* On the face of it; pertaining to a fact that is presumed to be true unless disproved by some evidence to the contrary (prima facie showing). At first sight, on the first appearance, so far as can be judged from the first disclosure, presumably, by all appearances, apparently, at first glance, sufficient on its face, satisfactory, adequate, legally sufficient.

Prima facie case A case as presented that will prevail until contradicted and overcome by contrary evidence; a case consisting of evidence that is sufficient to overcome a motion for a directed verdict and to get the case to the jury.

Prima facie evidence Evidence that is good and sufficient on its face; evidence that is sufficient to establish a given fact or group of facts and will remain sufficient unless rebutted or contradicted. See adequate, evidence.

Prima facie tort The intentional infliction of harm without justification, resulting in special damages.

Primal, *adj.* See primary (1); fundamental.

Primary, *adj.* **1.** First in order of importance or intention (primary obligation). Principal, chief, leading, overriding, key, cardinal, uppermost, supreme, greatest, predominant, vital, highest, paramount, major, top, senior, ruling, essential, star, utmost, basic, determining, most valuable, champion, prize, crowning, superior, exceptional, capital, hand-picked, preferred, rare, elite, blue-ribbon, elect, unique, first-class, priority, peerless, nonpareil, choice, superb, select, unequaled, best, eminent, foremost, prominent, transcendent, excellent, superlative, extraordinary, optimal, A-1, renowned, sovereign, governing, main, fundamental, prime, necessary, capital; innate, congenital, inherent, native, intrinsic; auspicious, suitable, fitting, opportune, convenient, seasonable. **2.** First in time (the primary step). Original, beginning, initial, inaugural, earliest, aboriginal, elementary, primitive, introductory, oldest, primordial, rudimentary, embryonic, germinal, genetic, authentic, basal, starting, fossil, dawning, opening, nascent, incipient. *Ant.* Secondary; subsequent.

Primary election, *n.* A preliminary election for the nomination of candidates for office or of delegates to a party convention. See election.

Primary jurisdiction doctrine Although a case is properly before a court, if there are issues requiring administrative discretion and expertise, the court can refrain from proceeding until the administrative agency acts. See jurisdiction, abstain.

Primary school, *n.* See school; education.

Prime 1. *adj.* Paramount, major, or prior (prime suspect). See primary. 2. *v.* To prepare someone (prime the witness). Educate, tutor, brief, guide, instruct, school, drill, coach, prep, breed, groom, ready. 3. *n.* The best condition (the prime of life). Flower, heyday, zenith, summit, top, pinnacle, height, perfection, vigor. 4. *n.* See prime rate.

Prime contractor General contractor; the party to a building contract who has responsibility for total construction and who enters into subcontracts for part of the work. See builder, entrepreneur, supplier, independent contractor.

Prime minister, *n.* See official, head, administrator.

Primer, *n.* See book (4); education.

Prime rate, *n.* The lowest rate of interest charged by a specific lender to its best customers for short-term, unsecured loans. See interest, rate.

Primitive, *adj.* See aboriginal, native; simple, innocent.

Primogeniture, *n.* The status of being the first-born among several children of the same parents; the superior or exclusive right of the oldest son to succeed to the entire estate of his ancestor. See inheritance, heir.

Primordial, *adj.* See ancient, original (2), primary (2).

Principal 1. *n.* The amount of debt not including interest; the capital sum of a debt or obligation, as distinguished from interest or other additions to it (payment of principal). Original investment, face amount, capital sum, main amount. 2. *n.* A superintendent (school principal). Head, headmaster, headmistress, leader, director, supervisor, administrator, captain, chief executive, manager, dean, proprietor, commander, chairman, chancellor. See also superior (1), official. 3. *n.* A chief actor or perpetrator of a crime, or an aider and abettor who is actually or constructively present at the commission of a crime (an indictment of the principals). See party (2), accessory (1), accomplice, actor. 4. *n.* Someone who permits or directs an agent to act for his or her benefit, subject to his or her control (the principal was liable for the agent's mistake). See employer, entrepreneur, financier. 5. *adj.* Greatest or foremost in importance or rank (principal means of support). Chief, major, primary, supreme, highest, prime, strongest, paramount, leading, first, prominent, central, cardinal, capital, pre-eminent, sovereign, crowning, uppermost, controlling, managing, governing, determining, predominating, predominant, fundamental, essential, key, matchless, superior, outstanding, basic.

Principal in the first degree The one who actually commits the crime.

Principal in the second degree The one who is actually or constructively present and aids in the commission of the crime.

Principle, *n.* 1. A fundamental truth or doctrine (an equitable principle). Rule, law, tenet, axiom, maxim, standard, creed, precept, code, fact, norm, parameter, opinion, theorem, way, corollary, rubric, hypothesis, criterion, test, policy, gospel, proposition, theory, truism, formula, element, basis, assumption, adage, self-evident statement, belief, philosophy, credo, model, cause, mode, rationale, explanation, motive, origin, genesis, workings. 2. Integrity (a woman of principle). Ethics, morality, trustworthiness, conscience, ideals, faithfulness, nobility, honor, righteousness, probity, fidelity, loyalty, conviction, virtue, incorruptibility, goodness, character, justice, scruples, constancy. *Ant.* Fallacy; dishonor.

Print, *v.* See engrave.

Prior 1. *adj.* Earlier (prior conviction). Preceding, first, former, foregoing, antecedent, past, anterior, aforementioned, quondam, erstwhile, earlier, precedent, prefatory, pre-existent, initial, next preceding, ex, latter, said, last, inaugural, precursive. See also previous. 2. *adj.* Superior in rank, right, or time (prior lien). See primary (1), predominant. 3. *n.* A monk who is next in dignity to an abbot; the chief of a convent.

Prior inconsistent statements A basis for impeaching the credibility of a witness: prior statements made by the witness that contradict statements of the latter on the stand. See evidence, inconsistent, impeach.

Prioritize, *v.* See rate (3), organize, plan; priority.

Priority, *n.* A legal preference or precedence (her lien has priority). Seniority, primacy, superiority, advantage, pre-eminence, prerogative, rank, consequence, urgency, tenure, pre-existence, first place, ascendancy, leverage.

Prior jeopardy See jeopardy, double jeopardy.

Prior restraint The imposition of restrictions on a publication before it is published. See restraint.

Prison, *n.* An institution for the imprisonment of persons convicted of serious crimes; a place for the confinement of persons as punishment imposed by law or otherwise in the course of the administration of justice (escape from prison). Penitentiary, correctional institution, reformatory, detention center, cell, penal institution, guardhouse, tower, penal colony, lockup, "cooler," "can," "clinker," brig. See also jail.

Prisoner, *n.* One who is deprived of his or her liberty; a person in confinement as punishment for crime (disciplinary proceedings against the prisoner). Convict, internee, trusty, jailbird, "con," felon, captive, hostage, recidivist. See also wrongdoer, inmate.

Pristine, *adj.* See aboriginal, native, original (2), primary (2); simple, innocent, clean, clear, blameless, honest.

Privacy, *n.* 1. See invasion of privacy. A person's right to be left alone; the right to restrict access to private information (failure to respect her privacy). Confidentiality, noninfringement, nonintrusion. 2. Concealment or seclusion (concocted in privacy). Withdrawal, retreat, sequestration, aloofness, clandestine manner, isolation, solitude, obscurity, independency, silence, shyness, hiding, separation, retirement.

Private 1. *adj.* Concerning or belonging to an individual; not official or public (private communication). Restricted, confined, off-the-record, intimate, unpublished, undisclosed, secret, unofficial, reserved, apart, closet, undercover, secluded, retired, sequestered, exclusive, bosom, nonpublic, not open, cloistered, peculiar, alone, classified, buried, singular, reclusive, furtive, inviolate, unfrequented, unique, privy, monastic, hushed, concealed, underground, invisible; obscure, dark. See also hidden, personal, confidential, mysterious. 2. *n.* An enlisted person of low rank in the military (she was promoted from private). Soldier, noncommissioned officer. See also sailor, military. *Ant.* Public, open; general.

Private bill, *n.* Legislation for the special benefit of an individual or of a small area of the state or nation. See bill, legislation.

Private enterprise, *n.* See business, commerce, entrepreneur, financier.

Privateer, *n.* A vessel, owned by a private individual, commissioned by a belligerent power to attack enemy ships. See vessel (1), military.

Private law, *n.* The law governing the relations between private individuals. See law, regulation.

Private nuisance A nuisance affecting a single individual or a definite small number of persons in the enjoyment of private rights that are not common to the public. See nuisance.

Private offering An issue of securities made to a limited number of persons who are so well informed concerning the affairs of the company that they do not require the protections afforded by the disclosure provisions of the Securities Act of 1933. See securities.

Private placement 1. A direct placement; the placement of a child for adoption by the parents or by their intermediaries and not through an adoption agency. See adopt (1), home. **2.** The sale of corporate stock to private persons outside of a public offering. See sale, securities.

Private ruling Advice from the Internal Revenue Service to an individual taxpayer on the tax consequences of a specific transaction that is contemplated or completed. See decision.

Privation, *n.* The lack of basic necessities and comforts; a taking away or withdrawal (endured the privation). Poverty, necessity, penury, bankruptcy, insolvency, straits, mendicancy, mendicity, loss, misery, indigence, distress, insufficiency, misfortune, want, destitution, inadequacy, shortage, deficiency, predicament, pauperism, plight, confiscation, deprivation, seizure, sequestration, dispossession, forfeiture, impoverishment. See also hardship. *Ant.* Affluence.

Privies, *n.* See privy (1), privity.

Privilege, *n.* A defense to a tort action that negates the tortious nature of the defendant's conduct (e.g., the privilege of self-defense); a special benefit or immunity enjoyed by a person, company, or class beyond the common advantages of other citizens; preferential treatment (doctor-patient privilege). Liberty, license, franchise, entitlement, concession, charter, power, authorization, leave, leverage, due, authority, claim, allowance, grant, warrant, favor, patent, exception, release, consent. See also prerogative, right (3), perquisites.

Privilege against self-incrimination The government must prove its criminal case without the aid of the defendant as a witness against himself or herself. See evidence, declaration.

Privileged, *adj.* Possessing or enjoying a privilege (privileged information). Protected, excused, immune, exempt, entitled to priority or precedence, franchised, favored, licensed, free, released, empowered, special, elite, allowed, warranted, sheltered, advantaged, inside, confidential, inaccessible, excluded, permitted, unaccountable, preeminent, exceptional, extraordinary. *Ant.* Burdened.

Privileged communications Statements made by persons within protected relationships (e.g., husband-wife, attorney-client, doctor-patient, priest-penitent), which the law protects from forced disclosure at the option of the person enjoying the privilege (e.g., spouse, client, patient, penitent). See communication.

Privileges and Immunities Clause Clauses in the U.S. Constitution that place the citizens of each state on the same footing with citizens of other states so far as the advantages resulting from citizenship are concerned. If a person from one state goes into another state, the person must be accorded the same privileges as citizens of the latter state.

Privity, *n.* A close and direct relationship between two or more persons that gives rise to legal consequences that do not apply to persons outside the relationship; a mutual or successive relationship to the same rights of property; an identity or mutuality of interest between parties; a relationship between a party to a suit and a person who was not a party but whose interest in the suit was such that the latter will be bound by the final judgment as if he or she was a party (privity of contract; the judgment binds those in privity with the defendant). Continuity of interest, identity of interest, connection, tie, link, nexus, derivative relationship.

Privity of contract The connection or relationship that exists between two or more contracting parties, e.g., X sells a car to Y, and Y then sells the car to Z. There is privity between X and Y and between Y and Z, but no privity between X and Z. See contract.

Privy 1. *n.* A person who is in privity with another; a party or partaker; one who has a part or interest in any action, matter, or thing (the decision bound the owner and her privies). See privity. **2.** *adj.* Participating in something private or secret (she was privy to the conspiracy). Informed of, aware of, apprised, acquainted with. See also cognizant.

Prize 1. *n.* A reward offered to a person who is the first to perform a condition or who performs it best (a cash prize). Cup, ribbon, trophy, premium, winnings, medal, accolade, jackpot, purse, honor, laurels, citation, windfall, medallion, treasure, title, decoration, bonus, plum, crown, guerdon, booty. **2.** *v.* To attach importance to (her opinion was highly prized by the manager). Value, esteem, honor, respect, cherish, appreciate, treasure, sought after, revere. **3.** *adj.* See outstanding (2), exceptional.

Probability, *n.* The likelihood of a proposition or hypothesis being true (the doctor was asked her opinion of the probability of success). Prospect, possibility, expectation, odds, outlook, plausibility, potentiality, gamble, eventuality, reasonableness, liability, promise. See also chance (3).

Probable, *adj.* Appearing to be founded in reason or experience; having more evidence for than against (defeat is the probable outcome). Likely, apparent, expected, plausible, promising, credible, seeming, colorable, believable, ostensible, foreseeable, logical, reasonable, favorable, viable, indubitable, conceivable, dependable, potential, close-to-certain, anticipated, verisimilar, presumptive. See also practicable, feasible. *Ant.* Implausible.

Probable cause A reasonable ground for a belief in the existence of supporting facts; the existence of circumstances that would lead a reasonably prudent person to believe that the accused person committed the crime charged.

Probably, *adv.* In all probability (the comment probably influenced the jury). More likely than not, likely, credibly, presumably, in all probability, very likely, doubtless, plausibly, by all appearances, indubitably.

Probate, *n.* A court procedure by which a will is proved to be valid or invalid (the costs of probate). Validation, authentication, substantiation, adjudication, verification, establishment, confirmation.

Probate Court, *n.* A court with jurisdiction over the probate of wills, the administration of estates, and in some states, the appointment of guardians and the adoption of children. Orphan's Court, Surrogate Court.

Probation, *n.* **1.** The conditional release to the community of a person convicted of a crime so long as there is compliance with certain conditions of good behavior under the supervision of a probation officer (a year of probation). **2.** A trial or test period for a new, transferred, or promoted employee to determine competence and suitability for the position (the probation status of the teacher).

Probationer, *n.* A convicted offender who is out on probation rather than in prison.

Probative, *adj.* Furnishing proof; serving to test (probative facts). Evidentiary, demonstrative. See also empirical.

Probative evidence Evidence that furnishes, establishes, or contributes toward proof. See evidence.

Probative value Tending to prove an issue; carrying a quality of proof.

Probe, *v., n.* See investigate, search (1), ask, cross-examine, trace, audit; investigation, examination, inquiry, inquest.

Probity, *n.* See honor (3), integrity.

Problem, *n., adj.* See question, mystery, conundrum, complication, crisis; difficult

(3), inflexible, particular (2).

Problematic, *adj.* See doubtful, debatable, inconclusive, moot, ambiguous.

Pro bono For the good; work or services performed free of charge. See gratuitous, charity, benevolence.

Pro bono publico For the public good; for the welfare of the whole.

Procedural, *adj.* Pertaining to the manner of proceeding or accomplishing something; pertaining to the manner in which rights are enforced, as distinguished from the law that gives or defines the rights (procedural delay). Mechanical, adjective; method, approach, practice, means, mode, course, scheme. *Ant.* Substantive.

Procedural due process Minimum standards of procedure such as notice, hearing, and the opportunity to respond before the government deprives an individual of life, liberty, or property. The standards may differ depending on factors such as the nature of the deprivation that is about to take place. See notice, hearing, procedure.

Procedural law A law that prescribes a method of enforcing rights or of obtaining redress for the invasion of rights. See adjective law.

Procedure, *n.* A method or process by which legal rights are enforced, as distinguished from substantive law which gives or defines the rights; the machinery as distinguished from the product; the machinery for carrying on a suit (they alleged that the procedure was unfair). Mode, manner, course, methodology, way, modus operandi, conduct, plan, routine, measures, steps, process, operation, adjective law. *Ant.* Substance.

Proceed, *v.* See advance (3); begin, commence; proceeds.

Proceeding, *n.* **1.** The form or manner of conducting business before a court, agency, or other organization (adjudicative proceeding). Steps, conduct, course, mode, process, procedure, method, system, progress, measure, way, methodology. **2.** A litigation (contempt proceeding). Case, action, prosecution, suit, trial, hearing, lawsuit, cause, inquest, inquiry. **3.** A sequence of events (an account of the proceedings). Happenings, affairs, actions, occurrences, agenda, goings-on, concerns, dealings, deeds, incidents, transactions, matters. **4.** A record of what takes place at a meeting (the proceedings are kept in the file). Minutes, memoranda, archives. See also report (1), record (2).

Proceeds, *n.* That which results or accrues from some possession or transaction (taxable proceeds). Yield, receipts, income, produce, issue, cash, sum, amount, outcome, profit, gain, revenue, net, gross, crop, earnings, reward, end, balance, remuneration, "take," "gate," assets, winnings.

Process 1. *n.* A series of actions, motions, or occurrences (a process of elimination). Procedure, method, sequence, course, plan, means, scheme, methodology, technique, moves, mode, practice, treatment, routine, system, line, steps, tactics, strategy, ritual, formula, praxis, evolution, unfolding, development, motion, flow. **2.** *n.* The means used by a court to acquire or exercise its jurisdiction over a person or over specific property (service of process). Notice, command, subpoena, direction to appear. **3.** *v.* To treat or handle (process the applications). Dispose of, organize, deal with, prepare, systematize, engineer; change, transform, convert, adapt. See also produce (2).

Process agent A person authorized to accept service of process on behalf of another. See agent.

Procession, *n.* See succession (2), chain (1), series, development (1), array, ceremony, celebration.

Process server A person authorized by law (e.g., a sheriff) to serve process papers on defendants.

Procès-verbal, *n.* An official record of what was said before a public officer or at a session.

Pro-choice, *adj.* Being in favor of the availability of abortion. See abortion, choice, choose.

Proclaim, *v.* To promulgate; to publish by an official act (proclaimed a new bidding procedure). Circulate, announce, broadcast, publicize, advertise, state, herald, air, disclose, reveal, inform, assert, utter, disseminate, enunciate, make known, expound, trumpet, profess, signal, release, notify, vent, propagandize, divulge, decree, enact, proselytize, sponsor, pronounce, annunciate, blazon, voice, shout, exclaim, blurt, cry out, bellow, make manifest. See also communicate, express (2), report (4). *Ant.* Suppress.

Proclamation, *n.* A formal and public declaration (Emancipation Proclamation). Avowal, edict, publication, announcement, promulgation, notice, fiat, notification, ruling, report, utterance, pronouncement, manifesto, decree, message, profession, statement, law, ordinance. See also communication.

Proclivity, *n.* See disposition (4), affinity, bias; lean.

Procrastinate, *v.* See defer (1), delay (1), loiter; loaf; doubt (1); hedge.

Procrastination, *n.* See delay (3); dilatory, fluctuating.

Procreate, *v.* See beget, produce (2).

Procreation, *n.* The producing of children. See birth.

Proctor, *n.* One appointed to manage the affairs of or represent another (specially designated proctor). Supervisor, steward, procurator, representative, delegate, monitor, manager, surrogate, caretaker, administrator, executor, middleman, go-between, solicitor, superintendent, instrument, substitute, spokesperson, lieutenant, proxy. See also agent, attorney, advocate.

Procuration, *n.* The act of designating someone as an agent; doing something as the agent of another (indorsement by procuration).

Procurator, *n.* One who acts for another. See proctor.

Procure, *v.* To cause a thing to be done; to obtain something (procure the release of the hostage). Instigate, effect, induce, persuade, initiate, contrive, bring about, manipulate, provoke, seize, accumulate, commandeer, secure, appropriate, take possession of, embezzle, gather, capture, elicit, attain, receive, earn. See also acquire, purchase.

Procurement, *n.* The act of obtaining or acquiring something (procurement contract). Acquisition, securing, purchasing, hiring, leasing, gaining, appropriation, seizure, buying, effecting, bringing about, taking over.

Procurer, *n.* One who procures. See pimp; parasite; prostitute.

Procuring cause The cause originating a series of events that results in the accomplishment of the object without a break in their continuity. Inducing cause, direct cause, efficient cause, proximate cause. See also cause.

Prod, *v.* See incite, provoke, induce, entice, encourage, persuade, press (1).

Prodigal, *adj.* Extravagant or wasteful (prodigal tendencies). Spendthrift, lavish, profligate, inordinate, profuse, squandering, excessive, generous, immoderate, unruly, intemperate, wanton, free, abundant overliberal, thriftless, careless, luxurious, profuse, impetuous, gluttonous, precipitate, dissipating. See also improvident, reckless, excess. *Ant.* Cautious.

Prodigious, *adj.* See big, great; extraordinary, exceptional, outstanding (2); agape.

Produce, *n.*, **produce,** *v.* **1.** *n.* The product of natural growth, labor, or capital; articles produced or grown from or on the soil (produce sold at market). Crop, harvest, staples, fruit, outgrowth, handiwork, vegetables, return. See also yield, proceeds. **2.** *v.* bring forward, exhibit, or devise (produce witnesses). Disclose, present, show, exhibit, supply, generate, furnish, yield, uncover, effectuate, create, manufacture, manifest, reveal, achieve, parade, realize, stage, breed, accomplish, devise, demonstrate, evidence, execute, initiate, beget, deliver, perform, fabricate, assemble, erect, invent, contrive, provoke, process, kindle, build, engender, unfold, fashion, materialize, effect, cause, procreate, concoct, give birth to.

Producer, *n.* One who produces, generates, or brings forth; the person who raises agricultural products and puts them in condition for the market (grain producer). Grower, initiator, miner, originator, fabricator, processor, industrialist. See also manufacturer, entrepreneur, owner.

Producing cause An efficient, existing, or contributing cause which, in natural and continuous sequence, produces the damage, injury, or other impact; that without which the result would not have occurred. See cause.

Product, *n.* Something produced by physical labor, intellectual effort, or natural processes (defective product). Thing, result, item, article, good, crop, fruit, commodity, merchandise, production, output, creation, invention, handiwork, effect, concoction, outcome, issue, stock, child, offspring, accomplishment. See also property, proceeds, yield, produce (1).

Production, *n.* The act of producing (the production of computers). Creation, assembling, construction, fabrication, making, preparation, origination, formation, performance, execution, materialization, revelation, demonstration, composition, presentation, manifestation, display, spectacle, ostentation, parade, exposure, arrangement, indication, exhibition. See also manufacture.

Productive, *adj.* See effective, gainful, fertile, pregnant (2), competent, dominant, active, efficient, strong (3), abundant, original.

Product liability The liability of a manufacturer, supplier, wholesaler, assembler, retail seller, or lessor of a defective product placed on the market, which causes damage or injury. Several causes of action can be used to impose such liability: negligence, strict liability in tort, deceit, breach of express warranty, breach of implied warranty of merchantability, breach of implied warranty of fitness for a particular purpose.

Profane, *adj.* **1.** Showing disrespect for God or for other sacred things (profane utterance). Blasphemous, sacrilegious, wicked, iconoclastic, obscene, evil, sinful, impious, ungodly, irreligious, coarse, abusive, ribald, desecrative, satanic, immoral, vulgar. See also irreverent. **2.** Not involving religious matters (profane considerations). Secular, worldly, lay, earthly, temporal, civil, terrestrial. *Ant.* Spiritual.

Profanity, *n.* Irreverence toward sacred things; blasphemous use of the name of God (public profanity). Desecration, impiety, sacrilege, iniquity, immorality, debasement, cursing, profanation, vulgarity, damning, defilement, outrage, malediction, swearing, billingsgate. See also blasphemy. *Ant.* Respect.

Profess, *v.* **1.** To make an open declaration (he professed to be an atheist). Allege, claim, assert, declare, acknowledge, certify, confirm, confess, announce, postulate, avow, warrant, contend, maintain, admit, depose, advance, utter, confess, proclaim, affirm, offer, reveal, pronounce, broadcast, publish, pledge, disclose. **2.** To pretend. See counterfeit (1), lie.

Profession, *n.* **1.** A vocation or occupation requiring special education and skill (legal profession). Field, trade, career, line, pursuit, discipline, employment, specialty, business, métier, craft, post, office, service, endeavor, job, situation, work, livelihood. **2.** A declaration (profession of innocence). Assertion, allegation, statement, avowal, certification, notification, guarantee, testimony, oath, confession, pledge, acknowledgment, promise, assurance, vow, confirmation, asseveration, representation, plea, word, contention, manifesto, claim.

Professional 1. *adj.* Pertaining to or characteristic of a profession (professional services). Specialized, unique, skilled, trained, degreed, qualified, experienced, knowledgeable, polished, efficient, pragmatic, expert, superior, veteran, gifted, thorough, model, excellent, dexterous, proficient, well-trained, businesslike, prime,

Professional

finished. See also learned, apt, competent, able, outstanding (2), exceptional. **2.** *n.* A person with considerable skill in his or her field (they all considered her a professional at poker). Specialist, practitioner, authority, maestro, wizard, "pro," old hand, prodigy, expert, connoisseur. *Ant.* Lay; novice.

Professional corporation (P.C.) A corporation organized by those performing personal services to the public, of the type that requires a license or other legal authorization. See corporation.

Professional responsibility, code of See code of professional responsibility, canon, ethics, principle (2), right (4).

Professor, *n.* See teacher, scholar; school.

Proffer, *v.* To offer or tender. See offer, bid.

Proficiency, *n.* See ability, competence.

Proficient, *adj.* See apt (3), expert (2), able, effective, competent, professional.

Profile, *n.* See outline, description, map.

Profit 1. *n.* The gross proceeds of a business transaction less the costs of the transaction; excess of revenue over expenses (taxable profits). Net proceeds, gain, realization, earnings, bottom line, advancement, remuneration, receipts, winnings, prize, benefit, windfall, advantage, value, boon, "take," dividend, surplus, increment, appreciation, premium, improvement, betterment. See also yield, income, proceeds. **2.** *v.* To obtain benefit or advantage (he profited from the experience). Improve, avail oneself of, promote, use, aid, reap, serve, earn, edify, contribute, utilize, further, assist. *Ant.* Loss; deteriorate.

Profitable, *adj.* See gainful, beneficial, lucrative.

Profit and loss (P & L), *n.* Gain or loss arising from goods bought or sold or from carrying on any other business.

Profit à prendre The right to take from the land of another through mining, logging, drilling, fishing, grazing; an interest in the land of another conferring rights of use and removal. See interest, right, removal.

Profiteering, *n.* Taking advantage of unusual or exceptional circumstances to make excessive profits (e.g., selling scarce goods at inflated prices during a war. See graft, manipulate.

Profligacy, *n.* See intemperance, debauchery, abandon (2), waste.

Profligate, *adj.* See prodigal, improvident; immoral, corrupt, wild, abandoned (2).

Pro forma, *adj.* As a matter of form; done in a perfunctory manner (a pro forma acceptance). For the sake of form or appearances, by ritual, as a formality, superficially, by habit, as a matter of course.

Profound, *adj.* See learned, important, cultivated; comprehensive, broad, extreme, acute.

Profuse, *adj.* See abundant, copious, many, big, excess, improvident, prodigal.

Profusion, *n.* See remainder (2); profuse.

Progeny, *n.* See descendants, family, offspring.

Prognosis, *n.*. See prophecy.

Prognostication *n.* See prophecy.

Program, *n., v.* See platform (1), plan (1), agenda, schedule (1), method, modus operandi, instrumentality, agency, policy; list, plan (2).

Progress, *n., progress, v.* See development (1), advancement (2), growth, production; emerge, develop, mature (1), advance (3, 4, 5), produce (2); augment, continue.

Progression, *n.* See development (1), advancement (2), growth; chain (1), series, succession (2), continuation.

Progressive, *adj.* Advancing; favoring reform (progressive hiring policy). Open-minded, liberal, forward, dynamic, flowing, moving, modern, corrective, remedial, successive, rising, up-to-date, activist, reformist, supporting change, accelerating, graduated, continuing, unbroken, proceeding, consecutive, left, intensifying, spreading, worsening, enlarging, increasing, malignant. *Ant.* Withdrawing, reactionary.

Progressive tax A type of graduated tax that applies higher tax rates as one's income increases.

Pro hac vice (P.H.V.) For this particular occasion (e.g., a lawyer is given permission to practice law in the jurisdiction for this case only).

Prohibit, *v.* To prevent; to forbid by law (the parolee was prohibited from leaving the state). Restrain, enjoin, block, hamper, interdict, impede, quell, veto, disallow, deny, suppress, foil, stop, frustrate, preclude, negate, prescribe, constrain, outlaw, withhold, foreclose, thwart, embargo, stay, arrest, repress, debar, counteract, traverse, revoke. See also obstruct, ban, bar. *Ant.* License.

Prohibition, *n.* **1.** Suppression or interdiction (prohibition of child labor). Prevention, veto, suppression, repression, inhibition, outlawing, hindrance, ban, embargo, negation, obstruction, disallowance, stay, stoppage, revocation, constraint, debarment, check, proscription, injunction, estoppel, barrier, repudiation, disqualification, forbiddance, exile, foreclosure, impediment, interference, checkmate, eradication, retardation, denial, preclusion. **2.** A law preventing the manufacture, sale, or transportation of intoxicating liquors except for medicinal purposes. *Ant.* Legalization.

Prohibitive, *adj.* See exorbitant, costly; impossible, onerous.

Project, *n.*, **project,** *v.* See plan (1) enterprise, campaign, activity, action, assignment; plan (2), gauge (1); foresee, anticipate; protrude.

Projectile, *n.* See weapon, arms.

Projection, *n.* See prophecy, assessment.

Proletariat, *n.* The class of unskilled laborers without property or capital; those with no place in the established order of society. See laborer, employee, slave.

Pro-life, *adj.* In favor of restrictions on access to abortion; opposed to abortion. See abortion, prohibitions.

Proliferate, *v.* See augment; beget; double, many.

Proliferation, *n.* See increase, growth, appreciation, development, accumulation.

Prolific, *adj.* See abundant, copious, gainful, rank (2).

Prolixity, *n.* Unnecessary and superfluous statement of facts in pleading or in evidence (an objection to the prolixity of the complaint). Wordiness, verbosity, meandering, redundancy, verbiage, circumlocution, tediousness, rambling, digression, diffuseness, tedious length, bombast, long-windedness. See also babble; balderdash. *Ant.* Brevity.

Prologue, *n.* See preamble; commencement.

Prolong, *v.* To extend the time (the medicine prolonged her life). Lengthen, stretch, protract, elongate, drag out, expand, preserve, prolongate, maintain, perpetuate, sustain, continue, increase, filibuster. See also extend. *Ant.* Abridge.

Promenade, *n.*, *v.* See passage (2); walk.

Prominence, *n.* See eminence, notoriety, reputation, superiority, honor (3), note (4).

Prominent, *adj.* See conspicuous, obvious, outstanding (2), elevated, notorious, popular, great, extraordinary.

Promiscuity, *n.* See intemperance, debauchery, lust.

Promiscuous, *adj.* See mixed; capricious, fortuitous; casual; wild; immoral, carnal, prurient, obscene.

Promise 1. *n.* A manifestation of an intention to act or to refrain from acting in a specified way so as to justify the promisee in understanding that a commitment has been made (promise to make the loan). Oath, declaration, affirmation, guarantee, assurance, word, undertaking, endorsement, stipulation, covenant, obligation, vow, attestation, profession, handshake, avowal, engagement, warrant, pact. See also commitment (2), pledge (1), contract (1), intent (1). **2.** *v.* To make a commitment (he promised to lend the money). Commit, swear, warrant, attest, stipulate, agree, aver, covenant, resolve, engage, ensure, bargain, consent, contract, assure, undertake, declare, testify, vow, affirm, subscribe, obligate. **3.** *v.* To give some basis for expecting (the trial promises to be controversial). Indicate, portend, suggest, encourage, presage, point to, show signs, foretell, hint; omen. See also augur. **4.** *n.* See hope (2), likelihood, chance (3).

Promisee, *n.* One to whom a promise has been made.

Promising, *adj.* See auspicious, expedient (1), seasonable, gainful, brilliant, learned.

Promisor, *n.* One who makes a promise.

Promissory estoppel A promise will be binding if (a) the promisor makes a promise that he or she should reasonably expect to induce action or forbearance of a definite and substantial character on the part of the promisee, (b) the promise does induce such action or forbearance, and (c) injustice can be avoided only by enforcement of the promise.

Promissory note A signed paper unconditionally promising to pay another a certain sum of money at a specified date or on demand. See note.

Promote, *v.* To contribute to the growth, enlargement, or prosperity of (the system promotes fraud). Encourage, incite, prompt, provoke, aid, further, advocate, encourage, facilitate, strengthen, augment, nourish, endorse, engender, help, support, urge, cultivate, upgrade, forward, champion, heighten, subscribe, subsidize, elevate, popularize, influence, espouse, foster, reward, intensify, advertise, enhance, enliven, push, recommend, succor, patronize, circulate, guarantee, sanction. See also back, abet, assist, advance. *Ant.* Frustrate.

Promoter, *n.* One who promotes, urges on, or encourages; one who takes the preliminary steps in the organization of a corporation (the promoters filed the articles of incorporation). Organizer, incorporator, advocate, planner, benefactor, financier, sponsor, aider, abettor, patron, patroness, founder, backer, prime mover, subsidizer, guarantor, cosigner, angel, champion, upholder, partisan, godfather, guardian, philanthropist, surety, insurer, protector, proponent; publicist, advertiser. *Ant.* Antagonist.

Promotion, *n.* See backing, indorsement (2), help (1); advancement (2).

Prompt 1. *adj.* Responding immediately (prompt delivery). Instant, instantaneous, punctual, quick, rapid, efficient, timely, summary, expeditious, speedy, direct, seasonable, swift, express, precipitate, hurried, fast, hasty, flying, brisk, fleet, galloping, early, without delay, ready, zealous, alive, energetic, agile. **2.** *v.* To give rise to or move to action (the order prompted reform). Incite, instigate, activate, promote, stir, bring on, urge, stimulate, motivate, prod, animate, foment, predispose, spur, press, lure, entice, persuade, impel, occasion, induce, influence, excite, inspire, goad, dispose, jog, encourage, push, drive, elicit, agitate, evoke. *Ant.* Dilatory; inhibit.

Promulgate, *v.* To announce officially. See proclaim, pronounce.

Promulgation, *n.* See declaration, proclamation, communication; decision, mandate.

Prone, *adj.* See liable (2), susceptible, likely.

Pronounce, *v.* To declare formally (pronounce sentence). Deliver, speak, utter, pass, announce, adjudicate, present, voice, frame, articulate, judge, vocalize, enunciate, promulgate, verbalize, proclaim, emphasize, hold, affirm, propound, order, dictate, broadcast. See also communicate, report (4).

Pronounced, *adj.* See conspicuous, manifest, clear, obvious.

Pronouncement, *n.* See declaration, proclamation, communication; decision, mandate.

Proof, *n.* The establishment of a fact by evidence; a logically sufficient reason for asserting the truth of a proposition (burden of proof). Establishment, certification, substantiation, confirmation, corroboration, verification, validation, documentation, assurance, authentication, certainty, demonstration, conviction, manifestation, testimony. See also evidence.

Proof of claim A statement under oath filed in a bankruptcy proceeding by a creditor, in which the latter sets forth the amount owed and sufficient detail to identify the basis for the claim. See claim, bankruptcy.

Proof of loss A formal statement given to an insurer by the policyholder concerning a loss suffered by the latter, providing enough information to enable the insurer to determine the extent of its liability under a policy or bond. See insurance, claim.

Propaganda, *n.* See dogma; information, education.

Propagandize, *v.* See manipulate; educate, instruct; persuade; diffuse, publish, circulate, communicate; convert (3).

Propagate, *v.* **1.** To spread (propagate the faith). See announce, circulate. **2.** To breed (propagate the species). See beget.

Propagation, *n.* See circulation, distribution; increase; beget.

Propel, *v.* See prompt (2), incite, launch; discharge (4).

Propensity, *n.* See disposition (4), preference, affinity, bias; favor (2).

Proper, *adj.* Appropriate or correct; reasonably sufficient (proper treatment). Fit, suitable, acceptable, orthodox, right, precise, well-chosen, accepted, becoming, fitted, normal, advantageous, exact, convenient, just, befitting, respectable, standardized, honest, tasteful. See also admissible, appropriate (3), apt (1), legitimate (1), legal, lawful. *Ant.* Inappropriate.

Proper party A party who has an interest in the subject matter of the litigation that may be conveniently settled therein; one who may be joined in the action but whose nonjoinder would not result in a dismissal.

Property, *n.* **1.** That which one can possess or own; every species of valuable right and interest; everything that is the subject of ownership, tangible or intangible, corporeal or incorporeal, real or personal (deprivation of property without due process of law). Possessions, realty, personalty, investments, movables, immovables, choses, capital, stock, paraphernalia, holdings, appointments, estate, domain, acquisitions, belongings, goods, real estate, things, titles, resources, valuables, funds. See also chattel, asset, effects, right. **2.** The quality or characteristic of a thing (the chemist studied the properties of the substance). Trait, component, attribute, feature, mark, idiosyncrasy, ingredient, earmark, individuality, badge, distinction, style, personality, peculiarity, constituent.

Property right Any type of right to specific property whether it is personal property or real property, tangible (e.g., house, car) or intangible (e.g., the right to work and earn a living, the right of a professional baseball player in his name, photograph, and image). See right.

Property settlement An agreement settling property rights between spouses incident to their separation or divorce. See agreement, separation agreement, division.

Property tax, *n.* A tax levied on real and personal property, the amount being dependent on the value of the property. See tax.

Prophecy, *n.* Prediction. Prognostication, forecast, anticipation, warning, divination, revelation, augury, omen, speculation, guess, conjecture, soothsaying. See also foresight, oracle, augur, witchcraft.

Prophesy, *v.* See foresee, augur, anticipate (1); promise (3).

Prophet, *n.* See oracle, teacher, scholar, master; prophecy.

Prophetic, *adj.* See imminent; prophecy.

Prophylactic, *adj.* See contraceptive, prevention, preventive; sanitary; remedy.

Propinquity, *n.* **1.** Kindred. See affinity (1). **2.** Proximity. See presence, vicinity; near.

Propitiate, *v.* See assuage, mitigate.

Propitious, *adj.* See auspicious, beneficial.

Proponent, *n.* The one who brings forth or propounds something (the proponent of an initiative). Sponsor, advocate, spokesperson, backer, defender, upholder, exponent, patron, enthusiast, subscriber, vindicator, booster, protector, partisan, adherent, propagandist. See also promoter, champion. *Ant.* Challenger.

Proportion, *n.* See extent, range, scope, measure; balance (4), harmony.

Proportional, *adj.* See proportionate, consonant, correlative, analogous.

Proportionate, *adj.* Being in proportion; adjusted to something else according to a certain rate of comparative relation (proportionate share of the costs). Proportional, balanced, just, equivalent, pro rata, uniform, harmonious, relative, equitable, scaled, due, symmetrical, parallel. See also commensurate, analogous. *Ant.* Disproportionate.

Proposal, *n.* A suggestion for examination; an offer (a proposal to fund the project through taxation). Plan, recommendation, proffer, tender, overture, trial balloon, program, idea, scheme, bid, proposition, stratagem, hypothesis, diagram, projection, motion, invitation, request, prospectus, thesis, resolution.

Propose, *v.* See offer, advance (6), nominate; proposal.

Proposition, *n.* **1.** An offer to do a thing (a deceptive proposition). Proposal, tender, prospectus, scheme, bid, motion, recommendation, suggestion, intention, overture, presentation, request. **2.** An assumption or theory (the proposition had little merit). Thesis, postulate, construct, premise, theory, motif, statement, resolution, question, issue. See also hypothesis.

Propound, *v.* To offer or propose for analysis. See offer, advance (6).

Proprietary 1. *adj.* Owned by a private person or company (proprietary school). See private, business. **2.** *adj.* Exclusively made or controlled by right (proprietary medicine). See exclusive. **3.** *adj.* Pertaining to ownership (proprietary interest). See ownership. **4.** *n.* One who has exclusive title. See proprietor, owner.

Proprietary function A function exercised by a municipal corporation for the peculiar or private benefit and advantage of the citizens of the municipality (e.g., operation of a public swimming pool); a function of a city that does not involve an exercise of sovereignty or in which the city is not acting as the agent or arm of the state in the exercise of sovereign powers; an activity that is commercial or chiefly for the private advantage of the community. See governmental functions.

Proprietor, *n.* One who has the legal right or exclusive title to anything; one who runs a small business (the proprietor of the shop). Holder, landlord, landlady, master, partner, proprietary, landowner, possessor, innkeeper, manager, supervisor, overseer, superintendent, skipper, director, administrator. See also owner, promoter.

Proprietorship, *n.* A form of small business, often owned and controlled by one person. See sole proprietorship, business, merchant.

Propriety, *n.* **1.** Conformity to standards and customs (the accountant questioned the propriety of the investment). Appropriateness, fitness, correctness, equity, utility, rightness, suitableness, decorum, aptness, accuracy, justness; courtesy, etiquette, respectability, morality, rectitude delicacy, seemliness, grace, taste, protocol. **2.** Property.

Propulsion, *n.* See impulse, force.

Pro rata, *adv., adj.* According to a certain rate, percentage, or proportion (the firm sought its pro rata share). Apportioned, distributed equitably. See also proportionate, commensurate.

Pro rata clause An insurance company will be liable only for the proportion of the loss represented by the ratio between its policy limits and the total limits of all available insurance. See insurance, ratio.

Prorate, *v.* To divide, share, or distribute proportionally (the cost was prorated among the participants). Split up, assess. See also allot, allocate, distribute (1), divide (2).

Prorogue, *v.* To suspend or terminate a legislative session. See end.

Prosaic, *adj.* See commonplace, pedestrian (2), barren.

Proscribe, *v.* To prohibit or condemn (proscribed child labor). Outlaw, repudiate, check, censure, reject, revoke, castigate, ban, damn, disapprove, boycott, anathematize, exclude, ostracize, forbid, interdict, excommunicate, embargo, curse, banish. *Ant.* Welcome.

Proscription, *n.* See prohibition, ban, exile, censure.

Prose, *n.* See language.

Pro se In his own behalf; appearing for or representing oneself.

Prosecute, *v.* To commence and carry an action through to its ultimate conclusion (the case was dismissed for failure to prosecute). Follow through, complete, finish, litigate, consummate, persist, pursue, advance, see through, maintain, execute, accuse, indict, arraign, charge, prefer charges, summon. *Ant.* Withdraw.

Prosecuting attorney See prosecutor, attorney.

Prosecution, *n.* **1.** In a criminal case, the judicial proceedings instituted to determine the guilt or innocence of a person accused of a crime (the prosecution of the defendant). Criminal proceedings, litigation, trial, suit. See also proceeding, action, hearing. **2.** The prosecuting attorney or the government in a criminal case. See prosecutor.

Prosecutor, *n.* The person who initiates and conducts criminal cases on behalf of the government or the people (the prosecutor requested a high bail). Prosecuting attorney, prosecution, government, district attorney, DA, state's attorney, public prosecutor, United States attorney, attorney general. See also attorney. *Ant.* Defense counsel.

Prosecutrix, *n.* A female prosecutor.

Proselytize, *v.* See persuade, influence, convert (3).

Prosequi, *v.* To follow up, pursue, or prosecute. See nolle prosequi.

Prospect, *n.* See likelihood, hope (2), chance (3), probability, presumption; view.

Prospective, *adj.* Looking forward; pertaining to the future (prospective losses). Anticipated, potential, foreseeable, eventual, looming, conceivable, coming, immediate, expected, imaginable, pending, threatening, approaching, ultimate, scheduled, in view, intended, subsequent, in the wind, close at hand, promising, overhanging, destined, awaited, presumed, in prospect. See also imminent, forthcoming. *Ant.* Retroactive.

Prospective damages Damages that have not yet accrued but which in the nature of things must necessarily or most probably will result from the acts or facts complained of; damages expected to follow. See damages.

Prospective law A law that applies only to cases that arise after the enactment of the law. See law.

Prospectus, *n.* A document published by a company or by its agent, setting forth the nature and objects of an issue of shares, debentures, or other securities created by the company, and inviting the public to subscribe to the issue; a document containing all material facts concerning a company and its operations, so that a prospective investor may make an informed decision as to the merits of an investment (misrepresentations in the prospectus). Announcement, statement, résumé, outline, syllabus, bulletin, digest, circular, abstract, scheme, plan, catalogue, précis, brief.　See also report (1), communication.

Prosper, *v.*　See advance (3, 4, 5), develop, mature (1), produce (2); augment.

Prosperity, *n.*　See affluence, luxury, property.

Prosperous, *adj.*　See affluent, lucrative, gainful, beneficial.

Prostitute 1. *n.*　A person who engages in sexual intercourse or other unlawful sexual acts for hire (accosted by a prostitute).　Whore, strumpet, trollop, harlot, hooker, gigolo, call girl, streetwalker, courtesan, hustler, madam, tart, woman of the street, woman of ill repute, "bitch," cocotte, concubine, slut, mistress, bawd.　See also paramour, parasite, suitor.　**2.** *v.*　To sell out; to degrade (prostitute her ability).　Belittle, pervert, contaminate, mar, defile, desecrate, lower, pander, dishonor, misapply, profane, demean, taint, humble, waste, sully, ruin.　See also corrupt (2), abuse, pollute.

Prostitution, *n.*　Engaging in sexual activities for hire (arrested for prostitution).　See prostitute, debauchery.

Prostrate, *v., adj.*　See grovel, cringe, pander; overcome; exhausted.

Prostration, *n.*　See exhaustion; depression, anguish, distress (3), affliction.

Protagonist, *n.*　See actor, advocate, champion, head, master, manager.

Pro tanto　For so much; partial payment made on a claim.　See partial.

Protect, *v.*　See preserve, oversee, secure, defend, fortify, guard, house; protection.

Protection, *n.*　The act of defending or shielding from harm; a system of providing security (insurance protection).　Custody, preservation, support, screen, safeguard, safekeeping, cover, aegis, maintenance, watch, sanctuary, patronage, asylum, shelter, immunity, wardship, buffer, preserve, guardianship, shade, fortification, oversight, defense, tutelage, shield, covering, helmet, coating, safety, armor, panoply, barricade, refuge, haven, salvation, bulwark, palladium, championship, keep, saving aid, preserver, patron, fence, harbor, convoy, precaution.　*Ant.* Exposure.

Protective, *adj.*　Intended to isolate, secure, or protect (protective custody).　Shielding, prophylactic, custodial, watchful, conservative, safeguarding, covering, vigilant, guiding, assisting, insulating, sheltering, solicitous, defensive, heedful.　See also paternal, preventive.

Protective custody　Being held under force of law for one's own protection.　See custody.

Protective order　A court order or decree designed to protect a person from further harassment.　See harass.

Protective tariff　A law imposing duties on imports with the purpose and effect of discouraging the importation of designated foreign products and hence of stimulating and protecting competing domestic products.　See duties, tax, tariff.

Protector, *n.*　See champion (1), advocate, promoter; police.

Protégé, *n.*　See student, beginner, partisan.

Pro tempore (pro tem), *adv.*　For the time being (president pro tem).　Temporarily, provisionally, for now, for a time, for the moment, fill-in, transitory, transitional, standby.　*Ant.* Permanent.

Protest, *n., protest,* *v.* **1.**　*n.*　A formal declaration of dissent or disapproval (the minister filed a protest).　Opposition, complaint, challenge, protestation, objection, remonstration, outcry, revolt, expostulation, resistance, argumentation, demurrer, demurral, remonstrance, strike, demonstration, negation, criticism, condemnation, defiance, contradiction, disclaimer, admonishment, argument, castigation, censure, correction, exception, warning, reproof, reprobation, blame, scolding, berating, boycott, dispute, disagreement.　**2.** *n.*　A certificate of dishonor of a negotiable instrument.　**3.** *v.*　To dissent strongly (she protested the denial).　Disapprove, oppose, complain, challenge, object, remonstrate, resist, defy, criticize, dispute, strike out at, expostulate, contest, picket, contravene, negate, disclaim, veto, take exception to, denounce, disaffirm, disagree, controvert, mutiny, contradict. **4.** *v.* To affirm (protest her innocence). Assert, avow, proclaim, announce, maintain, profess, annunciate, asseverate, allege, offer, propound. *Ant.* Acquiescence; acceptance; endorse; deny.

Protestants, *n.* Christians who do not follow the Roman Catholic Church or the Orthodox Church; those who adhered to the doctrine of Luther. See church, religion, assembly.

Prothonotary, *n.* A clerk of court. See clerk, official, officer.

Protocol, *n.* **1.** A brief summary of the text of a document; the first copy of a treaty. See compact (1). **2.** The etiquette of diplomacy and the ranking of officials. See ceremony, decorum, propriety.

Prototype, *n.* See model, ancestor.

Protract, *v.* See prolong, extend (1), delay.

Protracted, *adj.* See long, diffuse (2); continuous.

Protrude, *v.* To stick out. Bulge, swell, overhang, project.

Proud, *adj.* **1.** Dignified, independent (a proud judge). Self-respecting, principled, distinguished. **2.** Satisfied (proud of her performance). Pleased, glad, delighted, appreciative, content, gratified. See also happy. **3.** See arrogant, pompous, contemptuous.

Provable, *adj.* Susceptible of being proved (provable claim). Ascertainable, supportable, discoverable, verifiable, well-grounded, confirmable. See also demonstrable, empirical.

Prove, *v.* To establish a fact or position by sufficient evidence (failed to prove his case). Demonstrate, manifest, vindicate, confirm, uphold, substantiate, authenticate, bear out, validate, show, evince, justify, make known, uncover, unveil, exhibit, certify, bear witness, embody, make good, show to be true, attest, affirm, subscribe, ascertain, solidify, strengthen, guarantee, determine. See also corroborate, verify. *Ant.* Contradict.

Proven, *adj.* See authentic, certified.

Proverb, *n.* See moral (3), maxim.

Proverbial, *adj.* See familiar (2), commonplace, common, regular, customary.

Provide, *v.* To furnish or supply (provide necessities for his child). Maintain, stock, serve, equip, arm, donate, impart, outfit, produce, accommodate, endow, cater, plan, lend, bring, keep, procure, feed, clothe, fund, administer, make provision for. See also minister (3), nurture, necessaries. *Ant.* Neglect.

Provided, *conj.* On condition that. In the event that, with the proviso that, with the understanding that, subject to.

Providence, *n.* See foresight, prudence, judgment (2), precaution, caution (3), care; God, chance (2), destiny.

Provident, *adj.* See cautious, prudent, judicious, economical.

Providential, *adj.* See auspicious, beneficial, seasonable, happy.

Province, *n.* **1.** A division of the state or country. See district, zone. **2.** A sphere of expertise or authority. See domain (2).

Provincial, *adj.* See parochial, backward, narrow; awkward; local, country (2), idyllic.

Provision, *n.* **1.** Supplying (the provision of resources). Procurement, accommodation, servicing, catering, purveying, endowment, furnishment, donation, rigging, outfitting, giving, stockpiling, preparation. **2.** That which is supplied (provisions for the trip). Supplies, stock, resources, equipment, food, wherewithal, materiel, materials, gear, groceries, feed, machinery, inventory, edibles, staples, rations, means. **3.** A condition or clause (provision in the will). Term, article, proviso, stipulation, qualification, reservation, restriction, exception, limitation, prerequisite, obligation.

Provisional, *adj.* Temporary (provisional government). Transient, unsettled, pro tem, nonpermanent, limited, substitute, qualified, makeshift, stopgap, conditional, contingent, preliminary, tentative, precautionary, ad hoc. See also temporary, acting, interim. *Ant.* Permanent.

Proviso, *n.* A condition or stipulation in a document, agreement, or proposal (she accepted with the proviso that the time be extended). Limitation, exception, qualification, rider, clause, specification, reservation, prerequisite, obligation, term, modification, amendment, addition. See also condition (1), requirement.

Provocateur, *n.* See insurgent, anarchist, nihilist; agent.

Provocation, *n.* **1.** Inciting another to do a particular deed (provocation for the attack). Incitement, stimulation, inspiration, prompting, instigation, inducement, stimulus, motivation, agitation, fomentation, incentive, stimulant, causation, invitation, dare, arousing, inflaming, inflammation, enragement, aggravation, vexation, prodding, urge, goading, allurement, temptation, compulsion. **2.** See grievance (1).

Provocative, *adj.* See incendiary (2), outrageous; intriguing, attractive.

Provoke, *v.* **1.** To stimulate (she provoked the attack). Stir up, arouse, actuate, move, cause, prompt, challenge, instigate, generate, animate, force, enkindle, egg on, evoke, goad, allure, seduce, inveigle, impel, precipitate, occasion, compel, galvanize, create, quicken, elicit, rouse, produce, foment, agitate, prick, impassion, further. See also bait, incite. **2.** To anger (the noise provoked her). Enrage, exasperate, enflame, irritate, vex, rile, aggravate, madden, perturb, pester, persecute, infuriate, pique, humiliate, nettle, exacerbate, antagonize, disquiet, beset, taunt, irk, incense, plague, mortify, sting, ill-treat, misuse, insult, annoy, gall, aggrieve, discomfort, maltreat, hector, hound, try one's patience, discompose. See also badger, harass, offend. *Ant.* Block; assuage.

Provost, *n.* See officer, official, administrator, chief.

Prowess, *n.* See ability, facility (3), gift (2); courage.

Prowl, *v.* See search, pursue (2), trace (2), ferret.

Prowler, *n.* See intruder, wrongdoer.

Proximate, *adj.* Nearest; close in causal connection (proximate result). Next in order, immediate, direct, following, adjacent, touching, nearby, abutting, approaching, succeeding, contiguous, impending, coterminous, subsequent, neighboring, connected, prospective, tangential. See also near, imminent. *Ant.* Remote.

Proximate cause The defendant is the proximate cause of the plaintiff's injury (a) if it can be said that the defendant's acts or omissions were a substantial factor in producing the injury, or that but for these acts or omissions, the injury would not have occurred, and (b) the injury was the foreseeable consequence of the original risk created by the defendant's acts or omissions. Proximate cause is that cause which, in natural and continuous sequence, unbroken by any efficient intervening cause, produces the injury and without which the injury would not have occurred. See cause.

Proximity, *n.* **1.** The quality or state of being next in time, place, causation, influence, etc. (the proximity of the fire caused great concern). Immediate nearness, closeness, propinquity. See presence (1), vicinity; near. **2.** Kindred between two persons. See kindred (1).

Proxy, *n.* **1.** A person who is substituted for another in order to represent and act for the latter (she was his proxy at the meeting). Representative, delegate, broker, lieutenant, emissary, envoy, proctor, attorney, intermediary, factor. See also replacement, agent, surrogate. **2.** Written authorization that allows one to act for another (she gave him her proxy for the shareholder meeting).

Proxy marriage A valid marriage contracted or celebrated through agents acting on behalf of one or both absent parties. See marriage.

Prudence, *n.* Good judgment and carefulness (her prudence in canceling the trip). Precaution, attentiveness care, diligence, foresight, calculation, forethought, wisdom, sagacity, planning, circumspection, deliberation, perspicacity, vigilance, cunning, mindfulness, frugality, attention, providence, heedfulness, presence of mind, preparedness, husbandry, watchfulness, moderation, thrift, judiciousness. See also caution, judgment (2), discretion, common sense, maturity, experience, learning. *Ant.* Negligence.

Prudent, *adj.* Careful in adapting means to ends (a prudent accountant). Wise, circumspect, sagacious, sensible, provident, economical, wary, sound, guarded, frugal, practical, far-sighted, discriminating, calculating, astute, levelheaded, considerate, economical, sober, canny, politic, rational, sparing, expedient, sapient, shrewd, discerning, prudential, chary, mindful, moderate. See also acute (1) cautious, judicious, discreet. *Ant.* Reckless.

Prudential, *adj.* See prudent.

Prudish, *adj.* See particular (2), difficult (3), formal (3), inflexible, precise, proud.

Prune, *v.* See cut, abridge, diminish; removal.

Prurient, *adj.* Pertaining to a shameful or morbid interest in nudity, sex, or excretion (prurient appeal). Erotic, pornographic, obscene, indecent, lascivious, wanton, bawdy, salacious, lewd, voyeuristic, lecherous, lustful, satyric, vulgar, vile, lurid, licentious, carnal, debauched, dirty, unwholesome, dissipated, ribald, suggestive, carnal, promiscuous, blue, concupiscent. *Ant.* Chaste.

Pry, *v.* See eavesdrop, bug, intermeddle, interfere, encroach, impose.

Prying, *adj.* Meddlesome. Intrusive, "snoopy," snooping, eavesdropping, "nosy," meddling, overcurious, impertinent, quizzical. See also search.

Psalm, *n.* See music; bible.

Pseudo, *adj.* False or pretended (a pseudo professional). Spurious, counterfeit, fraudulent, superficial, phony, bogus, sham, simulated, mock, fake, feigned, self-styled, unreal, fictitious. See also false, illusory, fraud. *Ant.* Authentic.

Pseudonym, *n.* See alias, name.

Psyche, *n.* See mind (1), spirit (3), life.

Psychedelic, *adj.* See hallucination, drug.

Psychiatry, *n.* The medical science of treating mental illness. See doctor, medicine, treatment, insanity, mind, science, behavior.

Psychic, *n.*, *adj.* See oracle; augur, prophecy, clairvoyance; intangible, incorporeal.

Psychoanalyze, *v.* To treat mental illness by Freudian techniques.

Psychological, *adj.* See mental; emotional.

Psychology, *n.* The study of the mind and human behavior. See science, mind, behavior.

Psychopath, *n.* See maniac, deviant (2); insanity.

Psychosis, *n.* A severe mental disorder in which the patient departs from the normal pattern of thinking, feeling, and acting—often losing contact with reality. See illness, disease, insanity.

Psychosomatic, *adj.* Concerning the interrelationship of the mind and body.

Psychotic, *adj.* See mental, demented, insane, non compos mentis.

Pub, *n.* See inn; merchant, business, liquor.

Puberty, *n.* The earliest age at which persons are capable of begetting or bearing children—about 14 for boys and 12 for girls. See minor, majority, age, birth.

Public 1. *n.* The community at large (the public favored the change). Citizenry, society, population, body politic, rank and file, populace, electorate, everybody, people at large, inhabitants, silent majority, general public, nation, folk, masses, proletariat, country, city, mankind, voters, men, women, middle America. **2.** *adj.* Common to all or many; open to common use (public accommodations). Unrestricted, accessible, general, available, reachable, community, national, governmental, societal, statewide, unobstructed, city, civic, universal, catholic, popular, passable, civil, federal, communal, free, tax-supported. **3.** *adj.* Generally known (public knowledge). Notorious, well-known, manifest, patent, acknowledged, visible, exposed, plain, overt, evident, published, publicized, prominent, notable, naked, apparent, ventilated, egregious, avowed, aired, reported, divulged, obvious, frank, outward, unabashed, conspicuous, in sight, disseminated, propagated, broadcast. *Ant.* Individual; private; concealed.

Public assistance, *n.* Welfare, dole. See charity, benevolence, assistance.

Publication, *n.* **1.** Making something known to people (the publication of an opinion). Disclosure, presentation, revelation, circulation, printing, promulgation, broadcasting, notice, release, publishing, announcement, airing, dissemination, exposition, pronouncement, publicizing, advertisement, broadcast. **2.** Something that has been published (the publication was censored). Periodical, book, treatise, magazine, newspaper, circular, bulletin, volume, communication, flyer, serial, issue, piece, composition, article, opus, document, correspondence, diary, story, writing, tome, play, novel, report, manuscript, edition.

Public convenience and necessity Reasonable necessity to meet the convenience of the public; that which is fitting or suited to the public need. See convenience, convenient, necessity, adequate.

Public corporation An artificial person (e.g., municipality, government corporation) created for the administration of public affairs; an instrumentality of the government, founded and owned in the public interest, supported by public funds, and governed by those deriving their authority from the government. See corporation, government.

Public defender, *n.* An attorney appointed by a court or employed by a government agency, whose work consists primarily in defending indigent defendants in criminal cases. See attorney, assigned counsel.

Public disclosure of private fact See invasion of privacy.

Public domain, *n.* Property that is not protected by copyright, ownership, or other restrictions.

Public figures Those who have assumed a role of special prominence in society; those who occupy positions of persuasive power, who have thrust themselves to the forefront of particular public controversies in order to influence the resolution of the issues involved. See defamation, popular, notorious, conspicuous.

Public interest Something in which the public, the community at large, has some pecuniary interest, or some interest by which their legal rights or liabilities are affected; an interest shared by citizens generally in affairs of local, state, or national government. See interest.

Publicity, *n.* See fanfare, notoriety.

Publicize, *v.* See exhibit, notify, publish, proclaim, promote.

Public Law (PL), *n.* A law or statute that applies generally to the people of a nation or of a state; the law concerned with the organization of the state, the relations between the state and the people, the responsibilities of public officers, and the relationship between states (e.g., constitutional law, administrative law, criminal law, international law). See law, legislation.

Public nuisance An unreasonable interference with a right that is common to the general public; behavior that unreasonably endangers or interferes with the health, safety, peace, morals, comfort, or convenience of the general community. See nuisance.

Public official The holder of a public office that requires the exercise of some portion of the sovereign power. At the very least, public officials include those among the hierarchy of government employees who have, or appear to the public to have, substantial responsibility for or control over the conduct of governmental affairs. See official, officer.

Public prosecutor, *n.* See prosecutor, attorney.

Public purpose Governmental purpose; pertaining to a public service or use that affects inhabitants as a community and not merely as individuals; pertaining to the promotion of the public health, safety, morals, prosperity, and contentment of all the residents of a given political division such as a state. See purpose, government.

Public record Records that a government unit is required by law to keep or that are necessary to keep in the discharge of duties imposed by law. See record (4), report (1).

Public school, *n.* See school; education.

Public use 1. A use that confers some benefit or advantage to the public; public usefulness, utility, advantage, or what is productive of general benefit. See use. **2.** Any nonsecret use of a completed and operative invention in its natural and intended way.

Public utility, *n.* A business or service regularly supplying the public with some commodity or service that is of public consequence and need (e.g., electricity, gas, water, transportation, telephone); a privately owned and operated business whose services are provided to the public without discrimination and are so essential to the general public as to justify special franchises (e.g., the use of public property). See business, necessaries, essential.

Public welfare The prosperity, well-being, or convenience of the public at large or of the whole community as distinguished from the advantage of an individual or limited class; that which pertains to the primary social interests of safety, order, morals, economics, politics, etc. See convenience, welfare, safe, police.

Public works, *n.* See building, highway, river, park.

Publish, *v.* To make known; to make public (the statement was published when he showed it to his colleague). Circulate, utter, issue, put in circulation, announce, broadcast, promulgate, speak, advise the public, air, trumpet, disseminate, print, bring out, spread, advertise, disclose, herald, report, divulge, impart, exhibit, ventilate, publicize, blazon, express, distribute, inform. See also notify, communicate, promote. *Ant.* Suppress.

Publisher, *n.* One who by himself or herself, or through an agent, makes something publicly known; one in the business of manufacturing and selling books, magazines, or other literary productions. See merchant, promoter.

PUD See planned unit development.

Puddle, *n.* See pond, water.

Pudgy, *adj.* See corpulent, short (2).

Puerile, *adj.* Pertaining to childhood; childish. See juvenile (2).

Puff, *v.* See exaggerate, augment; puffing.

Puffery, *n.* See puffing, flattery, fanfare, decoration.

Puffing, *n.* **1.** A seller's expression of opinion that is not made as a representation of fact; a seller's exaggeration concerning the quality of goods (calling the product "fabulous" was mere puffing). Puffery, overpraise, overcommendation, inflation, magnification, overrating, build-up, smoke, sales talk, flattery, bombast, panegyric, hot air, hype. **2.** Secret bidding at an auction by or on behalf of the seller.

Pugnacious, *adj.* See belligerent, hostile, litigious, contentious.

Pull, *v., n.* See tow; bait (3), entice; extract (1); influence.

Pullback, pullout, *n.* See exit (2), removal, departure, emigration.

Pullman, *n.* A railroad sleeping car.

Pulpit, *n.* See platform; clergy, minister, religion.

Pulsate, *v.* See beat (3).

Pulse, *n.* See climate (2), disposition (4), manner; beat (3).

Pulverize, *v.* See destroy, break (2); rescind.

Pummel, *v.* See beat (1), batter, destroy.

Pump, *v.* See cross-examine; drain.

Pun, *n.* See joke.

Punch, *v.* See beat, batter, attack, assail.

Punctilious, *adj.* See precise (2), careful, deliberate; formal, particular, proper.

Punctual, *adj.* See expeditious, precise, dependable; seasonable.

Punctuate, *v.* See accent (2), emphasize.

Puncture, *v.* See break (2), pierce, enter (2).

Pundit, *n.* See oracle, expert (1), teacher, authority

Pungent, *adj.* See caustic, biting; delectable.

Punish, *v.* See amerce, fine (1), correct (3), castigate; abuse, batter, hurt.

Punishable, *adj.* Deserving of or liable to punishment (punishable by fine or imprisonment). Indictable, chargeable, impeachable, at fault. See also blameworthy, culpable. *Ant.* Innocent.

Punishment, *n.* Any fine, penalty, or confinement imposed by law for a crime, offense, or omission of a duty enjoined by law (she received the maximum punishment). Deprivation, retribution, chastisement, suffering, sentence, pain, condemnation, mulct, damages, sanction, denunciation, punitive measure, coercion, penance, castigation, forfeiture, price, amercement, infliction, tax, loss, disgrace, vengeance, reckoning, dressing down. See also discipline (2), correction, censure. *Ant.* Forgiveness.

Punitive, *adj.* Having the characteristic of punishment or a penalty (punitive measures). Penal, avenging, retaliatory, retributive. See also vindictive.

Punitive damages, *n.* See exemplary damages.

Punk, *n.* See wrongdoer.

Puny, *adj.* See small, anemic, slight (2); petty, inferior.

Pupil, *n.* See student, intern, beginner, amateur; scholar.

Puppet, *n.* See pawn (3), dummy, victim.

Pur autre vie For or during the life of another.

Purblind, *adj.* See blind; backward.

Purchase 1. *n.* The acquisition of title to property by a means other than descent; the voluntary transmission of property for consideration from one person to another (the purchase of land). Procurement, buying, assumption, redemption, realization, investment. **2.** *n.* That which one purchases (a unique purchase). See property (1). **3.** *v.* To obtain by paying a consideration (she purchased the estate). Buy, invest, bargain, secure, redeem, get, collect, ransom, pick up. See also acquire, procure. *Ant.* Sale; release.

Purchase money mortgage A mortgage or security device taken back to secure the performance of an obligation incurred in the purchase of the property. See mortgage, security interest.

Purchase money resulting trust When one person furnishes the money for the purchase of property with the title being placed in the name of another, the former is the equitable owner under a purchase money resulting trust. See trust, resulting trust, equitable owner.

Purchase money security interest A security interest (a) taken or retained by the seller of the collateral to secure all or part of its price, or (b) taken by a person who by making advances or incurring an obligation gives value to enable the debtor to acquire rights in or the use of the collateral if such value is in fact so used. See security interest.

Purchaser, *n.* One who acquires property by buying it for a consideration; one who has contracted to purchase property (the purchaser tried to withdraw from the sales agreement). Vendee, customer, investor, emptor. See also buyer, client (2), patron.

Pure, *adj.* **1.** Free from conditions or restrictions; absolute; homogeneous. See complete (2), absolute, outright, clear (2). **2.** Innocent or unblemished. See blameless, innocent, clear (4).

Pure accident An unavoidable accident; an unforeseeable event that is not due to carelessness or fault. See accident.

Purgation, *n.* Cleansing or exonerating oneself of suspicion of guilt by denying the charge on oath or by ordeal. See clear (4).

Purge 1. *v.* To clear or exonerate from a charge or imputation of guilt (the report purged him of any responsibility). See clear (5). **2.** *n.* Elimination (a purge of opponents from the committee). Separation, ejection, eviction, termination, displacement, withdrawal, liquidation, excommunication, unseating, exile, dismissal, discharge, shakeup, eradication, annihilation, banishment, suppression, witchhunt, destruction, evacuation, murder. See also removal, ouster. *Ant.* Accuse; restoration.

Purify, *v.* See fix (3), clear (5); bathe, disinfect, fumigate.

Purist, *n.* See fanatic, nonconformist.

Puritan, puritanical, *adj.* See parochial, narrow (2), draconian, strict (2), extreme (1), ascetic, formal (3), grave (3), inflexible, arbitrary, firm (2), plain, caustic; squeamish, particular (2); temperance.

Purity, *n.* **1.** Free from extraneous matter or anything debasing or contaminating (chemical tests to determine its purity). Cleanliness, integrity, wholesomeness, excellence, uniformity, genuineness, authenticity, healthfulness. **2.** Without guilt or fault. See innocence, moral (2), blameless.

Purloin, *v.* See pilfer, embezzle; larceny.

Purport, *n., ***purport,** *v.* **1.** *n.* The meaning, substance, or legal effect (the purport of the law). Intention, significance, end, design, gist, objective, bearing, spirit, drift, implication, rationale, sense, sum and substance, tenor, import, aim, essence, relevance, purpose. **2.** *v.* To claim (he purports to be a specialist). Insinuate, allege, pretend, pose, represent, misrepresent, feign, profess, assert, contend, imply, infer, intimate, suggest.

Purported, *adj.* See assumed.

Purpose, *n.* **1.** That which one seeks to accomplish (legislative purpose). Plan, aim, intent, end, object, project, design, ambition, target, rationale, motivation, resolve, wish, reason, proposal, scheme, rationalization, vision, desideratum, view, guiding principle, outcome, basis, destination, explanation, objective, raison d'être, aspiration. **2.** Resolve (want of purpose). Determination, persistence, will, perseverance, tenacity, steadfastness, constancy, zeal, volition, industry.

Purposeful, *adj.* See intentional, willful, deliberate (2), premeditated.

Purposely, *adv.* Consciously, knowingly (she purposely ignored the warning). Intentionally, deliberately, calculatedly, willfully, purposefully, by design, by choice, voluntarily, expressly, on purpose, designedly, decidedly, calmly, thoughtfully, with aforethought. *Ant.* Unintentionally.

Purpresture, *n.* An appropriation to private use of that which belongs to the public; an encroachment upon public rights and easements. See appropriation (1), encroach.

Purse, *n.* **1.** A sum of money available to the winner(s) of a contest (the purse was divided between the top two scorers). Prize, jackpot, kitty, premium, gift, award, reward, stake, ante. **2.** Available funds. See fund (2).

Pursuance, *n.* See execution (1), performance.

Pursuant, *adj.* In accordance with (pursuant to your instructions). Consistent with, according to, in the course of carrying out, commensurate with, following, pursuing, in line with, in agreement with.

Pursue, *v.* **1.** To aim for (to pursue a career in law). Strive, progress toward, go after, aspire, seek, try, labor, be intent on, struggle, court, desire, work toward, yearn for. **2.** To follow (the police pursued the suspect). Track, search, trail, hunt, stalk, ferret out, trace. See also chase. **3.** To continue (pursue one's studies). Carry on, persist, perform, engage in, progress, cultivate, operate, practice, undertake, prosecute, endure. See also execute (1), maintain, commence.

Pursuit, *n.* **1.** The act of chasing (hot pursuit). Quest, chase, campaign, effort, probe, struggle, following, inquiry, trail, investigation, exploration, prosecution, continuation, stalk, attempt, hunt, try. **2.** A hobby or occupation (her favorite pursuit). Employment, livelihood, trade, profession, work, craft, specialty, field, sphere, endeavor, calling, preoccupation, project, business, practice, career, venture, activity, undertaking, avocation, province, concern, plan, objective, aspiration, purpose, goal, target, object, end.

Pursuit of happiness An inalienable right that includes the right to follow one's individual employment preferences, liberty of conscience, freedom of contract, the privileges of family, and exemption from oppression and invidious discrimination.

Purulent, *adj.* See rotten.

Purveyor, *n.* See carrier, messenger.

Purview, *n.* **1.** The scope or extent of something (within the purview of the inquiry). Boundary, limit, jurisdiction, ambit, compass, field, comprehension, breadth, design, span, territory, domain, arena, orbit, experience, angle, dominion. **2.** The body of a statute; that part of a statute commencing with the words "Be it enacted"; the design, purpose, or scope of the statute.

Push 1. *v.* To shove. Press, jolt, cram, jam, jostle, elbow, squeeze, pack, bunch, swarm, butt, force, compress, poke, propel, ram. **2.** *v.* See promote, advocate. **3.** *v.* See provoke, incite. **4.** *n.* See ambition.

Pusher, *n.* One who engages in the illegal sale of drugs; a dealer. See drug, addict, wrongdoer.

"Pushover," *n.* See nonentity; boor, ass; coward; victim.

Pushy, *adj.* See assertive, obnoxious.

Pusillanimous, *adj.* See apprehensive, yellow (1), afraid; coward, cowardice.

Put 1. *n.* An option to sell a certain stock or commodity at a fixed price for a stated quantity within a stated period. **2.** *v.* See place (2); deposit; attribute (1).

Putative, *adj.* Alleged or reputed (putative spouse). Supposed, assumed, reported, imputed, speculative, purported, believed, conjectured. See also apparent, reputed, ostensible.

Putative father The alleged father of an illegitimate child. See father, paternity.

Putative marriage A marriage contracted in good faith and in ignorance (on one or both sides) of an impediment that renders the marriage unlawful. See marriage, impediment, annulment.

"Put-down," *n.* See slander, affront, abuse.

Putrid, *adj.* See foul, dirty, odious, rotten.

Puzzle, *n., v.* See conundrum, mystery, confusion; confuse, distract (2), surprise (1).

Pyramid, *v.* See accumulate, spread, augment.

Pyramiding, *n.* A device for increasing holdings of a stock by financing new holdings out of the increased margin of those already owned; the use of a small amount of money or of "paper profits" to finance buying stock. See plan (1), contrivance, machination.

Pyromania, *n.* The urge to start fires. See impulse, insanity, compulsion, arson.

Pyrrhic victory, *n.* A victory offset by a loss. See offset, counteract, neutralization; deception.

Q.B. See Queen's Bench.

Qua, *prep.* In the character or capacity of (the treasurer qua chairperson of the finance committee).

Quack, *n.* One who practices medicine without the qualifications (a reputed quack). Phony, incompetent, pretender, impostor, shyster, peddler "con man," counterfeiter, sham. See also charlatan, cheat, fraud, wrongdoer.

Quadrant, *n.* An angular measure of ninety degrees; a quarter of a circle; one of the quarters created by two intersecting roads or streets.

Quaere, *n.* A query or doubt. See question.

Quagmire, *n.* See morass, confusion, disorder, commotion, dilemma, mystery, conundrum, plight, complication, emergency.

Quaint, *adj.* See intriguing, attractive, peculiar, original, ancient, old, obsolete.

Quake, *v.* See beat (3).

Qualification, *n.* **1.** Quality or circumstance that is legally or inherently necessary to perform a function (qualification for office). Standard, requisite, prerequisite, ability, fitness, capacity, eligibility, suitability, skill, contacts, competence, readiness, adequacy, preparedness, aptitude, intelligence, insight, knowledge, proficiency. See also requirement. **2.** Restriction (accepted without qualification). Modification, exception, alteration, reservation, exemption, boundary, change, confinement, stipulation, exception. See also proviso, condition.

Qualified, *adj.* **1.** Eligible; possessing legal power or capacity (qualified voter). Entitled, capable, adapted, competent, worthy, suitable, fit, efficient, prepared, ready, knowledgeable, acceptable, sufficient, trained, equipped, adept, skillful, experienced, proficient, licensed, suited, certified, accomplished, authorized, versed, fitted, susceptible. See also learned, literary (2), cultivated, able, apt (3), expert (2). **2.** Restricted or imperfect (qualified right to enter). Confined, temporary, modified, conditioned, limited, provisional, guarded, delimited, equivocal, ambiguous, reserved, narrowed, dependent, defined. See also contingent, indefinite, doubtful, disputable. *Ant.* Unqualified; absolute.

Qualified indorsement An indorsement that restrains, limits, qualifies, or enlarges the liability of the indorser. See indorsement.

Qualified pension plan An employer-sponsored plan that meets the requirements of the Internal Revenue Code. The employer can deduct the contributions in the year made, and the employee is not taxed on these contributions until they are distributed. See pension.

Qualified privilege Conditional privilege; a privilege that can prevent tort liability so long as there was no actual malice. See privilege, liability, tort.

Qualify, *v.* **1.** To make oneself fit or prepared (qualify for the job). Train, license, prepare, comply with the standards, capacitate, empower, fit, legitimate, sanction, take the necessary steps, supply, coach, entitle, authorize, suit. See also certify, adapt, enable. **2.** To limit or restrict (she qualified her answer). Modify, moderate, narrow, diminish, confine, reduce, modulate, condition, accommodate, characterize, adjust, alter, temper, lessen, circumscribe, abate, assuage. See also

Qualify

define, limit (1). *Ant.* Disable; enlarge.

Qualifying, *adj.* See extenuating; qualify, qualification.

Quality, *n.* **1.** A character or nature of something; that which describes (the qualities of the drug). Trait, feature, component, peculiarity, eccentricity, idiosyncrasy, faculty, tendency, complexion, constitution, caliber, endowment, capacity, capability, proneness, singularity, mark, grade. See also property, character, essence, attribute (2). **2.** Excellence (a product of quality). Superiority, status, wonder, distinction, virtue, pre-eminence, standing, worth, nobility, competency, backbone, skill, potency, might, dignity, greatness. See also merit, quality (2), ability, perfection, eminence.

Qualm, *n.* See doubt (2), question, reservation (3), cloud (2), confusion (2), apprehension, fear.

Quandary, *n.* See dilemma, emergency, conundrum, mystery, crisis.

Quantity, *n.* See amount (1, 2), portion, extent, spread (1), measure, aggregate.

Quantum meruit "As much as he deserves." A theory of recovery on a contract implied in law in the absence of a specific contract. Valuable services are rendered or materials furnished by the plaintiff, and accepted, used, or enjoyed by the defendant under such circumstances that the plaintiff reasonably expected to be paid. The implied promise is to pay what the services or materials are reasonably worth in order to avoid unjust enrichment. See implied, implied contract, unjust enrichment.

Quarantine 1. *n.* Isolation of a person with a contagious disease; detention of a vessel coming from a place where a contagious or infectious disease is prevalent (quarantine of the afflicted patients). Sequestration, confinement, seclusion, cordon, detachment. See also segregation, separation, division. **2.** *v.* See sequester. *Ant.* Release.

Quare clausum fregit See trespass quare clausum fregit.

Quarrel, *n.* An angry dispute (she intervened in the quarrel). Altercation, clash, strife, contention, battle, exchange of recriminations, misunderstanding, squabble, feud, hassle, controversy, fracas, bickering, spat, dissension, dissidence, polemic, conflict, tumult, rupture, disturbance, donnybrook, rhubarb, vendetta, words, tiff, discord, row. See also argument, brawl, breach of the peace. *Ant.* Harmony.

Quarrelsome, *adj.* See contentious, litigious, disobedient, difficult (3), particular (2).

Quarry, *n.* See mine; game (2), animal; victim.

Quart, *n.* One-fourth of a gallon; two pints; .946 liter. See amount, portion.

Quarter, *n.* **1.** A fourth part of something (quarter of a pound). **2.** A section or region (she was seen in that quarter of the city). See zone, district. **3.** Lodging (living quarters). See home (1).

Quash, *v.* To vacate or overthrow (quash the indictment). Abate, void, annul, stop, stay, suppress, abolish, repress, invalidate, reverse, strike out, dissolve, exterminate, quell, subdue, terminate, dismiss, discard, extinguish, erase, countermand, overrule, abrogate, repudiate, withdraw, eradicate, nullify, cancel, destroy, crush, nolle prosequi, extirpate, repeal, defeat, delete, expunge. See also rescind. *Ant.* Sanction.

Quasi, *adj.* Somewhat the same, but different (quasi judicial officer). Apparent, semi, near, part, similar, seeming, almost, resembling, as if, pseudo, nominal. See also analogous, about.

Quasi contract An obligation created by the law to avoid unjust enrichment in the absence of an agreement between the parties. See contract, implied contract, unjust enrichment.

Quasi estoppel A party should be precluded from asserting, to another's disadvantage, a right or claim that is inconsistent with a position previously taken by the party. See estoppel.

Quasi in rem A court's power to reach a person's interest in property within the jurisdiction of the court. This is different from the court's power over the person of the defendant (in personam) or over the property or thing itself (in rem).

Quay, *n.* See dock, landing, harbor.

Queen, *n.* See sovereign (2), king, manager, tyrant; woman.

Queen's Bench (Q.B.) A high English common-law court during the reign of a queen.

Queer, *adj.* See odd, anomalous, peculiar, irregular, exceptional; gay.

Quell, *v.* See quash, restrain, inhibit, quiet, destroy, defeat; mitigate, assuage.

Quench, *v.* See satisfy; mitigate, assuage; quash, destroy, annul.

Querlous, *adj.* Habitually complaining; apt to find fault (querulous spouse). Fretful, whining, testy, carping, hypercritical, obstinate, irascible, hypersensitive, faultfinding, irritable, disparaging, petulant, censorious, dissatisfied, lamenting, disputatious, impatient, cross, hostile, antagonistic. See also contentious, litigious, difficult (3), particular (2). *Ant.* Docile.

Query, *v., n.* See ask, cross-examine; audit, search (1), investigate; question.

Quest, *n.* See endeavor (2), adventure, campaign, search.

Question 1. *n.* An interrogation put to a witness (she refused to answer the question). Query, probe, inquiry, examination, quiz, request, inquisition, scrutiny, inspection. **2.** *n.* The subject of a debate or inquiry (the question before the committee). Issue, topic, theme, problem, proposition, case, thesis, proposal, motion, hypothesis, matter, agenda, query, poser, puzzle, mystery. **3.** *n.* Doubt or controversy (there was some question about his qualifications). Uncertainty, contention, trouble, concern, qualm, misgiving, dispute, confusion, disbelief, objection, suspicion, hesitation, opposition, challenge, criticism, disapproval, protest, grievance, dissatisfaction, disagreement. **4.** *v.* See ask, cross-examine.

Questionable, *adj.* See debatable, disputable, doubtful, hypothetical, contingent, indefinite, ambiguous, suspicious; immoral, suggestive.

Question of fact See issue of fact.

Question of law See issue of law.

Queue, *n.* See chain (1).

Quia emptores A 1290 English statute that had the effect of facilitating the alienation of fee-simple estates; it ended subinfeudation, a process of carving out smaller estates by tenants ad infinitum.

Quibble, *v.* To pose a petty objection (they quibbled over the shape of the conference table). Carp, bicker, nitpick, split hairs, haggle, equivocate, doubletalk, dodge, shuffle, prevaricate, argue, spar, fence, cavil, trifle, exchange sophistries, raise specious arguments. See also complain (2), hedge.

Quick, *adj.* **1.** Readily convertible into cash (quick assets). See liquid. **2.** Capable of moving within the mother's womb; capable of surviving the trauma of birth (quick child). See alive (1), viable. **3.** Speedy (quick response). See prompt (1), expeditious, summary.

Quicken, *v.* See accelerate, expedite, precipitate (1), facilitate, raise (1).

Quickening, *n.* The first motion of the fetus in the womb felt by the mother, usually occurring about the middle of the term of pregnancy.

Quick-tempered, *adj.* See feverish, hot (2), querulous, litigious, contentious, excitable, inflexible, crabby, difficult (3).

Quick with child Having conceived. See birth, pregnant.

Quick-witted, *adj.* See active (3), alive (2), brilliant, learned.

Quiddity, *n.* See essence.

Quid pro quo, *n.* Something for something; giving one valuable thing for another (membership on the committee was the quid pro quo for the contribution).

Consideration, reciprocity, barter, interchange, trading; retaliation. See also exchange (2), offset (1).

Quiescent, *adj.* See dormant, silent (2), latent.

Quiet 1. *adj.* Free from interference (quiet enjoyment). Unmolested, undisturbed, untroubled, pacific, without disturbance, tranquil, peaceful, restful, without fear of litigation. **2.** *adj.* Reserved (quiet witness). Conservative, inconspicuous, undemonstrative, reticent, unobtrusive, dispassionate, inarticulate, shy, still, serene, tranquil, cool, impassive, gentle, collected, imperturbable, self-possessed, low-key, subdued, docile, steady, meet, stoical, patient, moderate, even-tempered, sedate, collected, humble. See also passive, bashful, silent (1). **3.** *v.* To still or pacify (quiet the crowd). Still, appease, silence, soothe, calm, temper, lull, muffle, tranquilize, palliate, curb, compose, arrest. See also mitigate. **4.** *v.* To render secure or unassailable (action to quiet title). Remove a cloud, resolve, litigate, strengthen, solidify, perfect, forestall, settle, finalize, remove doubt. *Ant.* Insecure; ostentatious; aggravate; challenge.

Quiet title action See action to quiet title.

Quietus, *n.* **1.** A final discharge or acquittance from a debt or obligation; that which silences claims. See discharge (1). **2.** Demise. See death.

Quintessence, *n.* See essence, gist.

Quirk, *n.* See eccentricity, exception, caprice, accident.

Quit, *v.* **1.** To surrender possession (quit the premises). Leave, retreat, abandon, evacuate, withdraw, flee, depart, forsake, yield, exit, emigrate; resign, disavow, abdicate. **2.** To stop (quit smoking). Discontinue, cease, forgo, halt, break off, desist, intermit, suspend. *Ant.* Enter; commence.

Quitclaim deed A deed of conveyance that passes any title, interest, or claim that the grantor may have without any assurance or warranty that the title is valid.

Quite, *adv.* See entirely; exclusively, absolutely.

Quiver, *v.* See beat (3).

Quixotic, *adj.* See impracticable, absurd, reckless, wild.

Quiz, *v.* See ask, cross-examine, audit, investigate.

Quizzical, *adj.* See odd, peculiar, irregular; mysterious; mock.

Quorum, *n.* The number of members who must be present in a deliberative body before business may be transacted (adjourned for want of a quorum). Quota, sufficient number. See also minimum.

Quota, *n.* An assigned goal; a proportional part (racial quota). Percentage, share, allocation, proportion, allotment, ration, parcel, limiting number, minimum acceptable, assignment, distribution, measure, quantity, cut, quotient. See also apportionment.

Quotation, *n.* **1.** A word-for-word reproduction from another source (quotation of the statute). Quote, repetition, restatement, excerpt, reference, report, selection. See also extract. **2.** A statement of price (upon hearing the quotation, he made the purchase). Quoted price, market price. See also bid, cost.

Quote, *n.,* *v.* See quotation (1), extract; cite (3); paraphrase.

Quotient verdict A verdict resulting from an agreement as follows: each juror writes down an amount for damages; all the amounts are then added together, and divided by the number of jurors. See verdict, agreement, damages.

Quo warranto A remedy to challenge the continued exercise of unlawful authority; a remedy brought by or on behalf of the state against a usurpation of public office.

Rabbi, *n.* See minister, clergy; church, religion.

Rabble, *n.* See mob, gang, people, outcast.

Rabid, *adj.* See extreme, ardent, emotional, wild, hysterical, hot.

Race 1. *n.* A major division of mankind, having in common certain physical peculiarities constituting a comprehensive class appearing to be derived from a distinct primitive source (pride in her race). Stock, breed, tribe, ancestry, stirps, parentage, ethnic stock, strain, clan, generation, people, nation, lineage, kin. See also genealogy, family. **2.** *n.* Contest (presidential race). Campaign, competition, run, chase, trial. **3.** *v.* To move rapidly in a contest of speed (race to the recorder's office). Dash, scramble, run, bolt, dart, compete, hurry, accelerate, hustle, rush, fly, pursue, gallop.

Race-notice recording statute A state law that provides that an unrecorded conveyance is invalid as against a subsequent purchaser for value who records without knowledge of the prior unrecorded instrument. The first to record in the chain of title without notice of a prior unrecorded deed or mortgage has superior rights.

Race recording statute A state law that provides that the party who records an instrument of conveyance has the better claim regardless of notice of prior unrecorded instruments. The first to record regardless of notice of an unrecorded deed or mortgage earlier in time has superior rights.

Racism, *n.* See segregation, injustice, bias, prejudice.

Racist, *adj.* See narrow (2), fanatic.

Rack, *n.* **1.** A frame. Lattice, scaffold, skeleton, trestle, grate. **2.** See pain.

Racket, *n.* **1.** An ongoing illegal operation to make money (gambling racket). Scheme, conspiracy, fraud, game, illegitimate enterprise, underworld, organized crime, embezzlement, illicit business. **2.** Loud noise (the racket created a nuisance). Commotion, clatter, din, rattle, fracas, clamor, disturbance, shouting, pandemonium, turbulence, babel. See also noise. *Ant.* Tranquillity (2).

Racketeer, *n.* A person participating in illegal money-making operations; someone violating the racketeering laws (conviction of the racketeer). Gangster, criminal, mobster, swindler, pirate, outlaw, offender, underworld figure, extortionist, bandit, miscreant, felon, blackmailer, forger, malefactor. See also wrongdoer.

Racketeering, *n.* An organized conspiracy to commit the crimes of extortion or coercion; activities of organized criminals who extort money from legitimate businesses by violence or other forms of threats; organized illegal enterprises such as gambling, narcotics traffic, or prostitution. See crime, extort, extortion.

Racy, *adj.* See suggestive, obscene, immoral; alive.

Radiance, *n.* See light; happiness.

Radiant, *adj.* See clear (3); happy, friendly, convivial, attractive, optimistic, positive; light.

Radiate, *v.* See emit, distribute, spread.

Radical, *n., adj.* See fanatic, nonconformist, partisan, insurgent; fundamental, essential, organic (1), intrinsic, comprehensive; extreme.

Radio, *v.*, *n.* See emit, communicate, publish, circulate; press (1).

Radius, *n.* See range (2), scope, area, zone.

Raffish, *adj.* See base (1, 2), gross (1), rude, common (3), gaudy; obscene, immoral.

Raffle, *n.* A kind of lottery in which each participant buys a ticket for an article put up as a prize, with the winner being determined by a random drawing. Sweepstakes, drawing. See also lottery, gambling.

Raft, *n.* See lot, mass.

Ragamuffin, *n.* See delinquent (3), juvenile (1), orphan, derelict, tramp, wrongdoer.

Rage 1. *v.* To be very angry. Boil, foam, rave, explode, fume, bristle, tremble, rant, simmer, blow up, stew, fulminate, seethe, go berserk, have a fit, storm, bluster, madden, chafe. **2.** *n.* See wrath, annoyance, passion, animus (2).

Ragged, *adj.* Torn, shabby. Untidy, frayed, tattered, jagged, seedy, worn, shredded, tacky. See also disheveled; dirty; exhausted, anemic; gaudy.

Raid, *v.* See attack, assault, plunder, rape (2).

Rail, *v.*, *n.* See decry, castigate; banister, fence.

Railing, *n.* See fence; banister; wall.

"Railroad," *v.* To force through over the objection of a minority (the bill was railroaded through the Senate). Push, accelerate, speed, hasten, shove, press.

Rain, *v.*, *n.* See inundate; climate, storm; water.

Rain check, *n.* See assurance; delay; receipt (1).

Raise, *v.* **1.** To bring about or produce (the pleadings raise the damage issue). Activate, prompt, launch, occasion, introduce, bring into question, stir up, provoke, stimulate, animate, quicken, incite, energize, kindle, revive, breed, create, arouse, present, engender, cause, cultivate, rear, develop, nurture. **2.** To intensify or elevate (raise her voice). Increase, uplift, heighten, animate, amplify, advance, strengthen, promote, extend, add to, magnify, enlarge, inflate, accelerate, augment, escalate, double, erect, jack up. See also lift (2). **3.** To gather together (raise revenue). Collect, muster, procure, accumulate, assemble, convene, amass, mobilize. *Ant.* Withdraw; reduce; disperse.

Raised check A negotiable instrument payable on demand, with a face amount that has been increased without authorization. See fraud.

Raison d'être, *n.* See reason (1), destination (1), design (2), end (1), cause.

Rake, *v.* See accumulate; trace, ferret, investigate.

Rake-off, *n.* An illegal payoff or bribe; a skimming of profits; a share of profits demanded, paid, or otherwise illegally taken. See bribe, corruption.

Rally, *v.*, *n.* See raise (3), muster, marshal (2), organize, group (2); revive; meeting, assembly.

Ram, *v.* See batter, beat, assault, attack.

Ramble, *v.* See wander, digress, stray, depart, deviate.

Rambling, *adj.* See circuitous, diffuse, itinerant, migratory; irregular, nonconforming, deviant (1).

Rambunctious, *adj.* See excitable, disobedient, inflexible, hot, prodigal, juvenile, feverish.

Ramification, *n.* See import (2), importance, consequence, effect (1).

Ramp, *n.* See grade (2).

Rampage, *n.* See commotion, eruption, violence, disturbance, fit, storm, plunder.

Rampant, *adj.* See wild, epidemic, flagrant, comprehensive, excess, offensive, extreme.

Ranch, *n.* See home, farm.

Rancid, *adj.* See foul (1), dirty, rotten.

Rancor, *n.* See malice, hostility, animus (2).

Random, *adj.* See casual, fortuitous, irregular, accidental, capricious, blind (1).

Range, *n.* **1.** A tract of land within which a large number of domestic animals graze (trespassing on his range). Meadowland, field, pasture. **2.** The extent or limit of something (range of ability). Boundary, compass, area, reach, scale, margin, sphere, power, distance, line, latitude, gamut, domain, purview, radius. See also scope, measure (1), extent.

Ranger, *n.* See keeper, warden; police; sailor.

Rank 1. *n.* Position in society or in an organization (rank of service). Status, class, place, dignity, standing, step, order, station, echelon, level, rung, caste, division, grade, notch, stage, interval, gradation, degree, tier, eminence, branch. **2.** *adj.* Too large in amount (rank with weeds). Excessive, profuse, overgrown, overabundant, wild, luxuriant, prolific. **3.** *adj.* Complete (rank injustice). Absolute, sheer, glaring, utter, downright, unmitigated, flagrant, gross, crass, atrocious, bald, blatant. **4.** *v.* See appraise, assess, judge (3), itemize, classify. **5.** *adj.* See rotten, foul.

Rank and file, *n.* See people, constituency, citizen, country (1), nation, member (1).

Rankle, *v.* See harass, outrage (2), disturb.

Ransack, *v.* See plunder; investigate, ferret, trace.

Ransom 1. *n.* The release of illegally detained persons or property for money; the money, price, or consideration paid or demanded for the return of a kidnapped person. Liberation, redemption, emancipation, discharge, rescue, deliverance, delivery, freedom, liberty; payoff, cost, payment. **2.** *v.* See save (1).

Rant, *v.* See babble, communicate; rage.

Rap, *v.* See batter, attack, assault; communicate; censure, defame.

Rapacious, *adj.* See avaricious; predatory; plunder, piracy.

Rape, *v.* **1.** To have sexual intercourse with a person without consent (a charge of rape). Molest, sexually assault, violate, debauch, force, attack, defile, deflower, ravish. See also abuse, seduce, corrupt. **2.** To plunder (rape the treasury). Raid, sack, loot, ravage, devastate, desecrate, maltreat.

Rapid, *adj.* See summary, prompt, expeditious, immediate.

Rapine, *n.* Feloniously taking another's personal property by violence. See plunder (3).

Rapport, *n.* See harmony, accord, affinity, agreement, cooperation, concord, community (3), goodwill (2).

Rapprochement, *n.* See reconciliation; rapport.

Rapscallion, *n.* See juvenile, delinquent (3), tramp, wrongdoer.

Rap sheet, *n.* Police arrest record. See record (2), report (1), crime.

Rapture, *n.* See happiness, heaven, passion, emotion, spirit (2).

Rare, *adj.* See seldom, intermittent, periodic; great (2), outstanding (2), extraordinary, exclusive; raw (2).

Rarefied, *adj.* See elevated; isolated.

Rarity, *n.* See novelty, marvel, mystery.

Rascal, *n.* See juvenile, delinquent, orphan, derelict, tramp, wrongdoer.

Rash, *adj.* See reckless, careless, impetuous, excitable, wild.

"Rat", *n.* See wrongdoer.

Ratable, *adj.* According to a measure with fixed proportions; proportional; capable of being rated or assessed; taxable (ratable property). See proportionate; tax.

Rate 1. *n.* Proportional or relative value, measure, or degree; the standard by which something is adjusted (rate of interest). Classification, worth, position, status, pace, gradation, velocity, station, rank, rating. **2.** *n.* Cost (rental rates). Payment, tariff, price, fare, tax, toll, quotation, rent, assessment. See also cost. **3.** *v.* To estimate value (rate the options). Rank, weigh, appraise, evaluate, gauge, compute, price, quantify, classify, grade, consider, regard, count, figure, arrange, sort, prioritize, label. See also assess, judge.

Rate base The fair value of a utility's property upon which a reasonable return is allowed. See worth.

Rate of exchange, *n.* The price at which the money of one country may be exchanged for the money of another; the price at which a bill drawn in one country upon another country can be bought or obtained in the former country. See money, currency, exchange.

Rate of return, *n.* The annual percentage of return on an investment. See yield.

Ratification, *n.* The confirmation of a prior act, with the effect of becoming bound by it (the ratification of her agent's transaction). Endorsement, acceptance, adoption, assent, certification, sanction, vindication, approval, approbation, imprimatur, validation, consent, acknowledgment, admission, authorization, corroboration. *Ant.* Repudiation.

Ratify, *v.* To make valid (he ratified her contract). Sanction, approve, consent, assent, authorize, endorse, embrace, subscribe, support, underwrite, acquiesce, verify, validate, substantiate, warrant, vindicate, attest, establish, corroborate, authenticate, agree, uphold, make good, concur, recognize, countersign. See also confirm (2), guarantee (2), insure, certify. *Ant.* Repudiate.

Rating, *n.* See rate (1), credit rating, classification.

Ratio, *n.* Proportion; the number resulting when one number is divided by another (the ratio of profits to employees). Relationship, fraction, interrelationship, apportionment, calculation, connection, extent, balance. See also rate, correlation, correspondence.

Ratio decidendi The ground, reason, or principle that is the basis of the decision; the dispositive point.

Ration, *n.*, *v.* See portion, allotment; allot.

Rational, *adj.* Based upon reason (a rational formula). Sensible, logical, sound, intelligent, reasonable, enlightened, balanced, well-grounded, sane, discerning, understanding, proper, practical, commonsensical, deductive, realistic, sober, analytical, self-composed, levelheaded, consistent, cognitive, discreet, lucid, plausible, perceptive, pragmatic, credible, fit, thoughtful, responsible, justifiable, sage, well-founded, clear-headed, self-possessed, circumspect, composed, dispassionate, moderate, cool, forceful, justified, legitimate, rightful, potent, competent, accurate, factual, scientific, strong, acknowledged, tested, efficacious, unexaggerated, persuasive, weighty, authentic, advisable. See also objective, judicious, feasible, practicable. *Ant.* Irrational.

Rationale, *n.* See reason (1), cause, basis (1).

Rationalization, *n.* See excuse (1), justification, defense.

Rationalize, *v.* See vindicate, excuse (2), justify.

Rattle, *n.*, *v.* See noise, racket; babble, confuse.

Raucous, *adj.* See disorderly, wild; noisy; noise, racket.

"Raunchy," *adj.* See vulgar, gaudy; obscene, filthy, dirty.

Ravage, *v.* See defile, rape, plunder.

Rave, *n.*, *v.* See tribute, indorsement (2); rage; promote; babble.

Ravenous, *adj.* See prodigal, avaricious, predatory.

Ravine, *n.* A long, deep, and narrow hollow worn by a stream or torrent of water; a long, deep pass through the mountains. Chasm, canyon, gulf, crevasse, gullet, valley, cleft.

Ravish, *v.* To have carnal knowledge of a woman by force. See rape, abuse, seize, outrage.

Ravishing, *adj.* See attractive, beautiful, outstanding, compelling, enjoyable; entice, seduce.

Raw, *adj.* **1.** Inexperienced (raw troops). Undisciplined, immature, green, new, unskilled, unsettled, naive, untrained, unprepared, crude, amateur, untested, ignorant, unsophisticated, unschooled, awkward, youthful, backwoods, clumsy. See also incompetent, maiden (1), novel, backward (1), innocent (2), illiterate. **2.** Unprocessed (raw meat). Unprepared, unbaked, uncooked, rare, unrefined, unembellished, plain, bare, exposed, bold, candid, frank, brusque, coarse, straightforward, straight, unadulterated, undiluted. See also naked (2), genuine, clean (2), honest, natural (5). *Ant.* Skilled; prepared.

Raw land Unimproved land.

Raw materials Goods (e.g., wood, steel) used in the manufacture of a product. See material (3).

Raze, *v.* To tear down or erase. See demolish, erase.

Razor, *n.* See weapon.

Re, *prep.* See concerning, in re.

Reach, *v., n.* See enter (2), approach (1), realize (2), appear (2); extend; contact (3); extent, range (2).

React *v.* See answer (5), acknowledge, rebut; act (5).

Reaction, *n.* See reply, acknowledgment, rebuttal; consequence (1), act (3); change; reversal, backfire, offset.

Reactionary, *adj.* Regressive. Conservative, ultraconservative, tory, diehard, right-wing, rigid.

Reactivation, *n.* See restoration.

Read, *v.* See comprehend, interpret, construe.

Readable, *adj.* See comprehensible, clear, precise.

Reading, *n.* See construction (1), definition.

Readjust, *v.* See adjust.

Readjustment, *n.* A voluntary readjustment of a corporation in financial trouble by the shareholders themselves, without outside intervention. See adjustment.

Ready 1. *adj.* Prepared (ready to proceed). Equipped, supplied, fit, available, waiting, primed, groomed, mobilized, set, in condition, eager, alert, prone, armed, in shape, arranged, placed, accessible, standing by, inclined, disposed, predisposed, willing, anxious, convenient, serviceable, punctual, present, mature, likely, on the verge of, apt, zealous, keen, on tap, in readiness. **2.** *v.* To prepare (the courtroom was readied for the trial). Place in order, equip, organize, arrange, complete, develop.

Reaffirm, *v.* See affirm.

Real, *adj.* **1.** Pertaining to land. See real estate. **2.** Authentic or genuine (real concern). Bona fide, certified, factual, valid, sincere, verifiable, actual, veracious, solid, honest, substantive, realistic, physical, natural, dependable, legitimate, unfeigned, conformed, truthful, objective, demonstrable, authorized, complete, unadulterated, positive, well-grounded, well-founded, intrinsic, inevitable, unquestionable, correct, licit, confirmed, perceptible, unvarnished, tangible, indisputable, existing, certain, absolute, internal. *Ant.* Personal; spurious.

Real estate, *n.* Land and anything permanently affixed to the land (deed to the real estate). Real property, fee, realty, ground, lot, earth, soil, surface, terrain, acreage, buildings, trees, minerals. *Ant.* Personalty.

Real estate broker See broker.

Real Estate Settlement Procedures Act (RESPA) A federal statute governing disclosure of settlement costs in the sale of residential (one to four-family) improved property that is to be financed by a federally insured lender.

Real evidence Evidence furnished by things themselves on view or inspection, as opposed to a description of them from the testimony of a witness. See evidence.

Realign, *v.* See adjust, adapt.

Realistic, *adj.* See reasonable, rational; natural, genuine, precise, authentic; practicable, functional, feasible.

Reality

Reality, *n.* See fact, fait accompli, veracity, validity.

Realization, *n.* See comprehension, apprehension; performance, enforcement; realize.

Realize, *v.* **1.** To convert property into money; to receive the returns from an investment (nothing was realized until the asset was sold). Enjoy, possess, reap, net, bring in, have in hand, produce, obtain, profit, clear. **2.** To achieve (realize the objective). Make real, actualize, accomplish, engineer, effectuate, fulfill, produce, succeed, carry through, perform, discharge, consummate, substantiate, implement, attain, manage, effect, complete, make good. **3.** To understand (realize the seriousness of the matter). Comprehend, apprehend, grasp, appreciate, discern, perceive, recognize, fathom, see, penetrate, discover, absorb, become cognizant of, conceive, know, seize, learn, assimilate.

Realized gain or loss The difference between the amount realized on the sale or other disposition of property and the adjusted basis of the property. See gain, loss.

Reallocate, *v.* See redistribute, allocate.

Realm, *n.* A country or province; sphere. See domain, zone.

Real party in interest The party who has the legal right under the applicable substantive law to enforce the claim in question; the one who has the right to control and receive the fruits from the litigation. See party.

Real property See real estate.

Realtor, *n.* A real estate broker or agent who is a member of the National Association of Realtors. See broker, agent.

Realty, *n.* See real estate.

Reap, *v.* See receive (1), acquire, realize; yield.

Reapportion, *v.* See redistribute, apportion; reapportionment.

Reapportionment, *n.* A realignment or change in legislative districts brought about by changes in population (mandated reapportionment). Reallotment, reclassification, reorganization, redistribution, equalization, rearrangement. See also apportionment.

Rear, *adv., n., v.* See back (3, 4), after; nurture, foster.

Reargument, *n.* A rehearing in which a party seeks to show a misapprehension of the facts or that a controlling law has been overlooked. See argument(1).

Rearm, *v.* See equip, strengthen, augment.

Rearrange, *v.* See redistribute, organize, plan, settle.

Reason 1. *n.* An inducement, motive, or ground for action (the reason for the termination). Inspiration, cause, incentive, impetus, explanation, rationale, purpose, aim, design, goal, provocation, basis, source, excuse, motivation, occasion, stimulation, justification, why, pretext, objective, object, ratiocination, mover, agent, instigation, end, target, rationalization, argument, reasoning, alibi, consideration, vindication, theory, intention, genesis, raison d'être, principle, apologia, foundation. **2.** *n.* The faculty of the mind that distinguishes truth from falsehood, good from evil, and which deduces inferences from facts or propositions (lost her reason). Insight, intelligence, logic, thinking, comprehension, conception, intuition, reasoning, rationality, sanity, lucidity, common sense, understanding, judgment, perception, analysis. **3.** *v.* To argue or exercise analytical powers (they were no longer able to reason with him). Discuss, deliberate, think, debate, confer, talk over, exchange views, advise, explain, weigh, theorize, persuade, convince, think or follow through, speculate, cogitate, analyze, deduce.

Reasonable, *adj.* Suitable under the circumstances; rational (reasonable precautions). Fair, moderate, fit, just, honest, equitable, logical, realistic, temperate, justifiable, wise, judicious, right, practical, sensible, perceptive, pragmatic, evenhanded, clear-headed, discriminating, plausible, sound, intelligent, even, credible, sane, understanding, objective, tolerable, sober, considered, legitimate, modest, reasoned, valid, aboveboard, manageable, proper, believable, prudent, diligent, careful, foresighted, viable, conscientious, attentive; common sense. *Ant.* Unreasonable.

Reasonable belief See probable cause.

Reasonable care That degree of care which a person of ordinary prudence would exercise in the same or similar circumstances; due care under the circumstances. See care, due care, due diligence.

Reasonable cause for an arrest Such a state of facts as would lead a person of ordinary care and prudence to believe and conscientiously entertain an honest and strong suspicion that the person is guilty of a crime. See crime, evidence.

Reasonable certainty Reasonable probability; facts that take the issue out of the arena of speculation; evidence that lays some foundation enabling the fact-finder to make a fair and reasonable estimate. See evidence, probability, speculation, speculative.

Reasonable doubt Doubt that would cause prudent people to hesitate before acting in matters of importance to themselves; doubt based on reason arising from evidence or the lack of evidence. See evidence, doubt.

Reasonable force That degree of force which is not excessive and is appropriate in protecting oneself or one's property. See force, excess, defense, property.

Reasonable grounds See probable cause, ground.

Reasonable man (person) A fictitious person of ordinary prudence under the circumstances. See reasonable care.

Reasoning, *n.* See reason (2), deduction (2); faculties; logical, analytic; contemplation.

Reassign, *v.* See redistribute, assign.

Reassurance, *n.* See assurance, commitment (2).

Rebate, *v.* To deduct or return money for stated reasons, e.g., prompt payment (the manufacturer will rebate shipping costs). Discount, refund, take off, decrease, mark down, "kick back," subtract, reimburse, cut, strike, reduce.

Rebel, *v.,* **rebel,** *n.* See challenge (1), resist, confront; fanatic, nonconformist, partisan (1); insurgent, revolutionary; nihilist.

Rebellion, *n.* Organized resistance, by force and arms, to the laws or operations of the government, committed by a subject (tax rebellion). Uprising, strike, insurrection, subversion, revolution, insurgency, upheaval, revolt, rising, coup d'état, noncompliance, disobedience, riot, sedition, treason, incitement, agitation, fomentation, insurgence, civil disorder, disloyalty, desertion, lawlessness, treachery, mutiny. See also insubordination, defiance, apostasy. *Ant.* Submission.

Rebellious, *adj.* See mutinous, insurgent (2), disobedient, contentious, litigious, difficult (3), wild, hostile, contumacious, nonconforming.

Rebirth, *n.* See rehabilitation, restoration, betterment, amelioration, increase.

Rebound, *v.* See recover, strengthen, build, augment, improve; ricochet.

Rebuff, *v.* See rebut, challenge (1), resist, confront, avoid; rebuke.

Rebuild, *v.* See recover, build, strengthen, augment, improve.

Rebuke, *v., n.* See reprimand, castigate, rebut, censure, discredit, disparage; correction.

Rebut, *v.* To refute or take away the effect of something (rebut the presumption). Contravene, rebuff, defeat, retaliate, deny, oppose, negative, contradict, respond, discredit, retort, overthrow, disprove, negate, counterclaim, refute, overturn, parry, counter, confute. See also answer (5). *Ant.* Substantiate.

Rebuttable presumption A presumption that holds good until evidence to the contrary is introduced; a presumption that can be overcome. See presumption,

Rebuttable presumption

evidence.

Rebuttal, *n.* A refutation (a weak rebuttal). Retort, retaliation, contradiction, disproof, negation, counterargument, denial, invalidation, upset, overthrow. See also answer. *Ant.* Confirmation.

Rebuttal evidence Evidence given to explain, counteract, or disprove facts given in evidence by the other side. See evidence, counteract.

Recalcitrant, *adj.* See inflexible, arbitrary, incorrigible, disobedient, difficult (3), particular (2), querulous, litigious, contentious, hostile.

Recall 1. *n.* A method of removing a public official from office before the end of his or her term, by a vote of the people (petition for recall). Repudiation, rescission, revocation, withdrawal, cancellation, dismissal, reconsideration, disqualification, veto, reversal. **2.** *v.* To summon back (recall the ambassador). Withdraw, remove, take back, return. **3.** *v.* To bring back to mind (the witness could not recall). Remember, retrace, recollect, recognize, revive, recapture, reminisce, restate, recreate, place, evoke. See also review, retain (2). *Ant.* Reinstatement; install; forget.

Recant, *v.* To withdraw and repudiate something formally and publicly (recant the testimony). See abjure, disaffirm.

Recap, *n.,* **recap,** *v.* See brief (2); paraphrase.

Recapitalization, *n.* An arrangement whereby stock, bonds, or other securities of a corporation are adjusted as to type, amount, income, or priority; reshuffling an existing corporation's capital structure.

Recapitulate, *v.* See review, paraphrase, repeat; abstract (3), brief (2).

Recapture, *v.* To recover or retake (they recaptured the vessel). Restore, regain, repossess, liberate, retrieve, rescue, reseize, countermand. See also reclaim, redeem, recall.

Recede, *v.* See disappear, withdraw (1), diminish.

Receipt, *n.* **1.** Written acknowledgment of having received something (receipt for the purchase). Admission of receipt, acknowledgment of payment, memo, slip, acquittance, release, stub, proof of purchase, sales slip, voucher, copy, stamp, ticket, discharge. See also certificate. **2.** Taking physical possession (receipt of goods). Reception, acceptance, custody, acquisition, arrival.

Receivable, *adj.* Awaiting collection whether or not it is currently due; pertaining to that which is due and owing a person (account receivable). See outstanding (1).

Receive, *v.* **1.** To accept into possession and control (receive the order). Obtain, accept, collect, acquire, get, realize, inherit, pocket, gross, reap, secure, net, derive, gain, seize, catch, win, assume. **2.** To obtain information about (receive the good news). Be informed, find out, hear about, comprehend, understand, learn. **3.** To allow entrance (receive into evidence). Tolerate, permit in, embrace, accept, admit, welcome, usher in, endure, suffer, absorb. *Ant.* Release; communicate; block.

Receiver, *n.* A person appointed by the court to manage property in litigation or the affairs of a bankrupt (the receiver of the company authorized the payment). Trustee, supervisor, depositary, recipient, overseer, superintendent, collector, holder; beneficiary, donee, fence. See also manager, guardian.

Receiver of stolen property A person who receives property, knowing that it has been stolen or otherwise unlawfully taken. See wrongdoer.

Receivership, *n.* The condition of a company or individual over whom a receiver has been appointed for the protection of its assets and for ultimate sale and distribution to creditors.

Recent, *adj.* See new, current, novel, present (3).

Receptacle, *n.* See vessel (2).

634

Reception, *n.* See acceptance; entertain.

Receptive, *adj.* See open (6), flexible, accessible, friendly.

Recess, *n.* An interval during which a body suspends business but usually without adjourning (the court announced a recess). Pause, break, interruption, withdrawal, cessation, stoppage, postponement, intermission, vacation, lull, respite, breather, halt, rest, hiatus, time-out. *Ant.* Continuation.

Recession, *n.* **1.** The act of ceding or falling back. See withdrawal. **2.** A slowdown or temporary setback in economic growth, less serious than a depression.

Recidivate, *v.* See revert, regress, lapse, return.

Recidivist, *n.* A habitual criminal (obtaining parole was difficult for the recidivist). Repeat criminal, incorrigible criminal, hardened criminal. See also offender, wrongdoer.

Recipe, *n.* See formula (1), method, means.

Recipient, *n.* See beneficiary, legatee; nominee, appointee; victim.

Reciprocal, *adj.* Given or owed mutually as between two persons (reciprocal obligation). Bilateral, interrelated, interchangeable, alternate, complementary, shared, interdependent, corresponding, linked, analogous, correlative, two-sided, parallel, common, correspondent. See also mutual. *Ant.* Independent.

Reciprocal Enforcement of Support Act See Uniform Reciprocal Enforcement of Support Act (URESA).

Reciprocal laws Laws of one state that extend rights and privileges to citizens of another state if the latter grants similar rights and privileges to the citizens of the first state. See mutuality.

Reciprocal wills Wills of two or more persons in which each person makes reciprocal testamentary provisions in favor of each other. This is done either in one will, in which case the will is both joint and reciprocal or it is done by separate wills. See will, mutual wills.

Reciprocate, *v.* See exchange (1), return (3).

Reciprocity, *n.* A mutual exchange of benefits or treatment between countries, states, companies, or individuals; the granting of a privilege on condition that a comparable privilege is returned (when the California lawyer moved to Texas she had to take the Texas bar exam, since there was no reciprocity between the states). Cooperation, reciprocation, interchange, correspondence, quid pro quo. See also mutuality.

Recision, *n.* The termination of a contract upon the occurrence of a certain kind of default by the other party (she exercised her right of recision when the consideration was not paid). See cancellation.

Recital, *n.* The formal statement or setting forth of some facts (the recitals in the deed). Description, recitation, narration, summary, account, chronicle, depiction. See also report (1), record (2); performance (3).

Recite, *v.* To state facts; to quote from something. See communicate, list; repeat.

Reckless, *adj.* Consciously failing to exercise due care without intending the consequences; wantonly disregarding the consequences of one's acts or omissions (reckless driving). Impulsive, rash, abrupt, unmindful, unwary, volatile, foolhardy, irresponsible, improvident, fickle, inconsiderate, negligent, unreasonable, irrational, hasty, neglectful, thoughtless, inattentive, ill-advised, indiscreet, venturesome, desperate, hotheaded, madcap, headlong, precipitous, injudicious, silly. See also careless, wild, heedless, impetuous, precipitate, oblivious. *Ant.* Circumspect.

Reckless disregard 1. Going ahead with the publication of a matter even though the defendant entertained serious doubts as to the truth of the matter, or when there were obvious reasons to doubt the veracity of the matter. **2.** Wanton disregard; conscious indifference to the safety of others; an "I don't care"

Reckless disregard

attitude. See disregard (2), neglect (2).

Reckless driving Gross negligence in driving; a conscious and intentional driving that the driver knows, or should know, creates an unreasonable risk of harm to others even though there is no intent to harm; driving in deliberate disregard for the safety of others. See deliberate, disregard (2), neglect (2); vehicle.

Reckless homicide Death resulting from a willful and wanton disregard of the consequences of one's acts or omissions. See homicide.

Reckon, *v.* See expect (1); measure (3), calculate, rate.

Reckoning, *n.* See redress, satisfaction (1); account (2), estimate.

Reclaim, *v.* To ask for the return of something; to restore (reclaim her job). Demand back, claim back, get back, regain, retrieve, save, redeem, rescue, reinstate, reform, recycle, reoccupy, repossess. See also recapture, recover. *Ant.* Relinquish.

Reclamation, *n.* Increasing the value of land by physically changing it (e.g., draining a swamp). See restoration.

Reclassify, *v.* See redistribute, classify.

Recline, *v.* See lie (4).

Recluse, *n.* See hermit; nonconformist; ascetic.

Reclusive, *adj.* See isolated, ascetic; bashful, awkward (2), quiet (2).

Recognition, *n.* **1.** Identification or comprehension (recognition of merit). Perception, detection, attention, tribute, remembrance, awareness, finding, knowledge, understanding, acceptance, notice, recollection, discovery, citation. See also comprehension, information (2), appreciation (2). **2.** An acknowledgment or confirmation. See ratification.

Recognizance, *n.* See obligation (2), personal recognizance, release; bail.

Recognize, *v.* **1.** To identify (he recognized the accused). Remember, recollect, discern, perceive, comprehend, pick out, espy, pinpoint, detect, discover, place, know, know again, distinguish, see, spot, sight. See also recall (3), observe. **2.** To accept (recognize his responsibilities). Acknowledge, embrace, admit, confess, yield, appreciate, bow to, approve, suffer, endure, realize, defer to, warrant, respect, grant, concede, endorse, uphold, ratify, validate, own.

Recoil, *v.* See cringe; resist; ricochet.

Recollect, *v.* See recall (3), retain (2), recognize (1); recollection.

Recollection, *n.* Remembrance; the recall of something to mind (recollection of the incident). Recognition, reconstruction, consciousness, impression, calling to mind, reminiscence, mental image. See also retrospect, memory; recall (3), recognize (1). *Ant.* Oblivion.

Recommend, *v.* To advise (she recommended the settlement). Counsel, suggest, advocate, prescribe, endorse, commend, countenance, guide, propose, caution, admonish, convince, support, favor, back, prefer, put forward, order, urge, condone, enjoin, vouch for, promote, underwrite, coax, dissuade, propound, acclaim, exhort, advance, applaud, encourage, sanction, bless.

Recommendation, *n.* See counsel (2), advice, admonition, approbation.

Recommit, *v.* See return, send.

Recompense, *n.* A reward for services; remuneration for goods or other property. See compensation.

Reconcilable, *adj.* See negotiable (2), arguable, debatable; malleable.

Reconcile, *v.* See settle (1), adapt, accommodate, harmonize, negotiate, arbitrate (3); judge (2), adjudge.

Reconciliation, *n.* The voluntary resumption of full marital relations; the renewal of amicable relations between persons who had been at odds; a statement showing the consistency of financial documents (the divorce proceedings were dismissed following the reconciliation). Restoration, conciliation, arrangement, rapprochement, adjustment, compromise, reunion, accommodation, mediation, appease-ment, peacemaking, correction, understanding, arbitration, concordat, release, ordering, working out, stabilization, normalization, ratification, propitiation, for-giveness, modification, conformity, rapport, negotiation, resolution, détente. See also harmony, pact, contract, agreement. *Ant.* Enmity.

Recondite, *adj.* See mysterious, complex (1), abstract, ambiguous.

Recondition, *v.* See fix (3), repair (1), correct, cure, improve; rehabilitation.

Reconfirm, *v.* See confirm.

Reconnaissance, *n.* See inspection, examination, inquiry; eavesdrop.

Reconsider, *v.* See review, recall (3), consider; retrospect.

Reconstruct, *v.* **1.** To recreate in the mind (the witness attempted to reconstruct the facts of the accident). Remember, recollect, review. See also recall, recog-nize; memory. **2.** To form again; to restore as an entity (reconstruct the building). Rebuild, revamp, duplicate, reassemble, reformulate, rehabilitate, rees-tablish, remodel, recompose, reclaim, redo, modernize, reforge, redesign, recast, mend, rejuvenate, reform, refurbish.

Reconstruction expert One who recreates the events of an accident from given facts. See expert, witness.

Record, *v., **record,** n.* **1.** *v.* To make an official note of; to enter in a book (record a deed). Write down, commit to writing, print, transcribe, file, docket, register, enroll, log, mark, set down, list, inscribe, note, copy, post, tape, calendar, chronicle, slate, line up, program, schedule, document, book, insert, tabulate. **2.** *n.* A written account of some act or event (court records). Register, roll, entry, history, account, journal, recording, certificate, diary, instrument, memorandum, list, dossier, transcript, annals, sheet, invoice, roster, calender, archive, program, directory, tablet, table, document, documentation, almanac, file, inventory, sched-ule, ledger, index, muster, directory, atlas, census, enumeration, tabulation, tally, slate, agenda, ticket, registry, affidavit, proceedings, scrapbook, minutes, cata-logue. **3.** *n.* The available facts (employment record). Experiences, occurrences, happenings, events, career, performance, résumé, background, achievements, con-duct, adventures, reputation.

Recorder, *n.* **1.** An officer appointed to record documents (Recorder of Deeds). Archivist, registrar, secretary, stenographer, historian, administrator, scribe, clerk. See also accountant. **2.** A magistrate with limited jurisdiction in some states.

Recording statutes Statutes that govern the manner of recording documents (e.g., deeds, mortgages) and the effect of such recording on creditors, subsequent purchasers, etc. See race recording statute, race-notice recording statute, notice recording statute.

Record notice When an instrument of conveyance or a mortgage is recorded in the appropriate public office, it is constructive notice of its contents to the whole world. See notice, constructive notice.

Recoup, *v.* **1.** To replace or make up for (recoup one's losses). Regain, restore, redeem, compensate, repay, make good, recapture, indemnify, correct, reimburse, refund, reclaim, reinstitute, satisfy, repossess, retrieve, fix, replevin, make amends for, reacquire, atone, win back, redress, remunerate. **2.** To set off or keep back. See deduct; deduction (1).

Recoupment, *n.* A reduction or rebate by the defendant of part of the plaintiff's claim because of a right in the defendant arising out of the same transaction; the right of the defendant to reduce or eliminate the plaintiff's demand either because the plaintiff has not complied with some cross obligation of the contract, which is the basis of the suit, or because the plaintiff has violated some duty imposed by law in making or performing that contract. See offset.

Recourse, *n.* **1.** Turning or appealing for help (recourse to the courts). Remedy, redress, measure, access, retreat, resource, device, haven, recipe, entreaty, application, solicitation, asylum, option, refuge. **2.** The right of a holder of a negotiable instrument to recover against a prior indorser or other party who is secondarily liable (the indorser was not liable for payment, since she signed "without recourse").

Recover, *v.* **1.** To obtain back (recover the property). Repossess, return, win back, collect, regain, recoup, replevin, salvage, redeem, retrieve, reacquire, revive, rescue, procure, resume, secure, retake, make good, compensate, replevy. See also reclaim, recapture, offset. **2.** To restore to a normal state (recover from the illness). Mend, revitalize, revive, recuperate, rehabilitate, resuscitate, convalesce, survive, rally, heal, recondition, regenerate. *Ant.* Lose; deteriorate.

Recovered, *adj.* See healthy, fit.

Recovery, *n.* **1.** That which is obtained by a court judgment (recovery of damages). Satisfaction, award, indemnification, restitution, redress, vindication, restoration, collection. See also indemnity. **2.** See rehabilitation; recover (2).

Recreant 1. See disloyal, corrupt (1). **2.** *n.* A coward.

Recreate, *v.* See recall (3); amuse.

Recreation, *n.* See diversion (2), amusement, hobby.

Recriminate, *v.* See accuse, blame, incriminate.

Recrimination, *n.* **1.** A charge made by an accused person against the accuser (bitter recriminations). Countercharge, counteraccusation, retort, rejoinder, reprisal, reproach, counterattack, revenge, retribution. See also retaliation. **2.** If the conduct of both husband and wife has been such as to furnish grounds for divorce, neither is entitled to relief.

Recruit, *v., n.* See conscript; enroll; induce; muster; enlistment; beginner, amateur, intern, assistant; sailor.

Rectify, *v.* To correct or define that which is erroneous or doubtful (rectify the mistake). Cure, square, adjust, reform, straighten, heal, regulate, redress, fix, better, amend, synchronize, attune, meliorate, rehabilitate, untangle, emend, revise, calibrate, improve, doctor, renovate, repair, clarify, enunciate, align. *Ant.* Aggravate.

Rectitude, *n.* See honor (3), integrity; virtue (1).

Rector, *n.* See minister, clergy; clerical; church, religion.

Rectory, *n.* The residence of a minister. See home.

Recuperate, *v.* See heal, remedy (2), correct (2), cure (2).

Recuperation, *n.* See rehabilitation.

Recur, *v.* See continue, repeat, return.

Recurrent, *adj.* See habitual, daily, chronic, constant (1).

Recusant, *n.* See nonconformist, dissenter.

Recusation, *n.* The disqualification of a judge because of prejudice or interest.

Redecorate, *v.* See repair (1), fix (3), improve.

Redeem, *v.* **1.** To recover ownership or buy back by making payment of a debt (the debtor redeemed her land just before the foreclosure sale). Recover, repurchase, repossess, retrieve, reclaim, regain, rescue, ransom, exchange, convert, replevy, replevin, liberate. **2.** To pay off (redeem a mortgage). Make good, satisfy, make amends, discharge, fulfill, abide by, adhere to, carry through, acquit, perform. *Ant.* Forfeit; incur.

Redeemable, *adj.* Subject to redemption or repurchase.

Redeemable bond A bond that the issuer may call back for payment before its maturity date. See bond.

Redemption, *n.* **1.** The realization of a right to have the title of property restored free and clear of a mortgage (or other encumbrance) once the obligation has been paid or performed; a buying back; a repurchase of notes, bonds, stock, bills, or other evidence of debt by paying their value to their holders (price of redemption). Restoration, repossession, indemnification, retrieval, reclamation, release, discharge, rescue. **2.** See emancipation, release (3), rescue.

Redemption period A time period, often provided by statute, during which a defaulted mortgage, land contract, deed of trust, etc., can be redeemed.

Redesign, *v.* See revise, repair, improve.

Redevelopment, *n.* See urban renewal.

Red herring, *n.* See pretext.

Redhibition, *n.* Avoiding a sale because of a vice or defect in the thing sold.

Redirect examination The examination of a witness by the party that conducted the direct examination of this witness, after the other side has cross-examined him or her. See cross-examine, question.

Redistribute, *v.* To reallocate (redistribute income). Reapportion, reassign, reclassify, redivide, rearrange, readminister.

Red-light district, *n.* An area containing brothels, "smut shops", etc. See zone, neighborhood, locality, prostitute, obscene.

Redlining, *n.* A pattern of discrimination in which financial institutions refuse to make mortgage loans, regardless of the credit record of an applicant, on property in specified areas because of alleged deteriorating conditions therein. See discrimination, bias.

Redo, *v.* See repeat, repair (1), fix (3), improve; organize.

Redound, *v.* See contribute, influence.

Redraft, *n.* A second note or bill drafted by the original drawer after the first draft has been dishonored and protested.

Redress 1. *n.* Satisfaction for an injury; damages or equitable relief (redress of grievances). Indemnification, amends, compensation, remedy, reparation, atonement, recompense, relief, restoration, correction, rectification, propitiation, appeasement, payment, repair, acquittal, retribution, help, assistance, cure. **2.** *v.* See correct (2), cure (2), heal.

Red tape, *n.* Excessive bureaucracy (the application process was a maze of red tape). Triviality, paperwork, rules, forms, routines, pettiness, steps, procedures, nonsense, protocol, Mickey Mouse, mumbo jumbo. See also bureaucracy.

Reduce, *v.* See diminish, condense, abridge.

Reductio ad absurdum Disproving an argument by showing that it leads to an absurd consequence. See argument (1), absurd.

Reduction, *n.* The process of making something smaller (reduction of principal). Decrease, limitation, shortening, abridgement, curtailment, deduction, abatement, withdrawing, cutback, abbreviation, condensation, shrinking, alleviation, narrowing, diminution, lessening, rollback, phaseout, depletion, retrenchment, attenuation, mitigation, tempering, compressing, weakening, minimizing, modulating, abstraction, attrition, erosion, contracting. *Ant.* Aggravation.

Reduction to practice Embodying an inventor's conception in such form as to render it capable of practical and successful use. See invention, novelty, patent.

Redundancy, *n.* Needless repetition; superfluous matter (she objected to the redundancies in the pleading). Superfluity, duplication, excess, profusion, surfeit, overabundance, reiteration, excessiveness, restatement, tautology, wordiness, verbosity, magnification, prolixity, verbiage, inflation, pleonasm, exaggeration. *Ant.* Compactness.

Redundant, *adj.* See superfluous, needless, frivolous, expendable (2), collateral (2), gratuitous (2).

"Reefer," *n.* See marijuana, drug.

Reek, *v.* See emit; foul.

Re-enact, *v.* See reconstruct, repeat, recall.

Re-enforce, *v.* See emphasize, accent.

Re-enter, *v.* See enter, return (1, 2).

Re-examine, *v.* See review, cross-examine, investigate, repeat; retrospection.

Refer, *v.* To direct, deliver, or make reference to (the case was referred to arbitration). Send, transmit, suggest, allude, transfer, connect, attribute, entrust, assign, advert, mention, consult, point, relegate, resort, invoke, indicate, credit, yield, go, turn. See also pertain.

Referee 1. *n.* A person to whom a judge refers a case, to take testimony and to file a report with the court (the referee conducted the hearing). Master, auditor, umpire, mediator, arbiter, moderator, conciliator, go-between, interceder, intervenor. **2.** *v.* See arbitrate, judge; negotiate.

Referee in bankruptcy An officer appointed by a court to exercise administrative and judicial functions in bankruptcy cases. See bankruptcy.

Reference, *n.* **1.** An indication or direction (she resented the reference to her criminal record). Mention, referral, intimation, quotation, notification, suggestion, imputation, innuendo, allusion, assignment, inkling, notation, introduction, specification, citation. **2.** A person who will provide information about the character and background of an applicant; a recommendation about an applicant's character or background (references available on request). Endorsement, voucher, commendation, statement, declaration, affirmation, testimonial, certificate, attestation, word, source, allegation, evidence. **3.** An authority relied upon in one's argument. See cite (2), authority (5).

Reference statute A statute that refers to other statutes and makes them applicable to the subject of the legislation; a statute that incorporates and adopts pre-existing statutes.

Referendum, *n.* Seeking approval from the electorate of a change in the state constitution or of a statute passed by the legislature (referendum on gun control legislation). Poll, ballot, plebiscite, mandate.

Refinance, *v.* To pay off existing debts with funds secured from new debts. See borrow (1), debt.

Refine, *v.* See clarify, define, limit (1), qualify (2); improve, advance; nurture, instruct (1).

Refined, *adj.* See cultivated, learned, civil (3).

Refinement, *n.* See dignity, delicacy, courtesy (2), character (1), worth (1).

Reflect, *v.* See deliberate (1); manifest (2), demonstrate; repeat, duplicate.

Reflection, *n.* See consideration (2), examination; imitation, copy.

Reflective, *adj.* See contemplative, preoccupied, engaged.

Reflex, *adj.* See mechanical (2), inadvertent, spontaneous.

Reform 1. *v.* To amend or correct (campaign to reform the jury system). Cure, rectify, remodel, improve, rewrite, reconstitute, reshape, renovate, rehabilitate, revise, salvage, repair, meliorate, ameliorate, enhance, better, redeem, restore, deliver, repent, elevate, cleanse, modify, reconstruct, fix, advance, develop, enrich, progress, recover. **2.** *n.* See betterment (2), amelioration, correction (2). *Ant.* Deteriorate.

Reformation, *n.* An equitable remedy to correct a writing so that it embodies the actual agreement between the parties. See reform.

Reformatory, *n.* A penal institution for youthful offenders. See jail (1).

Refractory, *adj.* See inflexible, incorrigible, difficult (3), querulous, particular (2).

Refrain, *v.* See avoid, abstain, desist, abandon, resist; forbearance.

Refresh, *v.* To revive (refresh her memory). Jog, strengthen, prompt, stimulate, revitalize, arouse, renew, energize, fortify, resuscitate, regenerate, freshen, restore, awake, brace, rouse, prod, remind, quicken, reanimate. See also animate. *Ant.* Weaken.

Refreshing, *adj.* See original, novel, intriguing, attractive, current, alive (2), ardent, delectable.

Refreshing the memory Using documents, memos, or books to bring more distinctly to mind the details of past events. See past recollection recorded, present recollection recorded, present recollection revived.

Refreshment, *n.* See food, necessaries; renewal, awakening.

Refrigerator, *n.* Cooler, icebox. See apparatus, equipment.

Refuge, *n.* See asylum, harbor (2).

Refugee, *n.* See alien (3), immigrant, outcast.

Refund, *v.* To repay or restore (the company refused to refund her down payment). Return, give back, redeem, settle, recompense, rebate, square, requite, indemnify, adjust, make restitution for, reimburse, remit, cover, replace. *Ant.* Withhold.

Refurbish, *v.* See repair (1), fix (3); cure, correct (2), improve.

Refusal, *n.* A rejection, a denial of what is asked or available (refusal to bargain). Veto, repudiation, nonconsent, rebuff, nonacceptance, defiance, turndown, disclaimer, resistance, unwillingness, dissent, disapproval, forswearing, repudiation, objection, negation, disclaimer, renunciation. *Ant.* Acceptance.

Refuse, *v.,* **refuse,** *n.* **1.** *v.* To reject (they refused to bargain). Object, decline, spurn, veto, resist, deny, abstain, rebuff, disapprove, bar, protest, prohibit, disavow, recoil, grudge, demur, not accept, withhold, forbid, dismiss, repudiate, forbear, bypass, abjure, reprobate, discountenance, renege, negative. **2.** *n.* Worthless matter (discharge of refuse into the river). Rubbish, waste, garbage, litter, remains, sediment, deposit, settlings, scum, junk, leftovers, filth, trash, dregs, sweepings, dirt, debris, leavings, scraps, fragments, spoilage, excrement, rubble, chaff, spillage, droppings, sludge, mud, feces, discards, riffraff, swill. *Ant.* Consent; valuables.

Refutation, *n.* See rebuttal, contradiction, answer, disagreement.

Refute, *v.* See rebut, contradict, answer (5), dispute (2), counter.

Regain, *v.* See recapture, reclaim, redeem.

Regale, *v.* See delight, amuse, satisfy (2), interest (5).

Regard 1. *v.* To consider (he was regarded with contempt). Think of, perceive, witness, look at, fancy, deem, eye, inspect, judge, suspect, peruse, scrutinize, contemplate, note, heed, view, believe, rate, estimate, find, appraise, investigate, study, analyze, reflect, review, cogitate, gauge, react, think over, ruminate, meditate, ponder, weigh, adjudge, be conscious of, look upon, reckon. **2.** *n.* Respect (held in high regard). Esteem, appreciation, admiration, note, distinction, favor, reverence, deference, recognition, honor, approval, affection, veneration, consideration, opinion, fame, judgment, eminence, homage, warmth, love, awe, praise. **3.** *n.* See concern (5). *Ant.* Ignore; disrespect; indifference.

Regardful, *adj.* See careful, cautious.

Regarding, *prep.* See about, in re; pertain, appertain.

Regardless, *adv., adj.* See nevertheless; careless, reckless.

Regenerate, *v.* See heal, remedy (2), correct (2), cure (2), improve, reinstate.

Regeneration, *n.* See awakening, renewal.

Regent, *n.* A governor or master; one who administers the government in the name of the king during the latter's minority or disability. See manager, director.

Regime, *n.* The prevailing authority or political system. See government.

Regimen, *n.* See plan (1), method, process, organization; government.

Regiment, *n.* See division (2); military; sailor.

Region, *n.* See zone, area.

Regional, *adj.* See local, domestic, parochial.

Register 1. *v.* To record formally (he failed to register on time). Enroll, enter, list, book, schedule, catalogue, chronicle, write, sign up, mark, enlist, check in, subscribe, post, join, calendar, inscribe, codify, docket. See also record (1), report (4). **2.** *n.* A book containing official facts (the expenses were entered in the register). **3.** *n.* See report (1), record (2).

Registered, *adj.* Entered or recorded in some official register, record, or list. See register (1), record.

Registrant, *n.* The person who registers. See applicant, candidate.

Registrar, *n.* An officer who is in charge of keeping records. See accountant, recorder, treasurer, clerk (2), officer, official.

Registrar of deeds Recorder; a public official in charge of recorded instruments affecting land title. See recorder, clerk (2), officer, official.

Registration, *n.* **1.** Inserting in an official record; formally applying (registration for the course). Recording, reservation, signing up, inscription, enrollment, filing, listing, enlistment, booking. See also inauguration; enroll, register. **2.** See certification.

Registration statement A statement disclosing financial data and other items of interest to potential investors, which must be filed by companies wishing to issue securities to the public or to trade securities in public markets. See securities, disclosure.

Registry, *n.* A book or document kept for recording or registering documents or facts. See record (2), report (1).

Regress, *v.* To go back or revert (he regressed to his earlier ways). Recede, reverse, backslide, deteriorate, relapse, fade, withdraw, ebb, wane, retrogress, recoil, subside, sink, fall back. See also revert, decline. *Ant.* Progress.

Regression, *n.* See deterioration, decline (3); regress.

Regressive tax A tax whose rate decreases as the amount being taxed increases; a tax bearing more heavily on poorer taxpayers. See tax.

Regret, *v., n.* See bemoan, suffer, cry (1); guilt (2), contrition, disgrace, embarrassment, anguish.

Regretful, *adj.* See contrite.

Regrettable, *adj.* See deplorable, grievous, distressing, abject; ill-fated, fatal.

Regroup, *v.* See organize; reorganization.

Regs. See regulations.

Regular, *adj.* **1.** Pertaining to a steady or uniform course, practice, or occurrence (regular maintenance). Routine, systematic, customary, recurring, steady, methodical, habitual, ordinary, commonplace, natural, standard, everyday, typical, prevalent, traditional, conventional, wonted, average, unchanged, periodical, periodic, set, daily, usual, continual, unceasing, matter-of-fact, accustomed, stock, popular, level, cyclic, frequent, automatic, symmetrical, predictable, orthodox, pat, unvaried, businesslike, routinized, established, seasonal, balanced, orderly, even. **2.** Conformable to law (regular on its face). See legal, correct (1). *Ant.* Sporadic; illegal.

Regular course of business The customary operation of a business; one's habitual or regular occupation.

Regularity, *n.* See symmetry, harmony, coherence, discipline.

Regularize, *v.* See organize, regulate.

Regularly, *adv.* At fixed intervals; in accordance with some consistent or periodical rule or practice (she was regularly entrusted with the records). Consistently, habitually, persistently, commonly, traditionally, customarily, continuously, continually, usually, ordinarily. *Ant.* Rarely.

Regulate, *v.* To adjust or control by rule, method, or principle (the agency regulates the quantity of material dumped in the river). Direct, fix, establish, govern, manage, supervise, prescribe, balance, handle, operate, steer, rectify, correct, modify, standardize, square, temper, order, systematize, pilot, normalize, arrange, dispose, coordinate, regularize, determine, adapt, codify, superintend, police, monitor, guide, oversee, discipline, conduct, marshal, set right. *Ant.* Neglect.

Regulation, *n.* **1.** A rule; a rule of an administrative agency, designed to explain or carry out the statutes or executive orders that govern the agency (Code of Federal Regulations). Directive, mandate, order, ordinance, command, code, dictum, instruction, canon, measure, edict, statute, prescript, enactment, legislation, act, bylaw, dictate, commandment. **2.** The act of controlling or managing (regulation of the economy). Regimentation, conduct, arrangement, standardization, administration, governance, adjustment, guidance, steering, handling, organization, coordination, disposition, supervision, fixing, balancing, establishment, superintendence, visitation, moderation.

Regulation Z A regulation of the Federal Reserve Board, implementing provisions of the Truth-in-Lending Act.

Regulator, *n.* See official, officer, agency, administrator.

Regurgitate, *v.* See repeat, paraphrase; disgorge.

Rehabilitate, *v.* See heal, remedy (2), correct (2), cure (2), right (5), improve, mitigate.

Rehabilitation, *n.* Restoration to a former capacity (rehabilitation programs in juvenile homes). Correction, renewal, restitution, development, reformation, amelioration, reorganization, conversion, salvation, replacement, indoctrination, mending, reinstatement, adjustment, revival, improvement, repair, regeneration, renovation, reconstruction, transformation, amendment, normalization, redemption, rejuvenation, convalescence, recovery, renascence, recuperation, remediation. See also awakening. *Ant.* Deterioration.

Rehabilitative alimony Alimony for a limited time until the recipient ex-spouse can get back on his or her feet and become self-sufficient. See alimony.

Rehash, *v.* See repeat, paraphrase.

Rehearing, *n.* A second consideration of a case for the purpose of calling to the attention of the court or agency any error, omission, or oversight in the first hearing. See hearing.

Rehearse, *v.* See prepare, practice (3), repeat, preparation.

Reign, *n., v.* See government, influence, rule (3).

Reimburse, *v.* To pay back (reimburse the travel expenses). Restore, repay, make whole, satisfy, compensate, refund, square, make restitution, requite, recompense, remit, remunerate, make amends, make good. See also indemnify.

Rein, *v.* See check (1), restrain.

Reinforce, *v.* See strengthen, augment, build, recover, equip.

Reinforcement, *n.* See increase, assistance; military.

Reinstate, *v.* To place again in a former state, condition, or office (reinstated as chairperson). Reconstitute, restore, reestablish, rehabilitate, resuscitate, renew, revamp, overhaul, cure, reclaim, revitalize, rejuvenate, remedy, repair, regenerate, reappoint, return, recreate, reopen, rehire, reinstall, reconnect. *Ant.* Remove.

Reinstatement, *n.* To place a case, insurance policy, etc., in the same position it was in before it was dismissed, canceled, or lapsed.

Reinsurance, *n.* A contract by which one insurance company agrees to indemnify another in whole or in part against loss or liability that the latter has incurred under a separate contract as the insurer of a third party. See insurance, indemnify.

Reinsured, *n.* An insurer who is insured against loss under its policies.

Reinsurer, *n.* An insurance company that insures other insurance companies.

Reissuable notes Bank notes that after having been once paid, may again be put into circulation. See note, securities.

REIT A real estate investment trust.

Reiterate, *v.* See repeat, paraphrase, emphasize, accent.

Reject, *v.*, **reject,** *n.* **1.** *v.* To refuse (the company rejected the offer). Decline, renounce, spurn, repudiate, discard, deny, repel, rebuff, jettison, disallow, repulse, turn from, dismiss, overrule, discredit, snub, blacklist, abandon, dump, eliminate, expel, discount, prohibit, ignore, rule out, banish, weed out, oppose, veto, neglect, contravene, remove, scrap, waive, disregard, forsake, eject, evict, disown, negative, brush aside, thwart, disapprove, blackball, traverse, boycott, preclude, disaffirm, dodge, forbid, disbelieve, disdain, quell, quash, kill, interdict, outlaw, discountenance, slough, junk, oust. **2.** *n.* That which is cast aside (a separate file for the rejects). Castaway, leftover, scrap, waste, castoff, outcast. See also refuse, tramp. *Ant.* Accept (1).

Rejection, *n.* Nonacceptance (rejection of the offer). Refusal, repudiation, veto, abnegation, proscription, rebuff, opposition, turndown, renunciation, omission, disallowance, challenge, abandonment, contempt, waiver, disdain, dissent, exile, scorn, disregard, disclaimer, denial, disagreement, rebuffing, dismissal, spurning, forbiddance, disavowal, exclusion, contradiction, eviction, prohibition, negation, elimination, repulse, discountenance, objection, hatred, interdiction, injunction, embargo, prevention, disapproval, reprobation, eradication. *Ant.* Approval.

Rejoice, *v.* See delight, enjoy (2), exult.

Rejoin, *v.* See reply, rebut, answer.

Rejoinder, *n.* The second pleading of the defendant, responding to the plaintiff's reply. See answer (1).

Rejuvenate, *v.* See animate, refresh, heal, cure (2), improve.

Relapse, *n.*, **relapse,** *v.* See deterioration, decline (2, 3), revert, regress.

Relate, *v.* **1.** To stand in some relation (the testimony related to the accident). Connect, bear upon, refer, concern, affect, interrelate, belong, pertain, appertain, is relevant, associate, identify, parallel, link, attach, coordinate, unite, ally, compare, join, couple, mingle, involve, respect, blind, juxtapose, wed. **2.** To communicate (the witness related her experience with the product). Describe, verbalize, recite, tell, repeat, go over, convey, express, notify, phrase, impart, recount, narrate, recapitulate, reveal, particularize, make known, utter, state, apprise, mention, represent, acquaint, portray, ventilate, articulate, broadcast, elucidate, detail. See also report (4), communicate. *Ant.* Isolate; conceal.

Related, *adj.* Connected; standing in relation (a related development). Tied, linked, germane, affiliated, kindred, dependent, interdependent, comparable, associated, leagued, reciprocal, interrelated, fellow, pertinent, akin, analogous, relevant, contingent, correspondent, coupled, matched, parallel, relative, annexed, correlative, applicable, federated, allied, subsidiary, fused, complementary, cognate, auxiliary, coliateral, implicated. *Ant.* Isolated.

Relation, *n.* **1.** A connection or association (an attempt to establish a relation between the product and the fire). Relationship, interconnection, dependency, bond, mutuality, link, alliance, correlation, similarity, rapport, association, affinity, applicability, tie-in, liaison, affiliation, nexus, reference, bearing, relevance. **2.** A person connected with another by blood or affinity. See consanguinity, affinity (1), kindred.

Relation back An act done at one time is considered by a fiction of the law to have been done at a prior time.

Relationship, *n.* See connection, relation (1); collaboration, cooperation; kindred (1), family, ancestry.

Relative 1. *n.* A person connected with another by blood or affinity. See consanguinity, affinity (1), kindred. **2.** *adj.* Considered in relationship to something else; germane (relative advantages). Comparable, proportional, parallel, related, apropos, analogous, reciprocal, commensurate, connected, relevant, collateral, kindred, associated, allied, correspondent, material, respecting, correlative, dependent, pertaining, interconnected, appropriate, concerning. *Ant.* Alien; independent.

Relator, relatrix, *n.* The person upon whose complaint or at whose instance certain writs are issued (State ex rel. John Jones v. Smith). See ex rel.

Relax, *v.* See ease (2), mitigate; enjoy.

Relaxant, *n.* That which relieves tension. See drug, diversion.

Relaxation, *n.* See reduction, remission; enjoyment, diversion.

Relaxed, *adj.* See patient (3).

Relay, *v.* See send, communicate.

Release 1. *v.* To set free; to discharge a claim that one has against another (the settlement released him from liability). Discharge, relinquish, liberate, clear, unburden, spare, acquit, dissolve, extricate, emancipate, exempt, relieve, disengage, unbind, undo, rescue, franchise, exonerate, redeem, unchain, remit, forgive, vindicate, untie. **2.** *v.* To allow something to be communicated (release the information). See publish. **3.** *n.* The giving up of a right, claim, or privilege (she signed the release). Relinquishment, discharge, concession, abandonment, waiver, liberation, dismissal, yielding, deliverance, acquittal, clearance, freedom, emancipation, exculpation, loosing, clearing, salvation, indemnity, pardon, exoneration, disengagement, amnesty, letting go, exemption, redemption, absolution, severance. *Ant.* Burden; conceal; assertion, confinement.

Release on own recognizance See personal recognizance.

Relegate, *v.* To turn over, refer, or remove (the employee was relegated to the position of a clerk). See assign (2), classify, expel.

Relent, *v.* See capitulate, yield, acquiesce.

Relentless, *adj.* See chronic, constant (1), continual, inflexible, indefatigable; mortal (2).

Relevance, *n.* See relation (1), affinity, connection; relevant.

Relevancy, *n.* Applicability to the issue at hand; the logical tendency of evidence to prove or disprove a material fact (an objection to the relevancy of the question). See applicable, relevant.

Relevant, *adj.* Applying to the matter in question; having a logical tendency to prove or disprove a material fact; having the tendency of making the existence of a fact more probable or less probable than it would otherwise be (relevant evidence). Germane, pertinent, connected, bearing, to the point, apt, allied, on target, admissible, suited, seasonable, apropos, compatible, at issue, suitable, pertaining, timely, apposite, correspondent, expedient, congruent, fitting, consistent, significant, associated, cognate. See also material, appropriate, applicable, important, related, *Ant.* Irrelevant.

Relevant market The area of effective competition.

Reliable, *adj.* Worthy of confidence (reliable witness). Trustworthy, reputable, unfailing, trusty, veracious, credible, responsible, dependable, true, steady, solid, sound, truthful, faithful, steadfast, honorable, authentic, secure, authoritative, substantiated, well-founded, genuine, believable, incontestable, well-grounded, honest, infallible, assured, unquestionable, indubitable, firm, established, confident, positive, guaranteed, demonstrated, unimpeachable, unhesitating, determined, sure, unwavering, staunch, stationary, constant, diligent, immutable, tenacious, well-built, anchored, rooted, persistent, undeviating, fastened, strong, stalwart, indissoluble, abiding, levelheaded, safe, definite, exact, irrefutable, stable, unequivocal, incontrovertible, strong, conscientious, scrupulous, legitimate, competent, able, professional, certain, tried, experienced. See also mature (2), accurate, loyal. *Ant.* Undependable.

Reliance

Reliance, *n.* A belief that motivates an act or an omission; dependence (she acted in reliance on the promise). Expectation, security, confidence, assurance, stock, conviction, credence, acceptance. See also faith, belief. *Ant.* Distrust.

Relic, *n.* See remainder; antique, memento, object (3); survival.

Relict, *n.* A widow or widower.

Reliction, *n.* An increase of the land by the permanent withdrawal or retrocession of the sea or river.

Relief, *n.* **1.** Deliverance from an injustice or wrong (seek relief from the courts). Redress, satisfaction, assistance, help, remedy, mitigation, rescue, succor, award, judgment, restoration, lightening, removal, reduction, amelioration, panacea, deliverance, aid, abatement, extrication, relaxation, alleviation, reparation, cessation, corrective, palliative, reprieve, release, assuagement, recompense, compensation, damages, freedom. **2.** Private or public assistance for the poor (on relief). Welfare, aid, dole, handout, charity, care, support, accommodation, ministry. *Ant.* Oppression; abandonment.

Relieve, *v.* **1.** To release from a position or duty (relieve a party from a judgment). Exempt, free, disburden, extricate, rid, deliver, emancipate, unload, relax, excuse, substitute, spare, reprieve, remit, replace, end, disengage. **2.** To improve or make less burdensome (the announcement relieved the tension). Lighten, moderate, allay, meliorate, aid, ease, succor, comfort, abate, assuage, subdue, pacify, reduce, soothe, mollify, dwindle, appease, interrupt. *Ant.* Impose; aggravate.

Religion, *n.* Belief in the existence of a superior being; a system of faith and worship practiced by a church, sect, or denomination; belief in a deity or deities (the practice of religion). Dogma, theology, canons, faith, divinity, cult, persuasion, devotion, affiliation, credo. See also church, creed, God, minister, clergy. *Ant.* Atheism.

Religious, *adj.* **1.** Pertaining to religion (religious beliefs). Spiritual, theological, sectarian, dogmatic, divine, denominational, sacred, parochial, reverential, churchly, clerical, angelic, godly, priestly, consecrated, unworldly, eternal, transcendent, celestial, sacrosanct, sanctified, devotional, orthodox, canonical, pious, devout. See also moral, intangible. **2.** Meticulous or rigid. See conscientious (2).

Relinquish, *v.* To give up or renounce (relinquish possession). Waive, turn over, release, abandon, yield, drop, forswear, disclaim, repudiate, vacate, cede, cast off, withdraw, abdicate, disavow, discontinue, surrender, jettison, resign, transfer, desert, evacuate, disown, quit, eliminate, leave, renege, retire, shed, desist, give up, concede, remise, forgo, reject, abjure, sacrifice. *Ant.* Claim.

Relish, *v.* See appreciate (3), enjoy (2), prefer (2).

Relocate, *v.* See move (2), enter, depart, leave (2); immigration, emigration.

Reluctance, *n.* See doubt (2), confusion (2), delay (3); caution, silence (1).

Reluctant, *adj.* See suspicious, doubtful (1); adverse; cautious.

Rely, *v.* See depend, trust (6).

Remain, *v.* See continue (1), last (2); loiter, delay.

Remainder, *n.* **1.** An estate that will take effect and be enjoyed after another estate is determined, spent, or terminated (contingent remainder). **2.** That which is left after everything or everyone else has been satisfied; the remaining portions (the will left the remainder of the estate to charity). Surplus, excess, residue, remnant, residuum, reservoir, overload, surplusage, glut, overflow, rest, carryover, residual, leftover, unused parts, scraps, reversion, trace, fragments, leavings, vestige, overage, store, spare, superfluity, surfeit, plethora, bonus, overrun, superabundance, balance.

Remainderman, *n.* The one who is entitled to the remainder of an estate after another estate has expired. See beneficiary.

Remains, *n.* See body (4), cadaver, corpse; refuse (2).

Remake, *v.* See reconstruct (2).

Remand, *v.* **1.** To send back for further action (the appellate court remanded the case to the trial court for a new hearing). Return, recommit, reassign. **2.** To return to custody (remanded for 6 months). See imprison.

Remark, *n., v.* See comment (1, 2), report, record, communication, communicate.

Remarkable, *adj.* See outstanding (2), extraordinary, exceptional, attractive, great; emotional, ardent, strong (2).

Remediable, *adj.* See salvageable, amenable, malleable.

Remedial, *adj.* Intended to correct wrongs and abuses (remedial action). Corrective, medicinal, compensatory, therapeutic, mending, cleansing, reformative, healing, restorative, alleviating, curative, salutary, correctional, prophylactic. *Ant.* Punitive.

Remedial statute A statute that provides a remedy or a means to enforce a right; a statute designed to correct an existing law or to redress an existing grievance.

Remediate, *v.* See correct (2), heal, cure (2), reconstruct (2), remedy (2).

Remedy 1. *n.* The means by which a right is enforced; the steps by which the violation of a right is prevented, redressed, or compensated (inadequate remedy at law). See procedure, procedural, adjective law. **2.** *v.* To relieve, cure, or correct (the order failed to remedy the condition). Mend, fix, redress, repair, set right, regulate, amend, rectify, improve, restore, calm, mollify, revive, straighten out, palliate, aid, meliorate, reverse, offset, soothe, "doctor," assuage, readjust, adjust, better, save, alleviate, mitigate, change, provide the antidote, assist, counteract, compensate for, rehabilitate, ease, neutralize. See also heal, correct (2), cure (2). *Ant.* Exacerbate (2).

Remember, *v.* See recall, retain (2), recognize (1); memory, recollection.

Remembrance, *n.* See memory, recollection, memento.

Remind, *v.* See caution (1), suggest, intimate (6), recall (3), refresh.

Reminisce, *v.* See recall (3); recognize (1).

Reminiscence, *n.* See recollection, retrospect; memory.

Reminiscent, *adj.* See suggestive (1); akin (2), related, analogous.

Remise, *v.* To give up or release. See relinquish.

Remiss, *adj.* Neglectful or careless (remiss in her duties). Derelict, slack, asleep, lax, disregardful, perfunctory, delinquent, negligent, tardy, inconsiderate, lazy, inattentive, absent-minded, undutiful, oblivious, indolent, laggard, thoughtless, reckless, heedless, slothful, imprudent, forgetful, rash, indifferent, shiftless, dilatory, idle, slipshod. *Ant.* Scrupulous.

Remission, *n.* **1.** The release or relinquishment of a debt. See discharge. **2.** A diminution or abatement of symptoms of a disease (mental illness in remission). Diminution, contraction, moderation, recess, ease, lessen, declining, lull, arrest, mitigation, decrease, hiatus, subsidence, reduction, suspension, alleviation, amelioration, interruption, abeyance, relief, interval, relaxation, loosening, waning, ebbing. *Ant.* Imposition; aggravation.

Remit, *v.* **1.** To send or pay (remit the money owed). Transmit, forward, dispatch, compensate, disburse, reimburse, tender, render, recompense, settle, liquidate, advance, present, proffer, make good, ship, indemnify, repay. **2.** To cancel or excuse (the fee was remitted). See forgive. **3.** To lessen (remit one's efforts). See diminish. *Ant.* Retain; impose; aggravate.

Remittance, *n.* Money sent. See payment.

Remitter, *n.* The relation back of a later defective title to an earlier valid one.

Remittitur, *n.* Diminishing or subtracting from a verdict that is excessive; the ordering of a new trial unless the plaintiff agrees to reduce the verdict by a stated amount.

Remnant, *n.* The remaining part or trace. See remainder (2).

Remonstrance

Remonstrance, *n.* A statement of reasons against something. See protest (1), objection.

Remonstrate, *v.* See protest (3), oppose, object.

Remorse, *n.* See contrition, guilt (2), anguish, embarrassment, disgrace.

Remorseful, *adj.* See contrite, ashamed.

Remorseless, *adj.* See cruel, callous, indifferent; mortal (2).

Remote, *adj.* **1.** At a distance; secluded (a remote part of the country). Distant, removed, inaccessible, isolated, faraway, separated, far-off, outlying, sequestered, segregated, apart, lonely, unreachable, forgotten, godforsaken, backwoods, unfrequented, forbidding, detached, foreign, abandoned, alien, private. **2.** Slight (remote possibility). Unlikely, insignificant, small, faint, trivial, improbable, dubious, imperceptible, minimal, inconsequential, implausible, meager, limited, slender, minute, superficial, doubtful, inconsiderable, negligible. *Ant.* Neighboring; substantial.

Remote cause An improbable, indirect, or speculative cause; a cause whose effect is uncertain, vague, or indeterminate; a cause whose effect does not necessarily follow. See cause, speculative.

Remote damages Unusual and unexpected results not reasonably to be anticipated from the accident. See damages, unforeseeable.

Removal, *n.* **1.** The transfer of a person or thing from one place to another; the transfer of a case from one court to another (removal of the state case to a federal court). Relocation, transference, transplantation, change of venue. **2.** An ouster (removal from office). Dismissal, displacement, discharge, withdrawal, dislocation, retirement, departure, ejection, banishment, deportation, renunciation, secession, suspension, disbarment, isolation, separation, blackballing, eviction, excommunication, dethronement, dislodgment, expulsion, repudiation, ostracism, divorce. **3.** The elimination (removal of the cancer). Eradication, deletion, obliteration, abolition, erasure, sequestration, purge, uprooting, stripping, amputation, cancellation, extermination, abolishment, destruction, liquidation, effacement, subtraction, prohibition, retreat, pullout, nullification, excavation, abstraction. *Ant.* Installation (2); preservation (3).

Remove, *v.* See withdraw (1), depart (1), transfer, move; rescind, cut, abridge, diminish; oust, expel.

Removed, *adj.* See remote (1), isolated, abandoned (1).

Remunerate, *v.* See compensate (1); pay, compensation.

Remuneration, *n.* Reward or salary. See compensation, pay.

Remunerative, *adj.* See gainful, lucrative, beneficial.

Renaissance, *n.* See renewal, restoration, betterment, rehabilitation, amelioration, increase, awakening, revival.

Renascense, *n.* See renaissance.

Rend, *v.* See break (2), divide; disturb, hurt.

Render, *v.* **1.** To pronounce or execute (render an accounting). State, deliver, hand down, convey, submit, present, furnish, give, impart, execute, hand over, proffer, provide, accomplish, communicate, report, agree on, administer, mete out, contribute, make available, grant, dispense, allot, yield, surrender. **2.** To cause to become (rendered unconscious). Bring about, create, produce. See cause, effect (2). **3.** To portray. See characterize.

Render judgment The official announcement of a judgment, either orally in open court or by memorandum filed with the clerk. After the judgment is rendered, it is entered in the record by the clerk. See judgment.

Rendezvous, *n.* An appointment; a place for an engagement. See meeting (3), conference, place (1), appointment (3).

Rendition, *n.* **1.** The return of a fugitive to the state in which he or she is accused of having committed a crime (interstate rendition). See extradition, return. **2.** See render.

Renegade, *n.* See nonconformist; traitor, insurgent (1), anarchist, wrongdoer.

Renege, *v.* See break (1), abandon (1), reject (1), rescind.

Renegotiate, *v.* See bargain, negotiate.

Renegotiation, *n.* Negotiating again; the review of contracts after performance to determine whether excess profits were made.

Renew, *v.* To restore; to make new again; to begin again (renew a lease). Regenerate, recommence, resume, revive, reestablish, recreate, replace, continue, resurrect, reinstitute, extend, retain, reintroduce, start over, reopen, reenter, reinstate, fix, rejuvenate, rehabilitate, revitalize, renovate, repair, recondition, refurbish, modernize, save, enhance, strengthen, resuscitate, salvage, redress, rebuild, perfect, redeem, overhaul, revise, improve, revamp. *Ant.* Cancel.

Renewal, *n.* A restoration or rehabilitation (urban renewal). Repair, enhancement, continuation, salvage, salvation, rebirth, revival, resumption, regeneration, renaissance, resurrection, restoration, reconstruction, return, repetition, reversal, reclamation, modernization, rescue, revision, renovation, readjustment, comeback. *Ant.* Deterioration.

Renounce, *v.* To make an affirmative repudiation (renounce all future claims). Repudiate, abandon, disclaim, disavow, forsake, divest, abjure, waive, forgo, relinquish, desert, give up, forswear, quit, desist, abdicate, eschew, dismiss, resign, discard, abnegate, reject, banish, disown, surrender, yield, defect, deny, retract, retire from, walk away from, decline, refuse, renege, demit, recant, cast off, cede, write off, repel, forbear, spurn, divorce, rebuff, lay down, let go, hand over, vacate, concede, backdown, capitulate, despair. *Ant.* Retain.

Renovate, *v.* See repair (1), fix (3), improve, reform, cure.

Renown, *n.* See notoriety, reputation, note (4), honor (3).

Renowned, *adj.* See notorious, popular, conspicuous, blatant, great, elevated, outstanding (2), exceptional.

Rent 1. *n.* Consideration paid for the use of property (a 10% rent increase). Fee, cost, payment, rental, price, assessment, dues, toll, proceeds, revenue. See also charge (9). **2.** *v.* To allow someone for a fee to use one's property (rent a car). Lease, sublease, let, sublet, hire, charter, farm. **3.** *adj.* See ragged.

Rent control, *n.* A government-imposed restriction or limitation upon the maximum rent that may be charged. See restraint (1), limitation (1).

Renter, *n.* See tenant, occupant.

Rent strike, *n.* An organized effort among tenants to withhold rent until conditions are improved, rent increases are lowered, etc. See strike, protest (1), coalition; union.

Renunciation, *n.* The abandonment of a right (renunciation of their claim). Rejection, giving up, relinquishment, desertion, repudiation, negation, cancellation, yielding, refusal, surrender, veto, self-denial, disclaimer, abdication, withdrawal, disapproval, waiver, recantation, expulsion, forbearance, spurning, resignation, repulsion, abjuration, disavowal, forswearing, eschewing, disaffirmation. *Ant.* Retention.

Reopen, *v.* To allow new evidence to be introduced in a trial that was completed. See revive, reinstate.

Reorder, *v.* See organize, revise.

Reorganization, *n.* The act or process of organizing again; a total adjustment made in the capital structure of a corporation, in which old securities and indebtedness are retired, and new securities and bonds issued (reorganization plan approved by the court). Restructuring, overhaul, recasting, realignment, revamping, conversion, rearrangement, revision, reconstitution, restoration, correction.

Reorganize, *v.* See organize, revise; improve, fix (3), repair.

Rep. *n.* See representative, legislator.

Repair, *v.* **1.** To renovate or mend (the landlord failed to repair the boiler). Fix, restore, improve, remedy, condition, revive, rebuild, patch, service, correct, heal, cure, meliorate, salvage, recondition, retouch, reassemble, refit, overhaul, rehabilitate, refurbish, set right, rectify, redress, better, rejuvenate, mend, revamp, alleviate, reform, remodel. **2.** To compensate for (repair the wrong). Satisfy, recompense, indemnify, square, remunerate, appease, make good, redeem, make amends, pay, pay back, repay. *Ant.* Aggravate.

Repairman, *n.* See merchant, laborer.

Reparable, *adj.* See salvageable; malleable, amenable.

Reparation, *n.* Payment for an injury; redress for a wrong done (reparation for the victim). Restitution, payment, indemnification, indemnity, satisfaction, remedy, atonement, retribution, compensation, propitiation, appeasement, amends, requital, damages, expiation, apology, refund.

Repartee, *n.* See reply, answer; joke.

Repartition, *n.* See partition, division.

Repatriation, *n.* The return to one's country; the regaining of nationality. See return.

Repay, *v.* **1.** To pay back (repay the loan). Refund, restore, return, reimburse, make restitution, settle, recompense, replace, balance, offset. See also indemnify. **2.** To retaliate (repay her enemies). Get even, avenge, square, vindicate, reciprocate, match, revenge, punish, strike back. *Ant.* Forgive.

Repeal 1. *n.* The express or implied abrogation or annulling of a pre-existing law by the enactment of a later law (repeal of the right-to-work legislation). Cancellation, removal, revocation, elimination, abolition, invalidation, termination, overruling, dissolution, voiding, abolishment, nullification, deletion, setting aside, doing away with, negation, withdrawal, vacating, waiver, obliteration, reversal, rescinding, quashing, countermand, repudiation, retraction, recall. **2.** *v.* See rescind. *Ant.* Approval; ratify.

Repeat, *v.* To say or perform again (he repeated the accusation). Reiterate, duplicate, renew, recite, reproduce, replicate, regurgitate, recount, recur, retell, echo, quote, reinform, reenact, imitate, belabor, retrace, rephrase, mimic, reassert, review, parrot, relapse, rehash, rerun, harp on, replay. See also paraphrase.

Repeated, *adj.* See habitual, continual, continuous.

Repeater, *n.* A person who commits and is convicted of crime after crime. See recidivist, habitual criminal.

Repel, *v.* See renounce, avoid (2), reject (1); displease, disrupt, disturb; harass.

Repellent, *adj.* See offensive, odious, repulsive.

Repent, *v.* See bemoan, suffer, cry (1); contrition, contrite.

Repentance, *n.* See contrition, guilt (2), embarrassment, anguish, anxiety, pain, depression.

Repentant, *adj.* See contrite, ashamed.

Repercussion, *n.* See import (2), impact, impression (2), consequence, effect, result.

Repertoire, *n.* See range (2); music; cinema.

Repetition, *n.* That which is repeated (a repetition of the offense). Reiteration, reproduction, reversion, recurrence, replication, restoration, duplication, restatement, remaking, redoing, déjà vu, echo, copy, tautology, reappearance, replica.

Repetitious, *adj.* See habitual, continuous, continual; commonplace, superfluous, needless.

Repetitive, *adj.* See repetitious.

Rephrase, *v.* See paraphrase, repeat, communicate; revise.

Replace, *v.* To provide a substitute or equivalent (the merchant replaced the defective product).   Change, switch, exchange, give satisfaction, restore, refund, cover, swap, supplant, displace, alter, retrieve, supersede, succeed, represent, subrogate, alternate, relieve.

Replaceable, *adj.* See expendable, extraneous.

Replacement, *n.* **1.** Substitution or restoration (replacement cost).   Equivalent, reconstitution, replica, compensation, reconstruction, relief, restitution, refund, reorganization. **2.** That which replaces (the replacement performed as well). Alternate, surrogate, substitute, understudy, delegate, proxy, agent, second, alternative, representative, envoy, successor.

Replacement insurance Insurance that provides that the loss will be measured by replacement of the property new.   If the property is actually replaced, the measure is the difference between the depreciated value and the replacement cost.

Replenish, *v.* See refresh, renew, strengthen, augment, improve.

Replete, *adj.* See full, abundant, complete.

Replevin, *n.* A possessory action designed to permit the party entitled to possession of personal property to recover it from the one who has wrongfully taken or detained it.   See recover (1), recapture, reclaim, possession, action.

Replevy, *v.* To regain possession of personal property through an action of replevin. See recover, recapture, possession.

Replica, *n.* See model, copy (1), imitation.

Replicate, *v.* See copy (2), repeat.

Replication, *n.* **1.** A reply made by the plaintiff to the defendant.   See reply. **2.** Reproduction.   See copy (1), imitation, model.

Reply 1. *n.* The plaintiff's response to the answer of the defendant (file a reply). Rejoinder, replication, return, counter, retort, refutation, reaction, comeback, retaliation, reciprocation, riposte.   See also acknowledgment, rebuttal. **2.** *v.* See answer (5), acknowledge, rebut.

Report 1. *n.* A formal account or descriptive statement (the report on the new rules).   Article, minutes, narration, history, story, chronicle, message, bulletin, release, summary, communiqué, review, memorandum, dossier, version, address, publication, transcript, sketch, brief, explanation, word, recital, tidings, intelligence, dispatch, telegram, advice, piece, exposition.   See also record (2), communication. **2.** *n.* Rumor (a report of wrongdoing).   Suggestion, whisper, gossip, hearsay, insinuation, scuttlebutt, hint, grapevine, news. **3.** *n.* A volume of court opinions.   See reports. **4.** *v.* To recite or give an account (he reported his findings to the commission).   Inform, circulate, broadcast, disclose, declare, impart, recount, detail, state, brief, relay, disseminate, relate, tell, air, apprise, transmit, advise, notify, divulge, announce, expound, specify, promulgate, reveal, present, show.   See also communicate, record (1), publish.

Reporter, *n.* **1.** The person who reports the decisions of a court of record; one who takes down and transcribes proceedings (court reporter).   See clerk, official. **2.** A volume of court opinions (Federal Reporter 2d). **3.** A loose-leaf service on a particular area of the law (CCH Labor Law Reporter). **4.** One who collects and reports the news (the reporter was sued for libel).   Journalist, member of the press, newspaperman, newspaperwoman, writer, investigator, columnist, pundit, editor.   See also press.

Reports, *n.* **1.** Volumes of court opinions (United States Reports; American Law Reports). **2.** Volumes of administrative decisions (ICC Reports).

Repose, *n.* See sleep, quiet, respite; composure, balance (5), self-confidence.

Repository, *n.* See warehouse, depository.

Repossess, *v.* See seize, possess; return; repossession.

Repossession, *n.* The taking back of property (repossession of the car by the seller).   Recapture, restoration, retrieval, seizure, recall, foreclosure, reacquisition, recovery.

Reprehend, *v.* See censure (2), reprimand.

Reprehensible, *adj.* See immoral, corrupt, culpable, blameworthy, odious.

Reprehension, *n.* See censure (1).

Represent, *v.* **1.** To speak or act with authority on behalf of another person (she represents the company). Replace, stand for, substitute for, appear for, be the agent for, be the envoy for, transact business for. **2.** To present or hold out as (the brochure represented the company as a going concern). Describe, depict, illustrate, show, portray, paint, characterize, exhibit, outline, record, express, sketch, designate, display, state, evoke, delineate, impersonate, masquerade, simulate. **3.** To exemplify (flashing yellow represents caution). Signify, symbolize, equal, stand for, personify, betoken, imply. See also mean (2).

Representation, *n.* **1.** The act of representing another (representation provided by the ACLU). See represent (1). **2.** A statement; any conduct that constitutes a statement of fact (false representation of the company's value). Version, declaration, allegation, explanation, assertion, report, portrayal, history, expression, designation, depiction, deposition, indication, illustration, painting, reflection. See also communication, description, account. **3.** See sample (1), model, archetype; manifestation.

Representative 1. *n.* One who stands in the place of and acts on behalf of another (trade representative). Spokesman, spokesperson, proxy, middleman, go-between, broker, solicitor, envoy, trustee, negotiator, surrogate, lieutenant, mouthpiece, intermediary, alternate, ombudsman, second, emissary, proctor, guardian, executor, administrator. See also agent, attorney, delegate. **2.** *n.* See legislator. **3.** *adj.* Acting as an example (a representative collection). Characteristic, typifying, typical, model, indicative, symbolic, archetypal, illustrative, sample, emblematic, exemplary, exemplifying, prototypical.

Repress, *v.* See inhibit, restrain, coerce, silence (2), quash.

Repression, *n.* See coercion, duress, control, tyranny, dominion.

Repressive, *adj.* See odious, arbitrary (2), strict (2), compulsory, forcible.

Reprieve, *n.* Temporary relief or postponement in carrying out a sentence (a 1-week reprieve). Stay, deferment, suspension, delay, respite, pause, interruption, extension, moratorium, adjournment, truce, alleviation, abeyance, remission, grace, clemency.

Reprimand 1. *v.* To censure someone (she reprimanded him for incompetence). Reprove, scold, berate, impugn, rebuke, chide, chastise, find fault with, reproach, criticize, upbraid, lecture, "dress down," denounce, revile, castigate, disparage, reprehend, take to task, condemn, trounce, flay, vituperate, decry, "chew out", tirade against, curse, inveigh against, remonstrate, denunciate, impeach, blame, accuse, correct, rail, call on the carpet, tongue-lash, disapprove, warn, object. **2.** *n.* See censure (1). *Ant.* Commend.

Reprisal, *n.* Action taken in retaliation (the attack was in reprisal for the insult). Retribution, punishment, recrimination, counterattack, repayment, reciprocation, revenge, vindication, compensation, eye for an eye, countermove, vengeance, return, indemnity, requital, counterblow, amends, satisfaction. *Ant.* Acquiescence.

Reproach, *v., n.* See reprimand, blame (3), accuse; censure, accusation, disgrace, embarrassment, discredit.

Reproachful, *adj.* See derogatory, contentious, querulous.

Reprobate 1. *n.* An immoral person. See offender, wrongdoer. **2.** *adj.* Depraved. See immoral.

Reproduce, *v.* See copy (2); beget; produce (2).

Reproduction, *n.* See copy (1), imitation, facsimile.

Reprove, *v.* See reprimand, censure (2), disparage.

Republic, *n.* A form of government in which the supreme authority lies with the voters who act through their elected representatives. See government.

Republican, *adj.* See party (3); republic.

Repudiate, *v.* See abandon (1), reject (1), abjure; repudiation.

Repudiation, *n.* Rejection; refusal to perform (repudiation of her obligations). Renunciation, disclaimer, abandonment, disavowal, cancellation, veto, contradiction, dismissal, protest, denunciation, dissent, defection, repeal, retraction, nullification, disregard, banishment, annulment, countermand, transgression, refutation, dishonoring, disagreement, evasion, revocation, voidance, abjuration, rescinding, abolition, withdrawal, breach, denial, forswearing, dishonor, violation, abrogation, reversal, neglect, spurning, protest, discarding, disaffirmation, invalidation, condemnation, contempt. *Ant.* Acceptance, performance.

Repugnance, *n.* See contempt (2), odium; repugnant.

Repugnant, *adj.* **1.** Arousing great dislike (repugnant odors from the factory). Repulsive, disgusting, foul, odious, abhorrent, repellent, obnoxious, offensive, fulsome, unsavory, nauseating, unpleasant, horrible, abominable, unpalatable, filthy, revolting, offending, icy, forbidding, displeasing, detestable, painful, objectionable, nauseous, stinking, gross, disgraceful, scandalous, horrid, obscene, disliked, noisome, grimy, reeking, sour, ghastly, monstrous, pornographic, bad, insipid, undesirable, appalling, dreadful, vile, contemptible, nasty, unappetizing, loathsome, hateful, unacceptable, aversive, hideous, unfriendly, inedible, displeasing, remote, unsightly, crude, sickening, insufferable, unclean, rancid, grotesque. **2.** Contradictory (repugnant terms in the will). See inconsistent. *Ant.* Agreeable; compatible.

Repulse, *v.* See reject (1), avoid (2), challenge (1), resist, confront, frustrate.

Repulsion, *n.* See contempt (2), odium; hostility, animus (2); repulsive.

Repulsive, *adj.* Causing disgust (repulsive behavior). Disgusting, foul, odious, abhorrent, repellent, obnoxious, offensive, fulsome, unsavory, nauseating, unpleasant, horrible, abominable, unpalatable, filthy, revolting, offending, icy, forbidding, displeasing, detestable, painful, objectionable, nauseous, stinking, gross, disgraceful, scandalous, horrid, obscene, disliked, noisome, grimy, reeking, sour, ghastly, monstrous, pornographic, bad, insipid, undesirable, appalling, dreadful, vile, contemptible, nasty, unappetizing, loathsome, hateful, unacceptable, aversive, hideous, unfriendly, inedible, displeasing, remote, unsightly, crude, sickening, insufferable, unclean, rancid, grotesque. *Ant.* Agreeable.

Reputable, *adj.* Having a good reputation; worthy of repute or distinction (reputable dealer). Respectable, respected, honest, scrupulous, impeccable, trustworthy, legitimate, unimpeachable, estimable, prominent, famed, revered, venerated, notable, dependable, righteous, trusted, well-thought-of, well-regarded, well-known, reliable, upright, celebrated, virtuous, incorruptible, uncorrupt, renowned, conscientious, above reproach, eminent, dignified. *Ant.* Corrupt.

Reputation, *n.* The estimation in which one is held; the sum total of how one is seen by others (a reputation for honesty). Name, status, standing, repute, regard, report, stature, mark, esteem, fame, character, notoriety, position, respect, honor, prominence, respectability, acclaim, distinction, recognition, consequence, celebrity, importance, station, rank, place, credit, footing, popularity, prestige.

Repute 1. *n.* See regard (2), reputation. **2.** *v.* To consider (reputed to be a mobster). Deem, assume, presume, regard, suppose, judge, reckon, estimate, view, think, fancy, gather, believe, see.

Reputed, *adj.* Popularly considered (reputed member of the mob). Assumed, presumed, estimated, putative, apparent, seeming, ostensible, likely, plausible, reported, supposed, accepted, rumored, alleged.

Request

Request **1.** *n.* A petition (request for an extension of time). Asking, entreaty, plea, want, solicitation, expression of desire, demand, supplication, prayer, imploration, requisition, begging, application, call, behest, favor, importuning, appeal, invocation, suggestion, motion, overture, suit, inquiry, requisition, summon, obtestation. **2.** *v.* See ask, petition (2).

Request for admission Discovery device: A written statement of facts is submitted to an adverse party who must admit or deny them. Admitted facts need not be proven at the trial. See admission, discovery.

Require, *v.* **1.** To direct or instruct (the order requires her to appear). Order, command, demand, compel, coerce, necessitate, oblige, obligate, force, dictate, impose, make mandatory, make compulsory, constrain, bid, enjoin, prescribe, decree, enforce, ordain. **2.** To be in need of (the engine requires constant repair). Call for, need, desire, be deficient in, lack, crave, covet, hunger for.

Requirement, *n.* An obligation (the requirements of office). Condition, precondition, necessity, mandate, directive, sine qua non, prerequisite, standard, requisite, dictate, rule, law, regulation, essential, fundamental, exigency, onus, call, injunction, constraint, commandment, ultimatum, imperative, qualification, proviso, compulsion, desideratum, fiat, direction, decree, need, imposition, responsibility, provision.

Requirement contract A contract in which the purchaser agrees to buy all of its needs of specified material from a particular supplier, and the latter agrees to fill all the purchaser's needs during the period of the contract. See contract.

Requisite, *adj.* See mandatory, necessary, essential, compulsory.

Requisition 1. *n.* A formal demand. See request. **2.** *v.* To insist upon. See demand.

Requite, *v.* See avenge, repay, return (3), exchange.

Res, *n.* The subject matter of a trust or will; a thing or object, a status, everything that is the object of a right. See object (3), item, entity, article (2), content (1).

Res adjudicata, *n.* See res judicata.

Rescind, *v.* To annul or cancel (rescind the contract). Avoid, invalidate, reject, abandon, abrogate, renege, abolish, withdraw, countermand, repeal, supersede, repudiate, void, neutralize, break off, veto, override, terminate, recant, nullify, negate, vitiate, discharge, revoke, reverse, counterorder, quash, undo, unmake, obliterate, dissolve, overrule, renounce, disavow, disestablish, destroy, abdicate, abjure, backtrack, disassociate, evacuate, remove, subtract, recant, vacate, relinquish, set aside, eject, evict, purge, nolle prosequi, expel, upset, sweep away. *Ant.* Validate.

Rescission, *n.* The undoing or cancellation of something (rescission of the contract). Unmaking, termination, withdrawal, repeal, abandonment, vitiation, retraction, repudiation, dissolution, destruction, erasure, overthrow, abolishment, deletion, nullification, revocation, annulment, voidance, disestablishment, renunciation, quashing, disavowal, suspension, discontinuation, recall, relinquishment, overriding, abnegation. See also reversal. *Ant.* Confirmation.

Rescue 1. *n.* The act of saving or helping (come to his rescue). Liberation, delivery, deliverance, aid, release, preservation, emancipation, assistance, salvation, succor, intervention, freeing, redemption, unbinding, unburdening, reclaiming, extricating, safeguarding, ransom, relief. **2.** *v.* See save (1). *Ant.* Abandonment; frustrate.

Rescue doctrine Danger invites rescue: One who negligently endangers a person can be liable to third parties who are injured in an attempt to save the person in danger, so long as the attempt is not reckless.

Research, *v., n.* See investigate, audit (2), canvass (1), cross-examine; learning, knowledge, education, information.

Resemblance, *n.* See correspondence, correlation, affinity (3), analogy; imitation, copy, facsimile.

Resemble, *v.* To look like. Parallel, be similar to, favor, appear like, duplicate, be akin to, sound like. See also correspond, copy.

Resent, *v.* To take offense; to be jealous of. Take umbrage at, sulk, be angry, be indignant, bear a grudge, take exception, frown. See also disapprove (2), abhor, revolt (2).

Resentful, *adj.* See angry, aggravated (2), hot (2); jealous, avaricious, suspicious.

Resentment, *n.* See animus (2), malice, hostility, wrath, annoyance; jealous, suspicious; doubt.

Reservation, *n.* **1.** The holding back or retention of a right or interest; a right created and retained by the grantor (reservation clause in the deed). **2.** A tract of land to which an American Indian tribe retains its original title or which is set aside for its use (special courts on the reservation). Enclave, settlement, enclosure, territory, tract, domain, preserve, reserve, region. See also zone. **3.** A doubt (she expressed reservations about the proposal). Misgiving, qualm, qualification, proviso, condition, limitation, stipulation, scruple, hesitancy, compunction, second thoughts, reluctance, uncertainty, skepticism, caveat, objection. See also doubt (2). **4.** An appointment (a reservation at the club). Engagement, booking, arrangement. See also appointment.

Reserve 1. *v.* To keep back or retain (reserve the right to enter at will). Retain, set aside, withhold, preserve, save, amass, conserve, postpone, husband, stockpile, bank, earmark, store, stock, cache, spare, shelve, deposit, maintain, hide, accrue, delay, accumulate. **2.** *n.* A fund set aside to cover future expenses, losses, or claims (insufficient reserves). Supply, funds, accumulation, stock, resource, cache, stockpile, nest egg, emergency fund, contingency fund. **3.** *n.* Military personnel awaiting active duty in an emergency (in the reserves). National Guard. See military, sailor. **4.** *n.* Restraint or formality (a noticeable reserve in the witness). Self-control, detachment, rigidity, composure, unresponsiveness, distance, condescension, coolness, secrecy, silence, reluctance, inhibition, aloofness, shyness, hesitancy, diffidence, evasiveness, reticence, self-restraint, coldness, taciturnity, unwillingness.

Reserve Board See Federal Reserve Board of Governors.

Reserve clause A clause in the contract of a professional athlete that gives the club a continuing and exclusive right to the services of the athlete. See contract, clause, limitation.

Reserved, *adj.* **1.** Kept or set apart for a designated purpose or person (reserved jurisdiction). Retained, saved, set apart, withheld, engaged. **2.** Restrained or aloof. See reserve (4), indifferent.

Reserved powers Powers not delegated to the federal government by the U.S. Constitution nor prohibited by it to the states are reserved to the states or to the people.

Reservist, *n.* A member of a military reserve. See military, division, sailor.

Reservoir, *n.* See accumulation, fund; vessel (2); water, sea.

Res gestae, *n.* An exclamation or utterance is admissible as an exception to the hearsay rule if it (a) is made at or near the time of the occurrence, e.g., an accident, (b) is made spontaneously without time to deliberate, and (c) is so influenced by the occurrence itself as to become a part thereof. See evidence, hearsay, admissible.

Reside, *v.* **1.** To be in residence; to occupy a fixed abode; to dwell permanently or continuously (reside in the district). Live, abide, sojourn, stay, remain, lodge, settle, squat, keep house, room, nestle, inhabit, camp, locate, colonize, situate, establish roots, encamp, nest, domicile. **2.** To inhere as a quality; to be vested as a right (tax powers reside with the legislature). Belong, lie, subsist, exist, be intrinsic, rest, be innate.

Residence, *n.* Living or remaining in a particular locality without the intent to stay there indefinitely. If this intent existed, the place would be a domicile. In some situations, however, the law treats residence and domicile as synonymous. (Although Boston is her home base, she has residences in Newton and on the Cape). Quarters, address, lodging, abode, accommodations, household, habitation. See also home.

Resident, *n.* One who resides or dwells in a place; one who occupies a dwelling within the state and establishes an ongoing physical presence therein (service by publication on residents). Dweller, inhabitant, addressee, lessee, tenant, denizen, native. See also occupant, citizen.

Resident agent A person in the jurisdiction who is authorized to accept service of process for another. See agent.

Resident alien A person who is not yet a citizen of this country, who has come here from another country with the intent to abandon his or her former citizenship and reside here. See alien.

Residential, *adj.* Pertaining to or suitable for residences (residential district). Noncommercial, nonindustrial, private, for homes.

Residual, *adj.* Pertaining to that which is left over (residual clause in the will). Surplus, remaining, balance, residuum, residue, extra, superfluous, spare. See also excess.

Residuary, *adj.* Pertaining to the remainder of an estate after all debts, claims, and other testamentary gifts are satisfied (residuary beneficiary). Surplus, spare, remaining, leftover, outstanding. See also residual, excess.

Residuary clause A clause in a will disposing that part of the estate which remains after everything else is paid or satisfied (e.g., debts, expenses, all other legacies). See will, remainder.

Residue, *n.* That which remains of a testator's estate after all debts and particular legacies have been discharged (a clause in the will disposing of any residue). Residual, surplus, leftover, spare, remains, balance, rest, residuum, scraps, ends, dregs, leavings, overflow. See also remainder.

Residuum, *n.* See residue.

Resign, *v.* See quit, retire (1), depart (1), leave (2), abdicate.

Resignation, *n.* **1.** Formal relinquishment of a job or office (the director accepted his resignation). Quitting, withdrawal, termination, resigning, yielding, rejection, abandonment, evacuation, retirement, surrender, vacation, forsaking, divestment, divorce, departure, notice, abdication. **2.** Passive submission. See acquiescence.

Resigned, *adj.* See passive (2), apathetic, indifferent, malleable, amenable (2), patient, isolated; reserve (4).

Resilience, *n.* See resolution (4).

Resilient, *adj.* See flexible, malleable, amenable (2), alive.

Res ipsa loquitur "The thing speaks for itself." An inference or rebuttable presumption of the defendant's negligence (unreasonableness) arises in the following circumstances: (a) The event producing the harm was of a kind that ordinarily does not occur in the absence of someone's negligence, (b) the event was caused by an agency or instrumentality within the defendant's exclusive control, and (c) the event was not due to any voluntary action or contribution on the part of the plaintiff. See negligence, neglect (2).

Resist, *v.* To oppose, usually by direct action; to prevail against (the committee resisted all budget cuts). Challenge, fight, strike, assault, combat, assail, repulse, check, contradict, balk, defy, frustrate, thwart, dissent, obstruct, counteract, repress, contest, recoil, confront, withstand, persist, stem, face, revolt, impede, disregard, retaliate, weather, endure, counteract, foil, strive against, battle, flout. *Ant.* Yield.

Resistance, *n.* Standing against or obstructing (resistance to the court order). Confrontation, opposition, rebellion, battle, revolution, strike, disobedience, defiance, revolt, insurrection, recalcitrance, rebuff, mutiny, counteraction, frustration, defense, stubbornness, insurgence, combat, oppugnancy, antagonism, noncompliance, obstinacy, intransigence, fight, contumacy, sedition, contention. See also insubordination. *Ant.* Acquiescence.

Resistant, *adj.* See mutinous, disobedient, contentious, litigious, querulous, wild, incorrigible, disorderly (1); resistance, resist, insubordination.

Res judicata, *n.* A final judgment rendered by a court of competent jurisdiction on the merits is conclusive as to the rights of the parties and their privies, and hence bars any subsequent action by them involving the same claim, demand, or cause of action.

Resolute, *adj.* See firm (2), decisive, diligent, precise (2), inflexible; courageous, indefatigable, strong, constant.

Resolution, *n.* **1.** A decision or solution (a resolution of the conflict). Clearing up, working out, conclusion, outcome, upshot, answer, decoding, sorting out, finding, explanation, interpretation, discovery, clarification, conciliation, key, justification, deciphering. **2.** A formal expression of the opinion or will of an official body without constituting a rule or law (concurrent resolution). Statement, declaration, proclamation, finding, presentation, announcement. **3.** A plan or objective (a resolution to improve his study habits). Determination, scheme, proposal, intent, intention, design, hope, goal, ambition, promise, aim, purpose, proposition, resolve, target, motion, project. **4.** The quality of being firm or unwavering (he lacked the resolution to succeed). Perseverance, firmness, zeal, dedication, patience, resolve, devotion, constancy, tenacity, determination, resilience, energy, heart, aggressiveness, steadfastness, fortitude, stubbornness, will, application, vigor, push, mettle, backbone, nerve, conviction, stick-to-itiveness. See also spirit, self-confidence, endurance, character (1), quality (2). *Ant.* Stalemate; silence; avoidance; indecision.

Resolve, *v., n.* See settle (1), judge (2), decide, intend, plan (3), aim; resolution (3, 4), objective (3).

Resonant, *adj.* See full, abundant, noisy, strong.

Resort 1. *v.* To go to or make use of (resort to the courts). Utilize, avail oneself of, employ, turn to, use as a resource, bring into play, exercise, have recourse to, adopt, fall back on, apply to. **2.** *v.* To go often. See frequent (2). **3.** *n.* Recourse (court of last resort). Hope, chance, help, assistance, possibility, back-up, option, appeal. **4.** *n.* A place for relaxation. See asylum (2).

Resource, *n.* **1.** That to which one can turn to for help (a resource available to meet current expenses). Reserve, source, expedient, belongings, means, aid. **2.** Assets (attachment of resources). Wealth, property, money, wherewithal, chattel, funds, income, capital, accounts, possessions, effects, revenue, finances, estate, inventory, cash, securities, portfolio, fixtures, stocks. **3.** Abilities (untapped resources). See capacity (2), experience (1), facility (3), gift (2), power, ability.

Resourceful, *adj.* See apt (3), capable, competent, able, original (3), brilliant, learned.

RESPA See Real Estate Settlement Procedures Act.

Respect, *v., n.* See honor, regard (2), appreciate (3); relation (1); appearance (3), attribute (2), characteristic (1), component.

Respectable, *adj.* See reputable, meritorious (2), good (2), honest, moral (2); proper, appropriate; appreciable.

Respectful, *adj.* See civil (3), judicious, discreet, cautious, amenable, kind, friendly, convivial, malleable.

Respecting, *prep.* See about, in re; pertain, appertain.

Respective, *adj.* Relating to particular persons or things (respective homes). Specific, individual, several, each to each, separate, corresponding, special.

Respiration, *n.* See breath; life.

Respite, *n.* A delay; the temporary suspension of the execution of a sentence (the court ordered a respite so that a new motion could be filed). Reprieve, continuation, forbearance, interval, lull, cessation, pause, recess, extension, postponement, stoppage, letup, adjournment, moratorium, intermission, hiatus, repose, breather, halt, stay, deferment, lapse, relaxation, grace, abeyance, cease-fire, shelving.

Resplendent, *adj.* See beautiful, attractive, great, enjoyable, outstanding (2), exceptional, extraordinary, deluxe, exorbitant, prodigal, abundant, flamboyant, gaudy, lush (2), fertile; luxury.

Respond, *v.* See answer (5), acknowledge, rebut, reply.

Respondeat superior "Let the master answer." The master, employer, or principal in certain cases is liable for what the servant, employee, or agent does or fails to do. The former is liable for the torts of the latter when committed within the course of employment. See agent, employee, course of employment, scope of employment.

Respondent, *n.* The party who answers a claim, allegation, or bill; the party against whom an appeal is brought (the respondent had 2 weeks to file a reply brief). Defendant, appellee, accused, responding litigant. See also party. *Ant.* Petitioner, appellant.

Response, *n.* See reply, acknowledgment, rebuttal.

Responsibility, *n.* The state of being answerable for an obligation; the obligation to answer for an act or to make restitution for an injury (responsibility for the accident). Accountability, liability, culpability, observance, commitment, conscience, moral duty, dependability, trust, trustworthiness, charge, guarantee, encumbrance, debt, bounden duty, function, blame, contract. See also burden (1), duty, onus.

Responsible, *adj.* **1.** Legally accountable or answerable (the principal is responsible for her agent's negligence). Liable, bound, obligated, subject, chargeable, beholden, guilty, blameworthy, culpable. See also accountable, amenable (1). **2.** Trustworthy. See conscientious, mature (2), reliable. **3.** See rational, competent (2).

Responsive, *adj.* Constituting an answer; nonevasive (responsive to market conditions). Reciprocal, reactive, answering, sympathetic, receptive, sensitive, understanding, replying, alert, open, awake. See also alive, conscious, accessible. *Ant.* Unresponsive.

Responsive pleading A pleading that joins issue and replies to a prior pleading of an opponent. See pleadings.

Rest 1. *v.* To indicate to the court that a party has presented all of the evidence he or she intends to submit at this time (the plaintiff rests). See end (2), cease. **2.** *n.* A brief pause. See recess. **3.** *n.* That which is left. See residue, remainder.

Restate, *v.* See paraphrase, repeat, communicate.

Restatements, *n.* A series of volumes authored by the American Law Institute (e.g., Restatement of Torts 2d). The books state the law in a given area, note emerging changes, and sometimes indicate changes in the law that the Institute would like to see. See digest (1).

Restaurant, *n.* See inn.

Restful, *adj.* See quiet, passive, patient (3), comfortable; lazy.

Rest home, *n.* See institution (1); home; charity.

Restitution, *n.* The restoration of something to its rightful owner; making good or giving an equivalent value for any loss, damage, or injury (court-ordered restitution to the victim as a condition of probation). Indemnification, compensation, satisfaction, replacement, atonement, redemption, repayment, redress, reimbursement, amends, remuneration, reparation, retrieval, reinstatement, indemnity, recoupment, adjustment, return, refund, restoral, rebate, reestablishment, repair, repossession, renovation, making whole, retribution, reversion, replevin. *Ant.* Dispossession.

Restive, *adj.* See feverish, apprehensive, concerned.

Restless, *adj.* See feverish, excitable, apprehensive, concerned, impatient, crabby, assertive.

Restoration, *n.* The return of something (restoration of the status quo). Replacement, reestablishment, restitution, reinsertion, rebirth, reappearance, renaissance, rebuilding, resumption, renewal, reconstruction, reversion, comeback, reanimation, resurrection, resurgence, rejuvenation, revival, rehabilitation, indemnification, remedy, remaking, redemption. *Ant.* Destruction.

Restore, *v.* See recover, build, strengthen, augment, improve, refresh, revive, renew.

Restrain, *v.* To restrict or limit (the order restrained the company from issuing the stock). Confine, narrow, destroy, obstruct, impede, hinder, stay, check, keep in check, hold back, repress, suppress, arrest, withhold, enjoin, curb, proscribe, inhibit, diminish, exclude, vanquish, fetter, harness, muzzle, bind, chain, wall, frustrate, reduce, detain, retard, impound, blockade, subdue, curtail, bridle, qualify, hobble, enchain, secure, cramp, encumber, immure, condition, delimit, box in, manacle, leash, abridge, jail, handicap, control, regulate, ban, forbid, immobilize, squelch, cloister, demarcate, bar, smother, govern, trammel, interdict, stop, gag, handcuff, bury, veil, stifle, conceal, terminate, end, overcome, cancel, strangle, choke, silence, delete, overpower, mute, censor, still, cover up, shroud, extinguish, overthrow, tame, keep private, circumscribe. *Ant.* Release.

Restraining order A form of injunction issued ex parte for the purpose of restraining the defendant from doing the threatened act, pending notice and hearing on an application for a temporary injunction. See order, injunction, temporary restraining order.

Restraint, *n.* **1.** Restriction or prohibition (prior restraint on publication). Confinement, abridgement, limitation, holding back, hindrance, obstruction, destruction, ban, suppression, repression, bar, blockage, interference, deterrence, interruption, embargo, prevention, injunction, arrest, elimination, stifling, servitude, stay, curb, detention, check, shackles, impediment, muzzle, barrier, stoppage, constraint, warning, censure, straitjacket, brake, interdiction, manacle, deterrent, veto, harness, retardation, boundary, circumscription, conscription, proviso, condition, precondition, proscription, exception, incarceration, imprisonment, handicap, caveat, reservation, rule, law, prescription, stipulation. **2.** Self-control (we were surprised at the victim's restraint). Reserve, self-possession, moderation, temperance, reticence, poise, self-discipline, judgment, equanimity, levelheadedness, self-composure, aplomb. *Ant.* Encouragement; excess.

Restraint of trade Contracts or combinations that tend to or are designed to eliminate or stifle competition, create a monopoly, artificially maintain prices, or otherwise hamper or obstruct the course of trade and commerce that would be carried on if left to the control of natural economic forces. See monopoly, cartel, competition, commerce, business.

Restraint on alienation A provision in a deed or other instrument of conveyance that prohibits the grantee from selling or transferring the property. See exchange (2), conveyance (1).

Restrict, *v.* To restrain within bounds. See restrain, check (1).

Restricted

Restricted, *adj.* See qualified (2), restrictive, limited (1), contingent, doubtful; confine.

Restriction, *n.* A limitation. See restraint (1), obstruction, limitation (1), limit (2).

Restrictive, *adj.* Tending to confine (restrictive order). Restraining, prohibitive, qualifying, obstructive, inhibitive, modifying, conditional, limiting, restricted, circumscribed, controlled, exclusive, segregated, repressive, constraining, deterrent, selective, definite, fixed, set, narrow, provisional, preventive. See also limited, qualified (2), contingent.

Restrictive covenant A clause in a deed limiting the use of the property; a clause in a contract limiting a party from performing similar work for a period of time in a certain geographic area after the termination of the contract. See limitation, clause.

Restrictive indorsement An indorsement that limits the further negotiability of the instrument. See indorsement, note.

Restructure, *v.* See revise; organize; improve, fix (3), repair; reorganization.

Result 1. *n.* The consequence of something (the result of the court's deliberations). Upshot, finding, decision, product, verdict, issue, judgment, conclusion, resolution, development, denouement, fallout, answer, harvest, aftermath, reward, outgrowth, fruit, turnout, crop, eventuality, by-product, side effect, sequel, aftereffect, reaction, impact, opinion, determination. See also effect (1), consequence (1), yield. 2. *v.* To occur as a consequence of (the negotiation resulted in a settlement). Conclude, spring, arise, follow, emerge, occur, happen, accrue, proceed, ensue, emanate, eventuate, issue. *Ant.* Cause; originate.

Resulting trust A trust implied in law from the intention of the parties to a given transaction; a trust that arises when a person makes a disposition of property under circumstances that raise the inference that he or she did not intend the transfer of a beneficial interest to the person taking or holding the property. See trust.

Resulting use A use raised by equity for the benefit of one who has made a voluntary conveyance to uses without any declaration of the use. See use.

Resume, *v.* See continue, renew.

Résumé, *n.* A brief summary (e.g., of one's prior experiences, education). See brief (2); record (2).

Resumption, *n.* See continuation, renewal; commencement.

Resurgence, *n.* See renewal, revival, awakening, restoration; rehabilitation, betterment.

Resurrect, *v.* See renew, revive, reinstate, return, heal, cure (2), correct (2), remedy (2).

Resurrection, *n.* See renewal, revival, awakening, rehabilitation, restoration, increase, betterment, amelioration.

Resuscitate, *v.* See heal, remedy (2), correct (2), cure (2), improve, reinstate, revive, renew.

Retail, *adj.* Sale directly to the consumer. See sale, commerce, business, merchant. *Ant.* Wholesale.

Retailer, *n.* A person engaged in making sales of goods to the ultimate consumer or user who is not in the business of reselling them. See merchant, entrepreneur, business.

Retain, *v.* 1. To engage the services of (retain an attorney). Employ, hire, secure, commission, book, consult, recruit. 2. To hold or preserve (retain possession). Maintain, secure, restrain, grasp, keep, withhold, clutch, remember, memorize, recollect, recall, detain, cling to, fix, hold fast, clench, restrict, absorb. *Ant.* Fire; lose.

Retained income That portion of profits which has not been paid out as dividends;

net income over the life of a corporation less all income distributions. See income, profit, net.

Retainer, *n.* **1.** The act of employing an attorney; the fee paid by a client to an attorney when the latter is hired; the contract between the client and attorney, stating the nature of the services to be rendered and the cost thereof. See fee (1), compensation, contract, hire (1). **2.** A servant. See employee.

Retaining lien The right of an attorney to retain possession of the client's property acquired by the attorney within the scope of his or her employment until the client pays the balance owed for professional services. See lien.

Retaliate, *v.* See avenge, repay, return (3); retaliation, punishment.

Retaliation, *n.* The return of like for like (in retaliation, the defendant hit the plaintiff back). Revenge, reprisal, repayment, recrimination, vengeance, requital, satisfaction, quid pro quo, getting even, reciprocation, counterattack, measure for measure, tit for tat, retribution, avengement. *Ant.* Pardon.

Retaliatory eviction An eviction by a landlord because the tenant has complained to the housing authority about conditions in the leased premises, the tenant has participated in a tenant's organization, etc. See eviction.

Retard, *v.* See hinder, frustrate, obstruct, delay, arrest (2, 3).

Retarded, *adj.* See infirm, ill, frail, weak, senile; disable.

Retention, *n.* See memory; custody, possession, accumulation; retain.

Rethink, *v.* See review, consider.

Reticence, *n.* See reserve (4), restraint (2).

Reticent, *adj.* See quiet (2), passive, bashful, silent; suspicious.

Retinue, *n.* See coterie.

Retire, *v.* **1.** To terminate employment or service upon reaching the age of retirement (retire from the company). Resign, stop working, withdraw, stand aside, relinquish, drop out, give up office. See also quit, abdicate. **2.** To take out of circulation (retire the notes). Redeem, pay off, call in, buy back, reclaim. **3.** To seclude oneself (retire to the office). Isolate, abandon, remove, retreat, resort.

Retiring, *adj.* See quiet (2), passive, bashful, silent.

Retort, *v., n.* See reply, rebut, answer; rebuttal, retaliation.

Retrace, *v.* See trace (2), repeat, return.

Retract, *v.* To take something back; to recant (the newspaper retracted its story). Reverse, withdraw, repudiate, disclaim, annul, repeal, disavow, void, cancel, unsay, rescind, forswear, abjure, disown, countermand, abolish, counterorder, deny, renege. *Ant.* Repeat.

Retraction, *n.* See removal, reversal, denial; retract.

Retreat, *v., n.* See withdraw, depart; exit (2), removal, departure (2); asylum (2), harbor (2).

Retrench, *v.* See diminish, curtail, delete, omit; withdraw; save (2), conserve.

Retrenchment, *n.* See decline (3), removal.

Retrial, *n.* See hearing; repeat.

Retribution, *n.* Something given or demanded in payment (retribution for the crime). Punishment, reprisal, vengeance, justice, restitution, retaliation, reckoning, satisfaction, requital, return, penalty, reparation, repayment, reward, measure for measure, quid pro quo, counterattack, comeuppance, recrimination, avengement. *Ant.* Forgiveness.

Retrieval, *n.* See restoration.

Retrieve, *v.* See get (1), convey, carry (1), recapture, reclaim, redeem, recover, correct, improve.

Retroactive, *adj.* Applying to the time prior to enactment; affecting or acting on things that are past (retroactive law). Retrospective, looking backward, having

Retroactive

prior effect, ex post facto. See also nunc pro tunc. *Ant.* Prospective.

Retrogress, *v.* See lapse (2), regress, revert, decline.

Retrogression, *n.* See lapse (3), oversight, removal.

Retrospect, *n.* Thinking of past events (in retrospect). Looking back, afterthought, review, reconsideration, hindsight, remembrance, reminiscence, recollection, reexamination, flashback.

Retrospective, *adj.* See retroactive, review (2).

Return 1. *v.* To bring, carry, or send back (the stolen goods were returned). Replace, reinstate, restore, deliver, reset, reinstall, reestablish, reposition, recover, reseat. **2.** *v.* To reappear (the pain returned). Repeat, come back, reoccur, recur, boomerang, go back, resurrect, echo. **3.** *v.* To pay back in kind (he returned the insult). Reciprocate, retaliate, compensate, requite, retort, answer, respond, reply, rebut, exchange, react, repay, revenge, refund, avenge, recompense, counter, acknowledge, redress, remedy. **4.** *v.* To report (return a verdict). Render, adjudicate, pronounce, announce, publish, hand down, impart, recite, reveal, proclaim, come to. See also communicate, report (4), record (1). **5.** *n.* Profit (an unexpected return on the investment). Yield, income, gain, reward, bonus, increase, inflation, appreciation, proceeds, harvest, benefit, revenue, gross, net, interest, compensation, rent, royalty, bounty. *Ant.* Take; disappear; forgive; conceal; loss.

Returnable, *adj.* Requiring a return; to be returned on a certain day.

Reunion, *n.* See meeting, conference, appointment (2); consortium (2), amalgamation.

Reunite, *v.* See join (1), convene, converge, pool (1).

Revalidate, *v.* See certify, assure.

Revaluation, *n.* The restoration of purchasing power to an inflated currency.

Revamp, *v.* See revise; organize; improve, fix (3), repair; reorganization.

Reveal, *v.* See expose (1), exhibit, bare (2), disclose, present (5), clarify, communicate, confess.

Revel, *v.* See delight, enjoy (2), exult; dissipate (1); revelry.

Revelation, *n.* See exposé, disclosure, communication, report; surprise.

Revelry, *n.* See celebration (2), spree, amusement, banquet, entertainment, game, sport, diversion.

Revenge, *n.* See retaliation, reprisal, recrimination (1).

Revenue, *n.* Return or yield from an investment, venture, job, collection effort, etc. (Internal Revenue Service). Receipts, gross, wages, proceeds, dividends, salary, interest, "take," payment, winnings, stipend, capital, fee, money, emolument. See also compensation, yield (2), profit (1), net, gain, return. *Ant.* Expenses.

Revenue bond A bond issued by a state or local government, repayable by the unit of government that issues it; a bond issued for and payable solely from a revenue-producing public project. See bond, securities; government.

Revenue Ruling (Rev.Rul.) An IRS official interpretation of the tax law as applied to specific transactions. See tax, decision, construction (1).

Revenue stamp A stamp affixed on a deed or other instrument of conveyancing to show the amount of federal tax on the sale of real property. See tax.

Reverberate, *v.* To bounce back. Echo, thunder, resound, vibrate, resonate, bellow, roar, ring, rumble, sound.

Revere, *v.* See honor (2), worship; tribute (2).

Revered, *adj.* See reputable, elevated, popular; holy; meritorious (2), great.

Reverence, *n.* See regard (2), affection, worship, love, fidelity.

Reverend, *adj.* See holy.

Reverent, *adj.* See holy, religious, serious, grave, formal.

Reverie, *n.* See dream, hallucination; preoccupation; contemplation; fantasize.

Reversal, *n.* The setting aside by an appellate court of a decision of a lower court (the Supreme Court's reversal of the district court's ruling). Annulment, voiding, repeal, voidance, about-face, overturning, nullification, rejection, revocation, setback, renunciation, upset, retraction, abolishment, withdrawal, undoing, overruling, disavowal, repudiation, nonapproval, turnabout, invalidation, countermand, flip-flop. See also neutralization, defeat (2), rescission, abjuration, abolition, elimination, cancellation. *Ant.* Affirmance.

Reverse 1. *v.* To set aside (reverse the judgment below). Overthrow, vacate, make void, annul, repeal, revoke, undo, void, capsize, recall, override, veto, negate, invert, withdraw, countermand, turn around, backtrack, renege, disavow, repudiate, contradict, retract, unmake, abrogate, nullify, invalidate, change, shift, disaffirm, swap, transpose. See also rescind, destroy, overrule, cancel. **2.** *n.* Opposite (the reverse is true). Antithesis, inverse, contrary, counterpart, converse, underside, counterpole, foil, antonym. See also contradiction, opposite, contrast. **3.** *n.* A setback (she suffered many reverses). See misfortune. *Ant.* Affirm; same; advantage.

Reverse discrimination, *n.* Prejudice or bias exercised against a person or class for the purpose of correcting a pattern of discrimination against another person or class. See discrimination, discriminate, bias, prejudice.

Reversible error Substantial error; error that reasonably might have prejudiced the party complaining about the error. See error, prejudice.

Reversion, *n.* The estate left in the grantor during the continuance of a particular estate; an interest created by law when the owner of real estate conveys an interest in it less than his or her own; the residue left in the grantor or his or her heirs after the termination of a particular estate (she kept the reversion when she conveyed a life estate in her home to her mother). See estate, interest, remainder, residue.

Reversionary interest The interest that a person has in the reversion of land or other property; a right to the future enjoyment of property that at present is being enjoyed by another; the property that reverts to the grantor after the expiration of an intervening interest. See remainder, interest, estate, expectancy.

Revert, *v.* To turn back; to return to (the land reverts to the owner after the life estate expires). Retreat, resume, come back; go, pass to; relapse, relive, recidivate, backslide, decay, backtrack. See also regress, lapse. *Ant.* Advance.

Review 1. *v.* To examine or go over a matter again (the appellate court agreed to review the decision of the lower court). Investigate, inspect, critique, correct, study, check, reexamine, evaluate, reconsider, analyze, weigh, assess, scrutinize, criticize, deliberate, recapitulate, reiterate, summarize. **2.** *n.* A consideration for the purpose of correction (judicial review). Reconsideration, examination, evaluation, analysis, study, retrospective, critique, assessment, scrutiny, inspection, appraisal, investigation.

Revile, *v.* See defame, disparage, attack, abuse, castigate, censure.

Revise, *v.* To correct or update (the legislature revised its probate code). Improve, rearrange, change, amend, rework, alter, overhaul, edit, "doctor," review, emend, remold, reconstruct, recast, rectify, rewrite, repair, straighten out, revamp, transform.

Revised Statutes (R.S.) A collection of statutes that have been revised, rearranged, and reenacted as a whole. See statute.

Revision, *n.* A correction or updating following a reexamination (revision of the statutes). Amendment, change, alteration, improvement, rewriting, modification, editing, rectification, reappraisal, redrafting, review, emendation, reformation.

Revitalization, *n.* See awakening, revival, renewal, rehabilitation.

Revitalize, *v.* See renew, revise, heal, correct (2), cure (2).

Revival, *n.* Renewing the legal force or effectiveness of something (revival of the cause of action). Restoration, resurrection, return, reestablishment, resumption, recovery, revitalization, resurgence, new beginning, renaissance, exhumation. *Ant.* Termination.

Revive, *v.* To renew; to make oneself liable again (revive the obligation by a new promise). Revivify, restore, reactivate, bring back to life, reawaken, reanimate, resurrect, revitalize, rejuvenate, rally, repeat, produce again, rekindle, enliven, resuscitate. See also renew. *Ant.* Renege.

Revivify, *v.* See revive, renew, heal, cure (2), correct (2).

Revocable, *adj.* Susceptible of being withdrawn or canceled (revocable letter of credit). Reversible. See also voidable. *Ant.* Unalterable.

Revocable trust A trust in which the maker or settlor reserves to himself or herself the right to revoke the trust. See trust.

Revocation, *n.* The destruction or voiding of something; the recall of some power, authority, or thing granted (revocation of the will). Termination, elimination, withdrawal, veto, killing, abolishment, reversal, disavowal, abolition, repeal, discontinuance, retraction, rescission, invalidation, disclaimer, abrogation, nullification, repudiation, annulment, negation, quashing, overruling, defeasance, voidance, relinquishment, dissolution. *Ant.* Confirmation.

Revoke, *v.* To make void (revoke the will). Recall, annul, cancel, terminate, abrogate, quash, veto, repudiate, relinquish, stop, ban, bar, dismiss, repeal, reverse, abolish, retract, nullify, vacate, counterorder, discard, renege, disclaim, overrule, take back, declare null and void, countermand, disallow, cast aside, expunge, negate, erase, kill, disavow. See also rescind, destroy, override. *Ant.* Validate.

Revolt 1. *n.* An attempt to overthrow the government (the revolt led to a charge of treason). Uprising, insurrection, rebellion, mutiny, insurgence, anarchy, revolution, mob rule, replacement, takeover, strike, putsch, treason, dissent, coup, coup d'état, insurgency, riot, defection, resistance, insubordination, upheaval, disorder, confrontation, opposition, subversion, secession, turbulence, chaos. **2.** *v.* To disgust (the display revolted her). Nauseate, repel, shock, appall, distress, offend, repulse, horrify, sicken, outrage, scandalize. *Ant.* Allegiance; amuse.

Revolting, *adj.* See offensive, odious, repulsive, obnoxious.

Revolution, *n.* **1.** The act of overthrowing a government. See mutiny, rebellion, insubordination, resistance, defiance, revolt (1). **2.** A transformation (industrial revolution). Metamorphosis, innovation, cataclysm, extensive change, modernization, upheaval. See also change (1). *Ant.* Loyalty; status quo.

Revolutionary, *n.* One who instigates or takes part in a revolution. Mutineer, rebel, malcontent, underground fighter, traitor, radical, agitator, terrorist, fifth column, saboteur, Weatherman, resistance, guerrilla, "contra," opposition, subversive, extremist, insurrectionist. See also anarchist, insurgent, nihilist; nonconformist. *Ant.* Follower.

Revolve, *v.* See turn (1), alternate; circulate.

Revolver, *n.* See gun, weapon, arms.

Revolving credit An arrangement that permits a buyer or borrower to purchase goods or to secure loans on a continuing basis so long as the outstanding balance in the account does not exceed a certain limit. See credit.

Rev.Rul. See Revenue Ruling.

Revue, *n.* See music, performance, entertainment, amusement.

Revulsion, *n.* See contempt (2), odium; hostility.

Reward, *n.* That which is given for some service or attainment (reward for evidence leading to arrest). Payment, remuneration, prize, bounty, acknowledgment, purse, return, emolument, token, consideration, accolade, tip, honorarium, fee, gratuity, premium, windfall, incentive, retaliation, requital, quid pro quo, kick-back, retribution. See also compensation, bonus.

Rework, *v.* See review, revise, improve, cure.

Rhapsody, *n.* See passion, emotion; extravaganza; music; lyric.

Rhetoric, *n.* See balderdash, prolixity, language, communication.

Rhetorical, *adj.* See flamboyant, gaudy, pompous, emotional, artificial.

Rhinestone, *n.* See gem; imitation.

"Rhubarb," *n.* See fight (1), quarrel, brawl, breach of the peace.

Rhythm, *n.* See music, accent; beat; lyric.

Ribald, *adj.* See obscene, filthy, immoral, corrupt, vulgar, common (3).

Ribbon, *n.* See belt (1), strip (3).

Rich, *adj.* See affluent, abundant; wealth, luxury.

Riches, *n.* See money, wealth, luxury, property.

Rickety, *adj.* See frail, weak, infirm, breakable, decrepit; dangerous.

Ricochet, *v.* To rebound. Bounce back, recoil, boomerang, backfire, deflect, deviate. See also jump.

Rid, *v.* See discharge, oust, erase, clear (5).

Riddance, *n.* See removal, emancipation, release (3).

Riddle, *n., v.* See conundrum, mystery, ambiguity; joke; pierce, cut, damage (2).

Ride, *v., n.* See travel, sail; voyage, junket; vessel (1), vehicle.

Rider, *n.* An amendment or addition (a rider to the proposed legislation). Attachment, extension, insertion, supplement, endorsement, addendum, appendage, adjunct, postscript, codicil, appendix, sequel, continuation.

Ridge, *n.* See mountain; grade (2); wrinkle (1), trench.

Ridicule, *v.* See disparage, mock (1), censure (2), slander (2), injure.

Ridiculous, *adj.* See absurd, odd (1), anomalous, irrational, wild, extraordinary, capricious, comic; clown.

Rife, *adj.* See epidemic (2), common, extensive.

Riffraff, *n.* See refuse, tramp, nonentity, ass.

Rifle, *n.* See gun, weapon, arms.

Rift, *n.* See break (3), breach (2); quarrel, argument, separation.

Rig, *v.* **1.** To manipulate (rig the market). Maneuver, control, prearrange, falsify, defraud, deceive, engineer, hoax, circumvent, "con," cheat, jockey, dupe, victimize, gerrymander, stock, tamper, juggle, influence. See also manipulate, exploit. **2.** See equip.

Rigging, *n.* See rope.

Right 1. *adj.* Morally correct; consonant with ethical principles or rules of positive law (she was right to reject the bribe). Righteous, honorable, aboveboard, de jure, just, noble, virtuous, licit, equitable, principled, within the law, exemplary, scrupulous, unimpeachable, fair, legal, decent, legitimate, upright, reasonable, valid, legalized, statutory, warranted, authorized, sanctioned, constitutional, privileged, justifiable, impartial, undeviating, designated, straightforward, rightful, punctilious, evenhanded, lawful, unerring, errorless, mandated, ordained, due, responsible, fitting. See also honest, moral (2), good (2). **2.** *adj.* Appropriate, favorable (the right approach). Accurate, precise, perfect, faultless, unmistaken, infallible, factual, truthful, on target, actual, wholesome, sound, positive, literal, real, admissible, exact, authentic, proper, seemly, advantageous, desirable, profitable, opportune, orderly, suitable, reasonable, conventional, propitious, beneficial, genuine, straight, apt, becoming, auspicious, de rigueur, normal, promising, ideal, unquestionable, accepted, satisfactory, irrefutable, sane, rational, well-grounded, healthy, absolute, direct, sensible, competent, preferable, fortunate, bona fide, deserving. **3.** *n.* A power, privilege, or immunity (the right to free speech). Claim, title, license, control, entitlement, authority, prescription, inheritance, freedom, authorization, jurisdiction, liberty, heritage, justification, stake, grant, permission, certification, confirmation, birthright, ownership, property. See also prerogative, interest. **4.** *n.* That which is moral or good (distinguish right from wrong). Virtue, merit, righteousness, morality, truth, principle, justice, equity, goodness, probity, fairness, integrity, rectitude, impartiality, uprightness, morals, veracity, fidelity, conformity, propriety. See also honor. **5.** *v.* To redress (right the wrong). Correct, make restitution for, recompense, restore, amend, vindicate, square, straighten, reform, repair, remedy, cure, rehabilitate, meliorate, rectify, avenge, retaliate, compensate. *Ant.* Illegal; wrong; impotence; evil; aggravate.

Righteous, *adj.* See right (1), moral (2); holy.

Rightful, *adj.* See just, justifiable, moral (2), good (2), honest, right (1).

Right of action The right to bring a suit. See action (1), cause of action.

Right of privacy See invasion of privacy; privacy.

Right of way, *n.* The right to pass over the land of another; an easement; a preference in asserting the right of passage at the same time and place as between two vehicles, or between a vehicle and a pedestrian. See passage (2), pass (8), easement.

Right-to-life, *adj.* See pro-life.

Right-to-work law, *n.* A state law that employees are not required to join a union as a condition of receiving or retaining a job. See union, employment, freedom.

Right wing, *n.* See reactionary.

Right-wrong test See insanity (4).

Rigid, *adj.* See inflexible, strict (2), arbitrary, absolute (1), callous, contumacious; firm, stationary.

Rigmarole, *n.* See balderdash, red tape; babble.

Rigor, *n.* See affliction; strict (2), firm.

Rigor mortis, *n.* One of the tests of death: a rigidity or stiffening of the muscular tissue and joints of the body. See death (1).

Rigorous, *adj.* See strict (2), extreme, formal, inflexible, firm, arbitrary, precise; meticulous, accurate.

Rile, *v.* See harass, disturb, exacerbate, outrage, provoke.

Rim, *n.* See border (1), boundary, exterior.

Ring, *n.* An exclusive combination of persons who seek an illegitimate or selfish end. See gang, coterie; noise.

Ringleader, *n.* See manager, master, foreman, head, principal, wrongdoer.

Rink, *n.* See arena, facility (2); sport; building.

Rinse, *v.* See bathe, water (2).

Riot 1. *n.* An unlawful assembly that has developed to the stage of violence; a designated number of persons (e.g., three or more), unlawfully assembled together and disturbing the peace by acting in a violent or tumultuous manner (inciting a riot). Fracas, donnybrook, uproar, affray, mutiny, revolt, disturbance, scuffle, chaos, melee, civil disorder, fray, turmoil, revolution, insurrection, commotion, insubordination, furor, scene, breach of the peace, rumpus, pandemonium, broil, rebellion, panic, flare-up, storm, carousal. **2.** *v.* To participate in a public disturbance (they rioted after the game). Rise up, rampage, fight, pillage, rebel, brawl, run amok, resist; celebrate, revel.

Riotous, *adj.* See wild, noisy, incorrigible.

Rip, *v.* See cut, part (1), divide; cheat.

Riparian rights Those rights incident to the ownership of land contiguous to and abutting flowing navigable waters such as streams or rivers; the rights of persons, through whose land a natural watercourse runs, to the benefit of the water as it passes through their land for all useful purposes to which it may be applied. See water, navigable, pass, passage.

Ripe, *adj.* Prepared or suitable (the time was ripe for intervention). Advanced, ready, prime, developed, favorable, timely, grown, provident, complete, perfect, fit, finished, conditioned, adult, seasoned, set, consummate, opportune, reliable, mellow, inclined. See also mature (2), seasonable, appropriate, justiciable. *Ant.* Premature.

Ripen, *v.* See mature (1), advance, develop.

Ripeness doctrine The constitutional mandate of case and controversy requires an appellate court to consider whether a case has matured or ripened into a controversy worthy of adjudication before it will determine the case. To warrant the issuance of a declaratory judgment, there must be a substantial controversy between parties having adverse legal interests of sufficient immediacy and reality. See justiciable, case and controversy, declaratory judgment.

"Rip-off," *n.* See cheat, larceny; exploit, deceive, manipulate.

Rise, *v., n.* See advance, advancement, growth, increase, develop, improve, ascend, ascent; resist, challenge (1), confront.

Rising, *adj.* See runaway (2).

Risk 1. *n.* The danger or hazard of a loss or injury (assumption of the risk). Speculation, vulnerability, exposure, liability, insecurity, uncertainty, susceptibility, endangerment, gamble, threat, shakiness. See also jeopardy, peril, hazard, danger, doubt. **2.** *v.* To expose to danger (risk losing the cargo). Jeopardize, chance, speculate, menace, threaten, venture, imperil; dare, tempt. See also expose (2), endanger, hazard (2). *Ant.* Security; protect.

Risk capital Money or property invested in a business venture. See investment, capital.

Risky, *adj.* See speculative, doubtful (1), insecure (2), contingent, capricious, indefinite, precarious, dangerous.

Risqué, *adj.* See obscene, suggestive, prurient, vulgar, immoral.

Rite, *n.* See worship, service (3), ceremony; God, holy, religious.

Ritual, *n.* See formality, custom, practice (1), ceremony, service (3).

Rival, *n., adj., v.* See competitor, adversary; competitive (1), opposite; compete.

Rivalry, *n.* See competition, opposition, contest (2).

River, *n.* A natural stream of water, of greater volume than a creek or rivulet, flowing in a more or less permanent bed or channel between defined banks or walls (public river). Tributary, stream, creek, rivulet, streamlet, brook, rill, feeder, fork, current, freshet, runnel, estuary, canal, inlet, waterway, cascade, watercourse.

"Roach," *n.* See marijuana.

Road, *n.* An open way or public passage. See highway, pass (8), passage (2).

Roadblock, *n.* See block (1), blockade, obstruction.

Roam, *v.* See wander, digress, walk.

Roar, *n., v.* See noise; yell.

Roast, *v.* See bake.

Rob, *v.* See robbery. Steal, seize, commandeer, appropriate, purloin, hold up, filch, shoplift, pirate, plunder, burglarize, swindle, peculate, loot, ransack, hijack, plagiarize, arrogate. See also pilfer, embezzle; larceny.

Robbery, *n.* Unlawfully taking an article of value from the person of another by the use of violence or fear (bank robbery). Aggravated theft, larceny by violence, holdup, piracy, theft, plunder, hijacking, shoplifting, commandeering, snatching, looting, pilferage, stealing, banditry; pillage, embezzlement, burglary, rapine, misappropriation, rape, seizure, expropriation, confiscation, abduction, capture, mugging. See also larceny, appropriation (1).

Robe, *n.* See clothes, apparel.

Robot, *n.* See automation; pawn (3), slave.

Robust, *adj.* See durable, healthy, able-bodied; alive (2); rude, vulgar.

Rock, *n.* Stone. Marble, limestone, boulder, granite, pebble, reef, flint, slate, gravel. See also earth; foundation, asylum.

Rocket, *n., v.* See weapon; aircraft; launch.

Rock 'n' roll, *n.* See music, entertainment.

Rocky, *adj.* See difficult, hazardous, dangerous.

Rod, *n.* A lineal measure of 5½ yards or 16½ feet.

Rodeo, *n.* See entertainment, amusement, sport, athletics, game, extravaganza.

Rogatory letters See letters rogatory.

Rogue, *n.* A vagrant or scoundrel. See crook, wrongdoer.

Role, *n.* See part (2), assignment (3), function, character, characterization, pretext.

Roll 1. *n.* The record of the proceedings of a court or public office. See record (2) judgment roll. **2.** *v.* To rob by force. See rob, robbery.

Rollback, *n.* See reduction, return.

Rollicking, *adj.* See happy, festive, wild.

Rolling over An extension or renewal of a short-term loan from one period to another. See loan, lend, extension.

Rollover paper Short-term notes that may be extended (rolled over) or converted to installment payments after the initial due date. See note, extend.

Romance, *n.* See love, affection; mystery, adventure (1); book (4); legend, dream, fiction.

Romantic, *adj.* See idyllic; impracticable, frivolous, insane, sentimental, emotional.

Romp, *n.* See sport (2), antic.

Rood of land The fourth part of an acre in square measure, or 1,210 square yards.

Roof, *n.* See ceiling (2).

"Rook," *v.* See cheat, deceive.

Room, *n.* See margin (2); chamber.

Room and board, *n.* See maintenance (1), necessaries, assistance, food, home.

Roomer, *n.* One who rents a room or rooms. See lodger, occupant.

Rooming house, *n.* See inn; home.

Roommate, *n.* See associate (2), partner, intimate (5).

Root, *n.* Foundation or source (the root of her difficulties). Cause, essence, origin, base, seat, reason, spring, footing, fount, occasion, principle, germ, fountainhead, nucleus, ground, premise, start, embryo, womb, mainspring, inception, commencement, rationale, seed, matrix. *Ant.* Result.

Rootless, *adj.* See itinerant, migratory, abandoned (1).

Root of title The conveyance that begins the chain of title to land. See chain of title.

Rope, *n.* Cord. Cable, wire, rigging, cordage, hawser, tackle. See also strand (2).

ROR Release on own recognizance. See personal recognizance.

Rorschach test, *n.* A method of detecting neurotic and psychotic traits by noting the patient's reaction to a set of ten cards containing standardized inkblots.

Roster, *n.* A roll or list of persons. See record (2), report (1).

Rostrum, *n.* See platform (2).

Rot, *v., n.* See decompose, perish, diminish, dissolve; lapse; balderdash.

Rotate, *v.* See turn (1), alternate; circulate, twist.

Rotation, *n.* See series, succession (2), chain (1).

Rote, *n.* See custom, practice, routine.

Rotten, *adj.* **1.** Decayed, unsound (rotten fruit). Rank, tainted, rancid, spoiled, decomposed, foul, purulent, diseased, putrid, stale, smelly, sour, unclean, fetid, moldering, contaminated, decomposing. See also odious. **2.** See corrupt.

Rotund, *adj.* See corpulent; round.

Rough, *adj.* See irregular; disheveled; violent, rude, wild, cruel, awkward, backward, assertive; approximate (3); difficult.

Roulette, *n.* See gambling, game.

Round, *adj.* **1.** Complete (round dozen). Full, entire, total, whole, unbroken, intact, uncut, undiminished, undivided, solid. **2.** Shaped like a sphere (round object). Circular, globelike, oval, ringed, spherical, global, curved, egg-shaped. *Ant.* Divided; square.

Roundabout, *adj.* See circular, ambiguous, indirect.

Rounded, *adj.* See complete, round (1).

Round lot A unit of trading on the New York Stock Exchange. For stocks it is 100 shares; for bonds, $1000 par value.

Round up, *v.* See congregate, assemble, accumulate.

Rouse, *v.* See animate, incite, initiate, provoke.

Rout, *n.*, *v.* See debacle; riot, defeat, overcome; withdraw, depart.

Route, *n.* **1.** A line of travel from one place to another. See course, highway, pass (8), passage (2). **2.** The means used to accomplish something. See agency (4), instrumentality.

Routine, *adj.*, *n.* See customary, common, commonplace, ordinary, habitual; procedure, method, plan (1), process.

Routinize, *v.* See regulate, classify, organize, frame (1).

Row, *n.*, *v.* See quarrel, dispute, argument; series, succession, chain (1); pattern.

Rowdy, *adj.* See disorderly, wild, noisy, incorrigible; wrongdoer.

Royal, *adj.* See elevated; arbitrary (2), pompous, arrogant; sovereign.

Royalty, *n.* Compensation for the use of property, expressed as a percentage of the receipts or as an account per unit produced; a payment made to an author or composer by a licensee, copyright holder, or assignee for each copy of his or her work sold; a payment made to an inventor for each article sold under his or her patent (a 15% royalty). See compensation (1), pay (1).

R.S. See Revised Statutes.

Rub, *v.*, *n.* See touch (1); bathe; obstacle.

Rubber check, *n.* A check that has been returned by the drawee bank because of insufficient funds in the account of the drawer.

Rubber-stamp, *v.* See approve, accept.

Rubbish, *n.* See balderdash; refuse.

Rubric, *n.* See name; class.

Ruby, *n.* See gem.

Ruckus, *n.* See commotion, riot.

Ruddy, *adj.* See healthy, able-bodied.

Rude, *adj.* Discourteous (rude behavior). Impolite, brazen, inconsiderate, uncouth, contemptuous, brutish, ignorant, abrupt, brusque, indecent, uncivil, offensive, coarse, gauche, brutal, disrespectful, bold, crude, illiterate, acrimonious, unmannerly, boorish, rough, inexperienced, raw, ill-bred, primitive, barbarian, brash, gruff, tumultuous, impertinent, indelicate, caustic, testy, sharp, ill-tempered, petulant, surly, brash, irascible, venomous, strident, inharmonious, vulgar, unrefined, savage, barbarous, untamed, tactless, harsh, fresh, untrained, obscene, violent, robust, crusty, insulting, clumsy, derisive, curt, biting, insolent, surly, profane, ill-mannered, pert, turbulent, impudent, uncivilized, inelegant, unpolished, vigorous, fierce, callow, awkward, cantankerous, trenchant. *Ant.* Gracious.

Rudiment, *n.* See cause, commencement, foundation.

Rudimentary, *adj.* See necessary, fundamental, primary, essential; inchoate.

Rue, *v.* See bemoan, suffer, cry (1).

Rueful, *adj.* See contrite; despondent, depressed.

Ruffian, *n.* See wrongdoer, crook.

Ruffle

Ruffle, *v., n.* See disturb; commotion, riot; decoration.

Rug, *n.* Cover, mat, carpet, pad, doormat, runner.

Rugged, *adj.* See irregular, disheveled; healthy, able-bodied; difficult, severe, extreme, onerous; rude.

Ruin, *v., n.* See destroy, exhaust, quash, collapse, corrupt; affliction, cataclysm, catastrophe.

Ruinous, *adj.* See bad, deleterious, adverse (4), fatal.

Rule 1. *n.* An established standard, guide, or regulation (rules for seeking a filing extension). Law, statute, ordinance, legislation, act, order, principle, decree, mandate, direction, dictate, fiat, ukase, instruction, prescription, injunction, pronouncement, demand, manifesto, imperative, restriction, declaration, bylaw, maxim, tenet, canon, formula, test, dogma, commandment, command, precept, procedure, practice, control, criterion, measurement, code, guide, protocol, method, embargo, habit, regimen, charge, measure, proposition, adage, doctrine, precedent, model, convention. **2.** *n.* The controlling authority (the queen's rule). Sovereignty, reign, dominion, administration, leadership, authority, government, command, power, presidency, management. **3.** *v.* To govern or control (the chairman ruled with an iron hand). Manage, administer, regulate, officiate, oversee, supervise, preside over, lead, dominate, domineer, head, reign, exercise authority, manipulate, master, police, superintend; persuade, influence, prevail, flourish, persist, predominate. **4.** *v.* To settle or decide a point of law (the court ruled that the defense does not apply). Resolve, adjudicate, settle, adjudge, determine, establish, declare, umpire, referee, arbitrate, judge, pass upon, decree, find, conclude, ascertain.

Rule absolute A rule that must be enforced forthwith. *Ant.* See rule nisi.

Rule against perpetuities No interest in property is good unless it must vest, if at all, not later than 21 years, plus the period of gestation, after some life or lives in being at the time of the creation of the interest. A rule that fixes the time within which a future interest must vest. The estate must vest within a time limited by a life or lives then in being and 21 years thereafter, together with the period of gestation necessary to cover cases of posthumous birth.

Rule in Shelley's case When in the same instrument a life estate is given to a person, followed by a remainder to this person's heirs, the heirs take nothing and the holder of the life estate gets an estate in fee. Where a person takes an estate of freehold, legally or equitably, under a deed, will, or other writing, and in the same instrument there is a limitation by way of remainder, either with or without the interposition of another estate, of any interest of the same legal or equitable quality to his heirs, or heirs of his body, as a class of persons to take in succession from generation to generation, the limitation to the heirs entitles the ancestor to the whole estate.

Rulemaking power The power of certain appellate courts, usually the highest appellate court within a given judicial system, to prescribe rules of procedure to be followed by lower courts within that judicial system.

Rule nisi An ex parte order directing the other party to show cause why the temporary order should not become permanent; a rule that becomes final unless cause can be shown against it.

Rule of four A case is deserving of review if four United States Supreme Court justices find that the case raises a legal question of general importance.

Rule of law A legal principle of general application; an enforceable pronouncement of government that directly or indirectly establishes a standard of conduct.

Rule of lenity When the intention of the legislature is not clear from the act itself, and reasonable minds might differ as to its intention, the court will adopt the less harsh meaning. See construction.

Rule of necessity Even though a judge has an interest in a case, he or she should still hear the case if it cannot otherwise be heard. The normal rule of disqualification does not apply if there is no other judge available to hear and determine the matter. See necessity.

Rule of reason The legality of restraints on trade is determined by weighing all the factors of the case (e.g., the history of the restraint, the evil believed to exist, the reason for adopting the particular remedy, and the purpose or end sought to be attained).

Ruler, *n.* See king, tyrant, authority (3), manager, director.

Rules of Appellate Procedure See Federal Rules of Appellate Procedure.

Rules of Civil Procedure See Federal Rules of Civil Procedure.

Rules of court Rules that regulate practice and procedure before a given court.

Rules of Criminal Procedure See Federal Rules of Criminal Procedure.

Rules of Decision Act The laws of the several states (except where the Constitution, treaties, or statutes of the United States otherwise require or provide) shall be regarded as rules of decision in trials at common law in the courts of the United States in cases where they apply.

Rules of Evidence See Federal Rules of Evidence.

Ruling 1. *n.* A judicial or administrative interpretation of a statute, constitution, order, regulation, treaty, or ordinance; a determination on the admissibility of evidence, on the granting or denial of a motion, etc. (Revenue Rulings). Decree, order, mandate, opinion, conclusion, sentence, edict, adjudication, pronouncement, award, finding, command, verdict, resolution, outcome, result. See also rule, decision. **2.** *adj.* Predominant or governing (ruling passion). See principal (5), primary (1).

Rum, *n.* See liquor, beverage.

Rumble, *v.* See yell.

Ruminate, *v.* See deliberate (1), consider (1), contemplate (1).

Rumination, *n.* See contemplation

Rummage, *v.* See investigate, ferret, trace; plunder.

Rumor, *n.* A current story passing from one person to another without any known authority as to its truth (a rumor that the plaintiff wrote the announcement). Grapevine, hearsay, gossip, whisper, supposition, idle talk, hints, canard, innuendo, "scuttlebutt," tale, unverified information. See also communication, report.

Rumpus, *n.* See noise, commotion, argument.

Run 1. *v.* To have legal effect during a period of time (the statute of limitations has run against the claim). **2.** *v.* To move rapidly (run to the corner). Bolt, fly, dash, hurry, sprint, jog, rush, scramble, zip, race, abscond, retreat, speed, escape, trot, decamp, zoom, skip. See also flee. **3.** *v.* To accompany (the covenant runs with the land). Go with, follow, travel, advance, progress, flow, function, track. **4.** *v.* To conduct or carry on (run a business). See manage (1). **5.** *n.* A sudden and widespread withdrawal of funds (a run on the bank).

Run-around, *n.* See red tape, bureaucracy, confusion.

Runaway 1. *n.* A person who runs away (runaway from the institution). Fugitive, escapee, breakaway, deserter, refugee, truant. **2.** *adj.* Expanding quickly (runaway prices). Rising, growing, increasing, advancing, ascending, mounting, soaring, accelerating. *Ant.* Inmate; declining.

Runaway shop An employer that moves its business to another location or that temporarily closes its business for anti-union purposes. See evasion, avoidance.

Run-down, *adj., n.* See dilapidated, exhausted, weak; brief (2).

Runner, *n.* **1.** One who solicits business for an attorney from accident victims. An ambulance chaser. **2.** One who assists the bail bondsman in presenting the defendant in court when required.

Running 1. *adj.* In operation; functioning (running policy). Active, open, operative, going, in play, moving, continuing, subsisting, enduring, pursuing. See also functional. **2.** *v.* See run (2).

Running account An open, unsettled account. See account.

Running of the statute of limitations The time mentioned in the statute of limitations has passed, and hence the action is barred. See statute of limitations.

Running with the land Passing with the transfer of the land.

Run-off, *n.* See refuse (2), remainder, residue.

Run-of-the-mill, *adj.* See pedestrian (2), commonplace, routine.

Runway, *n.* See pass (8), passage (2), highway.

Rupture, *n.* See break (3), contusion, division, divorce.

Rural, *adj.* **1.** Concerning the country. See agrarian. **2.** Provincial. Crude, unsophisticated, rustic, "hick," simple, bucolic, pastoral, rough. See also idyllic. *Ant.* Urban; cosmopolitan.

Ruse, *n.* See fake (2), device.

Rush, *v., n.* See run (2); accelerate; attack, assault; dispatch (3).

Russian roulette, *n.* A person spins the cylinder of a revolver with one bullet in it, and pulls the trigger while aiming the revolver at his or her own head.

Rust, *v., n.* See decompose; deterioration.

Rustic, *adj.* See idyllic, agrarian; rude.

Rustling, *n.* Stealing cattle. See larceny.

Rusty, *adj.* See raw (1); rotten.

Rut, *n.* See habit, custom; break (3), conduit; trench, wrinkle (1).

Ruthless, *adj.* See draconian, cruel, wild, gross, rude, inhuman.

Rylands v. Fletcher The English case that helped establish the principle that a defendant is strictly liable for harm resulting from a non-natural or abnormal use of land which causes increased danger to persons or property.

Sabbath, *n.* Seventh day of the week. See holy, religious; recess.

Sabbatical, *n.* See leave (5), furlough, vacation, holiday.

Saber, *n.* See weapon.

Sabotage, *n.* Willful destruction of property or interference with normal operations (sabotage of the company's plant). Disablement, impairment, undermining, malicious destruction, subversion, disruption, incapacitation, paralyzing, crippling, obstruction, vandalism. See also mutiny. *Ant.* Cooperation.

Saboteur, *n.* See revolutionary, nihilist.

Sack, *v.* See plunder, destroy, rob.

Sacrament, *n.* See ceremony, worship; holy, religious, church.

Sacred, *adj.* See holy, inviolate, religious; God, church.

Sacrifice, *v., n.* See yield, cede, relinquish; offering (2).

Sacrilege, *n.* The desecration of anything considered holy. See blasphemy, outrage (1).

Sacrilegious, *adj.* See profane (1), irreverent; blasphemy; rude.

Sacrosanct, *adj.* See holy, inviolate, religious; God, church.

Sad, *adj.* See depressed, depressing, despondent, serious (5), dismal, grave, barren, grievous.

Saddle, *v.* See encumber, burden (3).

Sadism, *n.* See cruelty; deviation, abuse, debauchery; sadistic.

Sadist, *n.* See tyrant, deviant (2); sadistic.

Sadistic, *adj.* Pertaining to a form of satisfaction, commonly sexual, derived from inflicting harm on another (sadistic attack). See cruel.

Sadness, *n.* See anguish, anxiety, pain, affliction, depression.

Sadomasochism, *n.* Pleasure derived from inflicting pain on others and on oneself. See deviant, cruelty.

Safari, *n.* See expedition, voyage.

Safe 1. *n.* A receptacle for the preservation of valuables (kept in the safe). Chest, strongbox, vault, depository, trunk, case, locker. See also vessel (2). **2.** *adj.* Secure from injury or damage (safe product). Guarded, sound, secure, covered, tested, harmless, innocuous, trustworthy, insured, unfailing, faithful, true, sheltered, impregnable, unassailable, defended, immune, impenetrable, inoculated, vaccinated, unthreatened, safeguarded, cloistered, carefree, composed, guaranteed, intact, invulnerable, reliable, riskless, sure, scrupulous, benign, whole, regulated, impregnable, screened, shielded, without risk, dependable, bulletproof. **3.** *adj.* Conservative (a safe approximation). Modest, cautious, responsible, timid, tame, circumspect. See also discreet, prudent. **4.** *adj.* Out of danger (safe in her home). Intact, unhurt, alive, unmolested, uninjured. *Ant.* Unsafe (2); risky (3); vulnerable (4).

Safeguard, *n., v.* See margin (2), security (2), precaution, protection, prudence; preservation; conserve, save (1), maintain (1), inoculate.

Safekeeping, *n.* See custody, preservation, shelter (1), protection, security (2), auspices, care.

Safety, *n.* See margin (2), protection, preservation, security (2), asylum.

Saga, *n.* See legend, report.

Sagacious, *adj.* See acute (1), learned, judicious, mature (2), brilliant, able, logical.

Sagacity, *n.* See judgment (2), discretion (2), maturity, common sense, learning, prudence.

Sage, *n., adj.* See teacher, scholar, authority (3, 4), master (1), oracle; learned, judicious.

Said, *adj.* Before mentioned (the said agreement). Aforesaid, previously mentioned, above mentioned, supra, already referred to.

Sail, *v.* To travel on water; to begin a voyage. Navigate, float, pilot, coast, cruise, embark, ship out.

Sailboat, *n.* See vessel (1).

Sailor, *n.* A seaman. Seafarer, navigator, voyager, shipmate, "sea dog," deck hand, captain, cadet, skipper, mate; soldier, serviceman, conscript, G.I., draftee, combatant, fighter, enlisted man, veteran, warrior, infantryman, hero, brave, knight. See also mariner; officer.

Saint, *n.* See patron; angel.

Saintly, *adj.* See holy, religious; charitable, benevolent.

Sake, *n.* See consideration (2), concern (5), interest (3); cause, end, reason.

Salable, *adj.* Fit for sale in the usual course of trade (salable goods). Merchantable, acceptable, in demand, needed, fashionable, staple, desirable, in vogue, vendible. See also fit (1), marketable. *Ant.* Unmarketable.

Salacious, *adj.* See obscene, filthy, suggestive, pornographic, wanton, wild.

Salary, *n.* A fixed periodical compensation paid for services rendered (garnishment of her salary). See compensation (1), income.

Sale, *n.* A contract in which the seller, in consideration of the payment or promise of payment of a certain price by the buyer, transfers title and possession of the thing sold to the buyer (retail installment sale). Exchange, trade, transaction, selling, auction, barter.

Sale on approval A conditional sale which becomes absolute only if the buyer approves or is satisfied with the goods.

Salesman, *n.* A person hired to sell goods or services. Salesperson, drummer, shopkeeper, clerk, huckster, dealer, traveling hawker, salesclerk, middleman, peddler, vendor, seller, solicitor. See also merchant, agent.

Sales tax, *n.* A tax imposed on the sale of goods, computed as a percentage of the purchase price. See tax.

Salient, *adj.* See conspicuous, outstanding, important, compelling, obvious.

Saliva, *n.* Spit. Spittle, slaver, foam, sputum, drool; expectorate, salivate, dribble, eject.

Salon, *n.* See chamber.

Saloon, *n.* A place where intoxicating liquors are sold and consumed. Tavern, bar, barroom, pub, cabaret, restaurant, establishment, beer parlor, cocktail lounge, bar and grill, hotel. See also inn.

Salutary, *adj.* See medical, remedial, beneficial, good, gainful.

Salute, *v., n.* See signal (3), gesture; address (2), entertain (2); homage, celebration, acclamation.

Salvage 1. *n.* That portion of goods or property which has been saved or remains after a casualty; property that is no longer useful but which has scrap value (salvage value). Remains, junk, debris, parts, leftovers; surplus, residue, residual, residuum; recovery, rescue operation, reclamation, retrieval, restoration, salvation, conservation. See also refuse. **2.** *v.* To rescue from loss (they were not able to salvage the documents). Recapture, save, retrieve, restore, rehabilitate, recover, redeem, recycle, regenerate, renew, ransom, repair, return.

Salvageable, *adj.* Pertaining to that which can be saved or corrected. Corrigible, redeemable, reformable, recoverable, curable, correctable, treatable. See also amenable, malleable.

Salvage value The value of an asset which remains after the useful life of an asset has expired.

Salvation, *n.* See preservation, protection, auspices; emancipation, release (3), rescue.

Salve, *n.* See ointment; remedy, cure.

Salvo Without prejudice to; excepting.

Samaritan, *n.* See good samaritan.

Same, *adj.* Equal, equivalent (same cause of action). Identical, selfsame, duplicate, interchangeable, synonymous, exact, repeat, twin; similar, of the kind, of the species, approximate, parallel, corresponding, on a par, analogous, alike; consistent, continuing, unvarying, enduring, lasting. *Ant.* Dissimilar.

Same evidence test Whether the facts alleged in the second indictment, if given in evidence, would have sustained a conviction under the first indictment; whether the same evidence would support a conviction in each case. See double jeopardy, crime, evidence.

Same offense The same criminal act, transaction, or omission. See double jeopardy, crime.

Sample 1. *n.* A small quantity of a commodity presented for inspection or examination as evidence of the quality of the whole (sale by sample). Specimen, exemplar, representation, paradigm, example, exemplification, sampling, pattern, case in point, exponent, embodiment, model, prototype, portion, standard, cross section, illustration, taste, instance, part. **2.** *v.* To test by examining a portion (sample the wine). Try out, taste, examine, judge, assess, evaluate, experience.

Sanatorium, *n.* See hospital, institution, home.

Sanctify, *v.* See anoint, dedicate, approve, honor (2); holy; disinfect.

Sanctimonious, *adj.* See pompous, arrogant, parochial, artificial, feigned, false (2).

Sanction 1. *v.* To confirm or assent (the board could not sanction the behavior). Concur, agree, accept, allow, acknowledge, authorize, validate, foster, indorse, charter, approve, encourage, ratify, certify, countenance, support, uphold, indulge, acquiesce, legitimize, legitimate, accede, enable, vouchsafe, subscribe, favor, accredit, warrant, notarize, abet, countersign; command, decree, order. **2.** *n.* Support or encouragement. See approval. **3.** *n.* A penalty for an infraction or violation. See punishment. *Ant.* Reject; renunciation; commendation.

Sanctity, See inviolability, virtue (1), integrity (1), honor (3).

Sanctuary, *n.* A place of refuge. See haven, asylum (2), church.

Sanctum sanctorum, *n.* See sanctuary.

Sane, *adj.* **1.** Of natural and normal mental condition; healthy in mind (sane at the time of the act). Lucid, balanced, sound, of sound judgment, in possession of one's faculties, mentally sound, compos mentis, clear-headed. See also healthy. **2.** Sensible (a sane resolution). See rational. *Ant.* Insane.

Sanguine, *adj.* See optimistic, happy, certain (2), active (2).

Sanitary, *adj.* Pertaining to health (sanitary conditions of the restaurant). Hygienic, healthful, aseptic, clean, uncontaminated, harmless, uninfected, unpolluted, salubrious, disinfected, prophylactic, sterile, germ-free, pasteurized, antiseptic. See also healthy, wholesome. *Ant.* Unhealthy.

Sanitation, *n.* Measures for promoting public health; removal or neutralization of elements injurious to public health (sanitation practices). Sterilization, immunization, vaccination, hygienics, decontamination, inoculation, cleanliness. See also health.

Sanitize, *v.* See fumigate, disinfect, bathe; clean.

Sanity, *n.* **1.** The normal condition of the human mind (evidence of his sanity). Sound understanding, normalcy, rationality, mental health, mental balance, clearheadedness, saneness, lucidity; reason, sense, levelheadedness, reasonableness, judgment, moderation. **2.** See coherence (1).

Sap, *v.* To weaken. See impair.

Sapient, *adj.* See acute (1), learned, judicious, mature (2), brilliant, able.

Sapphire, *n.* See gem; color (4).

Sarcasm, *n.* See contempt, caricature, slander, aspersion; mock (1).

Sarcastic, *adj.* See caustic, cutting, biting, offensive, malicious, cruel; mock (1).

Sardonic, *adj.* See derogatory, defamatory; sarcastic.

Sash, *n.* See strip (3), belt (1).

Sass, *n.* See insubordination, effrontery, insolence.

Satanic, *adj.* See inhuman, cruel, malicious, bad (2), animal (2).

Satchel, *n.* See baggage; vessel (2).

Satellite, *n.* See assistant, attendant, appendage.

Satiate, *v.* See fill, realize (2), consummate (1), satisfy, perfect (3).

Satire, *n.* See caricature; slander; joke.

Satirical, *adj.* See caustic, cynical, derogatory, defamatory, irreverent, comic, absurd, anomalous.

Satirize, *v.* See mock (1), exaggerate, slander.

Satisfaction. *n.* **1.** The discharge of an obligation (satisfaction of the judgment by paying the damages awarded). Payment, compensation, settlement, amends, redress, reimbursement, reparation, atonement, justice, requital, restitution, clearance, indemnification, expiation, vindication. See also indemnity. **2.** Fulfillment (satisfaction over the performance). Pleasure, contentment, joy, felicity, pride, delight, comfort, gratification; success, accomplishment, realization. See also enjoyment, happiness, diversion (2). *Ant.* Repudiation; discontent.

Satisfactory, *adj.* Good enough (satisfactory proof). See adequate, abundant.

Satisfy, *v.* **1.** To discharge a debt (he satisfied the judgment). Pay, repay, carry out, answer, reimburse, requite, fulfill, compensate, settle, annul, clear, make good, defray, appease, remunerate. See also indemnify. **2.** To please (satisfy the director). Satiate, appease, gratify, serve, delight, assuage, content, relieve, indulge, pacify, cheer, amuse. **3.** To convince (satisfy the jury). Persuade, answer, respond to, assure, reassure, remove the doubts of. *Ant.* Incur (1); antagonize (2).

Saturate, *v.* See inundate, fill, pack.

Saucy, *adj.* See rude, offensive, impertinent (2).

Saunter, *v.* See walk; loiter, loaf; meander.

Savage, *adj.* See cruel, wild, gross, base (2), bad, violent, emotional, deleterious, extreme, malicious, obscene.

Savant, *n.* See teacher, scholar, authority (3, 4), master (1), oracle; learned, judicious.

Save 1. *v.* To deliver from harm (save the drowning victim). Rescue, salvage, preserve, deliver, free, protect, spare, redeem, safeguard, ransom, help, shield, cover, secure. **2.** *v.* To set aside funds for budgetary purposes (save for future needs). Economize, retrench, accumulate, shelve, put away, store up, keep in reserve, cut expenses, husband, hoard, amass, stock, reserve. **3.** *prep., conj.* With the exception of. But, barring, except, excepting, minus, not counting, less. *Ant.* Imperil (1); squander (2).

Save harmless clause A provision in a document by which one party agrees to indemnify another as to claims and suits that may be asserted against him or her. See indemnity, insurance.

Saving, *n.* **1.** A reduction in cost (a saving of 5%). Discount, markdown, kickback, cut. See also rebate. **2.** Resources. See fund (2), money.

Saving clause A restriction in a statute that preserves certain rights, remedies, or privileges; a provision in a statute that provides that if part of the statute is declared unconstitutional, the rest is to remain in force if it is self-sustaining. See statute, preservation, separability clause, severable.

Saving to suitors clause A suitor asserting an in personam admiralty claim may elect to sue in a common-law state court through an ordinary civil action. In such an action, the state court must apply the same substantive law as would be applied had the suit been instituted in admiralty in federal court.

Savior, *n.* See patron, angel, God.

Savoir-faire, *n.* See delicacy, discretion (3), experience (1), facility (3), skill (1), ability.

Savory, *adj.* See delectable, attractive; reputable.

"Savvy," *v.*, *n.*, *adj.* See comprehend; comprehension; expert (2).

Saw, *v.*, *n.* See cut; observe; maxim; equipment, apparatus, instrument (2), device.

Sawed-off shotgun See gun, weapon.

Say, *v.* See communicate, pronounce, report (4).

Saying, *n.* See maxim, communication.

S.B. Senate Bill. See bill, legislation.

SBA See Small Business Administration.

Scab, *n.* One who takes the job of a worker on strike; one who works for lower wages than, or under conditions contrary to, those prescribed by a trade union. Strikebreaker, traitor.

Scaffold, *n.* See rack (1), platform (2).

Scald, *v.* See burn.

Scale, *n.*, *v.* See extent, range, scope, measure; series, chain (1), succession (2); climb, advance.

Scalper, *n.* One who buys tickets and then resells them at an inflated price; a small-scale speculator; a small operator who takes profits on slight fluctuations in the securities market.

"Scam," *n.* See fraud, artifice, deception, cheat.

Scamper, *v.* See run.

Scan, *v.* See investigate, audit (2), canvass (1), browse, observe.

Scandal, *n.* **1.** Damage to reputation (the incident brought scandal to the company). See disgrace, damage, damages. **2.** Shameful or disgraceful conduct (a scandal in the president's office). See offense, corruption, fault (1), wrong (1), delinquency, debauchery, lapse (3). **3.** Malicious gossip (many heard the scandal). See libel (1), slander. **4.** Outrage over wrongdoing (the scandal led to her resignation). Outcry, furor, storm, fuss, turmoil, commotion, disturbance, tumult. See also outrage (1).

Scandalize, *v.* See outrage (2).

Scandalous, *adj.* Shocking, defamatory, disgraceful (a scandalous scene). See offensive, immoral, corrupt (1), odious; irreverent; blasphemy.

Scandal sheet, *n.* See press; reporter (4); yellow (2), yellow journalism.

Scant, *adj.*, *v.* See insufficient, few, small (1), bare, deficient, minimal, nugatory; diminish, abridge.

Scanty, *adj.* See scant.

Scapegoat, *n.* See victim.

Scar, *n.*, *v.* See lesion, contusion, wound, cut; brand; mutilate, maim.

Scarce, *adj.* See few, insufficient, inadequate, small (1), minimal, marginal, nugatory, minor (1); deficient.

Scarcity, *n.* See dearth, absence (2), privation, want (1), need (1), deficiency, arrears.

Scare, *v.* See intimidate, disturb, menace (2).

Scared, *adj.* See apprehensive, yellow (1).

Scathing, *adj.* See caustic, biting, cutting, offensive, malicious, violent, extreme.

Scatter, *v.* See sprinkle, distribute, circulate, dissipate (2).

Scatterbrain, *n.*, **scatterbrained,** *adj.* See ass, idiot; wild, oblivious, remiss, careless, reckless.

Scavenge, *v.* See collect; investigate, ferret.

Scavenger, *n.* See tramp.

Scenario, *n.* See plan (1), schedule, outline.

Scene, *n.* See view (5), environment, neighborhood; eruption, commotion.

Scent, *n.* See aroma; fragrant.

Schedule 1. *n.* A list of events, times, assets, etc. (a schedule of assets and liabilities). Table, itinerary, register, catalogue, inventory, recipe, enumeration, index, program, roll, calendar. See also agenda, plan (1), outline, record (2). **2.** *v.* To arrange (the hearing was scheduled for noon). See organize (1).

Scheduled injury An injury for which a specific sum is payable under worker's compensation. See injury, workmen's compensation.

Scheme 1. *n.* A design or strategy to accomplish a purpose (scheme to defraud). See machination, duplicity, contrivance, fraud, deception, plan (1). **2.** *v.* To contrive (they schemed to take over the firm). See plot, conspire, manipulate, plan (2).

Schism, *n.* A separation into factions. See division (1).

Schizophrenia, *n.* A psychotic withdrawal from reality. See insanity.

"Schlock," *n.* Inferior merchandize. See defective, inferior.

"Schmuck," *n.* See boor, ass, idiot.

Scholar, *n.* A student; someone with considerable knowledge. Pupil, bookworm, professional, professor, reader, learner. See also student, teacher, authority (3, 4), master, oracle.

Scholarly, *adj.* See academic (2), learned, literary (2), cultivated.

Scholastic, *adj.* See scholarly.

School, *n.* **1.** An institution or place for instruction or education (public school). Academy, college, university, department, seminary, lyceum, center, faculty, institute, alma mater, boarding school, conservatory, correspondence school, gymnasium. **2.** A group following a particular person or approach (school of thought). Way of thinking, clique, style, method, creed, belief, denomination, ism, faith, crowd, dogma, system, apostles, successors, persuasion. See also coterie.

School board or committee An agency of municipal officers charged with the administration of the affairs of public schools. See official, officer, agency.

Schooling, *n.* See education.

Schoolteacher, *n.* See teacher.

Science, *n.* An organized body of knowledge, usually involving observation and testing. Discipline, knowledge, field, inquiry, skill, facility, area, subject, specialty, scholarship, learning, pursuit; biology, mathematics, chemistry, medicine, zoology, botany, engineering, physics, mechanics, thermodynamics, social science, economics, sociology. See also art.

Scienter Guilty knowledge; intent to deceive or manipulate. See fraud.

Scientific, *adj.* See empirical, mathematical, technical, precise (2), objective, physical, material, concrete.

Scintilla, *n.* A minute amount (scintilla of evidence). Trifle, spark, small particle, trace, shadow, jot, glimmer, fragment, smidgen, insignificant amount, modicum, fleck, touch, drop, splinter, hair, atom, grain, hint. See also iota, minimum. *Ant.* Abundance.

Scion, *n.* See descendant, issue, child, offspring.

Scire facias, *n.* A judicial writ founded on a matter of record, requiring the person against whom it is brought to show cause why the party bringing the writ should not have advantage of the record or why the record should not be annulled and vacated.

Scoff, *v.* See mock (1), slander, censure (2).

Scofflaw, *n.* See delinquent (3), wrongdoer.

Scold 1. *v.* To criticize severely (scold the child). See castigate, reprimand. **2.** *n.* A quarrelsome, vituperative person. Faultfinder, chider, shrew, complainer.

Scoop, *v.* See excavate, shovel, extract (1).

Scope, *n.* The range of a function or operation (scope of representation). Breadth, span, circle, orbit, field, latitude, ambit, compass, purview, area, sphere, sweep, spread, depth, realm, extension, bounds, space, circuit, length. See also range, extent, measure, zone.

Scope of employment Activities that fairly and reasonably may be said to be incident of the employment or logically and naturally connected with it; activities of an employee in furtherance of duties owed to the employer where the latter is exercising or could exercise control over what the employee does. See course of employment, agent, employee.

Scorch, *v.* See burn; castigate.

Score, *n., v.* See result (1); number; account; multitude; calculate, measure (3), rate; slander.

Scorn 1. *v.* To hold in contempt. See condemn (3), mock, castigate, censure, reprimand, slander. **2.** *n.* Arrogance, disdain, or ridicule. See contempt (2), disgrace, obloquy.

Scotch, *v.* See block, quash, hinder, destroy; liquor, beverage.

Scoundrel, *n.* A base, villainous, or dishonest person. See wrongdoer.

Scour, *v.* See investigate, ferret, trace; bathe.

Scourge, *n., v.* See punishment, disaster, affliction; batter, beat.

Scout, *v., n.* See observe, trace, spy, investigator.

Scrabble, *v.* See flounder, blunder.

Scramble, *v., n.* See commingle, associate (1); confuse; contest, collide, disturb, disorder.

Scrap, *n., v.* See refuse; part, division, iota; fight, argument; delete, cancel, jettison.

Scrappy, *adj.* See alive (2), healthy, able-bodied.

Scratch, *v.* See mar, damage, cut, deface, delete, cancel.

Scream, *v., n.* See yell; noise.

Screech, *v., n.* See yell; noise.

Screen, *v., n.* See disguise, conceal, hide; classify; filter; select (1); wall (1).

Screw, *v.* See twist (1); distort; affix (1), attach (2), connect (1); cheat, deceive, manipulate.

"Screw-up," *n.* See complication, block (1), bar (3), obstruction; blunder, confuse, destroy.

Scribble, *v.* See draw (1), communicate; handwriting.

Scribe, *n.* See clerk, secretary (3), recorder, accountant.

Scrimmage, *n.* See brawl, fight, commotion, argument; practice (3); contest.

Scrimp, *v.* See save (2), conserve, hoard.

Scrip, *n.* Something exchanged for money or a privilege; a document entitling the holder to something of value; temporary money.

Script, *n.* **1.** Something written; the original of an instrument or document. See manuscript, publication (2); schedule, plan. **2.** Cursive handwriting. See handwriting.

Scripture, *n.* See bible; religion, church, God.

Scrivener, *n.* One who copies; one who prepares written instruments or documents. Writer, scribe, conveyancer. See also clerk, recorder, accountant.

Scroll, *n.* **1.** A rolled paper or parchment containing writing or painting. **2.** A mark intended to take the place of a seal.

Scrooge, *n.* See stingy, avaricious.

Scrounge, *v.* See parasite; salvage; filch.

Scrub, *v.* See bathe, fumigate, disinfect.

Scrumptious, *adj.* See delectable, attractive, enjoyable.

Scruple, *n.* See reservation (3), doubt (2), apprehension, question, ethics, caution.

Scrupulous, *adj.* See precise (2), particular (2), difficult (3); critical (2); careful, cautious; moral (2), honest, good (2).

Scrutinize, *v.* See investigate, audit, watch, observe (3).

Scrutiny, *n.* See examination, investigation, inquiry, inquest, inspection.

Scuffle, *n.* See fight, commotion, brawl, riot.

Sculpture 1. *v.* See engrave, create, forge. **2.** *n.* Art created by shaping designs in relief or in the round. Statue, statuette, figurine, bust, monument, icon, bronze, image, effigy.

Scum, *n.* See refuse; tramp, outcast.

Scurrilous, *adj.* Base or foul-mouthed. See indecent, obscene, vulgar.

Scutage, *n.* A tax or payment given in lieu of military service.

"Scuttle," *v.* See jettison, abandon (1), reject.

"Scuttlebutt," *n.* See rumor, communication, report.

S.D. Southern District (e.g., S.D.N.Y. is the United States District Court in the Southern District of New York).

Sea, *n.* **1.** A great mass of water that surrounds land. Ocean, waters, gulf, lake, deep, bay, lagoon, bayou, river, sound, harbor, estuary, basin, brine. **2.** Abundance (sea of regulations). Swarm, profusion, great deal, flock, plethora, mountain, quagmire, torrent, ton.

Seafarer, *n.* See sailor.

Seal 1. *n.* An impression or sign to attest the execution of an instrument or to authenticate the document (corporate seal). Emblem, token, logo, imprint, stamp, imprimatur, certification, pledge, authentication, hallmark, trademark. See also badge. **2.** *v.* To fasten. See affix (1). **3.** *v.* To sanction. See certify, authorize. **4.** *v.* To close (seal the record). Conceal, secure, keep private, keep secret, board up, block up, shut, dam, lock, bolt, bar.

Sealing of record Not allowing the record of a criminal or juvenile delinquent to be examined except by court order or by designated officials. See record.

Seaman, *n.* A person who navigates or who assists in the navigation of ships. See sailor.

Séance, *n.* See meeting; contact; witchcraft.

Search 1. *n.* An examination of one's person, premises, vehicle, etc., for the purpose of discovering evidence of guilt (illegal search). Prying, probe, inspection, exploration, scrutiny, study, hunt, quest, pursuit, check, chase, perusal, going-over, analysis, questioning, research, patrol, tracking, inquisition, investigation, reconnaissance, observation, seeking evidence. **2.** *v.* See investigate, audit, pursue (2), trace (2), ferret, chase, cross-examine.

Searching, *adj.* See comprehensive; curious, prying, acute.

Search warrant, *n.* A written order issued by a judge or magistrate in the name of the government, directed to and authorizing a sheriff or other officer to search for and seize any property that constitutes evidence of a crime. See order, warrant.

Seashore, *n.* Land adjacent to the sea that is covered or left dry according to the movement of the tides. See shore.

Season, *n., v.* See age (1), epoch, interval, period; mitigate; discipline (4).

Seasonable, *adj.* Done within the agreed-upon time, or within a reasonable time if no time was agreed upon (seasonable acceptance). Timely, well-timed, propitious, opportune, acceptable, fit, apposite, correct, serviceable, due, appropriate, right, suited, fortunate, favorable, advantageous, felicitous, proper. *Ant.* Untimely.

Seasonal, *adj.* Carried on only at certain seasons or at fairly definite portions of the year (seasonal employment). See intermittent, periodic, fluctuating, irregular, inconsistent.

Seat, *n.* Headquarters; location of the principal government offices (county seat). Capital, nucleus, hub, venue, site, source, cradle, base, station, quarters, domicile, axis, core, residence, nest, locale.

Seaworthy, *adj.* Pertaining to a vessel that is properly constructed, prepared, manned, equipped, and provided for the trip intended. See fit (1).

SEC See Securities and Exchange Commission.

Secede, *v.* See depart (1), divide, dissolve.

Secession, *n.* Withdrawing from membership. See departure, division (1), rebellion, removal.

Seclude, *v.* See sequester, confine.

Secluded, *adj.* See isolated, abandoned (1).

Seclusion, *n.* See separation, quarantine (1), concealment, exile.

Second 1. *adj.* Coming after the first (second best). Runner-up, next, following, alternate, consequent, resultant, other, secondary, subsequent. **2.** *adj.* Subordinate (second to none). See inferior (1). **3.** *n.* A moment (hesitated for a second). See instant (3), moment. **4.** *v.* Support (second the motion). See advocate (2), promote, back. **5.** *n.* One who assists or supports another. See agent (1), assistant.

Secondary, *adj.* Of a subsequent or subordinate kind or class. See inferior, minor (2), second (1), dependent, ancillary, collateral, extraneous.

Secondary boycott A refusal to work for, purchase from, or handle the products of a secondary employer with whom the union has no dispute in order to force this employer to stop doing business with the primary employer with whom the union does have a dispute. A combination with the purpose and effect of coercing customers or suppliers, through fear of loss or bodily harm, to withhold or withdraw their business from the employer who is the primary subject of the attack. See boycott, union.

Secondary meaning doctrine Protection given geographic or descriptive terms that the producer has used to such an extent as to lead the general public to identify the producer or the product with the mark or term. A geographic or descriptive mark receives protection against copying if consumers have come to associate it with a particular manufacturer or source. See badge, protection.

Secondary school, *n.* See school, education.

Second-class, *adj.* See inferior (1), dependent, minor (2), ancillary, collateral, extraneous.

Second degree murder The unlawful taking of a human life with malice but without premeditation and deliberation. See murder, homicide.

Second fiddle, *n.* See subordination; inferior.

Second-guess, *v.* See censure (2).

Secondhand, *adj.* See indirect, circuitous; old, ancient; dilapidated, disheveled.

Second mortgage, *n.* A mortgage given on property that has a prior mortgage on it. See mortgage.

Second-rate, *adj.* See deficient, inferior, minor (2), dependent, ancillary, collateral, extraneous, expendable.

Secrecy, *n.* The state of being concealed (meeting held in secrecy). Confidentiality, stealth, incognito, darkness, silence, camouflage, seclusion, isolation, privacy, concealment, secretiveness, furtiveness, slyness, subterfuge, covertness, sneakiness, unobtrusiveness, shadiness, surreptitiousness, underhandedness, mystery, solitude, dark.

Secret 1. *adj.* Not made public (secret report). See hidden, clandestine, covert, private. **2.** *n.* That which is kept from the general public; a private matter (disclosure of the secret). Confidence, confidential matter, private affair, mystery, classified facts, privileged information. **3.** *n.* Formula (secret of success). Key, answer, recipe, method, essence.

Secretary, *n.* **1.** The corporate officer in charge of keeping records, giving and receiving notices, etc. See official, officer, recorder. **2.** The administrator or director of the executive department of the government. See head, manager, director, employer. **3.** A stenographer, typist, or scribe. See accountant, clerk.

Secrete, *v.* To hide away. See conceal, hide, cloak, disguise, sequester, confine.

Secretive, *adj.* See hidden; private; evasive, clandestine, covert.

Sect, *n.* A relatively small group having common beliefs or practices. See group (1), denomination (2); church, religion.

Sectarian, *adj.* **1.** Promoting a particular sect or faith. See religious. **2.** Factional. Doctrinaire, prejudiced, zealous, narrow, provincial, dogmatic, fanatic, orthodox. See also parochial, absolute.

Section, *n.* **1.** A portion or part. See part (1), division (2). **2.** A region. See area (1), zone.

Sector, *n.* See division (2), classification (2), class (1), zone, area (1).

Secular, *adj.* Pertaining to the present, temporal world; not religious (secular education). Nonreligious, lay, material, worldly, earthly, mundane, materialistic, civil. See also physical, profane. *Ant.* Spiritual.

Secure 1. *v.* To make certain the payment of a debt or the discharge of an obligation (secure the loan). Guarantee, insure, stand behind, warrant, stake, cosign, countersign. See also indemnify, pledge, back (1); defend; protection. **2.** *v.* To attach. See affix (1), fix (2), connect. **3.** *v.* To obtain possession of. See acquire. **4.** *adj.* Not exposed to danger. See safe (2). **5.** *adj.* Dependable. See reliable. **6.** *adj.* See firm, fixed.

Secured, *adj.* **1.** Supported or backed by security or collateral (secured debt). See secure (1). **2.** See fixed (2); safe.

Secured creditor A creditor who holds a special assurance of payment of his or her debt (e.g., via mortgage, collateral, lien). See lender, creditor, protection.

Secured transaction A transaction founded on a security agreement that creates or provides for a security interest. See security interest.

Securities, *n.* Evidences of debts or of property; evidences of obligations to pay money or of rights to participate in earnings or the distribution of other corporate property. Stocks, convertible debentures, negotiable paper, coupon, bill, warrants, negotiables. See also security, note, bond, instrument; exchange (3).

Securities and Exchange Commission (SEC) A federal agency that regulates the exchange of securities. See agency (2), administrative agency.

Security, *n.* **1.** A pledge, mortgage, deposit, lien, etc., given by a debtor to assure payment or performance of the debt, which gives the creditor a resource to be used in case of failure of the principal obligation (without security, he could not obtain the loan). Warranty, bail, surety, escrow, collateral, debenture, bond, note, pawn, token, deposit, assurance, stock. **2.** Protection (national security). Safety, defense, strength, shelter, fortification, bulwark, trust, stability, safeguards, police, arms, military, preservation, impregnability, maintenance, care, support, unassailability, immunity, independence, freedom from harm, invulnerability, confidence, reliance, dependability, sanctuary, guard. **3.** See peace.

Security agreement An agreement that creates or provides for a security interest. See security interest.

Security deposit Money deposited by a tenant with the landlord as security for full and faithful performance of the lease. See deposit (2).

Security guard, *n.* See police, patrol, caretaker, guardian.

Security interest An interest in property which provides that the property may be sold on default in order to satisfy the obligation for which the security interest is given. For example, a mortgage grants a security interest in real property. See interest, right.

Sedan, *n.* See vehicle.

Sedate, *adj.* See deliberate (3), quiet (1, 2), patient (3), reasonable, cautious, proper.

Sedative, *n.* See drug, medicine; sedate.

Sedentary, *adj.* See stationary, dormant, passive, quiet; lazy, apathetic.

Sediment, *n.* Matter that has been transported from its site of origin by water, ice, wind, gravity, or other natural means as a product of erosion; matter that settles to the bottom of liquid. See refuse (2), earth.

Sedition, *n.* A communication or agreement that has as its objective the stirring up of treason or certain lesser commotions; advocating the overthrow or reformation of the government by violence; defamation of the government. See rebellion, insubordination, defiance, mutiny, apostasy, riot, revolt, betrayal.

Seditious, *adj.* Promoting sedition (seditious speech). Revolutionary, treasonable, defiant, underground, rebel, riotous, rebellious, unruly, subversive, insubordinate, traitorous, incendiary, undermining, insurgent, disloyal, extremist. See also mutinous, disobedient, lawless. *Ant.* Loyal.

Seduce, *v.* To induce someone to engage in sexual intercourse; to lead astray (seduced by a false promise to marry). Lure, tempt, inveigle, allure, charm, cajole, bewitch, attract, enthrall, magnetize, persuade, tantalize, tease, excite, captivate, titillate, trap, snare; violate, deflower, debauch, ravish, abuse, corrupt, defile, pervert. See also entrap, entice; rape. *Ant.* Dissuade.

Seduction, *n.* The act of seducing. See bait (1, 3), invitation, appeal (3), interest (4, 5); seduce.

Seductive, *adj.* See attractive, intriguing, compelling, beautiful, irresistible, cogent.

Sedulous, *adj.* See firm (2), decisive, diligent, precise (2), indefatigable, strong, constant.

See 1. *v.* See observe, witness (2), comprehend. **2.** *n.* The circuit of a bishop's jurisdiction.

Seed, *n.* See root, foundation; commencement; birth (1).

Seedy, *adj.* See dilapidated, disheveled, dirty; obscene.

Seek, *v.* See attempt (3), desire (1), hope (1); apply (1), petition, appeal (4).

Seem, *v.* See appear (2).

Seeming, *adj.* See apparent, putative, colorable, reputed, ostensible, deceptive.

Seemly, *adj.* See moral (2), honest, good (2), proper; attractive, beautiful, intriguing.

Seen, *v.* See known.

Seep, *v.* See emit (2); enter (2), pierce.

Seer, *n.* See oracle; teacher; witchcraft.

Seethe, *v.* See rage; angry.

Segment, *n.,* **segment,** *v.* See portion, part, division, classification (2), class (1), zone, area; iota, scintilla; divide (1).

Segmented, *adj.* See isolated, separate (1); divide (1).

Segregate, *v.* See group (2), divide, expel, withdraw, depart (1), sequester; quarantine.

Segregation, *n.* Separation (racial segregation). Classification, isolation, grouping, partition, differentiation, exile, splitting up, allocation, detachment, segmentation; racism; apartheid, bigotry, discrimination, ostracism, ghettoization. See also division, separation, quarantine; bias, prejudice. *Ant.* Integration.

Seisin, seizin, *n.* Full and complete present ownership and possession of land; possession of real property under a claim of freehold estate.

Seize, *v.* **1.** To put into possession; to take possession forcibly (the police seized the weapon). Sequester, sequestrate, capture, snatch, grab, grasp, impound, assume, confiscate, take hold of, usurp, commandeer, embrace, levy, abstract, clasp, annex, arrogate, wrest, replevy, expropriate, dispossess. See also wrench (1), appropriate (1). **2.** Pirate or steal. See rob, plunder (1); larceny. **3.** To grasp the meaning of. See comprehend (1).

Seizure, *n.* **1.** To take possession of property (search and seizure). Capture, confiscation, impoundment, annexation, takeover, expropriation, abduction, arrogation, dispossession, interception, annexation, divestment, acquisition, grab, apprehension, impressment; kidnapping, arrest. See also appropriation. **2.** A sudden convulsion (medical attention following the seizure). Fit, paroxysm, stroke, attack, throe, spasm, visitation, crisis, cramp, spell.

Seldom, *adv.* Infrequently. Occasionally, rarely, hardly; uncommon. See also few, periodic, intermittent; exceptional.

Select 1. *v.* To take one's preference (select a jury). Pick, cull, adopt, specify, single out, settle upon, elect, favor, abstract, prefer, opt, determine, establish, decide, discriminate, screen, set apart, differentiate, winnow, appoint, excerpt. See also choose. **2.** *adj.* Exclusive (a select group). See primary (1), exceptional, outstanding (2), great.

Selection, *n.* See election, preference; decision; extract, quotation (1), part (1).

Selective, *adj.* See particular (2), precise; acute (1), cultivated.

Selectman, *n.* A municipal officer elected by towns to transact certain public business. See official, officer.

Self, *n.* See individual, person; spirit (3), mind.

Self-abnegation, *n.* See discipline (1), renunciation, composure, restraint; abnegate, charity, benevolence.

Self-asserting, *adj.* See assertive, decisive (2), positive (1).

Self-assurance, *n.* See composure, confidence (3), self-confidence.

Self-assured, *adj.* See assertive, certain (2), conscientious (2), decisive (2), optimistic, positive (1).

Self-centered, *adj.* See irresponsible, arrogant, pompous, immoderate, narrow (2).

Self-complacent, *adj.* See self-centered.

Self-composed, *adj.* See rational; self-assured.

Self-composure, *n.* See restraint (2); self-assurance.

Self-condemnation, *n.* See confession; condemn.

Self-confidence, *n.* Self-assurance. Poise, stability, aplomb, self-control, savoir-faire, equanimity. See also balance (5), confidence (3), composure, valor, resolution.

Self-confident, *adj.* See assured (4), assertive, decisive (2).

Self-conscious, *adj.* See bashful, backward, awkward, insecure.

Self-consciousness, *n.* See embarrassment, anxiety, insecurity.

Self-contained, *adj.* See whole, complete; self-executing.

Self-control, *n.* See balance (5), composure, discipline (1), reserve (4), restraint (2), temperance.

Self-controlled, *adj.* See dispassionate, patient (3); self-control.

Self-dealing, *n.* Acting out of self-interest when one should be acting in the interest of another. See misconduct; misappropriate; fraud; breach.

Self-deception, *n.* See delusion, hallucination, deception; innocence.

Self-defeating, *adj.* See inconsistent, contradictory, fallacious, irrational; ill-fated.

Self-defense, *n.* The protection of one's person against threatened injury from another; the use of force to repel impending peril to one's person or property. See defense, protection; danger.

Self-denial, *n.* See discipline (1), temperance, renunciation, ascetic.

Self-determination, *n.* See discretion (2), freedom, sovereignty, autonomy, liberty; independent.

Self-direction, *n.* See self-determination.

Self-discipline, *n.* See restraint (2), reserve (4), balance (5), composure, discipline (1).

Self-disgust, *n.* See guilt (2), contrition, embarrassment, disgrace.

Self-doubt, *n.* See insecurity (2); self-effacing.

Self-effacing, *adj.* See bashful, backward (2), insecure, quiet (2), amenable (2), flexible, passive; obedience.

Self-esteem, *n.* See arrogance; satisfaction; proud.

Self-evident, *adj.* See certain (3), clear (1), conclusive, convincing, distinct (1), known, manifest (1), naked (2), obvious, demonstrable (2), palpable.

Self-executing, *adj.* Immediately effective without the necessity of intervening action or legislation; requiring no affirmative action by a court. See whole, complete.

Self-explanatory, *adj.* See comprehensible, plain (1); self-evident.

Self-government, *n.* See freedom, sovereignty, autonomy, liberty, authority (1), emancipation, enfranchisement; free (3); sovereign (1).

Self-gratification, *n.* See debauchery, intemperance, luxury; spendthrift, prodigal.

Self-help, *n.* Acting on one's own; acting independently of the courts.

Self-importance, *n.* See arrogance.

Self-important, *adj.* See arrogant, pompous.

Self-imposed, *adj.* See voluntary, intentional.

Self-incrimination, *n.* Acts or declarations by which one incriminates oneself in a crime; giving criminal evidence against oneself. See confession; incriminate.

Self-indulgence, *n.* See debauchery, epicure, intemperance, luxury.

Self-indulgent, *adj.* See decadent, immodest, immoral; excess.

Self-insurance, *n.* Setting aside a fund to meet losses instead of insuring against such losses by purchasing insurance. See insurance.

Self-interest, *n.* See interest; bias, prejudice, one-sided, narrow (2), parochial.

Selfish, *adj.* See stingy, avaricious; pompous.

Self-mortification, *n.* See contrition; disgrace, embarrassment, temperance.

Self-possessed, *adj.* See rational.

Self-possession, *n.* See composure, restraint (2), quiet.

Self-preservation, *n.* See protection, preservation, defense, self-defense.

Self-reliance, *n.* See confidence (3); freedom, liberty, autonomy; self-confidence, valor.

Self-reproach, *n.* See contrition, guilt (2); disgrace, embarrassment.

Self-respect, *n.* See character (1), honor (3), integrity; proud.

Self-restrained, *adj.* See chaste (3); self-restraint.

Self-restraint, *n.* See balance (5), discipline (1); forbearance, reserve (4), composure, temperance.

Self-righteous, *adj.* See parochial, pompous, arrogant, artificial, narrow (2), arbitrary, one-sided; holy.

Self-rule, *n.* See freedom, sovereignty, autonomy, liberty, authority, emancipation, enfranchisement; free (4); sovereign (1).

Self-sacrifice, *n.* See benevolence, charity (3), renunciation, discipline (1), temperance, restraint; abregate.

Self-satisfied, *adj.* See certain (2), pompous, arrogant; self-evident.

Self-serving, *adj.* Serving one's own interests; tending to benefit oneself. See one-sided, narrow, parochial; bias.

Self-starter, *n.* See nonconformist; independent, catalyst.

Self-styled, *adj.* See nominal (1); pseudo; arrogant, pompous.

Self-sufficient, *adj.* See mature (2); whole, complete (2).

Sell, *v.* To dispose of by sale (an agreement to sell the stock). Peddle, vend, auction, hawk, retail, offer, trade, merchandise, wholesale, unload, traffic in, push, furnish, exchange, provide. *Ant.* Buy.

Seller, *n.* One who has contracted to sell (the seller warranted the product for a year). Vendor, salesperson, retailer, drummer, peddler, wholesaler, jobber, dealer, middleman, promoter, shopkeeper, huckster. See also merchant, agent. *Ant.* Purchaser.

Selling short The agreement to deliver at a future date a security or commodity the seller does not own but which he or she hopes to buy later at a lower price.

Semantics, *n.* See language, meaning, construction.

Semblance, *n.* See appearance, exterior, countenance, pretense, copy.

Semester, *n.* See term, division, interval; school, education.

Semiannual, *adj.* Twice a year. See double, two; periodic.

Semifinal, *adj.* Just before the last entry, event, or contest.

Seminar, *n.* See conference, meeting; group (1); education, school, teacher.

Seminary, *n.* An institution of education; a school to train members of the clergy. See school (1); education; church, religion.

Senate, *n.* The upper chamber of the legislative branch of government. See legislature.

Send, *v.* To deposit in the mail or deliver for transmission by other means, properly addressed and with postage or other cost of transmission (send the notice). Route, dispatch, relay, ship, forward, radio, telegram, direct, propel, fly, post, broadcast, transmit, hurl, convey, emit, export, cart, transplant, fling, throw. See also mail (2). *Ant.* Receive.

Senescent, *adj.* See senile; old, ancient.

Senile, *adj.* Suffering from a feebleness of mind and body because of old age (the court appointed a guardian for the severely senile person). Failing, feeble-minded, senescent, disoriented, doddering, infirm, doting, confused, decrepit, superannuated, waning, aging, weak, enfeebled; second childhood. *Ant.* Quick.

Senior, *adj.* **1.** Older (senior citizen). Elder, more advanced in years. See old, ancient. **2.** More experienced, or of higher rank. See chief, superior, veteran, expert. *Ant.* Junior.

Seniority, *n.* Precedence or preference over others similarly situated; the length of continuous, unbroken service; more years of service and hence the last to be laid off, the first to be promoted, etc. (seniority rights in the union contract). Tenure, longevity, longer service, station, rank, standing. See also priority.

Sensation, *n.* See emotion, passion; intuition, impulse; perception, comprehension; marvel, mystery.

Sensational, *adj.* See moving, emotional; great (2), outstanding (2), extraordinary, exceptional, intriguing, attractive, beautiful; yellow (2).

Sense, *v., n.* See touch (1); apprehend (1), comprehend (1), notice (2), discover (1); comprehension, perception; common sense, judgment (2); gist, essence, meaning; opinion.

Senseless, *adj.* See absurd, irrational; unconscious; oblivious.

Sensibility, *n.* See discretion (3); intuition, perception, judgment.

Sensible, *adj.* See functional, rational, logical, compelling, cogent; acute (1); conscious, cognizant.

Sensitive, *adj.* See acute (1), cogent, capable (2), able, alive (2), cultivated, civil (3), responsive.

Sensitivity, *n.* See mercy, charity, benevolence, consideration (3); intuition, perception; responsive.

Sensitize, *v.* See prepare (1), plan, adapt, accommodate (2), adjust.

Sensory, *adj.* See physical, material (2), corporeal.

Sensual, *adj.* See sensuous.

Sensuous, *adj.* See dissolute, carnal, suggestive, prurient, obscene; physical, corporeal; responsive.

Sentence 1. *n.* The judgment formally declaring the legal consequences of a determination of guilt in a criminal case (a sentence of 5 years). See punishment, adjudication. **2.** *v.* To impose a punishment (sentenced to 5 years). Penalize, pass judgment, commit, punish, fine, imprison; convict, condemn, denounce. See also incarcerate.

Sententious, *adj.* See concise, brief; pompous, arrogant, parochial, artificial, feigned.

Sentient, *adj.* See responsive, conscious, cognizant.

Sentiment, *n.* See emotion, passion, intuition, perception, impression, opinion, love; bias; communication.

Sentimental, *adj.* Maudlin. Mawkish, teary, tearful, nostalgic, gushy, pathetic, mellow, romantic, soupy, trite. See also emotional, impracticable.

Sentinel, *n.* See sentry, guardian, police, patrol, caretaker; military, sailor.

Sentry, *n.* See keeper.

Separability clause A clause providing that if one or more provisions of the contract are declared void, the balance of the contract remains in force (i.e., the invalid provisions are severable). See saving clause, severable.

Separable, *adj.* See severable.

Separate 1. *adj.* Individual (separate entity). Distinct, particular, disconnected, divorced, detached, unassociated, severable, separable, discrete, separated, severed, singular, unique, different, isolated, unrelated, segregated, alone, lone, single, specific, private, apart, diverse, diverging, disparate, exclusive, characteristic, solitary, removed, independent, quarantined, sequestered, split, unaffiliated, dissimilar, set apart; respective, own; irrelevant, impertinent, inapplicable. **2.** *v.* See part (3), divide, leave (2), withdraw, except (1), group (2), sequester, flee, depart (1). *Ant.* Joined; join.

Separate and apart A ground for divorce. See living separate and apart, divorce, ground.

Separate maintenance An allowance granted to a spouse, usually the wife, for her support and that of her children while no longer living with the other spouse. See maintenance, alimony, necessaries.

Separate property Property owned by a married person in his or her own right during marriage. See property.

Separate return A tax return filed by one spouse covering only his or her income. See tax.

Separation, *n.* **1.** A decision by a court (a) that two people can live separately while still remaining husband and wife, and (b) declaring the rights and obligations of the parties while they are separated (the court awarded a separation). Judicial separation, legal separation, limited divorce, separation from bed and board, divorce a mensa et thoro. **2.** A severance (separation into factions). Division, cleavage, rift, breakup, partition, rupture, alienation, uncoupling, split, dissolution, disconnection, apartheid, disengagement, segregation, disunion, sequestration, sunderance, splitting, estrangement, dichotomy, quitting, termination, isolation, disassociation, breach, detachment, removal, schism, bifurcation, fission,

Separation

segmentation, sorting, withdrawal, divergence, subdivision, departure, disintegration, dismemberment, divorce. *Ant.* Marriage; union.

Separation agreement A contract between spouses who have separated or who are about to separate, concerning child custody, property division, child support, alimony, etc. The parties may or may not be contemplating a divorce or legal separation. See contract.

Separation of powers The constitutional requirement that the three branches of government—judicial, legislative, executive—not encroach upon or usurp each other's powers; no branch of government should exercise the functions exclusively committed to another branch. See encroach, misappropriate; power.

Septic, *adj.* See rotten, poisonous.

Sequel, *n.* See outcome, corollary, consequence (1), conclusion (2); development, continuation.

Sequence, *n.* See chain (1), series, succession (2), development (1), advancement (2).

Sequester, *v.* **1.** To separate or isolate (sequester the jury). Confine, closet, segregate, cloister, seclude, quarantine, lock, shelter, retreat, hibernate, sequestrate, seal. See also divide, withdraw, depart (1). **2.** To take and hold property pending litigation. See seize (1).

Sequestration, *n.* The process by which property or funds are attached pending the outcome of the litigation. See appropriation (1), attachment (1), quarantine; confiscate, sequester.

Serendipitous, *adj.* See fortuitous, adventitious.

Serendipity, *n.* See chance (2), accident, destiny.

Serene, *adj.* See patient (3), quiet, cautious, passive; amicable, moderate (1), friendly.

Serf, *n.* See slave, servant, laborer; pawn (3), nonentity.

Sergeant, *n.* See military; sailor; officer, official; manager.

Serial, *adj.* Arranged in a series (serial publication). Continuous, in installments, consecutive, periodical, successive, tabulated, scheduled, recurring, continued.

Serial bonds A number of bonds issued at the same time but with different maturity dates and usually with varying interest rates for each maturity date. See bond.

Seriatim, *adv.* One by one. One following after another, separately, individually, severally. See also succession (2); successive.

Series, *n.* A related sequence of events or things (a series of mishaps). Cycle, regimen, progression, train, suit, row, order, calendar, line-up, circuit, routine, string, catenation, number, parade, course. See also chain (1), succession (2), development (1).

Series bonds A group of bonds usually issued at different times and with different maturities but under the authority of the same indenture. See bond.

Serious, *adj.* **1.** Sincere (a serious offer). Genuine, earnest, real, definite, considered, thoughtful, heartfelt, honest, fervent, purposeful, true. **2.** Severe (serious injury). Grim, grave, onerous, troublesome, alarming, precarious, critical. **3.** Crucial (a serious issue). See important. **4.** Perilous (a serious electrical failure). See dangerous. **5.** Solemn or grave (serious demeanor). Pensive, absorbed, reflective, grim, sedate, intent, weighty, dour, preoccupied, engrossed, dejected, staid, solemn, sober. **6.** Resolute (serious about winning). Determined, resolved, firm, conscientious, methodical, disciplined. **7.** Complex; requiring thought (serious problem). Onerous, burdensome, knotty, difficult, demanding, challenging, strenuous, painful. *Ant.* Feigned; mild; trivial; safe; frivolous; indifferent; simple.

Seriousness, *n.* See import (2), importance; serious.

Sermon, *n.* See speech (2), address (3); religious; reprimand.

Serpentine, *adj.* See circuitous, indirect, indefinite, diffuse (2), equivocal, fluctuating; devious, clandestine, collusive, deceptive; complex.

Servant, *n.* **1.** One employed to perform service, whose performance is controlled by or subject to the control of the master. See employee, agent (1). **2.** One hired to perform household duties. Maid, housekeeper, domestic, valet, steward, butler, waiter, waitress, cleaning man, flunky, bellboy, bus boy, carhop, chef, chauffeur, hired help. *Ant.* Master.

Serve, *v.* See help (2), assist; comply, follow (1), perform, observe (1); deliver (1); service of process.

Service 1. *n.* Duty or labor to be rendered by one person to another (services due under the contract). Work, employment, function, job, effort, performance. **2.** *n.* Helping hand (be of service). Benefit, usefulness, avail, advantage, profit, assistance, aid, help, boon, accommodation, enjoyment, abetment, advancement, favor, contribution, promotion, ministration, backing, advocacy, support. **3.** *n.* Ceremony (marriage service). Rite, formality, celebration, ritual, sacrament, observance. **4.** *n.* Armed forces. See military. **5.** *n.* A branch of public employment (civil service). See bureau, department, agency. **6.** *n.* Delivery of legal process. See service of process. **7.** *v.* To keep repaired (service the car). Condition, tune, restore, fix, maintain, mend, adjust, check, inspect.

Serviceable, *adj.* See functional, practicable, effective.

Service by publication The service of a summons or other process upon an absent or nonresident defendant by publishing the summons or other process as an advertisement in a designated newspaper. See service of process.

Service charge, *n.* An added cost for administration or handling. See charge (9), cost, increase.

Serviceman, *n.* See military, sailor.

Service mark, *n.* A word, name, or symbol used in the sale or advertising of services to identify the services of one person and to distinguish them from the services of others. A trademark, on the other hand, is used to identify goods or products. See badge, manifestation.

Service of process The delivery or other communication of writs, summonses, etc. The delivery or other acceptable communication of a formal notice to the defendant ordering him or her to appear in court in order to answer the allegations made by the plaintiff. See notice (1), jurisdiction, long arm statute.

Service station, *n.* See merchant, business.

Servient, *adj.* Subject to a service or servitude. A servient estate is one burdened with a servitude. See servitude (2).

Servile, *adj.* Obsequious. Groveling, slavish, subservient, menial, sycophantic, toadying, submissive, ingratiating, docile, compliant, cowering, fawning, sniveling. See also grovel; flatter, flattery; abject.

Servitude, *n.* **1.** The condition of being subjected to another person as a servant or slave. Slavery, subjugation, compulsory impressment, oppression, service, imprisonment, enthrallment, captivity, constraint, domination, serfdom, yoke, repression, obedience, subordination, shackles, hard labor, fetters, submissiveness, dependence, indenture, vassalage, chains, duress. See also bondage. **2.** A charge or burden resting on one estate for the benefit of another estate, similar to an easement.

Session, *n.* The sitting of a court, legislature, council, commission, etc., for the transaction of its business; the time during which such a body sits (joint session of Congress). See convention (2), conference.

Session laws The laws enacted by the state legislature during one of its sessions. The laws are usually printed chronologically as they are enacted rather than by subject matter. See law, rule.

Set, *adj., n., v.* See customary, conventional; inflexible, formal, particular (2), querulous, contentious; definite, firm; collection, array, group, coterie; apparatus, device; plan (1), composition, classification (1); affix, connect, fix, regulate, assign, establish.

Set aside, *v.* **1.** To reverse or cancel a judgment, order, etc. See rescind. **2.** See save (2).

Setback, *n.* **1.** A temporary or unexpected upset or loss. See defeat (2), loss. **2.** A distance from the curb, property line, or structure within which construction or building is prohibited.

Set down, *v.* To enter in a calendar or docket. See record (1), report (4), enter, communicate.

Setoff, *n.* A money demand by the defendant against the plaintiff based upon a debt that is independent of and unconnected with the plaintiff's cause of action. A defendant's remedy to discharge or reduce the plaintiff's demand by an opposite demand arising from a transaction that is extrinsic to the plaintiff's cause of action. See offset.

Set out, *v.* To recite or narrate facts. See describe, communicate.

Setting, *n.* See view (5), environment, place, neighborhood, border.

Settle, *v.* **1.** To make or arrange for final disposition; to adjust difficulties among disputants; to reach an agreement or compromise (they settled the lawsuit). Resolve, accommodate, work out, reach an understanding, solve, straighten out, mediate, reconcile, put to rest, mutually concede, clear up, agree, rectify, harmonize, unravel, talk out, mend. See also bargain, arbitrate, negotiate. **2.** To satisfy a debt (settle the account). See pay (2). **3.** To establish a residence (settle in Manchester). See reside (1), inhabit, occupy. **4.** To make a choice (settle on a time). See choose, select (1). **5.** To soothe or reduce (settle her nerves). See mitigate. *Ant.* Litigate; incur; withdraw; disagree; aggravate.

Settlement, *n.* A payment, adjustment, or compromise agreed upon among parties; a resolution of difficulties in lieu of litigation. See reconciliation, mediation, resolution, compromise, adjustment, payment (1), settle (1).

Settler, *n.* One who goes on land as a resident. See inhabitant, occupant.

Settlor, *n.* One who creates a trust; a trustor; the grantor or donor in a deed of settlement.

Setup, *n.*, **set up,** *v.* See plan (1), contrivance; establish.

Sever, *v.* To cut off from something. See divide, dissolve, cut.

Severability clause A clause in a statute or contract, stating that if portions of the statute or contract are declared invalid, the remaining portions shall continue to be effective if they are self-sustaining.

Severable, *adj.* Susceptible to division into independent parts (severable portions of the statute). Separable, detachable, divisible. See also separate (1). *Ant.* Interdependent.

Several, *adj.* **1.** More than two but not a large number (several options). See few. **2.** Distinct. See separate (1).

Several liability Liability that is separate and distinct from the liability of another. See liability.

Severally, *adv.* Apart from others (each injury severally caused permanent disability). Distinctly, separately, individually. *Ant.* Collectively.

Severalty, *n.* An estate in severalty is one held by a person in his or her own right without others being joined or connected. See estate.

Severance, *n.* Partition or departure (the severance of diplomatic relations). See separation (2).

Severance damages An award made to the owner of land to compensate for the decrease in value of the remainder of his or her land due to a partial condemnation or taking. See damages, condemn (2).

Severance pay Payment by an employer to an employee beyond his or her wages upon termination of the employment. See compensation.

Severe, *adj.* Difficult to be endured; extreme, violent, or grave (severe injury). See violent, serious (2), draconian, strict (2), dangerous, extreme (1).

Severity, *n.* See cruelty; importance, import (2).

Sewage, *n.* See refuse.

Sex, *n.* Gender, attraction. Differences, masculinity, femininity, reproduction, children, eros. See also lust, male, female, coitus, fornication, intercourse (2), marriage, gay.

Sexism, *n.* See bias, discrimination, chauvinism.

Sexton, *n.* See caretaker.

Sexual, *adj.* See carnal, prurient; sex.

Sexual intercourse, *n.* See coitus, fornication, intercourse (2).

Shabby, *adj.* See disheveled, dilapidated, dirty.

Shack, *n.* See home; outhouse, outbuilding.

Shackle, *v., n.* See encumber, burden (3), bind, confine, fetter.

Shade, *v., n.* See hide; protect; obscure; iota, scintilla.

Shadow, *n., v.* See cloud; iota, scintilla; ferret, pursue (2), trace (2), chase.

Shady, *adj.* See suspicious, illicit, improper, corrupt, covert, clandestine.

Shaft, *n.* See pass (8), passage (2), conduit (2); slander, abuse.

Shake, *v.* See brandish; disturb, frustrate, impair, incapacitate.

Shakedown, *n.* Extortion of money with threats of physical violence or arrest. See extortion.

Shakeup, *n.* See reorganization.

Shaky, *adj.* See weak, infirm, tender (5), breakable, frail, dilapidated, defective; speculative; suspicious, corrupt, improper, illicit.

Shall, *v.* Usually a word of command denoting obligation, although it is sometimes construed as permissive or directory. See compulsory, mandatory; obligation.

Shallow, *adj.* See narrow (2), parochial, cursory, casual (3), artificial, frivolous.

Sham 1. *adj.* Deceptive, without substance (sham transaction to avoid taxes). See false, fraudulent. **2.** *n.* A hoax. See fraud, deception, pretext.

Shambles, *n.* See confusion, disorder, commotion, catastrophe.

Shame, *n.* See guilt (2), contrition, embarrassment, disgrace, pain, odium.

Shameful, *adj.* See base, odious, offensive, corrupt (1), bad (2).

Shameless, *adj.* See immoral, wanton, abandoned (2), rude, obscene, carnal, suggestive.

Shanghai, *v.* To drug, intoxicate, trick, or otherwise force someone to become a sailor. See abduct, hijack, seize; kidnapping.

Shanty, *n.* See home.

Shape, *v., n.* See form (1, 4), design, plan, forge (2), organize, organization (2), composition, pattern, order.

Shapeless, *adj.* See indefinite, indeterminate, inchoate, ambiguous, abstract, obscure.

Shapely, *adj.* See attractive, beautiful; healthy, able-bodied.

Share 1. *v.* To have a portion of (the beneficiaries shared in the estate). Parcel out, partition, subdivide, apportion, partake, enjoy with others, measure, mete, participate in, split up, allot, assign. See also part (3), divide. **2.** *n.* A portion of something owned by a number of persons (taxable share). See part (1). **3.** *n.* A unit of stock representing ownership in a corporation. Security, holding, capital, asset. See also interest, ownership, claim (3), securities.

Sharecropper, *n.* A tenant farmer who lives and works on the land of another.

Sharecropper

His or her compensation is a portion of the crops minus any advances for seed, tools, food, etc. See farm, farmer; servitude.

Shareholder, *n.* See stockholder, owner.

Sharp, *adj.* See caustic, biting, cutting, malicious; clear, precise (1), comprehensible, direct (6); acute (1), able, brilliant, capable (2); debonair, chic.

Sharpen, *v.* To make sharper. Edge, grind, file, taper, hone, whet, strop, acuminate.

Shatter, *v.* See break (2), damage, destroy, impair.

Shave, *n.* **1.** Obtaining the property of another by oppression or extortion. **2.** Buying notes and other securities for money at a discount.

Shear, *v.* See cut; cheat, plunder, rape.

Shed, *n., v.* See outhouse, outbuilding; emit, circulate; reject (1), jettison.

Sheen, *n.* See light (1).

Sheepish, *adj.* See ashamed, abject (1), bashful, awkward (2), quiet (2).

Sheer, *adj.* See absolute (1), outright, definitive; thin; bluff (3).

Shell, *n., v.* See exterior; cave, cell, abyss; arms, weapon; attack, batter.

Shelley's Case See rule in Shelley's Case.

Shell game, *n.* See fraud, cheat; gambling.

Shelter 1. *n.* Home; protection from the weather (inadequate shelter). Lodging, house, abode, housing, dwelling, roof; safety, quarters, sanctuary, harbor, security, cover, refuge, safekeeping, preserve, retreat, concealment, hiding, privacy, shield, haven, cloister. See also home, asylum. **2.** *v.* To protect. See oversee, harbor (1), defend, guard.

Shelve, *v.* See postpone, defer; adjourn.

Shenanigan, *n.* See antic, mischief; joke; juvenile.

Shepherd, *n., v.* See keeper, manager, guardian; marshal (2), manage, minister.

Sheriff, *n.* See police, official, officer, marshal, keeper.

Sheriff's deed A deed given at a forced sale conducted by a sheriff in foreclosure of a mortgage. See deed, execution, forced sale.

Sherry, *n.* See liquor, beverage.

Shibboleth, *n.* See slogan, maxim, moral (3), badge.

Shield 1. *v.* To protect (shielded from harm). Safeguard, preserve, oversee, secure, shelter, fortify, guard, house. See also harbor (1), defend. **2.** *v.* To screen or cover. See hide, conceal. **3.** *n.* That which defends or safeguards. See protection.

Shield law A statute giving journalists the privilege to refuse to disclose information obtained while gathering news. See protection, press.

Shift 1. *n.* A change of place or character (shift in policy). Substitution, exchange, transfer, rearrangement, deviation, passing, replacement, digression, turnabout, switch, transformation, fluctuation, roaming, variation, maneuver, about-face, metamorphosis, vacillating, reassignment, movement. **2.** *v.* See alter, change.

Shifting, *adj.* Changing (shifting use). Varying, wavering, uncertain, transient, roaming, vacillating, alternating, drifting. See also capricious, fluctuating.

Shifting income Moving income to children and others in lower tax brackets.

Shiftless, *adj.* See dilatory, lazy, apathetic, derelict (2), incompetent; tramp, parasite.

Shifty, *adj.* See dishonest, deceptive, irresponsible, corrupt (1), derelict (2), disloyal, base.

Shill, *n.* One who participates in a confidence game by pretending to be a bystander or one of the victims. See decoy.

Shine, *n., v.* See light (1), emit; exceed, pass (3).

Ship 1. *v.* To transport (ship goods). See mail, forward (1), deliver, send. **2.** *n.*

A vessel employed in navigation. See vessel (1).

Shipment, *n.* **1.** The delivery of goods to a carrier and the issuance by the latter of a bill of lading therefor; the transportation of goods. See delivery, consignment. **2.** Goods to be delivered (the shipment arrived). See cargo, movables, property, goods.

Shipper, *n.* One who transports goods for a charge. See carrier.

Shirk, *v.* See avoid; evasion, malingerer, parasite.

Shirt, *n.* See clothes, apparel.

"Shiv," *n.* See weapon.

Shiver, *v.* See beat (3); cold (2).

Shock 1. *n.* A sudden agitation of the physical or mental sensibilities. A sudden depression of the vital forces of the entire body or a part of it, producing a profound impression upon the nervous system (suffered a severe shock). Trauma, stroke, collapse, paralysis, stupefaction, concussion; blow, jar, start, clash, turn, disturbance, torrent, earthquake, blast, disaster, cataclysm, smash, eruption, impact, bump; consternation, scare, horror, distress, turmoil, crackup, wonder, upset, breakdown, revulsion, agitation, faint, outrage, daze. **2.** *v.* To disturb greatly. See outrage (2), disturb.

Shocking, *adj.* See extraordinary, flagrant, odious, offensive, notorious, wanton (1), gross (1), grievous (2); agape.

Shoddy, *adj.* See inferior, base, artificial, meretricious.

Shoot, *v.* To hit or wound, usually with a firearm. Fire, strike, eject, kill, thrust, dart, injure, hurt, damage, toss, pelt, spring, catapult, fling, impel, riddle, shell, detonate, launch, bombard, explode, hurl, let fly. See also discharge (4).

Shop 1. *n.* A retail store. Store, stall, booth, department, boutique, bazaar, establishment, mart, emporium, supermarket, salon, factory, mill, studio, plant, office. See also business, merchant, market (1). **2.** *v.* To go to stores to purchase, or to consider purchasing, goods or services. Market, buy, window-shop, explore, hunt, browse. See also patronize.

Shop book Records of customer accounts containing original entries. See account (1), record (2), report.

Shop-book rule An exception to the hearsay rule, permitting the introduction into evidence of books of original entry made in the usual course of business. See evidence, hearsay, course of dealing.

Shopkeeper, *n.* See merchant, business.

Shoplifter, *n.* See thief, wrongdoer.

Shoplifting, *n.* Willfully taking possession of merchandise offered for sale in a store or business establishment, with the intent of converting the merchandise to the taker's own use without paying the purchase price. See larceny.

Shopper, *n.* See patron (1), customer, client (2).

Shopping mall, *n.* See shop (1), market (1), business, merchant.

Shop right rule The right of an employer to use an employee's invention in the employer's business without paying a royalty. See right, invention, copyright.

Shop steward A union official elected to represent members of a particular department. See union, manager, foreman, official, officer.

Shore, *n.* Land adjacent to the sea or other tidal waters. Coast, seacoast, beach, shoreline, bank, riverbank, brink, seaboard, littoral, waterside, waterfront, brim, margin, seaside, rim, strand, embankment.

Shoreline, *n.* See border, shore.

Shore up, *v.* See strengthen, augment, build.

Short 1. *adj.* Brief (short presentation). Succinct, laconic, terse, concise, scanty, abridged, curtailed, momentary, summary, straightforward, lean, condensed, hasty, fleeting, cursory, compact, abbreviated, direct, thumbnail, synoptic, short-lived, quick, to the point, compressed, crisp, pointed, elliptical. **2.** *adj.* Below average height (short tree). Small, truncated, stunted, low, dwarfish, pygmy, stubby, diminutive, little, lilliputian, miniscule, bantam, tiny. **3.** *adj.* Insufficient (short supply). See inadequate. **4.** *adj.* Brusque or testy (short with her opponent). See rude. **5.** *adv.* Suddenly (stopped the train short). Abruptly, precipitously, quickly, hurriedly, without warning, unexpectedly, by surprise. *Ant.* Extended; tall; sufficient; cordial; slowly.

Shortage, *n.* See dearth, deficiency, poverty.

Shortchange, *v.* See cheat (1).

Short-circuit, *v.* See impede.

Shortcoming, *n.* See deficiency, fault.

Short cut, *n.* See economy; save.

Shorten, *v.* See abridge, curtail.

Shortfall, *n.* See deficiency, failure, fault.

Short-handed, *adj.* See insufficient, inadequate, deficient.

Short-lived, *adj.* See temporary, brief (4), perishable.

Short sale The taxpayer sells borrowed property—usually stock—and repays the lender with substantially identical property either held on the date of the sale or purchased after the sale.

Short shrift, *n.* See summary.

Shortsighted, *adj.* See narrow (2), parochial, careless, reckless, rude.

Short swing profits Profits made by an insider through the sale or other disposition of corporate stock within 6 months after purchase.

Short-tempered, *adj.* See hot (2), feverish, violent, emotional.

Short-term, *adj.* See temporary, brief (4).

Short-term debt Debt evidenced by notes or drafts that are payable on demand or within a year of issuance. See debt.

Shot, *n.* See eruption; shoot.

Shotgun, *n.* See gun, weapon.

Shotgun instruction, *n.* See Allen charge.

Shotgun wedding, *n.* See duress, coercion; pregnant; marriage.

Shoulder, *v.* See bear (2), assume (1).

Shout, *v.*, *n.* See yell; noise.

Shove, *v.* See push (1).

Shovel 1. *n.* A scoop. Spoon, spade, trowel. **2.** *v.* To clear or dig. Remove, bail, furrow. See also excavate.

Show 1. *v.* To make apparent or clear by evidence. See demonstrate, prove. **2.** *v.* See display. **3.** *n.* A display. See production, exposition (2), array (2). **4.** *n.* A hoax or pretense. See pretext, fraud.

Show business, *n.* See entertainment, cinema, business.

Showcase, *v.* See exhibit, publish, promote.

Show cause order An order or decree to appear as directed and explain why the court should not take a proposed action.

Showdown, *n.* See confrontation, contest, crisis.

Shower, *v.*, *n.* See inundate, water; climate.

Showing, *n.* See production, performance, exposition (2), array (2).

Showoff, *n.* Snob, exhibitionist. Braggart, prig, extrovert, egotist, strutter, boaster. See also boor, ass; boast; pompous, arrogant.

Show-up, *n.* A one-to-one confrontation between a suspect and the witness to or victim of a crime.

Shrapnel, *n.* See arms, weapon, gun.

Shred, *n.* See iota, scintilla, part.

Shrewd, *adj.* See acute (1), able, apt (3), expert; deceptive, deceitful.

Shriek, *n., v.* See noise; yell.

Shrill, *v., n.* See yell; noise.

Shrimp, *n.* See nonentity, cipher (2).

Shrine, *n.* See grave (1); church; memorial; asylum.

Shrink, *v., n.* See decline, diminish, constrict; psychiatrist, doctor.

Shrinkage, *n.* See abridgement, reduction.

Shroud, *v., n.* See conceal, hide; wrapper; cloud (2); clothes.

Shrubbery, *n.* Bushes. Thicket, greenery, undergrowth, planting, growth, hedges. See also woods, timber.

Shudder, *v.* See beat (3).

Shuffle, *v.* See confuse, commingle; mixture.

Shun, *v.* See avoid, boycott (2), bar (4), expel, proscribe, circumvent.

Shut, *v.* See close (2), bar (4), block (2); connect (1).

Shut down, *v.* To stop work. See cessation, close (1, 2); union, strike.

Shut-in, *n.* See invalid (2), patient (1).

Shuttle, *v.* See move, travel.

Shy, *adj.* See bashful, awkward (2), quiet (2); amenable (2), flexible.

Shylock, *n.* See loansharking; usurious; lend, loan; stingy, avaricious.

Shyster, *n.* One who carries on a business or profession dishonestly. See charlatan, cheat (2), wrongdoer.

[sic] The error in the quotation was in the original ("the new atorney [sic] arrived late.").

Sick, *adj.* Afflicted with disease (sick from the poison). Ailing, confined, indisposed, unwell, sickly, queasy, lame, under the weather, unsound, injured, deranged, psychotic, neurotic, invalid, unhealthy, nauseated, burdened, delicate, squeamish, tired, disquieted, miserable, bored, weary, annoyed, distressed, crushed, upset, perturbed. See also frail, weak, infirm, insane, ill, anemic. *Ant.* Unaffected.

Sickening, *adj.* See repulsive, odious, offensive, obnoxious.

Sick leave, *n.* Period away from work allowed by an employer to an employee during the latter's sickness with or without pay but without loss of seniority. See fringe, fringe benefits.

Sickly, *adj.* See ill, sick, weak, infirm, anemic.

Sickness, *n.* An ailment that affects general soundness and health. See disease, illness.

Sick-out, *n.* See strike, union.

Side 1. *n.* Any of the bounding lines of a surface (the right side collapsed). Edge, margin, verge, flank, limit, brink, rim, periphery. See also border, boundary. **2.** *n.* One of two or more opposing positions, persons, or groups (their side made an excellent presentation). See party (1, 3), adversary, opponent. **3.** *n.* Point of view (their side of the argument). See opinion (2). **4.** *adj.* Subordinate (side issue). See inferior (1), accessory. **5.** *v.* To support (the judge sided with the plaintiff). See advocate (2), promote, back.

Side effect, *n.* See consequence, effect.

Sideline, *n.* See hobby, avocation, interest.

Sidestep, *v.* See divert, circumvent, avoid; evasion.

Sidetrack, *v.* See divert, deviate; avoid; impede.

Sidewalk, *n.* That part of a public street or highway designed for the use of pedestrians. Promenade, path, walkway, mall. See also course, pass (8), passage (2).

Siege, *n., v.* See blockade; surround; attack, assault, plunder.

Sift, *v.* See filter, drain; investigate, canvass (1), review.

Sigh, *v.* See suffer, bemoan, cry (1); whisper; mope.

Sight 1. *n.* The ability to see; the act of seeing (restoration of his sight). Vision, perception, view, viewing, appearance, glimpse, display, picture, look, gaze, image, spectacle, peek. **2.** *v.* To observe (she sighted the ship). See witness (2), observe.

Sight draft An instrument payable upon presentment. See draft.

Sightseeing, *n.* See travel, voyage, junket, amusement, entertainment.

Sign 1. *v.* To affix one's name to a writing or instrument (he signed under protest). Autograph, subscribe, initial, undersign, countersign, place one's John Hancock, inscribe, endorse, attest. **2.** *n.* A symbol, mark, or emblem (a sign of hostility). See manifestation, badge. **3.** *n.* A public announcement (a sign on the street). Billboard, placard, poster, bulletin, beacon, arrow, marker, guidepost, signal, signpost, landmark, name tag.

Signal 1. *n.* A marker or landmark. See sign (3), warning. **2.** *n.* See gesture, manifestation. **3.** *v.* To gesture. Flag, beckon, motion, wave, nod, salute. **4.** *adj.* Remarkable. See outstanding (2), extraordinary, exceptional.

Signatory, *n.* The person who signs; the nation that signs.

Signature, *n.* **1.** One's name in writing. Holograph, autograph, John Hancock, notarization, subscription, indorsement; logo, stamp, seal. **2.** Trait. See mark, characteristic, property.

Significance, *n.* See importance, import (2), essence, gist, implication.

Significant, *adj.* See crucial, decisive, important, dominant, effective, great, outstanding (2), pregnant.

Signify, *v.* To make known by signs or words. See communicate, mean (2).

Silence 1. *n.* Not speaking (they were suspicious of his silence). Quiet, muteness, hush, speechlessness, stillness, quietude, soundlessness, reticence; shyness, restraint, reluctance, timidity, modesty, reserve, secretiveness, evasion. **2.** *v.* To cause to stop (the report silenced her critics). Still, hush, muzzle, nullify, quell, allay, subdue, deaden, muffle, moderate, diminish, cut off, interrupt, decrease, gag, curb, quiet. See also kill, abate, mitigate, confute, defeat (1). *Ant.* Speech; enhance.

Silent, *adj.* **1.** Close-mouthed, reticent (the witness remained silent about the incident). Tightlipped, timid, uncommunicative, unresponsive, taciturn, mum, secretive, quiet, tongue-tied, inert, dumb, noncommittal, reserved, mysterious, diffident, close, unassertive, uninformative. **2.** Undeclared, inactive (silent partner). Unspoken, unexpressed, concealed, unstated, implied, unarticulated, hidden, insinuated, unpublished, covert, tacit, passive, dormant, latent, hibernating. **3.** Without noise (silent engine). Inaudible, muted, noiseless, still, hushed, speechless. *Ant.* Loquacious; explicit; loud.

Silent partner, *n.* An investor in a firm who takes no active part in its management but who shares in its losses and profits; a dormant partner; a partner whose name does not appear in the firm but who has an interest in it and shares in its losses and profits. See partner, dormant.

Silicosis, *n.* A condition of massive fibrosis of the lungs, marked by shortness of breath due to prolonged inhalation of silica dust. See disease, infirmity.

Silly, *adj.* See absurd, dumb, irrational, juvenile, reckless, frivolous.

Silo, *n.* See vessel (2); warehouse; shelter.

Silver, *n.* See mineral; gem; luxury, wealth.

Silver platter doctrine Evidence obtained illegally by state officials was formerly admissible in federal prosecutions if no federal officer had participated in the violation of the defendant's rights.

Silver spoon, *n.* See benefit (1); blood (1); birth (3); luxury, wealth.

Similar, *adj.* Having a general likeness although somewhat different; resembling in many respects (similar cases). Corresponding, equivalent, resembling, like, allied, conformable, reconcilable, analogous, akin, comparable, much the same, agreeing, approximate, kindred, congruent; duplicate, identical, twin, matching, parallel. *Ant.* Antithetic.

Similarity, *n.* See analogy, affinity (3), parity, copy, imitation.

Simmer, *v.* See burn.

Simpatico, *adj.* See kindred (2), concordant, concurrent (2).

Simple, *adj.* **1.** Not aggravated (simple assault). Not compounded, single, plain, bare, ordinary, bald, basic, elemental, mere, fundamental, pure, unembellished, sheer, straight, average, unmixed, commonplace, garden variety. **2.** Uncomplicated (a simple case). Straightforward, uninvolved, manageable, easy, unsophisticated, without confusion, understandable, transparent, controllable. See also innocent, lucid (2), comprehensible, intelligible, obvious. **3.** Unpretentious, sincere. See innocent. *Ant.* Aggravated; complex; sophisticated.

Simple interest, *n.* Interest paid on the initial amount invested and not on any earnings or interest thereon. See interest.

Simple-minded, *adj.* See innocent, juvenile; absurd, dumb.

Simple negligence The failure to exercise that degree of care and caution which an ordinary, prudent person would exercise under the circumstances. See negligence, neglect (2).

Simpleton, *n.* See ass, idiot, boor; child, juvenile.

Simplicity, *n.* See clarity, candor, innocence, integrity.

Simplify, *v.* See facilitate, clarify, interpret, abridge.

Simulate, *v.* **1.** To give the appearance of something (simulate an illness). See misrepresent, pretend, copy; facsimile. **2.** See approximate (2).

Simulated, *adj.* **1.** Contrived (simulated contract). See artificial, deceitful, feigned, false; fabricate; facsimile, copy. **2.** See approximate (2).

Simulation, *n.* **1.** Providing a false and deceptive appearance. See imitation, fraud. **2.** See approximate (2); copy, facsimile.

Simultaneous, *adj.* Pertaining to two or more occurrences or happenings taking place at the same time (simultaneous death). Coincident, concomitant, coeval, contemporaneous, contemporary, accompanying, synchronous, synchronal, coexisting. See also concurrent (1). *Ant.* Separate.

Sin, *n., v.* See wrong (1, 4), offense, crime, violation, intrusion, invasion; encroach, interfere.

Since, *adv.* See because; whereas.

Sincere, *adj.* See direct (6), faithful (1), honest, ardent, loyal, bona fide, genuine, accurate, serious (1).

Sincerely, *adv.* See faithfully.

Sincerity, *n.* See integrity, honor (3), candor, innocence (2); clarity.

Sinecure, *n.* A salaried position with little or no responsibility or work.

Sine die, *adv.* Without day; without assigning a day for a further meeting or hearing.

Sine qua non, *n.* An indispensable requisite or condition; that without which a thing cannot be done. See gist (1), condition (1), requirement; fundamental, necessary.

Sinewy, *adj.* See able-bodied, healthy, durable.

Sinful, *adj.* See immoral, corrupt, bad.

Sing, *v.* See music; melody.

Singe, *v.* See burn.

Single, *adj.* **1.** One only (single dwelling unit). Alone, unitary, sole, singular, individual, unique, distinctive. See also separate, distinct, whole, isolated. **2.** Unmarried. Bachelor, unattached, spinster, maiden, widow, widower, mateless; monastic, celibate. *Ant.* Multiple; married.

Single-handed, *adj.* See alone, single (1).

Single-minded, *adj.* See one-sided; diligent, earnest (2), ardent, conscientious, firm, inflexible.

Single publication rule A defendant can be sued only once for each mass publication of libel, but evidence of all sales can be introduced on the issue of damages. See defamation, publication, slander.

Singular, *adj.* Unusual or distinctive. See extraordinary, exceptional, great, outstanding (2); odd.

Singularity, *n.* See eccentricity, specialty (1), exception (3), mystery; identity.

Sinister, *adj.* See bad (2), corrupt, malicious, harmful.

Sink, *v.* See fall (2), wane, depreciate, diminish; submerge, inundate; excavate; debase.

Sinking fund, *n.* Assets, and the earnings therefrom, that are earmarked for the retirement of bonds or other long-term obligations. See fund, securities.

Sinless, *adj.* See blameless, innocent.

Sinner, *n.* See wrongdoer, offender, criminal.

Sinuous, *adj.* See circuitous, indirect, diffuse (2), complex, fluctuating, devious, deceptive.

Sip, *v.* See consume; eat.

Siphon, *n., v.* See conduit (2); drain (1), filter.

Sire, *v.* See beget.

Sissy, *n.* See coward.

Sister, *n.* See kindred, affinity (1), blood, family; woman; partner, associate.

Sister corporations Two corporations that have common or substantially common ownership by the same shareholders. See corporation, amalgamation.

Sit, *v.* To hold a session; to be organized and proceeding with the transaction of business (the Court of Appeals sits every other week). Assemble, hold court, gather, be convened, conduct business, convene, officiate, congregate, deliberate, reign. *Ant.* Adjourn.

Sit-down strike A strike in which the workers stay in the plant but refuse to work. See strike, union.

Site, *n.* A location or ground set apart for some specific use (construction site). See place (1), zone, environment.

Sit-in, *n.* See demonstrate (3), strike.

Sitting, *n.* See session, convention (2), meeting, conference.

Situate, *v.* To give a specific position. See locate (2); reside (1), inhabit, occupy.

Situation, *n.* **1.** Circumstances (precarious situation). Posture, condition, arrangement, predicament, incidence, environment, status, disposition, dilemma, ball game, state of affairs, quandary, station, fix. See also circumstances, case (3, 5), crisis. **2.** Employment. See job (1), business.

Situs, *n.* The place where a thing happened, is located, or is considered (the situs of property). See location, locality, place (1).

Six-shooter, *n.* See gun, weapon, arms.

Sizable, *adj.* See considerable (2), big, great, massive.

Size, *n., v.* See extent, range, scope, measure; classify, assess, appraise, judge (3).

Skating, *n.* See athletics, sport.

Skeleton, *n.* See anatomy; form (1), composition, brief (2), plan, outline.

Skeptic, *n.* See cynic; suspicious (2); nonconformist.

Skeptical, *adj.* See cynical, suspicious (2), doubtful; disloyal, false; contingent.

Skepticism, *n.* See doubt (2), reservation (3), cloud (2).

Sketch, *v., n.* See draw (1), draft (2), plan, describe, model, brief (2), outline.

Sketchy, *adj.* See indefinite, ambiguous, imperfect, inadequate, cursory, bare (1).

Skew, *v.* See misrepresent, distort, exaggerate.

Skid, *v.* To slide. Coast, slip, glide, veer. See also stray, wander, depart (2), digress.

Skiing, *n.* See athletics, sport.

Skill, *n.* **1.** Knowledge of the principles and processes of an art, science, or trade, combined with an ability to apply them in practice in a proper and approved manner (the skill of research). Dexterity, know-how, proficiency, aptitude, talent, cleverness, expertise, knack, intelligence, craft, cunning, inventiveness, competence, savoir-faire, technique, address, sophistication, gift, execution. See also facility (3), experience, ability. **2.** A trade. See job (1).

Skilled, *adj.* See expert (2), able, apt (3), competent, qualified, effective, mature (2).

Skillful, *adj.* See skilled.

Skim, *v.* See ricochet; browse, audit (2).

Skimp, *v.* See save (2), conserve, hoard; restrict.

Skin, *n.* Integument, dermis, epidermis, coat, covering, pelt, hide.

Skin diving, *n.* See athletics, sport.

Skinny, *adj.* See thin; anemic, exhausted.

Skip, *v.* See jump; avoid, flee, escape.

Skipper, *n.* See manager, director, head, master; sailor; navigate.

Skiptracing, *n.* A service that assists creditors in locating delinquent debtors.

Skirmish, *n.* See contest, dispute, fight, commotion.

Skirt, *v., n.* See avoid, escape; clothes, apparel; border, margin (1).

Skittish, *adj.* See apprehensive, excitable; bashful.

Sky, *n.* See air (1), environment; heaven; apex.

Skyjack, *v.* See hijack, abduct; kidnapping.

Skyscraper, *n.* See building (1).

Slack, *adj.* See lazy; negligent, heedless, careless; flexible; quiet.

Slacken, *v.* See diminish, mitigate, abate.

Slacker, *n.* See malingerer, parasite.

"Slam," *v.* See batter, beat; collide.

Slander 1. *n.* A tort with the following elements: (a) oral defamatory statement by the defendant, (b) of and concerning the plaintiff, (c) publication of the statement, (d) causing, (e) damages or harm to the plaintiff's reputation. See slander per se. If the statement is slander per se, the plaintiff does not have to prove special damages. Defamation, slur, aspersion, calumny, vilification, denigration, vituperation, denunciation, accusation, censure, character assassination, imprecation, obloquy, malediction, mortification, malicious fabrication, distortion, affront, backbiting, odium, reproach, scandal, revilement, insinuation, scurrility, belittlement, invective, malicious falsehood, misrepresentation, disparagement, injury, smear. **2.** *v.* To defame someone orally. Discredit, impugn, belittle, damn, tarnish, anathematize, denigrate, accuse, scandalize, libel, malign, degrade, incriminate, traduce, revile, abuse, disparage, blacken, slur, vilify, denounce, condemn, berate, criticize, curse, disgrace, dishonor, humiliate, satirize, attack, besmirch, undermine, detract, blemish, decry, hold up to shame, destroy, ridicule, soil, contaminate, stain, lampoon, run down, shame, humble, slight, stigmatize, backbite, brand. *Ant.* Praise.

Slander of title A false and malicious oral or written statement made in disparagement of a person's title to real or personal property, or of some right that causes special damages.

Slanderous, *adj.* See defamatory, derogatory, slander.

Slander per se Slander in itself that does not require proof of special damages. Statements (a) accusing the plaintiff of a crime, (b) adversely affecting the plaintiff's trade, occupation, profession, or calling, (c) accusing the plaintiff of having an offensive or loathsome disease, or (d) accusing the plaintiff of unchasti-

ty.
Slang, *n.* See language.
Slant, *n., v.* See grade (2); distort, misrepresent; bias; opinion.
Slap, *v.* See beat, batter, reprimand, slander.
Slash, *v.* See mutilate, maim, cut.
Slate, *n.* **1.** A list of candidates for office. See record (2), schedule (1). **2.** See rock, earth.
Slaughter, *v., n.* See murder, kill, homicide.
Slave 1. *n.* A person who is wholly subject to the will of and is owned by a master. Chattel, vassal, bondman, serf, lackey, peon, thrall, indentured servant, helot. See also servant, laborer, employee; servitude. **2.** *v.* To work very hard. See labor (2).
Slavery, *n.* The status of being totally subject to the power and control of another. Exploitation, captivity, enslavement, subjection, duress, disenfranchisement, subjugation, subordination, conquest, shackles, oppression, yoke, domination, serfdom, chains. See also servitude, bondage.
Slay, *v.* To take the life of. See kill; homicide.
Sleazy, *adj.* See gaudy, base, meretricious, inferior.
Sledgehammer, *n.* See weapon.
Sleek, *adj.* See debonair; oil, ointment.
Sleep, *n., v.* A natural and periodical loss of consciousness, usually occurring in the evening. Slumber, rest, nap, doze, catnap, snore, drowse, repose, retire, "sack out," nod off, turn in, hibernate, snooze; siesta. See also drowsy, bed.
Sleeping, *adj.* Inactive. See dormant, passive.
Sleet, *n.* See climate, cold.
Slender, *adj.* See thin, slight (2).
Sleuth, *n.* See spy, investigator.
Slice, *n., v.* See part, portion, divide, cut.
Slide, *v.* See skid; stray; fall; lapse.
Sliding scale, *n.* A payment schedule that varies according to another factor such as one's income. See measure.
Slight 1. *adj.* Small in intensity or quantity (slight chance of winning). See worthless, small (1), minimal, minor (2). **2.** *adj.* Thin or slender (too slight for sports). Delicate, fragile, puny, narrow, unstable, rickety, slim, petite, lean, light, small, feeble, frail. **3.** *v.* To treat with contempt or disrespect. See slander (2), neglect (1). **4.** *n.* A slur or insult. See slander (1). **5.** *v.* See ignore, neglect (1), avoid. **6.** *adj.* See gradual. *Ant.* Large; muscular; respect; commendation.
Slim, *adj.* See thin, slight (2), anemic.
Slimy, *adj.* See foul, repulsive, offensive, filthy, obnoxious; ointment.
Sling, *v.* See jettison, launch.
Slip, *v., n.* See skid, fall, blunder, mistake; diminish.
Slip law A legislative enactment that is separately and promptly published in a pamphlet or single-sheet format after its passage. See law, session laws.
Slip opinion An individual court opinion published separately soon after it is rendered. See opinion.
Slippery, *adj.* See precarious, dangerous, hazardous, capricious, insecure.
Slipshod, *adj.* See careless, casual, negligent, heedless; inferior, meretricious; disheveled.
Slit, *v.* See cut, divide; maim.
Sliver, *n.* See part, iota, scintilla.
"Slob," *n.* See boor, ass, idiot; parasite, malingerer.
Slogan, *n.* A motto. Saying, catch phrase, shibboleth, logo, "buzz word," battle cry, trademark, line, byword, watchword. See also maxim, moral (3); badge,

signature (1).

Slop, v. See splash, sprinkle.

Slope, n. See grade (2).

Sloppy, adj. See careless, inferior, dirty, disheveled.

"Sloshed," adj. See intoxicated, drunk; liquor.

Slot, n. See place, alcove; occupation.

Slothful, adj. See lazy, indifferent, apathetic, drowsy, exhausted, oblivious.

Slot machine, n. A gambling apparatus by which a person depositing money therein may, by chance, receive money or articles that are worth more or less than the money deposited. See gambling.

Slough 1. n. An arm of a river flowing between islands and the mainland, and separating the islands from one another. **2.** n. A stagnant swamp. **3.** v. To discard. See reject (1).

Slovenly, adj. See careless, negligent, indifferent, disorderly, disheveled.

Slow, adj., v. See late (3), overdue; deliberate (3), cautious; backward, awkward; check (1).

Slowdown, n. An organized effort by workers in a plant, by which production is slowed in order to bring pressure on the employer for better working conditions. See strike (1).

Sludge, n. See refuse (2), dirt, swamp.

Slug, v. See batter, beat, bludgeon.

Sluggish, adj. See dormant, lazy, drowsy, passive (2), silent (1).

Slum, n. A squalid, run-down section of a city, town, or village. Skid row, shanty town, ghetto, warren, depressed area. See also zone.

Slumber, v. See sleep.

Slumlord, n. The owner of deteriorating tenements in the slums. See landlord, owner, proprietor.

Slump, n., v. See collapse, fall, decline.

Slur, n., v. See innuendo, slander; overlook.

Slush, n. See refuse (2).

Slush fund, n. Money collected or spent for corrupt purposes.

Slut, n. See prostitute.

Sly, adj. See covert, clandestine, evasive, deceptive, deceitful, able, apt (3).

Smack, v., n. See batter, beat; noise; drug.

Small, adj. **1.** Not large in size or amount (a small contingent of Marines). Tiny, petite, little, diminutive, bantam, puny, miniscule, dwarfish, mini, minute, undersized, infinitesimal, lilliputian, short. See also minimal, marginal, nugatory, frivolous, minor (2); hidden. **2.** Thin or lean. See slight (2), thin, anemic. **3.** Insignificant. See insufficient, minor (2). **4.** Bigoted. See petty (3), narrow (2), parochial (2).

Small Business Administration (SBA) A federal agency that assists small businesses by providing counseling, loans, help in obtaining government purchases or service contracts, etc. See agency, assistance, business.

Small-claims court, n. A special court that provides expeditious, informal, and inexpensive adjudication of small claims. See court.

Smart, adj. See brilliant, acute (1); chic, debonair, current (3); active (3), alive (2); pain, tender (6).

Smart-alecky, adj. See assertive, obnoxious, pompous, arrogant.

Smart money, n. Punitive damages; damages provided by way of punishment or example (e.g., for gross misconduct). See exemplary damages.

Smash, v. See beat, stamp (2), batter; break (2), destroy.

"Smashed," adj. See intoxicated; liquor.

Smear, n., v. See innuendo, slander; pollute.

Smell, *n.* See aroma; breath; fragrant.

Smile, *v.* Grin. Beam, smirk. See also laugh; joke.

Smirch, *v.* See pollute; slander, damage; dirt.

Smirk, *v.* See frown; smile.

Smite, *v.* See beat, batter, attack, castigate, amerce.

Smog, *n.* See fog, dirt; climate.

Smoke, *n.* See fog; fire, burn; cigarette.

Smolder, *v.* See burn; fire.

Smooth, *adj., v.* See flat; debonair; quiet, patient (3); ordinary; promote, mitigate; malleable, flexible.

Smother, *v.* See suffocate, clog, constrict; hide, conceal.

Smudge, *v.* See pollute, damage (2).

Smug, *adj.* See pompous, arrogant.

Smuggle, *v.* See import, export; illegal.

Smuggling, *n.* Importing or exporting prohibited articles without paying the duties chargeable upon them.

Smut, *n.* Obscene material. See obscene; dirt, pollution.

Snack, *v., n.* See eat; food.

"Snafu," *n.* See confusion; complication.

Snag, *n.* See block, complication, obstruction, drawback.

Snap, *v., n.* See break; noise; yell; collapse; spirit (2).

Snappy, *adj.* See active (3), alive (2), ardent, indefatigable; current (3), chic.

Snare, *n.* See danger, peril, ambush.

Snarl, *v., n.* See menace; grouch, complain; complication, block, obstruction.

Snatch, *v.* See seize, capture; handle (2), touch (1).

Sneaky, *adj.* See clandestine, covert, deceptive, collusive, corrupt.

Sneer, *v.* See mock, slander; censure (2); frown; laugh.

Snicker, *v.* See mock, slander; laugh.

Snide, *adj.* See derogatory, defamatory, malicious, contemptuous.

Sniff, *n.* See breath; drug.

Snip, *v., n.* See cut (1); break (2); iota, scintilla, part.

Snipe, *v.* See shoot.

Sniper, *n.* See wrongdoer; military; sailor.

"Snitch," *n., v.* See informer, accuser; report (4), notify, communicate.

Snob, *n.* See showoff, boor, ass; pompous.

Snobbish, *adj.* See arrogant, pompous; patronize; contemptuous.

Snoop, *v.* See eavesdrop, bug, intermeddle, interfere, impose, encroach; check (2), investigate; prying.

Snooze, *v.* See sleep.

Snort, *v.* See breath; drug.

Snow, *n., v.* See climate; cold, storm; flatter.

Snub, *v.* See avoid, neglect (1), resist, rebut, challenge (1), confront, rebuke, slander.

Snug, *adj.* See comfortable; adequate.

Soak, *v.* See inundate, water; absorb.

Soap, *n.* See bathe.

Soar, *v.* See sail; flee, run (2), speed (2).

Sob, *v.* See cry (1), bemoan, suffer.

Sober, *adj.* **1.** Not intoxicated (still sober). Not drunk, abstemious, dry. **2.** Clear-headed or self-controlled (sober thinking). See rational, moderate (1), reasonable, logical, cautious. **3.** Somber. See grave, serious (5).

Sobriquet, *n.* See name, alias.

So-called, *adj.* See nominal (1), ostensible.

Soccer, *n.* See athletics, sport, contest.

Sociable, *adj.* See friendly, amicable, social (2), convivial, attractive, cooperative, benevolent.

Social, *adj.* **1.** Pertaining to society or groups (social responsibility). Societal, sociological, collective, communal, interdependent, common, human, civil. See also public (2); commune; community. **2.** Friendly (social visit). Neighborly, sociable, amiable, noncommercial, affable, hospitable. See also friendly, amicable, convivial; festive.

Social guest A person who goes on the property of another for companionship, diversion, and enjoyment of hospitality. See guest.

Socialize, *v.* See befriend, consort (2), associate (2), commingle; friendly, convivial; guest.

Society, *n.* **1.** An association or company of persons united by mutual consent and acting jointly for a common purpose. See organization (1), group, alliance (2). **2.** The community at large. See public (1), nation. **3.** See companionship, goodwill (2).

Sociopath, *n.* See maniac; insanity.

"Sock," *v.* See batter, beat; clothes, apparel.

Sodomy, *n.* Oral or anal copulation between humans, or between humans and animals. Unnatural sexual intercourse, bestiality, buggery, depravity, perversion, sexual deviation. See also lust, degradation, deviant, deviation.

Soft, *adj.* See flexible, malleable; amenable (2); charitable, kind; weak, frail.

Soften, *v.* See mitigate, assuage, abate, diminish; impair.

Soft-spoken, *adj.* See quiet (2), bashful, flexible, amenable (2); reserve (4).

Soil 1. *n.* Loose material from the earth's surface in which things grow. See earth (1); shrubbery, woods. **2.** *v.* To stain. See pollute. **3.** *v.* To malign or belittle. See slander (2).

Soil bank A federal program of conservation under which farmers are paid for not growing crops, or for growing noncommercial vegetation in order to preserve the quality of the soil and to avoid surpluses.

Sojourn, *v.* To visit a place temporarily. Vacation, reside, repose, stop over, rest, holiday, lay over.

Solace, *n., v.* See comfort, amenity; mitigate, assuage; improve.

Solar, *adj.* Pertaining to the sun.

Solatium, *n.* Damages allowed for injury to feelings. See damages; pain; compensation.

Sold, *v.* See sale.

Soldier, *n.* **1.** A person who serves in the army; an enlisted man or woman. See military, martial, sailor. **2.** A follower. See accomplice, assistant, partisan.

Sole, *adj.* Individual or single (sole cause). Singular, unattached, one and only, alone, exclusive, solitary, solo, particular, lone. See also separate, isolated, single (2), individual (1). *Ant.* Joint.

Solemn, *adj.* **1.** Imposing, grave. See serious, grave (2, 3). **2.** In regular or proper form. See formal, legal, proper, regular. **3.** Sacred. See religious (1), holy; church, God.

Solemnity, *n.* **1.** Seriousness (the solemnity of the occasion). Gravity, pomp, dignity, ceremony, intensity, momentousness, grandeur, consequence, tradition, urgency, staidness, majesty, importance. **2.** Solemn proceeding. See ceremony.

Solemnize, *v.* To perform with a ceremony; to make serious. See dedicate, honor (2), preside, moderate (2), handle (1), perform; solemnity, ceremony, memorial.

Sole proprietorship A form of business in which one person owns all the assets. See business, merchant, commerce; corporation.

Solicit, *v.* **1.** To appeal for something. See apply (1), petition, appeal (4). **2.** To approach someone for sex. Proposition, lure, accost, pimp, hustle, entice. See also incite, provoke, seduce, pander.

Solicitation, *n.* **1.** The act of enticing, inviting, promoting, requesting, urging, or ordering someone to commit a crime (solicitation of a bribe). **2.** A request for something (solicitation of funds). Petition, requisition, application, entreaty, appeal, inquiry, demand, motion, proposal, submission, proposition, bid, presentation, prayer, adjuration, supplication, asking. See also solicit.

Solicitor, *n.* **1.** One who solicits. **2.** A lawyer for a city, town, or government agency. See attorney. **3.** A British lawyer engaged in office work and litigation before some courts. For representation in other courts, particularly the higher courts, the solicitor refers the case to a barrister.

Solicitor General of the United States The lawyer in charge of representing the United States in the U.S. Supreme Court.

Solicitous, *adj.* See apprehensive, concerned; ardent, active (3), strong, emotional; ambitious.

Solicitude, *n.* See interest (3), concern (5), affection, love.

Solid, *adj.* See fixed, permanent, firm (2), inflexible; healthy, able-bodied; reliable, mature (2), loyal, genuine.

Solidarity, *n.* A unity of interests and goals. See cooperation.

Solidify, *v.* See strengthen, help (2), equip, augment, improve, promote, remedy, raise (2).

Solitary, *adj.* Isolated or alone (solitary travel). Outcast, sole, singular, unattended, apart, monastic, unaccompanied, cloistered, desolate, uninhabited, separated, without company, deserted, lonely, celibate, estranged, exclusive, forsaken, hermitic, solo, removed, private, detached. See also alone, barren, separate, remote (1), isolated, individual, single (2), independent, abandoned. *Ant.* Communal.

Solitary confinement, *n.* The separate confinement of a prisoner, with little or no contact with other prisoners; complete isolation. See jail, prison.

Solitude, *n.* See alone, privacy, separation, quarantine (1); expulsion.

Solo, *adj.* See solitary, alone, separate, individual, isolated, single (2), independent.

Solution, *n.* See resolution (1), clarification, answer (3), outcome; mixture, compound (3).

Solvable, *adj.* See salvageable, amenable, malleable.

Solve, *v.* See clarify, settle (1), construe, decide, judge (2), arbitrate.

Solvent, *adj.* Able to pay debts as they mature (a solvent concern). Sound, financially stable, reliable, creditworthy, solid, safe, responsible. *Ant.* Bankrupt.

Somatic, *adj.* See physical, material (2), corporeal.

Somber, *adj.* See grave (3), depressed, depressing, dark, despondent, abandoned (1), dismal, serious (2, 5).

Some, *adj.* See few.

Somebody, *n., pron.* See identity (1); notoriety, reputation, note (4).

Someplace, *adv.* See locality, location, place (1), zone, neighborhood.

Something, *pron., n.* See entity, goods, item, object (3), property (1).

Sometime, *adv., adj.* See interval (1), period, minute, month, age (1), epoch; previous.

Somewhere, *n., adv.* See locality, location, place (1), zone, neighborhood.

Somnambulism, *n.* Sleepwalking. See illness, disease.

Son, *n.* See child, juvenile, family, blood, man.

Song, *n.* See music; lyric.

Sonorous, *adj.* See flamboyant, pompous; noisy.

Soon, *adv.* Within a reasonable time. As soon as practicable, shortly, in due time, directly, forthwith, straightaway, promptly, presently, quickly, without delay, in a while.

Soot, *n.* See dirt, pollution.

Soothe, *v.* See mitigate, assuage, quiet, abate.

Soothing, *adj.* See extenuating, remedial; narcotic.

Soothsayer, *n.* See oracle.

Sophistical, *adj.* See fallacious, erroneous, deceptive.

Sophisticated, *adj.* See expert (2), able, apt (3), learned, mature (2); worldly, aristocratic, cultivated, chic, civil (3).

Sophistication, *n.* See maturity, experience (1), facility (3), skill (1); solemnity.

Sophistry, *n.* See error, fault (1), falsehood.

Sophomoric, *adj.* See juvenile; innocent; absurd.

Sorcery, *n.* See witchcraft.

Sordid, *adj.* See base, immoral, abandoned (2), corrupt, avaricious, dirty, obscene.

Sore, *n., adj.* See contusion, hurt, lesion, injury, wound, pain, affliction; aggrieved, painful.

Sororicide, *n.* The killing or murder of a sister. See homicide.

Sorority, *n.* See club (1), assembly, community, companionship, goodwill (2), affinity; school.

Sorrow, *n.* See anguish, anxiety, pain, affliction, depression; guilt (2), contrition, embarrassment.

Sorrowful, *adj.* See depressed, depressing, despondent, serious (5), contrite, ashamed.

Sorry, *adj.* See contrite, ashamed; depressed, depressing, despondent, serious (5).

Sort, *n., v.* See class (1), classification, kind (1); classify, codify, organize (1); essence, character (2).

Sortie, *n.* See invasion, attack, assault.

SOS, *n.* See warning; help.

So-so, *adj.* See marginal, pedestrian (2), ordinary, commonplace, household.

Soul, *n.* See mind (1), spirit (3), essence, foundation, character, identity; woman, man, person.

Sound 1. *v.* To have reference or relation to; to aim at (the action sounds in tort). See pertain, refer. **2.** *adj.* In good condition. See durable, healthy, able-bodied, fit (1). **3.** *adj.* Sensible. See logical, reasonable, rational. **4.** *adj.* Free from illness. See healthy, able-bodied. **5.** *n.* Noise. Outcry, clamor, tone, clatter, din, babel, sensation, commotion, uproar, moan, racket, cacophony, cry, whine, bark, reverberation, drone, squeal, shout, jingle, ring. See also noise.

Sound mind The faculties of perception and judgment are well-developed and not impaired by mental disorder. The ability to understand in a general way the nature and extent of the property to be disposed of, one's relationship to those who would naturally claim a substantial benefit from the will, and the practical effect of the will as executed. See sanity, sane.

Sour, *adj.* See foul, stale (1), rotten; crabby.

Source, *n.* **1.** The person or thing that originates, sets in motion, or is the primary agency in producing a course of action or result (source of conflict). See cause (1), root, author, agent, impulse. **2.** An informant. See informer.

Souvenir, *n.* See memento, trophy.

Sovereign 1. *adj.* Having supreme power (sovereign leader). Governing, absolute, imperial, ruling, authorized, independent, self-ruling, free, autonomous, self-governing, uncontrolled, dominant, royal, paramount, master, enthroned. **2.** *n.* A person, body, or state in which independent and supreme authority is vested. Monarch, king, ruler, tyrant, head, czar, autocrat, emperor, chief.

Sovereign immunity The sovereign (i.e., the state) cannot be sued without its consent. See immunity, immune.

Sovereignty, *n.* The supreme and absolute power by which any independent state is governed; supreme political authority; the power of self-government; the international independence of a state (an incident of sovereignty). Self-rule, dominion, self-determination, jurisdiction, autonomy, home rule, primacy, royalty. See also supremacy.

Space, *n.* See extent, range, scope, area, interval.

Spacious, *adj.* See abundant, broad, adequate, big, considerable; comfortable.

Span, *v., n.* See connect, extend, live, continue; extent, scope, range, measure, zone.

Spank, *v.* See correct (3), discipline (2, 4), beat.

Spar, *v.* See contend, contest, dispute.

Spare, *v., adj.* See save (1), relieve, forgive, waive, protect, defend; conserve, hoard; extra, supplemental; thin, anemic, exhausted.

Sparing, *adj.* See economical, prudent, careful; small, bare, minimal.

Spark, *n.* See catalyst; fire; life, spirit (2); light; iota; scintilla.

Sparkle, *n., v.* See clear (3), light; life, spirit (2); catalyst; revive, provoke, animate.

Sparse, *adj.* See insufficient, few, inadequate, small (1), minimal, marginal, nugatory, minor (2); deficient, thin.

Spartan, *adj.* See ascetic, strict (2), extreme (1), grave (3), formal (3).

Spasm, *n.* See fit (2), seizure (2).

Spasmodic, *adj.* See excitable, feverish; intermittent, periodic, fluctuating, irregular, temporary.

Spat, *n.* See argument, fight, quarrel.

Spawn, *v.* See beget, produce (2).

Speak, *v.* To utter words with the voice; to talk. See communicate.

Speaker, *n.* **1.** The president or chairperson of a legislative assembly (Speaker of the House). See head, legislator. **2.** The person talking. Orator, reader, talker, mouthpiece, spokesperson, lecturer.

Speaking demurrer A demurrer that is defective because it requires reference to facts that do not appear on the face of the pleading. See demurrer.

Spear, *n., v.* See weapon; pierce, cut.

Special, *adj.* **1.** Confined to a particular purpose (special session). Unique, limited, specific, idiosyncratic, distinct, blue-ribbon, select, personal, uncommon, rare, sui generis, atypical. See also extraordinary, odd, peculiar (1), exceptional. **2.** Distinctive or celebrated. See outstanding (2), important.

Special agent An agent delegated to do a single act. See agent (1). *Ant.* General agent.

Special appearance An appearance made in the litigation for the limited and sole purpose of testing the jurisdiction of the court. See appearance. *Ant.* General appearance.

Special damages Damages that are peculiar to the particular plaintiff; damages that are the natural, but not the necessary, result of the injury complained of. See damages.

Specialist, *n.* One who has extensively studied or has considerable experience in a particular area (medical specialist). Professional, master, veteran, authority, practitioner, connoisseur, maestro, buff, old hand, devotee, technician, scholar, skilled hand. See also doctor, expert (1). *Ant.* Amateur.

Specialize, *v.* See emphasize, accent, concentrate; specialty.

Specialty, *n.* **1.** An area or field that has been given special attention or study; a distinctive feature (her specialty is patent law). Specialization, concentration, hallmark, focus, major, talent, peculiarity, distinction, badge, ability, professionalism, vocation, genius, endowment, career, faculty, craft, earmark, virtuosity, quality, individuality, character, strength, forte, trademark, idiosyncrasy, stamp, claim to fame, quirk, oddity, dominant trait. **2.** A contract or obligation under seal. A writing that is sealed and delivered, containing an agreement (suit upon a specialty). See contract (1). **3.** A structure that is uniquely adapted to the business conducted upon it and which cannot be converted to other uses without the expenditure of substantial sums of money.

Special verdict A jury's answers to specific factual questions. See verdict.

Specie, *n.* **1.** Coined money; metallic money. See currency, money. **2.** Strictly, according to the exact terms (performance in specie). **3.** The thing itself; identity (delivery of the picture in specie).

Species, *n.* A type or category. See classification (2), kind.

Specific, *adj.* Precisely formulated or restricted (specific intent). Explicit, definite, exact, certain, distinctive, select, categorical, special, detailed, bounded, prescribed, unique, individual, pertinent, particular, particularized, specified, concrete, clear-cut, pointed, relevant, unmistakable, designated, circumscribed, plain, characteristic, different, determinate, uncommon, singular, indicative, manifest, determined, separate, qualified, distinguished, minute, tailored, endemic, inherent, intrinsic, unequivocal. *Ant.* General.

Specification, *n.* A statement or listing of the particulars required or involved (specification of errors). Enumeration, designation, stipulation, account, itemization, description, recital, checklist, directory, schedule, entry, roster, catalogue, recitation, inventory, index, clarification, docket, articulation, particularization, condition, proviso, specific, program.

Specific bequest A testamentary gift of specific personal property that may be satisfied only by delivery of this particular property. See bequest, gift.

Specific performance The remedy of performance of a contract in the specific form in which it was made or according to the precise terms agreed upon. This remedy is granted when damages would be an inadequate compensation for a breach of the contract. See performance, remedy.

Specify, *v.* To mention in explicit terms. See detail (1), itemize, communicate, recognize.

Specimen, *n.* A part of something intended to exhibit the kind and quality of the whole. See sample (1), model, instance.

Specious, *adj.* See feigned, fake (3), deceitful, deceptive, false, fallacious, baseless, erroneous.

Speck, *n.* See dirt, pollution; iota, scintilla.

Spectacle, *n.* See extravaganza, marvel, mystery, performance (3), grandeur, ceremony, celebration.

Spectacular, *adj.* See extraordinary, exceptional, outstanding (2), attractive.

Spectator, *n.* See witness (2), bystander, eyewitness.

Specter, *n.* See ghost, dream (1), hallucination.

Spectograph, *n.* A machine used for voiceprint analysis. See voiceprint, voice exemplars.

Spectrum, *n.* See range (2), scope, measure (1), extent; diversity.

Speculate, *v.* See fantasize; bet (2), hazard (2), risk (2), venture (2); estimate; invest (1), contemplate, think; speculation.

Speculation, *n.* **1.** Buying or selling with the expectation of profiting by a rise or fall in price (market speculation). Wager, chance, venture, trading, risk. See also gambling. **2.** Theorizing about a matter as to which the evidence is not sufficient for certain knowledge (speculation about the cause of the injury). Surmise, assumption, conjecture, inference, hypothesis, opinion, impression, guesswork, suspicion, intuition, premise, supposition, inkling, presumption; rumination, reasoning, thinking, contemplation, deliberation, examination, consideration. **3.** See risk (1), jeopardy, peril, hazard, danger, doubt.

Speculative, *adj.* Based on conjecture or guessing (speculative conclusions). Hypothetical, theoretical, imaginary, unproven, experimental, debatable, uncertain, abstract, suppositional, vague, improbable, unconfirmed, risky, chancy, undemonstrated, intuitive, indefinite, academic, questionable, uninsured, unsafe, problematical, contestable, dubious, tentative. *Ant.* Corroborated.

Speculative damages Anticipated damages that are contingent, conjectural, or improbable. See damages.

Speech, *n.* **1.** Talk, utterance, or oral expression. See language, communication, declaration. **2.** A lecture. Oration, eulogy, discourse, tirade, harangue, recital, pep talk, homily, diatribe, "spiel," sermon, talk, valedictory, dissertation. See also address (3).

Speechless, *adj.* See aback (1); silent (1), mute, quiet.

Speech or debate Any action within the sphere of legitimate legislative activity.

Speed 1. *n.* Swiftness (travel with speed). Quickness, alacrity, promptness, velocity, haste, rapidity, zeal, vim, vigor, fleetness, precipitousness, dispatch. **2.** *v.* To move quickly (speed past the truck). Hasten, rush, tear, dash, scoot, scurry, fly, shoot, zip, race, sprint, zoom, dart, gallop, hurry, accelerate, quicken, plunge, hustle. See also expedite, run. **3.** *n.* Amphetamine. See drug.

Speedometer, *n.* Odometer. See measure, gauge.

Speedy, *adj.* Characterized by swift motion or progress; expeditious (speedy resolution). Hasty, quick, fast, punctual, agile, precipitate, rapid, fleet, hurried, headlong, not delayed, with dispatch, brisk, summary. See also prompt (1), expeditious, immediate (1). *Ant.* Dilatory.

Speedy trial A trial as soon as the prosecution can prepare for it with reasonable diligence. Factors considered: (a) length of the delay, (b) government's justification for the delay, (c) whether and how the defendant asserted the right to a speedy trial, and (d) prejudice caused by the delay.

Spell, *n.* See fit, seizure.

Spellbinding, *adj.* See agape (1), extraordinary, great, outstanding (2).

Spend, *v.* **1.** To pay out. See pay (2), expend. **2.** To use up or exhaust. See consume (1).

Spendthrift 1. *n.* One who spends money profusely and improvidently. Prodigal squanderer, waster, big spender, profligate, wastrel. **2.** *adj.* See improvident, precipitate (2), prodigal. *Ant.* Tightwad; prudent.

Spendthrift trust A trust created to provide a fund for the maintenance of a beneficiary, and at the same time to secure it against his or her improvidence by turning over only a certain portion of the total amount at any given time. See trust.

Sphere, *n.* See area, zone, domain, experience.

Spice, *n.* See color (4), appeal (3).

"Spiel," *n.* See speech (2), address.

Spike, *n.* Nail. Stake, stud, rivet, pin.

Spill, *v.* See splash, sprinkle; inundate, flood; disclose.

Spin, *v.* See turn (1), alternate.

Spineless, *adj.* See weak, infirm, fluctuating, bashful, capricious; coward, cowardice; base.

Spin-off, *n.* A subsidiary organized by a parent corporation. Part of the assets of the parent is transferred to the subsidiary. The stock of the subsidiary is distributed to the shareholders of the parent without any surrender by them of their stock in the parent. See branch (1), corporation.

Spinster, *n.* A woman who has never been married. See woman.

Spire, *n.* See steeple.

Spirit, *n.* **1.** Underlying meaning or purpose (spirit of the law). See meaning, intent. **2.** Energy or enthusiasm (his spirit was contagious). Zeal, energy, enterprise, drive, courage, dash, vivacity, resolution, soul, passion, motivation, boldness, vigor, valor, fervor, élan, animation, esprit de corps, devotion, fire, style, vim, sparkle, warmth, audacity, fortitude, spunk, mettle. **3.** The soul. Intellect, immortality, essence, life force, personality, anima, psyche, ego. See also mind. **4.** Subjective mental state. See emotion. **5.** See climate (2).

Spirited, *adj.* See earnest (2), emotional, ardent, active (3), strong (2).

Spiritual, *adj.* **1.** Relating to religion or matters of the spirit. See religious (1), church, clergy, God. **2.** Pertaining to that which cannot be perceived by the senses. See intangible (1, 3), incorporeal.

Spit, *n.* See saliva.

Spite 1. *n.* Ill will toward another. See animus (2), hostility, wrath, malice. **2.** *v.* To irritate or vex someone. See provoke, harass, disturb, outrage (2).

Spite fence A fence of no beneficial use to the person erecting it and maintained solely to annoy the occupant of adjoining land.

Spiteful, *adj.* See cruel, malicious, hostile.

Splash, *v.* To splatter. Slop, spray, spill, swash, dash, slosh, spatter, squirt, besprinkle, daub, strew, shower. See also sprinkle.

Splatter, *v.* See splash, sprinkle.

Spleen, *n.* See malice, animus (2), hostility, wrath.

Splendid, *adj.* See exceptional, great, extraordinary, outstanding (2), irresistible, beautiful, elevated, attractive.

Splendor, *n.* See grandeur, solemnity.

Splice, *v.* See connect, join (1), affiliate; merger.

Splinter 1. *n.* A fragment. See part, iota, scintilla. **2.** *v.* See divide.

Splintered, *adj.* See split (3), separate, isolated.

Split 1. *v.* To separate. See divide. **2.** *n.* A disconnection or partition. See separation (2), division (1). **3.** *adj.* Broken or detached. Segmented, fractured, divided, dual, parted, halved, cracked, torn, cut, alienated, isolated, splintered, separated, ruptured, dissevered, bisected, bifurcated, cleft. **4.** *v.* See depart.

Split hairs See quibble.

Split income Allowing married couples to have their income taxed on a joint return at a rate equal to that which would apply if each spouse had one-half the amount and were taxed on a separate return. See income, tax.

Split-off, *n.* A new corporation set up by a parent corporation. The shares of the new corporation go to the shareholders of the parent. In exchange, these shareholders surrender some of their stock in the old corporation. See corporation, reorganization.

Split sentence A sentence that is active in part and suspended in part. See punishment, adjudication, cessation; waive.

Splitting a cause of action Dividing a single or indivisible cause of action into several parts or claims and bringing several actions thereon; commencing an action for only part of the cause of action. See action (1).

Split-up, *n.* The process whereby a corporation divides into two or more separate new corporations, giving the shareholders the shares of these new corporations and then going out of business. See corporation, reorganization.

Splurge, *n., v.* See spree; satisfy (2).

Spoil, *v.,* **spoils,** *n.* **1.** *v.* To cause harm. See damage (2), impair, destroy, pollute. **2.** *n.* Goods seized. See plunder (2).

Spokesman, spokesperson, *n.* See agent, representative, intermediary, advocate, attorney.

Spoliation, *n.* The destruction of evidence; the destruction or meaningful alteration of a document.

Sponge, *n., v.* See parasite; exploit; absorb.

Sponsor 1. *n.* One who makes a promise or gives security for another. See

Sponsor

promoter, champion (1), advocate. **2.** *v.* To back or guarantee. See finance (1), defend (1), back (1).

Sponsorship, *n.* See backing, indorsement.

Spontaneity, *n.* See impulse, intuition; spontaneous.

Spontaneous, *adj.* Arising on its own; unpremeditated (spontaneous support). Automatic, impulsive, mechanical, reflexive, visceral, instinctive, extemporaneous, natural, unprompted, impromptu, uninhibited, unplanned, intuitive, uncontrollable, unrehearsed, free, gratuitous, ad lib, independent, self-determined, off-the-cuff, irresistible, unwitting, immediate. See also fortuitous. *Ant.* Contrived.

Spontaneous combustion, *n.* See fire; burn.

Spontaneous declaration A spontaneous and unreflecting statement produced from a startling occurrence when there was no time to fabricate and the statement related to the circumstances of the occurrence. See res gestae, declaration, communication.

Spontaneous exclamation A statement or exclamation made immediately after some exciting occurrence by a participant or spectator asserting the circumstances of the occurrence as observed by him or her. See res gestae, proclamation, communication.

Spoof, *n., v.* See antic, joke; artifice; mimic.

Spoon-feed, *v.* See pander, satisfy, accommodate; gift.

Sporadic, *adj.* See odd (3), periodic, irregular, isolated, intermittent; seldom, casual (2).

Sport, *n.* **1.** A game involving competition and physical activity (the sport of tennis). Contest, tournament, play, hobby, recreation. See also athletics. **2.** Frivolity (done in sport). Fun, amusement, gaiety, teasing, jest, merriment, banter, lark, ridicule, diversion, entertainment, mirth, kidding, mockery. See also antic, joke.

Sports car, *n.* See vehicle.

Sportsmanship, *n.* See goodwill, fairness, justice, companionship.

Spot 1. *v.* To stain. See pollute, damage (2). **2.** *v.* To identify or detect. See recognize (1), watch (1). **3.** *n.* A blemish. See disgrace. **4.** *n.* A location or site. See place, location.

Spot-check, *v.* See check (2); irregular, casual, periodic.

Spotless, *adj.* See clean; blameless, innocent.

Spotlight, *v.* See accent, emphasize, exhibit, promote, publish, proclaim.

Spot price, *n.* The selling price of goods.

Spot zoning Granting a zoning classification to a piece of land that differs from that of the other land in the immediate area. See zoning, exception.

Spouse, *n.* One's wife or husband. Marriage partner, mate, consort, helpmate, companion, better half, matron, squaw. See also partner.

Spout, *v.* See discharge; sprinkle, splash.

Sprain, *v., n.* See twist (1); pain, injury, contusion.

Sprawl, *v.* See lie (4).

Spray, *v.* See sprinkle, distribute, splash, water, inundate.

Spread 1. *n.* The difference between two amounts (price spread). Span, stretch, distance, area, scope, length, expanse, compass, breadth, orbit, depth, measurement, dimension. **2.** *v.* To disperse or disseminate (spread the rumor). See distribute, communicate. **3.** *v.* To unfold (spread a cloth). Extend, open, stretch, unfurl, enlarge, unveil, bloom. **4.** *v.* To broaden (the animals spread the disease). Enlarge, mushroom, escalate, expand, multiply, accelerate, overgrow, flare, swell.

Spree, *n.* Indulgence. Frolic, overindulgence, outing, bout, spell, orgy, bacchanal, "bender," fling, splurge, revel, fit, carousal, carouse. See also celebration, antic,

710

intoxicated; junket, voyage.

Spring, *v.* See jump (1), run; emerge, shoot.

Sprinkle, *v.* To scatter (sprinkle the funds). Disperse, spray, strew, disseminate, shower, diffuse, pepper. See also distribute, splash.

Sprinkling trust A trust that calls for distribution of income to various beneficiaries at different times. See trust.

Sprint, *v.* See speed, run.

Sprout, *v.* See begin, develop, mature (1), advance.

Spry, *adj.* See active (3), alive (2); healthy, able-bodied; flexible, malleable.

Spunk, *n.* See spirit (2).

Spur, *v.* See incite, provoke, prompt.

Spurious, *adj.* Counterfeit or synthetic (spurious offer). See deceptive, fraudulent, fake (3), deceitful, feigned, false, fallacious, baseless, erroneous.

Spurn, *v.* See resist, reject (1), abjure, rebut, avoid, rebuke.

Spurt, *n., v.* See force (1), power, eruption, increase, emit, shoot, discharge.

Spy 1. *n.* A undercover agent who attempts to obtain secrets from a rival (a spy for the allies). Sleuth, scout, detective, informant, informer, investigator, provocateur, secret agent, operative, source. **2.** *v.* To watch or listen secretly (spy on the competitor). Search, probe, investigate, delve, ferret out, survey, eavesdrop, reconnoiter, inspect, discover, expose, scour, trace, dig, shadow, comb, track, watch, observe, pry, peer. See also inspection.

Squabble, *n., v.* See argument, quarrel, fight.

Squad, squadron, *n.* See group (1), division (2); military; sailor.

Squalid, *adj.* See dirty, foul, rotten, abject, base, vulgar.

Squall, *v., n.* See yell; storm, tempest.

Squander, *v.* See dissipate (1), waste (3), deplete, consume.

Square 1. *n.* An open area surrounded by streets. Park, plaza, green, close, quadrangle, common, court, place, block, tract, enclave, enclosure. **2.** *n.* An area measuring 24 × 24 miles. **3.** *v.* To straighten out. See adjust.

Squash, *v.* See compact (4), squeeze; destroy, debilitate, disable, deter.

Squat, *v.* To settle. Encamp, take up residence, inhabit, reside, pitch tent, dwell. See also locate (2).

Squatter, *n.* One who settles on another's land without legal title or authority. See occupant, possessor.

Squawk, *v.* See yell; protest (3).

"Squeal," *v.* See betray; informer.

Squeamish, *adj.* Delicate, oversensitive. Fastidious, prim, finicky, fussy, puritanical, queasy, prudish, dainty, shy, priggish. See also particular (2).

Squeeze 1. *v.* To apply pressure from all sides. Tighten, compress, concentrate, narrow, cut back, press together, digest, pinch, condense, decrease, clutch, wedge, constrict, crowd, hold, crush, embrace, hug, clasp. **2.** *n.* See extortion.

Squeeze-out, *n.* A merger effected for no valid business purpose, resulting in the elimination of a minority shareholder. Freeze-out. See also merger.

Squelch, *v.* See arrest, abort, quash, defeat, squeeze.

Squirm, *v.* See flounder.

Squirt, *v.* See sprinkle, water.

SSI Supplemental Security Income.

SSS Selective Service System.

Stab, *v.* See pierce, cut, enter (2); attack, assault (3); shoot.

Stability, *n.* See balance (4), harmony.

Stabilize, *v.* To keep steady; to prevent fluctuation (stabilize prices). Preserve, maintain, ground, continue, immobilize, root, hold fast, secure, balance, stiffen, fasten, counterbalance, calm, fix, brace, reinforce, moor, settle, anchor. See also mitigate, quiet. *Ant.* Destabilize.

Stable, *adj.* Firm; not easily shaken. See reliable, firm (2), fit (1), loyal, certain, credible, cogent, legitimate, rational.

Stack, *v., n.* See pack; lot, collection, mass.

Stadium, *n.* See arena, facility (2), building.

Staff, *n.* See coterie; associate (2), employee.

Stag, *adj.* For males only. See man.

Stage, *n., v.* See period; platform (2); drama; exhibit, perform, manipulate, manage, contrive.

Stagger, *v.* See flounder; surprise, confuse, amaze.

Staging, *n.* See platform (2).

Stagnant, *adj.* See barren, stale, dormant, lazy, commonplace, foul, rotten.

Stagnate, *v.* See loiter, loaf; decline (2), diminish, fall, wear, dissolve, decompose.

Staid, *adj.* See bashful, quiet, squeamish, prudent, cautious, grave (3), serious (5); permanent.

Stain, *n., v.* See dirt; pollute; slander, damage, cloud (2).

Stainless, *adj.* See clean.

Stairs, *n.* Steps. Flight, staircase, stairwell.

Stake 1. *n.* A deposit that shall be given to the one entitled to it upon the happening of a stated condition. See deposit, gambling, prize. **2.** *n.* A boundary marker used for land survey purposes. Standard, pole, pillar, peg, column, bar, pile, rod, stick, picket. **3.** *n.* See right, claim, interest (1). **4.** *v.* See back, finance (1). **5.** *v.* See bet (2), venture (2).

Stakeholder, *n.* A person who is or may be exposed to multiple liability as a result of adverse claims. One who holds assets in which he or she claims no interest and which are sought by rival claimants. A third party chosen by two or more persons to keep property or money on deposit and to deliver it to the one who eventually establishes the right to it.

Stakeout, *n.* See inspection, search (1); eavesdrop.

Stale, *adj.* **1.** Having lost its freshness or vitality (stale argument). Unasserted, sour, wasted, unfresh, dry, effete, rancid, spoiled, moldy, withered, aged, lifeless. **2.** Boring or hackneyed. See commonplace (2), household, pedestrian (2).

Stale check A check that has been outstanding too long. See check (4).

Stale claim or demand A claim or demand that has long remained unasserted. See claim.

Stalemate, *n.* See deadlock, blockade, block (1), obstruction; dilemma.

Stalk, *v.* See pursue (2), chase, ferret, trace (2).

Stall, *n., v.* See cell, alcove; market; avoid, quibble, delay; arrest, incapacitate, disable, check.

Stalwart, *adj.* See durable; healthy, able-bodied; firm (2), decisive, courageous, strong.

Stamina, *n.* See endurance, power, force, vigor, spirit (2).

Stammer, *v.* See flounder.

Stamp 1. *n.* A mark, design, or seal that indicates ownership or approval. An identifying or characterizing mark or impression (stamp of approval). See mark, brand, indorsement (2), badge, manifestation. **2.** *v.* To crush. Pulverize, granulate, grind, pound, smash, stomp, trample, step. See also batter, beat. **3.** *v.* To make a mark. See engrave.

Stampede, *v., n.* See run, speed (2), flee; confusion, disorder, commotion, hysteria, eruption.

Stamp tax The cost of stamps that must be affixed to legal documents such as deeds.

Stance, *n.* See manner; opinion, belief, bias.

712

Stand 1. *v.* To remain in force (the award was allowed to stand). See continue (1), prevail (2). **2.** *v.* To submit to (stand trial). Face, encounter, undergo, experience, tolerate, stomach, endure. See also bear (2). **3.** *n.* A position or point of view. See belief, opinion (2). **4.** *n.* A raised structure. See platform.

Standard 1. *n.* A yardstick or point of reference (well-known standard). See measure (1), criterion; maxim. **2.** *adj.* Customary (standard practice). See conventional (1), ordinary (1), habitual, regular. **3.** *adj.* See uniform.

Standard deduction A fixed deduction from taxable income, used by a taxpayer who does not wish to itemize deductions.

Standardization, *n.* See equalization; organization (2); balance (4), harmony.

Standardize, *v.* See regulate, stabilize, adjust, balance (3), harmonize, organize (1).

Standardized, *adj.* See normal (1), uniform.

Standard of care That degree of care which a reasonably prudent person should exercise under the same or similar circumstances. For professionals, the standard of care is the skill and learning commonly possessed by members of the profession in good standing, usually in the same or in a similar locality. See care, negligence.

Standard of proof See beyond a reasonable doubt, preponderance of evidence, clear and convincing evidence.

Stand-in, *n.* See agent (1), representative (1), replacement (2), dummy (1).

Standing 1. *n.* As an aspect of justiciability, standing to sue is the legal right to set judicial machinery in motion. The requirement that a party in a lawsuit have sufficient personal interest in the outcome so that the case is fairly, fully, and vigorously litigated. **2.** *n.* One's place in the community in the estimation of others. See reputation. **3.** *adj.* Continuing or established (standing order). Traditional, constant, lasting, perpetual, fixed, continued, unchanging, enduring, renewable, lasting, permanent, continuous, uninterrupted, unbroken.

Stand-off, *n.* See deadlock, tie (4); blockade, block (1), obstruction.

Standout, *n.* See expert, specialist, champion.

Standpoint, *n.* See opinion, belief, bias.

Staple 1. *n.* A main product. See commodity (1); necessaries, goods. **2.** *adj.* Major. See principal (5), primary.

Star, *adj., n., v.* See outstanding (2), extraordinary, great, exceptional; destiny, chance (2); notoriety, reputation, eminence; exceed.

Starboard, *n.* The right-hand side of a vessel when the observer faces forward. See vessel (1), marine, maritime, nautical.

Star Chamber, *n.* An early English court that illegally extended its jurisdiction and acted secretly, arbitrarily, and harshly. See court, tyranny.

Stare, *v.* See observe (3), watch, spy (2), notice.

Stare decisis Similar cases should be decided in the same way unless there is good reason for a court to do otherwise. To abide by or adhere to decided cases. See precedent (1).

Stark, *adj.* See barren, bare, naked; difficult, extreme, strict (2); flagrant, obvious, absolute.

Star page When reading a page from an opinion printed in an unofficial reporter, you may be told what the comparable page number is in the official reporter—by star paging.

Start, *v., n.* See commence, begin; establish, institute; commencement; jump.

Startle, *v.* See menace (2), amaze, surprise (1); disturb, harass; agape.

Starvation, *n.* See privation, poverty; dearth, absence (2), want (1), desire; destitute, hungry.

Starve, *v.* See die; starvation.

Stash, *v.* To hide or secrete away. See conceal, hoard.

State

State 1. *n.* A body of people occupying a definite territory and organized under one government. See nation, country (1). **2.** *n.* The background or shape of something. See circumstances, particulars, fact, detail (2), condition (1). **3.** *v.* To express, set down, or declare. See communicate.

State action A sufficiently close involvement, sponsorship, interdependence, or nexus between the state and the challenged action so that the action may be fairly treated as that of the state itself. Under color of state law.

Stated, *adj.* Determined, fixed, or settled (they meet at stated times). Decided, ordained, ruled, defined, ascertained, specified, stipulated, agreed upon, mandated, predetermined, accredited, validated, prescribed, verified, authoritative, certified, resolved. See also official; stipulate. *Ant.* Flexible.

Stated capital The amount of capital contributed by stockholders. The capital or equity of a corporation as it appears in the balance sheet. See capital, equity (3).

Stately, *adj.* See elevated, awesome, important, formal; grandeur, solemnity.

Statement, *n.* An oral or written assertion, or nonverbal conduct of a person intended as an assertion. See declaration, communication, report (1), record (2).

Statement of account A report issued periodically by a bank or creditor to a customer, setting forth transactions, charges, payments, the balance due, etc. See account, report (1).

State of mind A person's reasons and motives for acting or failing to act. See mind (1), opinion, belief, reason (1), motive.

State's attorney, *n.* An officer who represents the state in criminal cases. See prosecutor, attorney.

State's evidence, *n.* Testimony given by an accomplice or joint participant in the commission of a crime, which tends to incriminate the others. See evidence, accomplice.

Statesman, *n.* See manager, legislator, sovereign, administrator, delegate (2); discretion (3), prudence, discreet; brilliant, learned.

State's rights, *n.* A political philosophy favoring a limitation on federal power with corresponding increased autonomy for individual states.

Static, *adj.* See stationary, dormant, silent, latent.

Station 1. *n.* Social position or status. See rank (1), class, reputation. **2.** *n.* A location or post. See place (1). **3.** *v.* To situate or arrange. See place (2). **4.** *n.* See depot.

Stationary, *adj.* Immobile. Secure, rooted, motionless, stable. See also inflexible, firm, fixed.

Statistics, *n.* See number; fact; calculate.

Statue, *n.* See sculpture (2).

Stature, *n.* See eminence, note (4), regard (2), reputation, notoriety.

Status, *n.* **1.** Social position; standing, state, or condition; a person's legal relation to the rest of the community. See condition (2), rank (1), reputation. **2.** Prestige or esteem. See eminence, note (4), regard (2), notoriety.

Status crime or offense A crime or offense that consists not in proscribed action or inaction but in the accused's having a certain personal condition or being a person of a specified character. See crime, offense.

Status quo, *n.* The existing state of things at any given time. The present state of affairs, the existing condition, things as they were before the change.

Statute, *n.* An act of the legislature declaring, commanding, or prohibiting something. See legislation (2), law.

Statute of frauds No suit or action shall be maintained on certain classes of contracts or engagements unless there shall be a note or memorandum thereof in writing, signed by the party to be charged or by his or her authorized agent. See writing, signature.

Statute of limitations No suit, action, or criminal prosecution shall be maintained unless brought within a specified period of time. See bar (3, 4, 5).

Statute of uses A statute that converted the purely equitable title of persons entitled to a use into a legal title or absolute ownership with the right of possession. The statute "executed" the use. See use.

Statutes at large An official compilation of the acts and resolutions of each session of Congress. See legislation (2), law.

Statutory, *adj.* Relating to a statute; created or defined by a statute; conforming to a statute. See legislative.

Statutory crime A crime created by statute. See crime, offense. *Ant.* Common-law crime.

Statutory rape The unlawful sexual intercourse with a female under the age of consent (e.g., 16). Her actual consent is not a defense to the crime. See rape, coitus.

Staunch, *adj.* See indefatigable, diligent, strong (2), loyal, reliable.

Stave, *v.* See avoid, reject.

Stay 1. *n.* The suspension of a judicial proceeding or some phase of it by order of the court (the defendant was granted a stay). See interruption, abeyance. **2.** *v.* To stop (stay an order). See block (2), bar, postpone (1). **3.** *n.* A temporary visit. See sojourn.

Steadfast, *adj.* See loyal, reliable, faithful, constant.

Steady 1. *adj.* Kept at a uniform level or pace (steady course). See constant (1), firm (2). **2.** *adj.* Frequent (steady customer). See habitual. **3.** *adj.* Dedicated and resolute (steady in her work). See reliable, careful, serious. **4.** *adj.* Tranquil and calm (she remained steady). See patient (3). **5.** *v.* To calm or secure (steady the rope). See stabilize.

Steal, *v.* See rob, filch, embezzle; larceny.

Stealing, *n.* Taking the property of another without right; feloniously taking and carrying away the personal property of another with the intent to keep it. See larceny.

Stealth, *n.* Any secret, sly, or clandestine act. See secrecy.

Steam, *n.* See spirit (2); muggy.

Steamship, *n.* See vessel.

Steep, *adj.* See costly, high; bluff (3).

Steeple, *n.* A tower on a building. Spire, belfry, turret.

Steer, *v.* See navigate, regulate, manage, administer.

Steering committee, *n.* A committee that establishes or proposes an agenda for a larger body.

Stem, *v.* See block (2), bar, obstruct; derive (1), arise.

Stench, *n.* See odium; foul, rotten; fragrant, aroma.

Stenographer, *n.* See clerk (2), recorder; accountant.

Step 1. *pref.* Designates a relationship of affinity rather than blood (stepmother). **2.** *v.* To move by walking, climbing, etc. See walk. **3.** *n.* A grade or stage in a series. See rank (1), chain (1), series, succession (2), development (1). **4.** *n.* A move or act in the direction of a goal (step toward completion). Measure, phase, exploit, accomplishment, deed, action, milestone, installment, stroke, maneuver. See also formality (1).

Stepchild, *n.* The child of one of the spouses by a former marriage. See child, family.

Stepparent, *n.* The "mother" or "father" of a child born during a previous marriage of the other parent and hence not the natural parent of such child.

Stereo, *n.* See music; apparatus, equipment.

Stereotype, *n., v.* See cliché; commonplace, household, pedestrian (2); classify, generalize.

Sterile, *adj.* **1.** Incapable of reproducing (sterile couple). See barren (1); impotence. **2.** Unproductive or ineffective. See barren (2), worthless (1), fallow, abortive, dead (3), arid. **3.** Free from germs or bacteria. See sanitary, wholesome, clean.

Sterilization, *n.* **1.** The act or process by which one is rendered incapable of procreation (e.g., by tying the female Fallopian tubes, a vasectomy, castration). **2.** The act or process by which an article or instrument is rendered free of germs. See sanitary.

Sterilize, *v.* See sterilization; castrate; bathe, fumigate, disinfect.

Sterling, *adj.* See meritorious, genuine, outstanding.

Stern, *adj.* See strict (2), inflexible, firm, arbitrary, serious.

Stew, *v., n.* See bake; mope, complain (2), suffer; food.

Steward, *n.* **1.** One who represents another. See manager, agent (1). **2.** See shop steward.

Stick, *n., v.* See stake (2); bludgeon (1); pierce.

Stickler, *n.* **1.** An obstinate contender. Perfectionist, zealot, nitpicker, intransigent. **2.** An enigma. Puzzle, mystery, conundrum, riddle, teaser, problem. **3.** An arbitrator.

Stick-to-itiveness, *n.* See spirit (2), endurance, industry (2), determination (2), conviction (3), passion, resolution (4), vigor.

Sticky, *adj.* See muggy; awkward.

Stiff, *adj.* See formal, artificial; inflexible, strict (2), firm, stationary; awkward; cruel, draconian; excess.

Stiffen, *v.* See strengthen, augment.

Stifle, *v.* See suffocate, kill, eliminate, prevent, extinguish, abort (2), obstruct.

Stigma, *n.* See disgrace, slander; guilt (2), contrition.

Stigmatize, *v.* See dishonor (3), slander.

Stiletto, *n.* See weapon; cut, maim.

Still 1. *n.* A device used for separating alcoholic spirits from fermented substances. **2.** *adj.* Without movement. Motionless, immobile, unmoving, inactive, dormant, reposeful, idle, calm, unstirring, passive, static, quiescent, stationary, at rest, sedentary. **3.** *adj.* Quiet or unspoken. See silent (1, 2), bashful.

Stillborn child A child born dead or in such an early stage of pregnancy as to be incapable of living.

Stilted, *adj.* See formal, awkward; squeamish; pompous, arrogant.

Stimulant, *n.* See drug, liquor, catalyst.

Stimulate, *v.* See incite, animate, provoke, cause (2); strengthen, augment, foster, promote; catalyst.

Stimulus, *n.* See catalyst, motivation, motive, impulse, cause.

Sting, *v., n.* See pierce, injure, harass, provoke, incite; affliction, pain.

Stingy, *adj.* Cheap. Parsimonious, miserly, niggardly, tight, penurious, ungenerous, penny-pinching, tight-fisted. See also avaricious.

Stink, *n.* See odium; foul, rotten; aroma, fragrant.

Stint, *n., v.* See assignment, duty (1), job (2); limit.

Stipend, *n.* A salary; fixed or settled pay. See compensation (1), income.

Stipulate, *v.* To arrange or settle definitely (the lawyers stipulated that the defendant owned the car). Specify, agree, bargain, acknowledge, determine, designate, guarantee, assure, provide, fix, adjust, define, arrange, require, indicate, negotiate, cite, warrant, name. See also limit.

Stipulated, *adj.* See stated.

Stipulation, *n.* **1.** A voluntary agreement between opposing counsel concerning the disposition of some relevant matter so that evidence on the matter does not have to be introduced at the trial (a stipulation that the substance was heroin). See agreement (1). **2.** A requirement or prerequisite. See condition (1).

Stir, *v., n.* See incite, animate, provoke; commingle, confuse; commotion, disturbance.

Stirps, *n.* The person from whom a family is descended; stock; a source of descent or title. See per stirps; ancestor, ancestry.

Stitch, *n., v.* See pain; iota, scintilla; affix, connect.

Stock 1. *n.* An equity representing an ownership interest in a corporation; the capital or principal fund of a corporation formed by the contributions of subscribers or the sale of shares; all the wealth and resources of a corporation. See share (3), fund, resource. **2.** *n.* The goods or wares of a merchant kept for sale; the entire property used in business. Merchandise, supply, collection, reserve, provisions, commodities, line, stockpile, assets, wares, hoard, arsenal. See also inventory, goods, property. **3.** *v.* To supply See furnish, equip. **4.** *n.* See ancestry, lineage. **5.** *adj.* Banal, routine. See commonplace (2), common (1), pedestrian (2). **6.** *v.* See accumulate, hoard.

Stockade, *n.* See blockade, wall (1), obstruction.

Stockbroker, *n.* One who buys or sells stock as the agent of another. See agent.

Stock exchange, *n.* The place at which shares of stock are bought and sold. See exchange (3), market, securities.

Stockholder, *n.* A person who owns shares of stock in a corporation or joint-stock company. Shareholder, stockowner, investor. See also owner.

Stockholder's derivative action See derivative action.

Stockholder's equity A stockholder's proportionate share in the corporation's capital stock and surplus. See equity, ownership.

Stock insurance company An insurance company whose shares are held by the public and which pays dividends, in contrast with a mutual insurance company, whose assets are owned by policyholders who receive dividends when available. See insurance, business.

Stock in trade The inventory carried by a retail business for sale in the ordinary course of business. The tools and equipment owned and used by a tradesman. See inventory, goods, stock (2), equipment.

Stock market, *n.* An organized market or exchange where shares (stock) are traded (e.g., New York Stock Exchange). See exchange (3), market, securities.

Stock option The right to purchase a specified number of shares of stock at a specified price at specified times. See right, option.

Stockpile, *n., v.* See stock (2), goods, inventory; hoard, accumulate.

Stock redemption A partial or complete liquidation of corporate stock by the corporation. It generally consists of the purchase by the corporation of its own stock. See redemption; liquidate.

Stock split One share is split into a larger number of shares. A reverse split or a split-down occurs when a number of shares are combined to form a smaller number of shares. See reorganization, securities.

Stock swap In corporate reorganization, an exchange of stock in one corporation for the stock of another corporation. See reorganization, exchange.

Stocky, *adj.* See corpulent; healthy, able-bodied.

Stodgy, *adj.* See commonplace (2), pedestrian, formal, pompous, arrogant.

Stoic, *adj.* See quiet, silent, patient (3), indifferent.

Stoicism, *n.* See endurance; toleration; balance (5), composure, discipline (1), reserve (4), restraint (2).

Stomach, *n., v.* See anatomy; food; eat; abide; stand (2), bear (2).

Stomp, *v.* See stamp (2), batter, beat, attack.

Stone, *n., v.* See rock, earth, mountain; batter, attack, beat.

Stonewall, *v.* See avoid, delay, quibble.

Stooge, *n.* See pawn (3), accomplice, slave, attendant; informer; decoy.

"Stool pigeon," *n.* See informer; decoy.

Stoop, *v.* See grovel, cringe; condescend, patronize (2).

Stop 1. *v.* To cease movement; to restrain or foil (stop payment). See prevent, prohibit, ban, bar, end (2), arrest (3). **2.** *n.* A breaking off or interruption. See cessation.

Stop and frisk The temporary seizure and "patting down" of a person who behaves suspiciously and appears to be armed. See detain, check, arrest, investigate.

Stoppage, *n.* See cessation, prevention, bar, ban.

Stop-payment order An order by the drawer of a draft (check) ordering the drawee not to make payment on it. See order, draft, check.

Storage, *n.* Safekeeping of goods in a warehouse or other depository. Accumulation, storing, saving, collection, stockpiling. See also depository, warehouse; hoard.

Store 1. *v.* To keep merchandise for safe custody. See accumulate, hoard. **2.** *n.* A place where goods are deposited and sold by one engaged in buying and selling them. See market (1), merchant, business. **3.** *n.* A supply. See stock (2), inventory (2), accumulation (1).

Storehouse, *n.* See warehouse, depository.

Storekeeper, *n.* See merchant, business.

Storm 1. *n.* Violent weather conditions. Flood, rain, tumult, tempest, avalanche, blizzard, snowstorm, hurricane, gale, blast, cyclone, thunderstorm, tornado, hailstorm, squall, deluge, lightning, upheaval, downpour, typhoon. See also climate (1). **2.** *n.* See eruption, commotion, disturbance, violence, discharge (4). **3.** *v.* See attack, assault, batter; complain.

Stormy, *adj.* See violent, emotional, wild; storm (2).

Story, *n.* See legend, account, report (1), record (2).

Stout, *adj.* See corpulent; healthy, able-bodied.

Stouthearted, *adj.* See courageous, adventurous, ardent; reckless.

Straddle 1. *n.* Having an option to purchase or sell; the privilege of both a "put" and a "call" on the same commodity at the same time. **2.** *v.* See hedge, quibble.

Straggle, *v.* See stray (1), wander, deviate, digress.

Straight, *adj.* **1.** Forthright. See reliable, genuine, accurate, precise. **2.** Not curved. Undeviating, linear, taut, aligned, unswerving, level, horizontal, even, unbent, adjusted, square. See also direct (4), lineal, constant. **3.** Candid. Frank, forthright, straightforward, bold, direct, aboveboard. **4.** Arranged. Organized, balanced, aligned, neat, proper, coordinated, methodical, sorted, tidy.

Straighten, *v.* See organize (1), codify (1), classify; clear (5); correct (2), improve, heal, cure.

Straightforward, *adj.* See direct (6), outright, explicit, free, open (4), honest; abrasive, rude.

Straightjacket, *n., v.* See straitjacket.

Straight-line depreciation The cost or other basis of the asset, less its estimated salvage value, if any, is determined first. Then this amount is distributed in equal amounts over the period of the estimated useful life of the asset. See depreciate, depreciation.

Strain, *v., n.* See extend (1); labor (2); burden (2, 3), exhaust; hurt, injure; filter, drain; effort; injury; ancestry, family; kind.

Strained, *adj.* See artificial; formal; insecure, apprehensive, impatient.

Strait, *n.* See passage; difficulty, plight, dilemma, emergency.

Straitjacket, *n., v.* See restraint; chain (2), confine.

Strait-laced, *adj.* See squeamish, particular (2), formal (3), narrow, inflexible, proper, serious.

Strand 1. *n.* The shore or bank of the sea or a river. See shore. **2.** *n.* A thread. String, wire, fiber, tress, yarn, loose end, part, piece, rope, cable, line, ligament, hair, twine, whisker, curl. **3.** *v.* To leave in a difficult position. See abandon (1), reject (1).

Strange, *adj.* See anomalous, odd, novel, mysterious, foreign (3), peculiar, irregular, alien, odious, offensive.

Stranger, *n.* One with whom you are not acquainted. Foreigner, newcomer, third person, disinterested party, nonparty, bystander, outsider, immigrant, visitor, interloper, trespasser, intruder, auslander, guest, caller. See also alien. *Ant.* Intimate.

Strangle, *v.* See suffocate, constrict, kill, extinguish, destroy, quash, quiet, arrest.

Strangle hold, *n.* See restraint (1), obstruction.

Strangulate, *v.* See strangle.

Strap, *v., n.* See attach; beat, batter; rope.

Strapping, *adj.* See healthy, able-bodied, durable.

Stratagem, *n.* A dishonest scheme either by words or by action. See machination, deception, contrivance, fraud, plan.

Strategic, *adj.* See important, crucial; military; discreet, careful, prudent.

Strategy, *n.* See plan, agenda, schedule, machination, artifice, conspiracy, duplicity.

Stratify, *v.* See divide, classify.

Stratum, *n.* See class, classification, division, kind (1), zone.

Straw man, *n.* A "front"; a nominal party; one who lends his or her name only to a transaction; a fictitious or bogus argument. See dummy (1).

Stray 1. *v.* To wander off. Drift, roam, digress, go off course, go astray, range, deviate, lapse, straggle, jaunt, ramble, traverse, veer, prowl. **2.** *adj.* Lost or deserted. See abandoned (1). **3.** *n.* Someone who is lost or wandering. Waif, vagabond, itinerant, drifter, foundling. See also tramp, alien.

Streak, *n.* See characteristic, habit.

Stream, *n.* **1.** A watercourse having banks and channels through which waters flow at least periodically. See river. **2.** A continuous flow or movement (stream of protest). Torrent, current, surge, spate, tide, profusion, deluge, rush, run, outpouring, cascade, fountain, outpour, waterfall, bolt, discharge, flood, burst. See also eruption.

Streamline, *v.* See improve, correct, adjust, organize.

Street, *n.* An urban way or thoroughfare. See highway, pass (8), passage (2).

Streetcar, *n.* See vehicle; carry.

Strength, *n.* See power, ability, facility (3), gift (2); measure (1); passion, emotion, spirit (2), force (1), vigor, diligence (1), endurance, determination (2).

Strengthen, *v.* To fortify. Buttress, reinforce, increase, brace, boost, stiffen, toughen, heighten, invigorate, support, stimulate, shore up, bolster. See also help (2), equip, augment, raise (2), improve, remedy, promote.

Strenuous, *adj.* See difficult, onerous; active, ardent, diligent, indefatigable.

Stress, *v., n.* See emphasize, accent; weight, influence, importance, import; burden (2), pain, anguish, anxiety, apprehension.

Stretch, *v., n.* See extend (1), exaggerate, augment; burden; extent, interval.

Strew, *v.* See sprinkle, distribute.

Stricken, *adj.* See hurt, incapacitate, disable.

Strict, *adj.* **1.** Determined or governed by exact rules (strict adherence). See precise. **2.** Authoritarian. Austere, dictatorial, harsh, severe, despotic, exacting, cold, unyielding, uncompromising, stern, stringent, puritanical, absolute, stiff, autocratic, extreme, adamant, illiberal. See also inflexible, arbitrary, willful,

Strict

irreconcilable, strong (2), diligent, indefatigable, callous, firm (2), draconian. *Ant.* Liberal; indulgent.

Strict construction A close and rigid reading and interpretation of the law. A refusal to expand the law by implication. When there is doubt about whether the law should be read broadly or narrowly, the latter is generally preferred. When there is doubt as to whether language is more inclusive or less inclusive, the latter is generally preferred. See construction; narrow, limited.

Strict foreclosure If the amount due under a mortgage is not paid within a certain time, title to the property vests absolutely in the mortgagee without any equity of redemption or sale of the property. See foreclose.

Strict liability See absolute liability.

Strict liability in tort Elements of this tort: (a) A seller or person engaged in the business of selling products for use or consumption, (b) a defective product that is unreasonably dangerous to person or property, (c) causes, (d) harm, (e) to a user or consumer. Some courts have extended the last element to include bystanders.

Stricture, *n.* See limit (2), limitation, restraint (1), obstruction; aspersion.

Stride, *v., n.* See walk; advancement (2), development (1), growth.

Strident, *adj.* See noisy, wild, blatant; offensive.

Strife, *n.* See conflict (1), argument, contention, feud, fight (1).

Strike 1. *n.* The act of quitting or leaving work by a body of workers for the purpose of coercing the employer to accede to some demand that the workers have made, which has been rejected by the employer (injunction against the strike). Walkout, shutdown, boycott, job action, slowdown, work suspension, protest, labor dispute, stoppage, discontinuance, obstruction of work, interruption of work, blockade, sit-down strike, revolt, demonstration, rebellion. **2.** *v.* To hit. See beat (1), batter, pound (1); attack.

Strikebreaker, *n.* See scab.

Strike suit A shareholder derivative action begun with the hope of winning large attorney fees or private settlements, and with no intention of benefiting the corporation on behalf of which the suit is theoretically brought.

Striking, *adj.* See outstanding (2), exceptional, extraordinary, intriguing, attractive, beautiful.

String, *n.* See thread, rope.

Stringent, *adj.* See exigent, strict (2), firm, strong (2), difficult, draconian, inflexible.

Strip 1. *v.* To ransack or devastate. See plunder (1), exhaust. **2.** *v.* To undress. Disrobe, uncover, unwrap, denude, peel, expose, take off, remove, shed, scale. See also bare (2). **3.** *n.* A narrow piece of something. Ribbon, stripe, band, sash, tape, cordon. See also belt (1).

Strip mine, *n.,* **strip-mine,** *v.* See mine; excavate; removal; plunder, destroy.

Strive, *v.* See attempt (3), desire (1), hope (1).

Stroke, *v., n.* See caress, touch (1); pound (1), beat (1), batter; fit, seizure; accident.

Strong, *adj.* **1.** Lasting or sturdy (strong arms). See durable, perpetual, healthy, able-bodied. **2.** Intense or spirited (strong will). Fervent, zealous, vehement, ardent, assiduous, keen, deep, resolute, unyielding, persistent, tough, determined, vibrant, vivid, forceful, sturdy, animated, impassioned, fierce, staunch, courageous, aggressive, dynamic, strong-willed, steadfast, intent, eager, diligent, graphic, severe, pointed, rabid, hardy. **3.** Formidable (strong opponent). Major, challenging, effective, potent, convincing, sharp, brilliant, impressive, eloquent, penetrating, dedicated. **4.** See competent, capable, able, reasonable. **5.** See extreme, excess. *Ant.* Weak; meek; impotent; incompetent; temperate.

Strong-arm, *v.* See intimidate, coerce, compel, menace.

Stronghold, *n.* See wall, building, protection, asylum, blockade; home.

Struck, *v.* See pound (1), strike.

Structural, *adj.* See organic, essential, intrinsic, fundamental.

Structure 1. *n.* That which is built or constructed. See building (1). **2.** *n.* The formation, exterior, or shape of something. See form (1), composition, design (1), organization (2), pattern (1), plan (1). **3.** *v.* To plan, visualize, assemble, or put together. See plan, organize.

Struggle, *n., v.* See effort; conflict, contest, fight, feud; labor, attempt (3); flounder.

Strumpet, *n.* A whore. See prostitute.

Strut, *v.* See walk, swagger.

Stub, *n., v.* See receipt (1), certificate; refuse, remainder; collide.

Stubborn, *adj.* See inflexible, arbitrary, stationary, firm (2), particular (2), difficult (3); contentious, litigious.

Stud, *n.* See prostitute; able-bodied.

Student, *n.* A learner. Pupil, follower, undergraduate, apprentice, schoolgirl, schoolboy, coed, novice, trainee, protégé. See also scholar, amateur, beginner, intern, partisan; learned.

Studio, *n.* See home; market.

Studious, *adj.* See diligent, conscientious (2); learned, cultivated.

Study, *v., n.* See investigate, canvass (1), audit (2), observe (3), consider (1), deliberate (1); education; report, review.

Stultify, *v.* **1.** To render worthless or inefficient; to vitiate or neutralize. See suffocate, prevent, abort (2). **2.** To make a fool of; to make one out mentally incapacitated; to show to be insane. See slander (2).

Stumble, *v.* See flounder, fall, blunder, err.

Stumbling block, *n.* See blockade, block (1), clog, obstruction, complication.

Stump, *v.* See confuse, surprise (1); incapacitate.

Stumpage, *n.* The price paid for a license to cut and remove trees.

Stun, *v.* See surprise, amaze.

Stunned, *adj.* See agape.

Stunning, *adj.* See attractive, beautiful, outstanding (2), exceptional, extraordinary.

Stunt, *n., v.* See antic; act (3), artifice; check (1), inhibit, restrain.

Stupefy, *v.* See surprise (1), amaze; agape.

Stupendous, *adj.* See big, great, outstanding (2), extraordinary, exceptional, attractive, beautiful, enjoyable, brilliant.

Stupid, *adj.* See dumb, lunatic, absurd, juvenile, irrational, backward, worthless, barren, careless, heedless, frivolous.

Stupidity, *n.* See balderdash; stupid.

Stupor, *n.* Numbness. Coma, oblivion, daze, apathy, faint, inertia, torpor, anesthesia. See also trance.

Sturdy, *adj.* See durable, healthy, able-bodied, firm, strong.

Stutter, *v.* See flounder; delay (1).

Style 1. *n.* System, conduct. See manner, method, process, appearance (3). **2.** *n.* Grace. Savoir-faire, class, taste, charm, flair, polish, urbanity, culture, sophistication, suavity, elegance, panache, dash, refinement. **3.** *n.* Fashion. Craze, trend, fad, look, rage, custom, mold, currency. **4.** *v.* To designate or label. See name (2).

Stymie, *v.* See check, impede, block (2), quash.

Suable, *adj.* Capable of being or liable to be sued. See actionable.

Sua sponte On one's own motion; without prompting or suggestion; voluntarily.

Suave, *adj.* See cultivated, chic, debonair, aristocratic, worldly, mature (2), learned; prudent, discreet, judicious, careful.

Subagent, *n.* An agent appointed by an agent; a substituted agent. See agent (1).

Subaltern 1. *n.* An inferior or subordinate officer. See assistant, officer. **2.** *adj.* Subordinate. See inferior (1).

Subchapter S corporation A small business corporation permitted to be taxed as if it were an individual proprietorship. See corporation, business, tax.

Subcommittee, *n.* See board (1), body (3), group (1).

Subcontract, *n.* A contract made under a prior contract. A subordinate contract made between one or more of the original contracting parties and a third party called the subcontractor. See contract.

Subcontractor, *n.* One who takes a portion of a contract from the principal contractor or from another subcontractor. One who agrees with the contractor to perform part of the work that the contractor previously agreed to perform for another. See independent contractor, contractor, supplier, builder.

Subdivide, *v.* To split a part into smaller parts. See divide (1), part (3).

Subdivision, *n.* **1.** The act of dividing into smaller parts. See division (1), partition. **2.** One of the parts that has been so divided. See parcel (3), part (1). **3.** A type or category. See classification (2), kind.

Subdue, *v.* See quash, defeat, best (2); stabilize, mitigate, assuage.

Subdued, *adj.* See grave (3), quiet (2), serious, depressed, dark.

Subirrigate, *v.* To irrigate below the surface. See water (2).

Subjacent, *adj.* Underlying; located below or underneath; at a lower level but not directly beneath.

Subjacent support The right of land to be supported by the land that lies beneath it, distinguished from lateral or side support.

Subject, *n., adj.,* **subject,** *v.* **1.** *n.* One who owes allegiance to a nation and is governed by its laws (American subjects). See citizen. **2.** *n.* The theme or topic acted upon (subject of the legislation). See matter (1), issue (3), point (1), proposition (2). **3.** *n.* The recipient (the subject of the attack). See beneficiary, victim. **4.** *v.* To subjugate or dominate (the island was subjected to foreign control). See quash, defeat, best (2), conquer. **5.** *v.* To undergo (subjected to ridicule). See expose (2). **6.** *adj.* Susceptible (subject to arrest). See liable. **7.** *adj.* Conditioned (subject to further negotiations). See contingent.

Subjection, *n.* Being under the dominion of another; domination by another. See slavery, bondage.

Subjective, *adj.* See individual, personal, private, particular, confidential; partial (2), partisan (2).

Subject matter, *n.* That which is presented for consideration; the thing in dispute. See matter (1), issue (3), point (1), proposition (2).

Subject matter jurisdiction The court's power or competence to hear and determine this particular kind of case; judicial power over the nature of the action and the relief sought. See jurisdiction (1).

Subject to See liable.

Subjoin, *v.* See add, append.

Sub judice, *adv.* Under judicial consideration; undetermined; before a court.

Subjugate, *v.* See dominate, conquer, confine, bind, coerce, compel, intimidate, quash.

Sublease, *n.* The grant by the tenant of an interest in the leased premises that is less than his or her own interest, or that reserves a reversionary interest. Subletting, subrenting. See also lease.

Subletting, *n.* A leasing by the lessee of a whole or a part of the premises during a portion of the unexpired balance of his or her term. See lease.

Sublimate, *v.* See divert, direct (2, 3); fumigate, bathe.

Sublime, *adj.* See elevated, great, exceptional, extraordinary, outstanding (2).

Subliminal, *adj.* See unconscious.

Submarine, *adj., n.* See submerged; marine.

Submerge, *v.* To place under a liquid. Sink, immerse, dunk, descend, go down, bathe, baptize, plunge, submerse, souse, dive, drown, cover, deluge, engulf, overwhelm, swamp, saturate, waterlog, bury. See also water, inundate. *Ant.* Emerge.

Submerged, *adj.* **1.** Underwater. Immersed, submarine, flooded, undersea, drowned, below the surface, buried, inundated, under. **2.** Concealed or veiled. See hidden.

Submergence, *n.* The disappearance of land under water and the formation of a more or less navigable body over it.

Submission, *n.* **1.** A yielding to authority. See obedience, acceptance, compliance. **2.** Offering something for consideration. Referral, presentation, tender, giving, assignment, transfer, entrustment, surrender, handing in.

Submission bond The bond by which the parties agree to submit their matters to binding arbitration. See bond.

Submissive, *adj.* See passive, malleable, amenable (2), quiet (2), flexible, servile.

Submit, *v.* **1.** To commit to the discretion of another; to present for determination (submit the proposal). See offer (1). **2.** See yield, acquiesce, defer (2), capitulate, concede (2), accommodate (1), comply, allow (3).

Sub nomine Under the name; in the name of; under the title of.

Subnormal, *adj.* See defective, inferior, deficient, inadequate.

Subordinate 1. *n.* One who works under or is dependent on another. See employee, aid (3), assistant. **2.** *adj.* Collateral, subservient, lesser. See inferior (1), auxiliary, minor, contingent, junior.

Subordinated bonds or debentures Bonds or debentures that yield priority in liquidation to other (senior) debt of a corporation. Such bonds or debentures are usually not subordinate to general creditors but only to debt owed to a financial institution.

Subordination, *n.* The act or process by which a person's rights are ranked below the rights of others. Inferior status, subservience, second fiddle.

Subordination agreement An agreement by which the subordinating party agrees that its interests in property have a lower priority than the interest to which it is being subordinated. See contract, interest.

Suborn, *v.* To prepare, provide, or procure, usually in a secret or underhanded manner; to procure another to commit perjury; to procure another to commit a crime. See instigate, procure, incite, provoke, prompt, abet, aid.

Subornation of perjury Procuring another to take a false oath that would be perjury.

Subpar, *adj.* See defective, inferior, deficient, base, minor, contingent, junior.

Subpoena 1. *n.* A command to appear. See command (1), mandate (1), order (1). **2.** *v.* To command one's presence. See command (2), order (2).

Subpoena ad testificandum A subpoena to testify.

Subpoena duces tecum A process by which the court compels the production of documents or chattels.

Subrogate, *v.* See exchange (1); subrogation.

Subrogation, *n.* The substitution of a third party in place of the party having the claim, demand, or right against another party (the insurance company sought subrogation). Displacement, transfer, transference, exchange, switch, supplanting. See also replacement.

Subrogee, *n.* The person who succeeds to the rights of another through subrogation; the one who is subrogated.

Sub rosa, *adv.* Secret; not for publication. See confidential, private, clandestine, hidden.

Subscribe, *v.* **1.** To sign at the end; to attest (subscribe a will). See sign (1), attest. **2.** To agree to purchase; to agree to pay (subscribe to stock). See pledge (2), promise (2). **3.** To support or lend approval (subscribe to the notion). See advocate (2), consent (1), accept.

Subscribed capital The total amount of stock or capital for which there are contracts of purchase or subscriptions. See capital, share (3), securities.

Subscribed stock A stockholder's equity account showing the capital that will be contributed as the subscription price is collected. See equity, account, capital, share (3).

Subscriber, *n.* **1.** One who writes his or her name on a document to authenticate or attest it, or to bind himself or herself by it. See witness, party. **2.** One who has agreed to purchase securities of a corporation, either bonds or stocks. See buyer.

Subscribing witness One who witnesses or attests the signature of a party to a document, and in testimony thereof signs his or her own name to the document. See witness.

Subscription, *n.* See subscribe, authentication, attestation, signature (1), promise (1), consent (2), approval, certification, contract, pledge.

Subscription rights The rights of existing stockholders to purchase additional stock, usually at a price under market and in an amount proportionate to their existing holdings. See right, purchase.

Subsequent, *adj.* Following in time (subsequent development). Succeeding, ensuing, next, sequential, future, trailing, following, eventual, coming, proximate, posterior, later, consequent. See also after. *Ant.* Prior.

Subsequent condition See condition subsequent.

Subservant, *n.* The servant or agent of another servant or agent. See agent, subagent.

Subservient, *adj.* See servile, abject; ministerial; grovel, flatter, flattery.

Subside, *v.* See decline (2), diminish, abate.

Subsidence, *n.* See decline (3), diminution.

Subsidiary 1. *adj.* Under another's control (subsidiary job). See auxiliary, inferior (1), minor, contingent, junior. **2.** *n.* See branch (1), division, affiliate (1).

Subsidiary corporation One in which another corporation, the parent, owns at least a majority of the shares and thus has control. See branch (1), division, affiliate (1), corporation.

Subsidize, *v.* To support. See aid (1), finance (1), facilitate, back (1), promote.

Subsidy, *n.* A government grant to support a program or project that benefits the public. See backing, compensation (1), assistance, charity, aid (2).

Sub silentio Under silence; silently; without any notice being taken.

Subsist, *v.* See exist, last (2), abide, continue.

Subsistence, *n.* **1.** Means of support. See necessaries, maintenance (1), assistance. **2.** Something that has real existence. Reality, existence, occurrence, being, life, materiality.

Subsistent, *adj.* See real, authentic, bona fide; inherent, native (3), congenital.

Substance, *n.* **1.** The material or essential part of a thing. See essence (1), center (2), foundation (2), basis (1), intent. **2.** Affluence or wealth. See property (1), luxury, wealth. **3.** Element, ingredient, or matter. See element, component, part, material (3). **4.** Reality. Concreteness, materiality, cogency, strength, solidity, thickness, density, actuality, palpability, physicality, tangibility, body, substantiality, real content.

Substandard, *adj.* See defective, inferior, deficient, inadequate.

Substantial. *adj.* **1.** Actually existing; not seeming or imaginary; not elusive (substantial evidence). Firmly established, actual, corporeal, material, concrete, substantive, physical, tangible, veritable, objective, vital, true, genuine, authentic, positive, valuable, worthwhile, of real worth, solid, existent. **2.** Abundant (substantial supply). Ample, plentiful, considerable, large, bulky, marked, sizable, significant, appreciable, generous, hefty, grand, plenteous, massive, major, healthy, full, big, monumental. **3.** Strong. See durable.

Substantial compliance Compliance with the essential requirements. See compliance, performance.

Substantial damages Considerable in amount and intended as real compensation for a real injury. See damages. *Ant.* Nominal damages.

Substantial evidence Such evidence that a reasonable mind might accept as adequate to support a conclusion. See evidence.

Substantially, *adv.* Without material qualifications. Essentially, in the main, in substance, materially, in a substantial manner.

Substantial performance Honestly and faithfully performing the material and essential particulars, omitting technical and unimportant matters. See performance.

Substantiate, *v.* To establish the existence or truth of something by true and competent evidence. See prove, certify, corroborate, demonstrate (1).

Substantive, *adj.* **1.** See real, substantial (1), meritorious (1). **2.** See fundamental, essential.

Substantive due process Protection from arbitrary and unreasonable action. See due process of law, fairness, justice, right (4).

Substantive evidence Evidence presented for the purpose of proving a fact in issue, as opposed to evidence that seeks to discredit or impeach a witness, or to corroborate the testimony of a witness.

Substantive law Law that creates, defines, and regulates rights, as opposed to adjective, procedural, or remedial law that provides a method of enforcing rights. See law, rule.

Substitute 1. *v.* To put in the place of another person or thing. See exchange (1), replace. **2.** *n.* One who stands in the place of another. See agent (1), successor, surrogate, replacement (2), representative (1), attorney, dummy (1).

Substituted basis The basis of the value of an asset determined by reference to the basis in the hands of a transferor, donor, grantor, or by reference to other property held at any time by the person for whom the basis is to be determined. See basis (2), tax, worth (1), appraisal.

Substituted service Service of process on the defendant in a manner other than personal service within the jurisdiction (e.g., by publication, by mail, by personal service in another state, etc.). See service of process, service by publication.

Substitution, *n.* Serving in lieu of another; putting in place of. See exchange (2), agent (1), replacement (2).

Substitutional, substitutionary, *adj.* Pertaining to a clause in a will that provides for someone to take a gift in the event of the death of the original beneficiary before the period of disposition.

Substratum, *n.* See foundation, basis; earth.

Substructure, *n.* See foundation, basis.

Subsume, *v.* See classify, codify.

Subtenant, *n.* One who leases all or part of the rented premises from the original lessee for a term less than that held by the latter. See tenant, lease.

Subterfuge, *n.* A device for escape or concealment. See artifice, fraud, deception, device (2).

Subterranean, *adj.* **1.** Existing beneath the surface of the earth. Underground, nether, hypogeal, subterrestrial. **2.** See clandestine, hidden.

Subtle

Subtle, *adj.* **1.** Indirect or understated. Delicate, quiet, refined, attenuated, light, tenuous. **2.** See acute (1), able, apt.

Subtract, *v.* See abridge, diminish, withdraw, deduct.

Subtraction, *n.* **1.** See removal. **2.** The act of withholding or withdrawing from another that to which the latter is entitled.

Suburb, *n.* See zone, neighborhood, location; margin (1), border, frontier.

Subvention, *n.* See aid (2), help (1), charity.

Subversion, *n.* **1.** The act of overthrowing. See revolt (1), insubordination, mutiny, treason, defiance, apostasy, revolution, rebellion, resistance. **2.** Sabotage or disruption. See defeat (2), riot, corruption.

Subversive 1. *adj.* Pertaining to the overthrow of the government. See mutinous, insurgent (2); subversion. **2.** *n.* Radical. Rebel, incendiary, revolutionary, saboteur, collaborator, fifth columnist, insurgent, traitor, sympathizer.

Subvert, *v.* See destroy, defeat, quash; defile, corrupt.

Subway, *n.* See vehicle, carrier.

Succeed, *v.* See prevail (2), work (2), gain (2), pass (3), complete (1), perfect (3), attain, realize; follow (2), replace.

Success, *n.* See satisfaction (2), growth; coup, conquest, achievement, work (5), completion, performance, perfection (1); wealth, luxury, eminence, note (4), regard (2).

Successful, *adj.* See lucrative, beneficial, gainful, perfect (2), affluent, dominant, predominant, effective, fertile.

Succession, *n.* **1.** The devolution of title to property under the law of descent and distribution. The acquisition of rights upon the death of another. Persons who take by will or inheritance, as opposed to those who take by deed, grant, gift, purchase, or contract. See lineage, descent, devolution. **2.** Series or sequence (a succession of mishaps). Procession, run, train, line, row, order, round, catenation, continuance, cycle, rotation. See also chain (1), series, development (1). **3.** Promotion or induction (succession to the presidency). Assumption, taking over, elevation, attainment, inauguration, initiation, accession.

Succession duty or tax See inheritance tax.

Successive, *adj.* Following one after another in a line or series (successive defeats). Continuous, serial, uninterrupted, nonstop, in sequence, sequential, seriatim, contiguous, succeeding, progressive, subsequent, back-to-back, in order, in a row. See also succession (2).

Successor, *n.* One who takes the place of another who has left; one who follows another by succession; another corporation which, through amalgamation, consolidation, or other legal succession, becomes invested with rights and assumes the burdens of the first corporation. Heir, substitute, recipient, next in line, donee, grantee, beneficiary, usurper, descendant, issue. See also replacement (2).

Successor in interest One who follows another in ownership or control of property.

Successor trustee A trustee who follows or succeeds an earlier trustee. See trustee.

Succinct, *adj.* To the point. See concise, precise, cogent, brief.

Succor, *n.* See aid, help, assistance, maintenance.

Succulent, *adj.* See delectable; attractive, enjoyable.

Succumb, *v.* See capitulate, yield (2), quit (1), relinquish, acquiesce; die.

Such, *adj.* Of that type. Kindred, corresponding, similar, of that sort, of that kind, comparable, suchlike, analogous, twin, allied, matching.

"Sucker," *n.* See victim, pawn (3).

Sudden, *adj.* Unexpected (sudden storm). Without warning, unforeseen, instant, immediate, prompt, unannounced, abrupt, quick, instantaneous, precipitate, unanticipated, impetuous, hasty, meteoric, fleeting, speedy, brisk, expeditious, surprising, unpredictable, express, fleet. *Ant.* Planned.

Sudden emergency doctrine See emergency doctrine.

Sue, *v.* **1.** To commence or continue legal proceedings; to proceed with an action (sue for damages). See litigate, prosecute, appeal. **2.** See ask, petition.

Suffer, *v.* **1.** To feel pain (suffer from an injury). Groan, ache, bleed, wince, grieve, languish, gasp, despair, convulse, ail, agonize, be stricken, lose, bear a cross, feel distress, pine, sacrifice, experience a loss, break down, sweat. **2.** To allow or admit (suffer an act to be done). See permit (1). **3.** To endure (suffer the loss). Undergo, experience, encounter, weather, go through, stomach, taste, sustain, put up with, tolerate, withstand, digest. See also bear (2). **4.** To deteriorate (her performance suffered). See decline (2). *Ant.* Rejoice; reject; avoid; improve.

Sufferance, *n.* Negative authorization by not forbidding. See permission, consent (2).

Suffering, *n.* See anguish, anxiety, pain, depression, affliction, misfortune, injury, hardship.

Suffice, *v.* To meet the need. Be sufficient, be adequate, be enough, satisfy, pass muster. See also qualify.

Sufficiency, *n.* An adequate quality or quantity. Adequacy, amplitude, abundance, enough, surfeit, plenty, satisfaction, completeness, profusion, affluence, plethora, repletion, cornucopia, saturation, fullness. *Ant.* Paucity.

Sufficiency of the evidence Evidence that affords a substantial basis of fact from which the fact in issue can reasonably be inferred; evidence that would warrant the conclusion reached; evidence that is substantial; some admissible evidence on each element that a reasonable jury could accept. See evidence.

Sufficient, *adj.* Enough; as much as may be necessary. See adequate, abundant.

Sufficient cause 1. Reasonable or probable cause or that state of facts as would lead a person of ordinary caution to conscientiously entertain strong suspicion of the defendant's guilt. See probable cause, cause. **2.** Legal cause; a reason of a substantial nature specifically relating to and affecting the administration of an office and the performance of one's duties.

Suffocate, *v.* To kill by stopping respiration. Strangle, asphyxiate, stifle, smother, throttle, mute, silence, choke, garrote; subdue, quench, suppress, deaden, quell. See also extinguish, kill, destroy, quash, rescind, obstruct. *Ant.* Revive.

Suffrage, *n.* The right of voting. See vote, emancipation; franchise, charter.

Suggest, *v.* **1.** To propose. See recommend, offer, advance (6). **2.** To introduce indirectly (suggest an impropriety). Insinuate, hint, whisper, imply, denote, signify, adumbrate, lead to believe, indicate. See also intimate (6).

Suggestion, *n.* **1.** An idea or recommendation. See proposal, proposition. **2.** The presentation of an idea indirectly (suggestion of wrongdoing). Insinuation, suspicion, intimation, hint, glimmer, whisper, clue, inkling, taste, shade, inference, cue, allusion. See also innuendo, implication.

Suggestive, *adj.* **1.** Providing a hint; indirectly conveying an idea while appearing to be neutral or objective (suggestive question). Leading, provocative, stimulative, expressive, allusive, evocative, thought-provoking. See also demonstrative, descriptive, informative. **2.** Immodest or indecent. See obscene, immoral, carnal.

Suicide, *n.* The deliberate termination of one's life. Self-destruction, self-immolation, suttee, hara-kiri. See also death.

Sui generis, *adj.* Of its own kind or class. See peculiar (1), special (1), exceptional.

Sui juris, *adj.* In one's own right; not under any legal disability or guardianship.

Suit 1. *n.* A lawsuit. See cause (3), action (1). **2.** *n.* A collection or assembly.

See group (1). **3.** *v.* To please or delight. See satisfy (2), conform, accommodate (2). **4.** *n.* See apparel, clothes.

Suitable, *adj.* Fit and acceptable for the end in view. See appropriate (3), fit, proper, admissible, competent, worthy.

Suitcase, *n.* See baggage.

Suite, *n.* See home; coterie.

Suitor, *n.* **1.** A litigant. See petitioner, party (1). **2.** An admirer. Lover, boyfriend, date, pursuer, sweetheart, wooer, beau, flame, gallant, paramour.

Sulk, *v.* See mope, bemoan, cry (1).

Sullen, *adj.* See depressed, despondent; crabby, particular (2).

Sully, *v.* See pollute, corrupt.

Sultry, *adj.* See muggy; hot; prurient, carnal, lascivious.

Sum, *n.* **1.** The entirety. Total, whole, number, score, outcome, totality. See also aggregate. **2.** Cash. See money, currency. **3.** The heart or substance of something. See essence (1), gist (1).

Sum and substance See essence (1), gist (1).

Summarily, *adv.* Without ceremony or delay (dismissed summarily). Promptly, unhesitatingly, straightaway, arbitrarily, with dispatch, precipitately, speedily, on the spur of the moment, abruptly, on short notice, immediately, quickly, on the spot, presently, instantly, at once; shortly, concisely, crisply, compactly, emphatically. See also forthwith.

Summarize, *v.* See paraphrase; abridge, digest.

Summary 1. *adj.* Short, concise, and immediate; without a jury or full trial (summary proceeding). Peremptory, without delay, speedy, condensed, perfunctory, abridged, cursory, direct, sudden, instantaneous, succinct, token, hurried, fast, abbreviated, terse, lean, short, expeditious, shortened, to the point, laconic, short and sweet, quickly performed, brisk, elliptical, compressed. **2.** *n.* An abstract or digest (he read a summary of the report). See brief (2).

Summary judgment, Motion for A request that the court conclude that there is no genuine issue as to any material fact and that a judgment be rendered without the need for a trial. See judgment, decision.

Summary jurisdiction The jurisdiction of a court to give a judgment or to make an order itself forthwith (e.g., to commit to prison for contempt). The power of a court to act promptly without having to comply with all the procedural requirements that govern regular proceedings. See jurisdiction.

Summation, *n.* A summary or recapitulation of the evidence that a party (or its attorney) believes has been established or not established during the trial.

Summit, *n.* See apex; conference, meeting.

Summon, *v.,* **summons,** *n.* **1.** *v.* To notify a defendant to appear in court and answer the case brought against him or her. Signal, instruct, direct, subpoena, cite, command, beckon, send for, invite, serve, assemble, demand, bid, solicit, draft. See also muster, marshal (2). **2.** *n.* A document used to commence a civil action or special proceeding, commanding a person to appear in order to answer the complaint or charge brought against him or her. Citation, mandate, process, notification, command, direction, subpoena, writ, demand, edict, warrant, invocation, signal, requisition.

Sumptuous, *adj.* See delectable, attractive, enjoyable, exorbitant, excess, prodigal; luxury, wealth.

Sunday closing laws See blue laws.

Sunday school, *n.* See school; religion, religious, teacher, creed; establishment.

Sundown, *n.* See sunset, evening.

Sundries, *n.* Miscellaneous articles or items. See goods, property.

Sundry, *adj.* Various (sundry agenda items). Diverse, several, divers, multifaceted, myriad, miscellaneous, manifold, motley, assorted, numerous, different, heterogeneous, diversified, multifarious.

Sunny, *adj.* See clear (3); climate; light.

Sunrise, *n.* See morning.

Sunset, *n.* The time when the sun disappears. Dusk, night, sundown, eventide, twilight, nightfall, evening, gloaming; conclusion, termination, finale, curtain.

Sunset law A statute that requires administrative bodies to justify their existence to the legislature periodically.

Sunshine, *n.* Direct sunlight. Daylight, brightness, illumination, glow, glitter, dazzle, luminance, radiance, brilliance. See also light (1).

Sunshine law A law that requires open meetings of governmental agencies. See conference, meeting.

Super 1. *adj.* First-rate. Excellent, very good, peerless, nonpareil, extraordinary, champion, great, prize, prime, incomparable. See also outstanding (2), exceptional. **2.** *n.* See manager.

Superabundant, *adj.* See abundant, great, big, full, many, majority, mass (2), excess, prodigal.

Superannuated, *adj.* See old, ancient, obsolete, senile.

Superb, *adj.* See superior (2), outstanding (2), extraordinary, attractive, beautiful.

Supercilious, *adj.* See arrogant, pompous; contemptuous.

Supererogatory, *adj.* See gratuitous; excess, needless.

Superficial, *adj.* See cursory, casual (3), artificial; obvious; exterior.

Superfluous, *adj.* See expendable (2), extraneous, peripheral, gratuitous, immaterial.

Superhuman, *adj.* See draconian; extraordinary; religious.

Superimpose, *v.* See impose, add.

Superintend, *v.* To direct or control. See manage (1), direct (2).

Superintendent, *n.* One who directs or controls. See manager, director.

Superior 1. *n.* One who holds a higher rank with the power to command (she was his superior at the factory). Director, senior, principal, commander, commandant, master, leader, manager, chief, foreman, supervisor. **2.** *adj.* Belonging to a higher grade (superior quality). Excellent, first-class, better, top-notch, sterling, eminent, notable, extraordinary, marvelous, nonpareil, perfect, fine, distinguished, choice, inimitable, de luxe, noteworthy, peerless, matchless, capital, classic, worthy, high-quality, preferable, second-to-none, transcendent, prime, superlative, illustrious, paramount. **3.** *adj.* Pretentious (a superior attitude). Sanctimonious, snobby, lordly, arrogant, vainglorious, holier-than-thou, patronizing, high-and-mighty. *Ant.* Underling; inferior; humble.

Superiority, *n.* See power, supremacy, control (3).

Superlative, *adj.* See predominant, best, primary.

Supermarket, *n.* See merchant, business; food.

Supernatural, *adj.* See religious; intangible, incorporeal; mysterious.

Superpower, *n.* See sovereign, sovereignty, nation, country.

Supersede, *v.* To take the position of; to suspend or render unnecessary. See override, overcome (2), cancel (1), replace, displace, abolish, rescind, countermand, annul.

Supersedeas, *n.* A writ containing a command to stay the proceedings at law; a suspension of a judgment's effectiveness.

Supersedeas bond A bond required of one who petitions to set aside a judgment or execution. If the action is unsuccessful, the other party may be made whole from the bond. See bond.

Superseding, *adj.* Replacing. Neutralizing, canceling, voiding, substituting, overriding, dominant, principal, outweighing, paramount, preponderant, unseating.

Superseding

See also intervening.

Superseding cause The act of a third person or other force that by its intervention prevents the actor from being liable for the harm or injury that the actor's antecedent conduct was a substantial factor in bringing about. An intervening cause that is so extraordinary that the defendant could not have reasonably anticipated that the cause would intervene. See cause, intervening cause.

Superstition, *n.* See witchcraft, delusion; superstitious.

Superstitious, *adj.* Given to irrational beliefs. Naive, gullible, magical, obsessed, apprehensive, ingenuous, talismanic, fearful. See also innocent, juvenile, credulous.

Supervening cause A new effective cause which, operating independently of anything else, becomes the proximate cause of the accident. See cause, intervening cause, superseding cause.

Supervening negligence See last clear chance doctrine, negligence.

Supervise, *v.* To have general oversight over; to inspect. See manage (1), direct, oversee.

Supervision, *n.* Watching, guiding, or overseeing (supervision of the crew). Inspection, administration, management, superintendence, surveillance, guidance, control, stewardship, government, direction, oversight, dominion, guardianship, governance, regulation, care, leadership, steerage.

Supervisor, *n.* See manager, director, foreman, official, officer.

Supervisory, *adj.* Managing (supervisory control). Executive, overseeing, governing, administrative, directing, officiating.

Supine, *adj.* See weak, passive, indifferent, lazy; lie (4).

Supper, *n.* See food; eat.

Supplant, *v.* See replace, displace.

Supple, *adj.* See malleable, flexible, amenable.

Supplement, *n.* See addendum, attachment, accessory (2), increase.

Supplemental, *adj.* Pertaining to that which is added (supplemental revenue). Supplementary, additional, another, incidental, new, surplus, extraneous, further, more, spare, auxiliary. See also extra, ancillary.

Supplemental act A statute designed to improve an existing statute by adding something without changing the original text. See legislation.

Supplemental pleading A new pleading containing facts that have arisen since the filing of the last pleading. See pleading.

Supplementary, *adj.* Additional; adding or serving as a supplement. See supplemental, accessory (2), ancillary.

Supplementary proceedings New proceedings to help collect the judgment debt after an execution on the judgment has been issued (e.g., discovery of the judgment debtor's property from which to satisfy the judgment). See proceeding, collection.

Supplicant 1. *n.* One who makes a request; an aspirant. See party (1), applicant, candidate, petitioner, suitor. **2.** *adj.* Begging. Entreating, solicitous, beseeching, precatory, importunate, praying.

Supplicate, *v.* See appeal (4), apply (1), petition (2), beseech.

Supplier, *n.* One engaged in the business of making products available to consumers; all persons in the chain of production and distribution of a consumer product. Subcontractor, furnisher, caterer, provider, manufacturer, producer, wholesaler, retailer. See also contractor, independent contractor, builder.

Supplies, *n.* See provision (2), goods, inventory (2), commodity (1), material (3), equipment, property, effects.

Supply 1. *v.* To furnish what is wanted. See maintain (2), furnish, accommodate (1), finance (1). **2.** *n.* An available aggregate of things needed or demanded.

Stock, store, fund. See also inventory (2), provision (2), reserve (2).

Support 1. *v.* To provide a means of livelihood; to subsidize. See sustain (3), maintain (2), furnish, equip, accommodate (1), aid (1), finance (1), facilitate, strengthen, augment. **2.** *v.* To champion, promote, or affirm. See advocate (2), defend (1), back, corroborate, prove. **3.** *n.* The means of livelihood. See means, maintenance (1), assistance. **4.** *n.* Verification. See confirmation. **5.** *n.* Encouragement. See help (1), approbation.

Supportable, *adj.* See defensible, logical, justifiable, proper, admissible, believable.

Supporter, *n.* See champion, advocate, promoter.

Supportive, *adj.* See cooperative (2), beneficial, friendly, humanitarian, responsive, kind.

Suppose, *v.* See assume (2); deduce, reason (3).

Supposition, *n.* A conjecture based upon the possibility or probability that a thing could or may have occurred, without proof that it did occur. See hypothesis, assumption, conjecture, belief, opinion (2).

Supposititious, *adj.* See hypothetical, fallacious, false.

Suppress, *v.* To put a stop to a thing actually existing; to keep something from being used (suppress evidence). See restrain, quash, inhibit, censor (3), ban, bar, end.

Suppression, *n.* Control or concealment. See restraint (1), prohibition, obstruction.

Suppression hearing A pretrial proceeding in a criminal case, in which the defendant seeks to prevent the introduction of evidence alleged to have been seized illegally. See hearing.

Supra, *adv.* Above; ante.

Supremacy, *n.* The state of being in the highest position of power (supremacy of the court). Paramount authority, absolute rule, sovereign power, ascendancy, sway, mastery, domination, omnipotence, predominancy, primacy, leadership, championship, superiority, transcendency, pre-eminence, triumph, excellence, hegemony, dominance, lordship, supervision. See also sovereignty, grandeur, dominion.

Supremacy Clause Federal laws made in pursuance of the U.S. Constitution and treaties made under the authority of the United States have superiority over any conflicting provision of a state constitution or law.

Supreme, *adj.* Superior to all other things. See predominant, primary, best.

Supreme Being, *n.* See God, religion.

Supreme Court, *n.* An appellate court. In most states and in the federal judicial system, it is the highest court or court of last resort. In New York, it is a trial court with some appellate jurisdiction.

Supreme Court of Errors The former name of the highest appellate court in Connecticut.

Surcease, *v.* See cease, end (1), rescind, conclude (1), expire, dismiss.

Surcharge, *n.* **1.** The imposition of an additional tax, impost, or cost. Extra fee, penalty, burden. See also cost, tax. **2.** The imposition of personal liability on a fiduciary for willful or negligent misconduct in the administration of his or her fiduciary duties.

Sure, *adj.* See reliable, dependable, conscientious; certain (3), clear (1), indubitable, inevitable, incontestable.

Surely, *adv.* See absolutely.

Surety, *n.* One who promises to answer for the debt, default, or miscarriage of another; one who undertakes to pay money or to do any other act in the event that his or her principal fails to do so (damages for which the surety is liable). Sponsor, backer, indemnitor, insurer, cosigner, underwriter, bondsman, indorser, signatory, subscriber. See also guarantor, promoter, champion (1); indemnity.

Surety bond Obligation of a guarantor to pay a second party upon default by a third party in the performance the third party owes to the second party. See bond.

Suretyship contract See surety, surety bond, contract.

Surface 1. *n.* The exterior part (the surface of the land). Superficial part, external appearance, top, covering, facade, skin, outside, shell, finish, veneer, crust, superficies. See also face, exterior. **2.** *v.* To rise to the top (the material surfaced). Uncover, ascend, leak out, transpire. See also emerge, escape. *Ant.* Interior; submerge.

Surface waters Waters that diffuse over the surface of the ground, following no defined course or channel, and not gathering into or forming any more definite body of water than a mere bog or marsh.

Surfeit, *v., n.* See satisfy (2), fill, inundate, pack; flood, remainder (2).

Surge, *n., v.* See growth, development, flood, storm, increase; run.

Surgeon, *n.* One whose profession or occupation is to cure diseases, defects, or injuries of the body by manual operation; one who specializes in surgery. See doctor (1), surgery, medicine, treatment.

Surgeon General, *n.* The chief medical officer of the U.S. Public Health Service. See officer, medicine.

Surgery, *n.* The branch of medical science that uses mechanical or operative measures for healing diseases, deformities, or injuries; treatment by removal or repair of parts of the body. See treatment, medicine; medical.

Surgical, *adj.* See medical; treatment; surgery.

Surly, *adj.* See rude, hostile, caustic.

Surmise 1. *n.* Conjecture; an idea based on weak evidence. See opinion (2), hypothesis, conjecture, assumption. **2.** *v.* To infer or guess. See assume, estimate, deduce.

Surmount, *v.* See overcome, beat (2), override, defeat, conquer, prevail (2).

Surname, *n.* The family name. Last name, proper name, maiden name, cognomen. See also name.

Surpass, *v.* See beat (2), pass (3), exceed, overcome, best (2).

Surplus, *n.* That which remains of a fund appropriated for a particular purpose (accumulated surplus). See remainder (2); excess.

Surplusage, *n.* Extraneous, impertinent, superfluous, or unnecessary matter. Verbiage, verbosity, wordiness, redundancy, superfluity, excessiveness, overkill, irrelevance, immateriality, inappropriateness. See also verbose.

Surprise 1. *v.* To take or be taken unawares; to cause sudden confusion or perplexity (surprised by the evidence). Catch off guard, astonish, overwhelm, flabbergast, defy belief, stagger, ambush, stupify, boggle the mind, dumfound, electrify, nonplus, startle. See also amaze. **2.** *n.* An unforeseen event (the announcement was a surprise). Wonder, amazement, bolt, marvel, bombshell, astonishment, jolt, miracle, sensation, wonderment, awe, revelation, dismay, consternation, perplexity, stupefaction, incredulity. See also shock.

Surprised, *adj.* See agape; consternation, appalling, extraordinary, wild.

Surrender 1. *v.* To give back or repudiate. See abdicate, relinquish, waive, renounce. **2.** *v.* To give in or capitulate. See yield, quit, acquiesce, capitulate. **3.** *n.* The act of giving up. See abandonment, cession, abdication.

Surreptitious, *adj.* Stealthily or fraudulently done. See clandestine, hidden, dishonest, covert, corrupt (1), collusive, deceptive.

Surrogate 1. *n.* The judge or judicial officer with jurisdiction over probate, guardianship, etc. See judge (1). **2.** *n.* One who substitutes for another. See agent (1), replacement (2). **3.** *adj.* Alternate (surrogate mother). Proxy, acting, vicarious, foster, substitute, stand-in, provisional, representative.

Surrogate mother A woman who is artificially inseminated with the semen of a man who is not her husband, and who surrenders the baby at birth to the father and his wife. See parent.

Surrogate parent A nonparent who voluntarily assumes parental rights and responsibilities and hence stands in loco parentis to the child. See parent.

Surround, *v.* To enclose on all sides. Encompass, enfold, circle, hedge in, ring, fence in, envelop, girdle, hem, beleaguer, environ, gird, confine, belt. See also circumscribe.

Surrounding, *adj.* Neighboring. Connecting, proximate, environmental, enclosing, encircling, adjoining, touching, abutting, juxtaposed, contiguous, nearby.

Surroundings, *n.* Objects, circumstances, or forces that characterize an area. See environment, neighborhood, view (5), zone.

Surtax, *n.* An additional tax on top of what has already been taxed. A tax on a tax.

Surveillance, *n.* Observation, oversight (electronic surveillance). See inspection, supervision, administration, direction (2), management (1); eavesdrop.

Survey, *v.,* **survey,** *n.* **1.** *v.* To scrutinize or examine. To ascertain corners, boundaries, and divisions with distances and directions. See observe, appraise, investigate (3). **2.** *v.* To tabulate or poll. See canvass (1). **3.** *n.* The process by which a parcel of land is measured and its boundaries and contents ascertained. The description so obtained. See examination, review, exploration, map, record (2), outline.

Surveyor, *n.* One who makes surveys, determines the area of portions of the earth's surface, the length and direction of boundary lines, the contour of the surface.

Survival, *n.* Continuation of life or existence (survival of the cause of action). Sustenance, staying, continuing, lasting, durability, keeping alive; vestige, relic. See also longevity, endurance. *Ant.* Termination.

Survival action An action or cause of action that does not become extinguished with the death of the injured party.

Survive, *v.* To continue to live, exist, or be effective. See continue (1, 3), last (2), exist, abide, live (2).

Survivor, *n.* The one who outlives another. Widow, widower, orphan, descendant, posterity, heir, beneficiary.

Survivorship, *n.* **1.** Living after another has died. **2.** Becoming entitled to property by reason of surviving the death of one of the joint tenants.

Susceptible, *adj.* Capable of experiencing something; easily stirred. Vulnerable, prone, pliable, gullible, credulous, predisposed, exposed, open, unprotected, influenceable, impressionable, susceptive, responsive, sensitive, swayable. See also liable (2), formative, malleable, amenable, defenseless; emotional.

Suspect, *n.,* *adj.,* **suspect,** *v.* **1.** *n.* A person who is believed to have committed a crime. See accused. **2.** *v.* To have a slight or vague idea of something. See think, contemplate, consider (2). **3.** *v.* To be skeptical. See doubt (1). **4.** *adj.* Open to suspicion. See suspicious.

Suspect classification A classification based on race, religion, alienage, national origin, and sex. See bias; class, classification.

Suspend, *v.* **1.** To cause to cease for a time; to hold in abeyance. See postpone (1), defer (1); suspended. **2.** To remove or displace for a time. See dismiss (2), discharge (5). **3.** To invalidate. See rescind, quash, bar, ban. **4.** To hang. Swing, dangle, append, sling, oscillate, hitch, hook up, sway.

Suspended, *adj.* Postponed; temporarily inoperative; held in abeyance. Tabled, discontinued, shelved, withheld, not in force, up in the air, delayed, on ice, put off.

Suspended sentence A sentence that is formally given but not actually served at the time imposed.

Suspense, *n.* The state of being anxious and uncertain; expectation. See apprehension (3), anxiety, anguish.

Suspension, *n.* **1.** A temporary stop or delay. See interruption, cessation. **2.** A disbarment or dismissal. See removal (2, 3).

Suspensive condition A condition that depends either on a future or uncertain event or on an event that has actually taken place without its being yet known to the parties. See condition (1).

Suspicion, *n.* A belief or opinion based upon facts or circumstances that do not amount to proof. See conjecture, reservation (3), doubt (2), cloud (2); suggestion, indication, innuendo (2); intimate (6).

Suspicious, *adj.* **1.** Tending to arouse distrust (suspicious behavior). Questionable, shady, queer, odd, strange, open to question, doubtful, abnormal, peculiar, dubious, suspect, enigmatic, slippery, untrustworthy, unconvincing, equivocal, bizarre, eccentric, inexplicable, curious, idiosyncratic, different, unconventional, unorthodox, funny, perplexing. **2.** Skeptical (suspicious of reform). Dubious, apprehensive, leery, mistrustful, cynical, wary, incredulous, fearful, nervous, hesitant, qualmish, anxious, distrustful, disbelieving, suspecting. *Ant.* Aboveboard; trusting.

Sustain, *v.* **1.** To affirm (the court sustained the objection). See agree (2), approve. **2.** To support (the evidence sustains his version). See corroborate, prove, verify. **3.** To keep alive or nourish (sustained by his beliefs). Maintain, conserve, nurse, prolong, continue, feed, protect, save, bolster, strengthen, foster, support. See also nurture. **4.** To endure (sustain the burden). Undergo, tolerate, bear, brook, labor under, weather, withstand, hold out, suffer, experience, carry on under, abide, brave, countenance, accept. *Ant.* Reject; weaken; perish; escape.

Sustenance, *n.* See maintenance (1), assistance; necessaries, food.

Swagger, *v.* **1.** To strut. Parade, prance, sweep, stride, amble, bounce. See also walk. **2.** See boast.

Swallow, *v.* See eat; suffer (3), bear (2); absorb, consume.

Swamp 1. *n.* Wet, spongy land. Marshy ground, mire, bog, everglade, slough, fen, quagmire, marshland, bayou, ooze, slough, slue. See also morass. **2.** *v.* To engulf, flood, or overwhelm. See inundate, submerge.

Swank, *adj.* See chic, current; beautiful, attractive; flamboyant; cultivated, aristocratic.

Swap, *v.* See exchange, barter, bargain.

Swarm, *v., n.* See pack, mob, multitude, mass.

Swash, *v.* See splash.

Sway, *v.* See influence, persuade, impress (1); alternate (1), stray; flounder; suspend (4), dangle.

Swear, *v.* To take or administer an oath. See attest, affirm (2, 3); blasphemy.

Sweat, *n.* Perspiration, excretion; drudgery. Hard work, toil, slavery, slave labor, agony, torture. See also labor.

Sweat equity Equity created through the labor of the owner in making improvements to his or her property.

Sweater, *n.* See apparel, clothes.

Sweating, *n.* Questioning an accused through harassment or threats.

Sweep, *n., v.* See gesture, move (4); extent; bathe.

Sweeping, *adj.* Including in its scope many persons or objects. See comprehensive, broad (1).

Sweepstakes, *n.* In horse racing, the sum of the stakes for which the subscribers agree to pay for each horse nominated. See lottery, gambling.

Sweet, *adj.* See delectable; friendly.

Sweeten, *v.* See mitigate, assuage.

Sweetener, *n.* Something added as an inducement. Lure, impetus, stimulus, encouragement, incentive.

Sweetheart, *n.* See suitor; intimate (5); paramour.

Sweetheart contract A contract between a union and an employer, in which concessions are granted to one or the other for the purpose of keeping a rival union out. See contract, union.

Swell, *v.* To increase. See enlarge, augment, strengthen.

Swelling, *n.* See lesion, contusion, injury, hurt, cut, wound.

Swerve, *v.* See depart (2), skid, stray, wander, digress.

Swift, *adj.* Fast, express, precipitate, or hurried. See prompt, expeditious, immediate (1); speed (1).

Swill, *n.* See refuse; balderdash.

Swindle, *v.* To cheat and defraud with deliberate artifice; to exploit or victimize. See deceive, cheat, embezzle; larceny.

Swindler, *n.* One who defrauds others. See thief, wrongdoer.

Swing, *v.* See dangle, suspend (4); brandish; alternate; manipulate, perform.

Swirl, *v.* See twist, alternate, turn (1), circulate.

Switch, *v.* To substitute. See exchange (1); shift, alter, change.

Switchblade knife, *n.* See weapon; cut.

Swivel, *v.* See twist, alternate, turn (1).

Swollen, *adj., v.* See full; enlarge, augment.

Sword, *n.* See weapon; cut.

Sworn, *adj.* Verified. See certified; verify.

Sycophant, *n.* See parasite; ass, boor; flatter, flattery, grovel, cringe.

Syllable, *n.* See language.

Syllabus, *n.* **1.** See brief (2), outline, abstract (3). **2.** A brief statement summarizing the rulings of a court opinion. See digest (1), headnote.

Syllogism, *n.* The full, logical form of a single argument consisting of two premises and the conclusion. See logic.

Symbiosis, *n.* See association, relation (1), connection.

Symbol, *n.* That which stands for something else. Representation, sign, token, model, badge, picture, mark, trademark, emblem, manifestation, archetype, prototype, specimen, exemplification, character, figure, initials, monogram, logo, trait, code, signature, metaphor, allegory, depiction, cue.

Symbolic, *adj.* Relating to or expressed by a symbol. Illustrative, representational, metaphorical, suggestive, denotative, indicative, characteristic, emblematic, figurative, allusive, allegorical, exemplary, symbolistic. See also nominal (1).

Symbolic delivery The constructive delivery of the cumbersome or inaccessible subject matter of a sale or gift by the actual delivery of an article that is conventionally accepted as representative of the subject matter, or which renders access to it possible, or which is evidence of the purchaser's or donee's title to it.

Symbolic speech Conduct that expresses opinions or thoughts about a subject; actions that have as their primary purpose the expression of ideas (e.g., burning the U.S. flag). See action (2), act (3).

Symbolize, *v.* See represent (3), manifest (2), exhibit (1), express (2).

Symmetric, symmetrical, *adj.* See uniform, parallel, analogous, proportionate, consonant, correlative; symmetry.

Symmetry, *n.* Due proportion of several parts of a body to each other; harmonic relationship of parts. Congruity, uniformity, poise, regularity, order, orderliness, congruence, agreement, equilibrium, parallelism, evenness, parity. See also harmony, balance (4), conformity, correspondence (1). *Ant.* Asymmetry.

Sympathetic, *adj.* **1.** Approving (sympathetic strike). Pro, backing, supporting, simpatico, favorably disposed, fraternal. See also friendly. **2.** Compassionate (sympathetic judge). See benevolent, charitable, patient (3). **3.** Receptive. See open (6), flexible, accessible. *Ant.* Antagonistic.

Sympathetic strike A strike designed to show support for another strike by different employees. See boycott, strike (1).

Sympathize, *v.* See empathize, commiserate, appreciate (2).

Sympathy, *n.* See favor (2), consolation, mercy, charity (3, 4), consideration (3), passion, benevolence, toleration (1), affinity, cooperation, confederacy, goodwill (2), companionship, harmony, approval, acceptance, consent, assent.

Symphony, *n.* See music; harmony, affinity, agreement.

Symposium, *n.* See conference, assembly, meeting.

Symptom, *n.* See manifestation, characteristic (1), mark, harbinger, indication, warning, evidence, effect.

Symptomatic, *adj.* See characteristic (2), demonstrative, descriptive.

Synagogue, *n.* See church, religion; God.

Synchronize, *v.* See coordinate (1).

Synchronous, *adj.* See concurrent (1), simultaneous.

Syncretize, *v.* See settle (1), accommodate, adapt, negotiate, arbitrate (3).

Syndicalism, *n.* The theory, plan, or practice of trade-union action that aims, by general strike and direct action, to establish control over the means and processes of production by local worker organizations. See criminal syndicalism; racket, control.

Syndicate 1. *n.* A grouping or organization of individuals formed for the purpose of conducting and carrying out some particular business transaction; a group of investment brokers who together underwrite and distribute securities. See association (1). **2.** *n.* See enterprise (1). **3.** *v.* To merge or affiliate. See combine (1), associate (1).

Syndication, *n.* The act or process of forming a syndicate.

Syndrome, *n.* See pattern, manifestation.

Synod, *n.* See assembly, congress (2), congregation, meeting, conference; church, religion.

Synonymous, *adj.* Expressing the same or nearly the same idea. See equivalent, equal (2), identical, analogous.

Synopsis, *n.* See digest (1), brief (2), outline.

Synthesis, *n.* See integration (2), association (2), harmony, cooperation, merger, combination.

Synthesize, *v.* See coordinate, harmonize, combine (1).

Synthetic, *adj.* See counterfeit (2), deceptive, deceitful, bogus, artificial.

Syphilis, *n.* See venereal disease, disease.

System, *n.* A method, strategy, or procedure for accomplishing something. See plan (1), process, method, classification, organization, pattern, composition.

Systematic, *adj.* See coherent (1), regular, precise, efficient, complete (2), careful, deliberate.

Systematization, *n.* See organization (2), classification (1), distribution (1).

Systematize, *v.* See regulate, classify, organize, frame (1).

Tab, *n.* See bill (2).

Tabernacle, *n.* See church, religion, God; vessel (2).

Table 1. *v.* To suspend consideration of a pending matter. See postpone (1). **2.** *n.* A listing or graph. Chart, list, column, catalogue, itemization, blueprint, register, file. See also schedule, report (1), agenda. **3.** *n.* Desk, bench, bar, stand, trivet, kitchen table, workbench, secretary, counter.

Tableau, *n.* See description, view (5).

Table of cases An alphabetical list of opinions that will be covered or referred to in the body of the text.

Tablet, *n.* See medicine, drug, treatment.

Tabloid, *n.* See newspaper, press (1), journal.

Taboo, *n., adj.* See prohibition, limitation, ban; witchcraft; illicit.

Tabulate, *v.* See calculate, organize, classify.

Tabulation, *n.* See estimate (1), classification.

Tacit, *adj.* Inferred or understood without being openly expressed or stated; inferred by silence (tacit approval). See implied, silent (2).

Taciturn, *adj.* See silent (1), quiet (2), passive.

Tack 1. *v.* To annex some junior lien to a first lien, thereby acquiring priority over an intermediate one. See attach (2); lien. **2.** *n.* Strategy or policy. See course (1). **3.** *n.* Nail. Pin, brad, thumbtack, spike, peg.

Tacking, *n.* The process of obtaining title to land by adverse possession: The adverse possessor adds his or her period of possession to that of a prior adverse possessor in order to establish a continuous possession for the statutory period; joining or combining in order to avoid a bar or to fulfill a requirement. See adverse possession.

Tackle, *v., n.* See attempt (3); seize; equipment.

Tacky, *adj.* See gaudy, vulgar, flamboyant, blatant (2).

Tact, *n.* Grace, acumen. See discretion (3), delicacy, judgment, prudence.

Tactful, *adj.* See prudent, cautious, discreet, judicious.

Tactic, *n.* See machination, plan, artifice.

Tactile, *adj.* See physical, corporeal, material (2).

Tactless, *adj.* See blind (1), blatant (2), careless, rude, vulgar, flamboyant.

Tad, *n.* See child, juvenile; iota, scintilla.

Tag, *v., n.* See label; name.

Tail, *adj.* Limited, curtailed, or abridged (e.g., to a certain order of succession or to certain heirs). See fee tail.

Tail female When lands are given to a person and the female heirs of his or her body. The male heirs are not capable of inheriting it.

Tail male When lands are given to a person and the male heirs of his or her body. The female heirs are not capable of inheriting it.

Tailspin, *n.* See collapse.

Taint 1. *v.* To soil, weaken, or defile. See corrupt, pollute. **2.** *n.* A moral defect.

Taint

See fault (1), wrong (1).

Take 1. *v.* To attain or assume possession. See seize (1), plunder (1), rob, appropriate (1). **2.** *n.* That which is received; receipts. See gain, profit (1). **3.** *v.* See transfer, withdraw (1).

Take back, *v.* To repossess or invalidate. See rescind.

Take care of, *v.* See maintain (1, 2, 4), manage (2).

Take effect, *v.* To go into operation; to become operative or executed; to be in force. See vest, commence.

Take over, *v.* To assume control or management. See appropriate (1), confiscate.

Taking, *n.* Gaining possession; laying hold of something with or without removing it. See dispossession, seizure (1).

Tale, *n.* See legend, fiction.

Talent, *n.* See facility (3), skill, experience, ability, gift, address (4).

Talented, *adj.* See apt (3), brilliant, able, competent.

Talesman, *n.* A person summoned to act as a juror from among the bystanders in the court.

Talisman, *n.* See witchcraft.

Talk, *v., n.* See communicate, babble, converse (1), address (2, 3).

Talkative, *adj.* See garrulous; babble, prolixity; convivial, friendly, amicable.

Tall, *adj.* **1.** Elevated. High, statuesque, elongated, lanky, towering, huge, long-limbed, gangling, lofty. See also big, able-bodied, healthy. **2.** See outrageous, improbable, doubtful (2), absurd, irrational, wild.

Tally 1. *n.* A scorecard or reckoning. See account (1), record (2). **2.** *v.* To compute or register. See calculate (1), record (1).

Talmud, *n.* A work that embodies the civil and canonical law of the Jewish people.

Tame 1. *adj.* Domesticated, adapted, trained, or disciplined; timid. See passive, malleable, moderate (1). **2.** *v.* To adapt to human or domestic use. See domesticate. **3.** *v.* To subdue or tone down. See conquer, mitigate.

Tamper, *v.* To meddle so as to change something, usually with illegal or unauthorized results. See alter, corrupt (2), interfere, manipulate, distort, "doctor" (4).

Tampering with the jury See embracery.

Tandem, *adv.* One behind another. In a row. See chain (1); together.

Tangent, *n.* See deviation, detour.

Tangential, *adj.* See peripheral, extraneous (1), immaterial, gratuitous (2), marginal, minimal, minor (2), nugatory, frivolous.

Tangible, *adj.* Having or possessing physical form. See physical, material (2), corporeal, substantial (1).

Tangible evidence Evidence consisting of something that can be seen or touched. See evidence. *Ant.* Testimonial evidence.

Tangible property Corporeal property; property that can be felt or touched. See property.

Tangle, *n., v.* See disorder, confusion, commotion; twist; implicate.

Tangled, *adj.* See complex (1), difficult, mixed.

Tank, *n.* See vessel (2); weapon.

Tanker, *n.* See vessel (1).

Tantalize, *v.* See flirt, inveigle, bait (3), provoke, entice, seduce.

Tantalizing, *adj.* See intriguing, attractive, irresistible.

Tantamount, *adj.* See equivalent.

Tantrum, *n.* See fit (2).

Tap, tapping, *n.* See eavesdrop, inspection; touch; employ (2).

Tape, *n.* See belt (1), strip (3), record.

Tardy, *adj.* See late (3), overdue, delinquent (1), due (1), outstanding (1); lazy.

Tare, *n.* An allowance or deduction for the weight of the carton, box, bag, or other container.

Target, *n.* See objective (3), aim (3), intent, victim.

Tariff, *n.* The custom or duty paid on articles imported into the United States; a list or schedule of articles subject to such a custom or duty. See duties, fee (1), tax.

Tarnish, *v.* See pollute, debase, corrupt.

Tarry, *v.* See delay, loiter, dwell (2), hover (1), continue (1).

Tart, *n., adj.* See prostitute; caustic, rude.

Task, *n.* See assignment (3), function, job.

Task force, *n.* See committee, division.

Taskmaster, *n.* See tyrant, master, manager.

Taste, *v., n.* See enjoy, face, confront; scintilla, iota; preference, bias, favoritism; judgment, discretion (3), maturity, common sense.

Tasteful, *adj.* See attractive, beautiful, proper, civil, fit, appropriate; chic.

Tasteless, *adj.* See gaudy, flamboyant, vulgar, offensive; weak.

Tasty, *adj.* See delectable.

Tattered, *adj.* See disheveled, ragged.

Tattle, *v.* See babble; report, disclose.

Taunt, *v.* See mock (1), harass, censure, provoke; slander.

Tautology, *n.* Describing the same thing twice in one sentence in equivalent terms. See repetition; needless, superfluous.

Tavern, *n.* A place where liquor is consumed on the premises. See inn.

Tawdry, *adj.* See gaudy, flamboyant, vulgar, meretricious.

Tax 1. *n.* A pecuniary burden imposed on individuals, businesses, or property to support the government. Levy, assessment, tribute, impost, duty, excise, exaction, imposition, capitation, toll, tithe, rate, contribution, custom, Peter's pence, surtax. **2.** *v.* To place a burden on. See encumber, burden (3), exhaust, disable. *Ant.* Deduction; liberate.

Taxable, *adj.* Subject to taxation; liable to be assessed. Chargeable, assessable, exactable.

Taxable estate The gross estate of a decedent reduced by allowable deductions. See estate.

Taxable income The gross income of a business or the adjusted gross income of an individual minus deductions and exemptions. See income.

Taxable year The calendar year or the fiscal year upon which net taxable income is computed; the annual accounting period of the taxpayer.

Tax avoidance The minimization of one's tax liability by taking advantage of legally available tax-planning opportunities. See avoidance.

Tax benefit rule If an amount deducted from gross income in one taxable year is recovered in a later year, the recovery is income in the later year.

Tax certificate An instrument issued to the buyer of property at a tax sale, which entitles the holder to the property thus purchased if it is not redeemed within the period provided by law.

Tax credit A subtraction from the taxes owed or paid.

Tax deduction A subtraction from revenues and gains to arrive at taxable income. See deduction.

Tax deed Proof of ownership of land given to the purchaser by the government after the latter has taken the land from another person and has sold it for failure to pay taxes.

Tax evasion Illegally paying less taxes than the law permits. See fraud, evasion.

Tax exemption Immunity from the obligation of paying taxes in whole or in part.

See exemption, immunity.

Taxi, *n., v.* See vehicle, merchant, business; carry (1), transfer.

Tax lien A lien on real estate in favor of the government, which may be foreclosed for nonpayment of taxes. See lien.

Taxonomy, *n.* See classification.

Taxpayer, *n.* See citizen.

Tax roll The official record maintained by cities and towns listing the names of taxpayers and the assessed property. See record (2).

Tax sale The sale of property for nonpayment of taxes. See sale.

Tax shelter A device used by taxpayers to reduce or to defer the payment of taxes. See shelter, avoidance.

Teach, *v.* To impart knowledge by means of lessons. See instruct (1), nurture, discipline (4), prepare (1), educate, improve, correct.

Teacher, *n.* One who teaches or instructs. Instructor, lecturer, pedagogue, trainer, academician, schoolmarm, don, maestro, preceptor, coach, lector, tutor, schoolmaster, professor, fellow, educator, doctor, mentor, guide, guru, interpreter, informer, preacher. See also school, education, oracle.

Teaching, *n.* See education, discipline (1), information, judgment (2), discretion (3); teacher.

Team, *n.* See group, association (1).

Teammate, *n.* See partner, colleague, cohort.

Teamster, *n.* A truck driver. See operator; union.

Teamwork, *n.* Cooperative effort. See collaboration, cooperation, concert.

Tear, *v.* To split or pull into pieces (tear the will). Pull apart, rip, sever, shred, rive, slash, tatter. See also deface, cut, mutilate, destroy, extract (1).

Tease, *v.* See mock (1), harass, provoke, censure.

Technical, *adj.* Belonging or peculiar to an art or profession (her technical expertise). Skilled, scientific, specialized, qualified, vocational, professional, technological, occupational, particularized, trained, specific, intricate, detailed, esoteric, abstruse, arcane. See also empirical, mathematical, precise, mechanical.

Technical error An error that has not prejudiced the complaining party and hence is not a ground for reversal. See error, harmless error.

Technicality, *n.* A narrow or fine point; a matter of form or procedure; something that does not go to the heart or substance of the case.

Technician, *n.* See artisan, specialist, expert, laborer.

Technique, *n.* See modus operandi, method, means, art, mode.

Technology, *n.* See art, science.

Tedious, *adj.* See commonplace (2), pedestrian (2), superfluous, continual, habitual.

Tedium, *n.* See boredom.

Teeming, *adj.* See abundant, copious, excess.

Teen-age, *adj.* See juvenile, minor; adolescence.

Teeter, *v.* See alternate (1), stray (1), flounder.

Teetotaler, *n.* One who does not drink alcoholic beverages. See abstention, abstain.

Telecast, *v.* See publish, circulate, communicate.

Telegram, *n.* A message that is sent by telegraph. Wire, telex, cable, dispatch. See also communication.

Telegraph, *v.* To send a message by means of a system using electrical impulses. See send, communicate.

Telephone, *v.* See communicate, contact (3).

Telescope, *v.* See abridge, digest.

Tell, *v.* See communicate, disclose, confess, expose, describe; ascertain; command.

Teller, *n.* **1.** One who receives and pays out money; one who counts. Bank clerk, cashier. See also clerk (2), accountant, officer. **2.** Narrator. Raconteur, storyteller, chronicler, reporter.

Temerity, *n.* See effrontery, spirit (2), annoyance.

Temper, *v., n.* See mitigate, diminish, adjust; disposition (4), manner; fit (2), passion, emotion, storm, eruption.

Temperament, *n.* See disposition (4), manner, character, essence.

Temperamental, *adj.* See feverish, excitable, emotional, capricious.

Temperance, *n.* Restrained or moderate indulgence in one's appetites and passions. Moderation, self-restraint, puritanism, self-mortification, abstinence, self-denial, self-deprivation, nonindulgence, self-sacrifice, fasting, teetotalism, self-control, austerity, celibacy, sobriety, prohibition, frugality, patience, judiciousness, measure. See also forbearance. *Ant.* Intemperance.

Temperate, *adj.* See reserve (4), judicious, reasonable.

Temperative, *n.* See climate.

Tempest, *n.* **1.** A violent storm. Hurricane, blizzard, sandstorm, windstorm, squall, typhoon, thunderstorm, tornado, twister. See also storm. **2.** An outbreak or upheaval. See commotion, eruption, passion.

Tempestuous, *adj.* See violent, impetuous, reckless, emotional, feverish, hot.

Temple, *n.* A place dedicated to worship. See church.

Tempo, *n.* See measure (1); climate.

Temporal, *adj.* See secular, profane (2), civil (2), material (2), physical; imperfect, temporary.

Temporarily, *adv.* Existing or continuing for a limited time (temporarily absent). Quickly, momentarily, for a little while, fleetingly, for the moment, pro tem, transiently, for the time being, for now, in the interim. *Ant.* Permanently.

Temporary, *adj.* Lasting for a limited time (temporary nuisance). Fading, passing, provisional, momentary, fleeting, stopgap, not permanent, evanescent, flash-in-the-pan, ephemeral, mortal, soon past, nondurable, temporal, fugitive, elusive, short-lived, impermanent; substitute, pro tempore, standby. See also brief (4), perishable, interim (2). *Ant.* Perpetual.

Temporary alimony An interim order of payment to a spouse pending the final outcome of the action for divorce. See alimony.

Temporary disability A disability that lasts for a limited time only while the worker is undergoing treatment; the healing period during which the claimant is totally or partially unable to work due to injury, which continues as long as recovery or lasting improvement of the injured person's condition can reasonably be expected. See disability.

Temporary injunction A preliminary or provisional injunction; an injunction granted pendente lite. See injunction.

Temporary restraining order (TRO) An emergency remedy of brief duration issued pending a hearing on the application for an injunction. See injunction.

Temporize, *v.* See delay, postpone, quibble, hedge.

Tempt, *v.* See bait (3), entice, seduce.

Temptation, *n.* See bait (1), solicitation, invitation.

Tempting, *adj.* See attractive, compelling, intriguing, beautiful.

Tenable, *adj.* See cogent, logical, justifiable, defensible.

Tenacious, *adj.* See durable, indefatigable, diligent, strong (3), constant (3), reliable; inflexible, firm (2).

Tenacity, *n.* See decision (2), determination (2), diligence (1), endurance, spirit (2), resolution (4), self-confidence.

Tenancy, *n.* **1.** The interest in real property in one who holds it for temporary use and occupation; control and possession or occupancy of land under a lease. Holding, leasing, renting, occupancy, residence, lesseeship, share. **2.** A form of ownership. See joint tenancy, tenancy by the entirety, tenancy in common, ownership.

Tenancy by the entirety A tenancy that is created between a husband and wife by which they together hold title to the whole property with the right of survivorship so that when one dies, the other takes the whole property to the exclusion of the heirs of the deceased. A joint tenancy between husband and wife. See entirety, joint tenancy.

Tenancy in common A form of ownership whereby each tenant (i.e., owner) holds an undivided interest in the property. Each tenant in common has a right to possession of the property, but the share in the property may not be equal. There is no right of survivorship. When one dies, his or her share passes to his or her heirs and not to the other tenant(s) in common (unless the latter happen to be heirs).

Tenant, *n.* **1.** One who pays rent to possess or hold another's property for temporary use and occupation (landlord-tenant relationship). Lessee, occupier, renter, boarder, leaseholder, inhabitant, roomer. See also occupant, possessor, resident, lodger. **2.** One who has an ownership interest in land (tenant in common). See owner.

Tenant at sufferance One who after rightfully being in possession of leased premises continues after his or her right has terminated.

Tenant at will One who holds possession of premises by permission of the owner or landlord but without a fixed term.

Tenant by the entirety See tenancy by the entirety.

Tenant farmer, *n.* See farmer.

Tenant from year to year **1.** A tenant paying an annual rent but without an agreed-upon time or term for the tenancy. **2.** A tenant who holds over by express or constructive consent of the landlord after the expiration of a term for years.

Tenant in common See tenancy in common.

Tend, *v.* **1.** To have a leaning or tendency (the judge tends to impose stiff sentences). Be disposed, lean, verge, be likely, trend, head, incline, steer, predispose, be apt, move, aim. See also gravitate. **2.** To care for. See minister (3), manage (1), help, aid.

Tendency, *n.* See preference, affinity, disposition (4), aim.

Tender **1.** *v.* To offer payment or other performance. See offer (1). **2.** *n.* That which is offered. See offer (2), payment (1). **3.** *adj.* Compassionate, sympathetic, or caring. See affectionate; benevolent. **4.** *adj.* Unsophisticated. See juvenile (2). **5.** *adj.* Delicate. Fragile, vulnerable, frail, breakable, soft, susceptible, warm, gentle, sensitive, weak, insubstantial, precarious, shaky, pitiful, infirm. **6.** *adj.* Painful. Aching, sore, throbbing, inflamed, hurting, smarting, irritated, raw, swollen.

Tenderhearted, *adj.* See kind (2), affectionate; intimate, charitable, benevolent.

Tenderness, *n.* See love, affection (1), affinity, charity, benevolence.

Tender offer A take-over bid. An offer to purchase shares made by one company direct to the stockholders of another company. See offer.

Tender years doctrine In custody disputes, some courts will award custody of children of tender years to the mother unless she is unfit. See custody.

Tenement, *n.* **1.** An apartment building. See home (1). **2.** Everything that may be holden of a permanent nature.

Tenet, *n.* A doctrine or principle. See belief, creed, opinion.

Tennessee Valley Authority (TVA) A government-owned corporation that conducts a program of resource development for the advancement of economic growth in the Tennessee Valley region. Its activities include flood control, navigation development, electric power development, etc.

Tennis, *n.* See athletics, sport, contest.

Tenor, *n.* The meaning, spirit, or sense of something. See intent, essence (1), import, character, object.

Tense, *adj.* See apprehensive, concerned; feverish, excitable, inflexible, firm.

Tension, *n.* See burden (2), pain, anxiety, anguish, apprehension; traction.

Tent, *n.* See awning.

Tentative, *adj.* **1.** Provisional or experimental (tentative agreement). Conditional, dependent, contingent, temporary, exploratory, probative, pilot, under consideration, hypothetical, theoretical, subject to change, negotiable, speculative. **2.** Manifesting uncertainty or hesitancy (a tentative yes). Doubtful, unsure, indecisive, cautious, anxious, faltering, insecure, shy, wavering, wobbling, questionable. *Ant.* Final; firm.

Tentative trust See totten trust, trust.

Tenuous, *adj.* See tentative, weak, insecure, infirm, thin, petty, frivolous.

Tenure, *n.* A status given a teacher upon completing a trial period, protecting him or her from summary dismissal. A right, term, or mode of holding or occupying something. The manner in which an office is held, especially as to time (federal judges have life tenure). Term, duration, entitlement, occupation, incumbency, permanence, guarantee, security. See also longevity.

Tepid, *adj.* See indifferent, apathetic.

Tergiversate, *v.* See quibble, hedge.

Term, 1. *n.* A fixed period (4-year term). Interval, span, tenure, time, session, age, spell, incumbency, semester, course, stage, era, cycle, stretch, date, season, life. **2.** *n.* A phrase or expression (derogatory term). See word (1), language. **3.** *n.* A proviso, specification, or detail (a non-negotiable term). See condition (1), requirement, clause. **4.** *v.* To designate or label (he was termed a conservative). See label, characterize, name (2).

Terminable, *adj.* Capable of being terminated; ending upon the occurrence of a specified event (terminable interest). Limitable, conditional. See also defeasible. *Ant.* Perpetual.

Terminal, *n., adj.* See depot; final, definitive, conclusive, definite, fatal.

Terminate, *v.* To end; to put an end to. See cease, end (1), rescind, dissolve, annul, dismiss, conclude (1), expire.

Termination, *n.* See cessation, rescission, dismissal, conclusion (1), expiration, reversal.

Terminology, *n.* See language, word.

Term insurance, *n.* A form of pure life insurance having no cash surrender value and generally furnishing insurance protection for only a specified or limited period of time, though it is usually renewable from term to term. See insurance.

Terminus, *n.* A limit either of space or time. See boundary, conclusion (1), expiration.

Term of art The vocabulary or terminology of a particular art or science. Words or phrases that have a special or technical meaning. Jargon, computerese, vernacular; lingo, shoptalk, idiom, cant, argot, slang, patois. See also language, word, ambiguity.

Terra, *n.* Earth, soil, arable land. See ground (2), earth, park.

Terrace, *n.* See balcony; ground (2), field, park.

Terra firma, *n.* See terra.

Terrain, *n.* See terra, zone.

Terra transit cum onere Land passes with the incumbrances.

Terrazzo, *n.* Marble or stone flooring.

Terrestrial, *adj.* See earth, secular, profane (2), physical.

Terrible, *adj.* See bad, awesome, appalling, odious, repulsive, repugnant, offensive, contemptible, corrupt, base; odd (1), anomalous, acute (2).

Terrific, *adj.* See outstanding (2), great, beautiful, attractive, exceptional, extraordinary.

Terrify, *v.* See outrage (2), intimidate, disturb, disrupt, harass.

Territorial, *adj.* Having to do with a particular area or land. Geographical, regional, local. See also zone.

Territorial jurisdiction The territory over which a government or a subdivision thereof has jurisdiction. See jurisdiction.

Territory, *n.* **1.** A part of a country. See area (1), zone. **2.** A portion of the United States not within the limits of any state, which has its own branches of government but has not yet been admitted as a state. **3.** A geographical area under the jurisdiction of another country or sovereign power.

Terror, *n.* **1.** Apprehension of harm from some hostile or threatening event or manifestation. See fear (1), consternation, shock (1), apprehension (3), hysteria, outrage (1), indignity; agape. **2.** A hoodlum, brute, demon, spitfire, or rogue. See wrongdoer.

Terrorism, *n.* See privacy, coercion, threat, duress, blackmail, cruelty, arson, assassination, homicide.

Terrorist, *n.* One who uses systematic violence, intimidation, or intense fear to obtain his or her goals. See revolutionary, insurgent, nihilist, anarchist, wrongdoer.

Terrorize, *v.* See menace (2), dominate, intimidate, harass, outrage, disturb, disrupt.

Terse, *adj.* See brief, concise, clear; rude, cursory.

Test 1. *v.* To ascertain the truth, quality, or fitness of a thing; to evaluate. See investigate, assess, appraise. **2.** *n.* An inquiry or inspection. See examination, assessment (3), appraisal, criterion. **3.** *n.* Battle, struggle, or competition. See contest (2), fight.

Testacy, *n.* The state or condition of leaving a will at one's death. See testate.

Testament, *n.* **1.** A statement of principle. See belief (2), creed, opinion. **2.** A covenant or agreement. See contract (1). **3.** A document that disposes personal property at death. See will (1).

Testamentary, *adj.* Pertaining to a will.

Testamentary capacity The mental ability that must be present in order to make a will: Your mind and memory must be such that you know in a general way the character and extent of your property, you understand your relationship to the objects of your bounty and those who ought to be on your mind on the occasion of making the will, and you understand the nature and effect of the testamentary act. See capacity (1).

Testamentary disposition A disposition of property by way of gift, will, or deed, which is not to take effect unless the grantor dies or until that event. See disposition.

Testamentary trust A trust that is to take effect at the death of the settlor. See trust.

Testate 1. *n.* One who has died leaving a valid will. **2.** *adj.* Having made a valid will. *Ant.* Intestate.

Testator, *n.* One who has died leaving a valid will. See donor.

Testatrix, *n.* A female testator. See testator, donor.

Testify, *v.* To give evidence as a witness; to make a solemn declaration under oath. See attest, assert, corroborate.

Testimonial 1. *adj.* In the nature of testimony; elicited from a witness. **2.** *n.* A statement of one's qualities; a recommendation. See indorsement (2), tribute (2), affidavit, certification, ceremony.

Testimonial evidence Evidence elicited from a witness. See evidence. *Ant.* See documentary evidence, real evidence.

Testimonium clause In conveyancing, a clause of a deed or instrument: "In witness whereof, the parties to these presents have hereunto set their hands and seals." A clause in the instrument reciting the date on which the instrument was executed and by whom.

Testimony, *n.* Evidence given by a competent witness under oath or affirmation. See declaration, assertion, attestation, statement, affirmation (2), deposition, evidence, confirmation (2).

Test-tube baby, *n.* A baby conceived outside the womb.

Testy, *adj.* See crabby, impatient, contentious (1), litigious, querulous, difficult (3), rude, inflexible, feverish, hot.

Tête-à-tête, *n., adv.* See meeting (3), conference; private, confidential.

Text, *n.* See book (4), language, word (1).

Texture, *n.* See character, essence, kind (1); composition; touch.

Thank, *v.* See acknowledge (2); appreciate.

Thankful, *adj.* See appreciative; benevolent; happy.

Thankless, *adj.* See rude; ingratitude; worthless, barren, fallow.

Thaw, *v.* To melt. Liquefy, defrost, soften. See also dissolve, mitigate.

Theater, *n.* See cinema, drama.

Theatrical, *adj.* See emotional, ardent, moving, flamboyant, pompous, artificial.

Theft, *n.* The taking of property without the owner's consent. See larceny, dispossession, seizure (1).

Theft of services Obtaining services from another by deception, threat, coercion, stealth, mechanical tampering, or the use of a false token or device. See larceny, fraud.

Theme, *n.* See question (2), matter (1), issue (3), proposition (2); thread (3); article (1).

Thence, *adv.* From there. From that place, from that time, thenceforth, from that circumstance, therefrom, thereafter, ever since.

Theocracy, *n.* Government of a state by the assumed direction of a divinity.

Theology, *n.* See creed, belief, dogma; religion; church.

Theoretical, *adj.* See abstract (4), hypothetical, intangible, speculative.

Theorize, *v.* See assume, think, contemplate, plan, reason (3).

Theory, *n.* An explanation; systematic ideas or knowledge that explains facts. See hypothesis, doctrine, opinion (2), school (2).

Therapeutic, *adj.* See medical, remedial, healthy.

Therapist, *n.* See medicine, treatment, specialist, expert; doctor.

Therapy, *n.* See treatment; medicine, cure, remedy, doctor, drug.

Thereabout, *adv.* About that place. Approximately, thereby, about that time, somewhat, generally, close, nigh, roughly, near that place.

Thereafter, *adv.* After the last time mentioned. After that, afterward, subsequently, thenceforth, thereupon, ultimately, next, later, afterwards, from that time on. See also thence. *Ant.* Previously.

Thereby, *adv.* By that means. In consequence of that, by which, whereby, through which.

Therefore

Therefore, *adv.* For that reason. Consequently, thus, because of, in which case, hence, ergo, on that account, whence, on that ground, accordingly.

Thermometer, *n.* See measure; climate; instrument (2), device, apparatus, equipment.

Thermostat, *n.* See thermometer.

Thesis, *n.* See hypothesis, doctrine, question (2), matter (1), proposition (2), issue; book.

Thick, *adj.* See measure, extent, scope, range, broad, big, strong, extreme; dumb, absurd, juvenile.

Thicket, *n.* See shrubbery, timber, woods.

Thickness, *n.* See measure, extent, scope, range.

Thick-skinned, *adj.* See callous, blind (1), indifferent (2).

Thief, *n.* One who commits larceny or theft. Pirate, pickpocket, embezzler, burglar, shoplifter, defrauder, pilferer, kleptomaniac, cutpurse, confidence man. See also wrongdoer.

Thievery, *n.* See larceny, fraud.

Thin, *adj.* **1.** Widely distributed. Sparse, dispersed, inadequate, insufficient, deficient, scrawny, underweight, undersized, emaciated, watery, meager, slim, gaunt, narrow, feeble, gossamer, tenuous, diluted, superficial, translucent. See also frail, weak, exhausted, small, anemic. **2.** See narrow, limited.

Thin capitalization When the debt owed by a corporation is large in relationship to its capital structure, the corporation may be seen as thinly capitalized.

Thing, *n.* See goods, item, object (3), entity, property (1).

Thing in action A right to recover money or other personal property by a judicial proceeding.

Think, *v.* To believe, conclude, or call to mind. Contemplate, meditate, mull over, remember, conceive, imagine, deliberate, believe, muse, reflect, speculate, opine, regard, mean, propose, visualize, picture, envision, cerebrate, guess. See also consider (2).

Thinkable, *adj.* See possible, credible, believable, practicable, feasible.

Thinking, *n., adj.* See contemplation, judgment, reason (2), common sense; logical, rational, reasonable, practicable; judicious.

Thin-skinned, *adj.* See emotional, squeamish, particular (2), excitable, tender (5), weak, frail.

Third degree, *n.* Securing information from a suspect by prolonged questioning, the use of threats, actual violence, etc. See interrogation, examination, inquest, inquiry, audit.

Third degree charge See Allen charge.

Third-party beneficiary One for whose benefit a contract is made but who is not a party to the contract. See beneficiary.

Third-party complaint A complaint filed by the defendant against someone who is not presently a party to the lawsuit. See complaint.

Third-party practice A procedural device whereby the defendant may bring in additional parties.

Third-rate, *adj.* See inferior, base, meretricious

Thirst, *n.* See desire, affinity (2).

Thorn, *n.* See affliction.

Thorny, *adj.* See difficult, controversial, painful, distressing.

Thorough, *adj.* See comprehensive, broad, universal, complete (2), extensive, efficient, precise.

Thoroughfare, *n.* A street or passage through which one can travel. See highway, pass (8), passage (2).

Thoroughgoing, *adj.* See careful, comprehensive, broad, complete; blatant, flagrant, extreme.

Thought, *n.* See contemplation; opinion, belief, creed, dogma; aim, intent, objective.

Thoughtful, *adj.* See kind, charitable, benevolent, friendly; preoccupied, contemplative.

Thoughtless, *adj.* See rude, vulgar, indifferent, negligent.

Thrash, *v.* See beat, batter, defeat, best, conquer.

Thread, *n.* **1.** Cord. Yarn, fiber, wire, cable, string, tendril, strand, wisp, tape, hair, strip. **2.** A line running through the middle of a stream or road. **3.** Theme. Motif, subject, story line, nexus, matter, gist, drift, plot, train.

Threadbare, *adj.* See ragged, disheveled, dirty; commonplace, pedestrian (2), barren.

Threat, *n.* **1.** A communicated intent to inflict harm; a declaration of intent to injure another (threats made to the victim). Warning, notice, saber rattling, intimidation, commination. See also blackmail, coercion, duress, warning. **2.** A risk or menace (threat of rain). See danger, hazard, caveat.

Threaten, *v.* **1.** To warn or terrorize. See menace (2), intimidate, coerce, harass, promise (3). **2.** To be imminent. Loom, endanger, imperil, impend, jeopardize, tower over, presage, portend.

Threatening, *adj.* See imminent, dangerous.

Threshold, *n.* See commencement, inception; entrance; verge, border (1), boundary.

Thrift, *n.* See economy (2).

Thriftless, *adj.* See prodigal, improvident; waste.

Thrifty, *adj.* See economical, prudent, cautious; stingy.

Thrill, *v., n.* See animate, delight, satisfy (2), incite; emotion, passion, mystery, marvel, spirit, happiness.

Thrilling, *adj.* See moving, emotional, great, extraordinary, attractive, outstanding (2).

Thrive, *v.* See advance (3, 4, 5) mature (1), develop, improve.

Throb, *v.* See beat (3).

Throne, *n.* See sovereign, sovereignty.

Throng, *n.* See assembly, mob, congregation, group.

Through, *prep.* By means of (acting through the corporation). In consequence of, by the agency of, by reason of, via, per, on account of, as a consequence of, by the intermediary of, in the name of, as the agent of.

Through bill of lading A bill of lading used when more than one carrier is required for shipping. See bill of lading.

Throw, *v.* See jettison (1).

Throwback rule In a trust, the amount distributed in any tax year that is in excess of that year's distributable net income must be "thrown back" to the preceding year and treated as if it had then been distributed.

Throw out, *v.* See ignore, dismiss, abandon (1), rescind, quash.

Thrust, *v.* To push or drive with force. Lunge, push, propel, pierce, prod, press, plunge, poke, jab, stab, ram, stick. See also assault, force (4).

Thug, *n.* See criminal, wrongdoer.

Thumbnail, *adj.* See brief, concise, summary.

Thunder, *n., v.* See storm, eruption; yell.

Thunderous, *adj.* See big, great, extraordinary; noisy.

Thunderstorm, *n.* See storm; climate.

Thunderstruck, *adj.* See agape.

Thus, *adv.* **1.** In the way just indicated. In this fashion, in this way, like this, in this manner. **2.** See therefore.

Thwart, *v.* See impede, bar, ban, frustrate, defeat, rescind, devastate.

Ticket, *n.* A paper entitling the holder to a right or privilege; a pass, voucher, or coupon. See certificate, license (1); receipt (1).

Tickle, *v.* See amuse, satisfy (2), delight.

Ticklish, *adj.* See difficult, doubtful (1), insecure (2).

Tide, *n.* The rising and falling of the water of the sea, produced by the attraction of the sun and moon. Ebb tide, undertow, neap tide, riptide, wave, flow, current; outburst, stream, tendency, direction, movement.

Tideland, *n.* The land between the lines of the ordinary high and low tides, covered and uncovered by the ebb and flow thereof.

Tidewater, *n.* Water that falls and rises with the ebb and flow of the tide.

Tidings, *n.* See communication, information (2), notice (1).

Tidy, *adj.* See careful, precise (2), efficient, coherent, clean (2).

Tie 1. *v.* To fasten, secure, or bind. See annex (1), affix, connect. **2.** *v.* To restrict or restrain. See impede, check, clog, chain (2). **3.** *n.* A bond. See connection (2, 3), affinity. **4.** *n.* Each with the same number. Draw, dead heat, stand-off.

Tie-in, *n.* See relation (1), link (1), connection, association.

Tie-in arrangement The vendor will sell one product only on the condition that the buyer will also purchase another and different product.

Tier, *n.* See rank (1).

Tie-up, *n.* See blockage, blockade, block (1), delay; association, connection.

Tiff, *n.* See fight, argument.

Tight, *adj.* See compact (2), concise, insufficient, difficult; narrow, limited.

Tighten, *v.* To make tighter. Twist, stiffen, screw, stretch, make taut, secure, constrict.

Tightfisted, *adj.* See stingy, avaricious.

Tightlipped, *adj.* See mute, silent(1).

Tightrope, *n.* See danger, peril, hazard.

Tightwad, *n.* See stingy, avaricious.

Till, *v., n.* See farm (2); vessel (2).

Tillage, *n.* Land under cultivation. See agriculture, husbandry, farm.

Tilt, *n., v.* See grade (2); tip (3); fight, contest.

Timber, *n.* Logs, boards. Trees, lumber, kindling, forest, copse, thicket; truss, beam, joist. See also woods, shrubbery.

Time 1. *n.* The measure of duration. See period, interval (1), minute, month. **2.** *v.* To measure duration. Synchronize, keep time, mark time, count, adjust, schedule, record, clock.

Time bomb, *n.* A bomb that will detonate at a predetermined time. See crisis, emergency, plight, dilemma.

Time immemorial, *n.* An ancient time; time before legal records; time beyond memory; time long past.

Time is of the essence The failure to do what is required by the time specified is a breach of the contract.

Timeless, *adj.* See permanent, perpetual, incalculable, ancient, old.

Timely, *adj.* Seasonable, ripe, appropriate, convenient.

Time-out, *n.* See delay, interruption, break (3).

Timer, *n.* A clock. Watch, timepiece, chronometer. See also measure; instrument (2), device, apparatus.

Time-sharing, *n.* Joint lease or ownership of property that is used individually for designated periods of time.

Timetable, *n.* See schedule, agenda, plan (1).

Time-tested, *adj.* See certified, authentic, effective.

Timid, *adj.* See bashful, quiet (2), insecure (2); apprehensive; weak, infirm; yellow; coward, cowardice.

Timorous, *adj.* See timid.

Tinderbox, *n.* See crisis, emergency, plight, dilemma; vessel (2).

Tinge, *n.* See color (4); suggestion, indication.

Tinker, *v., n.* See blunder, damage; repair; artisan.

Tinsel, *adj.* See artificial, gaudy, flamboyant.

Tint, *n.* See color (4); suggestion, indication.

Tiny, *adj.* See small, thin; marginal, minimal, minor (2), nugatory, frivolous; iota, scintilla.

Tip 1. *n.* Money given a servant as an extra for services rendered. See gratuity (1), compensation (1). **2.** *n.* A hint or recommendation. See advice. **3.** *v.* To tilt or overturn. Lean, incline, topple, slope, upset, slant, overthrow, angle, bend, capsize, cant, upend.

Tip-off, *n.* See warning; suggestion.

Tipsy, *adj.* See intoxicated; drunkard.

Tirade, *n.* See address (3), speech (2); eruption, censure, obloquy.

Tire, *v.* See exhaust, wear (1); harass.

Tired, *adj.* See exhausted; commonplace (2), ordinary, household, pedestrian (2).

Tireless, *adj.* See indefatigable; diligent, active (3).

Tiresome, *adj.* See difficult, onerous; commonplace, ordinary, pedestrian (2).

Tissue, *n.* See ligament, anatomy.

Titanic, *adj.* See big, great.

Tit for tat, *n.* See retaliation, reprisal.

Tithe, *n.* A tenth part of one's income contributed for charitable or religious purposes. See tax (1).

Titillate, *v.* See interest (5), entice, entrap, bait (3), enamor, delight, satisfy.

Titillating, *adj.* See intriguing, attractive, outstanding (2).

Titillation, *n.* See appeal (3), affinity (2), interest (4).

Title 1. *n.* The means whereby the owner of land has the just possession of his or her property. The union of all the elements that constitute ownership. The evidence of one's ownership interest in property. See right (3), interest, instrument (1), prescription (1). **2.** *n.* A unit or part of a statute, usually one of its major subdivisions. See chapter (2). **3.** *v.* To label something. See name, label. **4.** *n.* A designation by which something is known. See caption, mark, manifestation. **5.** *n.* One's position or status. See rank, office.

Title insurance Insurance against loss or damage resulting from defects in the title to land, or from the enforcement of liens existing against it at the time of the insurance. See insurance, indemnity.

Title search An examination of the records of the registry of deeds, or other office that contains records of title documents, to determine whether there are any defects in the title.

Titular, *adj.* See honorary, nominal (1).

Toady, *v., n.* See grovel, cringe, flatter; parasite.

Tobacco, *n.* See cigarette.

Today, *n.* See now; immediately; period, interval (1).

Together, *adv.* In union with. Along with, in concert, collectively, en masse, all at once, in tandem, conjointly, mutually, as one, as a whole; simultaneously, coincidently, contemporaneously, concurrently.

To have and to hold The words in a conveyance that show the estate intended to be conveyed.

Toil, *v.* See labor (2).

Toilet, *n.* See bathroom.

Token 1. *n.* See mark, manifestation, badge, characteristic, clue. **2.** *adj.* Superficial. Minimal, symbolic, perfunctory, pretended, apathetic, slight, indifferent, for show, hollow. **3.** *n.* See memento.

Tolerable, *adj.* See bearable, defensible; adequate, ordinary, commonplace.

Tolerance, *n.* See benevolence, charity; endurance.

Tolerant, *adj.* See permissive, cooperative (2), amenable; liberal (2), open (6, 7), charitable, benevolent, patient (3).

Tolerate, *v.* **1.** To allow something not wholly approved of. See permit (1), suffer (2), countenance (1). **2.** To endure. Stomach, sustain, swallow, brook, undergo, put up with, forbear, take. See also bear (2), suffer (3), stand (2).

Toleration, *n.* **1.** Open-mindedness. Lack of prejudice, liberality, generosity, magnanimity, compassion, milk of human kindness, impartiality, humanity, live and let live, altruism. See also benevolence, charity, mercy. **2.** See clemency, forbearance.

Toll 1. *n.* A sum of money paid for the use of something. See fee (1), tax (1), cost, price. **2.** *v.* To suspend or stop temporarily. See arrest (3), postpone (1), defer (1). **3.** *n.* Disruption. See damage (1).

Tomb, *n.* An excavation in the earth or a rock, intended to receive the dead body of a human. See grave (1).

Tome, *n.* See book (4).

Tomfoolery, *n.* See antic; juvenile; balderdash.

Tomorrow, *n.* See future; period, interval (1).

Ton, *n.* A measure of weight. In the United States, it is fixed at 2,000 pounds avoirdupois.

Tone, *n.* See climate (2); character, disposition (4); music.

Tongue, *n.* See language.

Tongue-in-cheek, *adj.* See facetious.

Tongue-lashing, *n.* See obloquy, censure, correction (1).

Tongue-tied, *adj.* See silent (1), quiet, passive, bashful.

Tonic, *n.* See medicine; beverage; ointment; remedial.

Tonight, *n.* See soon; now; period, interval (1).

Tonnage, *n.* The capacity of a vessel for carrying freight, calculated in tons.

Tontine, *n.* A financial arrangement whereby the participants share in a fund, with each participant's share increasing upon the death or default of another until the final survivor receives everything.

Tool, *n.* See apparatus, instrument, equipment, device (1), agency (4).

Toothless, *adj.* See weak, deficient; barren.

Top, *n., v., adj.* See apex, ceiling; best; outstanding (2), primary, chief (2).

Topaz, *n.* See gem.

Top-heavy, *adj.* Overcapitalized; precarious.

Topic, *n.* See issue (3), matter (1), question (2), proposition (2).

Topical, *adj.* See current, relevant; local, parochial.

Topnotch, *adj.* See best (1), exceptional, extraordinary, outstanding (2).

Topography, *n.* See description; map, outline.

Topple, *v.* See trip (2), flounder, tip (3), overrule, collapse, capsize.

Topsy-turvy, *adj.* See disorderly (3), wild, complex (1), confusion.

Torah, *n.* See bible, law, religion.

Torch, *n.* See light; fire, burn.

Torment, *n.,* **torment,** *v.* See distress (3), anxiety, depression (1), anguish, pain, affliction, annoyance; disturb, provoke, abuse, intimidate, menace, harass.

Tormentor, *n.* See tyrant, wrongdoer.

Torn, *adj., v.* See disheveled, ragged; tear.

Tornado, *n.* See storm, climate.

Torpedo, *n., v.* See weapon, arms; destroy, quash, abort (2).

Torpedo doctrine See attractive nuisance doctrine.

Torrens title system A system for registration of land under which, upon the landowner's application, a court issues a certificate of title that states the status of the title.

Torrent, *n.* See river; eruption, flood.

Torrential, *adj.* See wild, violent.

Torrid, *adj.* See ardent, hot (2), emotional.

Torso, *n.* See body (5), anatomy.

Tort, *n.* A civil (as opposed to criminal) wrong (other than a breach of contract) that has caused harm to person or property. See wrong, violation.

Tortfeasor, *n.* A person who has committed a tort. See wrongdoer.

Tortious, *adj.* Pertaining to an act that will subject the actor to tort liability. See wrongful, negligent, malicious, illegal, illicit.

Tortuous, *adj.* **1.** Not direct; having many bends or turns (tortuous reasoning). Twisting, winding, circuitous, labyrinthine, zigzag, roundabout, ambiguous, convoluted, indirect, serpentine, meandering, sinuous. **2.** See devious, fraudulent, immoral, corrupt.

Torture 1. *v.* To inflict intense pain in order to punish, to extract information, or to derive sadistic pleasure. See abuse (1), intimidate, harass, beat, batter. **2.** *n.* Great pain; brutality. See distress (3), anxiety, annoyance, depression (1), anguish; cruelty, affliction.

Torturous, *adj.* Causing severe abuse or cruelty; excruciating. See cruel, painful; severe, difficult, extreme, inexcusable, grievous.

Toss, *v.* See jettison (1).

Total 1. *adj.* Not divided; lacking no part. See whole, complete (2), entire, full, gross (2). **2.** *n.* Sum; the amount reached by adding everything up. See entirety, aggregate. **3.** *v.* See calculate.

Total disability A disability, whether temporary or permanent, that prevents the employee from doing the substantial and material acts required in his or her usual occupation. See disability.

Totalitarian, *adj.* See tyranny, coercion, oppression; absolute, arbitrary (2).

Totality, *n.* See sum, aggregate, entirety; whole; absolutely.

Tote, *v.* See carry (1).

Totten trust A tentative trust during the grantor's lifetime, revocable at will. A deposit of a person's own money in his or her own name as trustee for another. See trust.

Totter, *v.* See flounder, trip (2).

Touch, *v.* **1.** To use part of one's body to make contact with something or someone (touch the lense). Handle, rub, stroke, pet, manipulate, paw, finger, caress, feel, probe, press, slap, graze, hit, pick up, brush, massage, smack, fondle, trifle with, rap, impinge, pat. **2.** To border, meet, or converge (the buildings touched). See abut. **3.** See concern (1).

Touching, *adj.* **1.** Stimulating. Affecting, heartbreaking, emotional, tender, soul-stirring, stirring, pathetic, breathtaking, poignant, mournful, appealing, striking, rousing, exciting, sad, dramatic, sentimental. See also, moving (1), compelling, intriguing, attractive. **2.** See adjoining, continuous.

Touchstone, *n.* See criterion, measure.

Touchy, *adj.* See difficult (3), feverish, squeamish; controversial, debatable.

Tough, *adj.* See durable, healthy, able-bodied, firm, strong; difficult, inflexible, grievous, onerous; cruel, callous.

Toughen, *v.* See strengthen, augment, discipline (4).

Tour, *n., v.* See voyage, junket, travel, assignment.

Tour de force, *n.* See exploit (2), act (3).

Tourism, *n.* See travel, voyage, junket, amusement, entertainment.

Tourist, *n.* See traveler, guest.

Tournament, *n.* See contest, game, sport, athletics.

Tourniquet, *n.* A device to control the flow of blood. See treatment.

Tout, *v.* See promote, solicit, petition (2), apply, beseech.

Tow, *v.* To pull or drag. Transport, haul, lug, hoist, trail, tug, entrain, trawl, tote, convey. See also carry.

Towage, *n.* **1.** The towing of vehicles. **2.** The fee charged for towing. See charge (8).

Toward, *prep.* In the direction of. In line with, on the way, straight for.

Tower, *n.* See building.

Towering, *adj.* See tall, big, great, superior (2), extraordinary, outstanding (2).

To wit, *adv.* That is to say. Namely.

Town, *n.* A civil and political division of a state, usually part of a county. See municipality, community (1, 2), people (1), zone.

Town house, *n.* See home.

Toxic, *adj.* See poisonous; rotten.

Toxicant, *n.* A toxic agent. See poison (1).

Toxin, *n.* Any diffusible alkaloidal substance; the poisonous products of pathogenic bacteria. See poison (1).

Toy, *v., n.* See flirt, pretend; amusement, horseplay, antic, diversion, sport (2), game (1).

Trace 1. *v.* To make a copy or facsimile of an original by following its lines through a transparent medium (trace the design). Draw, reproduce, graph, chalk, delineate, depict, duplicate, sketch, diagram, outline, chart. **2.** *v.* To follow (trace the stolen check). Trail, track, chase, shadow, spy on, pursue, ferret out, unearth, scent, probe, search, tail, dog, hound. See also investigate. **3.** *n.* See clue, mark, manifestation, evidence, iota.

Tracing, *n.* See copy, imitation; trace.

Track, *v., n.* See chase, pursue (2), ferret, trace (2); passage (2), pass (8), course (1); clue.

Tract, *n.* **1.** A relatively large piece of land. See lot (1). **2.** A pamphlet. See book (4).

Tractable, *adj.* See malleable, flexible, amenable (2).

Traction, *n.* Friction, adhesion, resistance, tension, pull.

Tractor, *n.* See vehicle.

Trade 1. *n.* Buying and selling for profit. See commerce, business (1, 2), market (2), exchange (2). **2.** *n.* What one does for a living; a job requiring manual skills. See occupation (1), career, practice (4), employment. **3.** *v.* See exchange (1), barter.

Trade fixture Personal property supplied and used by tenants in business, which they have a right to remove. See fixture.

Trade libel See disparagement; slander.

Trademark, *n.* A distinctive mark, motto, device, or emblem that a manufacturer stamps, prints, or otherwise affixes to the goods it produces so that they may be identified in the market and distinguished from others. See mark, badge, manifestation, label, identification, slogan.

Trade name A name used in trade to designate a particular business. See name (1), mark, manifestation, badge, caption.

Trader, *n.* One in the business of buying and selling goods for a profit. See merchant, jobber, entrepreneur, retailer.

Trade school, *n.* See school; education.

Trade secret, *n.* A business formula, pattern, device, or compilation of information known only by certain individuals in the business and used as an advantage over competitors. See secret (2).

Tradesman, *n.* A mechanic, craftsman, or artificer of any kind whose livelihood depends primarily on manual labor. See artificer, artisan, employee, laborer.

Trade union, *n.* See union, organization.

Tradition, *n.* See convention (3), custom (1), practice (1), precedent (1), legend, institution (2), heritage.

Traditional, *adj.* Handed-down; historic. Ancestral, unwritten, classic, orthodox, sanctioned, prevalent. See also conventional (1), common, habitual, historic.

Traduce, *v.* See decry, disparage, defame, slander.

Traffic 1. *n.* The sale or exchange of merchandise, bills, money, etc. See commerce, business (1, 2), intercourse (1), market (2). **2.** *v.* To transact business. See deal (2). **3.** *n.* The subjects of transportation on a route; the passage or flow of people, goods, vehicles, etc. See pedestrian (1), passenger, vehicle (1), delivery, cargo, intercourse (1).

Trafficking, *n.* Trading and dealing, usually in illegal goods. Smuggling, bootlegging, drug dealing. See also graft, profiteering.

Tragedy, *n.* See catastrophe, calamity, disaster.

Tragic, *adj.* See fatal, adverse (2), bad (4), deleterious.

Trail 1. *n.* A path. See course (1), pass (8), passage (2). **2.** *v.* To follow or pursue. See trace (2), chase, pursue (2), ferret. **3.** *v.* To lag behind. Dawdle, straggle, follow, poke, wander, fizzle, fade, disappear. See also loiter. **4.** *n.* A footprint or scent. See mark.

Trailer, *n.* See vehicle.

Train, *v., n.* See prepare (1), educate, discipline (4), improve, nurture; direct (3), chain (1); vehicle.

Trainee, *n.* See student, amateur, beginner, intern; scholar.

Trainer, *n.* See teacher.

Training, *n.* See practice (3), education, discipline (1).

Trait, *n.* See characteristic, property (2), quality.

Traitor, *n.* One who betrays a trust; one who commits treason. Judas, betrayer, snake, double-dealer, Benedict Arnold, informer, fifth columnist, turncoat, deserter, conspirator, apostate, mutineer, renegade. See also revolutionary, insurgent (1), anarchist, wrongdoer.

Traitorous, *adj.* See disloyal, corrupt, false.

Trajectory, *n.* See course, pass (8), passage (2).

Trammel, *v.* See hinder, confine, entrap.

Tramp 1. *n.* One who roams about from place to place begging or living without any visible means of support. Vagrant, hobo, loiterer, vagabond, wanderer, derelict, gypsy, nomad, exile, pariah, outcast, bum, itinerant, beachcomber, floater, transient, panhandler. See also prostitute. **2.** *v.* To roam or wander. See walk.

Trample, *v.* See stamp (2), batter, beat, quash, injure, harass, abuse.

Trance, *n.* Detachment from one's surroundings. Daze, dream, reverie, catalepsy, sleep, lethargy. See also stupor.

Tranquil, *adj.* See patient (3), quiet (1, 2), cautious; composure.

Tranquilize, *v.* See ease (2), mitigate, stabilize, assuage.

Tranquilizer, *n.* See drug, medicine, treatment.

Tranquillity, *n.* See peace, harmony, composure.

Transact, *v.* To have dealings (transact business). Carry on, bring about, negotiate, bring into existence, carry through, conduct, proceed, render, operate, execute, accomplish, prosecute, enact, exact, handle, achieve, manage, realize, administer, treat, exercise, practice, come to terms.

Transaction, *n.* The act of conducting something; that which is done or conducted. See event, occurrence, performance (1), deal (1), operation (1), activity, act (3), enterprise (1); transact.

Transactional immunity Absolute protection against prosecution for any event or transaction about which a witness is compelled to give testimony or furnish evidence. Immunity from prosecution for offenses to which compelled testimony relates. See use and derivative use immunity.

Transcend, *v.* See exceed, pass (3); beat (2).

Transcendent, *adj.* See extraordinary, exceptional, outstanding (2); anomalous; religious; incorporeal, intangible.

Transcribe, *v.* See record (1); copy; translate, interpret; transcript.

Transcript, *n.* That which has been written out or typed, such as from shorthand; a copy; a writing made from the original. See copy (1), record (2), duplicate (2).

Transcription, *n.* See transcript.

Transfer, *v.*, **transfer,** *n.* **1.** *v.* To convey or remove from one place or person to another (transfer title). Deliver, transport, send, deed, donate, give, assign, grant, pass, carry, delegate, cede, transmit, transplant, shift, consign, relegate, transpose, forward, devise, bequeath, will, lease, let, ship, relocate, displace. **2.** *n.* A delivery or conveyance. See delivery, assignment (1, 2), exchange (2), removal.

Transferable, *adj.* Pertaining to that which may pass with the rights of the original owner. Assignable, negotiable, transmissible; contagious.

Transferee, *n.* One to whom a transfer is made. See donee, beneficiary.

Transferor, *n.* One who makes a transfer. See donor.

Transferred intent 1. The defendant intends to commit acts that would constitute one intentional tort (e.g., assault), but in fact commits another intentional tort (e.g., battery). The law will conclude that the defendant had the intent to commit the latter tort. **2.** The defendant intended to commit an intentional tort against one person, but in fact the tort is committed against another person. The law will conclude that the defendant had the intent needed to commit the tort against the latter person.

Transfer tax A tax on the transfer of property (e.g., bonds, stock) between living persons. See tax.

Transfigure, *v.* See transform.

Transform, *v.* See change (2), modify (1), alter, convert.

Transformation, *n.* See change (1), modification, conversion (2), amendment.

Transfuse, *v.* See imbue, fill, inundate; medicine, treatment.

Transgress, *v.* See encroach, interfere, break (1); attack (1), assault (3); hinder, impede.

Transgression, *n.* See violation, intrusion, invasion, infraction, offense, wrong, lapse.

Transient 1. *adj.* Passing, momentary, or transitory. See brief (4), itinerant, temporary, provisional. **2.** *n.* One who wanders from place to place. See tramp (1), lodger.

Transit, *n.* Movement from one location to another. See move (4), carriage (1), removal (1), migration, delivery, passage (3).

Transition, *n.* See passage (3); change (1), modification, conversion (2), amendment, move (4); connection, link.

Transitional, *adj.* See provisional, temporary, acting, interim.

Transitory, *adj.* **1.** Pertaining to that which may pass or be changed from one place to another. Nonlocal. See also migratory, itinerant. **2.** Ephemeral, momentary, transient, or fleeting. See brief (4), temporary.

Transitory action A lawsuit that may be brought in one of several places. See action (1). *Ant.* Local action.

Translate, *v.* **1.** To reproduce a text from one language into another. Convert, decode, decipher. **2.** To explain. See interpret, construe. **3.** See change (2), modify (1), convert, alter.

Translation, *n.* See construction (1); transcript.

Transmigrate, *v.* See move (2), enter, depart, leave, flee; immigration, emigration.

Transmission, *n.* **1.** The act of sending or conveying. Transfer, passage, conveyance, transportation, broadcast, transference, passing, dispatch, forwarding. See also communication. **2.** A system in a car for transmitting power from the engine to the driving axle and wheels.

Transmit, *v.* To send or transfer from one person or place to another. See transfer (1), send, issue (1), communicate.

Transmitter, *n.* See instrument (2), equipment, apparatus, device.

Transmute, *v.* See change, alter, modify (1), convert.

Transnational, *adj.* See international, world.

Transparent, *adj.* See clear (1), definite (1), intelligible, manifest, palpable, comprehensible.

Transpire, *v.* See occur, arise (1), result (2).

Transplant, *v.* See transfer, move (2), enter, depart, leave; change, alter.

Transport, *v.,* **transport,** *n.* **1.** *v.* To carry or convey from one place to another. See carry (1), transfer (1), send, issue (1), communicate; banishment. **2.** *n.* A ship or aircraft. See vehicle (1).

Transportation, *n.* The movement of goods or persons from one place to another by a carrier. See move (4), carriage (1), removal (1), migration, delivery; exile (1).

Transpose, *v.* See alternate, turn (1), transfer, reverse; inverse, opposite.

Transsexual, *n.* A person whose sex has been surgically changed; one who desires to become a member of the opposite sex.

Trap 1. *n.* A device to catch a person or animal unawares. See artifice, device (1, 2), bait. **2.** *v.* To catch, snare, or trick. See cheat (1), deceive, entrap.

Trappings, *n.* See decoration, equipment, apparatus, device, apparel.

Trash, *n.* See refuse; balderdash; prostitute.

Trashy, *adj.* See gaudy, flamboyant; inferior, base, obscene, filthy.

Trauma, *n.* A physical injury caused by a blow or fall; a psychologically damaging emotional experience. See injury, shock (1), pain, wound, contusion, lesion, cut.

Traumatic, *adj.* **1.** Caused by or resulting from a wound or any external injury. **2.** Shocking. Startling, crippling, bewildering, perplexing, disorienting, scarring, wounding, disabling, upsetting.

Traumatize, *v.* See wound (1), injure; outrage (2), disturb.

Travail, *n.* **1.** Arduous work. See labor (2), slavery, cruelty, hardship. **2.** The act of childbearing. See birth (1).

Travel, *v.* To go from one place to another; to journey. Tour, junket, trek, globetrot, hitchhike, roam, cruise, traverse, commute, proceed, jaunt, advance, pass through, sightsee, emigrate, go. See also sail, wander, walk, visit; migration, voyage.

Traveler, *n.* One who passes from place to place. Voyager, hiker, nomad, migrant, vacationer, tripper, vagabond, gypsy, wayfarer, adventurer, drummer, globetrotter, commuter, hobo. See also tramp; itinerant.

Traveler's check, *n.* An instrument purchased from a bank, express company, etc., in various denominations, which can be used as cash upon the second signature by the purchaser.

Traverse, *n.,* **traverse,** *v.* **1.** *n.* A denial of material facts stated in an adverse pleading. See denial (1). **2.** *v.* To reject or contest. See deny. **3.** *v.* To pass from point to point. See travel, pass (4), sail, walk. **4.** *v.* To scrutinize. See investigate, observe (3); examination.

Travesty, *n.* See caricature, slander, deception, fraud, falsehood, error.

Treacherous, *adj.* See dangerous, precarious, hazardous, deceptive, insecure; disloyal, corrupt, mutinous, insurgent (2).

Treachery, *n.* Deliberate and willful betrayal of trust and confidence. See betrayal, fraud, corruption; disloyal.

Tread, *v.* See walk, stamp (2), quash, batter, beat.

Treason, *n.* Attempting by overt acts to overthrow the government of the state to which the offender owes allegiance; betraying the state into the hands of a foreign power; rendering aid and comfort to the enemy. A stab in the back. See betrayal, revolt (1), rebellion, insubordination, defiance, apostasy, mutiny; traitor.

Treasonable, *adj.* See insurgent (2), mutinous, disloyal, corrupt.

Treasure 1. *n.* Hidden or stored riches. See wealth. **2.** *v.* To cherish or venerate. Prize, esteem, consider precious, revere, hold dear, adore, appreciate, love.

Treasurer, *n.* An officer of an organization with responsibility over the receipt, custody, and disbursement of moneys or funds. Bursar, cashier, exchequer, teller, purser, depositary. See also controller, accountant, officer.

Treasure-trove, *n.* Money or precious metals found hidden in a private place. See windfall.

Treasury, *n.* **1.** A place or building in which revenues or wealth is stored; the agency charged with the receipt, custody, and disbursement of revenue or funds. See depository. **2.** Money or resources. See wealth, property (1), asset (1), fund (2).

Treasury bill Short-term obligations of the U.S. government. See securities.

Treasury stock Stock issued as fully paid to stockholders, and reacquired by the corporation.

Treat, *v., n.* See act (5), perform, manage, consider (2); minister (3), nurture, cure (2); enjoyment, satisfaction (2), happiness.

Treatise, *n.* See book (4), report, speech (2).

Treatment, *n.* All the steps taken to effect a cure of an injury or disease. Therapy, hospitalization, operation, medication, medical care, doctoring, regimen, first aid, nursing, antidote, prescription; ministry, handling, manipulation, management, application, behavior. See also process, procedure, medicine, surgery; doctor.

Treaty, *n.* A compact made between two or more nations. See compact (1).

Treble damages Damages tripled in amount. See damages.

Tree, *n.* See timber, woods, shrubbery.

Trek, *n., v.* See migration, voyage, wander, travel, walk.

Tremble, *v.* See beat (3); flounder.

Tremendous, *adj.* See great (2), outstanding, attractive, extraordinary, big, awesome.

Tremor, *n.* A vibration or trembling. See shock (1), fit.

Trench, *n.* A furrow or ditch. Excavation, fortification, ridge, dugout, tunnel, fosse, groove. See also conduit, course, cave, cell, mine.

Trenchant, *adj.* See effective, acute (1); clear (1), definite (1), palpable, direct (6); caustic, cutting, biting, malicious, offensive.

Trend, *n.* See style (3), direction (3), mode, pattern, bias.

Trendy, *adj.* See chic, current (3).

Trepidation, *n.* See fear, apprehension, anxiety, anguish.

Trespass 1. *n.* An unlawful interference with a person's property or rights. See trespass to land, trespass to chattels; infringement, intrusion, violation, invasion, wrong (1). **2.** *v.* See interfere, break (1), encroach; enter (2); attack (1), assault (3); hinder, impede.

Trespass ab initio A trespass from the beginning even though the entry was initially lawful. A subsequent wrong relates back and makes a previously innocent act unlawful.

Trespass de bonis asportatis See de bonis asportatis.

Trespasser, *n.* One who commits a trespass. Invader, gatecrasher. See also intruder, interloper, wrongdoer.

Trespass on the case See action on the case.

Trespass quare clausum fregit A common-law action for damages for an unlawful entry or trespass upon the plaintiff's land. "Trespass wherefore he broke the close."

Trespass to chattels A tort with the following elements: (a) personal property—chattel, (b) plaintiff is in possession of the chattel or is entitled to immediate possession, (c) intent to dispossess or to intermeddle with the chattel, (d) dispossession, impairment, or deprivation of use for a substantial time, (e) causation of the dispossession, impairment, or deprivation.

Trespass to land A tort with the following elements: (a) an act, (b) intrusion on land, (c) in possession of another, (d) intent to intrude, (e) causation of the intrusion. There are four kinds of intrusion covered: physically going on the land, remaining on the land, going to a prohibited part of the land, or failing to remove goods from the land.

Trespass vi et armis Trespass with force and arms. The common-law action for any injury committed by the defendant with direct and immediate force or violence against the person or property of the plaintiff.

Trial, *n.* **1.** A judicial examination and determination of issues between adverse parties. See hearing, action (1), contest (2). **2.** A test or evaluation. See inspection, examination, assessment (3), appraisal. **3.** Misfortune. See affliction, burden, hardship, ordeal (1).

Trial balance, *n.* A listing of debit and credit balances of all ledger accounts. See account, balance.

Trial brief A collection of all the documents, arguments, and strategies that an attorney plans to use at trial. A trial manual or trial book.

Trial by fire See ordeal (1).

Trial court A court of original jurisdiction; the first court to consider the litigation. See court.

Trial de novo A new trial where the whole case is retried as if no trial had taken place in the first instance.

Tribal, *adj.* See native, aboriginal; wild.

Tribal lands Lands within the boundaries of an Indian reservation held in trust by the federal government for the Indian tribe as a community. *Ant.* See allotment

(2).

Tribe, *n.* See family, group, kindred.

Tribulation, *n.* See anguish, anxiety, pain, affliction, hardship, depression, misfortune.

Tribunal, *n.* The place where a judge administers justice. See court (1).

Tributary, *n.* Any stream flowing directly or indirectly into a river. See river.

Tribute, *n.* **1.** Money paid by subjects to sustain the expenses of the estate. See tax (1). **2.** Praise or celebration. Eulogy, gratitude, acknowledgment, testimonial, respect, commendation, laudation, panegyric, memorial, award, kudos.

Trick, *v., n.* See deceive, betray, cheat; fraud, artifice, duplicity, deception, machination, contrivance.

Trickle, *v.* To move, flow, or fall slowly. Leak, squint, ooze, seep, dribble, pass. See also emit (2).

Tricky, *adj.* See difficult, debatable, complex; deceptive, clandestine, illicit, corrupt (1), collusive, fraudulent.

Tricycle, *n.* See vehicle.

Trident, *n.* See weapon, arms.

Tried, *adj.* See reliable, certain; attempt.

Trier of fact The jury. If there is no jury, the trier of fact is the trial judge. See jury, judge.

Trifle, *v., n.* See flirt; loiter; babble; trivia, red tape; iota, scintilla.

Trifling, *adj.* See petty (2), frivolous, nugatory, de minimis, minor (2).

Trifurcated, *adj.* Divided into three parts.

Trigger, *v.* See provoke, cause, incite, prompt (2).

Trigger-happy, *adj.* See hot, violent, feverish, deadly.

Trim, *v.* See cut, abridge; beautify, adjust, beat.

Trimester, *n.* Three-month periods; three academic semesters. See term.

Trimonthly, *adj.* Occurring every three months.

Trinity, *n.* A group of three. Trio, triangle, triad, threesome, triumvirate. See also group; God, religion.

Trio, *n.* See trinity, group.

Trip **1.** *n.* A journey or going from one place to another. See voyage; travel. **2.** *v.* To stumble. Fall, drop, misstep, topple, totter, lurch, slip, flop, sprawl, throw off balance, lose one's footing; miss, err, blunder. See also flounder.

Tripartite, *adj.* In three parts.

Tripe, *n.* See balderdash, refuse.

Triple, *adj.* See trinity.

Trite, *adj.* See commonplace (2), ordinary (2), pedestrian (2).

Triumph, *v., n.* See conquer, beat (2), overcome, best, exceed; supremacy, dominion; celebration; boast.

Triumphant, *adj.* See ardent, emotional, active (3), earnest (2), happy, great, extraordinary, champion.

Trivia, *n.* Useless details. Minutiae, pettiness, irrelevancies, trifles, side matters. See also red tape.

Trivial, *adj.* Of small worth or importance. See petty (2), frivolous, nugatory, incidental, commonplace.

Triviality, *n.* See trivia.

Trivialize, *v.* See debase, abase, defile, diminish.

TRO See temporary restraining order.

Trolley, *n.* See vehicle.

Trollop, *n.* See prostitute.

Troop, *n.* See military, sailor; group, division, company (2).

Trooper, *n.* See police, officer.

Trophy, *n.* A token or memento of victory. Prize, laurels, wreath, souvenir, ribbon, citation, honor, testimonial, relic, medal, cup. See also plunder (2); memento.

Tropical, *adj.* See muggy, hot; zone.

Trot, *v.* See run.

Troth, *n.* See faith.

Trouble, *n., v.* See plight, affliction, ordeal, pain, distress (3), misfortune, hardship, dilemma, emergency, conundrum, crisis, commotion, fight, riot; concern (2), burden (2, 3).

Troublemaker, *n.* See delinquent (3), wrongdoer.

Troublesome, *adj.* See distressing, offensive, difficult, complex (1), mysterious, painful, onerous, delinquent.

Trounce, *v.* See beat, batter, best (2), defeat.

Troupe, *n.* See group (1), company (2).

Trousers, *n.* See apparel, clothes.

Trousseau, *n.* See apparel, clothes; marriage, nuptial.

Trove, *n.* See treasure-trove.

Trover, *n.* A common-law action for the recovery of damages against a person who wrongfully interferes with, detains, or converts the goods of another. See conversion, trespass to chattels.

Truancy, *n.* See absence (1); delinquency.

Truant 1. *n.* One who willfully and unjustifiedly fails to attend school as required. Delinquent, absentee, evader, shirker, dodger, deserter, vagrant, goldbrick, "goof-off," idler, procrastinator; AWOL, absent without leave. See also derelict (3), wrongdoer, juvenile (1). **2.** *adj.* Lazy, neglectful, shiftless, unemployed, and apathetic. See derelict (2), juvenile (2).

Truce, *n.* A suspension or temporary cessation of hostilities; a cease-fire. See respite, reprieve, interruption, abeyance, compact (1), accommodation (2), cessation.

Truck, *n., v.* See vehicle; carry; exchange, barter, sell.

Truculent, *adj.* See cruel, deadly, violent, predatory, hostile, belligerent.

Trudge, *v.* See walk.

True, *adj.* **1.** Conformable to fact or to the actual state of things. See correct (1), accurate, credible, authentic, empirical, real, faithful (2), honest. **2.** Sincere and trustworthy. See faithful (1), loyal, reliable.

True bill, *n.* An endorsement made by a grand jury upon a bill of indictment when they are satisfied of the truth of the accusation and find sufficient evidence to warrant a criminal charge. See indictment.

True value The market value of the property at a fair and bona fide sale at private contract; the value of property in exchange for money. See market value.

Truism, *n.* See maxim, cliché, fact.

Trumpet, *v.* See promote, circulate, publish, yell; music.

Truncate, *v.* See curtail, cut, abridge.

Trunk, *n.* See vessel (2); package; baggage.

Trust 1. *n.* A right of property, real or personal, held by one party (the trustee) for the benefit of another (the beneficiary or cestui que trust). The creator of this right is the settlor. (A trust set up for her daughter). **2.** *n.* Reliance on the honesty or integrity of someone (a relationship of trust). See faith (1), confidence (1). **3.** *n.* An association of persons or companies having the intention and power, or the tendency to create a monopoly or otherwise to interfere with the free course of trade or transportation. See monopoly, pool (2), association (1). **4.**

Trust

n. Custody, care, and guardianship (the orphan was left in his trust). See custody (1). **5.** *n.* Responsibility (a public trust). See duty (1). **6.** *v.* To depend on (he trusted the report). Swear by, rely, believe in, count on, accept, take for granted, expect, have faith in, credit, accredit, subscribe to, turn to; hope, anticipate, foresee, envision, reckon, calculate. **7.** *v.* See entrust.

Trust company, *n.* A company formed for the purpose of accepting trusts committed to it and acting as trustee, executor, guardian, etc. See company, business.

Trust deed The deed by which one creates a trust or transfers property to a trust. See deed.

Trustee, *n.* The person or company holding property in trust. See fiduciary (1), guardian, custodian, agent (1).

Trust fund, *n.* A fund that is devoted to a particular purpose and cannot or should not be diverted therefrom. See fund.

Trust fund theory The imposition of fiduciary obligations. Officers, directors, or stockholders of a corporation that is going out of business will be treated as holding in trust for the benefit of creditors those corporate assets that have been improperly distributed or appropriated.

Trust indenture The document that contains the terms and conditions that govern the conduct of the trustee and the rights of the beneficiaries.

Trustor, *n.* See settlor.

Trust territory, *n.* A territory or colony placed under the administration of a country by the United Nations. See territory, zone.

Trustworthy, *adj.* See dependable, reliable, incorruptible, blameless, innocent (1), loyal.

Trusty, *n.* A prisoner who, because of good conduct, is given some measure of freedom in or around the prison, or responsibility over other inmates.

Truth, *n.* **1.** Agreement of thought and reality; eventual verification. See verity, fact, principle (1). **2.** Integrity. See honor (3), principle (2).

Truthful, *adj.* See accurate, authentic, credible, correct, honest, empirical, faithful, reliable, dependable, incorruptible, loyal.

Truth-in-lending Meaningful information provided to the consumer on the cost or other terms of credit. See disclosure.

Try 1. *v.* To examine judicially. See judge (2, 3), adjudicate. **2.** *v.* To undertake, put forth, or venture. See attempt (3), aim (2). **3.** *n.* An endeavor, turn, or effort. See attempt (2).

Trying, *adj.* See onerous, difficult, inconvenient, severe, extreme.

Tryout, *n.* See hearing, attempt.

Tryst, *n.* See adultery, meeting (3), affairs, infidelity, coitus.

Tub, *n.* See vessel (2).

Tube, *n.* See conduit; vessel (2).

Tug, *v.* See tow.

Tugboat, *n.* See vessel (1).

Tuition, *n.* See cost, charge (8), education, school.

Tumble, *v.* See fall; athletics.

Tumor, *n.* See disease, illness.

Tumult, *n.* See commotion, eruption, riot, hysteria, disorder, confusion.

Tumultuous, *adj.* See disorderly, noisy, wild, violent.

Tune, *n.* See music, harmony; lyric.

Tunnel, *n.* See passage (2), conduit, course.

Tunnel vision, *n.* See narrow (2), parochial, petty (3), partisan, blind, arbitrary.

Turbulence, *n.* See commotion, eruption, riot, violence, hysteria, disorder, confusion.

Turbulent, *adj.* See disorderly, noisy, wild, violent, mutinous, insurgent (2), hostile.

Turf, *n.* Grass. Sod, lawn, grassland, verdure, meadow, pasture; racetrack. See also neighborhood.

Turgid, *adj.* See pompous, arrogant, flamboyant, gaudy.

Turmoil, *n.* See commotion, eruption, riot, hysteria, disorder, confusion.

Turn 1. *v.* To spin or rotate (turn the knob). Swivel, shift, curve, reverse, roll over, gyrate, bend, invert, wheel, grind, twiddle, revolve, upend, zigzag, flex, deform, circle, overturn, transpose. **2.** *v.* To alter or convert (turn the solid into a liquid). Transform, mutate, change, recast, transmute, metamorphose, reconstruct, vary, reshape. **3.** *n.* An opportunity. See attempt (2), chance (4).

Turncoat, *n.* One who changes sides. See traitor.

Turning point, *n.* See determinant, crisis.

Turnkey, *n.* One who has responsibility over the keys in a prison or institution. See watchman.

Turn-key contract A contract or job in which the contractor agrees to do all the work, assume all the risk, and turn over a finished product so that nothing further need be done except "turn the key" and unlock the building or other structure for use.

Turnover, *n.* See reversal; inventory, sale.

Turnpike, *n.* See highway, pass (8), passage (2).

Turntable doctrine See attractive nuisance doctrine.

Turpitude, *n.* Inherent baseness, vileness, or depravity. See moral turpitude, corruption, violation, wrong (1), fault, debauchery, delinquency, ignominy, lapse (3).

Tussle, *n.* See contest, fight.

Tutelage, *n.* The state of being under a guardian; guardianship. See protection, direction (2), custody.

Tutor 1. *n.* One who instructs. See teacher. **2.** *v.* To train. See discipline (4), educate, instruct, improve.

T.V.A. See Tennessee Valley Authority.

Twice, *adv.* See double; two.

Twilight, *n.* See evening, sunset, nighttime; collapse.

Twin, *adj.* See double; two.

Twirl, *v.* See twist, alternate, turn (1); circulate.

Twist, *v.* **1.** To wind or interlace. Swathe, entwine, coil, wrap, knot, pivot, tangle, roll, wreathe, writhe, braid. See also turn (1), alternate, circulate. **2.** To disfigure or contort. See distort, misrepresent.

Twister, *n.* See storm.

Twitch, *v.* See beat (3).

Two, *n.* A pair. Couple, set, couplet, twosome; binary, both. See also double.

Two-faced, *adj.* See false, fake, dishonest, feigned, deceitful, deceptive, artificial, disloyal, corrupt, mutinous.

Tycoon, *n.* See entrepreneur, owner, manager, employer, master, chief (1).

Tying arrangement A person agrees to sell one product, the "tying product," only on the condition that the vendee also purchase another product, the "tied product."

Tyke, *n.* See child, juvenile; wrongdoer.

Type, *n.* See kind (1), model, class, measure, criterion.

Typhoon, *n.* See storm.

Typical, *adj.* See characteristic, representative, average (2), common, regular, habitual, conventional (1), ordinary (1).

Typify, *v.* See represent (3), mean (2).

Typist

Typist, *n.* See clerk (2), laborer, employee; clerical (2).

Tyrannical, *adj.* See arbitrary, absolute (1), cruel, severe, unreasonable.

Tyrannize, *v.* See intimidate, harass, abuse (1), hurt, menace, disturb.

Tyranny, *n.* Autocratic or despotic government; reign of terror. Absolutism, autocracy, dictatorship, despotism, iron rule. See also cruelty, coercion, oppression.

Tyrant, *n.* A ruler, legitimate or otherwise, who uses his or her power unjustly and arbitrarily. Despot, overlord, autocrat, czar, dictator, fascist, slave driver, sadist, bully, persecutor, inquisitor, Big Brother, authoritarian boss. See also oppressor, sovereign (2), head.

Ubiquitous, *adj.* Appearing to be everywhere at once. Omnipresent, pervading, ever-present, widespread, worldwide, prevalent. See also predominant, great, comprehensive, universal.

U.C.C. See Uniform Commercial Code.

U.C.C.C. See Uniform Consumer Credit Code.

U.C.M.J. See Uniform Code of Military Justice.

Ugly, *adj.* See homely; odious, corrupt.

Ukase, *n.* An official decree or proclamation. See law.

Ulterior, *adj.* Beyond what is seen; intentionally kept secret (ulterior motive). See hidden, clandestine.

Ultimate 1. *adj.* Basic. See essential, intrinsic, primary, fundamental. **2.** *adj.* Coming at the end. See final, definitive, conclusive. **3.** *adj.* Highest or greatest. See predominant, best, primary, maximum. **4.** *adj.* Outermost. See extreme (2). **5.** *n.* The peak. See apex, perfection. **6.** *n.* The utmost edge. See extreme (3).

Ultimate facts Facts essential to a cause of action or a defense; the facts on which the ultimate decision rests. See fact.

Ultimatum, *n.* The final demand or proposal made by a negotiator. See threat (1), blackmail, warning, requirement, condition (1).

Ultra, *adj., pref.* See extreme (1, 2), excess.

Ultraconservative, *adj.* See conservative, narrow (2), reactionary, extreme.

Ultrafiche, *n.* See microfiche.

Ultrahazardous, *adj.* See extrahazardous, dangerous, precarious, hazardous.

Ultramodern, *adj.* See chic, current (3); avant-garde.

Ultra vires Beyond the scope of the powers of a corporation, as defined by its charter or state law. See illegal, illicit, improper.

Umbrage, *n.* See pain, dissatisfaction, annoyance, offense.

Umbrella, *n.* See protection; awning.

Umpire, *n.* A third party who arbitrates disputes. See judge (1).

Unabashed, *adj.* See public (3).

Unable, *adj.* Without the power, skill, or credential (unable to appear). Helpless, powerless, incapable, incompetent, unsuitable, unfit, impotent; weak, inept, ineffective, inoperative. *Ant.* Capable.

Unabridged, *adj.* See complete (2), entire, full.

Unacceptable, *adj.* See inadmissible, ineligible, invalid (1), inexcusable, imperfect, inferior (2), repugnant (1).

Unaccessible, *adj.* See hidden, privileged.

Unaccommodating, *adj.* See difficult (1), incompatible (1).

Unaccompanied, *adj.* See bare (1), solitary.

Unaccountable, *adj.* See mysterious, privileged.

Unaccrued, *adj.* Not become due.

Unachievable, *adj.* See impossible, impracticable.

Unadorned, *adj.* See bare (1), mere, naked (2).

Unadulterated, *adj.* See natural (5), raw (2), real (2), literal (1), genuine, clean (2), honest, mere.

Unaffected, *adj.* See neutral, immune, chaste (3), natural (5), uneducated.

Unaffiliated, *adj.* See independent, separate, alien (2).

Unafraid, *adj.* See courageous.

Unalienable, *adj.* Not to be divided or separated. See inalienable, fixed; inviolability.

Unallowed, *adj.* See inadmissible, illegal, improper, inexcusable.

Unalterable, *adj.* See final, certain (3), inflexible, inevitable, indestructible, peremptory (1), irreconcilable.

Unaltered, *adj.* See natural (2), permanent.

Unambiguous, *adj.* Susceptible of but one meaning. See clear (1), definite (1), direct (6), manifest (1), palpable, precise (1), comprehensible, intelligible.

Unambiguously, *adv.* See clearly.

Unanimity, *n.* Agreement of all persons concerned. See harmony, accord (2), concert, concurrence, consensus.

Unanimous, *adj.* All in agreement; no one voting in the negative (unanimous approval). United, consonant, agreed, with one voice, uniform, harmonious, of one mind, solid, accordant. See also concurrent (2). *Ant.* Discordant.

Unannounced, *adj.* See sudden.

Unanticipated, *adj.* See sudden, fortuitous, precipitate (3); improbable.

Unappealable, *adj.* See final (1).

Unappetizing, *adj.* See offensive, odious, repugnant (1), repulsive.

Unarguable, *adj.* See conclusive.

Unarmed, *adj.* See defenseless.

Unarranged, *adj.* See casual (1).

Unarticulated, *adj.* See silent (2).

Unascertained, *adj.* Not certainly known or determined. See ambiguous.

Unassailable, *adj.* See certain (3), clear (1), safe (2), inalienable, incontestable, definitive, conclusive.

Unassertive, *adj.* See passive (2), silent (1).

Unassisted, *adj.* See alone.

Unassociated, *adj.* See separate (1), individual.

Unassuming, *adj.* See bashful, backward (2), ordinary.

Unattached, *adj.* See individual (1), single (2), sole, separate, solitary.

Unattainable, *adj.* See impossible, impracticable.

Unattended, *adj.* See unattached.

Unattractive, *adj.* See homely.

Unauthorized, *adj.* Done without authority; wrongful, unjustified, or unconstitutional. See ultra vires, illegal, wrong (2), improper, criminal, lawless, informal.

Unavailable, *adj.* Not available; dead, insane, or beyond reach of a summons. See frozen.

Unavailing, *adj.* See nugatory; needless.

Una voce, *adj., adv.* Without dissent; with one voice. See unanimous.

Unavoidable, *adj.* Incapable of being prevented. See inevitable, inescapable, act of God, necessary, imperative, compulsory, obligatory, compelling, fortuitous, peremptory (1), conclusive, accidental (1), irrevocable, mandatory; imminent.

Unavoidable accident See inevitable accident, act of God, accident.

Unaware, *adj.* See oblivious, blind (1); uneducated, ignorance.

Unbalanced, *adj.* See partisan (2), one-sided, partial (2); inconsistent (2), insecure (1), paranoid, lunatic (2), mental (2).

Unbar, *v.* See open (1, 4).

Unbearable, *adj.* See painful, grievous (1), odious, offensive, inexcusable.

Unbecoming, *adj.* See improper.

Unbelievable, *adj.* See impossible; extraordinary.

Unbending, *adj.* See inflexible.

Unbent, *adj.* See straight (2).

Unbiased, *adj.* See dispassionate, neutral, fair, equitable (1), equal (1), impartial, objective (2), open (7), just, honest, indifferent, liberal (2).

Unbind, *v.* See release (1), clear (5).

Unblemished, *adj.* See clean (1), perfect (2), blameless, incorruptible, innocent (1), inviolate.

Unborn, *adj.* Pertaining to human life in existence from fertilization till birth. See future, prenatal.

Unbounded, *adj.* See open-ended.

Unbreakable, *adj.* See indestructible, indivisible.

Unbridled, *adj.* See lawless (2); independent, clear (2), high (1).

Unbroken, *adj.* See continuous, continual, consecutive, permanent, whole (1), complete (2), entire, constant (1), direct (4), inviolate, round (1), flat, standing (3).

Unburden, *v.* See confide, release (1).

Unburdened, *adj.* See clear (2).

Uncalculating, *adj.* See innocent; reckless, precipitate (2).

Uncalled-for, *adj.* See gratuitous (2), frivolous, baseless, needless, unconscionable.

Uncanny, *adj.* See mysterious, odd.

Uncaring, *adj.* See callous, careless.

Unceasing, *adj.* See chronic, regular (1), constant (1), unlimited.

Unceremonious, *adj.* See informal.

Uncertain, *adj.* Unknown or vague. See mysterious, indeterminate, indefinite, tentative (2), doubtful (1), obscure (1), disputable, improbable, shifting, equivocal, debatable, insecure (2), hypothetical, contingent, capricious, casual (1), precarious, dangerous.

Uncertainty, *n.* See doubt (2), question (3), reservation (3), confusion (2); jeopardy, risk, danger, hazard, peril.

Unchain, *v.* See liberate, discharge (3), release (1), clear (5).

Unchained, *adj.* See free (1).

Unchallenged, *adj.* See consensual.

Unchangeable, *adj.* See final (1), certain (3).

Unchanged, *adj.* See regular (1).

Unchanging, *adj.* See durable, immemorial, permanent, standing.

Uncharacteristic, *adj.* See irregular, foreign (3), novel.

Uncharitable, *adj.* See narrow (2), cruel.

Uncharted, *adj.* See new.

Unchaste, *adj.* Impure in mind and conduct. See obscene, incontinent (1); infidelity.

Unchecked, *adj.* See dissolute, lawless (2), clear (2), independent, unlimited.

Uncivil, *adj.* See rude, impertinent (2), disorderly (1), indecent, contemptuous.

Uncivilized, *adj.* See lawless (2), rude, gross.

Unclaimed, *adj.* See derelict (1).

Unclean, *adj.* Dirty. Soiled, defiled, sooty, unwashed, infected, littered, unhealthy, smeared, impure, adulterated, putrid, slimy, unsanitary, noxious, stained, fouled. See also obscene, lascivious, immoral, corrupt (1), dirty, filthy, foul, rotten, repugnant, repulsive.

Unclean hands doctrine A court should not grant relief to a plaintiff who is a wrongdoer (e.g., through fraud, bad faith, or other misconduct) with respect to the subject matter in the suit.

Unclear, *adj.* See ambiguous, indefinite, indeterminate, difficult (1).

Unclog, *v.* See open.

Unclouded

Unclouded, *adj.* See clear (2), manifest.

Uncollected, *adj.* See outstanding (1).

Uncolored, *adj.* See honest, objective (2), impartial.

Uncomfortable, *adj.* See bashful, backward, awkward, insecure.

Uncommon, *adj.* See special (1), novel, exceptional, extraordinary, particular (1), specific, individual (1), odd (1), choice (3).

Uncommunicative, *adj.* See mute, silent (1), backward (2).

Uncompensated, *adj.* See gratuitous (1).

Uncomplicate, *v.* See facilitate.

Uncomplicated, *adj.* See simple (2), clear (1), ministerial.

Uncomplimentary, *adj.* See critical (2), rude.

Uncompromising, *adj.* See inflexible, draconian, strict (2), precise (2), particular (2), close (5), patient (2), irreconcilable.

Unconcealed, *adj.* See overt, obvious.

Unconcern, *n.* See indifference, neglect (2).

Unconcerned, *adj.* See indifferent; careless; content (2).

Unconditional, *adj.* See absolute, comprehensive, unlimited, outright, express, explicit, categorical, precise, definitive, binding, decisive, individual (1), peremptory (1).

Unconditional discharge A release without any terms or conditions attached.

Unconfined, *adj.* See open-ended, unlimited.

Unconfirmed, *adj.* See speculative, inconclusive.

Unconnected, *adj.* See distinct (2), outside (3), discrete, alien (2), collateral (2), irrelevant.

Unconscionable, *adj.* So one-sided as to be oppressive and unfair (unconscionable contract). Excessive, unreasonable, preposterous, exorbitant, unscrupulous, corrupt, monstrous, criminal, dishonorable, scheming, unethical, amoral, perverse, unjustifiable, inexcusable, undue, uncalled-for, shameless, overbearing, unequal, inordinate. See also immoderate, extreme (1), immoral, one-sided.

Unconscious, *adj.* Unaware of one's acts; not possessed of mind. See oblivious, involuntary, blind; natural (5); ignorance; mind (1).

Unconstitutional, *adj.* Contrary to the constitution. See illegal.

Unconstrained, *adj.* See clear (2), free (1), informal.

Uncontaminated, *adj.* See sanitary, clear (2).

Uncontested, *adj.* See consensual.

Uncontrollable, *adj.* Incapable of being controlled; ungovernable. See incorrigible, wild (3); involuntary, irresistible, spontaneous, inescapable, hysterical, difficult (3), deranged.

Uncontrollable impulse See irresistible impulse, insanity.

Uncontrolled, *adj.* See disorderly (1), lawless (2), involuntary, incontinent (1), sovereign (1).

Unconventional, *adj.* See novel, original (3), different, irregular, anomalous, peculiar (2), odd (1), nonconforming, deviant (1), exceptional, extraordinary, extreme (1), informal, suspicious (1), bluff (4).

Unconvincing, *adj.* See doubtful (1), inconclusive, disputable, suspicious (1).

Uncooked, *adj.* See raw (2).

Uncooperative, *adj.* See hostile, disobedient, negative (2).

Uncorroborated, *adj.* See baseless, inconclusive, frivolous.

Uncorrupted, *adj.* See blameless, chaste (3), clean (1), just, moral (2), good (2), honest, reputable.

Uncouple, *v.* See part (3).

Uncouth, *adj.* See rude, blatant (2), peculiar (2).

Uncover, *v.* See disclose, expose (1), discover, bare (2), exhibit (1), find (1), locate

(1), strip (2), betray (2), produce (2), surface (2).

Uncovered, *adj.* See naked.

Uncovering, *n.* See disclosure, discovery (2), betrayal (2).

Uncreative, *adj.* See pedestrian (2).

Uncritical, *adj.* See blind (1).

Uncurbed, *adj.* See clear (2), high (1).

Uncut, *adj.* See complete (2), full, gross (2), round (1).

Undamaged, *adj.* See inviolate.

Undecided, *adj.* See pending, debatable, doubtful (1), indeterminate, moot (2).

Undeclared, *adj.* See silent (2).

Undefiled, *adj.* See blameless, clear (4), inviolate.

Undefined, *adj.* See indeterminate, open-ended.

Undemonstrated, *adj.* See inconclusive, speculative, disputable.

Undemonstrative, *adj.* See passive (2), quiet (2).

Undeniable, *adj.* See certain (3), categorical (1), clear (1), cogent, definite, demonstrable, incontestable, indubitable, manifest (1), noncontestable, patent (1), obvious, outright, peremptory (1); indeed.

Undependable, *adj.* See irresponsible, insecure (1), precarious, variable, capricious.

Under, *prep.* **1.** Beneath. Below, underneath. See also subaltern, submerged. **2.** Subordinate to. Inferior to, secondary to, bound by, lower than, subject to, junior to, lesser than.

Under color of law See color of law, color of office.

Under control See control.

Undercover, *adj.* Operating in secret; underground. See clandestine, hidden, furtive, deceptive, confidential, private (1).

Undercover agent See undisclosed agent, agent (1), spy (1).

Undercurrent, *n.* **1.** A current of water or air below the surface. Riptide, undertow, crosstide, crosscurrent. **2.** An underlying force or tendency (an undercurrent of hostility). Tinge, vibration, undertone, suggestion, connotation, atmosphere, overtone, murmur, implication, aura, implication, flavor, quality.

Undercut, *v.* See impair, compromise (2).

Underestimate, *v.* See distort, err, blunder (2), misrepresent, diminish, discredit, color (3).

Undergo, *v.* See suffer (1), bear (2), sustain (4), stand (2), tolerate (2), expose (2).

Undergraduate, *n.* See student; school.

Underground 1. *adj.* See clandestine, seditious, private (1), hidden, subterranean. **2.** *adj.* See avant-garde. **3.** *n.* The underworld; terrorists. See criminal, wrongdoer, insurgent, nihilist, anarchist, revolutionary.

Undergrowth, *n.* See shrubbery, woods, timber.

Underhanded, *adj.* See fraudulent, corrupt (1), illicit, deceptive, dishonest, improper, covert, clandestine, collusive; fraud, secrecy.

Underline, *v.* See emphasize, accent.

Underling, *n.* See pawn (3), servant, employee; minor (2).

Underlying, *adj.* See intrinsic, inherent, congenital, organic (1), original (2).

Undermine, *v.* See demoralize, incapacitate, debilitate, disable, frustrate, impair, harm (2), deter, discredit, prejudice (2), pollute, slander (2).

Undermining, *adj.* See harmful, seditious; betrayal (1).

Undernourished, *adj.* See frail, hungry, weak, thin.

Underpin, *v.* See carry, corroborate.

Underpinning, *n.* See base (3), foundation (2), gravamen.

Underprivileged, *adj.* See destitute, indigent.

Under protest Waiving no rights; under duress. See protest (1, 2), duress (1).

Underrate, *v.* See disparage, discredit, demote.

Undersea, *adj.* See submerged.

Undersigned, *n.* The person or persons who have signed at the end of the document or at the bottom of the page. Signatory, subscriber, signer, attestant.

Undersized, *adj.* See small (1), thin (1).

Understand, *v.* To perceive, fathom, or internalize. See know, comprehend (1), digest (4), discover (1), deduce, construe, receive (2).

Understandable, *adj.* See intelligible, comprehensible, justifiable, lucid (2), simple (2).

Understandably, *adv.* See clearly.

Understanding 1. *n.* A meeting of the minds. See compromise, deal (1), pact, reconciliation, harmony, agreement, contract (1). **2.** *n.* Realization or grasp. See comprehension. **3.** *n.* Acumen or intelligence. See reason (2), judgment (2), mind (1), ability (2). **4.** *n.* Point of view. See opinion (2), impression, construction (1), deduction (2), information (2), recognition (1). **5.** *n.* The lack of prejudice; open-mindedness. See toleration (1), charity, benevolence, mercy, passion, consideration (3). **6.** *adj.* See conciliatory, responsive, rational, patient (3), humanitarian.

Understate, *v.* To minimize. See color (3), distort, misrepresent, diminish, condense, abridge, discredit, demote; subtle.

Understood, *adj.* See clear (1), distinct (1), intelligible, comprehensible, implied.

Undertake, *v.* To enter upon; to take upon oneself; to guarantee; to endeavor. See attempt (3), aim (3), pledge (2), commit (3), incur, promise (2), assume (1), commence, initiate, institute (1), launch, pursue, maintain (4), carry (2).

Undertaker, *n.* One whose business is to prepare the dead for burial. Mortician, embalmer, funeral director. See also merchant, business.

Undertaking, *n.* See assumption (1), pledge (1), promise (1), enterprise, assurance (1), commitment (2), contract (1), pursuit (2), part (2), intent (1), labor (1), occupation (1).

Under the influence See intoxicated.

Undertow, *n.* See tide, undercurrent (1).

Underwater, *adj.* See submerged.

Underweight, *adj.* See thin (1).

Underworld, *n.* See racket, racketeering, crime.

Underwrite, *v.* To insure life or property; to agree to sell bonds or other securities to the public, or to furnish the necessary money for such securities and to buy those that cannot be sold. See insure, back (1), finance (1), vouch, guarantee (2), recommend, confirm (2), ratify, promote; indorsement.

Underwriter, *n.* See insurer, guarantor, surety, promoter; backing.

Undesigned, *adj.* See casual (1), fortuitous, chance (5).

Undesirable, *adj.* See repulsive, odious, bad, improper, illicit, immoral, repugnant (1).

Undetailed, *adj.* See broad (1), indefinite, general.

Undetected, *adj.* See hidden, blind (2).

Undetermined, *adj.* See open-ended, pending, inconclusive, indeterminate, moot (2).

Undeveloped, *adj.* See dormant, inchoate, inadequate, partial (1), imperfect, backward (1).

Undeviating, *adj.* See constant (3), reliable, right (1), conscientious (2), precise (2), direct (4), straight (2), lineal, literal.

Undiluted, *adj.* See raw (2), honest.

Undiminished, *adj.* See complete (2), outright, healthy, round (1).

Undisciplined, *adj.* See wild, capricious, disobedient, disorderly (1), gross (1), raw (1).

Undisclosed, *adj.* Operating in secret; unannounced. See clandestine, hidden, deceptive, private (1), personal, confidential, blind (2).

Undisclosed agent A person who works as an agent without revealing his or her status as an agent. See agent (1).

Undisclosed principal One who acts through an agent at a time when a third party has no notice that the agent is acting for a principal. See employer, principal (4).

Undisguised, *adj.* See clear (1), overt, manifest, obvious.

Undisputed, *adj.* Uncontested; not questioned or challenged; stipulated; admitted. See certain, clear (1), noncontestable; acknowledge (1).

Undistinguished, *adj.* See ordinary (2), marginal, obscure (2).

Undistorted, *adj.* See honest, clear.

Undistributed, *adj.* Accumulated, set aside, not distributed, not paid out as dividends. See accumulate, collect (1).

Undistributed profits tax A tax imposed on the unreasonable accumulation of profits by a corporation that has sufficient surplus for expansion and other needs beyond the amount that it could but does not pay out in dividends. See tax.

Undisturbed, *adj.* See quiet (1).

Undivided, *adj.* Not divided. See complete (2), entire, full, gross (2), outright, joint, whole (1); unanimous, round (1).

Undivided profits Current undistributed earnings; profits not set aside as surplus or distributed as dividends.

Undo, *v.* See destroy, devastate, frustrate, rescind, reverse (1), overrule, part (3), release (1).

Undoing, *n.* See defeat (2), reversal, loss, misfortune, neutralization.

Undoubtedly, *adv.* See presumably.

Undress, *v.* See strip (2), bare (2).

Undue, *adj.* More than necessary; wrongful. See illegal, improper, wrong (2, 3), unconscionable, immoderate, gratuitous (2), exorbitant, disproportionate, excess, redundancy.

Undue influence Taking advantage of a person's weakness, infirmity, age, or distress in order to change that person's actions or decisions. Misuse of a position of confidence in order to take unfair advantage of another. Any unlawful or improper constraint that overpowers the will of another. See duress, coercion.

Undulate, *v.* See beat (3).

Undying, *adj.* See permanent, perpetual, indestructible.

Unearned, *adj.* **1.** Not acquired through or in exchange for labor or service. **2.** Undeserved. Uncalled-for, unnecessary, gratuitous, superfluous, unprovoked, excessive, redundant, groundless, unconscionable, wrongful, arbitrary, unauthorized, unfair.

Unearned income Income that has been received but not yet earned. See income.

Unearth, *v.* See expose (1), discover (1), exhume, ferret, find (1), locate (1), trace (2), learn.

Unease, *n.* See guilt (2), contrition, embarrassment, disgrace, care (2), fear (1).

Uneasy, *adj.* See impatient, insecure (2).

Uneconomical, *adj.* See improvident, impracticable.

Uneducated, *adj.* Unsophisticated; not formally educated but not necessarily illiterate. Naive, inexperienced, unworldly, green, innocent, unschooled, unaware, uninitiated, unversed, unlettered, ignorant, simple; ingenuous, unaffected, artless. See also illiterate.

Unembellished, *adj.* See naked (2), simple (1), raw (2).

Unemotional, *adj.* See indifferent (2), callous, casual.

Unemployed

Unemployed, *adj.* **1.** Without work. Jobless, laid off, fired, idle, inactive, unoccupied. See also destitute. **2.** Not being put to use. See dormant.

Unencumbered, *adj.* See clear (2), free (1), independent, exempt (2).

Unending, *adj.* See open-ended, constant (1), long, chronic, habitual, unlimited, permanent, daily.

Unendurable, *adj.* See obnoxious, onerous, offensive.

Unenforceable, *adj.* See invalid (1), nugatory.

Unenlightened, *adj.* See blind (1), uneducated, illiterate; ignorance.

Unentangled, *adj.* See clear (2).

Unequal, *adj.* **1.** Discriminatory. Prejudicial, biased, unjust, unfair, partial, predisposed, bigoted. See also one-sided, unconscionable. **2.** Disparate, variable, uneven, or not uniform. See disproportionate, irregular, different, opposite.

Unequaled, *adj.* See best, primary (1), exceptional, most.

Unequivocal, *adj.* Capable of being understood in only one way; unambiguous; categorical. See clear (1), certain, absolute, categorical (1), definite (1), specific, explicit, evident, express (1), distinct (1), concrete, demonstrable (2), lucid (2), cogent, conspicuous, reliable, incontestable, peremptory (1).

Unequivocally, *adv.* See clearly.

Unerring, *adj.* Incapable of error or failure; infallible. See certain (3), precise (2), correct (1), right (1).

Unessential, *adj.* See collateral (2).

Unestablished, *adj.* See inconclusive.

Unethical, *adj.* Disreputable or underhanded. In violation of standards of practice. See illegal, immoral, wrong (3), dishonest, corrupt (1), fraudulent, unconscionable; Code of Professional Responsibility, offense.

Uneven, *adj.* See irregular, disproportionate, unequal, odd (2), insufficient; disparity.

Unexacting, *adj.* See casual (3).

Unexaggerated, *adj.* See naked (2), raw, simple.

Unexceptionable, *adj.* Not subject to any objection or criticism. See blameless.

Unexceptional, *adj.* See commonplace, common (1), ordinary (2), pedestrian (2), natural (4).

Unexcited, *adj.* See patient (3), indifferent, casual.

Unexecuted, *adj.* See inchoate.

Unexpected, *adj.* See unforeseeable, fortuitous, chance (5), improbable, sudden, extraordinary, new, original (2), precipitate (3), incidental.

Unexpectedly, *adv.* See short (5).

Unexpired term The remainder of a period prescribed by law after a portion of such time has passed.

Unexplained, *adj.* See mysterious.

Unexpressed, *adj.* See silent (2).

Unfailing, *adj.* See reliable, certain (3), safe (2), permanent.

Unfair, *adj.* One-sided, biased, unreasonable, inequitable, exploitative, intolerant, unscrupulous, wrongful, underhanded, excessive. See also arbitrary (1), partial (2), unequal (1), wrong (2), unconscionable, unearned, corrupt (1); discriminate (1), discrimination.

Unfair competition Dishonest or fraudulent rivalry in trade and commerce (e.g., the imitation or simulation of the name, materials, or pattern used by another for the purpose of deceiving the public). See palming off.

Unfair labor practice Interference by an employer with the right of employees to form or join a union, to bargain collectively, or to engage in concerted activities for their mutual aid and protection. Refusal of an employer to bargain collectively in good faith.

Unfairness, *n.* See injustice, bias (1), grievance (1).

Unfaithful, *adj.* See disloyal, false, dishonest, deceptive, deceitful; bad faith; adultery.

Unfaithfulness, *n.* See betrayal (1).

Unfaltering, *adj.* See constant (3), patient (2), indefatigable.

Unfamiliar, *adj.* See foreign (3), outside (3), peculiar (2), novel; ignorance.

Unfashionable, *adj.* See obsolete.

Unfasten, *v.* See open (1, 2).

Unfathomable, *adj.* See mysterious, obscure (1); perpetual.

Unfavorable, *adj.* See injurious, deleterious, prejudicial, derogatory, ill (2).

Unfeasible, *adj.* See impracticable, impossible.

Unfeeling, *adj.* See callous, inhuman, cruel, malicious, mechanical (2).

Unfeigned, *adj.* See real (2).

Unfenced, *adj.* See open (4).

Unfetter, *v.* See clear (5), liberate.

Unfettered, *adj.* See clear (2), unlimited.

Unfinished, *adj.* Not brought to an end. See inchoate, imperfect, outstanding (1), partial (1), pending, defective.

Unfit, *adj.* Not suitable or qualified. See incompetent, negligent, inadequate, ineligible, infirm, careless, improper, unable, defective, irregular.

Unfitness, *n.* See disability (1), incapacity.

Unfixed, *adj.* See variable, fluctuating.

Unflagging, *adj.* See constant (3), diligent, indefatigable, strong (2), patient (2).

Unflappable, *adj.* See patient (3).

Unflinching, *adj.* See constant (3), courageous.

Unfocused, *adj.* See diffuse (2), ambiguous.

Unfold, *v.* See expose (1), bare (2), open (1), produce (2), spread (3), develop (2); development (1), growth.

Unforeseeable, *adj.* Not expected or foreseen (unforeseeable storm). Unanticipated, unexpected, surprise, startling, unpredicted, spontaneous, abrupt, accidental, out of the blue, unintentional, unplanned, unusual, unlooked-for, astonishing. See also fortuitous, sudden, precipitate (3), improbable, contingent; act of God, inevitable accident, accident. *Ant.* Foreseeable.

Unforeseen, *adj.* See chance (5), sudden, fortuitous, casual (1).

Unforgettable, *adj.* See outstanding (2), great, extraordinary.

Unforgivable, *adj.* See inexcusable.

Unfortunate, *adj.* See ill-fated.

Unfounded, *adj.* See fallacious, fictitious, baseless, erroneous, frivolous, invalid (1), precarious.

Unfrequented, *adj.* See remote (1).

Unfresh, *adj.* See commonplace, pedestrian (2).

Unfriendly, *adj.* See hostile, negative (3), repugnant (1), disaffected, ill (2).

Unfruitful, *adj.* See barren (2), dead (3).

Unfulfilled, *adj.* See executory, inchoate.

Unfurl, *v.* See exhibit (1), spread (3).

Ungenuine, *adj.* See bogus, false (2).

Ungodly, *adj.* See profane (1), irreverent.

Ungovernable, *adj.* See incorrigible, disorderly (1), disobedient, inflexible, hot (2), mutinous.

Ungrateful, *adj.* See ingratitude.

Ungrudging, *adj.* See liberal (3).

Unguarded, *adj.* See defenseless, open (4).

Unhampered, *adj.* See clear (2), unlimited.

Unhappy, *adj.* See depressed, despondent; hardship, pain.

Unharmed, *adj.* Uninjured. See safe (4), healthy, inviolate.

Unhealthy, *adj.* See harmful, injurious, poisonous, deleterious, dangerous, defective, unclean; ill (1), infirm, sick, frail, weak.

Unheard-of, *adj.* See outstanding (2), extraordinary; obscure (2).

Unhesitating, *adj.* See reliable.

Unhidden, *adj.* See clear (1), open (5).

Unholy, *adj.* See irreverent; blasphemy.

Unidentified, *adj.* See secret, private, mysterious, hidden.

Unification, *n.* See cooperation, concurrence (1), integration (2), organization (2).

Unified, *adj.* Made one. United, allied, confederated, uniform, combined, amalgamated. See also integrated, associated, joint.

Uniform 1. *adj.* Without change; equally applicable. Symmetrical, universal, similar, conforming, even, alike, undeviating, undiversified, correspondent, homogeneous, regular. See also consistent (1), equal (1), consonant, organic (3), unified, constant (1), identical, customary; flat; harmony. **2.** *n.* An official dress or outfit. Costume, garb, suit, silks, regalia, vestment, habit, attire. See also clothes, apparel.

Uniform Code of Military Justice (U.C.M.J.) The body of law that governs persons in their conduct as military personnel.

Uniform Commercial Code (U.C.C.) A law adopted by almost all states, governing commercial transactions (e.g., sale of goods, commercial paper, bank deposits, secured transactions).

Uniform Consumer Credit Code (U.C.C.C.) A law adopted by some states governing consumer credit, usury, rate ceilings, unfair credit practices, etc.

Uniform Gifts to Minors Act See Gifts to Minors Act.

Uniformity, *n.* See symmetry, harmony, balance (4), coherence, conformity, correspondence (1), identity (2), parity, purity.

Uniform laws Laws prepared or sponsored by the National Conference of Commissioners on Uniform State Laws and then proposed to the various state legislatures, which may adopt, modify, or reject them.

Uniform Reciprocal Enforcement of Support Act (URESA) A law adopted by most states, by which a party can commence a support proceeding in one state against a party in another state who has the support obligation.

Unify, *v.* To cause to be one; to unite. See consolidate, affiliate (2), organize, join (1), connect (1), cohere (1), pool (1).

Unilateral, *adj.* Affecting only one side; obligating only one side (unilateral concession). Lone, singular, independent. See also ex parte, one-sided. *Ant.* Bilateral, reciprocal.

Unilateral contract One party makes an express engagement or undertakes a performance without receiving in return any express engagement or promise of performance from the other. See contract.

Unilateral mistake A mistake or misunderstanding made by only one of the parties as to the terms or effect of a contract. See mistake.

Unimaginable, *adj.* See impossible, extraordinary.

Unimaginative, *adj.* See commonplace (2), pedestrian (2), limited (2), literal (2).

Unimpaired, *adj.* See clean (1), clear, entire, perfect (2).

Unimpeachable, *adj.* See clear (1), certain (3), definite (1), demonstrable, definitive, conclusive, believable, incontestable, literal (1), indubitable, incorruptible, blameless, correct (1), right (1), reliable, loyal, innocent (1), just, official (2).

Unimpeded, *adj.* See free (1).

Unimportant, *adj.* See petty, frivolous, nugatory, expendable, minor (2), de minimus, immaterial, impertinent (1), null and void.

Unimpressive, *adj.* See ordinary (2).

Unimproved, *adj.* Not improved, cultivated, or built upon to increase the value of something.

Unincorporated association A voluntary group of persons, without a charter, formed to promote a common enterprise or objective. See association.

Uninfected, *adj.* Not permeated with what is bad or harmful. Uncontaminated, untainted. See also clean, sanitary.

Uninformed, *adj.* See uneducated; ignorance.

Uninhabited, *adj.* See solitary, unoccupied, abandoned (1), void (3).

Uninhibited, *adj.* See spontaneous.

Uninitiated, *adj.* See uneducated; amateur, beginner.

Uninjured, *adj.* See healthy, safe.

Uninspired, *adj.* See ordinary (2), pedestrian (2).

Uninsured motorist coverage Insurance protection for those who are injured by motorists who cannot pay damages because they do not carry liability insurance. See insurance, indemnity.

Unintelligent, *adj.* See dumb, absurd, irrational; uneducated.

Unintelligible, *adj.* Not understandable. See obscure (1), incoherent, illegible, indefinite, mysterious.

Unintended, *adj.* See chance (5), accidental.

Unintentional, *adj.* See fortuitous, inadvertent, accidental, casual, unforeseeable, involuntary.

Uninteresting, *adj.* See ordinary (2), pedestrian (2), commonplace (2), barren (2).

Uninterrupted, *adj.* See constant (1), continual, continuous, consecutive, successive, standing (3), direct (4), lineal, fresh; continuity.

Uninvolved, *adj.* See disinterested, neutral, dispassionate; simple (2); innocent (1).

Union, *n.* **1.** An organization or workers formed to negotiate with employers on work issues. Trade union, labor organization, organized labor, brotherhood, shop, bargaining unit, craft union, local, guild, coalition, party, fraternity. **2.** A league or federation. See organization (1), association (1), pool (2), consortium (2). **3.** Wedlock. See marriage. **4.** A mixture or consolidation. See merger, combination, amalgamation. **5.** See conformity, cooperation, conjunction, connection (1), contact (1).

Union certification The process by which a government body declares that a particular union has qualified as the bargaining representative of a group of workers by reason of a majority vote.

Unionize, *v.* See organize (2).

Union security clause The clause in a union contract that establishes the status of the union in a plant.

Unique, *adj.* See different, distinct (2), peculiar, special (1), irregular, odd (1), isolated, separate (1), nonconforming, exclusive, novel, original (3), individual (1), particular (1), specific, single (1), only (1), professional (1), outstanding (2), extraordinary.

Uniqueness, *n.* See difference (1), identity, eccentricity, novelty.

Unison, *n.* See consensus, consort.

Unissued stock Stock of a corporation that has been authorized but is not outstanding.

Unit, *n.* **1.** A single thing of any kind. See component, item, part (1), division (2), class (1), element, section. **2.** A fixed quantity. See measure (1).

Unitary, *adj.* See single (1).

Unite, *v.* To act in concert; to combine. See join (1), concur, connect, incorporate (2), converge, cooperate, convene, lock, pool (1), relate (1), contact (4).

United, *adj.* See joint, concerted, cooperative (2), conglomerate (2), concurrent (2), concomitant, conjoint.

United States Usually means the federal government centered in Washington, D.C. (agency of the United States). See federal (2), national (1), nation, sovereign (2).

United States Code (U.S.C.) An official collection of permanent and public federal statutes organized by subject matter. The collection also includes the U.S. Constitution.

United States Code Annotated (U.S.C.A.) An unofficial collection of permanent and public federal statutes organized by subject matter, published by West. The collection also includes the U.S. Constitution.

United States Code Service (U.S.C.S.) An unofficial collection of permanent and public federal statutes organized by subject matter, published by Lawyers Cooperative Publishing Co. The collection also includes the U.S. Constitution.

United States Reports (U.S.) The official collection of opinions of the U.S. Supreme Court.

Unity, *n.* **1.** Oneness. Individuality, entirety, wholeness, singularity, homogeneity, integrality, undividedness, similitude, entity, consolidation, synthesis, affiliation, federation, unification. See also identity (2), association. **2.** See harmony, accord (2), peace, cooperation.

Universal, *adj.* Pertaining to all without exception (universal conscription). All-inclusive, widespread, catholic, pandemic, total, ecumenical, entire, unlimited, international, omnipresent, worldwide, all-embracing, endless. See also broad (1), comprehensive, common, generic, general, complete (2), conventional (1), normal (1). *Ant.* Limited.

Universe, *n.* See world.

University, *n.* An institution of higher learning consisting of an assemblage of colleges under one governance. See school (1), institution.

Unjust, *adj.* Contrary to right and justice; violating the rights enjoyed by others. See illegal, improper, dishonest, unfair, one-sided, arbitrary (1), partisan, unequal (1), wrong (2), corrupt (1), immoral; discriminate (1), discrimination.

Unjust enrichment A person has and retains a benefit that in equity and good conscience belongs to another.

Unjustifiable, *adj.* See inexcusable, unconscionable, invalid (1), disproportionate.

Unjustified, *adj.* See baseless, frivolous, illegal.

Unkempt, *adj.* See disheveled, ragged, dirty.

Unkind, *adj.* See rude, impertinent (2), callous, caustic.

Unknown, *adj.* **1.** Unidentified, unannounced, undiscovered, or undisclosed. See anonymous; hidden, clandestine; original (3). **2.** Inexplicable. See mysterious. **3.** Not determined. See indeterminate.

Unlawful, *adj.* Pertaining to that which is contrary to the law. See illegal, wrong (2), improper, illicit, criminal (2); injustice.

Unlawful assembly The meeting together of a designated number of persons (e.g., three or more) to the disturbance of the public peace and with the intention of cooperating in the forcible execution of some unlawful private enterprise. See breach of peace, riot.

Unlettered, *adj.* See illiterate, uneducated.

Unlicensed, *adj.* See illegal; contraband.

Unlike, *adj.* See alien (2), different, distinct (2); difference.

Unlikely, *adj.* See improbable, remote (2), outside (4).

Unlimited, *adj.* Boundless (unlimited power). Limitless, unrestricted, unfettered, unhampered, numberless, unceasing, unchecked, unconfined, vast, unending, untrammeled, free, open, untold, beyond measure, infinite, absolute, plenary, uncounted, arbitrary, complete, interminable, eternal, unrestrained, all-encompassing, totalitarian, total, immeasurable, inexhaustible, unqualified, unconditional. See also universal, broad (1), comprehensive, perpetual, open-ended, great (1), immoderate, categorical (1), abundant, clear (2), indefinite. *Ant.* Limited.

Unliquidated, *adj.* Not determined; not ascertained in amount.

Unliquidated claim A claim that has not been finally determined or calculated.

Unliquidated damages Damages that have not yet been calculated or determined in amount.

Unload, *v.* To discharge a cargo; to disburden or remove from (unload the vessel). Empty, discard, unpack, dump, slough; disentangle, lighten, ease, uplift, unsnarl, alleviate, disencumber, extricate, unlock, free. See also jettison, relieve (1), sell; landing.

Unlock, *v.* See open, unload.

Unlooked-for, *adj.* See unforeseeable.

Unloose, *v.* See clear (5), free.

Unlucky, *adj.* See ill-fated.

Unmake, *v.* See rescind.

Unmanageable, *adj.* See incorrigible, disobedient, disorderly (1), inflexible, difficult (3), querulous, contentious, litigious, impracticable.

Unmannerly, *adj.* See rude.

Unmarketable title A title of such character as to expose the purchaser to the hazards of litigation where there are outstanding possible interests in third persons. An ordinary prudent person with knowledge of the facts would not accept the title in the ordinary course of business even if the title in fact is not bad.

Unmarred, *adj.* See fit (1), complete (3), perfect.

Unmarried, *adj.* Not having a husband or wife at the time. See single (2).

Unmask, *v.* See disclose, expose (1), betray (2); detection.

Unmindful, *adj.* See careless, reckless, inadvertent, oblivious.

Unmistakable, *adj.* See clear (1), manifest, obvious, blatant (1), certain (3), categorical, demonstrable (2), naked (2), palpable, specific, outright, distinct (1), evident, express, intelligible, comprehensible, outstanding (2).

Unmistakably, *adv.* See clearly.

Unmitigated, *adj.* See chronic, categorical (1), rank (3), gross (1), mere.

Unmixed, *adj.* See entire, simple (1).

Unmodifiable, *adj.* See irrevocable.

Unmolested, *adj.* See safe; quiet (1).

Unmoved, *adj.* See callous, passive (2), still (2).

Unnatural, *adj.* Against nature; strange; brutal. See abnormal, anomalous, irregular, artificial, corrupt, deformed, deviate (1), peculiar (2), foreign (3), exceptional, extraordinary.

Unnaturalized, *adj.* See alien (2).

Unnatural offense An infamous offense against nature (e.g., see sodomy, buggery).

Unnecessary, *adj.* Not required by the circumstances of the case (unnecessary force). See gratuitous, collateral (2), immaterial, excess, extraneous, peripheral, optional; unearned; redundancy.

Unnecessary hardship A criterion for a variance if the property could be used for a permitted purpose only at a prohibitive expense, or if the restriction is so unreasonable as to constitute an arbitrary interference with the basic right of private property. See hardship.

Unneeded, *adj.* See needless.

Unnerve, *v.* See disturb, harass, menace (2).

Unnoticed, *adj.* See obscure (2).

Unobjectionable, *adj.* See blameless, fair, good (1).

Unobservant, *adj.* See careless, blind (1), heedless, oblivious, negligent.

Unobstructed, *adj.* See clear (2).

Unobtainable, *adj.* See impossible, impracticable.

Unobtrusive, *adj.* See bashful, quiet (2).

Unoccupied, *adj.* Not being used as a residence; no longer being used for the ordinary and accustomed purposes of the dwelling. Empty, tenantless, deserted, unpeopled, godforsaken, lonely, abandoned, forsaken. See also vacant; unemployed (1), dormant.

Unoffending, *adj.* See blameless.

Unofficial, *adj.* See informal, private (1).

Unopposed, *adj.* See consensual.

Unorganized, *adj.* See casual (3), complex (1).

Unoriginal, *adj.* See derivative; commonplace.

Unorthodox, *adj.* See nonconforming, irregular, deviant (1), peculiar (2), odd (1), suspicious (1); heresy.

Unpack, *v.* See unload.

Unpaid, *adj.* See delinquent (1), outstanding (1), due (1), overdue.

Unpalatable, *adj.* See odious, repugnant (1).

Unparalleled, *adj.* See best (1), leading (1), major (2), exceptional, extraordinary, outstanding (2), odd (1).

Unpardonable, *adj.* See inexcusable.

Unpatriotic, *adj.* See disloyal.

Unperformed, *adj.* See executory, inchoate.

Unperturbed, *adj.* See patient (3), passive (2).

Unplanned, *adj.* See casual, spontaneous, inadvertent, chance (5), accidental, unforeseeable.

Unpleasant, *adj.* See painful, distressing, obnoxious, repulsive, offensive.

Unpolished, *adj.* See gross (1), rude.

Unpolluted, *adj.* See clean (2), sanitary, healthy.

Unpopularity, *n.* See disrepute.

Unprecedented, *adj.* Having no precedent or example. See novel, unforeseeable, extraordinary, first, extreme (1), original (3).

Unpredictable, *adj.* See precarious, contingent, sudden, unforeseeable, irresponsible.

Unprejudiced, *adj.* See impartial, objective (2), just, neutral, liberal (2), independent, indifferent, open (7).

Unpremeditated, *adj.* See inadvertent, fortuitous, spontaneous, chance (5), casual, precipitate (3), unforeseeable.

Unprepared, *adj.* See precipitate (2); raw.

Unpretentious, *adj.* See natural (5), innocent (2), direct (6), ordinary (2).

Unpreventable, *adj.* See inevitable, inescapable, necessary, irresistible.

Unprincipled, *adj.* See delinquent (2), dishonest, false (2), illicit, illegal, base (2), corrupt (1), cruel, dissolute, fraudulent, immoral, improper.

Unproductive, *adj.* See barren (2), worthless (1), fallow, dead (3).

Unprofessional, *adj.* Violating the code of a profession or occupation; amateurish. See unethical, illegal, wrong (3), dishonest, immoral; malpractice.

Unprofitable, *adj.* See barren (2), fallow, worthless (1), dead (3).

Unpropitious, *adj.* See harmful.

Unprotected, *adj.* See helpless, insecure, susceptible, precarious.

Unproven, *adj.* See inconclusive, speculative.

Unprovoked, *adj.* See gratuitous (2), unearned.

Unpublished, *adj.* See hidden, private (1), silent (2).

Unqualified, *adj.* See ineligible, inadequate, insufficient; clear (1), naked (2), definite (1), comprehensive, certain (2), demonstrable, direct (6), gross (1), complete (2), outright, unlimited, peremptory (1), obligatory.

Unquestionable, *adj.* See certain (3), inevitable, indubitable, incontestable, right (2), clear (1), evident, believable, reliable, genuine, real (2), peremptory (1); certainty.

Unravel, *v.* See clarify, construe, interpret, settle, discover (1); divide (1); detection.

Unreachable, *adj.* See remote (1), impracticable, impossible.

Unreal, *adj.* See false (1), fictitious, illusory, impossible, hypothetical, deceptive.

Unrealistic, *adj.* See impracticable, absurd, insane, impossible, irregular.

Unreality, *n.* See delusion; unreal.

Unreasonable, *adj.* See negligence, negligent, irrational, capricious, arbitrary (1), illegal, wrong (3), baseless, extreme (1), great (1), improbable, improper, illogical, high (1), unconscionable, exorbitant, immoderate, impossible, impracticable, invalid (1), reckless.

Unrefined, *adj.* See raw (2); gross (1), rude, impertinent, common (3), bare (1).

Unreflecting, *adj.* See blind (1), careless.

Unregulated, *adj.* See free (1); unlimited.

Unrehearsed, *adj.* See spontaneous, fortuitous, accidental, unforeseeable.

Unrelated, *adj.* Dissimilar; unconnected (unrelated charge). See separate (1), irrelevant, extrinsic (2), foreign (3), impertinent, extraneous (1), alien (2).

Unrelenting, *adj.* See inflexible, constant (1), deadly, mortal (2), inhuman.

Unreliable, *adj.* See precarious, insecure (1), dangerous, deceptive, dishonest, hazardous, improper, irregular, irresponsible.

Unremitting, *adj.* See chronic, perpetual, continual, constant (1), inflexible, mortal (2), close (5).

Unreserved, *adj.* See complete (2), outright, categorical (1), direct (6), explicit, honest, peremptory (1).

Unresolved, *adj.* See indeterminate, pending, debatable, disputable, outstanding (1).

Unresponsive, *adj.* **1.** Being silent or not providing a direct answer; elusive. See silent (1), irrelevant, evasive. **2.** Phlegmatic, aloof, or taciturn. See passive, callous, reserve (4), dispassionate.

Unrest, *n.* See confusion, disorder, commotion, riot.

Unrestrained, *adj.* See unlimited, free, exempt (2), clear (2), independent, demonstrative (2), indefinite; irresponsible, immoderate, incontinent, precipitate (2), dissolute.

Unrestricted, *adj.* See unlimited, open-ended, open (4), general, public (2), peremptory (1), comprehensive, independent; combative (2).

Unrevealed, *adj.* See hidden, clandestine, blind (2).

Unrewarding, *adj.* See barren (2), worthless (1), fallow, dead (3).

Unrivaled, *adj.* See best (1), major (2), primary, extraordinary, great, outstanding (2).

Unruffled, *adj.* See patient (3), constant (3).

Unruly, *adj.* Difficult to manage or control; hyperactive. See incorrigible, disobedient, disorderly, prodigal, irregular, lawless, inflexible, mutinous, seditious, wild (2), wanton; insubordination.

Unsafe, *adj.* See dangerous, harmful, hazardous, deficient, deadly, speculative.

Unsalvageable, *adj.* See irreparable, irreconcilable.

Unsanctioned, *adj.* See illegal, improper.

Unsanitary, *adj.* See poisonous, unclean, unsafe.

Unsatisfactory, *adj.* See inadequate, insufficient, deficient, imperfect, inferior (2).

Unsavory, *adj.* See odious, offensive, repugnant, obnoxious.

Unschooled, *adj.* See illiterate, uneducated, raw (1).

Unscientific

Unscientific, *adj.* See irrational, invalid (1).

Unscramble, *v.* See clarify, interpret.

Unscreened, *adj.* See open (4).

Unscrupulous, *adj.* See corrupt (1), dishonest, fraudulent, immoral, depraved, delinquent (2), unconscionable.

Unseal, *v.* See open (1, 3); patent (1).

Unseasonable, *adj.* See improper, inconvenient.

Unseat, *v.* See oust, dismiss (2), discharge (5), purge, displace.

Unseaworthy, *adj.* Unable to withstand the perils of an ordinary voyage at sea. See inadequate, infirm, defective, negligent, incompetent, ineligible.

Unseemly, *adj.* See improper, indecent, illicit, delinquent, common (3), vulgar, offensive.

Unseen, *adj.* See hidden, furtive.

Unselfish, *adj.* See charitable, humanitarian, benevolent, liberal (3).

Unselfishness, *n.* See benevolence, charity.

Unsettle, *v.* See confuse, distract, outrage (2), harass.

Unsettled, *adj.* See overdue, outstanding (1), delinquent (1), doubtful, debatable, open-ended, inconclusive, moot (2), raw (1), precarious, juvenile (2), itinerant.

Unshackle, *v.* See liberate, release, discharge (3).

Unshakable, *adj.* See certain (3).

Unshaken, *adj.* See certain (2), dispassionate.

Unsightly, *adj.* See deformed, repugnant (1), repulsive.

Unskilled, *adj.* See incompetent, raw (1).

Unsnarl, *v.* See unload.

Unsolvable, *adj.* See irreconcilable.

Unsophisticated, *adj.* See innocent (2), simple (2), uneducated, backward (1), parochial (2), raw (1), juvenile (2).

Unsound, *adj.* See false, fallacious, defective, irrational, invalid (1), insane (2), wrong (2), erroneous, frail, lame, lunatic, sick, deficient, improper, infirm, rotten.

Unsound mind An infirmity of mind that renders one incapable of managing oneself or one's affairs. See insanity, infirm.

Unsparing, *adj.* See close (5), liberal (3).

Unspecified, *adj.* See indefinite, indeterminate.

Unspoiled, *adj.* See idyllic, innocent.

Unspoken, *adj.* See implied, silent (2).

Unspotted, *adj.* See blameless, innocent, clean.

Unstable, *adj.* See capricious, irresponsible, fluctuating, hazardous, infirm, perishable, breakable.

Unstated, *adj.* See silent (2), implied.

Unsteady, *adj.* See insecure (1), inconsistent, capricious, variable, dangerous, broken, dizzy.

Unstinting, *adj.* See benevolent, liberal (3), charitable.

Unstudied, *adj.* See informal, natural (5), spontaneous.

Unsubstantiated, *adj.* See baseless, inconclusive, frivolous, debatable, moot.

Unsuccessful, *adj.* See barren (2), nugatory, worthless.

Unsuited, *adj.* See anomalous, unsuitable.

Unsuitable, *adj.* See ineligible, improper, disproportionate, imperfect, impracticable, incompetent, incompatible, unable, indecent.

Unsullied, *adj.* See blameless, chaste (3), clean (1), clear, good (2).

Unsupportable, *adj.* See erroneous, invalid (1), baseless.

Unsure, *adj.* See insecure (2), precarious, tentative (2).

Unsurpassed, *adj.* See best (1), leading, most, paramount.

Unsuspected, *adj.* See blind (2), covert, oblivious.

Unsuspicious, *adj.* See credulous.

Unsustainable, *adj.* See erroneous, baseless, fallacious, invalid.

Unswerving, *adj.* See conscientious (2), loyal, direct (4), lineal, straight (2).

Unsympathetic, *adj.* See callous, incompatible, inhuman, inflexible.

Unsystematic, *adj.* See disorderly (3), capricious, inconsistent, casual (3).

Untainted, *adj.* See blameless, good (2), chaste (3), perfect (2).

Untamed, *adj.* See rude, wild.

Untangle, *v.* See clarify, interpret, liberate, rectify.

Untarnished, *adj.* See incorruptible, blameless, innocent.

Untenable, *adj.* See baseless, fallacious, doubtful, invalid (1), impossible, precarious.

Untested, *adj.* See maiden (1), novel, raw (1).

Unthinkable, *adj.* See irrational, impossible, improbable, wild, insane.

Unthinking, *adj.* See careless, negligent, improvident, irrational, inadvertent, mechanical.

Unthreatened, *adj.* See immune, safe (2).

Untidy, *adj.* See disheveled, ragged, dirty.

Untie, *v.* See liberate, dissolve, divide (1).

Untied, *adj.* See free (1), unlimited.

Untimely, *adj.* See inconvenient, improper, overdue.

Untiring, *adj.* See diligent, patient (2), indefatigable.

Untold, *adj.* See unlimited.

Untouched, *adj.* See inviolate, natural (2).

Untoward, *adj.* **1.** Unfavorable, unlucky, or ominous. See adverse, negative (2). **2.** Difficult to manage or control. See incorrigible. **3.** Unseemly. See improper. **4.** Unlooked-for. See unforeseeable.

Untrained, *adj.* See incompetent, raw (1), amateur.

Untrammeled, *adj.* See free (1), unlimited.

Untried, *adj.* See maiden (1), new, novel.

Untroubled, *adj.* See content (2), quiet (1).

Untrue, *adj.* See false, fallacious, dishonest, invalid (1), fictitious, erroneous, illusory, improper, fraudulent, deceptive, disloyal.

Untrustworthy, *adj.* See disloyal, corrupt (1), deceitful, irresponsible, derelict (2), dishonest, improper, insecure (1), suspicious (1).

Untruth, *n.* See error, falsehood.

Untruthful, *adj.* See dishonest, false (2), lying.

Untutored, *adj.* See illiterate, uneducated, common (3).

Unused, *adj.* See dormant.

Unusual, *adj.* Uncommon or rare. See extraordinary, abnormal, peculiar (2), anomalous, irregular, novel, new, original (3), exceptional, unforeseeable.

Unusual punishment See cruel and unusual punishment.

Unvaried, *adj.* See regular (1), same.

Unvarnished, *adj.* See real (2), honest, naked (2), literal.

Unveil, *v.* See expose (1), disclose, exhibit (1), bare (2), clarify, present (5), manifest (2), find (1).

Unversed, *adj.* See illiterate, uneducated, blind (1).

Unwanted, *adj.* See derelict (1), alien, abandoned.

Unwarranted, *adj.* See baseless, frivolous, disproportionate, immoderate, irregular, improper, illegal, lawless (1), inexcusable.

Unwary, *adj.* See careless, negligent, heedless, reckless, inadvertent.

Unwashed, *adj.* See unclean.

Unwavering, *adj.* See constant (3), indefatigable, certain (2), reliable, faithful, fixed, loyal, permanent.

Unwelcome, *adj.* See inadmissible; hostile.

Unwholesome, *adj.* Not fit; toxic; degrading. See unclean, harmful, poisonous, corrupt (1), immoral, injurious, deleterious, prurient, obscene.

Unwieldy, *adj.* See onerous, difficult.

Unwilling, *adj.* See involuntary; refusal.

Unwise, *adj.* See improvident, juvenile (2), careless, reckless.

Unwitting, *adj.* See spontaneous.

Unworkable, *adj.* See impracticable, impossible.

Unworldly, *adj.* See intangible; religious; uneducated.

Unworthy, *adj.* Not having suitable qualities, qualifications, or value. See worthless, frivolous, inferior (2), inadequate, immoral.

Unwritten, *adj.* See verbal, oral, parol, implied, traditional.

Unwritten law, *n.* The law observed and administered by the courts that has not been enacted or promulgated in the form of a statute or ordinance (e.g., unenacted portions of the common law, customs having the force of law, principles and maxims established by judicial precedents). See common law, natural law.

Unyielding, *adj.* See inflexible, chronic, firm (2), diligent, indefatigable, precise (2), strict, strong (2), permanent, particular (2), courageous; inescapable; barren (2), callous, irreconcilable.

UPA Uniform Partnership Act.

Upbeat, *adj.* See optimistic, happy.

Upbraid, *v.* See reprimand, censure, blame.

Upbringing, *n.* See education, nurture.

Upcoming, *adj.* See future.

Update, *v.* See amend, revise, improve.

Upend, *v.* See rescind.

Upgrade, *v.* See uplift, improve, advance, promote.

Upheaval, *n.* See eruption, commotion, riot, collapse.

Uphill, *adj.* See difficult, onerous.

Uphold, *v.* See defend, conserve, maintain, save.

Upkeep, *n.* See maintenance (1), conservation, overhead; repair.

Uplift, *v.* To elevate spiritually or emotionally. Advance, better, inspire, erect, lift, exalt, dignify, glorify, improve, refine, civilize, stimulate, encourage, exhilarate, canonize, hearten, ameliorate. *Ant.* Debase.

Upper, *adj.* More elevated, higher, or superior. See major (1, 2), predominant.

Upper-class, *adj.* See class; aristocracy.

Uppermost, *adj.* See predominant, major, primary, first.

Upright, *adj.* See good, honest.

Uprising, *n.* See riot, mutiny, insurrection, rebellion.

Uproar, *n.* See commotion; disturbance, eruption; confusion; emotion, passion, noise.

Uproot, *v.* See excise (2); destroy.

Upset, *v.* See defeat, rescind; disturb.

Upstanding, *adj.* See reputable, honest.

Upstart, *n.* Parvenu. Social climber, nouveau riche, pretender, snob, intruder.

Upsurge, *v.,* **Upsurge,** *n.* See increase.

Upswing, *n.* See improvement, betterment.

Uptight, *adj.* See apprehensive, concerned, feverish; destitute.

Up-to-date, *adj.* See progressive, current, chic.

Up-to-the-minute, *adj.* See present (3), current.

Urban, *adj.* Of or belonging to a city or town. See metropolitan.

Urbane, *adj.* See chic, debonair, civil (3), cultivated, worldly.

Urbanity, *n.* See discretion (3), delicacy, facility (3), experience (1), skill (1), ability.

Urban renewal, *n.* Redevelopment. Slum clearance, rehabilitation, restoration. See also renewal.

Urchin, *n.* See juvenile (1), orphan, child, minor; tramp, derelict (3), outcast.

URESA See Uniform Reciprocal Enforcement of Support Act.

Urge, *v.* See encourage (1), persuade, press (1), advocate, beseech, petition, entice, provoke.

Urgency, *n.* See exigency, emergency, crisis, importance, import (2).

Urgent, *adj.* See earnest (2), exigent, important, critical (1).

Urinal, *n.* See bathroom.

Urinalysis, *n.* A chemical analysis of urine. See examination.

Urn, *n.* See vessel (2).

Usable, *adj.* See fit, operative.

Usage, *n.* A custom that is widely known or established; a uniform practice or course of conduct; a repetition of acts; handling or manipulation. See practice (1), custom (1), procedure, formula (1), manner (1), method, convention (3).

Usance, *n.* The customary period for the payment of foreign bills of exchange.

U.S.C. See United States Code.

U.S.C.A. See United States Code Annotated.

U.S.C.S. See United States Code Service.

Use 1. *v.* To utilize or convert to one's service. See employ (2), manipulate. **2.** *n.* The application or employment of something; usage, or the fact of being used or employed habitually. The enjoyment of property that consists in its employment, occupation, exercise, or practice. Exploitation, utilization, operation, disposal, manipulation, administration, adoption, service, utility, usefulness, advantage, function, serviceability. **3.** *n.* The right of one person, called the cestui que use, to take the profits from land of which another has legal title. Beneficial interest or ownership. An estate vested since the statute of uses. See statute of uses. **4.** *n.* Value. See worth (1).

Use and derivative use immunity A witness is given immunity from the use of compelled testimony and the evidence derived therefrom; it cannot be used in a subsequent prosecution of the witness. See transactional immunity, immunity.

Useful, *adj.* Functional, accomplishing its purpose practically; serviceable; valuable. See practicable, effective, functional, operative, worthy; help (1).

Useful life The period of time for which an asset is capable of being used for the production of income.

Useless, *adj.* See worthless (1), barren, fallow, dead, abortive.

User, *n.* **1.** One who exercises or enjoys a right. See party, person. **2.** See addict (1).

Use tax An ad valorem tax on the use, consumption, or storage of tangible property. See tax.

Use variance An authorization to use land for a purpose that is proscribed by the zoning regulations. See zoning, exception (3).

Usher, usherette, *n.* Escort or doorkeeper. Guide, concierge, attendant, porter, conductor, guard, butler, maid, gatekeeper, director, companion. See also watchman.

Usual, *adj.* According to custom or usage. See customary, habitual, conventional (1), common (1), commonplace.

Usual course See regular course of business.

Usufruct, *n.* The right to use and obtain the profits from something vested in another so long as it is not altered or damaged thereby.

Usurious, *adj.* Pertaining to usury; charging excessive interest. See usury, predatory, excess, loansharking, avaricious; stingy; lend, loan.

Usurp, *v.* To seize and hold any office by force and without right; to assume the functions, rights, or powers of another without authority to do so. See misappropriate, assume (3), seize, interfere, depose (2), encroach, rob, impede, attack.

Usurpation, *n.* See usurp, assumption (3), seizure, pre-emption (1), infringement, deprivation, intrusion.

Usury, *n.* Laws on the charging of interest rates; lending money at an interest rate in excess of that authorized by law.

Utensil, *n.* See apparatus, instrument (2), device, equipment.

Uterine, *adj.* **1.** Born of the same mother but with a different father. **2.** Pertaining to the uterus.

Utilitarian, *adj.* See practicable, feasible, functional, effective, operative, beneficial.

Utility, *n.* **1.** Usefulness; the capability of being applied in a practical, advantageous way. See worth (1), use (2), help (1), convenience, profit (1), service (2). **2.** See public utility.

Utilize, *v.* See employ (2), manipulate, exploit.

Utmost, *adj.* See maximum, predominant, chief (2); outer.

Utopia, *n.* See heaven, perfection.

Utopian, *adj.* See impracticable, fictitious, illusory; perfect.

Utter 1. *v.* To put or send into circulation; to declare directly or indirectly by words or actions that an instrument is good; to offer a forged instrument and directly or indirectly claim that it is genuine (utter a forged check). See cheat (1), deceive, forge (1). **2.** *v.* To express aloud. See communicate, voice (2), publish. **3.** *adj.* Total or entire. See complete (2), absolute, gross (1).

Utterance, *n.* See communication, declaration, report (1, 2).

Uxoricide, *n.* The killing of one's wife. See homicide.

V.A. See Veterans Administration.

Vacancy, *n.* The condition or status of being empty, unfilled, or unoccupied. Gap, void, crater, opening, breach, crevice, hollowness, space, orifice, cleft, pore; position, opportunity. See also home, residence, habitation; job (1).

Vacant, *adj.* Empty, not in use, uninhabited, unfurnished, unutilized, and vacuous. See unoccupied, abandoned (1), void (3), dormant.

Vacate, *v.* **1.** To annul or set aside. See rescind, quash. **2.** To move out, surrender, or evacuate. See abandon (1), depart (1), retire (1).

Vacation, *n.* A time away from active duty or employment. Holiday, break, R & R, rest, release, time off, freedom, recuperation, interruption, pause, intermission, furlough, breather, sabbatical, leisure, trip, repose, excursion. See also leave (5), voyage, travel, junket.

Vacation of judgment The setting aside of a judgment on the ground that it was issued by mistake, inadvertence, surprise, excusable neglect, or fraud. See rescind; judgment.

Vacatur "Let it be vacated."

Vaccinate, *v.* See inoculate, prevent; treatment, medicine; cure (1); sanitation.

Vaccinated, *adj.* See safe, immune.

Vaccine, *n.* See medicine, prevention.

Vacillate, *v.* See alternate (1), stray (1), flounder; capricious.

Vacillating, *adj.* See variable, capricious.

Vacillation, *n.* See doubt (2); fluctuating, shift, capricious.

Vacuity, *n.* Emptiness. Void, hollowness, nihility, inanity, asininity, stupidity, imbecility, ignorance, mindlessness, trash, bunk, idiocy, nonsense, chatter, hogwash. See also balderdash, refuse, vacancy. *Ant.* Substance.

Vacuous, *adj.* See vacant, void (3), barren, lunatic, dumb, absurd.

Vacuum, *n.* See need (1), dearth, absence (2), want, deficiency, vacancy, abyss.

Vadium, *n.* Security by pledge of property. See pledge (1).

Vagabond 1. *n.* A vagrant or homeless wanderer without means of honest livelihood. See tramp (1). **2.** *adj.* Traveling, homeless. Transient, gypsy, bohemian, drifting, transitory, footloose, rootless, migratory, roving, peripatetic, wandering, nomadic, fly-by-night, shiftless, truant, disreputable.

Vagrancy, *n.* Going about from place to place without visible means of support, begging, etc. Drifting, wayfaring, roaming, hoboism, gallivanting, bumming around. See also loiter; tramp.

Vagrant 1. *n.* An idle wanderer with no visible means of support. See tramp (1). **2.** *adj.* Roaming or nomadic. See vagabond (2).

Vague, *adj.* Not susceptible of being understood. See ambiguous, indefinite, obscure; vagueness.

Vagueness, *n.* Unclarity. Obscurity, imprecision, unintelligibility, fuzziness, obfuscation, cloudiness, dimness, abstractness, dubiousness, indefiniteness, inexactness, haziness, opaqueness, uncertainty, inconstancy, confusion, incomprehensibility. See also ambiguity.

Vagueness doctrine A law that does not fairly inform a person of what is commanded or prohibited is unconstitutional.

Vain, *adj.* See arrogant, pompous; parochial, narrow; boast; barren, worthless.

Vainglorious, *adj.* See arrogant, pompous; boast.

Valedictory, *n.* See speech, address.

Valet, *n.* See servant (2), employee.

Valiant, *adj.* See courageous, strong, adventurous, alive (2), ardent.

Valid, *adj.* Having the force of law; legally sufficient. See effective (2), binding, lawful, legal, authentic, legitimate, genuine; validity.

Validate, *v.* To make valid, confirm, or sanction. See ratify, affirm (2), authorize, corroborate, certify.

Validity, *n.* Truthfulness, accuracy, and effectiveness. Authenticity, constitutionality, soundness, authority, veracity, genuineness, potency, correctness, substance, logic, applicability, weight, persuasiveness, cogency, strength, verifiability, factuality, significance, actuality, verity, morality, reality, truth, lawfulness. See also legality, legitimacy.

Valium, *n.* See drug; medicine, treatment.

Valley, *n.* An opening or depression between high lands. River basin, hollow, gap, cavity, dale, chasm, gulch, crater, glen, ravine, canyon, divide.

Valor, *n.* Courage or fortitude. Daring, bravado, virility, tenacity, boldness, bravery, endurance, "moxie," steadfastness, chivalry, audacity, prowess, gallantry, rashness, resolution, will power, self-confidence, self-reliance, determination, stamina, fortitude, spunk, "guts," nerve, toughness. See also spirit. *Ant.* Timidity.

Valuable, *adj.* Commanding or worth a good price. See beneficial, marketable, worthy, meritorious; costly.

Valuable consideration Some right, interest, profit, or benefit accruing to one party, or some forbearance, detriment, loss, or responsibility given, suffered, or undertaken by the other. See consideration.

Valuate, *v.* See appraise, judge (3), assess.

Valuation, *n.* Ascertaining the worth of a thing; the estimated worth of a thing. See assessment (1, 3), appraisal, estimate (1), examination, investigate, measure (1).

Value 1. *n.* The usefulness or utility of something in satisfying a human need. See worth (1), importance, appraisal, cost (1). **2.** *v.* See appraise, judge (3), assess.

Value-added tax, *n.* A tax on the increased value of goods at each stage as they move through production, manufacturing, and distribution to the marketplace. See tax.

Valueless, *adj.* See worthless (1), barren, dead.

Valve, *n.* See device (1).

Van, *n.* See vehicle.

Vandal, *n.* See wrongdoer, delinquent.

Vandalic, *adj.* Willfully or ignorantly destructive. See malicious.

Vandalism, *n.* Willful or ignorant destruction of property. See mischief, piracy; destroy.

Vandalize, *v.* See destroy, harm.

Vanguard, *n.* See forefront, avant-garde.

Vanish, *v.* See disappear, withdraw, dissolve, end.

Vanity, *n.* See arrogance, pretense; delusion.

Vanquish, *v.* See defeat, conquer, beat.

Vantage, *n.* See benefit (1), aid (2), mileage (2); dominion, superiority, authority, influence.

Vapid, *adj.* See void (3), barren, pedestrian (2), commonplace.

Vapor, *n.* See fog.

Vaporize, *v.* See distill (1).

Variable, *adj.* Changeable, alterable, or varied (variable price). Emotional, mercurial, vacillating, unsteady, faddish, elastic, modifiable, convertible, volatile, diverse, mutable, inconstant, undependable, transformable, adjustable, fickle, unfixed, interchangeable, intermittent, diversified, indefinite. See also fluctuating, capricious, irregular.

Variance, *n.* **1.** Permission to depart from the literal requirements of a zoning ordinance. See exception (3), dispensation, modification, change. **2.** A difference of opinion. See disagreement, argument, dispute. **3.** An inconsistency between two allegations or positions. See discrepancy, contradiction.

Variation, *n.* See modification, amendment, change.

Varied, *adj.* See multifarious, divers, sundry, multiple, mixed, many, different.

Variegate, *v.* See change (2), divide; diffuse.

Variety, *n.* Diversity, change; kind, class, grade (3), collection, multitude, classification; range (2), scope, extent, measure (1).

Various, *adj.* **1.** Diverse; heterogeneous; motley. See divers, sundry, multifarious, multiple, mixed, many, different, separate (1). **2.** Ample. See abundant.

Varnish, *v., n.* See beautify, color; pretense.

Vary, *v.* See change (2), alter, alternate; depart, divert.

Varying, *adj.* See fluctuating, variable.

Vase, *n.* See vessel (2).

Vasectomy, *n.* Resection of the ductus deferens. Sterilization of the male by surgical excision of part of the vas deferens. See contraceptive, sterilization.

Vassal, *n.* A feudal tenant or grantee. See slave (1).

Vast, *adj.* See big, great, incalculable, comprehensive, broad.

Vat, *n.* See vessel (2).

Vault, *n., v.* See depository, vessel (2); arc; jump, run.

Vaunt, *v.* See boast, exaggerate; arrogance, pompous.

Veer, *v.* See stray (1), wander, digress, skid, depart (2); fluctuating.

Vegetable, *n.* See food; nonentity.

Vegetate, *v.* See exist; loiter, mope.

Vegetation, *n.* See shrubbery, timber, woods.

Vehement, *adj.* See violent, emotional, earnest (2), ardent, demonstrative (2), strong (2).

Vehicle, *n.* **1.** A device used for transportation. Carrier, transport, conveyance, motor vehicle, car, rocket, ship, truck, wagon, bicycle, motorcycle, streetcar, automobile, trolley, sled, coach, tank, bus, subway, tractor, moped, tandem, three-speed, ten-speed, tricycle, unicycle, bike, bobsled, boxcar, buggy, cab, taxi, cable car, cart, caisson, camper, caravan, carriage, combine, common carrier, plane. See also vessel (1), aircraft. **2.** A medium or method. See agency (4), instrumentality, instrument (3).

Vehicular homicide Homicide caused by the illegal operation of a motor vehicle. See homicide.

Veil, *v.* See disguise (1), conceal, cloak; fortify, defend; protection.

Vein, *n.* **1.** A vessel carrying blood to the heart. Blood vessel, capillary, artery, venule, aorta. **2.** A continuous body of mineral or mineralized rock, filling a seam or fissure in the earth's crust, within defined boundaries in the general mass of the mountain. Seam, mine, bed, stria, stratum, lode, layer, thread, stripe, ridge, furrow, groove, line. **3.** Mood, character, or temperament. See disposition (4).

Vel non "Or not." See devisavit vel non.

Velocity, *n.* See speed, range (2), scope, extent, measure (1).

Venal, *adj.* Capable of being bought; mercenary. Greedy, covetous, grasping, selfish, corruptible, purchasable, avaricious, bribable. See also corrupt, dishonest.

Vend, *v.* See sell.

Vendee, *n.* See buyer.

Vendetta, *n.* A private blood feud. See war, fight, contention (2), feud.

Vendible, *adj.* Suitable for sale; merchantable. See marketable, salable, fit (1).

Vendor, *n.* See seller.

Vendue, *n.* An auction or public sale.

Veneer, *n.* See disguise (2), surface (1), face, exterior, pretense.

Venerable, *adj.* See reputable, meritorious, elevated, great, popular; holy.

Venerate, *v.* See honor (2).

Veneration, *n.* See worship; tribute (2).

Venereal disease, *n.* Diseases communicated through sexual intercourse. Syphilis, gonorrhea, chancroid.

Vengeance, *n.* See retaliation, retribution, punishment, violent.

Vengeful, *adj.* see vindictive, punitive.

Venial, *adj.* See petty, minor, excusable; justifiable.

Venire, *n.* A list of people summoned to appear as prospective jurors.

Venireman, *n.* A person summoned as a juror.

Venom, *n.* See malice, animus, poison.

Venomous, *adj.* See lethal, poisonous, harmful, malicious, deadly, vindictive.

Vent, *v., n.* See express, proclaim, communicate; communication, declaration.

Venter, *n.* The abdomen, belly, uterus, or womb. The maternal parentage of children.

Ventilate, *v.* See circulate, voice, report (4), expose.

Venture 1. *n.* An undertaking attended with risk; business speculation; a gamble or long shot. See enterprise (1), risk. **2.** *v.* To take chances. Dare, wager, strive, risk, jeopardize, gamble, tempt, speculate, bet, lay odds, plunge, imperil. See also hazard (2), endanger. **3.** *v.* To tender, put forward, or proffer. See offer (1).

Venturesome, *adj.* See ambitious, courageous, optimistic, adventurous; hazardous, dangerous, precarious, insecure.

Venue, *n.* The county or geographical area in which a court with jurisdiction may hear and determine a case. See zone, neighborhood.

Veracious, *adj.* See genuine, reliable, honest, authentic, credible, accurate; veracity.

Veracity, *n.* Accuracy, truthfulness (questions raised about the veracity of the report). Uprightness, rectitude, conscientiousness, candor, sincerity, meticulousness, frankness, straightforwardness, probity, factuality, precision, exactitude, believability, reality, integrity, openness, genuineness, authenticity, virtue, credibility, trustworthiness, verisimilitude, morality. See also verity, fact, principle (1), honor (3). *Ant.* Deception.

Verbal, *adj.* Concerned with words; expressed orally (verbal contract). Unwritten, spoken, said, uttered, word-of-mouth, stated, voiced, nuncupative, audible, informal, recited. See also parol, oral. *Ant.* Written.

Verbal act doctrine Where a declaration of an individual is so connected with his or her acts as to derive a degree of credit from this connection, independently of the declaration, the declaration becomes part of the transaction and is admissible.

Verbalize, *v.* See express (2), communicate, voice.

Verbiage, *n.* See surplusage, prolixity, balderdash.

Verbose, *adj.* Wordy. Prolix, long-winded, babbling, effusive, inflated, profuse, swollen, windy, chatty, repetitive, redundant, glib. See also pompous; surplusage; prolixity.

Verdict, *n.* The formal decision or finding of a jury, reported to the court (excessive verdict). Declaration, conclusion, award, pronouncement, assessment, determination, sentence, answer, evaluation; judgment, adjudication, decree, arbitration, settlement, order, edict, call, command; consensus, reading.

Verge, *n.* Margin or brink (verge of a solution). Edge, fringe, perimeter, frontier, curb, threshold, lip, confine. See also border (1), boundary.

Verification, *n.* See proof, evidence, confirmation; verify, corroborate.

Verify, *v.* **1.** To confirm by oath or affidavit (verify the accuracy of the amount). Substantiate, certify, validate, stand behind, vouch for, affirm, witness, demonstrate, bear out, authenticate, uphold, warrant, attest to, establish, accredit, guarantee, document, acknowledge. See also prove, corroborate. **2.** To test (verify the results). Evaluate, probe, examine, estimate, ascertain, analyze, weigh. See also appraise, assess, judge (3), investigate, review, audit.

Verily, *adv.* In very truth. Beyond doubt or question, in fact, certainly, truly, confidently, really.

Verisimilitude, *n.* See veracity; likelihood, probability.

Veritable, *adj.* See accurate, correct (1), real, bona fide.

Verity, *n.* Conformity to fact. True statement, actuality, reality, authenticity, truth; moral principle. See also validity, veracity.

Vermin, *n.* See refuse; tramp (1), wrongdoer, parasite.

Vermouth, *n.* See liquor, beverage.

Vernacular, *adj., n.* See common, informal, popular, vulgar; language, term of art.

Versatile, *adj.* See competent, expert (2), able, apt (3), qualified, effective, mature (2).

Verse, *n.* See poem.

Versed, *adj.* See qualified (1), able, expert (2), apt (3), learned, literary (2), cultivated.

Version, *n.* See opinion, description; revision; book (4).

Versus (vs.), *prep.* Against.

Vertical, *adj.* Up and down (vertical restraint). Upright, perpendicular. *Ant.* Horizontal.

Vertical integration The control of the production and distribution of goods from raw material to their sale to the ultimate consumer.

Vertical merger A merger between two companies that have a buyer-seller relationship with each other (i.e., one produces a product that is then sold to the other). See merger.

Vertical price fixing An attempt to control retail prices; resale price maintenance. See monopoly.

Vertigo, *n.* See confusion; dizzy.

Verve, *n.* See life (3), vigor, spirit, emotion.

Very, *adv.* In a very high degree. Exceedingly, positively, incalculably, greatly, decidedly, hugely, extremely, uncommonly, entirely, unusually, exceptionally. *Ant.* Slightly.

Vespers, *n.* See worship, prayer (2), ceremony.

Vessel, *n.* **1.** A vehicle used in navigation on water. Brig, craft, boat, barge, ferry, raft, tanker, tug, liner, flagship, steamer, freighter, ark, yacht, carrier, destroyer, houseboat, armada, battleship, man-of-war, gunboat, cruiser, submarine, canoe, clipper, coaster, common carrier, container ship, steamship, cruiser, dredge. See also vehicle (1). **2.** A container or tube. Can, urn, canister, vase, receptacle, pitcher, basin, cask, vial, pot, utensil, bowl, mug, tube, duct, artery, basket, hamper, bucket, box, bassinet, bin, bottle, jar, bunker, bushel, cage, caisson, carton, cartridge, chassis, cistern, vat, drum, tub, hogshead, butt, tun, kettle, caldron, casket, catchall, chute, glass. See also package, wrapper.

Vest, *v.* To give an immediate, fixed right of present or future enjoyment; to put into possession (the right to receive the funds vested upon reaching majority age).

Vest

Take effect, accrue, fix, clothe, furnish, endow, confer, grant, sanction, invest, hand over, empower, authorize, entrust. See also enable, entitle, assign. *Ant.* Divest.

Vested, *adj.* Fixed; not subject to be defeated by a condition (vested pension rights). Accrued, settled, not contingent, absolute, irrevocable, set, inalienable, immutable, established, inviolable, unquestionable, indisputable, protected, warranted, guaranteed. See also complete, permanent. *Ant.* Contingent.

Vested interest An interest in which there is a present fixed right either of present or of future enjoyment. See interest, right (3).

Vested remainder A remainder limited to a certain person at a certain time or upon the happening of a necessary event; an absolute right to become a possessory interest at the end of a prior particular estate. See remainder.

Vested right An immediate or fixed right to present or future enjoyment, which is not dependent on an uncertain event. See right (3).

Vestibule, *n.* See entrance; passage (2), course.

Vestige, *n.* See remainder (2), memento, memory.

Vestigial, *adj.* Pertaining to a trace or vestige (vestigial words).

Vestigial words Language remaining in a statute that has been rendered useless or meaningless by reason of later amendments.

Veteran 1. *n.* Any honorably discharged member of the military (a demonstration by the veterans). Vet, ex-serviceman, old soldier. **2.** *n.* An expert (a veteran at the plant). Master, professional, old hand, trouper, authority. See also expert (1), specialist. **3.** *adj.* Having considerable experience and skill (veteran court reporter). Polished, skilled, seasoned, versed, knowledgeable, proficient, trained, accomplished, adroit, "ace," prepared. See also able, apt (3). *Ant.* Neophyte.

Veterans Administration A federal agency that administers benefits to those who served in the armed forces and to their dependents (e.g., pension, health care, etc.).

Veterinarian, *n.* One who practices the art of treating diseases and injuries of animals. See specialist, expert; medicine.

Veto 1. *n.* A chief executive's refusal to assent to a proposed law enacted by the legislature. See rejection. **2.** *v.* To refuse to consent. See reject (1); rescind.

Vex, *v.* To disquiet or annoy. See harass, disturb, accost (1), outrage (2), exacerbate, provoke, assault, attack.

Vexation, *n.* A source of irritation; an injury or damage suffered as a result of the tricks of another. See annoyance, grievance, mischief, affliction, burden, nuisance, provocation, wrong (1).

Vexatious, *adj.* **1.** Without reasonable or probable cause or excuse (vexatious delay). Groundless, unwarranted, illusory, uncalled-for, without basis, baseless, fallacious, imaginary, chimerical, unneeded, unsupported, tenuous, irrational, illogical, ridiculous, unsubstantial, needless, unfounded, unnecessary, superfluous, dispensable, excess, redundant, expendable, gratuitous. **2.** Annoying. See offensive, distressing. *Ant.* Justified; innocuous.

Vexatious proceeding An action or proceeding instituted maliciously and without probable cause.

Vexing, *adj.* See offensive, distressing; difficult, painful; vexatious.

Via 1. *n.* Way or road. See highway, pass (8), passage (2). **2.** *prep.* By way of, by means of. See through.

Viability, *n.* Capability of living. That stage of fetal development when the life of the unborn child may be continued indefinitely outside the womb by natural or artificial life-supporting systems.

Viable, *adj.* **1.** Capable of living (viable child). Potential, sprouting, nascent, developing, growing. See also alive (1), live; viability. **2.** See feasible, practicable, logical, reasonable. *Ant.* Futile.

Vial, *n.* See vessel (2).

Vibrant, *adj.* See alive (2), active (2), ardent, strong.

Vibrate, *v.* See beat (3), reverberate.

Vicar, *n.* One who performs the functions of another. See agent (1).

Vicarious, *adj.* Experienced, endured, or substituting for another (vicarious punishment). Proxy, indirect, secondhand; delegated, commissioned. See also surrogate (3).

Vicarious liability Being responsible because someone else is responsible; indirect legal responsibility (e.g., an employer is liable for the negligence of its employee). See liability.

Vice 1. *pref.* In substitution for (vice-president). In the place of, in the stead of. **2.** *n.* Immoral conduct. See corruption, fault (1), wrong (1), delinquency, debauchery, lapse (3).

Vice consul, *n.* A consular officer who is subordinate to and temporarily substitutes for a consul or consul general. See delegate (2), officer.

Vice principal, *n.* An employee with authority to direct and supervise work, and authority to hire and discharge subordinate workers. See manager.

Vice versa, *adv.* In reverse order. Conversely, on the other hand, in inverted order, the other way around, contrariwise.

Vicinity, *n.* The state or quality of being near (in the vicinity of the crime). Nearness, neighborhood, propinquity, proximity, region, adjacent area, space, environs, area, surroundings, periphery, closeness, adjacency, bounds; nearby, not remote. See also presence (1); near.

Vicious, *adj.* Seriously tending to endanger safety (vicious tendencies). See corrupt (1), dangerous, bad (2), cruel, malicious.

Vicissitude, *n.* See chance (2), destiny; change, modification; experience (2).

Victim, *n.* The person who is the subject of a crime, tort, or other wrong (testimony by the victim against the accused). Target, complainant, innocent, bystander, casualty, sufferer, injured party, aggrieved, scapegoat, dupe, martyr, fatality, prey, deceased, wounded, injured, recipient, subject, object, patient, mark. See also pawn (3). *Ant.* Wrongdoer.

Victimize, *v.* See abuse, exploit (1), wrong (4), manipulate, rig, deceive, cheat.

Victimless crime A crime that involves only or primarily the criminal (e.g., illegal possession of drugs).

Victor, *n.* See champion (3).

Victorian, *adj.* See parochial, narrow (2); ascetic.

Victorious, *adj.* See dominant, predominant, effective, fertile, gainful, ascendant (2).

Victory, *n.* See conquest, dominion, coup, supremacy.

Vie, *n.* Life.

Vi et armis With force and arms.

View 1. *v.* See observe, watch (1). **2.** *v.* To judge. See consider, regard (1). **3.** *n.* Observation. See examination, inspection. **4.** *n.* Judgment. See belief, opinion (2). **5.** *n.* Scene (the view was obstructed). Panorama, vision, range, vista, spectacle, landscape, setting, outlook, image, perspective, scenery, picture. See also environment, neighborhood.

Viewer, *n.* See eyewitness, witness, bystander.

Viewpoint, *n.* See opinion, belief, manner.

Vigil, *n.* Remaining awake and on guard. See inspection; watch; vigilance.

Vigilance, *n.* A proper degree of activity in pursuing one's rights and opportunities (vigilance in discovering the fraud). Watchfulness, precaution, prudence, circumspection, discretion, heedfulness, providence, calculation, preparation, consideration, shrewdness, alertness, foresight, deliberation, apprehension, observance, attention, care, forethought, concern, keenness, regard, wariness, discrimination, mindfulness, conscientiousness. *Ant.* Laches.

Vigilant, *adj.* Attentive to discover and avoid danger (vigilant in the operation of the crane). See cautious, careful, prudent.

Vigilante, *n.* A member of a group that takes the law into its own hands in the apprehension and punishment of criminals. See usurp.

Vigor, *n.* Strength or spirit (the task was attacked with vigor). Vitality, power, forcefulness, potency, enthusiasm, fire, robustness, force, energy, steel, drive, might, stamina, zeal, passion, verve, sturdiness, ardor, gusto, prowess, effectiveness, vehemence, hardiness, vivacity, élan, zing, sparkle, animation, endurance, mettle, fervor, dash, liveliness, "spunk," health, intensity, impact, muscle. See also life (3). *Ant.* Frailty.

Vigorous, *adj.* See durable, healthy, able-bodied, indefatigable, diligent, strong (2), active (3).

Vile, *adj.* See malicious, bad, corrupt, odious, immoral, repulsive, filthy, obscene, vulgar.

Vilify, *v.* See defame, slander, censure, debase, reprimand.

Villa, *n.* See home, estate (3).

Village, *n.* A collective body of inhabitants. See community (1), city.

Villain, *n.* An evil person. See wrongdoer.

Villainous, *adj.* See immoral, base, corrupt, bad, malicious, cruel.

Villainy, *n.* See cruelty, tyranny, oppression, coercion.

Vim, *n.* See life (3), vigor, spirit, passion.

Vincible, *adj.* See susceptible, weak, insecure (1), precarious, helpless.

Vinculo matrimonii See divorce a vinculo matrimonii.

Vindicate, *v.* To clear of suspicion, blame, or doubt (the investigation vindicated him). Exonerate, free, acquit, absolve, exculpate, justify, corroborate, reprieve, discharge, rationalize, liberate, declare innocent, pardon, excuse, dismiss, bear out, support, advocate, bolster, uphold, maintain, champion. *Ant.* Convict.

Vindication, *n.* See pardon (1); vindicate.

Vindictive, *adj.* Characterized by desire for revenge (a vindictive response). Vengeful, malicious, retaliatory, hostile, resentful, retributive, venomous, spiteful, avenging, malevolent, retaliative, unrelenting, punitive, malignant, angry, unforgiving, hardhearted, unmerciful, bitter, inexorable, malign, evil, godless, implacable, antagonistic, base, unconciliatory. *Ant.* Magnanimous.

Vintage, *adj., n.* See old, ancient; superior (2), best; mature; liquor; yield (2).

Violate, *v.* See break (1), encroach, interfere; impede, hinder; attack (1), assault (3), corrupt, rape, debase, mock, slander, usurp.

Violation, *n.* Breach of a duty, right, or law (she was dismissed because of the violation). Infringement, mistreatment, wrong, desolation, illegality, disruption, misdemeanor, offense, felony, crime, evasion, lawbreaking, infraction, abuse, trespass, tort, encroachment, intrusion, inroad, interruption, plunder, dereliction, irreverence, disrespect, immorality, brutality, ignorance, fault, rape, delinquency, misfeasance, nonfeasance, malfeasance, misbehavior, misdeed, transgression, disregard, disobedience, breach of trust, destruction, adulteration, sin, sacrilege, defilement, corruption, contravention, maltreatment, dishonor, opposition, misuse. *Ant.* Compliance.

Violence, *n.* The unjust and unwarranted use of force (the argument led to street violence). Physical force, brute force, brutality, rage, ferocity, assault, vehemence, savagery, fierceness, fury, severity, destructiveness, madness, passion, abandon, onslaught, frenzy, craziness, anarchy, turbulence, uproar, rebellion, fire, hysteria, attack, outburst, rampage, bestiality, excessiveness, storm, bedlam, disruption, explosion, extremity, desecration, fracas, blood. See also eruption, riot, commotion, cruelty. *Ant.* Calmness.

Violent, *adj.* Characterized by physical force; tempestuous (violent confrontation). Stormy, savage, furious, vehement, passionate, cruel, fiery, destructive, inhuman, harsh, perilous, brutal, boiling, rabid, intense, unremitting, crazed, explosive, hot, raging, murderous, seething, berserk, surging, psychopathic, demonic, insane, headstrong, excruciating, stinging, racking, ferocious, intractable, unbridled, volcanic, howling, burning, wild, brutish, injurious, damaging, killing, deleterious, ruinous, barbaric, ruthless, irrational, unruly, merciless, bloodthirsty, lethal, calamitous, painful, tormenting, stern, frenetic, rash, catastrophic. *Ant.* Tranquil.

VIP, *n.* See chief (1).

Viperous, *adj.* See cruel, malicious, base, bad, vindictive.

Vires Powers or capabilities. See ultra vires.

Virgin, *adj.* See chaste; new, maiden (2); clean, innocent, blameless.

Virginity, *n.* See celibacy, abstention.

Virile, *adj.* See courageous, durable, able-bodied, healthy.

Virility, *n.* See vigor, life (3), force, power, passion.

Virtual, *adj.* In essence though not in actuality (virtual stranger in his home). Functioning as, essential, acting as, implicit, effective, tacit, implied, indirect, equivalent to, tantamount.

Virtue, 1. *n.* Integrity and character (her virtue was compromised). Righteousness, honesty, chastity, piety, incorruptibility, goodness, rectitude, morality, probity, purity, justice, faith, merit, fortitude, charity, principle, uprightness, modesty, decency, equity, impeccability, worthiness, excellence, intelligence, understanding, temperance, nobility, fair play, constancy, respectability, high-mindedness, purpose; blessing, strength, boon, gift, credit. See also integrity (1), honor (3). **2.** On the grounds of (success by virtue of her stamina). Because of, by reason of, on the basis of, on account of, owing to, in view of, by authority of, power. *Ant.* Weakness; in spite of.

Virtuoso, *n.* See expert (1), professional (2), artisan.

Virtuous, *adj.* See moral (2), honest, good (2), innocent, blameless, clean (1).

Virulent, *adj.* See harmful, deleterious, dangerous; hostile, vindictive.

Virus, *n.* See germ (1).

Visa, *n.* An official indorsement on a document, passbook, commercial book, etc., to certify that it has been examined and found correct or in due form; an indorsement on a passport giving the holder permission to enter or leave a country. See permission.

Visage, *n.* See countenance, face (1).

Vis-à-vis 1. *prep.* In relation to (income vis-à-vis losses). Contrasted with, in regard to, as distinguished from, compared to, in comparison with. **2.** *adv., adj.* Face to face (negotiating vis-à-vis). Eyeball to eyeball, side by side, in company, together, head to head.

Visceral, *adj.* See spontaneous, immediate, emotional, natural (3), involuntary.

Visible, *adj.* Open or perceptible (visible means of support). Discernible, evident, clear, distinct, conspicuous, patent, manifest, obvious, apparent, prominent, glaring, unmistakable, perceivable, noticeable, recognizable, discoverable, in view, palpable, marked, revealed, undisguised, plain, unhidden, detectable, salient, pronounced, blatant, inescapable. *Ant.* Concealed.

Vision, *n.* See sight (1), perception, judgment (2), foresight, discretion (3), maturity, prudence, education; dream (1), hallucination, fiction.

Visionary, *n.* See oracle, augur, clairvoyance (2), nonconformist, avant-garde.

Visit, *v.* **1.** To come, stay, or go temporarily (visited her father). Call upon, stop by, appear, look up, go to see, come to see, inspect, sojourn, travel to, drop in on. **2.** See cause, impose.

Visitation, *n.* **1.** Calling upon or being called upon (visitation rights of the noncustodial parent). **2.** Regulation or examination. See inspection, regulation (2).

Visitor, *n.* One who makes a visit. Transient, caller, company, tourist, patron, traveler, voyager, houseguest, vacationer. See also guest.

Vis major, *n.* An irresistible force; a greater or superior force; pertaining to a loss that results immediately from a natural cause without human intervention and which could not have been prevented by the exercise of reasonable care.

Vista, *n.* See view (5), environment, neighborhood.

Visual, *adj.* See apparent, clear, palpable.

Visualize, *v.* See contemplate, think, foresee, regard, fantasize, dream (1), realize (3).

Vital, *adj.* **1.** Essential (vital records). Life-and-death, basic, crucial, indispensable, key, chief, pivotal, important, critical, focal, needed, urgent, main, imperative, material, principal, elementary, paramount, pressing, significant, cardinal, serious, leading, compulsory. **2.** Pertaining to life (vital signs). Breathing, life-preserving, animating, living, biological, viable, quick. **3.** Energetic. See active (3). *Ant.* Minor; death; listless.

Vitality, *n.* See life (3), vigor, spirit, passion.

Vital statistics, *n.* Public records kept by the government on births, deaths, marriages, etc.

Vitiate, *v.* To destroy the legal efficacy and binding force of something (fraud vitiates the contract). See destroy, rescind, quash, impair.

Vitriolic, *adj.* See caustic, biting, cutting, malicious, hostile, derogatory.

Vituperate, *v.* See reprimand, condemn (3), castigate.

Vituperative, *adj.* See vitriolic.

Vivacious, *adj.* See active (3), alive (2), ardent.

Viva voce, *adv.*, *adj.* By word of mouth. With the living voice, orally.

Vivid, *adj.* See descriptive, clear.

Vivify, *v.* See animate, revive, initiate, incite.

Vivisection, *n.* The dissection of living animals for scientific reasons.

Viz Namely. That is to say, to wit.

Vocabulary, *n.* See language, word, communication.

Vocal, *adj.* See oral, verbal, parol; open (5), public, demonstrative.

Vocalize, *v.* See express (2), voice, communicate.

Vocation, *n.* One's regular occupation or business. See calling, business.

Vocational, *adj.* See technical.

Vociferous, *adj.* Making a loud outcry (vociferous dissenter). Clamorous, blatant, boisterous, vocal, shrill, uproarious, shouting, rackety, deafening, demanding, yelling, piercing, screeching, blustering, thundering, blaring. See also noisy. *Ant.* Subdued.

Vodka, *n.* See liquor, beverage.

Vogue, *n.* See style (3), caprice; chic, current (3).

Voice 1. *n.* Choice or vote (a voice in the election). Opinion, say, comment, part, preference, suffrage, expression, role, representation, option, participation. **2.** *v.* To make oneself heard (voice an opinion). Utter, express, articulate, reveal, announce, verbalize, pronounce, speak, divulge, ventilate, assert, disclose, declare, mention, broadcast, publish, air, vocalize. See also communicate. *Ant.* Suppress (2).

Voice exemplars A type of test in which one's voice is compared with the voice heard on a particular occasion.

Voiceprint, *n.* A "print" of one's voice produced by a spectograph for use in comparing such readings with the actual voice of the person.

Void 1. *adj.* Having no legal force or binding effect (void signature). Nugatory, null, ineffectual, unenforceable, inoperative, futile, invalid, cancelled, nonviable, useless, meaningless, vain, dead, annulled, unavailing, unproductive, powerless, ineffective, invalidated, rescinded, disestablished, inane, inconsequential, worthless, idle, incurable. **2.** *v.* To invalidate. See rescind, quash, destroy. **3.** *adj.* Lacking (void of meaning). Devoid, empty, unsupplied, deserted, bare, wanting, destitute, free, hollow, unfilled, barren, lacking, clear, blank. **4.** *n.* See vacancy. *Ant.* Valid; validate; replete.

Void ab initio Invalid from its inception or beginning. See ab initio.

Voidable, *adj.* Pertaining to that which may be avoided or declared invalid; pertaining to that which is defective but which remains effective until declared invalid (voidable contract). Subject to cancellation, capable of being declared void, revocable, reversible, nullifiable.

Voidable marriage A marriage that can be annulled because of its invalidity but which remains valid until a court declares it invalid. See marriage.

Voidable preference A preference given to a creditor of a bankrupt over other creditors in the same class.

Void for vagueness A law that is so obscure that a reasonable person could not determine what the law purports to command or prohibit. See vagueness.

Void judgment A judgment with no force or legal effect. See judgment.

Void marriage A marriage that was void from its inception; a marriage that is invalid whether or not a court declares its invalidity. See marriage.

Void on its face The invalidity of the document is relatively easy to determine upon inspection.

Voir dire, *n.* Jury selection; a preliminary examination of prospective jurors or witnesses to inquire into their competence. "To speak the truth."

Volatile, *adj.* See excitable, incendiary (2), outrageous, violent, ardent, emotional, feverish, demonstrative, angry, capricious.

Volcanic, *adj.* See volatile.

Volenti non fit injuria There is no cause of action for damages suffered by consent. See assumption of the risk.

Volition, *n.* See will, choice, discretion, freedom.

Volley, *n.* See eruption, discharge, storm, attack; noise.

Volume, *n.* See extent; book (4).

Voluminous, *adj.* See big, great, comprehensive, broad, copious.

Voluntary, *adj.* Proceeding from the free and unconstrained will of a person (voluntary payment). By choice, uncoerced, elective, without compulsion, by design, optional, willed, uncompelled, on purpose, chosen, gratuitous, unforced, unimpelled, volitional. See also premeditated, willful, intentional, deliberate (2), spontaneous, free. *Ant.* Coerced.

Voluntary manslaughter The intentional, unlawful killing of someone without malice or premeditation. See manslaughter, homicide; kill.

Voluntary nonsuit The plaintiff abandons his or her case and consents to the entry of a judgment against him or her. See nonsuit.

Volunteer 1. *n.* A person who provides services without any express or implied promise of remuneration. Unpaid worker, charity worker, gratuitous worker, good samaritan. See also patron, backer. **2.** *v.* To provide or be willing to provide services (volunteer to undergo the experiment). Step forward, present oneself, submit, put forward, donate, supply, contribute, tender. See also offer.

Voluptuous, *adj.* See carnal, physical, prodigal, wild, attractive, enjoyable, beautiful, delectable, abundant, big.

Vomit, *v.* See disgorge.

Voodoo, *n.* See witchcraft.

Voracious, *adj.* See avaricious; immoderate, excess.

Vote 1. *n.* The formal expression of one's will or choice (a vote for capital punishment). Ballot, preference, suffrage, franchise, say, plebiscite, election, referendum, judgment, decision, option, count, selection, pick, poll, opinion, determination. **2.** *v.* See choose, select (1).

Voter, *n.* A person who votes or who has the qualifications to vote. Elector, balloter; constituent, resident. See also citizen.

Voting stock A type of stock that gives the holder the right to vote for directors and on other matters. See share (3) securities.

Voting trust An agreement between stockholders and a trustee whereby the rights to vote the stock are transferred to the trustee. See trust.

Vouch, *v.* To give a personal assurance or to serve as a guarantee (vouch for the accuracy of the amount). Substantiate, verify, certify, stand behind, back, indorse, subscribe, sponsor, corroborate, affirm, pledge, acknowledge, authenticate, attest to, testify, confirm, warrant, countersign, underwrite, witness, sustain, support, assure, avow, sign for, declare, document, depose. *Ant.* Disassociate.

Voucher, *n.* **1.** A receipt or release that may serve as evidence of payment or that certifies the correctness of accounts. See acknowledgment, receipt, release (3). **2.** A document that serves to recognize a liability and to authorize the disbursement of cash.

Vouching-in, *n.* A device by the defendant to bring another party into the litigation. See implead.

Vouchsafe, *v.* See give, grant (3), sanction (1), yield, let (1), patronize, condescend.

Vow, *n.* See affirmation (2), pledge (2), commitment (2).

Vox populi, *n.* Popular sentiment. See voice, communication, public, citizen.

Voyage, *n.* A journey; the passage of a vessel from one place to another (foreign voyage). Trip, cruise, crossing, trek, flight, traverse, sail, transport, safari, tour, jaunt, pilgrimage, foray, expedition, outing, junket, commute, promenade, excursion, ride, stroll, hike, navigation.

Voyeur, *n.* A person who derives sexual satisfaction from observing the sexual organs or acts of others, usually from a secret vantage point. Peeping Tom, snooper; eavesdropper, fetishist.

Vs. Versus or against (Smith vs. Jones).

Vulgar, *adj.* **1.** Lacking refinement (vulgar presentation). Unsophisticated, ignorant, unrefined, gauche, crude, coarse, base, artless, tasteless, trite, uncultivated, gross, sensational, lowbred, uncouth, lacking taste, rough, impolite, low, ignoble, illiterate, ill-mannered, loutish, raw, uncivilized, inferior, boorish, tawdry, banal, lowbrow; humble, plebian, popular, mass, proletarian, ordinary. See also common (3). **2.** Lewd. See obscene, carnal, filthy, pornographic. *Ant.* Refined.

Vulnerable, *adj.* See precarious, defenseless, dependent (2), susceptible, liable (2), destitute; hazardous, dangerous; emotional; malleable, amenable (2), formative, weak, tender (5), breakable.

Vulture, *n.* See parasite, wrongdoer.

W

Wade, *v.* See walk.

Waffle, *v.* See hedge, quibble; flounder.

Wage, *n.* Payments made to a hired person for his or her services (wage freeze). See compensation (1), income.

Wage assignment A transfer to someone else of one's right to receive wages. See assignment.

Wage earner, *n.* See laborer, employee.

Wage earner's plan A type of partial bankruptcy in which a person keeps his or her property and pays off a court-established proportion of debt over a period of time under court supervision.

Wage garnishment See garnishment.

Wager 1. *n.* A contract in which the parties agree that they will gain or lose upon the happening of an uncertain event in which they have no interest other than this possibility of gain or loss. See gambling. **2.** *v.* See bet (2), venture (2), hazard (2).

Wagon, *n.* See vehicle.

Waif, *n.* That which nobody claims. Urchin, stray, foundling, gypsy, itinerant, vagrant, ragamuffin, gamin. See also abandoned.

Wail, *v.* See bemoan, suffer, cry (1).

Wait, *v.* To stay inactive while anticipating something (wait for the decision). Anticipate, linger, await, stay, mark time, abide, look for, loiter, look forward to, tarry, queue, dally; postpone, defer, procrastinate, pause, suspend, adjourn.

Waiter, *n.* See servant, employee.

Waive, *v.* To give up a right, claim, or privilege intentionally and voluntarily; to engage in conduct that warrants an inference that a right, claim, or inference is being relinquished (the state waived the fee). Surrender, forsake, forgo, forswear, cede, overlook, dismiss, dispense with, renounce, shelve, repudiate, disown, abjure, defer, throw away, abandon, disclaim, table, eliminate, stay, delay, postpone. See also forfeit, lapse (1), yield. *Ant.* Demand.

Waiver 1. *n.* The intentional and voluntary relinquishment of a known right or such conduct as warrants an inference of the relinquishment of such a right (waiver of the right to notice). Renunciation, refusal, abandonment, surrender, disclaimer, dismissal, rejection, forgoing, sacrifice, spurning. See also forfeiture. **2.** *n.* See alternate (1), stray (1); fluctuating. *Ant.* Claim.

Waiver of immunity See immunity.

Waiver of premium A provision in an insurance policy that the premium is waived upon the disability of the insured.

Waiver of tort An election by the plaintiff to treat the facts as establishing an implied contract and to sue on this theory rather than on a tort theory.

Wake, *n., v.* See consequence (1); animate, incite, provoke.

Waken, *v.* See animate, incite, provoke.

Walk, *v.* To move around on foot. Stroll, march, promenade, stride, amble, perambulate, trek, journey on foot, saunter, traipse, step, sprint, travel, ambulate,

Walk

tramp, roam, trudge, meander, gallivant, prowl, shuffle, pace, plod, hike, clump, lumber, wade, tread. See also limp, grovel, flounder. *Ant.* Ride.

Walkout, *n.* An organized withdrawal of employees from their place of employment because of a labor dispute. Work stoppage, job action, protest, picket, sick-out. See also strike.

Wall, *n.* **1.** An upright structure of solid material, intended to enclose, provide privacy, or protect (common wall). Fence, barricade, divider, partition, screen, separator, panel, barrier, side, division. **2.** Obstacle. See obstruction; impede.

Wallop, *v.* See beat, batter.

Wallow, *v.* See flounder; delight.

Wan, *adj.* See anemic, frail, weak, thin, exhausted.

Wander, *v.* To ramble without any certain course (the animals wandered onto her field). Roam, meander, range, travel, stroll, deflect, wind, veer, lapse, err, cruise, amble, trek, become lost, deviate, go off on a tangent, ramble, prowl. See also digress.

Wandering, *adj.* See itinerant, migratory; wander.

Wane, *v.* See decline, diminish, fall (2), disappear, abate, withdraw, wear (1).

Wangle, *v.* See manipulate.

Want 1. *n.* Lack (want of consideration). Deficiency, shortage, paucity, insufficiency, absence, shortness, default, scarcity, inadequateness, dearth; poverty, privation, destitution, necessity, insolvency, penury, bankruptcy. **2.** *v.* See desire.

Wanting, *adj.* See deficient, insufficient, inadequate, void (3); want.

Wanton, *adj.* **1.** Characterized by a conscious disregard of the consequences of one's acts or omissions; recklessly disregardful of the rights or safety of others (wanton destruction of property). Malicious, intentional, willful, careless, negligent, senseless, irresponsible, inconsiderate, immoderate, outrageous, precipitate, cruel, deliberate, malevolent, arbitrary, heedless, calculated, disregardful, thoughtless, capricious, rash, indifferent, ill-considered, mindless, stupid, injudicious. **2.** Lewd. See obscene.

War, *n.* Hostile contention by means of armed force carried on between nations, states, rulers, or among citizens in the same nation or state (civil war). Conflict, battle, combat, fighting, hostility, fight, slaughter, warfare, bloodshed, contest, struggle, engagement, crusade, showdown, clash, massacre, destruction, uprising, revolt, revolution, insurrection, confrontation, vendetta, blood feud, infighting, acrimony, enmity, bad blood, collision, Armageddon, carnage, donnybrook, brawl, opposition. *Ant.* Peace.

War crimes Crimes committed by countries in violation of international laws governing wars. See crime, atrocity.

Ward 1. *n.* A person placed by the court under the care of a guardian (he was declared a ward of the state). Dependent, unfortunate, incompetent, infant. See also charge (11). **2.** *n.* A division of a city or town. See zone. **3.** *n.* A unit of a hospital. Wing, section, pavilion, annex, dormitory, hall, room, suite, complex. See also hospital. **4.** *v.* To repel (ward off an attack). See prevent.

Warden, *n.* A guardian; a person in charge of a prison; a turnkey. See keeper, manager, watchman.

Ward of the court An infant or person of unsound mind who has come under the protective jurisdiction of the court.

Wardrobe, *n.* See apparel, clothes, uniform (2).

Ware, wares, *n.* See inventory, goods, effects, property, movables, paraphernalia.

Warehouse, *n.* A structure for the reception and storage of goods for compensation or profit. Storeroom, closet, storehouse, depository, arsenal, magazine, repository, depot, vault, armory. See also storage; hoard, accumulate.

Warehouseman's lien The right of a warehouseman to retain possession of the goods until storage charges have been paid. See lien.

Warehouse receipt A receipt issued by a warehouseman for goods received for storage in the warehouse. See receipt.

Warm, *adj.* See kind (2), affectionate, intimate (2); muggy; active (3), ardent.

Warmth, *n.* See love, affection (1), passion, spirit, vigor.

Warn, *v.* See caution (1), counsel (3); warning.

Warning, *n.* That which points out danger (warnings on the label). Caution, foreboding, forewarning, monition, caveat, sign, advice, signal, alarm, notice, notification, hint, indication, threat, flare, siren, alert, light, horn, yell, whistle, flag, beacon, guide, torch, landmark, arrow, prediction, intimation, apprisal, omen. See also admonition (1).

Warp, *v.* See distort, color (3), corrupt, prejudice.

Warrant 1. *v.* To engage or promise that certain facts are as they are represented to be (the dealer warrants the brakes for 2 years). Stand behind, pledge, guarantee, assure, insure, vouch for, attest, avow, assert, swear, aver, stipulate, plight, certify, underwrite, indorse, secure, sanction, authenticate, covenant, agree. **2.** *v.* To give sufficient reason for (the attack warrants a response). Justify, demand, necessitate, call for, legitimate, vindicate, require, provide grounds for. See also merit (2). **3.** *n.* An official order (arrest warrant). Summons, command, decree, directive, edict, mandate, precept, process, writ. **4.** *n.* An order by which the drawer authorizes one person to pay a particular sum of money. An option to purchase stock at a given price. Authorization, license, permission, authority, certification, allowance, charter, approval, voucher, commission, sanction, power, permit, right, credential, legalization, imprimatur, surety, assurance, validation, confirmation.

Warrant of arrest See arrest warrant.

Warranty, *n.* A promise that a proposition of fact is true (the dealer disclaimed all warranties). Pledge, assurance, guarantee, voucher, word, acknowledgment, representation, commitment, obligation, certification, insurance, indorsement, oath, bond, avowal, token, affirmation. *Ant.* Disclaimer.

Warranty deed A deed in which the grantor promises a good clear title. See deed.

Warranty, express See express warranty.

Warranty, implied See implied warranty.

Warranty of fitness for a particular purpose See fitness for a particular purpose.

Warranty of habitability An implied promise by a landlord that the premises are fit for habitation at the time of letting and will remain so during the term of the tenancy. See habitable.

Warranty of merchantability An implied promise that the goods are reasonably fit for the general purpose for which they were sold. See fit (1), merchantable, marketable.

Warranty of title An implied promise that the seller owns the item offered for sale. See title.

Warrior, *n.* See sailor; adversary, competitor.

Warsaw Convention A 1929 treaty on rules for international air travel (e.g., a limitation on liability). See compact (1).

Wary, *adj.* See suspicious, doubtful, cautious, careful, prudent.

Wash 1. *v.* To clean. Launder, brush, wipe, cleanse, shampoo, bathe, shower, scour, purify, mop, sponge, douche, purge, soak, soap, flush, rinse, lave, moisten, hose, swab. **2.** *n.* A shallow part of a river or arm of the sea.

Washout, *n.* See erosion, waste (1); failure.

Washroom, *n.* See bathroom.

Wash sale, *n.* The sale and purchase of the same or a similar asset within a short time period; a transaction involving no change in beneficial ownership; a fictitious kind of sale. See sale.

Waste 1. *n.* An abuse or destructive use of property by one in rightful possession (the owner charged the tenant with waste). Misuse, depletion, destruction, squandering, dissipation, impairment, needless consumption, decay, erosion, devastation, wreckage, plunder, eradication, decomposition, excessiveness, depredation, leveling, deterioration, extravagance, misapplication, prodigality, wastefulness, annihilation, breakup, neglect. **2.** *n.* Useless material. See refuse (2). **3.** *v.* To use or spend carelessly (she wasted her reserves). Squander, misuse, fritter away, exhaust, misemploy, consume needlessly, misspend, drain, use recklessly, expend, dissipate, throw away, deplete, strip, erode, diminish, emaciate, sap, disable, empty, atrophy, corrode, decay, evaporate, die, wither, disappear, melt, shrink, enfeeble, wash away. **4.** *v.* To devastate. See destroy. *Ant.* Conservation; valuables; preserve; rehabilitate.

Wasteful, *adj.* See prodigal, improvident, precipitate.

Wasteland, *n.* See desert (3); park (1); barren.

Wasting asset An asset with a limited useful life (e.g., an oil well) and hence subject to amortization or depletion. See asset, property.

Watch 1. *v.* To observe (he watched the stall collapse). Witness, see, observe, regard, notice, note, mark, scrutinize, oversee, view, survey, inspect, scan, contemplate, sight, discern, gaze, peek, perceive, read, explore, study, glimpse, spot, recognize, stare, attend, behold, eye, spy, peer at, examine, pore over. **2.** *v.* To guard. See oversee. **3.** *n.* A guard. See watchman. **4.** *n.* Surveillance. See inspection.

Watchdog, *n.* See guardian, watchman; conscience.

Watchful, *adj.* See careful, cautious, prudent.

Watchman, *n.* One who guards or patrols buildings or grounds. Custodian, guardian, sentry, defender, patrolman, lookout, sentinel, watchdog, picket, scout, protector; turnkey, warden, jailer, gatekeeper.

Water 1. *n.* H_2O; a colorless, tasteless liquid (subterranean water). Sea, ocean, lake, pond, pool, stream, river. **2.** *v.* To supply with water (water the crops). Irrigate, subirrigate, dampen, vaporize, humidify, hose, spray, douse, drench, submerge, immerse, saturate, plunge, dip, splash, sprinkle, moisten, wet, soak. See also wash, bathe.

Water closet, *n.* See bathroom.

Watercourse, *n.* A natural stream fed from permanent or natural sources (e.g., rivers, creeks, runs, rivulets). See river.

Water down, *v.* See dilute.

Watergate, *n.* See corruption.

Watermark, *n.* A mark indicating the highest point to which water rises or the lowest point to which it sinks.

Wave, *n., v.* See gesture; beat (3).

Waver, *v.* See doubt (1), flounder, stray (1), alternate (1).

Wavering, *adj.* See variable, capricious, indefinite, fluctuating.

Way, *n.* **1.** A route, road, or street (the way to Dorchester). See passage (2), course (1). **2.** A means of attaining a result (the way to succeed). See method. **3.** Behavioral pattern (aggravating ways). See habit. **4.** Preference (he always got his way). See will (3).

Wayfarer, *n.* See traveler, itinerant; tramp.

Waylay, *v.* See ambush, attack, intercept.

Ways and Means Committee A legislative committee with jurisdiction over the methods and sources for raising revenue.

Wayward, *adj.* See disobedient, inflexible, mutinous, seditious; irregular, capricious, variable.

W.D. Western District (e.g., W.D. Ky. refers to the U.S. District Court for the Western District of Kentucky).

Weak, *adj.* Infirm or feeble (a weak argument). Shaky, unsound, unsteady, fragile, impotent, lame, flimsy, puny, effete, effeminate, invalid, ineffective, thin, faint, brittle, diluted, wishy-washy, soft, enervated, delicate, ineffectual, timid, vulnerable, watery. See also breakable, infirm, frail, exhausted. *Ant.* Powerful.

Weaken, *v.* See debase, encumber, debilitate, wear (1), attenuate, disable.

Weakling, *n.* See coward; nonentity, nullity; boor.

Weakness, *n.* See defect, fault; disease; imperfect; affinity (2).

Wealth, *n.* Abundance of financial or material resources (considerable wealth). Capital, riches, assets, means, money, treasure, fortune, goods, bounty, prosperity, lucre, estate, affluence, reserves, cornucopia, plenitude, substance. See also luxury, property. *Ant.* Poverty.

Wealthy, *adj.* See affluent, abundant; luxury.

Wean, *v.* See withdraw, extract.

Weapon, *n.* A device for combat (deadly weapon). Arms, armaments, lethal instrument, gun, knife, artillery, cannon, firearm, bayonet, dagger, dirk, blade, BB gun, bazooka, tank, blade, bomb, bullet, cudgel, Molotov cocktail, mine, land mine, explosive, projectile, torpedo, grenade, missile, pistol, cap gun, ammunition.

Wear, *v.* **1.** To erode or impair (wear away). Corrode, deteriorate, fatigue, grind, waste, fray, shred, eat away, wash away, diminish, deplete, enfeeble, exhaust, tax, overburden. **2.** To carry on the body (wear a coat). Bear, don, display, put on, dress in, exhibit, manifest, costume, attire, parade. *Ant.* Rehabilitate; remove.

Wear and tear, *n.* Deterioration and depreciation in value due to ordinary and reasonable use. See maintenance, repair.

Wearisome, *adj.* See commonplace (2), pedestrian (2), common; onerous, difficult.

Weary, *adj.* See exhausted, indifferent.

Weasel, *v.* See hedge, quibble.

Weather, *n.* See climate, elements, environment.

Weave, *v.* See compose, create.

Web, *n.* See complex (2); conundrum, confusion, mystery; artifice, device, bait.

Wed, *v.* See marriage; contract, join (1).

Wedding, *n.* See marriage, nuptial, spouse; suitor.

Wedge, *v., n.* See force, push, device (2).

Wedlock, *n.* The state of marriage (born out of wedlock). Status of husband and wife, matrimony, connubiality, nuptial state, union.

Weed, *v.* See extract.

Weep, *v.* See bemoan, suffer, cry (1).

Weigh, *v.* See deliberate (1), investigate, review, consider, appraise, assess, judge (3), measure (3), gauge.

Weight, *n.* **1.** Influence, effectiveness, or power to influence judgment or conduct (weight of authority). Credibility, reliability, credit, clout, importance, substance, potency, merit, significance, hold, pressure, value, seriousness, emphasis, urgency, magnitude, consequence, concern, gravity, impact. See also influence, force. **2.** A pressure or load (the weight of responsibility). See burden (2). **3.** See amount, portion.

Weight of evidence The balance or preponderance of the evidence; the inclination of the greater amount of credible evidence to support one side of an issue rather than the other. See evidence.

Weighty, *adj.* See serious, important, cogent, severe.

Weird, *adj.* See mysterious, odd (1), abnormal, peculiar (2), novel.

Welcome, *v., adj.* See entertain (2), address (2); enjoyable, attractive, worthy, marketable.

Weld, *v.* See affix.

Welfare, *n.* **1.** The enjoyment of health and the common blessings of life (public welfare). Prosperity, happiness, well-being, success, benefit, profit, felicity, good fortune, affluence, ease, pleasure, soundness, luck, satisfaction, advantage. **2.** Public assistance, dole, financial aid. See also charity (1), relief (2). *Ant.* Destitution.

Well 1. *n.* A hole sunk into the earth in order to obtain water, oil, or other fluids from a subterranean supply (oil well). Shaft, abyss, hollow, crater, pit, crevasse; mine, spring, reservoir, fount, source, pump, line. **2.** *adv.* Satisfactorily (doing well). Sufficiently, agreeably, favorably, acceptably, smoothly, advantageously, adequately, properly, successfully, splendidly, superbly, commendably, nicely, skillfully, effectively, properly, admirably, excellently. **3.** *adj.* See healthy.

Well-adjusted, *adj.* See normal (3).

Well-advised, *adj.* See judicious, deliberate (2), cognizant.

Well-behaved, *adj.* See good (2).

Well-being, *n.* See comfort, health.

Well-bred, *adj.* See debonair, civil (3).

Well-built, *adj.* See healthy, able-bodied, reliable.

Well-chosen, *adj.* See proper.

Well-defined, *adj.* See clear (1), certain (1), conspicuous, definite, distinct (1), manifest, obvious, particular (1), intelligible, comprehensible.

Well-founded, *adj.* See convincing, credible, rational, legitimate (1), reliable, real (2), presumptive.

Well-grounded, *adj.* See real (2), reliable, right (2), certain (3), cogent, credible, informed, legitimate (1), rational, judicious.

Well-informed, *adj.* See learned, literary (2).

Well-knit, *adj.* See coherent (2).

Well-known, *adj.* See public (3), popular, outstanding (2), notorious (1), historic, reputable, blatant (1), customary.

Well-mannered, *adj.* See civil (3).

Well-marked, *adj.* See plain (1).

Well-meaning, *adj.* See harmless, innocent.

Well-read, *adj.* See learned, literary (2).

Well-regarded, *adj.* See reputable, popular.

Well-stocked, *adj.* See copious.

Well-suited, *adj.* See appropriate, proper, convenient.

Well-thought-of, *adj.* See reputable.

Well-to-do, *adj.* See affluent; abundant; wealth, luxury.

Well-trained, *adj.* See professional (1), apt, able.

Welshing, *n.* A form of larceny: receiving money for a bet by falsely telling the depositor that the intention is to return it along with any winnings derived therefrom. See larceny.

Welt, *n.* See wound, injury, contusion, lesion; batter.

Wench, *n.* See woman, servant, prostitute.

Wend, *v.* See walk, advance, continue, move.

Wept, *v.* See cry, suffer, bemoan.

WESTLAW A system of computerized legal research.

Wet, *adj., v.* See muggy; water, inundate.

Whack, *v.* See beat, batter.

Wharf, *n.* A structure on the shore or margin of navigable waters, alongside of which vessels can be brought for the sake of loading or unloading. Dock, marina, jetty, pier, slip, quay, berth, landing, mooring, port, harbor.

Wharfage, *n.* A fee paid for landing goods upon or loading them from a wharf.

Wharton rule An agreement by two persons to commit a crime cannot be prosecuted as a conspiracy where the crime necessarily requires the participation of two persons.

Wheedle, *v.* See entice, entrap, bait, seduce; avoid.

Wheel, *n., v.* See circle; turn (1), twist; device (1).

Whelp, *n.* A young mammal. See animal (1); child; juvenile.

Whenever, *adv., conj.* At whatever time. In any or every instance in which, every time that, whensoever.

Whereas, *conj.* That being the case. When in fact, considering that, because, since, inasmuch as, while, though, even though.

Whereby, *conj.* By means of which. By which, through which, by the help of which, in accordance with which, by means of which.

Whereupon, *conj.* Upon which. After which, at which time, in consequence of which.

Wherewithal, *n.* See means, property, wealth, asset, fund (2); implement (2), agency.

While, *conj.* During the time that (while driving). Pending, when, as long as, at the same time as; whereas; although.

Whim, *n.* Impulse or caprice (a decision based on the judge's whim). Passing fancy, quirk, personal notion, craze, dream, chimera, vagary, crotchet, passion, arbitrariness, mood, humor, freak, eccentricity, peculiarity, fantasy. See also caprice. *Ant.* Reasoning.

Whimper, *v.* See cry, mope, complain (2), bemoan.

Whimsical, *adj.* See capricious, inconsistent, facetious, comic; joke.

Whine, *v., n.* See mope, complain (2), bemoan, cry, suffer; noise.

Whip, *v.* See beat, batter, defeat.

Whiplash, *n.* A snapping of the neck when a person has his or her head thrown forward or back, or from side to side. Whiplash can cause a sprain, fracture, dislocation, etc. See injury, wound, cut, contusion.

Whipping, *n.* Punishment by thrashing or flogging. Beating, lashing, scourging, pounding, spanking, flagellation, slapping.

Whirl, *v.* See turn (1), alternate, twist, circulate.

Whisk, *v.* See move, run.

Whiskey, *n.* See liquor, beverage.

Whisper, *v.* To speak softly. Murmur, mumble, mutter, sigh.

Whistle, *n.* See noise.

Whit, *n.* See iota, scintilla.

White-collar crime A nonviolent crime committed by an individual or a company in the course of its business or occupation (e.g., embezzlement, price fixing). See crime.

White Slave Act A federal statute prohibiting the interstate and foreign transportation of women and girls for immoral purposes.

Whitewash, *v., n.* See cover (2), hide, conceal; justification, excuse.

Whole, *adj.* **1.** Entire or complete (the whole operation). Unabridged, undivided, uncut, full, integral, intact, unbroken, indivisible, all-inclusive, undiminished, inseparable, widespread, thorough, united, comprehensive, exhaustive, total, gross, utter, consummate, unqualified, thoroughgoing, without exception, inclusive, collective, composite, unconditional, sound, universal, all-embracing, absolute, sweeping; unanimous. See also aggregate. **2.** In good health. See healthy, able-bodied, durable. **3.** Faultless. See blameless.

Whole blood Kinship by descent from the same father and mother; the relationship of those who have both parents in common. See half blood, family, kindred

(1).

Wholehearted, *adj.* See complete (2), entire, full, whole (1), ardent, demonstrative, emotional, friendly.

Whole life insurance, *n.* Insurance for which premiums are collected as long as the insured may live. The amount of the premium remains the same, and the policy builds up cash reserves. See insurance, indemnity.

Wholesale, *adj.* **1.** Pertaining to a sale in large quantity to one who intends to resell; a sale to retailers rather than to consumers (wholesale dealer). See commercial; business. **2.** Widespread and indiscriminate (wholesale collapse). See extensive, comprehensive, broad.

Wholesaler, *n.* See supplier, contractor, merchant.

Wholesome, *adj.* **1.** Tending to promote health (wholesome food). Sound, sanitary, helpful, beneficial, salutary, good, whole, refreshing, healthful, nutritious, fresh, strengthening, hygienic, invigorating, robust, unharmed, strong. See also healthy, fit. **2.** Virtuous. See moral (2), good.

Wholly, *adv.* Not partially (wholly disabled). Entirely, completely, perfectly, exclusively, totally, fully, thoroughly, altogether, all, in every respect, in toto, purely, inclusively, comprehensively, through and through, collectively, unconditionally. See also absolutely. *Ant.* Somewhat.

Whore, *n.* A woman who practices illicit sexual intercourse either for hire or to gratify a depraved passion. See prostitute.

Wicked, *adj.* See bad, base, corrupt, malicious, cruel, odious, repulsive, offensive, obscene.

Wide, *adj.* See broad, comprehensive, big, extensive; indefinite, general.

Wide-awake, *adj.* See cautious, active (3), acute (1).

Widen, *v.* To increase in width (widen the road). Lengthen, expand, elongate, enlarge, stretch, spread, dilate, supplement, inflate, amplify, magnify, increase, add to. See also extend (1), augment. *Ant.* Reduce.

Wide-reaching, *adj.* See extensive, comprehensive, broad (1).

Widespread, *adj.* See extensive, comprehensive, broad (1), general, prevailing, epidemic (2), popular.

Widow, *n.* A woman who has lost her husband by death and who has not remarried. See woman, survivor.

Widower, *n.* A man who has lost his wife by death and who has not remarried. See man, survivor.

Widow's allowance The amount of money or property that a widow may claim from her husband's estate free from all claims.

Widow's election See election by spouse.

Width, *n.* See scope, range, extent, measure.

Wield, *v.* See exercise (2), manage, manipulate, brandish.

Wife, *n.* A woman united to a man by marriage. Spouse, mate, bride, companion, better half, consort. See also woman, partner. *Ant.* Husband.

Wiggle, *v.* See twist, turn, alternate.

Wild, *adj.* **1.** In a state of nature (wild dog). Undomesticated, feral, untamed, savage, unbroken; desolate, abandoned, natural. **2.** Uncontrolled (wild delinquent). Unrestrained, disorderly, frenzied, distracted, mad, fanatical, unruly, misbehaving, tumultuous, disobedient, boisterous, rebellious, unmanageable, bizarre, demented, insane, illogical, intractable, unrestricted, violent, crazy, hysterical, agitated, immoderate, disheveled, mutinous, frantic, destructive, turbulent, tempestuous, furious, explosive, volatile, rabid, lawless, rowdy, bacchanalian, wanton, reckless, negligent, extravagant, extreme, giddy, loose, stormy, intemperate, careless, unreasonable, irrational, irresponsible, unreliable, obdurate, undisciplined, headstrong, mulish, pigheaded, raving, rash, thoughtless. **3.** Uncivilized (wild behavior). See gross (1). *Ant.* Trained; discreet; calm.

Wild animal An animal in the state of nature; an animal of an untamable disposition. See animal.

Wildcat strike A strike called without authorization from the union or in violation of a no-strike clause in the collective bargaining agreement. See strike.

Wilderness, *n.* See desert (3), woods; timber.

Wildlife, *n.* See animal, game (2).

Wile, *n., v.* See artifice, fraud; cheat, seduce, entice, bait.

Will 1. *n.* An instrument by which a person makes a disposition of his or her property, which takes effect after his or her death but is revocable during his or her lifetime (the will was probated). Testamentary disposition, testament, devise, legacy, bequest. **2.** *n.* A determination (the will to succeed). Resolution, self-discipline, self-control, persistence, steadfastness, resolve, disposition, mind, will power, seriousness, intent, decree, commitment, backbone, decision, earnestness, mettle, single-mindedness, strength, conviction, courage, purposefulness. **3.** *n.* Desire (he let his will be known). Preference, inclination, behest, command, order, bidding, direction, pleasure, craving, yearning, intention, election, aspiration, choice, ambition, fancy, hope, decision, longing. **4.** *n.* The faculty of conscious and deliberate action (impaired will). Judgment, volition, self-control, decision, choice. **5.** *v.* Shall or must (the director will file quarterly reports).

Willful, *adj.* **1.** Proceeding from a conscious motion of the will (willful violation). Voluntary, not accidental, designed, conscious, purposeful, wanton, reckless, planned, calculated, volitional, studied, contemplated, willed. See also premeditated, intentional, deliberate (2). **2.** Stubborn, see inflexible, firm (2), unreasonable, arbitrary, absolute.

Willful misconduct of employee The intentional doing of something with knowledge that it is likely to result in serious injuries or with reckless disregard of its probable consequences. Mere incompetence or negligence is not enough to establish willful misconduct. See misconduct.

Willful neglect The intentional disregard of a plain or manifest duty without just cause or excuse. See neglect.

Willful negligence Intentionally doing an act of an unreasonable character in disregard of a known risk, which makes it highly probable that harm will follow. See negligence.

Willing, *adj.* See amenable, cooperative (2); earnest (2), active (3); willful, voluntary; willingly.

Willingly, *adv.* Of one's own free choice (willingly participated). Voluntarily, unreluctantly, without reluctance, without hesitation, without reservation, intentionally, freely, agreeably, eagerly, enthusiastically, happily, avidly, by choice, ungrudgingly. *Ant.* Coercively.

Will power, *n.* See discipline (1), will (2), resolution (4), determination (2).

Will substitute Devices that try to achieve what a will is designed to accomplish (e.g., life insurance, joint ownership of property).

Willy-nilly, *adv.* Whether or not desired. See unavoidable.

Wilt, *v.* See wear (1), diminish, debase.

Wily, *adj.* See devious, deceptive, deceitful.

"Wimp," *n.* See nonentity, boor.

Win, *v.* See gain (2), conquer, beat (2), overcome, defeat (1).

Wince, *v.* See cringe.

Windfall, *n.* Unexpected gain. Bonanza, good luck, boon, jackpot, prize, hit, fortune, discovery, bonus, treasure, godsend, gold mine, sudden profit. See also gift, benefit, reward

Winding, *adj.* See circuitous, tortuous.

Window, *n.* An opening in the wall of a building to admit light and air, and to furnish a view. Portal, aperture, porthole, dormer, lattice, transom.

Window-dressing, *n.* See pretense, decoration.

Windstorm, *n.* See storm.

Wind up, *v.* To settle the accounts and liquidate the assets of a business, for the purpose of making a distribution and dissolving the concern. See liquidate.

Wine, *n.* See liquor, beverage.

Wing, *n., v.* See ward (3), hospital; group, division; run.

Wink, *v.* See ignore, excuse (2), condone, forgive (2).

Winner, *n.* See champion (3), best.

Winning, *adj.* See attractive, intriguing, convivial, friendly.

Winter, *n.* See cold.

Wipe, *v.* See wash, bathe; destroy.

Wire, *n.* See rope, thread.

Wiretap, *v.* See eavesdrop; spy.

Wiry, *adj.* See able-bodied, healthy, durable.

Wisdom, *n.* See judgment (2), discretion (3), maturity, experience (1), common sense, prudence, learning, education.

Wise, *adj.* See judicious, mature (2), learned, cultivated, brilliant, able, capable (2), logical; arrogant.

Wish 1. *n.* An expression of desire (her wish was to return). Longing, hope, inclination, expectation, yearning, partiality, thirst, liking, passion, aspiration, yen, love, hunger, pining, craving, leaning, fancy, appetite, preference, disposition, predisposition, penchant, want, pleasure, petition, entreaty, proposal, appeal, request. **2.** *v.* See desire (1). *Ant.* Aversion.

Wishful, *adj.* See optimistic, auspicious; irrational, fictitious.

Wishy-washy, *adj.* See weak, capricious, thin, barren.

Wisp, *n.* See iota, scintilla.

Wistful, *adj.* See contemplative; despondent, depressing; desire (4), wish.

Wit, *n.* **1.** See judgment (2), discretion (3), prudence, learning, education. **2.** See joke, caricature. **3.** See to wit.

Witchcraft, *n.* Alleged intercourse with evil spirits. Sorcery, black magic, wizardry, voodooism, occultism, black art, magic, fetishism, hoodoo, Satanism, deviltry, casting spells, necromancy, enchantment.

Witchhunt, *n.* See purge (2).

With all faults See as is.

Withdraw, *v.* **1.** To take away (withdraw funds). Take back, draw out, deduct, subtract, retire, remove, recall, extract, draw back, take away, recede. **2.** To retreat (withdraw from the conference). See depart (1), sequester, divide (1). **3.** To cancel (he withdrew the last statement). See rescind. **4.** To draw off liquid. See drain (1).

Withdrawal, *n.* See departure, removal.

Withdrawn, *adj.* See bashful, quiet (2), remote, solitary.

Wither, *v.* See perish, diminish, fall (2), abate, decline, wear (1).

Withhold, *v.* To retain or conceal (withhold information). Keep, keep back, hold back, suppress, inhibit, repress, curb, deny, arrest, forbid, block, screen, camouflage, constrain, harness, censor, veil, mask, secrete, keep secret, control, limit, stay, impede, refuse, delay, muzzle, maintain, hide, leash, shackle. *Ant.* Release.

Withholding tax Tax collected by deductions from wages as they are paid. See tax.

Within, *prep.* Inside the limits of (within 2 days). Any time before, at or before, at the end of, before the expiration of, not beyond, not exceeding, not later than, not above, in the bounds of.

Without, *prep.* Lacking (without delay). In the absence of, free from, excluding, exclusive of, destitute of, no. *Ant.* With.

Without notice In good faith.

Without prejudice No rights or privileges are waived or lost. A dismissal without prejudice allows a new suit to be brought later on the same cause of action. *Ant.* See with prejudice.

Without recourse An indication by an indorser of a negotiable instrument that he or she declines to assume any responsibility for payment to subsequent holders. If the parties primarily liable refuse to pay, there can be no recourse to such an indorser. See recourse.

Without reserve No minimum auction price.

With prejudice, dismissal The judgment is conclusive of the rights of the parties; a dismissal having the same effect as a final adjudication, barring the right to bring or maintain an action later on the same claim or cause. *Ant.* See without prejudice.

With recourse An indication by the indorser of a negotiable instrument that he or she remains liable for the payment of the instrument. See recourse. *Ant.* See without recourse.

Withstand, *v.* See confront, resist, contest; last (2), live (2), abide, continue, bear (2), tolerate.

Witless, *adj.* See dumb, lunatic, absurd.

Witness 1. *v.* To subscribe one's name to a deed, will, or other document for the purpose of attesting its authenticity and proving its execution (witness a will). Authenticate, attest, corroborate, substantiate, depose, verify, acknowledge, validate, certify, give testimony, vouch for, countersign, swear, confirm, initial, sign, warrant, indorse, affirm. **2.** *v.* To see, hear, or experience something personally (she witnessed the crime). Observe, behold, note, mark, notice, take cognizance of, watch, recognize, have direct knowledge, perceive, spot, espy, discern, make out, spy, distinguish, scrutinize, inspect, sight, look on, attend, be present, see firsthand. **3.** *n.* One who, being present, personally sees or perceives a thing (the witness on the stand). Observer, eyewitness, reporter, bystander, informer, viewer, beholder, onlooker, watcher, spectator, corroborator. *Ant.* Overlook (2).

Wittingly, *adv.* With knowledge and by design. See knowingly.

Wizard, *n.* See oracle, expert, specialist, professional, teacher; witchcraft.

Wobble, *v.* See flounder, alternate (1), stray (1); capricious.

Woe, *n.* See distress (3), anxiety, anguish, depression (1), affliction, pain; hardship, misfortune.

Woeful, *adj.* See abject, deplorable, grievous.

Wolf, *n.* See wrongdoer.

Woman, *n.* Lady; feminine sex. Distaff, girl, dame, wife, sister, mistress, debutante, maid, spinster, bride, homemaker, head, widow, dowager, mademoiselle, madam. See also matron, maiden (2); maternal, maternity, pregnant (1).

Womb, *n.* See pregnant (1), maternity, woman.

Wonder, *n., v.* See mystery, marvel, surprise; deliberate (1), contemplate, consider (1), think.

Wonderful, *adj.* See exceptional, extraordinary, great, outstanding (2), enjoyable, attractive, beautiful, intriguing; agape.

Wondrous, *adj.* See wonderful.

Wont, *n.* See custom (1), manner, habit.

Woo, *v.* See entice, seduce, influence, pursue, chase.

Woods, *n.* Land covered with a large and thick collection of natural trees. Forest, grove, woodland, wilderness, jungle, timberland, thicket, bush, copse. See also shrubbery, timber. *Ant.* Desert.

Woozy, *adj.* See dizzy; confuse.

Word, *n.* **1.** A symbol indicating ideas; remark (slanderous words). Term, language, representation, sign, name, speech, phrase, letter, talk, expression, comment, utterance, cognomen, title, verbalization, usage, idea, thought, designation, idiom, appellation, dialogue, interview, audience, conference, colloquy. **2.** An assurance. See promise (1). **3.** News. See report (1, 2).

Word of art See term of art.

Wordy, *adj.* See verbose.

Work 1. *v.* To exert oneself for a purpose (she works at the factory). Toil, sweat, labor, be employed, practice, follow a trade, endeavor, drudge, slave, moil, exercise, operate, carry on, maneuver, manipulate, shape, fashion, strive, handle. **2.** *v.* To do something effectively (the computer works). Succeed, run, function, operate, prevail, achieve, prosper, accomplish, produce, generate, effectuate, manage, realize, fulfill, implement, execute, solve, transmit, bring about, cause, answer, decipher, effect, beget, dispatch. **3.** *n.* Physical or mental exertion for the attainment of some object (the value of her work). Manual labor, endeavor, effort, strain, pursuit, attempt, campaign, undertaking, job, task, craft, line, exercise, discipline, deed, assignment, drill, sweat, field, vocation, industry, avocation, toil, métier, chore, performance, grind, profession, production, struggle, function, drudgery, business, elbow grease, office, project, enterprise, occupation. **4.** *n.* An establishment for performing industrial labor (injury on the works of the company). Factory, mill, foundry, workshop, shop, plant, yard, workshop, assembly. **5.** *n.* An achievement (honored for her good works). Creation, composition, deed, feat, fruit, invention, handiwork, output. *Ant.* Idle; break down, inactivity; playground; failure.

Workable, *adj.* See feasible, practicable, functional, operative, working, running (1), effective (2).

Worker, *n.* **1.** One who accomplishes things. Practitioner, performer, doer. See also actor, party. **2.** See employee, laborer.

Workhouse, *n.* A place for the confinement of persons convicted of lesser offenses. See jail (1).

Working, *adj.* Functioning (working engine). Operating, running, going, performing, moving, usable, executing, conducting, acting. See also active (1), feasible, practicable. *Ant.* Defective.

Working capital, *n.* Cash and other quick assets required to carry on operations; the difference between current assets and current liabilities. See capital.

Working class, *n.* See class, proletariat, laborer, employee.

Workload, *n.* See assignment, capacity; schedule, agenda.

Workman, *n.* One who is employed in manual labor. See employee, laborer.

Workmanship, *n.* See skill, facility, quality, art, method, mode, production.

Workmen's compensation, *n.* A state system of providing fixed awards to employees or their dependents for employment-related accidents and diseases.

Workout, *n.* See practice (3), athletics.

Work product rule The following material is protected against discovery: private memoranda of attorneys, and mental impressions or personal recollections prepared or formed by an attorney in anticipation of litigation or for trial. Some documents and tangible things prepared in anticipation of litigation or for trial are discoverable if it can be shown that the party seeking discovery has substantial need of the materials and is unable without undue hardship to obtain the substantial equivalent of the materials by other means. If this showing of need is made, the attorney is still entitled to have protected from disclosure his or her mental impressions, conclusions, opinions, or legal theories concerning the litigation.

Work release program A program that allows an inmate to leave the institution

for employment during the day. The inmate returns to the prison each evening.
Workshop, *n.* See conference, meeting, education; business, facility, area.
Work stoppage, *n.* See strike.
World, *n.* **1.** Everyone (the order binds the world). All, anyone, each and every person, all persons, everybody, humankind, mankind, world at large, the public, all groups, human race, humanity. **2.** The earth. Planet, globe, universe, creation, cosmos; realm. See domain. **3.** Era. See period.
World Court, *n.* See International Court of Justice.
Worldly, *adj.* Pertaining to the present state of existence; materialistic (worldly pleasures). Temporal, earthly, secular, nonreligious, nonspiritual, terrestrial, carnal, profane, lay, material, physical, mundane, mercenary, sophisticated, greedy, callous, ambitious, shrewd, cosmopolitan, practical, covetous, hedonistic, blasé. *Ant.* Spiritual.
Worldwide, *adj.* See universal, comprehensive.
Worn, *adj.* See ragged, disheveled, old, ancient, exhausted, anemic; commonplace, pedestrian (2).
Worn-out, *adj.* See exhausted, commonplace, pedestrian (2).
Worried, *adj.* See apprehensive, concerned, impatient, insecure (2); anxiety.
Worrisome, *adj.* See distressing, offensive.
Worry, *n.*, *v.* See anxiety, apprehension (3), burden; mope, bemoan, cry (1), suffer; harass.
Worse, *adj.* See base, inferior, deficient, inadequate.
Worsen, *v.* See exacerbate, harm (2), decline (2), lapse (2).
Worship, *n.* A form of religious service showing reverence for a divine being; an assembly engaged in a religious exercise (public worship). Veneration, church service, prayer meeting, adoration, devotional, glorification, praise, adulation, homage, idolization, liturgy, rite, oblation, ritual, cult, celebration, honor, deference, genuflection, exhaltation, Mass, communion, laudation, deification. See also prayer (2), ceremony; God, holy, religious. *Ant.* Desecration.
Worst, *adj.*, *v.* See bad; contemptible; defeat.
Worth, *n.* **1.** The quality of a thing that gives it value; the sum of valuable qualities (its worth could not be calculated). Merit, benefit, excellence, virtue, importance, class, rate, utility, weight, significance, credit, usefulness, respectability, honor, esteem, perfection; market price, appraisal, valuation, estimation, cost. **2.** Wealth (net worth). Resources, assets, portfolio, property, belongings, accounts, money, stocks, bonds, receivables, fortune, riches, estate.
Worthless, *adj.* **1.** Having no value or use (worthless stock). Futile, valueless, useless, of no account, ineffectual, unproductive, barren, abortive, nugatory, inefficient, unprofitable, fruitless, unimportant, unusable, empty, trivial, pointless, piddling, inconsequential, meritless, unavailing, purposeless, slight, vain, inane, sterile, unsuccessful, superfluous, mediocre, impotent. See also frivolous, absurd. **2.** Base. See contemptible. *Ant.* Meritorious.
Worthwhile, *adj.* See worthy, beneficial, gainful, expedient (1).
Worthy, *adj.* Possessing merit (worthy of consideration). Deserved, valuable, merited, honorable, of high station, praiseworthy, acceptable, reliable, meritorious, fitting, dependable, estimable, reputable, suitable, commendable, apt, good, proper, unimpeachable, appropriate, virtuous, excellent, righteous, just, worthwhile, profitable, beneficial, upright, noble, befitting, blameless, due, creditable, exemplary. *Ant.* Worthless.
Would-be, *adj.* See nominal (1), ostensible, quasi; pseudo; candidate.
Wound 1. *v.* To inflict a cut or bruise (the shot wounded a bystander). Lacerate, lame, injure, stab, hurt, pierce, traumatize, scratch, harm, slash, tear, rend, puncture, gash; wrong, sting, offend, distress, torment, damage, affront, insult,

Wound

aggrieve, pain, mortify, embarrass. **2.** *n.* An injury to the body (treated for his wound). Laceration, fracture, bruise, trauma, blow, tear, abrasion, sore, slash, hurt, scratch. See also contusion, lesion, cut, injury.

Wrangle, *v.* See dispute (2), contend, fight (2); quarrel.

Wrap, *v.* See cover (2), enclose; surround; conceal.

Wraparound mortgage A method of refinancing whereby a new mortgage to cover a new loan is placed in a secondary position to the existing mortgage on the original loan. The entire loan is treated as a single obligation. See mortgage.

Wrapper, *n.* A cover. Jacket, envelope, case, blanket, covering, container, holder, sheath, receptacle, casing. See also package, vessel (2).

Wrath, *n.* Violent anger (the victim's wrath). Ire, rage, frenzy, passion, resentment, bitterness, irritation, hostility, vexation, animus, indignation, fury, exasperation, heat, choler, acrimony, gall, displeasure, virulence, spleen, acerbity, animosity, venom, bile, pique. *Ant.* Forbearance.

Wrathful, *adj.* See angry, violent, hysterical; wrath.

Wreak, *v.* See cause, impose, administer.

Wreathe, *v.* See twist, surround.

Wreck, *v.* To destroy or seriously damage (wreck the engine). Ruin, disable, smash, demolish, "total," ravage, level, break, raze, shatter, gut, dilapidate, wrack, desolate, bulldoze, eradicate, liquidate, spoil, dynamite, kill, waste, dismantle, exterminate, annihilate, finish. *Ant.* Salvage.

Wreckage, *n.* See refuse (2); wreck.

Wrench 1. *v.* To twist or pull (she wrenched the gun from the burglar). Wrest, pull, rip, tear, yank, force, wring. **2.** *n.* A strain and injury caused by twisting (a wrench in the knee). Strain, sprain, jolt, ache, pull, spasm, cramp, jerk. See also wound.

Wrest, *v.* See seize (1), wrench (1), force (4).

Wrestle, *v.* See fight, contest (1); athletics.

Wretch, *n.* See nonentity; victim; wrongdoer.

Wretched, *adj.* See abject, destitute.

Wretchedness, *n.* See pain, anxiety, anguish, affliction, depression.

Wring, *v.* See wrench (1), seize (1), force (4).

Wrinkle, *n.* **1.** A crease or furrow (wrinkles appearing on the face). Channel, hollow, depression, rut, cup, pocket, dimple, corrugation, ridge, groove. See also trench. **2.** An ingenious idea (a new wrinkle in computers). Gimmick, notion, device, trick, development, innovation, method.

Writ, *n.* An order issued from a court requiring the performance of a specified act, or giving authority to have it done (writ of habeas corpus). See order.

Write, *v.* See draw (1), draft (2), describe, record (1), create; writing.

Write-off, *n.* The removal of a worthless debt from the books of account. See deduction, removal.

Writer, *n.* See author.

Writhe, *v.* See twist, contort.

Writing, *n.* **1.** The expression of ideas by letters visible to the eye (an agreement in writing). Printing, handwriting, script, calligraphy, penmanship, chirography, longhand. **2.** A manuscript. See publication (2), book (4).

Writ of assistance A form of process used by an equity court to bring about a change in the possession of realty. The writ dispossesses the occupant and gives possession to the one adjudged entitled thereto by the court.

Writ of certiorari See certiorari.

Writ of entry An action to recover possession of land where the tenant or owner has been wrongfully dispossessed. See possession.

Writ of error coram nobis See coram nobis.

Writ of execution See execution (2).

Writ of habeas corpus See habeas corpus.

Writ of mandamus See mandamus.

Writ of prohibition A device by which a court may restrain an inferior tribunal from exercising jurisdiction over matters not legally within its cognizance or from exceeding its jurisdiction in matters properly before it.

Wrong 1. *n.* A violation of the right of another (wrongs committed against the tenant). Blunder, immorality, misdeed, omission, invasion, trespass, crime, tort, injustice, illegality, transgression, abuse, error, malice, dereliction, delinquency, abandonment, neglect, negligence, "screw-up," malfeasance, misfeasance, nonfeasance, outrage, corruption, atrocity, vice, malpractice, misdemeanor, felony, offense, infraction, turpitude, sin, villainy, wickedness, misdoing, abomination, iniquity. **2.** *adj.* Illegal (price fixing is wrong). Lawless, corrupt, disgraceful, sinful, immoral, degenerate, odious, detestable, illicit, delinquent, negligent, reckless, unfair, unjust, unethical, wrongful, contemptible, nasty, illegitimate, felonious, atrocious, shameful, lurid, dishonest, dishonorable, evil, vicious, blameworthy, larcenous, iniquitous, reprehensible, wicked, inexcusable, crooked, unwarranted, improper, inapt, unbecoming, awry, askew, unacceptable, inept, sordid, despicable, malicious, spiteful, malapropos, opprobrious, rotten, satanic, abominable. **3.** *adj.* Mistaken (wrong answer). Incorrect, false, mistaken, imprecise, amiss, erroneous, fallacious, untrue, faulty, inaccurate, awry, inexact, off base, illogical, ungrounded. **4.** *v.* To invade the right of someone (the report wronged her). Damage, injure, abuse, trespass, mistreat, violate, defame, slander, libel, desecrate, oppress, persecute, victimize, harm, malign, dishonor, cheat, encroach upon, defraud, prostitute, debase, aggrieve, exploit, impugn, misuse, defile. *Ant.* Justice; legal; correct; benefit.

Wrongdoer, *n.* One who invades the right of another (conscious wrongdoer). Culprit, trespasser, criminal, villain, sinner, outlaw, evildoer, malefactor, transgressor, lawbreaker, blackguard, convict, gangster, scoundrel, "con," embezzler, racketeer, fake, pretender, quack, terrorist, highwayman, desperado, gunman, insurgent, kidnapper, pirate, cutthroat, mugger, nihilist, anarchist, mafioso, subversive, bully, despot, tyrant, rapscallion, wicked person, tortfeasor, rascal, rogue, cur, reprobate, fiend, libertine, swindler, wretch, dastard, "bastard," troublemaker, incorrigible, dog, cheat, charlatan, assassin, arsonist, incendiary, shylock, usurer, loan shark, shyster, parasite, knave, miscreant, mobster. See also offender.

Wrongdoing, *n.* See mischief, wrong (1).

Wrongful, *adj.* Infringing some right; unjust (wrongful conduct). Reckless, unfair, heedless, wrong, illegal, negligent, tortious, criminal, felonious, bad, evil, illicit, misguided, wrong-headed, harmful, dangerous, lawless, unethical, unauthorized, illegitimate, malicious, mischievous, improper, immoral, underhanded, inequitable, undue, dishonest, misleading, fraudulent, meretricious, false, spurious, devious, mendacious, shameless, corrupt. *Ant.* Rightful.

Wrongful death action A suit brought on behalf of a deceased person's beneficiaries, alleging that the death was attributable to the tortious or wrongful act of another. See action (1), Lord Campbell Act.

Wrongful life action A suit against a doctor whose malpractice has resulted in the birth of a child (e.g., unsuccessful sterilization operation, failure to diagnose pregnancy in time for an abortion, failure to perform an abortion successfully). See action (1), birth.

Wrought, *v.* See made (1).

Wry, *adj.* See wrong, erroneous, disproportionate; distort.

X

ABCDEFGHIJKLMNOPQRSTUVW**X**YZ

X-ray, *n.* Radiograph. Skiagraph, roentgenogram.

Y

Yacht, *n.* See vessel (1); nautical.

Yahweh, *n.* See God.

Yank, *v.* See wrench (1), seize.

Yard, *n.* **1.** Three feet, 36 inches, .914 meter. **2.** Grounds of a building. Park, courtyard, lawn, compound, garden, curtilage. See also close (3), enclosure, ground (2).

Yardstick, *n.* See precedent (1), canon (2), measure (1), criterion, pattern (2).

Yarn, *n.* See thread, strand (2); legend, fiction.

Year, *n.* Twelve calendar months. 365 or 366 days; epoch, era, period, span, cycle, session. See also date (1), age (1).

Yearbook, *n.* See journal.

Yearly, *adj., adv.* See annual (1).

Yearn, *v.* See need (2), pursue (1), aim (2), desire (1).

Yearning, *n.* See desire (4), wish, will (3).

Yell, *v.* To howl. Bellow, whine, cry, yowl, squawk, squeal, bark, scream, holler, screech, shout, roar, laugh, wail, shriek, yelp, explode, boom, bang, thunder, reverberate. See also noise.

Yellow, *adj.* **1.** Cowardly (when he called him yellow, the fight began). Weak, frightened, scared, apprehensive, craven, faint-hearted, untrustworthy, pusillanimous, timorous, afraid, unreliable. **2.** Sensational (yellow journalism). Lurid, melodramatic, muckraking, scandal-mongering, cheap, sordid. *Ant.* Brave; sophisticated.

Yellow-dog contract, *n.* As a condition of employment, the employer requires the employee to promise not to join a union.

Yellow journalism, *n.* Distortion, exploitation, and sensationalism in reporting the news in order to increase profits.

Yelp, *v.* See yell.

Yen, *n.* See wish, desire.

Yes, *adv., n.* See approval, consent.

Yield 1. *v.* To give up or relinquish (yield to pressure). Succumb, submit, forgo, relent, bend, buckle under, break, surrender, comply, release, forsake, back down, resign, bow. See also accept (3), bear (1), acquiesce, allow (3), abdicate, acknowledge (1), quit (1), recognize (2), defer (2), refer, cede, abnegate, confess, accede, assent (2), capitulate, concede (2), abandon (1), conform (1), relinquish, waive, accommodate (1), comply, offer (1), agree (2), renounce, concur, consent (1), render, pay (3), leave (2), abide (1), grant (3). **2.** *n.* That which is produced (an impressive yield). Fruit, harvest, effect, earning, accrual, interest, payment, premium, increment, goods, commodities. See also income, profit (1), produce, product, proceeds, net, gain (1), revenue, return (5), result (1), outcome, output. *Ant.* Resist; input.

Yielding, *n., adj.* See abdication, resignation (1), obedience, conformity, release (3), concession (2), compliance (1), cession, consent (2), renunciation, abandonment; passive, flexible, permissive, malleable, amenable (2).

Yield to, *v.* See follow (1), observe (1).

Yoke, *n.* See slavery, servitude (1), fetter, bondage.

Young, *adj., n.* See new; juvenile (1), offspring, issue (4).

Younger, *adj.* See junior.

Youngster, *n.* See minor (1), child, juvenile (1), adolescence.

Youth, *n.* **1.** Children and young persons of both sexes. See child, minor (1), juvenile (1). **2.** The time between childhood and adulthood. See minority (1), adolescence.

Youthful, *adj.* **1.** Young in years (youthful appearance). Adolescent, juvenile, childlike, pubescent, developing. **2.** Inexperienced or frivolous. See juvenile (2), raw (1). **3.** Energetic. See active (3).

Youthful offender A youth who is treated as a delinquent in the juvenile or family courts and not as a criminal. See wrongdoer, delinquent.

Yowl, *v.* See yell.

Z

Zany, *adj.* See comic; absurd.

Zeal, *n.* See determination (2), diligence (1), vigor, enterprise (2), spirit (2), force (1), passion, love, emotion, industry (2), conviction (3), purpose (2), resolution (4), activity, loyalty.

Zealot, *n.* See fanatic, addict, partisan, aficionado, bigot, stickler (1).

Zealous, *adj.* See diligent, earnest (2), emotional, active, strong (2), ardent, hot (2), conscientious, ready (1), prompt (1).

Zeitgeist, *n.* See characteristic, essence, disposition (4).

Zenith, *n.* See prime (3), apex, culmination, ceiling (1).

Zero, *n.* See nil, nullity, nonentity, cipher (2).

Zero in, *v.* See concentrate (1), aim (1), center (3).

Zest, *n.* See spirit (2), life (3), vigor.

Zigzag, *n., v., adj.* See indirect, turn (1); meander; tortuous, circuitous.

Zilch, *n.* See nil, nullity, cipher (2), nonentity.

Zing, *n.* See vigor.

Zip, *n., v.* See speed (2), run (2).

Zipper, *v.* See attach (2).

Zombie, *n.* See corpse; boor.

Zone, *n.* An area or region that has been set aside and hence has distinctive characteristics (commercial zone). Division, subdivision, belt, tract, domain, province, territory, section, sector, expanse, locale, ward, barrio, ghetto, colony, site, borough, hemisphere, stretch, plot, terrain, quarter; orbit, sphere, bailiwick. See also enclosure, demarcation, precinct, scope, area (1), jurisdiction (2), location, locality, department, neighborhood, circuit, district, place (1); land (2); climate (1).

Zoning, *n.* The division of a city or community into districts in which regulations are imposed on the structure and architectural designs of buildings and the uses to which they may be put.

Zoo, *n.* See confusion.

Zoom, *v.* See speed (2), run (2).

†